GAAP 20

HANDBOOK OF POLICIES AND PROCEDURES

Joel G. Siegel, Ph.D., CPA
Marc H. Levine, Ph.D., CPA
Anique A. Qureshi, Ph.D., CPA, CIA
Jae K. Shim, Ph.D.

CCH
a Wolters Kluwer business

Editorial Staff

Developmental Editor ······· Sandra Lim

Production ······· Holly Whorton

This publication is designed to provide accurate and authoritative information in regard to the subject matter covered. It is sold with the understanding that the publisher is not engaged in rendering legal, accounting, or other professional services. If legal advice or other professional assistance is required, the services of a competent professional person should be sought.

—From a *Declaration of Principles* jointly adopted by a Committee of the American Bar Association and a Committee of Publishers and Associations

Portions of this work were published in previous editions.

In Chapter 1, "Reporting, Presentation, and Disclosures for the Income Statement," information and examples on the binomial option-pricing model are adapted from "Valuing Employee Stock Options Using a Lattice Model," by Les Barenbaum, Walt Schubert, and Bonnie O'Rourke, *The CPA Journal* (December 2004), pp. 16–20. Adapted with permission.

Printed in the United States of America

GAAP 2013 Handbook of Policies and Procedures

by Joel G. Siegel, Marc H. Levine, Anique A. Qureshi, and Jae K. Shim

GAAP 2013 Handbook of Policies and Procedures is an essential reference in applying generally accepted accounting principles in practice. It contains all of the important authoritative pronouncements on GAAP, financial reporting presentation requirements, required and recommended disclosures, and specialized accounting topics needed to evaluate and solve the day-to-day problems of accounting and disclosure.

Guidelines, checklists, diagrams, illustrations, examples from annual reports, and step-by-step instructions simplify complex accounting issues and give public and private accountants quick answers to accounting application questions.

2013 Edition

Coverage has been updated throughout the 2013 Edition of the *GAAP Handbook* to include the following:

- Accounting Standards Update (ASU) No. 2011-12 (December 2011), *Comprehensive Income* (Topic 220), *Deferral of the Effective Date for Amendments to the Presentation of the Reclassifications of Items Out of Accumulated Other Comprehensive Income in Accounting Standards Update No. 2011-05*

- Accounting Standards Update (ASU) No. 2011-11 (December 2011), *Balance Sheet* (Topic 210), *Disclosures about Offsetting Assets and Liabilities*

- Accounting Standards Update (ASU) No. 2011-09 (September 2011), *Compensation –Retirement Benefits – Multiemployer Plans* (Topic 715-80), *Disclosures about an Employer's Participation in a Multiemployer Plan*

- Accounting Standards Update (ASU) No. 2011-08 (September 2011), *Intangibles –Goodwill and Other* (Topic 350), *Testing Goodwill for Impairment*

- Accounting Standards Update (ASU) No. 2011-06 (July 2011), *Other Expenses* (Topic 720), *Fees Paid to the Federal Government by Health Insurers*

- Accounting Standards Update (ASU) No. 2011-05 (June 2011), *Comprehensive Income* (Topic 220), *Presentation of Comprehensive Income*

- Expanded discussion on nonmonetary transactions (Chapter 3)

- Updated information on the treatment of goodwill includes three new examples (Chapter 11)

- New disclosures on offsetting of assets and liabilities (Chapter 17)

- New 2011 annual report examples

Accounting Research Manager™

Accounting Research Manager is the most comprehensive, up-to-date, and objective online database of financial reporting literature. It includes all authoritative and proposed accounting, auditing, and SEC literature, plus independent, expert-written interpretive guidance.

Our Weekly Summary e-mail newsletter highlights the key developments of the week, giving you the assurance that you have the most current information. It provides links to new FASB, AICPA, SEC, PCAOB, EITF, and IASB authoritative and proposal-stage literature, plus insightful guidance from financial reporting experts.

Our outstanding team of content experts take pride in updating the system on a daily basis, so you stay as current as possible. You'll learn of newly released literature and deliberations of current financial reporting projects as soon as they occur! Plus, you benefit from their easy-to-understand technical translations.

With **Accounting Research Manager**, you maximize the efficiency of your research time while enhancing your results. Learn more about our content, our experts, and how you can request a FREE trial by visiting us at **http:// www.accountingresearchmanager.com.**

CCH Learning Center

CCH's goal is to provide you with the clearest, most concise, and up-to-date accounting and auditing information to help further your professional development, as well as a convenient method to help you satisfy your continuing professional education requirements. The CCH Learning Center® offers a complete line of self-study courses covering complex and constantly evolving accounting and auditing issues. We are continually adding new courses to the library to help you stay current on all the latest developments. The CCH Learning Center courses are available 24 hours a day, seven days a week. You'll get immediate exam results and certification. To view our complete accounting and auditing course catalog, go to: **http://cch.learningcenter.com.**

10/12

* CCH is registered with the National Association of State Boards of Accountancy (NASBA) as a sponsor of continuing professional education on the National Registry of CPE Sponsors. State boards of accountancy have final authority on the acceptance of individual courses for CPE credit. Complaints regarding registered sponsors may be addressed to the National Registry of CPE Sponsors, 150 Fourth Avenue North, Nashville, TN 37219-2417. Telephone: 615-880-4200.

* CCH is registered with the National Association of State Boards of Accountancy as a Quality Assurance Service (QAS) sponsor of continuing professional education. Participating state boards of accountancy have final authority on the acceptance of individual courses for CPE credit. Complaints regarding QAS program sponsors may be addressed to NASBA, 150 Fourth Avenue North, Suite 700, Nashville, TN 37219-2417. Telephone: 615-880-4200.

CONTENTS

WHAT THIS BOOK WILL DO FOR YOU

The *GAAP Handbook of Policies and Procedures* is a valuable reference in applying generally accepted accounting principles (GAAP) in practice. It can be used by either a certified public accountant (CPA) in the performance of his or her accounting and advisory functions to clients, or by accountants responsible for the accounting policies and procedures of a business entity. It also provides guidance in resolving any issues and problems that the accountant might be faced with day to day in applying GAAP. The book helps the professional accountant in determining what to look for, what to watch out for, what to do, and how to do it.

This volume will become an essential reference in assisting you in dealing with the complex, ever changing world of financial accounting. It provides many rules of thumb to guide you in evaluating and solving the problems of accounting and disclosure that a CPA encounters on the job. This is a practical, real-life, comprehensive, and useful working book. Its content includes informative rules, policies, and procedures applicable to public accountants at any level working for CPA firms and to private accountants working for large, medium, or small businesses. It may also be used as a training medium. The uses of this book are as varied as the topics presented.

This practical reference contains all of the important authoritative pronouncements on GAAP and is the most up-to-date source of such pronouncements. The GAAP pronouncements include Financial Accounting Standards Board (FASB) Accounting Standards Updates (ASUs) as well as statements, interpretations, technical bulletins, and concepts as well as the unsuperseded GAAP of the American Institute of CPAs (AICPA). This includes the Accounting Principles Board opinions, accounting research bulletins, and statements of position. Securities and Exchange Financial Reporting Releases are also covered when appropriate. Specialized industry accounting principles are included. Consideration is also given to Emerging Issues Task Force (EITF) Consensus Summaries. In general, the SEC follows EITF consensus opinions. In fact, the SEC Chief Accountant has stated that he would challenge any accounting principle that differs from the EITF consensus opinions. EITF issuances have the full effect of GAAP and are positioned in Category C of the GAAP hierarchy. Future developments in GAAP, such as FASB exposure drafts and proposed interpretations are considered.

This volume contains accounting principles, financial reporting presentation requirements, required and recommended disclosures, and specialized accounting topics to keep you on the forefront of GAAP. It avails you of instant answers to any accounting application question you may have in the course of your work and allows you to perform your duties correctly, productively, and successfully.

The book is comprehensive and detailed, so each topic is presented thoroughly. It includes examples, tables, exhibits, and practice aids to show how GAAP is practically applied. The material—clear, understandable, concise, current, and user friendly—is presented in a logical, sequential order to aid reader comprehension.

Guidelines, checklists, diagrams, illustrations, step-by-step instructions, and practical applications make this a valuable reference tool. Complex accounting issues are simplified. In some cases, flowcharts are presented to explain in clearer terms the practitioner's decision process in applying a pronouncement. For explanatory purposes, references including footnotes from annual reports are presented. Keep this book handy for easy reference and daily use.

In conclusion, the book explains and evaluates in easy-to-read terms promulgated GAAP. It analyzes how to apply GAAP to everyday business situations. The focus of this book is on the accounting practitioner working for a CPA firm rendering accounting and audit services to clients, the corporate accountant applying accounting rules and standards, and the CPA candidate whose future goals include a career in financial accounting.

Joel G. Siegel, Ph.D., CPA
Marc H. Levine, Ph.D., CPA
Anique Qureshi, Ph.D., CPA, CIA
Jae K. Shim, Ph.D.

ACKNOWLEDGMENTS

We express our deep gratitude and thanks to Sandra Lim and Holly Whorton for their outstanding editorial advice and assistance on this project. We appreciate their valuable contribution. In addition, we thank Alison I. Shim for her valued assistance in producing the necessary annual reports. Lastly, we thank Roberta M. Siegel for her invaluable input and editorial review.

DEDICATION

Roberta M. Siegel,
loving wife, colleague, and partner

Carol Levine,
dedicated wife and friend

Reva, Daniel, and Sori Levine,
loving children

Tessie and Samuel Levine,
my dear departed parents

Shaheen Qureshi,
loving and devoted wife

Mohammad Rafique Qureshi and Zakia Qureshi,
loving parents

Amera N. Ahmed, Uzma Qureshi, and Jawad Qureshi,
wonderful sisters and brother

Chung Shim,
dedicated wife

ABOUT THE AUTHORS

JOEL G. SIEGEL, Ph.D., CPA, is a retired professor of accounting at Queens College of the City University of New York. He was previously employed by Coopers and Lybrand, CPAs, and Arthur Andersen, CPAs. Dr. Siegel has acted as a consultant in accounting to many organizations, including Citicorp, International Telephone and Telegraph, United Technologies, American Institute of CPAs, and Person-Wolinsky Associates. Dr. Siegel is the author of 68 books and 300 articles on accounting topics. His books have been published by Prentice Hall, Richard Irwin, McGraw-Hill, Probus, Macmillan, Harper and Row, John Wiley, International Publishing, Barron's, Glenlake, American Management Association, Southwestern, and the American Institute of CPAs. His articles have been published in many accounting and financial journals, including *Financial Executive, The CPA Journal, Financial Analysts Journal, Practical Accountant, National Public Accountant, The Ohio Public Accountant, Massachusetts CPA Review, Michigan CPA, Virginia Accountant Quarterly, Today's CPA* (Texas Society of CPAs), *Delaware CPA,* and the *Journal of Corporate Accounting and Finance.* Dr. Siegel was the recipient of the Outstanding Educator of America Award. He is listed in *Who's Where Among Writers* and *Who's Who in the World.* He has served as chairperson of the National Oversight Board.

MARC H. LEVINE, Ph.D., CPA, is a financial accounting consultant and professor of accounting at Queens College. Dr. Levine was previously associated with Deloitte and Touche, CPAs. He has authored seven books, including those published for Warren, Gorham and Lamont, American Management Association, and Thomson and Trentop. He has authored 49 professional and academic articles in publications such as *The CPA Journal, Practical Accountant, National Public Accountant, Michigan CPA, Journal of Corporate Accounting, Accountants Record, Massachusetts CPA Review, Virginia Accountant Quarterly, Cost and Management, Management Accountant,* and *The Accountant.*

ANIQUE A. QURESHI, Ph.D., CPA, CIA, is a business consultant and professor of accounting at Queens College, Dr. Qureshi has written 10 books, and his articles have appeared in *The Journal of Business Research, CPA Journal, EDP Auditing, National Public Accountant, Internal Auditing,* and *International Journal of Computer Applications in Technology.*

JAE K. SHIM, Ph.D., is an accounting consultant to several companies and professor of accounting at California State University, Long Beach. He received his Ph.D. from the University of California at Berkeley. Dr. Shim has 40 books to his credit and has published more than 50 articles in accounting and financial journals, including *The CPA Journal, Advances in Accounting, International Accountant,* and *Financial Management.*

Part I
FINANCIAL
STATEMENTS

Chapter 1
Reporting, Presentation, and Disclosures for the Income Statement

CONTENTS

This chapter discusses the format of the income statement, major income statement categories, extraordinary and nonrecurring items, discontinued operations, research and development costs, deferred compensation arrangements, compensation expense arising under a stock option plan, insurance costs, and earnings per share calculation.

REVENUE, EXPENSES, GAINS, AND LOSSES

The four major components of an income statement, according to Statement of Financial Accounting Concepts (SFAC) No. 6, *Elements of Financial Statements*, are revenues, expenses, gains, and losses:

1. *Revenues* Actual or expected inflows of cash or other assets or reductions in liabilities resulting from producing, delivering, or providing goods or services constituting an entity's major or central operations.

2. *Expenses* Actual or expected outflows of cash or other assets or incurrences of liabilities resulting from producing, delivering, or providing goods or services constituting an entity's major or central operations.

3. *Gains* Increases in equity or net assets from peripheral or incidental activities of an entity and from all other transactions except those resulting from revenues or investments by shareholders or owners.

4. *Losses* Decreases in equity or net assets from peripheral or incidental activities of an entity and from all other transactions except those resulting from expenses or distributions to shareholders or owners.

Revenues

Revenue is recognized when:

☐ It is *realized* or *realizable* (goods or services are converted or convertible to cash or claims to cash or receivables), *and*

☐ It is earned (the earning process is complete or virtually complete when the entity has substantially completed what it must do to receive the benefits represented by the revenues).

Revenue from selling products is usually recognized on the date of delivery of goods to customers. Revenue from services performed is usually recognized when the services have been rendered and are billable. Revenue is usually recognized at point of delivery; however, problems can sometimes occur when trying to implement it.

Sales with Buyback Agreements

No sale is recognized when a company sells a product in one accounting period and agrees to buy it back in the next accounting period at a set price that includes not only the cost of inventory but also related holding costs. Although the legal title may transfer in such a transaction, the economic substance of the transaction is to leave the risk with the seller, and hence no sale is recognized.

Sales When Right of Return Exists

When a company experiences a high rate of return, it may be necessary to delay reporting sales until the right of return has substantially expired. The right of return may be specified in a contract or it may be a customary business practice involving "guaranteed sales" or consignments. Three methods are generally used to record sales when the right of return exists. First, the company may decide not to record any sale until the right of return has substantially expired. Second, the company may record the sale and estimated future returns. Finally, the company may record the sale and accounting for returns as they occur. According to FASB Accounting Standards Codification™ (ASC) 605-15-25-1, *Revenue Recognition: Products*, the company may recognize revenue at the time of sale only if *all* of the following six conditions are satisfied:

1. The price is fixed or determinable at the date of sale.

2. The obligation of the buyer to pay the seller is not contingent on resale of the product, or the buyer has paid the seller.

3. Theft or other damage to the product would not affect the buyer's obligation to the seller.

4. The product being acquired by the buyer for resale has economic substance apart from that provided by the seller.

5. Seller does not have significant future obligations to assist directly in the resale of the product by the buyer.

6. Future returns can be reasonably estimated.

Whereas revenue is generally recognized at the delivery date, under certain circumstances revenue may be recognized before the completion and delivery, such as in long-term construction contracts. Two methods have been used for recognizing revenues from long-term contracts. Under the *percentage-of-comple-*

tion method, revenues are recognized based on the progress of construction. The *completed contract method* recognizes revenue only when the contract is complete.

Expenses

Expenses are generally recognized when incurred. Expenses are "matched" against revenues and should be recorded in the same accounting period. Expenses that benefit several periods, such as depreciation, should be allocated systematically over relevant periods.

Gains and Losses

Gains and losses do not involve an earnings process and are typically recognized at the time of sale of assets, at disposition of liabilities, or when the price of certain assets changes. Gains or losses may also result from environmental factors, such as damage by fire, flood, or earthquake.

INCOME STATEMENT FORMATS

There are two generally accepted formats for preparing the income statement: the single-step format and the multistep format. The single-step format contains just two sections: Revenues Minus Expenses Equals Net Income. The revenue section includes sales revenue, interest income, gains, and all other types of revenues. The expense section includes cost of goods sold, selling and administrative expenses, interest expense, losses, and taxes. The single-step format does not emphasize any one type of revenue or expense. Potential problems with classifying revenues and expenses are thus eliminated. An example of a single-step income statement is shown in Exhibit 1-1. Entities that choose the single-step format for income statement presentation break out income tax expense separately at the bottom of the statement placing it directly after the caption "income before taxes." Although this is not strictly in accordance with the single-step concept, which requires income tax expense to be included in the expenses category, it is done to enhance the comparability of the entity's income statement to other entities.

Exhibit 1-1: Example of Single-Step Income Statement

XYZ Company
Income Statement
For the Year Ended December 31, 20X5

REVENUES	
Net sales	$3,000,000
Interest income	120,000
Dividend income	45,000
Rental income	36,000
Gain on sale	150,500
Total revenues	$3,351,500
EXPENSES	
Cost of goods sold	$2,000,000

XYZ Company
Income Statement
For the Year Ended December 31, 20X5

Selling expenses	700,000	
Administrative expenses	250,000	
Interest expense	65,000	
Loss on disposal	55,000	
Income tax expense	110,500	
Total expenses		3,180,500
NET INCOME		$ 171,000
Less: Net income attributable to the noncontrolling interest		(10,000)
Net income attributable to XYZ Company		161,000
EARNINGS PER SHARE (500,000 shares)		$ .34

A multistep income statement is used to emphasize certain sections and relationships. It contains separate sections for operating and nonoperating activities. Expenses are also classified by functions, such as merchandising or manufacturing (cost of goods sold), selling, and administration.

It is acceptable to combine the statement of income with the statement of retained earnings to produce a combined Statement of Income and Retained Earnings. The first part of the statement may be prepared using either the single-step or the multistep approach to derive net income. The beginning balance of retained earnings is added to net income. Dividends declared are deducted to arrive at ending retained earnings. An example of a combined Statement of Income and Retained Earnings using a multistep approach is shown in Exhibit 1-2.

Exhibit 1-2: Combined Statement of Income and Retained Earnings Using the Multistep Approach

XYZ Company
Combined Statement of Income and Retained Earnings
For the Year Ended December 31, 20X5

REVENUES		
Sales		$5,000,000
Less: Sales returns and allowances	$ 670,000	
Sales discounts	95,000	765,000
Net sales		4,235,000
COST OF GOODS SOLD		
Beginning inventory	$ 620,000	
Plus: Net purchases	1,300,000	
Merchandise available for sale	$1,920,000	
Less: Ending inventory	435,000	

XYZ Company
Combined Statement of Income and Retained Earnings
For the Year Ended December 31, 20X5

Cost of goods sold		1,485,000
Gross profit		$2,750,000
OPERATING EXPENSES		
Selling expenses		
Advertising	$ 35,000	
Rent	150,000	
Travel	87,000	
Sales salaries	320,000	
Depreciation	120,000	
Utilities	77,000	
Commissions	150,000	
Total selling expenses		939,000
ADMINISTRATIVE EXPENSES		
Legal expenses	$ 215,000	
Professional expenses	125,000	
Insurance	83,000	
Supplies	62,000	
Officers' salaries	250,000	
Miscellaneous office expenses	35,000	
Total administrative expenses		770,000
INCOME FROM OPERATIONS		$1,041,000
OTHER REVENUES AND GAINS		
Interest income	$ 370,000	
Dividend income	425,000	
Rental income	325,000	
Gain on sale	175,000	
Total		1,295,000
		$2,336,000
OTHER EXPENSES AND LOSSES		
Interest expense	$ 400,000	
Loss on disposal	395,000	
Total		$ 795,000
INCOME BEFORE TAXES		$1,541,000
Income tax expense (30%)		462,300
NET INCOME		$1,078,700
Less: Net income attributable to the noncontrolling interest		(25,000)
Net income attributable to XYZ Company		$1,053,700

XYZ Company
Combined Statement of Income and Retained Earnings
For the Year Ended December 31, 20X5

Beginning Retained Earnings	800,000
	$1,878,700
Less: Cash dividends declared and paid	(650,000)
Ending Retained Earnings	$1,228,700
EARNINGS PER SHARE (500,000 shares)	$ 2.16

NONRECURRING GAINS OR LOSSES

Nonrecurring gains or losses are items that are either unusual or infrequent. They are not considered extraordinary and are presented separately before tax prior to income from continuing operations. Examples are a loss on the sale of property, plant, and equipment as well as the cost of closing a warehouse as part of a business line. Disclosure should be made of the nature and effect of nonrecurring items.

RESEARCH AND DEVELOPMENT COSTS

Research is defined as testing to search for a new product, service, technique, or process. Research may also be undertaken to improve already existing products or services. Development is defined as translating the research into a design for a new product or process. Development may also encompass improvements made to existing products or processes.

ASC 730-10-05-1, *Research and Development: Overall*, requires the expensing of internally generated research and development costs as incurred. R&D costs are presented separately within income from continuing operations.

When research is performed under contract for a fee from a third party, a receivable is charged.

Equipment, facilities, materials, and intangibles (e.g., patents) bought that have alternative future benefit in R&D activities are capitalized. Any resulting depreciation or amortization expense on such assets (e.g., the depreciation on an R&D building) is presented as an R&D expense. When there is no future alternative use, the costs must be immediately expensed.

R&D costs include employee salaries directly tied to R&D efforts, and directly allocable indirect costs for R&D efforts.

If a group of assets is bought, proper allocation should be made to those applicable to R&D activities.

Accounting Standards Update 2009-03 (August 2009) (ASC 730, *Research and Development*), *SEC Update—Amendment to Various Topics Containing SEC Staff Accounting Bulletins,* states that a significant related-party relationship to an R&D arrangement exists when 10 percent or more of the entity providing the funds is owned by related parties (ASC 730-20-S99-1) (SAB Topic 5.B).

Research and Development Costs Acquired as Part of a Business Combination

ASC 730-10-14-4f, amends ASC 730-10-25-1 as it relates to research and development costs. ASC 730-10-14-4f requires that all research and development assets acquired in a business combination be initially recognized and measured at fair value, even if those assets do not have alternative future use.

If payments are made to others to undertake R&D efforts on the company's behalf, R&D expense is charged.

Exception: ASC 730-10-15-4, *Research and Development: Overall*, is not applicable to the extractive (e.g., mining) or regulated industries.

Examples of R&D activities are:

☐ Testing the feasibility of products.

☐ Engineering functions so the new product may satisfy manufacturing requirements.

☐ Developing models and prototypes before manufacturing.

☐ Formulating and designing product alternatives.

☐ Laboratory research conducted to uncover new knowledge.

☐ Pilot programs before operations commence.

The following are *not* R&D activities:

☐ Marketing research.

☐ Legal fees to secure a patent.

☐ Quality control during commercial production.

☐ Rearrangement and startup activities.

☐ Design changes due to changes in the season (e.g., winter to spring).

☐ Identifying and solving manufacturing problems during commercial production.

☐ Construction engineering.

☐ Routine or periodic alterations to existing products, operations, or production processes.

☐ Commercial applications of the product.

ASC 985-20-25, *Software: Costs of Software to Be Sold, Leased, or Marketed*, and ASC 985-20-25, *Software: Costs of Software to Be Sold, Leased, or Marketed*, provide special treatment for R&D costs incurred for computer software, whether leased, sold, or otherwise marketed. R&D costs for software development are expensed up until there is a working (program) model (technological feasibility). Technological feasibility is established when the enterprise has completed all planning, designing, coding, and testing activities necessary to establish that the product can be produced to meet its design specifications, features, functions, and technical performance requirements. Technological feasibility also involves ensuring that all risks have been identified. After a working model has been completed, the R&D production software costs are deferred to an asset and reflected at the lower of unamortized cost or net realizable value. If unamortized cost exceeds net realizable value, the write-down is charged against earnings. The write-down is not reversed for any subsequent recovery in value. Examples of these R&D production software costs incurred after the working model are refining subroutines, debugging, and alternative adaptations. After the software is available to the public (marketable), the R&D asset is amortized. The amortization expense is based on the greater of:

☐ Straight-line method amount.

☐ Percent of current-year revenue to total expected revenue from the product.

Note: The purchase price of software bought from others that has future benefit should be deferred and amortized over the period benefited.

Once the product is ready to be sold or otherwise marketed, the costs incurred for duplicating the computer software, documentation, and training materials from the product masters and for physically packing the product for distribution shall be capitalized as inventory. Cost of sales is charged when the related revenue from the sales of those units occurs.

Any costs incurred to maintain or provide customer support for the software once sold to the public are expensed to match against the associated revenue generated. Examples of such costs are costs to correct errors, make updates, and perform routine changes.

ASC 730-10-15-4 does not cover software costs associated with that developed by the company for others or created to use internally within the company. Further, the costs to develop a computer system that enhances the company's administrative or selling activities is not classified as an R&D cost.

According to ASC 730-20-25, *Research and Development: Research and Development Arrangements*, if a company contracts with others to fund R&D efforts, a determination must be made of the nature of the obligation. If the company is obligated to repay the funds regardless of R&D success, the company must first debit cash and credit liabilities at the time of borrowing and then debit R&D expense and credit cash at the time of R&D incurrence.

However, a liability does not exist if the transfer of financial risk to the party is substantive and real. If the financial risk related to the R&D is transferred because repayment depends only on the R&D having future economic benefit, the company treats its obligation as a contract to engage in R&D for others. In this instance, R&D costs are capitalized and revenue is recognized as earned and becomes billable under the agreement. Footnote disclosure should be made of the terms of the R&D agreement, amount of earned compensation, and costs incurred under the agreement.

In the event that loans or advances to the entity depend only on R&D results, such amounts are considered R&D costs to be charged to expense.

Stock issued for R&D should be recorded at the fair value of the stock issued or fair value of the R&D acquired, whichever is more clearly evident. If warrants, options, or other financial instruments are issued in connection with an R&D

contract, R&D expense is charged. In addition, the company records part of the proceeds to be provided by the other party as paid-in-capital based on their fair market value on the arrangement date.

According to ASC 730-20-25-13, *Research and Development: Research and Development Arrangements*, nonrefundable advance payments for goods or services that will be used for future research and development activities should be deferred and capitalized. Such amounts should be recognized as an expense as the related goods are delivered or the associated services are performed. If an entity does not anticipate the goods to be delivered or services to be rendered, the capitalized advance payment should be charged to expense.

Footnote disclosures with regard to research and development follow:

☐ Terms of R&D arrangements, such as options to buy, licensing, royalty basis, and funding commitments.

☐ Valuation basis.

☐ Fees earned from R&D contracts.

☐ Amortization method and time period.

COMPENSATION COST ARISING FROM SHARE-BASED PAYMENTS MADE TO EMPLOYEES

FASB Statement No. 123 (FAS-123), *Accounting for Stock-Based Compensation*, established fair value accounting as the preferential methodology of accounting for share-based compensation to employees. However, it also allowed companies to continue accounting for share-based compensation using the intrinsic method described in APB Opinion No. 25 (APB-25), *Accounting for Stock Issued to Employees*. Under the intrinsic method, many companies recorded no compensation at all for the share options that were issued to employees and exercised by them. In addition, pro forma disclosures of the entity's net income and earnings per share as if the fair-value method was used were also required. For many years, most entities continued to use the intrinsic method of accounting for stock-based compensation to employees. However, beginning in early 2001, serious financial company failures began to surface in several large companies, leading many to surmise that the failure to recognize compensation for employee stock option plans was clouding the communication of a company's performance and preventing users of financial statements from obtaining a faithful representation of the entity's financial health.

ASC 718-10-05, *Compensation—Stock Compensation: Overall*, eradicates this problem by eliminating the intrinsic value method. Some of the salient improvements of ASC 718-10-05 relating to employee share-based compensation are:

☐ The use of the intrinsic method described in APB-25 as an alternative to the fair value method in computing and recognizing share-based compensation cost is no longer acceptable.

☐ Share-based compensation must now be recorded for most entities in accounting for share options given to employees. Recognition of zero compensation cost in this situation is no longer possible.

☐ Generally accepted accounting principles (GAAP) are simplified in that there is only one way of accounting for compensatory share options and therefore comparability among financial statements will now be improved.

☐ Users of financial statements will be able to better understand the economic transactions affecting an entity and will be able to make better decisions as a result of having more accurate and precise information about the entity.

In general, ASC 718-10-55-4 requires that the total compensation cost that should be recognized be equal to the grant-date fair value of all share options that actually vest with employees. This amount is then allocated over the service period based on the amount of service performance that has been, or will be, rendered by employees. At grant date, the fair value of the share options "locks" and becomes impervious to subsequent changes in stock prices. In addition, the service period is generally the vesting period; that is, the period that extends from the date of grant to the date of vesting. ASC 718-10-35-3 and 30-16 also require that an entity estimate the number of share options that will be given to employees based on the services performed. This differs from FAS-123 in that the latter allowed entities to account for forfeitures as they occurred. In this updated version, compensation cost should be recognized only if performance by the employee is likely to occur. If it is unlikely that the employee performance will occur (such an expectation may occur, for example, because of expected resignations or other causes of turnover), compensation cost should not be accrued. ASC 718-10-35-3 requires that appropriate estimates of this expectation should be made. If at a subsequent time, for example, it is determined that the original estimates of the number of share options that are likely to be earned by employees were incorrect, a revision should be made. ASC 718-10-35-3 requires that the cumulative effect on current and prior periods of a change in the estimated number of share options for which service is expected to be, or has been, rendered should be recognized as compensation in the period of the change.

A nonpublic entity may be unable to estimate the fair value of it share options simply because it is not able to measure the expected volatility of its future share price. In this case, ASC 718-10-30-20 requires that the fair value calculation should be based on a value calculated using the historical volatility of an appropriate industry sector index instead of the entity's own share price volatility. If an entity issues an equity instrument with terms whose fair value (at the date of grant) cannot be reasonably estimated, it should be accounted for using the intrinsic method with remeasurement taking place at each reporting date through the date of settlement (i.e., exercise). In other words, recorded compensation expense must be adjusted based on the change in the intrinsic value of the equity instrument each reporting period. (Notwithstanding the aforementioned, the emphasis of this section is on public entities. For the remaining discussions on share-based payments, the guidance provided relates to public entities unless otherwise specified.)

Models Used to Value Employee Share Options

The models used to measure the fair value of share options do so at a single point in time, generally the date of grant. The assumptions underlying the fair value measurement are a function of information that is available at the time that the measurement is made. The following is a discussion of the models used to value share options.

The Black-Scholes-Merton Option-Pricing Model

The Black-Scholes-Merton Option-Pricing Model (OPM) was developed in 1973 by Fischer Black and Myron Scholes. The model provides the relationship between call option value and the five factors that determine the premium of an option's market value over its expiration value:

1. *Time to maturity* The longer the option period, the greater the value of the option.

2. *Stock price volatility* The greater the volatility of the underlying stock's price, the greater its value.

3. *Exercise price* The lower the exercise price, the greater the value.

4. *Stock price* The higher the price of the underlying stock, the greater the value.

5. *Risk-free rate* The higher the risk-free rate, the higher the value.

The formula is:

$$V = P[N(d_1)] - PV(E) [N(d_2)]$$

where:

V = current value of a call option

P = current stock price

$PV(E)$ = present value of exercise or strike price of the option, $E = E/e^{rt}$

   r = risk-free rate of return, continuously compounded for t time periods

   e = 2.71828

   t = number of time periods until the expiration date (e.g., 30 days means $t = 30/365 = 0.0822$)

$N(d)$ = probability that the normally distributed random variable Z is less than or equal to d

$d1$ = $\ln[P/PV(E)]/\sigma\sqrt{t} + \sigma\sqrt{t/2}$
   $\ln()$ = natural logarithm of the argument

σ = standard deviation per period of (continuously compounded) rate of return on the stock

$d2$ = $d1 - \sigma\sqrt{t}$

The formula requires readily available input data, with the exception of σ^2, or volatility. P, X, r, and t are easily obtained. The implications of the option model are as follows:

1. The value of the option increases with the level of stock price relative to the exercise price $[P/PV(E)]$, the time to expiration, and the time to expiration times the stock's variability ($\sigma\sqrt{t}$).

2. Other properties:

a. The option price is always less than the stock price.

b. The option price never falls below the payoff to immediate exercise (P − E or zero, whichever is larger).

c. If the stock is worthless, the option is worthless.

d. As the stock price becomes very large, the option price approaches the stock price less the present value of the exercise price.

EXAMPLE

The current price of Sigma Corporation's common stock is $59.375 per share. A call option on this stock has a $55 exercise price. It expires in 30 days. If the standard deviation of continuously compounded rate of return on the stock is 0.2968 and the risk-free rate is 5% per year, the value of this call option is determined as follows:

1. Calculate the time until the option expires in years:

   t in years = 30 days/365 days = 0.0822

2. Calculate the values of the other variables:

   $PV(E) = E/e^{rt} = \$55/e^{0.05 \times 0.0822} = \$54.774$

   $d1 = \ln[P/PV(E)]/\sigma\sqrt{t} + \sigma\sqrt{t}/2 = \ln[\$59.375/\$54.774]/$
   $(0.2968 \times \sqrt{0.0822}) + (0.2968 \times \sqrt{0.0822})/2 = 0.9904$

   $d2 = d1 - \sigma\sqrt{t} = 0.9904 - 0.2968 \times \sqrt{0.0822} = 0.9053$

3. Use a table for the standard normal distribution (to determine N(d1) and N(d2)):

   $N(d_1) = N(0.9904) = 0.8389$

   $N(d_2) = N(0.9053) = 0.8173$

4. Use those values to find the option's value:

   $V = P[N(d_1)] - PV(E)[N(d_2)]$
   $= \$59.375[0.8389] - \$54.774[0.8173]$
   $= \$5.05$

   This call option is worth $5.05, a little more than its value if it is exercised immediately, $4.375 ($59.375 − $55), as one should expect.

EXAMPLE

Another option on the same stock has an exercise price of $50 and expires in 45 days. The value of the call option is determined as follows:

1. Calculate the time until the option expires in years:

   t in years = 45 days/365 days = 0.1233

2. Calculate the values of the other variables:

   $PV(E) = E/e^{rt} = \$55/e^{0.05 \times 0.1233} = \$49.6927$

   $d_1 = \ln[P/PV(E)]/\sigma\sqrt{t} + \sigma\sqrt{t}/2 = \ln[\$59.375/\$49.6927]/$
   $(0.2968 \times \sqrt{0.1233}) + (0.2968 \times \sqrt{0.1233})/2 = 1.7602$

   $d_2 = d_1 - \sigma\sqrt{t} = 1.7602 - 0.2968 \times \sqrt{0.1233} = 1.6560$

3. Use a table for the standard normal distribution (to determine N(d1) and N(d2)):

$$N(d_1) = N(1.7603) = 0.9608$$

$$N(d_2) = N(1.6561) = 0.9511$$

4. Use those values to find the option's value:

$$V = P[N(d_1)] - PV(E)\,[N(d_2)]$$
$$= \$59.375[0.9608] - \$49.6927[0.9511]$$
$$= \$9.78$$

The call option is worth more than the other option ($9.78 versus $5.05) because it has a lower exercise price and a longer time until expiration.

Lattice-Based Models

The Black-Scholes-Merton Model is viewed by some as overstating the value of employee stock options, because the model does not take into account the essential differences between traditional exchange-traded stock options and those granted to employees. Unlike conventional options, employee options are subject to vesting schedules and forfeiture conditions and cannot be transferred. As a result, they are invariably exercised before their usual 10-year term expires. These characteristics reduce the value of an option.

Although the FASB does not specify a preference for a particular valuation technique or model in estimating the fair values of employee share options, it recognizes that a lattice-based method can take into account assumptions that reflect the conditions under which employee options are typically granted. The binomial model is the most commonly used lattice-based method, but other methods may be better suited to compensation programs that link vesting to specific performance objectives. Each of these models is outlined below:

☐ *Binomial* Unlike Black-Scholes-Merton, the binomial method divides the time from the option's grant date to the expiration date into small increments. Because the share price may increase or decrease during any interval, the binomial model takes into account how changes in price over the term of the option would affect the employee's exercise practice during each interval. The binomial model can also consider an option grant's lack of transferability, its forfeiture restrictions, and its vesting restrictions—even for options with more-complicated terms, such as in-dexed and performance-based vesting restrictions.

☐ *Trinomial* The trinomial model goes a step further by allowing for the underlying stock price either to remain unchanged or to move up or down. This is useful for valuing performance-based options that vest only if the stock price exceeds a certain level over time.

☐ *Multinomial* This model can take many more factors into account than either the binomial or trinomial framework. Such additional flexibility may be required to value options that cannot be exercised unless the underlying stock price exceeds the performance of one or more indices.

But when there are more than two such sources of uncertainty, a Monte Carlo simulation may be preferable, as it is easier to apply than lattice models.

Note: The new models are far less familiar to users than Black-Scholes-Merton, so individuals must spend considerable time figuring out how to use it. Black-Scholes-Merton is so widely used that there are lots of software packages, for laptops and handheld computers, to run the model.

The binomial model. Lattice-based option-pricing models, such as the binomial mode, can explicitly capture assumptions about employee exercise behavior over the life of each option grant, expected changes in dividends, and stock volatility over the expected life of the options, in contrast to the Black-Scholes-Merton model, which uses weighted average assumptions about option characteristics.

Exhibit 1-3 illustrates a simple two-year lattice model that portrays the expected price changes of the security, along with their chance of occurrence. Each node of the lattice reflects an expected share price at year-end. These expectations are developed through analysis of the security's historical volatility and its expected future volatility. Volatility, measured by the expected standard deviation of the returns of a security, then determines expected share price fluctuations over time. In turn, these potential share price fluctuations are a major factor in estimating option value.

Exhibit 1-3: Two-Year Binomial Lattice

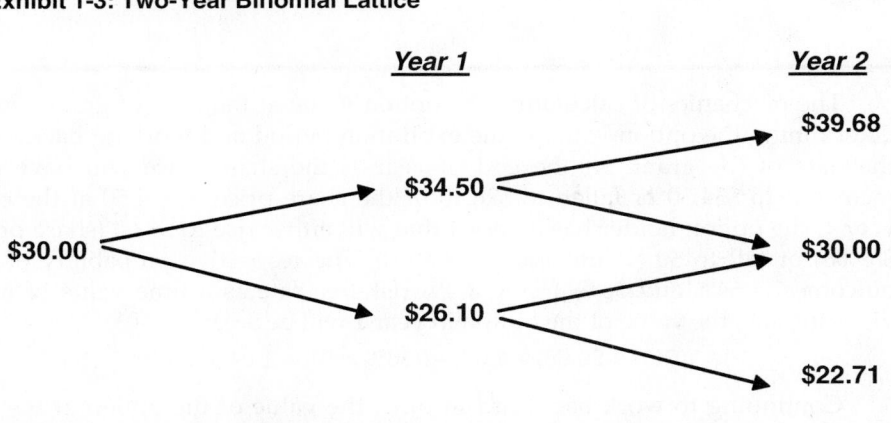

Exhibit 1-4 presents an example with a 64% probability that the price of the security will increase 15% (from $30.00 to $34.50) and a 36% chance that the price will decline by 13% (from $30.00 to $26.10). Assuming that the probabilities and percentage price increases are the same for each of the two years, if the price does go up to $34.50 in year 1, there is a 64% chance that it will go up again in year 2 (to $39.68) and a 36% chance that it will decline in year 2 (back to $30.00).

Exhibit 1-4 shows how option values are determined. Assuming that fully vested stock options have been granted with an exercise price of $30.00 and a term of two years, the holder of the option can buy shares of stock for $30.00 until the option expires in two years. If the share price increases in both years 1 and 2, the option holder will net $9.68 ($39.68 – $30.00) upon exercise of the option. If the share price stays at $30.00 a share or falls to $22.71 at the end of year 2, the option holder will not exercise, as the share price does not exceed the exercise price. If the share price has a value of $30.00 or less at the end of the two-year period, there is neither gain nor loss for the holder. The option simply expires unexercised. At the time of the option grant, the option clearly has value. It is more likely that the stock will have a value greater than $30.00 at the end of two years, and the holder will not suffer any loss if it does not.

Exhibit 1-4: Two-Year Binomial Lattice with Option Values

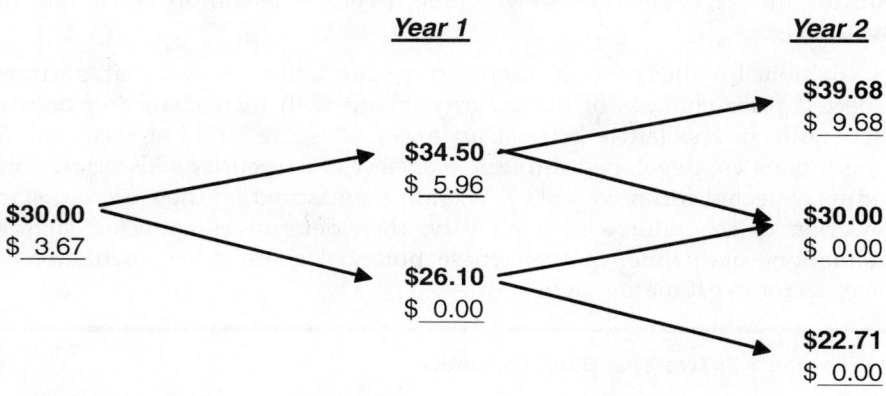

The mechanics of calculating the option value at the time of grant begin by determining the option value at the expiration period and working backward to the date of the grant. At the end of year 1, the share price will have either increased to $34.50 or fallen to $26.10. If the share price is $34.50 at the end of year 1, the option holder has an asset that will either rise to $9.68 (share price of $39.68) or fall to $0 (share price of $30.00). The respective probability of these outcomes is 64% and 36%. Using a 4% risk-free rate as a time value of money discount rate, the value of the option in year 1 will be $6.05:

$$[(64\% \times \$9.68) \div 1.04] + [(36\% \times \$0) \div 1.04] = \$5.96$$

Continuing to work backward in time, the value of the option at the grant date is based on the option values at the end of year 1. The calculation is the same as in the previous example, and yields an option value of $3.67, the present value of $5.96 and $0 weighted by the probabilities of each outcome occurring:

$$[(64\% \times \$5.96) \div 1.04] + [(36\% \times \$0) \div 1.04] = \$3.67$$

Thus, the option value is based on the expected share price at each node on the lattice. If the historical volatility is higher, and the future volatility is projected to be higher, other things being equal, the option will have more value; the higher the probability of an increase in stock price, the higher the value of the option. There is no real risk of loss to the option holder, who will simply not exercise the option if the stock price declines. Therefore, as long as there is a positive probability that the price will rise above the exercise price, the option has value.

The analysis above illustrates the value of transferable options at the grant date. Employee stock options, however, are not transferable, and this affects their value.

Nontransferability and early exercise   If the share price in the preceding example rises to $34.50, the option is then worth $5.96, factoring in the possibility of a rising price in year 2. If, however, the option cannot be sold, the option holder must choose between exercising the option at the end of year 1 and holding it until the end of year 2. If the holder opts to exercise the option at the end of year 1, the proceeds would be only $4.50.

Because they cannot sell the option in the open market, many employees will exercise their options early to realize a gain rather than take the chance that the share price will fall. In other words, the option is worth only $5.96 at the end of year 1 if it can be sold. There is a positive probability that the stock will rise in year 2 and be worth $9.68, but it also might decline and become worthless. Employees may prefer to take a profit of $4.50 rather than risk losing all the potential value. The result of the potential early exercise is that the grant date value of the option falls from $3.67 to $2.77:

$$[(64\% \times \$4.50) \div 1.04] + [(36\% \times \$0) \div 1.04] = \$2.77$$

The reduced option value is due to the increased likelihood of early exercise that nontransferability represents.

Other important share-based payment considerations   ASC 718-20-55-24 modifies FAS-95, *Statement of Cash Flows*, to require that excess tax benefits derived from the excess of tax deductible amounts over the compensation cost recognized in the accounting records be classified in the statement of cash flows as a financing cash inflow and as a cash outflow from operating activities. This would be true whether or not the entity's statement of cash flows is presented under the direct or indirect method. In the predecessor statement, the excess tax benefits were viewed as a reduction of taxes paid.

As previously noted, ASC 718-10-55-17 does not suggest a preference for the model that should be used in establishing the value of the employee share options granted. However, in valuing the share options award, it does require that an entity must establish defensible and reasonable estimates for each of the variables used in the model. As an example, the employee share option expected term, the contractual term of the instrument, the effects of employees' expected exercise, and postvesting termination behavior must all be estimated.

If the share options are not fully exercised (or not exercised at all), the amount that is deductible on the entity's tax return may be less than the compensation cost that was recognized in the accounting records. The deferred tax asset related to this situation must be resolved. ASC 718-740-35-5 requires that the deferred tax asset related to this deficiency (net of any related valuation allowance) should be offset against any remaining additional paid-in-capital from previous share option program awards. If any balance in the deferred tax asset account remains, it should be written off and charged to income tax expense.

EXAMPLE

FAIR VALUE METHOD

The stockholders of X Company approve a share option plan that grants share options to employees on January 1, 20A1, to purchase 100,000 shares of $.25 par value common stock. The exercise price of the stock is $18 per share and its current market price (on the date of grant) is $18. Assume that the lattice valuation share option-pricing model determines that the fair value of each share option is $8.50. It is also assumed that the expected forfeitures per year based on the entity's historical turnover rate is 2%. However, at the end of 20A3, it is believed that (based on actual experience and future expectations) the estimated forfeiture rate will improve (decrease) from 2% to 1% per year. Management, therefore, changes the estimated forfeiture rate for the entire award to 1% per year. The share options granted vest at the end of four years (explicit and requisite service period) and the options may be expected to be exercised at any time after this period. At the end of 20A4, it is determined that actual forfeitures averaged 1% per year, therefore no further adjustments are necessary. The total contractual term of the options is 10 years and the tax rate is 40%. All the share options are exercised the first day of the last year of the contract. The share price at the date of exercise is $36. The share options are considered nonqualified stock options for tax purposes. The journal entries to recognize compensation cost and all related transactions follow:

1. Estimate the number of share options that are expected to vest at the end of the four years on the date of grant (January 1, 20A1) based on the 2% annual forfeiture rate:

   100,000 share options × .98 (assuming a 2% expected forfeiture in 20A1) × .98 (20A2) × .98 (20A3) × .98 (20A4) = 92,237 share options

2. Compute the required compensation cost based on the data in this problem, assuming there is no revision in estimated forfeitures. The calculation for years 20A1–20A4 is shown below:

Year	Total Compensation Cost	Compensation Cost for the Year (Pre-Tax)	Cumulative Compensation Cost
20A1	$784,015 (92,237 × $8.50)	196,004 ($784,015/4)	196,004
20A2	$784,015	196,004	392,008
20A3	$784,015	196,004	588,012
20A4	$784,015	196,003 (rounded)	784,015

The entries that are required to be made to recognize the required compensation cost and associated deferred tax benefit for 20A1-A4 follow, assuming that the company determines that it will have sufficient taxable income in the future to realize the tax benefit.

20A1–20A4	Compensation cost	196,004	
	Paid-in-capital share options		196,004
	Deferred tax asset	78,402	
	Deferred tax benefit		78,402

Recognition of the deferred tax asset for the temporary difference related to compensation cost ($196,004 × .4).

The net-of-tax effect on income from recognizing compensation cost for 20A1–20A3 is $117,602 ($196,004–78,402) each year.

3. Now, assume instead, that at the end of 20A3, the estimated forfeiture rate used by management improves from 2% to 1%. The new estimated number of share options that are expected to vest at the end of the four years (on the date of grant) must be recalculated, based on the revised forfeiture rate of 1%:

100,000 share options × .99 (assuming an expected 1% forfeiture rate in 20A1) × .99 (20A2) × .99 (20A3) × .99 (20A4) = 96,060 share options

If the entity's estimate of forfeiture rate changes, FAS-123(R) requires that the change be accounted for as a change in estimate and its cumulative retrospective effect should be recognized in the period of the change. The year of the change in this situation is 20A3.

The calculation of compensation cost based on the revised forfeiture rate of X Company in year 20A3 is shown below. The revised forfeiture rate, as previously noted, should be accounted for as a change in estimate with cumulative retrospective effect taking place in year 20A3. For purposes of continuity, the data for years 20A1 and 20A2 are replicated as well. The final year of the service period, year 20A4, is also included.

Year	Total Compensation Cost	Compensation Cost for the Year (Pre-Tax)	Cumulative Compensation Cost
20A1	$784,015 (92,237 × $8.50)	196,004 ($784,015/4)	196,004
20A2	$784,015	196,004	392,008
20A3	$816,510 (96,060 × $8.50)	$ 220,375*	612,383
20A4	816,510	$204,127**	816,510

* ($816,510 × 3/4) – $392,008.

** $816,510/4 = $204,127.5 rounded down to $204,127 so that the cumulative compensation cost equals $816,510.

The computation to adjust for the new 1% forfeiture at December 31, 20A3 is shown below:

| Adjusted total compensation cost as of 12/31/20A3 | $816,510 (96,060 × $8.50) |

Adjusted cumulative cost that should exist as of 12/31/20A3 based on the revised forfeiture rate $612,383 ($816,510 × 3/4)

Share costs cumulatively recognized for 20A1–20A3   588,012 ($196,004 × 3)

Additional amount needed to cumulatively adjust accounts as of 12/31/20A3 $ 24,371

The following are the entries required to adjust for the new 1% forfeiture rate. The entry for 20A4 is also included.

12/31/20A3	Compensation cost	24,371	
	Paid-in-capital share options		24,371

Recognition of the adjustment needed to revise the previously recorded compensation cost to the lower forfeiture of 1%.

	Deferred tax asset	9,748	
	Deferred tax benefit		9,748

Recognition of the deferred tax asset for the temporary difference related to compensation cost (24,371 × .4).

20A4	Compensation cost	204,128	
	Paid-in-capital share options		204,128

Recognition of compensation cost for 20A4.

	Deferred tax asset	81,651	
	Paid-in-capital share options		81,651

Recognition of the deferred tax asset for the temporary difference related to compensation cost ($204,128 × .4).

After the end of the service period, actual forfeitures that took place should be determined to adjust the cumulative compensation cost for the number of shares that were vested. It is assumed in this illustrative example, that at the end of 20A4, when the award became vested, actual forfeitures actually averaged 1% per year. Therefore, no further adjustments are necessary. If the result is different, then a change to the cumulative compensation cost should be made.

Exercise of the Share Options

4. Assume that all the share options are exercised the first day of the last year (20B0) of the contractual term of the share options program. The share price at the date of exercise is $35. At the date of exercise, employees pay in the exercise price of $18 per share option and those proceeds, as well as the previously credited paid-in-capital share option

amounts, are now debited. The total is then credited to common stock and paid-in-capital in excess of par. The following entry illustrates this:

Cash	(96,060 × $18)	1,729,080	
Paid-in-capital share options		816,510	
Common stock	(96,060 × $.25)		24,015
Paid-in-capital in excess of par			2,521,575

Income Tax Considerations

5. Assume for purposes of this problem that X Company has already recognized its income tax expense for the period without considering the effects of the exercise of the employee share options that was described in the initial data. Also, assume that the company is able to deduct the difference between the market price per share and the exercise price on the date of exercise on its tax return. It may be recalled that this employee share option program is classified as a nonqualified plan. ASC 718-740-45-2 requires that realized benefits of income tax deductions in excess of the compensation cost that has already been recognized in the accounting records should be accounted for as a credit to additional paid-in-capital. X Company has sufficient taxable income to fully realize this tax deduction benefit. The amount of the tax deduction is computed based on the difference between the market price per share and the exercise per share on the date of exercise:

$$96{,}060 \text{ shares} \times (\$36 - \$18) = \$1{,}729{,}080$$

The tax benefit realized from this deduction is .4 ($1,729,080 × .4) = $691,632. The entries for the income tax effects related to the share option problem, made at the date of exercise, follow:

Deferred tax expense ($816,510 × .4)	326,604	
Deferred tax asset		326,604

Because all the share options were exercised, the benefit of the deferred tax asset related to the deductible share options can be realized at the date of exercise.

Current taxes payable	691,632	
Current tax expense		326,604
Additional paid-in-capital [($1,729,080 − $816,510) × .4] =		365,028

The credit made to additional paid-in-capital in this last entry represents the excess tax benefit due to the amount the entity may deduct on its tax return over the recognized compensation cost in the accounting records. Current tax expense and current taxes payable are also adjusted to recognize the tax benefit from the exercise of the share options.

It is important to note that if the share options were not exercised and expired, the recorded compensation cost would not have been reversed. According to ASC 718-740-35-5, resolving the deferred asset recorded on the accounting records requires that it first be written off against any additional paid-in-capital from excess tax benefits that remained on the accounting records from previously existing share option programs and with any remaining balance then accounted for as income tax expense on the income statement. (Additional information related to the tax aspects arising from share-based payments awards may be found under the heading "Tax Aspects" several sections after this.)

Cash Flow Considerations

6. Consider the implications of this problem on the statement of cash flows. ASC 718-20-55-24 (FAS-123(R)) amended FAS-95 to require that the tax benefits that have been realized as a result of excess deductible amounts on the entity's tax return over the cumulative recorded amounts in the accounting records must be shown as inflow of cash from financing activities and outflow of cash from operating activities. This is done regardless of the cash flow reporting format chosen by the entity—whether the direct or indirect method. The required disclosures relating to the problem are shown below on the Statement of Cash Flows in the last year of the contractual period (12/31/20B0)

Cash outflows from operating activities	
Excess tax benefits from employee share based option plan	($365,028)
Cash inflows from financing activities	
Excess tax benefits from employee share-based option plan	$365,028

Nonvested and Restricted Stock

Nonvested stock is stock that cannot be sold currently because the employee who was granted the shares has not yet met the vesting requirements needed to earn the right to the shares. Vesting of these shares is predicated on some sort of agreed upon consideration such as employee services. The fair value of a share of nonvested stock awarded to an employee is measured at the market price per share as if it was vested and issued on the grant date. If a restriction will be imposed after the employee has a vested right to awarded stock, the resulting shares are entitled "restricted." ASC 718-10-30-19 notes that these shares also should be measured at their fair value, which is the same amount for similarly restricted shares issued to third parties.

Employee Stock Purchase Plans

An employee stock purchase plan permits employees to buy stock at a discount. It is noncompensatory if the discount is minor (5% or less), most fulltime employees may participate, and the plan has no option features.

ASC 480-10-S99-4, *Distinguishing Liabilities from Equity: Overall*, covers the sponsor's balance sheet classification of capital stock with a put option held by any employee stock ownership plan.

ASC 718-40-15-3, 6 and 1 covers the employer's accounting for employee stock ownership plans.

Cash-Settled Share-Based Liability Awards

Some share-based compensation awards called Stock Appreciation Rights (SARs) require that an employer entity pay its recipient employee a cash amount based on only the increase in the market price of one share of the entity's stock over some previously established price. The total cash to be received by the employee is the product of the number of SARs earned times the increase. This type of arrangement is classified as a liability award. ASC 718-30-55-1 requires that the compensation cost of such a share-based payment agreement be based on the change in the award's fair value remeasured at each reporting date until the date of settlement. Depending on the amount of service that has been performed at the given reporting date, the compensation cost may be based on only a portion of the change.

According to Accounting Standards Update (ASU) No. 2010-05 (January 2010) (ASC 718, *Compensation—Stock Compensation*), *Escrowed Share Arrangements and the Presumption of Compensation*, in the case of a contract for escrowed stock that is forfeited if employees no longer work is deemed compensation. Escrowed shares may be given back to stockholders when certain conditions as to perform-ance are satisfied. In some cases, major stockholders may be involved in escrow stock contracts (ASC 718-10-S99-2).

In Accounting Standards Update (ASU) No. 2010-13 (April 2010) (ASC 718, *Compensation—Stock Compensation*), *Effect of Denominating the Exercise Price of a Share-Based Payment Award in the Currency of the Market in Which the Underlying Equity Security Trades*, liability classification is mandated in the case of a share-based payment award when the condition does not apply to service or perform-ance. A worker share-based award having an exercise price in a currency where a significant amount of the company's stock trades is not deemed a service or performance condition. Hence, liability presentation is not appropriate for the award when equity classification is required. Footnote disclosure should be made of the particulars of the award (ASC 718-10-25-14A).

Share-Based Compensation Plan Disclosures

The following disclosure parameters are adapted from ASC 718-10-50-1. They represent the salient disclosure requirements in connection with share-based compensation plans:

1. A general description of the share-based payment arrangement or arrangements, such as the terms of the award. This includes, for example, the:

   a. Service period or periods.

   b. Term of the share options.

   c. Number of authorized shares for awards.

   d. Method of measuring compensation expense from the share-based programs with employees.

2. For the current year for which an income statement is provided, the number and weighted-average exercise prices for the following categories of share options:

   a. Outstanding at the beginning and end of the year.

   b. Exercisable at the end of the year.

   c. Granted, exercised, forfeited, and expired during the year.

3. For each year for which an income statement is provided, the:

   a. Weighted-average grant-date fair value of equity options granted during the year.

   b. Total intrinsic value of options exercised.

   c. Total fair value of shares vested during the year.

4. For fully vested share options and share options expected to vest at the date of the latest balance sheet date, the:

   a. Number.

   b. Weighted-average exercise price.

   c. Aggregate intrinsic value.

   d. Weighted-average remaining contractual term of options (or shares) outstanding and currently exercisable options (or shares).

5. For each year for which an income statement is presented:

   a. A description of the method used during the year to estimate the fair value of the share-based program.

   b. A description of the significant assumptions used during the year to estimate the fair value of share-based compensation awards, including:

      (1) Expected term of share options. This should include a discussion of the method used to incorporate the contractual term of the instruments and employees' expected exercise and postvesting employment termination behavior into the fair value.

      (2) Expected volatility of the entity's shares and the method used to estimate it. If an entity uses a method that employs different volatilities during the contractual term, it must disclose the range of expected volatilities used and the weighted-average expected volatility.

      (3) Expected dividend rates. An entity that uses a method that employs different expected dividend rates during the contractual term shall disclose the range of expected dividends used and the weighted-average expected dividends.

      (4) Risk-free rates. An entity that uses a method that employs different risk-free rates shall disclose the range of risk-free rates used.

      (5) Discount for postvesting restrictions and the method for estimating it.

6. For each year for which an income statement is presented the:

  a. Total compensation cost for the share-based payment arrangement:

    (1) Recognized in income as well as its related total recognized tax benefit and

    (2) The total compensation cost capitalized as part of the cost an asset, if applicable.

  b. A description of significant modifications, including the:

    (1) Terms of the modifications.

    (2) Number of employees affected.

    (3) Total incremental compensation resulting from the modifications.

7. As of the latest balance-sheet date presented, the total compensation cost related to nonvested awards not yet recognized and the weighted-average period over which they are expected to be recognized.

8. If not separately disclosed elsewhere, the amount of cash received from exercise of share options and similar instruments granted under share-based payment arrangements and the tax benefit realized from stock options exercised during the annual period.

9. A description of the entity's policy, if any, for issuing shares upon share option exercise including the source of those shares (that is, new shares or treasury shares). If, as a result of its policy, an entity expects to repurchase shares in the following annual period, the entity shall disclose an estimate of the amount (or a range, if more appropriate) of shares to be repurchased during that period.

Tax Aspects

Compensation expense is deductible for tax purposes when paid but for book purposes when accrued. The recognition of compensation expense for financial accounting purposes over the requisite service period generates a cumulative amount on the accounting records that results in a future tax deduction. This is considered a deductible temporary difference under ASC 718-740-25-2, *Compensation—Stock Compensation: Income Taxes*. ASC 718-740-25-2 requires that the recorded deferred tax asset that is recognized as a result be evaluated for realization and be reduced by a valuation allowance account if evidence indicates that it is more likely than not that all or a part of the deferred tax asset will not be realized.

If the cumulative compensation expense recognized in the accounting records turns out to be less than the deduction reported on the entity's tax return, the amount of realized tax benefits that exceeds the recorded tax asset previously reported should be recognized as additional paid-in-capital.

DEFERRED COMPENSATION ARRANGEMENTS

ASC 710-10-05-6 covers the accounting and reporting requirements of deferred compensation contracts. Deferred compensation plans typically include such stipulations as continued employment over a predetermined time period, availability, and noncompetitive clauses. In a deferred compensation arrangement, expected benefits to be paid should be accrued as an expense and liability in the current year as the associated services are performed. If the plan is based on current and future employment, the accrued amount is based only on current-year services. Once the employee has performed all services required to have a vested right to receive the deferred compensation, the amount accrued should then be the discounted (present) value of future benefits to be paid to the worker. Accrued amounts start with the first day of employment.

If the plan pays benefits over the life of a beneficiary, the total liability depends on the life expectancy of the beneficiary or the estimated cost associated with the annuity contract to provide adequate amounts to pay the benefits.

Deferred compensation plans do not apply to pension or to post-retirement benefit plans.

EXAMPLE

An employee is hired on January 1, 20X2. The deferred compensation agreement stipulates a payment of $30,000 at the end of employment. The contract calls for employee services for at least nine months. It is expected that the employee will work three years. The discount rate is 12%.

At year-end 20X2, the employee is still working. Because the employee has worked nine months, he is eligible to cease employment and receive the deferred compensation. The accrual at year-end 20X2 is $23,916 ($30,000 × .79719), which represents the present value of the $30,000 payable at the end of two years at 12%. The two years is the initially expected service of three years less the one year (20X2) already elapsed. The entire amount of accrual is recorded as a deferred compensation cost in 20X2 because the worker is fully eligible by year-end.

Assuming the employee continues working to year-end 20X3, the accrued liability at December 31, 20X3, will be $26,786 ($30,000 × .89286), representing the discounted value of $30,000 at the end of one year at a 12% discount rate.

Thus, the cost to be recorded for 20X3 is $2,870 computed as follows:

Accrual at year-end 20X3	$26,786
Accrual at year-end 20X2	(23,916)
Compensation expense for 20X3	$ 2,870

ADVERTISING COSTS

ASC 720-35-25-1, *Other Expenses: Advertising Costs*, requires the expensing of advertising as incurred or when the advertising program first occurs. However, the cost of direct-response advertising may be deferred if the major purpose of the promotion is to elicit sales to customers who respond specifically to the advertising and for which future benefit exists. For example, the former condition is met if the response card is specially coded. The latter condition is satisfied if the resulting future revenues exceed the future costs to be incurred. The deferred advertising is amortized over the expected period of benefit using the revenue method (current-year revenue to total revenue). The cost of a billboard should also be deferred and amortized. Advertising expenditures incurred after revenue is recognized should be accrued. These advertising costs should be expensed when the related revenues are recognized.

Disclosures for advertising follow:

☐ Accounting policy for recording advertising (e.g., expense versus capitalize).

☐ Total advertising expense for each period.

☐ For direct-response advertising: description, amortization period, and amount capitalized each period; asset at each balance sheet date; and amortization expense.

SALES INCENTIVES

According to ASC 605-50-45-12 and 13, *Revenue Recognition: Customer Payments and Incentives*, resellers are allowed to report as a deduction from cost of sales the value of the consideration received for all sales incentive agreements associated with the vendor. Further, footnote disclosure is required by the reseller of the vendor's accounting policies with respect to sales arrangements.

Note: ASC 605-50-45-12 and 13 shifted vendor allowances from advertising expense to cost of sales. Thus, cash consideration received by a customer from a vendor is assumed to reduce the prices of the vendor's products or services, and thus reduce cost of sales when recognized. However, this presumption is overcome in the following two cases:

1. The customer should record the cash consideration received from the vendor as *revenue* if the consideration is for payment for assets or services delivered to the vendor by the customer.

2. The customer should record the consideration received by the vendor as a *reduction of cost of sales* if the receipt is because of a reimbursement of costs.

INSURANCE COSTS

The accounting for insurance costs relate to life insurance and casualty insurance.

Life Insurance

ASC 325-30-05-03, *Investments—Other: Investments in Insurance Contracts*, deals with the accounting for purchases of life insurance. As premiums are paid for a life insurance policy, the premiums may consist of two portions—one for insurance expense for the period applicable to the insurer's assumption of risk and the other for cash surrender value.

Cash surrender value of life insurance is the amount payable when the insured cancels the policy. The insured will obviously receive less than the premium paid. The amount to be received upon cancellation by the insured equals the cash value less borrowings against the policy less any fees associated with surrendering the policy. A change in the cash surrender value during the year is treated as an adjustment to the insurance premiums paid. The cash surrender value may also be used as collateral for a loan from the insurer. As per ASC 210-20-05-01, *Balance Sheet: Offsetting*, the cash value should be directly offset against the loans payable account in the balance sheet. Cash surrender value is usually presented under long-term investments. However, if the policy will be cashed in within the next year, the cash surrender value will be reported under current assets.

EXAMPLE

The difference between the premium paid and the amount attributable to the cash surrender value represents insurance expense. If the premium paid is $20,000 and $4,000 of that amount is attributable to the increase in cash surrender value, the journal entry is:

Life insurance expense	16,000	
Cash surrender value	4,000	
Cash		20,000

When the insured dies, the insurer pays the beneficiary the face value of the policy less any associated borrowings against the policy less any redemption fees.

If insurance premium payments are made in a policy that does not transfer risk to the insurer, the payments are considered deposits receivable and presented as an asset.

ASC 325-30-05-2 through 05-9 and 325-30-35-3 through 5, *Investments—Other: Investments in Insurance Contracts*, require that the determination of the amount realizable under an insurance contract (1) take into account any additional amounts (beyond cash surrender value) included in the policy's contractual terms and (2) be based on assumed surrender at the individual policy or certificate level. If it is probable that contractual restrictions would limit the amount that could be realized, such contractual limitations should be considered and any amounts recoverable at the insurance company's discretion should be excluded from the amount that could be realized.

ASC 715-60-05-15, 715-60-35-181 through 35-183, 715-60-55-178 and 55-180, 715-60-35-184 and 35-185, and 715-60-55-181, *Compensation—Retirement Benefits:*

Defined Benefit Plans—Other Postretirement, require an employer to recognize a liability for the postretirement benefit provided by a collateral assignment split-dollar life insurance arrangement. An asset may be recognized when appropriate.

Casualty Insurance

Casualty insurance is taken out for fire or flood losses. This insurance reimburses the policy holder for the fair market value of destroyed property. Insurance companies usually have a coinsurance provision so the insured is responsible for a portion of the loss. The insurance reimbursement formula assuming an 80% coinsurance provision follows:

$$\frac{\text{Face of Policy}}{.80 \times \text{Fair Market Value of Insured Property}} \times \text{Fair Value of Loss} = \frac{\text{Possible}}{\text{Reimbursement}}$$

The insurance recovery is based on the lower of the face of the policy, fair market value of the loss, or possible reimbursement.

EXAMPLE

Case	Face of Policy	Fair Market Value of Property	Fair Market Value of Loss
1	$ 8,000	$20,000	$12,000
2	3,000	5,000	5,000
3	30,000	30,000	12,000

Insurance reimbursement follows:

Case A: $\dfrac{\$8,000}{.8 \times \$20,000} \times \$12,000 = \$6,000$

Answer = $6,000

Case B: $\dfrac{\$3,000}{.8 \times \$5,000} \times \$5,000 = \$3,750$

Answer = $3,000

Case C: $\dfrac{\$30,000}{.8 \times \$30,000} \times \$12,000 = \$15,000$

Answer = $ 12,000

EXAMPLE

A blanket policy of $22,000 relates to machinery A and B. The fair values of the machinery are $45,000 and $25,000, respectively. Machinery B is partly destroyed, causing a fire loss of $5,000.

The policy allocated to machinery B is determined as follows:

	Fair Market Value	Policy
Machinery A	$45,000	$14,143
Machinery B	25,000	7,857
Total	$70,000	$22,000

Insurance reimbursement equals:

$$\frac{\$7,857}{.8 \times \$25,000} \times \$5,000 = \$1,964$$

Answer = $1,964

When there is fire damage, the destroyed asset must be removed from the accounts, with the ensuring fire loss recorded based on book value. The insurance reimbursement reduces the fire loss. The fire loss is presented as an extraordinary item (net of tax).

EXAMPLE

XYZ Company experienced a fire. Inventory costing $10,000 was completely destroyed. The inventory was not insured. Equipment costing $20,000 with accumulated depreciation of $2,000 and having a fair market value of $14,000 is fully destroyed. The policy is for $20,000. A building costing $60,000 with accumulated depreciation of $6,000 and having a fair market value of $40,000 is half destroyed. The face of the policy is $30,000. The journal entries to record the book loss are:

Fire loss	10,000	
Inventory		10,000
Fire loss	18,000	
Accumulated depreciation	2,000	
Equipment		20,000
Fire loss	27,000	
Accumulated depreciation	3,000	
Building		30,000

Insurance reimbursement totals $32,750, calculated as follows:

Equipment: $\dfrac{\$20,000}{.8 \times \$14,000} \times \$14,000 = \$25,000$

Answer = $14,000

Building: $\dfrac{\$30,000}{.8 \times \$40,000} \times \$20,000 = \$18,750$

Answer = $18,750

The journal entry for the insurance reimbursement is:

| cash | 32,750 | |
| Fire loss | | 32,750 |

The net fire loss is $22,250 ($55,000 − $32,750).

As per ASC 720-20-05-01, *Other Expenses: Insurance Costs,* amounts paid for retroactive insurance should be expensed immediately, and a receivable should be recorded at the same time for anticipated recoveries applicable to the underlying event.

Business Interruption Insurance

ASC 225-30-50-1, *Income Statement: Business Interruption Insurance,* requires disclosure of the event resulting in losses due to business interruption as well as the total amount received from insurance and where such amounts are presented in the income statement.

RESTRUCTURING CHARGES

Securities and Exchange Commission (SEC) Staff Accounting Bulletin No. 67 requires restructuring charges to be expensed and presented as an element in computing income from operations.

In general, an expense and liability should be accrued for employee termination benefits in a restructuring. Disclosure should be made of the group and the number of workers laid off.

An exit plan requires the recognition of a liability for the restructuring charges incurred if there is no future benefit to continuing operations. The expense for the estimated costs should be made on the commitment date of the exit plan. Expected gains from assets to be sold in connection with the exit plan should be recorded in the year realized. These gains are *not* allowed to offset the accrued liability for exit costs. Exit costs incurred are presented as a separate item as part of income from continuing operations. Disclosures associated with an exit plan include the terms of the exit plan, description and amount of exit costs incurred, activities to be exited from, method of disposition, expected completion date, and liability adjustments.

COSTS ASSOCIATED WITH EXIT OR DISPOSAL ACTIVITIES

ASC 420-10-05-3, *Exit or Disposal Cost Obligations: Overall,* replaces EITF Consensus Summary No. 94-3. ASC 420-10-05-3 applies to costs (e.g., certain employee service costs, lease termination costs) associated with a discontinued operation, restructuring, plant closing, or other exit or disposal activity. Such costs must be recognized as incurred based on fair value along with the related liability. Thus, the company must actually incur the liabilities before recognition may be made.

The fair value of a liability is the amount the liability can be settled for in a current transaction between willing parties, that is, other than in a forced or liquidation transaction. The best indication of fair value is quoted market prices in active markets.

In years after initial measurement, changes to the liability should be measured based on the credit-adjusted risk-free rate that was used to initially measure the liability. The cumulative effect of a change arising from revising either the timing or the amount of estimated cash flows shall be recognized as an adjustment to the liability in the year of change and reported in the same line item(s) in the income statements used when the associated costs were recognized initially. Changes arising from the passage of time shall be recognized as an increase in the carrying value of the liability and as an expense.

Examples of costs associated with the exit or disposal activity include contract termination costs, one-time employee termination benefits, and costs to consolidate facilities or relocate employees.

Costs applicable to exit or disposal activities are included in income from continuing operations unless they apply to discontinued operations. If there is an occurrence that discharges a company's duty to settle a liability for a cost applicable to an exit or disposal activity recognized in a previous year, the liability and the related costs are reversed.

Footnote disclosure includes:

☐ A description of the exit or disposal activity and the anticipated completion date.

☐ For each major type of cost applicable to the exit activity, the total cost anticipated, the amount incurred in the current year, and the cumulative amount to date.

☐ Reconciliation of the beginning and ending liability balances presenting the changes during the year applicable to costs incurred and charged to expense, costs paid or otherwise settled, and any modifications of the liability along with the reasons of doing so.

☐ Where in the income statement or the statement of activities the costs are presented.

☐ If a liability for a cost is not recorded because fair value is not reasonably estimated, that should be noted along with the reasons.

WEB SITE DEVELOPMENT COSTS

As per ASC 350-50-55-1, *Intangibles—Goodwill and Other: Website Development Costs*, Web site development is segregated into three stages (activities) that affect the accounting treatment for expenditures incurred. During the initial stage, planning, the costs incurred are expensed. Development is the second stage, and it is here that the costs for Web application and infrastructure as well as graphics development are capitalized and then amortized once the Web site is ready for its intended use. (Costs to develop the content for the Web site may be capitalized or expensed, depending on the circumstances.) In the third stage of postimplementation, work is performed after the site is put into service (e.g., security, training, administration) and related costs are expensed as incurred. Also in the third stage are expenditures for additional upgrades and features once the Web site is launched; such costs attributable are capitalized if the upgrades and enhancements furnish *additional functionality*.

INCOME STATEMENT PRESENTATION STARTING WITH INCOME FROM CONTINUING OPERATIONS

The income statement is shown in the following form beginning with income from continuing operations before taxes:

Income from continuing operations before taxes

Less: Taxes

Income from continuing operations

Discontinued operations

> Loss or gain from operations of discontinued component (including loss or gain on disposal)
>
> Less: Taxes
>
> Loss or gain from discontinued operations

Income before extraordinary item

Extraordinary item (net of tax)

Net income

> Less: Net income attributable to the noncontrolling interest
>
> Net income attributable to the controlling interest

ASC 260-10-50-1, *Earnings Per Share: Overall*, requires earnings per share disclosures for income from continuing operations, income before extraordinary items, and net income. If an entity has discontinued operations and extraordinary items as well, per share disclosures for those amounts may be shown either on the face of the income statement or in the notes to the financial statements.

Note: Equity in earnings of investees must be presented separately.

DISCONTINUED OPERATIONS AND RELATED DISPOSAL OF LONG-LIVED ASSET CONSIDERATIONS

ASC 205-20-45-3, *Presentation of Financial Statements: Discontinued Operations*, requires that a long-lived asset that is to be sold by a company should be classified as *held for sale* when the following considerations are satisfied. If they are not all met (except as permitted by exceptions), the long-lived asset should be reclassified as held and used. The six considerations are:

1. Management agrees and commits to a plan to sell the asset. It is assumed that management has the requisite authority to approve such a commitment.

2. The asset is available for immediate sale in its present condition, restricted only by conditions that are usual and customary for sales of such assets. For example, an entity commits to sell land and a related building complex. It is believed that the time necessary to vacate the building will take a month, an amount of time that is considered usual and customary for such assets. The assets would be considered available for immediate sale at the plan commitment date. However, this status would not exist if the sale were predicated on the completion of a new building that the entity was planning to move into. The entity could not vacate the old building until the new one was complete. This constraint implies that

the available-for-immediate-sale criterion would not have been met and could be met only when the construction of the new building was complete and ready to be moved into.

3. An active program has been initiated by the selling company to complete the sale.

4. Management considers the sale of the asset likely to occur. In addition, the time frame for recognition as a completed sales transaction is within one year unless circumstances beyond the entity's control would extend the period beyond this limit. For example, assuming that a leasing and finance company is currently holding equipment that has recently come off lease, it has not yet been decided whether the equipment should be sold or leased in the future. Because the form of the future transaction (sale or lease) has not yet been determined, the plan-of-sale criterion has not been met. (There is uncertainty as to whether the asset will be sold at all.) Exceptions to the one-year requirement are discussed in the following section.

5. The asset or group is currently being marketed at a price that is reasonable in relation to its fair value.

6. Based on information related to the plan to sell the asset or group, it is improbable that the plan will be withdrawn or that significant modifications will be made.

Exceptions to the One-Year Requirement That Must Exist for Held-for-Sale Classification

The following events and circumstances are considered beyond an entity's control and extend the period that is required by GAAP to complete the sale of a long-lived asset or group beyond one year:

☐ An entity commits to a plan to sell a long-lived asset or group and expects that others (other than a buyer) will impose conditions on the transfer that will extend the period required to complete the sale and that (1) these conditions cannot be influenced until after a firm purchase commitment is obtained, and (2) the receipt of the firm purchase commitment is expected to occur within one year. For example, it is assumed that a regional utility plans to sell a group of assets that represents a significant portion of its operation. This action requires regulatory approval and therefore is expected to require more than one year to complete the sale. The one-year sale period requirement clearly will not be satisfied. Nevertheless, because approval of the sale cannot commence until after a buyer is identified and has given a firm purchase commitment, and because the receipt of said purchase commitment is probable within one year, the criteria for extending the sale of the asset beyond one year are satisfied.

☐ A firm purchase commitment is obtained, and the buyer or others impose (unexpectedly) conditions on the transfer of the asset already classified as held for sale that will potentially extend the period required to consummate the sale. If (1) responsive actions to the delaying conditions have commenced or will commence on a timely basis, and (2) a favorable outcome to the delaying conditions is expected, then the period required to complete the sale of the asset may be extended beyond one year. For example, management commits to sell a plant and classifies the group of assets as held for sale. After a firm purchase commitment is obtained from the buyer, it is determined that extensive water damage exists as a result of long-term corrosion of the foundation that was previously unknown to the seller or buyer. The buyer requires that the seller repair the damage before the sale can be closed. However, it is estimated that the repairs will extend the period required to complete the sale beyond the one-year limit. The seller has already begun the repair of the damage and there is very little doubt that it will be completed to the total satisfaction of the buyer. The criteria for extending the sale of the asset beyond one year are satisfied.

☐ Circumstances arise that were previously considered unlikely during the initial one-year period. As a result, the long-lived asset that was classified as held for sale is not sold at the end of that period, and (1) the entity initiated actions to respond to a change in circumstances within the initial one-year period; (2) the asset is being actively marketed at a price that is considered reasonable given the change of circumstances; and (3) all the criteria for a held-for-sale classification have been met. For example, an asset is held for sale and is not sold at the end of the one-year period because market conditions that existed at the date of classification have deteriorated. The entity did not receive any reasonable offers to buy the asset during the initial period and, as a result, reduced its asking price. The asset continues to be marketed at a price that is reasonable given the downturn in market conditions. In these circumstances, the asset would continue to be classified as held for sale.

Other Held-for-Sale Considerations

If a newly acquired long-lived asset will be sold rather than held for use, it may be classified as such (held for sale) at the date of acquisition if (1) the one year requirement is met (unless the current circumstances satisfy the exception criteria) and (2) any other of the six criteria required for held-for-sale classification not met on that date are deemed likely to be met within a short period (usually three months) following acquisition.

If the six criteria required for held-for-sale classification are met in the subsequent events period (after the balance sheet date but before the financial statements are issued), the long-lived assets should continue to be classified as held and used in the financial statements when they are issued. If the asset is tested for recoverability on a held-and-used basis as of the balance sheet date, the estimates of future cash flows used in that test, including the cash flow from the future sale of the asset, should be considered as of the balance sheet date. This assessment made as of the balance sheet date should not be revised for a decision to sell the asset after the balance sheet date. In addition, if the carrying value of the asset exceeds its fair value at the balance sheet date, an impairment loss should be recognized.

Held-for-Sale Measurement Considerations

A held-for-sale long-lived asset or group should be measured *at the lower of its carrying amount or fair value less cost to sell* (see next paragraph). If newly acquired, the carrying value should be based on its fair value less cost to sell at the acquisition date. During the time it is classified as held for sale, a long-lived asset should not be depreciated.

Cost to sell includes broker commissions, legal and title transfer fees, and closing costs that must be incurred before legal title can be transferred. These costs do not include any expected future losses associated with the operations of the long-lived asset while it is classified as being held for sale. A loss should be recognized and result in a downward adjustment to the carrying value of a long-lived asset for any initial or subsequent write-down to fair value less cost to sell. The carrying value should be written up for any subsequent increase in fair value less cost to sell but may never exceed the cumulative loss previously recognized. The gain or loss that is realized from the actual sale of a long-lived asset (that has not been previously recognized) should be recognized at the date of sale.

EXAMPLE

X Corporation decides to sell one of its *components* (a component comprises operations and cash flows that can be clearly distinguished, operationally and for financial reporting purposes, from the rest of the entity; also see the discussion on components in the subsection titled "Discontinued Operations" presented later) on June 15, 20X1, and classifies this disposal group as "held for sale." At that date, the company reviews the fair value of the component to determine whether its carrying value needs to be adjusted downward. GAAP requires that a loss and downward adjustment to the carrying value of a long-lived asset group be recognized for any write-down to fair value less cost to sell. The carrying value of the component is $700,000 and its fair value is $700,000. The cost to sell is approximated to be $35,000. A loss of $35,000 and corresponding write-down of carrying value is computed in the following way. The fair value less cost to sell is $665,000 ($700,000 – $35,000), which is less than its carrying value ($665,000<$700,000). Therefore, the carrying value of the component is reduced only by the estimated cost to sell of $35,000. The loss to be recognized is $35,000 and the new carrying value of the disposal group is $665,000 ($700,000 –$35,000).

At the end of the year (December 31, 20X1), the company once again tests to see if the carrying value (adjusted) of the held-for-sale component exceeds fair value less cost to sell. The fair value of the component is now determined to be $685,000 and the estimated cost to sell remains at $35,000. The loss to be recognized is $15,000 ($665,000 – [$685,000 – $35,000]), and the new carrying value of the disposal group is determined to be $650,000. X Corporation would report a total loss for 20X1 relating to its decision to sell its component as $50,000 ($35,000 +$15,000).

Events and circumstances beyond the entity's control extend the period required to complete the sale of the component beyond one year. The fair value of the component at December 31, 20X2, has risen to $765,000. In addition, the estimated cost to sell remains at $35,000. A gain for the period should be recognized for $50,000 ([$765,000 – $35,000] – $650,000 = $80,000, but it is restricted to the previously recognized cumulative loss of $50,000 ($35,000 + $15,000). The adjusted carrying value of the component in this instance is $700,000 ($650,000 + $50,000). FAS-144 requires that a gain be recognized for any subsequent increase in fair value less cost to sell, but not in excess of the cumulative loss previously recognized for a write-down to fair value less cost to sell. Because the cumulative loss previously recognized (due to a write-down to fair value) was $50,000, the recognized recovery should be limited to this amount even though the fair value rose in excess of the original fair value ($700,000).

Changing the Decision to Sell

If an entity decides not to sell a long-lived asset that it previously had classified as held for sale, the asset should be reclassified as held and used and should be valued at the lower of its carrying value (before the asset was classified as held for sale and adjusted for any depreciation expense that would have been recognized had the assets been continuously classified as held and used) or fair value at the date of the subsequent decision not to sell. The adjustment to the carrying value should be included in income from continuing operations in the period in which the entity changed its decision not to sell. If a component of an entity is reclassified as held and used, it should be included in income from continuing operations for all periods presented.

If an entity decides to remove an individual asset or liability from a disposal group that was classified as held for sale, the remaining assets and liabilities of the disposal group should continue to be measured as a group, as long as the six held-for-sale criteria continue to be satisfied. If said criteria are not satisfied, the remaining assets should be measured individually at the lower of their carrying amounts or fair values less cost to sell at that date.

Discontinued Operations

For purposes of reporting discontinued operations, a component of an entity consists of operations and cash flows that can be clearly distinguished operationally and financially (from a reporting perspective) from the rest of the entity. A component of an entity may be (1) a reportable segment or an operating segment (ASC 280-10-50-10, *Segment Reporting: Overall*); (2) a reporting unit (ASC 350-20-55-1); (3) a subsidiary; or (4) asset group as discussed in this statement. For example, if an entity manufactures and markets consumer products that have several product groups each with different product lines and brands, a product group for that entity is the lowest level at which the operations and cash flow can be clearly distinguished operationally and financially from the rest of the entity. Each product group of the entity would be considered a component of an entity for purposes of reporting in discontinued operations. Other illustrations of components that would and would not qualify for component classification are discussed in the next section.

Classification as a Discontinued Operation

When a component of an entity has been disposed of or is classified as held for sale, its results of operations should be reported in the discontinued operations section of the entity's income statement if the two following criteria are met:

1. The operations and cash flows of the component have been or will be eliminated from the ongoing operations of the entity as a result of the disposal; and

2. The entity will not have any significant continuing involvement in the operations of the component after the disposal.

The following are examples of scenarios that do and do not qualify for discontinued operations reporting:

☐ An entity makes the decision to leave the electronics business and decides to sell its entire product group with its operations. Its electronics business is classified as held for sale at this date. After it is sold, the operations and cash flow of the product group will be eliminated from the ongoing operations of the entity and the entity will not have continuing involvement in the operations of the business. While the electronics business is classified as held for sale, it should be reported in the discontinued operation section of the income statement. If, on the other hand, the company decides not to discontinue its entire electronic business but to sell only the brands of the product group that are losing money, discontinued operations disclosure would not be warranted. The reason for this is that the failing brands are only a part of a larger cash-flow-generating product group of the entity and by themselves could not be so classified. Therefore, the losing brands do not represent a component of the entity and should not be disclosed as a discontinued operation.

☐ An entity owns and operates a group of small factories around the country that manufactures products for the home. For that entity, each factory represents the lowest level at which operations and cash flows as can be distinguished operational and for financial statement reporting purposes from the rest of the entity. In this situation, each factory represents a component of the entity. The entity decides to expand its operations and open a larger factory that replaces a smaller factory. The larger factory will continue to manufacture the products that the other smaller one did in addition to other related products that were not produced. Although each factory does represent a component of the entity, the closure of a smaller factory should not be reported in the discontinued operations of the entity, because the operations and cash flows from the manufacture of products for the home through the smaller factory will not be eliminated from the ongoing operations of the entity but will be perpetuated in the expanded factory.

☐ An entity that manufactures sporting goods has several divisions, one of which is a ski division that designs, manufactures, and distributes skis. Each division is the lowest level at which operations and cash flows can be easily distinguished from the ongoing operation of the entity. Therefore, the ski division is a component of the entity. The entity decides to remain in the ski business but outsource the manufacturing operations and commits itself to sell the ski-related manufacturing operations. At that date, the manufacturing facility is classified as held for sale. Because the ski manufacturing facility is only part of the larger cash-generating ski component and therefore by itself not a component of the entity, the manufacturing operations alone would not be disclosed as discontinued operations. In addition, even if the ski manufacturing operations qualified as a component of the entity, the decision to outsource the manufacturing operations alone would not be sufficient to include it in the discontinued operations section of the income statement, because this action would not eliminate the operations and cash flows of the ski division from the ongoing operations of the entity.

Reporting the Gain or Loss from Operations of the Discontinued Component

When the component of an entity either has been disposed of or is classified as held for sale, the income statement of the entity for the current and prior periods should report the results of operations of the component, including any gain or loss on disposal in the discontinued operations section of the income statement. The results of operations of a component classified as held for sale should be reported in discontinued operations in the period in which they occur. In addition, the results of operations less applicable income taxes (benefit) should be reported as a separate component of income after income from continuing operations and before extraordinary items and the cumulative effect of accounting changes if applicable. The following is an example of a format that may be followed:

Income from continuing operations before income taxes	$XXXX	
Income taxes	XXX	
Income from continuing operations		$XXXX
Discontinued operations (note X)		
Loss from operations of the discontinued Component Y (including loss on disposal of $XXX)		XXXX
Income tax benefit		XXX
Loss on discontinued operations		$XXXX
Net income		$XXXX
Less: Net income attributable to the noncontrolling interest		(XXX)
Net income attributable to the controlling interest		$XXX

The gain or loss on disposal may be disclosed either on the face of the income statement (as shown in the preceding example) or in the notes to the financial statements. If the disposal of a component of an entity took place in a prior period and adjustments to this previously reported amount must be made, it should be disclosed separately in the current period in discontinued operations. In addition, the nature and amount of such adjustments must be disclosed (e.g., the settlement of employee benefit plan obligations such as pension, post-employment benefits other than pensions, and other postemployment benefits that are directly related to the disposal transaction).

EXAMPLE

X Corporation's held-for-sale component (discussed in the example from the previous Held-for-Sale Measurement Considerations section) is sold on December 2, 20X3, and meets both criteria for discontinued operations disclosure. The proceeds of the sale of the component is $730,000 (sales price of $765,000 less cost to sell of $35,000). In addition, the results of operations of the discontinued component resulted in a loss of $360,000 during 20X3 (January 1 through December 2, 20X3). The gain on the sale of the discontinued component is $30,000 (net proceeds of $730,000 less carrying value of $700,000 at December 31, 20X2). For disclosure purposes, the loss from operations of the discontinued component nets to $330,000 ($360,000 – $30,000). It would be disclosed in the discontinued operations section of the entity's income statement as follows:

Income from operations before income taxes		$XXXX
Income taxes		XXX
Income from continuing operations		$XXXX
Discontinued operations (note X)		
Loss from operations of discontinued operations (including gain on disposal of $30,000)	$330,000	
Less income tax benefit (40% tax rate)	132,000	
Loss on discontinued operations		198,000

Other considerations. A recognized gain or loss from a disposal that is not considered a component of an entity should be included in income from continuing operations before income taxes. All long-lived assets that are classified as held for sale should be presented separately in the balance sheet. In addition, the assets and liabilities of a disposal group that are classified as held for sale must be presented separately in the asset and liability sections of the balance sheet. They should not be offset and presented as a single amount. The major classes of assets and liabilities classified as held for sale should be separately disclosed either on the face of the balance sheet or in the notes to the financial statements.

ASC 205-20-45-3, *Presentation of Financial Statements: Discontinued Operations*, and 360-10-55-42, *Property, Plant, and Equipment: Overall*, provide guidance on when a component of an entity should be reported in discontinued operations if the entity will have cash flows from, or continuing involvement in, the component that is disposed of or held for sale. Classification of a disposed component is appropriate only if the ongoing entity has *no* continuing direct cash flows and does *not* retain an interest, contract, or other arrangement to enable it to exercise significant influence over the disposed component's operating and financial policies after the disposal transaction.

Reporting and Disclosure—Long-Lived Asset or Disposal Group That Has Been Sold or Is Classified for Sale

The following data should be disclosed in the notes to the financial statements in the period in which a long-lived asset or disposal group either has been sold or is classified for sale:

☐ A description of the facts and data leading to the expected disposal, the expected manner and timing of that disposal, and if not separately presented on the face of the statement, the carrying amounts of the major classes of assets and liabilities included as part of a disposal group.

☐ The loss recognized for any initial or subsequent write-down to fair value less cost to sell or the gain recognized for any subsequent increase in fair value less cost to sell, but not in excess of the cumulative loss previously recognized as a result of a write-down to fair value. If the long-lived asset (disposal group) has been sold, the gain or loss not previously recognized from the sale should be recognized at the date of sale. If the gain or loss is not separately presented on the face of the income statement, the disclosure should include the caption in the income statement that includes that gain or loss.

☐ The amounts of revenue and pretax profit or loss reported in discontinued operations, if applicable.

☐ The reportable segment in which the long-lived asset or disposal group is reported, if applicable (ASC 280-10-50-1).

EXTRAORDINARY GAINS AND LOSSES

Extraordinary items are material in nature and are both infrequent (not expected to occur in the foreseeable future) and unusual (abnormal, not typical) given the environment of the company. The corporate environment considers such factors as industry attributes, geographic locality, regulatory requirements, economic characteristics, lines of business, and nature of operations. **Note:** An occurrence is not deemed unusual just because it is beyond management's control. Extraordinary items are presented net of tax. Earnings per share is shown on them. What is extraordinary for one company may not necessarily be extraordinary for another. In some cases, amounts reported for extraordinary items are based on estimates and may need adjustment in later years.

Materiality is a concern. In applying materiality, items should be examined individually rather than in the aggregate. However, if the items arise from one particular event, they may be combined.

Examples of extraordinary items follow:

☐ Gain on troubled debt restructuring.

☐ Gain on certain types of life insurance proceeds.

☐ Catastrophe and casualty losses (e.g., earthquake, fire).

☐ Loss arising from a prohibition because of a new law or regulation.

☐ Loss from governmental expropriation of property.

☐ Gain or loss on the disposal of a major part of the assets of the previously separate companies arising from a business combination that are disposed of within two years subsequent to the consummation date.

☐ Receipt of Federal Home Loan Mortgage Corporation participating preferred stock.

☐ Write-off of interstate operating rights of motor carriers.

Note: Losses on inventory and receivables relate to the normal operations of a business and thus are not extraordinary. However, such losses would be extraordinary if they arose from a catastrophe (e.g., hurricane) or from government seizure or government-forced destruction (e.g., the government forces a company to destroy its existing inventory of a certain chemical just proven to cause cancer).

The following items are *not* considered extraordinary:

☐ Impact of a strike.

☐ Modifications to long-term contracts.

☐ Costs incurred to defend against a takeover attempt as per ASC 225-20-55-4, *Income Statement: Extraordinary and Unusual Items*.

Disclosures required for extraordinary items include the nature of the transaction and the major considerations in determining the amounts.

FAS-4, *Reporting Gains and Losses from Extinguishment of Debt*, was repealed by ASC 470-50-45-1, *Debt: Modifications and Extinguishments*. As a result, gains and losses from early extinguishment of debt are no longer considered extraordinary. A recent study indicated that the bulk of extraordinary items reported by companies were, in fact, gains and losses from early extinguishment of debt. As a result, very few public companies have reported extraordinary items subsequent to passage of ASC 470-50-45-1.[*]

EARNINGS PER SHARE

ASC 260-10, *Earnings Per Share: Overall*, covers the computation, reporting, and disclosures associated with earnings per share. It requires public companies to present earnings per share on the face of the income statement. (Nonpublic entities are not required to present earnings per share.) If the entity's capital structure is simple—that is, it has no potentially dilutive securities—only basic earnings per share needs to be disclosed. However, if the capital structure is complex (it includes potentially dilutive securities), then presentation of both basic and diluted earnings per share is mandated.

---

[*] Henry, T.F., Holtzman, M.P., "Extraordinary Items Share Exclusive Company," *Journal of Accountancy*, May 2007, 80–83.

Basic earnings per share takes into account only the actual number of outstanding common shares during the period (and those contingently issuable in certain cases).

Diluted earnings per share includes the effect of common shares actually outstanding and the impact of convertible securities, stock options, stock warrants, and their equivalents if dilutive. Diluted earnings per share should not assume the conversion, exercise, or contingent issuance of securities having an antidilutive effect (increasing earnings per share or decreasing loss per share) because it violates conservatism.

According to ASC 260-10-05-5, *Earnings Per Share: Overall*, under the two-class method, the presentation of basic and diluted earnings per share for all participating securities is not required. ASC 260-10-45, 59A-60, 55 and 71-75 states that a participating security is one that may participate in undistributed earnings with common stock, whether that participation is conditional upon an event happening or not. The participation need *not* be a dividend, so any form of participation in earnings would qualify. Allocation of earnings is based on a predetermined formula with, at times, an upper limit on the extent of participation. EITF requires the two-class method to compute earnings per share for companies with participating securities or multiple classes of common stock.

Basic Earnings per Share

Basic earnings per share equals net income available to common stockholders divided by the weighted-average number of common shares outstanding. Net income available to common stockholders is net income less declared preferred stock dividends for the current year. If the preferred stock is noncumulative, preferred stock dividends are subtracted only if they are declared during the period. On the other hand, if the preferred stock is cumulative, the dividends are subtracted even if they are not declared in the current year. The weighted-average number of common shares outstanding is determined by multiplying the number of shares issued and outstanding for any time period by a fraction, the numerator being the number of months the shares have been outstanding and the denominator being the number of months in the period (e.g., 12 months for annual reporting).

EXAMPLE

On January 1, 20X2, 100,000 shares were issued. On October 1, 20X2, 10,000 of those shares were reacquired. The weighted-average common shares outstanding equals 97,500 shares, computed as follows:

1/1/20X2–9/30/20X2	$(100,000 \times 9/12)$	75,000
10/1/20X2–12/31/20X2	$(90,000 \times 3/12)$	22,500
Weighted outstanding common shares		97,500

EXAMPLE

On January 1, 20X2, 10,000 shares were issued. On April 1, 20X2, 2,000 of those shares were bought back. The weighted-average common stock outstanding is 8,500 shares computed as follows:

1/1/20X2–3/31/20X2	(10,000 × 3/12)	2,500
4/1/20X2–12/31/20X2	(8,000 × 9/12)	6,000
Weighted outstanding common shares		8,500

If a stock dividend or stock split has been issued for the period, it is presumed that such stock dividend or split was issued at the beginning of the period. Thus, stock dividends or stock splits are weighted for the entire period, regardless of the fact that they were issued during the period. Further, when comparative financial statements are prepared, the issuance of a stock dividend or stock split requires retroactive restatement of each previous year's earnings per share to give effect to the dividend or split for those prior years.

EXAMPLE

The following occurred during the year regarding common stock:

Shares outstanding—1/1	30,000
2-for-1 stock split—4/1	30,000
Shares issued—8/1	5,000

The common shares to be used in the denominator of basic EPS is 62,083 shares, computed as follows:

1/1–3/31	30,000 × 3/12 × 2	15,000
4/1–8/1	60,000 × 4/12	20,000
8/1–12/31	65,000 × 5/12	27,083
Total		62,083

EXAMPLE

On December 1, 20X2, a company declared and issued an 8% stock dividend on its 200,000 outstanding common shares. The number of common shares to be used in determining basic EPS is $216,000 (200,000 shares × 108%).

EXAMPLE

In 20X3, a 15% stock dividend occurs. The weighted-average shares used for previous years' computations has to be increased by 15% to make basic EPS comparable.

EXAMPLE

The following information is presented for a company:

Preferred stock, $10 par, 6% cumulative, 30,000 shares issued and outstanding	$300,000
Common stock, $5 par, 100,000 shares issued and outstanding	500,000
Net income	400,000

The company paid a cash dividend on preferred stock. The preferred dividend would therefore equal $18,000 (6% × $300,000). Basic EPS equals $3.82, computed as follows:

EARNINGS AVAILABLE TO COMMON STOCKHOLDERS

Net income	$400,000
Less: preferred dividends	(18,000)
Earnings available to common stockholders	$382,000

Basic EPS = $382,000/100,000 shares = $3.82.

EXAMPLE

On January 1, 20X2, Dauber Company had the following shares outstanding:

6% Cumulative preferred stock, $100 par value	150,000 shares
Common stock, $5 par value	500,000 shares

During the year, the following occurred:

- ☐ On April 1, 20X2, the company issued 100,000 shares of common stock.
- ☐ On September 1, 20X2, the company declared and issued a 10% stock dividend.
- ☐ For the year ended December 31, 20X2, the net income was $2,200,000.

Basic earnings per share for 20X2, equals $2.06 ($1,300,000/ 632,500 shares), calculated as follows:

EARNINGS AVAILABLE TO COMMON STOCKHOLDERS

Net income		$2,200,000
Less: preferred dividend	(150,000 shares × $6)	(900,000)
Earnings available to common stockholders		$1,300,000

WEIGHTED-AVERAGE NUMBER OF OUTSTANDING COMMON SHARES

1/1/20X2–3/31/20X2	(500,000 × 3/12 × 110%)	137,500

4/1/20X2–8/31/20X2	(600,000 × 5/12 × 110%)	275,000
9/1/20X2–12/31/20X2	(660,000 × 4/12)	220,000
Weighted-average outstanding common shares		632,500

Diluted Earnings per Share

If potentially dilutive securities are outstanding, such as convertible bonds, convertible preferred stock, stock options, or stock warrants, both basic and diluted earnings per share must be presented.

In the case of convertible securities, the *if-converted method* must be used. Under this approach, it is assumed that the dilutive convertible security is converted into common stock at the beginning of the period or date of issue, if later. If conversion is assumed, the interest expense (net of tax) that would have been incurred on the convertible bonds must be added back to net income in the numerator. Any dividend on convertible preferred stock would also be added back (dividend savings) to net income in the numerator. The add-back of interest expense (net of tax) on convertible bonds and preferred dividends on convertible preferred stock results in an adjusted net income figure used to determine earnings per share. Correspondingly, the number of common shares the convertible securities are convertible into (or their weighted-average effect if conversion to common stock actually took place during the year) must also be added to the weighted-average outstanding common shares in the denominator.

ASC 260-10-55-1, *Earnings Per Share: Overall*, provides that issued securities with embedded conversion features (e.g., contingently convertible debt or preferred stock) contingently exercisable upon the occurrence of a market-price condition should be part of the computation of diluted EPS irrespective of whether the market price trigger has been satisfied.

In the case of dilutive stock options, stock warrants, or their equivalent, the *treasury stock method* is used. Under this approach, there is a presumption that the option or warrant was exercised at the beginning of the period, or date of issue if later. The assumed proceeds received from the exercise of the option or warrant are assumed to be used to buy treasury stock at the average market price for the period. However, exercise is presumed to occur only if the average market price of the underlying shares during the period is greater than the exercise price of the option or warrant. This presumption ensures that the assumed exercise of a stock option or warrant will have a dilutive effect on the earnings-per-share computation. Correspondingly, the denominator of diluted earnings-per-share increases by the number of shares assumed issued owing to the exercise of options or warrants reduced by the assumed treasury shares purchased.

EXAMPLE

One hundred shares are under a stock option plan at an exercise price of $10. The average market price of stock during the period is $25. Exercise is presumed to occur because the average market price of the stock for the period

($25) is greater than the exercise price ($10). The assumed issuance of common shares is computed as 60, as follows:

Proceeds from assumed exercise of stock option plan:	100 shares × $10 =	$1,000
Number of shares needed from assumed exercise of stock option plan:		100 shares
Less: Number of shares of treasury stock assumed acquired ($1000/$25)		40 shares
Additional shares that must be issued to satisfy stock option holders		60 shares

Alternatively, the computation may be done using the following formula:

Assumed issuance of additional common shares under the Treasury Stock Method used to satisfy option holders

$$= \text{Average market price of Stock} - \text{Exercise Price/Average market price of the stock} \times \text{Number of shares under the stock option plan}$$

$$= \$25 - \$10/\$25 \times 100 \text{ shares}$$

$$= \$15/\$25 \times 100 \text{ shares}$$

$$= 60 \text{ shares}$$

If options are granted as part of a stock-based compensation arrangement, the assumed proceeds from the exercise of the options under the treasury stock method include deferred compensation and the resulting tax benefit that would be credited to paid-in-capital arising from the exercise of the options.

As a result of the if-converted method for convertible dilutive securities and the treasury stock method for stock option plans and warrants, the denominator of diluted-earnings-per-share computation equals the weighted-average outstanding common shares for the period plus the assumed issue of common shares arising from convertible securities plus the assumed shares issued because of the exercise of stock options or stock warrants, or their equivalent.

Exhibit 1-5 shows in summary form the earnings-per-share fractions.

Exhibit 1-5: Earnings-per-Share Fractions

BASIC EARNINGS PER SHARE =

$$\frac{\text{Net income available to common stockholders}}{\text{Weighted average number of common shares outstanding}}$$

DILUTED EARNINGS PER SHARE =

$$\frac{\text{Net income available to common stockholders + net of tax interest and/or } \pm \text{ dividend savings on convertible securities}}{\text{Weighted-average number of common shares outstanding + effect of convertible securities + net effect of stock options}}$$

EXAMPLE

This example assumes the same information about the Dauber Company given in the example from the previous section, Basic Earnings per Share. It is further assumed that potentially dilutive securities outstanding include 5% convertible bonds (each $1,000 bond is convertible into 25 shares of common stock) having a face value of $5,000,000. There are options to buy 50,000 shares of common stock at $10 per share. The average market price for common shares is $25 per share for 20X1. The tax rate is 30%.

Basic Earnings per Share

$$\frac{\text{Net income available to common stockholders}}{\text{Weighted-average number of common shares outstanding}} =$$

$$\frac{\$1,300,000}{632,500} = \$2.06$$

Diluted Earnings per Share

Income for diluted earnings per share:

Earnings available to common stockholders		$1,300,000
Interest expense on convertible bonds ($5,000,000 × .05)	$250,000	
Less: tax savings ($250,000 × .30)	(75,000)	
Interest expense (net of tax)		$ 175,000
Income for diluted earnings per share		$1,475,000
Shares outstanding for diluted earnings per share:		
Weighted-average outstanding common shares		632,500
Assumed issued common shares for convertible bonds (5,000 bonds × 25 shares)		125,000
Assumed issued common shares from exercise of option	50,000	
Less: assumed repurchase of treasury shares (50,000 × $10 = $500,000/$25)	(20,000)	30,000
Shares outstanding for diluted earnings per share		787,500

Diluted earnings per share for 20X1 is $1.87 ($1,475,000/787,500 shares). Diluted earnings per share must be disclosed because the two securities (the 5% convertible bond and the stock options) had an aggregately dilutive effect on earnings per share. That is, earnings per share decreased from $2.06 to $1.87. The required disclosures are indicated as follow:

EARNINGS-PER-SHARE DISCLOSURE

Basic earnings per share	$2.06
Diluted earnings per share	$1.87

Antidilutive Securities

In computing earnings per share, all antidilutive securities should be ignored. A security is considered to be antidilutive if its inclusion does not cause earnings per share to go down. In computing earnings per share, the aggregate of all dilutive securities must be considered. However, in order to exclude the ones that should not be used in the computation, it is necessary to ascertain which securities are individually dilutive and which ones are antidilutive. As was previously noted, a stock option will be antidilutive if the underlying average market price of the stock that can be purchased for the period is less than the exercise price of the option. A convertible security is antidilutive if the exercise of the convertible bond or preferred stock causes an increase in the earnings-per-share computation compared to that derived before the assumed conversion. In this situation, the additive effect to the numerator and denominator as a result of the conversion causes earnings-per-share to increase. In both of these situations, the antidilutive securities should be ignored in the calculation.

EXAMPLE

A company's net income for the year is $100,000. A 10% $2,000,000 convertible bond was outstanding all year that was convertible into 2,000 shares of common stock. The weighted-average number of shares of common stock outstanding all year was 200,000. The income tax rate was 30%.

BASIC EARNINGS PER SHARE

$$\frac{\$100,000}{200,000} = \$.50$$

DILUTED EARNINGS PER SHARE

$$\frac{\$100,000 + 200,000(1-30\%)}{200,000 + 2,000} = \frac{\$240,000}{202,000} = \$1.19$$

Because earnings per share increased as a result of the inclusion of the convertible bond, the bond is antidilutive and should be excluded from the calculation. Only basic earnings per share should be disclosed here.

EXAMPLE

Davis Company has basic earnings per share of $14 for 20X2. There were no conversions or exercises of convertible securities during the year. However, possible conversion of convertible bonds would have reduced earnings per share by $2. The impact of possible exercise of stock options would have increased earnings per share by $.38. Diluted earnings per share for 20X2 equals $12 ($14–$2). **Note:** The dilutive convertible bonds are considered in deriving diluted earnings per share, but the stock options are ignored because they have an antidilutive effect.

Share-Based Payment Transactions

ASC 260-10-45-61A, *Earnings Per Share: Overall*, provides guidance in calculating earnings per share for share-based payment awards with dividend rights. Unvested share-based payment awards that have nonforfeitable rights to dividends or dividend equivalents (whether paid or unpaid) are considered participating securities and are includable in the EPS calculation under the two-class method.

Earnings per Share and Specialized Disclosures on the Income Statement

When net income of a given period includes specialized activities disclosures, including income or loss from discontinued operations, extraordinary items, and the cumulative effect of change of accounting principle, earnings-per-share disclosure is required for each of these categories. GAAP requires that per-share amounts for each of these amounts be shown either on the face of the income statement or in the notes to the financial statements.

Business Combinations

If a subsidiary has been acquired under the purchase or acquisition methods during the year, the weighted-average shares outstanding for the year are used from the purchase date.

Disclosures

Basic earnings per share and diluted earnings per share (if required) for income from continuing operations and net income must be disclosed on the face of the income statement. In addition, the earnings-per-share effects associated with the disposal of a business segment, and extraordinary gains or losses, must be presented either on the face of the income statement or notes thereto.

A reconciliation is required of the numerators and denominators for basic and diluted earnings per share. Disclosure is also mandated for the impact of preferred dividends in arriving at income available to common stockholders.

Other disclosures include:

☐ Information on the capital structure.

☐ Assumptions made.

☐ Number of shares converted.

☐ Rights and privileges of securities, such as dividend and participation rights, call prices, and conversion ratios.

COMPREHENSIVE INCOME

ASC 220-10-15-2, *Comprehensive Income—Scope and Scope Exceptions*, requires companies (including investment companies) to report comprehensive income and its components in a complete set of financial statements. (The pronouncement does not apply to nonprofit entities.) ASC 220-10-45-7 retains the present reporting requirements for net income, including its major components (e.g., income from continuing operations, income from discontinued operations, and extraordinary items), but it considers net income a major element of comprehensive income. A restatement of prior years' financial statements is required when presented for comparative purposes.

Comprehensive income refers to the change in equity (net assets) arising from either transactions or other occurrences with nonowners. Excluded are investments and withdrawals by owners. Hence, a synonymous phrase for comprehensive income is total nonowner changes in equity. Comprehensive income consists of two components: net income and other comprehensive income. Other comprehensive income applies to all items of comprehensive income excluding net income. Thus, net income plus other comprehensive income equals total comprehensive income. Common other comprehensive income items include the following:

☐ Foreign currency items, including translation gains and losses, and gains and losses on foreign currency transactions designated as hedges of a net investment in a foreign entity;

☐ Holding losses or gains on available-for-sale securities;

☐ Gain or loss on a pension plan; and

☐ Changes in market value of a futures contract that is a hedge of an asset reported at fair value.

ASC 220-10-45-1, 1A, 1B, and 1C discuss the requirements for reporting comprehensive income. These sections require an entity to report comprehensive income either in a single continuous financial statement or in two separate but consecutive financial statements. GAAP has eliminated the option to present the components of other comprehensive income as part of the Statement of Stockholders' Equity.

If comprehensive income is presented in a single continuous financial statement, then two sections, net income and other comprehensive income, must be disclosed. If two separate but consecutive statements are shown, then an income statement is presented first followed by a statement of other comprehensive income. GAAP requires, in both choices, that the following be presented: (1) each component of net income along with total net income, (2) each component of other comprehensive income along with a total for other comprehensive income, and (3) a total amount for comprehensive income.

A sample presentation of the single continuous financial statement option follows:

X Company
Statement of Comprehensive Income
For the Year Ended December 31, 20X1

Revenues		$1,301,000
Expenses		(400,000)
Income from operations		$ 901,000
Other gains and losses		$ 95,000
Income before taxes		$ 996,000
Income tax expense		(196,000)
Net Income		$ 800,000
EPS:		
Basic and diluted	$0.79	
Other comprehensive income, net of tax		
Foreign currency translation gain	$40,000	
Unrealized loss on available-for-sale securities	(5,000)	
Loss on pension plan	(3,000)	
Other comprehensive income		$ 32,000
Comprehensive Income		$ 832,000

A sample presentation of the two statement options is shown below:

X Company
Statement of Income
For the Year Ended December 31, 20X1

Revenues		$1,301,000
Expenses		(400,000)
Income from operations		$ 901,000
Other gains and losses		$ 95,000
Income before taxes		$ 996,000
Income tax expense		(196,000)
Net Income		$ 800,000
EPS:		
Basic and diluted	$0.79	

X Company
Statement of Comprehensive Income
For the Year Ended December 31, 20X1

Net income		$800,000
Other comprehensive income, net of tax		
Foreign currency translation gain	$40,000	
Unrealized loss or gain on available-for-sale securities	(5,000)	
Loss on pension plan	(3,000)	

X Company
Statement of Comprehensive Income
For the Year Ended December 31, 20X1

Other comprehensive income	$ 32,000
Comprehensive Income	$ 832,000

ASC 220-10-45-11 notes that, for both presentations, the elements of other comprehensive income for the year may be presented on either a net-of-tax basis or a before-tax basis, with one amount for the tax effect of all the items of other comprehensive income. In addition, ASC 220-10-45-12 indicates that the amount of income tax expense or benefit allocated to each component of other comprehensive income, including reclassification adjustments, be presented in the statement in which these components are presented or in the notes to the financial statements.

At the end of the period, the total of other comprehensive income should be transferred to a component of stockholders' equity called accumulated other comprehensive income (AOCI) which should be presented in the Statement of Financial Position separately from retained earnings and additional paid in capital. ASC 220-10-45-14A requires that an entity present on the face of the financial statements or as a separate disclosure in the notes, the changes in the accumulated balances for each component of other comprehensive income included in AOCI. The presentation of these changes on the face of the financial statements, for example, may be presented as a reconciliation in the statement of changes in stockholders' equity.

A reclassification adjustment should be made so as not to double-count items reported in net income for the current year that have also been taken into account as part of other comprehensive income in a prior year. An example is the realized gain on an available-for-sale security sold in the current year when an unrealized (holding) gain was also included in other comprehensive income in a prior year. Besides an available-for-sale security, reclassification adjustments may apply to foreign currency translation. The reclassification adjustment associated with foreign exchange translation applies only to translation gains and losses realized from the sale or liquidation of an investment in a foreign entity.

Reclassification adjustments were allowed to be presented on the face of the financial statement in which other comprehensive income was reported or in the notes to the financial statements. Specifically, for all components of other comprehensive income, an entity was allowed to use either a gross display on the face of the comprehensive income financial statements or a net display (on the face of the statements) with the gross change presented in the notes. Accounting Standards Update 2011-05 changed the aforementioned requirement. Under the new rule, reclassification adjustments must be presented on the face of financial statements where the components of net income and other comprehensive income are presented (by line item). However, Accounting Standards Update 2011-12 issued an amendment deferring the effective date regarding the presentation of reclassification items. As a result of this deferral, until further notice, entities may follow the guidance prior to the issuance of Accounting Standards

Update 2011-05, which allowed reclassification details to be disclosed in the notes.

EXAMPLE

On January 1, 20X1, a company bought 1,000 shares of available-for-sale securities having a market price per share of $100. On December 31, 20X1, the available-for-sale securities had a market price of $150 per share. On January 1, 20X2, the securities were sold at a market price of $130. The tax rate is 30%.

The unrealized gain or loss included in other comprehensive income is computed as follows:

	Before Tax	Tax Effect at 30%	Net of Tax
20X1 (1000 × $50)*	$50,000	$15,000	$35,000
20X2 (1000 × $20**)	(20,000)	(6,000)	(14,000)
Total gain	$30,000	$ 9,000	$21,000

* $150 − $100 = $50
** $150 − $130 = $20

The presentation in the income statement for 20X1 and 20X2 follows:

	20X1	20X2
Net income		
Gross realized gains in available-for-sale securities		$30,000
Tax expense		9,000
Net realized gain		$21,000
Other comprehensive income:		
Unrealized gain or loss after tax	$35,000	(14,000)
Reclassification adjustment net of tax		(21,000)
Net gain included in other comprehensive income	$35,000	($35,000)
Total effect on comprehensive income	$35,000	($14,000)

In interim financial statements issued to the public, ASC 220-10-45-18 requires a company to present the components of net income and other comprehensive income, as well as total comprehensive income in condensed financial statements of interim periods.

DISCLOSURES ASSOCIATED WITH OPERATIONS

Disclosure should be provided about the company's primary products and services, including major markets by geographic area. This information enables a proper assessment of an entity's nature of operations. In addition, ASC 275-10-55-3, *Risks and Uncertainties: Overall*, requires disclosure of major risks and uncertainties facing the business. It also requires disclosure in the significant accounting policies footnote that the financial information presented is based on management's estimates and assumptions. Reference should also be made that actual results may differ from such estimates.

ANNUAL REPORT REFERENCES

Campbell Soup
2011 Annual Report

17. Stock-Based Compensation

In 2003, shareowners approved the 2003 Long-Term Incentive Plan, which authorized the issuance of 28 million shares to satisfy awards of stock options, stock appreciation rights, unrestricted stock, restricted stock/units (including performance restricted stock) and performance units. Approximately 3.2 million shares available under a previous long-term plan were rolled into the 2003 Long-Term Incentive Plan, making the total number of available shares approximately 31.2 million. In November 2005, shareowners approved the 2005 Long-Term Incentive Plan, which authorized the issuance of an additional 6 million shares to satisfy the same types of awards.

Awards under the 2003 and 2005 Long-Term Incentive Plans may be granted to employees and directors. The term of a stock option granted under these plans may not exceed ten years from the date of grant. Options granted under these plans vest cumulatively over a three-year period at a rate of 30%, 60% and 100%, respectively. The option price may not be less than the fair market value of a share of common stock on the date of the grant.

Pursuant to the 2003 Long-Term Incentive Plan, in July 2005 the company adopted a long-term incentive compensation program which provides for grants of total shareowner return (TSR) performance restricted stock/units, EPS performance restricted stock/units, and time-lapse restricted stock/units. Initial grants made in accordance with this program were approved in September 2005. Under the program, awards of TSR performance restricted stock/units will be earned by comparing the company's total shareowner return during a three-year period to the respective total shareowner returns of companies in a performance peer group. Based upon the company's ranking in the performance peer group, a recipient of TSR performance restricted stock/units may earn a total award ranging from 0% to 225% of the initial grant. Awards of EPS performance restricted stock/units will be earned based upon the company's achievement of annual earnings per share goals. During the three-year vesting period, a recipient of EPS performance restricted stock/units may earn a total award ranging from 0% to 100% of the initial grant. Awards of time-lapse restricted stock/units will vest ratably over the three-year period. In addition, the company may issue special grants of time-lapse restricted stock/units to attract and retain executives which vest ratably over various periods. Awards are generally granted annually in October. Annual stock option grants are not part of the long-term incentive compensation program for 2009, 2010, and 2011. However, stock options may still be granted on a selective basis under the 2003 and 2005 Long-Term Incentive Plans.

Total pre-tax stock-based compensation expense recognized in Earnings from continuing operations was $87 for 2011, $88 for 2010, and $84 for 2009. Tax related benefits of $32 were recognized for 2011, $33 were recognized for 2010 and $31 were recognized for 2009.

Information about stock options and related activity is as follows:

2011 (Options in thousands)		Weighted-Average Exercise Prices	Weighted-Average Remaining Contractual Life	Aggregate Intrinsic Value
Beginning of year	12,473	$ 26.47		
Granted	—	$ —		
Exercised	(3,737)	$ 26.97		
Terminated	(30)	$ 33.82		
End of year	8,706	$ 26.23	2.2	$ 59
Exercisable at end of year	8,706	$ 26.23	2.2	$ 59

The total intrinsic value of options exercised during 2011, 2010, and 2009 was $29, $33, and $30, respectively. As of January 2009, compensation related to stock options was fully expensed. The company measured the fair value of stock options using the Black-Scholes option pricing model.

The following table summarizes time-lapse restricted stock/units and EPS performance restricted stock/units activity:

	Shares/Units (Restricted stock/units in thousands)	Weighted-Average Grant-Date Fair Value
Nonvested at August 1, 2010	2,395	$35.05
Granted	1,585	$35.64
Vested	(1,113)	$35.74
Forfeited	(157)	$35.11
Nonvested at July 31, 2011	2,710	$35.11

The fair value of time-lapse restricted stock/units and EPS performance restricted stock/units is determined based on the number of shares granted and the quoted price of the company's stock at the date of grant. Time-lapse restricted stock/units are expensed on a straight-line basis over the vesting period, except for awards issued to retirement-eligible participants, which are expensed on an accelerated basis. EPS performance restricted stock/units are expensed on a graded-vesting basis, except for awards issued to retirement-eligible participants, which are expensed on an accelerated basis.

On July 1, 2011, the company issued approximately 400,000 special retention time-lapse restricted stock units to certain executives to support the successful execution of the company's shift in strategic direction and leadership transition. The awards vest over a two-year period. The grant-date fair value was $34.65 and is included in the table above.

As of July 31, 2011, total remaining unearned compensation related to nonvested time-lapse restricted stock/units and EPS performance restricted stock/units was $46, which will be amortized over the weighted-average remaining service period of 1.7 years. The fair value of restricted stock/units vested during 2011, 2010, and 2009 was $40, $32, and $47, respectively. The weighted-average grant-date fair value of restricted stock/units granted during 2010 and 2009 was $32.25 and $39.50, respectively.

The following table summarizes TSR performance restricted stock/units activity:

	Shares/Units (Restricted stock/units in thousands)	Weighted-Average Grant-Date Fair Value
Nonvested at August 1, 2010	3,581	$38.02
Granted	1,255	$43.18
Vested	(1,062)	$34.65
Forfeited	(343)	$39.74
Nonvested at July 31, 2011	3,431	$40.78

The company estimates the fair value of TSR performance restricted stock/units at the grant date using a Monte Carlo simulation. Assumptions used in the Monte Carlo simulation were as follows:

	2011	2010	2009
Risk-free interest rate	**0.59 %**	1.27 %	2.06 %
Expected dividend yield	**3.00 %**	3.06 %	2.46 %
Expected volatility	**23.71 %**	24.83 %	18.57 %
Expected term	**3 yrs.**	3 yrs.	3 yrs.

Compensation expense is recognized on a straight-line basis over the service period. As of July 31, 2011, total remaining unearned compensation related to TSR performance restricted stock/units was $53, which will be amortized over the weighted-average remaining service period of 1.7 years. In the first quarter of fiscal 2011, recipients of TSR performance restricted stock/units earned 100% of their initial grants based upon the company's TSR ranking in a performance peer group during a three-year period ended July 30, 2010. The total fair value of TSR performance restricted stock/units vested during 2011, 2010 and 2009 was $38, $31 and $58, respectively. The grant-date fair value of TSR performance restricted stock/units granted during 2010 and 2009 was $33.84 and $47.20, respectively. In the first quarter of 2012, recipients of TSR performance restricted stock/units will receive 0% of the initial grant based upon the company's TSR ranking in a performance peer group during the three-year period ended July 31, 2011.

Prior to fiscal 2009, employees could elect to defer all types of restricted stock awards. These awards were classified as liabilities because of the possibility that they may be settled in cash. The fair value was adjusted quarterly. As of

October 2010, these awards were fully vested. The total cash paid to settle the liabilities in 2011, 2010, and 2009 was not material.

The excess tax benefits on the exercise of stock options and vested restricted stock presented as cash flows from financing activities were $11 in 2011 and 2010 and $18 in 2009. Cash received from the exercise of stock options was $96, $139, and $72, for 2011, 2010, and 2009, respectively, and is reflected in cash flows from financing activities in the Consolidated Statements of Cash Flows.

Schlumberger
2011 Annual Report

13. Stock Compensation Plans

Schlumberger has three types of stock-based compensation programs: stock options, a restricted stock and restricted stock unit program (collectively referred to as "restricted stock") and a discounted stock purchase plan ("DSPP").

Stock Options

Key employees are granted stock options under Schlumberger stock option plans. For all of the stock options granted, the exercise price equals the average of the high and low sales prices of Schlumberger stock on the date of grant; an option's maximum term is ten years, and options generally vest in increments over four or five years. The fair value of each stock option grant was estimated on the date of grant using the Black-Scholes option-pricing model with the following weighted-average assumptions and resulting weighted-average fair value per share:

	2011	*2010*	*2009*
Dividend yield	**1.2%**	1.3%	1.2%
Expected volatility	**37%**	35%	34%
Risk free interest rate	**2.8%**	2.9%	2.2%
Expected option life in years	**6.9%**	6.9%	6.9%
Weighted-average fair value per share	**$31.38**	$24.13	$13.92

The following table summarizes information concerning options outstanding and options exercisable by five ranges of exercise prices as of December 31, 2011:

(Shares stated in thousands)

	Options Outstanding			Options Exercisable	
Exercise prices range	*Options Outstanding*	*Weighted-average remaining contractual life (in years)*	*Weighted-average exercise price*	*Options Exercisable*	*Weighted-average exercise price*
$19.04 - $32.46	2,764	0.99	$27.35	2,764	$27.35
$32.62 - $37.85	5,921	6.67	$37.43	2,109	$36.69
$39.08 - $55.69	6,116	5.00	$52.71	4,929	$53.45

(Shares stated in thousands)

	Options Outstanding			Options Exercisable	
Exercise prices range	Options Outstanding	Weighted-average remaining contractual life (in years)	Weighted-average exercise price	Options Exercisable	Weighted-average exercise price
$56.61 - $74.00	11,223	7.19	$65.09	4,199	$62.50
$83.89 - $110.78	14,003	8.02	$ 6.08	2,885	$89.48
	40,027	6.64	$63.84	16,886	$55.49

The weighted average remaining contractual life of stock options exercisable as of December 31, 2011 was 4.7 years.

The following table summarizes stock option activity during the years ended December 31, 2011, 2010 and 2009:

(Shares stated in thousands)

	2011		2010		2009	
	Shares	Weighted-average exercise price	Shares	Weighted-average exercise price	Shares	Weighted-average exercise price
Outstanding at beginning of year	**37,499**	**$55.33**	35,500	$50.30	32,301	$50.36
Granted	**9,528**	**$84.29**	8,283	$66.67	7,981	$40.87
Assumed in Smith transaction	–	$ –	581	$28.77	–	$ –
Exercised	**(5,470)**	**$42.36**	(5,962)	$37.60	(3,851)	$29.00
Forfeited	**(1,530)**	**$58.82**	(903)	$61.28	(931)	$58.82
Outstanding at year-end	**40,027**	**$63.84**	37,499	$55.33	35,500	$50.30

The aggregate intrinsic value of stock options outstanding as of December 31, 2011 was approximately $428 million.

The aggregate intrinsic value of stock options exercisable as of December 31, 2011 was approximately $278 million.

The total intrinsic value of options exercised during the years ended December 31, 2011, 2010 and 2009, was $246 million, $188 million and $103 million, respectively.

Restricted Stock

Restricted stock awards generally vest at the end of three years. There have not been any grants to date that are subject to performance-based vesting.

The following table summarizes information about restricted stock transactions:

(Shares stated in thousands)

	2011		2010		2009	
	Restricted Stock	Weighted Average Grant Date Fair Value	Restricted Stock	Weighted Average Grant Date Fair Value	Restricted Stock	Weighted Average Grant Date Fair Value
Unvested at beginning of year	2,223	$64.27	1,343	$62.75	1,701	$66.49
Granted	1,136	84.61	1,261	65.79	304	48.14
Vested	(767)	67.36	(286)	63.92	(580)	65.15
Forfeited	(159)	72.51	(95)	64.16	(82)	69.23
Unvested at end of year	2,433	$72.25	2,223	64.27	1,343	$62.75

Discounted Stock Purchase Plan

Under the terms of the DSPP, employees can choose to have a portion of their earnings withheld, subject to certain restrictions, to purchase Schlumberger common stock. The purchase price of the stock is 92.5% of the lower of the stock price at the beginning or end of the plan period at six-month intervals.

The fair value of the employees' purchase rights under the DSPP was estimated using the Black-Scholes model with the following assumptions and resulting weighted average fair value per share:

	2011	2010	2009
Dividend yield	1.2%	1.6%	1.1%
Expected volatility	28%	36%	44%
Risk free interest rate	0.2%	0.3%	0.3%
Weighted average fair value per share	$12.83	$10.30	$9.76

Total Stock-Based Compensation Expense

The following summarizes stock-based compensation expense recognized in income:

(Stated in millions)

	2011	2010	2009
Stock options	$176	$121	$118
Restricted stock	60	44	32
DSPP	36	33	36
	$272	$198	$186

At December 31, 2011, there was $527 million of total unrecognized compensation cost related to nonvested stock-based compensation arrangements of which $218 million is expected to be recognized in 2012, $152 million in 2013, $101 million in 2014, $53 million in 2015 and $3 million in 2016.

Corning Incorporated
2011 Annual Report

2. Restructuring, Impairment and Other Charges (Credits)

2011 Activity

During the fourth quarter of 2011, the Specialty Materials segment recorded an impairment charge related to certain assets used in the ion exchange process for the production of large cover glass. Although sales of Corning Gorilla Glass used in our large cover glass products increased in 2011 when compared to 2010, gross margins continue to be weak and sales volumes were significantly below our expectations in 2011 and both sales and margins are expected to be lower than forecasted in 2012. As a result, certain assets located in Japan used in the ion exchange process for the production of large cover glass were written down to estimated fair value in the fourth quarter of 2011 and an impairment loss of $130 million was recognized. This asset group includes machinery and equipment used in the ion exchange process and facilities dedicated to the ion exchange process.

The following table summarizes the restructuring, impairment and other charges (credits) as of and for the year ended December 31, 2011 (in millions):

	Reserve at January 1, 2011	Net Charges/ Reversals	Cash Payments	Reserve at December 31, 2011
Restructuring:				
Employee related costs	$ 15	$ (1)	$ (12)	$ 2
Other charges (credits)	12		(4)	8
Total restructuring activity	$ 27	$ (1)	$ (16)	$ 10
Impairment of long-lived asset:				
Assets to be held and used		$130		
Total impairment charges		$130		
Total restructuring, impairment and other charges		$129		

2010 Activity

Corning recorded credits of $329 million in 2010. During 2009, we had two events which impacted production at several of our LCD glass manufacturing facilities. In August 2009, an earthquake halted production at one of our LCD glass manufacturing facilities in Japan and in October 2009, production at our facility in Taichung, Taiwan was impacted by a power disruption. In the fourth quarter of 2010, we recorded $324 million in other credits in our Display segment as settlement of business interruption and property damage insurance claims resulting from these events.

The following table summarizes the restructuring, and other charges (credits) as of and for the year ended December 31, 2010 (in millions):

	Reserve at January 1, 2010	Non-cash adjustments	Net charges/ (reversals)	Cash Payments	Reserve at December 31, 2010
Restructuring:					
Employee related costs	$ 80	$ (2)	$ (5)	$ (58)	$ 15
Other charges (credits)	20			(8)	12
Total restructuring activity	$ 100	$ (2)	$ (5)	$ (66)	$ 27
Other charges (credits):					
Settlement of business interruption and property damage insurance claims			$(324)		
Total other credits			$(324)		
Total restructuring, impairment and other charges (credits)			$(329)		

Cash payments for employee-related costs were substantially completed in 2010. Payments for exit activities were substantially completed in 2011.

2009 Activity

Corning recorded net charges of $228 million in 2009. A summary of the charges follows:

> We recorded a charge of $228 million associated with a corporate-wide restructuring plan to reduce our global workforce in response to anticipated lower sales in 2009. The charge included costs for severance, special termination benefits, outplacement services, asset disposal costs, and the impact of a $32 million curtailment loss for postretirement benefits in 2009. Total cash expenditures associated with this plan are expected to be approximately $150 million with the majority of spending completed in 2010.

The following table summarizes the restructuring, and other charges (credits) as of and for the year ended December 31, 2009 (in millions):

	Reserve at January 1, 2009	Charges	Non-cash settlements	Cash Payments	Reserve at December 31, 2009
Restructuring:					
Employee related costs	$ 17	$ 203	$ (54)	$ (86)	$ 80
Other charges (credits)	17	6		(3)	20
Total restructuring activity	$ 34	$ 209	$ (54)	$ (89)	$ 100
Impairment of long-lived assets:					
Assets to be disposed of		$ 19			
Total impairment charges		$ 19			
Total restructuring, impairment and other charges		$ 228			

The year-to-date cost of these plans for each of our reportable segments was as follows (in millions):

Operating segment	Employee-related and other costs
Display Technologies	$ 31
Telecommunications	42
Environmental Technologies	28
Specialty Materials	17
Life Sciences	8
Corporate and All Other	102
Total restructuring, impairment and other charges	$ 228

3. Available-for-Sale Investments

The following is a summary of the fair value of available-for-sale securities (in millions):

	Amortized cost December 31,		Fair value December 31,	
	2011	2010	2011	2010
Bonds, notes and other securities:				
U.S. government and agencies	$ 1,150	$ 1,734	$ 1,155	$ 1,737
Other debt securities	6	11	9	15
Total short-term investments	$ 1,156	$ 1,745	$ 1,164	$ 1,752
Asset-backed securities	$ 57	$ 64	$ 35	$ 45
Total long-term investments	$ 57	$ 64	$ 35	$ 45

We do not intend to sell, nor do we believe it is more likely than not that we would be required to sell, the long-term investment asset-backed securities (which are collateralized by mortgages) before recovery of their amortized cost basis. It is possible that a significant degradation in the delinquency or foreclosure rates in the underlying assets could cause further temporary or other-than-temporary impairments in the future.

The following table summarizes the contractual maturities of available-for-sale securities at December 31, 2011 (in millions):

Less than one year	$ 835
Due in 1–5 years	320
Due in 5–10 years	0
Due after 10 years[1]	44
Total	$ 1,199

[1] Included in the maturity table is $35 million of asset-based securities that mature over time and are being reported at their final maturity dates.

The following table provides the fair value and gross unrealized losses of the Company's investments and unrealized losses that are not deemed to be other-than-temporarily impaired, aggregated by investment category and length of time that individual securities have been in a continuous unrealized loss position at December 31, 2011 and 2010 (in millions):

| | | December 31, 2011 | | | |
| | | 12 months or greater | | Total | |
	Number of securities in a loss position	Fair value	Unrealized losses[1]	Fair value	Unrealized losses[1]
Asset-backed securities	22	$ 35	$ (23)	$ 35	$ (23)
Total long-term investments	22	$ 35	$ (23)	$ 35	$ (23)

[1] Unrealized losses in securities less than 12 months were not significant.

Hormel Foods
2010 Annual Report

Note K. Stock-Based Compensation

The Company issues stock options and nonvested shares as part of its stock incentive plans for employees and non-employee directors. The Company's policy is to grant options with the exercise price equal to the market price of the common stock on the date of grant. Ordinary options vest over periods ranging from six months to four years and expire ten years after the date of the grant. The Company recognizes stock-based compensation expense ratably over the shorter of the requisite service period or vesting period. The fair value of stock-based compensation granted to retirement-eligible individuals is expensed at the time of grant.

A reconciliation of the number of options outstanding and exercisable (in thousands) as of October 31, 2010, and changes during the fiscal year then ended, is as follows:

	Shares	Weighted-Average Exercise Price	Weighted-Average Remaining Contractual Term	Aggregate Intrinsic Value
Outstanding at October 25, 2009	11,604	$ 30.86		
Granted	1,328	38.51		
Exercised	(1,808)	23.41		
Forfeited	(100)	37.20		
Outstanding at October 31, 2010	**11,024**	**$ 32.94**	**5.7 yrs**	**$ 62,959**
Exercisable at October 31, 2010	**6,582**	**$ 30.96**	**4.4 yrs**	**$ 98,488**

The weighted-average grant date fair value of stock options granted and the total intrinsic value of options exercised (in thousands) during each of the past three fiscal years is as follows:

	Fiscal Year Ended		
	October 31, 2010	October 25, 2009	October 26, 2008
Weighted-average grant date fair value	$ 9.09	$ 5.87	$ 10.38
Intrinsic value of exercised options	$ 32,378	$ 5,049	$ 27,669

The fair value of each ordinary option award is calculated on the date of grant using the Black-Scholes valuation model utilizing the following weighted-average assumptions:

	Fiscal Year Ended		
	October 31, 2010	October 25, 2009	October 26, 2008
Risk-free interest rate	3.4%	3.2%	4.0%
Dividend yield	2.2%	2.5%	1.8%
Stock price volatility	22.0%	22.0%	21.0%
Expected option life	8 years	8 years	8 years

As part of the annual valuation process, the Company reassesses the appropriateness of the inputs used in the valuation models. The Company establishes the risk-free interest rate using stripped U.S. Treasury yields as of the grant date where the remaining term is approximately the expected life of the option. The dividend yield is set based on the dividend rate approved by the Company's Board of Directors and the stock price on the grant date. The expected volatility assumption is set based primarily on historical volatility. As a reasonableness test, implied volatility from exchange traded options is also examined to validate the volatility range obtained from the historical analysis. The expected life assumption is set based on an analysis of past exercise behavior by option holders. In performing the valuations for ordinary option grants, the Company has not stratified option holders as exercise behavior has historically been consistent across all employee groups.

The Company's nonvested shares vest after five years or upon retirement. A reconciliation of the nonvested shares (in thousands) as of October 31, 2010, and changes during the fiscal year then ended is as follows:

	Shares	Weighted-Average Grant-Date Fair Value
Nonvested at October 25, 2009	98	$ 34.90
Granted	25	39.12
Vested	(20)	33.21
Nonvested at October 31, 2010	**103**	**$ 36.25**

The weighted-average grant date fair value of nonvested shares granted, the total fair value (in thousands) of nonvested shares granted, and the fair value (in thousands) of shares that have vested during each of the past three fiscal years is as follows:

	Fiscal Year Ended		
	October 31, 2010	October 25, 2009	October 26, 2008
Weighted-average grant date fair value	$ 39.12	$ 30.54	$ 38.97
Fair value of nonvested shares granted	$ 978	$ 865	$ 974
Fair value of shares vested	$ 664	$ 204	$ 43

Stock-based compensation expense, along with the related income tax benefit, for each of the past three fiscal years is presented in the table below:

	Fiscal Year Ended		
(in thousands)	October 31, 2010	October 25, 2009	October 26, 2008
Stock-based compensation expense recognized	$ 14,402	$ 12,054	$ 14,691
Income tax benefit recognized	(5,510)	(4,633)	(5,611)
After-tax stock-based compensation expense	$ 8,892	$ 7,421	$ 9,080

At October 31, 2010, there was $12.5 million of total unrecognized compensation cost from stock-based compensation arrangements granted under the plans. This compensation is expected to be recognized over a weighted-average period of approximately 2.3 years. During fiscal years 2010, 2009, and 2008, cash received from stock option exercises was $22.9 million, $2.4 million, and $11.3 million, respectively. The total tax benefit to be realized for tax deductions from these option exercises was $18.9 million, $1.3 million, and $10.6 million, respectively.

Shares issued for option exercises and nonvested shares may be either authorized but unissued shares, or shares of treasury stock acquired in the open market or otherwise. The number of shares available for future grants (in thousands) was 17,647 at October 25, 2010, 18,998 at October 25, 2009, and 7,161 at October 26, 2008.

Meadwestvaco
2010 Annual Report

M. Restructuring Charges

Year ended December 31, 2010

During 2005, the company launched a cost reduction initiative to improve the efficiency of its business model. During 2008, the company commenced a separate series of broad cost reduction actions to reduce corporate and business unit overhead expense and close or restructure certain manufacturing locations. Restructuring charges incurred during 2010 were pursuant to the 2008 program. Restructuring charges incurred during 2009 were pursuant to the 2008 and 2005 programs. Cumulative charges included in the results from continuing operations through December 31, 2010 since the inceptions of the 2005 and 2008 programs were $254 million and $247 million, respectively. Although these charges related to individual segments, such amounts are included in Corporate and Other.

For the year ended December 31, 2010, the company incurred pre-tax charges of $53 million from continuing operations in connection with employee separation costs, asset write-downs and other restructuring actions, of which $35 million is included in cost of sales and $18 million is included in selling, general and administrative expenses. The non-cash portion of these charges was $8 million. For the three months ended December 31, 2010, the company incurred pre-tax charges of $18 million of which $11 million is included in cost of sales and $7 million is included in selling, general and administrative expenses.

The following table and discussion present additional detail of the 2010 charges:

(In millions)	Employee Costs	Asset Write-downs and Other Costs	Total
Consumer Solutions	$ 32	$ 8	$ 40
Packaging Resources	0	4	4
Consumer & Office Products	1	1	2
All other	5	2	7
	$ 38	$ 15	$ 53

Consumer Solutions

During the year ended December 31, 2010, the Consumer Solutions segment had various restructuring actions in its manufacturing operations in Europe and the U.S. These actions resulted in pre-tax charges of $40 million, of which $32 million related to employee separation costs and $8 million related to asset write-downs and other restructuring actions.

Packaging Resources

During the year ended December 31, 2010, the Packaging Resources segment had various restructuring actions in its manufacturing operations in Brazil and the U.S. These actions resulted in pre-tax charges of $4 million related to asset write-downs and other restructuring actions.

Consumer & Office Products

During the year ended December 31, 2010, the Consumer & Office Products segment had various restructuring actions in its manufacturing operations in the U.S and Brazil. These actions resulted in pre-tax charges of $2 million, of which $1 million related to employee separation costs and $1 million related to asset write-downs and other restructuring actions.

All other

During the year ended December 31, 2010, the company recorded restructuring charges of $7 million, of which $5 million related to employee relocation costs and $2 million related to other restructuring actions.

Year ended December 31, 2009

For the year ended December 31, 2009, the company incurred pre-tax charges of $173 million from continuing operations in connection with employee separation costs, asset write-downs and other restructuring actions, of which $137 million is included in cost of sales and $36 million is included in selling, general and administrative expenses. Of these charges, $71 million related to the Consumer Solutions segment, $42 million related to the Packaging Resources segment, $6 million related to the Consumer & Office Products segment and $54 million was attributed to Corporate and Other. The non-cash portion of these charges was $126 million.

Year ended December 31, 2008

For the year ended December 31, 2008, the company incurred pre-tax charges of $52 from continuing operations in connection with employee separation costs, asset write-downs and other restructuring actions, of which $31 million is included in cost of sales, $19 million is included in selling, general and administrative expenses and $2 million is included in other income. Of these charges, $32 million related to the Consumer Solutions segment, $4 million related to the Packaging Resources segment, $4 million related to the Specialty Chemicals segment, $3 million related to the Consumer & Office Products segment and $9 million was attributed to Corporate and Other. The non-cash portion of these charges was $34 million.

Summary of restructuring accruals

The activity in the accrued restructuring balances was as follows for the year ended December 31, 2007 to the year ended December 31, 2010:

(In millions)	Employee Costs			Other Costs			Total		
	2005 Program	2008 Program	Total	2005 Program	2008 Program	Total	2005 Program	2008 Program	Total
Balance at December 31, 2007	16	0	16	13	0	13	29	0	29
Current charges	19	25	44	5	0	5	24	25	49
Payments	(21)	0	(21)	(13)	0	(13)	(34)	0	(34)
Balance at December 31, 2008	14	25	39	5	0	5	19	25	44
Current charges	0	57	57	4	11	15	4	68	72
Payments	(14)	(46)	(60)	(5)	(11)	(16)	(19)	(57)	(76)

(In millions)	Employee Costs 2005 Program	Employee Costs 2008 Program	Total	Other Costs 2005 Program	Other Costs 2008 Program	Total	Total 2005 Program	Total 2008 Program	Total
Balance at December 31, 2009	$ 0	$ 36	$ 36	$ 4	$ 0	$ 4	$ 4	$ 36	$ 40
Current charges	0	38	38	1	3	4	1	41	42
Payments	0	(42)	(42)	(1)	(3)	(4)	(1)	(45)	(46)
Balance at December 31, 2010	$ 0	$ 32	$ 32	$ 4	$ 0	$ 4	$ 4	$ 32	$ 36

N. Other Income, Net

Components of other income, net are as follows:

(In millions)	Years ended December 31, 2010	2009	2008
Interest income	$ (22)	$ (18)	$ (39)
Charges from early extinguishments of debt	6	23	0
Foreign currency exchange losses (gains)	4	(2)	25
Gains on sales of certain assets	0	(16)	(16)
Alternative fuel mixture credit[1]	0	(375)	0
Other, net	(2)	6	(2)
	$ (14)	$ (382)	$ (32)

[1] Through December 31, 2009, the U.S. Internal Revenue Code allowed an excise tax credit for alternative fuel mixtures produced by a taxpayer for use as a fuel in a taxpayer's trade or business.

United States Steel 2010 Annual Report

14. Stock-Based Compensation Plans

On April 26, 2005, U.S. Steel's stockholders approved the 2005 Stock Incentive Plan (the "2005 Stock Plan"). The aggregate number of shares of U.S. Steel common stock that may be issued through April 26, 2020 under the 2005 Stock Plan is 15,450,000 shares, of which 10,090,652 shares are available as of December 31, 2010 for future grants. Generally, a share issued under the Plan pursuant to an award other than a stock option will reduce the number of shares available under the Stock Plan by 1.64 shares. The purposes of the 2005 Stock Plan are to attract, retain and motivate employees and non-employee directors of outstanding ability, and to align their interests with those of the stockholders of U.S. Steel. The Compensation & Organization Committee of the Board of Directors (the Compensation Committee) administers the plan pursuant to which they may make grants of stock options, restricted stock, restricted stock units (RSU's), performance awards, and other stock-based awards. Also, shares related to awards (i) that are forfeited, (ii) that terminate without shares having been issued or (iii) for which payment is made in cash or property other than shares are again available for awards under the plan; provided, however, that shares delivered to U.S. Steel or withheld for purposes of satisfying the exercise price or tax withholding obligations shall not again be available for awards.

The following table summarizes the total stock-based compensation awards granted during the years 2010, 2009 and 2008:

	Stock Options	Restricted Stock	Restricted Stock Units	Performance Awards
2010 Grants	**612,270**	–	**359,960**	**105,640**
2009 Grants	1,026,580	–	564,210	116,410
2008 Grants	281,200	1,000	118,420	32,870

Stock-based compensation expense

The following table summarizes the total compensation expense recognized for stock-based compensation awards:

(In millions, except per share amounts)	Year Ended December 31, 2010	Year Ended December 31, 2009	Year Ended December 31, 2008
Stock-based compensation expense recognized:			
Cost of sales	$ 9	$ 10	$ 11
Selling, general and administrative expenses	20	27	24
Total	29	37	35
Related deferred income tax benefit	11	14	13
Decrease in net income	$ 18	$ 23	$ 22
Decrease in basic earnings per share	$ 0.13	$ 0.17	$ 0.19
Decrease in diluted earnings per share	$ 0.13	$ 0.17	$ 0.18

As of December 31, 2010, total future compensation cost related to nonvested stock-based compensation arrangements was $34 million, and the average period over which this cost is expected to be recognized is approximately 12 months.

Stock options

Compensation expense for stock options is recorded over the vesting period based on the fair value on the date of grant, as calculated by U. S. Steel using the Black-Scholes model and the assumptions listed below. The 2010, 2009 and 2008 awards vest ratably over a three-year service period and have a term of ten years. Options are issued at the market price on the date of the grant. Upon exercise of stock options, shares of U. S. Steel stock are issued from treasury stock.

Black-Scholes Assumptions	2010 Grants	2009 Grants	2008 Grants
Price per share of option award	$ 45.65	$ 29.81	$ 169.23
Expected annual dividends per share	$ 0.20	$ 0.20	$ 1.00
Expected life in years	5.0	4.5	4.5
Expected volatility	64%	62%	43%
Risk-free interest rate	2.1%	2.6%	3.2%
Average grant date fair value per share of unvested option awards as calculated from above	$ 24.31	$ 14.87	$ 64.51

The expected annual dividends per share are based on the latest annualized dividend rate at the date of grant; the expected life in years is determined primarily from historical stock option exercise data; the expected volatility is based on the historical volatility of U. S. Steel stock; and the risk-free interest rate is based on the U.S. Treasury strip rate for the expected life of the option.

The following table shows a summary of the status and activity of stock options for the year ended December 31, 2010:

	Shares	Weighted-Average Exercise Price (per share)	Weighted-Average Remaining Contractual Term (in years)	Aggregate Intrinsic Value (in millions)
Outstanding at January 1, 2010	2,220,957	$ 56.92		
Granted	612,270	45.65		
Exercised	(145,254)	29.93		
Forfeited or expired	(47,683)	45.31		
Outstanding at December 31, 2010	2,640,290	$ 56.00	9.1	$ 6
Exercisable at December 31, 2010	1,351,989	$ 65.76	5.3	–
Exercisable and expected to vest at December 31, 2010	2,552,699	$ 56.38	8.9	$ 5

The aggregate intrinsic value in the table above represents the total pretax intrinsic value (difference between our closing stock price on the last trading day of 2010 and the exercise price, multiplied by the number of in-the-money options). Intrinsic value changes are based on the fair market value of our stock. Total intrinsic value of options outstanding at December 31, 2009 was zero because generally the options were out-of-the-money at December 31, 2009.

During the years ended December 31, 2010, 2009 and 2008, the total intrinsic value of stock options exercised (i.e., the difference between the market price at exercise and the price paid by the employee to exercise the option) was $3 million, $0.3 million and $29 million, respectively. The total amount of cash received by U. S. Steel from the exercise of options during the year ended December 31, 2010 was $4 million and the related net tax benefit realized from the exercise of these options was immaterial.

Stock awards

Compensation expense for nonvested stock awards is recorded over the vesting period based on the fair value at the date of grant.

Restricted stock awards and RSU's vest ratably over three years. Their fair value is the market price of the underlying common stock on the date of grant.

Performance awards vest at the end of a three-year performance period as a function of U. S. Steel's total shareholder return compared to the total shareholder return of a peer group of companies over the three-year performance period. Performance awards can vest at between zero and 200 percent of the target award.

The following table shows a summary of the performance awards outstanding as of December 31, 2010, and their fair market value on the respective grant date:

Performance Period	Fair Value (in millions)	Minimum Shares	Target Shares	Maximum Shares
2010 - 2013	$ 6	–	105,640	211,280
2009 - 2012	$ 5	–	116,410	232,820
2008 - 2011	$ 7	–	32,870	65,740

The following table shows a summary of the status and activity of nonvested stock awards for the year ended December 31, 2010:

	Restricted Stock	Restricted Stock Units	Performance Awards[a]	Total	Weighted-Average Grant-Date Fair Value
Nonvested at January 1, 2010	47,178	608,870	190,605	846,653	$ 58.96
Granted	–	359,960	105,640	465,600	48.23
Vested	(45,859)	(212,298)	(33,767)	(291,924)	69.65
Performance adjustment factor[b]	–	–	(20,078)	(20,078)	143.60
Forfeited or expired	(1,319)	(22,799)	(569)	(24,687)	42.80
Nonvested at December 31, 2010	–	733,733	241,831	975,564	$ 49.30

[a] The number of shares shown for the performance awards is based on the target number of share awards.

[b] Consists of adjustments to vested performance awards to reflect actual performance. The adjustments were required since the original grants of the awards were at 100 percent of the targeted amounts.

The following table presents information on restricted stock, RSU's and performance awards granted:

	2010	2009	2008
Number of shares (or RSU's) granted	465,600	680,620	152,290
Weighted-average grant-date fair value per share	$ 48.23	$ 31.61	$ 174.28

During the years ended December 31, 2010, 2009, and 2008, the total fair value of shares vested was $20 million, $19 million, and $12 million, respectively.

Atwood Oceanics
2009 Annual Report

Note 3. Share-Based Compensation

We account for share-based compensation in accordance with ASC 718. Under ASC 718, share-based compensation cost is measured at the grant date, based on the calculated fair value of the award, and is recognized as an expense over the requisite service period (generally the vesting period of the equity grant).

On December 7, 2006, our Board of Directors adopted, and our shareholders subsequently approved on February 8, 2007, the Atwood Oceanics, Inc. 2007 Long-Term Incentive Plan, which, as amended, is referred to herein as the "2007 Plan." The effective date of the 2007 Plan was December 7, 2006, and awards may be made under the 2007 Plan through December 7, 2016. Under our 2007 Plan, up to 4,000,000 shares of common stock may be issued to eligible participants in the form of restricted stock awards or upon exercise of stock options granted pursuant to the 2007 Plan. We also have two other stock incentive plans approved by our shareholders, the Atwood Oceanics, Inc. Amended and Restated 2001 Stock Incentive Plan (the "2001 Plan") and the Atwood Oceanics, Inc. 1996 Incentive Equity Plan (as amended, the "1996 Plan"), under which there are outstanding stock options and restricted stock awards. However, no additional options or restricted stock will be awarded under the 2001 or 1996 plans.

A summary of share and stock option data for our three stock incentive plans as of September 30, 2009 is as follows:

	2007 Plan	2001 Plan	1996 Plan
Shares available for future awards or grants	2,781,749	–	–
Outstanding stock option grants	461,948	926,528	110,922
Outstanding unvested restricted stock awards	439,880	118,300	–

Awards of restricted stock and stock options have both been granted under our stock incentive plans as of September 30, 2009. We deliver newly issued shares of common stock for restricted stock awards upon vesting and upon exercise of stock options. All stock incentive plans currently in effect have been approved by the shareholders of our outstanding common stock.

We recognize compensation expense on grants of share-based compensation awards on a straight-line basis over the required service period for each award. Unrecognized compensation cost, net of estimated forfeitures, related to stock options and restricted stock awards and the relating remaining weighted average service period is as follows (in thousands, except average service periods):

	September 30,	
	2009	2008
Unrecognized Compensation Cost		
Stock options	**$ 3,738**	$ 4,414

| | September 30, | |
	2009	2008
Restricted stock awards	**7,329**	10,072
Total	**$11,067**	$14,486
Remaining weighted average service period (Years)	**2.1**	2.6

Stock Options

Under our stock incentive plans, the exercise price of each stock option must be equal to or greater than the fair market value of one share of our common stock on the date of grant, with all outstanding options having a maximum term of 10 years. Options vest ratably over a period from the end of the first to the fourth year from the date of grant under the 2007 and 2001 Plans and from the end of the second to the fifth year from the date of grant under the 1996 Plan. Each option is for the purchase of one share of our common stock.

The total fair value of stock options vested during years ended September 30, 2009, 2008 and 2007 was $2.7 million, $2.4 million and $2.1 million, respectively. The per share weighted average fair value of stock options granted during years ended September 30, 2009, 2008 and 2007 was $5.75, $20.34 and $11.82, respectively. We estimated the fair value of each stock option on the date of grant using the Black-Scholes pricing model and the following assumptions:

	Fiscal 2009	Fiscal 2008	Fiscal 2007
Risk-Free Interest Rate	**1.5%**	3.7%	4.5%
Expected Volatility	**42%**	46%	46%
Expected Life (Years)	**5.2**	5.3	5.3
Dividend Yield	**None**	None	None

The average risk-free interest rate is based on the five-year United States treasury security rate in effect as of the grant date. We determined expected volatility using a six year historical volatility figure and determined the expected term of the stock options using 10 years of historical data. The expected dividend yield is based on the expected annual dividend as a percentage of the market value of our common stock as of the grant date.

A summary of stock option activity for year ended September 30, 2009, is as follows:

	Number of Options (000s)	Weighted Average Exercise Price	Weighted Average Remaining Contractual Life (Years)	Aggregate Intrinsic Value (000s)
Outstanding at October 1, 2008	1,253	$18.82		
Granted	286	14.65		
Exercised	(20)	10.74		$ 355

	Number of Options (000s)	Weighted Average Exercise Price	Weighted Average Remaining Contractual Life (Years)	Aggregate Intrinsic Value (000s)
Forfeited	(20)	26.46		
Outstanding at September 30, 2009	1,499	$18.03	6.2	$25,846
Exercisable at September 30, 2009	960	$14.80	5.0	$19,651

Restricted Stock

We have also awarded restricted stock to certain employees and to our non-employee directors. The awards of restricted stock to employees are subject to a vesting period ranging from three to four years. Awards of restricted stock to non-employee directors prior to Amendment No. 1 to the 2007 Plan, which was approved by our shareholders on February 14, 2008, vested immediately, while awards granted subsequent to the adoption of Amendment No. 1 to the 2007 Plan are subject to a vesting period ranging from one to three years. All restricted stock awards granted to date are restricted from transfer for at least three or four years from the date of grant, whether vested or unvested. We value restricted stock awards at fair market value of our common stock on the date of grant.

A summary of restricted stock activity for the year ended September 30, 2009 is as follows:

	Number of Shares (000s)	Weighted Average Fair Value
Unvested at October 1, 2008	581	$32.50
Granted	173	14.65
Vested	(185)	20.06
Forfeited	(11)	32.58
Unvested at September 30, 2009	558	$31.09

Microsoft
2009 Annual Report

Note 3. Other Income (Expense)

The components of other income (expense) were as follows:

(In millions)			
Year Ended June 30,	2009	2008	2007
Dividends and interest	$ 706	$ 888	$1,319
Net recognized gains (losses) on investments	(125)	346	650

(In millions)			
Year Ended June 30,	2009	2008	2007
Net gains (losses) on derivatives	(558)	226	(358)
Net gains (losses) on foreign currency remeasurements	(509)	226	56
Other	(56)	(143)	(4)
Total	$(542)	$1,543	$1,663

Effective July 1, 2008, we began presenting gains and losses resulting from foreign currency remeasurements as a component of other income (expense). Prior to July 1, 2008, we included gains and losses resulting from foreign currency remeasurements as a component of sales and marketing expense. We changed our presentation because this better reflects how we manage these foreign currency exposures, as such gains and losses arising from the remeasurement of foreign currency transactions are incidental to our operations. For fiscal year 2009, $509 million of losses were reported as other income (expense). For fiscal years 2008 and 2007, $221 million and $86 million of gains, respectively, were previously recorded as a component of sales and marketing expense and have been recast as other income (expense).

Net recognized gains (losses) on investments included other-than-temporary impairments of $862 million, $312 million, and $25 million in fiscal years 2009, 2008, and 2007, respectively. Realized gains and losses from sales of available-for-sale securities (excluding other-than-temporary impairments) were $1.6 billion and $897 million, respectively, in fiscal year 2009, $751 million and $93 million, respectively, in fiscal year 2008, and $851 million and $176 million, respectively, in fiscal year 2007.

Schlumberger
2009 Annual Report

3. Charges and Credits

Schlumberger recorded the following Charges and Credits in continuing operations during 2009, 2008 and 2007:

2009

Second quarter of 2009:

- Schlumberger continued to reduce its global workforce as a result of the slowdown in oil and gas exploration and production spending and its effect on activity in the oilfield services sector. As a result of these actions, Schlumberger recorded a pretax charge of $102 million ($85 million after-tax), which is classified in Cost of revenue in the Consolidated Statement of Income. These workforce reductions were completed by the end of 2009.

- As a consequence of these workforce reductions, Schlumberger recorded pretax non-cash pension and other postretirement benefit curtailment charges of $136 million ($122 million after-tax). These costs are classified in Cost of revenue in the Consolidated Statement of Income. Refer to Note 19 – Pension and Other Benefit Plans for further details.

The following is a summary of these charges:

(Stated in millions)	Pretax	Tax	Net
Workforce reductions	$102	$(17)	$ 85
Postretirement benefits curtailment	136	(14)	122
	$238	$(31)	$207

2008

Fourth quarter of 2008:

- Due to the continuing slowdown in oil and gas exploration and production spending and its effect on activity in the oilfield services sector, Schlumberger took actions to reduce its global workforce. As a result of these actions, Schlumberger recorded a pretax charge of $74 million ($65 million after-tax), which is classified in Cost of revenue in the Consolidated Statement of Income.

- Schlumberger wrote off certain assets, primarily accounts receivable relating to one client with liquidity issues. Accordingly, Schlumberger recorded a pretax charge of $42 million ($28 million after-tax and noncontrolling interest). $32 million of the pretax charge is classified in Cost of revenue in the Consolidated Statement of Income, with the remaining $10 million classified in Interest and other income, net.

The following is a summary of these charges:

(stated in millions)	Pretax	Tax	Non-controlling Interests	Net
Workforce reduction	$ 74	$ (9)	$ –	$65
Provision for doubtful accounts	32	(8)	(6)	18
Other	10	–	–	10
	$116	$(17)	$(6)	$93

2007

Fourth quarter of 2007:

- Schlumberger sold certain workover rigs for $32 million, resulting in a pretax gain of $24 million ($17 million after-tax) which is classified in Interest and other income, net in the Consolidated Statement of Income.

Tyco International
2009 Annual Report

5. Other Expense, Net

Other expense, net was $7 million in 2009 compared to $224 million in 2008 and $255 million in 2007. Other expense, net in 2009 primarily relates to a $14 million charge recorded as a result of a decrease in the receivables due from Covidien and Tyco Electronics under the Tax Sharing Agreement, which was partially offset by income of $5 million relating to a gain on derivative contracts used to economically hedge the foreign currency risk related to the Swiss franc denominated dividends.

Other expense, net during 2008, includes $258 million on extinguishment of debt related to the consent solicitation and exchange offers and termination of the bridge loan facility offset by income of $6 million recorded in connection with the settlement of its 3.125% convertible senior debentures and related financial instruments. See Notes 12 and 14. The Company also recorded other-than-temporary impairments and realized losses on the sale of investments of $6 million related primarily to investments in corporate debt. See Note 9. Additionally, the Company recorded $40 million of income as a result of an increase in the receivables due from Covidien and Tyco Electronics under the Tax Sharing Agreement in connection with the adoption of the guidance pertaining to the accounting for uncertain income taxes. The Company also recorded $6 million of expense for other activity in accordance with the Tax Sharing Agreement during 2008.

During 2007, other expense, net consisted primarily of a $259 million loss on early extinguishment of debt incurred in connection with debt tender offers undertaken in connection with the Separation, for which no tax benefit is available. This charge consists primarily of premiums paid and the write-off of unamortized debt issuance costs and discounts. The total loss on early extinguishment of debt was $647 million, with $259 million included in continuing operations and $388 million allocated to Covidien and Tyco Electronics and included in discontinued operations.

Kellogg's
2008 Annual Report

Note 3. Exit or Disposal Activities

The Company views its continued spending on cost reduction initiatives as part of its ongoing operating principles to provide greater visibility in achieving its long-term profit growth targets. Initiatives undertaken are currently expected to recover cash implementation costs within a five-year period of completion. Each cost-reduction initiative is normally up to three years in duration. Upon completion (or as each major stage is completed in the case of multi-year programs), the project begins to deliver cash savings and/or reduced depreciation.

Cost summary

The Company recorded $27 million of costs in 2008 associated with exit or disposal activities comprised of $7 million of asset write offs, $17 million of severance and other cash costs and $3 million related to pension costs. $23 million of the 2008 charges were recorded in cost of goods sold within the Europe operating segment, with the balance recorded in selling, general and administrative (SGA) expense in the Latin America operating segment.

For 2007, the Company recorded charges of $100 million, comprised of $7 million of asset write offs, $72 million for severance and other exit costs including route franchise settlements, $15 million for other cash expenditures, and $6 million for a multiemployer pension plan withdrawal liability. $23 million of the total 2007 charges were recorded in cost of goods sold within the Europe operating segment results, with $77 million recorded in SGA expense within the North America operating results.

For 2006, the Company recorded charges of $82 million, comprised of $20 million of asset write offs, $30 million for severance and other exit costs, $9 million for other cash expenditures, $4 million for a multiemployer pension plan withdrawal liability, and $19 million for pension and other postretirement plan curtailment losses and special termination benefits. $74 million was recorded in cost of goods sold within SGA expense within corporate results. The Company's operating segments were impacted as follows (in millions): North America–$46; Europe–$28.

Exit cost reserves at January 3, 2009 were $2 million related to severance payments. Exit cost reserves were $5 million at December 29, 2007, consisting of $2 million for severance and $3 million for lease termination payments.

Specific initiatives

During the fourth quarter of 2008, the Company executed a cost-reduction initiative in Latin America that resulted in the elimination of approximately 120 salaried positions. The cost of the program was $4 million and was recorded in Latin America's SGA expense. The charge related primarily to severance benefits which were paid by the end of the year. There were no reserves as of January 3, 2009 related to this program.

The Company commenced a multi-year European manufacturing optimization plan in 2006 to improve utilization of its facility in Manchester, England and to better align production in Europe. The project resulted in an elimination of approximately 220 hourly and salaried positions from the Manchester facility through voluntary early retirement and severance programs. The pension trust funding requirements of these early retirements exceeded the recognized benefit expense by $5 million which was funded in 2006. During this program certain manufacturing equipment was removed from service.

All of the costs for the European manufacturing optimization plan have been recorded in cost of goods sold within the Company's Europe operating segment. The following tables present total project costs and a reconciliation of employee severance reserves for this initiative. All other cash costs were paid in the period incurred. The project was completed in 2008.

Project costs to date (millions)	Employee Severance	Other Cash Costs(a)	Asset Write-Offs	Retirement Benefits(b)	Total
Year ended December 30, 2006	$12	$ 2	$5	$9	$28
Year ended December 29, 2007	7	8	4	–	19
Year ended January 3, 2009	5	3	(3)	3	8
Total project to date	$24	$13	$6	$12	$55

(a) Primarily includes expenditures for equipment removal and relocation, and temporary contracted services to facilitate employee transitions.

(b) Pension plan curtailment losses and special termination benefits recognized under SFAS No. 88, "Accounting for Settlements and Curtailments of Defined Benefit Pension Plans and for Termination Benefits."

Employee severance reserves to date (millions)	Beginning of Period	Accruals	Payments	End of Period
Year ended December 29, 2007	$12	$7	$(19)	$
Year ended December 3, 2009	$	$5	$ (3)	$2

In October 2007, management committed to reorganize certain production processes at the Company's plants in Valls, Spain and Bremen, Germany. Commencement of this plan followed consultation with union representatives at the Bremen facility regarding the elimination of approximately 120 employee positions. This reorganization plan improved manufacturing and distribution efficiency across the Company's continental European operations, and has been completed as of the end of the Company's 2008 fiscal year.

All of the costs for European production process realignment have been recorded in cost of goods sold within the Company's Europe operating segment.

The following tables present total project costs and a reconciliation of employee severance reserves for this initiative. All other cash costs were paid in the period incurred.

Project costs to date (millions)	Employee Severance	Other Cash Costs(a)	Asset Write-Offs	Total
Year ended December 29, 2007	$2	$1	$ 1	$ 4
Year ended January 3, 2009	4	1	10	15
Total project costs	$6	$2	$11	$19

(a) Primarily includes expenditures for equipment removal and relocation, and temporary contracted services to facilitate employee transitions.

Employee severance reserves to date (millions)	Beginning of Period	Accruals	Payments	End of Period
Year ended December 29, 2007	$	$2	$	$2
Year ended January 3, 2009	$2	$4	$(6)	$

In July 2007, management commenced a plan to reorganize the Company's direct store-door delivery (DSD) operations in the southeastern United States. This DSD reorganization plan was intended to integrate the Company's southeastern sales and distribution regions with the rest of its U.S. DSD operations, resulting in greater efficiency across the nationwide network. The Company exited approximately 517 distribution route franchise agreements with independent contractors. The plan also resulted in the involuntary termination or relocation of approximately 300 employee positions. Total project costs incurred were $77 million, principally consisting of cash expenditures for route franchise settlements and to a lesser extent, for employee separation, relocation, and reorganization. Exit cost reserves were $3 million as of December 29, 2007 and were paid in 2008. This initiative is complete.

During 2006, the Company commenced several initiatives to enhance the productivity and efficiency of its U.S. cereal manufacturing network, primarily through technological and sourcing improvements in warehousing and packaging operations. In conjunction with these initiatives, the Company offered voluntary separation incentives, which resulted in the retirement of approximately 80 hourly employees by early 2007. During 2006, the Company incurred approximately $15 million of total up-front costs, comprised of approximately 20% asset write-offs and 80% cash costs, including $10 million of pension and other postretirement plan curtailment losses. These initiatives were complete by the end of 2007.

Also during 2006, the Company undertook an initiative to improve customer focus and selling efficiency within a particular Latin American market, leading to a shift from a third-party distributor to a direct sales force model. As a result of this initiative, the Company paid $8 million in cash during 2006 to exit the existing distribution arrangement.

During 2008 the Company finalized its pension plan withdrawal liability related to its North America snacks bakery consolidation which was executed in 2005 and 2006. The final liability was $20 million, $16 million of which was recognized in 2005 and $4 million in 2006; and was paid in the third quarter of 2008.

U.S. Steel
2008 Annual Report

13. Stock-Based Compensation Plans

On April 26, 2005, U. S. Steel's stockholders approved the 2005 Stock Incentive Plan (the "2005 Stock Plan"). The aggregate number of shares of U. S. Steel common stock that may be issued under the 2005 Stock Plan is 6,750,000 shares during the 10-year life of the plan. Generally, a share issued under the Plan pursuant to an award other than a stock option will reduce the number of shares available under the Stock Plan by 1.42 shares. The purposes of the 2005 Stock Plan are to attract, retain and motivate employees and non-employee directors of outstanding ability, and to align their interests with those of the stockholders of U. S. Steel. The Compensation & Organization Committee of the Board of

Directors (the Compensation Committee) administers the plan pursuant to which they may make grants of stock options, restricted stock, restricted stock units (RSU's), performance awards, and other stock-based awards. Also, shares related to awards (i) that are forfeited, (ii) that terminate without shares having been issued or (iii) for which payment is made in cash or property other than shares are again available for awards under the plan; provided, however, that shares delivered to U. S. Steel or withheld for purposes of satisfying the exercise price or tax withholding obligations shall not again be available for awards.

	Stock Options	Restricted Stock Awards	Restricted Stock Units	Performance Stock Awards
2008 Grants	281,200	1,000	118,420	32,870
2007 Grants	234,930	199,585	–	62,800
2006 Grants	344,490	229,380	–	95,400

Stock-based compensation

Effective January 1, 2006, U. S. Steel adopted the fair value recognition provisions of FAS No. 123(R), "Share-Based Payment," (FAS 123(R)) which requires the recognition of compensation expense for stock-based compensation awards based on the grant date fair value. U. S. Steel elected the modified prospective application method for adoption, and prior period consolidated financial statements were not restated.

Under this adoption method, compensation expense recognized in 2006 included compensation expense related to the May 2006 grants and the applicable amounts of compensation expense of all stock-based payments granted prior to, but not yet vested as of January 1, 2006 (based on the grant date fair value estimated in accordance with the original provisions of FAS No. 123). Prior to the adoption of FAS 123(R), no compensation expense had been recorded for stock options.

Stock-based compensation expense

The following table summarizes the total compensation expense recognized for stock-based compensation awards:

(In millions, except per share amounts)	Year Ended December 31, 2008	Year Ended December 31, 2007	Year Ended December 31, 2006
Stock-based compensation expense recognized:			
Cost of sales	$ 11	$ 7	$ 5
Selling, general and administrative expenses	24	16	11
Total	35	23	16
Related deferred income tax benefit	13	9	6
Decrease in net income	$ 22	$ 14	$ 10

(In millions, except per share amounts)	Year Ended December 31, 2008	Year Ended December 31, 2007	Year Ended December 31, 2006
Decrease in basic earnings per share	$0.19	$0.12	$0.08
Decrease in diluted earnings per share	$0.18	$0.12	$0.08

As of December 31, 2008, total future compensation cost related to nonvested stock-based compensation arrangements was $42 million, and the average period over which this cost is expected to be recognized is approximately 13 months.

Stock options

In accordance with FAS 123(R), compensation expense for stock options is recorded over the vesting period based on the fair value on the date of grant, as calculated by U. S. Steel using the Black-Scholes model and the assumptions listed below. The 2008, 2007 and 2006 awards vest ratably over a three-year service period and have a term of ten years. Options are issued at the market price on the date of the grant. Upon exercise of stock options, shares of U. S. Steel stock are issued from treasury stock.

Black-Scholes Assumptions	2008 Grants	2007 Grants	2006 Grants
Price per share of option award	$ 169.23	$ 108.50	$ 65.40
Expected annual dividends per share	$ 1.00	$ 0.80	$ 0.60
Expected life in years	4.5	5	5
Expected volatility	43%	43%	43%
Risk-free interest rate	3.2%	4.5%	4.8%
Average grant date fair value per share of unvested option awards as calculated from above	$ 64.51	$ 44.55	$ 27.05

The expected annual dividends per share are based on the latest annualized dividend rate at the date of grant; the expected life in years is determined primarily from historical stock option exercise data; the expected volatility is based on the historical volatility of U. S. Steel stock; and the risk-free interest rate is based on the U.S. Treasury strip rate for the expected life of the option.

The following table shows a summary of the status and activity of stock options for the year ended December 31, 2008:

	Shares	Weighted-Average Exercise Price (per share)	Weighted-Average Remaining Contractual Term (in years)	Aggregate Intrinsic Value (in millions)
Outstanding at January 1, 2008	1,347,927	$ 54.10		
Granted	281,200	169.23		

	Shares	Weighted-Average Exercise Price (per share)	Weighted-Average Remaining Contractual Term (in years)	Aggregate Intrinsic Value (in millions)
Exercised	(279,298)	39.96		
Forfeited or expired	(17,782)	97.53		
Outstanding at December 31, 2008	1,332,047	$ 80.79	6.5	–
Exercisable at December 31, 2008	826,767	$ 47.83	5.0	–
Exercisable and expected to vest at December 31, 2008	1,302,661	$ 79.56	6.4	–

The aggregate intrinsic value in the table above represents the total pre-tax intrinsic value (difference between our closing stock price on the last trading day of 2008 and the exercise price, multiplied by the number of in-the-money options). The aggregate intrinsic value shown for the stock options outstanding, those options exercisable, and those options exercisable and expected to vest at December 31, 2008 is reported at zero because generally the options were out-of-the-money at December 31, 2008. Intrinsic value changes are based on the fair market value of our stock. Total intrinsic value of options outstanding at December 31, 2007 was $90 million.

During the years ended December 31, 2008, 2007, and 2006, the total intrinsic value of stock options exercised (i.e., the difference between the market price at exercise and the price paid by the employee to exercise the option) was $29 million, $32 million, and $27 million, respectively.

The total amount of cash received by U. S. Steel from the exercise of options was $11 million during the year ended December 31, 2008, and the related net tax benefit realized from the exercise of these options was $11 million.

Stock awards

In accordance with FAS 123(R), compensation expense for nonvested stock awards is recorded over the vesting period based on the fair value at the date of grant.

Remaining outstanding performance restricted stock awards, a type of award granted prior to 2006, vested in three tranches, subject to U. S. Steel's satisfaction of certain performance criteria during 2005. In May 2006, the Compensation Committee determined that the performance criteria had been satisfied and a portion of the performance restricted stock awards vested (52,900 shares). In May 2007, 35,113 shares vested and the remaining 32,300 shares vested in May 2008.

Restricted stock awards and RSU's vest ratably over three years. The fair value of restricted stock awards and RSU's is the market price of the underlying common stock on the date of grant.

Performance stock awards vest at the end of a three-year performance period as a function of U. S. Steel's total shareholder return compared to the total shareholder return of peer companies over the three-year performance period. Performance stock awards can vest at between zero and 200 percent of the target award.

The following table shows a summary of the performance stock awards outstanding as of December 31, 2008, and their fair market value on the respective grant date:

Performance Period	Fair Value (in millions)	Minimum Shares	Target Shares	Maximum Shares
2008–2011	$7	–	32,870	65,740
2007–2010	$9	–	61,300	122,600
2006–2009	$6	–	87,433	174,866

The following table shows a summary of the status and activity of nonvested stock awards for the year ended December 31, 2008:

	Performance Restricted Stock Awards	Restricted Stock Awards	Restricted Stock Units	Performance Stock Awards[a]	Total	Weighted-Average Grant-Date Fair Value
Nonvested at January 1, 2008	32,300	336,679		151,525	520,504	$ 89.39
Granted	–	1,000	118,420	32,870	152,290	174.28
Vested	(32,300)	(127,206)	(37)	–	(159,543)	75.87
Forfeited or expired	–	(20,234)	(969)	(2,792)	(23,995)	101.29
Nonvested at December 31, 2008	–	190,239	117,414	181,603	489,256	

[a] The number of shares shown for the performance stock awards is based on the target number of share awards.

The following table presents information on performance restricted stock awards, restricted stock awards, RSU's and performance stock awards granted:

	2008	2007	2006
Number of shares (or RSU's) granted	152,290	262,385	324,780
Weighted-average grant-date fair value per share	$ 174.28	$ 115.53	$ 66.06

Textron
2008 Annual Report

Note 2. Discontinued Operations

In November 2008, we completed the sale of our Fluid & Power business unit to Clyde Blowers Limited, a U.K.-based worldwide leader in the areas of power, materials handling, intermodal transport and logistics, and pump technologies. This sale included our Gear Technologies, Hydraulics, Maag Pump and Union Pump product lines, along with each of their respective brands. We received approximately $527 million in cash, a six-year note with a face value of $28 million and up to $50 million based on final 2008 operating results that will be determined by the end of the first quarter of 2009, which will be primarily payable in a six-year note. We recorded an after-tax gain of $111 million for this sale. After taxes and other deal-related expenses are paid, we expect total net after-tax proceeds for the sale to be approximately $380 million, excluding any payments due to us related to the 2008 operating results.

In August 2006, we completed the sale of our Fastening Systems business to Platinum Equity, a private equity investment firm, for approximately $613 million in cash and the assumption of $16 million of net indebtedness and certain liabilities. There was no gain or loss recorded upon completion of the sale. Prior to the consummation of the sale of the Fastening Systems business, we recorded an impairment charge of $120 million in 2006 to record the business at the estimated fair value less cost to sell.

The Fluid & Power and Fastening Systems businesses met the discontinued operations criteria and have been included in discontinued operations for all periods presented in our Consolidated Financial Statements. The results of the Fluid & Power business were previously reported in the Industrial segment.

We generally use a centralized approach to the cash management and financing of our manufacturing operations and, accordingly, do not allocate debt or interest expense to our discontinued businesses. Any debt and related interest expense of a specific entity within a business is recorded by the respective entity. General corporate overhead previously allocated to the businesses for reporting purposes is excluded from amounts reported as discontinued operations.

The assets and liabilities of our discontinued businesses are as follows:

(In millions)	January 3, 2009	December 29, 2007
Accounts receivable, net	$ –	$125
Inventories	–	131
Other current assets	–	20
Property, plant and equipment, net	–	81
Goodwill	–	216
Other assets	10	26
Total assets of discontinued operations of Fluid & Power	10	599

(In millions)	January 3, 2009	December 29, 2007
Assets of discontinued operations of Fastening Systems	26	8
Total assets of discontinued operations	$ 36	$607
Accounts payable and accrued liabilities	$ 12	$178
Accrued postretirement benefits other than pensions	–	38
Other liabilities	24	115
Long-term debt	–	2
Total liabilities of discontinued operations of Fluid & Power	36	333
Liabilities of discontinued operations of Fastening Systems	115	134
Total liabilities of discontinued operations	$151	$467

Upon the sale of Fluid & Power, we retained sponsorship of a defined benefit pension plan for former employees and retirees of the U.K.-based businesses. No additional benefits can be earned under this plan, and future cash contributions to the plan are not expected to be significant. At January 3, 2009, the fair value of the plan assets totaled $198 million, and the projected benefit obligation totaled $188 million.

Revenue, results of operations and gains on disposal for our discontinued businesses are as follows:

(In millions)	2008	2007	2006
Revenue	$560	$610	$1,618
Income (loss) from discontinued operations before income taxes	34	51	(76)
Income taxes	3	15	16
Operating income (loss) from discontinued operations, net of income taxes	31	36	(92)
Gains on disposal, net of income taxes	111	2	–
Income (loss) from discontinued operations, net of income taxes	$142	$ 38	$ (92)

Note 17. Research and Development

Company-funded and customer-funded research and development costs are as follows:

(In millions)	2008	2007	2006
Company-funded	$ 476	$ 365	$ 351
Customer-funded	504	449	435
Total research and development	$ 980	$ 814	$ 786

Our customer-funded research and development costs primarily are related to U.S. Government contracts, including development contracts for the V-22, VH-71, H-1, Intelligent Battlefield Systems and Unmanned Aircraft Systems, and, prior to its termination, the ARH.

Through Bell/Agusta Aerospace Company LLC (BAAC), Bell Helicopter, Agusta S.p.A. and two of its affiliated companies (collectively, "Agusta") share certain Model BA609 development costs. On behalf of BAAC, Agusta will incur development costs to enhance its investment in BAAC. Agusta also may make cash contributions to reimburse portions of our development costs incurred on behalf of BAAC. Based on development costs incurred, we received $8 million, $11 million and $19 million in cash contributions from Agusta, which were recorded in income in 2008, 2007 and 2006, respectively.

During 2005, Bell Helicopter entered into four separate risk-sharing arrangements. Two of the arrangements are with commercial participants in the development of the Bell Model 429 aircraft. In 2007, one agreement was modified to reduce the amount of cash and in-kind development efforts required from the participant, with corresponding reductions in the entitlements the participant may obtain upon future Model 429 production and sales. The arrangements require contributions from the participants totaling $14 million, which are due once the development effort reaches certain predetermined milestones, as well as in-kind development contributions from one participant. The other two arrangements are with Canadian governmental organizations. These arrangements, which currently include the Model 429 aircraft and may potentially include certain future aircraft, each require cash contributions of up to CAD 115 million from the participants, based on a percentage of qualifying research and development costs incurred.

Each of the participants under these arrangements is entitled to payments from Bell Helicopter, with the commercial participants also entitled to discounts, based on future sales of the Model 429 aircraft. In addition, there are certain requirements related to production of future Model 429 aircraft in Canada. Based on the development activities completed and costs incurred, we have recorded income of $15 million, $22 million and $22 million in 2008, 2007 and 2006, respectively, related to these arrangements.

Cessna began developing the Citation Columbus, a wide-body, eight-passenger business jet in 2008. As part of the development of the jet, we entered into a risk-sharing arrangement with a supplier for the development of the aircraft. The arrangement requires contributions from the supplier of $50 million, which are due once the development effort reaches certain predetermined milestones. The contributions will be recognized as a reduction of research and development costs ratably as development costs are incurred. Based on development activities completed and costs incurred, contributions of $3 million were recognized as an offset to research and development expense in 2008. We have also contracted with several other suppliers to perform development efforts related to the Columbus aircraft on a fixed-price basis. Our obligations to these suppliers are based on the progress toward completion of certain predetermined milestones. The related development costs are accrued as the milestones are completed.

Based on the milestone progress achieved, we have recorded expense of $17 million in 2008 related to these arrangements.

In 2008, 2007 and 2006, we received, or were due to receive, $23 million, $33 million and $41 million, respectively, in cost reimbursements of company-funded amounts from our risk-sharing partners. Based on these reimbursements, our net company-funded costs totaled $453 million, $332 million and $310 million in 2008, 2007 and 2006, respectively.

Note 18. Guarantees and Indemnifications

Our Manufacturing group extends a variety of financial and performance guarantees to third parties as provided in the table below:

	January 3, 2009		December 29, 2007	
(In millions)	Maximum Potential Payment*	Carrying Amount of Liability	Maximum Potential Payment*	Carrying Amount of Liability
Performance guarantee	$331	$ –	$300	$ –
Guaranteed minimum resale contracts	30	3	30	3
Guarantees related to dispositions	17	19	17	29
Debt obligations of joint ventures	3	–	4	–

* These agreements include uncapped guarantees as described below.

Performance Guarantee

In 2004, through our Bell Helicopter business, we formed AgustaWestlandBell LLC (AWB LLC) with AgustaWestland North America Inc. (AWNA). This venture was created for the joint design, development, manufacture, sale, customer training and product support of the VH-71 helicopter, and certain variations and derivatives thereof, to be offered and sold to departments or agencies of the U.S. Government. In March 2005, AWB LLC received a $1.2 billion cost reimbursement-type subcontract from Lockheed Martin for the System Development and Demonstration phase of the U.S. Marine Corps Helicopter Squadron Program, which was increased to $1.4 billion in December 2008. We guaranteed to Lockheed Martin the due and prompt performance by AWB LLC of all its obligations under this subcontract, provided that our liability under the guaranty shall not exceed 49% of AWB LLC's aggregate liability to Lockheed Martin under the subcontract. AgustaWestland N.V., AWNA's parent company, has guaranteed the remaining 51% to Lockheed Martin. We have entered into cross-indemnification agreements with AgustaWestland N.V. in which each party indemnifies the other related to any payments required under these agreements that result from the indemnifying party's workshare under any subcontracts received. AWB LLC's maximum obligation is 50% of the total contract value, or $676 million, for a maximum amount of our liability under the guarantee of $331 million at January 3, 2009 through completion. Under the current phase of the contract, we do not believe that there is any performance risk with respect to the guarantee. In late January 2009, the Pentagon declared a Nunn-McCurdy Act breach for this program due to cost overruns, requiring recertification of the program. We do not have enough information at this time to make a determination of whether the program will be recertified; however, if the program were to be terminated, we do not believe that the guarantee will be triggered as it relates solely to performance under the subcontract.

Guaranteed Minimum Resale Contracts

We have a number of guaranteed minimum resale value contracts associated with certain past aircraft sales. If the fair value of an aircraft falls below a minimum guaranteed amount, we may be required to make a future payment to the customer or provide a minimum trade-in value toward a new aircraft. These agreements generally include operating restrictions such as maximum usage over the contract period or minimum maintenance requirements. We also have guaranteed the minimum resale value of certain customer-owned aircraft anticipated to be traded in upon completion of a model currently under development. These contracts expire as follows: $3 million in each year in 2009, 2010 and 2011, $19 million in 2012 and $2 million in 2013. Based upon the expected guarantees to be exercised under these arrangements, we had an accrued liability of $3 million as of both January 3, 2009 and December 27, 2007.

Guarantees Related to Dispositions

We indemnified the purchasers of the Fastening Systems and Fluid & Power businesses for remediation costs related to pre-existing environmental conditions to the extent they exist at the sold locations and certain retained litigation matters. We have estimated the fair value of these indemnifications at approximately $19 million. Potential payments under these obligations are not capped, and, as a result, the maximum potential obligation cannot be determined. During 2008 and 2007, we incurred approximately $2 million and $1 million, respectively, in remediation costs. We also have other obligations, some of which are capped, arising from sales of these and certain other businesses, including representations and warranties and related indemnities for environmental, health and safety, and tax and employment matters. The maximum potential payment related to other obligations that are capped is $17 million, while the maximum potential payment for the obligations that are not capped cannot be determined. At January 3, 2009, we do not believe there are any capped or uncapped matters that could have a significant adverse effect on our financial position, results of operations or liquidity.

Software Indemnifications

We enter into software license agreements with customers through our Overwatch Systems business. These software license agreements generally include certain provisions for indemnifying customers against liabilities if our software products infringe a third party's intellectual property rights. To date, we have not incurred any material costs as a result of such indemnifications and have not accrued any liabilities related to such obligations. The risk that we will be required to perform on any of these indemnifications is low.

Warranty and Product Maintenance Contracts

We provide limited warranty and product maintenance programs, including parts and labor, for certain products for periods ranging from one to five years. We estimate the costs that may be incurred under warranty programs and record a liability in the amount of such costs at the time product revenue is recognized. Factors that affect this liability include the number of products sold, historical and anticipated rates of warranty claims, and cost per claim. We assess the adequacy of our recorded warranty and product maintenance liabilities periodically and adjust the amounts as necessary.

Changes in our warranty and product maintenance liability are as follows:

(In millions)	2008	2007	2006
Accrual at beginning of year	$ 315	$ 310	$ 313
Provision	190	189	188
Settlements	(195)	(178)	(165)
Adjustments to prior accrual estimates*	(26)	(15)	(26)
Acquisitions and related adjustments	(4)	9	–
Accrual at end of year	$ 280	$ 315	$ 310

* Adjustments include changes to prior year estimates, new issues on prior year sales and currency translation adjustments.

Goodyear Tire and Rubber
2008 Annual Report

Note 3. Other (Income) and Expense

(In millions)	2008	2007	2006
Interest income	$(68)	$(128)	$(86)
Asset sales	(53)	(15)	(40)
Financing fees and financial instruments	97	106	40
General and product liability—discontinued products	30	15	26
Foreign currency exchange	57	31	(2)
Royalty income	(32)	(15)	(8)
Subsidiary liquidation loss	16	–	–
Fire loss expense	3	12	–
Miscellaneous	9	2	(7)
	$59	$ 8	$(77)

Interest income consisted primarily of amounts earned on cash deposits. The decrease in 2008 compared to 2007 was due primarily to lower average cash balances and interest rates during the year.

Net gains on asset sales in 2008 were $53 million ($50 million after-tax or $0.21 per share) and included a gain of $20 million on the sale of property in EMEA, a gain of $10 million on the sale of property, buildings and equipment in Asia Pacific Tire, a gain of $11 million on the sale of property in North American

Tire, a gain of $5 million on the sale of property and buildings in Latin American Tire, and net gains of $7 million on the sales of other assets in North American Tire.

Net gains on asset sales in 2007 were $15 million ($11 million after-tax or $0.05 per share) and included a gain of $19 million on the sale of our Washington, UK facility in EMEA, a gain of $19 million on the sale of warehouses and other property and equipment in North American Tire, a gain of $7 million on the sale of property in Asia Pacific Tire, and net gains of $6 million on the sales of other assets primarily in EMEA and North American Tire.

Net gains were partially offset by the loss of $36 million on the sale of substantially all of the assets of North American Tire's tire and wheel assembly operation in the fourth quarter of 2007. Net gains on asset sales in 2006 were $40 million ($31 million after-tax or $0.17 per share) and included a gain of $21 million on the sale of a capital lease in EMEA, a gain of $9 million on the sale of the Fabric business, and net gains of $10 million on the sales of other assets primarily in EMEA.

Financing fees and financial instruments in 2008 included $43 million related to the redemption of $650 million of long term debt, of which $33 million was a cash premium paid on the redemption, $9 million was deferred financing fee write-offs, and $1 million was bond discount write-offs. Also included was a $10 million charge related to the interest rate basis swap on our $1.2 billion term loan and a $5 million valuation allowance on our investment in The Reserve Primary Fund.

Financing fees and financial instruments in 2007 included $33 million related to the redemption of $315 million of long term debt, of which $28 million was a cash premium paid on the redemption, and $5 million was deferred financing fee write-offs. Also included was a $17 million charge related to the exchange offer for our outstanding 4% convertible senior notes and $14 million of debt issuance costs written-off in connection with our refinancing activities in April 2007.

General and product liability-discontinued products includes charges for claims against us related to asbestos personal injury claims, and for liabilities related to Entran II claims, net of probable insurance recoveries. During 2008, $3 million of expenses were related to Entran II claims and $27 million of net expenses were related to asbestos claims ($28 million of expense and $1 million of probable insurance recoveries). During 2007, $4 million of expenses were related to Entran II claims and $11 million of net expenses were related to asbestos claims ($25 million of expense and $14 million of probable insurance recoveries). During 2006, $9 million of expenses were related to Entran II claims and $17 million of net expenses were related to asbestos claims ($39 million of expense and $22 million of probable insurance recoveries).

During 2008, we incurred $57 million of foreign currency exchange losses primarily as a result of the weakening Canadian dollar, euro, South African rand and Australian dollar against the U.S. dollar.

During 2007, we incurred $31 million of foreign currency exchange losses primarily as a result of the strengthening euro, Chilean peso and Brazilian real against the U.S. dollar.

Royalty income increased in 2008 and included royalties from licensing arrangements related to divested businesses, including recognition of deferred income from a trademark licensing agreement related to our Engineered Products business that was divested in the third quarter of 2007.

We liquidated our subsidiary in Jamaica in the fourth quarter of 2008 and recognized a loss of $16 million primarily due to the recognition of accumulated foreign currency translation losses.

In 2007, there was a fire in our Thailand facility, which resulted in a loss of $12 million, net of insurance proceeds.

Included in 2006 miscellaneous income is a $13 million gain in Latin American Tire resulting from the favorable resolution of a legal matter.

Texas Instruments
2008 Annual Report

2. Restructuring Activities

We record severance-related expenses in accordance with the provisions of SFAS No. 112, Employer's Accounting for Post-Employment Benefits; SFAS No. 146, Accounting for Costs Associated with Exit or Disposal Activities and SFAS No. 88, Employers' Accounting for Settlements and Curtailments of Defined Benefit Pension Plans and for Termination Benefits. The determination of when we accrue for involuntary severance costs and which standard applies depends on whether the termination benefits are provided under an ongoing benefit arrangement as described in SFAS 112 or under a one-time benefit arrangement as defined by SFAS 146. We record involuntary severance-related expenses related to an ongoing benefit arrangement in accordance with the provisions of SFAS No. 112 once they are probable and the amounts are estimable. One-time, involuntary termination benefits are recorded under the provisions of SFAS No. 146 when the benefits have been communicated to employees. Voluntary termination benefits are accounted for under the provisions of SFAS No. 88 and are recorded when the employee accepts the offered benefit arrangement.

When the decision to commit to a restructuring plan requires an asset impairment review, we evaluate such impairment issues under the provisions of SFAS No. 144, Accounting for the Impairment or Disposal of Long-Lived Assets. Because the impairment is a direct result of the restructuring, the impairment amount is included in the restructuring expense line item in the income statement and is recorded as an adjustment of the basis of the asset, not as a liability relating to a restructuring charge. When we commit to a plan to abandon a long-lived asset before the end of its previously estimated useful life, we accelerate the recognition of depreciation to reflect the use of the asset over its shortened useful life. When an asset is to be sold, we write the carrying value down to its net realizable value and cease depreciation.

2008 and 2009 actions

In October 2008, we announced actions that, when complete, will reduce annualized expenses by more than $200 million in our Wireless segment, especially our cellular baseband operation. About 650 jobs are expected to be eliminated. The total restructuring charges related to this action will be approximately $110 million and are expected to be complete by June 2009.

In January 2009 we announced actions that include employment reductions to align our spending with demand that has weakened in the slowing economy. Our employment will be reduced 12 percent through 1,800 layoffs and 1,600 voluntary retirements and departures. The total restructuring charges for this action will be about $300 million and will continue through the third quarter of 2009. Combined with the Wireless actions described above, our annualized costs will be reduced by more than $700 million.

In the fourth quarter of 2008, we recognized $230 million in restructuring charges related to these actions, which included $121 million for a portion of the actions announced in January 2009 and $109 million for the Wireless actions announced in October 2008. The restructuring costs consisted of $218 million for severance and benefits costs and $12 million related to impairments of long-lived assets. We also fully impaired $24 million of assets that were held for sale related to a 2007 action discussed below.

As of December 31, 2008, $2 million has been paid for these actions to terminated employees for severance and benefits.

2007 actions

In January 2007, we announced plans to change how we develop advanced digital manufacturing process technology. Instead of separately creating our own core process technology, we work collaboratively with our foundry partners to specify and drive the next generations of digital process technology. Additionally, we stopped production at an older digital factory. These actions are complete and as a result, about 300 jobs were eliminated by year-end 2007.

Operating profit for 2007 included a charge of $52 million related to these actions, which consisted of severance and benefits costs of $31 million and acceleration of depreciation on the impacted facilities' assets of $21 million. These amounts have been reclassified from cost of revenue ($37 million), R&D ($14 million) and SG&A ($1 million) to the restructuring expense line on the income statement to conform to the 2008 presentation.

As of December 31, 2008, $19 million has been paid for these actions to terminated employees for severance and benefits.

Parker Hannifin
2008 Annual Report

Note 5. Earnings per Share

Earnings per share have been computed according to FASB Statement No. 128, "Earnings per Share." Basic earnings per share is computed using the weighted-average number of common shares outstanding during the year. Diluted earnings per share is computed using the weighted-average number of common shares and common share equivalents outstanding during the year. Common share equivalents represent the dilutive effect of outstanding stock-based awards.

The computation of income from continuing operations per share was as follows:

	2008	2007	2006
Numerator:			
Income from continuing operations	$ 949,466	$ 830,046	$ 638,276
Denominator:			
Basic-weighted-average common shares	168,285,487	174,643,327	178,816,787
Increase in weighted average from dilutive effect of exercise of stock-based awards	3,358,348	2,851,563	2,509,485
Diluted-weighted-average common shares, assuming exercise of stock-based awards	171,643,835	177,494,890	181,326,272
Basic earnings per share from continuing operations	$ 5.64	$ 4.75	$ 3.57
Diluted earnings per share from continuing operations	$ 5.53	$ 4.68	$ 3.52

For 2008, 2007 and 2006, 1.1 million, 2.5 million and 2.9 million common shares, respectively, subject to stock-based awards were excluded from the computation of diluted earnings per share from continuing operations because the effect of their exercise would be anti-dilutive.

Goodyear Tire
2007 Annual Report

Note 2. Costs Associated with Rationalization Programs

To maintain global competitiveness, we have implemented rationalization actions over the past several years to reduce excess and high-cost manufacturing capacity and to reduce associate headcount. The net rationalization charges included in Income (Loss) from Continuing Operations before Income Taxes and Minority Interest are as follows:

(In millions)	2007	2006	2005
New charges	$ 63	$ 322	$ 24
Reversals	(14)	(11)	(17)
	$ 49	$ 311	$ 7

The following table presents the roll-forward of the liability balance between periods:

(In millions)	Associate-Related Costs	Other Than Associate-Related Costs	Total
Balance at December 31, 2004	$ 39	$ 27	$ 66
2005 charges	22	2	24
Incurred	(34)	(7)	(41)
Reverse to the Statement of Operations	(10)	(7)	(17)
Balance at December 31, 2005	17	15	32
2006 charges	294	28	322
Incurred	(225)	(21)	(246)
Reversed to the Statement of Operations	(9)	(2)	(11)
Balance at December 31, 2006	77	20	97
2007 charges	36	27	63
Incurred	(45)	(39)	(84)
Reversed to the Statement of Operations	(12)	(2)	(14)
Balance at December 31, 2007	$ 56	$ 6	$ 62

Rationalization actions in 2007 consisted primarily of a decision to reduce tire production at two facilities in Amiens, France in our European Union Tire Segment. These actions are expected to be implemented in the second half of 2008 and will involve a reduction of up to 500 associates and the reduction of certain high-cost production. Other rationalization actions in 2007 relate to plans to reduce manufacturing, selling, administrative and general expenses through headcount reductions in several segments.

During 2007, net rationalization charges of $49 million ($41 million after-tax or $0.17 per share) were recorded. New charges of $63 million were comprised of $28 million for plans initiated in 2007, primarily related to associate severance costs, and $35 million for plans initiated in 2006, consisting of $9 million for associate severance costs and $26 million for other exit and non-cancelable lease costs. The net charges in 2007 also included the reversal of $14 million of charges for actions no longer needed for their originally intended purposes. Approximately 600 associates will be released under programs initiated in 2007, of which approximately 100 were released by December 31, 2007.

In 2007, $45 million was incurred for associate severance payments, and $39 million was incurred for noncancelable lease and other exit costs.

The accrual balance of $62 million at December 31, 2007 consists of $56 million for associate severance costs that are expected to be substantially utilized within the next twelve months and $6 million primarily for long term non-cancelable lease costs.

In addition to the above charges, accelerated depreciation charges of $37 million were recorded in CGS in 2007, primarily for fixed assets taken out of service in connection with the elimination of tire production at our Tyler, Texas and Valleyfield, Quebec facilities in our North American Tire Segment.

No significant additional rationalization charges are expected to be incurred related to rationalization plans announced in 2007.

Rationalization actions in 2006 consisted of plant closures in the European Union Tire Segment of a passenger tire manufacturing facility in Washington, United Kingdom, and in the Asia Pacific Tire Segment of the Upper Hutt, New Zealand passenger tire manufacturing facility. Charges were also incurred for a plan in North American Tire to cease tire manufacturing at our Tyler, Texas facility, which was substantially complete in December 2007, and a plan in Eastern Europe Tire to close our tire manufacturing facility in Casablanca, Morocco, which was completed in the first quarter of 2007. Charges were also recorded for a partial plant closure in the North American Tire Segment involving a plan to discontinue tire production at our Valleyfield, Quebec facility, which was completed by the second quarter of 2007. In conjunction with these charges we also recorded a $47 million tax valuation allowance. Other plans in 2006 included an action in the Eastern Europe Tire Segment to exit the bicycle tire and tube production line in Debica, Poland, retail store closures in the European Union Tire and Eastern Europe Tire Segments as well as plans in most segments to reduce selling, administrative and general expenses through headcount reductions, all of which were substantially completed.

For 2006, $311 million ($328 million after-tax or $1.85 per share) of net charges were recorded. New charges of $322 million are comprised of $315 million for plans initiated in 2006 and $7 million for plans initiated in 2005 for associate-related costs. The $315 million of charges for 2006 plans consisted of $286 million of associate-related costs, of which $159 million related to associate severance costs and $127 million related to non-cash pension and postretirement benefit costs, and $29 million of non-cancelable lease costs. The net charges in 2006 also included reversals of $11 million for actions no longer needed for their originally intended purposes. Approximately 4,800 associates will be released under programs initiated in 2006, of which approximately 3,900 were released by December 31, 2007.

In 2006, $98 million was incurred for associate severance payments, $127 million for non-cash pension and postretirement termination benefit costs, and $21 million for non-cancelable lease and other exit costs.

In addition to the above charges, accelerated depreciation charges of $81 million and asset impairment charges of $2 million were recorded in CGS related to fixed assets that will be taken out of service primarily in connection with the Washington, Casablanca, Upper Hutt, and Tyler plant closures. We also recorded charges of $2 million of accelerated depreciation and $3 million of asset impairment in SAG.

Rationalization charges in 2005 consisted of manufacturing associate reductions, retail store reductions, IT associate reductions, and a sales function reorganization in European Union Tire; manufacturing and administrative associate reductions in Eastern Europe Tire; and manufacturing and corporate support group associate reductions in North American Tire, all of which were substantially completed.

For 2005, $7 million ($2 million after-tax or $0.00 per share) of net charges were recorded, which included $24 million of charges recorded in 2005, of which $22 million were for associate-related costs for new plans initiated in 2005 and $2 million for plans initiated in prior years. These charges were partially offset by $17 million of reversals for rationalization charges no longer needed for their originally-intended purposes. The reversals consisted of $10 million of associate-related costs for plans initiated in prior years, and $7 million for noncancelable leases that were exited during the first quarter related to plans initiated in prior years. Approximately 740 associates have been released under the programs initiated in 2005 as of December 31, 2007.

In 2005, $33 million was incurred for associate severance payments, $1 million for cash pension settlement benefit costs and $7 million for non-cancelable lease costs.

Accelerated depreciation charges of $4 million were recorded for fixed assets that were taken out of service in connection with certain rationalization plans initiated in 2005 and 2004 in the European Union Tire Segment, of which $3 million was recorded as CGS and $1 million was recorded as SAG.

Kellog's
2007 Annual Report

Note 3. Exit or Disposal Plans

The Company views its continued spending on cost-reduction initiatives as part of its ongoing operating principles to provide greater reliability in meeting long-term growth targets. Initiatives undertaken must meet certain pay-back and internal rate of return (IRR) targets. Each cost-reduction initiative is normally one to three years in duration. Upon completion (or as each major stage is completed in the case of multi-year programs), the project begins to deliver cash savings and/or reduced depreciation, which is then used to fund new initiatives. To implement these programs, the Company has incurred various up-front costs, including asset write-offs, exit charges, and other project expenditures.

Cost summary

For 2007, the Company recorded total program-related charges of approximately $100 million, comprised of $7 million of asset write-offs, $72 million for severance and other exit costs including route franchise settlements, discussed on page 40, $15 million for other cash expenditures, and $6 million for a multiemployer pension plan withdrawal liability. Approximately $23 million of the total 2007 charges were recorded in cost of goods sold within the Europe operating segment results, with approximately $77 million recorded in SGA expense within the North America operating results.

For 2006, the Company recorded total program-related charges of approximately $82 million, comprised of $20 million of asset write-offs, $30 million for severance and other exit costs, $9 million for other cash expenditures, $4 million for a multiemployer pension plan withdrawal liability, and $19 million for pension and other postretirement plan curtailment losses and special termination benefits. Approximately $74 million of the total 2006 charges were recorded in cost of goods sold within operating segment results, with approximately $8 million recorded in SGA expense within corporate results. The Company's operating segments were impacted as follows (in millions): North America–$46; Europe–$28.

For 2005, the Company recorded total program-related charges of approximately $90 million, comprised of $16 million for a multiemployer pension plan withdrawal liability, $44 million of asset write-offs, $21 million for severance and other exit costs, and $9 million for other cash expenditures. All of the 2005 charges were recorded in cost of goods sold within the Company's North America operating segment.

Exit cost reserves were approximately $5 million at December 29, 2007, consisting principally of severance and lease termination obligations associated with projects commenced in 2007, which are expected to be paid out in 2008. At December 30, 2006 and December 31, 2005, exit cost reserves were approximately $14 million, and $13 million respectively, primarily representing severance costs that were substantially paid out in the following year.

Specific initiatives

In September 2006, the Company approved a multi-year European manufacturing optimization plan to improve utilization of its facility in Manchester, England and to better align production in Europe. Based on forecasted foreign exchange rates, the Company currently expects to incur approximately $55 million in total up-front costs, including $28 million recorded in 2006, and $19 million recorded in 2007, with the remainder to be incurred in 2008. The cost is comprised of approximately 90% cash expenditures and 10% non-cash asset write-offs. The cash portion of the total up-front costs results principally from management's plan to eliminate approximately 220 hourly and salaried positions from the Manchester facility by the end of 2008 through voluntary early retirement and severance programs. The pension trust funding requirements of these early retirements are expected to exceed the recognized benefit expense impact by approximately $5 million; most of this incremental funding occurred in 2006. During this program, certain manufacturing equipment will also be removed from service.

All of the costs for the European manufacturing optimization plan have been recorded in cost of goods sold within the Company's European operating segment. The following tables present total project costs to date and a reconciliation of employee severance reserves for this initiative. All other cash costs were paid in the period incurred.

Project costs to date (millions)	Employee Severance	Other Cash Costs[a]	Asset Write-Offs	Retirement Benefits[b]	Total
Year ended December 30, 2006	$12	$ 2	$5	$9	$28
Year ended December 29, 2007	7	8	4		19
Total project to date	$19	$10	$9	$9	$47

(a) Primarily includes expenditures for equipment removal and relocation, and temporary contracted services to facilitate employee transitions.

(b) Pension plan curtailment losses and special termination benefits recognized under SFAS No. 88, "Accounting for Settlements and Curtailments of Defined Benefit Pension Plans and for Termination Benefits."

Employee severance reserves to date (millions)	Beginning of Period	Accruals	Payments	End of Period
Year ended December 30, 2006	–	$12	–	$12
Year ended December 29, 2007	12	7	(19)	–
Total project to date		$19	($19)	

In October 2007, management committed to reorganize certain production processes between the Company's plants in Valls, Spain and Bremen, Germany. Commencement of this plan follows consultation with union representatives at the Bremen facility regarding the elimination of approximately 120 employee positions. This reorganization plan is specifically intended to improve manufacturing and distribution efficiency across the Company's continental European operations, and is expected to be completed by mid 2008. Based on forecasted foreign exchange rates, the Company expects to incur approximately $25 million of total project costs, comprised of approximately 50% asset write-offs and 50% employee separation benefits and other cash costs. The Company recorded $4 million of costs in 2007, with the remaining to be incurred in 2008.

All of the costs for European production process realignment have been recorded in cost of goods sold within the Company's European operating segment.

The following tables present total project costs to date and a reconciliation of employee severance reserves for this initiative. All other cash costs were paid in the period incurred.

Project cost to date (millions)	Employee Severance	Other Cash Costs(a)(a)	Asset Write-Offs	Total
Year ended December 29, 2007	$2	$1	$1	$4
Total project to date	$2	$1	$1	$4

(a) Primarily includes expenditures for equipment removal and relocation, and temporary contracted services to facilitate employee transitions.

Employee severance reserves to date (millions)	Beginning of Period	Accruals	Payments	End of Period
Year ended December 29, 2007	–	$2	–	$2
Total project to date		$2	–	

In July 2007, management commenced a plan to reorganize the Company's direct store-door delivery (DSD) operations in the southeastern United States. This DSD reorganization plan is intended to integrate the Company's southeastern sales and distribution regions with the rest of its U.S. direct store-door operations, resulting in greater efficiency across the nationwide network. In preparation for this initiative, in June 2007, the Company began to extend offers to exit approximately 517 distribution route franchise agreements with independent contractors, which were substantially accepted as of July 2007. The plan resulted in the involuntary termination or relocation of approximately 300 employee positions. Total project costs incurred were $77 million, principally consisting of cash expenditures for route franchise settlements and to a lesser extent, for employee separation, relocation, and reorganization. This initiative was substantially complete by the end of 2007.

All of the costs for the U.S. DSD reorganization plan have been recorded in selling, general, and administrative expense within the Company's North America operating segment. The following tables present total project costs to date. Exit cost reserves were approximately $3 million as of December 29, 2007, primarily related to lease termination costs. All other cash costs were paid in the period incurred.

Project cost to date (millions)	Route Franchise Settlements	Employee Severance	Other Cash Costs[a]	Retirement Benefit[b]	Asset Write-Offs	Total
Year ended December 29, 2007	$62	$1	$6	$6	$2	$77
Total project to date	$62	$1	$6	$6	$2	$77

[a] Primarily includes expenditures for equipment removal and relocation, and temporary contracted services to facilitate employee transitions.
[b] Estimated multiemployer pension plan withdrawal liability.

During 2006, the Company commenced several initiatives to enhance the productivity and efficiency of its U.S. cereal manufacturing network, primarily through technological and sourcing improvements in warehousing and packaging operations. In conjunction with these initiatives, the Company offered voluntary separation incentives, which resulted in the retirement of approximately 80 hourly employees by early 2007. During the fourth quarter of 2006, the Company incurred approximately $15 million of total up-front costs, comprised of approximately 20% asset write-offs and 80% cash costs, including $10 million of pension and other postretirement plan curtailment losses. These initiatives were complete by the end of 2007.

Also during 2006, the Company undertook an initiative to improve customer focus and selling efficiency within a particular Latin American market, leading to a shift from a third-party distributor to a direct sales force model. As a result of this initiative, the Company paid $8 million in cash during the fourth quarter of 2006 to exit the existing distribution arrangement.

To improve operational efficiency and better position its North American snacks business for future growth, during 2005, the Company undertook an initiative to consolidate U.S. bakery capacity, which was completed by the end of 2006. The project resulted in the closure and sale of the Company's Des Plaines,

Illinois facility in late 2005 and closure of its Macon, Georgia facility in April 2006, with sale occurring in September 2006. These closures resulted in the elimination of over 700 hourly and salaried employee positions, through the combination of involuntary severance and attrition. Related to this initiative, the Company incurred up-front costs of approximately $80 million in 2005, comprised of approximately one-half asset write-offs and one-half cash costs, including $16 million for the present value of a projected multiemployer pension plan withdrawal liability associated with closure of the Macon facility. The Company incurred approximately $31 million in up-front costs for 2006, comprised of approximately one-third asset write-offs and two-thirds cash costs, including a $4 million increase in the Company's estimated pension plan withdrawal liability to $20 million. This increase was principally attributable to investment loss experienced during 2005 in conjunction with increased benefit levels for all participating employers. The final calculation of this liability is pending full-year 2007 employee hours attributable to the Company's remaining participation in this plan, and is therefore subject to adjustment in early 2008. The associated cash obligation is payable to the pension fund over a 20-year maximum period; management has not currently determined the actual period over which the payments will be made. Except for this pension plan withdrawal liability, the Company's cash obligations attributable to this initiative were substantially paid out by year end 2006.

Boeing
2007 Annual Report

Note 3. Earnings Per Share

The weighted-average number of shares outstanding (in millions) for the years ended December 31, used to compute earnings per share are as follows:

	2007	*2006*	*2005*
Weighted-average shares outstanding	**750.5**	760.5	779.4
Participating securities	**8.8**	10.5	9.1
Basic weighted-average shares outstanding	**759.3**	771	788.5
Diluted potential common shares	**13.2**	16.6	14.4
Diluted weighted-average shares outstanding	**772.5**	787.6	802.9

The numerator used to compute diluted earnings per share is as follows:

	2007	*2006*	*2005*
Net earnings	**$4,074**	$2,215	$2,572
Expense related to diluted shares	**2**	27	
Total numerator	**$4,076**	$2,242	$2,572

Expense related to diluted shares in the amount of $2 and $27 in 2007 and 2006 represented mark-to-market adjustment of vested performance shares to employees terminated as of December 31, 2005.

Basic earnings per share is calculated by the sum of (1) net income less declared dividends divided by the basic weighted average shares outstanding and (2) declared dividends divided by the weighted average shares outstanding.

The weighted-average number of shares outstanding for the year ended December 31 (in millions), included in the table below, is excluded from the computation of diluted earnings per share because the average market price did not exceed the exercise/threshold price. However, these shares may be dilutive potential common shares in the future.

	2007	*2006*	*2005*
Stock options			0.2
Stock units		0.1	
Performance shares	**0.7**	4.0	24.9
Performance awards	**3.0**	1.4	
Share value trust	**25.8**	24.6	33.9

Note 4. Income Taxes

The components of earnings before income taxes were:

Years ended December 31,	*2007*	*2006*	*2005*
U.S.	**$5,901**	$3,067	$2,605
Non-U.S.	**217**	127	214
	$6,118	$3,194	$2,819

Income tax expense/(benefit) consisted of the following:

Years ended December 31,	*2007*	*2006*	*2005*
Current tax expense			
U.S. federal	**$1,260**	$193	$(276)
Non-U.S.	**139**	35	58
U.S. state	**164**	(58)	(86)
	1,563	170	(304)
Deferred tax expense			
U.S. federal	**487**	750	547
Non-U.S.	**(6)**	(6)	(120)
U.S. state	**16**	74	134
	497	818	561
Total income tax expense	**$2,060**	$988	$257

The following is a reconciliation of the U.S. federal statutory tax rate of 35% to our recorded income tax expense/(benefit):

Years ended December 31,	2007	2006	2005
U.S. federal statutory tax	35%	35%	35%
Global settlement with U.S. Department of Justice		6.7	
Foreign sales corporation/ extraterritorial income tax benefit		(5.8)	(5.6)
Research benefit	(2.4)	(0.7)	(1.2)
Federal audit settlement		(1.5)	(13.1)
State income tax provision, net of effect on U.S. federal tax	1.6	0.4	1.1
Change in valuation allowances	0.3		(3.2)
Other provision adjustments	(0.8)	(3.2)	(3.9)
Income tax expense	33.7%	30.9%	9.1%

Significant components of our deferred tax assets, net of deferred tax liabilities, at December 31 were as follows:

	2007	2006
Retiree health care accruals	$2,581	$3,257
Inventory and long-term contract methods of income recognition	209	640
Other employee benefits accruals	1,476	1,473
In-process research and development related to acquisitions	108	124
Net operating loss, credit, and charitable contribution carryovers (net of valuation allowance of $20 and $2)	275	319
Pension asset	(1,648)	(397)
Customer and commercial financing	(1,587)	(1,517)
Unremitted earnings of non-U.S. subsidiaries	(48)	(48)
Other net unrealized losses	(18)	37
Net deferred tax assets[1]	$1,348	$3,888

[1] Of the deferred tax asset for net operating loss and credit carryovers, $151 expires in years ending from December 31, 2008 through December 31, 2027 and $125 may be carried over indefinitely.

Net deferred tax assets at December 31 were as follows:

	2007	2006
Deferred tax assets	$ 9,640	$ 12,174
Deferred tax liabilities	(8,272)	(8,284)
Valuation allowance	(20)	(2)
Net deferred tax assets	$ 1,348	$ 3,888

We recorded net deferred tax liabilities of $11 and $171 in 2007 and 2006, which were primarily due to acquisitions.

As required under SFAS 123R, deferred tax liabilities of $79 and $306 were reclassified to Additional paid in capital in 2007 and 2006. This represents the tax effect of the net excess tax pool created during 2007 and 2006 due to share awards paid with a fair market value in excess of the book accrual for those awards.

Included in the net deferred tax assets at December 31, 2007 and 2006 are deferred tax assets in the amounts of $3,169 and $5,240 related to other comprehensive income.

Net income tax payments/(refunds) were $711, $28 and ($344) in 2007, 2006 and 2005, respectively.

We have provided for U.S. deferred income taxes and foreign withholding tax in the amount of $48 on undistributed earnings not considered permanently reinvested in our non-U.S. subsidiaries. We have not provided for U.S. deferred income taxes or foreign withholding tax on the remainder of undistributed earnings from our non-U.S. subsidiaries because such earnings are considered to be permanently reinvested and it is not practicable to estimate the amount of tax that may be payable upon distribution.

FASB Interpretation No. 48

Effective January 1, 2007, we adopted FIN 48 which prescribes a more-likely-than-not threshold for financial statement recognition and measurement of a tax position taken or expected to be taken in a tax return. This interpretation also provides guidance on derecognition of income tax assets and liabilities, classification of current and deferred income tax assets and liabilities, accounting for interest and penalties associated with tax positions, accounting for income taxes in interim periods and income tax disclosures. The cumulative effects of applying this interpretation have been recorded as a decrease of $11 to Retained earnings, an increase of $125 to Deferred income taxes and an increase of $136 to Income taxes payable as of January 1, 2007.

In conjunction with adoption of FIN 48, we classified uncertain tax positions as non-current income tax liabilities unless expected to be paid in one year. We also began reporting income tax-related interest income in Income tax expense in our Consolidated Statement of Operations. In prior periods, such interest income was reported in Other income. Within the Consolidated Statements of Operations, Other income included interest of $16 in 2006 and $100 in 2005 related to federal income tax settlements for prior years. Penalties and tax-related interest expense are reported as a component of Income tax expense. As of December 31 and January 1, 2007, the amount of accrued income tax-related interest and penalties included in the Consolidated Statement of Financial Position was as follows: interest of $143 and $63, and penalties of $17 and $1. The amounts of interest and penalties accrued during 2007 are $108 and $17 respectively.

We are subject to examination in the U.S. federal tax jurisdiction for the 1998-2007 tax years.

We are also subject to examination in major state and foreign jurisdictions for the 2001-2007 tax years, for which no individually material unrecognized tax benefits exist. During the third quarter of 2007 we received an Internal Revenue Service (IRS) audit report for the 2002-2003 tax years and have filed an appeal. We have also filed appeals with the IRS for the 1998-2001 tax years. We believe appropriate provisions for all outstanding issues have been made for all jurisdictions and all open years.

A reconciliation of the beginning and ending amount of unrecognized tax benefits is as follows:

Unrecognized Tax Benefits—January 1, 2007	**$1,097**
Gross increases—tax positions in prior periods	181
Gross decreases—tax positions in prior periods	(85)
Gross increases—current-period tax positions	89
Lapse of statute of limitations	(10)
Unrecognized Tax Benefits—December 31, 2007	**$1,272**

As of December 31 and January 1, 2007, the total amount of unrecognized tax benefits was $1,272 and $1,097, of which $1,032 and $905 would affect the effective tax rate, if recognized. These amounts are primarily associated with U.S. federal tax issues such as the tax benefits from the Foreign Sales Corporation/Extraterritorial Income (FSC/ETI) tax rules, the amount of research and development tax credits claimed, U.S. taxation of foreign earnings, and valuation issues regarding charitable contributions claimed. Also included in these amounts are accruals for domestic state tax issues such as the allocation of income among various state tax jurisdictions and the amount of state tax credits claimed.

It is reasonably possible that within the next 12 months we and the IRS will resolve some of the matters presently under consideration at appeals for 1998-2003 which may increase or decrease unrecognized tax benefits for all open tax years. Settlement could increase earnings in an amount ranging from $0 to $130 based on current estimates. Audit outcomes and the timing of audit settlements are subject to significant uncertainty.

The Research and Development credit expired on December 31, 2007. The credit provided a 2.4% and a 0.7% reduction in the 2007 and 2006 effective tax rate. Congress is currently considering bills that will extend the credit. If the Research and Development credit is not legislatively enacted there could be an unfavorable impact on our 2008 effective income tax rate.

International Business Machines Corporation
2007 Annual Report

Note P. Research, Development and Engineering

RD&E expense was $6,153 million in 2007, $6,107 million in 2006 and $5,842 million in 2005.

The company incurred expense of $5,754 million in 2007, $5,682 million in 2006 and $5,379 million in 2005 for scientific research and the application of scientific advances to the development of new and improved products and their uses, as well as services and their application. Within these amounts, software-related expense was $3,037 million, $2,842 million and $2,689 million in 2007, 2006 and 2005, respectively. In addition, included in the expense was a charge of $7 million and $1 million in 2006 and 2005, respectively, for acquired in-process R&D.

Expense for product-related engineering was $399 million, $425 million and $463 million in 2007, 2006 and 2005, respectively.

Note Q. 2005 Actions

In May 2005, management announced its plans to implement a series of restructuring actions designed to improve the company's efficiencies, strengthen its client-facing operations and capture opportunities in high-growth markets. The company's actions primarily included voluntary and involuntary workforce reductions, with the majority impacting the Global Services segments, primarily in Europe, as well as costs incurred in connection with the vacating of leased facilities. These actions were in addition to the company's ongoing workforce reduction and rebalancing activities that occur each quarter. The total charges expected to be incurred in connection with all second-quarter 2005 initiatives is approximately $1,771 million ($1,765 million of which has been recorded cumulatively through December 31, 2007). Approximately $1,631 million of the total charges require cash payments, of which approximately $1,453 million have been made as of December 31, 2007 and $73 million are expected to be made over the next 12 months.

Total pre-tax restructuring activity was as follows:

(in millions)	Pre-Tax Charges Recorded in Second-Qtr 2005	Asset Impairments	Liability Recorded in Second-Qtr 2005	Payments	Other**	Liability as of Dec 31, 2005
Workforce reductions	$1,574	–	$1,574	$(10,113)	$(107)	$454
Vacant space	141	–	141	(53)	(5)	83
Asset impairments	95	95	–	–	–	–
Total restructuring activity for second-quarter 2005 actions	**$1,810***	**$95**	**$1,715**	**$(10,166)**	**$(112)**	**$537†**

* $1,574 million recorded in SG&A expense and $236 million recorded in Other (income) and expense in the Consolidated Statement of Earnings.

** Consists of foreign currency translation adjustments ($38 million), net balance sheet reclassifications ($41 million) and reversals of previously recorded liabilities ($34 million) for changes in the estimated cost of employee terminations and vacant space, offset by approximately $1 million of accretion expense. The reversals were recorded primarily in SG&A expense.

† *$391 million recorded as a current liability in Accounts payable and accruals and $146 million as a noncurrent liability in Other liabilities in the Consolidated Statement of Financial Position.*

(in millions)	Liability As of Dec 31, 2005	Payments	Other*	Liability As of Dec 31, 2006	Payments	Other†	Liability As of Dec 31, 2007
Workforce reductions	$454	$(264)	$10	$199	$(65)	$11	$145
Vacant space	83	(37)	1	47	(21)	–	27
Total restructuring activity for second-quarter 2005 actions	**$537**	**$(302)**	**$11**	**$247****	**$(86)**	**$11**	**$171**††

* Consists of foreign currency translation adjustments ($37 million), net balance sheet reclassifications ($2 million), accretion expense ($7 million) and reversals of previous recorded liabilities ($35 million) for changes in the estimated cost of employee terminations and vacant space. These reversals, net of accretion expense, were primarily recorded in SG&A expense.

** $92 million recorded as a current liability in Accounts payable and accruals and $155 million as a noncurrent liability in Other liabilities in the Consolidated Statement of Financial Position.

† Consists of foreign currency translation adjustments ($20 million) and accretion expense ($6 million), partially offset by adjustments to previously recorded liabilities ($13 million) for changes in the estimated cost of employee terminations and vacant space and net balance sheet reclassification of $2 million. The adjustments and accretion expense were primarily recorded in SG&A expense.

†† $73 million recorded as a current liability in Accounts payable and accruals and $98 million as a noncurrent liability in Other liabilities in the Consolidated Statement of Financial Position.

Charges incurred for the workforce reductions consisted of severance/termination benefits for approximately 16,000 employees (14,500 of which were for the incremental second-quarter 2005 actions). All separations were substantially completed by March 31, 2006. The noncurrent portion of the liability associated with the workforce reductions relates to terminated employees who were granted annual payments to supplement their income in certain countries. Depending on individual country legal requirements, these required payments will continue until the former employee begins receiving pension benefits or is deceased. Cash payments made through December 31, 2007 associated with the workforce reductions were $1,342 million.

The vacant space accruals are primarily for ongoing obligations to pay rent for vacant space, offset by estimated sublease income, over the respective lease term of the company's lease agreements. The length of these obligations varies by lease with the longest extending through 2013.

In connection with the company's restructuring activities initiated in the second quarter of 2005, the company recorded pre-tax impairment charges for certain real estate assets of approximately $95 million during the year ended December 31, 2005. The principal component of such impairment charges resulted from the sale of a facility in Yasu-City, Japan, which closed during the third quarter of 2005. In connection with this sale, the company recorded an impairment charge to write the asset down to its fair value in the second quarter.

These restructuring activities had the following effect on the company's reportable segments.

(in millions)	Total Pre-Tax Charges Expected To Be Incurred	Cumulative Pre-tax Charges Recorded for 2nd-Qtr. 2005 Initiatives*
Global technology services	$ 722	$ 719
Global business services	444	444
Systems and technology	132	132
Software	98	98
Global financing	16	16
Total reportable segments	1,412	1,408
Unallocated corporate amounts	360	357
Total	**$1,771**	**$1,765**

* Includes $13 million and $35 million for reversals of previously recorded charges for the years ended December 31, 2007 and 2006, respectively, due to changes in the estimated cost of employee terminations and vacant space. These adjustments were primarily recorded in SG&A expense.

United States Steel Corporation
2007 Annual Report

7. Income and Dividends Per Common Share

Basic net income per common share is calculated by adjusting net income for dividend requirements of any outstanding preferred stock and is based on the weighted average number of common shares outstanding during the period.

Diluted net income per common share assumes the exercise of stock options, the vesting of stock awards and the conversion of any outstanding preferred stock, provided in each case the effect is dilutive. For the year ended December 31, 2007, 725,622 additional shares have been included in the computation of diluted net income per share. For the year ended December 31, 2006, 8,000,168 additional shares have been included in the computation of diluted net income per common share. Additional shares included in the calculation declined in 2006, as compared to prior years, following the conversion of all remaining preferred stock on June 15, 2006 (Note 18). For the year ended December 31, 2005, 16,499,945 additional shares have been included in the computation of diluted net income per common share. Net income was not adjusted for preferred stock dividend requirements since their conversion was assumed.

Computation of Income Per Common Share	2007	2006	2005
Net income applicable to common stock (in millions)	$ 879	$ 1,366	$ 892
Weighted average shares outstanding (in thousands):			
Basic	118,090	114,918	113,470
Diluted	118,815	122,918	129,970
Per share:			
Basic	$7.44	$11.88	$7.87
Diluted	$7.40	$11.18	$7.00

Quarterly dividends on common stock in 2007 were 20 cents per share for each quarter.

Quarterly dividends on common stock in 2006 were 10 cents per share for the first quarter, 15 cents per share for the second and third quarters, and 20 cents per share for the fourth quarter.

Quarterly dividends on common stock in 2005 were 8 cents per share for the first quarter and 10 cents per share for the second, third and fourth quarters.

8. Inventories

(In millions)	December 31, 2007	December 31, 2006
Raw materials	$ 798	$ 560
Semi-finished products	827	597
Finished products	548	368
Supplies and sundry items	106	79
Total	$2,279	$1,604

Current acquisition costs were estimated to exceed the above inventory values at December 31 by approximately $910 million in 2007 and $900 million in 2006. Cost of revenues was reduced and income from operations was improved by $29 million, $22 million and $22 million in 2007, 2006 and 2005, respectively, as a result of liquidations of LIFO inventories.

Inventory includes $88 million and $65 million of land held for residential/ commercial development as of December 31, 2007 and 2006, respectively.

U. S. Steel has coke swap agreements with other steel manufacturers de-signed to reduce transportation costs. U. S. Steel shipped approximately 810,000 tons and received approximately 900,000 tons of coke under the swap agreements during 2007. U. S. Steel shipped approximately 195,000 tons and received approximately 170,000 tons of coke under the swap agreements during 2006.

The coke swaps are recorded at cost in accordance with APB 29, "Accounting for Nonmonetary Transactions" and FAS No. 153, "Exchanges of Nonmonetary Assets." There was no income statement impact related to these swaps.

13. Stock-Based Compensation Plans

On April 26, 2005, U. S. Steel's stockholders approved the 2005 Stock Incentive Plan (the "2005 Stock Plan"). The aggregate number of shares of U. S. Steel common stock that may be issued under the 2005 Stock Plan is 6,750,000 shares during the 10-year life of the plan. Generally, a share issued under the Plan pursuant to an award other than a stock option will reduce the number of shares available under the Stock Plan by 1.42 shares. The purposes of the 2005 Stock Plan are to attract, retain and motivate employees and non-employee directors of outstanding ability, and to align their interests with those of the stockholders of U. S. Steel. The Compensation & Organization Committee of the Board of Directors (the Compensation Committee) administers the plan pursuant to which they may make grants of stock options, restricted stock, performance awards, and other stock-based awards. Also, shares related to awards (i) that are forfeited, (ii) that terminate without shares having been issued or (iii) for which payment is made in cash or property other than shares are again available for awards under the plan; provided, however, that shares delivered to U. S. Steel or withheld for purposes of satisfying the exercise price or tax withholding obligations shall not again be available for awards. There were no awards of stock options, restricted stock or performance awards under this plan in 2005; however, there were 344,490 stock options, 229,380 restricted stock awards and 95,400 performance awards granted in 2006 and 234,930 stock options, 199,585 restricted stock awards and 62,800 performance awards granted in 2007. Stock-based compensation awarded prior to 2006 was issued under the 2002 Stock Plan. Options are issued at the market price per share on the date of the grant.

Stock-based compensation

Prior to January 1, 2006, U. S. Steel accounted for stock-based compensation following the recognition and measurement principles of Accounting Principles Board Opinion No. 25, "Accounting for Stock Issued to Employees," (APB 25) and related interpretations. Effective January 1, 2006, U. S. Steel adopted the fair value recognition provisions of FAS No. 123(R), "Share-Based Payment," (FAS 123(R)) which requires the recognition of compensation expense for stock-based compensation awards based on the grant date fair value. U. S. Steel elected the modified prospective application method for adoption, and prior period consolidated financial statements were not restated.

Under this adoption method, compensation expense recognized in 2006 included compensation expense related to the May 2006 grants and the applicable amounts of compensation expense of all stock-based payments granted prior to, but not yet vested as of January 1, 2006 (based on the grant date fair value estimated in accordance with the original provisions of FAS No. 123 and previously presented in the pro forma footnote disclosures). Prior to the adoption of FAS 123(R), no compensation expense had been recorded for stock options.

Stock-based compensation expense

The following table summarizes the total compensation expense recognized for stock-based compensation awards:

(In millions, except per share amounts)	Year Ended December 31, 2007	Year Ended December 31, 2006
Stock-based compensation expense recognized:		
Cost of sales	$ 7	$ 5
Selling, general and administrative expenses	16	11
Total	23	16
Related deferred income tax benefit	9	6
Decrease in net income	$ 14	$ 10
Decrease in basic earnings per share	$0.12	$0.08
Decrease in diluted earnings per share	$0.12	$0.08

As of December 31, 2007, total future compensation cost related to nonvested stock-based compensation arrangements was $35 million, and the weighted-average period over which this cost is expected to be recognized is approximately 15 months.

The following table illustrates the effect on net income and earnings per share if U. S. Steel had applied the fair value recognition provisions of FAS 123(R) in the year ended December 31, 2005:

(In millions, except per share data)	Year Ended December 31, 2005
Net income	$ 910
Add: Stock-based employee compensation expense included in reported net income, net of related tax effects	–
Deduct: Total stock-based employee compensation expense determined under fair value methods for all awards, net of related tax effects	(8)
	$ 902
Pro forma net income	
Net income per share:	
As reported—basic	$7.87
—diluted	7.00
Pro forma—basic	7.79
—diluted	6.96

Stock options

In accordance with FAS 123(R), compensation expense for stock options is recorded over the vesting period based on the fair value on the date of grant, as calculated by U. S. Steel using the Black-Scholes model and the assumptions listed below. The 2005 awards vested over a one-year service period and have a term of eight years. The 2007 and 2006 awards vest ratably over a three-year service period and have a term of ten years. Upon exercise of stock options, shares of U. S. Steel stock are issued from treasury stock.

Black-Scholes Assumptions	2007 Grants	2006 Grants	2005 Grants
Grant date price per share of option award	$108.50	$65.40	$40.37
Expected annual dividends per share, at grant date	$ 0.80	$ 0.60	$ 0.40
Expected life in years	5	5	4
Expected volatility	43%	43%	44%
Risk-free interest rate	4.5%	4.8%	3.7%
Weighted average grant date fair value per share of unvested option awards as calculated from above	44.5	25.05	14.61

The expected annual dividends per share are based on the latest annualized dividend rate at the date of grant; the expected life in years is determined primarily from historical stock option exercise data; the expected volatility is based on the historical volatility of U.S. Steel stock; and the risk-free interest rate is based on the U.S. Treasury strip rate for the expected life of the option.

The following table shows a summary of the status and activity of stock options for the year ended December 31, 2007:

	Shares	Weighted-Average Exercise Price (per share)	Weighted-Average Remaining Contractual Term (in years)	Aggregate Intrinsic Value (in millions)
Outstanding at January 1, 2007	1,632,526	$ 40.82		
Granted	234,930	108.50		
Exercised	(492,096)	35.22		
Forfeited or expired	(27,433)	68.02		
Outstanding at December 31, 2007	1,347,927	$ 54.10	6.4	$90
Exercisable at December 31, 2007	920,870	$ 37.98	5.2	$76
Exercisable and expected to vest at December 31, 2007	1,323,417	$ 53.45	6.4	$89

During the years ended December 31, 2007, 2006, and 2005 the total intrinsic value of stock options exercised (i.e., the difference between the market price at exercise and the price paid by the employee to exercise the option) was $32 million, $27 million, and $19 million, respectively. The total amount of cash received by U. S. Steel from the exercise of options was $17 million during the year ended December 31, 2007, and the related net tax benefit realized from the exercise of these options was $7 million.

Stock awards

In accordance with FAS 123(R), compensation expense for nonvested stock awards is recorded over the vesting period based on the fair value at the date of grant.

Remaining outstanding performance restricted stock awards, a type of award granted prior to 2006, vest in three tranches, subject to U. S. Steel's satisfaction of certain performance criteria during 2005. In May 2006, the Compensation Committee determined that the performance criteria had been satisfied and a portion of the performance restricted stock awards vested (52,900 shares). In May 2007, 35,113 shares vested and the remaining shares (32,300) are scheduled to vest in May 2008, conditioned upon participants' continued employment.

Restricted stock awards vest ratably over three years. The fair value of restricted stock awards is the market price of the underlying common stock on the date of grant.

Performance stock awards vest at the end of a three-year performance period as a function of U.S. Steel's total shareholder return compared to the total shareholder return of peer companies over the three-year performance period. Performance stock awards can vest at between zero and 200 percent of the target award.

The following table shows a summary of the performance stock awards outstanding as of December 31, 2007:

Performance Period	Fair Value (in millions)	Minimum Shares	Target Shares	Maximum Shares
2006–2009	$6	–	88,725	177,450
2007–2010	**$9**	**–**	**62,800**	**125,600**

The following table shows a summary of the status and activity of nonvested stock awards for the year ended December 31, 2007:

	Performance Restricted Stock Awards	Restricted Stock Awards	Performance Stocks Awards[a]	Total	Weighted-Average Grant-Date Fair Value
Nonvested at January 1, 2007	72,100	225,756	95,400	393,256	$ 61.36
Granted	–	199,585	62,800	262,385	$115.53
Vested	(35,113)	(73,500)	–	(108,613)	$ 57.31
Forfeited or expired	(4,687)	(15,162)	(6,675)	(26,524)	$ 63.76
Nonvested at December 31, 2007	32,300	336,679	151,525	520,504	$ 89.39

[a] The number of shares shown for the performance stock awards is based on the target number of share awards.

The following table presents information on performance restricted stock awards, restricted stock awards and performance stock awards granted:

	2007	2006	2005
Number of shares granted	262,385	324,780	125,000
Weighted-average grant-date fair value per share	$115.53	$ 66.06	$ 40.37

During the years ended December 31, 2007, 2006, and 2005, the total fair value of shares vested was $6 million, $2 million, and $6 million, respectively.

Kellogg
2005 Annual Report

Note 3 Cost-reduction Initiatives

The Company undertakes cost-reduction initiatives as part of its sustainable growth model of earnings reinvestment for reliability in meeting longterm growth targets. Initiatives undertaken must meet certain pay-back and internal rate of return (IRR) targets. Each cost-reduction initiative is of relatively short duration, and normally begins to deliver cash savings and/or reduced depreciation during the first year of implementation, which is then used to fund new initiatives. To implement these programs, the Company has incurred various upfront costs, including asset write-offs, exit charges, and other project expenditures.

Cost summary

For 2005, the Company recorded total program-related charges of approximately $90 million, comprised of $16 million for a multiemployer pension plan withdrawal liability, $44 million of asset write-offs, and $30 million for severance and other cash expenditures. All of the charges were recorded in cost of good sold within the Company's North American operating segments.

For 2004, the Company recorded total program-related charges of approximately $109 million, comprised of $41 million in asset write-offs, $1 million for special pension termination benefits, and $15 million in severance and other exit costs, and $52 million in other cash expenditures such as relocation and consulting. Approximately $46 million of the total 2004 charges were recorded in cost of goods sold, with approximately $63 million recorded in selling, general, and administrative (SGA) expense. The 2004 charges impacted the Company's operating segments as follows (in millions): North America-$44, Europe-$65.

For 2003, the Company recorded total program-related charges of approximately $71 million, comprised of $40 million in asset write-offs, $8 million for special pension termination benefits, and $23 million in severance and other cash costs. Approximately $67 million of the total 2003 charges were recorded in cost of goods sold, with approximately $4 million recorded in SGA expense. The 2003 charges impacted the Company's operating segments as follows (in millions): North America-$36, Europe-$21, Latin America-$8, Asia Pacific-$6.

Exit cost reserves were approximately $13 million at December 31, 2005, consisting principally of severance obligation associated with projects commenced in 2005, which were expected to be paid out in 2006. At January 1, 2005 exit cost reserves were approximately $11 million, representing severance costs that were substantially paid out in 2005.

Specific initiatives

To improve operational efficiency and better position its North American snacks business for future growth, during 2005, management undertook an initiative to consolidate U.S. bakery capacity, resulting in the closure and sale of the Company's Des Plaines, Illinois facility in late 2005 and planned closure of its Macon, Georgia facility by mid 2006. As a result of this initiative, approximately 350 positions are expected to be eliminated in 2006. The Company incurred up-front costs of approximately $80 million in 2005 and expects to incur an additional $30 million in 2006 to complete this initiative. The total project costs are expected to include approximately $45 million in accelerated depreciation and other asset write-offs and $65 million of cash costs, including severance, removals, and a pension plan withdrawal liability. The pension plan withdrawal liability is related to trust asset under-performance in a multiemployer plan that covers the majority of the Company's union employees in the Macon bakery and is payable over a period not to exceed 20 years. The final amount of the pension plan withdrawal liability will not be determinable until early 2008. Results for 2005 include management's current estimate of this liability of approximately $16 million, which is subject to adjustment through early 2008 based on trust asset performance, employer contributions, employee hours attributable to the Company's participation in this plan, and other factors.

During 2004, the Company commenced an operational improvement initiative which resulted in the consolidation of meat alternatives manufacturing as its Zanesville, Ohio facility and the closure and sale of its Worthington, Ohio facility by mid 2005. As a result of this closing, approximately 280 employee positions were eliminated through separation and attrition. The Company recognized approximately $20 million of up-front costs related to this initiative in 2004 and recorded an additional $10 million of asset write-offs and cash costs in 2005.

During 2004, the Company's global rollout of its SAP information technology system resulted in accelerated depreciation of legacy software assets to be abandoned in 2005, as well as related consulting and other implementation expenses. Total incremental costs for 2004 were approximately $30 million. In close association with this SAP rollout, management undertook a major initiative to improve the organizational design and effectiveness of pan-European operations. Specific benefits of this initiative are expected to include improved marketing and promotional coordination across Europe, supply chain network savings, overhead cost reductions, and tax savings. To achieve these benefits, management implemented, at the beginning of 2005, a new European legal and operating structure headquartered in Ireland, with strengthened pan-European management authority and coordination. During 2004, the Company incurred various up-front costs, including relocation, severance, and consulting, of approximately $30 million. Additional relocation and other costs to complete this business transformation during the next several years are expected to be insignificant.

In order to integrate it with the rest of our U.S. operations, during 2004, the Company completed the relocation of its U.S. snacks business unit from Elmhurst, Illinois (the former headquarters of Keebler Foods Company) to Battle Creek, Michigan. About one-third of the approximately 300 employees affected by this initiative accepted relocation/reassignment offers. The recruiting effort to fill the remaining open positions was substantially completed by year-end 2004. Attributable to this initiative, the Company incurred approximately $15 million in relocation, recruiting, and severance costs during 2004. Subject to achieving certain employment levels and other regulatory requirements, management expects to defray a significant portion of these up-front costs through various multi-year tax incentives, beginning in 2005. The Elmhurst office building was sold in late 2004, and the net sales proceeds approximated carrying value.

During 2003, the Company implemented a wholesome snack plant consolidation in Australia, which involved the exit of a leased facility and separation of approximately 140 employees. The Company incurred approximately $6 million in exit costs and asset write-offs during 2003 related to this initiative.

Also in 2003, the Company also undertook a manufacturing capacity rationalization in the Mercosur region of Latin America, which involved the closure of an owned facility in Argentina and separation of approximately 85 plant and administrative employees during 2003. The Company recorded an impairment loss of approximately $6 million to reduce the carrying value of the manufacturing facility to estimated fair value, and incurred approximately $2 million of severance and closure costs during 2003 to complete this initiative. In 2004, the Company began importing its products for sale in Argentina from other Latin America facilities.

In Great Britain, management initiated changes in plant crewing to better match the work pattern to the demand cycle, which resulted in voluntary workforce reductions of approximately 130 hourly and salaried employee positions. During 2003, the Company incurred approximately $18 million in separation benefit costs related to this initiative.

Solectron
2005 Annual Report

NOTE 16. Discontinued Operations

During the fourth quarter of fiscal 2003 and first quarter of fiscal 2004, as a result of a full review of its portfolio of businesses, Solectron committed to a plan to divest a number of business operations that are outside its core competencies. These businesses are Dy 4 Systems Inc., Kavlico Corporation, Solectron's MicroTechnology division, SMART Modular Technologies Inc., Stream International Inc., Solectron's 63% interest in US Robotics Corporation, and Force Computers, Inc. The divestiture of these companies allows Solectron to offer a more focused and integrated set of supply chain solutions for its customers.

These businesses each qualify as a discontinued operation component of Solectron under SFAS No. 144, "Accounting for the Impairment or Disposal of Long-Lived Assets." Solectron has reported the results of operations and consolidated financial position of these businesses in discontinued operations within the consolidated statements of operations and the balance sheets for all periods presented. In addition, Solectron has excluded the cash flow activity from these businesses from the statements of cash flows for all periods presented.

The results from discontinued operations were as follows (in millions):

	Years Ended August 31		
	2005	2004	2003
Net Sales	$15.2	$1,264.9	$1,872.1
Cost of Sales	4.1	1061.8	1,598.1
Gross profit	1.1	203.1	274.0
Operating (income) expenses-net	(14.8)	109.4	606.5
Operating income (loss)	15.9	93.7	(332.5)
Interest income-net	–	1.4	1.5
Other income (expense)-net	0.9	(1.4)	(0.7)
Income (loss) before income taxes	16.8	93.7	(331.7)
Income tax expense	2.9	8.7	112.0
Income (loss) on discontinued operations, net of tax	$13.9	$ 85.0	$(443.7)

During fiscal 2005, net sales, gross profit, operating income (loss) and income tax expense from discontinued operations decreased for fiscal year 2005 as compared to fiscal year 2004 due to the fact that the final discontinued operation was sold in the first quarter of fiscal 2005. Furthermore, Solectron recorded a $10.1 million pre-tax gain from the sale of the discontinued operation in operating (income) expenses I net, in the first quarter of fiscal 2005. As a result of the disposition, Solectron transferred approximately $28.3 million from accumulated foreign currency translation gains included in accumulated other comprehensive losses within Stockholders Equity and recognized that amount as part of the pre-tax gain.

During fiscal 2004, Solectron completed the sale of six of its discontinued operations for net cash proceeds of approximately $508.0 million resulting in a pre-tax gain of $190.6 which is included in operating (income) expenses I net for the year ended August 31, 2004 as disclosed above. As a result of the disposition of these operations, Solectron transferred approximately $14.5 million from accumulated foreign currency translation losses, included in accumulated other comprehensive losses within stockholders' equity, and recognized that amount as part of the pre-tax gain.

The sale agreements for the divestitures contain certain indemnification provisions pursuant to which Solectron may be required to indemnify the buyer of the divested business for liabilities, losses, or expenses arising out of breaches of covenants and certain breaches of representations and warranties relating to the condition of the business prior to and at the time of sale. In aggregate, Solectron is contingently liable for up to $94.8 million for a period of 12 to 24 months subsequent to the completion of the sale. As of August 31, 2005, there were no significant liabilities recorded under these indemnification obligations. Additionally, Solectron may be required to indemnify a buyer for environmental remediation costs for a period up to 10 years and not to exceed $13 million. Solectron maintains an insurance policy to cover environmental remediation liabilities in excess of reserves previously established upon the acquisition of these properties. Solectron did not record any environmental charges upon disposition of these properties.

Furthermore, Solectron recorded approximately $0 million, $123.8 million and $62.8 million of restructuring and impairment costs (excluding goodwill impairment costs) related to discontinued operations which is also included in operating (income) expenses I net for the years ended August 31, 2005, 2004, and 2003, respectively, as disclosed above.

In fiscal 2003, approximately $370.1 million of restructuring and impairment costs (including goodwill) included in operating expenses determined in connection with Solectron's impairment test performed during the third and fourth quarter of fiscal 2003 was related to discontinued operations. See Note 15, "Goodwill and Intangible Assets," for further discussion of this impairment test.

Also in fiscal 2003, approximately $95.7 million was recorded in discontinued operations related to establishing a valuation allowance for deferred tax assets. See Note 10 "Income Taxes," for further discussion of income taxes.

The current and non-current assets and liabilities of discontinued operations as of August 31, 2005 and 2004, were as follows (in millions):

	August 31 2005	August 31 2004
Accounts receivable, net	$–	$18.3
Inventories	–	18.1
Total current assets of discontinued operations	$–	$36.4
Net property and equipment	$–	$10.1
Other assets	–	1.8
Total non-current assets of discontinued operations	$–	$11.9
Short-term debt	$–	8.9
Accounts payable	–	26.0
Accrued employee compensation	–	7.2

	August 31 2005	August 31 2004
Accrued expenses	–	4.3
Total current liabilities of discontinued operations	$–	$46.4
Total non-current liabilities of discontinued operations	$–	1.8

**Procter & Gamble
2006 Annual Report**

Note 8. Stock-Based Compensation

We have a primary stock-based compensation plan under which stock options are granted annually to key managers and directors with exercise prices equal to the market price of the underlying shares on the date of grant. Grants were made under plans approved by shareholders in 2001, 2003 and 2004. A total of 249 million shares of common stock were authorized for issuance under these plans of which 123 million remain available for grant. Grants issued since September 2002 are vested after three years and have a 10-year life. Grants issued from July 1998 through August 2002 are vested after three years and have a 15-year life, while grants issued prior to July 1998 are vested after one year and have a 10-year life. In addition to our key manager and director grants, we make other minor stock option grants to employees for which vesting terms and option lives are not substantially different.

As discussed in Note 1, effective July 1, 2005, we adopted SFAS 123(R) on a modified retrospective basis to account for our stock-based compensation plans. Total stock-based compensation expense for stock option grants was $526, $459 and $445 for 2006, 2005 and 2004, respectively. The total income tax benefit recognized in the income statement for these stock-based compensation arrangements was $140, $125 and $120 for 2006, 2005 and 2004, respectively. We also make minor grants of restricted stock, restricted stock units and other stock-based grants to certain employees. Total compensation cost for these restricted stock, restricted stock units and other stock-based grants, which are generally expensed at grant date, was $59, $65 and $46 in 2006, 2005 and 2004, respectively.

In calculating the compensation expense for options granted, we have estimated the fair value of each grant issued through December 31, 2004, using the Black-Scholes option-pricing model. Effective January 1, 2005, we utilize a binomial lattice-based model for the valuation of stock option grants. The utilization of the binomial lattice-based model did not have a significant impact on the valuation of stock options as compared to the Black-Scholes model. Assumptions utilized in the model, which are evaluated and revised, as necessary, to reflect market conditions and experience, are as follows:

Years ended June 30	2006	2005	2004
Interest rate	4.5%–4.7%	3.2%–4.5%	3.8%
Weighted average interest rate	4.6%	4.4%	–
Dividend yield	1.9%	1.9%	1.8%
Expected volatility	15%–20%	15%–20%	20%
Weighted average volatility	19%	20%	–
Expected life in years	9	9	8

Because lattice-based option valuation models incorporate ranges of assumptions for inputs, those ranges are disclosed for the period of time that lattice-based models were employed. Expected volatilities are based on a combination of historical volatility of our stock and implied volatilities of call options on our stock. We use historical data to estimate option exercise and employee termination patterns within the valuation model. The expected term of options granted is derived from the output of the option valuation model and represents the period of time that options granted are expected to be outstanding. The interest rate for periods within the contractual life of the option is based on the U.S. Treasury yield curve in effect at the time of grant.

In connection with the Gillette acquisition, we issued 70 million fully vested Procter & Gamble stock options valued at $1.22 billion to current and former Gillette employees in exchange for fully vested Gillette stock options. We also issued 9 million unvested Procter & Gamble stock options valued at $102 in exchange for Gillette stock options that were not yet vested as of the acquisition date. Vesting terms and option lives are not substantially different from our key manager option grants.

A summary of options under the plans as of June 30, 2006 and activity during the year then ended is presented below:

Options in Thousands	Options	Weighted Avg. Exercise Price	Weighted Avg. Remaining Contractual Life in Years	Aggregate Intrinsic Value (in millions)
Outstanding, beginning of year	287,183	$41.07		
Issued in Gillette acquisition	79,447	41.36		
Granted	33,904	59.97		
Exercised	(36,623)	32.54		
Canceled	(1,559)	55.38		
OUTSTANDING, END OF YEAR	362,352	43.71	7.3	$4,472
EXERCISABLE	252,689	39.04	5.7	4,196

The weighted average grant-date fair value of options granted was $16.30, $14.34 and $12.50 per share in 2006, 2005 and 2004, respectively. The total intrinsic value of options exercised was $815, $526 and $537 in 2006, 2005 and 2004, respectively. The total grant-date fair value of options that vested during 2006, 2005 and 2004 was $388, $532 and $620, respectively. We have no specific policy to repurchase common shares to mitigate the dilutive impact of options; however, we have historically made adequate discretionary purchases, based on cash availability, market trends and other factors, to satisfy stock option exercise activity.

At June 30, 2006, there was $647 of compensation cost that has not yet been recognized related to nonvested stock-based awards. That cost is expected to be recognized over a remaining weighted average period of 1.9 years.

Cash received from options exercised was $1,229, $455 and $555 in 2006, 2005 and 2004, respectively. The actual tax benefit realized for the tax deductions from option exercises totaled $242, $149 and $161 in 2006, 2005 and 2004, respectively.

Energizer Holders
2006 Annual Report

7. Share-Based Payments

The Company's 2000 Incentive Stock Plan (the Plan) was adopted by the Board of Directors in March 2000 and approved by shareholders, with respect to future awards which may be granted under the Plan, at the 2001 Annual Meeting of Shareholders. Under the Plan, awards of restricted stock, restricted stock equivalents or options to purchase the Company's common stock (ENR stock) may be granted to directors, officers and key employees. A maximum of 15.0 million shares of ENR stock was approved to be issued under the Plan. At September 30, 2006, 2005 and 2004, respectively, there were 3.7 million, 3.8 million and 4.2 million shares available for future awards.

Options under the Plan have been granted at the market price on the grant date and generally vest ratably over three to five years. These awards have a maximum term of 10 years. Restricted stock and restricted stock equivalent awards may also be granted under the Plan. Under the terms of the Plan, option shares and prices, and restricted stock and stock equivalent awards, are adjusted in conjunction with stock splits and other recapitalizations so that the holder is in the same economic position before and after these equity transactions.

The Company permits deferrals of bonus and salary and for directors, retainers and fees, under the terms of its Deferred Compensation Plan. Under this plan, employees or directors deferring amounts into the Energizer Common Stock Unit Fund are credited with a number of stock equivalents based on the fair value of ENR stock at the time of deferral. In addition, the participants were credited with an additional number of stock equivalents, equal to 25% for employees and 33 1/3% for directors, of the amount deferred. This additional company match vests immediately for directors and three years from the date of initial crediting for employees. Amounts deferred into the Energizer Common Stock Unit Fund, and vested company matching deferrals, may be transferred to other investment options offered under the plan. At the time of termination of employment, or for directors, at the time of termination of service on the Board, or at such other time for distribution which may be elected in advance by the participant, the number of equivalents then credited to the participant's account is determined and then an amount in cash equal to the fair value of an equivalent number of shares of ENR stock is paid to the participant. This plan is reflected in Other Liabilities on the Consolidated Balance Sheet.

On October 1, 2005, the Company adopted SFAS No. 123 (revised 2004), "Share-Based Payment" (SFAS 123R), using the "modified retrospective" method. Accordingly, prior year results have been adjusted to incorporate the effects of SFAS 123R. The impact to the Company's net earnings is consistent with the pro forma disclosures provided in previous financial statements as found in Note 18. The Consolidated Balance Sheets also reflect the adoption of SFAS 123R. At September 30, 2005, the cumulative impact was $13.5 to total deferred taxes, $45.8 to retained earnings and $73.2 to additional paid-in capital, which also reflects the reclassification of unearned compensation for restricted stock equivalents of $13.9. The Statements of Cash Flows for fiscal years prior to 2006 was adjusted in accordance with SFAS 123R to reflect excess tax benefits as an inflow from financing activities as reflected in Note 19.

Beginning with new grants in fiscal 2006, the Company used the straight-line method of recognizing compensation cost. In fiscal years prior to 2006, the Company used the accelerated method of recognizing compensation costs for awards with graded vesting. The accelerated method treated tranches of a grant as separate awards, amortizing the compensation costs over each vesting period within a grant.

Total compensation cost charged against income for the Company's share-based compensation arrangements was $16.0, $14.3 and $13.0 for the years ended September 30, 2006, 2005 and 2004, respectively, and was recorded in selling, general and administrative (SG&A) expense. The total income tax benefit recognized in the Consolidated Statement of Earnings for share-based compensation arrangements was $5.9, $5.3 and $4.8 for the years ended September 30, 2006, 2005 and 2004, respectively. Restricted stock issuance and shares issued for stock option exercises under the Company's share-based compensation program are generally issued from treasury shares.

Options

As of September 30, 2006, the aggregate intrinsic value of stock options outstanding and stock options exercisable was $176.0 and $140.8, respectively. The aggregate intrinsic value of stock options exercised for the years ended September 30, 2006, 2005 and 2004 was $34.0, $78.2 and $28.2, respectively. When valuing new grants, Energizer uses an implied volatility, which reflects the expected volatility for a period equal to the expected life of the option. No new option awards were granted in the year ended September 30, 2006. The weighted-average fair value of options granted in fiscal 2005 and 2004 was $15.27 and $14.81 per option, respectively. This was estimated at the grant date using the Black-Scholes option-pricing model with the following weighted-average assumptions:

	2005	2004
Risk-free interest rate	3.86%	3.92%
Expected life of option	6 years	7.5 years
Expected volatility of ENR stock	22.2%	19.4%
Expected dividend yield on ENR stock	–	–

As of September 30, 2006, there was $3.6 of total unrecognized compensation costs related to stock options granted, which will be recognized over a weighted-average period of approximately six months. For outstanding nonqualified stock options, the weighted average remaining contractual life is 5.1 years.

The following table summarizes nonqualified ENR stock option activity during the current year (shares in millions):

	Shares	Weighted-Average Exercise Price
Outstanding on October 1, 2005	4.76	$25.38
Exercised	(0.92)	23.33
Cancelled	(0.03)	28.57
Outstanding on September 30, 2006	3.81	25.85
Exercisable on September 30, 2006	2.79	$21.45

Restricted Stock Equivalents (RSE)

In October 2005, the Board of Directors approved two different grants of RSE. First, a grant to key employees, included approximately 73,000 shares that vest ratably over four years. The second grant for 80,000 shares was awarded to a group of key senior management and consists of two pieces: 1) 25% of the total restricted stock equivalents granted vest on the third anniversary of the date of grant; 2) the remainder vests on the date that the Company publicly releases its earnings for its 2008 fiscal year contingent upon the Company's compound annual growth in earnings per share (CAGR) for the three year period ending on September 30, 2008. If a CAGR of 10% is achieved, an additional 25% of the grant vests. The remaining 50% will vest in its entirety on the third anniversary of the grant date, only if the Company achieves a CAGR at or above 15%, with smaller percentages of that remaining 50% vesting if the Company achieves a CAGR between 11% and 15%. The total award expected to vest is amortized over the vesting period.

The following table summarizes RSE activity during the current year (shares in millions):

	Shares	Weighted-Average Grant Date Fair Value
Nonvested RSE at October 1, 2005	0.52	$36.76
Granted	0.15	52.81
Vested	(0.13)	33.43

	Shares	Weighted-Average Grant Date Fair Value
Cancelled	(0.01)	29.6
Nonvested RSE at September 30, 2006	0.53	$42.44

As of September 30, 2006, there was $11.6 of total unrecognized compensation costs related to RSE granted under the Plan, which will be recognized over a weighted-average period of approximately 2.7 years. The weighted-average fair value for RSE granted in 2006, 2005 and 2004 was $52.81, $48.90 and $38.77, respectively. The fair value of RSE vested in 2006, 2005 and 2004 was $6.9, $1.9 and $4.5, respectively.

Subsequent to year-end, in October 2006, the Board of Directors approved two grants of RSE. First, a grant to key employees, included approximately 108,225 shares that vest ratably over four years. The second grant for 303,000 shares was awarded to key senior management with similar performance and vesting requirements to the RSE award granted in 2005, as described above.

Other Share-Based Compensation

During the quarter ended December 31, 2005, the Board of Directors approved an award for officers of the Company. This award totaled 196,800 share equivalents and has the same features as the restricted stock award granted to senior management discussed above, but will be settled in cash and mandatorily deferred until the individual's retirement or other termination of employment. The total award expected to vest is amortized over the three year vesting period and the amortized portion is recorded at the closing market price of Energizer stock at each period end. As of September 30, 2006, there was $9.4 of total unrecognized compensation costs related to this award. The related liability is reflected in Other Liabilities in the Company's Consolidated Balance Sheet.

Emerson Electric
2005 Annual Report

14) Stock-Based Compensation

The Company's stock-based compensation plans include stock options and incentive shares.

Stock Options

The Company's Stock Option Plans permit key officers and employees to purchase common stock at specified prices. Options are granted at 100 percent of the market value of the Company's common stock on the date of grant, generally vest one-third each year and expire ten years from the date of grant. Compensation cost is recognized over the vesting period based on the number of options expected to vest. At September 30, 2005, approximately 8.1 million options remained available for grant under these plans.

Changes in shares subject to option during the year ended September 30, 2005, follow:

(shares in thousands)	Average Exercise Price per Share	Shares	Aggregate Intrinsic Value	Average Contractual Life
Beginning of year	$51.22	9,071		
Options granted	$63.61	2,213		
Options exercised	$47.39	(1,321)		
Options canceled	$57.53	(104)		
End of year	$54.44	9,859	$169	5.4 years
Exercisable at year end		7,371	$146	4.2 years

The weighted-average grant-date fair value per share of options granted was $12.77, $11.13 and $8.13 for 2005, 2004 and 2003, respectively. The total intrinsic value of options exercised was $26, $22 and $7 in 2005, 2004 and 2003, respectively. Cash received from option exercises under share option plans was $50, $37 and $13 and the actual tax benefit realized for the tax deductions from option exercises was $4, $2 and $1 for 2005, 2004 and 2003, respectively.

The fair value of each award is estimated on the grant date using the Black-Scholes option-pricing model. Weighted-average assumptions used in the Black-Scholes valuations for 2005, 2004 and 2003 are as follows: risk-free interest rate based on the five-year U.S. Treasury yield of 3.5 percent, 3.1 percent and 2.8 percent, dividend yield of 2.5 percent, 2.8 percent and 3.4 percent and expected volatility based on five-year historical volatility of 24 percent, 25 percent and 25 percent for 2005, 2004 and 2003, respectively. The expected life based on historical experience was five years for options.

Incentive Shares

The Company's Incentive Share Plans include performance share awards, which involve the distribution of common stock to key management personnel subject to certain conditions and restrictions. Compensation cost is recognized over the service period based on the number of shares expected to be ultimately issued. Performance share awards are accounted for as liabilities in accordance with FAS 123R. Compensation expense is adjusted at the end of each period to reflect the change in the fair value of the awards.

As of September 30, 2005, 3,443,855 rights to receive common shares were outstanding, which are contingent upon accomplishing certain Company performance objectives and the performance of services by the employees. A total of 1,044,995 of these rights (awarded primarily in 2001) will be issued primarily in shares of common stock of the Company and paid partially in cash in early 2006 as a result of achieving certain objectives at the end of 2005. The remaining 2,398,860 rights (awarded primarily in 2004) are contingent upon achieving certain Company performance objectives by 2007 and the performance of services by the employees.

The Company's Incentive Share Plans also include restricted stock awards, which involve the distribution of the Company's common stock to key management personnel subject to service periods ranging from three to ten years. The fair value of these awards is determined by the market price of the Company's stock at the date of grant. Compensation cost is recognized over the applicable service period. As of September 30, 2005, there were 1,583,431 shares of restricted stock awards outstanding, including 724,654 shares which will be distributed in early 2006.

Changes in awards outstanding but not yet earned under the Incentive Share Plans during the year ended September 30, 2005, follow:

(shares in thousands)	Shares	Average Grant Date Fair Value Per Share
Beginning of year	4,949	$62.54
Granted	223	$64.95
Earned/vested	(86)	$32.07
Canceled	(59)	$63.20
End of year	5,027	$63.16

The total fair value of shares earned/vested was $5, $24 and $5 under the Incentive Share Plans of which $2, $9 and $2 was paid in cash, primarily for tax withholding, in 2005, 2004 and 2003, respectively. As of September 30, 2005, approximately 0.8 million shares remained available for award under the Incentive Share Plans.

In addition to the stock option and incentive share plans, the Company issued 11,070 shares of restricted stock in 2005 under the Restricted Stock Plan for Non-Management Directors and 0.2 million shares remained available for issuance as of September 30, 2005.

Compensation cost for the stock option and incentive share plans was $100, $66 and $28 for 2005, 2004 and 2003, respectively. Total income tax benefit recognized in the income statement for these compensation arrangements during 2005, 2004 and 2003 were $33, $22 and $9, respectively. As of September 30, 2005, there was $149 of total unrecognized compensation cost related to nonvested awards granted under these plans, which is expected to be recognized over a weighted-average period of 2.4 years.

Genuine Parts
2005 Annual Report

5. Stock Options and Restricted Stock Awards

In 1999, the Company authorized the grant of options of up to 9,000,000 shares of common stock. In accordance with stock option plans approved by shareholders, options are granted to key personnel for the purchase of the Company's stock at prices not less than the fair market value of the shares on the dates of grant. Most options may be exercised not earlier than twelve months nor later than ten years from the date of grant.

Pro forma information regarding net income and earnings per share is required by SFAS No. 123, as amended, determined as if the Company had accounted for its employee stock options granted subsequent to December 31, 1994, under the fair value method of SFAS No. 123. The fair value for these options was estimated at the date of grant using a Black-Scholes option pricing model with the following weighted-average assumptions for 2005, 2004 and 2003, respectively: risk-free interest rates of 4.1%, 4.0%, and 4.0%; dividend yield of 3.2%, 3.7%, and 3.6%; annual volatility factor of the expected market price of the Company's common stock of 0.23, 0.23, and 0.25; an expected life of the options of 6, 8, and 8 years; and turnover of 4.0 to 4.4% based on the historical pattern of existing grants.

The Black-Scholes option valuation model was developed for use in estimating the fair value of traded options, which have no vesting restrictions and are fully transferable. In addition, option valuation models require the input of highly subjective assumptions including the expected stock price volatility. Because the Company's employee stock options have characteristics significantly different from those of traded options, and because changes in the subjective input assumptions can materially affect the fair value estimate, in management's opinion, the existing models do not necessarily provide a reliable single measure of the fair value of its employee stock options.

For purposes of pro forma disclosures under SFAS No. 123, as amended by SFAS No. 148, the estimated fair value of the options is amortized to expense over the options' vesting period. The following table illustrates the effect on net income and income per share if the fair value based method had been applied to all outstanding and unvested awards in each period:

(in thousands, except per share amounts) Year ended December 31,	2005	2004	2003
Net income, as reported	$437,434	$395,552	$334,101
Add: stock-based employee compensation expense related to option grants after January 1, 2003 included in reported net income, net of related tax effects	4,247	1,566	13
Deduct: Total stock-based employee compensation determined under fair value based method for all awards, net of related tax effects	(6,225)	(5,324)	(5,688)
Pro forma net income	$435,456	$391,794	$328,426
Income per share:			
Basic-as reported	$ 2.51	$ 2.26	$ 1.92
Basic-pro forma	$ 2.50	$ 2.24	$ 1.89
Diluted-as reported	$ 2.50	$ 2.25	$ 1.91
Diluted-pro forma	$ 2.49	$ 2.23	$ 1.88

A summary of the Company's stock option activity and related information is as follows:

	2005		2004		2003	
	Shares (000's)	Weighted Average Exercise Price	Shares (000's)	Weighted Average Exercise Price	Shares (000's)	Weighted Average Exercise Price
Outstanding at beginning of year	5,795	$31	6,913	$30	7,590	$29
Granted (1)	1,260	44	1,270	37	20	32
Exercised	(1,246)	28	(2,096)	29	(500)	23
Forfeited	(184)	29	(328)	32	(197)	31
Outstanding at end of year	5,589	$34	5,759	$31	6,913	$30
Exercisable at end of year	3,216	$32	3,092	$30	4,171	$29
Weighted-average fair value of Options granted during the year	$8.58		$6.94		$6.92	
Shares available for future grants	1,547		2,689		3,631	

(1) Total includes 91,000 and 124,000 Restricted stock Units (RSUS) granted in 2005 and 2004, respectively. The weighted average exercise price excludes RSUS.

Exercise prices for options outstanding as of December 31, 2005, ranged from approximately $21 to $37, except for 12,000 options granted in connection with a 1998 acquisition for which the exercise price is approximately $18. The weighted average remaining contractual life of options outstanding is approximately 6.5 years.

In 2004, the Company granted approximately 1,146,000 *Stock Appreciation Rights* (SARS) and 124,000 *Restricted Stock Units* (RSUS). In 2005, the Company granted approximately 1,169,000 *Stock Appreciation Rights* (SARS) and 91,000 *Restricted Stock Units* (RSUS). SARS represent a right to receive the excess, if any, of the fair market value of one share of common stock on the date of exercise over the grant price. RSUS represent a contingent right to receive one share of the Company's common stock at a future date provided certain pre-tax profit targets are achieved.

Walt Disney
2004 Annual Report

Note 10. Stock Incentive Plans

Under various plans, the Company may grant stock options and other equity based awards to executive, management and creative personnel at exercise prices equal to or exceeding the market price at the date of grant. Effective in January 2003, options granted for common stock become exercisable ratably over a four-year period from the grant date while options granted prior to January 2003 generally vest ratably over a five-year period from the grant date. All options expire 10 years after the date of grant. At the discretion of the Compensation Committee, options can occasionally extend up to 15 years after date of grant. Shares available for future option grants at September 30, 2004 totaled 57 million.

The following table summarizes information about stock option transactions (shares in millions):

	2004		2003		2002	
	Shares	Weighted Average Exercise Price	Shares	Weighted Average Exercise Price	Shares	Weighted Average Exercise Price
Outstanding at beginning of year	219	$26.44	216	$27.48	188	$29.54
Awards forfeited	(8)	24.40	(14)	44.41	(14)	33.64
Awards granted	27	24.61	30	17.34	50	21.99
Awards exercised	(11)	18.77	(3)	14.57	(2)	18.02
Awards expired	(6)	33.56	(10)	47.73	(6)	34.72
Outstanding at September 30	221	$26.50	219	$26.44	216	$27.48
Exercisable at September 30	132	$28.39	109	$27.86	88	$26.89

The following table summarizes information about stock options outstanding at September 30, 2004 (shares in millions):

	Outstanding			Exercisable	
Range of Exercise Prices	Number of Options	Weighted Average Remaining Years of Contractual Life	Weighted Average Exercise Price	Number of Options	Weighted Average Exercise Price
$10–$14	1	5.6	$14.59	1	$14.34
$15–$19	30	7.0	17.37	11	17.64
$20–$24	94	6.4	22.55	44	21.65
$25–$29	26	4.7	27.04	22	27.06
$30–$34	53	5.7	31.50	39	31.72
$35–$39	8	4.1	37.32	7	37.45
$40–$44	7	6.1	41.25	6	41.36
$45–$395	2	5.3	112.68	2	111.91
	221			132	

The weighted average fair values of options at their grant date during 2004, 2003 and 2002 were $9.94, $6.71, and $8.02, respectively. The weighted average assumptions used in the Black-Scholes option-pricing model used to determine fair value were as follows:

	2004	2003	2002
Risk-free interest rate	3.5%	3.4%	4.8%
Expected years until exercise	6.0	6.0	6.0
Expected stock volatility	40%	40%	30%
Dividend yield	0.85%	1.21%	0.96%

During the years ended September 30, 2004, 2003, and 2002, the Company granted restricted stock units of 5.4 million, 2.9 million, and 1.9 million, respectively, and recorded compensation expense of $66 million, $20 million, and $3 million, respectively. Units totaling 750,000 shares and 250,000 shares were awarded to four executives in 2002 and 2004, respectively, that vest upon the achievement of certain performance conditions. Otherwise, the units are not performance related and generally vest 50% two years from grant date and 50% four years from the grant date. Units are forfeited if the employee terminates prior to vesting.

Chapter 2
Revenue Recognition

CONTENTS

This chapter covers the accounting, reporting, and disclosures associated with revenue recognition for the sale of products or rendering of services. Revenue involves a gross increase in assets or decrease in liabilities. Revenue may be recognized at the time of sale or service, during production, at the completion of production, and at the time of cash receipt. Long-term construction contracts may be accounted for under the percentage-of-completion method or the completed contract method. When a right of return exists, revenue may or may not be recognized, depending on the circumstances. The recording of revenue in the case of warranty and maintenance contracts is also included. The accounting treatment of contributions is also discussed.

According to Accounting Standards Update (ASU) No. 2010-04 (January 2010) (ASC 855, *Subsequent Events*), *Accounting for Various Topics,* when financial statements are presented to the SEC they cannot be misleading; subsequent events must be disclosed. An earnings release does not represent financial statements being issued (ASC 855-10-S99-2).

When there is a business combination accounted for as a purchase, push-down accounting should be used. (ASC 805, *Business Combinations*) (ASC 805-50-S99-2).

SERVICE SALES REVENUE

Frequently, a transaction involves the sale of both a product and a service. It is therefore necessary to determine whether the transaction should be classified as primarily a service transaction, primarily a product transaction, or a transaction that is both a service transaction and a product transaction.

For transactions that have a product and service component, the following applies:

☐ A transaction should be classified as primarily a service transaction if the inclusion or exclusion of the product would not change the total price of the transaction.

☐ If the inclusion or exclusion of the service would not change the total transaction price, the transaction should be classified as primarily a product transaction.

☐ If the inclusion or exclusion of the service or product would change the total transaction price, that transaction should be split and the product component should be accounted for separately from the service component.

According to ASC 605-10-25-1, *Revenue Recognition: Overall*, revenue is generally recognized when:

☐ It is realized or realizable, and

☐ It has been earned.

Revenue from service transactions is recognized based on performance— performance over a period of time or as it applies to a single action or a series of actions. The following four methods should be used to recognize revenue from service transactions:

1. *The specific performance method* should be used if performance involves a single action and revenue is recognized when that action is completed. For example, a CPA is retained to prepare a tax return. Revenue is recognized when the single action of preparing the tax return is completed.

2. *The proportional performance method* is used when performance involves a series of actions. If the transaction involves an *unspecified number* of actions over a given period of time, an equal amount of revenue should be recognized at fixed intervals. The use of the straight-line method is recommended unless another method is deemed to be more appropriate.

If the transaction involves a *specified number of similar* or *essentially similar* actions, an equal amount of revenue should be recognized when each action is performed. If the transaction involves a *specified number* of *dissimilar* or *unique* actions, revenue should be recognized based on the following calculation:

$$\frac{\text{Direct costs involved in a single action}}{\text{Total estimated direct costs of the transaction}} \times \frac{\text{Total revenues from the}}{\text{entire transaction}}$$

3. *The completed performance method* should be used to recognize revenue upon completing the final (critical) action, without which the entire transaction would be considered incomplete.

4. *The collection method* is used to recognize revenue when there is significant uncertainty regarding the collection of revenue. Revenue should not be recognized until cash is collected.

The matching principle requires that expenses be matched to revenues. In other words, revenues should be recognized in the same period as their associated expenses. If expenses are expected to be recovered from future revenues, those expenses should be deferred. Three major categories of costs result from service transactions:

1. *Initial direct costs* are incurred to negotiate and obtain a service agreement. They include commissions costs, credit investigation costs, processing fees, and legal fees. They do not include indirect costs, such as rent and other administrative costs.

2. *Direct costs* result from performing the service. A strong correlation exists between performing the service and incurring direct costs.

3. *Indirect costs* are necessary to performing the service but cannot be classified as either initial direct costs or direct costs. Indirect costs include selling and administrative expenses, rent, depreciation, allowance for bad debts, and costs associated with negotiating transactions that are not consummated.

Indirect costs should always be expensed in the period in which they are incurred. No attempt should be made to match these costs with service revenue. The accounting treatment for initial direct costs and direct costs depends upon the method used for revenue recognition.

Initial direct costs and direct costs should be expensed at the time related revenue is recognized when using the specific performance or completed performance methods. In other words, initial direct costs and direct costs should be recorded as prepaid assets and expensed once the service has been performed. The same accounting treatment is used to expense initial direct costs under the proportional performance method. In contrast, direct costs should be expensed as incurred when using the proportional performance method. This is done because a strong relationship exists between the direct costs incurred and the completion of service. When the collection method is used to recognize revenue, both initial direct costs and direct costs should be expensed as incurred.

Sometimes, a loss is incurred in a service transaction. A loss should be recognized when initial direct costs and estimated total direct costs are greater than estimated revenues. This loss should first be used to reduce any prepaid assets (deferred costs); any remaining loss is then charged to an estimated liability account.

Frequently, service transactions involve nonrefundable initiation fees and installation fees. If it is possible to determine objectively the value of the right or privilege granted by the initiation fees, the fees should be recognized as revenue and the related direct costs expensed on the initiation day. On the other hand, if the value cannot be objectively determined, the fees should initially be considered unearned revenue and recorded as a liability. Revenue should be recognized from such initiation fees using one of the service revenue recognition methods.

The accounting treatment for equipment installation fees depends on whether the customer can purchase the equipment independent of installation. If so, the transaction should be considered a product transaction and installation fees accounted for as part of a product transaction. On the other hand, if both the equipment and its installation are essential for service and the customer cannot purchase the equipment separately, the installation fees should be considered unearned revenue. Unearned revenue should be recognized, and the cost of installation and equipment should be amortized over the estimated service period.

REVENUE RECOGNITION METHODS

The major methods of revenue recognition are:

- ☐ At realization.
- ☐ At the completion of production.
- ☐ During production.
- ☐ On a cash basis.

Realization

Revenue is recognized at the time goods are sold or services are performed. This method is used in most cases. When a sale is made, the earnings process is complete, and there is an exchange that can be objectively measured. Revenue is being recognized as accrued (earned). Realization is appropriate when:

- ☐ The selling price is ascertainable.
- ☐ Future costs are estimable.

EXAMPLE

In the year 2000, J&M Corporation sold a magazine to Magazines-R-Us Inc. The contract between the parties specified that J&M would receive royalties of 30% of all future revenues derived from the magazine. At December 31, 20X1, J&M reported royalties receivable of $100,000. During 20X2, J&M received royalty payments of $250,000. Magazines-R-Us reported revenues of $2,500,000 in 20X2 from the magazine. What amount should J&M report as royalty revenue from the magazine in its 20X2 income statement?

In this problem it is assumed that an accrual basis is being used because an alternative basis is not specified (e.g., cash; see subsequent discussion). Therefore, J&M Corporation should make the following accrual in 20X2 for royalty revenue expected to be collected from Magazines-R-Us:

$$30\% \times \$2,500,000 = \$750,000$$

The other three methods of revenue recognition are used when special circumstances exist. They are discussed next.

Completion of Production

Revenue is recognized at the completion of production (before sale or exchange) only if all of the following exist:

☐ A stable selling price,

☐ Interchangeable units, and

☐ An absence of significant marketing costs that prevents consummating the final transfer.

This method might be appropriate in the following cases:

☐ When accounting for construction contracts using the completed contract method. (Construction contracts are discussed in a separate section.)

☐ For agricultural products, byproducts, and precious metals.

During Production

Revenue may be recognized during production when:

☐ There exists an assured price for the product, such as arising from a written contract.

☐ The degree of completion can be accurately determined with each stage of the manufacturing process.

An example of the use of this approach is the percentage-of-completion method for long-term construction contracts. This is discussed in a later section.

Cash Basis

Under the cash basis method, revenue is recognized when cash is received. A service business does not have inventory and therefore may recognize revenue on either an accrual or a cash basis. A company selling merchandise must use accrual accounting unless:

☐ The collection period is uncertain or extended.

☐ Expenses were not estimated accurately at the time of sale.

☐ There is a risk of noncollection.

☐ The selling price cannot be determined reliably at time of sale.

If any of these exceptions exist, revenue is recorded only as cash is received under the installment sales method or the cost recovery method, discussed next.

There exists uncertainty of cash collection, forcing revenue recognition to be deferred until the actual receipt of money.

Installment Sales Method

An installment transaction takes place when a seller sells a product or conducts a service and the purchaser is to remit periodic payments over an extended time period. Installment sales should be segregated from regular sales. A seller will typically protect itself when making installment sales by keeping title to the product such as through a conditional sales agreement or mortgage.

If the installment method is appropriate, income recognition is deferred (delayed) until the period of cash collection. The seller recognizes both revenues and cost of goods sold at the time of sale, but the related unrealized gross profit is deferred to later years based on cash collection. Selling and administrative costs are immediately expensed.

Each payment received consists of both a recovery of cost and gross profit based on the same proportion as those components in the original sale. The gross profit rate equals installment sales revenue less cost of installment sales divided by installment sales revenue. Because gross profit ratios differ by product and department as well as by year, the company must maintain separate records of sales by year, product line, and department. Therefore, care must be taken to identify the year in which the receivable arose when accounting for cash collections.

Revenue recognition equals the cash received multiplied by the gross profit percentage. When collections are received, deferred gross profit is debited and revenue is credited. Any gross profit not collected is deferred in the balance sheet. Deferred gross profit equals the installment accounts receivable balance at year-end multiplied by the gross profit rate.

The interest charged to customers on installment sales is credited to interest income when cash is received. This is in addition to the gross profit recognized.

The current asset section of the balance sheet shows the following:

Installment accounts receivable (cost + profit)

Less: deferred gross profit (profit)

Net accounts receivable (cost)

Note: Deferred gross profit is a contra asset account.

The accounts receivable is a current asset because it is based on the normal operating cycle of the business (which may, of course, be more than one year in the case of installment sales).

EXAMPLE

Zieden Corporation began its business operations in the year 20X5. It accounts for revenue recognition using the installment method. Zieden's sales and collections for the year were $160,000 and $135,000, respectively. In addition, uncollectible accounts receivable of $15,000 were written off during 20X5. Zieden's gross profit rate is 40%. What amount should Zieden report as deferred revenue in its December 31, 20X5 balance sheet?

The installment method is primarily utilized when there is a high degree of uncertainty regarding cash collections. Under this method, revenue is recognized by determining the product of cash collected times the gross profit percentage for the period in which the sale was made. Any gross profit not collected is "deferred" on the balance sheet pending collection. When collections are subsequently made, realized gross profit is increased by debiting the deferred gross profit account:

Installment sales		$160,000
Less: collections	$135,000	
Uncollectible accounts written off	15,000	150,000
Installment receivables, December 31, 20X5		$ 10,000
Deferred revenue, December 31, 20X5: $10,000 × 40% =		$ 4,000

EXAMPLE

A company sells a product for $500 that costs $350. The gross profit percentage is 30%. Therefore, the company recognizes each collection as 70% recovery of cost and 30% as realized gross profit:

$$\frac{(500-350)}{500} = 30\%$$

$$\frac{350}{500} = 70\%$$

The journal entry for the sale follows:

Accounts receivable	500	
Installment sales		500
Cost of installment sales	350	
Inventory		350

At the end of the first year, the closing journal entry follows:

Installment sales	500	
Cost of installment sales		350
Unrealized gross profit		150

Assuming a collection of $200 is received, the journal entries are:

Cash	200	
Accounts receivable		200
Unrealized gross profit	60	

Realized gross profit		60

$200 × 30% = $60

The balance owed ($300) was defaulted upon and the merchandise was repossessed, having an inventory value of $180. The journal entry is:

Unrealized gross profit (30% × $300)	90	
Loss	30	
Inventory	180	
Accounts receivable		300

EXAMPLE

On January 2, 20X5 a company sold a product for $3,000,000. The cost of the product was $2,000,000. Collections received in 20X5 were $1,200,000. The installment method of revenue recognition is used. The amount of realized gross profit to be reported is:

Installment sales	$3,000,000
Less: cost of installment sales	2,000,000
Gross profit	$1,000,000

Gross profit percentage
$1,000,000/$3,000,000 = 33.3%

20X5 collections	$1,200,000

Realized gross profit, 12/31/20X5

$1,200,000 × 33.3% =	$ 400,000

EXAMPLE

Blake Company uses the installment sales method. The following information applies for 20X5:

Installment accounts receivable, 12/31/20X5	$ 450,000
Deferred gross profit, 12/31/20X5 (prior to recognizing realized gross profit for 20X5)	280,000
Gross profit on sales	35%

For 20X5, cash collections is computed as follows:

Installment sales for 20X5 $280,000/35%	$800,000
Installment accounts receivable, 12/31/20X5	450,000
Cash collections	$350,000

For 20X5, realized gross profit equals:

$350,000 × 35%	$122,500

EXAMPLE

On January 3, 20X2, a company sold equipment for $2,700,000, resulting in a gain of $1,900,000. Collections received during the year were $700,000. Deferred gross profit at year-end 20X2 is computed as follows:

Installment sales	$2,700,000
Cost of installment sales ($2,700,000 – $1,900,000)	800,000
Gross profit	$1,900,000

$$\text{Gross profit percent} = \frac{\text{Gross profit}}{\text{Sales}} = \frac{\$1,900,000}{\$2,700,000} = 70.4\%$$

Installment receivables	
$2,700,000 – $700,000	$2,000,000
Deferred gross profit, 12/31/20X2	
$2,000,000 × 70.4%	$1,408,000

EXAMPLE

Mavis Company uses the installment sales method to recognize revenue. The following information applies to installment sales for year-end 20X1 and 20X2:

	20X1	20X2
Installment receivables at year-end on 20X1 sales	$300,000	$150,000
Installment receivables at year-end on 20X2 sales	–	350,000
Installment sales	400,000	450,000
Cost of sales	200,000	300,000

The deferred gross profit on the December 31, 20X2, balance sheet is computed as follows:

Installment receivables at 12/31/20X2 on 20X1 sales	$150,000
20X1 gross profit rate	
($400,000 – $200,000/$400,000)	× 50%
	$ 75,000
Installment receivables at 12/31/20X1 on 20X2 sales	$350,000
20X2 gross profit rate	
($450,000 – $300,000/$450,000)	× 50%
	$116,667
Total deferred gross profit, 12/31/20X2	$191,667

Disclosure should be made of amounts to be collected within the next year by type of installment receivable.

With the installment sales method, bad debts are accounted for using the *direct write-off method.* Bad debts are recognized when the account becomes uncollectible. Because of the default on an installment sales contract, the merchandise will likely be repossessed. There must be a write-off of the accounts receivable and unrealized gross profit. The repossession loss or gain on the default of the contract is calculated as follows:

Loss (gain) = accounts receivable balance less unrealized gross profit less carrying value of repossessed goods

Any reconditioning costs for repossessed merchandise increase the loss or decrease the gain.

The value of the repossessed merchandise is based on its net realizable value and is presented in the inventory section of the balance sheet.

Cost Recovery Method

The cost recovery method should be used when extreme uncertainty exists as to cash collections from installment sales. With the cost recovery method, both sales and cost of sales are recorded at the time of sale. However, the related gross profit is not recognized until all costs have first been recovered—only then are the additional cash receipts included as profit. The only remaining expenses are those applicable to the collection process. Obviously, the cost recovery method is much more conservative than the installment sales method.

The installment sales method is commonly used for tax purposes.

LONG-TERM CONSTRUCTION CONTRACTS

The accounting, reporting, and disclosures for long-term construction contracts are provided in ASC 605-35-15, *Revenue Recognition: Construction-Type and Production-Type Contracts*; the AICPA Industry Audit and Accounting Guide entitled *Construction Contractors*; and ASC 605-35, *Revenue Recognition: Construction-Type and Production-Type Contracts*. If there are any revisions in revenue, cost, and profit estimates on contracts or in measuring the progress toward completion, they are considered changes in accounting estimates.

Contract Costs

The accounting for contract costs is similar to the reporting for inventory. As costs are incurred, they are charged to the construction-in-progress (CIP) account, which is an inventory account for a construction company presented under current assets. The CIP account is presented under current assets because the construction period represents the operating cycle of the business. CIP is charged for both direct and indirect construction costs on specific contracts. However, general and administrative expenses as well as selling expenses are expensed as incurred because they are not attributable to specific construction contracts. **Exception:** General and administrative costs may be included in CIP under the completed contract method, at the option of the company, if costs are being allocated, particularly in years when no contracts have been finished.

Contract costs include subcontractor charges billed to the contractor for work performed. The CIP account is charged for costs directly attributable to projects.

Costs incurred to date include precontract costs and costs incurred after the contract date. Precontract costs include design fees, learning costs for a new process, and any other expenditures likely to be recouped after the contract is signed. After the contract, the precontract costs are considered contract costs to date.

Some precontract costs, such as for materials and supplies, may be deferred to an asset called Deferred Contract Costs in expectation of a specific contract as long as recoverability is probable. If recoverability is not probable, the precontract costs must be immediately expensed. When excess goods are manufactured in expectation of future orders, related costs may be deferred to inventory if the costs are deemed recoverable.

After the status of a contract bid has been determined (accepted or rejected), all associated precontract costs should be reviewed. If the contract has been approved, the deferred precontract costs become included in contract costs. If the contract has been rejected, the precontract costs are immediately expensed unless there are other related contracts pending that might recoup these costs.

Back charges are billable costs for work conducted by one party that should have been done by the party billed. Such an arrangement is typically provided for in the contract between the parties. Back charges are accounted for by the contractor as a receivable from the subcontractor with a corresponding reduction in contract costs. The subcontractor accounts for the back charge as contract costs and as a payable.

In the event the back charge is disputed by the subcontractor, the contractor treats the cost as a claim. The claim is the amount exceeding the agreed upon price. The contractor records a receivable and the subcontractor records a payable for the likely amount to be paid under the dispute.

A change order is an amendment to the initial contract that alters its terms. As per ASC 605-35-05, if the price change is mutually agreed on by the contractor and customer, the contractor appropriately adjusts the applicable costs and revenue. However, under the completed contract method, costs applicable to unpriced change orders are deferred if it is probable that the total contract costs (including those subject to the charge order) will be recovered from contract revenues. Under the percentage-of-completion method, if it is probable that the unpriced change order costs will be recoverable, such costs are either deferred until the changed price has been agreed upon or immediately expensed, at the option of the company. However, if it is not probable that the unpriced change order costs will be recoverable, such costs are immediately expensed.

Contract Types

There are various types of construction contracts, including time and materials, unit price, fixed price, and cost type. A contract may also have a provision awarding a bonus for excellent performance or early completion.

Time-and-materials contracts reimburse the contractor for direct labor and direct material costs.

Unit-price contracts provide payment to the contractor based on the amount of units worked.

Fixed-price contracts usually have a constant price associated with them. They are not typically subject to adjustment such as because of increasing construction costs.

Cost-type contracts may be either cost without fee or cost plus fee. In the first type, the contractor recoups its costs. In the second type, the contractor receives payment for its costs plus a fixed fee. The fee is usually based on a profit margin, but it also may be based on such variables as total expected costs, uncertainty in estimating costs, risk of the project, or economic conditions. The costs of a contract should never exceed its net realizable value, because in that case the contract is not financially feasible. If accumulated costs exceed net realizable value during the term of the contract, a loss should be recognized immediately.

Aggregating and Segmenting Contracts

Highly similar contracts may be combined for accounting purposes. As specified in ASC 605-35-25-10, similarity in contracts may be indicated by a single customer or similar project management and be performed sequentially or concurrently, interrelated, or negotiated as a package deal.

The segmenting of a contract involves breaking the larger unit into smaller ones for accounting purposes so that revenues can be associated with different components or phases. As a result, different profitability margins may apply to each unit or phase. As per ASC 605-35-25-10, segmenting a project may be indicated when all of the following conditions are met: (1) The entire project can be explained by all of the components added together, (2) a contract bid price is made for the whole project and for its major elements, and (3) customer approval is received. Even though all of these criteria are not satisfied, the project may still be segmented if all of the following exist: (1) similarity in services and prices, (2) cost savings, (3) stability, (4) contractor with a track record, (5) explainable risk differences, (6) negotiation of each segment, and (7) logical and consistent segregation.

Contract Options

An addition or modification made to an existing contract arising from an option clause is accounted for as a separate contract if any of the following conditions exists: (1) the product or service contracted for is substantially different from that stipulated in the initial agreement, (2) the product or service to be provided for is similar to that in the original contract but explainable differences exist in contract price and costing, or (3) the price of the new product or service is distinct.

Claims

A claim is an amount exceeding the contract price that a contractor wants customers to pay because of customer delays, customer mistakes in specifications, sudden changes requested by the customer, or other unexpected causes resulting in higher costs to the contractor. The contractor may recognize additional revenue arising from these claims if justification exists and the amount can be reliably estimated. The revenue is recorded only to the degree that contract costs applicable to the claim have been incurred. ASC 605-35-25-30 provides the following guidelines to establish the ability to record the additional revenue: (1) the claim is objective and verifiable, (2) costs are identifiable or determinable, (3) additional costs incurred were not initially anticipated at the time of contract, and (4) the claim is legally justifiable. If these criteria are not satisfied, a contingent asset should be disclosed.

COMMON CONSTRUCTION CONTRACT METHODS

The two popular methods to account for construction contracts are the percentage-of-completion method and the completed contract method.

Percentage-of-Completion Method

When the percentage-of-completion method is used, a construction company records revenue as production activity takes place. The progress toward a construction project's completion may be based on costs, efforts expended, units of work, units of delivery, or some other reasonable measure of activity (e.g., engineering estimates). (However, the degree of completion should never be based on cash received or interim billings.) The gradual recognition of revenue acts to level out earnings over the years and is more realistic because revenue is occurring as performance occurs. It results in matching of expenses against revenue each period. The major disadvantage of this method is the reliance on estimates. According to ASC 605-35-05-7, the percentage-of-completion method should be used when the following conditions exist: (1) Reliable estimates of the degree of completion are possible, (2) the contractor is capable of meeting its contractual responsibilities, (3) the customer is expected to meet his or her contractual obligations, and (4) contractual terms are clear regarding the rights of the parties and the terms of payment. If these criteria are not satisfied, the completed contract method should be used (this method is discussed in the next section).

Revenue is recognized under the percentage-of-completion method based on the following cost-to-cost approach:

$$\frac{\text{Actual costs to date}}{\text{Total estimated costs}} \times \text{Contract price} = \text{Cumulative revenue}$$

Estimates of costs to complete should be analyzed periodically in light of current data. Such estimates may need revision because of increasing raw material costs, new union labor agreements, political strife with foreign suppliers, and delays.

Revenue recognized in previous years is subtracted from cumulative revenue to compute the revenue for the current year as follows:

Cumulative revenue (1–3 years)

Less: revenue recognized (1–2 years)

Revenue (Year 3–current year)

The expenses for the current year are subtracted from the revenue for the current year to determine the current year's profit as follows:

$$\text{Revenue} - \text{Expenses} = \text{Profit}$$

EXAMPLE

In year 3 of a contract, the actual costs to date were $100,000. Total estimated costs are $400,000. The contract price is $2,000,000. Revenues recognized in previous years (years 1 and 2) are $300,000.

$$\text{Cumulative revenue} = \frac{\$100,000}{\$400,000} \times \$2,000,000 = \$500,000$$

Cumulative revenue	$500,000
Prior years' revenue	$300,000
Current year revenue	$200,000

In the early years of a contract, costs may occur that distort the degree of completion. An example is materials bought shortly after the contract was signed but not to be used until later years. In this case, these types of costs may be excluded in calculating the percentage of completion based on the cost-to-cost approach.

Under the percentage-of-completion method, realized gross profit recognized each year is determined as follows:

Realized gross profit = (percentage of completion – total anticipated gross profit) – gross profit recognized to date

Journal entries under the percentage-of-completion method using hypothetical figures follow:

Construction in progress	60,000	
Cash		60,000
For construction costs incurred		
Progress billings receivable	90,000	
Progress billings on construction in progress		90,000
For periodic billings		
Cash	20,000	

Progress billings receivable		20,000
For collections		
Construction in progress	15,000	
Profit		15,000

Annual profit recognition based on percentage of completion during the year

In the final year of the project, the following additional entry is required to record the profit in the last year:

Progress billings on construction in progress (for total billings)

Construction in progress (for total cost plus profit)

Profit (for incremental profit for last year only)

If a loss on a construction contract is evident, it must be recognized immediately based on the conservatism principle. A loss account is charged and a current liability is credited for such expected loss. **Note:** Under the percentage-of-completion method, any gross profit (loss) reported in previous years must be added (deducted) from the total estimated loss. If a loss is expected on a contract that is part of a group of contracts, the group is treated as the accounting unit to determine the need, if any, of a loss provision. For example, a loss on one contract in the group may be offset by profits on other contracts in the group so that a loss need not be accrued.

If CIP minus progress billings on CIP is a debit, it is presented as a current asset, as previously stated, because the balance represents an inventory account for a construction company. In this case, costs exceed billings. If the net balance is a credit, the credit balance is reported as a current liability because billings exceed costs.

Assets cannot be offset against liabilities unless a right of offset is present. Hence, the net debit balances on construction contracts should not offset any net credit balances on other contracts.

EXAMPLE

The Levita Company is a construction entity with the following data relating to two particular jobs, which began during 20X5:

	Job X	Job Y
Contract price	$210,000	$150,000
Cost incurred during 20X5	120,000	140,000
Estimated cost to complete	60,000	20,000
Billed to customers during 20X5	75,000	135,000
Received from customers during 20X5	45,000	125,000

Assuming Levita uses the percentage-of-completion method of accounting for long-term contracts, what amount of gross profit (loss) should Levita report in its 20X5 income statement?

As was previously noted, under the percentage-of-completion method of accounting for long-term contracts, the amount of revenue that would be recognized in a given period during construction equals:

$$\frac{\text{Actual costs to date}}{\text{Total estimated costs}} \times \text{Contract price} = \text{Cumulative revenue}$$

With respect to job X, because the total actual costs incurred during 20X5 are $120,000 and estimated costs to complete are $60,000, the total estimated costs to complete the project at this time are $180,000. Therefore, the amount of revenue that would be recognized on this project would be:

$$\frac{\$120,000}{180,000} \times \$210,000 = \$140,000$$

Therefore, the amount of gross profit that would be recognized for project X would be:

Project X	
Revenue	$140,000
Less: construction costs actually incurred in 20X5	120,000
Gross profit for 20X5 for project X	$ 20,000

With respect to job Y, because the total actual costs incurred during 20X5 are $140,000 and estimated costs to complete are $20,000, the total estimated costs to complete the project at this time are $160,000. Given a contract price of $150,000, it appears, based on current data, that a loss will be recognized on the project overall. Therefore, the loss must be recognized immediately, regardless of whether the contract is completed or not. The loss that would be recognized would be:

Project Y		
Revenue—contract price		$150,000
Less: construction costs actually incurred in 20X5	$140,000	
Estimated costs to complete	20,000	160,000
Loss for project Y in 20X5		$ (10,000)

In total, assuming that Levita Company utilizes the percentage-of-completion method of recognizing revenue, gross profit of $10,000 [project X: $20,000 + project Y: $(10,000)] would be recognized from both jobs in year 20X5.

Completed Contract Method

Under the completed contract method for construction contracts, a construction company does not recognize revenue until the completion of the job. A contract is deemed substantially complete when remaining completion costs are insignificant. The completed contract method should be used only when it is inappropriate to use the percentage-of-completion method. The major benefit of this method is its basis on final results instead of on estimates. The major drawback is its failure to reflect current activity on a multiyear contract.

Under this method, construction costs (including direct costs and overhead) are charged to construction in progress. In the year the contract is completed, gross profit (loss) is recognized equal to the difference between the contract price and total costs.

If a loss on a construction contract is evident, it must be recognized immediately. Under the completed contract method, the total expected loss on the contract equals the total estimated contract costs less the total estimated contract revenue.

EXAMPLE

Hercules Construction Company has a debit balance in its CIP account of $400,000 for the costs incurred on this project. Although the company originally expected to make a profit on the contract, it is now apparent that there will be an estimated loss of $100,000 on the project at its completion. The appropriate journal entry for this loss is:

Estimated loss on construction project	100,000	
Construction in Progress		100,000

This entry reduces the CIP (inventory) account by $100,000. The loss is recognized in full immediately in the current year. If the estimated loss is accurate, future costs will be charged to the CIP account as incurred and the balance in that account will equal contract revenue.

Journal entries under the completed contract method using assumed figures follow:

Construction in progress	60,000	
Cash		60,000
For construction costs		
Progress billings receivable	90,000	
Progress billings on		
Construction in progress		90,000
For periodic billings		
Cash	20,000	
Progress billings receivable		20,000
For collections		

In the final year of the project, the following additional entry is required to record the profit in the last (completion) year:

Progress billings on construction in progress (for total billings)

Construction in Progress (for total costs)

Profit (profit for all the years)

EXAMPLE

In this example, data from the previous Levita Company example is used; however, the long-term construction jobs will be accounted for using the completed contract method. The following data relates to the two different construction jobs for Levita Construction during 20X5:

	Job X	Job Y
Contract price	$210,000	$150,000
Cost incurred during 20X5	120,000	140,000
Estimated cost to complete	60,000	20,000
Billed to customers during 20X5	75,000	135,000
Received from customers during 20X5	45,000	125,000

Assuming Levita now uses the completed contract method of accounting for long-term contracts, what amount of gross profit (loss) should Levita report in its 20X5 income statement?

The completed contract method strictly follows the revenue recognition principle, requiring that revenue should not be recognized until the earning process is fully completed. Therefore, the following computations for each project must be made.

Job X

For job X, costs of $120,000 were incurred in 20X5, with an estimated $60,000 in additional costs needed to complete the project in the future. Assuming that the contract price is $210,000, it appears that the gross profit should be recognized as $30,000 [210,000 − (120,000 + $60,000)]. However, because revenue is accounted for under the completed contract method, no gross profit is recognized at all. Zero gross profit is recognized because the contract was not completed this period.

Job Y

In job Y, actual costs of $140,000 were incurred, with an estimate of $20,000 needed to complete the project in the future. Thus, at this point, it is estimated that $160,000 of costs will be required to complete the job in total. On the basis of this current data, it appears that Levita will generate a loss of $10,000 on the overall contract. As was previously noted, if a loss on a construction contract is evident, it must be recognized immediately. Therefore, this loss must be disclosed and recognized in the company's income statement for 20X5 even though construction has not been completed. The disclosure that should be made is the same as the disclosure for the completed contract previously shown under the same circumstances. It is replicated here for the reader's convenience:

Job Y		
Revenue – contract price		$150,000
Less: construction costs actually incurred in 20X5	$140,000	
Estimated costs to complete	20,000	60,000
Loss for project Y in 20X5		$ (10,000)

Therefore, overall, the amount of gross profit that should be recognized in the Levita's income statement based on both jobs is a loss of $10,000 [job X: $0 + job Y: $(10,000)].

Long-term construction contracts require certain disclosures in the financial statements, including:

☐ Accounting method used and any change therein.

☐ Nature of claims and associated amounts.

☐ Significant commitments made.

☐ Changes in estimates and their impact on the financial statements.

☐ Approach in determining the percentage of completion when the percentage-of-completion method is used.

☐ Criteria used to ascertain when substantial completion has occurred.

GOVERNMENT CONTRACT ACCOUNTING

The percentage-of-completion method to account for contracts should be used when the buyer is financially sound enough to pay its obligations and the contractor is expected to complete all of its work. As per ASC 605-35, a company should apply earnings rates to all contract costs, including general and administrative expenses, to determine sales and operating earnings. A company should review earnings rates periodically to assess adjustments in contract values and estimated costs at completion. Any adjustment in earnings rates should be made over current and future years.

On cost-plus-fixed-fee government contracts, fees should usually be accrued as billable. If an advance payment is received from the government, it should *not* offset receivables unless the payment is for work in process. If any amounts are offset, proper disclosure is required.

If a government contract is subject to renegotiation, a renegotiation claim to which the contractor is responsible should be debited to sales and credited to a current liability account. Disclosure should be made of the basis to compute the expected refund.

If the government terminates a contract, contract costs included in inventory should be transferred to receivables. The claim against the government should be presented under current assets unless a long delay in receipt of payment is expected. A termination claim should be treated as a sale. A subcontractor's claim resulting from the termination should be included in the contractor's claim against the government. For example, a contractor has a termination claim receivable of $500,000, of which $100,000 arises from the contractor's obligation to the subcontractor. In this case a liability of $100,000 should be accrued. The termination claim is reduced by any inventory related to the contract that the contractor is retaining. Disclosure should be made of the particulars of terminated contracts.

All direct costs are included in contract costs, such as material, labor, and subcontracting. Indirect costs should be allocated to contracts on a rational basis. Allocable costs include contract supervision, tools, quality control, inspection, insurance, and repairs and maintenance. Learning and startup costs should be charged to existing contracts. The way to enter an expected loss on a contract is to debit a loss provision and credit a liability account.

REVENUE RECOGNITION WHEN A RIGHT OF RETURN EXISTS

ASC 605-15-15, *Revenue Recognition: Products*, deals with the accounting and disclosures when there is a right of return. However, the pronouncement is not applicable to real estate transactions, dealer leases, or service industries. Returns do not include exchanges for similar items in type, quality, and price. In some cases, the return privilege expires shortly after sale, such as with perishable food. In other situations, the return privilege has a longer time period, such as in textbook publishing.

If a buyer has the right to return a product, the seller cannot recognize revenue when sold unless all of the following exist:

- ☐ The buyer is obligated to pay for the product even if he or she loses it or the item becomes damaged.
- ☐ The acquisition of the product makes economic sense to the buyer.
- ☐ The seller is not obligated to provide future services in order for the buyer to resell the item.
- ☐ Selling price is known or determinable.
- ☐ The buyer must pay for merchandise even if he or she is not able to resell it. For example, a wholesaler buying goods from a manufacturer does not have the right to return the goods if he or she cannot find a retailer.
- ☐ There is a reasonable basis to estimate returns.

If all of these conditions are satisfied, the seller must make an appropriate provision (accrual) for expenses and losses related to possible returns of products by buyers. Further, sales and cost of sales should be reduced for estimated returns.

The provisions for estimated returns and cost of receiving these returns are contra accounts to accounts receivable. The deferred cost of sales is the inventory cost of items expected to be returned. The deferred cost of reacquiring returns may increase either deferred charges or inventory.

If any one of the foregoing is not satisfied, revenue must be deferred along with related costs until either all the criteria are met or the right of return stipulation has expired or changed from agreement. An alternative treatment to the deferral of revenue is just to have a memo entry of the sale. Another acceptable alternative treatment is to consider the transaction as a consignment.

EXAMPLE

On January 1, 20X1, a sale of $100,000 is made with a right of return. The related costs associated with this sale are $60,000. On May 4, 20X2, the right of return no longer applied. The journal entries are:

1/1/20X1

Cash	100,000	
Deferred revenue		100,000
Deferred expenses	60,000	
Cash		60,000

Alternatively, instead of a journal entry, a memo entry may have been made:

5/4/20X2

Deferred revenue	100,000	
Revenue		100,000
Expenses	60,000	
Deferred expenses		60,000

EXAMPLE

Davis Corporation expects that sales of $400,000 will be returned and the related cost of goods sold will be $250,000. It is anticipated that costs of $16,000 will be incurred to process the returns. The journal entry required to accrue sales returns follows:

Sales returns	400,000	
Inventory	250,000	
Processing expense for sales returns	16,000	
Allowance for expected returns		400,000
Cost of goods sold		250,000
Accrued expense to process sales returns		16,000

In predicting returns, the following must be considered:

☐ Time period awarded to return merchandise.

☐ Experience with the product in estimating returns.

☐ Obsolescence risk of goods.

☐ Transaction volume.

☐ Type of customer and relationship.

☐ Type of product.

☐ Product demand.

☐ Marketing policies.

A reasonable estimate of returned merchandise may be impaired if (1) the products are not homogeneous, (2) there is a lack of prior experience in estimating returns because the product is relatively new or circumstances have changed, (3) a lengthy time period exists for returns, or (4) the product has a high degree of obsolescence.

EXAMPLE

On February 6, 20X2, product sales of $500,000 were made. The cost of goods is $300,000. A 60-day return privilege exists. The expected return rate of merchandise is 10%. On March 17, 20X2, a customer returns goods having a selling price of $40,000. No other returns pertaining to the original product sales were received. The criteria for recognizing revenue when the right of return exists have been met. The journal entries follow:

2/6/20X2

Accounts receivable	500,000	
Sales		500,000
Cost of sales	300,000	
Inventory		300,000
Sales returns	50,000	
Allowance for sales returns $500,000 × 10% = $50,000		50,000
Inventory	30,000	
Cost of sales		
$50,000 × 60% (1–gross profit rate) = $30,000		

3/17/20X2

Allowance for sales returns	40,000	
Accounts receivable		40,000

4/7/20X2

Cost of sales	6,000	
Inventory		6,000*
Allowance for sales returns	10,000	
Sales returns		10,000

* Inventory assumed returned ($50,000 × 60%)

	$30,000
Less: amount returned ($40,000 × 60%)	24,000
Adjustment to inventory	$ 6,000

VENDOR CONSIDERATION TO CUSTOMER

ASC 605-50-05, *Revenue Recognition: Customer Payments and Incentives*, provides that when the vendor gives a customer something for buying the vendor's product, such consideration should reduce the vendor's revenue associated with that sale. **Exception:** The vendor's consideration represents a cost if the vendor receives a benefit and both of the following criteria are met:

1. The fair value of the benefit is determinable.

2. The vendor receives goods or services from the customer associated with the arrangement constituting an identifiable benefit. For example, the vendor would have bought the good or service from a third party if not provided by the customer.

As per ASC 605-50-25, a company may offer to customers certain sales incentives, such as rebates, free products or services, coupons, and discounts. When the sales incentive does *not* result in a loss on the sale of a product or service, the vendor recognizes the *cost* of the sales incentive at the later of the date the vendor recognized the related revenue or the date the sales incentive was offered. In the case of mail-in rebates and certain manufacturer coupons, the vendor should record a liability (deferred revenue) for those sales incentives.

In the event that a sales incentive *will* result in a loss on the sale of the product or service, the vendor should *not* recognize a liability for the sales incentive before the date the related revenue is recognized. The loss is computed by deducting cost of sales and the cost of the rebate from the selling price.

If a sales incentive is a reduction in, or refund of, the selling price of the product or service, it is classified as a reduction of revenue. If, however, the sales incentive is free merchandise or service delivered at the time of sale of another product, such as a gift certificate, the cost of the free product of service should be expensed.

As per ASC 605-45-45-22, *Revenue Recognition: Principal Agent Considerations*, service revenue includes *reimburseable expenses* billed to customers (e.g., travel expenses). Further, ASC 605-50-05, as mentioned above, requires that consideration, including warrants, issued to a customer be classified by the vendor as an offset to the amount of cumulative revenues recognized from that customer. If merchandise or service is delivered at the time of sale of another product, such as a gift certificate, the cost of the free product or service should be expensed.

Consideration from a vendor to a retailer reduces the vendor's selling prices of its products or services and thus reduces the vendor's revenue. **Exception:** The consideration is expensed by the vendor if both of the following conditions exist:

1. The vendor receives in turn an identifiable benefit in the form of goods or services from the retailer.
2. The fair value of the benefit can reasonably be estimated.

MULTIPLE DELIVERABLES

ASC 605-25-25, *Revenue Recognition: Multiple-Element Arrangements*, provides guidance on when and how to separate elements of an arrangement for the delivery or performance of multiple products, services, and rights where performance may occur at different points or over different time periods.

Accounting Standards Update (ASU) No. 2009-13 (October 2009) (ASC 605, *Revenue Recognition*), *Multiple-Deliverable Revenue Arrangements*, discusses revenue recognition policy. This ASU provides amendments to Subtopic 605-25 for separating consideration in multiple-deliverable arrangements. A selling price hierarchy is established to determine the selling price of a deliverable. The selling price used for each deliverable is based on vendor-specific evidence if available, third-party evidence if vendor-specific objective evidence is not available, or estimated selling price if neither of the two aforementioned evidence is not available.

Arrangement consideration should be allocated at the inception of the arrangement to all deliverables using the relative selling price method. This method allocates any discount in the arrangement proportionally to each deliverable on the basis of each deliverable's selling price.

A vendor must determine its best estimate of selling price consistent with that used to determine the price to sell the deliverable on a standalone basis.

The following should be disclosed by similar types of arrangements:

☐ Timing of revenue recognition for separate units of accounting.

☐ Description of multiple-deliverable arrangements, including nature and terms.

☐ Factors and estimates used to determine vendor-specific objective evidence, third-party evidence, or estimated selling price.

☐ Significant deliverables within its arrangements.

☐ General timing of delivery or performance.

(ASC 605-25)

REIMBURSEMENTS RECEIVED

ASC 605-45-45-22, requires businesses to record the recovery of reimbursable expenses (e.g., travel costs on services contracts) as revenue. **Note:** These costs are *not* to be netted as a reduction of cost.

MISCELLANEOUS REVENUE CONCERNS

ASC 605-20-25-14, *Revenue Recognition: Services*, requires barter transactions to be recorded at the fair value of the advertising surrendered.

ASC 605 provides guidance on the recognition, presentation, and disclosure of revenue.

ASC 605-45-45-19, *Revenue Recognition: Principal Agent Considerations*, requires that all shipping and handling costs billed to customers be recorded as sales.

ASC 605-50-25-13, *Revenue Recognition: Customer Payments and Incentives*, requires disclosure of the nature of the incentive programs including the amounts recognized in the income statement and their associated classification for each period presented. A company may agree to revenue arrangements that stipulate multiple payment streams for a single unit of accounting. For instance, a service provider may get an up-front payment when signing a service contract and then receive additional payments as services are provided to the customer.

If delivery of a single unit of accounting covers multiple accounting periods, a company must determine how to allocate the multiple payment streams applicable to the unit of accounting to those accounting periods.

Delivery or performance of a deliverable is deemed to have taken place when the seller has fulfilled its obligations applicable to that deliverable and the customer has realized the value of the deliverable.

SOFTWARE REVENUE RECOGNITION

According to ASC 985-605-25, *Software: Revenue Recognition*, revenue should be recognized when the contract for software does not involve major production, alteration, or customization, provided all of the following conditions are satisfied:

☐ Receipt of payment is probable.

☐ The selling price is fixed or known.

□ The software has been delivered.

□ The contract is enforceable.

Separate accounting is required for the service aspect of a software transaction if the following conditions exist:

□ A separate provision exists in the contract covering services so a price for such services is stipulated.

□ The services are not mandatory for the software transactions.

A software contract may include more than one component, such as add on software, upgrades, customer support after sale, and exchange or return privileges. The total selling price of the software transaction should be allocated to the contractual components, based on fair value. If fair value is not determinable, revenue should be deferred until it is determinable or until all components of the transaction have been delivered. **Note:** The four preceding revenue criteria must be satisfied before any allocation of the fee to the contractual elements may be made. Further, the fee for a contractual component is determinable if the element is sold separately.

ASC 985-605, *Software: Revenue Recognition*, which modifies ASC 985-605-25, requires revenue to be recognized under the residual method if (1) fair market values are determinable for undelivered items in a multiple-element agreement that is not recorded using long-term contract accounting, (2) objective evidence of fair value does not exist for one or more of the delivered elements in the arrangement, and (3) all other revenue recognition criteria are met. Using the residual method, the arrangement fee is recorded as follows:

□ Deferral is made of the total fair value of undelivered elements.

□ The difference between the total arrangement fee and the deferred amount for the undelivered items is recognized as revenue applicable to the delivered elements.

Accounting Standards Update 2009-14 (October 2009) (ASC 985, *Software*), *Certain Revenue Arrangements That Include Software Elements*, relates to the accounting for revenue arrangements consisting of tangible products and software.

A vendor must sell a particular element separately to assert vendor-specific objective evidence for that element. If a vendor does not have vendor-specific objective evidence for the undelivered element in an arrangement, the revenue for both the delivered and undelivered elements are combined into one unit of accounting. Any revenue associated to the delivered products is then deferred and recognized at a later date, which, in most instances, is as the undelivered elements are delivered by the vendor.

The update does not affect software revenue arrangements that do not include tangible products. In addition, the update changes the accounting model for revenue arrangements that include both tangible products and software elements.

If software contained on the tangible product is essential to the tangible products' functionality, the software is excluded from the scope of the software revenue guidance. This exclusion includes essential software that is sold with the product and undelivered software elements that relate to the tangible product's essential software.

The effective date for this update is for fiscal years beginning on or after June 15, 2010 (ASC 985-605).

CONTRIBUTIONS

ASC 958-605-05-3, 605-10-15-3 and 720-25-25-1 are the primary authoritative sources for accounting for contributions.

Contributions are a voluntary and unconditional conveyance of assets or cancellation of liabilities by one entity to another entity, in a nonreciprocal relationship, where one entity does not have an ownership interest in the other entity. These entities may be either for profit or not for profit. Cash as well as other monetary and nonmonetary assets, services, or unconditional promises to give those assets or services qualify as contributions.

ASC 958-605-25 and 11-15, 958-30-25-4 and 958-205-45-4 distinguish between donor-imposed restrictions and donor-imposed conditions. If a donor limits the way a contribution is to be used (such as to build a hospital building), it is considered a *restriction*, and the revenue from such a contribution and any related expenses should be recognized immediately. In contrast, if the donor imposes a condition, such as that the donee-entity must raise matching funds, that *condition* must be satisfied before revenue may be recorded.

A promise by a donor may be either unconditional or conditional. A promise is considered unconditional if the donor has no right to take back the donated asset and the contribution would be available after some time or on demand. Unconditional promises to give contributions should be recognized immediately. A conditional promise is contingent upon the occurrence of a future event. If that event does not occur, the donor is not bound by the promise. A vague promise is deemed conditional. Conditional promises should be recorded only when their conditions have been fulfilled. A conditional promise may be treated as an unconditional promise only if the possibility that the condition will not be met is remote.

A promise to give may be either written or oral. Of course, evidence of the promise must exist before any amount is recorded. Such evidence may consist of information about the donor, such as the donor's name and address, the amount that the donor promised to give, when the amount will be given (e.g., payment schedule), when the promise was made, and to whom was the promise to give made. A public announcement by the donor may be made. The donor may make partial payments. The donee may have taken actions relying on the promise. If a promise to give is recorded, it should be recorded at fair value. If the promised amount is not expected to be collected within a year, the use of discounted cash flow may be appropriate. If discounted cash flow is used, the interest should be treated as contribution income rather than as interest income.

Contributions received should be recorded at fair value by debiting the asset and crediting revenue. Quoted market prices or market prices for similar assets, appraisal by an independent expert, or valuation techniques such as discounted cash flows should be used to determine fair value. The value of contributed services should also be based on quoted market prices for those services. An increase in the fair value of nonmonetary assets resulting from the performance services may alternatively be used to measure the fair value of services.

Both skilled and unskilled contributed services should be recognized if nonmonetary assets are created or enhanced. Contributed services should also be recognized if specialized skills are provided by the donor and those skills would have to be purchased by the donee if they were not donated.

ASC 958-605-50 requires certain disclosures in the financial statements of recipients of contributions. For unconditional promises to give, the amount of receivables due within one year, in one to five years, and in more than five years should be disclosed along with the amount for allowance for uncollectible unconditional promises receivable. For conditional promises to give, disclosure is required of the promised amounts and a description of the promise. Promises with similar characteristics may be grouped together. Disclosure should also be made in the financial statements that describes the nature and extent of contributed services, restrictions or conditions set, and the programs or activities that utilized contributed services. Entities are encouraged to disclose the fair value of services received but not recorded as revenues.

When donations are made of works of art, historical items, and other such valuable assets, the recording of such assets is optional if the following conditions are satisfied:

☐ The assets added to collections are held for public exhibition, education, or research.

☐ The assets are protected, preserved, and kept unencumbered.

☐ The proceeds from the sale of such assets are used to obtain other items for the collection.

Contributed collection items should be recorded as revenues or gains and as assets if collections are capitalized. Certain disclosures are required if collections are not capitalized, including the cost of collection items purchased, the proceeds from the sale of collection items, and the proceeds from insurance recoveries of lost or destroyed collection items.

The donor should recognize an expense and a corresponding decrease in assets, or an increase in liabilities, at fair value, in the period in which the contribution is made. If the fair value differs from the book value, a gain or loss on disposition should be recognized, as appropriate.

RESEARCH AND DEVELOPMENT REVENUES

As per ASC 605, when a company is providing continuing services for product development, nonrefundable upfront technology license fees are deferred. Such fees are recorded as revenue over the product development periods, based on expected total development costs. If a company is not furnishing continuing services, revenue is recognized when the payment is due.

Accounting Standards Update (ASU) No. 2010-17 (April 2010) (ASC 605, *Revenue Recognition*), *Milestone Method*, applies to recognizing revenue for research and development efforts based on the achievement of a milestone or event happening. The milestone method is when a company records a milestone payment as revenue. A payment may be contingent on the happening of a future event.

A company can record as revenue a substantive contingent consideration when a milestone is achieved if it satisfies the following conditions (ASC 605-28-25-2A):

- The vendor has accomplished the milestone.
- The earned consideration applies to prior performance.
- The consideration is reasonable. (ASC 605-28-25-1 and 25-2)

A milestone should be deemed substantive in full. There may be multiple milestones involved, and if so, each milestone should be appraised separately to ascertain whether it is substantive. It is possible that a situation can exist when there are substantive and nonsubstantive milestones (ASC 605-28-25-3).

Disclosure should be made of the arrangement, each contingent milestone, whether the milestone is substantive, and the amount of revenue recorded for the milestone (ASC 605-28-50-2).

EQUITY INSTRUMENTS RECEIVED FOR LICENSING FEES

ASC 505-50-05, *Equity: Based Payments to Non-Employees*, stipulates that a company should record the fair value of equity instruments as revenue when received for providing merchandise or services.

WARRANTY AND MAINTENANCE CONTRACTS

Extended warranty and product maintenance contracts are frequently offered by retailers as separately priced items in addition to their products. Accounting for *separately priced* extended warranty and maintenance contracts is given by ASC 605-20-25-1. Warranty and maintenance contracts that are *not* separately priced should be accounted for as *contingencies.*

Extended warranty contracts provide protection beyond the scope of the manufacturer's warranty or beyond the period of the original warranty. Product maintenance contracts provide services to maintain a product for a specified duration. Service may be provided at fixed intervals, or a specified number of times, or as required to keep the product operational.

Revenue and incremental direct costs from separately priced extended warranty and product maintenance contracts should be initially deferred. Revenue should be recognized on a straight-line basis over the contract period. Related incremental direct costs should be expensed in proportion to revenue recognized. Incremental direct costs result from obtaining the contract; these costs would not otherwise have been incurred. Other costs, such as the cost of services performed, general and administrative expenses, and costs of contracts not consummated, should be expensed when incurred.

Losses from such contracts should be recognized when the estimated costs of providing the service plus the unamortized portion of acquisition costs exceed corresponding unearned revenue. To determine loss, contracts should be grouped in a consistent manner, similar to the pool-of-risk concept in ASC 944-20, *Financial Services-Insurance: Insurance Activities*; that is, losses are not recognized on individual contracts but rather on a group of similar contracts. Loss is recognized by first reducing unamortized acquisition costs; if this is not adequate, a liability should be recorded.

BARTER TRANSACTIONS

Barter transactions are generally recorded at the fair market value of the assets surrendered. A company can record advertising barter revenue only up to the amount of similar previous cash transactions and can use only cash-based advertising with like features (e.g., time length, web page, positioning). In the case of Internet barter transactions, each transaction should be treated individually.

ANNUAL REPORT REFERENCES

Caterpillar
2008 Annual Report

C. Sales and Revenue Recognition

Sales of Machinery and Engines are generally recognized when title transfers and the risks and rewards of ownership have passed to customers or independently owned and operated dealers. Typically, where product is produced and sold in the same country, title and risk of ownership transfer when the product is shipped. Products that are exported from a country for sale typically pass title and risk of ownership at the border of the destination country.

No right of return exists on sales of equipment. Replacement part returns are estimable and accrued at the time a sale is recognized.

We provide discounts to dealers and original equipment manufacturers (OEM) through merchandising programs that are administered by our marketing divisions. We have numerous programs that are designed to promote the sale of our products. The most common dealer programs provide a discount when the dealer sells a product to a targeted end user. OEM programs provide discounts designed to encourage the use of our engines. The cost of these discounts is estimated based on historical experience and known changes in merchandising programs and is reported as a reduction to sales when the product sale is recognized.

Our standard invoice terms are established by marketing region. When a sale is made to a dealer, the dealer is responsible for payment even if the product is not sold to an end customer and must make payment within the standard terms to avoid interest costs. Interest at or above prevailing market rates is charged on any past due balance. Our policy is to not forgive this interest. In 2008 terms were extended to not more than one year for $544 million of receivables, which represent approximately 1% of consolidated sales. In 2007 and 2006, terms were extended to not more than one year for $219 million and $49 million of receivables, respectively, which represent less than 1% of consolidated sales

Sales with payment terms of two months or more were as follows:

| | (Dollars in millions) | | | | | |
| | 2008 | | 2007 | | 2006 | |
Payment Terms (months)	Sales	Percent of Sales	Sales	Percent of Sales	Sales	Percent of Sales
2	$ 4,130	8.6%	$ 2,830	6.8%	$ 2,557	6.6%
3	2,786	5.8%	2,067	4.9%	711	1.8%
4	866	1.8%	526	1.3%	336	0.9%
5	1,062	2.2%	965	2.3%	1,222	3.1%
6	561	1.2%	4,549	10.8%	8,583	22.1%
7–12	4,469	9.3%	293	0.7%	274	0.7%
	$13,874	28.9%	$11,230	28.8%	$13,683	35.2%

Revenues of Financial Products primarily represent the following Cat Financial revenues:

☐ Retail (end-customer) finance revenue on finance leases and installment sale contracts is recognized over the term of the contract at a constant rate of return on the scheduled outstanding principal balance. Revenue on retail notes is recognized based on the daily balance of retail receivables outstanding and the applicable effective interest rate.

☐ Operating lease revenue is recorded on a straight-line basis in the period earned over the life of the contract.

☐ Wholesale (dealer) finance revenue on installment contracts and finance leases is recognized over the term of the contract at a constant rate of return on the scheduled outstanding principal balance. Revenue on wholesale notes is recognized based on the daily balance of wholesale receivables outstanding and the applicable effective interest rate.

☐ Loan origination and commitment fees are deferred and then amortized to revenue using the interest method over the life of the finance receivables.

Recognition of income is suspended when collection of future income is not probable. Accrual is resumed, and previously suspended income is recognized, when the receivable becomes contractually current and/or collection doubts are removed. Cat Financial provides wholesale inventory financing to dealers. See Notes 7 and 8 for more information.

Sales and revenue recognition items are presented net of sales and other related taxes.

Monsanto
2002 Annual Report

Revenue Recognition

The company derives most of its revenue from three main sources: sales of agricultural chemical products; sales of branded conventional seed and branded seed with biotechnology traits; and royalties and license revenues from licensed biotechnology traits and genetics.

Revenues for agricultural chemical products are recognized when title to the products is transferred and the goods are deemed delivered to customers. The company recognizes revenue on products it sells to distributors when according to the terms of the sales agreements, delivery has occurred, performance is complete, no right of return exists, and pricing is fixed or determinable at the time of sale.

Revenues from all branded seed sales are recognized when the title to the products is transferred, at which time the goods are deemed delivered. When the right of return exists, sales revenues are reduced at the time of sale to reflect expected returns, which are estimated based on historical experience and current market conditions.

In 2000, Monsanto adopted Staff Accounting Bulletin (SAB) No. 101, *Revenue Recognition in Financial Statements*, the Securities and Exchange Commission's (SEC) interpretation of accounting guidelines on revenue recognition. The adoption of SAB 101 primarily affected the company's recognition of license revenues from corn and soybean biotechnology traits sold through third-party seed companies. Monsanto restated license revenues in 2000, recognizing them when a grower purchases seed. The previous practice was to recognize the license revenue when the third-party seed company sold the seed into the distribution system. SAB 101 required companies to report any change in revenue recognition related to adopting its provisions as an accounting change in accordance with Accounting Principles Board (APB) Opinion No. 20, Accounting Changes. Monsanto recognized the cumulative effect of a change in accounting principle as a loss of $26 million, net of taxes of $16 million, effective Jan. 1, 2000.

Starting in the third quarter of 2001, Monsanto changed its marketing approach on certain trait fees. It replaced the technology fee paid by growers who plant *YieldGard* insect-protected corn, *Roundup Ready* corn and *Roundup Ready* soybeans, with a royalty paid by the seed companies that are licensed to market those products. This change resulted in trait revenues being recognized earlier—from the first half of 2002 to the second half of 2001, which had a $0.34 positive effect on 2001 diluted earnings per share, or $90 million on net income, and a comparable negative effect on 2002 results. Royalties are recorded when earned, usually when the third-party seed companies sell their seeds containing Monsanto traits. License revenues are earned on certain traits, primarily cotton and canola biotechnology traits in certain geographic locations, and are recognized when growers purchase the seed containing the Monsanto trait.

Additional conditions for recognition of revenue are that the collection of sales proceeds be reasonably assured based on historical experience and current market conditions, that pricing is fixed or determinable, and that there are no further performance obligations under the sale, or royalty or license agreement.

During 2001, to reduce credit exposure in Latin America, Monsanto began to collect payments on certain customer accounts in grain. In accordance with Emerging Issues Task Force (EITF) Issue 99-19, *Reporting Revenue Gross As a Principal and Net As an Agent,* the company recorded revenues of approximately $65 million in the Seeds and Genomics segment during the year ended Dec. 31, 2001, for the sale of grain received as payment on account from customers. Revenue on sale of grain was virtually offset by cost of sales; there was minimal contribution to gross profit. During 2002, the company changed this program so Monsanto no longer takes ownership of the grain, thereby eliminating the subsequent sale of grain and the associated inventory risk. Such payments in grain, negotiated at the time Monsanto's products were sold to the customers, were valued at the prevailing grain commodity prices on that day. By entering into forward sales contracts with grain merchants, Monsanto protects itself from the commodity price exposure from the time a contract is signed with a customer until the grain is collected from the customer by a grain merchant on Monsanto's behalf.

Abbott Laboratories
2002 Annual Report

Revenue Recognition—Revenue from product sales is recognized upon passage of title and risk of loss to customers (when product is delivered to common carrier for shipment to domestic customers). Provisions for discounts, rebates and sales incentives to customers, and returns and other adjustments are provided for in the period the related sales are recorded. Sales of product rights are recorded as revenue upon disposition of the rights. Sales incentives to customers are generally not material. Revenue from license of product rights, or for performance of research or selling activities, is recorded over the periods earned.

Merck and Co.
2002 Annual Report

Revenue Recognition—Revenues from sales of Merck human health products are recognized upon shipment of product. Revenues are recorded net of provisions for rebates, discounts and returns, which are established at the time of sale.

Medco Health revenues consist principally of sales of prescription drugs through managed prescription drug programs, either from its home delivery pharmacies or its networks of contractually affiliated retail pharmacies, and are recognized when those prescriptions are dispensed. Medco Health evaluates client contracts using the indicators of Emerging Issues TaskForce Issue No. 99-19, Reporting Gross Revenue as a Principal vs. Net as an Agent, to determine whether it acts as a principal or as an agent in the fulfillment of prescriptions through the retail pharmacy network. Where Medco Health acts as a principal, revenues are recognized on a gross reporting basis at the prescription price (ingredient cost plus dispensing fee) negotiated with clients, including the portion of the price allocated by the client to be settled directly by the member (copayment). This is because Medco Health (a) has separate contractual relationships with clients and with pharmacies, (b) is responsible to validate and most economically manage a claim through its claims adjudication process, (c) commits to set prescription prices for the pharmacy, including instructing the pharmacy as to how that price is to be settled (copayment requirements), (d) manages the overall prescription drug relationship with the patients, and (e) has credit risk for the price due from the client. Where Medco Health adjudicates prescriptions at pharmacies that are under contract directly with the client and there are no financial risks to Medco Health, such revenue is recorded using net reporting as service revenues, at the amount of the administrative fee earned by Medco Health for processing the claim. Rebates, guarantees, and risk-sharing payments paid to clients and other discounts are deducted from revenue as they are earned by the client. Other contractual payments made to clients are generally made upon initiation of contracts as implementation allowances, which may, for example, be designated by clients as funding for their costs to transition their plans to Medco Health or as compensation for certain data or licensing rights granted by the client to Medco Health. Medco Health considers these payments to be an integral part of its pricing of a contract and believes that they represent only a variability in the timing of cash flow that does not change the underlying economics of the contract. Accordingly, these payments are capitalized and amortized as a reduction of revenue on a straight-line basis over the life of the contract where the payments are refundable upon cancellation of the contract or relate to non-cancelable contracts. Amounts capitalized are assessed periodically for recoverability based on the profitability of the contract.

Medco Health revenues also include service revenues consisting principally of administrative fees earned from clients and other non-product related service revenues, including from sales of data to pharmaceutical manufacturers and health care organizations. Administrative fees are earned for services that are comprised of claims processing, eligibility management, benefits management, pharmacy network management and other related customer services and are recognized when the prescription is dispensed. Other non-product related service revenues are recorded by Medco Health when performance occurs and collectibility is assured.

Textron
2002 Annual Report

Revenue Recognition

Revenue is generally recognized when products are delivered or services are performed. With respect to aircraft, delivery is upon completion of manufacturing, customer acceptance and the transfer of the risk and rewards of ownership.

Revenue under fixed-price contracts is generally recorded as deliveries are made. Certain long-term fixed-price contracts provide for periodic delivery after a lengthy period of time over which significant costs are incurred or require a significant amount of development effort in relation to total contract volume.

Revenues under those contracts and all cost-reimbursement-type contracts are recorded as costs are incurred. Certain contracts are awarded with fixed-price incentive fees. Incentive fees are considered when estimating revenues and profit rates, and are recorded when these amounts are reasonably determined. Long-term contract profits are based on estimates of total sales value and costs at completion. Such estimates are reviewed and revised periodically throughout the contract life. Revisions to contract profits are recorded when the revisions to estimated sales value or costs are made. Estimated contract losses are recorded when identified.

Revenues under the V-22 low-rate initial production contract are recorded as costs are incurred, primarily due to the significant engineering effort required over a lengthy period of time during the initial development stage in relation to total contract volume. Under the low-rate production releases, Textron continues to manufacture aircraft which may subsequently be modified for engineering changes. Beginning with new production releases in 2003, the development effort will be substantially completed. As a result, revenue on new production releases will be recognized as units are delivered.

Revenue from certain qualifying non-cancelable aircraft and other product lease contracts are accounted for as sales-type leases. The present value of all payments (net of executory costs and any guaranteed residual values) is recorded as revenue, and the related costs of the product are charged to cost of sales. Generally, this lease financing is through Textron Finance and the associated interest is recorded over the term of the lease agreement using the interest method. Lease financing transactions which do not qualify as sales-type leases are accounted for under the operating method wherein revenue is recorded as earned over the lease period.

Finance revenues include interest on finance receivables which is recognized using the interest method to provide a constant rate of return over the terms of the receivables. Finance revenues also include direct loan origination costs and fees received, which are deferred and amortized over the contractual lives of the respective receivables using the interest method. Unamortized amounts are recognized in revenues when receivables are sold or pre-paid. Accrual of interest income is suspended for accounts that are contractually delinquent by more than three months, unless collection is not doubtful. In addition, detailed reviews of loans may result in earlier suspension if collection is doubtful. Accrual of interest is resumed when the loan becomes contractually current, and suspended interest income is recognized at that time.

Sears, Roebuck and Co.
2002 Annual Report

Revenue Recognition

In-store revenues from merchandise sales and services, including delivery fees, are reported net of estimated returns and allowances and customer rebates, and are recognized when the related goods are shipped and all significant obligations of the Company have been satisfied. The reserve for returns and allowances is calculated as a percentage of sales based on historical return percentages. Commissions earned on sales made by licensed businesses are also included as a component of merchandise sales and services.

During 2002, the Company adopted the provisions of Emerging Issues Task Force ("EITF") Issue 01-9, "Accounting For Consideration Given By A Vendor To A Customer". This EITF issue established requirements for the recognition, measurement and display of certain sales incentives and impacted the Company's presentation of rebates provided to customers. As a result of adopting EITF Issue 01-9, net sales and cost of sales decreased by $88 million in 2002 and $89 million in 2001 and 2000, respectively.

Revenues from product installation and repair services are recognized as the services are provided. Additionally, the Company sells extended service contracts with terms of coverage between 12 and 60 months. Revenues from the sale of these contracts are deferred and amortized over the lives of the contracts while the service costs are expensed as incurred. Incremental costs directly related to the acquisition of such contracts are deferred and charged to expense in proportion to the revenue recognized.

The Company direct markets merchandise through catalogs and online via websites. Revenue is recognized for these items when the merchandise is delivered to a customer unless the terms of the sale are FOB shipping point, in which the revenue is recognized upon shipment. The Company also direct markets insurance (credit protection, life and health) and clubs and services memberships. Deferred revenue is recorded when the member is billed (upon expiration of any free trial period), and revenue is recognized over the insurance or membership period. Membership revenue associated with clubs and service memberships is recognized on a straightline basis.

The Company is responsible for providing warranty coverage on certain hardline products. Based on historical warranty claims, the Company accrues the estimated costs of the warranty coverage at the time of sale. A rollforward of the warranty reserve is as follows:

Millions	*2002*	*2001*
Beginning balance	$114	$109
Warranty expense	233	255
Warranty claims	(216)	(250)
Ending balance	$131	$114

The Company recognizes finance charges and fee income on credit card receivables according to the contractual provisions of the credit agreements, and such charges and income are recorded until an account is charged off, at which time uncollected finance charge and fee revenue are recorded as a reduction of credit revenues. The Company provides an allowance for estimated uncollectible finance charge and fee revenues in the provision.

Honeywell International
2002 Annual Report

Sales Recognition

Product and service sales are recognized when persuasive evidence of an arrangement exists, product delivery has occurred or services have been rendered, pricing is fixed or determinable, and collection is reasonably assured. Sales under long-term contracts in the Aerospace and Automation and Control Solutions segments are recorded on a percentage-of-completion method measured on the cost-to-cost basis for engineering-type contracts and the units-of-delivery basis for production-type contracts. Provisions for anticipated losses on long-term contracts are recorded in full when such losses become evident. Revenues from contracts with multiple element arrangements are recognized as each element is earned based on the relative fair value of each element and when there are no undelivered elements that are essential to the functionality of the delivered elements. Amounts allocated to each element are based on its objectively determined fair value, such as the sales price for the product or service when it is sold separately or competitor prices for similar products or services.

Xerox
2002 Annual Report

Revenue Recognition: In the normal course of business, we generate revenue through the sale and rental of equipment, service, and supplies and income associated with the financing of our equipment sales. Revenue is recognized when earned. More specifically, revenue related to sales of our products and services is recognized as follows:

Equipment: Revenues from the sale of equipment, including those from sales-type leases, are recognized at the time of sale or at the inception of the lease, as appropriate. For equipment sales that require us to install the product at the customer location, revenue is recognized when the equipment has been delivered to and installed at the customer location. Sales of customer installable and retail products are recognized upon shipment or receipt by the customer according to the customer's shipping terms. Revenues from equipment under other leases and similar arrangements are accounted for by the operating lease method and are recognized as earned over the lease term, which is generally on a straight-line basis.

Service: Service revenues are derived primarily from maintenance contracts on our equipment sold to customers and are recognized over the term of the contracts. A substantial portion of our products are sold with full service maintenance agreements for which the customer typically pays a base service fee plus a variable amount based on usage. As a consequence, we do not have any significant product warranty obligations, including any obligations under customer satisfaction programs.

Supplies: Supplies revenue generally is recognized upon shipment or utilization by customer in accordance with sales terms.

Revenue Recognition Under Bundled Arrangements: We sell most of our products and services under bundled contract arrangements, which contain multiple deliverable elements. These contractual lease arrangements typically include equipment, service, supplies and financing components for which the customer pays a single negotiated price for all elements. These arrangements typically also include a variable component for page volumes in excess of contractual minimums, which are often expressed in terms of price per page, which we refer to as the "cost per copy." In a typical bundled arrangement, our customer is quoted a fixed minimum monthly payment for (1) the equipment, (2) the associated services and other executory costs and (3) the financing element. The fixed minimum monthly payments are multiplied by the number of months in the contract term to arrive at the total fixed minimum payments that the customer is obligated to make ("Fixed Payments") over the lease term. The payments associated with page volumes in excess of the minimums are contingent on whether or not such minimums are exceeded ("Contingent Payments"). The minimum contractual committed copy volumes are typically negotiated to equal the customer's estimated copy volume at lease inception. In applying our lease accounting methodology, we consider the Fixed Payments for purposes of allocating to the fair value elements of the contract. We do not consider the Contingent Payments for purposes of allocating to the elements of the contract or recognizing revenue on the sale of the equipment, given the inherent uncertainties as to whether such amounts will ever be received. Contingent Payments are recognized as revenue in the period when the customer exceeds the minimum copy volumes specified in the contract.

When separate prices are listed in multiple element customer contracts, such prices may not be representative of the fair values of those elements, because the prices of the different components of the arrangement may be modified through customer negotiations, although the aggregate consideration may remain the same. Therefore, revenues under these arrangements are allocated based upon estimated fair values of each element. Our revenue allocation methodology first begins by determining the fair value of the service component, as well as other executory costs and any profit thereon and second, by determining the fair value of the equipment based on comparison of the equipment values in our accounting systems to a range of cash selling prices or, if applicable, other verifiable objective evidence of fair value. We perform extensive analyses of available verifiable objective evidence of equipment fair value based on cash selling prices during the applicable period. The cash selling prices are compared to the range of values included in our lease accounting systems. The range of cash selling prices must support the reasonableness of the lease selling prices, taking into account residual values that accrue to our benefit, in order for us to determine that such lease prices are indicative of fair value. Our interest rates are developed based upon a variety of factors including local prevailing rates in the marketplace and the customer's credit history, industry and credit class. These rates are recorded within our pricing systems. The resultant implicit interest rate, which is the same as our pricing interest rate, unless adjustment to equipment values is required, is then compared to fair market value rates to assess the reasonableness of the fair value allocations to the multiple elements.

Determination of Appropriate Revenue Recognition for Leases: Our accounting for leases involves specific determinations under Statement of Financial Accounting Standards No. 13 "Accounting for Leases" ("SFAS No. 13") which often involve complex provisions and significant judgments. The two primary criteria of SFAS No. 13 which we use to classify transactions as sales-type or operating leases are (1) a review of the lease term to determine if it is equal to or greater than 75 percent of the economic life of the equipment and (2) a review of the minimum lease payments to determine if they are equal to or greater than 90 percent of the fair market value of the equipment. Under our current product portfolio and business strategies, a non-cancelable lease of 45 months or more generally qualifies as a sale. Certain of our lease contracts are customized for larger customers, which results in complex terms and conditions and requires significant judgment in applying the above criteria. In addition to these, there are also other important criteria that are required to be assessed, including whether collectibility of the lease payments is reasonably predictable and whether there are important uncertainties related to costs that we have yet to incur with respect to the lease. In our opinion, our sales-type lease portfolios contain only normal credit and collection risks and have no important uncertainties with respect to future costs. Our leases in our Latin America operations have historically been recorded as operating leases since a majority of these leases are terminated significantly prior to the expiration of the contractual lease term. Specifically, because we generally do not collect the receivable from the initial transaction upon termination or during any subsequent lease term, the recoverability of the lease investment is deemed not to be predictable at lease inception. We continue to evaluate economic, business and political conditions in the Latin American region to determine if certain leases will qualify as sales-type leases in future periods.

The critical estimates and judgments that we consider with respect to our lease accounting are the determination of the economic life and the fair value of equipment, including the residual value. Those estimates are based upon historical experience with all our products. For purposes of estimating the economic life, we consider the most objective measure of historical experience to be the original contract term, since most equipment is returned by lessees at or near the end of the contracted term. The estimated economic life of most of our products is five years since this represents the most frequent contractual lease term for our principal products and only a small percentage of our leases have original terms longer than five years. We believe that this is representative of the period during which the equipment is expected to be economically usable, with normal service, for the purpose for which it is intended. We continually evaluate the economic life of both existing and newly introduced products for purposes of this determination. Residual values are established at lease inception using estimates of fair value at the end of the lease term. Our residual values are established with due consideration to forecasted supply and demand for our various products, product retirement and future product launch plans, end of lease customer behavior, remanufacturing strategies, used equipment markets if any, competition and technological changes.

The vast majority of our leases that qualify as sales-type are non-cancelable and include cancellation penalties approximately equal to the full value of the leased equipment. Certain of our governmental contracts may have cancellation provisions or renewal clauses that are required by law, such as (1) those dependant on fiscal funding outside of a governmental unit's control, (2) those that can be cancelled if deemed in the taxpayer's best interest or (3) those that must be renewed each fiscal year, given imitations that may exist on entering multi-year contracts that are imposed by statute. In these circumstances and in accordance with the relevant accounting literature, we carefully evaluate these contracts to assess whether cancellation is remote or the renewal option is reasonably assured of exercise because of the existence of substantive economic penalties for the customer's failure to renew. Certain of our commercial contracts for multiple units of equipment may include clauses that allow for a return of a limited portion of such equipment (up to 10 percent of the value of equipment). These return clauses are only available in very limited circumstances as negotiated at lease inception. We account for our estimate of equipment to be returned under these contracts as operating leases.

Aside from the initial lease of equipment to our customers, we may enter subsequent transactions with the same customer whereby we extend the term. We evaluate the classification of lease extensions of sales-type leases using the originally determined economic life for each product. There may be instances where we have lease extensions for periods that are within the original economic life of the equipment.

These are accounted for as sales-type leases only when the extensions occur in the last three months of the lease term and they otherwise meet the appropriate criteria of SFAS No. 13. All other lease extensions of this type are accounted for as direct financing leases.

We generally account for lease extensions that go beyond the economic life as operating leases because of important uncertainties as to the amount of servicing and repair costs that we may incur.

Yahoo!
2002 Annual Report

Revenue Recognition. The company's revenues are derived principally from services, which include marketing services, fees, and listings.

Marketing services revenues are primarily generated from the sale of banner, sponsorship, text-link advertisements, including sponsored search advertisements, and transaction revenues. Banner advertising agreements typically range from one week to three years. The Company recognizes marketing services revenues related to banner advertisements as "impressions" are delivered by the Company. "Impressions" are defined as the number of times that an advertisement appears in pages viewed by users of the Yahoo! network. Sponsorship advertising agreements have longer terms than banner advertising agreements, typically ranging from three months to three years, and often involve multiple element arrangements that may include placement on specific properties, exclusivity and content integration. Sponsorship advertisement revenues are recognized as "impressions" are delivered or ratably over the contract period, where applicable, and when collection of the resulting receivable is reasonably assured. Text-link advertisements, including sponsored searches, are recognized as the net amount earned in the period in which the "click-throughs" occur. "Click-throughs" are defined as the number of times a user clicks on an advertisement or search result. Transactions revenues include service fees for facilitating transactions through the Yahoo! network, principally from the Company's commerce properties. Transactions revenues are recognized when there is evidence that the qualifying transactions have occurred and collection of the resulting receivable is reasonably assured. The Company recognizes revenue on these arrangements in accordance with Securities and Exchange Commission Staff Accounting Bulletin No. 101 ("SAB 101"), "Revenue Recognition in Financial Statements." In all cases, revenue is recognized only when the price is fixed or determinable, persuasive evidence of an arrangement exists, the service is performed, and collectibility of the resulting receivable is reasonably assured. Revenues from sponsored search and media from the Company's agreement with Overture Services, Inc. ("Overture") are included in marketing services for the years ended December 31, 2002 nd 2001. Revenues from Overture amounted to 14% of net revenues for the year ended December 31, 2002. No one customer accounted for 10% or more of net revenues during 2001 and 2000.

Periodically, the Company engages in barter transactions for marketing services. Barter revenue is recognized over the periods in which the Company completes its obligations under the arrangement. In January 2000, the Company adopted Emerging Issues Task Force Issue No. 99-17 ("EITF 99-17"), "Accounting for Advertising Barter Transactions," which requires advertising barter transactions to be valued based on similar cash transactions that have occurred within six months prior to the barter transaction. Barter revenues represented 2%, 7%, and 7% of total revenues for 2002, 2001 and 2000, respectively. During 2002, 2001 and 2000, the Company delivered approximately 3.5 billion, 1.6 billion and 1.1 billion impressions, respectively, under barter arrangements where fair value was not determinable under EITF 99-17 and, accordingly, revenue was not recognized.

Fees revenues consist of revenues generated from a variety of consumer and business fee-based services, including Yahoo! SBC DSL and Dial, Yahoo! Personals, Small Business Services, Yahoo! Mail and Yahoo! Enterprise Solutions. With the exception of Yahoo! Portal Solutions, revenues are recognized in the month in which the services are performed, provided that no significant Company obligations remain and collection of the resulting receivable is reasonably assured. Revenues from Yahoo! Portal Solutions consist of software license and service revenues, which are principally platform and maintenance services. Yahoo! Portal Solutions revenue is recognized in accordance with Statement of Position No. 97-2, "Software Revenue Recognition" and Statement of Position 98-9, "Modification of SOP No. 97-2 with Respect to Certain Transactions." License revenues are recognized when persuasive evidence of an arrangement exists, delivery of the license has occurred, the fee is fixed or determinable, and collection is probable. License revenues from Portal Solutions were not material to the Company as they represented less than 1% of total net revenue for all periods presented. Platform services are sold as a subscription and are recognized ratably over the subscription period. Platform services are priced based on the specific content or service purchased by the customer. These services are optional and renewable annually at fixed renewal rates. Maintenance is generally sold under annual contracts with fixed renewal rates. Maintenance revenue is recognized ratably over the contract period. Yahoo! Portal Solutions revenues have represented less than 10% of total net revenues in all periods presented.

Listings revenues consist of revenues generated from a variety of consumer and business listings-based services, including access to the HotJobs database and classifieds such as Yahoo! Autos, Yahoo! Real Estate and other Search and Directory services. Revenues are recognized in the month in which the services are performed, provided that no significant Company obligations remain and collection of the resulting receivable is reasonably assured.

Deferred revenue primarily comprises contractual billings in excess of recognized revenue and payments received in advance of revenue recognition.

NCR
2002 Annual Report

Revenue Recognition   NCR's revenue recognition policy is consistent with the requirements of Staff Accounting Bulletin No. 101 (SAB 101), "Revenue Recognition in Financial Statements," Statement of Position No. 97-2 (SOP 97-2), "Software Revenue Recognition," and other applicable revenue recognition guidance and interpretations. In general, the Company records revenue when it is realized, or realizable, and earned. The Company considers these requirements met when persuasive evidence of an arrangement exists, the products or services have been provided to the customer, the sales price is fixed or determinable and collectibility is reasonably assured.

For the Company's solutions, computer hardware and software revenue is recognized upon shipment, delivery, installation or customer acceptance of the product, as defined in the customer contract. Typically, NCR does not sell its software products without the related hardware as the software products are embedded in the hardware. The Company's typical solution requires no significant production, modification or customization of the software or hardware that is essential to the functionality of the products other than installation for its more complex solutions. For these complex solutions, revenue is deferred until the installation is complete.

As a solutions provider, the Company's sales arrangements often include services in addition to hardware and software. These services could include hardware maintenance, upgrade rights, customer support and professional consulting services. For sales arrangements that include bundled hardware, software and services, NCR accounts for any undelivered service offering as a separate element of a multiple-element arrangement. These services are typically not essential to the functionality of the hardware and software. Amounts deferred for services are determined based upon vendor-specific objective evidence of the fair value of the elements as prescribed in SOP 97-2. For these services, revenue is typically recognized ratably over the period benefited or when the services are complete. If the services are essential to the functionality of the hardware and software, revenue from the hardware and software components is deferred until the essential services are complete.

NCR's customers may request that certain transactions be on a bill and hold basis. For these transactions, the Company recognizes revenue in accordance with SAB 101 and the criteria established by the Securities and Exchange Commission.

Boeing
2002 Annual Report

Contract accounting   Contract accounting is used predominantly by the Military Aircraft and Missile Systems and Space and Communications segments. The majority of the business conducted in these segments is performed under contracts for the U.S. Government and foreign governments that extend over a number of years.

The process to estimate the total contract cost-revenue relationship results in the development of gross margin and cost of sales percentages. These percentages are utilized in the recognition of earnings and are significant factors in contract accounting. The amount reported as cost of sales is determined by applying the estimated cost of sales percentages to the amount of revenue recognized for each contract.

Revenues under contracts with fixed prices are generally recognized as deliveries are made. For certain fixed-price contracts that require substantial performance over an extended period before deliveries begin, revenues are recorded based on the attainment of performance milestones. Revenues under contracts with terms that reimburse for costs incurred plus an agreed upon profit are recorded as costs are incurred. Contracts may contain provisions to earn incentive and award fees if targets are achieved. Incentive and award fees that can be reasonably estimated are recorded over the performance period of the contract. Incentive and award fees that cannot be reasonably estimated are recorded when awarded.

Program accounting   The Company uses program accounting for its 7-series commercial airplane products. Program accounting is a method of accounting for the costs of certain products manufactured for delivery under production type contracts where profitability is realized over multiple contracts and years. Under program accounting, inventoriable production costs (including overhead), program tooling costs and warranty costs are accumulated and charged to revenue by program instead of by individual units or contracts. A program consists of the estimated number of units (accounting quantity) of a product to be produced in a continuing, long-term production effort for delivery under existing and anticipated contracts. To establish the relationship of revenue to cost of sales, program accounting requires estimates of (a) the number of units to be produced and sold in a program, (b) the period over which the units can reasonably be expected to be produced, and (c) their expected selling prices, production costs, program tooling, and warranty costs for the total program.

The Company recognizes revenue for commercial airplanes when a unit is completed and accepted by the customer. The revenue recognized is the price negotiated with the customer including special features adjusted by an escalation formula. The amount reported as cost of sales is determined by applying the estimated cost of sales percentage for the total remaining program to the amount of revenue recognized for the quarter.

Chapter 3
Balance Sheet Reporting and Disclosures: Assets

CONTENTS

This chapter discusses generally accepted accounting principles (GAAP) for assets. It includes a discussion of accounts and loans receivable, inventory, prepaid expenses, fixed assets, capitalized interest, exchange of assets, impairment of assets, involuntary conversion, intangibles, and transfer of financial assets. Promulgated GAAP for current assets is provided in ASC 210-10-45-1 through 45-3, *Balance Sheet: Overall*. Current assets have a life of one year or the normal operating cycle of the business, whichever is greater. The accounting policies and any restrictions on current assets must be disclosed.

Assets are recorded at the price paid plus normal incidental costs necessary to bring that asset into existing use and location. Examples of incidental costs include installation, freight, insurance, tooling, testing, instruction, flooring, and taxes. As a general rule, costs incurred before an asset is put into use for the first time is capitalized to the asset. If an asset is bought in exchange for the issuance of stock, the asset is recorded at the fair value of the stock issued. If the fair value is not known, such as in the case of a closely held company, the asset is presented at its appraised value. If an asset is acquired because of the incurrence of long-term debt, the asset is recorded at the present (discounted) value of future payments.

EXAMPLE

Equipment is bought in exchange for making ten $30,000 payments at an interest rate of 10%. The asset should be recorded at:

$$\$30,000 \times 6.145^* = \$184,350$$

The asset is recorded at the principal amount excluding the interest payments.

*Factor using the present value of an ordinary annuity table for $n = 10$, $i = 10\%$.

Some assets are recorded at net realizable value, which equals the amount of cash expected to be obtained for them in the ordinary course of business less any direct costs associated with their conversion to cash.

CASH

Cash includes money, available cash funds on deposit, and bank drafts. Petty cash is typically presented with other cash accounts.

Note: Bank overdrafts are presented under current liabilities, typically accounts payable. Bank overdrafts are usually not offset against the cash account. However, offsetting is allowed for two or more accounts at the same bank.

Note: Certificates of deposit and similar types of deposit are classified as temporary investments rather than cash because they contain restrictions or penalties if cashed in before maturity. However, cash restricted as to withdrawal or use for other than current operations will not be presented as a current asset.

Cash *restricted* for specified purposes may be segregated and may be presented as a current asset if it is the basis to pay a current liability. If not, the restricted cash will be presented under noncurrent assets. Further, cash may be presented as a noncurrent asset if it is to be used to pay long-term debt, or if the cash is to be used to buy or construct a noncurrent asset.

The amount of cash constituting a compensating balance has to be segregated and presented under noncurrent assets if the related debt is noncurrent. If, however, the debt is current, the compensating balance may be shown separately as a current asset.

The cash surrender value of life insurance policies is classified under noncurrent investments unless the policy will be cashed in within one year from the balance sheet date.

Any restrictions or commitments on cash must be disclosed. Compensating balance requirements must be noted.

Footnote disclosure is required of off-balance-sheet risk of loss as applied to cash, such as possible theft of cash in an unsecured location or high crime area. Such disclosure would be required of a company keeping more than $100,000 in a bank account and therefore having off-balance-sheet risk, because amounts on deposits exceeding $100,000 are not insured by the Federal Deposit Insurance Corporation.

RECEIVABLES

Receivables may consist of accounts receivable, notes receivable, trade acceptances, travel advances and loans receivable. Postdated checks and IOUs are classified as receivables.

Nontrade receivables include advances to officers and employees, advances to subsidiaries or affiliated companies, receivables from stockholders, third-party instruments, deposits owed the company (e.g., deposits to cover product damages or guarantees of performance), interest and dividends receivable, and claims against others (e.g., insurance recoveries, tax refunds, returned items, damaged goods in transit by carrier). Nontrade receivables should be segregated from trade receivables in the balance sheet. **Note:** ARB No. 43, chapter 1A, covers receivables from officers, employees, or affiliated companies.

Unearned discounts (excluding for cost or volume), finance charges, and interest included in the face of receivables should be subtracted therefrom to determine net receivables.

Accounts Receivable

Accounts receivable are presented in the balance sheet at net realizable value. Net realizable value equals the gross receivable less the allowance for bad debts. Bad debts may be recognized under the allowance method or direct write-off method. The *allowance method* recognizes bad debt expense in the year of sale. The bad debt provision may be based on either a percentage of credit sales or an aging of the ending accounts receivable balance. A company may estimate bad debt percentage based on several factors, such as past experience, the experience of other companies in the industry, or current economic conditions. The allowance method is the only one required in financial reporting. The *direct write-off* method records bad debt expense only when a customer's balance is uncollectible. This method is not allowed for financial reporting purposes because it does not match expenses against sales in the year of sale. However, the direct write-off method is required for tax reporting purposes.

An accrual should also be made in the year of sale for estimated returns and allowances due to product deficiency. Collection expenses may be accrued by debiting collection expenses and crediting allowance for collection expenses. An allowance for trade discounts should also be provided. The allowance account is a contra to gross accounts receivable to determine net accounts receivable.

EXAMPLE

If a company sells on terms of 4/15, net 30, and 30% of its customers take advantage of the discount on sales of $90,000, the allowance for discounts will be $1,080 ($90,000 × .30 × .04).

EXAMPLE

Harris Company presents the following data related to its accounts receivable for 20X2:

Accounts receivable, 1/1/20X2	$325,000
Credit sales	1,350,000
Sales returns	37,500
Accounts written off	20,000
Collections from customers	1,075,000

Gross accounts receivable equals $542,500, computed as follows:

Accounts receivable—1/1/20X2	$325,000
Credit sales	1,350,000
Sales returns	(37,500)
Accounts written off	(20,000)
Customer collections	(1,075,000)
Total	$ 542,500

EXAMPLE

Mavis Company's allowance for bad debts has a credit balance of $48,000 at December 31, 20X1. During 20X2, the company wrote off customer accounts of $192,000. The aging of accounts receivable shows that a $200,000 allowance account is needed at December 31, 20X3.

Bad debts for 20X3 should be $344,000, computed as follows:

Allowance—12/31/20X1	$ 48,000
Accounts written off in 20X2	(192,000)
Debit balance before year-end adjustment	$ (144,000)
Desired credit balance (based on aging)	200,000
Year-end adjustment (increase in expense)	$ 344,000

EXAMPLE

Erlach Company computed its net value of accounts receivable at December 31, 20X2 as $162,500 based on aging the receivable. Additional information for 20X2 follows:

Allowance for bad debts—1/1/20X2	$ 15,000
Uncollectible accounts written off	9,000
Uncollectible accounts recovered	1,000
Accounts receivable—12/31/20X2	175,000

Bad debts for 20X2 will be $5,500, computed as follows:

Allowance—1/1/20X2	$ 15,000
Accounts written off	(9,000)
Recovery of accounts written off	1,000
Balance before adjustment	7,000

Desired allowance balance ($175,000 − $162,500)	12,500
Bad debts	$ 5,500

The *pledging* of accounts receivable involves using accounts receivable as *security* for a loan. The company retains title to the receivable but must disclose the pledging agreement in the footnotes. The agreement usually stipulates that as collections are received they must be used to reduce the loan. The pledged accounts receivable must be identified as such in the current asset section. The related debt must be identified as being collateralized by the pledged receivable. Customers whose accounts have been pledged are usually not informed of it. They continue to mail their payments to the company.

An *assignment* of account receivable involves using the receivable as collateral for a loan. Typically, less than the face value of the receivable (e.g., 80%) will be advanced to the borrower by the lender, depending on the credit worthiness of the borrower and the quality of the customer base. Accounts receivable that are assigned are presented in the current asset section and are required to be disclosed as such. The assignment of accounts receivable usually involves both a finance charge and interest on the note. Prepaid finance charges are deferred and amortized over the period of the agreement.

EXAMPLE

Levsee Company assigns $1,000,000 of its accounts receivable to Levine Bank as collateral for a loan of $800,000 made by the bank on January 1. The loan agreement provides that Levsee's credit customers will not be notified of the arrangement and the company will continue to collect payments on account as usual. Levine Bank charges a finance charge of 2% of the accounts receivable assigned and Levsee is required to pay 10% interest on the amount borrowed. The bank requires that collections on the accounts receivable that were assigned and interest payments on the outstanding debt be remitted monthly.

The following are the entries made by Levsee Company:

Issuance of the note for the loan of $800,000:

Cash	780,000	
Finance expense (2% × $1,000,000)	20,000	
Notes payable		800,000

Sales discounts and sales returns for the month of January were $1,000 and $2,000, respectively:

Sales discounts	1,000	
Sales returns	2,000	
Accounts receivable		3,000

Collections of accounts receivable net of discounts and returns for the month of January amounted to $500,000:

Cash	500,000	
Accounts receivable		500,000

Remitted collections on accounts receivable plus interest owed on note to Levine Bank for the month of January are as follows:

Notes payable	500,000	
Interest expense	6,667 (800,000 × 10% × 1/12)	
Cash		506,667

During February, $25,000 was written off as uncollectible:

Allowance for doubtful accounts	25,000	
Accounts receivable		25,000

Remaining collections of receivables net of uncollectible accounts amounted to $472,000 for February. The balance of the note payable plus accrued interest for the month was remitted to Levine Bank by Levsee Company:

Cash	472,000	
Accounts receivable		472,000
Note payable	300,000	
Interest expense	2,500 (300,000 × 10% × 1/12)	
Cash		302,500

In a *factoring* arrangement, accounts receivable are, in effect, sold to a financial institution (factor). Title is transferred. Notification is usually made to customers, and remissions are made directly to the factor. Factoring is accomplished usually without recourse, meaning the risk of uncollectibility of the customer's account resides in the lender (factor). Interest is based on how long it is expected to take the factor to collect on customer balances. A fee is also assessed based on expected bad debts. The factor usually does the billing and collection. The difference between the factored receivable and the amount received constitutes a gain or loss as follows:

Cash

Loss (or gain)

    Accounts receivable

EXAMPLE

ABC Company sells its receivable without recourse to a factor. The total face value of the accounts receivable is $100,000. There is a 4% allowance provided. The interest rate is 12% and is to apply to a 60-day period before collection is expected. A 2% fee is provided for expected uncollectible balances. An 8% holdback is stipulated for expected customer returns of merchandise. The amount of merchandise actually returned was $3,000. The remaining holdback will be paid by the factor after the return privilege period expires. The journal entries for this factoring arrangement follow:

Cash	88,000	
Allowance for bad debts	4,000	
($100,000 × .04)		
Interest expense	2,000	
($100,000 × .12 × 60/360)		

Factoring fee ($100,000 × .02)	2,000	
Factor's holdback receivable	8,000	
($100,000 × .08)		
Bad debts expense		4,000
Accounts receivable		100,000

Note: As an alternative, $4,000 may be charged to a loss on sale of receivable account based on the total interest and factoring charges.

Sales returns and allowances	3,000	
Factor's holdback receivable		3,000
Cash*	5,000	
Factor's holdback receivable		5,000

* When the return privilege period expires, the remaining holdback is due the borrower amounting to $5,000 ($8,000 – $3,000).

Footnote disclosure for accounts receivable includes:

☐ Receivables arising from major sources such as trade, officers, and employees.

☐ Year-end receivable balance and amounts received by the transferor during the period.

☐ Receivables that have been billed or unbilled.

☐ Loss contingencies on receivables.

☐ Collateralized or pledged receivables.

☐ Significant concentration of credit risk arising from receivables.

☐ Related-party receivables.

☐ Losses on receivables after year-end but before the financial statements are issued.

Note that in Accounting Standards Update (ASU) No. 2011-02 (April 2011) (ASC 310, *Receivables*), *A Creditor's Determination of Whether a Restructuring Is a Troubled Debt Restructuring*, in appraising if a restructuring is of troubled debt, the creditor must conclude that both the restructuring is a concession and the debtor is having financial problems.

Notes Receivable

A note receivable may be discounted at the bank to obtain the proceeds before the maturity date. The amount of cash (proceeds) received by the holder when the note is discounted equals the face value of the note plus interest income to maturity to obtain the maturity value less the discount based on the maturity value. The bank discount equals the maturity value of the note multiplied by the discount rate for the time period the note will be held by the bank. If the note is discounted with recourse, the company is contingently liable if the note is not paid. The discounted notes receivable account is a contra to notes receivable.

EXAMPLE

A $10,000, six-month note having a 12% interest rate is discounted at the bank after being held for two months. The bank discount rate is 15%. The cash received is:

Principal	$10,000
Interest ($10,000 × 6/12 × .12)	600
Maturity value	$10,600
Bank discount ($10,600 × 4/12 × .15)	530
Proceeds	$10,070

The journal entry is as follows:

Cash	10,070	
Notes receivable discounted		10,000
Interest income		70

EXAMPLE

Blake Company bought from David Company a $10,000, 8%, five-year note involving five equal annual year-end payments of $2,505. The note was discounted at 9% to Blake. At the purchase date, the note's present value was $9,743. Interest income earned over the life of the note will be $2,783, computed as follows:

Total cash receipts $2,505 × 5	$12,525
Less: acquisition cost of note	9,743
Interest revenue over life of note	$ 2,782

An installment note receivable should *not* be offset against a related bank debt in a note monetization situation.

A note received in payment for common stock issued should usually be deducted in the stockholders' equity section of the balance sheet.

Footnote disclosure for notes receivable include the amount of notes receivable discounted, description of the notes, face amount of the notes, and interest rate on the notes.

According to Accounting Standards Update (ASU) No. 2010-18 (April 2010) (ASC 310, *Receivables*), *Effect of a Loan Modification When the Loan Is Part of a Pool That Is Accounted for as a Single Asset*, it is possible that a purchased loan may have poor credit quality. An acquired asset that has similar risk attributes (e.g., credit risk) may be treated as a pool, which is considered an accounting unit. Pooled loans do not involve allocation of the purchase discount to the specific loans; one pool rate applies to all the loans. The loan pool is evaluated for any impairment.

In some cases, modification of a loan may be considered a reworking of troubled debt. A loan modification for a pool does not constitute a loan removal from the pool, even when the loan restructuring is deemed troubled debt. Note that a troubled debt restructuring does not apply to a modification of a worker contract or lease modification (ASC 310-40-15-11).

In determining whether a loan impairment exists, anticipated future cash flows should be taken into account. In addition, the cost of purchased assets should be allocated based on fair market value at the time of acquisition (ASC 310-30-15-6).

If a loan is refinanced, except for a troubled debt restructuring, that loan is not considered a new loan (ASC 310-30-35-13).

A loan is only taken out of a pool if it is written-off or if assets are obtained in exchange for the loan. A removal of a loan should be at book value (ASC 310-30-40-1).

Loans Receivable

ASC 310-20-05-2, *Receivables: Nonrefundable Fees and Other Costs*, is applicable to both the incremental direct costs incurred in originating a loan and internally incurred costs that are directly related to loan or loan commitment activity. Loan origination fees are netted with the related loan origination costs and are accounted for as follows:

☐ For loans held for resale, the net cost is deferred and recognized at the time the loan is sold.

☐ For loans held for investment purposes, the net cost is deferred and amortized over the term of the loan by the interest method.

Loan commitment fees are initially deferred and recognized in earnings as follows:

☐ If the commitment is exercised, the fee is recognized over the term of the loan by the interest method.

☐ If the commitment expires without exercise, the fee is recognized at the expiration date.

☐ If, based on past experience, exercise of the commitment is remote, the fee is amortized over the term of the commitment by the straight-line method.

IMPAIRMENT OF LOANS

ASC 310-10-35-13, *Receivables: Overall*, is the primary authoritative guideline for recognizing impaired loans. A loan is a contractual right to receive cash either on demand or at a fixed or determinable date. Loans include accounts receivable and notes only if their term is longer than one year. If it is probable (likely to occur) that some or all of the principal or interest will not be collected, the loan is considered impaired. Any loss on an impaired loan should be recognized immediately by debiting bad debt expense and crediting the valuation allowance.

Creditors may exercise their judgment and use their normal review procedures in determining the probability of collection.

Determining the Value of an Impaired Loan

If a loan is considered impaired, the loss is the difference between the investment in loan and the present value of the future cash flows discounted at the loan's effective interest rate. The investment in loan will generally be the principal and the accrued interest. Future cash flows should be determined using reasonable and supportable assumptions and projections. The discount rate will generally be the effective interest used at the time the loan was originally made. As a practical matter, the loan's value may be determined using the market price of the loan, if available. The loan's value may also be determined using the fair value of the collateral, less estimated costs to sell, if the loan is collateralized and the collateral is expected to be the sole source of repayment.

EXAMPLE

On December 31, 20X0, Debtor Inc. issues a five-year, $100,000 note bearing a 10% interest, payable annually, to Creditor Inc. The market interest rate for such loans is 12%. The present value of the principal, $100,000 discounted at 12% for five years, is $56,742. The present value of the interest payments of $10,000 (10% of $100,000) per year for five years discounted at 12% is $36,048. Therefore, the present value of the loan is $92,790. Discount on notes receivable is $7,210, and it will be amortized using the effective interest method. Creditor Inc. will record the note as follows:

Notes receivable	100,000	
Discount on notes receivable		7,210
Cash		92,790

The following table shows the amortization of the discount and the increase in the carrying amount of the note:

Year	Interest Income	Cash Received	Discount Amortization	Discount Remaining	Carrying Amount
12/31/X0				7,210	92,790
12/31/X1	11,135	10,000	1,135	6,075	93,925
12/31/X2	11,271	10,000	1,271	4,804	95,196
12/31/X3	11,424	10,000	1,424	3,380	96,620
12/31/X4	11,594	10,000	1,594	1,786	92,214
12/31/X5	11,786	10,000	1,786	0	100,000

On December 31, 20X2, Creditor Inc. determines that it is probable that Debtor Inc. will only be able to repay interest of $8,000 per year (instead of $10,000 per year) and $70,000 (instead of $100,000) of the principal at maturity. This constitutes a loan impairment, and a loss should be recorded immediately. The present value of future cash flows should be discounted for three years at the historical effective interest rate of 12%. The present value of $70,000 discounted at 12% for three years is $49,824, and the present value of interest payments of $8,000 discounted at 12% for three years is $19,215. The total present value of future cash flows is $69,039:

Carrying amount of investment in loan on 12/31/X2	$95,196
Present value of future cash flows from loan	69,039
Loss due to impairment	$26,157

The entry to record the loss is as follows:

Bad debt expense	26,157	
Allowance for doubtful accounts		26,157

Evaluating Loan Collectibility

A loan is considered impaired if it is probable that the creditor will be unable to collect the entire principal and interest. The definition of *probable* is consistent with the definition given in ASC 450-20-25-2, *Contingencies: Loss Contingencies*. *Probable* does not mean certainty or virtual certainty; it means only that the impairment is likely to occur.

GAAP does not provide any specific guidance on how to determine collectibility of loans. Normal loan review procedures utilized by the creditor may be used to determine the collectibility of loans. The following items may be considered in making such judgments:

☐ The materiality of the loan amount.

☐ Previous loss experience.

☐ Reports of total loan amounts by borrower.

☐ Regulatory reports.

☐ Internal reports (e.g., "watch list," past due reports, loans to insiders, and listing of overdrafts).

☐ Borrower experiencing financial problems (e.g., operating losses, insufficient working capital, or inadequate cash flows).

☐ Borrower in unstable industry or country.

☐ Loans secured by collateral that is not readily marketable or is subject to decline in value.

☐ Compliance exception reports.

☐ Loan files containing missing or inadequate current financial data on borrowers or guarantors.

A loan is *not* considered impaired if:

☐ There is an insignificant delay or shortfall in collecting payments.

☐ The creditor expects, despite a delay, to collect the full amount plus accrued interest.

Income Recognition

Interest income from an impaired loan may be recognized using several methods, such as the cash basis method, the cost recovery method, or some combination. GAAP does not specifically recommend or prescribe a method for measuring, recording, or disclosing interest income from impaired loans (ASC 310-10-35-40). Use of some accounting methods, or the creditor charging off some part of the loan, may lead to recording an investment in an impaired loan at less than the present value of expected future cash flows. Hence, no additional impairment would need to be recognized.

Disclosure Requirements

The following information should be disclosed either in the body of the financial statements or in the notes that accompany them:

☐ The total investment in impaired loans as of the balance sheet date, including (1) the amount of investments for which there is a related valuation allowance, and (2) the amount of investments for which there is no valuation allowance.

☐ The creditor's policy for recognizing interest revenue on impaired loans, including the recording of cash receipts.

☐ For each period that is presented, the average recorded investment in impaired loans, the related interest income recognized while the loans were impaired, and, if possible, the amount of interest income recognized using the cash basis while the loans were impaired.

According to ASC 310-10-35-13, *Receivables: Overall*, the total allowance for credit losses related to impaired loans should be disclosed, including the beginning and ending valuation allowance account balance, additions charged to operations, direct write-downs charged against the valuation allowance, and recoveries of amounts previously charged off, if any.

In Accounting Standards Update (ASU) No. 2010-20 (July 2010), *Receivables* (ASC 310, *Receivables*), *Disclosures about the Credit Quality of Financing Receivables and the Allowance for Credit Losses*, the following should be disclosed:

• Allowance for credit losses from the beginning to year-end;

• Major purchases and sales of financing receivables;

• Nonaccrual of financing receivables;

• Investment in financing receivables;

• Aging of receivables;

• Receivables that have been impaired;

• Financing receivables that have defaulted;

• Troubled debt restructurings and their impact on the allowance for credit losses; and

• Indicators of credit quality.

LENDING TO OR FINANCING THE ACTIVITIES OF OTHERS

ASC 310-10-35-47, *Receivables: Overall*, states that a company has a loan or trade receivable not held for sale when the expectation is to hold the loan or receivable for the foreseeable future or until the maturity date. These loans and receivables are to be reflected at the principal balance after adjustment for any charge-offs, bad debt provisions, deferred loan fees, and unamortized discounts or premiums for purchased loans.

A company must recognize credit losses attributable to off-balance-sheet exposures by debiting loss and crediting the associated liability.

A nonmortgaged loan held for sale should be presented at the lower of cost or fair value.

Footnote disclosure should be made of the company's accounting policies regarding its loans and trade receivables as well as its policies for credit losses and doubtful accounts, collateralized assets and their carrying values, accounting treatment for nonaccrual and past-due loans and trade receivables, foreclosed or repossessed assets, lease financings, classification policies, recognition method for interest income on loans and trade receivables, measurement and recognition for loan losses, and the gain or loss on the sale of loans and trade receivables.

INVENTORY

The accounting, reporting, and disclosures associated with inventory are provided by various authoritative pronouncements, including ASC 250-10-55-1, *Accounting Changes and Error Corrections: Overall*, and ASC 330-10-55-3, *Inventory: Overall*.

Inventories consist of merchandise to be sold for a retailer. Inventories for a manufacturing company include raw materials, work in process (partially completed goods), finished goods, operating supplies, and ordinary maintenance parts.

Inventories are presented under current assets. However, if inventory consists of slow-moving items or excessive amounts that will not be sold within the normal operating cycle of the business, such excess amounts should be classified as noncurrent assets.

Inventory includes direct and indirect costs associated with preparing inventory for sale or use. Therefore, the cost of inventory to a retail store includes the purchase price, taxes paid, delivery charges, storage, and insurance. A manufacturer includes in its cost of inventory the direct materials (including the purchase price and freight-in), direct labor, and factory overhead (including factory utilities, rent, and insurance).

Inventory should be valued at the lower of cost or market value. The value of inventory may decrease because of being out-of-date, deteriorated, or damaged or because of price-level changes. Specialized inventory methods also exist including retail, retail lower of cost or market, retail last-in, first-out (LIFO), and dollar value LIFO.

Footnote disclosure for inventory includes the valuation basis method, inventory categorization by major type, unusual losses, and inventory pledged or collateralized.

Purchases may be recorded gross or net of any cash discount, whether or not taken. If the discount is not taken, purchase discount lost is charged and is considered a financial expense.

ASC 845-10-05-8, *Nonmonetary Transactions: Overall*, addresses the situation in which one company both sells inventory to and buys inventory from another company in the same line of business. Such purchase and sale agreements may be under single or separate contracts.

Invoice issuance or the exchange of offsetting cash payments is not a consideration in deciding if two or more inventory transactions with the same counterparty should be considered as a single nonmonetary inventory transaction.

If an inventory transaction is legally contingent upon the performance of another inventory transaction with the same counterparty, the two are in contemplation of each other and should be combined.

An inventory transaction that does not legally depend on the performance of another inventory transaction is appraised based on the following factors to ascertain whether those transactions were made in contemplation of one another:

☐ The counterparties engaged in the inventory purchase and sale transactions at the same time.

☐ The contractual terms are at off-market rates at the inception of the agreements.

☐ The counterparties have a specific legal offset right applicable to the inventory purchase and sale transactions.

☐ There exists certainty of the occurrence of reciprocal inventory transactions.

As per ASC 845-10-05, *Nonmonetary Transactions: Overall*, nonmonetary exchange transactions of finished goods for work-in-process or raw materials in the same line of business are not exchange transactions that have commercial substance. However, a transaction is recognized at fair value if reasonable determination of fair value is possible and the transaction has commercial substance. All other nonmonetary exchanges of inventory in the same line of business (e.g., exchange of raw materials or work-in-process for raw materials, transfer of finished goods for finished goods) are accounted for at the carrying amount of the transferred inventory.

Purchase Contract Commitments

If a loss occurs on a purchase contract commitment, it should be recorded in the current year.

EXAMPLE

In 20X2, XYZ Company entered into a purchase contract to buy 10,000 units of product X at $2 per foot. At year-end, the price of the product declined to $1.50 per foot. The loss of $.50 per foot must be immediately recognized. The journal entry is:

Loss on purchase commitment–Unrealized	5,000	
Estimated liability resulting from purchase commitments loss		5,000
10,000 units × $.50 = $5,000		

Freight Terms

If items are bought on terms of free-on-board (FOB) shipping point, title passes to the buyer when the goods are shipped by the seller. If items are bought on terms of FOB destination, title passes to the purchaser when the merchandise is received by the buyer.

EXAMPLE

Akel Company's inventory at December 31, 20X2, was $2,000,000 based on a physical count priced at cost and before any adjustments due to the following:

☐ Merchandise costing $60,000 was shipped FOB shipping point from the vendor on December 30, 20X2, but was received on January 4, 20X3.

☐ Goods in the shipping area were excluded from inventory even though shipment was not made until January 6, 20X3. The merchandise was billed to the customer FOB shipping point on December 29, 20X2. It had a cost of $140,000.

The amount of inventory to be reported on the December 31, 20X2, balance sheet is $2,200,000 ($2,000,000 + $60,000 + $140,000).

Consigned Goods

Consigned goods are included in the consignor's inventory in the balance sheet. The consignee holds the inventory as an agent to sell it on behalf of the consignor. When the consigned goods are sold, the sale is credited by the consignor. The consignee records commission revenue.

EXAMPLE

The following items were included in Travis Company's inventory account at December 31, 20X2:

Goods held on consignment by Travis	$10,000
Goods bought, in transit, shipped FOB shipping point	24,000
Goods out on consignment at sales price, including 30% markup on selling price	30,000

Travis Company's inventory account at December 31, 20X2, should be reduced by $19,000, computed as follows:

Goods held on consignment belonging to consignor	$10,000
Goods out on consignment $30,000 × .30	9,000*
Total reduction	$19,000

* The goods out on consignment are appropriately considered the property of Travis. However, they must be included in ending inventory at cost. Therefore, inventory should be reduced by the 30% markup on selling price.

The goods in transit bought FOB shipping point are correctly included in inventory.

Financing Product Arrangements

ASC 470-40-05-2, *Debt: Product Financing Arrangements*, states that a financing arrangement may be entered into for the sale and repurchase of inventory. Such an arrangement is reported as a borrowing, not a sale. In many situations, the product is kept on the company's (sponsor's) premises. In addition, a sponsor may guarantee the debt of the other company.

Typically, most of the financed product is ultimately used or sold by the sponsor. However, in some instances, minimal amounts of the product may be sold by the financing entity to other parties.

The company that provides financing to the sponsor is typically a creditor, nonbusiness entity, or trust. In a few cases, the financing entity may have been set up solely to furnish financing to the sponsor.

The sponsor should footnote the terms of the product financing arrangement.

Examples of the different forms of financing arrangements follow:

☐ The sponsor has another entity purchase the good on its behalf and agrees to repurchase the product from the other entity, usually over a specified time period at predetermined prices. The repurchase price includes the original selling price plus carrying and financing costs.

☐ The sponsor sells the product to another business and agrees to reacquire the product or one identical to it.

☐ The sponsor controls the distribution of the product that has been purchased by another company.

☐ A financing entity procures the funds remitted to the sponsor by borrowing from a financial institution, using the newly bought merchandise as collateral.

Regardless of the arrangement, the company (sponsor) either commits to repurchase the product at established prices over a designed time period or commits to resale prices to third parties. Although a financing institution may sell small amounts of the product, ASC 470-40-15-2 requires that most of the product be used or sold by the sponsor.

When the sponsor sells the good to the other company and in a related transaction commits to rebuy it, the sponsor records a liability when the proceeds are received. A sale should not be recorded and the product should be retained as inventory on the sponsor's books. (A product financing arrangement, irrespective of its legal form, is a financing deal, not a sale or purchase by the sponsor.)

When another company purchases the merchandise for the sponsor, inventory is debited and a liability is credited at the date of acquisition. The sponsor accrues the carrying and financing costs.

EXAMPLE

On January 1, 20X3, a sponsor borrows $50,000 from another and gives the inventory as collateral for the loan. The entry is:

Cash	50,000	
Liability		50,000

On December 31, 20X3, the sponsor pays back the other company. The collateralized inventory is returned. The interest rate is 10% and storage charges total $600. The entry is:

Liability	50,000	
Interest expense	500	
Holding charges	600	
Cash		51,100

EXAMPLE

A sponsor sells goods costing $5,000 to a purchaser for $6,000 and commits to repurchase the same goods for $6,200 in 60 days. The sponsor's journal entries are:

Cash (or receivable)	6,000	
Liability		6,000
Inventory under PFA*	5,000	
Inventory		5,000

* PFA = product financing arrangement.

EXAMPLE

A sponsor arranged for the purchaser to buy goods costing $6,000 from a third party and commits to purchase that inventory from the purchaser for $6,200 in 60 days. The sponsor's journal entry is:

Inventory under PFA	6,000	
Liability		6,000

EXAMPLE

A sponsor sells goods costing $900 to a purchaser for $1,000 and commits to a resale price of $1,200 to outside parties. The sponsor's journal entries are:

Cash (or receivable)	1,000	
Liability		1,000
Inventory under PFA	900	
Inventory		900

EXAMPLE

A sponsor arranges for a purchaser to buy inventory from an outside party for $850 and guarantees the resale price to outside parties for $1,000. The sponsor's journal entry is:

Inventory under PFA	850	
Liability		850

Financing Product Arrangements—Other Considerations

Product financing arrangements require the sponsor to purchase the product at specified prices that are not subject to change, except for fluctuations due to finance and holding costs. The payments that the other company will receive are established by the financing arrangement. These costs (which will be paid by sponsor) are required to be adjusted to cover all fluctuations in costs incurred by the other entity in purchasing and holding the product. This includes interest costs as well.

The requirement that the sponsor purchase the inventory at predetermined prices may be met if any of the following circumstances exists:

☐ The specified prices in the financing arrangement are in the form of resale price guarantees, under which the sponsor agrees to make up any difference between the specified price and resale price for products sold to third parties.

☐ The sponsor is not required to purchase the product but has an option that compels it to do so (e.g., the sponsor is penalized if it does not exercise the option to purchase the product).

☐ The sponsor is not required to purchase the product, but the other entity has an option whereby it can require the sponsor to purchase the product.

Lower of Cost or Market Value

Inventory is valued at the lower of cost or market value applied on a total inventory basis, a category basis, or an individual basis. However, the individual basis is the most popular because it generates the most conservative valuation of inventory and is the only basis acceptable for tax purposes. Whichever approach is chosen, it must be applied consistently.

In general, market is defined as replacement cost. Replacement cost is the cost to "replace" the product at a given point in time; for example, the cost to buy or manufacture the product at fiscal year-end. However, in computing the lower-of-cost-or-market valuation, replacement cost is constrained by an "upper limit" and "lower limit" (see the steps below).

The lower-of-cost-or-market valuation is computed by applying the following steps:

1. Market is initially viewed as the replacement cost of the product. (See Exhibit 3–1.)

2. Market cannot exceed the upper limit of net realizable value (net realizable value equals selling price less costs to complete and dispose) shown in Exhibit 3–1. If it does, the upper limit is selected.

3. Market cannot be less than the lower limit of net realizable value less a normal profit margin. If it is, the lower limit is selected.

4. Replacement cost is selected as market when it lies between the upper and lower limits.

5. After the market value is selected, compare it to cost. The lower of the two constitutes the lower-of-cost-or-market valuation.

Exhibit 3–1: Diagram of Lower of Cost or Market Value

EXAMPLE

Company ABC uses the lower of cost or market value method on an item-by-item basis. The valuation of each product follows:

Product	Cost	Replacement Cost	Upper Limit	Lower Limit	Answer
M	$10	$14	$18	$12	$10
N	28	24	22	14	22
O	36	30	32	24	30
P	40	24	36	32	32
Q	12	10	24	14	12

With respect to Q, replacement cost is initially selected as the market value. However, since the replacement cost of $10 is below the lower limit, the lower limit of $14 is chosen as the market value. This value ($14) is then compared to cost and the lower of the two ($12) is selected as the final lower-of-cost-or-market valuation.

The write-down of inventory to market is charged to the cost of goods sold and credited to inventory. Alternatively, if it is desired to separately record the inventory holding loss, a loss account and inventory valuation account must be utilized. The loss account, known as "Loss to reduce inventory to lower of cost or market," is shown separately on the income statement, if material. An account, termed "Allowance to reduce inventory to market," is credited for the loss and is presented as a reduction to inventory (contra inventory account) on the balance sheet.

The lower-of-cost-or-market-value method is not used with LIFO because under LIFO current costs are matched against current revenue. Further, as a general rule, once a company uses LIFO for tax return preparation, it must use LIFO for book purposes (LIFO conformity rule).

Note: Inventories may be stated at market value when market value exceeds cost in exceptional cases, such as when:

☐ Immediate marketability exists at quoted prices and units are interchangeable (e.g., certain agricultural and mineral products, and precious metals).

☐ No basis exists for cost apportionment (e.g., meat packing industry), or there is some other inability to determine approximate costs.

In these cases, inventory is stated at market price less disposal costs. When inventory is valued above cost, revenue is recognized before sale. Appropriate disclosure should be made when inventory is carried above cost.

Retail Method

The *retail method* is followed by department stores and other large retail businesses that stock merchandise at retail selling price. The retail method may be used to estimate period-end inventory at cost by using a cost-to-retail (selling price) ratio. It may also be used for year-end financial statements when a physical count of inventory at retail is taken. In using the retail method, the ending inventory is determined at selling price and then converted to cost. Additionally, if a lower-of-cost-or-market valuation is needed, then net markups (markups less markup cancellations) would be added to the cost-to-retail ratio and net markdowns (markdowns less markdown cancellations) would be excluded. On the other hand, if a cost valuation is required both would be added to the cost-to-retail ratio. With the retail method, separate calculations may be made for departments within the business that experience substantially lower or higher profit margins. The retail method may be used based on FIFO, last-in, first-out (LIFO), or average cost methods.

Retail Lower-of-Average-Cost-or-Market-Value (Conventional Retail) Method

The *retail lower-of-cost-or-market-value method* is a variation of the retail method and is preferable to it because it results in a lower (conservative) inventory balance. In deriving the cost or retail ratio, markups are taken into account but not markdowns.

The following example shows the difference in calculation between the retail method and the retail lower of cost or market value method.

EXAMPLE

Retail Lower-of-Cost-or-Market-Value Method

		Cost	Retail	
Inventory—1/1		$32,000	$ 60,000	
Purchases		60,000	120,000	
Purchase returns		(10,000)	(20,000)	
Purchase discount		(4,000)		
Freight in		2,000		
Markups	$50,000			
Markup cancellations	(10,000)			
Net markups			40,000	
Total		$80,000	$200,000	40%
Markdowns		$44,000		
Markdown cancellations		(4,000)		
Net markdowns			40,000	
Cost of goods available		$80,000	$160,000	50%
Deduct:				
Sales		$80,000		
Less:				
Sales returns		(10,000)		
Net sales			70,000	
Inventory—retail			$90,000	
Retail method:				
At cost 50% × $90,000			$45,000	
Retail lower-of-cost-or-market-method:				
At cost 40% × $90,000			$ 36,000	

Retail LIFO

In determining ending inventory, the approach of the retail method is practiced. Markups and markdowns are both considered in computing the cost-to-retail ratio. However, this ratio excludes beginning inventory. A decline in inventory during the period is subtracted from the most recently added layers in the inverse order of addition. Inventory is restated based on a retail price index.

EXAMPLE

Retail price indices follow: 20X0, 100; 20X1, 104; and 20X2, 110.

20X1	Cost	Retail			
Inventory—Jan. 1 (base inventory)	$ 80,000	$130,000			
Purchases	$240,000	$410,000			
Markups		10,000			
Markdowns		(20,000)			
Total (excluding beginning inventory)	$240,000	$400,000	60%		
Total (including beginning inventory)	$320,000	$530,000			
Sales		389,600			
20X1 inventory—end at retail		$140,400			
Cost Basis					
20X1 inventory in terms of 20X0 prices					
$140,400 ÷ 1.04		$135,000			
20X0 base	$ 80,000	130,000	$130,000 × 1.04	$135,200	
20X1 layer in 20X0 prices		$ 5,000			
20X1 layer in 20X1 prices		$ 5,200	$ 5,000 × 1.04	5,200	
				$140,400	
20X1 LIFO cost 60% × $5200	3,120				
20X2	$ 83,120	$140,400			
Inventory—Jan. 1	$ 83,120	$140,400			
Purchases	$260,400	$430,000			
Markups		20,000			
Markdowns		(30,000)			
Total (excluding beginning inventory)	$260,400	$420,000	62%		

20X1	Cost	Retail		
Total (including beginning inventory)	$343,520	$560,400		
Sales		408,600		
20X2 inventory—end at retail		$151,800		
Cost Basis				
20X2 inventory in 20X0 prices $151,800 ÷ 1.10		$138,000		
20X0 base	$ 80,000	130,000	$130,000 × 1.10	$143,000
Excess over base year		$ 8,000		
20X1 layer in 20X2 prices 3,120		5,000	$ 5,000 × 1.10	5,500
20X2 layer in 20X0 prices		$ 3,000		
20X2 layer in 20X2 prices		3,300	$ 3,000 × 1.10	3,300
20X2 increase in 20X2 prices LIFO cost 62% × $3,300	2,046			
	$ 85,166	$ 151,800		$151,800

Dollar Value LIFO

Dollar value LIFO extends the historical cost principle. This method groups (pools) dollars rather than units. Any decrease in inventory is subtracted from the last year.

Dollar value LIFO has the following steps:

☐ Restate ending inventory in the current year into base dollars through use of a price index.

☐ Deduct the year-0 inventory in base dollars from the current year's inventory in base dollars.

☐ Multiply the incremental inventory in the current year in base dollars by the price index to derive the incremental inventory in current dollars.

☐ Derive the reportable inventory for the current year by adding to the year-0 inventory in base dollars the incremental inventory for the current year in current dollars.

EXAMPLE

At December 31, 20X2, Company ABC had a year-end inventory of $150,000, and the price index is 1.20. On January 1, 20X2, the base inventory was $110,000. The December 31, 20X2 inventory is calculated as follows:

12/31/20X2 inventory in base dollars ($150,000/1.2)	$125,000
1/1/20X2 beginning base inventory	110,000
20X2 increment in base dollars	$ 15,000
× Price index	× 1.2
Increment in current year dollars	$ 18,000
Inventory in base dollars	$110,000
Increment in current year dollars	18,000
Reportable inventory	$128,000

Base Stock Method

The base stock method presumes there will be a minimum base stock of inventory each year. Amounts over the base are costed under such inventory methods as FIFO, LIFO, average cost. A decrease in inventory is charged against earnings based on current cost. This method is not allowed on the tax return.

Costs Excluded from Inventory

Idle capacity costs, abnormal spoilage costs, double freight charges, and rehandling costs may require write-off immediately in the current year rather than allocation as a component of inventory valuation. Inventory cost does not include selling expenses. Selling expenses and interest incurred to finance inventory are period costs (charged directly against earnings as incurred). However, general and administrative expenses can be inventoried when they apply to manufacturing operations. It is a violation of GAAP to exclude all overhead from inventory costing. Thus, the direct costing method for inventory valuation is not accepted for financial reporting purposes.

ASC 330-10-30-7, *Inventory: Overall*, requires the immediate expensing of abnormal amounts of idle facility expense, freight, handling, and wasted material (spoilage). Further, allocation of fixed production overhead to the costs of conversion must be based on the normal capacity of the manufacturing facilities.

Standard Costing

Inventory may be valued based on standard cost as long as it is adjusted at the end of the accounting period to actual cost for financial reporting purposes. Proper disclosure is required. Insignificant variances between standard cost and actual cost are adjusted to cost of goods sold. Significant variances must be adjusted to a loss or gain account.

Relative Sales Value Method

Relative sales (or net realizable) values may be used as a basis to assign costs to inventory that is bought or produced in groups. This is because costs cannot be determined individually. The method is appropriate for allocating costs to joint products, real estate lots, and lump-sum purchases.

EXAMPLE

Joint products X and Y arise from the same manufacturing process up to the split-off point. The units produced for X and Y are 10,000 and 50,000, respectively. The selling prices per unit for X and Y are $3 and $1.20, respectively. The joint cost is $63,000. Allocated cost based on relative sales value follows:

Joint Product	Units Produced	Selling Price	Sales Value	Allocated Cost
X	10,000	$3.00	$30,000	$21,000
Y	50,000	1.20	60,000	42,000
Total				$63,000

EXAMPLE

XYZ Company bought inventory comprising four items of product for $115,000. At the time of purchase, the appraised values and relative percents were as follows:

		Percent
Product A	$ 11,000	.09
Product B	30,000	.25
Product C	50,000	.42
Product D	29,000	.24
Appraised value	$120,000	1.00

The costs of each type of product allocated based on relative appraisal value percentages were:

Product A .09 × $115,000	$ 10,350
Product B .25 × $115,000	28,750
Product C .42 × $115,000	48,300
Product D .24 × $115,000	27,600
Total cost allocation	$115,000

Stripping Costs

ASC 930-330-25, *Extractive Activities—Mining: Inventory*, states that stripping costs incurred by mining companies to find and remove overburden and waste materials are variable production costs and included in inventory.

Research and Development

According to ASC 730-10-25-2, *Research and Development: Overall*, supplies inventory used in R&D activities should be expensed unless there is an alternative future use or benefit. If the company uses its supplies or materials for R&D

efforts, such inventory is charged as an R&D expense. On the other hand, if R&D activities result in salable inventory, inventory is debited and R&D expense credited. An exception is where supplies used in research and development activities are acquired as part of a business combination or an asset acquisition. In that instance, supplies are to be measured at fair value and be subject to annual impairment reviews as discussed in Chapter 1, "Reporting, Presentation, and Disclosures for the Income Statement."

Terminated Contracts

If inventory was bought for a particular customer who has since canceled the order, or the contract has been terminated for some other reason, the inventory should be written down to recognize a loss in value, if any.

Discontinued Operations

Inventories used in discontinued operations of a business must be written down to net realizable value. The write-down is included as an element of the gain or loss on disposal of the discontinued activity.

Taxes

For tax return preparation purposes, the tax law requires manufacturers to defer the following costs related to inventory: warehousing costs, accounting and data service costs, and such personnel costs as recruiting and hiring. The tax law requires large retailers and wholesalers (having gross receipts of $10 million or more) to defer the following costs related to inventory: handling and unloading charges, incidental purchasing costs, assembling and processing costs, and storage costs.

Deferred taxes arising from temporary differences result when inventory is accounted for differently on the books and the tax return.

Disclosures

The following should be footnoted with regard to inventory:

- ☐ The cost basis to determine inventory valuation.
- ☐ Inventory method used.
- ☐ Nature of any accounting changes (e.g., change in method) and their effect upon earnings.
- ☐ Inventory classification and categorization.
- ☐ Unusual losses associated with inventory, such as in applying the lower-of-cost-or-market-value rule and losses on purchase commitments.
- ☐ Excessive exposure to risk (e.g., health hazards, safety concerns, limited supply availability, labor strife).

PREPAID EXPENSES

Prepaid expenses result from prepaying cash or incurring a liability. Prepaid expenses are presented under current assets even though they are not expected to be converted into cash, because the prepaid items would have required the use of current assets if they were not paid in advance. Prepaid expenses include insurance, rent, advertising, taxes, interest, and office supplies. However, prepayments that will not be charged to operations within one year or the normal operating cycle of the business, whichever is greater, are classified under deferred charges or other assets. Prepaid expenses expire and become expenses because of usage, events, or the passing of time. Prepaid expenses should be amortized on a ratable basis over their life.

LONG-TERM INVESTMENTS

Long-term investments include securities of other companies (e.g., stocks, bonds, long-term notes); amounts held within special funds, such as sinking funds, and the cash surrender value of life insurance that will not be cashed in within the next year; and investments in tangible plant assets not being currently used in the operations of the entity (e.g., land held for future value appreciation). Long-term investments are discussed in detail in Chapter 10.

FAIR VALUE OPTION FOR LONG-TERM NOTES RECEIVABLE

Under the fair value option (see the Fair Value Option for Financial Assets and Financial Liabilities section in Chapter 4 for more details on this topic), companies now have the option to record receivables as well as most other financial instruments in their accounts at the fair value. The FASB hoped that this option would increase the relevancy of the financial statements. If the fair value option is chosen for a given financial instrument, all unrealized holding gains and losses relating to that instrument must be recorded in net income until ownership of the instrument ceases. If a company chooses the fair value option for a financial instrument such as a long-term notes receivable, it is required to record any change in the fair value of the receivable each period as part of the entity's unrealized holding gains or losses. The latter is then reported as in the entity's net income. Each period, thereafter, the entity's notes receivable must be reevaluated for any change in fair value and that change must be recorded in net income.

FIXED ASSETS

GAAP for the accounting, reporting, and disclosures associated with fixed assets are included in the AICPA's Accounting Principles Board Opinion No. 6 (APB 6) dealing with depreciation; APB 12, paragraphs 4 and 5, *Disclosure of Depreciable Assets and Depreciation* (ASC 360-10-50); ARB 43, chapter 9A, *Depreciation and High Costs* (ASC 360-10-35-4).

When bought, a fixed asset is recorded at its fair value or the fair value of the consideration given, whichever is more clearly evident. The basis of accounting for a fixed asset is its cost, which includes expenditures necessary to put it into location or initially use it (e.g., delivery, installation, sales taxes, testing, breaking in, setup, assembling, trial runs, foundation). However, abnormal costs are not charged to the asset but rather expensed, such as for repairs of a fixed asset that was damaged during shipment because of mishandling.

If a fixed asset is to be disposed of, it should not be depreciated. Further, it should be recorded at the lower of its book value or net realizable value. Net realizable value equals fair value less costs to sell. Expected costs to sell beyond one year should be discounted. Idle or obsolete fixed assets should be written down and reclassified as other assets. The loss on the write-down is presented in the income statement.

Expenditures incurred that increase the capacity, life, or operating efficiency of a fixed asset are capitalized. However, insignificant expenditures are usually expensed as incurred.

Additions to an existing asset are deferred and depreciated over the shorter of the life of the addition or the life of the building. Rearrangement and reinstallation costs should be deferred if future benefit exists. Otherwise, they should be expensed. If fixed assets are obsolete, they should be written down to salvage value, recognizing a loss, and reclassified from property, plant, and equipment to other assets.

If two or more assets are purchased at a lump-sum price, cost is allocated to the assets based on their fair market values.

A liability secured by a fixed asset should not be offset.

A deposit on a fixed asset to be bought within one year is still presented as a long-term asset.

Self-Constructed Assets

Self-constructed assets are recorded at the *incremental or direct costs* to build (material, labor, and variable overhead) assuming idle capacity. Fixed overhead is excluded unless it increases because of the construction effort. However, self-constructed assets should not be recorded at an amount in excess of the outside cost.

EXAMPLE

Incremental costs to self-construct equipment are $80,000. The equipment could be bought from outside for $76,000. The journal entry is:

Equipment	76,000	
Loss	4,000	
Cash		80,000

EXAMPLE

Mavis Company uses its excess capacity to build its own machinery. The associated costs are direct material of $80,000, direct labor of $20,000, variable overhead of $10,000, and fixed overhead of $5,000. The cost of the self-constructed machine is $110,000. The fixed overhead is excluded because it is not affected by the construction effort.

Donation of Fixed Assets

As per ASC 958-605-15-4 and 25-2, a donated fixed asset should be recorded at its fair value by debiting fixed assets and crediting contribution revenue.

ASC 958 states that the company donating a nonmonetary asset recognizes an expense for the fair value of the donated asset. The difference between the book value and fair value of the donated asset represents a gain or loss.

EXAMPLE

Harris Company donates land costing $50,000 with a fair value of $70,000. The journal entry is:

Contribution expense	70,000	
Land		50,000
Gain on disposal of land		20,000

If a company pledges unconditionally to give an asset in the future, contribution expense and payable are accrued. This includes a conditional promise that has satisfied all conditions and, in effect, is now unconditional. However, if the pledge is conditional, an entry is not made until the asset is, in fact, transferred. If it is unclear whether the promise is conditional or unconditional, the former is presumed.

Writing Up Fixed Assets

It is prohibited to write up fixed assets except for a discovery on a natural resource, in a business combination accounted for under the purchase method, or in a quasi-reorganization. If a natural resource is discovered on land, such as oil or coal, the appraised value is charged to the land account and then depleted using the units of production method.

Land and Land Improvements

The cost of land includes closing costs (e.g., attorney fees, recording fees), costs to get land in condition for intended use (e.g., grading, draining, filling), assumption of any liens or encumbrances on the property, and costs to remove an old structure to build on the property. For example, if an old building is torn down to make way for the construction of a new building, the demolition costs are charged to land.

Land held for investment, speculation, or a future plant site should be classified under investments rather than fixed assets.

Land held for resale by a real estate company is considered inventory.

Land improvements such as fences, driveways, sidewalks, and parking lots are deferred and depreciated over their useful lives.

Repairs

Ordinary repairs such as a tune-up for a delivery truck are expensed, because they only benefit less than one year.

Extraordinary repairs are deferred to the fixed asset because they benefit more than one year. An example is a new motor for a salesperson's automobile. Extraordinary repairs either increase the asset's life or make the asset more useful. Capital expenditures enhance the quality or quantity of services to be obtained from the asset.

ASC 360-10-45, *Property, Plant, and Equipment: Overall,* prohibits using the accrue-in-advance method to account for planned major maintenance activities in annual reports.

Environmental

As per ASC 410-30-25-16, *Asset Retirement and Environmental Obligations: Environmental Obligations,* the costs to prevent, contain, or remove environmental contamination should be expensed. **Exception:** These costs can be deferred to the fixed asset in the following cases:

☐ The costs increase the asset's life or capacity or improve its efficiency or safety.

☐ The costs are incurred to prepare the property for sale.

According to ASC 410-30-45-6, *Asset Retirement and Environmental Obligations: Environmental Obligations,* the cost to treat property bought having an asbestos problem should be deferred to the asset. Disclosure should be made of the asbestos problem and related costs to correct.

Depreciation

If a fixed asset is bought during the year, there will be fractional year depreciation requiring proration.

EXAMPLE

On April 1, 20X2, a fixed asset costing $30,000 with a salvage value of $2,000 and a life of 10 years is bought.

Depreciation for 20X2 using the sum-of-the-years'-digits method is:

$$4/1/20X2–12/31/20X2 \quad {}^{10}/_{55} \times \$ 28,000 \times {}^{9}/_{12} = \$ 3,818$$

Depreciation for 20X3 using the sum-of-the-years'-digits method is:

1/1/20X3 – 3/31/20X3 10/55 × $28,000 × 3/12	$1,273
4/1/20X3 – 12/31/20X3 9/55 × $28,000 × 9/12	3,436
	$4,709

Depreciation expense for 20X3 under the double declining balance method is:

Year	Computation	Depreciation	Book Value
0			$30,000
4/1/20X2-12/31/20X2	9/12 × $30,000 × 20%	$4,500	25,500
20X3	$25,500 × 20%	5,100	20,400

It is also an acceptable GAAP to provide depreciation based on the *group and composite methods.* The group method is used for similar assets and the composite method is used for dissimilar assets, but both methods are usually accepted. One accumulated depreciation account applies for the whole group:

$$\text{Depreciation rate} = \text{Depreciation/Gross cost}$$

For the accounting period:

$$\text{Depreciation expense} = \text{Depreciation rate} \times \text{Gross cost}$$
$$\text{Depreciable life} = \text{Depreciable cost/Depreciation}$$

When one asset in the group is sold, the entry is:

Cash (proceeds received)

Accumulated depreciation (balancing figure)

Fixed asset (cost)

No gain or loss is recorded on the sale. The only occurrence in which a gain or loss would be recorded is when all of the assets are sold.

EXAMPLE

Computations under the composite depreciation method follow:

Asset	Cost–	Salvage =	Depreciable Cost/Life =		Depreciation
X	$ 50,000	$10,000	$ 40,000	10	$ 4,000
Y	80,000	4,000	76,000	5	15,200
Z	104,000	8,000	96,000	6	16,000
	$234,000	$22,000	$212,000		$35,200

Composite rate =   Depreciation/Cost = $35,200/$234,000 = 15%

Composite life =   Depreciable cost/Depreciation

          = $212,000/$35,200 = 6 years

The entry to record depreciation is:

Depreciation expense	35,200	
Accumulated depreciation		35,200

The journal entry to sell asset X for $43,000 is:

Cash	43,000	
Accumulated depreciation	7,000	
Fixed asset		50,000

Accounting for the Impairment of Long-Lived Assets and Related Considerations

Historically, FASB Statement No. 144 (FAS-144) (ASC 360-10-05-4) was issued primarily because its predecessor statement, FASB Statement No. 121 (FAS-121),

Accounting for the Impairment of Long-Lived Assets and for Long-Lived Assets to Be Disposed Of, did not address the accounting and reporting for a segment of a business classified as a discontinued operation in APB Opinion No. 30, *Reporting the Results of Operations—Reporting the Effects of Disposal of a Segment of a Business, and Extraordinary, Unusual and Infrequently Occurring Events and Transactions* (ASC 220-20-45-10). Before FAS-144 (ASC 360-10-05-4), then, two accounting standards existed for the disposal of long-lived assets. In issuing FAS-144 (ASC 360-10-05-4), the FASB decided to unify the accounting and disclosure parameters into a single model predicated on the conceptual guidance for assets to be disposed of enumerated in FAS-121. In addition, FAS-144 (ASC 360-10-05-4) broadened the presentation of discontinued operations to include more disposal transactions and terminated the practice of recognizing future operating losses before they occur when measuring discontinued operations. By virtue of these and other changes, similar events relating to the disposal of long-lived assets are now accounted for in the same manner. Clearly, this represents an improvement in financial reporting. This section discusses the accounting, reporting, and disclosure requirements for impaired long-term assets to be held and used, and for long-lived assets to be disposed of as required by FAS-144 (ASC 360-10-05-4).

FAS-144 (ASC 360-10-05-4) continues FAS-121 requirements regarding recognition and measurement of impaired long-term assets. It is applicable to a company's long-term assets to be retained or to be disposed of, which include noncurrent prepaid assets, lessor long-term assets leased under operating leases, lessee capital leases, and deferred exploration costs under the successful efforts method. When a long-term asset is an element of a group of other assets and debt not covered by this Statement, the Statement is applicable to the group. In this case, the group is the accounting unit for the long-term asset. With regard to long-term assets to be kept and utilized, this *asset group* constitutes the minimum level for which identifiable cash flows are principally independent of the cash flows of other asset and liability groups. With regard to long-term assets to be disposed of, this *disposal group* refers to the net assets (assets less liabilities) to be disposed of in one transaction. An example of a liability associated with a disposed asset is a pollution-related obligation of a disposed plant.

ASC 360-10-05-4 does not relate to the following:

- ☐ Unproved natural resources accounted for under the successful efforts method.
- ☐ Financial instruments.
- ☐ A financial institution's long-lived customer connections, such as servicing assets.
- ☐ Deferred tax charges.
- ☐ Goodwill.
- ☐ Capitalized acquisition costs of policies.
- ☐ Unamortized intangible assets.

In addition, ASC 360-10-05-4 does not alter the accounting for individual assets not included in asset groups falling under this Statement, such as inventory, accounts receivable, accounts payable, and noncurrent debt.

Long-Term Assets to Be Retained and Used

ASC 360-10-05-4 provides GAAP for long-lived assets to be held and used with regard to recognizing and measuring impairment loss, recoverability tests including predicting future cash flows, asset grouping, and formulating the new cost basis. Fair value determination and reporting and disclosure requirements are also discussed.

Recognizing and measuring the impairment loss. An impairment is recognized when the book (carrying) value of a long-term asset group is greater than its fair value. The impairment loss is recorded only when the carrying value of the asset group is not recoverable. To ascertain recoverability, a threshold test, commonly referred to as the recoverability test, must first be failed before an impairment loss may be recognized. The recoverability test is failed (indicating a lack of recoverability) when the book value of the asset group is more than the total undiscounted (gross) cash flows expected to arise from the use and ultimate disposition of the asset group. If the recoverability test is failed, an impairment loss is recognized. The impairment loss is equal to the carrying value of the asset group less its fair value. This evaluation of carrying value should be made on the date of the recoverability test (which could be made on a date other than the end of a reporting period).

EXAMPLE

The following information is provided for an asset group:

Carrying value	$100,000,000
Fair value	80,000,000
Sum of the undiscounted cash flows	95,000,000

Because the carrying value is greater than the sum of the undiscounted cash flows, a nonrecoverability situation is evident. (The recoverability test is failed.) The impairment loss to be recognized equals $20,000,000 ($100,000,000–$80,000,000). **Note:** The impairment loss is *not* $5,000,000 ($100,000,000–$95,000,000) or $15,000,000 ($95,000,000–$80,000,000).

EXAMPLE

The following data is provided for another asset group:

Carrying value	$100,000,000
Fair value	106,000,000
Sum of the undiscounted cash flows	93,000,000

Because the carrying value is greater than the sum of the undiscounted cash flows, a nonrecoverability situation exists. However, an impairment loss is *not* recognized because the carrying value if the asset group is not greater than its fair value.

EXAMPLE

Carrying value	$100,000,000
Fair value	92,000,000
Sum of the undiscounted cash flows	104,000,000

Because carrying value does not exceed the sum of the undiscounted cash flows, a recoverability situation exists (the recoverability test is passed). As such, no impairment loss is recognized.

Recoverability test. A recoverability test must be made when it is deemed that the carrying value of the asset group may lack recoverability. The following may be indicative of such a situation:

☐ An operating or cash flow loss for the reporting period occurs, coupled with either a past history of such losses or anticipated future losses for the asset group.

☐ There is a material negative development in how the asset group is being utilized.

☐ A major impairment occurs in the physical condition of the asset group.

☐ A probability of more than 50% exists that the asset group will be sold or disposed of much earlier than its expected useful life.

☐ The market value of the asset group drastically declines.

☐ The total costs incurred for the asset group (e.g., actual construction costs) far exceed the expected costs.

☐ A major business-related government or legal development could have a significant adverse effect on the value of the asset group. An example is new government regulations restricting the business use of the long-lived assets.

In performing a recoverability test, the CPA may need to appraise the existing depreciation method and estimates for property and plant and equipment as well as the amortization periods for intangibles.

A change in useful life arising from such evaluation should be taken into account in formulating the estimates of future cash flows used to test the asset group for recoverability. **Caution:** A change in the accounting method for an asset arising from this review can occur only after this test has been applied.

Asset grouping. To determine and record an impairment loss, the asset group should be based on the minimum level that identifiable cash flows are predominantly independent of the cash flows of other assets and liabilities. In a few situations, a long-lived asset may not have identifiable cash flows predominantly independent of the cash flows of other assets and liabilities and other asset groups. An example is the central administrative office of the business entity. In such a case, the long-term asset group should encompass all of the company's assets and liabilities.

Goodwill may be considered for impairment in the asset group only if the group is or includes a reporting unit. Thus, goodwill must be tested for impairment at the reporting unit level, and only after the other assets of the reporting unit have been tested for impairment based on other authoritative pronouncements. ASC 350-20-35, *Intangibles—Goodwill and Other: Goodwill*, requires that goodwill be tested for impairment at the reporting unit level, which is one level below an operating segment. It is prohibited that goodwill be part of a lower-level asset group that incorporates only a segment of a reporting unit. However, future cash flow projections used to test the recoverability of the lower-level asset group cannot be modified for the impact of the goodwill omission from the group.

With the exception of goodwill, the carrying values of net assets in the group not falling under the dictates of ASC 360-10-05-4 must be adjusted per relevant GAAP before testing for the recoverability of the asset group.

The impairment loss for the asset group should be proportionately allocated to the specific assets of the group, based on relative carrying values. However, a particular asset in the group cannot be reduced for an amount that will bring it below its fair value, provided such value is ascertainable without unreasonable effort and cost.

EXAMPLE

Travis Manufacturing Company is testing its plant with other assets for recoverability purposes as an asset group. This group includes long-lived assets W, X, Y, Z, inventory (at lower of cost or market value), and other current assets and liabilities not falling under ASC 360. The total carrying value of the asset group of $6,000,000 is not recoverable. The fair value of the asset group is $5,200,000. The impairment loss of $800,000 ($6,000,000 – $5,200,000) is allocated to the long-term assets of the group as follows:

Asset Group (Dollars in Thousands)	Carrying Value	Proportionate Allocation Percentage	Allocated Impairment Loss	Adjusted Carrying Value
Current assets	$1,700			$1,700
Liabilities	(400)			(400)
Long-lived assets:				
Asset W	1,400	30%	$(240)	1,160
Asset X	1,500	32%	(256)	1,244
Asset Y	1,200	25%	(200)	1,000
Asset Z	600	13%	(104)	496
Total long-lived assets	4,700	100%	(800)	3,900
Total	$6,000	100%	$(800)	$5,200

EXAMPLE

In the event that the fair value of a specific long-lived asset of the asset group is ascertainable without undue effort and cost, and the fair value is more than the adjusted carrying value of that particular asset after an impairment loss is initially allocated, the excess impairment loss initially allocated to that asset would be reallocated to the other long-lived assets of the group. Assume the fair value of asset Y is $1,030,000. The excess impairment loss of $30,000 ($1,030,000–$1,000,000) initially allocated to that asset (based on the adjusted carrying value of $1,000,000) is reallocated to the other long-lived assets of the group proportionately based on the adjusted carrying amounts of those assets as follows:

Long-lived Assets (Dollars in Thousands)	Adjusted Carrying Value	Reallocation Proportionate Percentage	Reallocation of Excess Impairment Loss	Adjusted Carrying Value After Reallocation
Asset W	$1,160	40%	$(12)	$1,148
Asset X	1,244	43%	(13)	1,231
Asset Z	496	17%	(5)	491
Subtotal	2,900	100%	(30)	2,870
Asset Y	1,000		30	1,030
Total	$3,900		$ 0	$3,900

Formulating the new cost basis. After the impairment loss is recorded, the adjusted carrying value becomes the new cost basis of the long-term asset. A later recovery in market value of the impaired asset cannot be recorded, because the cost of the asset will be recovered through its use and cannot be written up above its new cost basis. A written-down fixed (intangible) asset should be depreciated (amortized) based on its new cost basis over the period of benefit.

Projecting future cash flows to test the recoverability of a long-lived asset. The estimation of future cash flows for testing the recoverability of the asset group represents the net cash flows directly related to, and resulting from, the utilization and ultimate disposition of the asset group. Interest expense is excluded from this calculation. In cash flow estimation, the company should take into account its reasonable assumptions and evidence about how the asset group will be used. If alternative steps to recover the carrying value of an asset group are being thought of, or there is a range of projected cash flows tied to a likely considered action, the business must take into account the probability of possible outcomes. In this regard, a probability-weighted method should be used in assessing the likelihood of potential results. This approach is explained in the following example. A range of possible projected cash flows take into account future sales price, quantity sold, volume produced, and production costs.

Varying scenarios are considered. Management assessments should take into account the probabilities of the best, worst, and most likely courses of action.

EXAMPLE

At December 31, 20X1, a production plant having a carrying value of $100,000,000 is being evaluated for recoverability. The two alternative action strategies for recovering the carrying value of the plant are to sell in either three years or at the end of its remaining useful life of 12 years. Cash flows applicable to the production plant are clearly identifiable from cash flows of other assets. The following information shows the range and probability of possible estimated cash flows expected to result from the use and eventual disposition of the facility:

Course of Action: Sell in 3 Years (in Millions)

Projected Cash Flow (Use)	Projected Cash Flow (Disposition)	Estimated Cash Flow	Probability	Probability-Weighted Cash Flows
$15	$65	$80	25%	$20
20	65	85	60%	51
25	65	90	15%	13.5
Total				$84.5

Course of Action: Sell in 12 Years (in Millions)

Projected Cash Flow (Use)	Projected Cash Flow (Disposition)	Estimated Cash Flow	Probability	Probability-Weighted Cash Flows
$70	$2	$72	25%	$18
100	2	102	60%	61.2
120	2	122	15%	18.3
Total				$97.5

In deriving the future cash flows used to test the plant for recoverability, it is decided that there is a 70% likelihood that the plant will be sold after 3 years but a 30% probability that it will be used for its remaining estimated life of 12 years. The probability computation to derive the final estimated future cash flows considering the weighted-average probabilities of the alternative scenarios follows:

(Cash flows in Millions)

Course of Action	Probability-Weighted Cash Flows	Probability Assessment	Expected Cash Flows
Sell in 3 Years	$84.5	70%	$59.2
Sell in 12 Years	97.5	30%	29.3
			88.5

The undiscounted future cash flows using probability analysis of the alternative scenarios is $88,500,000. Hence, the plant's carrying amount of $100,000,000 is not recoverable. **Note:** The alternatives of selling or using an asset are not necessarily independent of each other. Consequently, a business might opt for the action resulting in a much higher future cash flow. If such is the case, management typically will use the probable future cash flows applicable just to that particular scenario. In the preceding example, that option would be to sell in 12 years because its probability-weighted cash flows of $97,500,000 is higher than the other option of selling in 3 years of $84,500,000.

The company must make cash flow projections to test recoverability of a long-term asset for its remaining useful life. The remaining useful life of an asset group is based on that of the *primary asset* in the group. The primary asset is defined as the major long-term depreciable tangible asset or the intangible asset being amortized that is the most important component asset in the asset group in terms of cash flow generation. (Thus, the primary asset cannot be land or an intangible asset not subject to amortization.) To determine which is the primary asset, consideration should be given to the following:

☐ The remaining useful life of the asset compared to other group assets.

☐ The replacement cost of the asset.

☐ The likelihood that other assets would have been bought without the primary asset.

If the primary asset does not have the longest remaining life of the group assets, future cash flow projections for the group are based on the assumed sale of the group at the end of the remaining useful life of the primary asset.

Projected cash flows applied to the recoverability test for long-term assets in use (including significantly constructed or developed assets) should be based on the current service potential of the asset on the test date. Service potential considers, in addition to remaining useful life, cash-flow-generating capacity and, if applicable, output potential. The estimates include cash flows related to future costs required to upkeep the existing service potential of the long-term asset, including any component parts. Excluded from the estimates of cash flows are future capital expenditures to increase service potential.

Future cash flow estimates for recoverability testing of long-lived assets being developed should depend on the anticipated service potential when development is significantly finished. Deferred interest costs for self-construction should be included. The capitalization period should end when the asset is substantially finished and available for use.

Determining fair value. The fair value of an asset (liability) is the purchase (settlement) price in an arm's-length transaction currently made. If an active market price does not exist, other reasonable valuation approaches may be used, such as the prices of similar assets. A present value approach is often suitable in fair value estimation. Two present value approaches are used to derive the fair value of an asset (liability). In the first method, expected present value is derived based on multiple cash flow scenarios applying to a range of potential outcomes and a risk-free interest rate. In the second approach, one set of estimated cash flows and one interest rate based on the risk level are used in fair value determination. **Note:** The first technique is preferred when timing and amount uncertainties exist.

If individuals in the market make certain assumptions regarding fair value estimation, that should be incorporated. If not, the company should use its own assumptions. For a more detailed discussion on determining fair value measurement, see "Fair Value Measurements" in Chapter 4.

Reporting and disclosure—impairment of long-lived assets. The impairment loss on a long-term asset held and used is a component of income from continuing operations before income taxes in the income statement. The following should be footnoted for an impairment loss:

☐ A description of the impaired asset along with impairment circumstances.

☐ The technique used to compute fair value.

☐ If not shown by itself in the income statement, the amount of the impairment loss and where such loss is included in the income statement.

☐ The business segment associated with the impaired asset.

Long-Lived Assets to Be Disposed of Other Than by Sale

A long-lived asset to be disposed of other than by sale may occur*:

☐ As a result of abandonment;

☐ In exchange for a similar productive long-lived asset; or

☐ In a distribution to owners in the form of a spin-off.

Such assets should be classified as held and used until they are actually disposed of. A brief discussion of each of these scenarios follows.

An asset to be abandoned is considered disposed of when it ceases to be used. When a long-lived asset ceases to be used, the carrying value of the asset should equal its salvage value (if any). Only in unusual circumstances would the fair value of a long-lived asset to be abandoned be zero while it is being used. If a determination is made by an entity to abandon a long-lived asset before the end of its useful life, the entity must revise the asset's depreciation estimates to reflect its shortened useful life. In general, a long-lived asset that has been temporarily idled should not be accounted for as if abandoned. A disposal may also occur as a result of exchanging a long-lived asset for a similar productive long-lived asset or through a distribution to owners in a spin-off. While classified as held and used, if the asset (or group) is tested for recoverability, the estimates to be used should be based on the use of the asset for its remaining life, assuming that the disposal transaction will not occur. At time of disposal, if the carrying value of the asset (or group) exceeds its fair value, an impairment loss should be recognized in addition to any impairment losses required to be recognized while the asset is being held and used.

---

* For a discussion of the accounting and required disclosures of long-lived assets or disposal groups that have been sold or are classified for sale, see Chapter 1.

Capitalized Interest

In almost all cases, interest on borrowed funds is expensed. However, there is one exception in that interest on borrowings is deferred to the asset account and amortized when the following exist:

☐ Self-made assets for the company's own use.

☐ Assets for sale or lease built as discrete, individual projects. An example is real-estate development. **Note:** If land is being prepared for a specific use in the company, the cost of buying the land meets the test for capitalized interest.

☐ Assets bought for the entity's own use by agreements requiring a down payment or process payments.

☐ Assets received from a gift or grant in which donor restrictions exist.

Interest is *not* capitalized for:

☐ Assets in use or ready for use.

☐ Assets manufactured in large quantity or on a continual basis.

☐ Assets not in use and not being prepared for use.

Interest capitalization is based on the average accumulated expenditures for that asset. The interest rate used is generally based on the:

☐ Interest rate on the specific borrowing.

☐ Weighted-average interest rate for corporate debt.

Interest capitalization begins when the following commences:

☐ Interest is being incurred.

☐ Expenditures are being incurred.

☐ The asset is being made ready for use in terms of construction or when administrative and technical activities before construction are taking place. Consideration should also be given to costs related to labor problems and litigation.

The capitalization period ends when the asset is substantially finished and ready for use. When an asset has individual components, such as cooperative units, the capitalization period of interest costs related to one of the separate units ends when the particular unit is significantly complete and usable. Interest capitalization does not continue when construction ends, except for temporary and unexpected delays.

When the total asset must be completed to be useful, interest capitalization continues until the total asset is substantially complete. An example is a production facility where sequential manufacturing activities must occur.

Foreign currency losses on gains associated with debt funds denominated in a foreign currency may *not* be capitalized.

ASC 835-20-30, *Interest: Capitalization of Interest*, requires disclosure of both the interest capitalized and expensed. The following are tips in solving interest capitalization problems under ASC 835-20-30; they are fully demonstrated in a comprehensive problem following the enumeration:

☐ The amount of interest that is required to be capitalized under ASC 835-20-30 is the amount of interest that could have been avoided if the qualifying assets on which the interest is based had not been constructed. This amount of interest is sometimes referred to as avoidable interest. However, the amount of interest that is actually capitalized may never exceed the actual interest cost incurred by the entity for the period.

☐ To calculate the amount of interest cost that should be capitalized for a given accounting period, the average accumulated expenditures (AAE) for the period must be computed. These expenditures are weighed based on the time that they were incurred.

☐ In computing the amount of interest that should be capitalized, the following interest rates should be utilized in weighing the AAE:

— For the portion of the AAE represented by the specific borrowings incurred to acquire qualifying assets, the interest rates on those borrowings should be used to determine the amount of interest to be capitalized.

— For the remaining portion of the AAE of the period (excess of AAE over the amount of specific borrowings), computation should be based on the average interest rate incurred on other borrowings of the entity that are outstanding during the period.

The average rate incurred on the other borrowings of the period are weighed based on the magnitude of the specific debt outstanding and their respective interest rates.

EXAMPLE

Assume X Company begins construction on a new building on January 1, 20X2. In addition, X obtained a $100,000 loan to finance the construction of the building on January 1, 20X2 at an annual interest rate of 10%. The company's other outstanding debt during 20X2 consists of two notes of $600,000 and $800,000 with interest rates of 11% and 14.5%, respectively. Expenditures that were made on the building project follow:

Expenditures	
January 1	$200,000
April 1	300,000
July 1	400,000
December 1	120,000

Step 1

The AAE is computed:

$ 200,000 × 12/12 (January–December)	= $200,000
300,000 × 9/12 (April–December)	= 225,000
400,000 × 6/12 (July–December)	= 200,000
120,000 × 1/12 (December)	= 10,000
$1,020,000	AAE = $635,000

Step 2

The average interest rate is computed based on the other outstanding debt of the entity other than specific borrowings:

$ 600,000 × 11%	=	$ 66,000
800,000 × 14.5%	=	116,000
$1,400,000		$182,000

Average interest rate: = $182,000/$1,400,000

= 13%

Step 3

The interest that could be avoided is computed based on the AAE:

AAE	Interest That Should Be Capitalized (Based on AAE)
$100,000 (specific borrowing) × 10% =	$10,000
535,000 ($635,000 − 100,000) × 13% =	69,550
$635,000	$79,550

Step 4

Actual interest costs incurred during the year are computed:

$100,000 × 10% =	$ 10,000
600,000 × 11% =	66,000
800,000 × 14.5% =	116,000
Total	$192,000

Because the interest that could have been avoided if the building was not constructed (based on the AAE) is less than X's actual interest cost, the actual interest cost should be capitalized. Otherwise, the avoidable interest would be capitalized.

The journal entry is as follows:

Building ($200,000 + 300,000 + 400,000 + 120,000) + (79,550)	1,099,550	
Interest Expense	100,450	
Cash		1,200,000

ASC 835-20-15-5, *Interest: Capitalization of Interest*, provides that an investor's qualifying assets, for purposes of capitalizing interest, include equity funds, loans, and advances to investees accounted for by the equity method. Therefore, an investor has to capitalize interest costs on such qualifying assets if, during that period, the investee undergoes activities needed to begin its planned major operations and such activities include the use of funds to purchase qualifying assets for its operations. The investor does not capitalize any interest costs on or subsequent to the date the investor actually starts the planned major operations.

This Statement uses the term *investor* to mean both the parent and consolidated subsidiaries. Hence, all qualifying assets of a parent company and its consolidated subsidiaries are subject to the interest capitalization rule. However, there is no impact on the accounting or reporting of capitalized interest cost in an investee's separate financial statements.

Nonmonetary Transactions

Nonmonetary transactions involve the exchange of nonmonetary assets, such as inventories, plant and equipment, or property. In general, in a nonmonetary exchange, the asset received is recorded at the amount given up for it. Typically, this would include the fair value of the asset given up. In addition, an amount of cash, called boot, may also be included to equalize the fair value of the exchange. If cash is paid, the amount of fair value given up is increased. If cash is received, the amount of fair value given up is reduced. In addition, a gain or loss may be recognized on the transfer or disposal. It is the difference between the fair value and book value of the asset given up.

Nonmonetary transactions may or may not have commercial substance (see expanded discussion below). If a loss is computed, regardless of whether the transaction has commercial substance, it should always be recognized. If a gain is computed and the transaction has commercial substance, the gain is fully recognized. However, if the transaction lacks commercial substance, a gain may or may not be recognized based on the circumstances. In general, if the transaction lacks commercial substance and the amount of cash given or received is greater than or equal to 25% of the total fair value of the exchange, ASC 845-10-25-6 requires that the whole transaction should be considered monetized. That is, both parties to the transaction must recognize the full fair value of the assets exchanged and recognize all gains fully. On the other hand, if the amount of cash received is less than 25% of the total fair value received, a pro rata gain should be recognized based on the ratio of cash received to the total fair value received. However, if the amount paid is less than 25% of the total amount given up, then no gain is recognized. If no cash is involved, no gain is recognized.

ASC 845-10-50-1 requires note disclosure for a period in which an entity engages in one or more nonmonetary exchanges consisting of a description of: the nature of the transaction(s), the method to account for transferred assets, and the gain or loss on the exchanges. ASC 845-10-05-6 addresses nonmonetary transactions and covers the accounting for exchanges or distributions of fixed assets.

When Does a Transaction Have Commercial Substance?

Commercial substance occurs when future cash flows change as a result of an exchange of nonmonetary assets resulting in the modification of the economic positions of the two parties involved.

EXAMPLE

X Company exchanges machinery for Y Company's land. It is probable that the timing and dollar amount of cash flows from the land received will be materially different from the equipment's cash flows. Hence, both companies now have different economic positions indicating an exchange with commercial substance.

Even in the case of a similar exchange of assets (machine for a machine), there may arise a change in economic position. Assuming that the life of the machine received is much longer than that of the machine given up, the cash flows for the machines can be materially different. Consequently, there is commercial substance to the transaction and a gain or loss on the transaction is recorded. On the other hand, if the difference in cash flows is *not* significant, then the company is in the same economic position as before. In this case, the transaction does not have commercial substance and a loss is recognized immediately. However, as noted above, a gain is recognized in certain circumstances. This will be discussed further in the illustrations that follow.

Business entities must appraise the cash flow features of the assets exchanged to ascertain whether there is commercial substance to the transaction. In determining whether future cash flows change, it is required to either (1) analyze whether cash flows are affected from the exchange versus without it, or (2) determine whether the timing, amount, and risk of cash flows resulting from the asset received is different from the cash flows applicable with the asset given up. Another consideration is whether the entry-specific value of the asset received differs from that transferred, and whether the difference is significant, relative to the fair values of the assets exchanged.

Commercial Substance Exists

The cost of a nonmonetary asset received in exchange for another nonmonetary asset is typically recorded at the fair value of the asset given up plus cash paid or less cash received. In addition, any computed gain or loss on the disposal of the asset is always recognized. The fair value of the asset acquired should be used only if it is more clearly evident than the fair value of the asset given up.

EXAMPLE

XYZ Company exchanged autos plus cash for land. The autos have a fair value of $100,000. They cost $130,000 with accumulated depreciation of $50,000 so the book value is $80,000. Cash paid is $35,000. The cost of the land to XYZ equals:

Fair value of autos exchanged	$100,000
Cash paid	35,000
Cost of land	$135,000

The journal entry for the exchange transaction is:

Land	135,000	
Accumulated depreciation—autos	50,000	
Autos		130,000
Cash		35,000
Gain on disposal of autos		20,000

The gain equals the fair value of the autos less their book value as computed below:

Fair value of autos—given up		$100,000
Book value		
Cost of autos	$130,000	
Less: accumulated depreciation	50,000	80,000
Gain		$ 20,000

However, if the autos had a fair value of $78,000 rather than $100,000, there would be a loss recognized of $2,000 ($80,000 less $78,000). In either situation, the company is in a different economic position and thus the transaction has commercial substance. Hence, as noted, the gain or loss is recognized.

EXAMPLE

ABC Company exchanges its old equipment for new. The used equipment has a book value of $40,000 (cost $60,000 less accumulated depreciation of $20,000) with a fair value of $30,000. The list price of the new equipment is $80,000. The trade-in allowance is $45,000. Assuming that commercial substance exists, cash to be paid equals:

List price of new equipment	$80,000
Less: trade-in allowance	45,000
Cash to be paid	$35,000

The cost of the new equipment equals:

Fair value of old equipment—given up	$30,000
Cash due	35,000
Cost of new equipment	$65,000

The journal entry to record this exchange transaction is:

Equipment	65,000	
Accumulated depreciation	20,000	
Loss on disposal of equipment	10,000	
Equipment—old		60,000
Cash		35,000

The loss is computed as follows:

Fair value of old equipment	$30,000
Book value of old equipment	40,000
Loss	$10,000

Because assets should not be valued in excess of their cash equivalent price, the loss is recognized immediately instead of being added to the cost of the newly acquired asset.

Commercial Substance Does Not Exist

Exchanges *lacking* commercial substance may exist, as in the real estate industry. In real estate, for example, there may be a "swap" of real estate properties.

When a transaction lacks commercial substance, and a loss occurs, it is fully recognized. However, ASC-10-25-6 indicates a gain should be recognized in only certain situations. First, if cash is received or paid, the transaction should be tested for the 25% rule. That is, as was previously discussed, if the amount of cash is significant, that is, 25% or more of the total fair value of the exchange, then the entire transaction is considered to be monetized and is recorded at fair value (cash equivalent value). Thus, a computed gain would be fully recognized. Second, if the cash is less than 25%, then pro rater recognition of the gain (ASC 845-30-6) would be applied by the receiver of the cash (boot) only and the payer would not recognize any gain at all.

EXAMPLE

A Company and B Company both have undeveloped land for which the cash flows from the land properties to be exchanged are not materially different. Because of this, commercial substance does not exist. Both companies are in the same economic position after the swap as before. **Caution:** The asset given up may be impaired. In consequence, if the book value is more than fair value, an impairment should be recorded first provided the impairment test is satisfied.

SOLUTION

Avis Car Rental has mostly Chrysler automobiles. Avis contracts with Hertz Car Rental to exchange a group of Chrysler cars that are basically similar to Hertz's General Motors models. The Chrysler autos to be exchanged have a fair value of $320,000 and a book value of $270,000 (cost $300,000 less accumulated depreciation of $30,000). The General Motors cars have a fair value of $340,000. Avis pays $20,000 cash besides the Chrysler models exchanged. Avis has a total gain of $50,000 and pays cash of $20,000. Since $20,000/($20,000 + $320,000) is less than 25% (of the total fair value amount paid), the gain is completely deferred. The calculations are shown below:

If the cash paid was 25% or more of the total, the entire gain would have been recognized. If cash was received and it represented 25% or more of the total amount received, the entire gain would also be recognized. If, on the other hand, the cash amount received was less than 25% of the total, a pro rata amount of the gain would have been recognized.

Fair value of Chrysler autos exchanged	$320,000
Book value of Chrysler autos exchanged	270,000
Total unrecognized gain	$ 50,000

In this situation, Avis still has an auto fleet essentially generating the same cash flows as the autos given up even though they are different models. Thus, the transaction does *not* have commercial substance. As indicated above, the total gain is deferred, and the basis for the GM cars is decreased. The computation of the basis of the GM automobiles follows:

Book value of Chrysler cars	$270,000
Cash paid	20,000
Basis of GM cars	290,000

An alternative calculation is:

Fair value of GM cars	$340,000
Less: unrecognized gain	50,000
Basis of GM cars	$290,000

Avis prepares the following journal entry to record this transaction:

Autos (GM)	290,000	
Accumulated depreciation	30,000	
Autos (Chrysler)		300,000
Cash		20,000

The gain that lowered the basis of the new autos will be recorded when those cars are sold to an external party. The reduced basis means higher net income because of lower depreciation expense in later years while the autos are held.

Note: If fair values for either the asset received or the asset given up are *not* reliably measureable, the book value of the asset received is recorded at the cost of the asset given up (plus cash paid). Another exception to the fair value rule is for an exchange that facilitates customer sales. An example is when a business exchanges its inventory for that of another business because its inventory has the same features as the other business (e.g., size, color), which makes the inventory items easier to sell to an outside customer. In this situation, the earnings process for the inventory is not deemed complete, and there will be *no* recognition of gain.

EXAMPLE

Because of a change in product processing, X Company trades its outdated machinery for new machinery that can be used in the new product processing. Because of the specialized nature of the machinery being exchanged, the fair values of the assets being exchanged are *not* reliably measurable. The old machinery has a book value of $19,000 (cost $32,000 less accumulated depreciation $13,000). The new machinery has a list price of $32,000. The trade-in allowance on the old machinery is $25,000. The cash to be paid equals:

List price of new machinery		$32,000
Less: trade-in allowance for used machinery		25,000
Cash to be paid		$ 7,000
The cost of the new machinery equals:		
Cash to be paid		$ 7,000
Book value of old machinery—given up		19,000
Cost of new machinery		$26,000
The journal entry for the exchange follows:		
Machinery—new	26,000	
Accumulated depreciation	13,000	
Machinery—old		32,000
Cash		7,000

Reminder: As was noted, if the fair values for either the asset obtained or relinquished are *not* reliably measurable, the business uses the book value of the old asset plus the cash paid as the cost basis for the new asset.

Accounting for Barter Transactions Involving Barter Credits

A barter transaction may relate to an exchange of goods, services or barter credits. With respect to the latter, for example, the asset inventory may be exchanged for barter credits.

ASC 845-10-05-10, *Nonmonetary Transactions: Overall*, stipulates that ASC 845-10-05-2, *Nonmonetary Transactions: Overall*, should be applied to an exchange of a nonmonetary asset for barter credits. With respect to barter credits, it is assumed that the fair value of the asset exchanged is more reliably measureable than the fair value of the barter credits received. As a result, the barter credits received should be recorded at the fair value of the asset exchanged. In ascertaining the fair value asset surrendered, it is assumed that the fair value of the asset does not exceed its book value.

In the event the book value of the asset surrendered is greater than its fair value, an impairment should be recorded before making the entry for the exchange. As an example, inventory being exchanged in a barter transaction should be reflected at the lower of cost or market value before recording the barter transaction.

At year-end, the recorded amount of barter credits should be appraised for impairment. An impairment loss is recognized when the book value of remaining barter credits is greater than its fair value, or in the event it is probable that what is left of the barter credits will not be used.

Involuntary Conversion

An involuntary conversion of nonmonetary assets to monetary assets may arise because of fire, flood, theft, or condemnation. The destruction is followed by replacement of the involuntarily converted assets. An example is a building destroyed by a fire and the insurance proceeds received used to buy a similar building.

An *extraordinary gain or loss* is usually recorded for the difference between the insurance proceeds and the book value of the demolished asset. The new building is recorded at its purchase price.

Caution: A contingency arises if the old fixed asset is damaged in one year but the insurance recovery is not received until a later year. A contingent gain or loss is recognized in the period the old fixed asset was damaged. The gain or loss may be reflected for book and tax reporting in different years, resulting in a temporary difference mandating interperiod income tax allocation.

Asset Retirement Obligations

ASC 410-20-15-2, *Asset Retirement and Environmental Obligations: Asset Retirement Obligations,* requires companies to record a liability when a retirement obligation is incurred, provided fair value can be reasonably estimated even though it is years before the asset's planned retirement. The asset retirement obligation must be measured and recorded along with its associated asset retirement cost. However, the pronouncement's requirements do *not* apply to a liability arising from an asset's improper operation or functioning. An example is a machine resulting in environmental remediation. Asset retirements may be from sale, recycling, abandonment, or disposal. However, if the entity only has the intent or a plan for an asset disposal, that in and of itself does not require recognition.

ASC 410-20-15-2 applies to tangible long-term assets, including individual ones, similar asset groups, and major parts of assets. A company may be legally liable for the purchase, development, construction, or usual operation of the fixed asset.

A company must record the fair value of a liability for an asset retirement obligation as incurred. When the initial obligation arises, the company books a liability and defers the cost to the long-term asset for the same amount. After the initial recognition, the liability will change over time so the obligation must be accreted to its present value each year. The long-term asset's capitalized cost is depreciated over its useful life. When the liability is settled, the company either settles the liability for the amount recorded or will have a settlement gain or loss.

The asset retirement obligation is recorded at its fair value. In determining the fair value, the first valuation (provided it is ascertainable) is the amount by which the obligation could be settled in a current transaction in an *active market* between willing parties (not in a forced or liquidating transaction). Quoted market prices are the best basis for fair value measurement. If quoted market prices are unavailable, fair value can be estimated based on the best data available. Examples are the prices of similar liabilities and the use of present value techniques.

Fair value also can be estimated based on an alternative market value valuation, such as the discounted (present) value of projected future cash flows needed to pay the obligation. Projected cash flows are based on various assumptions, such as technology and the inflation rate. The present value technique is typically the best method to use when quoted market prices are unavailable.

The long-lived asset is charged with the asset retirement costs. Thus, the entry consists of debiting the long-term asset and crediting the asset retirement obligation. The asset is then depreciated, including the deferred (capitalized) retirement costs and interest attributable to the accretion of the asset retirement obligation arising from the passage of time.

There will be an increase in the carrying value of long-term assets because of the inclusion of asset retirement costs. Note that closure costs may be incurred during the asset's life. Further, carrying values of the assets will increase because assets bought with a related retirement obligation will be shown on a gross rather than net basis.

Any incremental liability incurred in a later year is an additional layer of the original obligation. Each layer is initially measured at fair value. For example, the contamination-related costs each year of a nuclear plant represents a separate layer for measurement and recognition.

In years after initial measurement, a business recognizes the yearly change in the asset retirement obligation owing to the passage of time, and modifications to the timing and original projection of undiscounted cash flows.

The entity may experience retirement obligations at the beginning of the asset's life or during its operating life. An example of the former is a production facility that experiences a removal obligation when it starts operations (e.g., oil production facility). An example of the latter is a mine that experiences a reclamation obligation gradually over its life as digging in the mine takes place over the years. Further, an asset retirement obligation may arise because of new governmental regulations or laws affecting the asset, such as newly enacted environmental restrictions.

The interest method of allocation is used to reflect changes in the asset retirement obligation. The interest rate is multiplied by the liability balance at the beginning of the year. The interest rate used is the one existing when the liability, or part thereof, was *initially* measured. The ensuing *accretion expense* increases the carrying value of the liability each year. Accretion expense is presented in the income statement as an operating item.

Changes in the timing or initial estimated undiscounted cash flows shall be recognized as an addition or reduction of the asset retirement obligation and the associated asset retirement cost deferred to the long-lived asset. Upward adjustments to the undiscounted estimated cash flows is discounted based on the *current* credit-adjusted risk-free rate. However, downward revisions are discounted using the rate existing when the initial liability was recognized. If asset retirement costs change because of revised estimated cash flows, we must adjust the asset retirement cost allocated to expense in the year(s) affected.

If an asset has an indeterminate service life, sufficient data to estimate a range of potential settlement dates for the obligation might not be available. In such cases, the liability is initially recognized in the year in which adequate information exists to estimate a range of potential settlement dates required to use a present value approach to estimate fair value.

Uncertainty of whether performance will be required does not defer recognizing a retirement obligation. Instead, that uncertainty is considered in the measurement of the fair value of the liability through assignment of probabilities to cash flows.

Any difference between the actual retirement costs and the asset retirement obligation is a gain or loss on retirement presented in the income statement.

ASC 410-20-25-4 through 25-6, *Asset Retirement and Environmental Obligations: Asset Retirement Obligations*, is an interpretation of ASC 410-20-25, *Asset Retirement and Environmental Obligations: Asset Retirement Obligations*. It provides that a company shall identify its asset retirement obligations. If the business has adequate data to reasonably estimate the fair value of an asset retirement obligation, it must record the liability as incurred. There exists reasonable estimation to an asset retirement obligation if (1) the fair value of the obligation is embodied in the asset's purchase price, (2) there is an active market for the obligation's transfer, or (3) adequate data is present to use an expected present value method. An expected present value method incorporates uncertainty regarding the timing and method of settlement into the fair value measurement. However, in some instances, adequate information about the timing and settlement method may not be available to reasonably approximate fair value.

A company would have sufficient information to use an expected present value method and, thus, an asset retirement obligation would be reasonably estimable when *either* of the following two conditions is present:

1. Data exists to reasonably estimate the settlement method, settlement date, and the probabilities with potential settlement methods and dates. The following may be considered in making these determinations: estimated life of asset, intent of management, prior practice, and industry policy.

2. The settlement method and date for the obligation has been stated by others, such as by contract, regulation, or law. In this case, the settlement method and date are known so the only uncertainty is whether performance will be required. Uncertainty concerning whether performance will be required does *not* defer asset retirement obligation recognition, because (a) there is a legal duty to conduct retirement activities and (b) it does not prevent reasonable estimation of fair value (this is because the only uncertainty is whether performance will be mandated).

Present Value Method

In using the present value method, the company must discount future estimated cash flows based on a credit-adjusted risk-free rate (e.g., rate on a zero-coupon U.S. Treasury Security) increased for the company's actual credit risk. After the final rate is decided on, the present value of cash flow calculation must reflect any relevant probabilities, uncertainties, and assumptions. Multiple cash flow and probability scenarios are used based on a range of possible outcomes.

EXAMPLE

A long-lived asset's carrying cost includes a $250,000 original cost plus the capitalized retirement cost of $53,426, which equals the initial liability amount. The business entity incurs an obligation to retire the asset upon installation. The asset retirement obligation is based on the following data:

Original cost $250,000
Credit-adjusted risk-free rate at date of installation   8%

Depreciation is based on the straight-line method for a five-year period of benefit.

The four possible alternative estimated market-based cash flows in year 5 to settle the obligation, along with their related probabilities are:

Scenario	Projected Cash Outflow (Year 5)	Probability
1	$100,000	30%
2	80,000	35%
3	70,000	15%
4	50,000	20%
Total probability		100%

The computation of the capitalized retirement cost of $53,426 follows:

Scenario	Projected Cash Outflow (Year 5)	Probability	Weighting
1	$100,000	30%	$30,000
2	80,000	35%	28,000
3	70,000	15%	10,500
4	50,000	20%	10,000
Expected cash outflow			$78,500
Present value for year 0 at 8%			$53,426*

* $78,500 × present value of $1 factor for n = 5, i = 8%
  $78,500 × .68058 = $53,426

The retirement entry for the long-term asset, based on the assumption that actual cash flows to settle the retirement liability are the same as those projected follows:

Accumulated depreciation	303,426	
Asset retirement liability	78,500	
Long-term asset		303,426
Cash		78,500

The annual accounting for the long-lived asset and the asset retirement obligation follows:

		Computation of the Long-Term Asset and Obligation			
Installment	Asset	Accumulated Depreciation	Book Value	Liability	Net Balance Sheet
Install	$303,426	–	$303,426	$53,426	$250,000
1	303,426	$60,685[a]	242,741	57,700[b]	185,041
2	303,426	121,370	182,056	62,316	119,740
3	303,426	182,055	121,371	67,301	54,070
4	303,426	242,740	60,686	72,685	(11,999)
5	303,426	303,426	0	78,500	(78,500)
Retirement	(303,426)	(303,426)			

[a] $303,426 divided by 5 years = $60,685
[b] $53,426 × 1.08 = $57,700

The depreciation expense and interest expense (accretion) follow:

	Computation of Depreciation and Interest Expense		
Year	Depreciation	Interest Expense	Net Income Statement
1	$60,685	$ 4,274[c]	$ 64,954
2	60,685	4,616	65,301
3	60,685	4,985	65,670
4	60,685	5,384	66,069
5	60,686	5,815	66,501
Total	$303,426	$25,074	$328,500

[c] $53,426 × 8% = $4,274

Asset Impairment. The carrying value of an asset being analyzed for impairment includes the deferred asset retirement costs. Projected future cash flows for the asset retirement obligation shall exclude the undiscounted cash flows used to test the asset for recoverability and the discounted cash flows used to derive the asset's fair value. If the fair value of the asset is based on a quoted market price and such price reflects the costs to retire the asset, the market price shall be increased by the fair value of the asset retirement obligation when measuring for impairment.

Disclosures

The following footnote disclosures are required:

☐ A description and valuation of legally restricted assets to settle the obligation.

☐ A description of both the asset retirement liability and the associated long-term asset.

☐ If the fair value of an asset retirement liability is not subject to reasonable estimation, that fact should be noted along with the reasons.

☐ Reconciliation of the asset retirement obligation balance for the year. This reconciliation shows the beginning and ending carrying values of the asset retirement obligation presenting separately the changes related to the liability incurred as well as settled in the current year, accretion expense, and adjustments made to projected cash flows.

The fair value of a conditional asset retirement obligation must be recognized before the event that either mandates or waives performance occurs. Further, a clear requirement that gives rise to an asset retirement debt coupled with a low likelihood of required performance still requires liability recognition.

Disclosure

The following should be footnoted in connection with fixed assets:

☐ Fixed assets by major category. Category may be in terms of nature or function.

☐ A description of depreciation method and estimates used.

☐ Fixed assets subject to pledges, liens, or other commitments.

☐ Fixed assets held to be disposed of and any anticipated losses. The reasons why such assets are to be disposed of should be provided. Disclosure includes expected disposal dates, carrying amounts of such assets, and business segments affected.

☐ Contracts to buy new fixed assets.

☐ Fixed assets that are fully depreciated but still in use.

☐ Idle fixed assets.

☐ Amount of capitalized interest.

NATURAL RESOURCES

Natural resources are wasting assets, such as petroleum, timber, and minerals. They are characterized as being subject to complete removal and being replaced only by an act of nature. Natural resources are subject to depletion. Depletion is the physical exhaustion of a natural resource from usage. From an accounting perspective, it consists of the process of allocating the cost of the natural resource over its anticipated useful life and is similar to depreciation except that it relates to a natural resource instead of a fixed asset. Depletion is generally based on the *units of production method.* An estimate is required of how much of the natural resource will be extracted in terms of tons, barrels, units, or other measure. The cost of the natural resource is divided by the total recoverable units to arrive at the depletion per unit. The depletion cost equals the units extracted for the year multiplied by the depletion per unit. A change in estimate requires the use of a new depletion rate per unit. Accumulated depletion reduces the cost of the natural resource in the noncurrent asset section of the balance sheet. When a natural resource is extracted from the ground, an inventory account is debited and accumulated depletion (or the natural resource account, itself) is credited.

When the inventory is sold, cost of goods sold is debited and the inventoy account is credited. For example, if depletion on a coal mine equals $20,000, the entry would be to debit coal inventory (for $20,000 and credit accumulated depletion (or land rights) for $20,000. When the coal inventory is sold, we debit cost of goods sold for $20,000 and credit coal inventory for that amount.

The basis on which depletion is computed is called the depletion base. The depletion base is generally made up of four components, consisting of the following:

1. *Acquisition cost of the depletable property* Property may be acquired in hope of finding natural resources or may already have been determined to have proved resources on it. Alternatively, the property may also be leased, with subsequent royalties being paid to the owner if resources are found on it.

2. *Exploration costs* When the rights to explore the property are secured (through acquisition or lease), exploration costs are incurred to determine the existence of natural resources. For most natural resources, the costs of exploration are expensed in the period in which they are incurred. However, for certain industries, such as oil-and gas-producing enterprises, certain specialized guidelines prevail (see Chapter 18 for greater detail). For example, oil and gas entities may choose between the successful efforts method or full cost method of accounting for exploration costs. In the successful efforts approach, only those exploratory costs related to successful wells are capitalized. Exploratory costs related to unsuccessful wells are expensed. In the full cost method, exploratory costs related to both successful wells and unsuccessful wells are capitalized as part of the depletion base.

3. *Development costs* These are the costs incurred in extracting the natural resource from the ground, making it ready for production or sale. Costs incurred on machinery and equipment that can be used for different wells or mines are generally not considered part of the depletable base and should be separately depreciated as they are utilized. On the other hand, intangible costs incurred on specific wells or mines which cannot be of benefit to any other should be considered part of that resource's depletion base. Such costs primarily include the costs incurred to dig, physically secure, and utilize the wells, mines, tunnels, shafts.

4. *Restoration costs* After extraction of the natural resource, companies generally incur significant costs to restore the natural resource to its original or natural state. Restoration costs are asset retirement obligations, which are explained in detail in the prior section of this chapter.

In summary, the components of the depletion base of a natural resource upon which depletion should be computed include (1) acquisition costs, (2) capitalized exploratory costs, (3) development costs, and (4) restoration costs.

EXAMPLE

In January 20X2, LevSe Company incurred costs of $3,500,000 in connection with the acquisition of a mineral mine. In addition, $200,000 of development costs were incurred in preparing the mine for production. It is estimated that 1,200,000 tons of ore will be removed from the mine over its useful life, at which point it is estimated that the company can sell the property for $250,000. LevSe is legally required to restore the mineral mine to a suitable condition after all the minerals are extracted. To this end, it estimates that the present value of the asset retirement obligation is $100,000. During 20X2, 30,000 tons of ore were extracted and sold. On its 20X2 income statement, what amount should LevSe report as the depletion component of Cost of Goods Sold?

DEPLETION BASE	
Acquisition cost	$3,500,000
Development costs	200,000
Restoration costs (asset retirement obligation)	100,000
Estimated salvage value	(250,000)
Depletion base	$3,550,000
20X2 production	30,000 tons
Depletion rate: $3,550,000/1,200,000 tons	$ 2.96/ton
Depletion costs—20X2 $2.96 × 30,000 tons	$ 88,800

INTANGIBLE ASSETS

Intangible assets have a life of one year or more and lack physical substance (e.g., goodwill) or reflect a right granted by the government (e.g., trademarks, copyrights) or by another company (e.g., license fee, franchise). Intangibles generally have a high degree of uncertainty concerning future benefits. Intangibles should be recorded at cost. Intangibles may be internally generated or they may be purchased. Intangibles acquired from others should be separately reported.

The cost at which intangibles are recorded depends on whether the intangible was developed internally or acquired from others. In general, expenses internally incurred to develop an identifiable intangible asset (e.g., patents, trademarks, and copyrights) should be expensed except for the direct costs of securing the intangible such as registration fees, attorney fees, design fees, etc. These are capitalized. Research and development costs, should be expensed when incurred except when arising from a business combination or asset purchase. Unidentifiable internally developed intangibles, such as goodwill, should not be recorded. Such an asset is recognized only if it is purchased from another entity.

When an intangible is purchased from another entity, its value equals the cash or fair value of the consideration given. The present value of payments on the liability incurred or the fair value of the stock issued may also be used to value externally acquired intangibles. When a group of assets is acquired, the identifiable intangible assets are allocated a part of the total cost based on the fair values of the individual assets in the group. The unidentifiable intangible assets, acquired as part of a group of assets, are valued at the excess of costs assigned to identifiable tangible and intangible assets, net of liabilities assumed.

EXAMPLE

Purchase price		$150,000
Fair value of assets acquired:		
Tangible assets		
Equipment	$ 20,000	
Land	80,000	
Identifiable intangible assets		
Copyrights	35,000	
Patents	40,000	
Total assets	175,000	
Less: liabilities assumed	(65,000)	110,000
Unidentifiable intangible assets		$ 40,000

In a business combination accounted for under the acquisition method ASC 805-20-30-1, the acquirer recognizes at fair value, the identifiable intangible assets acquired if they meet either the separability or contractual legal criterion. The separability criterion is met when the items are exchangeable and can be traded by the acquirer company. Examples include unpatented technology, customer lists, databases and trade secrets, including secret formulas. The contractual legal criterion relates to whether the holder obtains legal rights associated with the intangible. Examples meeting this criterion include trademarks, patents, construction permits, and licensing agreements.

As was noted, any costs to develop and maintain intangibles should generally be charged against earnings. For example, the costs incurred to develop a name (e.g., McDonald's) are expensed. Costs, such as legal costs associated with registering or successfully defending a patent, are capitalized. The costs of purchasing an externally developed patent should also be capitalized.

Patents are limited life intangibles which give the holder exclusive rights for a period of 20 years. It would, therefore, be inappropriate to amortize a patent for a period greater than 20 years. Copyrights are granted for the life of the creator plus 70 years. The useful life of copyrights is typically much shorter. Franchises and licenses are also limited life intangibles although it is possible for them to have indefinite lives. In general, limited life intangibles should be amortized over the shorter of their useful lives or legal lives. Trademarks and trade names have legal protection for a period of 10 years and may be renewed for an indefinite number of times. They are, therefore, considered to be indefinite life intangibles. Indefinite life intangibles have unlimited lives and should not be amortized. Organization costs, which include initial corporation, legal, and accounting fees that are incurred in connection with establishing an entity, are required to be expensed as incurred.

As per ASC 350-30-35-21, *Intangibles—Goodwill and Other: General Intangibles Other than Goodwill*, acquired or internally developed intangible assets having indefinite lives that have been separately recognized and are inseparable from each other owing to being operated as a single unit should be combined in one accounting unit when the impairment test is applied.

Companies must disclose information about how recognized intangible assets would aid financial statement users to determine how a company's ability to renew or extend an arrangement impacts the company's anticipated cash flows associated with the asset.

Disclosure should be made of the:

☐ Weighted-average period at acquisition or renewal before the next renewal or extension.

☐ Accounting policy for costs incurred to renew or extend an intangible asset's term.

☐ In the event renewal or extension costs are capitalized, the total cost incurred to renew or extend the term of a recognized intangible asset.

GOODWILL

Goodwill is theoretically equal to the discounted value (present value) of future excess earnings of a company over other companies in the industry.

In purchasing a new business, a determination is needed of the estimated value of the goodwill. Two possible methods are:

☐ Capitalization of earnings.

☐ Capitalization of excess earnings.

EXAMPLE

The following data are provided for a company being considered for purchase:

Expected average annual earnings	$ 25,000
Expected fair value of net assets excluding goodwill	$180,000
Normal rate of return	10%

Goodwill is estimated as follows under the capitalization of earnings method:

Total asset value implied ($25,000/10%)	$250,000
Estimated fair value of assets	180,000
Estimated goodwill	$ 70,000

Assuming the same information, except that the capitalization of excess earnings method is used with a capitalization rate of 20%, goodwill is estimated at:

Expected average annual earnings	$25,000
Return on expected average assets ($180,000 × 10%)	18,000

Excess earnings	$ 7,000
Goodwill ($7,000/.20)	$35,000

EXAMPLE

The net worth of XYZ Company excluding goodwill is $600,000, and total profits for the last five years were $550,000. Included in the latter figure are extraordinary gains of $40,000 and nonrecurring losses of $30,000. A 15% return on net worth is considered normal for the industry. The capitalization of excess earnings is 30%. What is the estimated goodwill?

Profits for 5 years	$550,000
Less: extraordinary gains	(40,000)
Add: nonrecurring losses	30,000
Adjusted 5-year earnings	$540,000
Average earnings ($540,000/5 years)	$108,000
Normal earnings ($600,000 × .15)	90,000
Excess annual earnings	$ 18,000
Excess earnings capitalized at 30%: $18,000/.30 =	$ 60,000

Goodwill may be recorded in a business combination accounted for under the acquisition method (ASC 805-30-30). Goodwill is calculated as the excess of the fair consideration transferred (generally the purchase price) over the fair value of net assets acquired. When the fair value of net assets acquired exceeds the fair value of consideration transferred, a bargain purchase occurs. A gain on a bargain purchase is reported in the consolidated income statement.

The prior rules for business combinations (ASC 805-10-65), which are grandfathered for acquisitions closing on or before December 15, 2008, reported a bargain purchase as a proportional reduction to acquire noncurrent assets with any remainder treated as an extraordinary gain.

ASC 350, *Intangibles—Goodwill and Other*, relates to financial accounting and reporting for intangibles purchased individually or with a group of other assets but not to those bought in a business combination, because they are covered in ASC 805. These intangibles are initially measured and recorded at fair value. The optimal measure of fair value is quoted market prices in active markets. If such is not available, valuation may be based on multiples of revenue or profits or a similar performance measure, if appropriate. The pronouncement also provides GAAP to account and report goodwill and other intangibles subsequent to purchase. Goodwill and intangible assets with unlimited lives are not amortized but instead tested for impairment at least once a year. In the event there is no factor (e.g., legal, economic, regulatory, competition) that limits an intangible's useful life, such intangible is considered to have an indefinite life. Intangible assets having finite useful lives are amortized over their useful lives. However, the arbitrary limitation of 40 years no longer applies.

Goodwill for each reporting unit must be tested each year for impairment. A reporting unit is defined as an operating segment or one level below an operating segment. If certain events occur, more than one annual impairment test is required. An impairment test can be performed at any date, as long as it is consistently used each year. However, different reporting units may be tested for impairment at different dates.

There are two steps in applying the impairment test. The initial step is to determine whether there is *potential* impairment. The book value of the reporting unit (including goodwill) is compared to its fair value. No impairment exists if fair value exceeds book value. If this is the case, the second step is not undertaken. However, if the reporting unit's fair value is below its book value there is an impairment and step 2 must be followed.

EXAMPLE

Step 1

Book value	$150
Fair value	190

No impairment exists. Do *not* proceed to step 2.

EXAMPLE

Step 1

Book value	$190
Fair value	150

An impairment exists. Proceed to step 2.

In the second step, the amount of impairment, if any, is measured. A comparison is made between book value of goodwill to the *implied fair value of goodwill*. Implied fair value of goodwill may be obtained by comparing the fair value of the reporting unit to the book value of its net identifiable assets excluding goodwill. If the implied fair value of goodwill is more than book value, no impairment loss exists and no entry is made. However, if the implied fair value of goodwill is below book value of the entity's goodwill, an impairment loss must be recognized for the difference. After an impairment loss for goodwill is recorded, the downwardly adjusted book value becomes the intangible's new cost basis, which means the new accounting basis cannot be written up for a recovery in fair value.

EXAMPLE

Step 1

The fair value of the reporting entity's net assets is $6,100, and the carrying value is $6,300 (shown in the following figures). Because the fair value is below the carrying value, step 2 must be undertaken:

Current assets	$2,000
Fixed assets (net)	1,600
Goodwill	3,000
Current liabilities	100
Noncurrent liabilities	200

Net Assets = $2,000 + 1,600 + 3,000 – 100 200 = $6,300

Net identifiable assets less goodwill = $6,300 – 3,000 = $3,300

If the fair value of the reporting unit is $6,100, the implied value of goodwill is $2,800, derived as follows:

Fair value of reporting unit	$6,100
Less: net identifiable assets less goodwill	3,300
Implied value of goodwill	$2,800

EXAMPLE

Step 2

Book value of goodwill	$3,000
Implied fair value of goodwill	2,800

An impairment loss of $200 has to be recognized. The new adjusted cost basis is $2,800. If there is a recovery in fair value in a subsequent period above $2,800, it cannot be recorded.

EXAMPLE

Step 2

Book value of goodwill	$2,800
Implied fair value of goodwill	3,000

No impairment loss should be recorded.

If goodwill and another asset of a reporting unit are tested for impairment at the same time, the other asset shall be tested for impairment before goodwill.

Goodwill should be tested for impairment at least annually. For example, ASC 350-20-35-30 notes that if an event, circumstance, or occurrence results in a probability that would make it more likely than not that a reporting unit's fair value would be below its book value, then the reporting unit should be tested for impairment between annual tests. Examples of such events follow:

☐ Unexpected actions by competitors.

☐ Serious lawsuits filed against the company or an adverse change in the business climate.

☐ Key senior executives quit.

☐ Anticipation that a reporting unit will be sold or disposed of.

☐ Recently issued government regulations or laws having a negative effect on the company.

☐ Applying the recoverability test of a major *asset group* within a reporting unit.

☐ Accounting for a goodwill impairment loss by a subsidiary that is part of a reporting unit. (Subsidiary goodwill is tested for impairment at the subsidiary level using the subsidiary's reporting unit.)

If only a part of goodwill is assigned to a business to be sold or disposed of, the remainder of the goodwill in the reporting unit must be tested for impairment using the adjusted carrying value.

Additional discussion on accounting for the impairment of goodwill may be found in Chapter 11 (Treatment of Goodwill). Goodwill impairment losses are presented as a separate line item in the income statement.

In Accounting Standards Update (ASU) No. 2010-28 (December 2010) (ASC 350, *Intangibles–Goodwill and Other*), *When to Perform Step 2 of the Goodwill Impairment Test for Reporting Units with Zero or Negative Carrying Amounts*, goodwill of a reporting unit must be examined for impairment between annual tests if there is an occurrence or circumstance that would more likely than not reduce the fair market value of a reporting unit below its carrying value.

In Accounting Standards Update (ASU) No. 2011-08 (September 2011), *Intangibles—Goodwill and Other* (Topic 350), *Testing Goodwill for Impairment*, a company has the option to first appraise qualitative data to ascertain if the existence of circumstances results in a determination that it is more likely than not that the fair value of a business unit is below its carrying value. If the company determines it is not more likely than not that the fair value of a reporting unit is less than its carrying value, then using the two-step impairment test is not required. However, if the company decides otherwise, then it must conduct the first step by computing the fair value of the reporting unit and comparing the fair value with the carrying value of the business unit. If the carrying amount is more than the fair value, the entity must perform the second step of the goodwill impairment test to measure any impairment loss. **Note:** A company has the option to bypass the qualitative appraisal for any reporting unit in any year and go directly to conducting the first step of the two-step goodwill impairment test. A company may resume doing the qualitative evaluation in any later year.

The following are footnote disclosures for goodwill and other intangible assets:

☐ Amortization period and expected amortization expense for the next five years.

☐ Amount of any significant residual value.

☐ Amount of goodwill included in the gain or loss on disposal of all or a part of a reporting unit.

☐ Method in deriving fair value.

☐ The book values of intangible assets by major class for intangibles subject to amortization and separately for those not subject to amortization. An intangible asset class is a group of similar intangibles either based on their use in the company's operations or by their nature.

☐ Description of impaired intangible assets and the causes for such impairment.

☐ Information relating to the changes in the carrying values of goodwill over the year both in total and by reporting unit.

☐ Total amount of impairment losses and where presented in the income statement.

Internally generated costs to derive a patented product are expensed (e.g., research and development incurred in developing a new product). The patent account is charged for registration fees, legal fees in successfully defending the patent in court, and the cost of buying competing products. The patent account is amortized over its useful life not exceeding 20 years.

When an intangible asset is worthless, it should be written off as either a nonrecurring loss or extraordinary loss, depending on its nature and recurrence.

Leaseholds are rentals paid in advance and are amortized over the life of the lease.

Leasehold improvements are improvements to leased property and are amortized over the life of the property or of the lease, whichever is shorter. If a lease contains a renewal option, it is included in the life of the lease unless exercise of the option is uncertain, in which case it is ignored.

ASC 840-10-35-9, *Leases: Overall*, requires that leasehold improvements acquired in a business combination or purchase after a lease's inception are amortized over the *lesser* of the asset's useful life or the lease term that includes reasonably assured lease renewals as determined on the acquisition date of the leasehold improvement. However, leasehold improvements not considered at or near the beginning of a lease and placed in service a significant time period subsequent to the lease's inception are amortized over the *shorter* of the useful life of the asset or a term that includes required lease periods and renewals that are reasonably assured at the date the leasehold improvements are purchased.

FAIR VALUE OF FINANCIAL ASSETS

ASC 820-10-35-15A and 35-55[A-B] states that irrespective of the valuation technique, a company must include suitable risk adjustments that market participants would use for nonperformance and liquidity risks. When markets are not active, brokers may rely on models with inputs based on information available to the broker. An income approach (e.g., present value) may be used to maximize the use of relevant observable inputs to value a financial asset that is *not* actively traded. A discount rate adjustment technique may be used to determine fair value of a financial asset at the measurement date. Risks considered in the discount rate include liquidity risk (e.g., difficulty selling an asset under present market conditions) and nonperformance risk (e.g., collateral value risk, default risk).

Fair Value Accounting

The SEC Office of the Chief Accountant and FASB staff clarified fair value accounting in a news release, which states that management may use internal assumptions, such as expected cash flows including appropriate risk premiums, to measure fair value when suitable market evidence is non-existent. In some cases, unobservable inputs (level 3) may be more appropriate then observable inputs (level 2). An example is when significant adjustments are needed to available observable inputs it may be better to use an estimate based mostly on unobservable inputs. Fair value determination often involves judgment. In some situations, multiple inputs from different sources may give the best indication of fair value. In this case, expected cash flows may be taken into account with other relevant data.

Broker quotes may be an input to measure fair value; however, they are not necessarily determinative if an active market does not exist for the security. When markets are less active, brokers may rely more on models with inputs based on information available to the broker. Less reliance should be placed on quotes not reflecting market transactions. The nature of the quote should also be considered such as if it indicates a price or binding offer.

Disorderly transactions are not determinative in measuring fair value. Fair value measurement assumes orderly transactions among market participants. Distressed or forced liquidation sales are not orderly transactions.

If prices in an inactive market are not reflective of current prices for similar assets, adjustments may be needed to determine fair value.

In determining if a market is inactive, the spread between the asking price of sellers and the bid price of buyers should be considered as well as the number of "bidding" parties. A significant increase in the spread and a small number of bidders indicate an inactive market.

In determining if another-than-temporary impairment of the financial asset exists, the following should be examined:

☐ Intent and ability of the holder to keep its investment in the issuer for a time period adequate to allow for a recovery in market value.

☐ The length of time and degree to which the market value has been less than cost.

☐ The issuer's financial condition and short-term prospects.

☐ The expected recovery period.

LEEWAY IN VALUING FINANCIAL ASSETS

In determining whether a market is not active and a transaction is not distressed, the FASB has given companies greater leeway in valuing assets and reporting losses on banks' balance sheets and income statements. A bank's assets may now be valued at what they could be sold for in an "orderly" sale in an inactive market between market participants at the measurement date as distinguished from a forced liquidation or distressed sale. The new guidelines will allow banks to avoid reporting some losses on securities. The change in how companies record impaired assets they do not currently plan to sell allows for the splitting off of credit losses from non-credit losses arising from such reasons as fluctuating interest rates. The latter will not have to be counted toward net income or loss. Banks will benefit because their asset values would be higher and so would earnings.

Assets would be valued at what banks project they might sell for in the future, instead of the current distressed environment. In effect, the mark-to-market rules are relaxed for banks' toxic assets.

To avoid a write-down as an impairment loss on an asset, management must assert it has the intent and ability to hold on to an asset until its value recovers. Under new rules, a company could avoid a write-down by stating it intends to hold the asset and it is more likely than not it will.

Once an asset is other than temporarily impaired, only losses related to the underlying creditworthiness would impact earnings and regulatory capital. Losses associated with market conditions would be disclosed and accounted for elsewhere.

More weight should be given when transactions are in a market operating in an orderly manner and less weight should be given to an inactive market.

The effective date for the pronouncement is the second quarter of 2009. Early adoption for the first quarter of 2009 is allowed.

OTHER ASSETS

The other assets section is the last classification of assets presented on the balance sheet. It is sometimes labeled *deferred charges* instead of other assets. Other assets is an all-inclusive heading representing those assets that do not fit into other asset categories. Other assets include long-term prepaid expenses (e.g., rent, insurance), deferred taxes, noncurrent receivable, and possibly restricted cash. Long-term prepaid expenses and deferred charges are amortized over the period benefited. Some deferred charges usually have no cash realizability in the event of corporate bankruptcy because they represent past expenditures of cash and cannot be sold to satisfy a bankruptcy judgment.

ANNUAL REPORT REFERENCES

Sysco Corp.
2011 Annual Report

4. Fair Value Measurements

Fair value is defined as the price that would be received to sell an asset or paid to transfer a liability in an orderly transaction between market participants at the measurement date (i.e. an exit price). The accounting guidance includes a fair value hierarchy that prioritizes the inputs to valuation techniques used to measure fair value. The three levels of the fair value hierarchy are as follows:

- *Level 1*—Unadjusted quoted prices for identical assets or liabilities in active markets;

- *Level 2*—Inputs other than quoted prices in active markets for identical assets and liabilities that are observable either directly or indirectly for substantially the full term of the asset or liability; and

- *Level 3*—Unobservable inputs for the asset or liability, which include management's own assumption about the assumptions market participants would use in pricing the asset or liability, including assumptions about risk.

Sysco's policy is to invest in only high-quality investments. Cash equivalents primarily include time deposits, certificates of deposit, commercial paper, high-quality money market funds and all highly liquid instruments with original maturities of three months or less. Short-term investments consist of commercial paper with original maturities of greater than three months but less than one year. These investments are considered available-for-sale and are recorded at fair value. As of July 3, 2010, the difference between the fair value of the short-term investments and the original cost was not material. There were no short-term investments as of July 2, 2011. Restricted cash consists of investments in high-quality money market funds.

The following is a description of the valuation methodologies used for assets and liabilities measured at fair value.

- Time deposits, certificates of deposit and commercial paper included in cash equivalents are valued at amortized cost, which approximates fair value. These are included within cash equivalents as a Level 2 measurement in the tables below.

- Commercial paper included in short-term investments is valued using broker quotes that utilize observable market inputs. These are included as a Level 2 measurement in the tables below.

- Money market funds are valued at the closing price reported by the fund sponsor from an actively traded exchange. These are included within cash equivalents and restricted cash as Level 1 measurements in the tables below.

- The interest rate swap agreements, discussed further in Note 8, "Derivative Financial Instruments," are valued using a swap valuation model that utilizes an income approach using observable market inputs including interest rates, LIBOR swap rates and credit default swap rates. These are included as a Level 2 measurement in the tables below.

The following tables present the company's assets measured at fair value on a recurring basis as of July 2, 2011 and July 3, 2010:

| | Assets Measured at Fair Value as of July 2, 2011 | | | |
	Level 1	Level 2	Level 3	Total
	(In thousands)			
Assets:				
Cash and cash equivalents				
Cash equivalents	$141,350	$ 163,465	$—	$ 304,815
Restricted cash	110,516	—	—	110,516
Other assets				
Interest rate swap agreements	—	13,482	—	13,482
Total assets at fair value	$251,866	$176,947	$—	$428,813

| | Assets Measured at Fair Value as of July 3, 2010 | | | |
	Level 1	Level 2	Level 3	Total
	(In thousands)			
Assets:				
Cash and cash equivalents				
Cash equivalents	$225,400	$199,047	$—	$424,447
Short-term investments	—	23,511		23,511
Restricted cash	124,488	—	—	124,488
Other assets				
Interest rate swap agreements	—	11,045	—	11,045
Total assets at fair value	$349,888	$233,603	$—	$583,491

The carrying values of accounts receivable and accounts payable approximated their respective fair values due to the short-term maturities of these instruments. The fair value of Sysco's total debt is estimated based on the quoted market prices for the same or similar issue or on the current rates offered to the company for debt of the same remaining maturities. The fair value of total debt approximated $2,919.4 million and $2,774.9 million as of July 2, 2011 and July 3, 2010, respectively. The carrying value of total debt was $2,668.5 million and $2,480.6 million as of July 2, 2011 and July 3, 2010, respectively.

Energizer Holdings
2010 Annual Report

(6) Goodwill and Intangible Assets

Goodwill and intangible assets deemed to have an indefinite life are not amortized, but reviewed annually for impairment of value or when indicators of a potential impairment are present. The Company monitors changing business conditions, which may indicate that the remaining useful life of goodwill and other intangible assets may warrant revision or carrying amounts may require adjustment. As part of our business planning cycle, we performed our annual impairment test in the fourth quarter of fiscal 2011, 2010 and 2009. During fiscal 2011, we consolidated the Playtex and Wet Shave strategic business units, which were both part of our Personal Care reporting segment, to form a single business unit. During our annual impairment testing in fiscal 2011, we tested goodwill for impairment for both Wet Shave and Playtex individually and in the aggregate, in addition to testing the goodwill associated with the Energizer reporting unit in our Household Products segment. There were no indications of impairment of goodwill noted during this testing. Going forward, we will test goodwill for impairment for two reporting units, the combined Personal Care reporting unit and the Energizer reporting unit.

In addition, we completed impairment testing on indefinite-lived intangible assets other than goodwill, which are trademarks/brand names used in our various product categories. No impairment was indicated as a result of this testing. However, the recorded values of such intangible assets from more recent acquisitions, such as the Playtex acquisition, are often more susceptible to an impairment risk, if operating results or macroeconomic conditions deteriorate. Playtex indefinite-lived intangible assets, exclusive of goodwill, represent more than 75% of total indefinite-lived intangible assets, exclusive of goodwill. We utilized a discounted cash flow model using an excess earnings valuation technique to test the Playtex trademarks for impairment. Key assumptions included a discount rate of 9% and a terminal growth rate of 3%. While no impairment was indicated during this testing, the indicated fair value for two trademarks, *Playtex* and *Wet Ones,* were relatively close to the carrying value at 114% of the carrying value (approximately $650) for the *Playtex* trademark and 107% of the carrying value (approximately $200) for the *Wet Ones* trademark.

The following table represents the carrying amount of goodwill by segment at September 30, 2011:

	Household Products	Personal Care	Total
Balance at October 1, 2010	$ 37.2	$1,279.2	$1,316.4
ASR acquisition	–	161.9	161.9
Cumulative translation adjustment	(0.3)	(2.7)	(3.0)
Balance at September 30, 2011	$ 36.9	$1,438.4	$1,475.3

The Company had indefinite-lived trademarks and tradenames of $ 1,703.6 at September 30, 2011 and $ 1,704.4 at September 30, 2010. Changes in indefinite-lived trademarks and tradenames are due primarily to changes in foreign currency translation.

Total amortizable intangible assets at September 30, 2011 are as follows:

	Gross Carrying Amount	Accumulated Amortization	Net
Tradenames / Brands	$ 18.9	$ 10.2	$ 8.7
Technology and patents	76.0	39.4	36.6
Customer-related / Other	165.3	36.0	129.3
Total amortizable intangible assets	$ 260.2	$ 85.6	$ 174.6

Amortizable intangible assets, with a weighted average remaining life of approximately thirteen years, are amortized on a straight-line basis over expected lives of 3 years to 20 years.

Amortization expense for intangible assets totaled $21.6 for the current year. Estimated amortization expense for amortizable intangible assets for the years ending September 30, 2012, 2013, 2014, and 2015, is approximately $22.6, $20.4, $17.4, and $15.1, respectively, $15.1 and $14.8 for the years ending September 30, 2016 and 2017 and $9.9 thereafter.

(7) Income Taxes

The provisions for income taxes consisted of the following for the years ended September 30:

	2011	2010	2009
Currently payable:			
United States - Federal	$ 34.0	$ 67.0	$ 91.7
State	4.6	8.4	8.6
Foreign	79.8	66.3	55.4
Total current	118.4	141.7	155.7
Deferred:			
United States - Federal	36.4	(7.8)	(12.5)
State	2.4	(0.3)	(0.5)
Foreign	(12.4)	6.8	4.8
Total deferred	26.4	(1.3)	(8.2)
Provision for income taxes	$ 144.8	$ 140.4	$ 147.5

Meritor
2010 Annual Report

15. Long-Term Debt

Long-Term Debt, net of discounts where applicable, is summarized as follows (in millions):

	September 30,	
	2011	2010
8-3/4 percent notes due 2012	$ 84	$ 84
8-1/8 percent notes due 2015	250	250
10-5/8 percent notes due 2018	246	245
4.625 percent convertible notes due 2026[1]	300	300
4.0 percent convertible notes due 2027[1]	200	200
Lines of credit and other	8	9
Unamortized gain on interest rate swap termination	14	18
Unamortized discount on convertible notes	(68)	(77)
Subtotal	1,034	1,029
Less: current maturities	84	—
Long-term debt	$ 950	$1,029

[1] The 4.625 percent and 4.0 percent convertible notes contain a put and call feature, which allows for earlier redemption beginning in 2016 and 2019, respectively (see *Convertible Securities* below).

Debt Securities. On March 3, 2010, the company completed a public offering of debt securities consisting of the issuance of $250 million 8-year fixed rate 10-5/8 percent notes due March 15, 2018. The offering was made pursuant to a shelf registration statement filed with the Securities and Exchange Commission on November 20, 2009, which became effective December 23, 2009 (the "Shelf Registration Statement"), registering $750 million aggregate debt and/or equity securities that may be offered in one or more series on terms to be determined at the time of sale. The notes were issued at a discounted price of 98.024 percent of their principal amount. The proceeds from the sale of the notes, net of discount, were $245 million and were primarily used to repurchase $175 million of the company's previously outstanding $276 million 8-3/4 percent notes due 2012.

On March 23, 2010, the company completed the debt tender offer for its 8-3/4 percent notes due March 1, 2012. The notes were repurchased at 109.75 percent of their principal amount. The repurchase of $175 million of 8-3/4 percent notes was accounted for as an extinguishment of debt and, accordingly, the company recognized a net loss on debt extinguishment of approximately $13 million, which is included in interest expense, net in the consolidated statement of operations. The loss on debt extinguishment primarily relates to the $17 million paid in excess of par to repurchase the $175 million of 8-3/4 percent notes, partially offset by a $6 million gain associated with the acceleration of previously deferred unamortized interest rate swap gains associated with the 8-3/4 percent notes.

On June 15, 2010, the company purchased in the open market $17 million of its 8-3/4 percent notes due March 1, 2012. The notes were repurchased at 104.875 percent of their principal amount. On June 17, 2010, the company purchased in the open market $1 million of its 8-1/8 percent notes due September 15, 2015. The notes were repurchased at 94.000 percent of their principal amount.

Revolving Credit Facility. On February 5, 2010 the company signed an agreement to amend and extend the revolving credit facility, which became effective on February 26, 2010. Pursuant to the revolving credit facility as amended, the company had a $539 million revolving credit facility at September 30, 2010 which excluded approximately $28 million of commitments that were unavailable due to the bankruptcy of Lehman Brothers in 2008. On March 31, 2011, the company exercised the accordion feature of the agreement, which allowed it to increase the size of the revolving credit facility with an additional revolving credit loan with a new lender in the amount of $30 million. On April 13, 2011 the company exercised an additional $15 million of the accordion feature. On June 23, 2011, $143 million of the revolving credit facility (including $2 million available under letters of credit) matured for banks that elected not to extend their original commitments (non-extending banks). The remaining revolving credit facility balance of $441 million matures in January 2014. The availability under this facility is dependent upon various factors, including principally performance against certain financial covenants. At September 30, 2011 and September 30, 2010, there were no borrowings outstanding under the revolving credit facility. The $441 million revolving credit facility includes $100 million of availability for the issuance of letters of credit. At September 30, 2011, no amount was outstanding on the letters of credit. At September 30, 2010, $26 million of letters of credit were outstanding under this facility.

Availability under the revolving credit facility is subject to a collateral test, pursuant to which borrowings on the revolving credit facility cannot exceed 1.0x the collateral test value. The collateral test is performed on a quarterly basis and under the most recent collateral test, the full amount of the revolving credit facility was available for borrowing at September 30, 2011. Availability under the revolving credit facility is also subject to certain financial covenants based on (i) the ratio of the company's priority debt (consisting principally of amounts outstanding under the revolving credit facility, U.S. accounts receivable securitization and factoring programs, and third-party non-working capital foreign debt) to EBITDA and (ii) the amount of annual capital expenditures. The company is required to maintain a total priority debt-to-EBITDA ratio, as defined in the agreement, of (i) 2.25 to 1 as of the last day of each fiscal quarter commencing with the fiscal quarter ended September 30, 2011 through and including the fiscal quarter ended June 30, 2012 and (ii) 2.00 to 1 as of the last day of each fiscal quarter thereafter through maturity. At September 30, 2011, the company was in compliance with all covenants under its credit agreement with a ratio of approximately 0.19x for the priority debt-to-EBITDA covenant.

Borrowings under the revolving credit facility are collateralized by approximately $671 million of the company's assets, primarily consisting of eligible domestic U.S. accounts receivable, inventory, plant, property and equipment, intellectual property and the company's investment in all or a portion of certain of its wholly-owned subsidiaries.

Borrowings under the revolving credit facility are subject to interest based on quoted LIBOR rates plus a margin, and a commitment fee on undrawn amounts, both of which are based upon the company's current credit rating for the senior secured facility. At September 30, 2011, the margin over LIBOR rate was 425 basis points and the commitment fee was 50 basis points.

Certain of the company's subsidiaries, as defined in the credit agreement, irrevocably and unconditionally guarantee amounts outstanding under the amended revolving credit facility. Similar subsidiary guarantees are provided for the benefit of the holders of the publicly-held notes outstanding under the company's indentures (see Note 26).

Letter of Credit Facilities. The company entered into a five-year credit agreement dated as of November 18, 2010 with Citicorp USA, Inc., as administrative agent and issuing bank, the other lenders party thereto and the Bank of New York Mellon, as paying agent. Under the terms of this credit agreement, as amended, the company has the right to obtain the issuance, renewal, extension and increase of letters of credit up to an aggregate availability of $30 million. This facility contains covenants and events of default generally similar to those existing in the company's public debt indentures. At September 30, 2011, $30 million of letters of credit were outstanding under this facility. In addition, the company had $2 million of letters of credit outstanding through other letters of credit facilities at each of September 30, 2011 and 2010.

Convertible Securities. In February 2007, the company issued $200 million of 4.00 percent convertible senior unsecured notes due 2027 (the 2007 convertible notes). In March 2006, the company issued $300 million of 4.625 percent convertible senior unsecured notes due 2026 (the 2006 convertible notes). The 2007 convertible notes bear cash interest at a rate of 4.00 percent per annum from the date of issuance through February 15, 2019, payable semi-annually in arrears on February 15 and August 15 of each year. After February 15, 2019, the principal amount of the notes will be subject to accretion at a rate that provides holders with an aggregate annual yield to maturity of 4.00 percent. The 2006 convertible notes bear cash interest at a rate of 4.625 percent per annum from the date of issuance through March 1, 2016, payable semi-annually in arrears on March 1 and September 1 of each year. After March 1, 2016, the principal amount of the notes will be subject to accretion at a rate that provides holders with an aggregate annual yield to maturity of 4.625 percent.

In May 2008, the FASB issued guidance contained in Accounting Standards Codification (ASC) Topic 470-20, "Debt with Conversion and Other Options" which applies to all convertible debt instruments that have a "net settlement feature," which means that such convertible debt instruments, by their terms, may be settled either wholly or partially in cash upon conversion. This topic requires issuers of convertible debt instruments that may be settled wholly or partially in cash upon conversion to separately account for the liability and equity components in a manner reflective of the issuers' nonconvertible debt borrowing rate.

This guidance impacted the company's accounting for the 2006 convertible notes and the 2007 convertible notes. On October 1, 2009, the company adopted this guidance and applied its impact retrospectively to all periods presented. Upon adoption, the company recognized the estimated equity component of the convertible notes of $108 million ($69 million after tax) in additional paid-in capital. In addition, the company allocated $4 million of unamortized debt issuance costs to the equity component and recognized this amount as a reduction to additional paid-in capital. The company also recognized a discount on convertible notes of $108 million, which is being amortized as non-cash interest expense over periods of ten and twelve years for the 2006 convertible notes and 2007 convertible notes, respectively.

Upon recognition of the equity component of the convertible notes, the company also recognized a deferred tax liability of $39 million as the tax effect of the basis difference between carrying and notional values of the convertible notes. The carrying value of this deferred tax liability was offset with certain net deferred tax assets in the first quarter of fiscal year 2009 for determining valuation allowances against those deferred tax assets (see Note 21).

At September 30, 2011 and 2010, the carrying amount of the equity component recognized upon adoption was $67 million. The following table summarizes the principal amounts and related unamortized discount on convertible notes (in millions):

	September 30, 2011	September 30, 2010
Principal amount of convertible notes	$ 500	$ 500
Unamortized discount on convertible notes	(68)	(77)
Net carrying value	432	423

The following table summarizes other information related to the convertible notes:

	2006 Convertible Notes	2007 Convertible Notes
Total amortization period for debt discount (in years):	10	12
Remaining amortization period for debt discount (in years):	5	8
Effective interest rates on convertible notes:	7.0 %	7.7 %

The following table summarizes interest costs recognized on convertible notes (in millions):

	Year Ended September 30,		
	2011	2010	2009
Contractual interest coupon	$ 22	$ 22	$ 22
Amortization of debt discount	9	8	8
Total	$ 31	$ 30	$ 30

Conversion Features—Convertible Securities. The 2007 convertible notes are convertible into shares of the company's common stock at an initial conversion rate, subject to adjustment, equivalent to 37.4111 shares of common stock per $1,000 initial principal amount of notes, which represents an initial conversion price of approximately $26.73 per share. If converted, the accreted principal amount will be settled in cash and the remainder of the company's conversion obligation, if any, in excess of such accreted principal amount will be settled in cash, shares of common stock, or a combination thereof, at the company's election. Holders may convert their notes at any time on or after February 15, 2025. The maximum number of shares of common stock the 2007 convertible notes are convertible into is approximately 7 million.

The 2006 convertible notes are convertible into shares of the company's common stock at an initial conversion rate, subject to adjustment, equivalent to 47.6667 shares of common stock per $1,000 initial principal amount of notes, which represents an initial conversion price of approximately $20.98 per share. If converted, the accreted principal amount will be settled in cash and the remainder of the company's conversion obligation, if any, in excess of such accreted principal amount will be settled in cash, shares of common stock, or a combination thereof, at the company's election. Holders may convert their notes at any time on or after March 1, 2024. The maximum number of shares of common stock the 2006 convertible notes are convertible into is approximately 14 million.

Prior to February 15, 2025 (2007 convertible notes) and March 1, 2024 (2006 convertible notes), holders may convert their notes only under the following circumstances:

- during any calendar quarter, if the closing price of the company's common stock for 20 or more trading days in a period of 30 consecutive trading days ending on the last trading day of the immediately preceding calendar quarter exceeds 120 percent of the applicable conversion price;

- during the five business day period after any five consecutive trading day period in which the average trading price per $1,000 initial principal amount of notes is equal to or less than 97 percent of the average conversion value of the notes during such five consecutive trading day period;

- upon the occurrence of specified corporate transactions; or

- if the notes are called by the company for redemption.

Redemption Features—Convertible Securities. On or after February 15, 2019, the company may redeem the 2007 convertible notes, in whole or in part, for cash at a redemption price equal to 100 percent of the accreted principal amount plus any accrued and unpaid interest. On each of February 15, 2019 and 2022, or upon certain fundamental changes, holders may require the company to purchase all or a portion of their 2007 convertible notes at a purchase price in cash equal to 100 percent of the accreted principal amount plus any accrued and unpaid interest.

On or after March 1, 2016, the company may redeem the 2006 convertible notes, in whole or in part, for cash at a redemption price equal to 100 percent of the accreted principal amount plus any accrued and unpaid interest. On each of March 1, 2016, 2018, 2020, 2022 and 2024, or upon certain fundamental changes, holders may require the company to purchase all or a portion of their 2006 convertible notes at a purchase price in cash equal to 100 percent of the accreted principal amount plus any accrued and unpaid interest.

The 2007 and 2006 convertible notes are fully and unconditionally guaranteed by certain subsidiaries of the company that currently guarantee the company's obligations under its senior secured credit facility and other publicly-held notes (see Revolving Credit Facility above).

Accounts Receivable Securitization. In September 2009 the company entered into a new, two-year, $125 million U.S. receivables financing arrangement which is provided on a committed basis by a syndicate of financial institutions led by Ally Commercial Finance LLC (formerly, GMAC Commercial Finance LLC). In October 2010, the company extended the expiration of the program to October 2013 (see Note 6). The weighted average interest rate on borrowings under this arrangement was approximately 6.25 percent at September 30, 2011. At September 30, 2011 and 2010, no amount was outstanding under this program. This program does not have specific financial covenants; however, it does have a cross-default provision to the company's revolving credit facility agreement.

Interest Rate Swap Agreements. In March 2010, the company entered into an interest rate swap agreement that effectively converted $125 million of the company's 8-1/8 percent notes due 2015 to variable interest rates. The swap had been designated as a fair value hedge and the impact of the changes in its fair values was offset by an equal and opposite change in the carrying value of the related notes. Under the terms of the swap agreement, the company received a fixed rate of interest of 8-1/8 percent on notional amounts of $125 million and paid a variable rate based on U.S. dollar six-month LIBOR plus a spread of 4.61 percent. The payments under the swap agreement coincided with the interest payment dates on the hedged debt instrument, and the difference between the amounts paid and received is included in interest expense, net. In July 2010, the company terminated the interest rate swap agreement and received proceeds from the termination of approximately $7 million.

The unamortized fair value adjustment of the notes associated with terminated interest rate swaps was $14 million and $18 million at September 30, 2011 and 2010, respectively. The fair value adjustment of the notes is classified as long-term debt in the consolidated balance sheet and is amortized to earnings as a reduction of interest expense over the remaining term of the debt.

Leases. The company has various operating leasing arrangements. Future minimum lease payments under these operating leases are $16 million in 2012, $13 million in 2013, $12 million in 2014, $11 million in 2015, $11 million in 2016 and $28 million thereafter.

Qualcomm
2011 Annual Report

Note 2. Fair Value Measurements

Fair value is defined as the exchange price that would be received for an asset or paid to transfer a liability (an exit price) in the principal or most advantageous market for the asset or liability in an orderly transaction between market participants as of the measurement date. Applicable accounting guidance provides an established hierarchy for inputs used in measuring fair value that maximizes the use of observable inputs and minimizes the use of unobservable inputs by requiring that the most observable inputs be used when available. Observable inputs are inputs that market participants would use in valuing the asset or liability and are developed based on market data obtained from sources independent of the Company. Unobservable inputs are inputs that reflect the Company's assumptions about the factors that market participants would use in valuing the asset or liability. There are three levels of inputs that may be used to measure fair value:

- Level 1 includes financial instruments for which quoted market prices for identical instruments are available in active markets.

- Level 2 includes financial instruments for which there are inputs other than quoted prices included within Level 1 that are observable for the instrument.

- Level 3 includes financial instruments for which fair value is derived from valuation techniques in which one or more significant inputs are unobservable, including the Company's own assumptions.

Assets and liabilities are classified based on the lowest level of input that is significant to the fair value measurements. The Company reviews the fair value hierarchy classification on a quarterly basis. Changes in the observability of valuation inputs may result in a reclassification of levels for certain securities within the fair value hierarchy.

The following table presents the Company's fair value hierarchy for assets and liabilities measured at fair value on a recurring basis at September 25, 2011 (in millions):

	Level 1	Level 2	Level 3	Total
Assets				
Cash equivalents	$2,495	$2,129	$—	$4,624
Marketable securities				
U.S. Treasury securities and government-related securities	14	508	—	522
Corporate bonds and notes	—	6,018	—	6,018
Mortgage- and asset-backed securities	—	667	11	678

	Level 1	Level 2	Level 3	Total
Auction rate securities	—	—	124	124
Non-investment-grade debt securities	—	3,656	16	3,672
Common and preferred stock	1,061	728	—	1,789
Equity mutual and exchange-traded funds	845	—	—	845
Debt mutual funds	1,327	476	—	1,803
Total marketable securities	3,247	12,053	151	15,451
Derivative instruments	—	24	—	24
Other investments(1)	152	—	—	152
Total assets measured at fair value	$5,894	$14,206	$151	$20,251
Liabilities				
Derivative instruments	$—	$122	$—	$122
Other liabilities(1)	152	—	7	159
Total liabilities measured at fair value	$152	$122	$7	$281

(1) Level 1 measurements are comprised of the Company's deferred compensation plan liability and related assets, which are invested in mutual funds.

Marketable Securities. With the exception of auction rate securities, the Company obtains pricing information from quoted market prices, pricing vendors or quotes from brokers/dealers. The Company conducts reviews of its primary pricing vendors to determine whether the inputs used in the vendor's pricing processes are deemed to be observable.

The fair value of U.S. Treasury securities and government-related securities, corporate bonds and notes and common and preferred stock are generally determined using standard observable inputs, including reported trades, quoted market prices, matrix pricing, benchmark yields, broker/dealer quotes, issuer spreads, two-sided markets and/or benchmark securities.

The fair value of debt and equity mutual funds is reported as published net asset values. The Company assesses the daily frequency and size of transactions at published net asset values and/or the fund's underlying holdings to determine whether fair value is based on observable or unobservable inputs.

The fair value of highly rated mortgage- and asset-backed securities is derived from the use of matrix pricing (prices for similar securities) or, in some cases cash flow pricing models with observable inputs, such as contractual terms, maturity, credit rating and/or securitization structure, to determine the timing and amount of future cash flows. Certain mortgage- and asset-backed securities, principally those that are rated below AAA, may require use of significant unobservable inputs to estimate fair value, such as default likelihood, recovery rates and prepayment speed.

The fair value of auction rate securities is estimated by the Company using a discounted cash flow model that incorporates transaction details such as contractual terms, maturity and timing and amount of future cash flows, as well as assumptions related to liquidity, default likelihood and recovery, the future state of the auction rate market and credit valuation adjustments of market participants. Though certain of the securities held by the Company are pools of student loans guaranteed by the U.S. government, prepayment speeds and illiquidity discounts are considered significant unobservable inputs. These additional inputs are generally unobservable, and therefore, auction rate securities are included in Level 3.

Derivative Instruments. Derivative instruments include foreign currency option and forward contracts to manage foreign exchange risk for certain foreign currency transactions and certain balances denominated in a foreign currency, and written put options to repurchase shares of the Company's common stock at fixed prices. Derivative instruments are valued using standard calculations/ models that are primarily based on observable inputs, such as foreign currency exchange rates, the Company's stock price, volatilities and interest rates. Therefore, derivative instruments are included in Level 2.

Other Liabilities. Other liabilities included in Level 3 are comprised of put rights held by third parties representing interests in certain of the Company's subsidiaries (Note 7). These put rights are valued with a standard option pricing model using significant unobservable inputs.

Activity between Levels of the Fair Value Hierarchy. There were no significant transfers between Level 1 and Level 2 during fiscal 2011 or 2010. When a determination is made to classify an asset or liability within Level 3, the determination is based upon the significance of the unobservable inputs to the overall fair value measurement. The following table includes the activity for marketable securities and other liabilities classified within Level 3 of the valuation hierarchy (in millions):

	2011			2010	
	Auction Rate Securities	Other Marketable Securities	Other Liabilities	Auction Rate Securities	Other Marketable Securities
Beginning balance of Level 3	$126	$18	$—	$174	$31
Total realized and unrealized gains (losses):					
Included in investment income, net	—	2	(1)	—	5
Included in other comprehensive income	2	(1)	—	7	(1)
Purchases	4	6	—	—	—
Issuances	—	—	8	—	—
Settlements	(8)	(6)	—	(55)	(21)

	2011			2010	
	Auction Rate Securities	Other Marketable Securities	Other Liabilities	Auction Rate Securities	Other Marketable Securities
Transfers into Level 3	—	8	—	—	4
Ending balance of Level 3	$124	$27	$7	$126	$18

The Company recognizes transfers into and out of levels within the fair value hierarchy at the end of the fiscal month in which the actual event or change in circumstances that caused the transfer occurs. Transfers into Level 3 in fiscal 2011 and 2010 primarily consisted of debt securities with significant inputs that became unobservable as a result of an increased likelihood of a shortfall in contractual cash flows or a significant downgrade in credit ratings.

Nonrecurring Fair Value Measurements. The Company measures certain assets at fair value on a nonrecurring basis. These assets include cost and equity method investments when they are deemed to be other-than-temporarily impaired, assets acquired and liabilities assumed in an acquisition or in a nonmonetary exchange, and property, plant and equipment and intangible assets that are written down to fair value when they are held for sale or determined to be impaired. During fiscal 2011, goodwill with a carrying amount of $154 million was written down to its implied fair value of $40 million, resulting in an impairment charge of $114 million (Note 4). The implied fair value was based on significant unobservable inputs, and as a result, the fair value measurement was classified as Level 3. During fiscal 2011, 2010 and 2009, the Company did not have any other significant assets or liabilities that were measured at fair value on a nonrecurring basis in periods subsequent to initial recognition.

Arvinmeritor
2010 Annual Report

11. Net Property and Impairment of Long-Lived Assets

Property is stated at cost. Depreciation of property is based on estimated useful lives, generally using the straight-line method. Estimated useful lives for buildings and improvements range from 10 to 50 years, and estimated useful lives for machinery and equipment range from 3 to 20 years. Significant improvements are capitalized and disposed or replaced property is written off. Maintenance and repairs are charged to expense in the period they are incurred. Company-owned tooling is classified as property and depreciated over the shorter of its expected life or the life of the related vehicle platform, generally not to exceed three years.

In accordance with the FASB guidance on property, plant and equipment, the company reviews the carrying value of long-lived assets, excluding goodwill, to be held and used, for impairment whenever events or changes in circumstances indicate a possible impairment. An impairment loss is recognized when a long-lived asset's carrying value is not recoverable and exceeds estimated fair value.

At December 31, 2008, management determined certain impairment reviews were required due to declines in overall economic conditions including tightening credit markets, stock market declines and significant reductions in current and forecasted production volumes for light and commercial vehicles. As a result, the company recognized pre-tax, non-cash impairment charges of $209 million in the first quarter of fiscal year 2009, primarily related to the LVS businesses, which are presented in discontinued operations and accordingly, $195 million is included in loss from discontinued operations in the consolidated statement of operations (see Note 3). The remaining impairment charges were for specific long-lived assets in the company's Commercial Truck segment ($8 million) and a certain corporate long-lived assets ($6 million). The charges recorded in the company's Commercial Truck segment were for specific land and buildings and other assets (primarily machinery and equipment) of $5 million and $3 million, respectively. The estimated fair value of long-lived assets was calculated based on probability weighted cash flows taking into account current expectations for asset utilization and life expectancy. In addition, liquidation values were considered where appropriate, as well as indicated values from divestiture activities.

During fiscal year 2010, the company recognized $2 million of asset impairment charges for specific European assets in the company's Aftermarket & Trailer segment.

Net property at September 30, 2010 and 2009 is summarized as follows:

(in millions)	September 30, 2010	2009
Property at cost:		
Land and land improvements	$ 42	$ 46
Buildings	267	254
Machinery and equipment	909	913
Company-owned tooling	150	163
Construction in progress	40	38
Total	1,408	1,414
Less accumulated depreciation	(1,019)	(969)
Net property	$ 389	$ 445

12. Other Assets

Other assets are summarized as follows:

(in millions)	September 30, 2010	2009
Non-current deferred income tax assets (see Note 22)	$ 23	$ 27
Investments in non-consolidated joint ventures (see Note 13)	164	125
Assets for uncertain tax positions (see Note 22)	4	11
Prepaid pension costs (see Note 21)	8	9

(in millions)	September 30,	
	2010	2009
Unamortized debt issuance costs (see Note 16)	32	24
Capitalized software costs, net	21	21
Asbestos-related recoveries (see Note 23)	55	47
Note receivable due from EMCON, net of discount	–	16
Other	30	26
Other assets	$ 337	$ 306

In the second quarter of fiscal year 2010, the company paid approximately $16 million of costs associated with the issuance of debt securities and the amendment and extension of its revolving credit facility (see Note 16). These costs were recognized as a long-term asset and are being amortized as interest expense over the term of the underlying debt instruments.

The note receivable from EMCON was recorded net of a discount to reflect the difference between the stated rate per the agreement of 4 percent and the effective interest rate of approximately 9 percent. The discount was being amortized over the term of the note as interest income. EMCON underwent a change in control during the company's second quarter of fiscal year 2010, and therefore, the note became immediately payable. The company received $22 million during the second quarter of fiscal year 2010, which represented the full amount of the note plus accrued interest. Upon receipt of the full outstanding amount of the note, the company recognized the remaining unamortized discount of $6 million to current period income. This amount is included in interest expense, net in the accompanying consolidated statement of operations.

In accordance with FASB ASC Topic 350-40, costs relating to internally developed or purchased software in the preliminary project stage and the post-implementation stage are expensed as incurred. Costs in the application development stage that meet the criteria for capitalization are capitalized and amortized using the straight-line basis over the estimated economic useful life of the software.

Walt Disney
2010 Annual Report

16. Fair Value Measurement

Fair value is defined as the amount that would be received for selling an asset or paid to transfer a liability in an orderly transaction between market participants and requires that assets and liabilities carried at fair value be classified and disclosed in the following three categories:

- Level 1—Quoted prices for identical instruments in active markets

- Level 2—Quoted prices for similar instruments in active markets; quoted prices for identical or similar instruments in markets that are not active; and model-derived valuations in which all significant inputs and significant value drivers are observable in active markets

- Level 3—Valuations derived from valuation techniques in which one or more significant inputs or significant value drivers are unobservable

The Company's assets and liabilities measured at fair value on a recurring basis are summarized in the following table by the type of inputs applicable to the fair value measurements.

| Description | Fair Value Measurements at October 2, 2010 | | | |
	Level 1	Level 2	Level 3	Total
Assets				
Investments	$ 42	$ 42	$ 2	$ 86
Derivatives[1]				
Interest rate	–	231	–	231
Foreign exchange	–	404	–	404
Residual Interests	–	–	54	54
Liabilities				
Derivatives[1]				
Interest rate	–	(22)	–	(22)
Foreign exchange	–	(490)	–	(490)
Other derivatives	–	–	–	–
Other	–	–	(1)	(1)
Total	$ 42	$ 165	$ 55	$ 262

[1] The Company has a master netting arrangements by counterparty with respect to certain derivative contracts. Contracts in a liability position totaling $206 million have been netted against contracts in an asset position in the Consolidated Balance Sheet.

The fair value of Level 2 investments is primarily determined by reference to market prices based on recent trading activity and other relevant information including pricing for similar securities as determined by third-party pricing services.

The fair values of Level 2 derivatives, which consist of interest rate and foreign currency hedges, are primarily determined based on the present value of future cash flows using internal models that use observable inputs such as interest rates, yield curves and foreign currency exchange rates. Counterparty credit risk, which is mitigated by master netting agreements and collateral posting arrangements with certain counterparties, did not have a material impact on derivative fair value estimates.

Level 3 residual interests consist of our residual interests in securitized vacation ownership mortgage receivables and are valued using a discounted cash flow model that considers estimated interest rates, discount rates, prepayment, and defaults. There were no material changes in the residual interests in fiscal 2010.

The Company also has assets and liabilities that are required to be recorded at fair value on a non-recurring basis when certain circumstances occur. During fiscal 2010, the Company recorded impairment charges of $249 million on film productions which are reported in "Costs and expenses" in the Consolidated

Statement of Income. The film impairment charges compared our estimated fair value using discounted cash flows, which is a level 3 input, to the unamortized cost of the films that had aggregate carrying values of $591 million prior to the impairment.

Fair Value of Financial Instruments

In addition to the financial instruments listed above, the Company's financial instruments also include cash, cash equivalents, receivables, accounts payable and borrowings.

The fair values of cash and cash equivalents, receivables, available-for-sale investments, derivative contracts and accounts payable approximated the carrying values. The estimated year end fair values of the Company's total borrowings (current and noncurrent) subject to fair value disclosures, determined based on broker quotes or quoted market prices or interest rates for the same or similar instruments are $13.7 billion and $12.6 billion at October 2, 2010 and October 3, 2009, respectively.

Transfers of Financial Assets

Through December 4, 2008, the Company sold mortgage receivables arising from the sales of its vacation ownership units under a facility that expired on December 4, 2008 and was not renewed. The Company sold $17 million and $147 million of mortgage receivables during the years ended October 3, 2009, and September 27, 2008, respectively. These sales of mortgage receivables resulted in gains on securitized sales of vacation ownership interests totaled $4 million and $32 million for fiscal 2009 and fiscal 2008, respectively.

The Company continues to service the sold receivables and has a residual interest in those receivables. As of October 2, 2010, the outstanding principal amount for sold mortgage receivables was $309 million and the carrying value of the Company's residual interest, which is recorded in other long-term assets, was $54 million.

The Company repurchases defaulted mortgage receivables at their outstanding balance. The Company did not make material repurchases in the years ended October 2, 2010 or October 3, 2009. The Company generally has been able to sell the repurchased vacation ownership units for amounts that exceed the amounts at which they were repurchased.

The Company also provides credit support for up to 70% of the outstanding balance of the sold mortgage receivables which the mortgage receivable acquirer may draw on in the event of losses under the facility. The Company maintains a reserve for estimated credit losses related to these receivables.

Credit Concentrations

The Company continually monitors its positions with, and the credit quality of, the financial institutions that are counterparties to its financial instruments and does not anticipate nonperformance by the counterparties. In 2008, Lehman Brothers Commercial Corporation defaulted on a $91 million trade settlement. The Company is pursuing collection of this amount, but has fully reserved the amount.

The Company does not expect that it would realize a material loss, based on the fair value of its derivative financial instruments as of October 2, 2010, in the event of nonperformance by any single derivative counterparty. The Company enters into transactions only with derivative counterparties that have a credit rating of A- or better. The Company's current policy regarding agreements with derivative counterparties is generally to require collateral in the event credit ratings fall below A- or in the event aggregate exposures exceed limits as defined by contract. In addition, the Company limits the amount of investment credit exposure with any one institution.

The Company does not have material cash and cash equivalent balances with financial institutions that have a credit rating of less than A-. As of October 2, 2010, the Company's balances that exceeded 10% of cash and cash equivalents with individual financial institutions were 30% compared to 38% as of October 3, 2009.

The Company's trade receivables and financial investments do not represent a significant concentration of credit risk at October 2, 2010 due to the wide variety of customers and markets into which the Company's products are sold, their dispersion across geographic areas, and the diversification of the Company's portfolio among issuers.

Alliance One International
2009 Annual Report

Note E—Goodwill and Other Intangibles

In accordance with SFAS No. 142, "Goodwill and Other Intangible Assets," the Company tests the carrying amount of goodwill annually as of the first day of the last quarter of the fiscal year and whenever events or circumstances indicate that impairment may have occurred. The Company evaluated its goodwill for impairment during fiscal 2009, 2008 and 2007 and determined that no impairment was required.

The carrying value of other intangible assets as of March 31, 2009 represents customer relationship, production and supply contracts and internally developed software. These intangible assets were determined by management to meet the criterion for recognition apart from goodwill and have finite lives. The Company uses judgment in assessing whether the carrying amount of its intangible assets is not expected to be recoverable over their estimated remaining useful lives. Amortization expense associated with these intangible assets was $3,412, $2,048 and $2,833 for the years ended March 31, 2009, 2008 and 2007, respectively.

The Company began implementing a new ERP system in fiscal 2008 and capitalized certain costs into intangible assets within the consolidated balance sheet in accordance with generally accepted accounting principles. As of March 31, 2009, the Company had incurred $12,025 of capitalizable costs associated with the ERP implementation and $313 of capitalizable costs related to other internally developed software projects. The ERP system was placed in service in the United States, Brazil and the United Kingdom during fiscal 2009. Amortization of the final accumulated costs of these locations began in fiscal 2009 over a five-year useful life.

Goodwill and Intangible Asset Rollforward:

	Unamortizable Goodwill	Amortizable Intangibles			
	Other Regions Segment	Customer Relationship Intangible	Production and Supply Contract Intangibles	Internally Developed Software Intangible	Total
Weighted average remaining useful life in years as of March 31, 2009	–	16	7	5	
March 31, 2007 balance: Gross carrying amount	$4,186	$33,700	$10,815	$ –	$ 48,701
Accumulated amortization	–	(3,159)	(10,433)	–	(13,592)
Net balance	4,186	30,541	382	–	35,109
Additions	–	–	–	6,330	6,330
Amortization expense and purchase accounting tax adjustments	(1,392)	(1,685)	(363)	–	(3,440)
March 31, 2008 balance	$2,794	$28,856	$19	$ 6,330	$ 37,999
Additions	–	–	7,844	7,446	15,290
Amortization expense	–	(1,685)	(289)	(1,438)	(3,412)
March 31, 2009 balance	$2,794	$27,171	$ 7,574	$12,338	$ 49,877

Estimated Intangible Asset Amortization Expense:

For Fiscal Years Ended	Customer Relationship Intangible	Production And Supply Contract Intangible	Internally Developed Software Intangible*	Total
2010	$ 1,685	$1,010	$ 2,699	$ 5,394
2011	1,685	1,087	2,699	5,471
2012	1,685	1,165	2,699	5,549
2013	1,685	1,243	2,699	5,627

For Fiscal Years Ended	Customer Relationship Intangible	Production And Supply Contract Intangible	Internally Developed Software Intangible*	Total
2014	1,685	1,243	1,353	4,281
Later	18,746	1,826	189	20,761
	$27,171	$7,574	$12,338	$47,083

* Estimated amortization expense for the internally developed software is based on costs accumulated as of March 31, 2009. These estimates will change as new costs are incurred and until the software is placed into service in all locations.

KB Home
2009 Annual Report

Note 10. Goodwill

The Company had a goodwill balance of $68.0 million at November 30, 2007, which consisted of $24.6 million and $43.4 million related to its Central and Southeast homebuilding reporting segments, respectively.

In accordance with ASC 350, the Company tested goodwill for potential impairment annually as of November 30 and between annual tests if an event occurred or circumstances changed that would more likely than not reduce the fair value of a reporting unit below its carrying amount. During 2008 and 2007, the Company determined that it was necessary to evaluate goodwill for impairment between annual tests due to deteriorating conditions in certain housing markets and the significant inventory impairments the Company identified and recognized in those years in accordance with ASC 360.

Based on the results of its impairment evaluation performed in the second quarter of 2008, the Company recorded an impairment charge of $24.6 million in that quarter related to its Central reporting segment, where it determined all of the goodwill previously recorded was impaired. The annual goodwill impairment test performed by the Company as of November 30, 2008 resulted in an impairment charge of $43.4 million in the fourth quarter of 2008 related to its Southeast reporting segment, where it determined all of the goodwill previously recorded was impaired. The goodwill impairment charges in 2008 were recorded at the Company's corporate level because all goodwill was carried at that level. As a result of those impairment charges, the Company had no remaining goodwill at November 30, 2008 or November 30, 2009.

The process of evaluating goodwill for impairment involved the determination of the fair value of the Company's reporting units. Inherent in such fair value determinations were certain judgments and estimates relating to future cash flows, including the Company's interpretation of current economic indicators and market valuations, and assumptions about the Company's strategic plans with regard to its operations. Due to the uncertainties associated with such estimates, actual results could differ from such estimates.

In performing its impairment analysis, the Company developed a range of fair values for its homebuilding and financial services reporting units using a discounted cash flow methodology and a market multiple methodology. For the financial services reporting unit, the Company also used a comparable transaction methodology.

The discounted cash flow methodology established fair value by estimating the present value of the projected future cash flows to be generated from the reporting unit. The discount rate applied to the projected future cash flows to arrive at the present value was intended to reflect all risks of ownership and the associated risks of realizing the stream of projected future cash flows. The discounted cash flow methodology used the Company's projections of financial performance for a five-year period. The most significant assumptions used in the discounted cash flow methodology were the discount rate, the terminal value and expected future revenues, gross margins and operating margins, which varied among reporting units.

The market multiple methodology established fair value by comparing the Company to other publicly traded companies that were similar to it from an operational and economic standpoint. The market multiple methodology compared the Company to those companies on the basis of risk characteristics in order to determine its risk profile relative to those companies as a group. This analysis generally focused on quantitative considerations, which included financial performance and other quantifiable data, and qualitative considerations, which included any factors which were expected to impact future financial performance. The most significant assumptions affecting the market multiple methodology were the market multiples and control premium. The market multiples the Company used were: (a) price to net book value and (b) enterprise value to revenue (for each of the homebuilding reporting units). A control premium represents the value an investor would pay above minority interest transaction prices in order to obtain a controlling interest in the respective company. The comparable transaction methodology established fair value similar to the market multiple methodology, and utilized recent transactions within the industry as the market multiple. However, no control premium was applied when using the comparable transaction methodology because those transactions represented control transactions.

Microsoft
2009 Annual Report

Note 10. Goodwill

Changes in the carrying amount of goodwill for fiscal years 2009 and 2008 by segment were as follows:

(In millions)	Balance as of June 30, 2007	Acquisitions	Purchase Accounting Adjustments and Other	Balance as of June 30, 2008	Acquisitions	Purchase Accounting Adjustments and Other	Balance as of June 30, 2009
Client	$77	$77	$(1)	$153	$1	$(77)	$77
Server and Tools	580	90	68	738	233	67	1,038

(In millions)	Balance as of June 30, 2007	Acquisitions	Purchase Accounting Adjustments and Other	Balance as of June 30, 2008	Acquisitions	Purchase Accounting Adjustments and Other	Balance as of June 30, 2009
Online Services Business	552	5,775	(53)	6,274	447	(64)	6,657
Microsoft Business Division	3,132	1,073	(14)	4,191	–	(264)	3,927
Entertainment and Devices Division	419	354	(21)	752	58	(6)	804
Total	$4,760	$7,369	$(21)	$12,108	$739	$(344)	$12,503

None of the amounts recorded as goodwill are expected to be deductible for tax purposes. The purchase price allocations for all of the acquisitions are preliminary for up to 12 months after the acquisition date and are subject to revision as more detailed analyses are completed and additional information about fair value of the assets and liabilities become available. Any change in the fair value of the net assets of the acquired company within this timeframe will change the amount of the purchase price allocable to goodwill. Changes in goodwill amounts resulting from foreign currency translations are included in "purchase accounting adjustments and other" in the above table.

We test goodwill for impairment annually at the reporting unit level using a fair value approach, in accordance with the provisions of SFAS No. 142, Goodwill and Other Intangible Assets. During the second quarter of fiscal year 2009, we changed the date of our annual impairment test from July 1 to May 1. The change was made to more closely align the impairment testing date with our long-range planning and forecasting process. We believe the change in our annual impairment testing date did not delay, accelerate, or avoid an impairment charge. We have determined that this change in accounting principle is preferable under the circumstances and does not result in adjustments to our financial statements when applied retrospectively. During fiscal year 2009, the annual impairment test was performed as of July 1, 2008 and was performed again as of May 1, 2009.

Omnova Solutions
2009 Annual Report

Note K—Property, Plant and Equipment, Net

	November 30,	
	2009	2008
	(Dollars in millions)	
Land	$8.0	$ 7.8
Building and improvements	103.8	101.0

| | November 30, | |
	2009	2008
Machinery and equipment	402.7	395.6
Construction in progress	6.8	9.9
	521.3	514.3
Accumulated depreciation	(379.4)	(360.6)
Property, Plant and Equipment, Net	$141.9	$153.7

Depreciation expense was $21.8 million, $22.0 million and $18.6 million in 2009, 2008 and 2007, respectively. Included in depreciation and amortization expense is $17.6 million, $17.7 million and $14.7 million in 2009, 2008 and 2007, respectively, related to depreciation of manufacturing facilities and equipment.

As of November 30, 2009 and 2008, the Company had $3.0 million and $4.6 million, respectively, of unamortized software costs included in machinery and equipment, primarily related to an Enterprise Resource Program (ERP) system, which the Company began implementing during 2005. Amortization expense of software costs was $1.7 million, $1.5 million and $1.1 million in 2009, 2008 and 2007, respectively. The Company is amortizing these costs over five years.

During 2009, the Company recorded asset impairment charges of $1.1 million related to assets that will no longer be utilized by the Company due to moving certain production to other facilities.

Marathon Oil
2008 Annual Report

17. Fair Value Measurements

As defined in SFAS No. 157, fair value is the price that would be received to sell an asset or paid to transfer a liability in an orderly transaction between market participants at the measurement date. SFAS No. 157 describes three approaches to measuring the fair value of assets and liabilities: the market approach, the income approach and the cost approach, each of which includes multiple valuation techniques. The market approach uses prices and other relevant information generated by market transactions involving identical or comparable assets or liabilities. The income approach uses valuation techniques to measure fair value by converting future amounts, such as cash flows or earnings, into a single present value amount using current market expectations about those future amounts. The cost approach is based on the amount that would currently be required to replace the service capacity of an asset. This is often referred to as current replacement cost. The cost approach assumes that the fair value would not exceed what it would cost a market participant to acquire or construct a substitute asset of comparable utility, adjusted for obsolescence.

SFAS No. 157 does not prescribe which valuation technique should be used when measuring fair value and does not prioritize among the techniques. SFAS No. 157 establishes a fair value hierarchy that prioritizes the inputs used in applying the various valuation techniques. Inputs broadly refer to the assumptions that market participants use to make pricing decisions, including assumptions about risk. Level 1 inputs are given the highest priority in the fair value hierarchy while Level 3 inputs are given the lowest priority. The three levels of the fair value hierarchy are as follows.

☐ Level 1—Observable inputs that reflect unadjusted quoted prices for identical assets or liabilities in active markets as of the reporting date. Active markets are those in which transactions for the asset or liability occur in sufficient frequency and volume to provide pricing information on an ongoing basis.

☐ Level 2—Observable market-based inputs or unobservable inputs that are corroborated by market data. These are inputs other than quoted prices in active markets included in Level 1, which are either directly or indirectly observable as of the reporting date.

☐ Level 3—Unobservable inputs that are not corroborated by market data and may be used with internally developed methodologies that result in management's best estimate of fair value.

We use a market or income approach for recurring fair value measurements and endeavor to use the best information available. Accordingly, valuation techniques that maximize the use of observable inputs are favored. Financial assets and liabilities are classified in their entirety based on the lowest priority level of input that is significant to the fair value measurement. The assessment of the significance of a particular input to the fair value measurement requires judgment and may affect the placement of assets and liabilities within the levels of the fair value hierarchy.

The following table presents net financial assets and liabilities accounted for at fair value on a recurring basis as of December 31, 2008:

(In millions)	Level 1	Level 2	Level 3	Level 4
Derivative instruments:				
Commodity	$107	$ 6	$(55)	$58
Interest rate	–	–	29	29
Foreign currency	–	(75)	–	(75)
Total derivative instruments	107	(69)	(26)	12
Other assets	2	–	–	2
Total at fair value	$109	$(69)	$(26)	$14

Deposits of $121 million in broker accounts covered by master netting agreements are included in fair values of commodity derivatives. Derivatives in Level 1 are exchange-traded contracts for crude oil, natural gas, refined products and ethanol measured at fair value with a market approach using the close-of-day settlement prices for the market. Derivatives in Level 2 are measured at fair value with a market approach using broker quotes or third-party pricing services, which have been corroborated with data from active markets. Level 3 derivatives are measured at fair value using either a market or income approach.

Generally at least one input is unobservable, such as the use of an internally generated model or an external data source.

Commodity derivatives in Level 3 include a $72 million liability related to two U.K. natural gas sales contracts that are accounted for as derivative instruments and a $52 million asset for crude oil options related to sales of Canadian synthetic crude oil. The fair value of the U.K. natural gas contracts is measured with an income approach by applying the difference between the contract price and the U.K. forward natural gas strip price to the expected sales volumes for the shorter of the remaining contract term or 18 months. These contracts originated in the early 1990s and expire in September 2009. The contract prices are reset annually in October based on the previous twelve-month changes in a basket of energy and other indices. Consequently, the prices under these contracts do not track forward natural gas prices. The crude oil options, which expire December 2009, are measured at fair value using a Black-Scholes option pricing model, an income approach that utilizes prices from an active market and market volatility calculated by a third-party service.

The interest rate derivatives are measured at fair value using quotes from our counterparties which are compared to internal calculations made using rates posted by a pricing service. Because we are unable to independently verify those rates directly to the market, such inputs are considered Level 3.

The following is a reconciliation of the net beginning and ending balances recorded for derivative instruments classified as Level 3 in the fair value hierarchy.

(In millions)	December 31, 2008
Beginning balance	
Total realized and unrealized losses:	$(355)
Included in net income	210
Included in other comprehensive income	1
Purchases, sales, issuances and settlements, net	118
Ending balance	$ (26)

The change in unrealized losses included in net income related to instruments held at December 31, 2008, was an addition of $299 million for 2008. Amounts reported in net income are classified as sales and other operating revenues or cost of revenues for commodity derivative instruments, as net interest and other financing income for interest rate derivative instruments and as cost of revenues for foreign currency derivatives, except those designated as hedges of future capital expenditures. Amounts related to foreign currency derivatives designated as hedges of future capital expenditures accumulate in other comprehensive income and are amortized to depletion, depreciation and amortization over the life of the capital asset.

The following table summarizes financial instruments, excluding the derivative financial instruments reported above, by individual balance sheet line item at December 31, 2008 and 2007.

| | December 31, | | | |
| | 2008 | | 2007 | |
(In millions)	Fair Value	Carrying Amount	Fair Value	Carrying Amount
Financial assets				
Receivables from United States Steel, including current portion	$ 438	$ 492	$ 500	$ 507
Other noncurrent assets[a]	286	113	1,140	899
Total financial assets	724	605	1,640	1,406
Financial liabilities				
Long-term debt, including current portion[b]	5,683	6,880	7,176	6,947
Total financial liabilities	$5,683	$6,880	$7,176	$6,947

[a] Includes restricted cash, cost method investments and miscellaneous long-term receivables or deposits.
[b] Excludes capital leases.

Our current assets and liabilities accounts contain financial instruments, the most significant of which are trade accounts receivables and payables. We believe the carrying values of our current assets and liabilities approximate fair value, with the exception of the current portion of receivables from United States Steel and the current portion of our long-term debt which is reported above. Our fair value assessment incorporates a variety of considerations, including (1) the short-term duration of the instruments (e.g., less than 1 percent of our trade receivables and payables are outstanding for greater than 90 days), (2) our investment-grade credit rating, and (3) our historical incurrence of and expected future insignificance of bad debt expense, which includes an evaluation of counterparty credit risk.

The fair value of the receivables from United States Steel is measured using an income approach that discounts the future expected payments over the remaining term of the obligations. Because this asset is not publicly-traded and not easily transferable, a hypothetical market based upon United States Steel's borrowing rate curve is assumed and the majority of inputs to the calculation are Level 3. The industrial revenue bonds are to be redeemed on or before the tenth anniversary of the USX Separation per the Financial Matters Agreement.

The majority of our restricted cash represent cash accounts that earn interest; therefore, the balance approximates fair value. Other financial assets included in our other noncurrent assets line include cost method investments and miscellaneous long-term receivables or deposits. Fair value for the cost method investments is measured using an income approach. Estimated future cash flows, obtained from our internal forecasts or forecasts from the partially owned companies, are discounted to obtain the fair value.

Over 90 percent of our long-term debt instruments are publicly-traded. A market approach, based upon quotes from major financial institutions is used to measure the fair value of such debt. Because these quotes cannot be independently verified to the market they are considered Level 3 inputs. The fair value of our debt that is not publicly-traded is measured using an income approach. The future debt service payments are discounted using the rate at which we currently expect to borrow. All inputs to this calculation are Level 3.

Long-term receivables and deposits are also measured using an income approach. The expected timing of payments are scheduled and then discounted using a rate deemed appropriate.

General Electric
2008 Annual Report

Note 17. Assets and Liabilities of Businesses Held for Sale

On January 7, 2009, we exchanged our GE Money businesses in Austria and Finland, the credit card and auto businesses in the U.K., and the credit card business in Ireland for a 100% ownership interest in Interbanca S.p.A., a leading Italian corporate bank. Assets and liabilities of $7,887 million and $636 million, respectively, were classified as held for sale at December 31, 2008; we recognized a $184 million loss, net of tax, related to the classification of the assets held for sale at the lower of carrying amount or estimated fair value less costs to sell.

On December 24, 2008, we committed to sell a portion of our Australian residential mortgage business, including certain underlying mortgage receivables, and expect to complete this sale during the first quarter of 2009. Assets of $2,669 million were classified as held for sale at December 31, 2008 (liabilities were insignificant); we recognized a $38 million loss, net of tax, related to the classifications of the assets held for sale at the lower of carrying amount or estimated fair value less costs to sell.

Summarized financial information is shown below.

December 31 (In millions)	2008
ASSETS	
Cash and equivalents	$ 35
Financing receivables—net	9,915
Intangible assets—net	394
Other	212
Assets of businesses held for sale	$10,556
LIABILITIES	
Liabilities of businesses held for sale	$ 636

U.S. Steel
2008 Annual Report

5. Assets Held for Sale

On September 26, 2007, U.S. Steel and Canadian National Railway Company (CN) announced that they had entered into an agreement under which CN will acquire the majority of the operating assets of Elgin, Joliet and Eastern Railway Company (EJ&E) for $300 million. Under the agreement, U.S. Steel will retain railroad assets, equipment, and employees that support Gary Works in northwest Indiana. The transaction was approved by the U.S. Surface Transportation Board on December 24, 2008 and was completed on January 31, 2009. As of December 31, 2008 and 2007, the assets of EJ&E that were to be sold, consisting primarily of property, plant and equipment, were classified as held for sale in accordance with FAS No. 144, "Accounting for Impairment or Disposal of Long-Lived Assets" (FAS 144).

Before U.S. Steel's October 31, 2007 acquisition of USSC, Cleveland Cliffs Inc. (Cliffs), now Cliffs Natural Resources Inc., and Stelco received and accepted a non-binding offer dated June 6, 2007 from Consolidated Thompson Iron Mines Limited (Consolidated) to purchase USSC's 44.6 percent interest and Cliffs' 26.8 percent interest in Wabush for a purchase price of $64.3 million plus two year warrants to purchase three million shares of Consolidated common stock. On August 30, 2007, ArcelorMittal Dofasco, Inc (Dofasco) purported to exercise a right of first refusal under the Participants Agreement dated as of January 1, 1967 governing Wabush. At December 31, 2007, USSC's investment in Wabush was classified as held for sale in accordance with FAS 144. On March 4, 2008, following several months of unsuccessful negotiations over many of the major terms of the purchase and sale, USSC and Cliffs informed Dofasco that they were withdrawing from further negotiations. At December 31, 2008, USSC's investment in Wabush was no longer classified as held for sale (see Note 27).

In December 2008, U.S. Steel decided to exit the drawn-over-mandrel (DOM) tubular products business. A pre-tax charge of $28 million was taken in the fourth quarter 2008 associated with this action principally to write down to fair value equipment associated with the DOM business that is now classified as held for sale.

Textron
2008 Annual Report

Note 10. Fair Values of Assets and Liabilities

In September 2006, the FASB issued SFAS No. 157, "Fair Value Measurements," effective for financial statements issued for fiscal years beginning after November 15, 2007. SFAS No. 157 replaces multiple existing definitions of fair value with a single definition, establishes a consistent framework for measuring fair value and expands financial statement disclosures regarding fair value measurements. This Statement applies only to fair value measurements that already are required or permitted by other accounting standards and does not require any new fair value measurements. In February 2008, the FASB delayed until the first quarter of 2009 the effective date of SFAS No. 157 for nonfinancial assets and liabilities that are not recognized or disclosed at fair value in the financial statements on a recurring basis.

The adoption of SFAS No. 157 for our financial assets and liabilities in the first quarter of 2008 did not have a material impact on our financial position or results of operations. Our nonfinancial assets and liabilities that meet the deferral criteria include goodwill, intangible assets, property, plant and equipment, and other long-term investments, which primarily represent collateral that is received by the Finance group in satisfaction of troubled loans. We do not expect that the adoption of SFAS No. 157 for these nonfinancial assets and liabilities will have a material impact on our financial position or results of operations.

In accordance with the provisions of SFAS No. 157, we measure fair value at the price that would be received to sell an asset or paid to transfer a liability in an orderly transaction between market participants at the measurement date. The Statement prioritizes the assumptions that market participants would use in pricing the asset or liability (the "inputs") into a three-tier fair value hierarchy. This fair value hierarchy gives the highest priority (Level 1) to quoted prices in active markets for identical assets or liabilities and the lowest priority (Level 3) to unobservable inputs in which little or no market data exist, requiring companies to develop their own assumptions. Observable inputs that do not meet the criteria of Level 1, and include quoted prices for similar assets or liabilities in active markets or quoted prices for identical assets and liabilities in markets that are not active, are categorized as Level 2. Level 3 inputs are those that reflect our estimates about the assumptions market participants would use in pricing the asset or liability, based on the best information available in the circumstances. Valuation techniques for assets and liabilities measured using Level 3 inputs may include methodologies such as the market approach, the income approach or the cost approach and may use unobservable inputs such as projections, estimates and management's interpretation of current market data. These unobservable inputs are utilized only to the extent that observable inputs are not available or cost-effective to obtain.

Assets and Liabilities Recorded at Fair Value on a Recurring Basis

The table below presents the assets and liabilities measured at fair value on a recurring basis at January 3, 2009 categorized by the level of inputs used in the valuation of each asset and liability:

(In millions)	Total	Quoted Prices in Active Markets for Identical Assets or Liabilities (Level 1)	Significant Other Observable Inputs (Level 2)	Significant Unobservable Inputs (Level 3)
Assets				
Manufacturing group				
Foreign currency exchange contracts	$ 2	$ –	$ 2	$ –
Total Manufacturing group	2	–	2	–
Finance group				
Derivative financial instruments, net	112	–	112	–

(In millions)	Total	Quoted Prices in Active Markets for Identical Assets or Liabilities (Level 1)	Significant Other Observable Inputs (Level 2)	Significant Unobservable Inputs (Level 3)
Interest-only securities	12	–	–	12
Total Finance group	124	–	112	12
Total assets	$126	$ –	$114	12
Liabilities				
Manufacturing group				
Cash settlement forward contract	$ 98	$98	$ –	$ –
Foreign currency exchange contracts	84	–	84	–
Total Manufacturing group	182	98	84	–
Total liabilities	$182	$98	$ 84	$ –

Valuation Techniques

Manufacturing Group

Foreign currency exchange contracts are measured at fair value using the market method valuation technique. The inputs to this technique utilize current foreign currency exchange forward market rates published by third-party leading financial news and data providers. This is observable data that represent the rates that the financial institution uses for contracts entered into at that date; however, they are not based on actual transactions so they are classified as Level 2. We record changes in the fair value of these contracts, to the extent they are effective as hedges, in other comprehensive income. If a contract does not qualify for hedge accounting or is designated as a fair value hedge, changes in the fair value of the contract are recorded in income.

Cash settlement forward contracts on our common stock are used to manage the expense related to stock-based compensation awards. The use of these forward contracts modifies compensation expense exposure to changes in the stock price with the intent of reducing potential variability. These contracts are measured at fair value using the market method valuation technique. Since the input to this technique is based on the quoted price of our common stock at the measurement date, it is classified as Level 1. Gains or losses on these instruments are recorded as an adjustment to compensation expense.

Finance Group

Interest-only securities are generally retained upon the sale of finance receivables to qualified special purpose trusts. These interest-only securities are initially recorded at the allocated carrying value, which is determined based on the relative fair values of the finance receivables sold and the interests retained. We estimate fair value upon the initial recognition of the retained interest based on the present value of expected future cash flows using our best estimates of key assumptions—credit losses, prepayment speeds, forward interest rate yield curves and discount rates commensurate with the risks involved. These inputs are classified as Level 3 since they reflect our own assumptions about the assumptions market participants would use in pricing these assets based on the best information available in the circumstances as there is no active market for these assets. We review the fair values of the interest-only securities quarterly using a discounted cash flow model and updated assumptions and compare such amounts with the carrying value. When a change in fair value is deemed temporary, we record a corresponding credit or charge to other comprehensive income for any unrealized gains or losses. If a decline in the fair value is determined to be other than temporary, we record a corresponding charge to income. During 2008, we recognized impairment charges of $15 million and $6 million related to the Distribution Finance revolving securitization and the Aviation Finance securitization trust, respectively, due to changes in our assumptions.

The Finance group's derivative contracts are not exchange-traded. Derivative financial instruments are measured at fair value utilizing widely accepted, third-party developed valuation models. The actual terms of each individual contract are entered into a valuation model, along with interest rate and foreign exchange rate data, which is based on readily observable market data published by third-party leading financial news and data providers. Credit risk is factored into the fair value of derivative assets and liabilities based on the differential between both our credit default swap spread for liabilities and the counterparty's credit default swap spread for assets as compared to a standard AA-rated counterparty; however, this had no significant impact on the valuation as of January 3, 2009 as most of our counterparties are AA-rated and the vast majority of our derivative instruments are in an asset position.

Changes in Fair Value for Unobservable Inputs

The table below presents the change in fair value measurements for our interest-only strips for which we used significant unobservable inputs (Level 3) during 2008:

(In millions)	
Balance, beginning of year	$ 43
Net gains for the year:	
Increase in securitization gains on sale of finance receivables	66
Change in value recognized in finance revenues	2
Reclassification to finance receivables held for investment	(19)
Impairment charges	(21)
Collections	(59)
Balance, end of year	$ 12

Assets Recorded at Fair Value on a Nonrecurring Basis

The table below presents the assets measured at fair value on a nonrecurring basis for the Finance group at January 3, 2009 categorized by the level of inputs used in the valuation of each asset:

(In millions)	Total	Quoted Prices in Active Markets for Identical Assets (Level 1)	Significant Other Observable Inputs (Level 2)	Significant Unobservable Inputs (Level 3)
Finance receivables held for sale	$1,658	$ –	$ –	$1,658
Impaired loans	191	–	–	191
Total assets	$1,849	$ –	$ –	$1,849

Finance receivables held for sale are recorded at the lower of cost or fair value. Due to our current plan to exit the non-captive commercial finance business through a combination of orderly liquidation of receivables as they mature and selected sales, we classified $1.7 billion of finance receivables as held for sale. The finance receivables held for sale as of January 3, 2009 include asset-based revolving lines of credit, dealer inventory financing and golf and resort mortgages. The majority of the finance receivables held for sale were identified at the individual loan level. Golf and resort mortgages classified as held for sale were identified as a portion of a larger portfolio with common characteristics based on the intention to balance the sale of certain loans with the collection of others to maximize economic value. Finance receivables held for sale are recorded at fair value on a nonrecurring basis during periods in which the fair value is lower than the cost value. Upon initial reclassification of these receivables held for sale we estimated the fair value to be $293 million less than the carrying value, net of the $44 million allowance for loan losses attributable to these portfolios. This net adjustment was recorded within special charges in the fourth quarter of 2008.

There are no active, quoted market prices for our finance receivables. The estimate of fair value was determined based on the use of discounted cash flow models to estimate the exit price we expect to receive in the principal market for each type of loan in an orderly transaction, which includes the sale of both pools of similar assets, and the sale of individual loans. The models we used incorporate estimates of the rate of return, financing cost, capital structure and/or discount rate expectations of current market participants combined with estimated loan cash flows based on credit losses, payment rates and credit line utilization rates. Where available, the assumptions related to the expectations of current market participants were compared to observable market inputs, including bids from prospective purchasers, and certain bond market indices for loans of similar perceived credit quality. Although we utilize and prioritize these market observable inputs in our discounted cash flow models, these inputs are rarely derived from markets with directly comparable loan structures, industries and collateral types. Therefore, all valuations of finance receivables held for sale involve significant management judgment, which can result in differences between our fair value estimates and those of other market participants.

Loan impairment is measured by comparing the expected future cash flows discounted at the loan's effective interest rate, or the fair value of the collateral if the loan is collateral dependent, to its carrying amount. If the carrying amount is higher, we establish a reserve based on this difference. This evaluation is inherently subjective, as it requires estimates, including the amount and timing of future cash flows expected to be received on impaired loans and the underlying collateral, which may differ from actual results. Impaired nonaccrual loans are also included in the table above since the measurement of required reserves on these loans is significantly dependent on the fair value of the underlying collateral. Fair values of collateral are determined utilizing either appraisals, industry pricing guides, input from market participants, our recent experience selling similar assets or internally developed discounted cash flow models.

Assets and Liabilities Not Recorded at Fair Value

The carrying amounts and estimated fair values of our financial instruments that are not reflected in the financial statements at fair value are as follows:

(In millions)	January 3, 2009		December 29, 2007	
	Carrying Value	Estimated Fair Value	Carrying Value	Estimated Fair Value
Manufacturing group:				
Debt	$(2,438)	$(2,074)	$(1,998)	$(2,021)
Finance group:				
Finance receivables held for investment	5,665	4,828	7,363	7,378
Retained interest in securitization, excluding interest only strips	188	178	160	160
Investment in other marketable securities	95	78	20	20
Debt	(7,549)	(6,663)	(7,336)	(7,309)

In accordance with disclosure requirements, debt and finance receivables held for investment in the table above exclude leases. Fair value for the Manufacturing group debt is determined using market observable data for similar transactions. We utilize the same valuation methodologies to determine the fair value estimates for finance receivables held for investment as described above for finance receivables held for sale.

Retained interests represent our subordinated interest in finance receivables sold to qualified special purpose trusts. These interests are classified as held-to-maturity and recorded at the allocated carrying value, which is determined based on the relative fair values of the finance receivables sold and the interests retained. We estimate fair value upon the initial recognition of the retained interest based on the present value of expected future cash flows using our best estimates of key assumptions—credit losses, prepayment speeds, forward interest rate yield curves and discount rates commensurate with the risks involved. These inputs reflect our own judgment regarding the assumptions market participants would use in pricing these assets based on the best information available in the circumstances as there is no active market for these assets.

Investments in other marketable securities represent notes receivable issued by securitization trusts that purchase timeshare notes receivable from timeshare developers. These notes are classified as held-to-maturity and are held at cost. The estimate of fair value was based on observable market inputs for similar securitization interests in markets that are currently inactive.

In 2008, approximately 80% of the fair value of term debt for the Finance group was determined based on observable market transactions. The remaining Finance group debt was determined based on discounted cash flow analyses using observable market inputs from debt with similar duration, subordination and credit default expectations. The fair values of short-term borrowings are assumed to approximate their carrying values.

Goodyear Tire & Rubber
2008 Annual Report

Note 7. Goodwill and Other Intangible Assets

The following table presents the net carrying amount of goodwill allocated by reporting unit, and changes during 2008:

(In millions)	Balance at December 31, 2006	Purchase Price Allocation	Divestitures	Translation & Other Adjustments	Balance at December 31, 2007
North American Tire	$ 94	$ –	$ –	$ –	$ 94
Europe, Middle East and Africa Tire	547	28	(1)	(52)	522
Asia Pacific Tire	72	–	–	(5)	67
	$713	$28	$(1)	$(57)	$683

In March 2008, we acquired an additional 6.12% ownership interest in our tire manufacturing subsidiary in Poland by purchasing outstanding shares held by minority shareholders for $46 million. As a result of the acquisition, we recorded goodwill totaling $28 million.

The following table presents the net carrying amount of goodwill allocated by reporting unit, and changes during 2007:

(In millions)	Balance at December 31, 2006	Purchase Price Allocation	Divestitures	Translation & Other Adjustments	Balance at December 31, 2007
North American Tire	$ 95	$ –	$ (1)	$ –	$ 94
Europe, Middle East and Africa Tire	500	–	(2)	49	547
Asia Pacific Tire	67	–	–	5	72
	$ 662	$ –	$ (3)	$ 54	$ 713

We reduced the carrying amount of goodwill by $11 million during 2007 primarily as a result of the adoption of FIN 48 and the release of a tax valuation allowance recorded in the purchase price allocation in prior years.

The following table presents information about other intangible assets:

(In millions)	2008			2007		
	Gross Carrying Amount[1]	Accumulated Amortization[1]	Net Carrying Amount	Gross Carrying Amount[1]	Accumulated Amortization[1]	Net Carrying Amount
Intangible assets with indefinite lives	$128	$ (6)	$122	$131	$ (9)	$122
Trademarks and patents	36	(21)	15	46	(23)	23
Other intangible assets	29	(6)	23	31	(9)	22
Total Other intangible assets	$193	$ (33)	$160	$208	$(41)	$167

[1] Includes impact of foreign currency translation.

Intangible assets are primarily comprised of the right to use certain brand names and trademarks on a non-competitive basis related to our global alliance with Sumitomo Rubber Industries, Ltd.

Amortization expense for intangible assets totaled $3 million in 2008, and $4 million in both 2007 and 2006. We estimate that annual amortization expense related to intangible assets will be approximately $3 million during each of the next five years and the weighted average remaining amortization period is approximately 21 years.

At December 31, 2008, as a result of certain impairment indicators including the decrease in our market capitalization, as well as the economic outlook in the United States, we performed an interim goodwill impairment analysis for our North American Tire business unit. Our annual impairment analysis for 2008 and 2007 as well as our interim analysis for North American Tire at December 31, 2008, indicated no impairment of goodwill or other intangible assets with indefinite lives. In addition, there were no events or circumstances that indicated the impairment test should be re-performed for goodwill for segments other than North American Tire or for other intangible assets with indefinite lives for any segment at December 31, 2008.

Note 8. Other Assets

We have funded approximately 10% of the obligations under our Supplemental Pension Plan as of December 31, 2008 (approximately 33% at December 31, 2007) using a trust. The trust invests in debt and equity securities and funds current benefit payments under the Supplemental Pension Plan. No contributions were made to the trust in 2008 or 2007. The debt securities have maturities ranging from January 15, 2009 through September 1, 2036. The fair value of the trust assets was $7 million and $21 million at December 31, 2008 and 2007, respectively, and was included in Other Assets. We have classified the trust assets as available-for-sale. Accordingly, gains and losses resulting from changes in the fair value of the trust assets are deferred and reported in AOCL. At December 31, 2008, AOCL included an unrealized holding loss on the trust assets of $2 million after-tax and an unrealized holding gain of $2 million after-tax at December 31, 2007.

We owned 3,421,306 shares of Sumitomo Rubber Industries, Ltd. ("SRI") at December 31, 2008 and 2007 (the "Sumitomo Investment"). The fair value of the Sumitomo Investment was $29 million and $31 million at December 31, 2008 and 2007, respectively, and was included in Other Assets. We have classified the Sumitomo Investment as available-for-sale. At December 31, 2008, AOCL included gross unrealized holding gains on the Sumitomo Investment of $13 million ($14 million after-tax), compared to $14 million ($15 million after-tax) at December 31, 2007.

In March 2008, we acquired an additional 6.12% ownership interest in our tire manufacturing subsidiary in Poland by purchasing outstanding shares held by minority shareholders for $46 million. In October 2008, we acquired the remaining 25% ownership interest in Goodyear Dalian Tire Company Ltd., our tire manufacturing and distribution subsidiary in China. The amount of our additional investment and the impact on our results of operations and financial position were not material. We finalized purchase accounting in 2008 for both acquisitions.

In January 2006, we acquired the remaining 50% ownership interest in our South Pacific Tyres ("SPT") joint venture. In connection with the acquisition we paid approximately $40 million and repaid approximately $50 million of outstanding loans. As a result of the acquisition, we recorded goodwill of approximately $12 million and indefinite lived intangible assets of $10 million. The purchase price was allocated based on 50% of the assets acquired and liabilities assumed.

Dividends received from our consolidated subsidiaries were $209 million, $562 million and $247 million in 2008, 2007 and 2006, respectively. Dividends received from our affiliates accounted for using the equity method were $3 million, $3 million and $5 million in 2008, 2007 and 2006, respectively.

In the third quarter of 2008, we sought redemption of $360 million invested in The Reserve Primary Fund. Due to reported losses in its investment portfolio and other liquidity issues, the fund ceased honoring redemption requests. The Board of Trustees of the fund subsequently voted to liquidate the assets of the fund and approved periodic distributions of cash to its shareholders. The plan of liquidation is subject to the supervision of the SEC under an exemption order granted to the fund. In the fourth quarter of 2008, we received partial distributions of $284 million. At December 31, 2008, $71 million, net of a $5 million valuation allowance, was classified as Prepaid expenses and other current assets, which represent the remaining funds still to be redeemed by The Reserve Primary Fund.

Note 9. Property, Plant and Equipment

(In millions)	2008			2007		
	Owned	Capital Leases	Total	Owned	Capital Leases	Total
Property, plant and equipment, at cost:						
Land	$ 429	$ 4	$ 433	$ 441	$ 5	$ 446
Buildings	1,847	62	1,909	1,992	64	2,056
Machinery and equipment	10,604	93	10,697	10,564	92	10,656
Construction in progress	748	–	748	596	–	596
	13,628	159	13,787	13,593	161	13,754
Accumulated depreciation	(8,213)	(97)	(8,310)	(8,236)	(93)	(8,329)
	5,415	62	5,477	5,357	68	5,425
Spare parts	157	–	157	173	–	173
	$5,572	$ 62	$5,634	$5,530	$ 68	$5,598

The range of useful lives of property used in arriving at the annual amount of depreciation provided are as follows: buildings and improvements, 5 to 45 years; machinery and equipment, 3 to 30 years.

PPG
2007 Annual Report

5. Property

(millions)	Useful Lives (years)	2007	2006
Land and land improvements	5-30	$ 401	$ 366
Buildings	20-40	1,272	1,182
Machinery and equipment	5-25	5,487	5,201
Other	3-20	507	435

(millions)	Useful Lives (years)	2007	2006
Construction in progress		166	207
Total[1]		$7,833	$7,391

[1] *Interest capitalized in 2007, 2006 and 2005 was $11 million, $7 million, and $5 million, respectively.*

6. Investments

(millions)	2007	2006
Investments in equity affiliates	$181	$182
Marketable equity securities		
Trading (See Note 14)	80	77
Available for sale	9	13
Other	30	71
Total	$360	$343

The Company's investments in equity affiliates are comprised principally of 50% ownership interests in a number of joint ventures that manufacture and sell coatings, glass and chemicals products, the most significant of which produce fiber glass products and are located in Asia.

In addition, we have a fifty-percent ownership interest in RS Cogen, L.L.C., which toll produces electricity and steam primarily for PPG and its joint venture partner. The joint venture was formed with a wholly-owned subsidiary of Entergy Corporation in 2000 for the construction and operation of a $300 million process steam, natural gas-fired cogeneration facility in Lake Charles, La., the majority of which was financed by a syndicate of banks. PPG's future commitment to purchase electricity and steam from the joint venture approximates $25 million per year subject to contractually defined inflation adjustments for the next fifteen years. The purchases for the years ended December 31, 2007, 2006 and 2005 were $25 million, $24 million and $25 million, respectively.

Summarized financial information of our equity affiliates on a 100 percent basis, in the aggregate, is as follows:

(millions)	2007	2006
Working capital	$ 56	$ 31
Property, net	804	715
Short-term debt	(75)	(50)
Long-term debt	(389)	(348)
Other, net	25	64
Net Assets	$421	$412

(millions)	2007	2006	2005
Revenues	$555	$601	$549
Net earnings	$ 60	$ 66	$ 25

PPG's share of undistributed net earnings of equity affiliates was $74 million and $63 million as of December 31, 2007 and 2006, respectively. Dividends received from equity affiliates were $20 million, $16 million and $19 million in 2007, 2006 and 2005, respectively.

As of December 31, 2007 and 2006, there were unrealized pretax gains of $4 million and $3 million, respectively, and as of December 31, 2005 there were pretax losses of $1 million recorded in "Accumulated other comprehensive loss" in the accompanying consolidated balance sheet related to marketable equity securities available for sale. During 2007, PPG sold certain of these investments resulting in recognition of pretax gains of $2 million and proceeds of $8 million. During both 2006 and 2005, PPG sold certain of these investments resulting in recognition of pretax gains of $1 million and proceeds of $3 million.

7. Goodwill and Other Identifiable Intangible Assets

The change in the carrying amount of goodwill attributable to each reportable business segment for the years ended December 31, 2007 and 2006 was as follows:

(millions)	Performance Coatings	Industrial Coatings	Optical and Specialty Materials	Glass	Total
Balance, Jan. 1, 2006	$ 814	$243	$ 2	$48	$1,107
Goodwill from acquisitions	84	25	48	–	157
Currency translation	45	17	5	6	73
Balance, Dec. 31, 2006	$ 943	$285	$55	$54	$1,337
Goodwill from acquisitions	55	7	(3)	–	59
Currency translation	53	18	5	4	80
Balance, Dec. 31, 2007	$1,051	$310	$57	$58	$1,476

The carrying amount of acquired trademarks with indefinite lives as of December 31, 2007 and 2006 totaled $144 million.

The Company's identifiable intangible assets with finite lives are being amortized over their estimated useful lives and are detailed below.

(millions)	Dec. 31, 2007			Dec. 31, 2006		
	Gross Carrying Amount	Accumulated Amortization	Net	Gross Carrying Amount	Accumulated Amortization	Net
Acquired technology	$448	$(188)	$260	$389	$(155)	$234
Other[1]	355	(147)	208	328	(124)	204
Balance	$803	$(355)	$468	$717	$(279)	$438

[1] *Consists primarily of customer-related intangibles*

Aggregate amortization expense was $58 million, $43 million and $32 million in 2007, 2006 and 2005, respectively. The estimated future amortization expense of identifiable intangible assets during the next five years is (in millions) $55 in 2008, $54 in 2009, $53 in 2010, $44 in 2011 and $40 in 2012. These amounts do not include amortization expense resulting from the SigmaKalon acquisition, which was completed on January 2, 2008. See Note 2, "Acquisitions" for more information.

8. Business Restructuring and Asset Impairment

During 2006, the Company finalized plans for certain actions to reduce its workforce and consolidate facilities and recorded a charge of $37 million for restructuring and other related activities, including severance costs of $35 million and loss on asset impairment of $2 million. These amounts were net of $5 million of amounts accrued in 2006 that were reversed later that year as a result of actions not being taken or being completed at a cost that was less than the estimated amount accrued. Of the $37 million restructuring charge recorded in 2006, $2 million related to the automotive glass businesses has been reclassified and is presented as discontinued operations in the accompanying consolidated statement of income. All actions related to the 2006 restructuring charge were substantially completed by the end of the second quarter of 2007.

The following table summarizes the details through December 31, 2007.

(Millions, except no. of employees)	Severance Costs	Asset Impairments	Total Charge	Employees Covered
Industrial coatings	$ 28	$ 1	$ 29	353
Performance coatings	7	1	8	193
Optical and specialty materials	1	–	1	33
Glass	4	–	4	190
Reversal	(5)	–	(5)	(112)
Total	$ 35	$ 2	$ 37	657
2006 Activity	(26)	(2)	(28)	(531)
Balance as of Dec. 31, 2006	$ 9	$ –	$ 9	126

(Millions, except no. of employees)	Severance Costs	Asset Impairments	Total Charge	Employees Covered
2007 Activity	(9)	–	(9)	(126)
Balance as of Dec. 31, 2007	$ –	$ –	$ –	–

In 2002, the Company recorded a charge of $81 million for restructuring and other related activities. The workforce reductions covered by this charge have been completed; however, as of December 31, 2007, $2 million of this reserve remained to be spent. This reserve relates to a group of approximately 75 employees in Europe, whose terminations were concluded under a different social plan than was assumed when the reserve was recorded. Under the terms of this social plan, severance payments will be paid to these 75 individuals through 2008.

In the fourth quarter of 2005, the Company evaluated our fine chemicals operating segment for impairment in accordance with SFAS No. 144, "Accounting for the Impairment of Long-Lived Assets", and determined that indicators of impairment were present for certain long-lived assets at our fine chemicals manufacturing plant in the United States. In measuring the fair value of these assets, the Company utilized an expected cash flow methodology to determine that the carrying value of these assets exceeded their fair value. We also wrote down the assets of a small fine chemical facility in France to their estimated net realizable value. The Company recorded an asset impairment charge related to these fine chemicals assets of $27 million pretax in 2005, which has been reclassified and is presented as a reduction to income from discontinued operations in the accompanying consolidated statement of income for the year ended December 31, 2005.

Sherwin-Williams
2007 Annual Report

Note 3. Goodwill, Intangible and Long-Lived Assets

During 2007, the Company recognized $93.3 million of goodwill in the acquisitions of Nitco, MAB, Napko, Columbia, Life Shield and Flex group. There was no goodwill recognized in the acquisitions of PISA and VHT. Trademarks of $37,180 were recognized in the acquisition valuations of Nitco, MAB, Napko, Columbia, VHT and Flex group. Covenants not to compete of $10,028 were obtained in the acquisitions of Nitco, MAB, Napko, Columbia and VHT. The covenants not to compete are being amortized over five years from date of acquisition. Customer lists and a distribution platform valued at $25,930 were recognized in the acquisitions of Nitco, MAB, Napko, Columbia and VHT. The customer lists and distribution platform are being amortized over periods of three and one-half to eight years. Additional identified intangible assets of product formulations ($3,680) and other intangible assets ($1,000) were recognized as part of the acquisitions of Nitco, MAB, Columbia and VHT. The additional acquired identified intangible assets are being amortized over periods of three to eight years depending on the estimated useful life of the asset. No significant residual value was estimated for any of the acquired identified intangible assets. No intangible assets were identified in the Life Shield acquisition.

During 2006, the Company recognized goodwill in the acquisition of Dobco of $29,038. Identifiable intangible assets, consisting of intellectual property of $7,617 and a customer list of $3,377, were also recognized in the acquisition of Dobco. The intellectual property is being amortized over 15 years and the customer list is being amortized over 5 years. No significant residual value was estimated for these assets.

During 2005, the Company recognized goodwill in the acquisition of KST of $14,476. Identifiable intangible assets, consisting of trademarks of $2,500 and a covenant not to compete of $300, were also recognized in the acquisition of KST. Acquired intangible assets subject to amortization are being amortized over three years. No significant residual value was estimated for these assets. In 2005, goodwill was reduced by $4,944 relating to the disposition of the Company's majority interest in Kinlita (see Note 2).

In accordance with FAS No. 144, whenever events or changes in circumstances indicated that the carrying value of long-lived assets may not be recoverable or the useful life had changed, impairment tests were performed. Undiscounted cash flows were used to calculate the recoverable value of long-lived assets to determine if such assets were impaired. Where impairment was identified, a discounted cash flow valuation model, incorporating discount rates commensurate with the risks involved for each group of assets, was used to determine the fair value for the assets to measure any potential impairment.

During 2007 in the Consumer Group, a reduction of $660 in the carrying values of certain manufacturing equipment and an impairment of $856 in certain assets held for disposal were charged to Cost of goods sold and Other general expense—net, respectively. An impairment test was performed due to changes in the manner in which the manufacturing equipment was used and changes in the disposition plan for the assets held for disposal.

During 2006, reductions in the carrying values of certain manufacturing equipment of $421 in the Consumer Group and $463 in the Global Group were charged to Cost of goods sold. An impairment test was performed due to changes in the manner in which these assets were used.

During 2005, an impairment test was performed for capitalized software costs due to the replacement and significant changes in the utilization of certain software. A reduction in the carrying value of capitalized software costs of $259 was charged to Selling, general and administrative expenses in the Global Group. Assets related to a customer sales incentive program were tested for impairment due to lower than anticipated sales performance, resulting in a reduction in carrying value and a charge of $1,656 to Net sales in the Consumer Group.

Goodwill and trademarks with indefinite lives are required by FAS No. 142 to be periodically tested for impairment. October 1 has been established for the annual impairment review. Fair values are estimated separately for goodwill and trademarks with indefinite lives using a discounted cash flow valuation model, incorporating discount rates commensurate with the risks involved for each group of assets.

The annual impairment review performed as of October 1, 2007 resulted in reductions in the carrying values of goodwill of $15,176 and trademarks with indefinite lives of $947. The goodwill impairment was reported as a separate line item in the Statements of Consolidated Income in accordance with FAS No. 142 and is included in the Consumer Group ($4,215) and the Global Group ($10,961). The trademark impairments were charged to Selling, general and administrative expenses in the Consumer Group ($175) and the Paint Stores Group ($172), and to Cost of goods sold in the Global Group ($600). The impairments related primarily to lower-than-anticipated cash flow in certain acquired businesses and lower-than-anticipated sales of certain acquired brands.

The annual impairment review performed as of October 1, 2006 resulted in reductions in the carrying values of certain trademarks with indefinite lives of $1,383, which was charged to Selling, general and administrative expenses in the Consumer Group ($1,300) and the Paint Stores Group ($83). The impairments related to lower-than-anticipated sales of certain acquired brands.

The annual impairment review performed as of October 1, 2005, and an additional impairment review performed in the fourth quarter of 2005 due to updated cash flow projections, resulted in a reduction in the carrying value of goodwill of $22,000 and trademarks with indefinite lives of $755. The goodwill impairment was reported as a separate line item in the Statements of Consolidated Income in accordance with FAS No. 142 and is included in the Consumer Group. The impairment of trademarks with indefinite lives of $755 was charged to Cost of goods sold in the Consumer Group ($653) and Selling, general and administrative expenses in the Paint Stores Group ($102). The impairment of goodwill and trademarks with indefinite lives was due to lower-than-anticipated projected sales and cash flow relating to the elimination of a portion of a paint program with a major retailer.

Amortization of finite-lived intangible assets is as follows for the next five years: $21,410 in 2008, $20,250 in 2009, $18,060 in 2010, $15,380 in 2011 and $14,020 in 2012. A summary of changes in the Company's carrying value of goodwill by reportable operating segment is as follows:

Goodwill	Paint Stores Group	Consumer Group	Global Group	Consolidated Totals
Balance at January 1, 2005	$205,698	$661,506	$33,240	$900,444
Acquisitions		14,476		14,476
Impairment charged to operations		(22,000)		(22,000)
Sale of operations			(4,944)	(4,944)
Currency and other adjustments	(549)	(1,615)	1,562	(602)
Balance at December 31, 2005	205,149	652,367	29,858	887,374
Acquisitions		29,038		29,038

Goodwill	Paint Stores Group	Consumer Group	Global Group	Consolidated Totals
Currency and other adjustments			52	(52)
Balance at December 31, 2006	205,149	681,405	29,910	916,464
Acquisitions	69,071	12,371	11,874	93,316
Impairment charged to operations		(4,215)	(10,961)	(15,176)
Currency and other adjustments	30	74	1,905	2,009
Balance at December 31, 2007	$274,250	$689,635	$32,728	$996,613

A summary of the Company's carrying value of intangible assets is as follows:

	Finite-Lived Intangible Assets			Trademarks with Indefinite Lives	Total Intangible Assets
	Software	All-Other	Subtotal		
December 31, 2007					
Weighted-average amortization period	10 years	10 years	10 years		
Gross	$71,480	$189,751	$261,231	$269,866	$531,097
Accumulated amortization	(28,488)	(116,161)	(144,649)	(35,304)	(179,953)
Net value	$42,992	$73,590	$116,582	$234,562	$351,144
December 31, 2006					
Weighted-average amortization period	10 years	12 years	11 years		
Gross	66,739	152,848	219,587	234,176	453,763
Accumulated amortization	(28,303)	(103,469)	(131,772)	(36,069)	(167,841)
Net value	$38,436	$49,379	$87,815	$98,107	$285,922
December 31, 2005					
Weighted-average amortization period	10 years	8 years	9 years		
Gross	$63,853	$141,561	$205,414	$232,631	$438,045
Accumulated amortization	(25,324)	(87,250)	(112,574)	(34,528)	(147,102)
Net value	$38,529	$54,311	$92,840	$198,103	$290,943

Black & Decker
2007 Annual Report

Note 5. Goodwill and Other Identified Intangible Assets

The changes in the carrying amount of goodwill by reportable business segment, in millions of dollars, were as follows:

	Power Tools & Accessories	Hardware & Home Improvement	Fastening & Assembly Systems	Total
Goodwill at January 1, 2006	$369.0	$463.6	$283.1	$1,115.7
Acquisition	84.2	–	–	84.2
Activity associated with prior year acquisition	(17.0)	–	–	(17.0)
Currency translation adjustment	0.9	0.2	11.6	12.7
Balance at December 31, 2006	437.1	463.8	294.7	1,195.6
Acquisition	–	–	0.5	0.5
Activity associated with prior year acquisition	(4.1)	–	–	(4.1)
Currency translation adjustment	3.4	0.6	16.9	20.9
Balance at December 31, 2007	$436.4	$464.4	$312.1	$1,212.9

The carrying amount of acquired intangible assets included in other assets at the end of each year, in millions of dollars, was as follows:

	2007	2006
Customer relationships		
(net of accumulated amortization of $10.3 in 2007 and $5.1 in 2006)	$ 53.0	$ 54.2
Technology and patents		
(net of accumulated amortization of $7.0 in 2007 and $4.9 in 2006)	14.2	17.1
Trademarks and trade names		
(net of accumulated amortization of $3.7 in 2007 and $1.9 in 2006)	208.4	207.0
Total intangibles, net	$275.6	$278.3

Trademarks and trade names include indefinite-lived assets of $193.9 million at December 31, 2007 and 2006, respectively.

Expense associated with the amortization of intangible assets in 2007, 2006, and 2005 was $9.1 million, $7.3 million, and $3.5 million, respectively. At December 31, 2007, the weighted-average amortization periods were 13 years for customer relationships, 10 years for technology and patents, and 10 years for trademarks and trade names. The estimated future amortization expense for identifiable intangible assets during each of the next five years is $9.1 million.

ArvinMeritor
2006 Annual Report

4. Goodwill

Goodwill is reviewed for impairment annually or more frequently if certain indicators arise. If business conditions or other factors cause the profitability and cash flows of the reporting unit to decline, the company may be required to record impairment charges for goodwill at that time. The goodwill impairment review is a two-step process. Step one consists of a comparison of the fair value of a reporting unit with its carrying amount. An impairment loss may be recognized if the review indicates that the carrying value of a reporting unit exceeds its fair value. Estimates of fair value are primarily determined by using discounted cash flows and market multiples on earnings. If the carrying amount of a reporting unit exceeds its fair value, step two requires the fair value of the reporting unit to be allocated to the underlying assets and liabilities of that reporting unit, resulting in an implied fair value of goodwill. If the carrying amount of the goodwill of the reporting unit exceeds the implied fair value, an impairment charge is recorded equal to the excess.

The impairment review is highly judgmental and involves the use of significant estimates and assumption. These estimates and assumptions have a significant impact on the amount of any impairment charge recorded. Discounted cash flow methods are dependent upon assumption of future sales trends, market conditions and cash flows of each reporting unit over several years. Actual cash flows in the future may differ significantly from those previously forecasted. Other significant assumptions include growth rates and the discount rate applicable to future cash flows.

In fiscal year 2006, our light vehicle emissions technologies reporting unit continued to face significant challenges, including higher raw material costs, intense pricing pressures and increased competition. These factors were greater than previously anticipated and partially offset the expected benefits from the company's fiscal year 2005 restructuring actions. In addition, higher stainless steel prices and recent downturns in production at certain North American manufacturers are expected to further negatively impact the financial performance of this reporting unit in fiscal year 2007. These combined factors resulted in a decline in the fair value of the light vehicle emissions technologies reporting unit in fiscal year 2006.

Step one of the company's fiscal 2006 annual goodwill impairment review indicated the carrying value of its LVS emissions technology reporting unit exceeded its fair value. The fair value of this reporting unit was estimated using a probability weighted average cash flow analysis. This analysis considered multiple cash flow scenarios, including earnings multiples and the expected present value of future cash flows. The company is currently in the process of completing the step two analysis and expects to have this completed in the first quarter of fiscal year 2007. However, the company recorded a $310 million non-cash goodwill impairment charge in the fourth quarter of fiscal year 2006 as its best estimate of the impairment loss. This estimate could change upon completion of the step two analysis in fiscal year 2007.

In response to the challenges LVS emissions technologies continues to face, the company has identified restructuring plans to downsize certain underperforming facilities and realign its emissions technologies manufacturing footprint to utilize assets more efficiently, improve operations and lower costs. The total estimated cost of these actions is $50 million, of which approximately $40 million is expected to be cash costs. This restructuring program will be executed over the next 12 to 36 months. No amounts have been recorded for this restructuring program at September 30, 2006.

A summary of the changes in the carrying value of goodwill, by segment, is as follows (in millions):

	LVS	CVS	Total
Balance at September 30, 2005	$368	$433	$801
Goodwill impairment charge	(310)	–	(310)
Goodwill written off due to the sale of off-highway brakes (see Note 6)	–	(7)	(7)
Other, primarily foreign currency translation	12	7	19
Balance at September 30, 2006	$ 70	$433	$503

Liberate Technologies
2005 Annual Report

Note 7. Restricted Cash

Our restricted cash balance was $4.4 million as of May 31, 2005 and $10.9 million as of May 31, 2004. Restricted cash consists primarily of certificates of deposit established at our banking institutions in connection with lease-related letters of credit. As part of the facilities lease for our former headquarters in San Carlos, California and our current headquarters in San Mateo, California, we were required to establish irrevocable letters of credit in the amounts of $8.8 million and $975,000, respectively, as security deposits. In order to secure our obligations to our bank under these letters of credit, we established certificates of deposit in the same amounts. At the request of our bank, we have provided additional security of $500,000 to secure our obligations under the $8.8 million letter of credit. In April 2005, our restricted cash decreased by $5.9 million due to our former landlord drawing against the letter of credit for unpaid rent, which the restricted cash was securing. In June 2005, we re-established a new letter of credit and certificate of deposit securing the letter of credit to stay in compliance with the lease terms for our former headquarters in San Carlos. We also have restricted cash deposits related to a lease obligations and bank relationship in the UK of approximately $182,000 as of May 31, 2005 and $522,000 as of May 31, 2004. We also hold approximately $86,000 of restricted cash in connection with potential obligations related to the closure of an overseas branch office.

Woodhead Industries
2004 Annual Report

3. Accounts Receivable

We reduce our accounts receivable balance to account for reserves for doubtful accounts, sales returns, warranties and allowances. The table below shows the activity in our accounts receivable reserves during the fiscal years:

	2004	*2003*	*2002*
Beginning balance	**$1,287**	$1,250	$1,844
Charged to costs and expenses	**382**	189	20
Write-offs	**(191)**	(240)	(180)
Price adjustments charged to net sales	**(53)**	88	(434)
Ending balance	**$1,531**	$1,287	$1,250

Solectron
2003 Annual Report

Note 2 Cash, Cash Equivalents and Short-Term Investments

Cash, cash equivalents and short-term investments (related to continuing operations and including restricted amounts) as of August 31, 2003 and 2002, consisted of the following:

	Cash and Cash Equivalents	Short-term Marketable Securities
Fiscal 2003	(in millions)	
Cash	$ 717.3	$ 19.9
Money market funds	543.5	–
Certificates of deposit	–	–
Market auction securities	–	21.9
U.S. government securities	–	–
Corporate obligations	210.9	5.6
Other	–	–
Total	$1,471.7	$47.4
Fiscal 2002		
Cash	$ 937.7	$ –
Money market funds	692.8	–
Certificates of deposit	24.8	11.4
Market auction securities	157.8	75.2
U.S. government securities	30.6	130.4
Corporate obligations	–	73.0
Other	41.7	42.2
Total	$1,885.4	$332.2

Solectron had $65.5 and $235.4 million of restricted cash, cash equivalents and short-term investment as of August 31, 2003 and 2002, respectively. Restricted cash, cash equivalents and short-term investments are restricted as collateral for specified obligations under certain lease agreements and certain interest payments on the 7.25% subordinated ACES debentures due November 15, 2006. Short-term investments are carried at fair market value, which approximates cost. Realized and unrealized gains and losses for the fiscal years ended August 31, 2003 and 2002 were not significant.

C. Inventories

Inventories related to continuing operations as of August 31, 2003 and 2002, consisted of:

	2003	2002
	(in millions)	
Raw materials	$ 957.8	$1,298.5
Work-in-process	236.1	228.2
Finished goods	221.0	295.4
Total	$1,414.9	$1,822.1

Inventoriable expenses, packages and supplies and turkey products amounting to approximately $82.6 million at October 31,1998, and $84.5 million at October 25, 1997, are stated at cost determined by the last-in, first-out method and are $27.4 million and $27.2 million lower in the respective years than such inventories determined under the first-in, first-out method.

Floride Rock Industries
2005 Annual Report

2. Asset Retirement Obligation

Effective October 1, 2002, the Company adopted SFAS No. 143, "Accounting for Asset Retirement Obligations" (SFAS No. 143). The statement applies to legal obligations associated with the retirement of long-lived assets that result from the acquisition, construction, development and (or) normal use of the asset.

SFAS No. 143 requires that the fair value of a liability for an asset retirement obligation be recognized in the period in which it is incurred if a reasonable estimate of fair value can be made. The fair value of the liability is added to the carrying amount of the associated asset and this additional carrying amount is amortized over the life of the asset. The liability is accreted at the end of each reporting period through charges to operating expenses. If the obligation is settled for other than the carrying amount of the liability, the Company will recognize a gain or loss on settlement. Previously, the Company accrued for such costs on units of production basis over the estimated reserves.

The Company cannot reasonably estimate the fair value of the asset retirement obligation related to substantially all of its concrete products segment and all of its cement segment since the Company is unable to estimate the date the obligation would be incurred or the cost of the obligation. For the aggregates segment, an asset retirement obligation was provided where the Company has a legal obligation to reclaim the mining site.

All legal obligations for asset retirement obligations were identified and the fair value of these obligations were determined as of October 1, 2002. Upon the adoption of the new standard, the Company recorded the current fair value of its expected cost of reclamation. The cumulative effect of the change related to prior years resulted in income recognized in the first quarter of fiscal 2003 of $514,000 before taxes and $333,000 after taxes. The current and long-term portions of the asset retirement obligation are recorded in Accrued Liabilities, Other and Other accrued liabilities, respectively in the accompanying consolidated balance sheets.

The analysis of the asset retirement obligation for the years ended September 30 is as follows (in thousands):

	2005	2004
Balance at beginning of period	$9,033	$8,649
Additional liabilities	1,736	213
Accretion of expenses	404	361
Payment of obligations	(2113)	(190)
Balance at end of period	$9,060	$9,033

National Semiconductor
2005 Annual Report

Note 7: Asset Retirement Obligations

We adopted SFAS No. 143, "Accounting for Asset Retirement Obligations," at the beginning of fiscal 2004. This statement requires that the fair value of a legal liability for an asset retirement obligation be recorded in the period in which it is incurred if a reasonable estimate of fair value can be made. Upon recognition of a liability, the asset retirement cost is recorded as an increase in the carrying value of the related long-lived asset and then depreciated over the life of the asset. Our asset retirement obligations arise primarily from contractual commitments to decontaminate machinery and equipment used at our manufacturing facilities at the time we dispose of or replace them. We also have leased facilities where we have asset retirement obligations from contractual commitments to remove leasehold improvements and return the property to a specified condition when the lease terminates. As a result of our evaluation of our asset retirement obligations, we recorded a $2.1 million noncurrent liability for asset retirement obligations and a $0.4 million increase in the carrying value of the related assets, net of $1.0

million of accumulated depreciation at the beginning of fiscal 2004. The cumulative effect that was recorded in the first quarter of fiscal 2004 upon the adoption of this accounting standard resulted in a charge of $1.9 million, including a tax effect of $0.2 million.

At the time we adopted SFAS No. 143, we did not recognize any asset retirement obligations associated with the closure or abandonment of the manufacturing facilities we own. Our legal asset retirement obligations for manufacturing facilities arise primarily from local laws and statutes that establish minimum standards or requirements for companies in that locale in the event it were to shut down or otherwise exit or abandon a manufacturing facility. We intend to operate our manufacturing facilities indefinitely and are therefore unable at any one time to reasonably estimate the fair value of any legal obligations we may have because of the indeterminate closure dates. However, we announced in July 2005 that we plan to close our assembly and test facility in Singapore and consolidate its production volume into our other assembly and test facilities in Malaysia and China. The majority of the activities associated with the closure is expected to take place over the next nine to twelve months. We do not expect to incur any significant asset retirement costs in excess of amounts accrued associated with the closure of this facility.

Nike
2005 Annual Report

Note 4—Identifiable Intangible Assets and Goodwill
Adoption of FAS 142

The Company adopted FAS 142 effective June 1, 2002. In accordance with FAS 142, goodwill and intangible assets with indefinite lives are not amortized but instead are measured for impairment at least annually in the fourth quarter, or when events indicate that an impairment exists. Intangible assets that are determined to have definite lives are amortized over their useful lives.

As required by FAS 142, the Company performed impairment tests on goodwill and other intangible assets with indefinite lives, which consisted only of certain trademarks, as of June 1, 2002. As a result of the impairment tests, the Company recorded a $266.1 million cumulative effect of accounting change for the year ended May 31, 2003. Under FAS 142, goodwill impairment exists if the net book value of a reporting unit exceeds its estimated fair value. The Company estimated the fair value of its reporting units by using a combination of discounted cash flow analyses and comparisons with the market values of similar publicly traded companies.

Included in the Company's $266.1 million impairment charge was a $178.5 million charge related to the impairment of the goodwill associated with the Bauer NIKE Hockey ("Bauer") and Cole Haan reporting units. These reporting units are reflected in the Company's Other operating segment. Since the Company's purchase of Bauer in 1995, the hockey equipment and apparel markets have not grown as fast as expected and the in-line skate market has contracted significantly. As a result, the Company determined that the goodwill acquired at

Bauer had been impaired. The goodwill impairment at Cole Haan reflected the significantly lower fair value calculated on the basis of reduced operating income in the year following the September 11, 2001 terrorist attacks.

The remaining $87.6 million of the impairment charge relates to trademarks associated with Bauer. Under FAS 142, impairment of an indefinite-lived asset exists if the net book value of the asset exceeds its fair value. The Company estimated the fair value of trademarks using the relief-from-royalty approach, which is a standard form of discounted cash flow analysis typically used for the valuation of trademarks. The impairment of the Bauer trademarks reflects the same circumstances as described above related to the Bauer goodwill impairment.

The following table summarizes the Company's identifiable intangible assets and goodwill balances as of May 31, 2005 and May 31, 2004:

	May 31, 2005			May 31, 2004		
	Gross Carrying Amount	Accumulated Amortization	Net Carrying Amount	Gross Carrying Amount	Accumulated Amortization	Net Carrying Amount
	(In millions)					
Amortized intangible assets:						
Patents	$29.2	$(10.9)	$18.3	$27.9	$(11.9)	$16.0
Trademarks .	54.8	(16.4)	38.4	14.1	(11.5)	2.6
Other	21.4	(13.5)	7.9	17.0	(10.8)	6.2
Total	105.4	$(40.8)	64.6	59.0	$(34.2)	24.8
Unamortized intangible assets- Trademarks .			$341.5			$341.5
Total			$406.1			$366.3
Goodwill			$135.4			$135.4

Amortization expense of identifiable assets with definite lives, which is included in selling and administrative expense, was $9.3 million, $12.0 million and $3.6 million for the years ended May 31, 2005, 2004, and 2003, respectively. The estimated amortization expense for intangible assets subject to amortization for each of the succeeding years ending May 31, 2006 through May 31, 2010 is as follows: 2006: $9.4 million; 2007: $8.5 million; 2008: $8.0 million; 2009: $6.7 million; 2010: $5.9 million.

On August 11, 2004, the Company acquired Official Starter LLC and Official Starter Properties LLC (collectively "Official Starter"). As a result of the acquisition, $39.0 million was allocated to amortized trademarks and $4.6 million was allocated to other amortized intangible assets. The weighted average amortization period is nine years in total and approximately 10 years and three years for amortized trademarks and other amortized intangible assets, respectively. See Note 15 for additional information related to the acquisition.

ConAgra Foods
2005 Annual Report

7. Asset Impairments and Casualty Loss

During fiscal 2005, the company determined that it would close a manufacturing facility within its Food Ingredients segment and recognized a charge of $15.0 million to reduce the carrying amounts of the related long-lived assets to their fair values.

As a result of a fire at a manufacturing facility in fiscal 2005, the company recognized a charge, net of insurance recoveries, of $10.0 million in the Foodservice Products segment for the loss of inventory and property, plant and equipment.

In fiscal 2005, the company determined the carrying values of its investments in two unrelated joint ventures were other than temporarily impaired and therefore recognized pre-tax impairment charges totaling $71.0 million ($65.6 million after tax). The pre-tax charges are reflected in equity method investment earnings (loss) in the statement of earnings. The extent of the impairments was determined based upon the company's assessment of the recoverability of its investments, including an assessment of the investees' ability to sustain earnings which would justify the carrying amount of the investments.

During fiscal 2005, the company recorded a pre-tax charge of $10.0 million for an impairment of a brand and related assets in the Retail Products segment.

Darden Restaurants
2005 Annual Report

Note 3 Restructuring and Asset Impairment Activities

Asset impairment charges related to the decision to relocate or rebuild certain restaurants amounted to $900, $5,667 and $4,876 in fiscal 2005, 2004 and 2003, respectively. Asset impairment credits related to assets sold that were previously impaired amounted to $2,786, $1,437 and $594 in fiscal 2005, 2004 and 2003, respectively. During fiscal 2005, we also recorded charges of $6,407 for the write-down of carrying value of two Olive Garden restaurants, one Red Lobster restaurant and one Smokey Bones restaurant. The Smokey Bones restaurant was closed subsequent to fiscal 2005 while the two Olive Garden restaurants and one Red Lobster restaurant continued to operate. All impairment amounts are included in asset impairment and restructuring charges in the consolidated statements of earnings.

During fiscal 2004, we recorded pre-tax asset impairment charges of $36,526 for long-lived asset impairments associated with the closing of six Bahama Breeze restaurants and the write-down of the carrying value of four other Bahama Breeze restaurants, one Olive Garden restaurant and one Red Lobster restaurant, which continued to operate. We also recorded a restructuring charge of $1,112 primarily related to severance payments made to certain restaurant employees and exit costs associated with the closing of the six Bahama Breeze restaurants in accordance with SFAS No. 146, "Accounting for Costs Associated with Exit or Disposal Activities." Below is a summary of the restructuring costs for fiscal 2005:

	Balance at May 29, 2004	Additions	Cash Payments	Balance at May 30, 2005
One-time termination benefits	$ 49	$–	$ (49)	$–
Less termination costs	–	–	–	–
Other exit costs	311	–	(311)	–
	$360	$–	$(360)	$–

The results of operations for all restaurants closed in fiscal 2005, 2004 and 2003 are not material to our consolidated results of operations and, therefore, have not been presented as discontinued operations.

Hewlett Packard
2004 Annual Report

Note 6: Goodwill and Purchased Intangible Assets

Goodwill

Goodwill allocated to HP's business segments as of October 31, 2003 and changes in the carrying amount of goodwill for the fiscal year ended October 31, 2004 are as follows:

	HP Services	Enterprise Storage and Servers	Software	Enterprise Systems Group	Personal Systems Group	Imaging and Printing Group	HP Financial Services	Total
	In millions							
Balance at October 31, 2003	$5,522	$ –	$ –	$5,390	$2,324	$1,508	$150	$14,894
Reallocation	–	4,794	596	(5,390)	–	–	–	–
Goodwill acquired during the period	740	11	168	–	–	–	–	919
Goodwill adjustment	8	5	(5)	–	3	2	2	15
Balance at October 31, 2004	$6,270	$4,810	$759	$ –	$2,327	$1,510	$152	$15,828

The goodwill reallocation shown in the table above relates to the reorganization of HP's business segments discussed in Note 18. The goodwill formerly included in the Enterprise Systems Group was allocated between ESS and Software based on a relative fair value approach.

The goodwill adjustment shown in the table above relates primarily to revisions of acquisition related tax estimates, that resulted in additions to goodwill, offset partially by the reduction of a restructuring liability and asset impairments associated with the fiscal 2002 and 2001 pre-acquisition Compaq restructuring plans. The reduction of the restructuring liability and asset impairments adjusted original estimates to actual costs incurred at various locations throughout the world.

On November 1, 2002, HP adopted SFAS No. 142, which requires that goodwill no longer be amortized and instead be tested for impairment on a periodic basis.

Based on the results of its annual impairment tests, HP determined that no impairment of goodwill existed as of August 1, 2004 or August 1, 2003. However, future goodwill impairment tests could result in a charge to earnings. HP will continue to evaluate goodwill on an annual basis as of the beginning of its fourth fiscal quarter, and whenever events and changes in circumstances indicate that there may be a potential impairment.

If the provisions of SFAS No. 142 had been in effect for all periods presented, HP's net earnings (loss) and net earnings (loss) per share would have been unchanged for fiscal 2004 and 2003. For fiscal 2002, the net loss, basic net loss per share and diluted net loss per share would have been $796 million, $0.32 and $0.32, respectively, which represents an improvement on reported net loss, basic net loss per share and diluted net loss per share of $107 million, $0.04 and $0.04, respectively.

Purchased Intangible Assets

HP's purchased intangible assets associated with completed acquisitions at October 31 are composed of:

	2004			2003		
	Gross	Accumulated Amortization	Net	Gross	Accumulated Amortization	Net
In millions						
Customer contracts, customer lists and distribution agreements	$2,340	$(637)	$1,703	$2,040	$(371)	$1,669
Developed and core technology and patents	1,704	(775)	929	1,663	(457)	1,206
Product trademarks	93	(44)	49	84	(25)	59

	2004			2003		
	Gross	Accumulated Amortization	Net	Gross	Accumulated Amortization	Net
Total amortizable purchased intangible assets	4,137	(1,456)	2,681	3,787	(853)	2,934
Compaq trade name	1,422	–	1,422	1,422	–	1,422
Total purchased intangible assets	$5,559	$(1,456)	$4,103	$5,209	$(853)	$4,356

Amortization expense related to finite-lived purchased intangible assets was approximately $603 million in fiscal 2004, $563 million in fiscal 2003, and $295 million in fiscal 2002.

HP performs an annual impairment test for its purchased intangible asset with an indefinite life, the Compaq trade name. Based on the results of its annual impairment tests, HP determined that no impairment of the Compaq trade name existed as of August 1, 2004 or August 1, 2003. However, future impairment tests could result in a charge to earnings. HP will continue to evaluate the purchased intangible asset with an indefinite life on an annual basis as of the beginning of the fourth quarter, and whenever events and changes in circumstances indicate that there may be a potential impairment.

The finite-lived purchased intangible assets consist of customer contracts, customer lists and distribution agreements, which have weighted average useful lives of approximately eight years, and developed and core technology, patents, and product trademarks, which have weighted average useful lives of approximately six years.

Estimated future amortization expense related to finite-lived purchased intangible assets at October 31, 2004 is as follows:

Fiscal year:	In millions
2005	$ 574
2006	530
2007	462
2008	396
2009	321
Thereafter	398
Total	$2,681

Clorox
2005 Annual Report

Changes in the carrying amount of goodwill for the fiscal years ended June 30, 2005 and 2004, by operating segment are summarized below. Goodwill is reported net of accumulated amortization of $345 and $357 at June 30, 2005 and 2004, respectively.

	Household Group	Specialty Group	International	Corporate	Total
Balance at June 30, 2003 (as reported)	$125	$ 381	$155	$69	$730
Segment realignment (Note 18)	298	(298)	–	–	–
Balance at June 30, 2003 (as realigned)	423	83	155	69	730
Acquisitions and sales . . .	–	–	6	–	6
Translation adjustments and other	(2)	–	8	–	6
Balance at June 30, 2004 . .	421	83	169	69	742
Henkel exchange	–	(15)	–	–	(15)
Translation adjustments and other	5	–	11	–	16
Balance at June 30, 2005 . .	$ 426	$ 68	$180	$69	$743

Changes in trademarks and other intangible assents for the fiscal years ended June 30, 2005 and 2004 are summarized below. The intangible assents, which are subject to amortization are reported net of accumulated amortization of $164 and $152 at June 30, 2005 and 2004, respectively, of which $38 and $28, respectively, related to technology. The estimated amortization expense for these intangible assents is $11 for each of the fiscal years 2006, 2007, 2008, 2009 and 2010.

	Trademarks and other intangible assets subject to amortization			Trademarks not subject to amortization	Total
	Technology	Other	Sub-Total		
Net balance at June 30, 2003	$105	$31	$136	$515	$651
Acquisitions	1	–	–	2	3
Translation adjustments and other	–	(4)	(4)	(2)	(6)
Amortization	(9)	(6)	(15)	–	(15)
Net balance at June 30, 2004	97	21	118	515	633
Henkel exchange	–	–	–	(32)	(32)
Translation adjustments and other	–	1	1	9	10
Amortization	(10)	(2)	(12)	–	(12)

	Trademarks and other intangible assets subject to amortization			Trademarks not subject to amortization	Total
	Technology	Other	Sub-Total		
Net balance at June 30, 2005	$87	$20	$107	$492	$599
Weighted average life (in years)	13	19	14		14

The Company performed its annual review of intangible assets in the third fiscal quarter and no instances of impairment were identified. Business valuations of the Colombia and Venezuela reporting units were performed, as these businesses operate under continuing economic and political uncertainties. The fair value for Colombia was only slightly in excess of the carrying amount. The Company is closely monitoring any events, circumstances, or changes in the businesses that might imply a reduction in the fair value and might lead to additional impairments. The Company will continue to test annually for impairment in the third fiscal quarter unless there are indications during an interim period that intangible assents may have become impaired.

H.J. Heinz
2005 Annual Report

5. Goodwill and Other Intangible Assets

Effective May 2, 2002, the Company adopted SFAS No. 142, "Goodwill and Other Intangible Assets." Under this standard, goodwill and intangibles with indefinite useful lives are no longer amortized. This standard also requires, at a minimum, an annual impairment assessment of the carrying value of goodwill and intangibles with indefinite useful lives. The reassessment of intangible assets, including the ongoing impact of amortization, and the assignment of goodwill to reporting units was completed during the first quarter of Fiscal 2003.

The Company completed its transitional goodwill impairment tests during the second quarter of Fiscal 2003 and, as a result, recorded a transitional impairment charge that was calculated as of May 2, 2002, and recorded as an effect of a change in accounting principle for Fiscal 2003, of $77.8 million. There was no tax effect associated with this charge. The charge, which relates to certain of the Company's reporting units, has been reflected in its segments as follows: Europe $54.6 million, Asia/Pacific $2.7 million, and Other Operating Entities $20.5 million.

The transitional impairment charge resulted from application of the new impairment methodology introduced by SFAS No. 142. Previous accounting rules incorporated a comparison of carrying value to undiscounted cash flows, whereas new rules require a comparison of carrying value to discounted cash flows, which are lower. Under previous requirements, no goodwill impairment would have been recorded on May 2, 2002.

The annual impairment tests are performed in the fourth quarter of each fiscal year unless events suggest an impairment may have occurred in the interim.

Changes in the carrying amount of goodwill for the fiscal year ended April 27, 2005 by reportable segment are as follows:

	North American Consumer Products	U.S. Foodservice	Europe	Asia/ pacific	Other Operating Entities	Total
	(Thousands of dollars)					
Balance at April 28, 2004 ..	$923,949	$179,544	$670,935	$165,646	$19,850	$1,959,914
Acquisitions .	–	52,008	1,541	21,662	4,735	79,946
Purchase accounting Adjustments	(11,099)	(1,185)	35,895	(298)	586	23,899
Disposal	(2,548)	–	(474)	–	(483)	(35,05)
Translation adjustments	7,414	–	55,865	20,915	903	85,093
Impairment ..	–	–	–	–	(6,848)	(6,848)
Balance at April 27, 2005 ..	$917,706	$230,367	$763,758	$207,925	$18,743	$2,138,499

During Fiscal 2005, the Company acquired a controlling interest in Shanghai LongFong Foods, Appetizers And, Inc., and certain assets from ABAL, S.A. de C.V. Preliminary purchase price allocations have been recorded for each of these acquisitions. The Company expects to finalize the purchase price allocations related to these acquisitions during Fiscal 2006 upon completion of third-party valuation procedures. During the fourth quarter of Fiscal 2005, the Company finalized the purchase price allocation related to the Fiscal 2004 acquisition of Unifine Richardson B.V., within the North American Consumer Products segment. The purchase accounting adjustment in the Europe segment primarily represents a correction to the deferred income tax liabilities related to the Fiscal 2001 acquisition of CSM Nederland NV.

The impairment in the above table, which was classified within cost of products sold, was recognized due to a deterioration of current and expected operating results of a consolidated joint venture following a recall in Fiscal 2004. The Company reached an agreement with third parties, the proceeds of which were offset by the impairment and other damages incurred to date. No other goodwill impairment charges were recognized in Fiscal 2005.

Trademarks and other intangible assets at April 27, 2005 and April 28, 2004, subject to amortization expense, are as follows:

	April 27, 2005			April 28, 2004		
	Gross	Accum Amort	Net	Gross	Accum Amort	Net
			(Thousands of dollars)			
Trademarks	$221,019	$ (61,616)	$159,403	$188,927	$ (50,505)	$(138,422)
Licenses	208,186	(123,911)	84,275	208,186	(118,504)	89,682
Others	155,481	(68,081)	87,400	123,394	(63,156)	60,238
	$584,686	$(253,608)	$331,078	$520,507	$(232,165)	$288,342

Amortization expense for trademarks and other intangible assets subject to amortization was $18.4 million, $17.1 million, and $20.4 million for the fiscal years ended April 27, 2005, April 28, 2004, and April 30, 2003, respectively. Based upon the amortizable intangible assets recorded on the balance sheet as of April 27, 2005, amortization expense for each of the next five fiscal years is estimated to be approximately $18 million.

Intangible assets not subject to amortization at April 27, 2005 and April 28, 2004, were $492.2 million and $505.5 million, respectively, and consisted solely of trademarks.

John Deere 2004 Annual Report

15. Goodwill and Other Intangible Assets-Net

Upon the adoption of FASB Statement No. 142, Goodwill and Other Intangible Assets, at the beginning of fiscal year 2003, goodwill was no longer amortized and will be written down in the future only for impairments. Goodwill is reviewed for impairment by reporting unit based on fair values annually or as events and circumstances change.

Pro forma net income and net income per share, excluding goodwill amortization, were as follows with dollars in millions except per share amounts:

	2004	2003	2002
Net income as reported	$1,406	$643	$319
Goodwill amortization, net of tax			35
Pro forma net income	$1,406	$643	$372
Basic net income per share:			
Net income as reported	$5.69	$2.68	$1.34
Goodwill amortization, net of tax			.22
Pro forma net income	5.69	2.68	1.56
Diluted net income per share:			
Net income as reported	$5.56	$2.64	$1.33
Goodwill amortization, net of tax			.22
Pro forma net income	$5.56	$2.64	$1.55

The amounts of goodwill by operating segment were as follows in millions of dollars:

	2004*	2003
Agricultural equipment	$101	$94**
Commercial and consumer equipment	299	305
Construction and forestry	574	473
Total goodwill	$974	$872

* The change in goodwill between years for construction and forestry was primarily due to $73 million goodwill from the additional acquisition and consolidation of Nortrax (see Note 1). The remaining changes are due to fluctuations in foreign currency exchange rates.
** Restated to include special technologies group (see Note 27).

The components of other intangible assets are as follows in millions of dollars:

	2004	2003
Amortized intangible assets:		
Gross patents, licenses and other	$12	$9
Accumulated amortization	(8)	(6)
Net patents, licenses and other	4	3
Unamortized intangible assets:		
Intangible asset related to minimum pension liability	18	250
Total other intangible assets—net	$22	$253

Other intangible assets, excluding the intangible pension asset, are stated at cost less accumulated amortization and are being amortized over 17 years or less on the straight-line basis. The intangible pension asset is remeasured and adjusted annually. The decrease in the intangible pension asset is a result of the decrease in the minimum pension liability due primarily to voluntary company contributions to the pension plan and the return on plan assets. The amortization of other intangible assets is not significant.

Ciena
2004 Annual Report

(4) Goodwill and Long Lived Asset Impairments

Goodwill Impairment

Effective November 1, 2001, Ciena adopted SFAS 142 and ceased to amortize goodwill. On adoption of SFAS 142, Ciena determined that its operations represented a single reporting unit. Ciena completed an impairment review of the goodwill associated with its reporting unit during the three months ended January 31, 2002. Ciena compared the fair value of its reporting unit at November 1, 2001 to the carrying value including goodwill for the unit at November 1, 2001, and determined that the carrying value, including goodwill, did not exceed the unit's fair value. As a result, no impairment charge was required on adoption.

Prior to the reorganization of Ciena into operating segments during fiscal 2004, the fair value of Ciena's goodwill was tested for impairment on an annual basis, and between annual tests if an event occurred or circumstances changed that would, more likely than not, have reduced the fair value of Ciena on an enterprise level, rather than a segment level, below its carrying value. Due to Ciena's reorganization into operating segments, SFAS 142 requires that Ciena assign goodwill to its reporting units. Ciena has determined its operating segments and reporting units are the same. In accordance with SFAS 142 Ciena tests each reporting unit's goodwill for impairment on an annual basis, which Ciena has determined to be the last business day of September each year, and between annual tests if events occur or circumstances change that would, more likely than not, reduce the fair value of the reporting unit below its carrying value. The following table summarizes the changes and reorganization assignment in the carrying amount of Ciena's goodwill to its reporting units as of October 31, 2004 for fiscal 2002, fiscal 2003 and fiscal 2004 (in thousands):

	CNG	MESG	TSG*	DNG	BBG	Total
Balance as of November 1, 2001						178,891
Goodwill acquired during fiscal 2002						590,895
Impairment losses						(557,286)
Balance as of October 31, 2002						212,500
Goodwill acquired during fiscal 2003						123,539
Balance as of October 31, 2003						336,039
Purchase adjustments						(121)
Assignment as of January 31, 2004	$151,121	$97,924	–	$86,873	–	$335,918
Goodwill acquired during fiscal 2004	–	120,574	–	–	326,241	446,815
Purchase adjustments	–	(289)	–	(1,858)	(259)	(2,406)

	CNG	MESG	TSG*	DNG	BBG	Total
Impairment losses	(93,321)	(129,009)	–	–	(149,382)	(371,712)
Reorganization assignment	(57,800)	(89,200)	147,000	–	–	–
Balance as of October 31, 2004	$ –	$ –	$147,000	$85,015	$176,600	$408,615

* CNG and MESG were combined to form TSG during October fiscal 2004.

During fiscal 2004 Ciena performed its annual testing to determine and measure goodwill impairment on a reporting unit basis, and with the assistance from independent valuation experts management performed an assessment of the fair value of Ciena's reporting units and their intangible assets as of September 27, 2004. Ciena compared the fair value of each of its reporting units to each reporting unit's carrying value including goodwill and determined that the carrying value, including goodwill, of CNG, MESG, and BBG exceeded their respective fair values as of September 27, 2004. As a result, Ciena assessed the fair values of CNG, MESG, and BBG assets, including identified intangible assets, and liabilities and derived an implied fair value for the reporting unit's goodwill. Since the carrying amount of the goodwill assigned to CNG, MESG and BBG was greater than the implied fair values, an impairment loss of $93.3 million, $129.0 million, and $149.4 million for CNG, MESG, and BBG, respectively, was recognized in fiscal 2004.

The fair value of Ciena's reporting units were determined using the average of the outcomes from the following valuation methods: market multiples; comparable transactions; and discounted cash flows. A control premium of 15% to 20% was added to the valuation results for each reporting unit. Ciena determined the estimated fair value of identifiable intangible assets of its reporting units using discounted cash flows. The cash flow periods used ranged from one to seven years, applying annual growth rates of 5% to 118%. Ciena used discount rates of 10% to 30% based on the specific risks and circumstances associated with the identified intangible asset or other non-goodwill assets or liability being evaluated. The assumptions supporting the estimated cash flows for identified intangible assets and other non-goodwill assets and liabilities, including the discount rate, reflects management's estimates. The discount rate was based upon Ciena's weighted average cost of capital as adjusted for the risks associated with its operations.

During fiscal 2002 and fiscal 2003, Ciena, with the assistance from independent valuation experts, performed an assessment of the fair value of Ciena's single reporting unit and its intangible assets as of September 27, 2002 and September 26, 2003, respectively. Ciena compared its fair value to its carrying value including goodwill and determined that its carrying value, including goodwill, exceeded fair value as of September 27, 2002 but did not exceed fair value as of September 26, 2003. As a result, during fiscal 2002 Ciena assessed the fair value of its assets, including identified intangible assets, and liabilities and derived an implied fair value for its goodwill. Since the carrying amount of goodwill was greater than its implied fair value, an impairment loss of $557.3 million was recognized in fiscal 2002.

During fiscal 2002 fair value of Ciena was determined using the average market price of Ciena's common stock over a 10-day period before and after September 27, 2002 and a control premium of 25%. During fiscal 2003 the fair value of Ciena was determined using the average market price of Ciena's common stock over a 10-day period before and after September 26, 2003 and a control premium of 25%. Ciena determined the estimated fair value of identified intangible assets and non-goodwill intangible assets and liabilities using dis-counted cash flows. The cash flow periods used were eight years, applying annual growth rates of 10% to 86%. Ciena used discount rates of 10% to 32% based of the specific risks and circumstances associated with the identified intangible asset or other non-goodwill assets or liability being evaluated. The assumptions supporting the estimated cash flows for identified intangible assets and other non-goodwill assets and liabilities, including the discount rate, reflects management's estimates. The discount rate was based upon Ciena's weighted average cost of capital as adjusted for the risks associated with its operations.

Long-Lived Asset Impairment—Equipment, Furniture, and Fixtures

During fiscal 2002, fiscal 2003, and fiscal 2004, Ciena recorded impairment losses of $127.3 million, $17.6 million, and $15.9 million, respectively, related to excess equipment, furniture, and fixtures that were classified as held for sale as a result of Ciena's restructuring activities.

Long-Lived Asset Impairment—Other Intangible Assets

As part of Ciena's review of financial results for fiscal 2002, fiscal 2003, and fiscal 2004, Ciena performed an assessment of the carrying value of Ciena's other intangible assets. The assessment was performed pursuant to SFAS 144 in fiscal 2003 and fiscal 2004 and pursuant to SFAS 121 in fiscal 2002. No impairments were required in fiscal 2002 or fiscal 2004. During fiscal 2003 Ciena recorded a charge of $29.6 million, related to the impairment of acquired MetroDirector K2 developed technology. The method used for determining fair value was the held-for-use model, two-step method. This charge was based on the amount by which the carrying amount of the developed technology exceeded its fair value. Fair value was determined based on discounted future cash flows derived from the developed technology, which had separately identifiable cash flows. The cash flow periods used were five years, applying a first year growth rate of 5% with subsequent declines of between 10% and 20% in the following years. The discount rate used was 21.0%. The assumptions supporting the estimated future cash flows, including the discount rate reflect management's best estimates. The discount rate was based upon Ciena's weighted average cost of capital as adjusted for the risks associated with its operations.

Chapter 4
Balance Sheet Presentation and Disclosures: Liabilities

CONTENTS

This chapter discusses the accounting, reporting, and disclosures associated with liabilities covered in ASC 210-10-45-5 through 45-12 and 470-10, *Balance Sheet: Overall*. Topics include loss contingencies, compensated absences, termination benefits, troubled debt restructuring, refinancing of current to noncurrent debt, callable obligations by creditors, issuance of bonds, calling debt, imputing interest on noninterest notes payable, environmental liabilities, and offsetting of liabilities.

INTRODUCTION TO LIABILITIES

A liability is liquidated from either the use of an asset or the incurrence of another liability. Liabilities may arise from a contract, by law, by a judicial decision, or by another means.

Current liabilities are those to be paid or liquidated from current assets or created from other current liabilities. Current liabilities are due on demand or within one year or the normal operating cycle of the business, whichever is greater. Current liabilities may arise in which:

☐ The payee and amount are known.

☐ The payee is not known but the amount may be reasonably estimated.

☐ The payable is known but the amount must be estimated.

☐ The liability arises from a loss contingency.

The current portion of long-term debt to be paid within the next year or the amount that is due on demand is classified as a current liability.

Refundable deposits are classified as current liabilities if the company intends to refund the money within the next year.

Agency liabilities are amounts withheld by the company from employees or customers for taxes owed to federal, state, or local taxing agencies. They are listed as current liabilities.

A company may offer potential customers premiums (something free or for a minimal charge, such as samples) to stimulate product sales. The customer may be required to return evidence of purchase of certain products (e.g., box top) to get the premium. A nominal cash payment may be necessary. A current liability arises for the amount of anticipated redemptions in the next year. If the premium and redemption period is for more than one year, an estimated liability must be allocated to the current and noncurrent portions.

EXAMPLE

XYZ Company offers its customers a camera in exchange for 20 boxtops and $3. The camera costs the company $18. It is expected that 60% of the boxtops will be redeemed. The following journal entries are required:

1. To record the purchase of 10,000 cameras at $18 each:

Inventory of premium cameras	180,000	
Cash		180,000

2. To record the sale of 400,000 boxes of the company's major product at $3 each:

Cash	1,200,000	
Sales		1,200,000

3. To record the actual redemption of 120,000 boxtops, the receipt of $3 per 20 boxtops, and the delivery of the cameras:

Cash [(120,000/20 × $3)]	18,000	
Premium expense	90,000	
Inventory of premium cameras [(120,000/20) × $18]		108,000

4. To record end-of-year adjusting entry for estimated liability for outstanding offers (boxtops):

Premium expense	90,000	
Estimated liability		90,000
Computation:		
Total boxtops sold		400,000
Total estimated redemptions (60%)		240,000
Boxtops redeemed		120,000
Estimated future redemptions		120,000

Cost of estimated claims outstanding
(120,000/20) × ($18 − 3) = $90,000

Note: The premium expense account is presented as a selling expense. The inventory of premium cameras account balance is presented as a current asset, and the estimated liability account is reported as a current liability.

EXAMPLE

On November 30, 20X6, a consignee received 1,000 units on consignment. The cost and selling price per unit were $60 and $85, respectively. The commission rate is 8%. At December 31, 20X6, the units in inventory were 200. The amount to be presented as a payable for consigned goods at year-end 20X6 is computed as follows:

Units sold (1,000 − 200)	800
× Amount to be remitted per unit ($85 − $6.80)	× $78.20
Payable	$62,560

ASC 470-10-45-9 covers the classification of demand notes with repayment terms. Obligations due on demand or within one year are classified as current debt even if liquidation is not anticipated within that period.

ASC 470-10-45-4, *Debt: Overall*, deals with the balance sheet classification of borrowings outstanding under revolving credit agreements that include both a subjective acceleration clause and a lock-box agreement. If the borrowings reduce the debt outstanding, the borrowings are classified as current liabilities.

EXAMPLE

Shapiro Company presented the following, liabilities at year-end 20X2:

Accounts payable	$100,000
Notes payable, 10%, due 7/1/20X3	600,000
Contingent liability	150,000
Accrued expenses	20,000
Deferred income tax credit	25,000
Bonds payable, 9%, due 5/1/20X3	500,000

The contingent liability represents a reasonably possible loss arising from a $400,000 lawsuit against Shapiro. In the opinion of legal counsel, the lawsuit is expected to be resolved in 20X4. The range of loss is $200,000 to $600,000. The deferred income tax credit is expected to reverse in 20X4.

At year-end 20X2, current liabilities equal $1,220,000, computed as follows:

Accounts payable	$ 100,000
Notes payable, due 5/1/20X3	600,000
Accrued expenses	20,000
Bonds payable, due 5/1/20X3	500,000
Total	$1,220,000

EXAMPLE

Morgan Company requires nonrefundable advance payments with special orders for equipment built to customer specifications. The following data were provided for 20X2:

Customer advances 1/1/20X2	$300,000
Advances related to canceled orders during the year	80,000
Advances for orders shipped during the year	160,000
Advances received with orders during the year	200,000

The amount to be presented as a current liability for customer advances at year-end 20X2 is computed as follows:

Balance—1/1/20X2	$300,000
Add: advances received with orders	200,000
Less: advances related to orders canceled	(80,000)
Less: advances for orders shipped	(160,000)
Balance—12/31/20X2	$260,000

EXAMPLE

Schwartz Company requires an advance payment for orders specially designed for particular customers. Such advances are not refundable. Relevant information for 20X2 follows:

Customer advances—1/1/20X2	$69,000
Advances associated with canceled orders	30,000

Advances received with orders	90,000
Advances applied to orders shipped	85,000

On December 31, 20X2, the current liabilities associated with customer advances was $44,000, computed as follows:

Balance—1/1/20X2	$69,000
Add: advances received with orders	90,000
Less: advances applicable to orders shipped	(85,000)
Less: advances related to canceled orders	(30,000)
Balance—12/31/20X2	$44,000

EXAMPLE

On December 31, 20X2, Fox Company received 200 units of a product on consignment from Jacoff Company. The cost of the product is $50 each, and the selling price per unit is $75. Fox's commission is 8%. At December 31, 20X2, 10 units were in stock. The payable for consigned goods to be shown under current liabilities is $13,110, computed as follows:

Units sold (200 – 10)	190
Per unit owed ($75 selling price less $6 commission)	× $69
Total	$13,110

EXAMPLE

As of December 31, 20X2 before adjustment for the following items, accounts payable had a balance of $700,000:

☐ A check to a supplier amounting to $40,000 was recorded on December 30, 20X2. The check was mailed on January 3, 20X3.

☐ At December 31, 20X2, the company has a $30,000 debit balance in its accounts payable to a supplier due to an advance payment for a product to be produced.

The accounts payable to be presented on the December 31, 20X2 balance sheet is computed as follows:

Unadjusted balance	$700,000
Unmailed check	40,000
Customer with debit balance	30,000
Adjusted balance	$770,000

Debt is classified as noncurrent if it is to be refinanced with another long-term issue or extinguished from noncurrent assets (e.g., sinking fund). It is not to be paid from current assets or the incurrence of current liabilities.

Long-term debt should be recorded at the present value discounted of future payments using the market rate of interest.

Derivatives and liabilities arising from the transfer of financial assets are recorded at fair market value.

In a deferred interest-rate-setting agreement that is an important element in the original issuance, amounts paid or received because of such agreement should be treated as a premium or discount on the initial debt and amortized over the term of the debt. In a deferred interest rate arrangement, the issuing company sells its debt at a fixed rate but also contracts to set an interest rate at a later date based on some index. As a result, the set interest rate will differ from the fixed interest rate during the designated period.

If a borrowing arrangement permits the debtor to redeem the debt instrument within one year, it is presented under current liabilities. However, the debt is classified as noncurrent if the letter of credit agreement satisfies the following criteria:

☐ The financing agreement does not terminate within one year.

☐ The refinancing is on a long-term basis.

☐ The lender cannot cancel the agreement unless there is a clearly ascertainable violation.

If debt is tied to a certain index or market value of a commodity so that a contingent payment will be due at maturity, a liability must be recorded for the amount by which the contingent payment exceeds the amount initially assigned to the contingent payment feature.

In a joint venture, there may be take-or-pay or through-put contracts to construct capital facilities (e.g., factory building). The debt is incurred by the joint venture, but the individual companies buy the goods (take-or-pay contract) or services (through-put contract) arising from the project. The goods or services are paid for periodically, irrespective of whether the items are delivered or not. A minimum amount of goods or services is usually provided for. Such agreements require disclosure.

An indirect guarantee of indebtedness of others is an assurance obligating one company (the first company) to transfer money to a second company upon the occurrence of some happening, whereby the funds are available to creditors of the second company, and those same creditors have a legal right to collect from the first company debt owed by it to the second company.

ASC 470-10-35, *Debt: Overall*, stipulates that notes maturing in three months having a continual extension option for up to five years may be classified after taking into account the intentions of the parties and the issuer's ability to pay the debt. If the source of repayment is current, the debt should be classified as current. However, if the source of repayment is noncurrent, the debt is noncurrent in nature. Interest should be computed based on the interest method. Debt interest costs should be deferred and amortized over the outstanding period of the debt. If excess accrued interest arises from paying the debt before maturity, it should be used to adjust interest expense. **Note:** classification of the debt need not be the same as the period used to compute periodic interest cost.

EXAMPLE

A company has an escrow account from which it pays property taxes on behalf of customers. Interest less a 5% service fee is credited to the mortgagee's account and is used to reduce future escrow payments. Additional data are as follows:

ESCROW ACCOUNTS LIABILITY—BEGINNING OF YEAR	$500,000
Receipt of escrow payments	800,000
Payment of property taxes	450,000
Interest earned on escrow funds	65,000

At year-end, the escrow accounts liability equals $911,750, determined as follows:

Balance—1/1	$500,000
Receipt of escrow payments	800,000
Payment of property taxes	(450,000)
Interest earned net of service fee ($65,000 × 95%)	61,750
Balance—12/31	$911,750

Disclosures for debt include:

☐ Type of debt (e.g., debentures, secured).

☐ Major classes of debt.

☐ Pledging or collateral requirements.

☐ Stated interest rate.

☐ Restrictive covenants (e.g., dividends limitations, working capital requirements).

☐ Maturity value, maturity period, and maturity date.

☐ Open lines of credit.

☐ Conversion options.

☐ Unused letters of credit.

☐ Sinking fund requirements.

☐ Amounts due to related parties.

☐ Amounts due to officers.

FAIR VALUE MEASUREMENTS

ASC 820-10-05, *Fair Value Measurements and Disclosures: Overall*, provides the definition of fair value, gives guidance on fair value measurements, and cites suitable disclosures in the financial statements of the measures of fair value used. Fair value is a market-based measurement. A fair value measurement reflects current market participant assumptions regarding future inflows of the asset and future outflows of the liability. A fair value measurement should take into account features of the specific asset or liability such as condition and location.

In deriving fair value, exchange price should be examined. This is the market price at the measurement date in an "orderly transaction" between the parties to sell the asset or transfer the liability. Specifically, focus is on the price at the measurement date that would be received to sell the asset or paid to transfer the liability (an exit price), not the price that would be paid to buy the asset or received to assume the liability (an entry price). In addition, the asset or liability may be independent (e.g., financial instrument, operating asset), or there may be a group of assets or liabilities (e.g., asset group, reporting unit).

To consider the assumptions of market participants in fair value measurements, ASC 820-10-05 provides a hierarchy of fair value that differentiates between (1) assumptions based on market data obtained from independent outside sources to the reporting entity (observable inputs) and (2) assumptions by the reporting entity itself (unobservable inputs). The use of unobservable inputs allows for situations in which there is minimal or no market activity for the asset or liability at the measurement date. In this scenario, the reporting entity need not perform all possible efforts to obtain information concerning market participant assumptions. However, the entity must not ignore information of reasonably available market participant assumptions. Valuation techniques used to measure fair value shall maximize the use of observable inputs and minimize the use of unobservable inputs.

Market participant assumptions include risk, such as risk in a specific valuation method to measure fair value (e.g., pricing model) or input risks to the valuation technique. An adjustment for risk should be made in a fair value measurement when market participants would include risk in the pricing of the asset or liability. Market participant assumptions should consider the impact of a restriction on the sale or use of an asset that influences its price.

A fair value measurement for a liability should take into account the risk that the obligation will not be fulfilled (nonperformance risk). In evaluating this risk, the reporting entity's credit risk should be considered.

The fair value of a position in a financial instrument (including a block) that is actively traded should be measured by multiplying the quoted price of the instrument by the quantity held (within Level 1 of the fair value hierarchy). The quoted price must not be adjusted because of the size of the position relative to trading volume (blockage factor).

A fair value measurement assumes the transaction takes place in the principal market for the asset or liability. The principal market is one in which the reporting entity would sell the asset or transfer the liability with the greatest volume and activity level. If there is no principal market, then the most advantageous market should be used. The most advantageous market is one in which the reporting entity would sell the asset or transfer the liability with the price that maximizes the amount that would be received for the asset or minimizes the amount that would be paid to transfer the liability after considering transaction costs.

The price in the principal (or most advantageous) market used to measure fair value should not be adjusted for transaction costs. On the other hand, transportation costs for the asset or liability should be included in the fair value measurement.

In measuring fair value, valuation techniques in conformity with the market, income, and cost approaches should be used. Under the "market approach," prices for market transactions for identical or comparable assets or liabilities are used. An example of a market approach is matrix pricing. This is a mathematical method used primarily to value debt securities without solely relying on quoted prices for the particular securities. This method relies on the relationship of the securities to other benchmark quoted securities. Under the "income approach," valuation techniques are used to convert future amounts (e.g., profits, cash flows) to a present value amount. For example, future cash flows are discounted to their present value amount using the present value tables. The measurement is based on market expectations of the future amounts. Examples of these valuation techniques are present value determination, option pricing models, and the multiyear excess earnings method (to value goodwill). The "cost approach" is based on the amount that would be required to replace an asset's service capability (current replacement cost). An example is the cost to purchase or build a substitute asset of comparable utility after adjusting for obsolescence.

Depending on the circumstances, a single or multiple valuation technique may be needed. For example, a single valuation method would be used to value an asset using quoted prices in an active market for identical assets, whereas a multiple valuation method would be used to value a reporting unit.

Input availability and reliability associated with the asset or liability may influence the selection of the best-suited valuation method.

The fair value hierarchy prioritizes the inputs to valuation techniques used to measure fair value into three broad levels. The levels range from the highest priority, which is assigned to quoted prices (unadjusted) in active markets for identical assets or liabilities (Level 1), to the lowest priority, which is assigned to unobservable inputs (Level 3).

Level 2 inputs are those (except quoted prices included within Level 1) that are observable for the asset or liability, either directly or indirectly. If the asset or liability has a specified (contractual) term, a Level 2 input must be observable for substantially the full term of the asset or liability. Included as Level 2 inputs are:

☐ Quoted prices for similar assets or liabilities in active markets.

☐ Quoted prices for similar or identical assets or liabilities in markets that are not active namely in markets having few transactions, noncurrent prices, price quotations that vary significantly, or very limited public information.

☐ Inputs excluding quoted prices that are observable for the asset or liability. Examples are interest rates observable at often quoted intervals, default rates, credit risks, loss severities, volatilities, and prepayment speeds.

☐ Inputs derived in most part from observable market data by correlation or other means.

Adjustments to Level 2 inputs vary depending on factors specific to the asset or liability. Those factors include the location or condition of the asset or liability, market volume and activity level, and the extent to which the inputs relate to comparable items to the asset or liability. A major adjustment to the fair value measurement may result in a Level 3 measurement.

Level 3 inputs are unobservable for the asset or liability. Unobservable inputs are used to measure fair value to the extent that observable inputs are unavailable. This allows for cases in which there is little or no market activity for the asset or liability at the measurement date. Unobservable inputs reflect the reporting entity's own assumptions about the assumptions (e.g., risk) that market participants would use in pricing the asset or liability.

If an input used to measure fair value is based on bid and ask prices, the price within the bid-ask spread that is most representative of fair value shall be used to measure fair value regardless of where in the fair value hierarchy the input falls.

Disclosures are mandated for fair value measurements to improve financial statement user understanding. Quantitative disclosures using a tabular format are required in all periods (annual and interim). Qualitative (narrative) disclosures are required about the valuation methods used to measure fair value. Disclosures of fair value in measuring assets and liabilities emphasizes the inputs used to measure fair value and the impact of fair value measurements on profit or change in net assets.

For assets and liabilities measured at fair value on a recurring basis in periods after initial recognition (e.g., trading securities), disclosures should be made to allow financial statement users to appraise the inputs used to formulate fair value measurements. To achieve this, the following should be disclosed in annual and interim periods for each major category of asset and liability:

1. Fair value measurements at the reporting date.

2. The level within the fair value hierarchy in which the fair value measurements in their entirety fall, segregating the fair value measurements using quoted prices in active markets for identical assets or liabilities (Level 1), major other observable inputs (Level 2), and significant unobservable inputs (Level 3).

3. For fair value measurements using major unobservable inputs (Level 3), a reconciliation of the beginning and ending balances, separately presenting changes during the period attributable to the following:

   a. Total gain or loss (realized and unrealized), segregating those gains or losses included in earnings (or changes in net assets) as well as where those gains or losses are presented in the financial statements.

   b. Purchases, sales, issuances, and settlements (net).

   c. Transfers in or out of Level 3. An example is a transfer because of a change in the observability of major inputs.

4. For annual reporting only, the valuation techniques used to measure fair value and a discussion of any changes in those techniques.

For assets and liabilities that are measured at fair value on a nonrecurring basis in periods after initial recognition such as impaired assets, disclosure should be made of:

1. The level within the fair value hierarchy in which the fair value measurements fall.

2. Fair value measurements recorded during the period and the reasons for those measurements.

3. For fair value measurements using significant unobservable inputs (Level 3), a description of the inputs and the data used to develop them.

4. For annual reporting only, the valuation methods used and any changes in them to measure similar assets and liabilities in prior years.

ASC 820, *Fair Value Measurement*, provides guidance for estimating fair value when the volume and activity level for the asset or liability have significantly decreased. This includes guidance on identifying circumstances that indicate a transaction is not orderly. Fair value is the price that would be received to sell an asset or paid to transfer a liability in an orderly transaction (i.e., not a forced liquidation or distressed sale) between market participants at the measurement date under current market conditions.

If the reporting entity decides there has been a major decrease in the volume and level of activity for the asset or liability relative to normal market activity for the asset or liability, transactions or quoted prices may not be determinative of fair value. Further analysis is needed, and a significant adjustment to the transaction or quoted prices may be necessary to estimate fair value. Significant adjustments also may be needed in other situations (for instance, when a price for a similar asset requires significant adjustment to make it more comparable to the asset being measured or when the price is old).

Even in cases where there has been a significant decrease in the volume and level of activity for the asset or liability regardless of the valuation technique used, the objective of a fair value measurement remains the same. Determining the price at which willing market participants would transact at the measurement date under current market conditions if there has been a significant decrease in the volume and level of activity for the asset or liability depends on the facts and circumstances and requires the use of judgment. However, a reporting entity's intention to hold the asset or liability is not relevant in estimating fair value. Fair value is a market-based measurement, not an entity-specific measurement.

Even if there has been a significant decrease in the volume and level of activity for the asset or liability, it is not appropriate to conclude that all transactions are not orderly (that is, distressed or forced).

Accounting Standards Update (ASU) No. 2011-04 (May 2011) (ASC 820, *Fair Value Measurement*), *Amendments to Achieve Common Fair Value Measurement and Disclosure Requirements in U.S. GAAP and IFRS*, provides the following amendments to ASC 820:

- The concepts of highest and best use and valuation in a fair value measurement are only relevant in measuring the fair value of nonfinancial assets, *not* financial assets or liabilities.

- A company should measure the fair value of its own equity instrument from the point of view of a holder of that instrument.

- A company should disclose quantitative data concerning unobservable inputs used to measure fair value classified in Level 3.

- The application of discounts or premiums in a fair value measurement applies to the unit of account for the asset or liability being measured at fair value.

In the case of a Level 3 fair value hierarchy, disclosure should be made of the valuation processes as well as the sensitivity of the fair value measurement to changes in unobservable inputs and any interrelationships between them.

FAIR VALUE OPTION FOR FINANCIAL ASSETS AND FINANCIAL LIABILITIES

ASC 825-10-05, 10-10 and 10-15, *Financial Instruments: Overall*, allows companies to measure many financial instruments and some other items at fair value. The pronouncement is effective as of the beginning of the company's first fiscal year beginning after November 15, 2007. Most provisions of the pronouncement solely apply to businesses that choose the fair value option. The eligible items for the fair value measurement option are:

1. Recognized financial assets and financial liabilities excluding
   (a) financial assets and financial liabilities recognized under leases,
   (b) financial instruments classified by the issuer as an element of stockholders' equity such as a convertible bond with a noncontingent beneficial conversion feature,
   (c) investment in a subsidiary or variable interest entity that must be consolidated,
   (d) deposit liabilities that can be withdrawn on demand of banks, and
   (e) employers' plan obligations or assets for pension and postretirement benefits.

2. Nonfinancial insurance contracts and warranties that can be settled by the insurer by paying a third party for goods or services.

3. Firm commitments applying to financial instruments such as a forward purchase contract for a loan not readily convertible to cash.

4. Written loan commitment.

5. Host financial instruments arising from separating an embedded nonfinancial derivative instrument from a nonfinancial hybrid instrument.

GAAP permits a company to choose to measure eligible items at fair value at stipulated election dates. Included in earnings at each reporting date are the unrealized (holding) gains and losses on items for which the fair value option has been elected.

The fair value option is irrevocable (except if a new election date occurs) and is applied solely to entire instruments (not portions of those instruments or specified risks or specific cash flows). In most cases, the fair value option may be applied instrument-by-instrument including investments otherwise accounted for under the equity method.

These parameters (ASC 825-10-15, 4-5) apply to all companies with trading and available-for-sale securities.

Upfront costs and fees applicable to items for which the fair value option is selected are expensed as incurred.

Electing the Fair Value Option

A company may elect the fair value option for all eligible items only on the date that one of the following occurs:

1. The company first recognizes the eligible item.

2. The company engages in an eligible firm commitment.

3. There is a change in the accounting treatment for an investment in another company because the investment becomes subject to the equity method or the investor no longer consolidates a subsidiary because a majority voting interest no longer exists, although the investor still retains some ownership interest.

4. Specialized accounting treatment no longer applies for the financial assets that have been reported at fair value such as under an AICPA Audit and Accounting Guide.

5. An event mandates an eligible item to be measured at fair value on the event date but does not require fair value measurement at each subsequent reporting date.

Events

Some events that require remeasurement of eligible items at fair value, initial recognition of eligible items, or both, and thus create an election date for the fair value option are:

☐ Consolidation or deconsolidation of a subsidiary or variable interest entity.

☐ Business combination.

☐ Sale of a portion of a consolidated subsidiary; any previously recorded noncontrolling interest must be measured at fair value.

☐ Major debt modification.

Instrument Application

The fair value option may be selected for a single eligible item without electing it for other identical items except for the following:

1. If the fair value option is selected for an eligible insurance contract, it must be applied to all claims and obligations under the contract.

2. If the fair value option is selected for an investment under the equity method, it must be applied to all of the investor's financial interests in the same entity that are eligible items.

3. If multiple advances are made to one borrower under a single contract (e.g., construction loan) and the individual advances lose their identity and become part of the larger loan, the fair value option must be applied to the larger loan balance but not to the individual advances.

4. If the fair value option is selected for an insurance contract for which integrated or nonintegrated contract features or riders are issued at the same time or later, the fair value option must be applied also to those features or coverage.

The fair value option does not usually have to be applied to all financial instruments issued or bought in a single transaction. For example, an investor in stock or bonds may apply the fair value option to some of the stock shares or bonds issued or acquired in a single transaction. In this case, an individual bond is considered the minimum denomination of that debt security. A financial instrument that is a single contract cannot be broken down into parts when using the fair value option. However, a loan syndication may consist of in multiple loans to the same debtor by different creditors. Each of the loans is a separate instrument, and the fair value option may be selected for some of the loans but not others.

An investor in an equity security may choose the fair value option for its entire investment in that security including any fractional shares.

Balance Sheet

Companies must report assets and liabilities measured at the fair value option in a way that separates those reported fair values from the book (carrying) values of similar assets and liabilities measured with a different measurement attribute. To achieve this, a company must either:

☐ Report the aggregate fair value and nonfinancial fair value amounts in the same line items in the balance sheet and, in parenthesis, disclose the amount measured at fair value included in the aggregate amount.

☐ Report two separate line items to display the fair value and nonfair value carrying amounts.

Statement of Cash Flows

Companies must classify cash receipts and cash payments for items measured at fair value based on their nature and purpose.

Disclosures

Disclosures of fair value are required in annual and interim financial statements.

When a balance sheet is presented, the following must be disclosed:

1. The reasons why the company selected the fair value option for each allowable item or group of similar items.

2. In the event the fair value option is chosen for some but not all eligible items within a group of similar items, management must describe those similar items and the reasons for partial election. In addition, information must be provided so that financial statement users can comprehend how the group of similar items applies to individual line items on the balance sheet.

3. For every line item on the balance sheet that includes an item or items for which the fair value option has been selected, management must provide information on how each line item relates to major asset and liability categories. In addition, management must provide the aggregate carrying amount of items included in each line item that are not eligible for the fair value option.

4. To be disclosed is the difference between the aggregate fair value and the aggregate unpaid principal balance of loans, long-term receivables, and long-term debt instruments with contractual principal amounts for which the fair value option has been chosen.

5. In the case of loans held as assets for which the fair value option has been selected, management should disclose the aggregate fair value of loans past due by 90 days or more. If the company recognizes interest revenue separately from other changes in fair value, disclosure should be made of the aggregate fair value of loans in the nonaccrual status. Disclosure should also be made of the difference between the aggregate fair value and aggregate unpaid principal balance for loans that are 90 days or more past due or in nonaccrual status.

6. Disclosure should be made of investments that would have been reported under the equity method if the company did not elect the fair value option.

When an income statement is presented, the following must be disclosed:

1. An enumeration of how dividends and interest are measured and where they are presented in the income statement.

2. Gains and losses from changes in fair value included in profit and where they are shown.

3. For loans and other receivables, the estimated amount of gains and losses (including how they were calculated) included in earnings associated with changes in instrument-specific credit risk.

4. For liabilities with fair values that have been materially impacted by changes in the instrument-specific credit risk, the estimated amount of gains and losses from fair value changes (including how they were calculated) applicable to changes in such credit risk, and the reasons for those changes.

Other disclosures include the methods and assumptions used in fair value estimation. Also to be disclosed is qualitative information about the nature of the event as well as quantitative information, including the impact on earnings of initially electing the fair value option for an item.

Eligible Items at Effective Date

A company may select the fair value option for eligible items at the effective date. The difference between the book (carrying) value and the fair value of eligible items chosen for the fair value option at the effective date must be removed from the balance sheet and included in the cumulative-effect adjustment. These differences include: (1) valuation allowances (e.g., loan loss reserves); (2) unamortized deferred costs, fees, discounts and premiums; and (3) accrued interest associated with the fair value of the eligible item.

A company that selects the fair value option for items at the effective date must provide, in the financial statements that include the effective date, the following:

1. The impact on deferred tax assets and liabilities of selecting the fair value option.

2. The reasons for choosing the fair value option for each existing eligible item or group of similar items.

3. The amount of valuation allowances removed from the balance sheet because they applied to items for which the fair value option was selected.

4. The schedule presenting the following by line items in the balance sheet: (a) before tax portion of the cumulative-effect adjustment to retained earnings for the items on that line and (b) fair value at the effective date of eligible items for which the fair value option is selected and the book (carrying) amounts of those same items immediately before opting for the fair value option.

5. In the event the fair value option is selected for some but not all eligible items within a group of similar eligible items, a description of similar items and the reasons for the partial election. In addition, information should be provided so financial statement users can comprehend how the group of similar items applies to individual items on the balance sheet.

Available-for-Sale and Held-to-Maturity Securities

Available-for-sale and held-to-maturity securities held at the effective date are eligible for the fair value option at that date. In the event that the fair value option is selected for any of those securities at the effective date, cumulative holding (unrealized) gains and losses must be included in the cumulative-effect adjustment. Separate disclosure must be made of the holding gains and losses reclassified from accumulated other comprehensive income (for available-for-sale securities) and holding gains and losses previously unrecognized (for held-to-maturity securities).

ASC 825, *Financial Instruments*, states that disclosures are required about fair value of financial instruments for interim periods of public companies. A company must disclose in the body or notes to the summarized financial information the fair value of all financial instruments for which it can practically estimate fair value, whether recognized or not recognized in the balance sheet.

Fair value information disclosed in the notes shall be presented along with the related carrying amount of the asset or liability. Disclosure shall also be made of the method(s) and major assumptions used to estimate fair value of financial instruments and describe any changes in method(s) and significant assumptions.

Accounting Standards Update (ASU) No. 2009-05 (August 2009) (ASC 820, *Fair Value Measurements and Disclosures*), *Measuring Liabilities at Fair Value*, provides information on the following:

☐ Offers guidance for identifying fair value in an active market. The best indication of fair value is the price in an active market. The quoted price is a Level 1 measurement. If a quoted priced for an identical liability is not present, fair value may be measured based on the prevailing price for an identical liability traded as an asset. An income method using present value or a market method may also be used (ASC 820-10-35-41).

☐ Discusses the measurement of fair value. In measuring fair value, there is a presumption of an exchange of debt in an orderly way. In reality, the transfer of liabilities is rare; certain liabilities are traded as assets (ASC 820-10-35-16A).

☐ States that observable inputs should be maximized and unobservable inputs should be minimized (ASC 820-10-35-16C).

☐ Specifies that in measuring the fair value of a liability, the quoted price of the asset should not be adjusted for any limitation on its sale (ASC 820-10-35-16D).

☐ States that in valuing a liability, an independent input applicable to a limitation on liability transfer should not be included (ASC 820-10-35-16E).

☐ Explains that a Level 1 valuation for a liability is the quoted price in an active market. If the quoted price is adjusted, the liability has a lower level measured fair value associated with it (ASC 820-10-35-41A).

☐ Discusses Level 2 inputs, which, when modified, vary based on asset or liability characteristics. Factors include asset or liability status and location, activity and volume levels, and comparability of inputs (ASC 820-10-35-50).

Accounting Standards Update (ASU) No. 2010-06 (January 2010) (ASC 820, *Fair Value Measurements and Disclosures*), *Improving Disclosures about Fair Value Measurements*, provides that a transfer between Levels 1 and 2 must be footnoted along with the reasons. (ASC 820-10) Gross information should be furnished for Level 3 items such as for sales. Each type of asset and liability must have a disclosure as to how fair value was determined. Valuation methods should be disclosed including inputs used (ASC 820-10-50-2).

ESTIMATED LIABILITIES AND CONTINGENCIES

GAAP (ASC 410-50-05-5) requires that a loss contingency be accrued if both of the following conditions are satisfied:

1. At year-end, it is probable (likely to occur) that an asset was impaired or a liability was incurred.

2. The amount of loss may be reasonably estimated.

Examples of loss contingencies are pending or threatened lawsuits, warranties or defects, assessments and claims, expropriation of property by a foreign government, environmental remediation guarantees of indebtedness, and agreement to repurchase receivables that have been sold. The accrual is required because of the conservatism principle.

The journal entry to record a probable loss contingency is:

Expense (loss)

    Estimated liability

EXAMPLE

On December 31, 20X2, warranty expenses are estimated at $30,000. On March 2, 20X3, actual warranty costs paid were $27,000. The journal entries are:

12/31/20X2	Warranty expense	30,000	
	Estimated liability		30,000
3/2/20X3	Estimated liability	27,000	
	Cash		27,000

If a probable loss cannot be estimated, it should be footnoted.

If there is a loss contingency at year-end but no asset impairment or liability incurrence exists (e.g., uninsured equipment), footnote disclosure should be made.

If there is a loss contingency occurring after year-end but before the audit report date, subsequent event disclosure should be made. An explanatory paragraph should be provided regarding the contingency.

If the loss amount is within a range, the accrual should be based on the best estimate within that range. If no amount within the range is better than any other amount, the minimum amount (not maximum amount) of the range should be accrued. There should be disclosure of the maximum loss. If later events indicate that the minimum loss initially accrued is insufficient, an additional loss must be accrued in the year this becomes evident. This accrual is treated as a change in estimate.

EXAMPLE

XYZ Company is involved in a tax dispute with the Internal Revenue Service (IRS). As of December 31, 2001, XYZ Company believed that an unfavorable outcome is probable and the amount of loss may be in the range of $2.5 million to $3.5 million. After year-end, when the 2001 financial statements had been issued, XYZ Company settled with the IRS and accepted an offer of $3 million.

Because a range of loss is involved, it is appropriate to accrue the minimum amount or $2.5 million for 2001 year-end.

If there exists a reasonably possible loss (more than remote but less than likely), no accrual should be made. However, footnote disclosure is required. The disclosure includes the nature of the contingency and the estimated probable loss or range of loss. In the event an estimate of loss cannot be made, that fact should be stated.

A remote contingency (slight chance of occurring) is typically ignored, with no disclosure required. **Exceptions:** Disclosure is made of agreements to repurchase receivables, indebtedness guarantees (direct or indirect), and standby letters of credit.

EXAMPLE

A company cosigned a loan guaranteeing the indebtedness if the mortgagee defaults on it. The likelihood of default is remote. This is an exception to the rule that remote contingencies need not be disclosed, because it represents a guarantee of indebtedness and thus requires disclosure.

No accrual is made for general (unspecified) contingencies, such as for self-insurance and hurricane losses. However, footnote disclosure and appropriation of retained earnings can be made for such contingencies. To be accrued, the future loss must be specific and measurable, such as freight or parcel post losses.

Gain contingencies can never be booked because doing so violates conservatism. However, footnote disclosure should be made.

Warranty obligations are contingencies and estimates. They may be based upon prior experience, experience of other firms in same industry, or estimates by specialists, such as engineers. If the warranty liability cannot be reasonably estimated, then significant uncertainty exists as to whether a sale should be reported, and another method, such as the installment sales method, cost recovery method, or some other method of revenue recognition used.

Unasserted claims exist when the claimant has elected not to assert the claim or because the claimant lacks knowledge of the existence of the claim. If it is probable that the claimant will assert the unasserted claim, and it is either probable or reasonably possible that the outcome will be unfavorable, the unasserted claim should be disclosed in the financial statements.

Contingent consideration in a business combination relates to an additional amount paid by the acquirer to the shareholders of the acquiree when certain conditions (such as meeting futures earnings targets) are met. Under ASC 805-30-25-5 through 25-7, the acquisition method requires that the contingency be measured at fair value and a liability be recorded at the closing date. Subsequent changes in fair value of contingent consideration are recorded in earnings.

Estimated liability needs to be recorded when a company offers customers something free or for a minimal charge to increase product sales. The customer may be required to provide proof of purchase to get the free product. Sometimes a nominal cash payment is also required.

EXAMPLE

XYZ Company includes a coupon in each cereal box that it sells. Customers may redeem 10 coupons and $5.00 in exchange for a toy that costs XYZ Company $10.00. Approximately 70% of the coupons are expected to be redeemed. This promotion began on December 1, 2001 and the company sold 200,000 boxes of cereal. As of December 31, 2001, no coupons had been redeemed. The estimated liability for coupons is calculated as follows:

Total coupons issued	200,000
Percentage expected to be redeemed	70%
Coupons expected to be redeemed	140,000
Number of coupons per toy	10
Number of toys to be distributed	14,000
Liability per toy	$ 5
Total liability for coupons	$70,000

EXAMPLE

In December 20X1, Mavis Company started to include one coupon in each box of popcorn. A customer will receive as a promotion a toy if 10 coupons and $1 are received. The toy costs $2.50. It is expected that 80% of the coupons will be exchanged. During December, 200,000 boxes of popcorn were sold, with no coupons being redeemed yet because the promotion just started. At year-end 20X1, the estimated liability for coupons is computed as follows:

Total coupons issued	200,000
Percentage of coupons expected to be redeemed	× 80%
To be redeemed	160,000
Number of toys to be distributed: 160,000/10 coupons =	16,000
Estimated liability for coupons—12/31/20X1:	
16,000 × $1.50* =	$24,000

* The liability is $2.50 cost per each toy less $1 to be received, or $1.50 per toy.

RISKS AND UNCERTAINTIES

The AICPA's Accounting Standard Executive Committee issued ASC 270-10-05, *Interim Reporting: Overall*. It requires disclosure of risks involving the nature of operations, use of estimates, and business vulnerability. With regard to the nature of operations, disclosure should be made of the company's major products and services, including by geographic locations. The relative importance of operations in multiple markets should also be discussed. Disclosure should be made of estimated accounts on which estimates are sensitive to near-term changes, such as technological obsolescence. Disclosure of corporate vulnerability to concentrations includes lack of diversification (e.g., customer base, suppliers, lenders, geographic areas, government contracts). An entity whose revenue is concentrated in certain products or services must make disclosure. Disclosure of information about significant concentrations of credit risk is also required for all financial instruments. Disclosure is mandated when concentrations exist for labor, supplies, materials, or other services which are necessary for an enterprise's operations. Overreliance on licenses and other rights should be noted.

Disclosure is required when a change in estimate would have a material effect on the financial statements. Examples of items requiring disclosure according to ASC 275-10-50-15 include:

☐ Rapid technological obsolescence of assets.

☐ Inventory subject to perishability, changing fashions, and styles.

☐ Capitalization of certain costs, such as for computer software or motion picture production.

☐ Insurance companies' deferred policy acquisition costs.

☐ Litigation-related liabilities and contingencies due to obligations of other enterprises.

☐ Valuation allowances for commercial and real estate loans, and allowances for deferred tax assets.

☐ Amounts of long-term obligations, such as for pension obligations and other benefits.

☐ Amounts of long-term contracts.

☐ Proceeds or expected loss on disposition of assets.

☐ Nature and amount of guarantees.

When an entity is vulnerable to concentration-related risks, disclosure is required if the concentration existed at the date of financial statements, the entity may suffer significantly because of the concentration risk, and it is reasonably possible that concentration-risk-related events will occur in the near future.

Uncertainties with labor unions should be noted. For organizations with significant concentrations of labor subject to collective bargaining agreements, the disclosure should include:

☐ The percentage of the labor force covered by a collective bargaining agreement.

☐ The percentage of the labor force covered by a collective bargaining agreement where the agreement will expire within one year.

COMPENSATED ABSENCES

ASC 710-10-15-3, *Compensation—General: Overall*, states that compensated absences include sick leave, vacation time, and holidays. The pronouncement also applies to sabbatical leaves related to past services rendered. The pronouncement does not apply to deferred compensation, postretirement benefits, severance (termination) pay, stock option plans, and other long-term fringe benefits (e.g., disability, insurance).

An estimated liability based on current salary rates should be accrued for compensated absences when all of the following criteria are satisfied:

- ☐ Employee services have been rendered.
- ☐ Employee rights have vested, meaning the employer is obligated to pay the employee even though he or she leaves the employment voluntarily or involuntarily.
- ☐ Probable payment exists.
- ☐ The amount of estimated liability can be reasonably determined.

If the conditions are met but the amount cannot be determined, no accrual can be made. However, there should be footnote disclosure.

Accrual for sick leave is required only when the employer allows employees to take accumulated sick leave days off regardless of actual illness. No accrual is made if workers may take accumulated days off only for actual illness, because losses for these are usually insignificant in amount. An employer should not accrue a liability for nonvesting rights for compensated absences expiring at the end of the year they are earned, because no accumulation is involved. However, if unused rights do accumulate, a liability should be accrued.

EXAMPLE

Estimated compensation for future absences is $40,000. The journal entry is:

Expense	40,000	
Estimated liability		40,000

If, at a later date, a payment of $35,000 is required, the journal entry is:

Estimated liability	35,000	
Cash		35,000

EXAMPLE

Blumenfrucht Corporation has a plan for compensated absences providing workers with 8 and 12 paid vacation and sick days, respectively, that may be carried over to future years. Instead of taking their vacation pay, the workers may select payment. However, no payment is allowed for sick days not taken. At year-end 20X2, the unadjusted balance of the liability for compensated absences was $34,000. At year-end 20X2, it is estimated that there are 110 vacation days and 80 sick leave days available. The average per-day pay is $125. On December 31, 20X2, the liability for compensated absences is $13,750 ($125 per day × 10 days). There is no accrual for unpaid sick days because payment of the compensation is not probable.

ASC 710-10-25-4, *Compensation—General: Overall*, states that compensation costs applicable to an employee's right to a sabbatical or other similar arrangement should be accrued over the mandatory service years.

DEFERRED COMPENSATION AGREEMENT

An accrual should be made over the service years of active employees for deferred compensation starting with the agreement date. Examples of deferred compensation agreements are a covenant not to compete, continued employment for a specified period, and availability to render services after retirement. The total amount accrued at the end of the employee's service years should at least equal the discounted value of future payments to be made. The annual journal entry to record deferred compensation is:

Deferred compensation expense	XXX	
Deferred compensation liability		XXX

ACCOUNTING FOR SPECIAL TERMINATION BENEFITS (EARLY RETIREMENT)

An accrual of a liability for employee termination benefits in the period that management approves the termination benefit package is required if the following circumstances are met:

☐ The benefits that terminated employees will receive have been agreed on and have been accepted by management prior to the financial statement date.

☐ Employees are made aware of the termination agreement prior to the issuance of the financial statements.

☐ The termination benefit plan provides the following data: (a) the number of employees to be terminated, (b) their job categories, and (c) the location of their jobs.

☐ Significant changes to the plan are not likely, so that completion of the plan may be expected in a short time.

The termination plan may include both individuals who have been involuntarily terminated and those who have voluntarily decided to leave their current employ. The latter may have been coaxed into leaving with the promise of higher termination benefits. The accrued liability should be based on the number of employees who will be terminated and the benefits that will be paid to both involuntarily and voluntarily terminated employees. The amount of the accrual equals the down payment plus the present value discounted of future payments.

When it can be objectively measured, the impact of changes on the employer's previously accrued expenses related to other employee benefits directly associated with employee termination should be included in measuring termination expense.

EXAMPLE

On January 1, 20X3, an incentive is offered for early retirement. Employees are to receive a payment of $100,000 today, plus payments of $20,000 for each of the next 10 years. Assume a discount rate of 10%. The journal entry is:

Expense	222,900	
Estimated liability		222,900
Down payment		$100,000
Present value of future payments ($20,000 × 6.145)*		122,900
Total		$222,900

* Present value factor for $n = 10$, $i = 10\%$ is 6.145.

TROUBLED DEBT

Frequently, during depressed economic times, debtors may be unable to pay their creditors. Because of the debtor's financial difficulties, it may be necessary for a creditor to grant a concession that otherwise would not have been considered. The accounting of debtors and creditors for troubled debt is based on the guidance of two FASB statements:

☐ ASC 310-40 and 470-60, *Receivables: Troubled Debt Restructurings by Creditors*.

☐ ASC 310-10-35-1 and 35-53, *Receivables: Overall*.

The latter statement modifies the former with respect to accounting by a creditor for modification of loan terms. When a troubled loan materializes, the creditor is required first to recognize a loss on impairment of the debt. After this, either the terms of the loan are modified or the loan is settled on terms that are not favorable to the creditor.

The concept of impairment of loans will be discussed first, followed by the restructuring of troubled debt.

Accounting by Creditors for Impairment of a Loan

ASC 310-10-35-1 and 35-53 requires that impairment of a loan by a creditor be recognized when it is probable that a creditor will be unable to collect all that is contractually owed, including both principal and interest. A loan, for example, that is modified in a troubled debt restructuring is considered impaired. A temporary delay of payment, however, is not considered an impairment. In addition, a loan should not be considered impaired if the creditor expects to collect all amounts that are due including any accrued interest for any delay in payment that may have occurred.

When a loan is classified as being impaired, measurement of the impairment is based on the expected new future cash flows discounted using the original historical contractual rate, not the rate specified in the restructuring agreement. If, on the other hand, the loan is collateralized or has a market price, the amount of impairment may be measured with the assistance of those amounts. For example, if foreclosure is probable, the impairment of the loan may be based on the fair market value of the collateral. The difference between the book value of the impaired loan and the amount of impairment should be recorded by debiting the bad debts expense account with a corresponding credit to a valuation allowance account. If a change occurs in the amount or timing of the new expected cash flow subsequent to the measurement of impairment, the creditor should recalculate the amount of impairment and adjust the valuation account in the period in which this change becomes known.

When the impairment is recognized using the present value of new expected cash flows, the creditor should recognize interest income using the effective interest method. Any changes in the initial impairment resulting from changes in the amount or timing of cash flows should be recorded as an entry in the bad debt expense, and allowance valuation accounts. This includes any changes that are based on the modifications of the market value of the loan or its collateral.

Disclosure should be made, as of the balance sheet date, of the recorded investment in loans for which impairment has been recognized less the allowance for related loan losses. In addition, each period for which an income statement is presented, an analysis should be disclosed of any changes in the valuation allowance account. The creditor's income recognition policy with respect to loan impairment should also be shown.

EXAMPLE

On January 1, 20X0, X Financing Company loaned $1,000,000 to Y Company. The loan was issued in the form of a 6-year zero-interest-bearing note due on December 31, 20X5, generating an effective yield of 8%. As a result, Y Company was paid proceeds of $630,170 This amount was computed in the following way:

$$\$1,000,000 \times \text{present value of \$1 discounted for 6 years at 8\%}$$
$$= \$1,000,000 \times .63017$$
$$= \$630,170$$

The following entry would be made on January 1, 20X0, by the creditor, X Financing Company, when the note was accepted and the proceeds issued to the Y Company, the debtor:

Notes receivable	1,000,000	
Discount on notes receivable		369,830
Cash		630,170

The following table shows the amortization of the discount on the note by X Financing Company over the life of the note.

Date	Interest Revenue (8%)	Discount Amortized	Carrying Value of the Note
1/1/20X0			$ 630,170
12/31/20X0	$50,414*	$50,414	680,584
12/31/20X1	54,447	54,447	735,031
12/31/20X2	58,802	58,802	793,833
12/31/20X3	63,507	63,507	857,340
12/31/20X4	68,587	68,587	925,927
12/31/20X5	74,073**	74,073	1,000,000

---

* $630, 170 \times 8\%$
** Understated by \$1 due to rounding.

On December 31, 20X3, because of a downturn in the economy and depression in the industry of Y Company, X Financing Company, after a comprehensive review of all available evidence at its disposal, determined that it was probable that Y Company would pay back only \$400,000 of the loan at maturity. These facts indicated to X Financing Company that the loan was impaired and that a loss should be recorded immediately.

ASC 310-10-35-1 and 35-53 requires that X Financing Company compute the present value of the new expected cash flows at the original contractual effective rate of interest. Based on present value calculations, this amount is \$342,936, computed in the following way:

$$\$4,000,000 \times \text{present value of \$1 discounted for 2 years at 8\%}$$
$$= \$4,000,000 \times .85734$$
$$= \$342,936$$

The impairment loss is the difference between the recorded value of the loan and the new expected present value of future cash flows from it. The impairment loss to X Financing Company is calculated as follows:

Carrying value of loan to creditor at Dec. 31, 2003	\$857,340
Less: present value of new expected cash flows of \$400,000 discounted for 2 years at 8%	342,936
Impairment loss to X Financing Company	\$514,404

The entry to record the impairment of the loan on the accounting records of X Financing is:

Bad debts expense	514,404	
Allowance for impairment of note		514,404

No entry is made on the accounting records of the debtor entity, Y Company, for the impairment of the loan.

Troubled Debt Restructuring

ASC 310-40 and 470-60 states that in a troubled debt situation the debtor is having significant financial problems and receives partial or full relief of the debt by the creditor. The relief may be in the form of any of the following:

☐ Creditor/debtor agreement.

☐ Repossession or foreclosure.

☐ Relief dictated by law.

The types of troubled debt restructuring include:

☐ Debtor transfers to creditor receivables from third parties or other assets in part or in full satisfaction of the obligation.

☐ Debtor transfers to creditor stock to satisfy the debt.

☐ Modification of debt terms, such as through extending the maturity date, reducing the balance due, or reducing the interest rate.

In restructuring, an extraordinary gain is recognized by the debtor, but either an ordinary or extraordinary loss is recognized by the creditor, depending on how unusual or infrequent the occurrence is. In most cases, it is an ordinary loss.

The extraordinary gain of the debtor equals the difference between the fair market value of the assets exchanged and the book value of the debt, including accrued interest. In addition, there may arise a gain on the disposal of the assets exchanged equal to the difference between the fair market value and the book value of the transferred assets. This gain or loss is not from the restructuring but instead an ordinary gain or loss arising from asset disposal.

EXAMPLE

A debtor transferred assets having a fair market value of $7,000 and a book value of $5,000 to satisfy a debt with a carrying value of $8,000. The gain on restructuring is $1,000 ($8,000 – $7,000), and the ordinary gain is $2,000 ($7,000 – $5,000).

If a debtor transfers an equity interest to the creditor, the debtor records the stock issued at its fair market value, not the recorded value of the debt relieved. The difference between these values is recorded as an extraordinary gain.

Any adjustment in the terms of the initial obligation is accounted for prospectively. A new interest rate is computed based on the new terms. The interest rate is then used to allocate future payments as a reduction in principal and interest. When the new terms of the agreement result in the total future payments being less than the book value of the debt, the debt is reduced, with a restructuring gain being recorded for the difference. ASC 310-40 and 470-60 requires that the gain on restructuring be based on the undiscounted restructured cash flows. Future payments are considered a reduction of principal only. Interest expense is not recognized.

There may be a mix of concessions offered to the debtor. This may arise when assets or equity are transferred for part satisfaction of the debt, with the balance subject to the modification of the terms. The two steps are:

1. Reduce the debt by the fair market value of the asset or equity transferred.

2. The balance of the debt is treated as an adjustment of the terms for accounting purposes.

Any direct costs (e.g., attorney fees) incurred by the debtor in the equity transfer reduce the fair market value of the equity interest. Any other costs reduce the gain on restructuring. If no gain is involved, direct costs are expensed.

Footnote disclosure by the debtor should be made of the terms surrounding the restructuring, gain on restructuring in aggregate and per-share amounts, and contingently payable amounts and terms.

The creditor's loss is the difference between the fair market value of assets received and the carrying value of the investment. When credit terms are modified, the following occurs:

☐ ASC 310-10-35-1 and 35-53 requires that the creditor's loss be based on the new expected cash flows discounted at the original contractual effective interest rate. The FASB believes that because loans are recorded initially at discounted amounts, the ongoing assessment for impairment should be made in a similar manner. (The debtor's gain on restructuring, as was previously noted, should be based on undiscounted amounts as required by ASC 310-40 and 470-60.)

☐ Direct costs are immediately expensed.

☐ Assets are recorded at fair market value.

☐ Interest revenue is recorded for the excess of total future payments over the carrying value of the receivable. Interest revenue is determined using the effective interest method.

☐ An ordinary loss is recognized for the difference between the carrying value of the receivable and the total payments.

☐ Any cash received in the future is treated as investment recovery.

The creditor does not recognize contingent interest until the contingency no longer exists and interest has been earned.

Any change in interest rates is treated as a change in estimate.

The following should be footnoted:

☐ Description of restructuring provisions (e.g., time period, interest rate).

☐ Outstanding commitments.

☐ Receivables by major category.

EXAMPLE

The debtor owes the creditor $80,000 and, owing to financial difficulties, may be unable to make future payments. Footnote disclosure is required.

EXAMPLE

The debtor owes the creditor $70,000. The creditor relieves the debtor of $10,000, with the balance payable at a future date. The journal entries follow:

Debtor		
Accounts payable	10,000	
Extraordinary gain		10,000
Creditor		
Ordinary loss	10,000	
Accounts receivable		10,000

EXAMPLE

The debtor owes the creditor $90,000. The creditor commits to accept a 30% payment in full satisfaction of the obligation. The journal entries are:

Debtor

Accounts payable	63,000	
Extraordinary gain		63,000

Creditor

Ordinary loss	63,000	
Accounts receivable		63,000

EXAMPLE

The following information applies to the transfer of property arising from a troubled debt restructuring:

Book value of liability liquidated	$300,000
Fair market value of property transferred	170,000
Book value of property transferred	210,000

The extraordinary gain on restructuring equals:

Book value of liability liquidated	$300,000
Less: fair market value of property transferred	170,000
Extraordinary gain	$130,000

The ordinary gain (loss) on the transfer of the property equals:

Book value of property transferred	$210,000
Fair market value of property transferred	170,000
Ordinary loss	$ 40,000

Impairment of Loans

ASC 310-10-35-1 through 35-53 and 310-10-50-1 through 50-26, apply to the accounting, reporting, and disclosures by a creditor for the impairment of a loan. They require creditors to determine the impaired value of a loan typically based on the discounted value of expected net cash flows associated with the loan. In addition to accounting for ensuing losses, appropriate footnote disclosure should be made. A number of methods may be used to determine how much impairment has occurred, including:

☐ Present value of anticipated future cash flows discounted at the loan's effective interest rate.

☐ The loan's market price.

☐ The face value of the collateral (assuming probable foreclosure).

The creditor records the impaired value of the loan as a debit to bad debts expense and a credit to the valuation allowance.

The creditor may recognize income on an impaired loan using the cost recovery method, cash basis method, or a combination.

The creditor should disclose, either in the body or footnotes to the financial statements, the following:

☐ Total investment in impaired loans along with valuation allowances.

☐ Method used and interest revenue recorded on impaired loans.

☐ Credit losses incurred.

REFINANCING SHORT-TERM DEBT TO LONG-TERM DEBT

According to ASC 470-10-45-12A, *Debt: Overall*, a short-term debt should be reclassified as a long-term debt when either of the following conditions apply:

1. After year-end but before the audit report date, the short-term debt is rolled over into a long-term debt, or an equity security is issued in substitution.

2. Before the audit report date, the company contracts to refinance the current debt on a long-term basis and all of the following conditions are satisfied:

   — Agreement is for a period of one year or more.

   — No provision of the agreement has been violated.

   — The parties are financially sound and therefore able to satisfy all of the requirements of the agreement.

When debt is reclassified from short term to long term because of conditions described in item 1, it should be classified under long-term liabilities, not stockholders' equity, even if equity securities were subsequently issued in substitution of the debt.

If short-term debt is excluded from current liabilities, the amount of short-term debt excluded from current liabilities should be the minimum amount expected to be refinanced based on conservatism.

Caution: The exclusion from current liabilities cannot exceed the net proceeds of debt or security issuances, or amounts available under the refinancing agreement. The latter amount must be adjusted for any restrictions in the contract that limit the amount available to pay off the short-term debt. If a reasonable estimate is not ascertainable from the agreement, the full amount must be classified as current debt. Further, a refinancing intent may be absent if the contractual provisions permit the lender or investor to establish unrealistic interest rates, security, or other related terms.

The refinancing of one short-term obligation with another is not sufficient to demonstrate the ability to refinance on a long-term basis.

ASC 470-10-55-1, *Debt: Overall*, stipulates that if cash is paid for the short-term debt, even if long-term debt of a similar amount is issued the next day, the short-term debt should be presented under current liabilities because cash was paid.

Footnote disclosure is required of the amount excluded from current liabilities. Disclosure is also mandated for the contractual terms and any noncurrent debt or equity securities issued or expected to be issued in substitution of the short-term debt.

CALLABLE OBLIGATIONS BY THE CREDITOR

ASC 470-10-45-11, *Debt: Overall*, deals with long-term debt callable or payable on demand by the creditor. If the debtor violates the debt agreement, and the long-term obligation therefore becomes callable, the debt must be included as a current liability, except if one of the following conditions exists:

☐ The creditor waives or loses his or her right to require repayment for a period exceeding one year from the balance sheet date. Refer to ASC 470-10-45 and 55.

☐ There exists a grace period under which it is probable that the debtor will cure the violation.

ASC 470-10-50-3, *Debt: Overall*, defines a subjective acceleration clause as one allowing the lender unilaterally to accelerate all or part of a noncurrent debt. For example, the lender in its sole discretion may accelerate repayment of the debt if it is believed that the borrower is experiencing significant profitability or cash difficulties. If it is probable that the acceleration provision will be enforced by the lender, the amount of the noncurrent debt likely to be accelerated should be classified as a current liability by the debtor. However, if acceleration by the lender is only reasonably possible, footnote disclosure is sufficient. If a remote possibility exists as to acceleration, no disclosure is needed.

An objective acceleration clause in a long-term debt agreement includes objective criteria to assess calling all or part of the debt. Examples are setting forth a minimum cash position or a minimum current ratio. If there is a violation of an objective acceleration provision, most noncurrent debts become callable immediately by the lender, or are callable after some predetermined grace period. In such cases, the creditor may demand repayment of all or part of the debt due as per the contract.

Footnote disclosure is required for the reasons and circumstances surrounding callable obligations and their balance sheet classification. Subsequent event disclosure is required when the violation occurs after year-end but before the audit report date.

Other reference sources are ASC 470-10-45-9 and 45-10, and ASC 470-10-45-3 through 45-6.

INDUCEMENT OFFER TO CONVERT DEBT TO EQUITY

ASC 470-20-05-10, *Debt: Debt with Conversion and Other Options*, states if convertible debt is converted into stock because of an inducement offer in which the debtor changes the conversion privileges (e.g., conversion ratio, issuance of warrants, or cash compensation), the debtor must record the inducement as an expense of the current period. However, it is not an extraordinary item. The conversion expense equals the fair market value of the securities and other consideration transferred in excess of the fair market value of the securities issuable based on the original conversion term. It is measured at the date the inducement offer is accepted by the convertible bondholders (usually the conversion or agreement date). The FASB views the inducement given as a compensatory payment to convertible bondholders for converting their securities to stock. If the additional inducement comprises stock, the market value of the stock is credited to common stock at par value, with the excess over par credited to paid-in-capital and with the offsetting-debit-to-debt conversion expense. If the additional inducement is assets, the market value of the assets is credited with an offsetting-charge-to-debt conversion expense. For example, the inducement may be in the form of cash or property. ASC 470-20-05-10 applies only to induced conversions that may be exercised for a limited time period.

EXAMPLE

On April 1, 20X1, a company issued $500,000 8% bonds at face value. Each $1,000 bond is convertible into 15 shares of common stock having a par value of $30. On July 1, 20X3, the company offers to increase the conversion rate to 18 shares per $1,000 bond to induce conversion through this "sweetener." The debtholders accept this offer. At this date, the market value of the stock is $50 per share. Therefore, the additional consideration given as an inducement to the holders of the $500,000 bonds will be $75,000, computed as follows:

($500,000/$1,000) = 500 bonds

500 bonds × 3 shares per $1,000 band = 1500 shares

Fair market value of additional consideration equals

1500 shares × $ 50 = 75,000

The journal entry for the conversion is:

Bonds payable	500,000	
Debt conversion expense	75,000	
Common stock (9,000 shares* × $30)		270,000
Paid-in-capital		305,000

* 500 bonds × 18 shares per bond = 9,000 shares

EXAMPLE

A company has outstanding $400,000 of convertible bonds issued at par value. Each $1,000 bond is convertible into 12 shares of $20 par value common stock. To induce bondholders to convert, the company increased the conversion rate from 12 shares per $1,000 bond to 16 shares per $1,000 bond. When the market price of the stock was $25, one bondholder converted his $1,000 bond. The amount of incremental consideration is $100 (4 additional shares × $25). The journal entry is:

Bonds payable	1,000	
Debt conversion expense	100	

Common stock (16 shares × $20)	320
Paid-in-capital	780

EXAMPLE

A bondholder is holding a $10,000 face value convertible bond that was issued at par. Each $1,000 bond is convertible into 50 shares of stock having a par value of $12. To induce conversion, the company offers the bondholder land having a fair market value of $1,500 at the date of conversion. The cost of the land is $1,200. The journal entries associated with the induced conversion are:

Land	300	
Gain		300

To increase land to fair value to use as inducement:

Bonds payable	10,000	
Debt conversion expense	1,500	
Land		1,500
Common stock (500* shares × $12)		6,000
Paid-in-capital		4,000

* $10,000/$1,000 = 10 bonds.

10 bonds × 50 shares = 500 shares.

If the debtor places cash or other assets in an irrevocable trust to be used only to pay interest and principal on the obligation, disclosure is required of the particulars concerning the transaction and the amount of debt considered extinguished.

ASC 470-20-30-27 and 30-28, states that interest costs associated with convertible debt instruments recognized in periods subsequent to their initial recognition should constitute the borrowing rate a company would have incurred had it issued a comparable debt instrument without the embedded conversion option. That objective is achieved by requiring issuers to separately account for the liability and equity components of convertible debt instruments.

The following steps should be used to *initially* measure the convertible debt:

1. Determine the carrying value of an instrument's liability component using a fair value measurement of a similar liability (including embedded features, if any, other than the conversion option) that has no related equity component.

2. Determine the carrying value of the instrument's equity component corresponding to the embedded conversion option by subtracting the liability component's fair value from the initial proceeds applicable to the total convertible debt instrument.

Appraise the total convertible debt instrument if its embedded features, other than the conversion option, are substantive at the issuance date. If, at issuance, the company concludes that it is *probable* that a convertible instrument's embedded feature will not be exercised, that embedded feature is considered to be nonsubstantive and would not impact the initial measurement of an instrument's liability component.

Transaction costs incurred with third parties except the investors that directly relate to convertible debt issuance should be allocated to the liability and equity components in the same proportion as the allocation of proceeds and accounted for as costs of issuing debt and equity, respectively.

A temporary tax basis difference associated with the liability component may occur. Additional paid-in-capital should be adjusted when deferred taxes are initially recognized for the tax impact of the temporary difference.

The principal amount of the liability component over its initial fair value must be amortized to interest cost using the interest method.

A liability component's anticipated life is not impacted by embedded features determined to be nonsubstantive when the convertible debt was issued.

If a conversion option has to be reclassified from stockholders' equity to a liability measured at fair value, the difference between the amount that has been recognized in equity and the fair value of the conversion option at the date of reclassification should be accounted for as an adjustment to stockholders' equity. On the other hand, when a conversion option accounted for in stockholders' equity is reclassified as a liability, gains or losses recognized to account for that conversion option at fair value while classified as a liability should *not* be reversed if later the conversion option is reclassified back to stockholders' equity. The reclassification of a conversion option does not impact the accounting for the liability component.

The following should be disclosed:

☐ Conversion price and the number of shares used to calculate the total consideration to be delivered on conversion.

☐ Effective interest rate on the liability component.

☐ Amount of interest cost applicable to both the contractual interest coupon and discount amortization on the liability component.

☐ Carrying value of the equity component.

☐ Principal amount of the liability component, its amortized discount, and its carrying value.

☐ Remaining years for which the discount on the liability will be amortized.

☐ Amount by which the instrument's if-converted value is more than the principal amount, irrespective of whether the instrument is currently convertible.

☐ Term of derivative transactions, reasons to enter into derivative transactions, and number of shares underlying derivative transactions.

Accounting Standards Update (ASU) No. 2009-15 (ASC 470, *Debt*), *Accounting for Own-Share Lending Arrangements in Contemplation of Convertible Debt Issuance or Other Financing*, which is based on EITF Issue No. 09-1, provides information on the following:

☐ Provides accounting and reporting advice for bonds and other types of preferred stock with conversion attributes. These include convertible bonds, bonds with detachable warrants, forfeiture of interest, and conversions that are induced. (ASC 470-20-05-1)

☐ Is applicable in the following instance. A firm that has a high cost of borrowed shares may contract for share lending separately transacted but along with a convertible bond issuance. The share lending contract allows investors to hedge the conversion option. (ASC 470-20-05-12A)

☐ Provides guidance when, in a share-lending contract, the firm issues loaned shares to an investment bank for a small charge. This fee typically equals the par value of the common stock, which is usually below the market value of the loaned securities. At maturity, the loaned shares are returned to the company. (ASC 470-20-05-12B)

☐ Offers guidance for properly recording a share-lending contract. When issued, a share-lending contract is recorded at market value and recorded at issuance cost with an adjustment to paid-in-capital. (ASC 470-20-25-20A)

ACCOUNTING FOR BONDS PAYABLE

The yield on a bond may be calculated based on either the simple yield or yield to maturity (effective interest) methods:

$$\text{Simple yield} = \text{Nominal interest/Present value of bond}$$

$$\text{Yield to maturity} = \frac{\text{Nominal interest} + \text{Discount/Years (or} - \text{Premium/Years)}}{(\text{Present value} + \text{Maturity value})/2}$$

Simple yield is less accurate than yield to maturity.

EXAMPLE

A $300,000, 8%, 10-year bond is issued at 98%.

$$\text{Simple yield} = \frac{\text{Nominal interest}}{\text{Present value of bond}}$$

$$\frac{\$24,000}{\$294,000} = 8.16\%$$

$$\text{Yield to maturity} = \frac{\text{Nominal interest} + \text{Discount/Years}}{(\text{Present value} + \text{Maturity value/2})}$$

$$\frac{\$24,000 + \$6,000/10}{(\$294,000 + \$300,000)/2} = 8.2\%$$

If a bond is sold at a discount, yield will exceed the nominal interest rate. However, if a bond is sold at a premium, yield will be less than the nominal interest rate.

A bond discount or premium may be amortized using either the straightline method or the effective interest method (scientific amortization). The latter method is preferred because it results in a better matching of periodic expense with revenue. Under the straight-line method, the amortization per period results in a fixed dollar amount but at a varying effective rate. Under the effective interest method, the amortization per period results in a constant rate of interest but a varying dollar amount.

The amortization entry under the effective interest method is:

Interest expense (Yield × Carrying value of bond at the beginning of the year)

Discount (for balance)

Cash (nominal interest rate × face value of bond)

In the early years, using the effective interest method results in a lower amortization amount relative to the straight-line method (either for discount or premium).

EXAMPLE

On January 1, 20X3, a $200,000 bond is issued at $194,554. The yield rate is 5% and the nominal interest rate is 4%. The effective interest method is used. A schedule for the first two years follows:

Date	Debit Interest Expense	Credit Cash	Credit Discount	Book Value
1/1/20X3				$194,554
12/31/20X3	$9,727	$8,000	$1,727	196,281
12/31/20X4	9,814	8,000	1,814	198,095
12/31/20X5	9,905	8,000	1,905	200,000

Note: Interest expense is increasing because the carrying value of the bond is increasing.

On December 31, 20X3, the journal entry is:

Interest expense	9,727	
Cash		8,000
Discount		1,727

EXAMPLE

On January 1, 20X2, a company issued 10% bonds with a face value of $600,000 for $560,000 to yield 11%. Interest is payable semi-annually on January 1 and July 1. The effective interest method of amortization is used. The journal entries for 20X2 are:

1/1/20X2

Cash	560,000	
Discount on bonds payable	40,000	
Bonds payable		600,000

7/1/20X2

Interest expense		
(11% × $560,000 × 6/12)	30,800	
Cash (10% × $600,000 × 6/12)		30,000
Discount on bonds payable		800

The book value of the bonds on July 1, 20X2, after the preceding entry is as follows:

Bonds payable	$600,000
Less: discount on bonds payable	
($40,000 – $800)	39,200
Book value	$560,800

12/31/20X2

Interest expense		
(11% × $560,800 × 6/12)	30,844	
Cash (10% × $600,000 × 6/12)		30,000
Discount on bonds payable		844

EXAMPLE

Cohen Company has outstanding an 8%, 10-year, $200,000 bond. The bond was initially issued to yield 7%. Amortization is based on the effective interest method. On July 1, 20X1, the carrying value of the bond was $211,943. The unamortized premium on the bond on July 1, 20X2, was $10,779 computed as follows:

Unamortized premium—7/1/20X1		
($211,943 – $200,000)		$11,943
Less: amortized premium for the year-ended		
7/1/20X2:		
Nominal interest ($200,000 × 8%)	$16,000	
Effective interest ($211,943 × 7%)	14,836	1,164
Unamortized premium—7/1/20X2		$10,779

Bonds payable may be issued between interest dates at a premium or discount. If a bond is issued between interest dates, the journal entry is:

Cash

Discount (or credit premium)

   Bonds payable

   Interest expense

EXAMPLE

On April 1, 20X2, a $500,000, 8% bond with a five-year life dated 1/1/20X2, is issued at 106%. Interest is payable on 1/1 and 7/1. The company uses the straight-line amortization method. The journal entries are:

4/1/20X2

Cash ($530,000 + $10,000)	540,000	
Bonds payable		500,000
Premium on bonds payable ($500,000 × 6%)		30,000
Interest expense ($500,000 × 8% × 3/12)		10,000

7/1/20X2

Interest expense	20,000	
Cash		20,000
Premium on bonds payable	1,578	
Interest expense		1,578

4/1/20X2 – 1/1/20X7 = 4 years, 9 months = 57 months

$30,000/57 = $526 per month (rounded)

4/1/20X2 – 7/1/20X2 = 3 months

3 months × $526 = $1,578

12/31/20X2

Interest expense	20,000	
Interest payable		20,000
Premium on bonds payable	3,156	
Interest expense		3,156

6 months × $526 = $3,156

1/1/20X3

Interest payable	20,000	
Cash		20,000

Bonds Payable is presented in the balance sheet at its book value in the following manner:

   Bonds payable

   Add: premium on bonds payable

   Less: discount on bonds payable

   Carrying value

Bond issue costs are the expenditures incurred in issuing bonds, such as legal, accounting, underwriting, commissions, registration, engraving, and printing fees. Bond issue costs should preferably be deferred and amortized over the life of the bond. They are presented as a deferred charge. However, two alternative acceptable methods exist to account for bond issue costs: to expense such costs immediately or to treat them as a reduction of bonds payable.

Serial bonds (bonds maturing in installments) may be issued as if each series were a separate bond issue or as one issue having varying maturity dates. In most cases, each series has the same interest rate and yield but different issue prices, depending upon their maturity period. One discount or premium account exists for all the bonds in the series. The effective interest method is used in determining amortization of the discount or premium.

The price of a bond is calculated as follows:

☐ The face value is discounted using the present value of $1 table.

☐ Interest payments are discounted using the present value of ordinary annuity of $1 table.

☐ Yield is used as the discount rate.

EXAMPLE

A $100,000 10-year bond is issued at an 8% nominal interest rate. Interest is payable semiannually. The yield rate is 10%. The present value of $1 table factor for $n = 20$, $i = 5\%$ is 12.46221. The price of the bond is

Present value of principal $100,000P × .37689	$37,689
Present value of interest payments $4,000 × 12.46221	49,849
Present value	$87,538

The issuance of convertible bonds usually allows the company to issue the securities at a lower interest rate with fewer restrictions compared to a conventional bond. When issued, the face value of the convertible bond usually will be more than the market value of the stock into which it is convertible. Further, at issuance no value is assigned to the conversion feature. The sale is only recorded as the issuance of debt. The conversion price is typically set at about 15% more than the market price of the stock when the convertible bond is issued. Unless attributable to antidilution, the conversion price remains the same. There may be a call feature allowing the issuer to call the bonds back before maturity. As the value of the stock increases, so does the value of the convertible bond. When the market value of the shares associated with the convertible bond exceeds the face value of the debt, the holder will benefit by converting the debt into shares. Alternatively, in such a situation the issuer may force conversion. If the market price of the stock remains the same or goes down, the holder of the convertible bond will not convert it into the stock. This is referred to as an overhanging bond. In other words, a holder will not convert if the market value of the common stock is less than the face value of the convertible bond. When this occurs, the issuer has a number of options, such as exercising the call feature and paying the bondholders the face amount of the bond, providing an inducement in the form of additional consideration to convert, or waiting until maturity to pay the principal of the debt. In bankruptcy, the convertible bond is subordinate to nonconvertible debt.

The strongly preferred and widely used method to account for the conversion of a bond into stock is the book value of bond method. A drawback to the book value method is that it fails to recognize in the accounting for the conversion the total value of the equity security issued. Although much less desirable, in a few exceptional cases when justified, the market value of bond or market value of stock method might be used. **Special Note:** The market value method is rarely used in practice and may be precluded under ASC 470-50-05, *Debt: Modifications and Extinguishments.*

Under the book value of bond method, there is no gain or loss reported on bond conversion, because the book value of the bond is the basis to credit equity. The entry to record the conversion using this method follows:

Bonds payable: At face value

Premium on bonds payable: Unamortized amount

   Discount on bonds payable: Unamortized amount

   Common stock: At par value of shares issued

   Paid-in-capital: For the difference between the book value of the bonds and the par value of common stock

Under the market value methods, gain or loss arises because the book value of the bond differs from the market value of the bond or market value of the stock, which is the basis to credit the equity account.

EXAMPLE

A $200,000 bond with an unamortized premium of $17,000 is converted to common stock. There are 200 bonds ($200,000/$1,000). Each bond is convertible into 100 shares of stock. Therefore, there are 20,000 shares of common stock to be issued. Par value per share is $8. The market value of the stock is $12 per share. The market value of the bond is 115%.

   Using the book value of bond method, the journal entry for the conversion is:

Bonds payable	200,000	
Premium on bonds payable	17,000	
Common stock (20,000 × $8)		160,000
Premium on common stock		57,000

   Using the market value of stock method, the journal entry is:

Bonds payable	200,000	
Premium on bonds payable	17,000	
Loss on bond conversion	23,000	
Common stock (20,000 × $8)		160,000
Premium on common stock (20,000 × $4)		80,000
20,000 shares × $12 = $240,000		

   Using the market value of bond method, the journal entry is:

Bonds payable	200,000	
Premium on bonds payable	17,000	
Loss on bond conversion	13,000	

Common stock (20,000 × $8)	160,000
Premium on common stock	70,000

$200,000 × 115% = $230,000

EXAMPLE

On July 1, 20X3, Klemer Company converted $1,000,000 of its 10% convertible bonds into 25,000 shares of $3 par value common stock. On the date of the conversion, the book value of the bonds was $1,200,000; the market value of the bonds was $1,250,000 and the market price of the stock was $54 per share. Using the preferred book value of bond method, the journal entry would be:

Bonds payable	1,000,000	
Premium on bonds payable	200,000	
Common Stock (25,000 × $3)		75,000
Paid-in-capital		1,125,000

EXAMPLE

A convertible bond having a face value of $80,000 with an unamortized discount of $5,000 is converted into 10,000 shares of $6 par value stock. Under the book value method, the journal entry for the conversion is:

Bonds payable	80,000	
Discount on bonds payable		5,000
Common stock (10,000 × $6)		60,000
Paid-in-capital		15,000

ASC 470-20-35-11, *Debt: Debt with Conversion and Other Options*, states that if the debt agreement specifies that accrued interest at the conversion date is forfeited by the bondholder, such accrued interest (net of tax) since the last interest date to the date of conversion should be treated as interest expense, with a corresponding credit to capital, because it is considered an element of the cost of the securities issued.

ASC 470-20-55-68, *Debt: Debt with Conversion and Other Options*, states that equity securities issued on the conversion of a debt instrument that has a substantive conversion feature at the issue (commitment) date should be treated for accounting purposes as a conversion if the debt security becomes convertible because the issuer has exercised a call option. In this case, gain or loss is not recorded. However, in the event that there is no substantive conversion feature at the issue date, the conversion should be treated as a debt extinguishment if the debt security becomes convertible because of the issuer's exercise of a call option based on the debt instrument's original conversion terms. In this situation, the fair value of the equity security should be treated as a part of the price of reacquiring the debt. In determining if a conversion feature is substantive, consideration should be given to assumptions and available market data.

Other authoritative sources of GAAP with regard to convertible debt may be found in ASC 815-15-55, *Derivatives and Hedging: Embedded Derivatives*.

EARLY EXTINGUISHMENT OF DEBT

ASC 860-50-35-3 and 35-5 through 35-7, *Transfers and Servicing: Servicing Assets and Liabilities*, ASC 860-50, *Transfers and Servicing: Servicing Assets and Liabilities*, and ASC 470-50-45, *Debt: Modifications and Extinguishments*, cover the accounting, reporting, and disclosures associated with retiring debt. Long-term debt may be called before its maturity date and new debt issued instead at a lower interest rate. On the other hand, the company may just retire the long-term debt early because it has excess funds and wants to avoid paying interest charges and having debt on its balance sheet. (A call provision allows the issuer the right to retire all or part of the debt prior to the maturity date, typically at a premium price.)

If a defeasance clause exists instead of a call provision, the issuer may satisfy the obligation and receive a lien release without retiring the debt. In a defeasance arrangement, the old debt is satisfied under law with a gain or loss being recognized.

According to ASC 860-50-35-3, when financial assets are transferred, any resulting debt or derivatives must be measured initially at fair value. The amortization of a servicing liability is proportionate based on the time period associated with the net servicing loss or gain. A change in fair value must be also considered. Disclosure is required of the nature of any limitations placed on assets set aside to pay debt payments.

ASC 860-50-35-3 also addresses the issue of a debtor becoming secondarily liable, such as because of a third-party assumption and a creditor's release. In this case, the original party is considered a guarantor. It is necessary to recognize a guarantee obligation based on the likelihood that the third party will pay. The guarantee obligation must initially be recognized at fair value. The guarantee obligation serves either to reduce the gain or increase the loss on debt extinguishment.

In an advance refunding arrangement, new debt is issued to replace the old debt issue that cannot be called. The amount received from issuing the new debt is used to buy high-quality investments, which are retained in an escrow account. The income earned on the investments in the escrow account is used to pay the interest and/or principal on the existing debt for a period ending on the date the existing debt is callable. When the call of the existing date occurs, the balance in the escrow account is used to pay the call premium. Any residual remaining is used to pay any interest due on the existing debt as well as the principal balance.

The reacquisition price for debt includes the call premium and any other associated costs (e.g., prepayment penalties, reacquisition costs) to buy back the debt. If the extinguishment is based on the issuance of securities, the reacquisition price is the fair value of the securities issued. The net carrying amount of the debt extinguished is its book value (including any associated unamortized discount or premium) and any other issuance costs (e.g., accounting, underwriter's commissions, legal). Any unamortized bond issue costs reduce the carrying value. ASC 470-50-15-2, *Debt: Modifications and Extinguishments*, stipulates that the gain or loss on extinguishment is based on either the fair value of the stock issued in exchange for the debt or the value of the debt extinguished, whichever is more clearly evident.

The gain or loss on the retirement of debt equals the difference between the retirement price and the carrying value of the bonds. The gain or loss on an extinguishment of debt is an ordinary item.

Debt is considered extinguished when the debtor is relieved of the principal liability and will most likely not need to make future payments. This occurs when either the debtor pays the debt or reacquires the debt in the securities market, or the debtor is legally discharged and it is probable that the debtor will not need to make future payments as guarantor of the obligation. The latter occurs when the debtor is legally discharged as the primary obligor but is secondarily liable for the debt.

EXAMPLE

A $300,000 bond payable with an unamortized bond discount of $7,000 is called at 90%. The journal entry is:

Bonds payable	300,000	
Discount on bonds payable		7,000
Cash (90% × $300,000)		270,000
Gain		23,000

EXAMPLE

On January 1, 20X3, a company called 500 outstanding, 8%, $1,000 face value bonds at 108%. The unamortized bond premium on this date was $25,000. The journal entry is:

Bonds payable	500,000	
Premium on bonds payable	25,000	
Loss	15,000	
Cash ($500,000 × 108%)		540,000

EXAMPLE

A bond having a face value of $300,000 and an unamortized discount of $8,000 is called at 102%. Unamortized deferred issue costs representing legal and accounting fees are $12,000. The journal entry for the extinguishment is:

Bonds payable	300,000	
Loss	26,000	
Cash ($300,000 × 102%)		306,000

Discount on bonds payable	8,000
Deferred issue costs	12,000

No gain or loss arises from an early extinguishment of a fully owned subsidiary's mandatory preferred stock by the parent company. It should be accounted for as a capital transaction. On the other hand, if a subsidiary has an outstanding third-party debt instrument that is purchased by the parent, a gain or loss is reported in consolidation equal to the difference between the carrying value of the debt on the subsidiary books and the purchase price paid by the parent. This accounting is also applicable if it is the parent that issued the debt and it is the subsidiary that purchases it.

There should be footnote disclosure in one footnote or cross-referenced footnotes concerning the extinguishment as follows:

☐ Description of the extinguishment transaction including the funding used for it.

☐ Direct and indirect guarantees of indebtedness of others (this includes a situation in which the debtor is released as the primary obligor but is contingently liable).

When a debtor contracts with a holder of its debt to redeem the obligation within one year for a predetermined amount, it is classified as a current liability. The debtor recognizes a loss when the contract becomes legally binding on the parties. However, a gain is not recognized until the redemption actually occurs.

Conversion Spread

As per ASC 470-20-40-12, *Debt: Debt with Conversion and Other Options*, an issuer should take into account only the *cash* payment when calculating a gain or loss on extinguishment of a liability or convertible debt if the accreted value is settled in cash and the embedded equity instrument (excess conversion spread) is *not* taken into account in calculating the gain or loss.

ASC 310-20-35-13, *Receivables: Nonrefundable Fees and Other Costs*, relates to modifications in mortgage loan payments.

EXTINGUISHMENT OF TAX-EXEMPT DEBT

ASC 840-30-35-31, *Leases: Capital Leases*, stipulates that if a modification is made to a rental because of a lessor's refunding of tax-exempt debt and the lessee receives the ensuing advantages and the modified lease qualifies as a capital lease to the lessee or a direct financing lease to the lessor, the change in the lease may qualify as a debt extinguishment. If so, the lessee adjusts the lease debt to its discounted value of future minimum lease payments based on the modified (new) arrangement. The discount rate used is the interest rate associated with the new lease contract. An ensuing gain or loss is considered as being associated with an early debt extinguishment resulting in an ordinary gain or loss. Meanwhile, the lessor adjusts its lease receivable account for the difference between the discounted value of payments associated with the old and modified (new) agreement. The ensuing gain or loss is recognized in the current year's income statement.

IMPUTING INTEREST ON NONINTEREST NOTES PAYABLE

ASC 835-30-05, *Interest: Imputation of Interest*, covers notes with no stated rate of interest. If the face value of a note differs from the consideration given or received, an interest calculation is required to avoid profit misstatement. Interest is imputed on noninterest-bearing notes, on notes with unreasonably low interest rates relative to market rates, and notes with face values substantially different from the prevailing selling prices of such notes.

If a note is issued just for cash, the note is recorded at the cash exchanged regardless of whether the interest rate is realistic or of the amount of the face value of the note. The present value of the note at the issue date is presumed to be the cash transacted.

If a note is exchanged for property, goods, or services, it is assumed that the interest rate is fair and appropriate. However, if the interest rate is not reasonable and adequate, the note must be recorded at the fair market value of the goods or services or at an amount approximating fair value. If fair value is nonascertainable for the product or service, the discounted present value of the note must be used.

The imputed interest rate is the one in which an independent borrower or lender would have engaged in a similar transaction. In determining the imputed interest rate, consideration should be given to such factors as credit rating, tax effect, collateral requirements, and restrictions.

It is the "going" interest rate the borrower would have paid for financing in an arm's-length transaction. There are several considerations involved in determining an appropriate interest rate, such as prevailing market interest rates, the prime interest rate, security pledged, loan restrictions, issuer's financial position, tax rate, and tax planning issues.

EXAMPLE

ABC Company sells equipment to XYZ Company on January 1, 20X4, in exchange for a $50,000 noninterest-bearing note due December 31, 20X5. There is no established price for this equipment, and the prevailing interest rate for this type of note is 10%. The present value of $1 at 10% for 2 years is 0.826446. Interest income will be recognized by ABC Company each year and the discount amortized.

Date	Interest Income	Discount Amortized	Carrying Amount
1/1/20X4			$41,322
12/31/20X4	$4,132	4,132	45,454
12/31/20X5	4,546*	4,546	50,000

* $1 adjustment for rounding

GAAP guidance on the imputation of interest (ASC 835-30-05) applies to long-term payables and receivables. Short-term payables and receivables are usually recorded at face value because the additional work of amortizing a discount or premium on a short-term note does not justify the information benefit derived.

In addition, it is not applicable to receivables or payables in the ordinary course of business, amounts not requiring repayment, security deposits, parent/subsidiary transactions, and customary lending of banks and other similar financial institutions.

The difference between the face value of a note and its present value constitutes a discount or premium, which is to be an increment or decrement to interest over the life of the note. The present value of the payments of the note depends on the imputed interest rate.

Discount or premium is amortized using the interest method, which results in a constant interest rate. Amortization equals the interest rate multiplied by the present value of the note payable at the beginning of the period.

The borrower recognizes interest expense while the lender recognizes interest revenue. Issuance costs are accounted for as a deferred charge.

The presentation of the note payable or note receivable in the balance sheet follows:

Notes payable (face amount)

Less: discount

Equals present value (principal)

Notes receivable (face amount)

Add: premium

Equals present value (principal)

EXAMPLE

On January 1, 20X3, a fixed asset is purchased for $40,000 cash and the incurrence of a $60,000, five-year, noninterest-bearing note payable. An imputed interest rate equals 10%. The present value factor for $n = 5$, $i = 10\%$ is .62. The journal entries follow:

1/1/20X3

Fixed asset ($40,000 + $37,200)	77,200	
Discount	22,800	
Notes payable		60,000
Cash		40,000

Present value of note = $60,000 × .62

= $37,200

On 1/1/20X3, the balance sheet presents:

Notes payable	$60,000
Less: discount	22,800
Present value	$37,200

12/31/20X3

Interest expense	3,720	
Discount		3,720

10% × $37,200 = $3,720

On 1/1/20X4, the balance sheet presents:

Notes payable	$60,000
Less: discount ($22,800 − $3,720)	19,080
Present value	$40,920

12/31/20X4

Interest expense	4,092	
Discount		4,092

10% × $40,920 = $4,092

EXIT OR DISPOSAL ACTIVITIES

ASC 420-10-05, *Exit or Disposal Cost Obligations: Overall*, relates to costs (e.g., operating lease termination costs, one-time termination benefits to current employees, costs to consolidate facilities or relocate workers) associated with a restructuring, discontinued operation, plant closing, or other exit or disposal activity. Restructurings include altering the management structure, relocating business operations, closing a location, and ceasing a business line. These costs are recognized as incurred (*not* at the commitment date to an exit plan) based on fair value along with the related liability. Therefore, the company must actually incur the liabilities before recognition may be made. If fair value cannot reasonably be estimated, recognizing the liability must be postponed to such time.

The fair value of a liability is the amount the liability can be settled for in a current transaction between willing parties, that is, other than in a forced or liquidated transaction. The best reflection of fair value is quoted market prices in active markets. If such is unavailable, fair value should be estimated based on the best data available.

The initiation date of an exit or disposal activity is when management obligates itself to a plan to exit or otherwise dispose of a long-lived asset, if the activity includes worker termination.

In years following initial measurement, changes to the liability should be measured based on the credit-adjusted risk-free rate that was used to initially measure the liability. The cumulative effect of a change due to revising either the timing or the amount of estimated cash flows shall be recognized as an adjustment to the liability in the year of change and reported in the same line items in the income statements used when the related costs were recognized initially. Changes due to the passage of time shall be recognized as an increase in the carrying value of the liability and as an expense (e.g., accretion expense).

Examples of costs attributable to exit or disposal activities are included in income from continuing operations unless they apply to discontinued operations.

If an event arises that discharges a company's obligation to settle a liability for a cost associated with an exit or disposal activity recognized in a prior year, the liability and the related costs are reversed.

The liability to end a lease or other legal agreement prior to the end of its term is measured at its fair value when the company cancels the contract. The estimated liability for future costs to be incurred is measured at its fair value when the business no longer uses its right under the contract such as using rented property. In the case of an operating lease, the obligation's fair value at the date the entity no longer uses the property is computed on the basis of the balance of the lease payments less any expected sublease rentals. However, the remaining rentals cannot be reduced to less than zero.

Consideration is given to when and how much a liability for one-time termination benefits is, based on whether employees are obligated to work until they are let go in order to be eligible for termination benefits and, if such is the case, whether workers will be kept to work beyond a minimum retention period. The minimum retention period cannot be more than the legal notification period or, in the event none exists, 60 days.

For situations in which workers do not have to work until they are let go to obtain termination benefits or will not be retained to work beyond a minimum retention period, the obligation for termination benefits is recorded at fair value at the date of communication.

If workers must work until they are terminated so as to obtain benefits and will be kept to work beyond the minimum retention period, the liability is initially measured at the communication date, based on the fair value as of the termination date but recorded ratably over future service years.

ASC 420-10-15-3, *Exit or Disposal Cost Obligations: Overall*, generally requires the recognition of costs related to one-time employee termination benefits at the communication date and contract termination costs at the cease-use date.

The following should be footnoted:

☐ A description of the exit or disposal activity and the expected completion date.

☐ The place in the income statement or statement of activities where exit or disposal costs are presented.

☐ If a liability for a cost is not recorded because fair value is not reasonably estimated, that should be noted along with the reasons.

☐ For each major kind of cost attributable to the exit activity, the total cost expected, the amount incurred in the current year, and the cumulative amount to date.

☐ Reconciliation of the beginning and ending liability balances presenting the changes during the year associated to costs incurred and charged to expense, costs paid or otherwise settled, and any adjustments of the liability along with the reasons for doing so.

Third-Party Credit Enhancement

ASC 820-10-25-1, 25-2 and 50-4A discusses liabilities issued with an inseparable third-party credit enhancement. Debt securities may be issued with a third-party credit enhancement. An example is a financial guarantee from an unrelated third party who guarantees the issuer's payment obligations. That guarantee may be purchased by the issuer who combines it with the debt and issues the combined security to an investor. In issuing debt combined with the guarantee, the issuer can obtain a lower interest rate and/or receive higher proceeds.

This guidance applies to an issuer's accounting for debt issued with an inseparable third-party credit enhancement that is measured or disclosed at fair value.

There should be disclosure of the credit enhancement. An issuer should not include the effect of the third-party credit enhancement in the fair value measurement of the liability. Therefore, the fair value measurement is determined taking into account the issuer's credit standing (without considering the third-party guarantor's credit standing). The unit of accounting for debt does not include the guarantee (or other third-party credit enhancement), and the guarantee does not represent an asset of the issuer. The guarantee is for the investor's benefit.

ENVIRONMENTAL LIABILITIES

In determining a loss contingency to accrue for environmental liabilities, the following should be taken into account:

☐ Type and degree of hazardous waste at a site.

☐ Remediation approaches available and remedial action plan.

☐ Level of acceptable remediation.

☐ Other responsible parties and their extent of liability.

Securities and Exchange Commission Staff Accounting Bulletin No. 92 requires full disclosure of environmental problems, how environmental liabilities are determined, "key" factors associated with the environment as it affects the business, and future contingencies. Depending on the circumstances, a liability and/or footnote disclosure would be required. Examples of environmental importance requiring accounting or disclosure recognition based on the facts follow:

☐ Information on site remediation projects, such as current and future costs, and remediation trends. (Site remediation may include hazard waste sites.)

☐ Contamination due to environmental health and safety problems.

☐ Legal and regulatory compliance issues, such as with regard to cleanup responsibility.

☐ Water or air pollution.

ASC 410-30-45, *Asset Retirement and Environmental Obligations: Environmental Obligations*, stipulates that if a liability for environmental losses is required, it should be reduced only when there is probable realization of recovery from a third party. However, both the liability and probable recovery must be shown separately. The present value of payments associated with a liability may be recognized only when the future cash flows are reliably determinable in amount and timing. If the liability is discounted, so must be the anticipated recovery. Disclosure is required of the gross cash flows and the discount rate used to determine present value.

According to ASC 410-30-55-18, *Asset Retirement and Environmental Obligations: Environmental Obligations*, in general, environmental contamination treatment costs should be expensed. However, in the following cases only, the company may elect to either expense or capitalize the costs:

☐ The expenditures made are to get the property ready for sale.

☐ The expenditures prevent or lessen environmental contamination that may result from *future* activities of property owned.

☐ The expenditures extend the life or capacity of the asset or enhance the safety of the property.

Other authoritative guidance for the accrual and disclosure of environmental liabilities include ASC 450-20-25, 4-5, *Contingencies: Loss Contingencies*, ASC 210-20-45, *Balance Sheet: Offsetting*, and ASC 410-30-45-6, *Asset Retirement and Environmental Obligations: Environmental Obligations*.

Environmental costs should be allocated across departments, products, and services.

DISCLOSURE OF LONG-TERM OBLIGATIONS

According to ASC 440-10-50-2, *Exit or Disposal Cost Obligations: Overall*, the following must be disclosed with respect to long-term obligations for each of the five years following the balance sheet date:

☐ The total payments for unconditional purchase obligations that have been recognized on the purchaser's balance sheet. An unconditional purchase obligation is a duty to transfer a fixed or minimum amount of funds at a later date or to transfer products or services at constant or minimum prices.

☐ The combined aggregate amount of maturities and sinking fund requirements for all long-term borrowings.

☐ The amount of redemption requirements for all issues of capital stock that are redeemable at fixed or determinable prices on fixed or determinable dates.

FAIR VALUE OPTION FOR ISSUED DEBT INSTRUMENTS

The fair value option was created to increase the relevancy of financial statements. Under this option (see the "Fair Value Option for Financial Assets and Financial Liabilities" section in this chapter for greater details), companies can now value their own liabilities as well as most other financial instruments in their accounts at the fair value. If the fair value option is chosen for a given financial instrument, all unrealized holding gains and losses relating to that instrument must be recorded in net income until the debt is retired. If a company chooses the fair value option for debt instruments that it issued (e.g., bonds payable), it is required to record any change in the fair value of these instruments each period as part of the entity's unrealized holding gains or losses. This amount is then reported in the entity's net income for the period. Changes in overall market interest rates, for example, would affect the fair value of an entity's debt. In addition, a change in the credit rating of the company would have a similar affect. Each period, the entity's bonds payable must be reevaluated for any change in fair value and that change must be recorded in net income.

COMMITMENTS

Footnote disclosure may be required of commitments, including their description and amount. Examples of such commitments are those associated with forward exchange contracts; employment agreements; agreements not to acquire another company, to reduce debt by a certain amount, not to issue debt, and not to issue debt exceeding a specified amount; agreements to maintain a minimum ratio (e.g., current ratio); and agreements to purchase a specified amount of assets.

EXAMPLE

On January 1, 20X3, Walter Company entered into a three-year noncancelable contract to buy up to 600,000 units of a product each year at $.15 per unit with a minimum annual guarantee purchase of 150,000. At year-end 20X3, 280,000 units of inventory were in stock. It is expected that each unit can be sold as scrap for $.04 per unit. The estimated loss on the purchase commitments to be recorded in 20X3 is:

(150,000 units × 2 years remaining on contract × $.11 unit cost) = $33,000

ASC 952-605-25, *Franchisors: Revenue Recognition*, provides disclosures as well as recognition and measurement provisions that require a liability to be recorded for certain guarantees at fair value.

OFFSETTING ASSETS AND LIABILITIES

In most cases, debts owed between two parties, a debtor and creditor, may be offset. However, a right to set off may be prohibited or restricted under federal or state bankruptcy law if the debtor is filing for bankruptcy. When related assets and liabilities are offset because of a right of setoff, they are shown in the balance sheet as a net amount.

ASC 210-20-45-1, *Balance Sheet: Offsetting*, indicates that an asset may be used to offset a liability if all of the following conditions are satisfied:

☐ The reporting entity intends to set off.

☐ A contractual right of setoff exists.

☐ The setoff is legal.

☐ Each of the two parties owes a determinable amount.

Note: A setoff right is a debtor's legal right to discharge an obligation owed another by applying against the obligation funds the other party owes the debtor.

An asset and liability may still be offset if they are in different currencies or have different interest rates associated with them. However, if the maturities of the asset and liability differ, only the company with the earlier maturity may offset.

A government security can be used to offset a tax obligation only if the security can be used as a direct offset of taxes due.

ASC 210-20-05, *Balance Sheet: Offsetting*, may allow for the offsetting of fair value amounts associated with forward, multiple swap, option, and conditional or exchange contracts in a master netting arrangement. In other words, the fair value of contracts with a loss may offset the fair value of contracts with a gain. Reference may be made to EITF Consensus Summary No. 86–25, *Offsetting Foreign Currency Swaps*.

ASC 210-20-45-11, *Balance Sheet: Offsetting*, discusses when amounts recognized as payables in repurchase contracts may be used to offset the amounts attributable to receivables in reverse repurchase agreements. Once a decision is made to offset or not to offset, it must be applied consistently. An offset of the payables and receivables is allowed if all of the following conditions are satisfied:

☐ The reporting company will use the same account at the clearing financial institution at the settlement date to transact the cash inflows and cash outflows associated with the contracts.

☐ There are adequate funds available at the settlement date for each party.

☐ The agreements are executed with the same counterparty.

☐ A master netting arrangement is involved.

☐ The settlement dates are the same for both agreements.

☐ The underlying securities are in "book entry" form.

An insurance recovery cannot be used to offset the associated litigation liability, because they do not involve the same two parties. **Recall:** A condition for setoff is that the two parties have a receivable and payable of determinable amounts.

A seller is not allowed to offset an installment note receivable against a bank debt with recourse, irrespective of whether the debt has a put option associated with it, making the debt a secured nonrecourse obligation.

ANNUAL REPORT REFERENCES

Sara Lee
2011 Annual Report

Note 12—Debt Instruments

The composition of the corporation's long-term debt, which includes capital lease obligations, is summarized in the following table:

In millions	Maturity Date	2011	2010
Senior debt			
Euro denominated - 2.25% note	2012	434	375
6.25% notes	2012	–	1,110
3.875% notes	2013	500	500
10% zero coupon notes ($19 million face value)	2014	15	14
10% - 14.25% zero coupon notes ($105 million face value)	2015	72	64
2.75% notes	2016	400	–
4.1% notes	2021	400	–
6.125% notes	2033	500	500
Total senior debt		2,321	2,563
Obligations under capital lease		3	3
Other debt		81	43
Total debt		2,405	2,609
Unamortized discounts		(5)	(6)
Hedged debt adjustment to fair value		9	26
Total long-term debt		2,409	2,629
Less current portion		(473)	(2)
		$1,936	$2,627

On September 7, 2010, the corporation completed a tender offer for any and all of its 6 1/4% Notes due September 15, 2011, of which $1.11 billion aggregate principal amount was outstanding. At the time of expiration of the tender offer, $653.3 million of the 6 1/4% notes had been validly tendered. On September 8, 2010, the corporation announced that it was redeeming the remaining $456.7 million of aggregate principal outstanding of the 6 1/4% Notes. This debt was redeemed on October 8, 2010. The corporation recognized a total charge of $55 million in 2011 associated with the early extinguishment of this debt. This charge is reported on the Debt extinguishment costs line of the Consolidated Income Statement. In September 2010, the company issued $400 million 2.75% Notes due in September 2015 and $400 million 4.1% Notes due in September 2020, the proceeds of which were used to fund a portion of the redemption of the 6 1/4% Notes. The remaining portion of the redemption of the 6 1/4% Notes in the second quarter of 2011 was funded by cash on hand and the net proceeds from commercial paper issuances.

In March, 2010, a subsidiary of the corporation issued € 300 million of debt, which is scheduled to mature in March 2012. The notes were issued at a fixed rate of 2.25% but have effectively been converted into variable rate debt using interest rate swap instruments. The proceeds were used to retire € 285 million of debt that was scheduled to mature in 2011. Payments required on long-term debt during the years ending 2012 through 2016 are $473 million, $521 million, $20 million, $77 million and $405 million, respectively. The corporation made cash interest payments of $123 million, $131 million and $156 million in 2011, 2010 and 2009, respectively.

In June 2011, the corporation amended its $1.85 billion five-year revolving credit facility that was set to expire in December 2011. The amendment lowered the dollar amount of the facility to $1.2 billion and extended the maturity date to the earlier of June 4, 2013 or the date on which the spin-off of the international beverage business is consummated. The credit facility has an annual fee of 0.05% as of July 2, 2011. Pricing under this facility is based on the corporation's current credit rating. As of July 2, 2011, the corporation did not have any borrowings outstanding under the credit facility. This agreement supports commercial paper borrowings and other financial instruments. The corporation had $150 million of letters of credit under this facility outstanding as of July 2, 2011. The corporation's credit facility and debt agreements contain customary representations, warranties and events of default, as well as, affirmative, negative and financial covenants with which the corporation is in compliance. One financial covenant includes a requirement to maintain an interest coverage ratio of not less than 2.0 to 1.0. The interest coverage ratio is based on the ratio of EBIT to consolidated net interest expense with consolidated EBIT equal to net income plus interest expense, income tax expense, and extraordinary or non-recurring non-cash charges and gains. For the 12 months ended July 2, 2011, the corporation's interest coverage ratio was 7.0 to 1.0.

Selected data on the corporation's short-term obligations follow:

In millions	2011	2010	2009
Maximum month-end borrowings	$605	$132	$461
Average borrowings during the year	323	69	289
Year-end borrowings	238	47	20
Weighted average interest rate during the year	2.36%	2.67%	3.60%
Weighted average interest rate at year-end	1.34	2.69	6.68

Walt Disney
2011 Annual Report

9. Borrowings

The Company's borrowings at October 1, 2011 and October 2, 2010, including the impact of interest rate swaps designated as hedges, are summarized below:

				2011				
				Interest rate and Cross-Currency Swaps(2)				
	2011	2010	Stated Interest Rate(1)	Pay Floating	Pay Fixed	Effective Interest Rate(3)	Swap Maturities
Commercial paper borrowings	$ 1,583	$1,190	0.15%	$—	$—	0.15%	
U.S. medium-term notes	8,400	6,815	4.84%	1,050	—	3.87%	2012–2018
European medium-term notes	91	273	1.65%	91	—	0.87%	2013

| | 2011 | 2010 | Stated Interest Rate[1] | Interest rate and Cross-Currency Swaps[2] | | Effective Interest Rate[3] | Swap Maturities |
				Pay Floating	Pay Fixed		
							2011
Other foreign currency denominated debt	1,020	965	0.86%	1,020	—	0.79%	2013
Capital Cities/ABC debt	114	115	8.75%	—	—	6.09%	
Other[4]	458	536	—	—	—	—	
	11,666	9,894	3.68%	2,161	—	2.94%	
Disneyland Paris (DLP) and Hong Kong Disneyland Resort (HKDL): DLP - CDC loans	1,440	1,417	5.04%	—	—	5.11%	
DLP - Credit facilities & other	116	228	4.55%	—	—	5.83%	
DLP - Other advances	425	468	3.04%	—	—	3.10%	
HKDL - Borrowings	330	473	3.25%	—	—	2.81%	
	2,311	2,586	4.39%	—	—	4.45%	
Total borrowings	13,977	12,480	3.80%	2,161	—	3.21%	
Less current portion	3,055	2,350	2.69%	50	—	2.17%	
Total long-term borrowings	$10,922	$10,130		$2,111	—		

[1] The stated interest rate represents the weighted-average coupon rate for each category of borrowings. For floating rate borrowings, interest rates are based upon the rates at October 1, 2011; these rates are not necessarily an indication of future interest rates.

[2] Amounts represent notional values of interest rate and cross-currency swaps as of October 1, 2011.

[3] The effective interest rate includes the impact of existing and terminated interest rate and cross-currency swaps on the stated rate of interest and reflects the estimated market interest rate for certain Disneyland Paris borrowings as of the time that they were modified during the 2005 Financial Restructuring. Other adjustments to the stated interest rate such as purchase accounting adjustments and debt issuance costs did not have a material impact on the overall effective interest rate.

[4] Includes market value adjustments for debt with qualifying hedges totaling $284 million and $315 million at October 1, 2011 and October 2, 2010, respectively.

Commercial Paper

At October 1, 2011, the Company had $1.6 billion of commercial paper debt outstanding. In February 2011, the Company entered into a new four-year $2.25 billion bank facility with a syndicate of lenders. This facility, in combination with an existing $2.25 billion bank facility that matures in 2013, is used to support commercial paper borrowings. These bank facilities allow for borrowings at LIBOR-based rates plus a spread, which depends on the Company's public debt rating and can range from 0.33% to 4.50%. The Company also has the ability to issue up to $800 million of letters of credit under the new facility, which if utilized, reduces available borrowings under this facility. As of October 1, 2011, $315 million of letters of credit had been issued of which $47 million was issued under this facility. The Company's bank facilities contain only one financial covenant, relating to interest coverage, which the Company met on October 1, 2011 by a significant margin. The Company's bank facilities also specifically exclude certain entities, including Disneyland Paris, Hong Kong Disneyland Resort and Shanghai Disney Resort, from any representations, covenants, or events of default.

Shelf Registration Statement

At October 1, 2011, the Company had a shelf registration statement which allows the Company to issue various types of debt instruments, such as fixed or floating rate notes, U.S. dollar or foreign currency denominated notes, redeemable notes, global notes, and dual currency or other indexed notes. Issuances under the shelf registration will require the filing of a prospectus supplement identifying the amount and terms of the securities to be issued. Our ability to issue debt is subject to market conditions and other factors impacting our borrowing capacity.

U.S. Medium-Term Note Program

At October 1, 2011, the total debt outstanding under U.S. medium-term note programs was $8.4 billion. The maturities of current outstanding borrowings range from 1 to 82 years and stated interest rates range from 0% to 7.55%.

European Medium-Term Note Program

At October 1, 2011, the Company had a European medium-term note program for the issuance of various types of debt instruments such as fixed or floating rate notes, U.S. dollar or foreign currency denominated notes, redeemable notes and index linked or dual currency notes. The size of the program is $4.0 billion. The remaining capacity under the program is $3.9 billion, subject to market conditions and other factors impacting our borrowing capacity. The remaining capacity under the program replenishes as outstanding debt under the program matures. At October 1, 2011, the outstanding debt under the program was $91 million, which matures in 2013 and has a stated interest rate of 1.65%. The Company has outstanding borrowings under the program denominated in Japanese Yen (JPY).

Other Foreign Currency Denominated Debt

In connection with the acquisition of Club Penguin Entertainment, Inc. in July 2007, the Company executed a credit agreement denominated in Canadian dollars (CAD) and borrowed CAD328 million ($317 million at October 1, 2011 exchange rate). The loan bears interest at CAD LIBOR plus 0.225% (1.42% at October 1, 2011) and matures in 2013. In July 2008, the Company executed a loan agreement denominated in JPY and borrowed JPY54 billion ($703 million at October 1, 2011 exchange rate). The loan bears interest at Japanese LIBOR plus 0.42% (0.61% at October 1, 2011) and matures in 2013.

Capital Cities/ABC Debt

In connection with the Capital Cities/ABC, Inc. acquisition in 1996, the Company assumed various debt previously issued by Capital Cities/ABC, Inc. At October 1, 2011, the outstanding balance was $114 million, matures in 2021 and has a stated interest rate of 8.75%.

Disneyland Paris Borrowings

	October 1, 2011	October 2, 2010
CDC senior debt	$322	$326
CDC subordinated debt - original and 1994 financing	369	373
CDC subordinated debt - Walt Disney Studios Park financing	749	718
CDC loans	1,440	1,417
Credit facilities and other	116	228
Other advances	425	468
	$1,981	$2,113

Disneyland Paris—Caisse des Dépôts et Consignations (CDC) loans. Pursuant to Disneyland Paris's original financing and the terms of a 1994 financial restructuring, Disneyland Paris borrowed funds from the CDC, a French state bank. As of October 1, 2011, these borrowings consisted of approximately € 237 million ($322 million at October 1, 2011 exchange rate) of senior debt and € 272 million ($369 million at October 1, 2011 exchange rate) of subordinated debt. The senior debt is collateralized primarily by the Disneyland Park, certain hotels, and land assets of Disneyland Paris with a net book value of approximately € 1.1 billion ($1.5 billion at October 1, 2011 exchange rate), whereas the subordinated debt is unsecured. Interest on the senior and subordinated debt is payable semiannually. Of these CDC loans, € 466 million ($633 million at October 1, 2011 exchange rate) bear interest at a fixed rate of 5.34%. The remaining CDC loans of € 42 million ($58 million at October 1, 2011 exchange rate) bear interest at a fixed rate of 6.33%. The loans mature from fiscal year 2012 to fiscal year 2024.

Disneyland Paris also executed a credit agreement with the CDC to finance a portion of the construction costs of Walt Disney Studios Park. As of October 1, 2011, approximately € 551 million ($749 million at October 1, 2011 exchange rate) of subordinated loans were outstanding under this agreement. The loans bear interest at a fixed rate of 5.15% per annum.

The loans mature between fiscal years 2015 and 2028. Pursuant to the 2005 Financial Restructuring, the CDC agreed to conditionally defer and convert to subordinated long-term borrowings, if operating results do not achieve specified levels, interest payments up to a maximum amount of € 20 million ($27 million at October 1, 2011 exchange rate) per year for fiscal year 2005 through fiscal year 2012 and € 23 million ($31 million at October 1, 2011 exchange rate) for each of the fiscal years 2013 and 2014. Disneyland Paris has deferred € 20 million of interest originally payable for each of fiscal year 2005 and 2006 as well as € 7 million of accrued interest on these amounts (collectively € 47 million). Disneyland Paris did not defer any CDC interest for fiscal years 2007 and 2008. Disneyland Paris deferred € 20 million ($27 million at October 1, 2011 exchange rate) of interest related to fiscal year 2009 and 2010, deferred € 15 million ($21 million at October 1, 2011 exchange rate) of interest related to fiscal 2011, and will defer the remaining € 5 million ($7 million at October 1, 2011 exchange rate) related to fiscal 2011 in the first quarter of fiscal 2012. The interest deferral related to fiscal 2011 is subject to third party confirmation of Disneyland Paris's operating results.

Disneyland Paris—Credit facilities and other. Pursuant to Disneyland Paris's original financing with a syndicate of international banks and the terms of a 1994 financial restructuring, Disneyland Paris borrowed funds which are collateralized primarily by the Disneyland Park, the hotels, and land assets of Disneyland Paris with a net book value of approximately € 1.1 billion ($1.5 billion at October

1, 2011 exchange rate). At October 1, 2011, the total balance outstanding was € 85 million ($116 million at October 1, 2011 exchange rate). The loans mature between fiscal years 2012 and 2013 and bear interest at a rate of EURIBOR plus 3% (4.55% at October 1, 2011).

Disneyland Paris—Other advances. Advances of € 304 million ($413 million at October 1, 2011 exchange rate) bear interest at a fixed rate of 3.0%. The remaining advances of € 9 million ($12 million at October 1, 2011 exchange rate) are collateralized by certain hotel assets and bear interest at EURIBOR plus 3% (4.55% at October 1, 2011). The advances are expected to mature between fiscal years 2012 and 2017.

Disneyland Paris has in its debt agreements certain annual financial performance objectives and limits on investing and financing activities. In fiscal 2011, Disneyland Paris did not meet its annual performance objectives and must defer € 25 million of royalties and management fees payable to the Company and € 20 million of interest payable to the CDC. Additionally, as a result of the fact that the performance objectives were not met, certain of Disneyland Paris's investment activities are further limited by the debt agreements.

Disneyland Paris is also subject to certain financial covenants and believes that it is in compliance with such covenants with the assistance of the Company's agreement, as permitted under the debt agreements, to defer an additional € 9 million of royalties payable to the Company into subordinated long-term borrowings.

The deferrals discussed above and compliance with these financial covenants are subject to final third-party review as provided in Disneyland Paris's debt agreements.

Hong Kong Disneyland Resort—Borrowings. Hong Kong Disneyland Resort has an unsecured loan facility of HK$2.6 billion ($330 million at October 1, 2011 exchange rate) from the HKSAR that is scheduled to mature on dates through September 12, 2030. The interest rate on this loan is subject to biannual revisions, but is capped at an annual rate of 6.75% (until March 12, 2014), 7.625% (until March 12, 2022) and 8.50% (until September 12, 2030). As of October 1, 2011, the rate on the loans was 3.25%.

Hong Kong Disneyland Resort Capital Realignment Plan

In July 2009, the Company entered into a capital realignment and expansion plan (the Plan) for Hong Kong Disneyland Resort with the HKSAR. See Note 7 for further details of the Plan. Total borrowings excluding market value adjustments, have the following scheduled maturities:

	Before International Theme Parks Consolidation	International Theme Parks	Total
2012	$2,857	$188	$3,045
2013	1,871	166	2,037
2014	1,466	47	1,513
2015	67	132	199

	Before International Theme Parks Consolidation	International Theme Parks	Total
2016	1,504	45	1,549
Thereafter	3,617	1,733	5,350
	$11,382	$2,311	$13,693

The Company capitalizes interest on assets constructed for its parks, resorts, and other property and on theatrical productions. In 2011, 2010, and 2009, total interest capitalized was $91 million, $82 million, and $57 million, respectively. Interest expense, net of capitalized interest, for 2011, 2010, and 2009 was $435 million, $456 million and $588 million, respectively.

Atwood Oceanics
2010 Annual Report

Note 5. Long-Term Debt

A summary of long-term debt is as follows (in thousands):

	September 30, 2010	2009
2007 credit facility, bearing interest (market adjustable) at approximately 1.1% and 1.9% per annum at September 30, 2010 and September 30, 2009, respectively	$ 180,000	$ 200,000
2008 credit facility, bearing interest (market adjustable) at approximately 1.8% and 2.2% per annum at September 30, 2010 and September 30, 2009, respectively	50,000	75,000
	$ 230,000	$ 275,000

During October 2007, we entered into a credit agreement with several banks, with Nordea Bank Finland plc, New York Branch, as Administrative Agent for the lenders, as well as Lead Arranger and Book Runner (as amended from time to time, the 2007 Credit Agreement). The 2007 Credit Agreement provides for a secured 5-year $300 million revolving loan facility with maturity in October 2012, subject to acceleration upon certain specified events of default, including but not limited to: delinquent payments, bankruptcy filings, breaches of representation or covenants, material adverse judgments, guarantees or security documents not in full effect, non-compliance with the Employee Retirement Income Security Act of 1974, defaults under other agreements including existing credit agreements, and a change in control. In addition, the 2007 Credit Agreement contains a number of limitations on our ability to: incur liens; merge, consolidate or sell assets; pay cash dividends; incur additional indebtedness; make advances, investments or loans; and transact with affiliates.

Loans under this facility bear interest at varying rates ranging from 0.70% to 1.25% over the Eurodollar Rate, depending upon the ratio of outstanding debt to earnings before interest, taxes and depreciation. The 2007 Credit Agreement supports the issuance, when required, of standby letters of credit. The collateral for the 2007 Credit Agreement consists primarily of preferred mortgages on three of our active drilling units (the *Atwood Eagle,* the *Atwood Hunter* and the *Atwood Beacon*). Under the 2007 Credit Agreement, we are required to pay a fee ranging from 0.225% - 0.375% per annum on the unused portion of the credit facility and certain other administrative costs. As of September 30, 2010, we have approximately $120 million of funds available to borrow under this credit facility, with standby letters of credit in the aggregate amount of approximately $0.1 million outstanding.

During November 2008, we entered into a new credit agreement with several banks with Nordea Bank Finland plc, New York Branch as Administrative Agent for the lenders, as well as Lead Arranger and Book Runner (as amended from time to time, the 2008 Credit Agreement). The 2008 Credit Agreement provides for a secured 5-year $280 million reducing revolving loan facility with maturity in November 2013, subject to acceleration upon certain specified events of default, including but not limited to: delinquent payments, bankruptcy filings, breaches of representation or covenants, material adverse judgments, guarantees or security documents not in full effect, non-compliance with the Employee Retirement Income Security Act of 1974, defaults under other agreements including existing credit agreements, such as our 2007 Credit Agreement, and a change in control. In addition, the 2008 Credit Agreement contains a number of limitations on our ability to: incur liens; merge, consolidate or sell assets; pay cash dividends; incur additional indebtedness; make advances, investments or loans; and transact with affiliates.

The 2008 Credit Agreement requires a mandatory quarterly commitment reduction of $7 million beginning at the earlier of three months after delivery of either semisubmersible drilling unit currently under construction or December 31, 2011. The commitment under this facility may be increased up to $20 million for a total commitment of $300 million. Loans under the 2008 Credit Agreement will bear interest at 1.50% over the Eurodollar Rate. The collateral for the 2008 Credit Agreement consists primarily of preferred mortgages on three of our drilling units (the *Atwood Falcon,* the *Atwood Southern Cross,* and the *Atwood Aurora*). Under the 2008 Credit Agreement, we are required to pay a fee of 0.75% per annum on the unused portion of the credit facility and certain other administrative costs. As of September 30, 2010, we have approximately $230 million of funds available to borrow under this credit facility, with standby letters of credit in the aggregate amount of approximately $1.4 million outstanding.

The 2008 Credit Agreement and the 2007 Credit Agreement contain various financial covenants that, among other things, require the maintenance of a leverage ratio, not to exceed 5.0 to 1.0, an interest expense coverage ratio not to be less than 2.5 to 1.0 and a required level of collateral maintenance whereby the aggregate appraised collateral value shall not be less than 150% of the total credit facility commitment. As of September 30, 2010, our leverage ratio was 0.14, our interest expense coverage ratio was 61.3 and our collateral maintenance percentage was in excess of 150%. We were in compliance with all financial covenants under the 2008 Credit Agreement and the 2007 Credit Agreement at September 30, 2010 and at all times during the year ended September 30, 2010. Subsequent to September 30, 2010, we borrowed an additional $70 million under the 2008 Credit Agreement, bringing the total amount outstanding under that agreement to $120 million as of November 22, 2010. No additional funds have been borrowed under the 2007 Credit Agreement subsequent to September 30, 2010.

Humana
2010 Annual Report

11. Debt

The carrying value of long-term debt outstanding was as follows at December 31, 2010 and 2009:

(in thousands)	2010	2009
Long-term debt:		
Senior notes:		
$500 million, 6.45% due June 1, 2016	$ 535,342	$ 540,907
$500 million, 7.20% due June 15, 2018	508,005	508,799
$300 million, 6.30% due August 1, 2018	321,622	323,862
$250 million, 8.15% due June 15, 2038	266,892	267,070
Total senior notes	1,631,861	1,640,638
Other long-term borrowings	36,988	37,528
Total long-term debt	$ 1,668,849	$ 1,678,166

Senior Notes

Our senior notes, which are unsecured, may be redeemed at our option at any time at 100% of the principal amount plus accrued interest and a specified make-whole amount. The 7.20% and 8.15% senior notes are subject to an interest rate adjustment if the debt ratings assigned to the notes are downgraded (or subsequently upgraded) and contain a change of control provision that may require us to purchase the notes under certain circumstances.

We had been parties to interest-rate swap agreements to exchange the fixed interest rate under our senior notes for a variable interest rate based on LIBOR. As a result, the carrying value of the senior notes had been adjusted to reflect changes in value caused by an increase or decrease in interest rates. During 2008, we terminated all of our swap agreements. The cumulative adjustment to the carrying value of our senior notes was $103.4 million as of the termination date which is being amortized as a reduction to interest expense over the remaining term of the senior notes, resulting in a weighted-average effective interest rate fixed at 6.08%. The unamortized carrying value adjustment was $83.8 million as of December 31, 2010 and $92.9 million as of December 31, 2009.

Credit Agreement

In December 2010, we replaced our 5-year $1.0 billion unsecured revolving credit agreement which was set to expire in July 2011 with a 3-year $1.0 billion unsecured revolving agreement expiring December 2013. Under the new credit agreement, at our option, we can borrow on either a competitive advance basis or a revolving credit basis. The revolving credit portion bears interest at either

LIBOR or the base rate plus a spread. The spread, currently 200 basis points, varies depending on our credit ratings ranging from 150 to 262.5 basis points. We also pay an annual facility fee regardless of utilization. This facility fee, currently 37.5 basis points, may fluctuate between 25 and 62.5 basis points, depending upon our credit ratings. The competitive advance portion of any borrowings will bear interest at market rates prevailing at the time of borrowing on either a fixed rate or a floating rate based on LIBOR, at our option.

The terms of the new credit agreement include standard provisions related to conditions of borrowing, including a customary material adverse event clause which could limit our ability to borrow additional funds. In addition, the credit agreement contains customary restrictive and financial covenants as well as customary events of default, including financial covenants regarding the maintenance of a minimum level of net worth of $5,257.9 million at December 31, 2010 and a maximum leverage ratio of 3.0:1. We are in compliance with the financial covenants, with actual net worth of $6,924.1 million and a leverage ratio of 0.8:1, as measured in accordance with the credit agreement as of December 31, 2010. In addition, the new credit agreement includes an uncommitted $250 million incremental loan facility.

At December 31, 2010, we had no borrowings outstanding under the credit agreement. We have outstanding letters of credit of $10.4 million secured under the credit agreement. No amounts have ever been drawn on these letters of credit. Accordingly, as of December 31, 2010, we had $989.6 million of remaining borrowing capacity under the credit agreement, none of which would be restricted by our financial covenant compliance requirement. We have other customary, arms-length relationships, including financial advisory and banking, with some parties to the credit agreement.

Other Long-Term Borrowings

Other long-term borrowings of $37.0 million at December 31, 2010 represent junior subordinated debt of $36.1 million and financing for the renovation of a building of $0.9 million. The junior subordinated debt, which is due in 2037, may be called by us without penalty in 2012 and bears a fixed annual interest rate of 8.02% payable quarterly until 2012, and then payable at a floating rate based on LIBOR plus 310 basis points. The debt associated with the building renovation bears interest at 2.00%, is collateralized by the building, and is payable in various installments through 2014.

Sherwin-Williams
2008 Annual Report

Note 7—Debt

Long-Term Debt

	Due Date	2008	2007	2006
7.375% Debentures	2027	$137,047	$137,044	$137,041
7.45% Debentures	2097	146,967	146,960	146,954

	Due Date	2008	2007	2006
1.0% to 13.5% Promissory Notes	Through 2015	19,713	9,450	7,881
		$303,727	$293,454	$291,876

Maturities of long-term debt are as follows for the next five years: $13,570 in 2009; $8,904 in 2010; $8,537 in 2011; $401 in 2012 and $402 in 2013. Interest expense on long-term debt was $31,973, $39,272, and $40,552 for 2008, 2007 and 2006, respectively.

Among other restrictions, the Company's Notes, Debentures and revolving credit agreement contain certain covenants relating to liens, ratings changes, merger and sale of assets, consolidated leverage and change of control as defined in the agreements. In the event of default under any one of these arrangements, acceleration of the maturity of any one or more of these borrowings may result. The Company was in compliance with all covenants for all years presented.

On October 6, 1997, the Company issued $50,000 of debt securities consisting of 5.5% notes, due October 15, 2027, with provisions that the holders, individually or in the aggregate, may exercise a put option that would require the Company to repay the securities. Prior to 2006, individual debt security holders exercised put options on $46,905 of these debt securities. During 2006, additional put options were exercised on $2,995 of these debt securities. Put options on the remaining balance of $100 of these debt securities were exercised in 2008.

Effective December 24, 1997, the Company filed a shelf registration with the Securities and Exchange Commission (SEC) covering $150,000 of unsecured debt securities with maturities greater than nine months from the date of issue. Effective September 8, 1998, the Company filed a universal shelf registration statement with the SEC to issue debt securities, common stock and warrants up to $1,500,000. Both shelf registrations expired in December 2008. There were no borrowings outstanding or issuance of common stock or warrants under either registration during all years presented.

Short-term borrowings. At December 31, 2008, 2007 and 2006, borrowings outstanding under the domestic commercial paper program totaled $83,064, $299,191 and $338,805, respectively, and were included in Short-term borrowings. The weighted-average interest rate related to these borrowings was 2.6%, 5.5% and 5.5% at December 31, 2008, 2007 and 2006, respectively. Borrowings outstanding under various foreign programs at December 31, 2008 of $33,374 with a weighted-average interest rate of 9.5%, December 31, 2007 of $107,891 with a weighted–average interest rate of 8.9% and December 31, 2006 of $30,973 with a weighted-average interest rate of 4.7% were included in Short-term borrowings.

On April 17, 2006, the Company entered into a three-year credit agreement, which was amended on April 25, 2006 and May 8, 2006. This credit agreement gives the Company the right to borrow and to obtain the issuance, renewal, extension and increase of a letter of credit up to an aggregate availability of $250,000. On May 23, 2006, the Company entered into a five-year credit agreement, which was amended on July 24, 2006. This credit agreement gives the Company the right to borrow and to obtain the issuance, renewal, extension and increase of a letter of credit up to an aggregate availability of $250,000. On April 26, 2007 and on August 28, 2007, which was amended on September 17, 2007 and September 25, 2007, the Company entered into two additional five-year credit agreements. This additional credit gives the Company the right to borrow and to obtain the issuance, renewal, extension and increase of a letter of credit up to an aggregate availability of $500,000. The total credit agreements aggregate $1,000,000. At December 31, 2008, $400,000 of this amount was outstanding, with a weighted-average interest rate of 2.8%. At December 31, 2007, $250,000 of this amount was outstanding, with a weighted average interest rate of 5.0%. At December 31, 2006, there were no borrowings outstanding under any of these credit agreements.

The Company has a five-year senior unsecured revolving credit agreement. The agreement was amended in 2008 to extend the maturity date from July 20, 2009 to July 20, 2010. A $500,000 letter of credit subfacility amendment to the agreement was reduced to $300,000 in 2008. The Company uses the revolving credit agreement primarily to satisfy its commercial paper program's dollar for dollar liquidity requirement. The Company's commercial paper program maximum borrowing capability is $910,000. The maximum borrowing capability will be reduced to $845,000 effective July 20, 2009. There were no borrowings outstanding under the revolving credit agreement during all years presented.

On February 1, 2006, the Company sold or contributed certain of its accounts receivable to SWC Receivables Funding LLC (SWC), a consolidated wholly-owned subsidiary. SWC entered into an accounts receivable securitization borrowing facility with a third party program agent. Under this program, SWC could borrow up to $500,000 and secure such borrowings by granting a security interest in certain eligible accounts receivable and related security. At December 31, 2007 and 2006, SWC had no borrowings outstanding under this program. On July 11, 2008, SWC terminated the accounts receivable securitization borrowing facility with a third party program agent and SWC was dissolved. There were no outstanding borrowings under the facility at the time it was terminated and no termination penalties were incurred.

Note 8. Other Long-Term Liabilities

The operations of the Company, like those of other companies in our industry, are subject to various federal, state and local environmental laws and regulations. These laws and regulations not only govern current operations and products, but also impose potential liability on the Company for past operations. Management expects environmental laws and regulations to impose increasingly stringent requirements upon the Company and the industry in the future. Management believes that the Company conducts its operations in compliance with applicable environmental laws and regulations and has implemented various programs designed to protect the environment and promote continued compliance.

The Company is involved with environmental investigation and remediation activities at some of its current and former sites (including sites which were previously owned and/or operated by businesses acquired by the Company). In addition, the Company, together with other parties, has been designated a potentially responsible party under federal and state environmental protection laws for the investigation and remediation of environmental contamination and hazardous waste at a number of third-party sites, primarily Superfund sites. In general, these laws provide that potentially responsible parties may be held jointly and severally liable for investigation and remediation costs regardless of fault. The Company may be similarly designated with respect to additional third-party sites in the future.

The Company initially provides for estimated costs of environmental-related activities relating to its past operations and third-party sites for which commitments or clean-up plans have been developed and when such costs can be reasonably estimated based on industry standards and historical experience. These estimated costs are determined based on currently available facts regarding each site. If the best estimate of costs can only be identified as a range and no specific amount within that range can be determined more likely than any other amount within the range, the minimum of the range is provided. At December 31, 2008, the aggregate unaccrued maximum of the estimated range of possible outcomes is $114,927 higher than the minimum.

The Company continuously assesses its potential liability for investigation and remediation-related activities and adjusts its environmental-related accruals as information becomes available upon which more accurate costs can be reasonably estimated and as additional accounting guidelines are issued. Actual costs incurred may vary from these estimates due to the inherent uncertainties involved including, among others, the number and financial condition of parties involved with respect to any given site, the volumetric contribution which may be attributed to the Company relative to that attributed to other parties, the nature and magnitude of the wastes involved, the various technologies that can be used for remediation and the determination of acceptable remediation with respect to a particular site.

Included in Other long-term liabilities at December 31, 2008, 2007, and 2006 were accruals for extended environmental-related activities of $128,179, $133,333 and $133,610, respectively. Estimated costs of current investigation and remediation activities of $52,555, $60,447 and $39,529 were included in Other accruals at December 31, 2008, 2007 and 2006, respectively.

Five of the Company's currently and formerly owned manufacturing sites accounted for the majority of the accrual for environmental-related activities and the unaccrued maximum of the estimated range of possible outcomes at December 31, 2008. At December 31, 2008, $135,161, or 74.8 percent of the total accrual, related directly to these five sites. In the aggregate unaccrued maximum of $114,927 at December 31, 2008, $74,944, or 65.2 percent, related to the five manufacturing sites. While environmental investigations and remedial actions are in different stages at these sites, additional investigations, remedial actions and monitoring will likely be required at each site.

Management cannot presently estimate the ultimate potential loss contingencies related to these sites or other less significant sites until such time as a substantial portion of the investigation at the sites is completed and remedial action plans are developed. In the event any future loss contingency significantly exceeds the current amount accrued, the recording of the ultimate liability may result in a material impact on net income for the annual or interim period during which the additional costs are accrued. Management does not believe that any potential liability ultimately attributed to the Company for its environmental-related matters will have a material adverse effect on the Company's financial condition, liquidity, or cash flow due to the extended period of time during which environmental investigation and remediation takes place. An estimate of the potential impact on the Company's operations cannot be made due to the aforementioned uncertainties.

Management expects these contingent environmental related liabilities to be resolved over an extended period of time. Management is unable to provide a more specific time frame due to the indefinite amount of time to conduct investigation activities at any site, the indefinite amount of time to obtain environmental agency approval, as necessary, with respect to investigation and remediation activities, and the indefinite amount of time necessary to conduct remediation activities.

FIN No. 47, "Accounting for Conditional Asset Retirement Obligations—an Interpretation of FASB Statement No. 143," requires a liability be recognized for the fair value of a conditional asset retirement obligation if a settlement date and fair value can be reasonably estimated. The Company recognizes a liability for any conditional asset retirement obligation when sufficient information is available to reasonably estimate a settlement date to determine the fair value of such a liability. The Company has identified certain conditional asset retirement obligations at various current and closed manufacturing, distribution and store facilities. These obligations relate primarily to asbestos abatement, hazardous waste Resource Conservation and Recovery Act (RCRA) closures, well abandonment, transformers and used oil disposals and underground storage tank closures. Using investigative, remediation and disposal methods that are currently available to the Company, the estimated costs of these obligations were accrued and are not significant. The recording of additional liabilities for future conditional asset retirement obligations may result in a material impact on net income for the annual or interim period during which the costs are accrued. Management does not believe that any potential liability ultimately attributed to the Company for its conditional asset retirement obligations will have a material adverse effect on the Company's financial condition, liquidity, or cash flow due to the extended period of time over which sufficient information may become available regarding the closure or modification of any one or group of the Company's facilities. An estimate of the potential impact on the Company's operations cannot be made due to the aforementioned uncertainties.

United Technologies
2007 Annual Report

Note 8. Borrowings and Lines of Credit

Short-term borrowings consist of the following:

(in millions of dollars)	2007	2006
Domestic borrowings	$ 1	$ 6
Foreign bank borrowings	1,084	401
Commercial paper	–	450
	$1,085	$857

The weighted-average interest rates applicable to short-term borrowings outstanding at December 31, 2007 and 2006 were 7.2% and 5.9%, respectively. At December 31, 2007, approximately $2.0 billion was available under short-term lines of credit with local banks at our various domestic and international subsidiaries.

At December 31, 2007, we had credit commitments from banks totaling $2.5 billion. We had a credit commitment of $1.5 billion under a revolving credit agreement, which serves as a backup facility for the issuance of commercial paper. As of December 31, 2007, there were no borrowings under this revolving credit agreement. We also have a $1.0 billion multi-currency revolving credit agreement that is to be used for general corporate funding purposes, including acquisitions. As of December 31, 2007, approximately $503 million had been borrowed under this revolving credit agreement to fund corporate expenses and international acquisitions. This credit agreement expires November 2011.

In December 2007, we issued $1.0 billion of long-term debt, the proceeds of which were primarily used to repay commercial paper borrowings. We generally use our commercial paper borrowings for general corporate purposes including financing acquisitions and the repurchase of our stock. The terms of the long-term debt issued in December 2007 were as follows:

Principal (in millions of dollars)	Rate	Maturity
$1,000	5.375%	December 15, 2017

We may redeem the notes, in whole or in part, at our option at any time at a redemption price in U.S. dollars equal to the greater of 100% of the principal amount of the notes to be redeemed or the sum of the present values of the remaining scheduled payments of principal and interest on the notes to be redeemed, discounted to the redemption date on a semiannual basis at the adjusted treasury rate plus 25 basis points. The redemption price will also include interest accrued to the date of redemption on the principal balance of the notes being redeemed.

In May 2006, we issued $1.1 billion of long-term debt, the proceeds of which were used to repay commercial paper borrowings. The long-term debt issued in May 2006 is comprised of two series of notes as follows:

Principal (in millions of dollars)	Rate	Maturity
$600	6.05%	June 1, 2036
$500	LIBOR + .07%	June 1, 2009

We may redeem the notes due in 2009, in whole or in part, at any time at a redemption price in U.S. dollars equal to 100% of the principal amount, plus interest accrued. We may redeem the notes due in 2036, in whole or in part, at our option at any time, at a redemption price in U.S. dollars equal to the greater of 100% of the principal amount of the notes to be redeemed or the sum of the present values of the remaining scheduled payments of principal and interest on the notes to be redeemed, discounted to the redemption date on a semiannual basis at the adjusted treasury rate plus 15 basis points. The redemption price will also include interest accrued to the date of redemption on the principal balance of the notes being redeemed. The three month LIBOR rate as of December 31, 2007 was approximately 4.7%.

In April 2005, we issued $2.4 billion of long-term debt, the proceeds of which were used primarily to support the funding of the Kidde acquisition. The long-term debt is comprised of three series of notes as follows:

Principal (in millions of dollars)	Rate	Maturity
$ 600	4.375%	May 1, 2010
$1,200	4.875%	May 1, 2015
$ 600	5.400%	May 1, 2035

We may redeem the notes of any series, in whole or in part, at our option at any time, at a redemption price in U.S. dollars equal to the greater of 100% of the principal amount of the notes of the series to be redeemed or the sum of the present values of the remaining scheduled payments of principal and interest on the notes of the series to be redeemed as described below, discounted to the redemption date on a semiannual basis, at the adjusted treasury rate described below plus 10 basis points for the 4.375% notes, 15 basis points for the 4.875% notes and 15 basis points for the 5.400% notes. In each case, the redemption price will also include interest accrued to the date of redemption on the principal balance of the notes being redeemed.

Total long-term debt consists of the following:

(in millions of dollars)	Weighted-Average Interest Rate	Maturity	2007	2006
Notes and other debt denominated in:				
U.S. dollars	6.0%	2008–2036	$7,942	$6,947
Foreign currency	5.7%	2008–2019	56	29
ESOP debt	7.7%	2008–2009	65	98
			8,063	7,074
Less: Long-term debt currently due			48	37
			$8,015	$7,037

Principal payments required on long-term debt for the next five years are: $48 million in 2008, $953 million in 2009, $1,123 million in 2010, $538 million in 2011, and $504 million in 2012.

In July 2007, we replaced our existing shelf registration statement by filing with the SEC a universal shelf registration statement for an indeterminate amount of securities for future issuance, subject to our internal limitations on the amount of debt to be issued under this shelf. As of December 31, 2007, we had issued $1.0 billion of long-term debt under this shelf registration statement.

The percentage of total debt at floating interest rates was 18% and 17% at December 31, 2007 and 2006, respectively.

Hercules Incorporated
2007 Annual Report

7. Debt

A summary of debt follows:

	2007	2006
Term B loan due 2010[a]	$261.0	$375.0
6.60% notes due 2027	15.9	100.0
11.125% senior notes due 2007	–	16.1
6.75% senior notes due 2029[b]	250.0	250.0
8% convertible subordinated debentures due 2010[c]	2.3	2.4
6.5% junior subordinated deferrable interest debentures due 2029[d]	215.1	214.1
Term loans at rates ranging from 5.814% to 7.2978% due in varying amounts through 2011[e]	49.9	28.1
Other	1.8	9.8
	796.0	995.5
Less: Current debt obligations	33.7	35.8
Long term debt	762.3	959.7

[a] The term loan, a component of the Company's Senior Credit Facility, matures on October 8, 2010 and bears interest at LIBOR + 1.50%, with the Company holding the option to reset interest rates for one, two, three or six month periods. The weighted average rate was 6.71% as of December 31, 2007. The Senior Credit Facility is also comprised of a $150 million committed revolving credit facility (the "Revolving Facility") which matures on April 8, 2009. The Senior Credit Facility is secured by liens on the Company's assets (including real, personal and intellectual properties) and is guaranteed by substantially all of the Company's current and future wholly-owned domestic subsidiaries (see Note 25).
As of December 31, 2007, the Company had $47.9 million of outstanding letters of credit under the Revolving Facility. The remaining $102.1 million was available for use.
The Company's Senior Credit Facility requires quarterly compliance with certain financial covenants, including a leverage ratio and an interest coverage ratio, and established limitations on the permitted amount of capital expenditures and dividends.
[b] The senior notes are guaranteed by each of Hercules' current and future wholly-owned domestic restricted subsidiaries.
[c] The convertible subordinated debentures are convertible into common stock at $14.90 per share and are redeemable at the option of the Company at varying rates.

(d) The 6.5% junior subordinated deferrable interest debentures due 2029 (the "6.5% debentures") had an initial issue price of $741.46 and have a redemption price of $1,000. The 6.5% debentures were initially issued to Hercules Trust II ("Trust II"), a subsidiary trust established in 1999. Trust II had issued, in an underwritten public offering, 350,000 CRESTS℠ Units, each consisting of a 6.5% preferred security of Trust II and a warrant (exercisable through 2029) to purchase 23.4192 shares of the Company's common stock for the equivalent of $42.70 per share. The preferred securities and the warrants were separable and were initially valued at $741.46 and $258.54, respectively. The Company and Trust II accreted the difference between the initial valuation of the 6.5% debentures and the preferred securities and the redemption value of $1,000 over the term of the 6.5% debentures and the preferred securities. In connection with the Company's dissolution and liquidation of Trust II in December 2004, Trust II distributed the 6.5% debentures to the holders of the preferred securities and the preferred securities were cancelled. The CRESTS℠ Units now consist of the 6.5% debentures and the warrants.

(e) Includes loans issued by Hercules Tianpu for which Hercules has provided a guarantee for 55% of the outstanding balances. The loans are denominated in renminbi and U.S. Dollar-equivalents and include a short-term loan payable due in 2008 for approximately $17.2 million and a long-term loan payable due in 2011 for approximately $25.2 million.

At December 31, 2007, Hercules had available and unused foreign lines of credit totaling $35.1 million and $31.0 million, respectively.

Debt maturities are $33.7 million in 2008, $12.2 million in 2009, $263.1 million in 2010, $6.1 million in 2011 and $480.9 million thereafter.

Total interest expense incurred for the years ended December 31, 2007, 2006 and 2005 was $69.7 million, $71.5 million and $89.8 million, respectively. The total amounts capitalized for the aforementioned periods were $1.1 million, $0.3 million and $0.4 million, respectively.

Rockwell Automation
2004 Annual Report

6. Debt

Short-term debt consists of the following (in millions):

	September 30, 2004	September 30, 2003
Current portion of long-term debt	–	$8.4
Other borrowings	0.2	0.3
Short-term debt	$0.2	$8.7

Long-term debt consists of the following (in millions):

	September 30, 2004	September 30, 2003
6.15% notes, payable in 2008	$353.7	$360.4
6.70% debentures, payable in 2028	250.0	250.0
5.20% debentures, payable in 2098	200.0	200.0
Other borrowings	–	8.4

	September 30,	
Unamortized discount	(46.0)	(46.4)
Total	757.7	772.4
Less current portion	–	8.4
Long-term debt	$757.7	$764.0

In September 2002, we entered into an interest rate swap contract (the Swap) that effectively converted our $350.0 million aggregate principal amount of 6.15% notes, payable in 2008, to floating rate debt based on six-month LIBOR. The floating rate was 4.27 percent at September 30, 2004 and 3.52 percent at September 30, 2003. The fair value of the Swap, based upon quoted market prices for contracts with similar maturities, was $3.7 million at September 30, 2004 and $10.4 million at September 30, 2003. As permitted by SFAS No. 133, *Accounting for Derivative Instruments and Hedging Activities* (SFAS 133), as amended, we have designated the Swap as a fair value hedge. Accordingly, the fair value of the Swap was recorded in other assets on the Consolidated Balance Sheet at September 30, 2004 and 2003. The carrying value of the underlying debt was increased to $353.7 million at September 30, 2004 and $360.4 million at September 30, 2003 in accordance with SFAS 133.

At September 30, 2004, we had $675.0 million of unsecured committed credit facilities, with $337.5 million expiring in October 2004 and $337.5 million expiring in October 2005. These facilities were available for general corporate purposes, including support for our commercial paper borrowings. On October 26, 2004, we entered into a new five-year $600.0 million unsecured revolving credit facility. It replaced both the facility expiring on that date and the facility expiring in October 2005 (which we cancelled on that date). Borrowings under our new credit facility bear interest based on short-term money market rates in effect during the period such borrowings are outstanding. The terms of our credit facility contain a covenant under which we would be in default if our debt to capital ratio were to exceed 60 percent. In addition to our $600.0 million credit facility, short-term unsecured credit facilities available to foreign subsidiaries amounted to $130.4 million at September 30, 2004. There were no significant commitment fees or compensating balance requirements under any of our credit facilities.

Interest payments were $40.9 million during 2004, $54.7 million during 2003, and $63.1 million during 2002.

Corning
2004 Annual Report

10. Other Liabilities

Other accrued liabilities follow (in millions):

	December 31,	
	2004	*2003*
Current liabilities:		
Wages and employee benefits	$291	$238

Other accrued liabilities follow (in millions):		
Asbestos settlement	315	282
Income taxes	153	88
Other current liabilities	417	466
Other accrued liabilities	$1,176	$1,074
Non-current liabilities:		
Asbestos settlement	$144	$136
Customer deposits	197	
Other non-current liabilities	374	276
Other liabilities	$715	$412

Asbestos Settlement

The current liability represents the cost of our investment in PCE and the fair value of the 25 million shares of Corning common stock as of December 31, 2004, which will be contributed to the Plan when it becomes effective. As the timing of this obligation's settlement is controlled by a third party (not Corning), this portion of the PCC liability is considered a "due on demand" obligation. Accordingly, this portion of the obligation has been classified as a current liability, even though it is possible that the contribution could be made in 2006 or later. The non-current liability represents the net present value of cash payments as of December 31, 2004, which will be contributed to the Plan in six installments beginning one year after the Plan is effective. Refer to Note 7 (Investments) for additional information on the asbestos settlement.

Customer Deposits

During 2004, in response to the rapid growth of the liquid crystal display (LCD) market, Corning held discussions with several of its customers to discuss how to meet this demand. Corning and these customers have typically entered into multi-year supply agreements for the purchase and sale of glass substrates. These agreements provide for Corning to supply a percentage of the customers' requirements and include mechanisms for forecasting and ordering. As part of its discussions, Corning has sought improved payment terms, including deposits against orders, to provide a greater degree of assurance that we are effectively building capacity to meet the needs of a rapidly growing industry.

In 2004, Corning and a Taiwanese customer entered into a long-term purchase and supply agreement (as amended) in which the Display Technologies segment will supply LCD glass to the customer over a five-year period. As part of the agreement, the customer will make advance cash deposits of $460 million to Corning through 2006 for a portion of the contracted glass to be purchased. Corning received a total of $204 million of deposits against orders in 2004 and expects to receive an additional $171 million in 2005.

In the event the customer does not make all customer deposit installment payments or elects not to purchase the agreed upon quantities of product, subject to specific conditions outlined in the agreement, Corning may retain certain amounts of the customer deposit. Likewise, if Corning does not deliver agreed upon product quantities, subject to specific conditions outlined in the agreement, Corning may be required to return certain amounts of the customer deposit.

11. Debt

(In millions):

	December 31,	
	2004	*2003*
Short-term borrowings, including current portion of long-term debt		$ 26
Short-term borrowings		
Current portion of long-term debt	$ 478	120
Total	$ 478	$ 146
Long-term debt		
Euro notes, 5.625%, due 2005	$ 189	$ 173
Debentures, 7%, due 2007, net of unamortized discount of $15 million in 2004 and $20 million in 2003	85	80
Convertible notes, 4.875%, due 2008	96	96
Convertible debentures, 3.50%, due 2008	297	665
Notes, 6.3%, due 2009	150	150
Euro notes, 6.25%, due 2010	408	374
Debentures, 6.75%, due 2013	100	100
Debentures, 5.90%, due 2014	200	
Zero coupon convertible debentures, 2%, due 2015, redeemable and callable in 2005	272	385
Debentures, 6.20%, due 2016	200	
Debentures, 8.875%, due 2016	81	82
Debentures, 8.875%, due 2021	82	83
Debentures, 7.625%, due 2024	1	100
Medium-term notes, average rate 8.1%, due through 2025	175	178
Debentures, 6.85%, due 2029	150	150
Other, average rate 3.4%, due through 2015	206	172
Total long-term debt	2,692	2,788
Less current portion of long-term debt	478	120
Long-term debt	$2,214	$2,668

Based on borrowing rates currently available to us for loans with similar terms and maturities, the fair value of long-term debt was $2.8 billion at December 31, 2004.

The following table shows debt maturities by year at December 31, 2004 (in millions):

2005	2006	2007	2008	2009	Thereafter
$478	$16	$104	$411	$166	$1,517

We have convertible debt of $297 million due November 1, 2008 that is convertible into approximately 31 million shares of common stock at an effective conversion price of $9.675 per share. The debentures are available for conversion into 103.3592 shares of Corning common stock for each $1,000 debenture. The debentures are issued at par and pay interest of 3.5% semi-annually on May 1 and November 1 of each year. Effective November 8, 2004, we may call the debentures at any time, at specified redemption prices. The holder can convert the debenture into Corning common stock at any time prior to maturity or redemption.

We have $272 million of zero coupon convertible debentures outstanding. The initial price of the debentures was $741.92 with a 2% annual yield. Interest is compounded semi-annually with a 25% conversion factor. The debentures mature on November 8, 2015, and are convertible into approximately 3 million shares of Corning common stock at the rate of 8.3304 shares per $1,000 debenture. We may call the debentures at any time on or after November 8, 2005. The debentures may be put to us for $819.54 on November 8, 2005 and $905.29 on November 8, 2010. We have the option of settling this obligation in cash, common stock, or a combination of both. The holder can convert the debenture into Corning common stock at any time prior to maturity or redemption. The zero coupon convertible debentures are presented in the above table as due in 2005 which is the earliest possible redemption date.

We also have $96 million of convertible subordinated notes bearing interest at 4.875%, due in 2008. The notes are convertible into 6 million shares of Corning common stock at a conversion price of approximately $16 per share.

We have full access to a $2.0 billion revolving line of credit with a syndicate of banks. The line of credit expires in August 2005. There were no borrowings under the agreement at December 31, 2004. The revolving credit agreement provides for borrowing of U.S. dollars and Euro currency at various rates and supports our commercial paper program when available. The facility includes a covenant requiring us to maintain a total debt to total capital ratio, as defined, not greater than 60%. At December 31, 2004, this ratio was 41%.

Debt Retirements

During the years ended December 31, 2004, 2003, and 2002, we retired a significant portion of our outstanding debentures as part of a debt reduction program. The debt was retired through a combination of cash repurchases and exchanges for Corning common stock. The following table summarizes the activities related to our debt retirements (in millions):

	Book Value of Debentures Retired	Cash Paid	Shares Issued	Gain (Loss)
2004 activity:				
Convertible debentures, 3.5%, due 2008	**$368**	**$37**	**38**	**$(36)**
Zero coupon convertible debentures, 2%, due 2015	119	117		
Total 2004 activity	**$487**	**$154**	**38**	**$(36)**
2003 activity:				
Zero coupon convertible debentures, 2%, due 2015	$1,239	$1,121	6	$20
Euro notes, 5.625%, due 2005	67	68		(1)
Total 2003 activity	$1,306	$1,189	6	$19
2002 activity:				
Zero coupon convertible debentures, 2%, due 2015	$493	$308		$175
Euro notes, 5.625%, due 2005	1	1		1
Total 2002 activity	$494	$309		$176

In addition to the above repurchases, during 2004 we repaid approximately $99 million of our 7.625% debentures as a result of certain bond holders exercising their early repayment option. The remaining balance of the bonds that were not repaid will mature in 2024.

Kimberly Clark
2004 Annual Report

Note 4. Debt

Long-term debt is composed of the following:

	Weighted-Average Interest Rate	Maturities	December 31 2004	2003
			(Millions of dollars)	
Notes and debentures	5.77%	2005–2038	$2,309.8	$2,342.9
Industrial development revenue bonds	2.58%	2006–2037	300.7	381.3
Bank loans and other financings in various currencies	7.22%	2005–2031	272.9	194.9
Total long-term debt			2,883.4	2,919.1
Less current portion			585.4	185.4
Long-term portion			$2,298.0	$2,733.7

Fair value of total long-term debt, based on quoted market prices for the same or similar debt issues, was approximately $3.0 billion and $3.1 billion at December 31, 2004 and 2003, respectively. Scheduled maturities of long-term debt for the next five years are $585.4 million in 2005, $64.8 million in 2006, $336.7 million in 2007, $19.7 million in 2008 and $5.1 million in 2009.

At December 31, 2004, the Corporation had $1.2 billion of revolving credit facilities. These facilities, unused at December 31, 2004, permit borrowing at competitive interest rates and are available for general corporate purposes, including backup for commercial paper borrowings. The Corporation pays commitment fees on the unused portion but may cancel the facilities without penalty at any time prior to their expiration. Of these facilities, $600 million expires in September 2005 and the balance expires in November 2009.

Debt payable within one year is as follows:

| | December 31 | |
	2004	2003
	(Millions of dollars)	
Commercial paper	$ 526.3	$533.5
Current portion of long-term debt	585.4	185.4
Other short-term debt	103.0	145.4
Total	$1,214.7	$864.3

At December 31, 2004 and 2003, the weighted-average interest rate for commercial paper was 2.3 percent and 1.0 percent, respectively.

Lockheed Martin
2002 Annual Report

Note 9—Debt

The Corporation's long-term debt is primarily in the form of publicly issued, fixedrate notes and debentures, summarized as follows:

Type (Maturity Dates) (In millions, except interest rate data)	Range of Interest Rates	2002(a)	2001
Notes (2003–2022)	6.5–9.0%	$3,099	$3,114
Debentures (2011–2036)	7.0–9.1%	4,198	4,198
ESOP obligations (2003–2004)	8.4%	82	132
Other obligations (2003–2016)	1.0–10.5%	178	67
		7,557	7,511
Less current maturities		(1,365)	(89)
		$6,192	$7,422

(a) Amounts exclude a $25 million adjustment to the fair value of long-term debt relating to the Corporation's interest rate swap agreements which will not be settled in cash.

In 2003, the Corporation decided to issue irrevocable redemption notices to the trustees for two issuances of callable debentures totaling $450 million. One notice was for $300 million of 7.875% debentures due on March 15, 2023, which were callable on or after March 15, 2003. The second was for $150 million of 7.75% debentures due on April 15, 2023, which were callable on or after April 15, 2003. The Corporation expects to repay amounts due on March 15, 2003 and April 15, 2003, respectively. Therefore, the $450 million of debentures to be redeemed has been included in current maturities of long-term debt on the consolidated balance sheet at December 31, 2002. The Corporation expects to incur a loss on the early repayment of the debt, net of state income tax benefits, of approximately $16 million, or $10 million after tax.

In the fourth quarter of 2002, the Corporation recorded $150 million of debt related to its guarantee of certain borrowings of Space Imaging (see Note 8). The debt was recorded due to the Corporation's assessment regarding Space Imaging's inability to attract the necessary funding sufficient to repay the borrowings, which are due on March 30, 2003. The debt is included in other obligations above and has been classified as current maturities of long-term debt in the Corporation's consolidated balance sheet.

In September 2001, the Corporation redeemed approximately $117 million of 7% debentures ($175 million at face value) due in 2011 which were originally sold at approximately 54% of their principal amount. The debentures were redeemed at face value, resulting in an unusual loss, net of state income tax benefits, of $55 million which was included in other income and expenses. The loss reduced net earnings by $36 million ($0.08 per diluted share).

In July 2001, COMSAT, a wholly-owned subsidiary of the Corporation, redeemed $200 million in principal amount of the 8.125% Cumulative Monthly Income Preferred Securities (MIPS) previously issued by a wholly-owned subsidiary of COMSAT. The MIPS were redeemed at par value of $25 per share plus accrued and unpaid dividends to the redemption date. The redemption did not result in an unusual gain or loss on the early repayment of debt.

Also in 2001, the Corporation repaid approximately $1.26 billion of notes outstanding which had been issued to a wholly-owned subsidiary of General Electric Company. The notes would have been due November 17, 2002. The early repayment of the notes did not result in an unusual gain or loss on the early repayment of debt.

In December 2000, the Corporation purchased approximately $1.9 billion in principal amount of debt securities included in tender offers for six issues of notes and debentures. The repurchase of the debt securities resulted in a loss, net of income tax benefits, of $156 million which was included in other income and expenses. The loss reduced net earnings by $95 million ($0.24 per diluted share).

The Corporation has entered into interest rate swaps toswap fixed interest rates on approximately $920 million of its long-term debt for variable interest rates based on LIBOR. At December 31, 2002, the fair values of interest rate swap agreements outstanding, as well as the amounts of gains and losses recorded during the year, were not material.

The registered holders of $300 million of 40 year debentures issued in 1996 may elect, between March 1 and April 1, 2008, to have their debentures repaid by the Corporation on May 1, 2008.

A leveraged employee stock ownership plan (ESOP) incorporated into the Corporation's salaried savings plan borrowed $500 million through a private placement of notes in 1989. These notes are being repaid in quarterly installments over terms ending in 2004. The ESOP note agreement stipulates that, in the event that the ratings assigned to the Corporation's long-term senior unsecured debt are below investment grade, holders of the notes may require the Corporation to purchase the notes and pay accrued interest.

These notes are obligations of the ESOP but are guaranteed by the Corporation and included as debt in the Corporation's consolidated balance sheet.

At December 31, 2002, the Corporation had in place a $1.5 billion revolving credit facility; no borrowings were outstanding. This credit facility will expire in November 2006. Borrowings under the credit facility would be unsecured and bear interest at rates based, at the Corporation's option, on the Eurodollar rate or a bank Base Rate (as defined). Each bank's obligation to make loans under the credit facility is subject to, among other things, the Corporation's compliance with various representations, warranties and covenants, including covenants limiting the ability of the Corporation and certain of its subsidiaries to encumber assets and a covenant not to exceed a maximum leverage ratio. In October 2002, the Corporation terminated its $1.0 billion 1-year credit facility.

The Corporation's long-term debt maturities for the five years following December 31, 2002 are: $1,365 million in 2003; $141 million in 2004; $15 million in 2005; $783 million in 2006; $33 million in 2007; and $5,220 million thereafter.

Certain of the Corporation's other financing agreements contain restrictive covenants relating to debt, limitations on encumbrances and sale and lease-back transactions, and provisions which relate to certain changes in control.

The estimated fair values of the Corporation's long-term debt instruments at December 31, 2002, aggregated approximately $9.0 billion, compared with a carrying amount of approximately $7.6 billion. The fair values were estimated based on quoted market prices for those instruments that are publicly traded. For privately placed debt, the fair values were estimated based on the quoted market prices for similar issues, or on current rates offered to the Corporation for debt with similar remaining maturities. Unless otherwise indicated elsewhere in the notes to the financial statements, the carrying values of the Corporation's other financial instruments approximate their fair values.

In June 2000, the Corporation paid $207 million to settle its share of obligations of Globalstar, L.P. (Globalstar) under a revolving credit agreement on which Lockheed Martin was a partial guarantor. At the same time, Loral Space, under a separate indemnification agreement between the Corporation and Loral Space, paid Lockheed Martin $57 million. In light of the uncertainty of the Corporation recovering the amounts paid on Globalstar's behalf from Globalstar, the Corporation recorded an unusual charge in the second quarter of 2000, net of state income tax benefits, of approximately $141 million in other income and expenses. The charge reduced net earnings for 2000 by $91 million ($0.23 per diluted share).

Interest payments were $586 million in 2002, $707 million in 2001 and $947 million in 2000.

Sherwin Williams
2004 Annual Report

Note 6—Exit or Disposal Activities

Management is continually re-evaluating the Company's operating facilities against its long-term strategic goals. Prior to January 1, 2003, upon commitment to a formal shutdown plan of an operating facility, provisions were made for all estimated qualified exit costs in accordance with EITF No. 94-3. Effective January 1, 2003, the Company recognizes liabilities associated with exit or disposal activities as incurred in accordance with SFAS No. 146. Qualified exit costs primarily include post-closure rent expenses, incremental post-closure costs and costs of employee terminations. Adjustments may be made to liabilities accrued for qualified exit costs if information becomes available upon which more accurate amounts can be reasonably estimated. Concurrently, property, plant, and equipment is tested for impairment in accordance with SFAS No. 144 and, if impairment exists, the carrying value of the related assets is reduced to estimated fair value. Additional impairment may be recorded for subsequent revisions in estimated fair value. No significant revisions occurred during 2004, 2003, or 2002.

The following table summarizes the activity and remaining liabilities associated with qualified exit costs:

Exit Plan	Balance at December 31, 2003	Provisions in Cost of Goods Sold	Actual Expenditures Charged to Accrual	Adjustments to Prior Provisions in Other Expense - Net	Balance at December 31,2004
Automotive finishes distribution facility shutdown in 2004:					
Severance and related costs		$297	$(185)	$(112)	

Exit Plan	Balance at December 31, 2003	Provisions in Cost of Goods Sold	Actual Expenditures Charged to Accrual	Adjustments to Prior Provisions in Other Expense - Net	Balance at December 31,2004
Other qualified exit costs		903	(683)	96	$316
Consumer manufacturing facility shutdown in 2004:					
Other qualified exit costs		1,500	(1,810)	310	
Consumer manufacturing facility shutdown in 2001:					
Other qualified exit costs	$2,058		(186)	(25)	1,847
Other qualified exit costs for facilities shutdown prior to 2001	12,854		(650)	(232)	11,972
Totals	$14,912	$2,700	$(3,514)	$37	$14,135

Exit Plan	Balance at December 31, 2002	Provisions in Cost of Goods Sold	Actual Expenditures Charged to Accrual	Adjustments to Prior Provisions in Other Expense - Net	Balance at December 31, 2003
Consumer manufacturing facility shutdown in 2001:					
Severance and related costs	$133		$(133)		
Other qualified exit costs	2,790		(641)	$(91)	$2,058
Paint Stores manufacturing facility shutdown in 2001:					
Other qualified exit costs	333		(105)	(228)	
Other qualified exit costs for facilities shutdown prior to 2001	13,221		(700)	333	12,854
Totals	16,477		$(1,579)	$14	$14,912

Exit Plan	Balance at December 31, 2001	Provisions in Cost of Goods Sold	Actual Expenditures Charged to Accrual	Adjustments to Prior Provisions in Other Expense - Net	Balance at December 31, 2002
Consumer manufacturing facility shutdown in 2001:					
Severance and related costs	$1,454		$(1,321)		$133
Other qualified exit costs	1,946		(256)	$1,100	2,790
Paint Stores manufacturing facility shutdown in 2001:					
Severance and related costs	710		(667)	(43)	
Other qualified exit costs	290			43	333
Other qualified exit costs for facilities shutdown prior to 2001	15,479		(1,420)	(838)	13,221
Totals	$19,879		$(3,664)	$262	$16,477

During 2004, a formal plan was approved to close a leased distribution facility in the Automotive Finishes Segment. During 2003, a formal plan was approved to close a manufacturing facility in the Consumer Segment and the useful lives of the assets were reduced in accordance with SFAS No. 144. Both facilities were closed during 2004. In accordance with SFAS No. 146, noncancelable rent, post-closure severance and other qualified exit costs were accrued at the time of closing. No formal shutdown plans were approved during 2002.

Less than 7 percent of the ending accrual for qualified exit costs at December 31, 2004 related to facilities shutdown prior to 2002 that are expected to be incurred by the end of 2005. The remaining portion of the ending accrual primarily represented post-closure contractual and demolition expenses related to certain owned facilities which are closed and being held for disposal or involved in ongoing environmental-related remediation activities. The Company cannot reasonably estimate when such matters will be concluded to permit disposition.

Chapter 5
Balance Sheet Reporting:
Stockholders' Equity*

CONTENTS

Stockholders' equity in a corporation is composed of five components:

1. Capital stock.

2. Additional paid-in capital.

3. Retained earnings.

4. Accumulated other comprehensive income (loss).

5. Noncontrolling interest.

In general, treasury stock is accounted for as a reduction of stockholders' equity.

Capital stock represents monies paid or to be paid into the corporation by investors who purchase shares of stock. Each share of stock represents a unit of ownership in the corporation. Capital stock also includes shares to be issued at a later date, such as stock options and warrants, and stock dividends distributable.

---

* This chapter was co-authored by David Erlach, Ph.D., J.D., M.B.A., Instructor of Accounting at Queens College, CUNY.

Legal capital is typically defined by state law and represents how much capital the company must have in order to protect the creditors. It usually includes the par value, stated value, and true no par value of all common and preferred stock issued. *Additional paid-in-capital* represents additional monies paid into the corporation by investors above the par value of shares issued, sale of donated treasury stock, and a variety of other sources that will be discussed in this chapter. (If stock is issued below par value, paid-in-capital is reduced.) *Retained earnings* represents income that the corporation has accumulated as a result of its day-to-day operating activities. *Accumulated other comprehensive income (loss)* represents the total of other comprehensive income (or loss) that has accumulated to date by an entity. Other comprehensive income (loss) is part of comprehensive income and is closed at the end of the period to accumulated other comprehensive income. (See the "Comprehensive Income" section in Chapter 1 for a full discussion on this topic.)

Stockholders' equity represents the cumulative net contributions by stockholders plus accumulated earnings less dividends. Stockholders' equity is synonymous with net worth, or net assets (assets less liabilities). This chapter discusses the accounting, financial statement presentation, and disclosures associated with preferred and common stock, stock retirement, treasury stock, dividends, appropriation of retained earnings, stock splits, stock warrants (including fractional share warrants), and quasi-reorganization.

PREFERRED STOCK

The capital stock component of stockholders' equity consists of two types of stock: preferred and common. *Common stock* has one major characteristic that preferred stock does not: voting rights; preferred stockholders usually do not have voting rights, but they enjoy other characteristics. *Preferred stock* may have a "participation" feature. *Participating* preferred stock is entitled to partake in dividend payments in excess of its predetermined dividend rate, on a proportionate basis using the total par values of the preferred and common shares outstanding. *Nonparticipating* preferred stock does *not* partake in excess dividends.

Preferred stock may be *cumulative*. If dividends are not declared by the board of directors in a particular year, the dividends accumulate. These "backlogged" dividends are termed dividends in arrears. Dividends in arrears must be paid before any dividends are paid to noncumulative preferred stock or to common stock. If preferred stock is *noncumulative*, the bypassed dividends do *not* accumulate.

Preferred stock has *preference* over common stock in the event of corporate liquidation. Preferred stockholders will receive the "liquidation value," sometimes stated as par value, before any monies are disbursed to common stockholders.

Convertible preferred stock may be exchanged for common stock through use of a stipulated conversion ratio. (As the market price of the common stock changes, so does the related convertible preferred stock.) When preferred stock is converted to common stock, any excess of preferred contributed capital over the par value is credited to paid-in-capital; any deficit is debited to retained earnings.

EXAMPLE

Siegel Company issued 10,000 shares of $100 par value convertible preferred stock for $120 per share. The conversion is based on one share of preferred stock for four shares of common stock. The par value of the common stock is $18 per share. All preferred shares were converted into common shares. The journal entry for the conversion is:

Convertible preferred stock (10,000 × $100)	1,000,000	
Additional paid-in-capital: excess of par preferred stock (10,000 × $20)	200,000	
Common stock (40,000 × $18)		720,000
Additional paid-in-capital: excess of par common stock (balance)		480,000

Preferred stock usually has no maturity date. However, there may be a call feature. *Callable preferred stock* may be redeemed at the stipulated call price at a predetermined date by the issuing company. The call (redemption) price is typically slightly more than the initial issue price. ASC 810-10-40-1, *Consolidation: Overall*, deals with the early extinguishment of a subsidiary's mandatorily redeemable preferred stock.

Preferred stock issued for services or property should be recorded at the market price of the stock issued. If market price of the stock is not known, the services or property should then be reported at their fair market value.

EXAMPLE

Erlach Company issued 2,000 shares of $10 par value preferred stock as compensation for 1,500 hours of legal services performed billable at $100 per hour. The market price of the stock is $60 per share. The journal entry is:

Compensation expense (2,000 shares × $60)	120,000	
Common stock (2,000 shares × $10)		20,000
Paid-in-capital (2,000 shares × $50)		100,000

The *costs to issue* stock include accounting and legal fees, printing charges, underwriting commissions, Securities and Exchange Commission (SEC) filing fees, and promoting costs for the issue. The prevalent accounting treatment is to charge such costs against paid-in-capital as incurred. However, costs incurred to defend against a takeover attempt of the company are expensed. Payments made to stockholders to induce them *not* to buy additional shares are also expensed.

When increasing rate preferred stock is issued, it should be recorded at its fair value, including the periodic increases in value in the early years due to dividends not being paid or paid at below market rates.

As per generally accepted accounting principles (GAAP), full disclosure must be made of:

- ☐ Par, stated, or assigned value of preferred stock.
- ☐ Number of shares authorized, issued and outstanding.
- ☐ The amount of dividends in arrears, per share and in the aggregate.
- ☐ Liquidation values in the aggregate for preferred stock.
- ☐ The amounts of dividends in arrears, per share and in the aggregate.
- ☐ Call and conversion features—ASC 505-10-50, *Equity: Overall*, mandates footnote disclosure of call features and a five-year redemption schedule associated with preferred stock.
- ☐ Restrictions placed on issuance of stock.
- ☐ Participation rights.

ASC 860-20-55-21, *Transfers and Servicing: Sales of Financial Assets*, covers the sale of preferred stock with a put option in which the buyer may later transfer the securities back to the issuer at a fixed price. If the exercise of the put option is *probable*, the transaction is accounted for as a borrowing. In such a case, the difference between the selling price and the price of the put is amortized from the issue date to the first permissible put date. If the exercise of the put option is *not* probable, the transaction is accounted for as a straight sale.

ASC 860-10-10, *Transfers and Servicing: Overall*, applies to the sale of put options on the issuer's stock that require or permit cash settlement. This transaction is accounted for as a liability marked to fair value, with any resulting gain or loss included in the income statement.

COMMON STOCK

Common stockholders have a residual interest in the corporation. They receive the benefits of success but also bear the ultimate risk of loss. Owning common stock guarantees neither dividends nor assets upon dissolution. In general, common stockholders control the management of the corporation and profit the most if the company is successful. If a corporation has authorized only one class of capital stock, that issue must be common stock. That is, a corporation cannot exist without a basic ownership interest.

Accounting for the issuance of common stock is simplistic. The following generic entry illustrates accounting for the issuance of common stock:

Cash (full amount of the proceeds)	xxx	
Common stock (par value shares issued)		xxx
Additional paid-in capital: excess of par (excess, if any)		xxx

If common and preferred shares are issued as a *unit* (e.g., three shares of common and one share of preferred), the proceeds received are allocated based on the relative market values of the securities.

Disclosure for common stock should include unusual voting rights, dividend rates, restrictions on dividends, rights and privileges of stockholders, shares authorized and issued, outstanding shares, and commitments to issue additional shares.

ASC 505-10-45-2, *Equity: Overall*, applies to the classification of a contribution to an entity's equity in the form of a note receivable. Such a note should usually be presented as a reduction of equity. However, if the note is to be collected in cash before the financial statements are issued or available to be issued, it may be reported as an asset.

ASC 815-40-25 covers the sale of put options on the issuer's common stock. The proceeds received from issuing the puts should be reported as equity. Disclosure should also be made of the fair value of the put.

ASC 815-40-25 deals with the accounting for derivative financial instruments indexed to, and potentially settled in, a company's own stock.

ASC 505-60-25 and 845-10-25 covers spin-offs or other distributions of loans receivable to shareholders.

ACCOUNTING FOR STOCK SUBSCRIPTIONS

It is not uncommon for a company to use stock subscription contracts to sell its stock to investors. In order to purchase the stock, the investor must sign a subscriptions contract and agree to buy a number of shares at a given price. The subscriptions contract specifies the required payment schedule for the shares as well as the manner in which defaults are handled. Generally, subscribed shares are not issued until the corporation receives full payment for them. However, many states consider subscribed common or preferred stock to be equivalent to outstanding common or preferred stock. That is, investors who have signed valid, bona fide subscription contracts have the same rights and privileges as stockholders who hold outstanding shares of stock. Another use of the stock subscription plan is for a company to sell its own stock directly to its employees through a stock purchase plan.

EXAMPLE

Levine Corporation receives subscriptions for 12,000 shares of $14, $10 par value common stock on September 10, 20X9. The subscriptions contract requires a 40% down payment. On October 10th, two months later, the company receives the balance due on one half the subscription shares and issues 6,000 shares to those investors who have fully paid for their stock. The entries are shown below:

September 10, 20X9

Subscriptions receivable	(12,000 × $14) 168,000	
Common stock subscribed		(12,000 × $10) 120,000
Paid-in capital in excess of par		(12,000 × $4) 48,000
Cash	($168,000 × 40%) 67,200	
Subscription receivable		67,200

October 10, 20X9

Cash	(12,000 × 50% × ($14 − [40% × $14]) 50,400	
Subscriptions receivable		50,400

Common stock subscribed	(12,000 × 50% × $10) 60,000	
Common stock		60,000

The Common Stock Subscribed account is reported on the balance sheet in the stockholders' equity section in the entity's capital stock section below common stock. The Common Stock Subscribed account indicates the intent of the entity to issue the applicable common stock after the subscription is fully paid. When this happens, the subscribed stock is converted into common stock. Although the Subscriptions Receivable account is, in fact, a special receivable, it is reported as a contra-stockholders' equity account on the balance sheet. The reason is it is questionable whether this receivable will ever be collected by the issuing corporation since it may be difficult to obtain deficiency judgments against defaulting subscribers. Therefore, general practice follows the policy of presenting the subscriptions receivable account as a reduction to stockholders' equity at the bottom of the stockholders' equity section. ASC 505-10-45-2 notes the following in this regard:

> An enterprise may receive a note, rather than cash, as a contribution to its equity from the sale of capital stock or a contribution to paid-in capital. The issue is whether an enterprise should report the note receivable as a reduction of shareholders' equity or as an asset.

> The Task Force reached a consensus that reporting the note as an asset is generally not appropriate, except in very limited circumstances when there is substantial evidence of ability and intent to pay within a reasonably short period of time. Some Task Force members would require collateralization or payment of the note prior to issuance of the financial statements to permit asset recognition.

> The SEC requires that public companies report notes received in payment for the enterprise's stock as a deduction from shareholders' equity. Task Force members confirmed that the predominant practice is to offset the notes and stock in the equity section. However, such notes may be recorded as an asset if collected in cash prior to issuance of the financial statements.

> The SEC Observer stated that, for registrants, exceptions to the general rule would be very rare.

Although the aforementioned citation focuses on the receipt of a note rather than the receipt of a signed subscriptions contract, the guidance is also appropriate for a subscriptions contract receivable account. It is interesting to note that the SEC also requires that public companies report notes received in payment for the enterprise's stock as a deduction from shareholders' equity.

ACCOUNTING FOR DEFAULTS OF STOCK SUBSCRIPTIONS

Subscribers of stock may, on occasion, default on payment. There are several alternatives available to the entity in this situation and these generally follow the parameters permitted by the state in which the entity is incorporated. The following illustrates several alternatives of accounting for subscription defaults by corporations. However, it is not a comprehensive list of alternatives.

In each of the following examples, a single subscriber of 200 shares defaults after making a 40% down payment on the shares. It is assumed that the defaulting subscriber is one of the subscribers from the prior illustration who paid 40% of his or her subscriptions contract but has not yet remitted the remaining 60% of the total.

EXAMPLE 1

The company returns the full down payment to the defaulting subscriber. The entry simply consists of a reversal of the original entry made when the shares were subscribed.

Common stock subscribed	(200 × $10) 2,000	
Paid-in capital in excess of par	(200 × $4) 800	
Subscriptions receivable		(200 × $14 × 60%) 1,680
Cash		(200 × $14 × 40%) 1,120

EXAMPLE 2

The company issues shares equal to the amount of the down payment made by the defaulting subscriber.

Amount paid-in by the defaulting subscriber: 200 × $14 × 40% = $1,120

Contract price of a share: $14

Number of shares issued to the defaulting subscriber: $1,120/$14 = 80 shares.

Common stock subscribed	(200 × $10) 2,000	
Paid-in capital in excess of par	(200 × $4) 800	
Subscription receivable		(200 × $14 × 60%) 1,680
Common stock		(80 × $10) 800
Paid-in capital in excess of par		($1,120 – $800) 320

EXAMPLE 3

The company requires that the full amount paid-in by the defaulting subscriber be forfeited in accordance with state law.

Common stock subscribed	(200 × $10) 2,000	
Paid-in capital in excess of par	(200 × $4) 800	
Subscription receivable		(200 × $14 × 60%) 1,680
Paid-in capital from forfeiture		(200 × $14 × 40%) 1,120

In this case, no cash is returned to the defaulting subscriber; it is forfeited and kept by the corporation.

TREASURY STOCK

Treasury stock is a term used to refer to shares of stock that have been issued and then reacquired by the issuing corporation. These shares are in shareholders' hands, and the corporation buys them in the market. The corporation holds the shares temporarily and then reissues them. Treasury stock may be kept on a first-in, first-out (FIFO) or average cost basis. While the corporation is holding on to these shares, the shares are said to be "in the treasury" and lose all their rights and characteristics while there. For example, treasury stock does not have the right to vote or to partake in dividends.

The reasons for acquiring treasury stock are diverse. The acquisition may be an effort to thwart a takeover attempt. It may be to support the market value of the shares. When the firm reacquires its own shares, the supply in the market is naturally reduced. With a sufficient demand, market price will then increase. Earnings per share will also become more attractive, because although treasury shares are considered issued shares, they are not considered to be outstanding while they are in the treasury. Another common reason for purchasing treasury shares is to reallocate ownership without issuing additional shares.

In some cases, the corporation laws require an appropriation of retained earnings equal to the cost of treasury stock on hand.

Treasury stock is presented on the balance sheet as a deduction from stockholders' equity and should not be presented as an asset. According to GAAP, it is not acceptable to show the stock of a corporation held in its own treasury as an asset.

The two most popularly used methods of accounting for treasury stock are the cost and par value methods. The former method is frequently used, whereas the latter method is used only in very limited circumstances. Both methods of accounting and presentation are comprehensively illustrated and explained below.

Under the cost method, the acquisition of treasury stock is recorded at the cost of the acquired shares. The journal entry is:

Treasury stock	xxxx	(shares × price per share)
Cash		xxxx (shares × price per share)

Correspondingly, the entry to record the reissuance of treasury shares requires a credit to treasury stock equal to the cost of the shares. If the reissuance is for an amount greater than the original cost of the treasury shares, a credit for the excess should be made to an account, titled Additional Paid-in-Capital: Treasury Stock. If the reissuance is for less than the original cost of the treasury shares, then this Additional Paid-in-Capital account would be debited for the difference.

However, Additional Paid-in-Capital may only be debited to the extent of its balance. This balance may be viewed as the result of "coming out ahead" rather than "falling behind" in the purchase and reissuance activities by an entity of its own treasury stock. After it is used up, any remaining deficiency as a result of selling the treasury stock should be debited to retained earnings.

A comprehensive illustration demonstrating the cost method of accounting for treasury stock follows:

EXAMPLE

If 15,000 shares of $25 par value common stock are issued for $30 at the beginning of the year and 3,000 of these shares are purchased for the treasury at $35 per share later that year, the entry for the acquisition of the treasury stock using the cost method is:

Treasury stock	105,000	(3,000 × $35)
Cash		105,000

If 500 of the treasury shares are reissued for $36 per share, the entry is:

Cash	18,000	
Treasury stock		17,000 (500 × $35)
Additional paid-in-capital: treasury stock		500

In the same year, if another 500 shares of the treasury stock are reissued for $20, the entry is:

Cash	10,000 (500 × $20)	
Additional paid-in-capital: treasury stock	500 (full balance)	
Retained earnings	7,000	
Treasury stock		17,500

Although the reissue price of $20 (above) is below par value (and cost), a discount on the issuance is not recorded. A discount occurs only when original issuance capital is sold below par. (Very few states allow stock to be issued below par.) This transaction is a reissuance of treasury stock.

If the remaining 2,000 shares of treasury stock are retired, all the original issuance capital relating to the treasury stock must be removed. In addition, the retired shares take on the status of authorized but unissued shares.

Common stock	50,000	(2,000 × $25)
Additional paid-in-capital: excess of par	10,000	(2,000 × $5)
Retained earnings	10,000	(deficiency)
Treasury stock		70,000 (2,000 × $35)

If there was a balance in the Additional Paid-in-Capital: Treasury Stock account, that amount should be utilized fully before debiting retained earnings. That is, if the balance in the Additional Paid-in-Capital: Treasury Stock is insufficient to balance the transaction, then retained earnings would be debited for the deficiency. In the above example, there is no balance in the Additional Paid-in-Capital: Treasury Stock account, so retained earnings is debited for the full deficiency instead.

If company stock is donated back to a corporation, the guidance of ASC 985-605-30-2, *Software: Revenue Recognition*, prevails. ASC 985-605-30-2 requires that if a donation from a nongovernmental entity such as a stockholder occurs, the transaction should be recorded as revenue at the fair value of the donation and be disclosed in the "Other revenues or gains" section of the donee's income statement.

EXAMPLE

If 1,000 shares of an entity's stock are donated back to the entity by a wealthy stockholder when the shares are selling for $15 per share, the receiving corporation makes the following entry:

Treasury stock	15,000	(1,000 shares × $15)
Revenue from donated treasury stock		15,000

If the 1,000 shares are reissued later that year for $16 per share, the entry is:

Cash	16,000	(1,000 × $16)
Treasury stock		15,000
Additional paid-in-capital: treasury stock		1,000

ASC 505-30-30, *Equity: Treasury Stock*, deals with the accounting for a purchase of treasury shares at a price significantly in excess of the current market price of the shares and the income statement classification of costs incurred in defending against a takeover attempt.

Footnote disclosures associated with treasury stock include the circumstances when it is presented as an asset, and amounts of treasury stock associated with rights and privileges.

The second method for recording treasury stock transactions is the *par value method*. The par value method accounts for treasury stock as if the shares are retired substantively (in substance) but not formally (actual retirement in accordance with law). Under this method, the treasury stock account is charged with the par (or stated) value of the shares involved. Other paid-in-capital accounts are proportionately reduced based on amounts recorded when the shares were issued. The balance in the common or preferred stock account remains the same.

The entries for accounting for treasury stock transactions under the par value method are illustrated below.

The same data is used that was given in the illustration of the cost method of accounting for treasury stock except that the initial acquisition of treasury stock occurs in two separate purchases instead of one. The first is for 1,500 shares of treasury stock at $35 per share and the second is for 1,500 shares at $28 per share.

Using the par value method, the entry for the first treasury stock acquisition is:

Treasury stock	37,500 (1,500 × $25)
Addition paid-in-capital: excess of par	7,500 (1,500 × $5)
Retained earnings	7,500
Cash	52,500 (1,500 × $35)

Recording the acquisition of 1,500 shares of treasury under the par value method requires debits to the treasury stock and additional paid-in-capital accounts for the amounts per share they were credited when the stock was originally issued (e.g., par: $25, additional paid-in-capital: excess of par: $5). It should be noted that 15,000 shares of $25 par value common stock were issued for $30 at the beginning of the year. (See the illustration for the cost method of accounting for treasury stock.)

The acquisition of another 1,500 shares of treasury stock at $28 requires the following entry:

Treasury stock	37,500 (1,500 × $25)	
Additional paid-in-capital: excess of par	7,500 (1,500 × $5)	
Cash		42,000 (1,500 × $28)
Additional paid-in-capital: treasury stock		3,000

If 500 shares of the treasury stock are sold for $36, the entry is:

Cash	18,000 (500 × $36)	
Treasury stock		12,500 (500 × $25)
Additional paid-in-capital: excess of par		5,500

The reissuance of treasury stock under the par value method thus is viewed as a virtual new issuance of stock, hence, the credit to additional paid-in-capital: excess of par.

If another 500 shares are sold at $20 per share, which is below the cost and par value of the issue, the entry recorded is:

Cash	10,000 (500 × $20)	
Retained earnings	2,500	
Treasury stock		12,500 (500 × $25)

As in the cost method, no discount on the issuance of stock occurs.

If the remaining 2,000 shares of treasury stock are retired, the entry is:

Common stock	50,000	
Treasury stock		50,000 (500 × $25)

This entry is simplistic because in the par value method all original issuance capital was removed from the accounts when the treasury stock is acquired. When actual retirement occurs, as shown above, all that is needed is a negation of the common stock and treasury stock accounts.

Under the par value method, treasury stock is presented as a contra account to the common stock it applies to under the capital stock section of stockholders' equity.

Some state laws prohibit the purchase of treasury stock unless earnings available for dividends exist; consequently, the retained earnings account must be restricted in an amount equal to the cost of treasury stock being held. This restriction must be disclosed by a note to the financial statements.[*] The underlying theory here is that when a corporation purchases treasury stock, it is paying money to its own shareholders. This is viewed as being tantamount to a divi-

---

[*] Kieso & Weygandt, pp. 812–813

dend. Consequently, the amount otherwise available for the distribution of dividends is restricted.

DIVIDENDS

There are a variety of dividends that a corporation can distribute. This section discusses cash dividends, stock dividends, property dividends, scrip dividends, and liquidating dividends.

A cash dividend is based on the number of outstanding shares (issued shares less treasury shares). As an example, a corporation has 7,000 shares of $50 par value, 8% preferred stock outstanding. Eight hundred shares are in the treasury. Dividends will be declared and paid only on the 6,200 shares that are actually in shareholders' hands. The dividend per share is $4, computed as 8% of the $50 par value. The total amount of dividends is $24,800 (6,200 shares × $4 per share). The following entry would be recorded on the date of declaration:

Retained earnings	24,800	
Cash dividends payable		24,800

No entry is made at the date of record. On the date of distribution, the following entry would be made:

Cash dividends payable	24,800	
Cash		24,800

An alternative treatment is to debit a dividends account in lieu of retained earnings. The dividends account would be closed out at the end of the accounting period against the retained earnings account. With this treatment, everything nets out the same as the treatment in the illustration, but by utilizing a dividends account, there is a specific record of dividends declared that can be utilized during the accounting period.

Cumulative preferred stockholders have priority in receiving first any dividends in arrears, and then any current year dividend. If preferred stock is fully participating, the first dividend payment (after arrearages) goes to preferred stockholders in the amount stipulated, stated either as a dollar amount per share or as a percentage of par value. Next, common stockholders receive a total amount to the extent available based on the same per share percentage that the participating preferred stockholders got. Thereafter, the amounts to be paid are on a pro rata basis to each class of stock based on the par value of the shares outstanding. Partially participating preferred stockholders share in the manner specified.

EXAMPLE

At December 31, 20X1, and 20X2, Simon Corp. had outstanding 2,000 shares of $100 par value 7% cumulative preferred stock and 10,000 shares of $10 par value common stock. At December 31, 20X1, preferred dividends in arrears were $6,000. The cash dividends declared in 20X2 were $22,000. The amount of dividends for 20X2 associated with the preferred and common stock is calculated as follows:

Total cash dividends declared		$22,000
Preferred stockholders receive:		
20X1 dividends in arrears	6,000	
20X2 dividends (2,000 × $7)	14,000	20,000
Balance to common stockholders		$2,000

A *stock dividend* arises when the corporation distributes additional shares of its own stock to its current stockholders. The number of shares to be distributed is phrased in terms of a percentage of the number of shares outstanding at the declaration date. For example, if a corporation has 120,000 shares outstanding when it declares a 10% stock dividend, the dividend will consist of 12,000 shares, and there will be 132,000 shares outstanding once the dividend shares are distributed. If the stock dividend is less than 20% to 25% of the outstanding shares at the date of declaration, retained earnings will be reduced in an amount equal to the market price of the shares at the date of declaration. This is referred to as a small stock dividend. If the stock dividend is greater than 20% to 25% of the outstanding shares at the date of declaration, retained earnings will be reduced in an amount equal to the par or stated value of the shares at the date of declaration. This is referred to as a large stock dividend. The area between 20% and 25% is considered a gray area. Accounting for stock dividends entails the use of an account called common stock dividend distributable. This is not a liability account. It is shown in the paid-in-capital section of stockholders' equity. It is a stockholders' equity account, which consists of the product of the number of shares declared and par value. It is disclosed in the capital stock section of stockholders' equity after common stock, because it represents the number of shares that will become common stock after the date of distribution.

EXAMPLE

A 5% stock dividend is declared on 6,000 shares of $6 par value common stock. The market price is $8 per share on the date of declaration. On the date of declaration, the following entry is made:

Retained earnings (300 shares × $8)	2,400	
Common stock dividend distributable (300 shares × $6)		1,800
Additional paid-in-capital: excess of par		600

The following entry would be made on the date of distribution:

Common stock dividend distributable	1,800	
Common stock		1,800

Assuming that the dividend was 30%, on the date of declaration, the following entry would be made:

Retained earnings (1,800 shares × $6)	10,800	
Common stock dividend distributable		10,800

The following entry would be made to record the distribution of the shares:

Common stock dividend distributable	10,800	
Common stock		10,800

A *property dividend*, also called a "dividend in kind," is payable in assets of the corporation other than cash (e.g., inventory, securities). Property dividends are formally defined as a nonreciprocal transfer of nonmonetary assets between an enterprise and its owners; they should be recorded at the fair value of the asset transferred, and a gain or loss should be recognized on the disposition of the asset ASC 845-10-30. Disclosure should be made of the nature of the distribution and the accounting basis for the transferred assets.

The accounting for a property dividend entails a journal entry that will adjust the asset to be distributed to its market value at the date of declaration. For example, if the fair value of the asset is higher than the book value, the following would be the format for this entry:

Asset	xxx	
Gain on appreciation of asset		xxx

The following entry would record the declaration of the property dividend:

Retained earnings	xxx	
Property dividends payable		xxx

When the asset is distributed, the following entry is made:

Property dividends payable	xxx	
Asset		xxx

Exception: Property distributions in a reorganization or liquidation should be based on recorded amounts less any required reduction for impairment in value.

A *scrip (liability) dividend* is payable in the form of a liability such as a note payable. This type of dividend may occur when a business has financial difficulties and wants to defer payment of the dividend. Interest expense is accrued. However, the interest is *not* part of the dividend.

EXAMPLE

On January 1, 20X3, a liability dividend of $100,000 is declared in the form of a one-year, 10% note. The journal entry at the declaration date is:

Retained earnings	100,000	
Scrip dividends payable		100,000

When the scrip dividend is paid, the entry is:

Scrip dividends payable	100,000	
Interest expense	10,000	
Cash		110,000

A *liquidating dividend* is any dividend that is not based on earnings but instead is a reduction of paid-in-capital. A liquidating dividend is a return of paid-in-capital and requires full disclosure. Paid-in-capital is debited and dividends payable is credited. The existence of a liquidating dividend does not necessarily mean that the company is going out of business. However, a company that decides to halt operations may declare a final, liquidating dividend. The accounting for a liquidating dividend is based on the state laws where the business is incorporated. A liquidating dividend is *not* taxable to the recipient but rather reduces the basis in the investor's shares.

According to Accounting Standards Update (ASU) No. 2010-01 (ASC 505, *Equity*), *Accounting for Distributions to Shareholders with Components of Stock and Cash*, the stock part of a stockholder distribution that permits investors to receive stock or cash with a possible restriction of the cash to be received is deemed an issuance of shares; it is not considered a stock dividend. EPS computation will include these distributions. The effective date for this accounting is December 15, 2009 (ASC 505-20-15-2; 15-3; and 15-3A).

RESTRICTIONS OF RETAINED EARNINGS

It is not uncommon for a corporation's board of directors to decide that a portion of the entity's retained earnings should be restricted and made unavailable for dividend declarations. The restriction is a communication mechanism that alerts financial statement users that the company's retained earnings balance, because of current circumstances, is partially (or totally) blocked and cannot be used for dividend declaration. The restrictions may be prompted by legal constraints, contractual terms, future plans that the board of directors has for the company, or unexpected material uses of cash that makes the declaring of cash dividends currently impossible.

Examples include restrictions due to bond indentures, plant expansion designs, and treasury stock acquisition restrictions based on state law. The disclosure of such restrictions of retained earnings may take the form of a note (the most common), a parenthetical notation, or a recorded journal entry in the company's accounts, which results in a portion of its retained earnings balance being transferred to an appropriated retained earnings account. The latter disclosure (i.e., appropriation entry) is infrequently used because of the potential for confusion caused by simultaneous presentation of two retained balances on the balance sheet of the entity: one unrestricted—available for dividend declaration—and the other restricted—not available for dividend declaration.

EXAMPLE

Note Disclosure: A company's bond indentures require that $50,000 of retained earnings be restricted annually until all principal and interest payments on its outstanding bonds are satisfied. At the end of 20X1, the company is in compliance with its bond agreements. Currently, $500,000 of retained earnings is cumulatively restricted and unavailable for dividend declaration.

STOCK SPLITS

A corporation may have a superlative history of performance. The financial statements show a positive trend, and retained earnings are sizable. This will cause a high demand for this corporation's stock in the market. A share of stock with a $50 par value could attain a market value of $150 or more. On the surface, a corporation whose stock is performing so well in the market seems attractive. In reality, a market value that is too high will prove debilitating to the issuing company. The phenomenon that results is that there will actually be a chill on trading in that company's shares because the investment is not affordable. The corporation would like the market price to be lower, so that trading in its shares becomes more affordable and new investors are attracted. Further, the brokerage commission and/or dealer spread per share for a round lot (100 shares) is typically lower than for an odd lot (less than 100 shares).

In this situation, the corporation may engage in an accounting mechanism called a *stock split*. The size of a stock split is stated in the form of a ratio. The following illustration will demonstrate the effect of a 2 : 1 stock split. The corporation will call in all of the outstanding shares of $50 par value stock and reissue to each shareholder double the number of shares initially held, but with half of the original par value—in this example, $25. This will cause the presplit market price of $150 to drop to approximately $75. Now the corporation's shares will become a lot more affordable than before the split. The corporation will have achieved its aim of increasing trading in its shares and attracting new investors.

A stock split does not affect the balance in any account. The total par value of the shares outstanding is the same after the stock split as it was before. The stock split requires a memorandum entry in the general journal and in the relevant stock account. For example:

April 30	Memorandum: Issued additional 5,000 shares of Capital Stock in a 2 : 1 stock split. There are now 10,000 shares of Capital Stock outstanding with a par value of $25 per share.

A stock split has no impact on the financial statements except for a description of the stock shown on the balance sheet and disclosure of the cause.

EXAMPLE

A company had 200,000 shares outstanding at the beginning of the year. On March 1, it issued a 15% stock dividend. On May 1, the company purchased 40,000 of its shares. On November 1, a 2-for-1 stock split was issued. On December 31, there will be 380,000 shares outstanding, computed as follows:

	Shares
Balance—1/1	200,000
3/1—Stock dividend (200,000 × 15%)	30,000
5/1—Purchased treasury stock	(40,000)
Subtotal	190,000

11/1—Stock split	190,000
Balance—12/31	380,000

A reverse stock split achieves the opposite effects of a stock split by increasing the par value and market price per share.

STOCK WARRANTS

Stock warrants are certificates entitling the holder to acquire shares of stock at a predetermined price for a predetermined period of time. A corporation may decide to sell stock warrants as part of a bond sale to make the securities more attractive to the potential investor and to justify a lower interest rate. A *nondetachable* warrant is one that must be traded with the related security as a package. In other words, the issue is accounted for as convertible debt. The value of the nondetachable warrant is built into the price of the related security. A *detachable* warrant is one that can be traded separately from the bond. Consequently, the warrant has its own market value separate from that of the attached security. An allocation must be engaged in to account for the valuation of these warrants apart from the related bonds, and they are accounted for as additional paid-in-capital according to ASC 470-20-25-2, *Debt: Debt with Conversion and Other Options*. The method of first resort for this allocation is the *proportional* method if the market price of both the bond and warrant is determinable. If the market value of the bonds or their detachable warrants cannot be determined, the *incremental* method is used for this allocation.

EXAMPLE

A $10,000 par value bond with nondetachable stock warrants is issued at $12,000. The entry is as follows:

Cash	12,000	
Bonds payable		10,000
Premium on bonds payable		2,000

The warrants are detachable. The fair market value (FMV) of the bonds without the warrants is determined to be $9,500, and the FMV of the warrants is $3,000. The proportional method would produce the following allocation:

1. FMV of bonds	$ 9,500
FMV of warrants	13,000
Total FMV	$12,500

2. $\dfrac{\$9,500}{\$12,500} \times \$12,000 = \$9,120$ allocated to bonds

3. $\dfrac{\$3,000}{\$12,500} \times \$12,000 = \$2,880$ allocated to warrants

The following journal entries would be necessary:

Cash	9,120	
Discount on bonds payable	880	
Bonds payable		10,000
Cash	2,880	
Additional paid-in-capital: stock warrants		2,880

If the FMV of the stock warrants was $1,500, but the FMV of the bonds could not be determined, the incremental method would be used for the allocation. If the proceeds for the entire sale were $12,000, and $1,500 is the FMV of the warrants, the difference of $10,500 will be accounted for as the FMV of the bonds. The following journal entries would be necessary:

Cash	10,500	
Bonds payable		10,000
Premium on bonds payable		500
Cash	1,500	
Additional paid-in-capital: stock warrants		1,500

If stock warrants expire or lapse, the entry requires a debit to paid-in-capital: stock warrants and a credit to additional paid-in-capital: expired stock warrants.

EXAMPLE

On December 31, 20X3, a company issued 2,000 of its 12%, 8-year, $1,000 face value bonds with detachable stock warrants, at par. Each bond has a detachable warrant for one common share at an option price of $40 per share. After issuance, the bonds had a market value of $2,100,000, and their warrants had a market value of $200,000. At year end 20X4, the bonds payable will be reported at $1,826,087, computed as follows:

Proceeds of issuance ($1,000 × 2,000)		$2,000,000
Allocated to warrants:		
Market value of bonds	$2,100,000	
Market value of warrants	200,000	
Total market value	$2,300,000	

$$\text{To warrants:} \quad \frac{\$\,200,000}{\$\,2,300,000} \times 2,000,000 = 173,913$$

Bonds payable—12/31/20X4	$1,826,087

Note: A holder may become a stockholder by exercising the warrant and continue as a bondholder.

Disclosures associated with stock warrants include conversion terms and exercise prices.

EITF Consensus Summary No. 86–35 relates to debentures with detachable stock purchase warrants.

RESTRICTED (NONVESTED) STOCK

(**Note:** The section "Nonvested and Restricted Stock" in Chapter 1, "Reporting, Presentation, and Disclosures for the Income Statement," refers to restricted stock as stock that is fully vested and outstanding shares whose sale is restricted for a specified time by a company. Restricted stock is more commonly used and refers here to nonvested shares granted to employees that are restricted from being sold by an employee until the restriction period (vesting period) has ended.)

Many companies have issued restricted (nonvested) stock as part of their share-based compensation to employees. In other situations, they have completely replaced the issuance of stock options (see Chapter 1, "Reporting, Presentation, and Disclosures for the Income Statement") with restricted stock plans, although the former still remains the more popular of the two.

Restricted stock plans are compensatory stock award plans where employees are given shares of stock in a company. However, the shares are restricted from being sold or transferred until vesting takes place. In addition, other vesting constraints or restrictions may exist, such as vesting of shares, based on successful performance during the service period measured, for example, by the company reaching some predetermined level of gross profit, earnings, or earnings per share. If the constraints on the restricted stock plans are violated, the employee forfeits his or her rights to the shares. Restricted shares also would be forfeited if an employee is terminated before completion of the service or vesting period.

Companies issue restricted stock awards to employees and use them as a replacement for stock option plans because:

- ☐ Employees receiving restricted stock are owners of the company. As both employees and owners of the entity, they manifest a greater degree of commitment, motivation, and loyalty to the company than those who are not.

- ☐ Employees who receive restricted stock are more likely to perceive congruency with management's goals and objectives and strive to accomplish them.

- ☐ Stock options do not encourage commitment and loyalty on the part of the recipient to the issuing corporation. Instead, they encourage the employee to take the necessary steps to raise the company's stock price in the relative short term in order to make a large profit, sell the stock, and personally benefit from any resulting gains. These employees frequently make risky decisions that may not be in the best interest of the company for the sole purpose of increasing the short-term price of stock. On the other hand, employees holding restricted stock are more interested in the company's long-term objectives and strive to benefit the company.

- ☐ Unlike stock options, restricted stock does not become worthless. If the stock price underlying a stock option plan does not exceed the exercise price, the stock options may not have value. However, restricted stock retains some value. For example, assume a company grants a stock option plan to certain executive employees of the company. The shares covered by the plan are currently selling at $6 and the exercise price of the stock option under the plan is $5. If the fair value of the stock drops to $4, then the employees' stock options are virtually worthless. Although the restricted stock's value may have decreased by one third, it does not become worthless.

Under GAAP, the total compensation expense that must be recorded when restricted stock is issued is the fair value of an unrestricted share of the same class of stock at the date of grant multiplied by the number of shares that will be issued under the plan. Any changes in the fair value of the stock subsequent to the date of grant should not influence total compensation expense. Compensation expense should be accrued over the service period required by the plan. Similar to a stock option plan, the measurement date of a restricted stock program is the date of grant.

The accounting for restricted stock is illustrated below:

> Assume the Levine and Siegel Company establishes a restricted stock award plan to be granted to certain managerial executives of their entity. On July1, 2012, the Board of Directors grants 750,000 shares of the company's $3 par value common stock to employees, which requires a three-year vesting period. That is, the shares are subject to forfeiture if the employees quit or are terminated within three years from the date of grant. The fair value of the shares at the date of grant is $10. Assume the Levine and Siegel Company has a December 31 year-end.

Solution

The service (and vesting period) is three years in this problem. If the employees who are part of this award program quit or are terminated within three years from the date of grant, they forfeit their rights to the granted stock.

The measurement date of the plan is the date of grant (July 1, 2012). The fair value is $10 per share and 750,000 shares will be issued under the plan. At the date of grant, the product of these numbers should be used to compute the total compensation expense of the restricted stock program.

Total compensation = 750,00 shares of common stock × $10 = $7,500,000

Since the service period is 3 years, we must divide $7,500,000 by the 3 years to determine the compensation expense per year.

Compensation expense per year: $7,500,000/3 years = $2,500,000

The required entries are:

December 31, 2012	Compensation expense 1,250,000 ($ 2,500,000/2)
	Additional paid-in capital—Restricted Shares 1,250,000
December 31, 2013—	
December 31, 2014	Compensation expense 2,500,000
	Additional paid-in capital—Restricted Shares 2,500,000
June 30, 2015	Compensation expense 1,250,000 ($2,500,000/2)
	Additional paid-in capital—Restricted Shares 1,250,000

After the required three-year service period (vesting period) is ended (July 1, 2012—June 30, 2015), the shares are issued to those employees who are part of the awards program. The entry for the distribution of the shares is shown below:

July 1, 2015	Additional paid-in capital—Restricted Shares	7,500,000	
	Common stock (750,000 × $3)		2,250,000
	Additional paid-in capital—In excess of par		5,250,000

Related entries for forfeiture of shares or required disclosures, for example, are comparable to those of other share-based compensation plans. These are shown in the stock option plan illustration in Chapter 1, "Reporting, Presentation, and Disclosures for the Income Statement." For example, if a managerial employee is terminated in the illustration above, the employee's shares are forfeited. This event is accounted for as a change in accounting estimate that must be recorded in the year of the forfeiture. The remaining total compensation expense, without the forfeited portion, should then be re-allocated over the remaining service period.

FRACTIONAL SHARE WARRANTS

A fractional share warrant is a warrant that is redeemable for a fractional share of stock. Consequently, more than one fractional warrant is required in order for the holder to acquire one full share.

EXAMPLE

A corporation has 2,000 shares of $10 par value stock outstanding. Each share has a market value of $18. A 15% stock dividend is declared. The number of dividend shares is 300 (2,000×15%). Included in the 300 shares are 200 fractional share warrants, each equaling one fourth of a share of stock. Thus, the dividend consists of 50 fractional shares and 250 regular shares. The journal entry at the date of declaration would be:

Retained earnings (300 shares × $18)	5,400	
Stock dividends distributable (250 shares × $10)		2,500
Fractional share warrants (50 shares × $10)		500
Additional paid-in-capital: excess of par		2,400

The journal entries at the date of issuance are:

Stock dividends distributable	2,500	
Common stock		2,500
Fractional share warrants	500	
Common stock		500

If only 60% of the fractional share warrants were turned in, the journal entry would be:

| Fractional share warrants | 300 | |
| Common stock | | 300 |

STOCK RIGHTS

Stock rights allow current stockholders to buy additional shares of the company's stock to maintain their proportionate interest in the company. This is usually referred to as the preemptive right. In some cases, existing stockholders can purchase the newly issued shares at a discount and at either no or reduced fees.

No entry is made upon the issuance of stock rights. There is only a memorandum notation. When stock rights are exercised, common stock increases by the par value of the shares issued, and additional paid-in-capital increases for the excess of the issue price over the par value of the shares issued. If stock rights are redeemed by the issuing company, the effect is the same as if a cash dividend had been paid. For example, if 10,000 rights were redeemed at $.20 per right, stockholders' equity would be reduced by $2,000.

REVERSE SPINOFFS

According to ASC 505-60-05-4, *Equity: Spinoffs and Reverse Spinoffs*, a transaction should be treated as a reverse spinoff if the substance of the transaction is most realistically represented for shareholders by treating a legal spinee as the accounting spinnor.

INDEXED TO STOCK

ASC 815-40-15, 5-8, *Derivatives and Hedging Relating to Contracts in Entitys' Own Equity*, provides that if an instrument (or embedded feature) that has the characteristics of a derivative instrument is indexed to an entity's own stock, the company still needs to appraise if it is classified in stockholders' equity (or would be classified in stockholders' equity if it were a freestanding instrument).

A company shall appraise if an equity-linked financial instrument (or embedded feature) is indexed to its own stock using the following two-step approach:

☐ Step 1: Appraise the instrument's contingent exercise provisions, if any.

☐ Step 2: Evaluate the instrument's settlement provisions.

REDEEMABLE EQUITY INSTRUMENTS

In Accounting Standards Update 2009-04 (August 2009) (ASC 480, *Distinguishing Liabilities from Equity*), *Accounting for Redeemable Equity Instruments—Amendment to Section 480-10-S99*, preferred securities redeemable for cash or other assets are to be classified outside of permanent capital if they are redeemable (1) at a fixed or determinable price on a fixed or determinable date, (2) at the holder's option, or (3) upon the occurrence of an event that is not solely within the control of the issuer. There is a major difference between a security with mandatory redemption or whose redemption is outside the control of the issuer and conventional equity capital. The SEC believes accountants should highlight the future cash obligations attached to this type of security to distinguish it from permanent capital.

Equity instruments with redemption features that are not solely within the control of the issuer must be classified as "temporary equity."

According to the SEC, the initial carrying amount of a redeemable equity instrument should be its issuance date fair value.

For share-based payment arrangements with employees, the amount presented in temporary equity at each balance sheet date should be based on the redemption provisions of the instrument and should take into consideration the proportion of consideration received in the form of employee services.

Disclosures are required for redeemable equity instruments as follows:

☐ For a redeemable equity instrument that is not adjusted to its redemption amount, the reasons why it is not probable that the instrument will be redeemable.

☐ Description of the accounting method used to adjust the redemption amount of a redeemable equity instrument.

☐ If the registrant decides to accrete changes in the redemption amount of a redeemable equity instrument, the redemption amount of the equity instrument as if it were currently redeemable.

☐ Amount credited to equity of the parent upon the subsidiary's deconsolidation.

(ASC 480-10-S99)

QUASI-REORGANIZATION

A quasi-reorganization gives a "new start" to a company with a deficit in retained earnings. It is undertaken to avoid a bankruptcy. The assets and liabilities are revalued, and the deficit in retained earnings is eliminated via a reduction of paid-in-capital. The date of the quasi-reorganization should be disclosed.

As per ASC 852-20-25, *Reorganizations: Quasi-Reorganizations*, in a quasi-reorganization:

1. The approval of the stockholders and creditors is required.

2. Net assets are almost always written down (a write-up is possible) to fair market value. If a write-down is unavailable, a conservative estimate must be made. Significant subsequent adjustments to such estimates should be charged or credited to paid-in-capital.

3. Paid-in-capital is debited to reduce the deficit in retained earnings. If paid-in-capital is not sufficient, the capital stock account will be debited.

4. Retained earnings will acquire a zero balance and will bear the date of the quasi-reorganization for 10 years subsequent to the reorganization (ASC 852-20-35-2). This puts readers on notice that the company's retained earnings have undergone a readjustment and are not representative of historic earnings and dividends.

The basic entry for a quasi-reorganization is:

Paid-in-capital	xxx
Capital stock (if required)	xxx

Assets	xxx
Retained Earnings	xxx

Caution: If potential losses exist at the readjustment date but the amounts of losses cannot be determined, there should be a provision for the maximum probable loss. If estimates used are subsequently shown to be incorrect, the difference goes to the paid-in-capital account.

Note: New or additional common stock or preferred stock may be issued in exchange for existing indebtedness. Thus the current liability account would be debited for the indebtedness and the capital account credited.

A parent with subsidiaries must not wind up with a credit balance in retained earnings when losses and deficits have been charged to paid-in-capital.

Any deferred tax liabilities as well as any tax loss carryforwards should be reported as an adjustment to paid-in-capital when they are recognized in a year after the quasi-reorganization.

EXAMPLE

A business shows the following balances before a quasi-reorganization:

Current assets	$200,000	Capital stock	$1,600,000
Fixed assets	600,000	Paid-in-capital	300,000
		Retained earnings	(1,100,000)
	$800,000		$800,000

Current assets are overvalued by $40,000, and fixed assets are overvalued by $150,000. The entries for a quasi-reorganization are:

Quasi-reorganization	190,000	
Current assets		40,000
Fixed assets		150,000
Quasi-reorganization	1,100,000	
Retained earnings		1,100,000
Paid-in-capital	300,000	
Quasi-reorganization		300,000
Common stock	990,000	
Quasi-reorganization		990,000

Noncontrolling interest (also referred to as minority interest) represents the portion of stockholders' equity owned by the less than 50% shareholders. This will arise in consolidated statements when there are one or more subsidiaries with outside ownership. Under ASC 810-10-45-6, noncontrolling interest is reported in stockholders' equity, separate from the stockholders' equity of the controlling interest.

DISCLOSURE

Disclosure should be made of the following regarding stockholders' equity: dividend and liquidation preferences, unusual voting rights, conversion features (e.g., dates, rates), participation rights, sinking fund provisions, agreements to issue additional shares, dividends in arrears, call features associated with redeemable stock, and any other relevant rights or privileges of stockholders.

Under ASC 810-10-50-1A, in consolidated financial statements, a parent with one or more less than wholly owned subsidiaries must disclose the following either in the consolidated statement of changes in stockholders' equity or in the notes to the consolidated financial statement: a reconciliation of equity at the beginning and end of the period split between equity (net assets) attributable to the controlling interest and equity attributable to the noncontrolling interest. That reconciliation must separately disclose net income, transactions with owners, and each component of comprehensive income.

ASC 505-10-50-3 and 50-6, *Equity: Overall*, states that companies should disclose important conversion features of contingently convertible securities and the potential impact of conversion. Useful quantitative and qualitative disclosures include:

- ☐ A description of events that would result in conversion.

- ☐ Conversion rights and timing.

- ☐ The conversion price and number of shares to be converted.

- ☐ Circumstances resulting in an adjustment in a contingency.

- ☐ The transaction manner to settle a conversion (e.g., cash, shares, combination of both).

- ☐ Whether and how contingently convertible securities have been included in computing diluted earnings per share.

- ☐ A description of derivative transactions entered into as a result of the issuance of contingently convertible securities (e.g., the terms of derivative transactions, number of shares underlying the derivatives, and potential effect of the issuance of contingently convertible securities).

In Accounting Standards Update (ASU) No. 2010-21 (August 2010), *Accounting for Technical Amendments to Various SEC Rules and Schedules* (ASC 505-10-S99-1), in a note or statement, there should be an appraisal of changes in other stockholders' equity and noncontrolling interests. The beginning balance should be reconciled to the ending balance for each period; and disclosure should be provided of the change in ownership interest in a subsidiary.

Under ASC 470-10-S99-1, the parent company should provide its investment in its subsidiaries based on its proportionate share of a subsidiary's net assets. In the situation of redeemable preferred stock, there should be a description of its redemption terms (e.g., sinking fund) and the rights. A company should consolidate majority owned entities; and disclosure should be provided of noncontrolling interests in consolidated subsidiaries.

SUMMARY

An illustrative stockholders' equity section of the balance sheet appears as follows:

Capital stock:		
Preferred stock	$1,000,000	
Common stock	3,000,000	
Common stock subscribed	300,000	
Common stock dividend distributable	30,000	
Stock options	100,000	
Stock dividends	50,000	
Total capital stock		$4,480,000
Additional paid-in-capital		
In excess of par value: common stock	$120,000	
From treasury stock transactions	80,000	
Total additional paid-in-capital		200,000
Retained earnings		
Appropriated	$100,000	
Unappropriated	600,000	
Total retained earnings		700,000
Subtotal		$5,380,000
Less: treasury stock at cost		(300,000)
Noncontrolling interest		200,000
Accumulated other comprehensive income		1,000,000
Total Stockholders' equity		$6,280,000

An illustrative statement of retained earnings follows:

Balance—1/1/20X3	$400,000
Less: correction of error (prior period adjustment)	(100,000)
Balance—restated—1/1/20X3	$300,000
Add: net income	550,000
Less: dividends	(150,000)
Balance—12/31/20X3	$700,000

ANNUAL REPORT REFERENCES

Sara Lee
2011 Annual Report

Note 7—Common Stock

Changes in outstanding shares of common stock for the past three years were:

Shares in thousands	2011	2010	2009
Beginning balances	662,118	695,658	706,359
Stock issuances			
Stock option and benefit plans	3,211	1,055	38
Restricted stock plans	1,992	1,741	543
Reacquired shares	(80,221)	(36,417)	(11,390)
Other	–	81	108
Ending balances	587,100	662,118	695,658

Common stock dividends and dividend-per-share amounts declared on outstanding shares of common stock were:

In millions except per share data	2011	2010	2009
Common stock dividends declared	$275	$299	$306
Dividends per share amount declared	$0.46	$0.44	$0.44

During 2010, the corporation's Board of Directors had authorized a $3.0 billion share repurchase program. In March of 2010, the corporation repurchased 36.4 million shares at a cost of $500 million under this program using an accelerated share repurchase program (ASR). The ASR provides for a final settlement adjustment at termination in either shares of common stock or cash based on the final volume weighted average stock price. In 2011, the corporation paid $13 million as a final settlement on the ASR. During 2011, the corporation also repurchased 80.2 million shares at a cost of $1.3 billion.

As of July 2, 2011, the remaining amount authorized for repurchase is $1.2 billion of common stock under an existing share repurchase program, plus 13.5 million shares of common stock that remain authorized for repurchase under the corporation's prior share repurchase program. However, the corporation does not expect to continue with any further share repurchases.

Note 8—Accumulated Other Comprehensive Income

The components of accumulated other comprehensive income are as follows:

In millions	Cumulative Translation Adjustment	Net Unrealized Gain (Loss) on Qualifying Cash Flow Hedges and Other	Pension/Post-retirement Liability Adjustment	Accumulated Other Comprehensive Income (Loss)
Balance at June 28, 2008	$ 539	$ 21	$(411)	$ 149
Measurement date adjustment	–	–	3	3
Amortization of net actuarial loss and prior service credit	–	–	1	1
Net actuarial loss arising during the period	–	–	(299)	(299)
Postretirement plan amendments	–	–	55	55

In millions	Cumulative Translation Adjustment	Net Unrealized Gain (Loss) on Qualifying Cash Flow Hedges and Other	Pension/Post-retirement Liability Adjustment	Accumulated Other Comprehensive Income (Loss)
Other comprehensive income (loss) activity	(561)	(32)	79	(514)
Balance at June 27, 2009	(22)	(11)	(572)	(605)
Disposition of Godrej J.V.	14	–	–	14
Amortization of net actuarial loss and prior service credit	–	–	19	19
Net actuarial loss arising during the period	–	–	(323)	(323)
Pension plan curtailment	–	–	27	27
Pension and postretirement plan amendments	–	–	(4)	(4)
Other comprehensive income (loss) activity	(96)	10	46	(40)
Balance at July 3, 2010	(104)	(1)	(807)	(912)
Disposition of Household & Body Care businesses	55	–	–	55
Amortization of net actuarial loss and prior service credit	–	–	16	16
Net actuarial gain arising during the period	–	–	326	326
Pension plan curtailment	–	–	25	25
Other comprehensive income (loss) activity	277	7	(50)	234
Balance at July 2, 2011	$228	$6	$(490)	$(256)

Note 9—Stock-Based Compensation

The corporation has various stock option, employee stock purchase and stock award plans. At July 2, 2011, 101.9 million shares were available for future grant in the form of options, restricted shares or stock appreciation rights out of 118.7 million shares originally authorized. The corporation will satisfy the requirement for common stock for share-based payments by issuing shares out of authorized but unissued common stock.

Stock Options The exercise price of each stock option equals the market price of the corporation's stock on the date of grant. Options can generally be exercised over a maximum term of 10 years. Options generally cliff vest and expense is recognized on a straightline basis during the vesting period.

All stock options will be impacted by the spin-off. Option holders will have a choice to continue to hold their options pursuant to their normal terms or to accelerate their vesting on the spin-off date with a six month window to exercise.

The fair value of each option grant is estimated on the date of grant using the Black-Scholes option-pricing model and the following weighted average assumptions:

	2011	2010	2009
Weighted average expected lives	7.2 years	8.0 years	8.0 years
Weighted average risk-free interest rates	2.08%	3.03%	3.1%
Range of risk-free interest rates	1.91 - 2.66%	3.02 - 3.15%	3.1%
Weighted average expected volatility	28.0%	27.2%	22.1%
Range of expected volatility	27.3 - 30.0%	27.2 - 27.6%	22.1%
Dividend yield	2.9%	4.4%	3.0%

The corporation uses historical volatility for a period of time that is comparable to the expected life of the option to determine volatility assumptions.

A summary of the changes in stock options outstanding under the corporation's option plans during 2011 is presented below:

Shares in thousands	Shares	Weighted Average Exercise Price	Weighted Average Remaining Contractual Term (Years)	Aggregate Intrinsic Value (in millions)
Options outstanding at July 3, 2010	20,036	$15.79	4.7	$16
Granted	2,318	15.49	-	-
Exercised	(3,106)	16.41	-	-
Canceled/expired	(1,436)	14.67	-	-
Options outstanding at July 2, 2011	17,812	$15.73	4.6	$66
Options exercisable at July 2, 2011	12,041	$17.06	2.9	$29

Tyco International
2011 Annual Report

17. Shareholders' Equity

Dividends

Prior to May 2011, the Company paid dividends in the form of a return of share capital from the Company's registered share capital. These payments were made free of Swiss withholding taxes. The Company now makes dividend payments from its contributed surplus equity position in its Swiss statutory accounts. These payments are also made free of Swiss withholding taxes. Unlike payments made in the form of a reduction to registered share capital, which are required to be denominated in Swiss francs and converted to U.S. dollars at the time of payment, payments from the contributed surplus account may effectively be denominated in U.S. dollars. At the next annual general meeting of shareholders, the Board of Directors intends to propose certain changes affecting the contributed surplus account on the Swiss statutory balance sheets to comply with Swiss tax regulation.

Under Swiss law, the authority to declare dividends is vested in the shareholders, and on March 9, 2011, the Company's shareholders approved an annual dividend on the Company's common shares of $1.00 per share, which will be paid from contributed surplus in four installments of $0.25 per share. As a result, the Company recorded an accrued dividend of $468 million as of March 9, 2011 and a corresponding reduction to contributed surplus. The first installment of $0.25 was paid on May 25, 2011 to shareholders of record on April 29, 2011. The second installment of $0.25 was paid on August 24, 2011 to shareholders of record on July 29, 2011. The third installment of $0.25 will be paid on November 17, 2011 to shareholders of record on October 28, 2011. The Company records its accrued dividend in accrued and other current liabilities in the Company's Consolidated Balance Sheet.

On March 10, 2010, the Company's shareholders approved an annual dividend on the Company's common shares of 0.90 Swiss Francs ("CHF") per share, which was paid in the form of a return on capital in four installments of CHF 0.22, CHF 0.22, CHF 0.23 and CHF 0.23 to shareholders on record on May 14, 2010, July 30, 2010, October 29, 2010 and January 28, 2011, respectively. As a result, the Company recorded an accrued dividend of CHF 428 million as of March 10, 2010, which approximated $399 million based on the exchange rate in effect on that date. The accrued dividend was recorded in accrued and other current liabilities in the Company's Consolidated Balance Sheet as of March 26, 2010 and as a corresponding reduction of common shares, which reduced the par value of the Company's common shares from CHF 7.60 to CHF 6.70. The installments were paid in U.S. dollars converted from Swiss Francs at the USD/ CHF exchange rate in effect shortly before the payment dates.

On May 14, 2010, the Company acquired all of the outstanding equity of BHS. BHS shareholders who received Tyco common stock as consideration in the merger were included in the first installment of dividend payments that were paid on May 26, 2010. As a result, the Company recorded an accrued dividend of CHF 32 million as of May 14, 2010, which was approximately $28 million based on the exchange rate in effect on that date.

On March 12, 2009, the Company's shareholders approved an annual dividend on the Company's common shares of CHF 0.93 per share, which was paid in the form of a return on capital in four installments of CHF 0.23, CHF 0.23, CHF 0.23 and CHF 0.24 on May 27, 2009, August 26, 2009, November 24, 2009 and February 24, 2010, respectively. The Company recorded an accrued dividend of CHF 440 million as of March 12, 2009, which approximated $377 million based on the exchange rate in effect on that date. On the Company's Consolidated Balance Sheet, this amount was recorded as a reduction of common shares, which reduced the par value of the Company's common shares from CHF 8.53 to CHF 7.60. The installments were paid in U.S. dollars converted from Swiss Francs at the USD/CHF exchange rate in effect shortly before the payment dates.

Common Stock

As of September 30, 2011, the Company's share capital amounted to CHF 3,258,632,435, or 486,363,050 registered common shares with a par value of CHF 6.70 per share following the cancellation of 28,088,101 registered shares which had been approved at the March 9, 2011 annual general meeting. Until March 9, 2013, the Board of Directors may increase the Company's share capital by a maximum amount of CHF 1,628,100,000 by issuing a maximum of 243,000,000 shares. In addition, (i) the share capital of the Company may be increased by an amount not exceeding CHF 321,127,717 through the issue of a maximum of 47,929,510 shares through the exercise of conversion and/or option or warrant rights granted in connection with bonds, notes or similar instruments and (ii) the share capital of the Company may be increased by an amount not exceeding CHF 321,127,717 through the issue of a maximum of 47,929,510 shares to employees and other persons providing services to the Company. Although the Company states its par value in Swiss francs, it continues to use the U.S. dollar as its reporting currency for preparing its Consolidated Financial Statements.

Change in Domicile

Effective March 17, 2009, the Company changed its jurisdiction of incorporation from Bermuda to the Canton of Schaffhausen, Switzerland. In connection with the Change of Domicile and pursuant to the laws of Switzerland, the par value of the Company's common shares increased from $0.80 per share to CHF 8.53 per share (or $7.21 based on the exchange rate in effect on March 17, 2009). The Change of Domicile was approved at a special general meeting of shareholders held on March 12, 2009. The following steps occurred in connection with the Change of Domicile, which did not result in a change to total Shareholders' Equity:

(1) approximately 21 million shares held directly or indirectly in treasury were cancelled;

(2) the par value of common shares of the Company was increased from $0.80 to CHF 8.53 through an approximate 1-for-9 reverse share split, followed by the issuance of approximately eight fully paid up shares so that the same number of shares were outstanding before and after the Change of Domicile, which reduced share premium and increased common shares; and

(3) the remaining amount of share premium was eliminated with a corresponding increase to contributed surplus.

Share Repurchase Program

The Company's Board of Directors approved the $1.0 billion 2011 share repurchase program, the $1.0 billion 2010 share repurchase program and the $1.0 billion 2008 share repurchase program, in April 2011, September 2010 and July 2008, respectively. During the year ended September 30, 2011, the Company repurchased approximately 30 million shares for approximately $1.3 billion under these programs, which reduced the amount of common shares outstanding and decreased the dividends declared on the Consolidated Statement of Shareholders' Equity as of September 30, 2011. During the year ended September 24, 2010, the Company repurchased approximately 24 million shares for approximately $900 million under the 2008 share repurchase program, which reduced the amount of common shares outstanding and decreased the dividends declared on the Consolidated Statement of Shareholders' Equity as of September 24, 2010. Both the 2008 and 2010 share repurchase programs were completed during the year ended September 30, 2011. As of September 30, 2011, approximately $700 million remained outstanding under the 2011 share repurchase program. See Note 27.

	2011 Share Repurchase Program		2010 Share Repurchase Program		2008 Share Repurchase Program	
	Shares (in millions)	Amounts ($ in billions)	Shares (in millions)	Amounts ($ in billions)	Shares (in millions)	Amounts ($ in billions)
Approved Repurchase Amount						
Repurchases		$ 1.0		$ 1.0		$ 1.0
Fiscal 2011	6.0	0.3	24.0	1.0		
Fiscal 2010	N/A	N/A	—	—	24.3	0.9
Fiscal 2009	N/A	N/A	N/A	N/A	—	—
Fiscal 2008	N/A	N/A	N/A	N/A	2.5	0.1
Remaining Amount Available		$ 0.7		—		—

Carnival
2010 Annual Report

Note 9. Shareholders' Equity

Carnival Corporation's Articles of Incorporation authorize its Board of Directors, at its discretion, to issue up to 40 million shares of preferred stock. At November 30, 2010 and 2009, no Carnival Corporation preferred stock had been issued and only a nominal amount of Carnival plc preference shares had been issued.

In June 2006, the Boards of Directors authorized the repurchase of up to an aggregate of $1 billion of Carnival Corporation common stock and Carnival plc ordinary shares subject to certain restrictions. On September 19, 2007, the Boards of Directors increased the remaining $578 million general repurchase authorization back to $1 billion (the "Repurchase Program"). During fiscal 2008, we purchased 0.6 million shares of Carnival Corporation common stock and 1.3 million ordinary shares of Carnival plc under the Repurchase Program. During 2010 and 2009, there were no repurchases of Carnival Corporation common stock or Carnival plc ordinary shares under the Repurchase Program. At January 28, 2011, the remaining availability under the Repurchase Program was $787 million. The Repurchase Program does not have an expiration date and may be discontinued by our Boards of Directors at any time.

In addition to the Repurchase Program, the Boards of Directors have authorized the repurchase of up to 19.2 million Carnival plc ordinary shares and up to 31.5 million shares of Carnival Corporation common stock under the "Stock Swap" programs described below. We use the "Stock Swap" programs in situations where we can obtain an economic benefit because either Carnival Corporation common stock or Carnival plc ordinary shares are trading at a price that is at a premium or discount to the price of Carnival plc ordinary shares or Carnival Corporation common stock, as the case may be. This economic benefit is used for general corporate purposes, which could include repurchasing additional treasury stock under the Repurchase Program. All Carnival plc share repurchases under both the Repurchase Program and the "Stock Swap" authorization require annual shareholder approval.

In fiscal 2009 and 2008, we sold 450,000 shares and 633,000 shares of Carnival Corporation common stock for $9 million and $15 million of net proceeds, respectively. In fiscal 2009 and 2008, substantially all of these net proceeds were used to fund the repurchase of 450,000 shares and 633,000 shares of Carnival plc ordinary shares, respectively. In these offerings, we sold Carnival Corporation common stock in the U.S., only to the extent we were able to purchase shares of Carnival plc in the UK on at least an equivalent basis under the "Stock Swap" program.

In fiscal 2010 and 2009, we also sold 14.8 million shares and 5.8 million shares of Carnival plc ordinary shares held as treasury stock for $545 million and $187 million of net proceeds, respectively. In fiscal 2010 and 2009, substantially all of these net proceeds were used to fund the repurchase of 14.8 million shares and 5.8 million shares of Carnival Corporation common stock, respectively. In these UK offerings, we sold Carnival plc ordinary shares held in treasury, only to the extent we were able to purchase shares of Carnival Corporation in the U.S. on at least an equivalent basis under the "Stock Swap" program.

At November 30, 2010, there were 38.9 million shares of Carnival Corporation common stock reserved for issuance substantially all pursuant to its employee benefit and dividend reinvestment plans. In addition, Carnival plc shareholders have authorized 18.6 million ordinary shares for future issuance under its employee benefit plans.

At November 30, 2010 and 2009, accumulated other comprehensive (loss) income was as follows:

	November 30,	
(in millions)	2010	2009
Cumulative foreign currency translation adjustments, net	$ (99)	$ 565
Unrecognized pension expenses	(91)	(99)
Unrealized loss on marketable security	(16)	(16)
Net (losses) gains on cash flow derivative hedges	(48)	12
	$ (254)	$ 462

Omnova Solutions
2010 Annual Report

Note E. Accumulated Other Comprehensive Income (Loss)

The components of Accumulated Other Comprehensive Income (Loss) are as follows:

	Years Ended November 30,		
(Dollars in millions)	2010	2009	2008
Foreign currency translation adjustments	$ –	$ (1.4)	$ (4.8)
Unrecognized loss on interest rate swap	(4.2)	(4.6)	(3.7)

(Dollars in millions)	Years Ended November 30,		
	2010	2009	2008
Employee benefit plans	(81.6)	(77.1)	(25.1)
Accumulated other comprehensive loss	$ (85.8)	$ (83.1)	$ (33.6)

The amounts included in Accumulated Other Comprehensive Loss during 2010 and 2009 relating to the Company's employee benefit plans were as follows:

(Dollars in millions)	Pension		Health Care	Total
	Domestic	Foreign		
2010				
Net Actuarial (Loss) Gain				
Net actuarial (loss) gain incurred during the period	$ (10.3)	$ (.1)	$ (.4)	$ (10.8)
Amortization included in net periodic expense (income)	4.1	.1	(2.3)	1.9
Net change in net actuarial gain	$ (6.2)	$ –	$ (2.7)	$ (8.9)
Prior Service Cost				
Amortization included in net periodic expense (income)	$ .6	$ –	$ (.3)	$ .3
Curtailment loss	1.3	–	–	1.3
Net change in prior service costs	$ 1.9	$ –	$ (.3)	$ 1.6
2009				
Net Actuarial (Loss) Gain				
Net actuarial (loss) gain incurred during the period	$ (50.9)	$ (.1)	$ .5	$ (50.5)
Amortization included in net periodic expense (income)	1.6	(.1)	(2.4)	(.9)
Change in measurement date	.3	–	(.6)	(.3)
Net change in net actuarial gain	$ (49.0)	$ (.2)	$ (2.5)	$ (51.7)
Prior Service Cost				
Amortization included in net periodic expense (income)	$ (.1)	$ –	$ (.3)	$ (.4)
Change in measurement date	.1	–	–	.1
Net change in prior service costs	$ –	$ –	$ (.3)	$ (.3)

Qualcomm
2010 Annual Report

Note 7. Capital Stock

Preferred Stock. The Company has 8,000,000 shares of preferred stock authorized for issuance in one or more series, at a par value of $0.0001 per share. In conjunction with the distribution of preferred share purchase rights, 4,000,000 shares of preferred stock are designated as Series A Junior Participating Preferred Stock, and such shares are reserved for issuance upon exercise of the preferred share purchase rights. At September 26, 2010 and September 27, 2009, no shares of preferred stock were outstanding.

Preferred Share Purchase Rights Agreement. The Company has a Preferred Share Purchase Rights Agreement (Rights Agreement) to protect stockholders' interests in the event of a proposed takeover of the Company. Under the original Rights Agreement, adopted on September 26, 1995, the Company declared a dividend of one preferred share purchase right (a Right) for each share of the Company's common stock outstanding. Pursuant to the Rights Agreement, as amended and restated on December 7, 2006, each Right entitles the registered holder to purchase from the Company a one one-thousandth share of Series A Junior Participating Preferred Stock, $0.0001 par value per share, subject to adjustment for subsequent stock splits, at a purchase price of $180. The Rights are exercisable only if a person or group (an Acquiring Person) acquires beneficial ownership of 20% or more of the Company's outstanding shares of common stock without approval of the Board of Directors. Upon exercise, holders, other than an Acquiring Person, will have the right, subject to termination, to receive the Company's common stock or other securities, cash or other assets having a market value, as defined, equal to twice such purchase price. The Rights, which expire on September 25, 2015, are redeemable in whole, but not in part, at the Company's option prior to the time such Rights are triggered for a price of $0.001 per Right.

Stock Repurchase Program. On March 1, 2010, the Company announced that it had been authorized to repurchase up to $3.0 billion of the Company's common stock. The stock repurchase program has no expiration date. When stock is repurchased and retired, the amount paid in excess of par value is recorded to paid-in capital. During fiscal 2010, 2009 and 2008, the Company repurchased and retired 79,789,000, 8,920,000 and 42,616,000 shares of common stock, respectively, for $3.0 billion, $284 million and $1.7 billion, respectively, before commissions and excluding $14 million of premiums received related to put options that were exercised in fiscal 2008. At September 26, 2010, approximately $1.7 billion remained authorized for repurchase under the Company's stock repurchase program.

At September 26, 2010, September 27, 2009 and September 28, 2008, no put options remained outstanding. During fiscal 2008, the Company recognized gains of $6 million in investment income due to decreases in the fair values of put options, including premiums received of $14 million.

Dividends. The Company announced increases in its quarterly dividend per share of common stock from $0.14 to $0.16 on March 11, 2008, from $0.16 to $0.17

on March 3, 2009, and from $0.17 to $0.19 on March 1, 2010. Cash dividends announced in fiscal 2010, 2009 and 2008 were as follows (in millions, except per share data):

	2010		2009		2008	
	Per Share	Total	Per Share	Total	Per Share	Total
First quarter	$ 0.17	$ 284	$ 0.16	$ 264	$ 0.14	$ 228
Second quarter	0.17	279	0.16	264	0.14	227
Third quarter	0.19	309	0.17	282	0.16	261
Fourth quarter	0.19	305	0.17	283	0.16	266
	$ 0.72	$ 1,177	$ 0.66	$ 1,093	$ 0.60	$ 982

On October 13, 2010, the Company announced a cash dividend of $0.19 per share on the Company's common stock, payable on December 22, 2010 to stockholders of record as of November 24, 2010, which will be reflected in the consolidated financial statements in the first quarter of fiscal 2011.

Rowan Companies
2010 Annual Report

Note 8. Stockholders' Equity

Stock-Based Incentive Plans

Under the 2009 Rowan Companies, Inc. Incentive Plan (the "Plan"), the Compensation Committee of the Company's Board of Directors is authorized to grant employees and nonemployee directors, through May 2019, incentive awards covering up to 4,500,000 shares of Rowan common stock. The awards may be in the form of stock options, stock appreciation rights, restricted stock awards, restricted stock units, and performance-based awards, in which the number of shares issued is dependent on the achievement of certain long-term market or performance conditions over a specified period. As of December 31, 2010, there were 2,523,946 shares available for future grant under the Plan.

Restricted stock, stock appreciation rights and options granted by the Company generally have multiple vesting dates. The Company recognizes compensation cost for stock-based awards on a straight-line basis over the requisite service period for the entire award. Compensation cost charged to expense under all stock-based incentive awards is presented below (in thousands):

	Year ended December 31,		
	2010	2009	2008
Restricted stock and units	$ 13,379	$ 10,334	$ 11,580
Stock appreciation rights	2,678	855	–
Stock options	239	378	1,302
Performance-based awards	(718)	1,467	2,952
Total compensation cost	$ 15,578	$ 13,034	$ 15,834

Restricted Stock—Restricted stock represents a full share of Rowan common stock issued with a restrictive legend that prevents its sale until the restriction is later removed. In general, the shares vest and the restrictions lapse in one-third increments each year over a three-year service period, or in some cases, cliff vest at the end of a two- or three-year service period. The Company measures compensation related to each share based on the market price of the common stock on the date of grant. Restricted stock activity for the year ended December 31, 2010, is summarized below:

	Shares	Weighted-average grant-date fair value per share
Nonvested at January 1, 2010	987,730	$ 22.46
Granted	480,401	27.49
Vested	(433,013)	24.33
Forfeited	(43,489)	23.73
Nonvested at December 31, 2010	991,629	$ 24.01

The fair value of shares vested (measured at the vesting date) in 2010, 2009 and 2008 was $12.6 million, $3.2 million and $6.4 million, respectively. As of December 31, 2010, unrecognized compensation cost for nonvested restricted stock totaled $15.6 million, which is expected to be recognized over a weighted-average period of 1.8 years.

Restricted Stock Units—Restricted stock units ("RSUs") are rights to receive a specified number of shares of Rowan common stock or an equivalent value in cash. RSUs are typically granted to nonemployee directors and generally cliff vest at the end of a one-year service period; however, shares are not issued until the director terminates service to the Company. The Company measures compensation related to each unit based on the market price of the underlying common stock on the grant date. RSU activity for the year ended December 31, 2010, is summarized below:

	Units	Weighted-average grant-date fair value per share
Outstanding at January 1, 2010	124,934	$ 33.84
Granted	45,472	31.34
Outstanding at December 31, 2010	170,406	$ 33.17
Vested at December 31, 2010	124,934	$ 33.84

In 2009, the Company issued 13,205 shares of common stock with a fair value of $0.3 million in connection with the settlement of vested RSUs. No RSUs were settled in either 2010 or 2008. As of December 31, 2010, unrecognized compensation cost for nonvested RSUs totaled $0.5 million, which is expected to be recognized over a weighted-average period of 0.4 years.

Performance-Based Awards—The Committee may grant awards in which payment is contingent upon the achievement of certain market or performance-based conditions over a period of time specified by the Committee. Payment of such awards may be in Rowan common stock or cash as determined by the Committee. The number of awards granted is expressed as the number of shares that would be issued in the event the "target" goal is attained. The number of shares actually issued may range from zero to 200% of the target share amount.

Performance-based criteria may include total shareholder return ("TSR"), return on investment ("ROI"), or return on capital employed ("ROCE"), among others. Under the TSR criterion, the number of shares that may be issued is based on the Company's TSR ranking among an industry peer group at the end of the performance period. Fair value is estimated at the grant date using the Monte Carlo simulation model, which considers the probabilities of the Company's ending TSR at each rank, the number of shares issuable at each rank, and the expected stock price subject to each rank to determine the probability-weighted expected payout. A TSR criterion is deemed a "market condition" under GAAP. Compensation expense for awards with a market condition is reduced only for estimated forfeitures; no adjustment to expense is otherwise made, regardless of the number of shares issued, if any.

The per-share fair value of awards with ROI or ROCE criteria is equal to the market price of the stock on the date of grant. The Company initially recognized such compensation expense based on the number of shares that would vest in the event the target goal is met, subject to reduction for estimated forfeitures, on a straight-line basis over the performance period. ROI and ROCE criteria are deemed "performance conditions" under GAAP. Compensation expense for awards with performance conditions is remeasured annually based on the Company's progress towards achieving the target goal and is recognized for only the actual number of shares that vest; in the event such awards do not vest for any reason, all previously recognized expense, if any, would be reversed.

Performance-based award activity for the year ended December 31, 2010, is summarized below:

	Number of shares issuable at target	Weighted-average grant-date fair value per share
Unearned awards outstanding at January 1, 2010	159,416	$ 41.08
Granted	–	–
Vested	(24,180)	37.79
Lapsed, unearned	(50,221)	37.79
Unearned awards outstanding at December 31, 2010	85,015	$ 43.96

Unearned awards outstanding at December 31, 2010, consisted of 85,015 shares (net of 41,985 forfeitures) granted in 2008, under which from zero to 170,030 shares of Rowan common stock will be issued in April 2011 based upon an equal weighting of the Company's TSR ranking as compared to an industry peer group and its ROCE over the three-year period then ended.

No shares vested in 2009 or 2008 in connection with performance-based awards. As of December 31, 2010, unrecognized compensation cost for outstanding performance-based awards totaled $0.1 million, which is expected to be recognized over a weighted-average period of 0.3 years.

Stock Options and Appreciation Rights—Stock options granted to employees generally become exercisable in one-third or one-quarter annual increments over a three or four-year service period at a price not less than 100% of the market price of the Company's common stock on the date of grant.

Stock appreciation rights ("SARs") give the holder the right to receive, at no cost, shares of Rowan common stock, or cash at the discretion of the Committee, equal in value to the excess of the market price of the stock on the date of exercise over the strike price, which is the market price of the stock on the date of grant. SARs granted to employees become exercisable in one-third annual increments over a three-year service period.

Unexercised options and SARs expire ten years after the grant date.

Fair values of options and SARs granted were determined using the Black-Scholes option pricing model with the following weighted-average assumptions. (SARs were granted in only 2010 and 2009; options were granted in only 2008 and prior years):

	2010	2009	2008
Expected life in years	6.0	6.0	5.0
Risk-free interest rate	2.725%	2.375%	2.500%
Expected volatility	50.16%	52.86%	48.96%
Weighted-average grant-date per-share fair value	$14.00	$9.03	$7.01

Stock option activity for the year ended December 31, 2010, is summarized below:

	Number of shares under option	Weighted-average exercise price	Weighted-average remaining contractual term (in years)	Aggregate intrinsic value (in thousands)
Outstanding at January 1, 2010	1,836,250	$ 22.50		
Exercised	(350,512)	19.52		
Forfeited or expired	(13,839)	20.87		
Outstanding at December 31, 2010	1,471,899	$ 23.23	3.1	$ 17,576
Exercisable at December 31, 2010	1,371,899	$ 23.81	2.7	$ 15,629

The total intrinsic value of options exercised was $3.6 million in 2010, $1.1 million in 2009 and $10.7 million in 2008. As of December 31, 2010, unrecognized compensation cost related to stock options totaled $0.2 million, which is expected to be recognized over a weighted-average period of 1.0 years.

SARs activity for the year ended December 31, 2010, is summarized below:

	Number of shares under SARs	Weighted-average exercise price	Weighted-average remaining contractual term (in years)	Aggregate intrinsic value (in thousands)
Outstanding at January 1, 2010	513,834	$ 17.39		
Granted	328,362	27.80		
Forfeited	(14,011)	22.51		
Outstanding at December 31, 2010	828,185	$ 21.43	8.6	$ 11,056
Exercisable at December 31, 2010	171,278	$ 17.39	8.2	$ 2,979

As of December 31, 2010, unrecognized compensation cost related to SARs totaled $5.2 million, which is expected to be recognized over a weighted-average period of 1.8 years.

Limitation on Payments of Dividends

Rowan's debt agreements contain financial covenants that limit the amount of dividends the Company may distribute to its stockholders. Under the most restrictive of such covenants, approximately $427 million was available for distribution at December 31, 2010. Subject to this and other restrictions, the Board of Directors will determine payment, if any, of future dividends or distributions in light of conditions then existing, including the Company's earnings, financial condition and cash requirements, opportunities for reinvesting earnings, general business conditions and other factors.

Note 9. Pension and Other Postretirement Benefit Plans

Rowan sponsors defined benefit pension plans covering substantially all of its employees, and provides health care and life insurance benefits upon retirement for certain employees.

Casey's General Store
2009 Annual Report

3. Preferred and Common Stock

Preferred stock. The Company has 1,000,000 authorized shares of preferred stock, none of which has been issued.

Common stock. The Company currently has 120,000,000 authorized shares of common stock. Dividends paid totaled $0.30, $0.26, and $0.20 per share for the years ended April 30, 2009, 2008, and 2007, respectively.

Common share purchase rights. On June 14, 2009, the Shareholder Rights Plan, providing for the distribution of one common share purchase right for each share of common stock outstanding was allowed to expire under its own terms and was not extended.

Stock option plans. Under the Company's stock option plans, options may be granted to non-employee directors, certain officers, and key employees to purchase an aggregate of 5,260,000 shares of common stock. Options for 494,164 shares were available for grant at April 30, 2009, and options for 678,000 shares (which expire between 2009 and 2018) were outstanding. All stock option shares issued are previously unissued authorized shares. Any additional option share requirements in the future will require approval by the shareholders of the Company. Additional information is provided in the Company's 2009 proxy statement.

On June 6, 2003, stock options totaling 307,000 shares were granted to certain officers and key employees. These awards vested on June 6, 2006; subsequent to adoption of FAS 123R, and compensation expense was recognized ratably over the vesting period.

On July 5, 2005, stock options totaling 234,000 shares were granted to certain officers and key employees. These awards will vest on July 5, 2010, and compensation expense is being recognized ratably over the vesting period.

On June 25, 2007, stock options totaling 246,000 shares were granted to certain officers and key employees. These awards will vest on June 25, 2010, and compensation expense is being recognized ratably over the vesting period.

The 2000 Stock Option Plan allows the grant of employees' options with an exercise price equal to the fair market value of the Company's stock on the date of grant and expire ten years after the date of grant. Vesting is generally over a three to five-year service period. The non-employee Directors' Stock Option Plan allows the grant of directors' options with an exercise price equal to the average of the last reported sale prices of shares of common stock on the last trading day of each of the twelve months preceding the award of the option. The term of such options is ten years from the date of grant, and each option is exercisable immediately upon grant. The aggregate number of shares of Common Stock that may be granted pursuant to the Director Stock Plan may not exceed 200,000 shares, subject to adjustment to reflect any future stock dividends, stock splits, or other relevant capitalization changes. On May 1, 2009, stock options totaling 16,000 shares were granted to the members of the Board of Directors.

The following table shows the stock option activity during the periods indicated:

	Number of shares	Weighted average exercise price
Balance at April 30, 2006	961,050	$15.29
Granted	14,000	22.36
Exercised	(223,550)	13.16
Forfeited	(22,000)	14.80
Balance at April 30, 2007	729,500	$16.10
Granted	260,000	26.77
Exercised	(156,950)	13.40
Forfeited	(49,000)	23.16
Balance at April 30, 2008	783,550	$19.74

	Number of shares	Weighted average exercise price
Granted	12,000	26.51
Exercised	(93,550)	14.39
Forfeited	(24,000)	23.80
Balance at April 30, 2009	**678,000**	**$20.45**

At April 30, 2009, all outstanding options had an aggregate intrinsic value of $4,241 and a weighted average remaining contractual life of 5.8 years. The vested options totaled 270,000 shares with a weighted average exercise price of $15.20 per share and a weighted average remaining contractual life of 3.8 years. The aggregate intrinsic value for the vested options as of April 30, 2009 was $3,081. The aggregate intrinsic value for the total of all options exercised during the year ended April 30, 2009 was $1,151, and the total fair value of shares vested during the year ended April 30, 2009 was $100.

The fair value of the 2009 stock options granted was estimated utilizing the Black Scholes valuation model. The grant date fair value for the May 1, 2008 options was $8.30. The significant assumptions follow:

	May 1, 2008
Risk-free interest rate	4.3%
Expected option life	8.9 years
Expected volatility	37%
Expected dividend yield	1.7%

The expected option life of each award granted was based upon historical experience of employees' exercise behavior. Expected volatility was based upon historical volatility levels of the Company's common stock over a similar length of time. Expected dividend yield was based on expected dividend rate. Risk-free interest rate reflects the yield of a zero coupon U.S. Treasury over the expected option life.

Total compensation costs recorded for the years ended April 30, 2009, 2008 and 2007 were $1,256, $1,432, and $526, respectively, for the stock option awards. As of April 30, 2009, there was $955 of total unrecognized compensation costs related to the 2000 Stock Option Plan for stock options that are expected to be recognized ratably through 2011.

At April 30, 2009, the range of exercise prices was $11.20–$26.92 and the weighted average remaining contractual life of outstanding options was 5.8 years. The number of shares and weighted average remaining contractual life of the options by range of applicable exercise prices at April 30, 2009 were as follows:

Range of Exercise Prices	Number of Shares	Weighted Average Exercise Price	Weighted Average Remaining Contractual Life (Years)
$11.20–13.07	58,500	$11.82	2.1
14.07–17.64	177,500	14.54	3.5
20.68–26.92	442,000	23.97	7.3
	678,000		

Jacobs Engineering Group
2009 Annual Report

12. Common and Preferred Stock

Jacobs is authorized to issue two classes of capital stock designated "common stock" and "preferred stock" (each has a par value of $1.00 per share). The preferred stock may be issued in one or more series. The number of shares to be included in a series as well as each series' designation, relative powers, dividend and other preferences, rights and qualifications, redemption provisions, and restrictions are to be fixed by the Board of Directors at the time each series is issued. Except as may be provided by the Board of Directors in a preferred stock designation, or otherwise provided for by statute, the holders of shares of common stock have the exclusive right to vote for the election of Directors and all other matters requiring stockholder action. The holders of shares of common stock are entitled to dividends if and when declared by the Board of Directors from whatever assets are legally available for that purpose.

In December 2000, the Board of Directors of Jacobs approved the Amended and Restated Rights Agreement dated December 20, 2000 (the "Rights Agreement"). The Rights Agreement is intended to protect the rights of our shareholders in the event of an unsolicited takeover attempt. It is not intended to prevent a takeover of the Company on terms that are favorable and fair to all shareholders, and the Rights Agreement will not interfere with any merger approved by the Board of Directors. Pursuant to the terms of the Rights Agreement, each outstanding share of common stock has attached to it one stock purchase right (a "Right"). Each Right entitles holders of common stock to purchase, in certain circumstances generally relating to a change in control of Jacobs, one four-hundredths of a share of our Series A Junior Participating Cumulative Preferred Stock, par value $1.00 per share (the "Series A Preferred Stock") at the exercise price of $175.00 per share, subject to adjustment. Alternatively, the Right holder may purchase shares of common stock having a market value equal to two times the exercise price, or may purchase shares of common stock of the acquiring corporation having a market value equal to two times the exercise price.

The Series A Preferred Stock confers to its holders, rights as to dividends, voting, and liquidation which are in preference to common stockholders. The Rights are nonvoting, are not presently exercisable, and currently trade in tandem with the common shares. In accordance with the Rights Agreement, we may redeem the Rights at $0.0025 per Right. The Rights will expire on December 20, 2010, unless earlier exchanged or redeemed.

Sherwin-Williams
2009 Annual Report

Note 11—Capital Stock

At December 31, 2009, there were 300,000,000 shares of common stock and 30,000,000 shares of serial preferred stock authorized for issuance. Of the authorized serial preferred stock, 3,000,000 shares are designated as cumulative redeemable serial preferred and 1,000,000 shares are designated as convertible serial preferred stock (see Note 12). An aggregate of 13,381,449, 14,884,028 and 16,477,802 shares of common stock at December 31, 2009, 2008 and 2007, respectively, were reserved for future grants of restricted stock and the exercise and future grants of option rights (see Note 13). Common shares outstanding shown in the following table included 475,628 shares of common stock held in a revocable trust at December 31, 2009, 2008 and 2007, respectively. The revocable trust is used to accumulate assets for the purpose of funding the ultimate obligation of certain non-qualified benefit plans. Transactions between the Company and the trust are accounted for in accordance with the Deferred Compensation—Rabbi Trusts Subtopic of the Compensation Topic of the ASC, which requires the assets held by the trust be consolidated with the Company's accounts.

	Common Shares in Treasury	Common Shares Outstanding
Balance at January 1, 2007	89,419,575	133,565,287
Shares tendered as payment for option rights exercised	18,593	(18,593)
Shares issued for exercise of option rights		2,345,069
Shares tendered in connection with grants of restricted stock	125,022	(125,022)
Net shares issued for grants of restricted stock		247,500
Treasury stock purchased	13,200,000	(13,200,000)
Balance at December 31, 2007	102,763,190	122,814,241
Shares tendered as payment for option rights exercised	4,706	(4,706)
Shares issued for exercise of option rights		1,275,151
Shares tendered in connection with grants of restricted stock	93,569	(93,569)
Net shares issued for grants of restricted stock		294,000
Treasury stock purchased	7,250,000	(7,250,000)
Balance at December 31, 2008	**110,111,465**	**117,035,117**
Shares tendered as payment for option rights exercised	**9,743**	**(9,743)**

	Common Shares in Treasury	Common Shares Outstanding
Shares issued for exercise of option rights		1,075,395
Shares tendered in connection with grants of restricted stock	88,461	(88,461)
Net shares issued for grants of restricted stock		424,561
Treasury stock purchased	9,000,000	(9,000,000)
Balance at December 31, 2009	119,209,669	109,436,869

Note 12—Stock Purchase Plan and Preferred Stock

As of December 31, 2009, 23,520 employees contributed to the Company's ESOP, a voluntary defined contribution plan available to all eligible salaried employees. Participants are allowed to contribute up to the lesser of twenty percent of their annual compensation or the maximum dollar amount allowed under the Internal Revenue Code. Prior to July 1, 2009, the Company matched one hundred percent of all contributions up to six percent of eligible employee contributions. Effective July 1, 2009, the ESOP was amended to change the Company match to one-hundred percent on the first three percent of eligible employee contributions and fifty percent on the next two percent of eligible contributions. Such participant contributions may be invested in a variety of mutual funds or a Company common stock fund and may be exchanged between investments as directed by the participant. Effective January 1, 2007, the ESOP was amended to permit participants to diversify both future and prior Company matching contributions previously allocated to the Company common stock fund into a variety of mutual funds.

The Company made contributions to the ESOP on behalf of participating employees, representing amounts authorized by employees to be withheld from their earnings on a pre-tax basis, of $70,025, $72,812 and $71,691 in 2009, 2008 and 2007, respectively. The Company's matching contributions to the ESOP charged to operations were $44,587, $54,001 and $52,683 for 2009, 2008 and 2007, respectively.

At December 31, 2009, there were 17,579,750 shares of the Company's common stock being held by the ESOP, representing 16.0 percent of the total number of voting shares outstanding. Shares of Company common stock credited to each member's account under the ESOP are voted by the trustee under instructions from each individual plan member. Shares for which no instructions are received are voted by the trustee in the same proportion as those for which instructions are received.

On August 1, 2006, the Company issued 500,000 shares of convertible serial preferred stock, no par value (Series 2 Preferred stock) with cumulative quarterly dividends of $11.25 per share, for $500,000 to the ESOP. The ESOP financed the acquisition of the Series 2 Preferred stock by borrowing $500,000 from the

Company at the rate of 5.5 percent per annum. This borrowing is payable over ten years in equal quarterly installments. Each share of Series 2 Preferred stock is entitled to one vote upon all matters presented to the Company's shareholders and generally votes with the common stock together as one class. The Series 2 Preferred stock is held by the ESOP in an unallocated account. As the value of compensation expense related to contributions to the ESOP is earned, the Company has the option of funding the ESOP by redeeming a portion of the preferred stock or with cash. Contributions are credited to the members' accounts at the time of funding. The Series 2 Preferred stock is redeemable for cash or convertible into common stock or any combination thereof at the option of the ESOP based on the relative fair value of the Series 2 Preferred and common stock at the time of conversion.

At December 31, 2009, 2008 and 2007, there were no allocated or committed-to-be released shares of Series 2 Preferred stock outstanding. In 2009, the Company elected to fund the ESOP with cash. The Company redeemed 107,980 and 108,482 shares of the Series 2 Preferred stock for cash in 2008 and 2007, respectively.

Walt Disney
2009 Annual Report

12. Shareholders' Equity

As of the filing date of this report, the Board of Directors had not yet declared a dividend related to fiscal 2009. The Company paid a $648 million dividend ($0.35 per share) during the second quarter of fiscal 2009 related to fiscal 2008. The Company paid a $664 million dividend ($0.35 per share) during the second quarter of fiscal 2008 related to fiscal 2007. The Company paid a $637 million dividend ($0.31 per share) during the second quarter of fiscal 2007 related to fiscal 2006.

During fiscal 2009, the Company repurchased 5 million shares of Disney common stock for $138 million. During fiscal 2008, the Company repurchased 139 million shares of Disney common stock for $4.5 billion. During fiscal 2007, the Company repurchased 202 million shares of Disney common stock for $6.9 billion. On May 1, 2007, the Board of Directors of the Company increased the share repurchase authorization in place to repurchase 179 million additional shares. The repurchase program does not have an expiration date.

In April 2008, the Company redeemed $1.3 billion of convertible senior notes. Pursuant to the redemption, substantially all of the notes were converted into 45 million shares of the Company's common stock.

The par value of the Company's outstanding common stock totaled approximately $26 million.

The Company also has 1.0 billion shares of Internet Group stock at $.01 par value authorized. No shares are issued and outstanding.

Accumulated other comprehensive income (loss), net of tax,[1] is as follows:

	October 3, 2009	*September 27, 2008*
Market value adjustments for hedges and investments	**$ 18**	$ 78
Foreign currency translation and other	**105**	137
Unrecognized pension and postretirement medical expense	**(1,767)**	(296)
Accumulated other comprehensive loss[1]	**$(1,644)**	$(81)

[1] Accumulated other comprehensive income(loss) and components of other comprehensive income(loss) are recorded net of tax using a 37% estimated statutory tax rate.

Johnson & Johnson
2008 Annual Report

12. Accumulated Other Comprehensive Income

Components of other comprehensive income/(loss) consist of the following:

(Dollars in millions)	Foreign Currency Translation	Unrealized Gains/ (Losses) on Securities	Employee Benefit Plans	Gains/ (Losses on Derivatives & Hedges	Total Accumulated Other Comprehensive Income/(Loss)
January 1, 2006	$(520)	70	(320)	15	(755)
2006 changes					
Net change due to hedging transactions	–	–	–	17	
Net amount reclassed to net earnings	–	–	–	(23)	
Net 2006 changes	362	(9)	(1,710)	(6)	(1,363)
December 31, 2006	$(158)	61	(2,030)	9	(2,118)
2007 changes					
Net change due to hedging transactions	–	–	–	(78)	
Net amount reclassed to net earnings	–	–	–	24	
Net 2007 changes	786	23	670	(54)	1,425
December 30, 2007	$628	84	(1,360)	(45)	(693)
2008 changes					

(Dollars in millions)	Foreign Currency Translation	Unrealized Gains/ (Losses) on Securities	Employee Benefit Plans	Gains/ (Losses on Derivatives & Hedges	Total Accumulated Other Comprehensive Income/(Loss)
Net change due to hedging transactions	–	–	–	94	
Net amount reclassed to net earnings	–	–	–	72	
Net 2008 changes	(2,499)	(59)	(1,870)	166	(4,262)
December 28, 2008	$(1,871)	25	(3,230)	121	(4,955)

Total comprehensive income for 2008 includes reclassification adjustment gains of $41 million realized from the sale of equity securities and the associated tax expense of $14 million.

Total comprehensive income for 2007 includes reclassification adjustment gains of $7 million realized from the sale of equity securities and the associated tax expense of $2 million.

Total other comprehensive income for 2006 includes reclassification adjustment gains of $13 million realized from the sale of equity securities and the associated tax expense of $4 million.

The tax effect on the unrealized gains/(losses) on the equity securities was an expense of $14 million, $46 million and $33 million in 2008, 2007 and 2006, respectively. The tax effect related to employee benefit plans was $1,090 million, $349 million and $891 million in 2008, 2007 and 2006, respectively. The tax effect on the gains/(losses) on derivatives and hedges are losses of $70 million in 2008, gains of $24 million in 2007, and losses of $4 million in 2006. See Note 15 for additional information relating to derivatives and hedging.

The currency translation adjustments are not currently adjusted for income taxes as they relate to permanent investments in international subsidiaries.

Sherwin-Williams
2008 Annual Report

Note 10—Capital Stock

At December 31, 2008, there were 300,000,000 shares of common stock and 30,000,000 shares of serial preferred stock authorized for issuance. Of the authorized serial preferred stock, 3,000,000 shares are designated as cumulative redeemable serial preferred and 1,000,000 shares are designated as convertible serial preferred stock (see Note 11). An aggregate of 14,884,028, 16,477,802 and 19,125,460 shares of common stock at December 31, 2008, 2007 and 2006, respectively, were reserved for future grants of restricted stock and the exercise and future grants of option rights (see Note 12). Common shares outstanding shown in the following table included 475,628 shares of common stock held in a revocable trust at December 31, 2008, 2007 and 2006, respectively. The revocable trust is used to accumulate assets for the purpose of funding the ultimate obligation of certain non-qualified benefit plans. Transactions between the Company and the trust are accounted for in accordance with EITF No. 97-14, "Accounting for Deferred Compensation Arrangements Where Amounts Earned Are Held in a Rabbi Trust and Invested," which requires the assets held by the trust be consolidated with the Company's accounts.

	Common Shares in Treasury	Common Shares Outstanding
Balance at January 1, 2006	83,795,302	135,139,381
Shares tendered as payment for option rights exercised	23,832	(23,832)
Shares issued for exercise of option rights		3,691,704
Shares tendered in connection with grants of restricted stock	441	(441)
Net shares issued for grants of restricted stock		358,475
Treasury stock purchased	5,600,000	(5,600,000)
Balance at December 31, 2006	89,419,575	133,565,287
Shares tendered as payment for option rights exercised	18,593	(18,593)
Shares issued for exercise of option rights		2,345,069
Shares tendered in connection with grants of restricted stock	125,022	(125,022)
Net shares issued for grants of restricted stock		247,500
Treasury stock purchased	13,200,000	(13,200,000)
Balance at December 31, 2007	102,763,190	122,814,241
Shares tendered as payment for option rights exercised	4,706	(4,706)
Shares issued for exercise of option rights		1,275,151
Shares tendered in connection with grants of restricted stock	93,569	(93,569)
Net shares issued for grants of restricted stock		294,000
Treasury stock purchased	7,250,000	(7,250,000)
Balance at December 31, 2008	110,111,465	117,035,117

Note 11—Stock Purchase Plan and Preferred Stock

As of December 31, 2008, 24,745 employees contributed to the Company's ESOP, a voluntary defined contribution plan available to all eligible salaried employees. Participants are allowed to contribute, on a pretax basis only, up to the lesser of 20 percent of their annual compensation or the maximum dollar amount allowed under the Internal Revenue Code. Such participant contributions may be invested in a variety of mutual funds or a Company common stock fund and may be exchanged between investments as directed by the participant. The Company matches current contributions up to 6 percent of annual compensation. Effective January 1, 2007, the ESOP was amended to permit participants to diversify both future and a portion of prior Company matching contributions previously allocated to the Company common stock fund into a variety of mutual funds.

The Company made contributions to the ESOP on behalf of participating employees, representing amounts authorized by employees to be withheld from their earnings on a pre-tax basis, of $72,812, $71,691 and $66,032 in 2008, 2007 and 2006, respectively. The Company's matching contributions to the ESOP charged to operations were $54,001, $52,683 and $48,123 for 2008, 2007 and 2006, respectively.

At December 31, 2008, there were 17,991,799 shares of the Company's common stock being held by the ESOP, representing 15.4 percent of the total number of voting shares outstanding. Shares of Company common stock credited to each member's account under the ESOP are voted by the trustee under instructions from each individual plan member. Shares for which no instructions are received, along with any unallocated shares held in the ESOP, are voted by the trustee in the same proportion as those for which instructions are received.

On August 1, 2006, the Company issued 500,000 shares of convertible serial preferred stock, no par value (Series 2 Preferred stock) with cumulative quarterly dividends of $11.25 per share, for $500,000 to the ESOP. The ESOP financed the acquisition of the Series 2 Preferred stock by borrowing $500,000 from the Company at the rate of 5.5 percent per annum. This borrowing is payable over ten years in equal quarterly installments. Each share of Series 2 Preferred stock is entitled to one vote upon all matters presented to the Company's shareholders and generally votes with the common stock together as one class. The Series 2 Preferred stock is held in an unallocated account by the ESOP until the value of compensation expense related to the Company's contributions is earned at which time contributions are credited to the members' accounts. The Series 2 Preferred stock is redeemable for cash or convertible into common stock or any combination thereof at the option of the ESOP based on the relative fair value of the Series 2 Preferred and common stock at the time of conversion. At December 31, 2008, 2007 and 2006, there were no allocated or committed-to-be-released shares of Series 2 Preferred stock outstanding. The ESOP redeemed 107,980, 108,482 and 66,785 shares of the Series 2 Preferred stock for cash in 2008, 2007 and 2006, respectively.

On August 27, 2003, the Company issued 350,000 shares of convertible serial preferred stock (Series 1 Preferred stock) with cumulative quarterly dividends of $10.00 per share for $350,000 to the ESOP. The ESOP financed the acquisition of the Series 1 Preferred stock by borrowing $350,000 from the Company at the rate of 4.5 percent per annum. Each share of Series 1 Preferred stock was entitled to one vote upon all matters presented to the Company's shareholders and generally voted with the common stock together as one class. The Series 1 Preferred stock was held in an unallocated account by the ESOP until the value of compensation expense related to the Company's contributions was earned at which time contributions were credited to the members' accounts. The ESOP redeemed 34,702 shares of the Series 1 Preferred stock for cash in 2006.

General Mills
2008 Annual Report

Note 10. Stockholders' Equity

Cumulative preference stock of 5.0 million shares, without par value, is authorized but unissued.

On December 10, 2007, our Board of Directors approved the retirement of 125.0 million shares of common stock in treasury effective December 10, 2007. This action reduced common stock by $12.5 million, reduced additional paid-in capital by $5,068.3 million, and reduced common stock in treasury by $5,080.8 million on our Consolidated Balance Sheets.

In fiscal 2007, our Board of Directors approved an authorization to repurchase up to 75 million shares of our common stock. This replaced a prior authorization, which permitted us to repurchase shares up to a treasury share balance of 170 million. Purchases under the new authorization can be made in the open market or in privately negotiated transactions, including the use of call options and other derivative instruments, Rule 10b5-1 trading plans, and accelerated repurchase programs. The authorization has no preestablished termination date. During fiscal 2008, we repurchased 23.9 million shares for an aggregate purchase price of $1.4 billion, of which $0.1 million settled after the end of our fiscal year. During fiscal 2007, we repurchased 25.3 million shares for an aggregate purchase price of $1.4 billion, of which $64.4 million settled after the end of our fiscal year. In fiscal 2006, we repurchased 18.8 million shares of common stock for an aggregate purchase price of $892.4 million. A total of 39.8 million shares were held in treasury as of May 25, 2008.

In October 2004, Lehman Brothers Holdings Inc. (Lehman Brothers) issued $750.0 million of notes, which were mandatorily exchangeable for shares of our common stock. In connection with the issuance of those notes, an affiliate of Lehman Brothers entered into a forward purchase contract with us, under which we were obligated to deliver to such affiliate between 14.0 million and 17.0 million shares of our common stock, subject to adjustment under certain circumstances. We delivered 14.3 million shares in October 2007, in exchange for $750.0 million in cash from Lehman Brothers. We used the cash to reduce outstanding commercial paper balances.

The forward purchase contract was considered an equity instrument. The $42.6 million fee we paid for the forward purchase contract was recorded as a reduction to stockholders' equity in fiscal 2005. The following table provides details of other comprehensive income:

In millions	Pretax	Tax	Net
Fiscal 2006:			
Foreign currency translation	$ 72.9	$ –	$ 72.9

In millions	Pretax	Tax	Net
Minimum pension liability	37.7	(13.7)	24.0
Other fair value changes:			
Securities	2.3	(0.8)	1.5
Hedge derivatives	(14.5)	5.4	(9.1)
Reclassification to earnings:			
Hedge derivatives	44.1	(16.1)	28.0
Other comprehensive income	$142.5	$(25.2)	$117.3
Fiscal 2007:			
Foreign currency translation	$193.8	$ –	$193.8
Minimum pension liability	(33.5)	12.7	(20.8)
Other fair value changes:			
Securities	2.0	(0.7)	1.3
Hedge derivatives	11.4	(4.9)	6.5
Reclassification to earnings:			
Hedge derivatives	22.8	(8.3)	14.5
Other comprehensive income	$196.5	$ (1.2)	$195.3
Fiscal 2008:			
Foreign currency translation	$246.3	$ –	$246.3
Minimum pension liability	61.4	(22.0)	39.4
Other fair value changes:			
Securities	1.5	(0.6)	0.9
Hedge derivatives	59.6	(21.3)	38.3
Reclassification to earnings:			
Hedge derivatives	(64.5)	23.5	(41.0)
Amortization of losses and prior service costs	20.6	(8.1)	12.5
Other comprehensive income	$324.9	$(28.5)	$296.4

Except for reclassifications to earnings, changes in other comprehensive income are primarily non-cash items.

Accumulated other comprehensive income (loss) balances, net of tax effects, were as follows:

In millions	May 25, 2008	May 27, 2007
Foreign currency translation adjustments	$ 648.4	$ 402.1
Unrealized gain (loss) from:		
Securities	4.8	3.9
Hedge derivatives	(39.2)	(36.5)
Pension, other postretirement, and postemployment benefits:		
Net actuarial loss	(400.4)	(448.5)

In millions	May 25, 2008	May 27, 2007
Prior service costs	(36.9)	(40.7)
Accumulated other comprehensive income(loss)	$ 176.7	$(119.7)

Omnova Solutions
2007 Annual Report

Note F. Accumulated Other Comprehensive Loss

The components of Accumulated other comprehensive loss are as follows:

	Years Ended November 30,		
(dollars in millions)	2007	2006	2005
Foreign currency translation adjustments	$8.2	$4.9	($ 0.6)
Unrecognized loss on interest rate swap	(2.5)		
Employee benefit plans	(9.6)	(29.5)	(60.6)
Accumulated comprehensive loss	($3.9)	($24.6)	($61.2)

The amounts included in Accumulated other comprehensive loss during 2007 and 2006 relating to the Company's employee benefit plans were as follows:

(dollars in millions)	Pension Plans	Health Care Plans	Total
2007			
Net Actuarial (Loss) Gain			
Net actuarial gain incurred during the period	$11.1	$4.1	$15.2
Amortization of net actuarial (loss) gain included in net periodic pension expense	3.6	(2.5)	1.1
Net change in net actuarial gain	$14.7	$1.6	$16.3
Prior Service Cost			
Prior service costs incurred during the period		$2.9	$2.9
Amortization of prior service costs included in net periodic pension expense	0.8	(0.2)	0.6
Net change in prior service costs	$0.8	$2.7	$3.5
2006			
Net Actuarial (Loss) Gain			
Amount recognized upon the adoption of SFAS No. 158	($51.5)	$26.3	($25.2)

(dollars in millions)	Pension Plans	Health Care Plans	Total
Prior Service Cost			
Amount recognized upon the adoption of SFAS No. 158	($3.6)	($0.7)	($4.3)

In 2006, the fair value of plan assets of the Company's funded defined benefit plan exceeded the accumulated benefit obligation, and accordingly, the Company reversed its minimum pension liability of $0.3 million. Additionally, as of November 30, 2006, the Company adopted the recognition and disclosure provisions of SFAS No. 158 as described in Note B. As a result of adopting SFAS No. 158, the Company recognized in its balance sheet the underfunded status of its defined benefit plans, measured as the difference between the fair value of plan assets and the benefit obligation (the projected benefit obligation for pension plans and the accumulated post-retirement benefit obligation for other post-retirement plans). As a result, as of November 30, 2006, the Company recognized liabilities of $3.0 million for its defined benefit pension plans and $19.9 million for its retiree health care plan and also recognized in Accumulated other comprehensive loss a net actuarial loss of $25.2 million and prior service costs of $4.3 million. The net difference between these liabilities and assets and liabilities previously recorded, approximately $29.8 million, was charged to Accumulated other comprehensive loss as required by SFAS No. 158.

Amgen
2007 Annual Report

7. Stockholder's Equity

Stock repurchase program

A summary activity under our stock repurchase program for the years ended December 31, 2007, 2006 and 2005 is as follows (in millions):

	2007		2006		2005	
	Shares	Dollars	Shares	Dollars	Shares	Dollars
First quarter	8.8	$537	46.6	$3,374	26.8	$1,675
Second quarter	73.9[1]	4,463	13.0	876	12.1	70
Third quarter	2.5[1]	–	7.3	505	9.5	769
Fourth quarter	1.8	100	3.3	245	14.8	1,236
Total	87.0	$5,100	70.2	$5,000	63.2	$3,750

[1] The total number of shares repurchased during the three months ended June 30, 2007 excludes 2.5 million shares received in July 2007 in connection with the final settlement of a block trade entered into in May 2007, which is discussed in Note 6, "*Financing Arrangements*" above.

As of December 31, 2007, $6.4 billion was available for stock repurchases under the $5.0 billion repurchase authorization received from the Board of

Directors in July 2007 and amounts remaining from the Board of Director's previous authorization in December 2006. The manner of purchases, the amount we spend, and the number of shares repurchased will vary based on a variety of factors including the stock price and blackout periods in which we are restricted from repurchasing shares, and may include private block purchases as well as market transactions.

Accumulated other comprehensive income

The components of accumulated other comprehensive income as of December 31, 2007 is as follows (in millions):

	Before-Tax	Tax Impact	After-Tax
Unrealized losses on foreign currency hedges	$(69)	$26	$(43)
Reclassification adjustments for losses realized in net income	(4)	2	(2)
Unrealized gains on available-for-sale securities	62	(23)	39
	(11)	5	(6)
Cumulative foreign currency translation gain	89	(30)	59
	$78	$(25)	$53

Other

In addition to common stock, our authorized capital includes 5 million shares of preferred stock, $0.0001 par value, of which 0.7 million shares have been reserved and designated Series A Preferred Stock. At December 31, 2007 and 2006, no shares of preferred stock were issued or outstanding.

At December 31, 2007, we had reserved 252 million shares of our common stock, which may be issued through our option and stock purchase plans, through conversion of our convertible notes and through our warrants.

FMC
2007 Annual Report

Note 15. Stockholders' Equity

The following is a summary of our capital stock activity over the past three years:

(number of shares in thousands)	Common Stock	Treasury Stock
December 31, 2004	90,244	15,460
Stock options and awards	1,702	–
Stock for employee benefit trust, net	–	(546)
December 31, 2005	91,946	14,914
Stock options and awards	1,046	(980)
Stock for employee benefit trust, net	–	(474)

(number of shares in thousands)	Common Stock	Treasury Stock
Repurchases of common stock, net	–	2,896
December 31, 2006	92,992	16,356
Stock options and awards	–	(1,132)
Stock for employee benefit trust, net	–	(2)
Repurchases of common stock, net	–	2,640
December 31, 2007	92,992	17,862

At December 31, 2007, 8.6 million shares of unissued FMC common stock were reserved for stock options and awards.

Accumulated other comprehensive gain (loss) consisted of the following:

(in millions)	December 31, 2007	2006
Deferred (loss) gain on derivative contracts	$(1.6)	$(15.7)
Pension and other postretirement liability adjustment	(46.1)	(45.6)
Other comprehensive income (loss), net	(47.7)	(61.3)
Foreign currency translation adjustments	37.8	4.2
Accumulated other comprehensive gain (loss)	$(9.9)	$(57.1)

In 2006, the Board of Directors approved the initiation of a quarterly cash dividend of $0.09 per share which was paid in April, July, and October of 2006, and January of 2007. In April 2007, the Board announced its plan to increase the quarterly dividend by 17 percent from $0.09 to $0.105. We declared dividends aggregating $30.9 million to our shareholders of record during the year 2007, and $7.9 million of this amount is included in "Accrued and other liabilities" on the consolidated balance sheet as of December 31, 2007.

In 2006, the Board of Directors also authorized the repurchase of up to $150 million of our common stock. In April 2007, we announced a new $250 million authorization, replacing the original $150 million program. Although the new repurchase program does not include a specific timetable or price targets and may be suspended or terminated at any time, we expect the program will be accomplished over the next two years. During the year ended December 31, 2007, we repurchased 2,474,839 of our shares at an aggregate of approximately $110 million, including 536,422 shares for approximately $20 million under the old program and 1,938,417 shares for approximately $90 million under the new program. We also reacquire shares from time to time in connection with the vesting and exercise of awards under our equity compensation plans.

See Note 1 for information regarding the stock split.

Shares of common stock repurchased and contributed to a trust for an employee benefit program (net of shares resold as needed to administer the plan) were 2,070 net shares contributed, 470,880 net shares contributed, and 528,644 net shares contributed in 2007, 2006 and 2005, respectively, at a cost of approximately $0.1 million, $17.3 million, and $14.9 million, respectively.

Archer Daniels Midland Co.
2006 Annual Report

Note 7—Shareholders' Equity

The Company has authorized one billion shares of common stock and 500,000 shares of preferred stock, each without par value. No preferred stock has been issued. At June 30, 2006 and 2005, the Company had approximately 16.3 million and 21.5 million shares, respectively, in treasury. Treasury stock of $238 million at June 30, 2006, and $315 million at June 30, 2005, is recorded at cost as a reduction of common stock.

The Company's employee stock compensation plans provide for the granting of options to employees to purchase common stock of the Company pursuant to the Company's 1996 Stock Option Plan, 1999 Incentive Compensation Plan, and 2002 Incentive Compensation Plan. These options are issued at market value on the date of grant and expire five to ten years after the date of grant. The vesting requirements of awards under the plans range from four to nine years based upon the terms of each option grant.

The Company's 1999 and 2002 Incentive Compensation Plans provide for the granting of restricted stock awards at no cost to certain officers and key employees. The awarded shares are made in common stock and vest at the end of a three-year restriction period. During 2006, 2005 and 2004, 2.4 million, 2.5 million, and 1.1 million common shares, respectively, were granted as restricted stock awards. At June 30, 2006, there were 1.1 million and 12.9 million shares available for future grants pursuant to the 1999 and 2002 plans, respectively.

Compensation expense for option grants and restricted stock awards granted to employees is generally recognized on a straight-line basis during the service period of the respective grant. Certain of the Company's option grants and restricted stock awards continue to vest upon the recipient's retirement from the Company and compensation expense related to option grants and restricted stock awards granted to retirement eligible employees is recognized in earnings on the date of grant. Total compensation expense for option grants and restricted stock awards recognized during 2006 and 2005 was $67 million and $29 million, respectively. Total compensation expense for restricted stock awards recognized during 2004 was $7 million.

The fair value of each option grant is estimated as of the date of grant using the Black Scholes single option pricing model. The volatility assumption used in the Black-Scholes single option pricing model is based on the historical volatility of the Company's stock. The volatility of the Company's stock was calculated based upon the monthly closing price of the Company's stock for the eight-year period immediately prior to the date of grant. The average expected life represents the period of time that option grants are expected to be outstanding. The risk-free rate is based on the rate of U.S. Treasury zero-coupon issues with a remaining term equal to the expected life of option grants. The assumptions used in the Black-Scholes single option pricing model are as follows:

	2006	*2005*	*2004*
Dividend yield	**2%**	2%	2%
Risk-free interest rate	**4%**	4%	4%
Stock volatility	**31%**	27%	28%
Average expected life (years)	**8%**	9%	9%

A summary of option activity during 2006 is presented below:

	Shares	*Weighted-Average Exercise Price*
	(In thousands, except per share amounts)	
Shares under option at June 30, 2005 .	10,523	$13.19
Granted	3,210	21.56
Exercised	(3,005)	12.48
Forfeited or expired	(792)	15.29
Shares under option at June 30, 2006 .	9,936	$15.94
Exercisable at June 30, 2006	1,623	$12.13

The weighted-average remaining contractual term of options outstanding and exercisable at June 30, 2006, is 7 years and 4 years, respectively. The aggregate intrinsic value of options outstanding and exercisable at June 30, 2006 is $252 million and $47 million, respectively. The weighted-average grant-date fair values of options granted during 2006, 2005, and 2004 were $7.52, $5.41, and $4.72 respectively. The total intrinsic values of options exercised during 2006, 2005, and 2004 were $60 million, $33 million, and $18 million, respectively. Cash proceeds received from options exercised during 2006, 2005, and 2004 were $30 million, $31 million, and $39 million, respectively.

At June 30, 2006, there was $33 million of total unrecognized compensation expense related to option grants. Amounts to be recognized as compensation expense during the next five fiscal years are $10 million, $9 million, $7 million, $4 million, and $2 million, respectively.

The fair value of restricted shares is determined based on the market value of the Company's shares on the grant date. The weighted-average grant-date fair values of shares granted during 2006 and 2005 were $22.04 and $15.73, respectively.

A summary of restricted shares activity during 2006 is presented below:

	Shares	Weighted-Average Exercise Price
	(In thousands, except per share amounts)	
Non-vested at June 30, 2005	4,434	$14.35
Granted	2,447	22.04
Vested	(930)	11.33
Forfeited	(326)	15.93
Non-vested at June 30, 2006	5,625	$18.11

At June 30, 2006 there was $33 million of total unrecognized compensation expense related to restricted shares. Amounts to be recognized as compensation expense during the next three fiscal years are $22 million, $10 million, and $1 million, respectively. The total fair value of restricted shares vested during 2006 was $11 million.

Note 8—Accumulated Other Comprehensive Income (Loss)

The following table sets forth information with respect to accumulated other comprehensive income (loss):

	Foreign Currency Translation Adjustment	Deferred Gain (Loss) on Hedging Activities	Minimum Pension Liability Adjustment	Unrealized Gain (Loss) on Investments	Accumulated Other Comprehensive Income (Loss)
			(In thousands)		
Balance at June 30, 2003	$(123,001)	$14,174	$(141,463)	$83,332	$(166,958)
Unrealized gains (losses)	97,044	14,292	19,227	250,876	381,439
(Gains) losses reclassified to net earnings		(22,834)		(11,042)	(33,876)
Tax effect		3,379	(9,330)	(91,699)	(97,650)
Net of tax amount .	97,044	(5,163)	9,897	148,135	249,913
Balance at June 30, 2004	(25,957)	9,011	(131,566)	231,467	82,955
Unrealized gains (losses)	8,528	9,677	53,274	33,655	(1,414)
(Gains) losses reclassified to net earnings		(14,292)		(35,889)	(50,181)
Tax effect		1,705	19,685	(16,133)	5,257
Net of tax amount .	8,528	(2,910)	(33,589)	(18,367)	(46,338)
Balance at June 30, 2005	(17,429)	6,101	(165,155)	213,100	36,617

	Foreign Currency Translation Adjustment	Deferred Gain (Loss) on Hedging Activities	Minimum Pension Liability Adjustment	Unrealized Gain (Loss) on Investments	Accumulated Other Comprehensive Income (Loss)
			(In thousands)		
Unrealized gains (losses)	107,356	(43,095)	212,315	(23,868)	253,708
(Gains) losses reclassified to net earnings		(9,677)		(16,653)	(26,330)
Tax effect		21,749	(78,053)	6,680	(49,624)
Net of tax amount .	107,356	(30,023)	134,262	(33,841)	177,754
Balance at June 30, 2006	$89,927	$(23,922)	$(30,893)	$179,259	$214,371

BJ Services
2006 Annual Report

14. Stockholders' Equity

Common Stock

On January 31, 2006, our stockholders approved a charter amendment increasing the authorized number of shares of common stock from 380,000,000 shares to 910,000,000 shares.

Dividends

Our Board of Directors approved a 2 for 1 stock split to be effected in the form of a stock dividend payable on September 1, 2005 to stockholders of record as of August 18, 2005. Common shares and earnings per share amounts have been restated for all prior periods presented to reflect the increased number of common shares outstanding. From its initial public offering in 1990 until 2004, we did not pay any cash dividends to our stockholders. On July 22, 2004, we announced the initiation of a regular quarterly cash dividend. During fiscal 2005, we paid cash dividends in the amount of $.04 per common share on a quarterly basis and $51.9 million in the aggregate annual amount. On July 28, 2005 our Board of Directors approved a 25% increase in the quarterly cash dividend and declared a cash dividend of $.05 per common share. During fiscal 2006, we paid dividends totaling $64.3 million. We anticipate paying cash dividends in the amount of $.05 per common share on a quarterly basis in fiscal 2007. However, dividends are subject to approval of our Board of Directors each quarter, and the Board has the ability to change the dividend policy at any time.

Stockholder Rights Plan

We have a Stockholder Rights Plan (the "Rights Plan") designed to deter coercive takeover tactics and to prevent an acquirer from gaining control of the Company without offering a fair price to all of our stockholders. The Rights Plan was amended September 26, 2002, to extend the expiration date of the Rights to

September 26, 2012 and increase the purchase price of the Rights. Under this plan, as amended, each outstanding share of common stock includes one-eighth of a preferred share purchase right ("Right") that becomes exercisable under certain circumstances, including when beneficial ownership of common stock by any person, or group, equals or exceeds 15% of the Company's outstanding common stock. Each Right entitles the registered holder to purchase from the Company one one-thousandth of a share of Series A Junior Participating Preferred Stock at a price of $520, subject to adjustment under certain circumstances. As a result of stock splits effected in the form of stock dividends in 1998, 2001, and 2005, one Right is associated with eight outstanding shares of common stock. The purchase price for the one-eighth of a Right associated with one share of common stock is effectively $65. Upon the occurrence of certain events specified in the Rights Plan, each holder of a Right (other than an "Acquiring Person," as defined under the Rights Plan) will have the right, upon exercise of such Right, to receive that number of shares of common stock of the Company (or the surviving corporation) that, at the time of such transaction, would have a market price of two times the purchase price of the Right. We have not issued any shares of Series A Junior Participating Preferred Stock.

Treasury Stock

On December 19, 1997, our Board of Directors authorized a stock repurchase program of up to $150 million. Through a series of increases, the stock repurchase program was now authorized to repurchase up to $2.2 billion. Repurchases are made at the discretion of management and the program will remain in effect until terminated by our Board of Directors. We purchased 48,366,000 shares at a cost of $499.0 million through fiscal 2004. During fiscal 2005, we purchased a total of 3,982,000 shares at a cost of $98.4 million. During fiscal 2006, we purchased a total of 31,725,882 shares at a cost of $1,133.3 million. As of September 30, 2006, remaining authority to repurchase Common Stock is $469.3 million. Treasury shares have been utilized for our various stock plans as described in Note 13. A total of 1,509,000 treasury shares were used at a cost of $21.2 million in fiscal 2006, 3,655,000 treasury shares were used at a cost of $45.2 million in fiscal 2005, and 7,126,000 treasury shares were used at a cost of $60.1 million in fiscal 2004.

Subsequent to September 30, 2006, we have purchased 668,889 shares for $20.0 million through November 30, 2006 under our stock repurchase program as discussed in Note 14 of the Notes to the Consolidated Financial Statements. We have authority remaining to purchase up to an additional $449.3 million in stock as of November 30, 2006.

Qlogic
2006 Annual Report

Note 7. Stockholders' Equity

Capital Stock

The Company's authorized capital consists of 1 million shares of preferred stock, par value $0.001 per share, and 500 million shares of common stock, par value

$0.001 per share. The preferred stock, of which no shares have been issued, includes 200,000 shares designated as Series A Junior Participating Preferred Stock (Series A Preferred Stock). As of April 2, 2006 and April 3, 2005, the Company had 195.3 million and 192.8 million shares of common stock issued, respectively. At April 2, 2006, 40.0 million shares of common stock were reserved for the exercise of issued and unissued common stock options and 2.9 million shares were reserved for issuance in connection with the Company's Employee Stock Purchase Plan.

Treasury Stock

In October 2002, the Company's Board of Directors approved a stock repurchase program that authorized the Company to repurchase up to $100 million of the Company's outstanding common stock for a two-year period. In June 2004, the Company's Board of Directors approved a new stock repurchase program that authorized the Company to repurchase up to an additional $100 million of the Company's outstanding common stock for a two-year period. As of July 3, 2005, the Company had repurchased the entire amount authorized pursuant to these programs, including 3.5 million shares for an aggregate purchase price of $55.0 million during the first quarter of fiscal 2006.

In August 2005, the Company's Board of Directors approved a third stock repurchase program that authorized the Company to repurchase up to an additional $350 million of the Company's outstanding common stock for a two-year period. As of January 1, 2006, the Company had completed the repurchase of the entire $350 million authorized pursuant to this program, representing an aggregate of 20.7 million shares of common stock.

In November 2005, the Company's Board of Directors approved a fourth stock repurchase program that authorized the Company to repurchase up to an additional $200 million of the Company's outstanding common stock for a two-year period. During fiscal 2006, the Company repurchased 0.6 million shares of common stock under this program for an aggregate purchase price of $10.0 million.

In May 2006, the Company repurchased an additional 1.1 million shares of common stock for an aggregate purchase price of $20.0 million.

The repurchased shares have been recorded as treasury shares and will be held until the Company's Board of Directors designates that these shares be retired or used for other purposes.

Stockholder Rights Plan

On June 4, 1996, the Board of Directors of the Company unanimously adopted a Stockholder Rights Plan (the Rights Plan) pursuant to which it declared a dividend distribution of preferred stock purchase rights (a Right) upon all of the outstanding shares of the common stock.

The Rights dividend was paid on June 20, 1996 to the holders of record of shares of common stock on that date at the rate of one-sixteenth of one whole Right per one share of common stock, as adjusted pursuant to the Company's stock splits. Each share of common stock presently outstanding that had been issued since June 20, 1996 also includes one-sixteenth Right, and each share of common stock that may be issued after the date hereof and prior to the Distribution Date (as defined below) also will include one-sixteenth Right.

The Rights become exercisable (i) the 10th business day following the date of a public announcement that a person or a group of affiliated or associated persons (an Acquiring Person) has, with certain exceptions, acquired beneficial ownership of 15% or more of the outstanding shares of common stock, or (ii) the 10th business day following the commencement of, or announcement of an intention to make a tender offer or exchange offer the consummation of which would result in the person or group making the offer becoming an Acquiring Person (the earlier of the dates described in clauses (i) and (ii) being called the Distribution Date).

The Rights held by an Acquiring Person or its affiliates are not exercisable. All shares of common stock that will be issued prior to the Distribution Date will include such Rights. The Rights will expire at the close of business on June 4, 2006 (the Scheduled Expiration Date), unless prior thereto the Distribution Date occurs.

Pursuant to the Rights Plan, as amended to date, each Right entitles the registered holder, on and after the Distribution Date and until redemption of all Rights, to purchase from the Company 1/100th of one whole share (a Unit) of the Company's Series A Preferred Stock. The purchase price is $425.00 per Unit. In the event of certain acquisitions involving the Acquiring Person, directly or indirectly, the holder of each Right will be entitled to purchase for $425.00 certain shares or assets of the Company or an Acquiring Person that have a market value of $850.00 at such time.

The Company has 200,000 whole shares of Series A Preferred Stock authorized, of which no shares are issued or outstanding at April 2, 2006. Each Unit would entitle the holder to (A) one vote, voting together with the shares of common stock; (B) in the event the Company's assets are liquidated, a payment of one dollar ($1.00) or an amount equal to the payment to be distributed per share of common stock, whichever is greater; and (C) in the event of any merger, consolidation or other transaction in which shares of common stock are exchanged, a payment in an amount equal to the payment received per share of common stock. The number of Rights per share of common stock is subject to adjustment in the event of stock splits, stock dividends and similar events.

Owens-Illinois
2002 Annual Report

12. Convertible Preferred Stock

Annual cumulative dividends of $2.375 per share are payable in cash quarterly. The convertible preferred stock is convertible at the option of the holder at any time, unless previously redeemed, into shares of common stock of the Company at an initial conversion rate of 0.9491 shares of common stock for each share of convertible preferred stock, subject to adjustment based on certain events. The convertible preferred stock may be redeemed only in shares of common stock of the Company at the option of the Company at predetermined redemption prices plus accrued and unpaid dividends, if any, to the redemption date.

Holders of the convertible preferred stock have no voting rights, except as required by applicable law and except that among other things, whenever accrued and unpaid dividends on the convertible preferred stock are equal to or exceed the equivalent of six quarterly dividends payable on the convertible preferred stock such holders will be entitled to elect two directors to the Company's board of directors until the dividend arrearage has been paid or amounts have been set apart for such payment. In addition, certain changes that would be materially adverse to the rights of holders of the convertible preferred stock cannot be made without the vote of holders of two-thirds of the outstanding convertible preferred stock. The convertible preferred stock is senior to the common stock with respect to dividends and liquidation events.

Ann Taylor
2002 Annual Report

3. Preferred Securities

In April and May of Fiscal 1996, the Company completed the sale of an aggregate of $100,625,000 of 8 1/2% Company-Obligated Mandatorily Redeemable Convertible Preferred Securities (the "preferred securities") issued by its financing vehicle, Ann Taylor Finance Trust, a Delaware business trust (the "Trust"). On June 29, 1999, the Trust redeemed all of the outstanding preferred securities. All but $100,000 of the liquidation amount of the preferred securities was tendered for conversion into an aggregate of 7,675,076 shares of Company common stock prior to the redemption date, at a conversion price of $13.10 per share of common stock, or 3.817 shares of common stock per $50 liquidation amount of the security. Holders of preferred securities that were not tendered for conversion received 105.95% of the liquidation amount of the preferred securities redeemed, plus accrued distributions.

Champion Enterprises
2002 Annual Report

Note 9—Redeemable Convertible Preferred Stock

On April 2, 2002 the Company issued $25 million of Series C cumulative convertible preferred stock and a warrant which was initially exercisable based on approximately 1.1 million shares of common stock at a strike price of $12.04 per share. The net proceeds of this issuance of $23.8 million were used to fund a portion of the cash collateral for the letters of credit discussed above. The preferred stock is carried net of issuance costs which are being amortized over a period of two years from the date of issuance by charges to paid-in-capital. At December 28, 2002 the redemption value of the Series C shares outstanding totaled $25.0 million.

In accordance with the terms of the warrant, on August 6, 2002 the number of shares under warrant and the strike price were reset at 2.2 million shares and

$10.02 per share, respectively. Beginning on April 2, 2003, the warrant strike price will increase annually by $0.75 per share. The warrant expires on April 2, 2009 and is exercisable only on a non-cash, net basis, whereby the warrant holder would receive shares of common stock as payment for the net gain upon exercise.

The Series C preferred stock has a seven-year term and a 5% annual dividend that is payable quarterly, at the Company's option, in cash or common stock. The original terms provided the holder the right to convert all or any part of the preferred stock into Champion common stock at a price of $9.6295 per share until June 29, 2003, at which time the conversion price would be reset to equal 115% of the average market price of Champion common stock as of June 29, 2003, provided that the conversion price could not be less than $5.66 nor more than $10.83. Subsequent to year end, on January 31, 2003, the terms of the Series C preferred stock were amended to accelerate the modification of the conversion price to $5.66 and the preferred shareholder agreed to convert $16.25 million of the Series C cumulative convertible preferred stock by March 12, 2003. Upon conversion, 2.9 million shares of common stock were issued.

In July 2001, the Company issued $20 million of Series B-1 cumulative convertible preferred stock. The proceeds from issuance totaled $18.5 million, net of issuance costs. The rights and preferences of the Company's Series B-1 preferred stock, were amended on March 29, 2002 to provide, among other things, for mandatory redemption on March 29, 2004. Such redemption may be made for either common stock or cash, at the Company's option. Additionally, the commencement date of the holder's optional redemption period for the outstanding Series B-1 preferred stock was changed to April 2, 2002, from July 2003, and the expiration date of the holder's rights to purchase an additional $12 million of Series B-1 preferred stock was extended to December 31, 2004 from March 2003. Optional redemptions may be made only for common stock and are subject to a common stock price of $5.66 per share. During 2002, the holder redeemed $15 million of the Series B-1 cumulative convertible preferred stock for 2.6 million shares of common stock. The Series B-1 preferred stock has a 5% annual dividend, which is payable quarterly in either cash or common stock, at Champion's option. At December 28, 2002 the redemption value of the Series B-1 shares outstanding totaled $5.0 million.

During 2002 and 2001, Champion paid quarterly dividends on the preferred stock by issuing 105,000 and 49,000 shares of the Company's common stock, respectively.

Bowater
2002 Annual Report

Note 20. Exchangeable Shares

In conjunction with the 1998 acquisition of Avenor, Bowater's indirect wholly-owned subsidiary, Bowater Canada Inc. ("BCI"), issued 3,773,547 shares ($183.6 million) of no par value Exchangeable Shares. Since 1998, BCI has issued an additional 1,359,620 Exchangeable Shares ($66.2 million) upon the redemption of Avenor's 7.50% Convertible Unsecured Subordinated Debentures and 5,505 Exchangeable Shares ($0.3 million) for conversions prior to the redemption. BCI issued an additional 856,237 Exchangeable Shares ($39.9 million) in connection with the 2001 acquisition of Alliance. The Exchangeable Shares are exchangeable at any time, at the option of the holder, on a one-for-one basis for shares of Bowater Common Stock. Through December 31, 2002, 4,346,137 Exchangeable Shares ($211.4 million) had been exchanged for the same number of Bowater common shares and 5,524 Exchangeable Shares ($0.3 million) cancelled. Holders of Exchangeable Shares have voting rights substantially equivalent to holders of Bowater Common Stock and are entitled to receive dividends equivalent, on a per-share basis, to dividends paid by Bowater on its Common Stock. On December 31, 2002, 1,643,248 Exchangeable Shares ($78.3 million) were outstanding.

Note 21. Treasury Stock

At December 31, 2002, Bowater held 11,617,494 shares of its Common Stock as treasury stock to pay for employee and director benefits and to fund its Dividend Reinvestment Plan. The shares are valued at their acquisition cost of $486.3 million. As of December 31, 2001, we held 11,619,812 shares at a cost of $486.4 million.

In May 1999, the Board of Directors authorized the repurchase of up to 5.5 million shares of Bowater's Common Stock in the open market, subject to normal trading restrictions. We made no purchases under the program during 2002 or 2001. During 2000, we purchased 2,125,900 shares of Common Stock at a cost of $103.7 million. Since the beginning of the program, we purchased 3.1 million shares at a total cost of $155.5 million.

Eli Lilly
2005 Annual Report

Changes in certain components of shareholders' equity were as follows:

	Additional Paid-in Capital	Retained Earnings	Deferred Costs-ESOP	Common Stock in Treasury	
				Shares (in thousands)	Amount
Balance at January 1, 2003	$2,610.0	$8,500.1	$(123.3)	1,008	$109.5
Net income		2,560.8			
Cash dividends declared per share: $1.36		(1,465.4)			
Retirement of treasury shares	(289.1)			(3,180)	(291.2)
Purchase for treasury				2,976	276.8
Issuance of stock under employee stock plans	150.4			148	9.1
ESOP transactions	13.6		4.7		
Reclassification	125.1	(125.1)			

	Additional Paid-in Capital	Retained Earnings	Deferred Costs-ESOP	Common Stock in Treasury	
				Shares (in thousands)	Amount
Balance at December 31, 2003	2,610.0	9,470.4	(118.6)	952	104.2
Net income		1810.1			
Cash dividends declared per share: $1.45		(1555.9)			
Retirement of treasury shares	(17.4)			(271)	(17.6)
Issuance of stock under employee stock plans	110.7			262	17.2
Stock-based compensation	53.0				
ESOP transactions	13.2		6.7		
Acquisition of AME	349.9				
Balance at December 31, 2004	3,119.4	9,724.6	(111.9)	943	103.8
Net income		1,979.6			
Cash dividends declared per share: $1.54		(1,677.0)			
Retirement of treasury shares	(381.7)			(6,874)	(386.0)
Purchase for treasury				6,704	377.9
Issuance of stock under employee stock plans	172.9			161	8.4
Stock-based compensation	403.5				
ESOP transactions	9.7		5.6		
Balance at December 31, 2005	$3,323.8	$10,027.2	$106.3	934	$104.1

As of December 31, 2005, we have purchased $2.46 billion of our announced $3.0 billion share repurchase program. We acquired approximately 6.7 million and 3.0 million shares in 2005 and 2003 under this program.

We have 5 million authorized shares of preferred stock. As of December 31, 2005 and 2004, no preferred stock has been issued.

We have funded an employee benefit trust with 40 million shares of Lilly common stock to provide a source of funds to assist us in meeting our obligations under various employee benefit plans. The funding had no net impact on shareholders' equity as we consolidated the employee benefit trust. The cost basis of the shares held in the trust was $2.64 billion and is shown as a reduction in shareholders' equity, which offsets the resulting increases of $2.61 billion in additional paid-in capital and $25 million in common stock. Any dividend transactions between us and the trust are eliminated. Stock held by the trust is not considered outstanding in the computation of earnings per share. The assets of the trust were not used to fund any of our obligations under these employee benefit plans in 2005, 2004, or 2003.

We have an ESOP as a funding vehicle for the existing employee savings plan. The ESOP used the proceeds of a loan from us to purchase shares of common stock from the treasury. The ESOP issued $200 million of third-party debt, repayment of which was guaranteed by us (see Note 6). The proceeds were used to purchase shares of our common stock on the open market. Shares of common stock held by the ESOP will be allocated to participating employees annually through 2017 as part of our savings plan contribution. The fair value of shares allocated each period is recognized as compensation expense.

Under a Shareholder Rights Plan adopted in 1998, all shareholders receive, along with each common share owned, a preferred stock purchase right entitling them to purchase from the company one one-thousandth of a share of Series B Junior Participating Preferred Stock (the Preferred Stock) at a price of $325. The rights are exercisable only after the Distribution Date, which is generally the 10th business day after the date of a public announcement that a person (the Acquiring Person) has acquired ownership of 15 percent or more of our common stock. We may redeem the rights for $.005 per right, up to and including the Distribution Date. The rights will expire on July 28, 2008, unless we redeem them earlier.

The rights plan provides that, if an Acquiring Person acquires 15 percent or more of our outstanding common stock and our redemption right has expired, generally each holder of a right (other than the Acquiring Person) will have the right to purchase at the exercise price the number of shares of our common stock that have a value of two times the exercise price.

Alternatively, if, in a transaction not approved by the board of directors, we are acquired in a business combination transaction or sell 50 percent or more of our assets or earning power after a Distribution Date, generally each holder of a right (other than the Acquiring Person) will have the right to purchase at the exercise price the number of shares of common stock of the acquiring company that have a value of two times the exercise price.

At any time after an Acquiring Person has acquired 15 percent or more but less than 50 percent of our outstanding common stock, the board of directors may exchange the rights (other than those owned by the Acquiring Person) for our common stock or Preferred Stock at an exchange ratio of one common share (or one one-thousandth of a share of Preferred Stock) per right.

Cisco Systems
2005 Annual Report

9. Shareholders' Equity

Stock Repurchase Program

In September 2001, the Company's Board of Directors authorized a stock repurchase program. As of July 30, 2005, the Company's Board of Directors had authorized the repurchase of up to $35 billion of common stock under this program. During fiscal 2005, the Company repurchased and retired 540 million shares of Cisco common stock at an average price of $18.95 per share for an aggregate purchase price of $10.2 billion. As of July 30, 2005, the Company had repurchased and retired 1.5 billion shares of Cisco common stock for an average price of $18.15 per share for an aggregate purchase price of $27.2 billion since inception of the stock repurchase program, and the remaining authorized amount for stock repurchases under this program was $7.8 billion with no termination date.

The purchase price for the shares of the Company's common stock repurchased was reflected as a reduction to shareholders' equity. In accordance with Accounting Principles Board Opinion No. 6, "Status of Accounting Research Bulletins," the Company is required to allocate the purchase price of the repurchased shares as a reduction to retained earnings and common stock and additional paid-in capital.

Shareholders' Rights Plan

In June 1998, the Board of Directors approved a Shareholders' Rights Plan ("Rights Plan") which was intended to protect shareholders' rights in the event of an unsolicited takeover attempt. On March 24, 2005, the Board of Directors approved an amendment to the Company's Rights Agreement to advance the Final Expiration Date of the Rights under the Rights Plan pursuant to the Rights Agreement from the close of business on June 19, 2008 to March 28, 2005, effectively terminating the Rights Plan as of the close of business on March 28, 2005.

Preferred Stock

Under the terms of the Company's Articles of Incorporation, the Board of Directors may determine the rights, preferences, and terms of the Company's authorized but unissued shares of preferred stock.

Comprehensive Income

The components of comprehensive income are as follows (in millions):

Years Ended	July 30, 2005	July 31, 2004	July 26, 2003
Net income	$5,741	$4,401	$3,578
Other comprehensive income:			
Changes in unrealized gains and losses on investments, net of tax benefit (expense) of $(61), $42, and $(150) in fiscal 2005, 2004, and 2003, respectively	(25)	(77)	352
Other	10	19	29
Other comprehensive income before minority interest	$5,726	4,343	3,959

Years Ended	*July 30, 2005*	*July 31, 2004*	*July 26, 2003*
Change in minority interest	**77**	(84)	–
Total	**$5,803**	$4,259	$3,959

The Company consolidates its investment in a venture fund managed by SOFTBANK as it is the primary beneficiary as defined under FIN 46(R). During fiscal 2005, SOFTBANK's aggregate minority share of the venture fund decreased by $77 million, from $84 million as of July 31, 2004 to $7 million as of July 30, 2005, as a result of a noncash distribution of the venture fund assets to its partners.

Oracle
2005 Annual Report

Stockholders' Equity

Stock Repurchases

Our Board of Directors has approved a program to repurchase shares of our common stock to reduce the dilutive effect of our stock option and stock purchase plans. From the inception of the stock repurchase program in 1992 to May 31, 2005, a total of 1.8 billion shares have been repurchased for approximately $20.4 billion. We repurchased 114.8 million shares for $1.3 billion, 117.8 million shares for $1.5 billion and 270.4 million shares for $2.7 billion in fiscal 2005, 2004 and 2003, respectively. At May 31, 2005, approximately $1.9 billion was available to repurchase shares of our common stock pursuant to the stock repurchase program.

Shareholder Rights Plan

On December 3, 1990, the Board of Directors adopted a Shareholder Rights Plan. The Shareholder Rights Plan was amended and restated on March 31, 199 and subsequently amended on March 22, 1999. Pursuant to the Shareholder Rights Plan, we distributed Preferred Stock Purchase Rights as a dividend at the rate of one Right for each share of our common stock held by stockholders of record as of December 31, 1990. The Board of Directors also authorized the issuance of Rights for each share of common stock issued after the record date, until the occurrence of certain specified events. The Shareholder Rights Plan was adopted to provide protection to stockholders in the event of an unsolicited attempt to acquire us. As a result of stock splits, each share of common stock now has associated with it one-sixth of a Right.

The Rights are not exercisable until the earlier of: (1) then days (or such later date as may be determined by the Board of Directors) following an announcement that a person or group has acquired beneficial ownership of 15% of our common stock or (2) ten days (or such later date as my be determined by the Board of Directors) following the announcement of a tender offer which would result in a person or group obtaining beneficial ownership of 15% or more of our outstanding common stock, subject to certain exceptions (the earlier of such dates being called the Distribution Date). The Rights are initially exercisable for one-six thousand seven hundred fiftieth of a share of our Series. A Junior Participating Preferred Stock at a price of $125 per one-six thousand seven hundred fiftieth of a share, subject to adjustment. However, if: (1) after the Distribution Date we are acquired in certain types of transactions, or (2) any person or group (with limited exceptions) acquires beneficial ownership of 15% of our common stock, then holders of Rights (other than the 15% holder) will be entitled to receive upon exercise of the Right, common stock (or in case we are completely acquired, common stock of the acquirer) having a market value of two times the exercise price of the Right.

We are entitled to redeem the Rights, for $0.00148 per Right, at the discretion of the Board of Directors, until certain specified times. We may also require the exchange of Rights, at a rate of one and one-half shares of common stock, for each Right, under certain circumstances. We also have the ability to amend the Rights subject to certain limitations.

Accumulated Other Comprehensive Income

The following table summarizes the components of accumulated other comprehensive income, net of income taxes:

		May 31,	
(in millions)	*2005*	*2004*	*2003*
Foreign currency translation adjustment	$301	$190	$115
Unrealized loss on derivatives	(51)	(37)	(14)
Unrealized gain on investments	9	3	26
Minimum benefit plan liability adjustment	(16)	–	–
Accumulated other comprehensive income .	$243	$156	$127

Settlement of Forward Contract

In fiscal 1998, we entered into a forward contract to sell 36.0 million shares of our common stock at $4.42 per share plus accretion, subject to adjustments over time. The forward contract had a stated maturity of February 13, 2003 and was accounted for as an equity instrument. The forward contract collateralized our master lease facility that provided for the construction or purchase of up to $182.0 million of property and improvements to be leased by us. In fiscal 2003, we settled the forward contract with a cash payment of $166.3 million, which was recorded as a reduction to additional paid in capital, and exercised as option to purchase the leased properties for approximately $168.3 million.

Saks
2005 Annual Report

Note 11—Shareholders' Equity

On March 15, 2004, the Company's Board of Directors declared a special one-time cash dividend of $2.00 per common share to shareholders of record as of April 30, 2004. The Company reduced Retained Earnings and Additional Paid-in Capital for the $285,551 dividend, and $283,126 was paid out on or after May 17,

2004. The remaining portion of the dividend will be paid prospectively as restricted shares vest.

As a result of the special one-time dividend, the Human Resources Committee of the Company's Board of Directors exercised its discretion under anti-dilution provisions of the employee stock plans to adjust the exercise price of stock options and number of shares subject to outstanding stock options to reflect the change in the share price on the ex-dividend date (April 28, 2004). The effect of this anti-dilution adjustment is presented below:

	As of ex-dividend date		As of January 31, 2004
	Prior to Adjustment	After Adjustment	
Options outstanding	19,313	21,645	20,503
Options exercisable	14,381	16,117	14,738
Weighted average exercise price:			
Options outstanding	$15.80	$14.10	$15.66
Options exercisable	$17.23	$15.39	$17.12

On April 8, 2003, the Company announced that its Board of Directors had authorized a 25,000 share increase in the Company's share repurchase program, bringing the total number of authorized shares to 35,000. During 2004, 2003, and 2002, the Company repurchased 62,03, 79,04 and 700 shares under the programs for an aggregate amount of $78,818, $74,543, and $7,111, respectively. There were 15,689 shares available for repurchase activity were 4,750 shares subject to a price settlement agreement containing a cap and a floor. The Company settled the maturity of this agreement in June 2004 for $6,579, which served to reduce Shareholders' Equity.

Each outstanding share of common stock has one preferred stock purchase right attached. The rights generally become exercisable ten days after an outside party acquires, or makes an offer for, 20% or more of the common stock. Each right entitles its holders to buy 1/200 share of Series C Junior Preferred Stock at an exercise price of $278 per 1/100 of a share, subject to adjustment in certain cases. The rights expire in March 2008. Once exercisable, if the Company is involved in a merger or other business combination or an outside party acquires 20% or more of the common stock, each right will be modified to entitle its holder (other than the acquirer) to purchase common stock of the acquiring company or, in certain circumstances, common stock having a market value of twice the exercise price of the right.

National Semiconductor
2005 Annual Report

Shareholders' Equity

Stocksplit

On May 13, 2004, we completed a two-for-one stock split of our common stock. The stock split was payable in the form of a 100 percent stock dividend and entitled each shareholder of record on April 29, 2004, to receive one share of common stock for each outstanding share of common stock held on that date. All information about capital stock accounts, share and per share amounts included in the accompanying consolidated financial statements for fiscal 2004 and 2003 have been retroactively adjusted to reflect this stock split.

Stock Purchase Rights

Each outstanding share of common stock carries with it a stock purchase right. If and when the rights become exercisable, each right entitles the registered holder to purchase one two-thousandth of a share of series A junior participating preferred stock at a price of $60.00 per one one-thousandth share, subject to adjustment. The rights are attached to all outstanding shares of common stock and no separate rights certificates have been distributed. If any individual or group acquires 20 percent or more of our common stock or announces a tender or exchange offer which, if completed, would result in that person or group owning at least 20 percent of our common stock, the rights become exercisable and will detach from the common stock. If the person or group actually acquires 20 percent or more of the common stock (except in certain cash tender offers for all of the common stock), each right will entitle the holder to purchase, at the right's then-current exercise price, our common stock in an amount having a market value equal to twice the exercise price. In addition, if, after the rights become exercisable, we merge or consolidate with or sell 50 percent or more of our assets or earning power to another person or entity, each right will then entitle the holder to purchase, at the right's then-current exercise price, the stock of the acquiring company in an amount having a market value equal to twice the exercise price. We may redeem the rights at $0.005 per right at any time prior to the acquisition by a person or group of 20 percent or more of the outstanding common stock. Unless they are redeemed earlier, the rights will expire on August 8, 2006.

Stock Repurchase Program

We began to repurchase stock in fiscal 2004 pursuant to a stock repurchase program announced in July 2003. During September and October 2003, we repurchased a total of 25.4 million shares of our common stock for $400 million. A portion (15.0 million shares) of the shares was repurchased through a privately negotiated transaction with a major financial institution and the remainder was purchased in the open market. We began another $400 million stock repurchase program in March 2004 and at the end of fiscal 2004, we had repurchased an additional 7.0 million shares of our common stock for $142.5 million, of which 730,988 shares were purchased through a privately negotiated transaction with a major financial institution, with the remainder purchased in the open market. We continued this repurchase program in fiscal 2005. At the time we completed this repurchase program in March 2005, we had repurchased a total of 15.4 million shares of our common stock in fiscal 2005 for $257.5 million. Of these shares, 1.5 million shares were repurchased for $30.0 million in June 2004 upon the final settlement of an advance purchase contract originally entered into with a financial institution in April 2004. Under the terms of the advance purchase contract, we made an advance cash payment of $60.0 million in May 2004 that enabled us to repurchase shares of our common stock at a fixed price on specified settlement dates. The advance payment was recorded as a note receivable and a credit to additional paid-in capital. The remaining 13.9 million shares of common stock were repurchased in the open market for $227.5 million during the second, third and fourth quarters of fiscal 2005.

In March 2005, we announced that our Board of Directors had approved another $400 million stock repurchase program similar to our prior stock repurchase programs. As of May 29, 2005, we had repurchased a total of 4.9 million shares of common stock for $96.0 million under this new repurchase program. Of these shares, 1.2 million were purchased for $25.0 million through an advance purchase contract with a major financial institution with terms similar to the prior advance purchase contract. As of May 29, 2005, we had $304.0 million remaining available for future common stock repurchases. All stock repurchased has been cancelled and is not held as treasury stock.

Dividends

During fiscal 2005, we paid $14.1 million in dividends. In June 2005, the Board of Directors declared a cash dividend of $0.02 per outstanding share of common stock, which was paid on July 11, 2005 to shareholders of record at the close of business on June 20, 2005.

Varian
2005 Annual Report

Note 14. Stockholders' Equity and Stock Plans

On April 2, 1999, stockholders of record of VAI on March 24, 1999 received in the Distribution (described in Note 1) one share of the Company's common stock for each share of VAI common stock held on April 2, 1999. Each stockholder also received one preferred stock purchase right ("Right") for each share of common stock distributed, entitling the stockholder to purchase one one-thousandth of a share of Participating Preferred Stock, par value $0.01 per share, for $200.00 (subject to adjustment), in the event of certain changes in the Company's ownership. The Participating Preferred Stock is designed so that each one one-thousandth of a share has economic and voting terms similar to those of one share of common stock. The Rights will expire no later than March 2009. As of September 30, 2005, no Rights were eligible to be exercised and none had been exercised through that date.

Omnibus Stock Plan

Effective April 2, 1999, the Company adopted the Stock Plan under which shares of common stock can be issued to officers, directors, consultants and key employees. The maximum number of shares of the Company's common stock available for awards under the Stock Plan was initially 4,200,000 plus 4,512,000 shares granted in substitution for other options in connection with the Distribution (described in Note 1). During fiscal year 2002, the Company's stockholders approved an amendment of the Stock Plan to increase the number of shares of common stock reserved for issuance under the Stock Plan by 1,000,000. During fiscal year 2005, the Company's stockholders approved an amendment of the

Stock Plan to increase the number of shares of common stock reserved for issuance under the Stock Plan by an additional 5,000,000.

The Stock Plan is administered by the Compensation Committee of the Company's Board of Directors. The exercise price for stock options granted under the Stock Plan may not be less than 100% of the fair market value at the date of the grant. Options granted are exercisable at the times and on the terms established by the Compensation Committee, but not later than ten years after the date of grant. Options granted generally become exercisable in cumulative installments of one-third each year commencing one year following the date of grant.

At September 30, 2005, options with respect to 5,354,000 shares were available for grant under the Stock Plan.

	Fiscal Year Ended					
	September 30, 2005		October 1, 2004		October 3, 2003	
	Shares	Weighted-Average Exercise Price	Shares	Weighted-Average Exercise Price	Shares	Weighted-Average Exercise Price
(shares in thousands)	3,640	$25.54	4,429	$20.65	4,358	$18.64
Outstanding at beginning of fiscal year	512	$36.66	567	$38.76	520	$31.36
Granted	(806)	$18.01	(1,310)	$14.46	(422)	$12.70
Exercised	(100)	$37.21	(46)	$33.10	(27)	$27.18
Cancelled or expired .	3,246	$28.80	3,640	$25.54	4,429	$20.65
Shares exercisable at end of fiscal year . .	2,381	$26.00	2,730	$22.48	3,334	$17.57

Outstanding and Exercisable Options at September 30, 2005					
	Options Outstanding			Options Exercisable	
Range of Exercise Prices	Shares	Weighted-Average Remaining Contractual Life	Weighted-Average Exercise Price	Shares	Weighted-Average Exercise Price
	(in thousands)	(in years)		(in thousands)	
$8.25–$12.69 . .	448	3.2	$9.73	448	$9.73
$12.69–$27.57 .	848	4.9	$23.12	841	$23.08
$27.57–$35.50 .	908	6.2	$32.95	805	$33.13
$35.50–$54.94 .	1,042	7.2	$38.01	287	$39.91
Total	3,246	5.8	$28.80	2,381	$26.00

In November 2004, the Company granted 24,850 shares of restricted (nonvested) common stock to its executive officers under the Stock Plan. These shares, which were issued upon grant, remain restricted for three years from the grant date and will vest only if the employee is still actively employed by the Company on the vesting date. An aggregate of approximately $0.9 million, representing the fair market value of the restricted shares on the date of the grant, was recorded as deferred compensation (included as a component of stockholders' equity) and is being recognized by the Company as stock-based compensation expense ratably over the three-year vesting period. During fiscal year 2005, the Company recognized approximately $0.2 million in stock-based compensation expense relating to these restricted stock grants.

Under the terms of the Stock Plan, on the first business day following each annual meeting of the Company's stockholders, each person then serving as a non-employee director is automatically granted stock units having an initial value of $25,000, which vest upon the director's termination of service as a director and are paid out as soon as possible thereafter in shares of the Company's common stock. The non-employee director will not have rights as a stockholder with respect to the stock units until such shares are paid out. The stock units are not transferable, except to the non-employee director's designated beneficiary or estate in the event of his or her death. During fiscal year 2005, the Company granted stock units with an aggregate value of $0.2 million to non-employee members of its Board of Directors (of which there were six) and recognized the total value of $0.2 million as stock-based compensation expense at the time of grant.

Employee Stock Purchase Plan

During fiscal year 2000, the Company's Board of Directors approved the ESPP for which the Company set aside 1,200,000 shares of common stock for issuance. In February 2003, the Company's stockholders approved the ESPP.

Under the ESPP, eligible Company employees may set aside, through payroll deductions, between 1% and 10% of eligible compensation for purchases of the Company's common stock. The participants' purchase price is the lower of 85% of the stock's market value on the enrollment date or 85% of the stock's market value on the purchase date. Enrollment dates occur every six months and purchase dates occur each quarter.

During fiscal years 2005, 2004 and 2003 employees purchased approximately 118,700 shares for $3.9 million, 136,600 shares for $3.9 million and 161,000 shares for $3.8 million, respectively. As of September 30, 2005, a total of approximately 478,000 shares remained available for issuance under the ESPP.

Stock Repurchase Programs

In February 2005, the Company's Board of Directors approved a stock repurchase program under which the Company was authorized to repurchase up to $145 million of its common stock. This authorization was conditioned upon the closing of the sale of the Electronics Manufacturing Business, and upon becoming effective replaced the prior repurchase authorization approved in May 2004. The sale of the Electronics Manufacturing business closed on March 11, 2005, and the repurchase authorization became effective on that date and replaced the previous (May 2004) repurchase authorization. During fiscal year 2005, the

Company repurchased and retired approximately 4.0 million shares for an aggregate cost of approximately $145 million. As of September 30, 2005, the Company had fully utilized its authorization under this program.

In May 2004, the Company's Board of Directors authorized the Company to repurchase up to 1,000,000 shares of its common stock until September 30, 2007. During fiscal year 2005, the Company repurchased and retired approximately 802,000 shares at an aggregate cost of $33.6 million. During fiscal year 2004, the Company repurchased and retired approximately 192,000 shares for an aggregate cost of approximately $7.5 million. As described in the preceding paragraph, this repurchase authorization was replaced upon the closing of the sale of the Electronics Manufacturing Business on March 11, 2005, and the remaining approximately 6,000 shares under this authorization were no longer available for repurchase.

In November 2002, the Company's Board of Directors authorized the Company to repurchase up to 1,000,000 shares of its common stock until October 1, 2004. During fiscal years 2004, 2003 and 2002, the Company repurchased and retired 597,000 shares for an aggregate cost of $24.2 million, 353,000 shares for an aggregate cost of $10.4 million and 50,000 shares for an aggregate cost of $1.6 million, respectively.

Shaw Group
2005 Annual Report

Common Stock

We have one class of common stock. Each outstanding share of common stock which has been held for four consecutive years without an intervening change in beneficial ownership entitles its holder to five votes on each matter properly submitted to our shareholders for their vote, waiver, release or other action. Each outstanding share of common stock that has been held for less than four consecutive years entitles its holder to only one vote.

On July 31, 2001, we distributed a dividend of one Preferred Share Purchase Right, or Right, for each share of our common stock outstanding on that date. The Rights, which expire on July 9, 2011, are designed to deter coercive or unfair takeover tactics, and are, therefore, intended to enable all of our shareholders to realize the long-term value of their investment. We anticipate that the Rights will encourage anyone seeking to acquire our company to negotiate with the Board of Directors prior to attempting a takeover. The Rights, which are governed by a Rights Agreement dated July 9, 2001 between us and Wachovia Corporation, as Rights Agent, should not interfere with a merger or other business combination approved by our Board of Directors.

The Rights are attached to our common stock and are exercisable only if a person or group (an "Acquiring Person") either (i) acquires 15% or more of our common stock or (ii) commences a tender offer, the which would result in the acquisition of 15% or more of the common stock. The Board of Directors is authorized to reduce the 15% threshold to not less than 10% of the common stock.

In the event the Rights become exercisable, each Right will entitle shareholders (other than the Acquiring Person) to buy one one-hundredth of a share of a new series of junior participating preferred stock ("Preferred Shares") at an exercise price of $170.00, or which is subject to certain anti-dilution adjustments. Each one one-hundredth of a Preferred Share will give the stockholder approximately the same dividend, voting and liquidation rights as would one share of common stock.

Prior to the acquisition of 15% or more of our common stock, the Rights are redeemable for $0.01 per Right at the option of the Board of Directors.

In lieu of Preferred Shares, each Right holder (other than the Acquiring Person) will be entitled to purchase from us at the Right's then-current Exercise Price, shares of our common stock having a market value of twice such Exercise Price. In addition, if we are acquired in a merger or other business combination transaction after a person has acquired 15% or more of our outstanding common stock, each Right will entitle its holder to purchase at the Right's then-current Exercise Price, a number of the acquiring company's common shares having a market value of twice such Exercise Price, in lieu of acquiring Preferred Shares.

Georgia Pacific
2002 Annual Report

Note 13. Common and Preferred Stock

The Corporation's authorized capital stock consists of (i) 10 million shares of Preferred Stock and 25 million shares of Junior Preferred Stock, of which no shares were issued at December 28, 2002 and December 29, 2001, and (ii) 400 million shares of Georgia-Pacific common stock of which 250,238,000 shares and 230,095,000 shares were issued at December 28, 2002 and December 29, 2001, respectively. In addition, the Corporation's authorized capital stock consists of 250 million shares of The Timber Company Common Stock. As a result of the merger of The Timber Company with Plum Creek Timber Company in 2001, the Corporation redeemed all of the outstanding shares of common stock of The Timber Company. Accordingly, no shares of The Timber Company Common Stock were issued at December 28, 2002 and December 29, 2001.

At December 28, 2002, the following authorized shares of common stock were reserved for issue:

2002 Outside Director Stock Option Plan	250,000
2000 Fort James conversions	6,636,409
2000 Employee Stock Purchase Plan	5,792,666
1999 Unisource conversions	259,061
1999 Wisconsin Tissue conversions	22,344
1997 Long-Term Incentive Plan	15,177,129
1995 Outside Directors Stock Plan	262,403
1995 Shareholder Value Incentive Plan	4,331,503
Common stock reserved	32,731,515

2002 Outside Director Stock Option Plan

The Corporation reserved 250,000 shares of Georgia-Pacific common stock for issuance under the 2002 Outside Director Stock Option Plan. This Plan provides for the issuance of non-qualified stock options to nonemployee directors of the Corporation. On February 1, 2002, each nonemployee director was granted 4,000 stock options at an exercise price of $24.80 per share. These option grants vest ratably over a three-year period and will expire and cease to be exercisable ten years after the date of grant.

1997 Long-Term Incentive Plan

The Corporation reserved 16,000,000 shares of Georgia-Pacific Group stock for issurance under the 1997 Long-Term Incentive Plan (the "Georgia-Pacific Group Plan"). The Georgia-Pacific Group Plan authorizes grants of stock options, restricted stock and performance awards.

Options granted under the plan have a 10-year term and vest ratably over a three-year period.

Performance rights granted under the Plan provide for the issuance of common stock upon achievement of a relative total shareholder return ("TSR"), as defined, during a three-year performance period. The performance rights provide for issuance of up to 200% of a specified target number of shares, depending upon the achieved TSR. Shares issued pursuant to the award have vesting requirements following the performance period of up to five years. At the time performance shares are awarded, the average of the high and low market value of the stock is added to common stock and additional paid-in capital and is deducted from shareholders' equity (longterm incentive plan deferred compensation). The long-term incentive plan deferred compensation of $3.8 million, $1.1 million and $0.5 million at the aforementioned respective award dates is being amortized over the vesting (restriction) period.

Performance shares of 92,000, 37,536, and 20,124 were granted in 2000, 2001 and 2002, respectively. The Corporation granted performance rights with a target of 157,000 shares, 591,000 shares and 837,350 shares in 2000, 2001 and 2002, respectively. No amounts have been reflected as compensation expense related to these grants because, based on current conditions, achievement of performance criteria is not considered probable.

Employee Stock Purchase Plan

The Corporation reserved 9,000,000 shares of Georgia-Pacific Group stock under the 2000 Employee Stock Purchase Plan (the "2000 Purchase Plan"), which offers employees the right to subscribe for shares of the Georgia-Pacific Group at a subscription price equal to 90% of the lower of the average price per share on the first day or the last day of the purchase period. The purchase period for the initial one-year period began on July 1, 2000 and ended on June 30, 2001. The Corporation issued 1,511,298 shares of Georgia-Pacific Group stock at a purchase price of $24.10 for the initial one-year period. The 2000 Purchase Plan was extended, and the next purchase period began on July 1, 2001 and ended on June 30, 2002. The Corporation issued 1,696,036 shares of Georgia-Pacific Group stock at a purchase price of $22.11 per share. The Purchase Plan was extended, and the next purchase period began on December 12, 2002 and ends on December 11, 2003. An employee may terminate his or her subscription at any time before he or she pays the full price of the shares subscribed and will receive in cash the full amount withheld, without interest.

1995 Outside Directors Stock Plan

The Corporation reserved 400,000 shares of Georgia-Pacific Group stock for issurance under the 1995 Outside Directors Stock Plan (the "Directors Plan"), which provides for the issuance of shares of common stock to nonemployee directors of the Corporation on a restricted basis. Each nonemployee director was issued 1,304 restricted shares, 625 restricted shares and 647 restricted shares of Georgia-Pacific Group stock in 2002, 2001 and 2000, respectively.

In 2001, as a result of The Timber Company spin-off and merger with Plum Creek, 33,212 restricted shares of The Timber Company were exchanged or canceled and 40,183 restricted shares of Georgia-Pacific were issued.

Effective May 6, 1997, accrual of additional retirement benefits under the Corporation's retirement program for directors ceased, and the accrued benefits of each of the current nonemployee directors (the present value of which totaled $1,303,889 as of May 6, 1997) were converted into a grant of an equivalent number of shares of restricted stock under the Directors Plan. The total number of shares issued related to this conversion was 15,702.

Employee Stock Option Plans

The 1995 Shareholder Value Incentive Plan (the "SVIP") provides for the granting of stock options having a term of either $5^1/_2$ or 10 years to officers and key employees. Under the amended and restated SVIP, no further grants may be made under the plan. Options having a term of 10 years become exercisable in $9^1/_2$ years unless certain performance targets tied to the Corporation's common stock performance are met, in which case the holder could exercise such options after 3, 4 or 5 years from the grant date. Options having a term of $5^1/_2$ years may be exercised only if such performance targets are met in the third, fourth or fifth year after such grant date. At the time options are exercised, the exercise price is payable in cash or by surrender of shares of common stock already owned by the optionee. All shares were vested as of February 2000.

Unisource Conversions

In connection with the acquisition of Unisource, the Corporation converted certain stock options awarded under a former Unisource stock option plan ("Unisource stock options") into Georgia-Pacific Group stock options. The conversion was intended to ensure that the aggregate intrinsic value of the Unisource stock options was preserved and the ratio of the exercise price per Unisource stock option to the market value per share of Georgia-Pacific Group stock was not reduced. Unisource stock options to purchase 2,633,459 shares had original grant dates ranging from November 10, 1994 through May 19, 1999 with a 10-year term, and vest ratably over three-year and five-year periods. These Unisource stock options were converted into options to purchase 629,648 shares of Georgia-Pacific Group stock at prices ranging from $31.88 to $91.58 per share. The vesting provisions and option periods of the original grants remained the same following such conversion. The value of these options at the acquisition date was $9.4 million and was included as part of the purchase price paid for Unisource.

Wisconsin Tissue Conversions

In connection with the formation of Georgia-Pacific Tissue, the Corporation converted certain outstanding stock options awarded under a Chesapeake stock option plan ("Chesapeake stock options") into Georgia-Pacific Group stock options. The conversion was intended to ensure that the aggregate intrinsic value of the Chesapeake stock options was preserved and the ratio of the exercise price per Chesapeake stock option to the market value per share of Georgia-Pacific Group stock was not reduced. Chesapeake stock options to purchase 172,250 shares had original grant dates ranging from August 11, 1997 through April 16, 1999, with a vesting period of three years and a 10-year term.

These Chesapeake stock options were converted into options to purchase 92,960 shares of Georgia-Pacific Group stock at prices ranging from $36.20 to $50.36 per share. The vesting provisions and option periods of the original grants remained the same following such conversion. The stock options' total value of $1.3 million was included in the asset purchase price on the date the Corporation formed Georgia-Pacific Tissue.

Fort James Conversions

In connection with the acquisition of Fort James as described in Note 3, the Corporation converted certain stock options awarded under a former Fort James stock option plan ("Fort James stock options") into Georgia-Pacific Group stock options. The conversion was intended to ensure that the aggregate intrinsic value of the Fort James stock options was preserved and the ratio of the exercise price per Fort James stock option to the market value per share of Georgia-Pacific Group stock was not reduced. Fort James stock options to purchase 7,399,316 shares had original grant dates ranging from February 11, 1991 through August 15, 2000 with a 10-year term. These Fort James Stock options were converted into options to purchase 10,348,501 shares of Georgia-Pacific Group stock at prices ranging from $9.59 to $36.76 per share. The options became fully vested as of the acquisition date with the same option period of the original grants. The value of these options at the acquisition date was $120 million and was included as part of the purchase price paid for Fort James.

The Corporation also converted 15,000 Fort James stock appreciation rights to receive cash into 20,981 Georgia-Pacific Rights with prices of $17.61 and $28.06. The rights became fully vested as of the acquisition date and maintained their original option dates of February 11, 2000 and January 6, 1999 with a 10 year term. The related compensation expense is being recorded based on changes in the quoted market price of the underlying stock until the rights are exercised or expire.

Long-Term Appreciation Plan

The Long-Term Appreciation Plan (the "LTAP") provides for the granting of stock appreciation rights ("SARs") to key employees of the Corporation. Benefits paid under this plan will be made in cash, not common stock. The Corporation issued 2.37 and 2.35 million SARs under the LTAP in 2002 and 2001 with an exercise price of $24.44 and $29.47, respectively. The SAR exercise price was based on the underlying fair value of Georgia-Pacific Group common stock at the grant date. The SARs vest over three years. Compensation expense for the SARs is based on the difference between the current fair market value of Georgia-Pacific Group common stock and the fair market value at the date of grant. Compensation expense recorded in 2002 and 2001 related to these SARs was deminimus.

Additional information relating to the Corporation's existing employee stock options is as follows:

| | Year Ended December 28, 2002 | |
	Shares	Weighted Average Exercise Price
Options outstanding at December 29, 2001	20,151,717	$29.05
Options granted/converted	3,097,617	24.54
Options exercised/surrendered	(200,788)	21.32
Options canceled	(842,651)	37.68
Options outstanding at December 28, 2002	22,205,895†	28.41
Options available for grant at December 28, 2002	4,354,903	
Total reserved shares	26,560,798	
Options exercisable at December 28, 2002	17,493,917	28.54
Option prices per share:		
Granted/converted	$24–$27	
Exercised/surrendered	$9–$29	
Canceled	$10–$92	

† Options outstanding by exercise price:

| | Outstanding | | | Exercisable | |
	Number of Options	Remaining Life (in years)	Average Exercise Price	Number of Options	Average Exercise Price
$9.59–$14.20	133,240	1.2	$10.60	133,240	$10.60
$14.43–$20.11	1,443,728	2.8	$17.48	1,443,728	$17.48
$22.03–$32.17	18,416,978	4.8	$27.66	14,306,719	$28.15
$35.99–$50.36	2,075,671	5.0	$41.37	1,473,952	$41.32
$59.44–$91.58	136,278	3.7	$66.17	136,278	$66.17

	Year Ended December 29,				
	2001			2001	
	Georgia-Pacific Group			The Timber Company	
	Shares	Weighted Average Exercise Price		Shares	Weighted Average Exercise Price
Options outstanding at December 31, 2000	22,522,345	$28.53		4,909,699	$22.46
Options granted/ converted	2,027,800	29.47		(2,806,737)	22.71
Options exercised/ surrendered	(3,503,152)	23.71		(2,086,679)	22.13
Options canceled	(895,276)	40.84		(16,283)	21.85
Options outstanding at December 29, 2001	20,151,717[†]	29.05		–	–
Options available for grant at December 29, 2001	6,885,449			–	
Total reserved shares	27,037,166				
Options exercisable at December 29, 2001	18,449,373	24.71			
Option prices per share:					
Granted/converted		$29			$21–$25
Exercised/surrendered		$9–$33			$21–$25
Canceled		$9–$92			$21–$25

	Year Ended December 29,				
	2000			2000	
	Georgia-Pacific Group			The Timber Company	
	Shares	Weighted Average Exercise Price		Shares	Weighted Average Exercise Price
Options outstanding at January 1, 2000	10,788,269	$29.97		4,967,650	$22.33
Options granted/ converted	12,740,475	27.39		624,250	22.50
Options exercised/ surrendered	(561,407)	22.15		(659,601)	21.56
Options canceled	(444,992)	39.70		(22,600)	22.17
Options outstanding at December 30, 2000	22,522,345	28.53		4,909,699	22.46
Options available for grant at December 30, 2000	7,738,885			2,164,200	

	Year Ended December 29,				
	2000			2000	
	Georgia-Pacific Group			The Timber Company	
	Shares	Weighted Average Exercise Price		Shares	Weighted Average Exercise Price
Total reserved shares	30,261,230			7,073,899	
Options exercisable at December 29, 2000	17,650,283	26.35		4,052,772	22.30
Option prices per share:					
Granted/converted	$9–$42			$23	
Exercised/surrendered	$9–$50			$21–$25	
Canceled	$26–$92			$21–$25	

Shareholder Rights Plan

On December 16, 1997, shareholders approved an amended and restated Share-holder Rights Plan (the "Rights Agreement") pursuant to which preferred stock purchase rights (the "Rights") are issued on each outstanding share of Georgia-Pacific Group stock (a "Georgia-Pacific Group Right"), which will entitle the holders thereof to purchase shares of Series B Junior Preferred Stock under the conditions specified in the Rights Agreement.

The Rights will expire on December 31, 2007, unless earlier redeemed by the Corporation or extended. The Rights would be exercisable only if a person or group acquires 15% or more of the total voting rights of all then outstanding shares of common stock of the Corporation or commences a tender offer that would result in such person or group beneficially owning 15% or more of the total voting rights of all then outstanding shares of common stock of the Corporation. In such event, each Right would entitle the holder to purchase from the Corporation one one-hundredth of a share of Series B Junior Preferred Stock (a "Series B Unit") at a purchase price of $175 (the "Series B Unit Purchase Price"), subject to adjustment.

Thereafter, in the event one of several specified events (generally involving transactions by an acquirer in the Corporation's common stock or a business combination involving the Corporation) occurs, each Georgia-Group Right will entitle its holder to purchase, for the Series B Unit Purchase Price, a number of shares of common stock of such entity or purchaser with a market value equal to twice the applicable purchase price. Because of the nature of the dividend, liquidation and voting rights of each class of Junior Preferred Stock related to the Rights, the economic value of one Series B Unit should approximate the eco-nomic value of one share of Georgia-Pacific Group stock.

Capital Stock

The Corporation does not hold any Georgia-Pacific Group stock in Treasury as of December 28, 2002 and December 29, 2001.

During 2000, the Corporation purchased on the open market approximately 1.7 million shares of Georgia-Pacific stock at an aggregate price of $62 million ($36.47 average per share). The Corporation also purchased on the open market approximately 3.3 million shares of The Timber Company stock at an aggregate price of $78 million ($23.64 average per share), all of which were held as treasury stock at December 30, 2000.

At the end of November 2000, the Corporation acquired Fort James (as described above and in Note 3) and issued 21.5 million shares of Georgia-Pacific treasury stock and 32.2 million newly issued shares of Georgia-Pacific stock as part of that transaction. During 2001, the Corporation issued an additional 190,000 shares of Georgia-Pacific Stock as part of this transaction.

Note 14. Accumulated Other Comprehensive Loss

The Corporation's accumulated other comprehensive loss includes the following:

In millions	Foreign Currency Items	Derivative Instruments	Minimum Pension Liability Adjustment	Accumulated Other Comprehensive Loss
December 30, 2000	$(14)	$–	$(2)	$(16)
Activity, net of taxes	(29)	(30)	(43)	(102)
December 29, 2001	(43)	(30)	(45)	(118)
Activity, net of taxes	154	25	(580)	(401)
December 28, 2002	$111	$(5)	$(625)	$(519)

Qualcomm
2005 Annual Report

Note 7. Capital Stock

Preferred Stock

The Company has 8,000,000 shares of preferred stock authorized for issuance in one or more series, at a par value of $0.0001 per share. In conjunction with the distribution of preferred share purchase rights, 4,000,000 shares of preferred stock are designated as Series A Junior Participating Preferred Stock and such shares are reserved for issuance upon exercise of the preferred share purchase rights. At September 25, 2005 and September 26, 2004, no shares of preferred stock were outstanding.

Preferred Share Purchase Rights Agreement

The Company has a Preferred Share Purchase Rights Agreement (Rights Agreement) to protect stockholders' interests in the event of a proposed takeover of the Company. Under the original Rights Agreement, adopted on September 26, 1995, the Company declared a dividend of one preferred share purchase right (a Right) for each share of the Company's common stock outstanding. Pursuant to the Rights Agreement, as amended and restated on September 26, 2005, each Right entitles the registered holder to purchase from the Company a one one-thousandth share of Series A Junior Participating Preferred Stock, $0.0001 par value per share, subject to adjustment for subsequent stock splits, at a purchase price of $180. The Rights are exercisable only if a person or group (an Acquiring Person) acquires beneficial ownership of 15% or more of the Company's outstanding shares of common stock without Board approval. Upon exercise, holders, other than an Acquiring Person, will have the right, subject to termination, to receive the Company's common stock or other securities, cash or other assets having a market value, as defined, equal to twice such purchase price. The Rights, which expire on September 25, 2015, are redeemable in whole, but not in part, at the Company's option prior to the time such rights are triggered for a price of $0.001 per Right.

Stock Repurchase Program

On March 8, 2005, the Company authorized the repurchase of up to $2 billion of the Company's common stock under a program with no expiration date. During fiscal 2005, the Company repurchased and retired 27,083,000 shares of common stock for $953 million and sold put options under this program. At September 25, 2005, the Company had two outstanding put options, with expiration dates of December 7, 2005 and March 21, 2006, that may require the Company to purchase 11,500,000 shares of its common stock upon exercise for $411 million (net of the option premiums received). Any shares repurchased upon exercise of the put options will be retired. The recorded values of the put option liabilities totaled $7 million at September 25, 2005. During fiscal 2005, the Company recognized $16 million in investment income due to decreases in the fair values of the put options and $15 million in investment income from premiums received on a put option that expired unexercised. At September 25, 2005, $636 million remained authorized for repurchases under this program.

On February 10, 2003, the Company had authorized the repurchase of up to $1 billion of the Company's common stock over a two-year period. The Company did not repurchase any of the Company's common stock under this program during fiscal 2004; however, the Company did sell put options. The Company repurchased all of the put options during fiscal 2004. The net gain recorded in investment income during fiscal 2004 related to the put options, including premiums received, was $5 million.

During fiscal 2003, the Company repurchased and retired 9,831,000 shares of common stock for $166 million and sold put options. The put options expired worthless during fiscal 2003. The $7 million in premiums received from the put options were recorded as paid-in capital.

Dividends

On March 2, 2004, the Company announced an increase in its quarterly dividend from $0.035 to $0.050 per share on common stock. On July 13, 2004, the Company announced an increase in its quarterly dividend from $0.050 to $0.070 per share on common stock.

On March 8, 2005, the Company announced an increase in its quarterly dividend from $0.070 to $0.090 per share on common stock. Cash dividends announced in fiscal 2005 and 2004 were as follows (in millions, except per share data):

	2005		2004	
	Per Share	*Total*	*Per Share*	*Total*
First quarter	$0.070	$115	$0.070[1]	$112
Second quarter	0.070	115	0.050	81
Third quarter	0.090	147	—[2]	—
Fourth quarter	0.090	147	0.070	114
Total	$0.320	$524	$0.190	$307

[1] In the first quarter of fiscal 2004, the Company announced two dividends of $0.035 per share which were paid in the first and second quarters of fiscal 2004.

[2] The Company paid a dividend of $0.05 per share in the third quarter of fiscal 2004 that had been announced in the second quarter of fiscal 2004.

On October 10, 2005, the Company announced a cash dividend of $0.09 per share on the Company's common stock, payable on January 4, 2006 to stockholders of record as of December 7, 2005, which will be reflected in the first quarter of fiscal 2006.

Rockwell Collins
2004 Annual Report

12. Shareowners' Equity

Common Stock

The Company is authorized to issue one billion shares of common stock, par value $0.01 per share, and 25 million shares of preferred stock, without par value, of which 2.5 million shares are designated as Series A Junior Participating Preferred Stock for issuance in connection with the exercise of preferred share purchase rights. At September 30, 2004, 13.4 million shares of common stock were reserved for issuance under various employee incentive plans.

Preferred Share Purchase Rights

Each outstanding share of common stock provides the holder with one Preferred Share Purchase Right (Right). The Rights will become exercisable only if a person or group acquires, or offers to acquire, without prior approval of the Board of Directors, 15 percent or more of the Company's common stock. However, the Board of Directors is authorized to reduce the 15 percent threshold for triggering the Rights to not less than 10 percent. Upon exercise, each Right entitles the holder to 1/100th of a share of Series A Junior Participating Preferred Stock of the Company (Junior Preferred Stock) at a price of $125, subject to adjustment.

Upon acquisition of the Company, each Right (other than Rights held by the acquirer) will generally be exercisable for $250 worth of either common stock of the Company or common stock of the acquirer for $125. In certain circumstances, each Right may be exchanged by the Company for one share of common stock or 1/100th of a share of Junior Preferred Stock. The Rights will expire on June 30, 2011, unless earlier exchanged or redeemed at $0.01 per Right. The rights have the effect of substantially increasing the cost of acquiring the Company in a transaction not approved by the Board of Directors.

Treasury Stock

The Company repurchased shares of its common stock as follows:

(in millions)	2004	2003	2002
Amount of share repurchases	$179	$154	$102
Number of shares repurchased	5.8	6.8	4.5

At September 30, 2004, the Company is authorized to repurchase an additional $165 million of outstanding common stock.

Accumulated Other Comprehensive Loss

Accumulated other comprehensive loss consists of the following:

	September 30	
(in millions)	2004	2003
Minimum pension liability adjustment, net of taxes of $234 for 2004 and $301 for 2003	$(399)	$(513)
Foreign currency translation adjustments	3	(3)
Foreign currency cash flow hedge adjustment	(1)	–
Accumulated other comprehensive loss	$(397)	$(516)

Navistar
2004 Annual Report

18. Common Shareowners' Equity

Changes in certain shareowners' equity accounts are as follows:

Millions of dollars	2004	2003	2002
Common Stock and Additional Paid in Capital			
Beginning of year	**$2,118**	$2,146	$2,139
Tax Benefit related to exercise of stock options	7	2	7
Net premium for call options	**(27)**	(25)	–
Amounts due from officers and directors	**2**	(5)	–
Other	**4**	–	–
End of year	**$2,096**	$2,118	$2,146
Retained Earnings (Deficit)			
Beginning of year	**$(833)**	$(731)	$(190)
Net income (loss)	**247**	(21)	(538)
Sale of treasury stock to pension funds	–	(73)	–

Millions of dollars	*2004*	*2003*	*2002*
Other	**(18)**	(8)	(3)
End of year	**$(604)**	$(833)	$(731)
Common Stock Held in Treasury			
Beginning of year	**$(219)**	$(487)	$(507)
Issuance of common stock and other	**63**	271	34
Treasury stock adjustment	**(20)**	(3)	(14)
End of year	**$(176)**	$(219)	$(487)

Common Stock

The company has authorized 110 million shares of common stock with a par value of $0.10 per share. There were 70.0 million and 68.8 million shares of common stock outstanding, net of common stock held in treasury, at October 31, 2004 and 2003, respectively.

Loans to officers and directors are recorded as a reduction of shareowners' equity. These loans accrue interest at the applicable federal rate (as determined by Section 1274(d) of the Internal Revenue Code) on the purchase date for loans of stated maturity, compounded annually, are unsecured obligations and have a nine-year term. Principal and interest is due at maturity and the loan may be prepaid at any time at the participant's option. Loans to officers and directors, which were made primarily to finance the purchase of company shares, totaled $5 million at October 31, 2003 and $3 million at October 31, 2004. Effective July 31, 2002, the company no longer offers such loans.

Common stock held in treasury totaled 15,210,154 shares at October 31, 2002, 6,841,059 shares at October 31, 2003, and 5,495,580 shares at October 31, 2004. In November 2002, the company completed the sale of a total of 7,755,030 shares of its common stock held in treasury, par value $0.10 per share, at a price of $22.566 per share, for an aggregate purchase price of $175 million to three employee benefit plan trusts of International. The securities were offered and sold in reliance upon the exemption from securities registration afforded by Section 4(2) of the Securities the company's retirement plans in 2003. In January 2003, the company filed a registration statement for the resale of the common stock by the employee benefit plan trusts. The remainder of the changes in treasury stock is primarily the result of the issuance of stock upon the exercise of options by employees.

Accumulated Other Comprehensive Loss

The components of accumulated other comprehensive income (loss) as of October 31 are as follows, in millions:

	Minimum Pension Liability Adjustments	Foreign Currency Translation Adjustments and Other	Accumulated Other Comprehensive Loss
2004	**$(737)**	**$(52)**	**$(787)**
2003	(737)	(41)	(778)
2002	(681)	(16)	(697)

The minimum pension liability adjustment is recorded on the Statement of Financial Condition net of deferred income taxes of $454 million and $445 million at October 31, 2004 and 2003, respectively.

In the Statement of Comprehensive Income, the tax effects of foreign currency translation and other adjustments were not material for each of the years in the three year period ended October 31, 2004.

Raytheon
2002 Annual Report

Note J: Equity Security Units

In May 2001, the Company issued 17,250,000, 8.25% equity security units for $50 per unit totaling $837 million, net of offering costs of $26 million. Approximately $20 million of the offering costs were allocated to equity and $6 million were allocated to the mandatorily redeemable equity securities. The net proceeds of the offering were used to reduce debt and for general corporate purposes. Each equity security unit consists of a contract to purchase shares of the Company's common stock on May 15, 2004 which will result in cash proceeds to the Company of $863 million, and a mandatorily redeemable equity security, with a stated liquidation amount of $50, due on May 15, 2006 which will require a cash payment by the Company of $863 million. The contract obligates the holder to purchase, for $50, shares of common stock equal to the settlement rate. The settlement rate is equal to $50 divided by the average market value of the Company's common stock at that time. The settlement rate cannot be greater than 1.8182 or less than 1.4903 shares of common stock per purchase contract. Using the treasury stock method, there is no effect on the computation of shares for diluted earnings per share if the average market value of the Company's common stock is between $27.50 and $33.55 per share. The mandatorily redeemable equity security represents an undivided interest in the assets of RC Trust I, a Delaware business trust formed for the purpose of issuing these securities and whose assets consist solely of subordinated notes issued by the Company. During 2002, the average market value of the Company's common stock was $35.41 per share, therefore, the Company included 1.4 million shares in its computation of shares for diluted earnings per share. The contract requires a quarterly distribution, which is recorded as a reduction in additional paid-in capital, of 1.25% per year of the stated amount of $50 per purchase contract. Cash paid for the quarterly distribution on the contract was $11 million and $6 million in 2002 and 2001, respectively. The mandatorily redeemable equity security pays a quarterly distribution, which is included in interest expense, of 7% per year of the stated liquidation amount of $50 per mandatorily redeemable equity security until May 15, 2004. Cash paid for the quarterly distribution on the mandatorily redeemable equity security was $60 million and $31 million in 2002 and 2001, respectively. On May 15, 2004, following a remarketing of the mandatorily redeemable equity securities, the distribution rate will be reset at a rate equal to or greater than 7% per year.

Note K: Stockholders' Equity

The changes in shares of common stock outstanding were as follows:

(In thousands)	
Balance at December 31, 1999	338,760
Common stock plan activity	1,337
Treasury stock activity	523
Balance at December 31, 2000	340,620
Issuance of common stock	46,809
Common stock plan activity	1,230
Treasury stock activity	6,773
Balance at December 31, 2001	395,432
Issuance of common stock	**9,218**
Common stock plan activity	**3,638**
Treasury stock activity	**(79)**
Balance at December 31, 2002	**408,209**

The Company issued 5,100,000 shares of common stock in 2002 to fund the Company Match and Company Contributions, as described in Note O, Pension and Other Employee Benefits. The Company also issued 4,118,000 shares of common stock in 2002 in connection with other activity in the Company's employee stock ownership plan. The Company issued 855,000 shares of common stock and 6,809,000 shares out of treasury in 2001 to fund the Company Match and Company Contributions, as described in Note O, Pension and Other Employee Benefits.

In May 2001, the Company issued 14,375,000 shares of common stock for $27.50 per share. In October 2001, the Company issued 31,578,900 shares of common stock for $33.25 per share. The proceeds of the offerings were $1,388 million, net of $56 million of offering costs, and were used to reduce debt and for general corporate purposes.

Basic earnings per share (EPS) is computed by dividing net income by the weighted-average shares outstanding during the period. Diluted EPS reflects the potential dilution that could occur if securities or other contracts to issue common stock were exercised or converted into common stock or resulted in the issuance of common stock that then shared in the earnings of the entity.

The weighted-average shares outstanding for basic and diluted EPS were as follows:

(In thousands)	2002	2001	2000
Average common shares outstanding for basic EPS	**401,444**	356,717	338,407
Dilutive effect of stock options, restricted stock, and equity security units	**6,587**	4,606	2,711
Shares for diluted EPS	**408,031**	361,323	341,118

Stock options to purchase 23.7 million, 20.5 million, and 22.3 million shares of common stock outstanding at December 31, 2002, 2001, and 2000, respectively, did not affect the computation of diluted EPS. The exercise prices for these options were greater than the average market price of the Company's common stock during the respective years.

Stock options to purchase 17.9 million, 15.5 million, and 10.1 million shares of common stock outstanding at December 31, 2002, 2001, and 2000, respectively, had exercise prices that were less than the average market price of the Company's common stock during the respective periods and are included in the dilutive effect of stock options, restricted stock, and equity security units in the table above.

In 2001, the Company eliminated its dual class capital structure and reclassified its Class A and Class B common stock into a single new class of common stock. The Company also effected a 20-for-1 reverse-forward stock split that resulted in holders of fewer than 20 shares of common stock being cashed out of their holdings.

In 1995, the Board of Directors authorized the repurchase of up to 12 million shares of the Company's common stock to allow the Company to repurchase shares from time to time when warranted by market conditions. In 1998, the Board of Directors ratified and reauthorized the repurchase of 2.5 million shares that remained under the original authorization. There have been 11.8 million shares purchased under these authorizations through December 31, 2002. There were no shares repurchased under this program during 2002, 2001, and 2000.

In 1999, the Board of Directors authorized the repurchase of up to an additional 6 million shares of the Company's common stock over the next three years. There have been no shares repurchased under this program.

In 1998, the Board of Directors authorized the purchase of up to 5 million shares of the Company's common stock per year to counter the dilution due to the exercise of stock options. There were no shares repurchased under this program during 2002, 2001, and 2000.

The Board of Directors is authorized to issue up to 200,000,000 shares of preferred stock, $0.01 par value per share, in multiple series with terms as determined by the Board of Directors.

In 1997, in connection with the merger with Hughes Defense, the Company adopted a shareholder rights plan. The plan protects the Company and its stockholders against hostile takeover tactics. The rights entitle the holder, other than a potential acquirer, to purchase shares of the Company's common stock at a 50 percent discount to the market price if certain triggering events occur, such as the acquisition of 15 percent or more of the Company's common stock by a person or group.

IBM
2002 Annual Report

N Stockholders' Equity Activity

In the fourth quarter of 2002, in connection with the PwCC acquisition, IBM issued 3,677,213 shares of restricted stock valued at approximately $254 million and recorded an additional $30 million for stock to be issued in future periods as part of the purchase price consideration paid to the PwCC partners. See Note C, "Acquisitions/Divestitures" for further information regarding this acquisition and related payments made by the company. Additionally, in the fourth quarter of 2002, in conjunction with the funding of the company's U.S. pension plan, the company issued an additional 24,037,354 shares of common stock from treasury shares valued at $1,871 million.

Stock Repurchases

From time to time, the Board of Directors authorizes the company to repurchase IBM common stock. The company repurchased 48,481,100 common shares at a cost of $4,212 million and 50,764,698 common shares at a cost of $5,293 million in 2002 and 2001, respectively. In 2002 and 2001, the company issued 979,246 and 1,923,502 treasury shares, respectively, as a result of exercises of stock options by employees of certain recently acquired businesses and by non-U.S. employees. At December 31, 2002, $3,864 million of Board-authorized repurchases remained. The company plans to purchase shares on the open market from time to time, depending on market conditions. The company also repurchased 189,797 common shares at a cost of $18 million and 314,433 common shares at a cost of $31 million in 2002 and 2001, respectively, as part of other stock compensation plans.

In 1995, the Board of Directors authorized the company to repurchase all of its outstanding Series A 7-1/2 percent callable preferred stock. On May 18, 2001, the company announced it would redeem all outstanding shares of its Series A 7-1/2 percent callable preferred stock, represented by the outstanding depositary shares (10,184,043 shares). The depositary shares represent ownership of one-fourth of a share of preferred stock. Depositary shares were redeemed as of July 3, 2001, the redemption date, for cash at a redemption price of $25 plus accrued and unpaid dividends to the redemption date for each depositary share. Accordingly, these shares are no longer outstanding. Dividends on preferred stock, represented by the depositary shares, ceased to accrue on the redemption date. The company did not repurchase any shares in 2000.

Employee Benefits Trust

In 1997, the company created an employee benefits trust to which the company contributed 10 million shares of treasury stock. The company was authorized to instruct the trustee to sell such shares from time to time and to use the proceeds from such sales, and any dividends paid or earnings received on such stock, toward the partial payment of the company's obligations under certain of its compensation and benefit plans. The shares held in trust were not considered outstanding for earnings per shares purposes until they were committed to be released. The company did not commit any shares for release from the trust during its existence nor were any shares sold from the trust. The trust would have expired in 2007. Due to the fact that the company had not used the trust, nor was it expected to need the trust prior to its expiration, the company dissolved the trust, effective May 31, 2001, and all of the shares (20 million on a split-adjusted basis) were returned to the company as treasury shares. Dissolution of the trust did not affect the company's obligations related to any of its compensation and employee benefit plans or its ability to settle the obligations. In addition, the dissolution is not expected to have any impact on net income. At this time, the company plans to fully meet its obligations for the compensation and benefit plans in the same manner as it does today, using cash from operations.

Accumulated Gains and (Losses) Not Affecting Retained Earnings*

(dollars in millions)	Net Unrealized Gains/ (Losses) on Cash Flow Hedge Derivatives	Foreign Currency Translation Adjustments	Minimum Pension Liability Adjustment**	Net Unrealized Gains/ (Losses) on Market Securities	Accumulated Gains/ (Losses) Not Affecting Retained Earnings
December 31, 2000	$ –	$ (73)	$ (218)	$ (78)	$ (369)
Cumulative effect on January 1, 2001	219	–	–	–	219
Change for period	77	(539)	(308)	92	(678)
December 31, 2001	296	(612)	(526)	14	(828)
Change for period	(659)	850	(2,765)	(16)	(2,590)
December 31, 2002	$(363)	$238	$(3,291)	$(2)	$(3,418)

* Net of tax.
** Reclassified to conform with 2002 presentation.

Net Change in Unrealized (Losses)/Gains on Marketable Securities (Net of tax)

(dollars in millions) at December 31:	2002	2001
Net unrealized losses arising during the period	$(13)	$(154)
Less: Net gains/(losses) included in net income for the period	3*	(246)*
Net change in unrealized (losses)/gains on marketable securities	$(16)	$ 92

* Includes write-downs of $36 million and $287 million in 2002 and 2001, respectively.

CORNING
2003 Annual Report

17. Shareholders' Equity

Preferred Stock. We have 10 million authorized shares of Preferred Stock, par value $100 per share.

Series A Junior Participating Preferred Stock

Of the authorized shares, we have designated 2.4 million shares as Series A Junior Participating Preferred Stock for which no shares have been issued.

In June 1996, the Board of Directors approved the renewal of the Preferred Share Purchase Right Plan, which entitles shareholders to purchase 0.01 of a share of Series A Junior Participating Preferred Stock upon the occurrence of certain events. In addition, the rights entitle shareholders to purchase shares of common stock at a 50% discount in the event a person or group acquires 20% or more of our outstanding common stock. The preferred share purchase rights became effective July 15, 1996 and expire July 15, 2006.

Series C Mandatory Convertible Preferred Stock

In July and August 2002, we issued 5.75 million shares of 7% Series C mandatory convertible preferred stock having a liquidation preference of $100 per share, plus accrued and unpaid dividends, and resulting in gross proceeds of $557 million. The mandatory convertible stock has an annual dividend rate of 7%, payable quarterly in cash. The first dividend payment date was November 16, 2002. The dividends are also payable immediately upon conversion to Corning common stock. At the time we issued the Series C convertible stock, a one-time dividend was declared for all dividends that will be payable from issuance through the mandatory conversion date of August 16, 2005. We secured the payment of the dividends through the issuance of a promissory note and used a portion of the proceeds from the sale of the Series C preferred stock to purchase $117 million of U.S. treasury securities that were pledged as collateral to secure the payments on the promissory note. As a result, net proceeds of the offering were $440 million.

The Series C preferred stock will automatically convert on the mandatory conversion date of August 16, 2005, into between 50.813 and 62.5 shares of Corning common stock, depending on the then current market price. At any time prior to the mandatory conversion date, holders may elect to convert in whole or part of their shares of Series C preferred stock into 50.813 shares of common stock plus an amount of cash equal to the market value at that time of the pro rata share of the collateral portfolio that secures the promissory note. At December 31, 2003, approximately 4.9 million shares of the Series C preferred stock had been converted into 248.8 million common shares.

As the closing price of Corning common stock was $1.60 on July 31, 2002, the holder could immediately convert the Series C preferred stock and obtain a value of $101.72 (50.813 shares valued at $1.60 plus $20.42 in future dividends) indicating that the preferred stock contains a beneficial conversion feature of $1.72 per preferred share. The beneficial conversion totaled approximately $10 million and was charged to additional paid in capital. The beneficial conversion was also deducted from earnings attributable to common shareholders in the 2002 earnings per share calculations.

Common Stock. In July 2003, we completed an equity offering of 45 million shares of common stock generating net proceeds of approximately $363 million. This offering's net proceeds were used to reduce debt through open market repurchases, public tender offers or other methods, and for general corporate purposes. We invest the net proceeds in short-term, interest bearing, investment grade obligations until they are applied as described.

In May 2003, we completed an equity offering of 50 million shares of common stock generating net proceeds of approximately $267 million. We used the net proceeds of this offering and approximately $356 million of existing cash to reduce debt through a public tender offer in the second quarter of 2003 as discussed in Note 14 (Long-Term Debt and Loans Payable). On July 9, 2001, we announced the discontinuation of the payment of dividends on our common stock. Dividends paid to common shareholders in 2001 totaled $112 million.

Treasury Stock. We did not repurchase any of our common stock in 2003. On July 22, 2002, we repurchased 5.5 million shares of our common stock for $23 million in a privately negotiated transaction.

Accumulated Other Comprehensive Income (Loss). Components of other comprehensive income (loss), accumulated in shareholders equity, are reported net of income taxes, follow (in millions):

	Foreign Currency Translation Adjustment	Minimum Pension Liability Adjustment	Net Unrealized Gains (losses) on Investments	Net Unrealized Gains (losses) on Cash flow Hedges	Accumulated Other Comprehensive (Loss) income
December 31, 2000	$(168)		41		$(127)
Foreign currency translation adjustment	(31)				(31)
Unrealized loss on investments (net of tax of $17 million)			(27)		(27)
Realized gains on securities (net of tax of $12 million)			(18)		(18)
Cumulative effect of adoption of SFAS No. 133				$3	3
Unrealized derivative gain on cash flow hedges (net of tax of $7 million)				11	11

	Foreign Currency Translation Adjustment	Minimum Pension Liability Adjustment	Net Unrealized Gains (losses) on Investments	Net Unrealized Gains (losses) on Cash flow Hedges	Accumulated Other Comprehensive (Loss) income
Reclassification adjustments on cash flow hedges (net of tax of $2 million)				(4)	(4)
December 31, 2001	(199)		(4)	10	(193)
Foreign currency translation adjustment	208				208
Minimum pension liability adjustment		$(173)			(173)
Unrealized gain on investments (net of tax of $1 million)			1		1
Realized loss on securities (net of tax of $3 million)			5		5
Unrealized derivative loss on cash flow hedges (net of tax of $17 million)				(27)	(27)
Reclassification adjustments on cash flow hedges (net of tax of $6 million)				9	9
December 31, 2002	9	(173)	2	(8)	(170)
Foreign currency translation adjustment	239				239
Minimum pension liability adjustment[*]		26			26
Unrealized gain on investments (net of tax of $2 million)			4		4
Realized gain on securities (net of tax of $2 million)			(3)		(3)
Unrealized derivative loss on cash flow hedges (net of tax of $4 million)				(30)	(30)

	Foreign Currency Translation Adjustment	Minimum Pension Liability Adjustment	Net Unrealized Gains (losses) on Investments	Net Unrealized Gains (losses) on Cash flow Hedges	Accumulated Other Comprehensive (Loss) income
Reclassification adjustments on cash flow hedges (net of tax of $4 million)				32	32
December 31, 2003	$ 248	$ (147)	$ 3	$ (6)	$ 98

(*) Includes adjustments from Dow Corning.

SOLECTRON
2003 Annual Report

Note 16. Restructuring

Beginning in the second quarter of fiscal 2001, Solectron recorded restructuring and impairment costs as it has continued to rationalize operations in light of customer demand declines and the current economic downturn. The measures, which included reducing the workforce, consolidating facilities and changing the strategic focus of a number of sites, was largely intended to align Solectron's capacity and infrastructure to anticipated customer demand as well as to rationalize its footprint worldwide. The restructuring and impairment costs include employee severance and benefit costs, costs related to leased facilities that will be abandoned and subleased, owned facilities no longer used by us which will be disposed of, costs related to leased equipment that has been or will be abandoned, and impairment of owned equipment that will be disposed of. For owned facilities and equipment, the impairment loss recognized was based on the fair value less costs to sell, with fair value estimated based on existing market prices for similar assets. Severance and benefit costs and other costs associated with restructuring activities initiated prior to January 1, 2003 were recorded in compliance with Emerging Issues Task Force (EITF) Issue No. 94-3, "Liability Recognition for Certain Employee Termination Benefits and Other Costs to Exit an Activity." Severance and benefit costs associated with restructuring activities initiated on or after January 1, 2003 are recorded in accordance with SFAS No. 112, "Employer's Accounting for Postemployment Benefits," as Solectron concluded that it had a substantive severance plan. For leased facilities that will be abandoned and subleased, the estimated lease loss accrued represents future lease payments subsequent to abandonment less any estimated sublease income. In order to estimate future sublease income, Solectron works with an independent broker to estimate the length of time until it can sublease a facility and the amount of rent it can expect to receive. As of August 31, 2003, the majority of the facilities Solectron plans to sublease have not been subleased and, accordingly, estimates of expected sublease income could change based on factors that affect Solectron's ability to sublease those facilities such as general economic conditions and the real estate market, among others.

See also Note 17, "Goodwill and Other Intangible Assets," for discussion of intangible asset and goodwill impairment charges.

Fiscal 2003

The employee severance and benefit costs included in these restructuring charges relate to the elimination of approximately 9,500 full-time positions worldwide and all such positions have been eliminated under this plan. Approximately 57% of the positions eliminated were in the Americas region, 31% were in Europe and 12% were in Asia/Pacific. Facilities and equipment subject to restructuring were primarily located in the Americas and Europe. For leased facilities that will be abandoned and subleased, the lease costs represent future lease payments subsequent to abandonment less estimated sublease income. For owned facilities and equipment, the impairment loss recognized was based on the fair value less costs to sell, with fair value based on estimates of existing market prices for similar assets.

During fiscal 2003, Solecton recorded restructuring and impairment costs of $469.6 million related to continuing operations. The following table summarizes these charges (in millions):

	2003	Nature
Impairment of equipment	$67.4	non-cash
Impairment of facilities	80.0	non-cash
Impairment of other assets	26.9	non-cash
Impairment of equipment, facilities and others	$174.3	cash
Severance and benefit costs	234.0	cash
Loss on leased equipment	2.3	cash
Loss on leased facilities	24.3	cash
Other exit costs	34.7	
Total	$469.6	

Fiscal 2002

The employee severance and benefit costs included in these restructuring charges relate to the elimination of approximately 15,000 full-time positions worldwide and all such positions have been eliminated under this plan. Approximately 69% of the positions eliminated were in the Americas region, 20% were in Europe and 11% were in Asia/Pacific. The employment reductions primarily affected employees in manufacturing and back office support functions within the Global Operations business unit. Facilities and equipment subject to restructuring were primarily located in the Americas and Europe within the Global Operations business unit. For leased facilities that will be abandoned and subleased, the lease costs represent future lease payments subsequent to abandonment less estimated sublease income. For owned facilities and equipment, the impairment loss recognized was based on the fair value less costs to sell, with fair value based on estimated of existing market prices for similar assets.

During fiscal 2002, we recorded restructuring and impairment costs related to this plan of $615.9 million related to continuing operations. The following table summarizes these charges (in millions):

	2003	Nature
Impairment of equipment	$127.8	non-cash
Impairment of facilities	81.0	non-cash
Impairment of IT software and other assets	162.5	non-cash
Impairment of equipment, facilities and others	$371.3	cash
Severance and benefit costs	119.8	cash
Loss on leased equipment	23.8	cash
Loss on leased facilities	80.3	cash
Other exit costs	20.7	
Total	$615.9	

Fiscal 2001

The employee severance and benefit costs included in these restructuring charges relate to the elimination of approximately 11,800 full-time positions worldwide and all such positions have been eliminated under this plan. Approximately 67% of the positions eliminated were in the Americas region, 23% were in Europe and 10% were in Asia/Pacific. The employment reductions primarily affected employees in manufacturing and back office support functions within the Global Operations business unit. Facilities and equipment subject to restructuring were primarily located in the Americas and Europe within the Global Operations business unit. For leased facilities that will be abandoned and subleased, the lease costs represent future lease payments subsequent to abandonment less estimated sublease income. For owned facilities and equipment, the impairment loss recognized was based on the fair value less costs to sell, with fair value based on estimates of existing market prices for similar assets.

During fiscal 2001, we recorded restructuring and impairment costs related to this plan of $517.3 million related to continuing operations. The following table summarizes these charges (in millions):

	2001	Nature
Impairment of equipment	$188.2	non-cash
Impairment of facilities	37.7	non-cash
Impairment of other assets	42.2	non-cash
Impairment of equipment, facilities and others	$268.1	
Severance and benefit costs	70.0	cash
Loss on leased equipment	117.5	cash
Loss on leased facilities	56.4	cash
Other exit costs	5.3	cash
Total	$517.3	

The following table summarizes the continuing operations restructuring accrual activity in all fiscal years presented (in millions):

	Severance and Benefits	Lease Payments on Facilities	Lease Payments on Facilities	Other	Total
Balance of accrual at September 1, 2000	$ –	$ –	$ –	$ –	$ –
FY2001 Provision	70.0	56.4	117.5	5.3	249.2
FY2001 Cash payments	(70.0)	(5.5)	(5.0)	(0.9)	(81.4)
Balance of accrual at August 31, 2001	–	50.9	112.5	4.4	167.8
FY2002 Provision	119.8	84.2	30.3	20.7	255.0
FY2002 Provision adjustments	–	(3.9)	(6.5)	–	(10.4)
FY2002 Cash payments	(113.7)	(67.1)	(51.9)	(24.8)	(257.5)
Balance of accrual at August 31, 2002	6.1	64.1	84.4	0.3	154.9
FY2002 Provision	234.0	24.3	2.3	34.7	295.3
FY2002 Provision adjustments	–	1.0	–	–	1.0
FY2002 Cash payments	(166.0)	(51.7)	(57.3)	(24.5)	(299.5)
Balance of accrual at August 31, 2003	$74.1	$37.7	$29.4	$10.5	$151.7

Accruals related to restructuring activities were recorded in accrued expenses in the accompanying consolidated balance sheet.

Chapter 6
Statement of Cash Flows

CONTENTS

A statement of cash flows is required as part of a full set of financial statements. It must be prepared in conformity with generally accepted accounting principles (GAAP). The statement is not required if the financial statements are prepared on a basis of accounting other than GAAP. The statement must be included in both annual and interim financial statements.

This chapter discusses the requirements of ASC 230, *Statement of Cash Flows* (ASC 230-10-45-18 and 45-27). ASC 958-205, *Not-for-Profit Entities: Presentation of Financial Statements*, requires the statement of cash flows for not-for-profit entities.

The statement presents the net effect of cash flows on the company's *cash*. It includes a reconciliation of beginning and ending cash. The total amount of cash at the beginning and end of year presented in the statement of cash flows should match the totals presented in the balance sheet. The statement presents cash flows from operating, investing, and financing activities. Separate disclosure must be made for noncash investing and financing transactions. Generally, these disclosures are presented in narrative form in a separate schedule appended at the bottom of the Statement of Cash Flows. They also may be disclosed in a note to the financial statements or in a supplementary schedule.

The statement of cash flows provides many benefits to the preparers and users of the statement, such as the following:

- ☐ Enables the assessment of the amounts, timing, and uncertainty surrounding future cash flows.
- ☐ Furnishes a reconciliation between net income and cash flow from operations.
- ☐ Provides the net effects of operating transactions on profit and cash flow.
- ☐ Indicates the impact on the company's financial status of its investing and financing transactions.
- ☐ Shows the company's ability to obtain financing.
- ☐ Provides important information about the entity's cash receipts and cash payments for the period.
- ☐ Shows the company's ability to generate recurring cash earnings.
- ☐ Evaluates the company's ability to pay debt when due.
- ☐ Allows for the evaluation of the company's ability to pay its expenses and conduct normal operations.
- ☐ Shows the entity's ability to pay dividends.
- ☐ Provides the reasons for the change in cash and cash equivalents for the period.

It is prohibited to present cash flow per share because doing so will give the false impression that such a statistic is as important as earnings per share. Further, the term *funds* should not be used, because it is ambiguous and easily misinterpreted.

CASH

Cash consists of currency and coin on hand, as well as deposits not restricted by the bank, that is, checking and generally savings accounts. Although banks could restrict the withdrawal of savings account funds, they generally do not. Cash also includes negotiable items such as cashier's checks, personal checks, certified checks, and money orders. In addition, it includes other accounts having demand deposit characteristics and allowing for customer deposit or withdrawal at will without penalty, such as unrestricted certificates of deposit. However, cash does not consist of items such as postage stamps (office supplies), post-dated checks (receivables), restricted certificates of deposit (short-term investments), and travel advances (prepaid expenses), which are sometimes misclassified as cash.

Securities and Exchange Commission Regulation S-X, Rule 5-02(1), provides that amounts held in bank accounts that are unavailable for immediate withdrawal (e.g., compensating balances) should be considered as cash for the purposes of preparing the statement of cash flows. Any restrictions on withdrawal should be disclosed.

RECONCILIATION OF NET INCOME TO CASH FLOW FROM OPERATIONS

A reconciliation of net income to cash flow from operations is required whether the direct method or indirect method is used. The reconciliation presents the various adjustments required to net income. Under the direct method, the operating section presents gross cash receipts and gross cash payments from operating activities, with a reconciliation of net income to cash flow from operations in a separate schedule accompanying the statement of cash flows. The cash flow from operations derived in this separate schedule must agree with the cash flow from operations in the operating section of the statement of cash flows.

Under the indirect method, gross cash receipts and gross cash payments from operating activities are not presented. Instead, only the reconciliation of net income to cash flow from operations may be presented either in the body of the operating section or in a separate schedule. If presented in a separate schedule, the net cash flow from operating activities is presented as a single line item in the operating section. The reconciling adjustments to derive cash flow from operations include adding back noncash expenses to and deducting noncash revenues from net income. Examples of these adjustments include adding back depreciation and depletion expense, adding back pension expense arising from a deferred pension liability, adding back bad debts, adding back accrued warranty expense, adding back tax expense arising from a deferred tax liability, adding back the loss on a fixed asset, adding back compensation expense arising from an employee stock option plan, deducting the amortization of deferred revenue, deducting the amortization of bond premium, subtracting tax expense arising from a deferred tax asset, subtracting the gain on the sale of a fixed asset, subtracting pension expense associated with a deferred pension asset, subtracting unrealized gains on trading securities, and subtracting income from investments under the equity method. Irrespective of whether the direct method or the indirect method is used, there must be separate disclosure of income taxes and interest paid during the year.

Exhibit 6-1 presents an illustrative reconciliation of net income to cash flow from operations. It shows the adjustment process for the various reconciling items.

Exhibit 6-1: Illustrative Reconciliation of Net Income to Cash Flow from Operations

Net income

Adjustments required to convert net income to the cash basis:

Add: noncash expenses (depreciation, depletion, amortization expense, loss on sale of fixed assets)

Less: noncash revenues (amortization of deferred revenue, amortization of bond premium, gain on sale of fixed assets)

Add (deduct) changes in current assets

   Add: decrease in current asset accounts

   Less: increase in current asset accounts

Add (deduct) changes in current liabilities

   Add: increase in current liability accounts

   Less: decrease in current liability accounts

Cash provided by operations

Note: A decrease in a current asset account results in an increase in cash flow. An example is a collection on accounts receivable. An increase in a current asset account results in a cash payment, such as the purchase of inventory. An increase in a current liability results in a cash receipt, such as the receipt of a short-term advance. A decrease in a current liability account results in a cash payment, such as a payment on an account payable.

EXAMPLE

XYZ Company reports net income of $50,000, depreciation expense of $4,000, amortization of patents of $500, amortization of deferred revenue of $3,000, loss of the sale of a fixed asset of $2,000, a decrease in accounts receivable of $8,000, a decrease in prepaid expenses of $1,000, a decrease in accounts payable of $6,000, and an increase in accrued liabilities of $4,000. Based on this information, a reconciliation of net income to cash flow from operations is prepared:

Reconciliation

Net income	$50,000
Add: noncash expenses	
Depreciation expense	4,000
Amortization expense	500
Loss on sale of fixed asset	2,000
Less: noncash revenue	
Amortization of deferred revenue	(3,000)
Decrease in accounts receivable	8,000
Decrease in prepaid expenses	1,000
Decrease in accounts payable	(6,000)
Increase in accrued liabilities	4,000
Cash provided by operations	$60,500

The topic of reconciliation is discussed more fully in the following sections on the direct and indirect methods.

DIRECT METHOD

The *direct method* is preferred by ASC 230-10-45-25, *Statement of Cash Flows: Overall.* Under this method, companies present cash flows from operating activities by major categories of gross receipts and gross payments and the resulting net amount. A company using the direct method should report separately operating cash receipts and operating cash payments. These cash flows from operations are discussed in the section of this chapter titled "Operating Activities."

Note: The only difference between the direct method and the indirect method is the presentation in the operating activities section of the statement of cash flows. The investing and financing sections are identical under both methods and are disclosed using the "direct method" presentation.

The direct method enables the user to comprehend better the relationship between the company's profit and its cash earnings. To this end, the FASB requires that an entity prepare, in addition to the direct method presentation of cash flows from operating activities, a reconciliation of net income to net cash flows from operating activities. This reconciliation is identical in form and content to the presentation of cash flows from operating activities using the indirect method (see indirect approach). It should be disclosed either in a separate schedule or at the bottom of the cash flows statement.

The direct method shows that the amount of net cash received or used in operating activities during the year equals the difference between the total amount of gross cash receipts and total gross cash payments applying to operating activities.

It is helpful to show how to convert income statement amounts for the direct method presentation from the accrual basis to cash basis. Three typical conversion formulas are:

1. Net sales + beginning accounts receivable – ending accounts receivable write-offs of accounts receivable = cash received from customers.

2. Cost of sales + ending inventory + beginning accounts payable – beginning inventory – ending accounts payable = cash paid to suppliers.

3. Operating expenses + ending prepaid expenses + beginning accrued expenses – beginning prepaid expenses – depreciation and amortization – ending accrued expenses payable – bad debt expense = cash paid for operating expenses.

EXAMPLE

A company's cost of sales for the year 20X2 was $300,000. During the year, the inventory increased by $60,000 and accounts payable to suppliers decreased by $50,000. The amount paid to suppliers to be reported in the statement of cash flows under the direct method is $410,000, computed as follows:

Cost of sales	$300,000
Add: increase in inventory	60,000
Add: decrease in accounts payable	50,000
Cash paid to suppliers	$410,000

INDIRECT (RECONCILIATION) METHOD

Although the direct method is preferred, the *indirect method* is used much more frequently by companies in financial reporting. In the indirect method, a company computes net cash flow from operating activities *indirectly* by adjusting an entity's net income or net loss to derive net cash flow from operations. Essentially, the presentation of net cash flow from operations is nothing more than a reconciliation of the entity's accrual income to net cash provided by operating activities. As previously noted, this reconciliation is also a required disclosure if a company chooses to use the direct approach. The indirect method emphasizes changes in most current asset and current liability accounts as they apply to operating activities. This was discussed in the reconciliation section of this chapter. **Caution:** Changes in current assets and current liabilities relating to investing or financing activities (e.g., short-term loans or short-term notes payable not involving sales of goods or services) should be presented as investing or financing activities, as applicable.

The amounts paid for interest and income taxes must be disclosed either on the face of the statement of cash flows or in the notes. If explained in the footnotes, they may appear in the relevant footnote on long-term debt or income taxes or may be discussed in a separate footnote dealing with supplemental cash flow disclosures.

A disadvantage of the indirect method is possible user confusion as to where the cash was received or paid to. The indirect method shows only adjustments to accrual basis net income to cash flow from operations in the operating activities section.

An illustrative format of the statement of cash flows under the indirect method is presented in Exhibit 6-2.

Exhibit 6-2: Illustrative Indirect Method Presentation

Operating activities:

Net income

Adjustments

Cash flow provided from operating activities

Investing activities:

Cash received from investing activities

Cash paid for investing activities

Net cash flow provided (used) by investing activities

Financing activities:

Cash received from financing activities

Cash paid for financing activities

Net cash flow provided (used) by financing activities

Net increase (decrease) in cash

Schedule of noncash investing and financing activities

EXAMPLE

Levine Company used the following data in the preparation of its 2005 statement of cash flows:

	December 31	January 1
Accounts receivable, net	$14,000	$11,100
Prepaid rent expense	4,100	6,200
Accounts payable	11,200	9,700

Levine's 2005 net income is $75,000. In ascertaining the amount that Levine should include as net cash provided by operating activities in the statement of cash flows, the following rule should be adhered to when the indirect method is used: In converting net income to net cash flow from operating activities, the following additions and subtractions must be made: net income + decreases in current assets accounts (other than cash) – increases in current assets accounts (other than cash) + increases in current liability accounts – decreases in current liability accounts + noncash expenses (e.g., depreciation, bond discount amortization) – noncash revenues (e.g., gain on sale of plant assets, bond premium amortization).

COMPUTATION

Net income	$75,000
Add (subtract)	
Increase in net accounts receivable	
$14,000 – $11,100	(2,900)
Decrease in prepaid rent expense:	
$6,200 – $4,100	2,100
Increase in accounts payable:	
$11,200 – $9,700	1,500
Net cash provided by operating activities, 2005	$75,700

GROSS VERSUS NET CASH FLOWS

In the investing and financing sections of the statement, gross cash inflows should be shown separately from gross cash outflows for similar items. In general, a company cannot net the cash inflows and cash outflows for similar items. (**Note:** There are a few exceptions in which netting is permitted, such as when the items involve fast turnover, are significant in amount, and have short maturities, such as transactions involving long-term investments, loans, and debts having a maturity of three months or less.) For example, in the investing section, the acquisition of a fixed asset would be a use of cash (say, $100,000), whereas the sale of a fixed asset (say, $60,000) would be a source of cash. Separate presentation of both the cash inflow and cash outflow aids reader comprehension and realism of the financial statements. The netting of the two (net cash outflow of $40,000) distorts what is really happening. In the financing section, the issuance of long-term debt (say, $80,000) would be a source of cash, but paying back the debt principal (say, $50,000) would be an application of cash. Both the cash inflows and cash outflows must be presented separately. A company is not allowed to present the net effect as a net source of cash of $30,000.

EXAMPLE

Carol Company reported net income of $150,000 for 2005. The following changes occurred in several of the company's balance sheet accounts:

Equipment	$12,500 increase
Accumulated depreciation	$20,000 increase
Note payable	$15,000 increase

In addition, three pertinent activities took place:

1. Depreciation expense for the year was $26,000.

2. In December 2005, Carol purchased equipment costing $25,000, with $10,000 down and the issuance of a 12% note payable of $15,000.

3. During 2005, Carol sold equipment costing $12,500, with accumulated depreciation of $6,000 for a gain of $2,500.

What is the net cash used in investing activities that should be reported by Carol?

In general, the cash flows from investing activities of an enterprise include transactions involving long-term assets and include the acquisition and disposal of investments and long-lived assets and the extension and collection of loans. There- fore, in Carol Company's 2005 statement of cash flows, the net cash used in investing activities should be computed in the following way:

Sale of equipment (cash inflow)	
($12,500 − $6,000 + $2,500)	$9,000
Acquisition of equipment (cash outflow)	(10,000)
Net cash used in investing activities, 2005	$(1,000)

In Carol's 2005 statement of cash flows, net cash flow provided by operating activities would be computed as follows:

Net income	$150,000
Add (subtract):	
Depreciation expense	26,000
Gain on sale of equipment	(2,500)
Net cash provided by operating activities	$173,500

EXAMPLE

During 2005, Dran Inc. had the following transactions related to its financial operations:

☐ Proceeds from the sale of stock of treasury stock (carrying amount at cost, $21,500)	$25,000
☐ Carrying amount of convertible preferred stock in Dran Inc., converted in common shares	30,000
☐ Distribution in 2005 of cash dividend declared in 2004 to preferred stockholders	15,500
☐ Payment for the early retirement of long-term bonds payable (carrying amount $185,000)	187,500

What is the net cash flow used in Dran's financing operations?

In general, the financing activities of an entity relate to liability and stockholder equity items and include obtaining cash from creditors and repaying these amounts and obtaining capital from owners and providing them in return with dividends as well returning their investments (reacquisition of capital stock).

In Dran's statement of cash flows for 2005, therefore, the net cash flow used in its financing operations should be computed as follows:

Proceeds from the sale of treasury stock (cash inflow)	$25,000
Cash dividend distributed in 2005 (cash outflow)	(15,500)
Payment for the early retirement of bonds payable	(187,500)
Net cash used in financing activities, 2005	$(178,000)

OPERATING ACTIVITIES

Operating activities apply to producing or selling merchandise or performing services. Under the direct method, items applying to the income statement are presented in the operating activities section.

Cash inflows from operating activities include:

☐ Cash receipts from sales or servicing, such as from customers, licensees, and lessees.

☐ Interest and dividend receipts.

☐ Proceeds received from an insurance policy.

☐ Refunds from suppliers.

☐ Sale of trading securities.

☐ Award received from a lawsuit.

☐ Other operating receipts.

Cash outflows from operating activities include:

☐ Cash paid to buy materials and merchandise purchases.

☐ Cash paid for services.

☐ Payment of general and administrative expenses.

☐ Employee salary payments.

☐ Payments to suppliers.

☐ Insurance payments.

☐ Advertising and promotion payments.

☐ Payment for lawsuit damages.

☐ Cash refunds such as to customers for inferior goods.

☐ Interest payments.

☐ Income tax payments.

☐ Cash purchase of trading securities.

☐ Payment of duties, fines, and penalties.

☐ Charitable contribution payments.

☐ Other operating cash payments.

☐ Amortization of acquisition date fair value adjustments under either the purchase or acquisition methods.

There may be further breakdowns of operating cash receipts and cash payments to improve financial reporting. For example, a producer may divide cash paid to vendors into payments to buy merchandise and payments for selling expenses.

ASC 230-10-45-17, provides that a cash payment to pay off an asset retirement obligation should be presented under operating activities.

Exhibit 6-3 illustrates the presentation of cash flows from operating activities using the direct method.

As stated before, with the direct method, the reconciliation of earnings to cash flow from operations is presented in a separate schedule.

Exhibit 6-3: Cash Flows from an Operating Activities Section Under the Direct Method

Cash inflows:		
Cash received from customers	$600,000	
Dividend and interest receipts	100,000	
Award received from a lawsuit	200,000	
Cash inflows from operating activities		$900,000
Cash outlays:		
Cash paid to vendors	$300,000	
Cash paid to employees	50,000	
Interest paid	20,000	
Income taxes paid	80,000	
Payment of insurance	30,000	
Advertising outlays	70,000	
Purchase of trading securities	150,000	
Cash outlays from operating activities		700,000
Net cash flow from operations		$200,000

Under the indirect method, as previously noted, the operating section presents only the reconciliation of net income to cash flow from operations based on adjustments for noncash revenue and noncash expense items as well as changes in current asset and current liability accounts affecting operating activities.

INVESTING ACTIVITIES

Investing activities include making and collecting loans; purchasing and selling property, plant, and equipment; and buying or selling available-for-sale or held-to-maturity securities in other companies. **Note:** Trading securities are considered operating activities.

Cash inflows from investing activities include:

☐ Proceeds received from selling fixed assets.

☐ Selling available-for-sale or held-to-maturity securities in other companies.

☐ Collecting on loans made to debtors, principal portion.

Cash outlays for investing activities include:

☐ Acquiring fixed assets.

☐ Buying available-for-sale or held-to-maturity securities of other companies.

☐ Granting loans to borrowers.

☐ Cash purchases of businesses in a business combination.

Note: Cash flows for investing activities should include only advance payments, the down payment, or other payments at the date when fixed assets are bought, or shortly before or after. If there are principal payments on an installment loan at later dates, such payments are included in financing activities. Any noncash element of a transaction to buy a fixed asset, such as through debt incurrence, is disclosed in a supplementary schedule titled "Noncash Investment and Financing Activities."

Tip: If a company is bought or sold under the purchase method to account for a business combination, any cash paid or received is considered an investing activity. The fair market value of any assets acquired or liabilities incurred in such a transaction would be presented in the schedule of noncash investing and financing activities.

FINANCING ACTIVITIES

Financing activities include issuing or repurchasing a company's own stock (common stock or preferred stock), paying cash dividends to stockholders, and issuing or paying back short-term or long-term debt.

Cash inflows from financing activities include:

☐ Funds received from issuing the company's own short-term or long-term debt (e.g., bonds payable, notes payable, or mortgage payable).

☐ Funds received from selling the company's own equity securities. (**Note:** This also includes the subsequent reissuance of treasury stock.)

Cash outflows for financing activities include:

☐ Purchase of treasury stock.

☐ Cash dividend payments. (**Note:** Dividends declared but unpaid and stock dividends are noncash transactions and are presented in a supplementary schedule titled "Noncash Investing and Financing Activities.")

☐ Retiring or paying off the principal on short-term or long-term debt. (This includes payments of principal on capital lease obligations.)

☐ Other principal payments to long-term creditors.

☐ Payment of debt issue costs.

☐ Subsidiary dividends paid to noncontrolling interest shareholders.

Caution: Gains or losses from the early extinguishment of debt are part of the cash flow related to the repayment of the amount borrowed as a financing activity. Such gains or losses are not an element of net cash flow from operating activities.

MULTICLASSIFICATION

If a cash receipt or cash payment relates to more than one classification (e.g., operating, investing, and financing), classification is based on the major activity involving the cash flow. For example, the acquisition and sale of machinery is usually deemed an investing outlay. Further, the purchase and sale of equipment used by the business or rented out typically is considered an investing activity. However, if the business intends to use or rent the equipment for a short time period and then sell it, this would be considered an operating activity.

NONCASH INVESTING AND FINANCING ACTIVITIES

There must be separate supplementary disclosure in a section (schedule) following the statement of cash flows or in the notes in narrative form presenting investing and financing activities that affect assets and liabilities but do not impact cash flow. In addition, though a transaction having cash and noncash components should be discussed, only the cash aspect should be presented in the statement of cash flows. In other words, if a transaction is part cash and part noncash, the cash part is reported in the cash flow statement while the noncash portion is disclosed in narrative form or in a schedule of noncash activities. Examples of noncash investing and financing activities are buying property in exchange for a mortgage payable and/or common stock, purchasing an intangible asset with the issuance of preferred stock, converting long-term debt into common stock, converting preferred stock to common stock, converting long-term notes receivable to held-to-maturity securities, conducting nonmonetary exchange of assets, and acquiring an asset though a capital lease. The following are also noncash investing and financing activities: stock issue costs not paid in cash, third-party financing, stock dividends, and property dividends. An illustrative presentation follows:

NONCASH INVESTING AND FINANCING ACTIVITIES:

Purchase of land by issuing a mortgage payable	$100,000
Conversion of a bond payable to common stock	$400,000

SPECIAL ITEMS IN THE INCOME STATEMENT

Extraordinary items, cumulative effect of a change in principle, and income from discontinued operations do not have to be broken out separately in the statement of cash flows. These items may be classified under operating, investing, or financing activities as appropriate. For example, an extraordinary loss due to a lawsuit would be presented under operating activities. An extraordinary gain on the early extinguishment of debt would be shown under financing activities. An extraordinary loss on equipment due to a fire would be presented as an investing activity.

AGENCY ARRANGEMENTS

Some changes in certain current assets and liabilities do not affect net income or cash earnings. An example is a company that collects sales taxes from customers that it must remit to the government. This type of agency transaction is an operating activity and results in cash inflow and then cash outflow. Although the company does not receive any benefit for tax collection and remittance, it must still present the transaction in the operating section of the statement of cash flows.

HEDGING TRANSACTIONS

Cash inflow and outflow may relate to futures contracts, swap agreements, or option contracts designed to hedge specific transactions, such as the purchase or sale of goods. The cash flow arising from the hedge transaction should be classified in the same manner as the cash flow associated with the hedge item (e.g., inventory). Disclosure should be made of the company's accounting treatment for hedged events and transactions.

FOREIGN CURRENCY CASH FLOWS

A company may have foreign operations and foreign currency translations. For accounting purposes in treating foreign currency cash flows, the exchange rate at the time of the cash flow should be used in reporting the currency equivalent. Alternatively, the weighted-average exchange rate may be used if there is an immaterial difference relative to using the actual currency exchange rate. The weighted-average exchange rate may be suitable for revenues and expenses. The effect of changes in the exchange rate on cash balances held in foreign currencies is presented as a separate item when reconciling the change in cash and cash equivalents for the year. Further, noncash exchange gains and losses presented in the income statement should be shown as a separate item when reconciling net income to cash flow from operations. Footnote disclosure should be made of the exchange rate to convert cash flows.

CASE STUDIES

Case Study A

X Company provides the following financial statements:

X Company
Comparative Balance Sheets
December 31
(in millions)

	20X2	*20X3*
ASSETS		
Cash	$47	$40
Accounts receivable	35	30
Prepaid expenses	2	4
Land	35	50
Building	80	100
Accumulated depreciation	(6)	(9)
Equipment	42	50
Accumulated depreciation	(7)	(11)
Total assets	$228	$254
LIABILITIES AND STOCKHOLDERS' EQUITY		
Accounts payable	$16	$20
Long-term notes payable	20	30
Common stock	100	100
Retained earnings	92	104
Total liabilities and stockholders' equity	$228	$254

X Company
Income Statement
For the Year Ended December 31, 20X3
(in millions)

Revenue		$300
Operating expenses (excluding depreciation)	$200	
Depreciation	7	207
Income from operations		$ 93
Income tax expense		32
Net income		$61

Additional information is as follows:

☐ Cash dividends paid totaled $49.

☐ The company issued long-term notes payable for cash.

☐ Land, building, and equipment were acquired for cash.

The statement of cash flows can now be prepared under the indirect method as follows:

X Company
Statement of Cash Flows
For the Year Ended December 31, 20X3
(in millions)

Cash flow from operating activities:		
Net income		$61
Add (deduct) items not affecting cash:		
Depreciation expense	$7	
Decrease in accounts receivable	5	
Increase in prepaid expenses	(2)	
Increase in accounts payable	4	14
Net cash flow from operating activities		$75
Cash flow from investing activities:		
Purchase of land	$(15)	
Purchase of building	(20)	
Purchase of equipment	(8)	(43)
Cash flow from financing activities:		
Issuance of long-term notes payable	$10	
Payment of cash dividends	(49)	(39)
Net decrease in cash		$(7)

A financial analysis of the statement of cash flows reveals that the profitability and operating cash flow of X Company improved. This indicates good earnings performance as well as the fact that earnings are backed up by cash. The decrease in accounts receivable may reveal better collection efforts. The increase in accounts payable is a sign that suppliers are confident in the company and willing to give interest-free financing. The acquisition of land, building, and equipment points to a growing business undertaking capital expansion. The issuance of long-term notes payable indicates that part of the financing of assets is through debt. Stockholders will be happy with the significant dividend payout of 80.3% (dividends divided by net income, or $49/$61). Overall, there was a decrease in cash of $7, but this should not cause alarm because of the company's profitability and the fact that the cash was used for capital expansion and dividend payments. The dividend payout should be reduced from its high level and the funds reinvested in the profitable business. Also, the curtailment of dividends by more than $7 would result in a positive net cash flow for the year. Cash flow is needed for immediate liquidity needs.

Case Study B

Y Company presents the following statement of cash flows:

Cash flows from operating activities:
Net income $134,000

Add (deduct) items not affecting cash		
Depreciation expense	$21,000	
Decrease in accounts receivable	10,000	
Increase in prepaid expenses	(6,000)	
Increase in accounts payable	35,000	60,000
Net cash flow from operating activities		$194,000
Cash flows from investing activities:		
Purchase of land	$(70,000)	
Purchase of building	(200,000)	
Purchase of equipment	(68,000)	
Cash used by investing activities		(338,000)
Cash flows from financing activities:		
Issuance of bonds	$150,000	
Payment of cash dividends	(18,000)	
Cash provided by financing activities		132,000
Net decrease in cash		$(12,000)

An analysis of the statement of cash flows reveals that the company is profitable. Also, cash flow from operating activities exceeds net income, which indicates good internal cash generation. The ratio of cash flow from operating activities to net income is a solid 1:45 ($194,000/$134,000). A high ratio is desirable because it shows that earnings are backed up by cash. The decline in accounts receivable could indicate better collection efforts. The increase in accounts payable shows that the company can obtain interest-free financing. The company is definitely in the process of expanding for future growth, as evidenced by the purchase of land, building, and equipment. The debt position of the company has increased, indicating greater risk. The dividend payout was 13.4% ($18,000/$134,000). Stockholders look positively on a firm that pays dividends. The decrease in cash flow for the year of $12,000 is a negative sign.

COMPREHENSIVE EXAMPLES

The Cash Flow Statement Using the Direct Method

Cherry Inc.
Balance Sheets
December 31

	20X2	20X1
ASSETS		
Current Assets		
Cash	$16,225	$28,125
Accounts receivable	56,400	60,800
Notes receivable—Lou Company	13,900	5,700
Interest receivable	725	400

	20X2	20X1
Inventory	74,750	91,650
Total current assets	$162,000	$186,675
Property and Equipment		
Land	30,000	30,000
Building	160,000	160,000
Machinery	27,500	20,000
Fixtures	9,250	9,250
Autos	5,500	11,750
	$232,250	$231,000
Accumulated depreciation	97,975	92,500
	$134,325	$138,500
Other Assets		
Cash surrender value of insurance policy	11,475	9,675
Deferred costs	675	1,350
	12,150	11,025
TOTAL ASSETS	$308,475	$336,200
LIABILITIES AND STOCKHOLDERS' EQUITY		
Current Liabilities		
Notes payable	$20,000	$25,000
Current portion of serial bonds	36,000	33,750
Accounts payable	85,425	89,700
Accrued liabilities		
Wages	5,500	4,075
Interest	925	700
Payroll taxes	650	475
Income taxes	2,175	1125
Total current liabilities	$150,675	$154,825
Serial long-term debt, less current portion	90,250	121,250
TOTAL LIABILITIES	240,925	276,075
Stockholders' Equity		
Common Stock	10,000	10,000
Retained Earnings	57,550	50,125
TOTAL STOCKHOLDERS' EQUITY	$67,550	$60,125
TOTAL LIABILITIES AND STOCKHOLDERS' EQUITY	$308,475	$336,200

Cherry Inc.
Statement of Income
Year Ended December 31, 20X2

REVENUES

Sales	$368,600
Gain on sale of auto	125
Interest income	1200
	$369,925

COST OF SALES

Raw materials	157,600
Labor	16,450
Transportation-in	8,350
	$182,400

GROSS PROFIT	$187,525

SELLING AND ADMINISTRATIVE EXPENSES

Administrator's salaries	44,800
Sales employees salaries	24,200
Office salaries	25,800
Payroll taxes	9,325
Rent expense	12,925
Office expenses	5,400
Life insurance of administrators	2,100
Fees to outside professionals	2,950
Telephone expenses	2,350
Utilities expenses	4,675
Maintenance expense	3,350
Insurance expense	7,150
Uncollectible accounts expense	10,000
Amortization expense	675
Depreciation expense	9,425
Miscellaneous taxes	1,600
Interest expense	7,325
	$174,050

Income before income taxes	$13,475
Income taxes	4,050
NET INCOME	$9,425
RETAINED EARNINGS—BEGINNING OF THE YEAR	50,125
DIVIDENDS PAID	(2,000)
RETAINED EARNINGS—END OF THE YEAR	$57,550

Additional Data for Cherry Inc.

☐ Lou Company repaid $1,800 of its $5,700 receivable during the year. At December 31, 20X2, the Lou Company borrowed an additional $10,000.

☐ Cherry Company purchased machinery in exchange for a $2,500 down payment and a $5,000 note. The first payment on the machinery note is due in 20X3.

☐ An auto with an original cost of $6,250 and accumulated depreciation of $4,000 was sold for $2,375.

☐ The notes payable indicated in the current liabilities section have original maturities of less than three months.

Statement of Cash Flows—Direct Method

CASH FLOWS FROM OPERATING ACTIVITIES		
Collections from customers	$363,000	(1)
Interest received	875	(2)
Cash paid to suppliers and employees	(316,600)	(3)
Interest paid	(7,100)	(4)
Income taxes paid	(3,000)	(5)
Net cash provided by operating activities	$37,175	
NET FLOWS FROM INVESTING ACTIVITIES		
Purchase of machinery	(2,500)	
Proceeds from sale of auto	2,375	
Loans made to Lou Company	(10,000)	
Collections of loans	1,800	
Net cash used by investing activities	(8,325)	
CASH FLOWS FROM FINANCING ACTIVITIES		
Short-term payment of debt	(5,000)	
Long-term payment of debt	(33,750)	
Dividends paid	(2,000)	
Net cash used by financing activities	(40,750)	
Net decrease in cash	(11,900)	
Cash at the beginning of year	28,125	
Cash at end of year	$16,225	

Supplemental Disclosures

Noncash investing and financing activities	
Purchase of $7,500 of machinery paid for in part with a $5,000 note	$5,000

Analysis of Captions in the Statement of Cash Flows—Direct Method

(1) Collections from customers

Sales from the income statement	$368,600
Increase in accounts receivable	(5,600)
Total	$363,000

(2) Interest received

Interest income	$1,200
Increase in interest receivable	(325)
Total	$875

(3) Cash paid to suppliers and employees

Cost of sales	$182,400
Selling and administrative cost	174,050
Deduct for interest—separately disclosed	(7,325)
Deduct noncash expenditures	
Depreciation	(9,425)
Amortization	(675)
Increase in cash surrender value of insurance policy	1800
Uncollectible accounts expense	(10,000)
Decrease in inventory	(16,900)
Decrease in payables	4,275
Increase in compensation and payroll taxes	(1,600)
Total	$316,600

(4) Interest paid

Interest expense on income statement	$7,325
Increase in interest payable	(225)
Total	$7,100

(5) Income taxes paid

Income taxes per income statement	$4,050
Increase in income taxes payable	(1,050)
Total	$3,000

ASC 230-10-45-17 requires that if an enterprise uses the direct method to present cash flow from operating activities, it also must provide in a separate schedule the reconciliation of net income to net cash flow provided by operating activities. This reconciliation represents the identical form and content of the indirect method. The reconciliation shown next should be presented at the bottom of the statement of cash flows when the direct method is used or in a separate schedule.

Reconciliation

Net income	$9,425
Adjustment to reconcile net income to net cash provided by operating activities	
Depreciation	9,425
Amortization	675
Gain on sale of auto	(125)
Cash surrender value of insurance	(1,800)
Uncollectible accounts expense	10,000
Increase in accounts receivable	(5,600)
Increase in interest receivable	(325)
Decrease in inventories	16,900
Decrease in accounts payable	(4,275)
Increase in accrued liabilities	2,875
Net cash provided by operating activities	$37,175

ASC 230, *Statement of Cash Flows*

This example illustrates the direct and indirect methods of preparing the statement of cash flows.

The comparative balance sheet of CF Inc. is as follows:

CF Inc.
Comparative Balance Sheet
As of 12/31/20X2 and 12/31/20X1

	12/31/02	*12/31/01*
ASSETS		
Cash	268,120	10,000
Accounts receivable	20,000	17,000
Short-term investments	15,000	25,000
Inventory	85,000	75,000
Prepaid rent	5,000	17,000
Prepaid insurance	4,500	3,000
Office supplies	2,500	500
Land	100,000	250,000
Building	800,000	80,000
Less: Accumulated depreciation	(220,000)	(150,000)
Equipment	750,000	500,000
Less: Accumulated depreciation	(180,000)	(160,000)
Patent	30,000	50,000
Total assets	1,680,120	1,437,500
LIABILITIES AND EQUITY		
Accounts payable	350,000	400,000

	12/31/02	12/31/01
Taxes payable	8,000	3,000
Wages payable	25,000	15,000
Short-term notes payable	75,000	75,000
Long-term notes payable	65,000	85,000
Bonds payable	500,000	500,000
Premium on bonds payable	80,000	90,000
Common stock	260,000	170,000
Paid-in-capital in excess of par	80,000	60,000
Retained earnings	292,620	95,000
Total liabilities and equity	1,735,620	1,493,000

The income statement of CF Inc. is as follows:

CF Inc.
Income Statement
For Year Ended 12/31/20X2

Sales revenue		1,350,000
Cost of goods sold		(800,000)
Gross margin		550,000
Operating expenses		
Selling expenses	(120,000)	
Administrative expenses	(195,000)	
Depreciation/amortization	(110,000)	
Total operating expenses		(425,000)
Income from operations		125,000
Other revenues and expenses		
Gain on sale of land	60,000	
Gain on sale of short-term investments	35,000	
Dividends revenue	6,600	
Interest expense	(80,000)	
Total other revenues and expenses		21,600
Income before taxes		146,600
Income taxes (30%)		(43,980)
Net income		102,620
Dividends—common stock		95,000
Addition to retained earnings		197,620

    The first step in preparing the statement of cash flows is to analyze the changes in the balance sheet accounts:

Change in:	
Cash	258,120
Accounts receivable	3,000
Short-term investments	(10,000)
Inventory	10,000
Prepaid rent	(12,000)
Prepaid insurance	1,500
Office supplies	2,000
Land	
	(150,000)
Building	–
Less: Accumulated depreciation	(70,000)
Equipment	250,000
Less: Accumulated depreciation	(20,000)
Patent	(20,000)
Accounts payable	(50,000)
Taxes payable	5,000
Wages payable	10,000
Short-term notes payable	–
Long-term notes payable	(20,000)
Bonds payable	–
Premium on bonds payable	(10,000)
Common stock	90,000
Paid-in-capital in excess of par	20,000
Retained earnings	197,620

The statement of cash flows using the direct method may now be prepared as follows:

CF Inc.
Statement of Cash Flows—Direct Method
For Year Ended 12/31/20X2

CASH FLOWS FROM OPERATING ACTIVITIES

Cash received from customers	1,347,000	(1)
Dividends received	6,600	
Cash paid to suppliers	(860,000)	(2)
Cash paid for operating expenses	(296,500)	(3)
Taxes paid	(38,980)	(4)
Interest paid	(90,000)	(5)
Net cash from operating activities		68,120

CASH FLOWS FROM INVESTING ACTIVITIES

Sale of short-term investment	45,000
Sale of land	210,000

Purchase of equipment	(250,000)	
Net cash from investing activities		5,000
CASH FLOWS FROM FINANCING ACTIVITIES		
Issuance of common stock	110,000	
Payment of principal on long-term debt	(20,000)	
Payment of dividends	95,000	
Net cash from financing activities		185,000
Net change in cash		258,120
Beginning cash balance		10,000
Ending cash balance		268,120

The supporting computations are as follows:

(1)	Sales revenue	1,350,000	
	– Increase in accounts receivable	(3,000)	
	Cash received from customers		1,347,000
(2)	Cost of goods sold	800,000	
	+ Increase in inventory	10,000	
	+ Decrease in accounts payable	50,000	
	Cash paid to suppliers		860,000
(3)	Operating expenses	425,000	
	– Depreciation/amortization expense	(110,000)	
	– Decrease in prepaid rent	(12,000)	
	+ Increase in prepaid insurance	1,500	
	+ Increase in office supplies	2,000	
	– Increase in wages payable	(10,000)	
	Cash paid for operating expenses		296,500
(4)	Income taxes (30%)	43,980	
	– Increase in tax payable	(5,000)	
	Taxes paid		38,980
(5)	Interest expense	80,000	
	+ Decrease in bond premium	10,000	
	Interest paid		90,000

Whenever the direct method is used, ASC 230 requires reconciliation of net income to net cash from operating activities:

Reconciliation

Net income		102,620
Adjustments		
+ Depreciation/amortization expense	110,000	
− Amortization of bond premium	(10,000)	
− Gain on sale of land	(60,000)	
− Gain on sale of investment	(35,000)	
− Increase in accounts receivable	(3,000)	
− Increase in inventory	(10,000)	
+ Decrease in prepaid rent	12,000	
− Increase prepaid insurance	(1,500)	
− Increase in office supplies	(2,000)	
− Decrease in accounts payable	(50,000)	
+ Increase in taxes payable	5,000	
+ Increase in wages payable	10,000	
Total adjustments		(34,500)
Net cash from operating activities		68,120

Alternatively, the statement of cash flows using the indirect method may be prepared as follows:

CF Inc.
Statement of Cash Flows—Indirect
Method For Year Ended 12/31/20X2

CASH FLOWS FROM OPERATING ACTIVITIES

Net income		102,620
Adjustments		
+ Depreciation/amortization expense	110,000	
− Amortization of bond premium	(10,000)	
− Gain on sale of land	(60,000)	
− Gain on sale of investment	(35,000)	
− Increase in accounts receivable	(3,000)	
− Increase in inventory	(10,000)	
+ Decrease in prepaid rent	12,000	
− Increase prepaid insurance	(1,500)	
− Increase in office supplies	(2,000)	
− Decrease in accounts payable	(50,000)	
+ Increase in taxes payable	5,000	
+ Increase in wages payable	10,000	
Total adjustments		(34,500)
Net cash from operating activities		68,120

CASH FLOWS FROM INVESTING ACTIVITIES

Sale of short-term investment	45,000	
Sale of land	210,000	
Purchase of equipment	(250,000)	
Net cash from investing activities		5,000

CASH FLOWS FROM FINANCING ACTIVITIES

Issuance of common stock	110,000	
Payment of principal on long-term debt	(20,000)	
Payment of dividends	95,000	
Net cash from financing activities		185,000
Net change in cash		258,120
Beginning cash balance		10,000
Ending cash balance		268,120

As per ASC 230-10-45-18, cash inflows and cash outflows for transactions in securities, and other assets bought only for *resale* and carried at market value in a *trading account* of banks, dealers, and brokers must be classified in the operating section of the statement of cash flows. A similar treatment is afforded for loans acquired for resale and carried at market value. They are also presented in the operating section of the statement.

Exception: Securities, other assets, or loans bought solely for investment purposes are presented in the investing section.

A statement of cash flows need not be prepared for a defined pension plan that is reporting under ASC 715-30, *Compensation—Retirement Benefits: Defined Benefit Plans—Pension*.

A statement of cash flows is not required for investment companies or for a common collective investment trust fund provided that the following conditions are satisfied:

☐ The entity prepared a statement of changes in net assets.

☐ The investments held are very liquid and expressed at market value.

☐ The entity's debt position is either minimal or none.

According to ASC 230-10-45-27, financial institutions may present net cash inflows and outflows for collections of loans, principal, deposit repayments, withdrawal of deposits, deposits with other financial institutions (e.g., credit unions, banks, savings institutions), time deposits, and client loans.

ASC 230-10-45-27 permits an entity that satisfies certain criteria to classify the cash flow arising from a hedging transaction in the same section of the cash flow statement as the hedged item (e.g., investing activity, financing activity). Appropriate disclosure should also be made of the accounting policy.

ANNUAL REPORT REFERENCES

Marathon Petroleum
2011 Annual Report

19. Supplemental Cash Flow Information

(In millions)	2011	2010	2009
Net cash provided by operating activities included:	$ 5	–	$ 2
Interest paid (net of amounts capitalized)	617	11	11
Income taxes paid to taxing authorities[a]			
Non-cash investing and financing activities:	$ 81	–	–
Property, plant and equipment contributed by Marathon Oil	26	32	77
Capital lease obligations increase	–	80	–
Preferred stock received in asset disposition			

[a] U.S. federal and most state income taxes were paid by Marathon Oil for periods prior to the Spinoff.

The consolidated statements of cash flows exclude changes to the consolidated balance sheets that did not affect cash. The following is a reconciliation of additions to property, plant and equipment to total capital expenditures:

(In millions)	2011	2010	2009
Additions to property, plant and equipment	$1,185	$1,217	$2,891
Acquistions[a]	74	–	–
Increase (decrease) in capital accruals	53	(51)	(312)
Total capital expenditures	$1,312	$1,166	$2,579

[a] Speedway's $74 million acquisition of 23 convenience stores in 2011. See Note 15.

The following is a reconciliation of contributions from (distributions to) Marathon Oil:

(In millions)	2011	2010	2009
Contributions from (distributions to) Marathon Oil per consolidated statements of cash flows	$ (783)	$ (1,330)	207
Net non-cash contributions from (distributions to) Marathon Oil	57	(118)	(158)
Contributions from (distributions to) Marathon Oil per consolidated statements of stockholders' equity / net investment	(726)	(1,448)	49

See Note 4 for information regarding non-cash contributions from (distributions to) Marathon Oil.

Anheuser-Busch
2007 Annual Report

9. Supplemental Cash Flow Information

Accounts payable include $120 million and $105 million of outstanding checks at December 31, 2007 and 2006, respectively. Supplemental cash flow information for the three years ended December 31 is presented in the following table (in millions).

	2007	*2006*	*2005*
Cash paid during the year			
Interest, net of interest capitalized	$ 454.8	$ 433.2	$ 436.0
Income taxes	$ 936.6	$ 920.2	$ 814.7
Excise taxes	$2,298.9	$2,252.3	$2,217.3
Change in working capital			
(Increase)/Decrease in current assets:			
Accounts receivable	$ (85.0)	$ (38.8)	$ 14.7
Inventories	(28.6)	(40.4)	35.8
Other current assets	(17.4)	(4.6)	6.9
Increase/(Decrease) in current liabilities:			
Accounts payable	38.2	176.8	54.7
Accrued salaries, wages and benefits	31.5	91.9	(40.5)
Accrued taxes	(27.7)	(22.8)	3.8
Accrued interest	12.2	0.5	(1.5)
Other current liabilities	3.5	17.1	(2.9)
Derivatives fair value adjustment	(7.4)	6.1	(9.8)
Working capital adjustment for acquisition/disposition	(1.4)	3.0	(10.9)
Impact of FIN 48 adoption	58.6	–	–
Net (increase)/decrease in working capital	$ (23.5)	$ 188.8	$ 50.3

General Electric
2005 Annual Report

Note 25. Supplemental Cash Flows Information

Changes in operating assets and liabilities are net of acquisitions and dispositions of principal businesses.

Amounts reported in the "Payments for principal businesses purchased" line in the Statement of Cash Flows is net of cash acquired and included debt assumed and immediately repaid in acquisitions.

Amounts reported in the "All other operating activities" line in the Statement of Cash Flows consists primarily of adjustments to current and noncurrent accruals and deferrals of costs and expenses, adjustments for gains and losses on assets, increases and decreases in assets held for sale and adjustments to assets.

Non-cash transactions include the following: in 2005, NBC Universal acquired IAC's 5.44% common interest in VUE for a total purchase price that included $115 million of non-cash consideration, representing the fair value of future services to be performed by NBC Universal (see note 16); in 2004, the issuance of GE common stock valued at $10,674 million in connection with the acquisition of Amersham and the issuance of NBC Universal shares valued at $5,845 million in connection with the combination of NBC and VUE; and in 2003, the acquisition of Osmonics, Inc. for GE common stock valued at $240 million.

December 31 (in millions)	2005	2004	2003
GE			
NET DISPOSITIONS (Purchases) OF GE SHARES FOR TREASURY			
Open market purchases under share repurchase program	$(5,024)	$(203)	$(340)
Other purchases	(1,844)	(1,689)	(837)
Dispositions	2,024	5,885	1,903
	$(4,844)	$(3,993)	$726
GECS			
ALL OTHER OPERATING ACTIVITIES			
Net change in assets held for sale	$2,192	$84	$1,168
Amortization of intangible assets	459	519	618
Realized gains on sale of investment securities	(381)	(204)	(205)
Other	(1,205)	(2,711)	(1,941)
	$1,065	$(2,312)	$(360)
NET INCREASE IN GECS FINANCING RECEIVABLES			
Increase in loans to customers	$(315,697)	$(342,357)	$(263,815)
Principal collections from customers—loans	267,728	305,846	238,518
Investment in equipment for financing leases	(23,728)	(22,649)	(22,518)

December 31 (in millions)	2005	2004	2003
Principal collections from customers— financing leases	21,770	19,715	18,909
Net change in credit card receivables	(21,391)	(20,651)	(11,483)
Sales of financing receivables	54,144	44,816	36,009
	$(16,954)	$(15,280)	$(4,687)
ALL OTHER INVESTING ACTIVITIES			
Purchases of securities by insurance activities	$(9,264)	$(7,474)	$(7,942)
Dispositions and maturities of securities by insurance activities	10,892	9,305	9,509
Proceeds from principal business dispositions	209	472	3,337
Other	2,807	2,807	1,199
	$4,644	$6,083	$6,103
NEWLY ISSUED DEBT HAVING MATURITIES LONGER THAN 90 DAYS			
Short-term (91 to 365 days)	$4,675	$3,940	$3,661
Long-term (longer than one year)	60,176	53,641	55,661
Proceeds-nonrecourse, leveraged lease	203	562	791
	$65,054	$58,143	$60,113
REPAYMENTS AND OTHER REDUCTIONS OF DEBT HAVING MATURITIES LONGER THAN 90 DAYS			
Short-term (91 to 365 days)	$(38,132)	$(41,443)	$(38,756)
Long-term (longer than one year)	(10,746)	(3,443)	(3,664)
Proceeds-nonrecourse, leveraged lease	(831)	(652)	(782)
	(49,709)	(45,538)	(43,202)
ALL OTHER FINANCING ACTIVITIES			
Proceeds from sales of investment contracts	$15,743	$11,079	$766
Redemption of investment contracts	(16,934)	(14,476)	(480)
	$(1,191)	$(3,397)	$286

Anheuser Busch
2004 Annual Report

9. Supplemental Cash Flow Information

Accounts payable include $111 million of outstanding checks at both December 31, 2004 and 2003. Supplemental cash flows information for the three years ended December 31 is presented in the following table (in millions).

	2004	2003	2002
Cash paid during the year:			
Interest, net of interest capitalized	**$390.3**	$369.0	$343.0
Income taxes	**$962.3**	$952.2	$788.7
Excise taxes	**$2,229.1**	$2,169.4	$2,119.5
Noncash investing activity:			
Issuance of treasury stock related to wholesaler acquisition (1)	**$ –**	$72.6	$ –
Change in working capital:			
(Increase)/decrease in current assets:			
Accounts receivable	**$(26.7)**	$(39.0)	$(9.5)
Inventories	**(102.8)**	(23.9)	28.2
Other current assets	**(21.6)**	(60.5)	53.3
Increase/(decrease) in current liabilities:			
Accounts payable	**101.1**	107.1	41.6
Accrued salaries, wages and benefits	**2.5**	1.4	31.7
Accrued taxes	**(10.2)**	(17.9)	19.9
Other current liabilities	**18.4**	(21.1)	(42.0)
Derivatives fair value adjustment	**(91.3)**	77.2	17.7
Working capital adjustment for acquisition	**(51.0)**	9.3	–
Net (increase)/decrease in working capital	**$(181.6)**	$32.6	$140.9

Note 1: Recorded as a reduction in treasury stock for the company's average cost of the shares ($28.5) and an increase in capital in excess of par value for the remainder ($44.1).

Alcoa
2005 Annual Report

Cash payments for interest and income taxes follow:

	2005	2004	2003
Interest	$386	$318	$352
Income taxes	413	294	303

The details related to acquisitions follow.

	2005	2004	2003
Fair value of assets acquired	$373	$7	$275
Liabilities assumed	(102)	(5)	(80)
Minority interests	190	–	224
Stock issued	–	–	(410)
Cash paid	461	2	9
Less: cash acquired	–	–	–
Net cash paid	$461	$2	$9

Chevron Texaco
2003 Annual Report

Note 4. Information Relating to the Consolidated Statement of Cash Flows

"Net decrease in operating working capital" is composed of the following:

	Year ended December 31		
	2003	*2002*	*2001*
(Increase) decrease in accounts and notes receivable	$(265)	$(1,135)	$2,472
Decrease (increase) in inventories	115	185	(294)
Decrease (increase) in prepaid expenses and other current assets	261	92	(211)
Increase (decrease) in accounts payable and accrued liabilities	242	1,845	(742)
(Decrease) increase in income and other taxes payable	(191)	138	(582)
Net decrease in operating working capital	$162	$1,125	$643
Net cash provided by operating activities includes the following cash payments for interest and income taxes:			
Interest paid on debt (net of capitalized interest)	$467	$533	$873
Income taxes paid	$5,316	$2,916	$5,465
Net (purchases) sales of marketable securities consist of the following gross amounts:			
Marketable securities purchased	$(3,563)	$(5,789)	$(2,848)
Marketable securities sold	3,716	5,998	2,665
Net sales (purchases) of marketable securities	$153	$209	$(183)

The 2003 "Net Cash Provided by Operating Activities" includes an $890 "Decrease in other deferred charges" and a decrease of the same amount in "Other" related to balance sheet reclassifications for certain pension-related assets and liabilities, in accordance with the requirements of FAS 87, "Employers' Accounting for Pensions."

The major components of "Capital expenditures" and the reconciliation of this amount to the capital and exploratory expenditures, excluding equity in affiliates, presented in the Management's Discussion and Analysis of Financial Condition and Results of Operations (MD&A) are detailed in the following table.

	Year ended December 31		
	2003	*2002*	*2001*
Additions to properties, plant and equipment[1]	$4,953	$6,262	$6,445
Additions to investments	687	1,138	2,902[2]
Current-year dry-hole expenditures	132	252	418
Payments for other liabilities and assets, net	(147)	(55)	(52)

| | Year ended December 31 | | |
	2003	*2002*	*2001*
Capital expenditures	**5,625**	7,597	9,713
Expensed exploration expenditures	**315**	303	393
Payments of long-term debt and other financing obligations, net	**286**[3]	2	210[3]
Capital and exploratory expenditures, excluding equity affiliates	**6,226**	7,902	10,316
Equity in affiliates' expenditures	**1,137**	1,353	1,712
Capital and exploratory expenditures, including equity affiliates	**$7,363**	$9,255	$12,028

[1] Net of noncash items of $1,183 in 2003, $195 in 2002 and $63 in 2001.
[2] Includes $1,500 for investment in Dynegy preferred stock.
[3] Deferred payments of $210 related to 1993 acquisition of an interest in the Tengizchevroil joint venture were made in 2003 and 2001.

Visteon
2003 Annual Report

15 Cash Flows

The reconciliation of net (loss) to cash flows provided by operating activities is as follows:

(in millions)	2003	2002	2001
Net (loss)	$(1,213)	$(352)	$(118)
Adjustment to reconcile net (loss) to cash flows from operating activities:			
Cumulative effect of change in accounting, net of tax	–	265	–
Depreciation and amortization	674	631	666
Asset impairment charges	436	–	–
Loss on divestitures	–	26	–
Earnings of affiliated companies in excess of dividends remitted	(20)	(28)	(12)
Benefit for deferred income taxes	(56)	(142)	(143)
Sale of receivables	5	10	–
Changes in assets and liabilities:			
Decrease (increase) in accounts receivable and other current assets	(39)	276	(197)
Decrease in inventory	143	85	86
Increase (decrease) in accounts payable, accrued and other liabilities	(13)	49	(185)
Increase in postretirement benefits other than pensions	376	258	256

(in millions)	2003	2002	2001
Other	77	23	83
Cash flows provided by operating activities	$370	$1,101	$436

Cash paid for interest and income taxes was as follows:

(in millions)	2003	2002	2001
Interest	$94	$120	$131
Income taxes	75	80	44

Copart
2003 Annual Report

(15) Noncash Financing and Investing Activities

In fiscal 2002, the Company acquired $18,487,000 of intangible assets and $9,505,900 of tangible assets through the issuance of common stock in conjunction with the New Castle, Delaware; Savannah, Georgia; Tifton, Georgia; Haslet, Texas and Greencastle, Pennsylvania acquisitions and purchase of land at the Baton Rouge, Louisiana location. In fiscal 2002, the Company received 21,670 shares of common stock as payment for the exercise of 148,000 shares of common stock under the 1992 Stock Option Plan. The Company retired these shares upon receipt. In fiscal 2001, the Company acquired $774,600 of intangible assets and $88,100 of tangible assets through the issuance of common stock in conjuction with the Shreveport, Louisiana acquisition.

H. J. Heinz
2005 Annual Report

	2005	2004	2003
	(Dollars in thousands)		
Cash Paid During the Year for:			
Interest	$209,888	$169,671	$282,366
Income taxes	$381,443	$221,043	$155,843
Details of Acquisitions:			
Fair value of assets	$187,108	$126,082	$30,391
Liabilities*	48,179	13,235	11,489
Cash paid	138,929	112,847	18,902
Less cash acquired	12,380	–	5,348
Net cash paid for acquisitions	126,549	$112,847	$13,554

	2005	2004	2003
Non-cash activities:			
Net assets spun-off	$ –	$ –	$1,644,195

* Includes obligations to sellers of $5.5 million and $4.6 million in 2005 and 2004, respectively.

Chiron
2003 Annual Report

Note 3–Supplemental Cash Flow Information

	2003	2002	2001
	(In thousands)		
Interest paid	$2,310	$876	$749
Income taxes paid	$70,240	$132,124	$134,827
Noncash investing and financing activities:			
Acquisitions:			
Cash acquired	$92,178	$18,208	–
Fair value of all other assets acquired	1,074,668	53,682	–
Liabilities assumed	(141,110)	(4,980)	–
Reduction of income taxes payable	–	1,739	–
Income taxes payable	(17,741)	–	–
Net deferred tax asset (liability)	(60,170)	8,425	–
Carrying value of original investment	–	(310)	–
Acquisition costs not yet paid as of December 31, 2003 and 2002	(40,930)	(707)	–
Total cash paid	$906,895	$76,057	$ –
Capital Lease:	$157,500	$ –	$ –
Exercise of common stock warrant	$ –	$ –	$18,513

National Semiconductor
2005 Annual Report

Note 15. Supplemental Disclosure of Cash Flow Information and Noncash Investing and Financing Activities

(IN MILLIONS)	2005	2004	2003
SUPPLEMENTAL DISCLOSURE OF CASH FLOW INFORMATION			
Cash paid for:			
Interest	$1.4	$1.3	$1.5
Income taxes	$76.1	$15.4	$17.6

(IN MILLIONS)	2005	2004	2003
SUPPLEMENTAL SCHEDULE OF NONCASH INVESTING AND FINANCING ACTIVITIES			
Issuance of stock for employee benefit plans	$ –	$0.9	$0.8
Issuance of common stock to directors	$1.0	$0.4	$0.3
Issuance of common stock in connection with the final installment payment of the purchase price paid to DigitalQuake	$ –	$0.6	$ –
Unearned compensation relating to restricted stock issuance	$2.6	$3.1	$0.5
Restricted stock cancellation	$1.4	$1.4	$1.1
Change in unrealized gain on cash flow hedges	$ –	$0.2	$0.2
Change in unrealized gain on available-for-sale securities	$(0.3)	$(3.4)	$(34.9)
Minimum pension liability	$13.5	$(24.3)	$57.5
Effect of investee equity transactions	$ –	$ –	$4.7
Acquisition of software license under long-term contracts	$ –	$19.7	$16.4
Repurchase of common stock upon settlement of an advance repurchase contract	$30.0	$ –	$ –

Chapter 7
Other Financial Statement Types and Related Items

CONTENTS

Interim financial statements are issued during the year, usually quarterly, to gauge periodically the entity's financial health and operating performance. Personal financial statements are discussed in this chapter; they reveal the net worth of an individual or family and may be used in loan applications. The accounting procedures for incorporating a business and for contemplating a start-up venture are also covered. Finally, the accounting and disclosure requirements for divestitures are presented.

INTERIM FINANCIAL REPORTS

ASC 270-10, *Interim Reporting: Overall*, covers interim financial reporting. Interim reporting is presenting financial information for a period less than one year. Each interim period is viewed as an integral part of the annual period. Interim financial reports may be issued semiannually, quarterly, or monthly. Complete financial statements or summarized information may be presented. Typically, interim reports include the operating results of the current interim period and the cumulative year-to-date figures, or last 12 months to date. Comparisons are usually made to results of comparable interim periods for the previous year. The authors recommend the following format:

ABC Company
Interim Financial Information
For Quarter Ending March 31, 20X3 and Comparable Periods

	Current Quarter		Twelve Months to Date	
	Three Months Ending	Three Months Ending	One Year Ending	One Year Ending
Accounts Listed	3/31/20X3	3/31/20X2	3/31/20X3	3/31/20X2

Quarterly reports are much less detailed than annual reports, often presenting condensed information. Interim statements do not have to be audited. Each page should be labeled "Unaudited."

Interim results should be based on those accounting principles used in the last year's annual report unless a change in accounting has been made subsequently. Further, accounting policies do not have to be disclosed in interim reports unless there has been a change in an accounting policy (principle or estimate).

Income statement information is required in interim reports. However, it is recommended but not required to present a balance sheet and cash flow statement at interim dates. If these statements are not reported, the company must disclose significant changes in liquid assets, working capital, noncurrent liabilities, and stockholders' equity.

Extraordinary items, nonrecurring items, and gain or loss on the disposal of a business segment are recognized in the interim period in which they occur.

Earnings per share determination for interim purposes is handled in a fashion similar to annual reporting.

Materiality should be related to the full fiscal year. However, an item not disclosed in the annual financial statement because of immateriality would still be presented in the interim report if it is material to that interim period.

Revenue and Expense Recognition

Sales or service revenue should be recorded as earned in the interim period. If an advance is received in the first quarter that benefits the whole year, it should be proportionately allocated over all quarters affected.

Expenses should be deducted in the interim period as incurred. Expenses are matched to related revenue in the same interim period. Matching expenses to revenue includes cost of material used, salaries and fringe benefits, rent, utilities, and warranty expense. Yearly expenses (e.g., insurance, pension, year-end bonuses) should be proportionately allocated to the interim periods affected on some rational basis (e.g., time, activity, benefit derived). For example, insurance premiums and property taxes should be allocated among the interim periods based on time expired. Some expenses (e.g., bad debts) are subject to year-end adjustment.

Gains or losses that would not be deferred at year-end should be reflected in the interim period in which they arise. It is prohibited to defer a gain or loss to a later interim period unless the deferral would have been allowed in annual reporting.

Inventory

In estimating interim inventory, the gross profit method may be used when interim physical inventory counts do not take place (or in the case of a fire). The method, assumptions, and reconciling adjustments must be disclosed.

ASC 330-10-55-2 covers recognition of inventory market declines at interim reporting dates. If a permanent loss occurs in inventory value in the interim period, it should be recognized immediately. A recovery in a later interim period is recognized as a gain. The gain from price recovery in a later interim period cannot exceed the previously recognized loss. Temporary losses in inventory value are not recognized, because no loss is anticipated for the annual period. In other words, temporary losses are viewed as seasonal price fluctuations.

If a temporary liquidation occurs in the last-in, first-out (LIFO) base with replacement anticipated by year-end, the cost of sales should be based on replacement cost.

EXAMPLE

The historical cost of an inventory item is $30,000 with an anticipated replacement cost of $36,000. The entry is:

Cost of sales	36,000	
Inventory		30,000
Reserve for liquidation of LIFO base		6,000

The reserve for liquidation of LIFO base is a current liability.

At the time of inventory replenishment at year-end, the journal entry is:

Reserve for liquidation of LIFO base	6,000	
Inventory	30,000	
Cash		36,000

Disclosure should be made of unusual accounting for computing interim inventories such as LIFO estimations.

If quantity (volume) discounts are granted to buyers that depend on expected annual purchases, an apportionment is required to the interim period based on the following ratio:

Purchases in the interim period/Total estimated annual purchases

If a standard cost system is used, variances that are expected to reverse by year-end may be deferred to a liability or asset account. However, if variances are not expected to reverse by year-end, they should be recognized in the interim period in which they arose.

Taxes

ASC 740-270, *Income Taxes: Interim Reporting*, covers the accounting for income taxes in interim statements, including the accounting for changes in tax rates.

The federal and local income tax provision for an interim period includes current and deferred taxes and should be cumulative for year-to-date. For example, the total tax expense for the first half of the year should be shown in the second quarter. Further, the second quarter's tax expense may also be presented for the three-month period of the second quarter.

Tax expense is based on income using the anticipated annual effective tax rate. The tax rate should take into account annual earnings, tax rates, tax credits, and alternative tax treatments. The tax rate should be based on continuing operations. A modification may be required to the anticipated annual effective tax rate at the end of each interim period based on new information:

$$\text{Effective tax rate} = \frac{\text{Expected annual income tax expense}}{\text{Expected annual before tax income}}$$

Extraordinary items and prior period adjustments should be shown net of tax in the interim period in which they occur.

The effect of a change in tax law should be recognized in the interim periods affected only after the effective date of the law.

Accounting Changes

ASC 250-10-05, *Accounting Changes and Error Corrections: Overall*, deals with the reporting of accounting changes in interim financial statements. A change in accounting principle made in an interim period shall be reported by retrospective application. If retrospective application to prechange interim periods is not practical, the desired change may only be made as of the beginning of a subsequent fiscal period. Disclosure should be made of the effect of the change in accounting method on income from continuing operations, net income, and related per-share amounts for postchange interim periods. Disclosure should be provided of the nature and justification of the change in principle.

Prior-Period Adjustments

ASC 250-10-45-26, *Accounting Changes and Error Corrections: Overall*, covers prior-period adjustments. Prior-period adjustments in interim reports are presented as follows:

- ☐ Net income of the current period should include the part of the effect applicable to current operations.
- ☐ Earnings of the affected interim periods of the current year should be restated to include the portion related thereto.
- ☐ If the prior-period adjustment impacts previous years, it should be included in the profit of the first interim period of the current year.

Criteria to be satisfied for prior-period adjustments in interim periods are identifiable to a previous interim period, subject to estimate, and material.

Prior-period adjustments for interim reporting include correction of errors, renegotiation proceedings, settlement of a lawsuit or claim, and utility revenue in connection with rate-making issues.

Disclosures

Minimum disclosure in interim reports is as follows:

☐ Revenue, tax expense, extraordinary items, and net income.

☐ Earnings per share.

☐ Seasonal revenue and costs.

☐ Material changes in tax expense, including reasons for significant differences between tax expense and income subject to tax.

☐ Information on disposal of a business segment.

☐ Commitments, contingencies, and uncertainties.

☐ Significant changes in financial position and cash flows.

Other disclosures peculiar to interim reporting are:

☐ Seasonal factors bearing on interim results. Seasonal companies should present supplementary information for the current and preceding 12-month periods ending at the interim date so that proper evaluation of the seasonal impact on interim results may be revealed.

☐ Significant items affecting the interim period.

☐ Whether a business combination took place and the financial effects thereto.

☐ Material adjustments to the fourth quarter if such quarter is not presented in the annual report.

☐ A change in the anticipated effective tax rate.

PERSONAL FINANCIAL STATEMENTS

Personal financial statements may be prepared for an individual or family to reveal financial position. Personal financial statements show both business and personal interests. Accrual accounting must be followed. Such statements may be used in financial planning, in loan applications, and for governmental compliance mandates.

The statement of financial condition is prepared as follows:

☐ No segregation is made between current and noncurrent classifications.

☐ Assets are presented at estimated current values and are listed in liquidity (maturity) order. Current values may be based on appraisals, present value of future cash flows, and inflation-adjusted historical cost. If assets are jointly owned, the person's beneficial interest should be presented. Receivables should be presented at the discounted amounts expected to be collected using the appropriate interest rate. The investment in life insurance is at the cash value of the policy less the amount of any loans against it. Option prices may not be available to value options. In such a case, the estimated current value may be based on the asset values subject to option, taking into account exercise prices and option periods. Intangible assets are presented at the present value of future net cash flows to be derived from them. Nonforfeitable rights to receive future sums should be presented at their discounted amounts.

☐ Liabilities are presented at current amounts in maturity order. Liabilities are typically shown at principal plus accrued interest due.

☐ Estimated taxes payable are presented as a liability, including provision for unpaid taxes of prior years. The tax obligation is reduced by withholding and estimated tax payments.

EXAMPLE

An illustrative Statement of Financial Condition follows:

Mr. and Mrs. Paul Jones
Statement of Financial Condition
December 31, 20X2

ASSETS	
Cash	$ 7,000
Interest and dividend receivable	1,000
Trading securities	12,000
Equity interest in a closely held business	5,000
Cash surrender value of life insurance	2,000
Real estate	185,000
Personal property	40,000
Total assets	$252,000
LIABILITIES	
Credit cards	$ 13,000
Income taxes payable	14,000
Loans payable	20,000
Mortgage payable	50,000
Total liabilities	$ 97,000
Estimated taxes on the differences between estimated current values of assets and liabilities	28,000
Net worth	$127,000
Total liabilities and net worth	$252,000

Preparation of a statement of changes in net worth is optional. Items increasing net worth include income, increases in the current value of assets, decreases in the current amounts of liabilities, and decreases in estimated taxes on the difference between estimated current asset values and liability amounts and their tax bases. Of course, items decreasing net worth are the opposite.

Comparative financial statements are optional.

The following should be footnoted:

☐ Individuals or family involved.

☐ Nature of joint ownership of assets.

☐ Information about receivables and payables, including collateral, maturities, and interest rates.

☐ Noncancellable commitments, such as particulars of leasing arrangements.

☐ Major investments by type.

☐ Listing of intangibles with anticipated lives.

☐ Approach followed in computing current values.

☐ Method and assumptions used in determining income taxes.

☐ Nonforfeitable rights (e.g., pension rights).

☐ Face amount of life insurance.

☐ Names of companies/industries and estimated current values of any significant investments relative to other assets.

☐ Percentage equity in a closely held company, including the type of business activities, summarized financial information, and accounting basis used.

INCORPORATION OF A BUSINESS

If an unincorporated business incorporates and issues equity and debt securities in exchange for the assets of the unincorporated entity, the following accounting procedures are followed:

☐ Assets are brought forth at fair market value.

☐ Current liabilities are recognized at face value while noncurrent liabilities are recorded at present value.

☐ Stock issued is recorded at par value.

☐ The gain or loss is not recorded on the issuance of stock in exchange for the unincorporated entity's assets.

The journal entry follows:

Current assets

Noncurrent assets

Current liabilities

Noncurrent liabilities

Common stock

Paid-in-capital

DIVESTITURES

As per ASC 845-10-05-6, *Nonmonetary Transactions: Overall*, a gain or loss cannot be recognized on a corporate divestiture. However, disclosure should be made of the nature and terms of the divestiture.

If there is an exchange of stock held by a parent in a subsidiary for stock of the parent company itself held by stockholders in the parent, there is a non-pro rata split-off of the business segment because a reorganization is recorded at fair value. However, if there is a split-off of a targeted company distributed on a pro rata basis to the one holding the applicable targeted stock, it should be recorded at historical cost, as long as the targeted stock did not arise in contemplation of the later split-off. If the contemplated situation did in fact exist, the transaction is recorded at fair value. In a split-off, there is a distribution of shares in the business segment, with the investor's shares being exchanged on a pro rata basis for the shares of the new company. In a split-off, the transaction is, in effect, the purchase of treasury stock. Retained earnings is not changed.

In a spin-off, there is a distribution of the segment's shares to the investor's shareholders without the holders surrendering their shares.

In some cases, a split-off or spin-off may be treated as a discontinued operation of a business segment.

EXAMPLE

X Company declares and pays a dividend to stockholders of 200,000 shares of common stock of Y Company. The investment in Y Company at the date of spin-off under the equity method was $900,000.

The journal entries follow:

Retained earnings	900,000	
Property dividends payable		900,000
To record the declaration of the property dividend.		
Property dividends payable	900,000	
Investment in Y Company		900,000
To record the payment of the property dividend.		

Note that in a spin-off no gain or loss is recorded.

The same information is assumed except that in exchange for the 200,000 shares of Y Company, X Company's stockholders give up 50,000 shares of X Company's common stock. The journal entry at the split-off date is:

Treasury stock	900,000	
Investment in Y Company		900,000

To reflect the purchase of treasury stock in exchange for the investment in Y Company.

In a split-up, there is a transfer of the operations of the original entity to at least two *new* entities.

EXAMPLE

L Company transfers Division A to M Company (a newly formed company) and its Division B to N Company (a newly formed company). L Company had only divisions A and B, so it terminates in existence. L Company shareholders receive a half share in M Company and a half share in N Company for each one share of L Company.

Divisions A and B have the same book value of net assets.

Prior to the transfer, L Company's assets were $1,000,000, liabilities were $600,000, and equity was $400,000.

The liquidation entry to record the termination of L Company is:

Liabilities	600,000	
Stockholders' equity	400,000	
Assets		1,000,000

The entry to record M Company and N Company (the newly formed companies) would be identical based on the information given in this example. The entry is:

Assets	500,000	
Liabilities		300,000
Paid-in-capital		200,000

ANNUAL REPORT REFERENCES

Campbell Soup
2005 Annual Report

22 Quarterly Data (unaudited)

2005	First	Second	Third	Fourth
Net sales	**$2,091**	**$2,223**	**$1,736**	**$1,498**
Cost of products sold	**1,245**	**1,321**	**1,035**	**890**
Net earnings	**230**	**235**	**146**	**96**
Per share—basic				
Net earnings	**0.56**	**0.57**	**0.36**	**0.23**
Dividends	**0.17**	**0.17**	**0.17**	**0.17**
Per share—assuming dilution				
Net earnings	**0.56**	**0.57**	**0.35**	**0.23**
Market place				
High	**$27.13**	**$30.52**	**$29.74**	**$31.60**
Low	**$25.21**	**$26.68**	**$27.35**	**$29.53**

2004	First	Second	Third	Fourth
Net sales	$1,909	$2,100	$1,667	$1,433
Cost of products sold	1,108	1,212	995	872
Net earnings[1]	211	235	142	59
Per share—basic				
Net earnings	0.51	0.57	0.35	0.14
Dividends	0.1575	0.1575	0.1575	0.1575
Per share—assuming dilution				
Net earnings	0.51	0.57	0.34	0.14

2004	First	Second	Third	Fourth
Market place				
High	$27.90	$27.39	$28.70	$28.13
Low	$23.26	$24.92	$26.15	$25.03

[1] Net earnings in the fourth quarter include a restructuring charge of $22 or $.05 per share. (See Note 5 to the Consolidated Financial Statements.)

International Game Technology
2004 Annual Report

19. Selected Quarterly Financial Data (Unaudited)

Years ended September 30,	First	Second	Third	Fourth
(In thousands, except per share amount and stock prices)				
2004				
Total revenues	$608,061	$636,084	$618,887	$621,720
Gross profit	321,066	339,109	338,257	320,817
Operating income	202,243	206,012	211,082	194,987
Income from continuing operations	116,658	117,684	141,102	54,309
Net income	176,324	116,942	141,102	54,309
Diluted earnings per share	$0.50	$0.32	$0.38	$0.15
Stock price				
High	$36.96	$45.78	$46.82	$38.17
Low	$28.09	$34.65	$33.45	$28.72
2003 (2)				
Total revenues	$489,632	$529,088	$561,921	$547,496
Gross profit	247,331	269,943	279,043	298,588
Operating income	150,054	160,052	173,563	182,273
Income from continuing operations	84,747	89,020	99,886	101,639
Net income	91,587	87,114	103,685	108,341
Diluted earnings per share (1)	$0.26	$0.25	$0.30	$0.31
Stock price (1)				
High	$19.82	$21.80	$25.38	$28.87
Low	$16.31	$18.52	$19.68	$24.50
2002 (2)				
Total revenues	$301,493	$461,286	$483,619	$482,114
Gross profit	136,402	227,902	235,990	242,599
Earnings (losses) of unconsolidated affiliates	33,865	(748)	(345)	(302)
Operating income	97,790	132,015	142,771	143,874
Income from continuing operations	51,790	70,328	78,420	54,174
Net income	51,790	73,900	82,628	62,847
Diluted earnings per share (1)	$0.18	$0.20	$0.23	$0.18
Stock price (1)				
High	$17.76	$17.52	$16.11	$17.52

Years ended September 30,	First	Second	Third	Fourth
Low	$10.28	$15.20	$13.44	$12.39

(1) Stock price and per share amounts for all periods presented have been adjusted to reflect the four-for-one stock split effected June 18, 2003.

(2) Certain operations acquired with Anchor that were not a strategic fit with IGTA's core business strategy were sold or held for sale, and therefore reclassified to discontinued operations for all periods presented.

Black & Decker
2002 Annual Report

Note 19: Quarterly Results (Unaudited)

(Dollars in Millions Except Per Share Data) Year Ended December 31, 2002	First Quarter	Second Quarter	Third Quarter	Fourth Quarter
Sales	$951.7	$1,125.3	$1,085.2	$1,231.8
Gross margin	306.9	378.5	380.7	451.8
Net earnings	33.0	66.1	54.9	75.7
Net earnings per common share— basic	$.41	$.82	$.68	$.94
Net earnings per common share— assuming dilution	$.41	$.81	$.68	$.94
Year Ended December 31, 2001				
Sales	$962.0	$1,049.7	$1,039.2	$1,194.7
Gross margin	325.6	339.5	342.8	391.1
Net earnings (loss)	33.1	41.7	46.2	(13.0)
Net earnings (loss) per common share—basic	$.41	$.52	$.57	$(.16)
Net earnings (loss) per common share—assuming dilution	$.40	$.51	$.57	$(.16)

Results for the third quarter of 2002 included a restructuring charge of $38.4 million ($22.3 million net of tax). Results for the fourth quarter of 2002 included a restructuring charge of $12.3 million ($9.4 million net of tax).

Results for the fourth quarter of 2001 included a restructuring charge of $99.8 million ($70.6 million net of tax).

As more fully described in Note 1, effective January 1, 2002, the Corporation adopted EITF 01-9. Upon the adoption of EITF 01-9, previously reported amounts were restated and resulted in a reduction of sales (and an offsetting reduction of selling expenses) of $17.0 million, $20.7 million, $23.8 million, and $26.0 million for the first, second, third, and fourth quarters of 2001, respectively.

As more fully described in Note 1, effective January 1, 2002, the Corporation adopted SFAS No. 142. Results for the first, second, third, and fourth quarters of 2001 each include goodwill amortization of $6.6 million. Net earnings (loss), adjusted to exclude goodwill amortization in the first, second, third, and fourth quarters of 2001, would have been $39.7 million, $48.3 million, $52.8 million, and $(6.4) million, respectively, Net earnings (loss) per common share–basic, adjusted to exclude goodwill amortization in the first, second, third, and fourth quarters of 2001, would have been $.49, $.60, $.65, and $(.08), respectively. Net earnings (loss) per common share–assuming dilution, adjusted to exclude goodwill amortization in the first, second, third, and fourth quarters of 2001, would have been $.48, $.59, $.65, and $(.08), respectively.

Earnings per common share are computed independently for each of the quarters presented. Therefore, the sum of the quarters may not be equal to the full year earnings per share amounts.

Whirlpool 2002
Annual Report

18 Quarterly Results of Operations (Unaudited)

Millions of dollars, except per share data	Dec. 31	Sept. 30	Jun. 30	Three Months Ended Restated Mar. 31
2002				
Net sales	$2,947	$2,759	$2,737	$2,574
Cost of products sold	$2,266	2,114	2,103	1,982
Earnings from continuing operations	14	101	63	84
Net earnings (loss)	(29)	101	63	(529)
Per share of common stock				
Basic earnings from continuing operations	$0.20	$1.48	$0.93	$1.25
Basic net earnings (loss)	(0.43)	1.48	0.93	(7.86)
Diluted earnings from continuing operations	$0.20	$1.46	$0.91	$1.21
Diluted net earnings (loss)	(0.42)	1.46	0.91	(7.63)
Dividends	$0.34	$0.34	$0.34	$0.34
Significant after-tax items included in the quarterly net earnings (loss):				
Restructuring and related charges (Note 13)	$(84)	$(11)	$(19)	$(8)
Impairment charge related to minority investment (Note 7)	–	–	(22)	–
Goodwill write-off of an Asian entity (Note 3)	(9)	–	–	–
Product recalls (Note 14)	(6)	–	–	–
Discontinued operations (Note 5)	(43)	–	–	–
Cumulative effect of a change in accounting principle (Note 3)	–	–	–	(613)

The net loss (and related per share amounts) for the restated first quarter as shown above differ from the originally filed amounts due to the adoption of SFAS No. 142, as discussed in Note 3.

Millions of dollars, except per share data	Dec. 31	Sept. 30	Jun. 30	Three Months Ended Restated Mar. 31
2001				
Net sales	$2,647	$2,594	$2,585	$2,517
Cost of products sold	1,989	1,988	1,989	1,959
Earnings (loss) from continuing operations	21	(94)	74	33
Net earnings (loss)	21	(94)	53	41
Per share of common stock				
Basic earnings (loss) from continuing operations	$0.31	$(1.40)	$1.12	$0.49
Basic net earnings (loss)	0.31	(1.40)	0.80	0.62
Diluted earnings (loss) from continuing operations	$0.31	$(1.40)	$1.10	$0.49
Diluted net earnings (loss)	0.31	(1.40)	0.78	0.61
Dividends	$0.34	$0.34	$0.34	$0.34
Significant after-tax items included in the quarterly net earnings (loss):				
Restructuring and related charges (Note 13)	$(91)	$(11)	$(14)	$(40)
Product recalls (Note 14)	3	(184)	–	–
Discontinued operations (Note 5)	–	–	(21)	–
Cumulative effect of a change in accounting principle (Note 1)	–	–	–	8

United States Steel
2004 Annual Report

3. Divestiture

On June 30, 2003, U.S. Steel completed the sale of the coal mines and related assets of U.S. Steel Mining Company, LLC (Mining Sale) to PinnOak Resources, LLC (PinnOak), which is not affiliated with U.S. Steel, thereby ending U.S. Steel's participation in coal mining operations. PinnOak acquired the Pinnacle No. 50 mine complex located near Pineville, West Virginia and the Oak Grove mine complex located near Birmingham, Alabama. In conjunction with the sale, U.S. Steel and PinnOak entered into a long-term coal supply agreement, which runs through December 31, 2006.

The gross proceeds from the sale were $55 million and resulted in a pretax gain on disposal of assets of $13 million in the second quarter of 2003. In addition, EITF 92-13, "Accounting for Estimated Payments in Connection with the Coal Industry Retiree Health Benefit Act of 1992" requires that enterprises no longer having operations in the coal industry must account for their entire obligation related to the multiemployer health care benefit plans created by the Act as a loss in accordance with FAS No. 5, "Accounting for Contingencies." Accordingly, U.S. Steel recognized the present value of these obligations in the amount of $85 million, resulting in the recognition of an extraordinary loss of $52 million, net of tax of $33 million.

Raytheon
2002 Annual Report

Note C: Acquisitions and Divestitures

In December 2002, the Company acquired JPS Communications, Inc. for $10 million in cash. Assets acquired included $2 million of accounts receivable and $2 million of inventories. The Company also recorded $4 million of intangible assets and $2 million of goodwill in connection with this acquisition. Also in December 2002, the Company announced an agreement to acquire Solipsys Corporation, subject to regulatory approval. There can be no assurance that this transaction will be consummated.

In 2001, the Company sold a majority interest in its aviation support business for $154 million in cash and retained $47 million in trade receivables and $66 million in preferred and common equity in the business. The Company also sold its recreational marine business for $100 million. The net gain resulting from these dispositions was $74 million.

In 2000, the Company sold its flight simulation business for $160 million, its optical systems business for $153 million, and other non-core business operations for $17 million. The net gain resulting from these dispositions was $35 million.

The Company merged with the defense business of Hughes Electronics Corporation (Hughes Defense) in December 1997. In October 2001, the Company and Hughes Electronics agreed to a settlement regarding the purchase price adjustment related to the Company's merger with Hughes Defense. Under the terms of the merger agreement, Hughes Electronics agreed to reimburse the Company approximately $635 million of its purchase price, with $500 million received in 2001 and the balance received in 2002. The settlement resulted in a $555 million reduction in goodwill. The $135 million receivable was included in prepaid expenses and other current assets at December 31, 2001.

Unisys
2002 Annual Report

Substantially all of the company's investments at equity consist of Nihon Unisys, Ltd., a publicly traded Japanese company ("NUL"). NUL is the exclusive supplier of the company's hardware and software products in Japan. The company considers its investment in NUL to be of a long-term strategic nature. For the years ended December 31, 2002, 2001 and 2000, total direct and indirect sales to NUL were approximately $270 million, $340 million and $530 million, respectively. At December 31, 2002, the company owned approximately 28% of NUL's common stock that had a market value of approximately $171 million. The company's share of NUL's earnings or losses are recorded semiannually on a quarter-lag basis in their income (expense), net in the company's statement of income. During the years ended December 31, 2002, 2001 and 2000, the company recorded equity income or (loss) related to NUL of $(11.8) million, $10.4 million and $8.2 million, respectively. The year ended December 31, 2002, included $21.8 million related to the company's share of an early retirement charge recorded by NUL. The company has approximately $176 million of retained earnings that represents undistributed earnings of NUL.

Summarized financial information for NUL as of and for its fiscal years ended March 31 is as follows:

(Millions) (Unaudited)	2002	2001	2000
Year ended March 31			
Revenue	**$2,451.8**	$2,819.2	$2,835.2
Gross profit	**646.0**	815.5	903.2
Pretax income (loss)	**(101.2)**	85.7	68.3
Net income (loss)	**(62.4)**	44.0	32.8
At March 31			
Current assets	**1,257.6**	1,304.9	1,564.1
Noncurrent assets	**892.3**	709.6	826.9
Current liabilities	**936.3**	913.7	1,015.6
Noncurrent liabilities	**851.2**	357.0	504.6
Minority interests	**10.7**	11.0	11.4

The company owns 51% of Intelligent Processing Solutions Limited ("iPSL"), a UK-based company, which provides high-volume payment processing. iPSL is fully consolidated in the company's financial statements. The minority owners' interests are reported in other long-term liabilities ($52.8 million and $48.6 million at December 31, 2002 and 2001, respectively) and in other income (expense), net in the company's financial statements.

Nucor
2002 Annual Report

15. Acquisitions and Dispositions

On July 22, 2002, Nucor's wholly owned subsidiary, Nucor Steel Decatur, LLC, purchased substantially all of the assets of Trico Steel Company, LLC ("Trico") for a purchase price of $117,700,000. The purchase price included approximately $86,000,000 of Trico's debt that was assumed by Nucor. Located in Decatur, Alabama, the sheet steel facility originally began operations in 1997 and has an annual capacity of approximately 1,900,000 tons. This acquisition was not material to the consolidated financial statements and did not result in material goodwill or other intangible assets.

On December 9, 2002, Nucor purchased substantially all of the assets of Birmingham Steel Corporation ("Birmingham Steel") for a cash purchase price excluding transaction costs of approximately $615,000,000, including $116,900,000 in inventory and receivables. Primary assets purchased are Birmingham Steel's four operating mills in Birmingham, Alabama; Kankakee, Illinois; Jackson, Mississippi; and Seattle, Washington with an estimated combined annual capacity of approximately 2,000,000 tons. Other included assets are the corporate office located in Birmingham, Alabama; the mill in Memphis, Tennessee, which is currently not in operation; the assets of Port Everglades Steel Corporation; the assets of the Klean Steel Division; and Birmingham Steel's ownership in Richmond Steel Recycling Limited. This acquisition was financed with proceeds from the issuance of $350,000,000 of 4.875% notes due in 2012 and internal cash flows.

The following table summarizes the estimated fair values of the assets acquired and liabilities assumed of Birmingham Steel as of the date of acquisition:

Current assets	$122,868,464
Property, plant and equipment	515,016,742
Other assets	550,000
Total assets acquired	638,435,206
Current liabilities	(13,690,000)
Deferred credits and other liabilities	(3,121,443)
Total liabilities assumed	(16,811,443)
	$621,623,763

Kellogg
2002 Annual Report

Note 2 Acquisitions and Dispositions

Keebler acquisition

On March 26, 2001, the Company acquired Keebler Foods Company in a cash transaction valued at $4.56 billion. The acquisition was accounted for under the purchase method and was financed through a combination of short-term and long-term debt.

The components of intangible assets included in the final allocation of purchase price are presented in the following table. During 2001, these intangibles were amortized based on an estimated useful life of 40 years. As a result of the Company's adoption of SFAS No. 142 on January 1, 2002 (refer to Note 1), these intangibles are no longer amortized after 2001, but are subject to annual impairment reviews.

(millions)	
Trademarks and tradenames	$1,310.0
Direct store door (DSD) delivery system	590.0

(millions)	
Goodwill	2,938.5
	$4,838.5

The final purchase price allocation includes $71.3 million of liabilities related to management's plans, as of the acquisition date, to exit certain activities and operations of the acquired company, as presented in the table below. Cash outlays related to these exit plans were approximately $28 million in 2001 and approximately $24 million in 2002, with the remaining amounts to be spent principally during 2003.

(millions)	Employee Severance Benefits	Employee Relocation	Lease and Other Contract Termination	Facility Closure Costs	Total
Total reserve at acquisition date:					
Original estimate	$59.3	$8.6	$12.3	$10.4	$90.6
Purchase accounting adjustments	(10.3)	(7.1)	(.5)	(1.4)	(19.3)
Adjusted	$49.0	$1.5	$11.8	$9.0	$71.3
Amounts utilized during 2001	(23.9)	(.8)	(.4)	(2.9)	(28.0)
Amounts utilized during 2002	(17.9)	(.1)	(1.8)	(4.2)	(24.0)
Remaining reserve at December 28, 2002	**$7.2**	**$.6**	**$9.6**	**$1.9**	**$19.3**

Exit plans are being announced as individual initiatives are implemented. In August 2002, management announced plans to consolidate certain functions in Battle Creek, Michigan, primarily research, technology, and financial services. As a result, approximately 70 positions in Elmhurst, Illinois, were relocated or eliminated. During November 2002, the Company commenced the process of consolidating ice cream cone and pie crust manufacturing operations from several facilities to a single facility in Chicago, Illinois. Other major initiatives begun in 2002 included the reconfiguration of Keebler's DSD system in the southeastern United States to accommodate Kellogg snack product volume, which has resulted in early termination of leases on approximately 100 small vans and separation of approximately 85 sales representatives and support personnel.

Exit plans implemented during 2001 included separation of approximately 0 Keebler administrative employees and the closing of a bakery in Denver, Colorado, eliminating approximately 440 employee positions. During June 2001, the Company communicated plans to transfer portions of Keebler's Grand Rapids, Michigan, bakery production to other plants in the United States during the next

12 months. As a result, approximately 150 employee positions were eliminated, partly through a voluntary retirement program.

During April 2002, the Company sold certain assets of Keebler's Bake-Line private-label unit, including a bakery in Marietta, Oklahoma, to Atlantic Banking Group, Inc. for approximately $65 million in cash and a $10 million note to be paid at a later date. In January 2003, the Company sold additional private-label operations for approximately $14 million in cash. For both of these transactions, the carrying value of net assets sold, including allocated goodwill, approximated the net sales proceeds.

The following table includes the unaudited pro forma combined results as if Kellogg Company had acquired Keebler Foods Company as of the beginning of either 2001 or 2000, instead of March 26, 2001. Net sales have been restated for the retroactive application of EITF Issue No. 01-09 (refer to Note 1) effective January 1, 2002.

(millions, except per share data)	2001	2000
Net sales	$8,049.8	$8,270.1
Earnings before extraordinary loss and cumulative effect of accounting change	$438.0	$517.9
Net earnings	$429.6	$517.9
Net earnings per share (basic and diluted)	$1.06	$1.28

The pro forma results include amortization of the intangibles presented above and interest expense on debt assumed issued to finance the purchase. The pro forma results are not necessarily indicative of what actually would have occurred if the acquisition had been completed as of the beginning of each of the fiscal periods presented, nor are they necessarily indicative of future consolidated results.

International Paper
2002 Annual Report

Note 7 Businesses Held for Sale and Divestitures

In 2000, International Paper announced a divestment program following the acquisition of Champion and the completion of a strategic analysis to focus on its core businesses of paper, packaging and forest products. Through December 31, 2002, more than $3 billion had been realized under the program, including cash and notes received plus debt assumed by the buyers.

Businesses Held for Sale

Certain smaller businesses that are being marketed for sale in 2003 remained in the divestment program at December 31, 2002. The Decorative Products Division was also included in this program prior to its sale in the third quarter of 2002.

Sales and operating earnings for each of the three years ended December 31, 2002, 2001 and 2000 for these businesses, as well as for other businesses sold through their respective divestiture dates were:

In millions	2002	2001	2000
Sales	$323	$1,134	$2,886
Operating Earnings	$10	$39	$154

The sales and operating earnings for these businesses are included in "Speciality Businesses and Other" of the company's industry segment information in Item 7. Management's Discussion and Analysis of Financial Condition and Results of Operations. The assets of businesses held for sale, totaling $128 million at December 31, 2002 and $219 million at December 31, 2001, are included in Assets of businesses held for sale in current assets in the accompanying consolidated balance sheet. The liabilities of businesses held for sale, totaling $44 million at December 31, 2002 and $77 million at December 31, 2001, are included in Liabilities of businesses held for sale in current liabilities in the accompanying consolidated balance sheet. The decreases in these balances since December 31, 2001 reflect divestitures in 2002.

In June 2002, International Paper announced that it would discontinue efforts to divest its Arizona Chemical and Industrial Papers businesses after sales efforts did not generate acceptable offers, and made a decision to operate these two businesses. As a result of these actions, Assets and Liabilities of businesses held for sale as of December 31, 2001 were reduced by $429 million and $138 million, respectively, with increases in the related corresponding asset and liability accounts in the accompanying consolidated balance sheet. Operating results for these businesses are included in the Specialty businesses and Other segment for all periods presented.

Divestitures:

Net (Gains) Losses on Sales and Impairments of Businesses Held for Sale

In the fourth quarter of 2002, International Paper recorded a $10 million pre-tax credit ($4 million after taxes) to adjust estimated accrued costs of businesses previously sold. In the third quarter of 2002, International Paper completed the sale of its Decorative Products operations to an affiliate of Kohlberg & Co. for approximately $100 million in cash and a note receivable with a fair market value of $13 million. This transaction resulted in no gain or loss as these assets had previously been written down to fair market value. Also during the third quarter of 2002, a net gain of $3 million before taxes ($1 million after taxes) was recorded related to adjustments of previously recorded costs of businesses held for sale.

During the second quarter of 2002, a net gain on sales of businesses held for sale of $28 million before taxes and minority interest ($96 million after taxes and minority interest) was recorded, including a pre-tax gain of $63 million ($40 million after taxes) from the sale in April 2002 of International Paper's oriented strand board facilities to Nexfor Inc. for $250 million, and a net charge of $35 million before taxes and minority interest (a gain of $56 million after taxes and minority interest) relating to other sales and adjustments of previously recorded estimated costs of businesses held for sale. This net pre-tax charge included:

(1) a $2 million net loss associated with the sales of the Wilmington carton plant and CHH's distribution business;

(2) an additional loss of $12 million to write down the net assets of Decorative Products to the amount subsequently realized on sale;

(3) $11 million of additional expenses relating to the decision to continue to operate Arizona Chemical, including a $3 million adjustment of previously estimated costs incurred in connection with the prior sale effort and an $8 million charge to permanently close a production facility; and

(4) a $10 million charge for additional expenses relating to prior divestitures.

The impairment charge recorded for Arizona Chemical in the fourth quarter of 2001 (see below) included a tax expense based on the form of sale being negotiated at that time. As a result of the decision in the second quarter of 2002 to discontinue sale efforts and to hold and operate Arizona Chemical in the future, this provision was no longer required. Consequently, special items for the second quarter include a gain of $28 million before taxes and minority interest, with an associated $96 million benefit after taxes and minority interest. The net 2002 gains, totaling $41 million, discussed above are included in Net gains (losses) on sales and impairments of businesses held for sale in the accompanying consolidated statement of earnings.

In the fourth quarter of 2001, a pre-tax impairment loss of $582 million ($524 million after taxes) was recorded including $576 million to write down the net assets of Arizona Chemical, Decorative Products and Industrial Papers to an estimated realizable value of approximately $550 million, and $6 million of severance for the reduction of 189 employees in the Chemical Cellulose Pulp business. Also in the fourth quarter, International Paper sold its Mobile, Alabama Retail Packaging facility to Ampac, resulting in a pre-tax loss of $9 million.

In the third quarter of 2001, International Paper sold Masonite to Premdor Inc. of Toronto, Canada, resulting in a pre-tax loss of $87 million, its Flexible Packaging business to Exo-Tech Packaging, LLC, resulting in a pre-tax loss of $31 million, and its Curtis/Palmer hydroelectric generating project in Corinth, New York to Trans Canada Pipelines Limited, resulting in a pre-tax gain of $215 million. Also, in the third quarter, a pre-tax impairment loss of $50 million ($32 million after taxes) was recorded to write down the Chemical Cellulose assets to their expected realizable value of approximately $25 million.

In the second quarter of 2001, a pre-tax impairment loss of $85 million ($55 million after taxes) was recorded to reduce the carrying value of the Flexible Packaging assets to their expected realizable value of approximately $85 million based on preliminary offers received.

The 2001 losses discussed above, totaling $629 million, are included in Net (gains) losses on sales and impairments of businesses held for sale in the accompanying consolidated statement of earnings.

Structured Transactions

In connection with a sale of forestlands in the state of Washington in 2001, International Paper received notes having a value of approximately $480 million on the date of sale. During 2001, International Paper transferred the Notes to an unconsolidated entity in exchange for a preferred interest in that entity valued at approximately $480 million, and accounted for this transfer as a sale of the Notes for financial reporting purposes with no associated gain or loss. Also during 2001, the entity acquired approximately $561 million of other International Paper debt obligations for cash. At December 31, 2001, International Paper offset, for financial reporting purposes, the $480 million of International Paper debt obligations held by the entity since International Paper had, and intended to effect, a legal right to net settle these two amounts.

In December 2002, International Paper acquired an option to purchase the third party's interest in the unconsolidated entity and modified the terms of the entity's special loss allocation between the third party and International Paper. These actions required the entity to be consolidated by International Paper at December 31, 2002, resulting in increases in installment notes receivable (included in Deferred charges and other assets) of $480 million, Long-term debt of $460 million and Minority interest of $20 million.

Also, in connection with the sale of the oil and gas properties and fee mineral and royalty interests in 2001, International Paper received a non-controlling preferred limited partnership interest valued at approximately $234 million. The unconsolidated partnership also loaned $244 million to International Paper in 2001. Since International Paper has, and intends to effect, a legal right to net settle these two amounts, we have offset for financial reporting purposes the preferred interest against the note payable.

International Paper
2002 Annual Report

Note 9—Sale of Limited Partnership Interests

During 1993, International Paper contributed assets with a fair market value of approximately $900 million to two newly formed limited partnerships, Georgetown Equipment Leasing Associates, L.P. and Trout Creek Equipment Leasing, L.P. These partnerships are separate and distinct legal entities from International Paper and have separate assets, liabilities, business functions and operations. However, for accounting purposes, these assets continue to be consolidated, with the minority shareholders' interests reflected as minority interest in the accompanying consolidated financial statements. The purpose of the partnerships is to invest in and manage a portfolio of assets including pulp and paper equipment used at the Georgetown, South Carolina and Ticonderoga, New York mills. This equipment is leased to International Paper Yunder long-term leases. Partnership assets also include floating rate notes and cash. During 1993, outside investors purchased a portion of our limited partner interests for $132 million and also contributed an additional $33 million to one of these partnerships.

At December 31, 2002, International Paper held aggregate general and limited partner interests totaling 69% in Georgetown Equipment Leasing Associates, L.P. and 66% in Trout Creek Equipment Leasing, L.P.

Chapter 8
Disclosures

CONTENTS

This chapter discusses the disclosures required of companies, including those related to accounting policies, segmental information, related parties, contingencies, long-term purchase contract obligations, inflation, and derivatives. The financial reporting and disclosure requirements of development stage companies are also presented. Changes bearing upon the comparability of financial statements should also be disclosed. Comparative statements aid reader comprehension of the significance of trends and their impact on the business.

According to Accounting Standards Update (ASU) No. 2010-04 (January 2010), *Accounting for Various Topics—Technical Corrections to SEC Paragraphs*), financial statements presented to the SEC cannot be misleading. Subsequent events must be disclosed. An earnings release does not represent financial statements being issued.

When there is a business combination accounted for as a purchase, push-down accounting should be used.

DISCLOSURE OF ACCOUNTING POLICIES

ASC 235-10-05 and 50-3, *Notes to Financial Statements: Overall*, covers the disclosure of accounting policies. Accounting policies include accounting principles and their methods of application in the preparation of financial statements, including:

- ☐ Choosing between alternative generally accepted accounting principles (GAAP).
- ☐ Unusual or innovative applications of GAAP.
- ☐ Accounting methods peculiar to a particular industry.

A company's major accounting policies should be disclosed in the first footnote or in a section called "Summary of Significant Accounting Policies," which appears before the footnotes. Examples of accounting policies to be disclosed include inventory method, construction contract method, depreciation method, consolidation basis, amortization method and period for intangibles, method to account for bad debts, foreign currency translation process, recognition of franchise revenue, method to amortize deferred revenue, definition of cash equivalents in preparing the cash flow statement, description of how deferred taxes are calculated, method to account for unconsolidated investees, and accounting policies for pension plans.

If more than one accounting method is used (e.g., different depreciation methods), the one disclosed in the footnote should be the primary method. Accounting policy disclosures need not duplicate information presented elsewhere in the financial statements.

Disclosure of accounting policies should not repeat what is stated elsewhere in other footnotes or within the face of the financial statements. However, reference may be made to other footnotes. In most cases, accounting policies are expressed broadly, with specifics disclosed in other notes or in the body of the financial statements.

In Accounting Standards Update (ASU) No. 2011-11 (December 2011), *Balance Sheet* (Topic 210), *Disclosures about Offsetting Assets and Liabilities,* a company shall disclose information to assist readers of its financial statements of the impact of netting arrangements such as rights of setoff of its assets and liabilities.

Nonprofit entities must disclose their significant accounting policies. Financial statements not requiring a description of the accounting policies followed include unaudited interim statements (unless a change in principle was adopted after the preparation of the last year-end financial statement) and financial statements issued only for internal use.

SEGMENTAL REPORTING

Segmental reporting aids in evaluating a company's financial statements by revealing growth prospects, including earning potential, areas of risk, and financial problems. It facilitates the appraisal of both historical performance and expected future performance. ASC 280-10-05-2, *Segment Reporting: Overall,* requires that the amount reported for each segment item be based on what is used by the *chief operating decision maker* in formulating a determination as to how many resources to assign to a segment and how to appraise the performance of that segment. The term *chief operating decision maker* may apply to the chief executive officer or chief operating officer or to a group of executives. **Note:** The term of *chief operating decision maker* may apply to a function and not necessarily to a specific person. This is a management approach rather than an industry approach in identifying segments. The segments are based on the company's organizational structure, revenue sources, nature of activities, existence of responsible managers, and information presented to the Board of Directors.

Revenues, gains, expenses, losses, and assets should be allocated to a segment only if the chief operating decision maker considers doing so in measuring a segment's earnings for purposes of making a financial or operating decision. The same is true with regard to allocating to segments eliminations and adjustments applying to the company's general-purpose financial statements. Any allocation of financial items to a segment should be rationally based.

In measuring a segment's earnings or assets, the following should be disclosed for explanatory purposes:

☐ Measurement or valuation basis used.

☐ Differences in measurements used for the general-purpose financial statements relative to the financial information of the segment.

☐ A change in measurement method relative to prior years.

☐ A symmetrical allocation, meaning an allocation of depreciation or amortization to a segment without a related allocation to the associated assets.

Segmental information is required in annual financial statements. Some segmental disclosures are required in interim financial statements. Segmental information is not required for unconsolidated subsidiaries or investees accounted for under the equity method.

An operating segment is a distinct revenue-producing component of the business for which internal financial data are produced. Expenses are recognized as incurred in that segment. **Note:** A start-up operation would qualify as an operating segment even though revenue is not being earned. An operating segment is periodically reviewed by the chief operating decision maker to evaluate performance and to determine what and how many resources to allocate to the segment.

A reportable segment requiring disclosure is one that is an operating segment and meets certain percentage tests, discussed later in this section. If a segment does not generate revenue or insignificant revenue, it is *not* an operating segment to be reported. An example is corporate headquarters.

An aggregation may be made of operating segments if they are similar in terms of products or services, customer class, manufacturing processes, distribution channels, legal entity, regulatory control, geographical area, and government contract.

The accounting principles used in preparing segmental information should be the same as those used in preparing the financial statements. However, intercompany transactions (which are eliminated in consolidation) are included for segmental reporting purposes, and for applying the 10% and 75% rules discussed later. Segmental information may be provided in the body of the financial statements, in separate schedules, or in footnotes. Most companies report segmental data in separate schedules.

Disclosures should be made of how reporting segments were determined (e.g., customer class, products, services, geographical areas). Disclosure should be given identifying those operating segments that have been aggregated. The following should be disclosed for each reportable segment:

☐ Nature and identification of products or services.

☐ Sales to unaffiliated customers.

☐ Method used to allocate costs.

☐ Tax effects.

☐ Geographic areas of operations.

☐ Interest revenue and interest expense.

☐ Unusual items included in segmental earnings.

☐ Book values of identifiable assets.

☐ Capital expenditures.

☐ Aggregate depreciation, depletion, and amortization expense.

☐ Effect of a change in method on a segment's operating earnings.

☐ Other profitability measures, such as contribution margin.

☐ Transfer pricing method. (Sales or transfers to other industry segments should be noted, including the accounting basis.)

☐ Equity in unconsolidated subsidiaries or investees.

Disclosures should be in both dollars and percentages.

A reportable segment is determined by:

☐ Grouping by industry line.

☐ Identifiable products or services.

☐ Significant segments to the company in the entirety.

If any one of the following exists, a segment must be reported on:

☐ Revenue, including unaffiliated and intersegment sales or transfers, is 10% or more of total revenue of all operating segments.

☐ Operating profit or loss is 10% or more of the greater, in absolute amount, of the combined operating profit (or loss) of all industry segments with operating profits (or losses).

☐ Identifiable assets are 10% or more of total assets of all operating segments.

Operating segments that are not reportable should be combined and disclosed in the "all other" category. Disclosure should be made of the sources of revenue for these segments.

EXAMPLE

A company reports the following information for its reportable segments:

Segment	Total Revenue	Operating Profit	Identifiable Assets
1	$500	$50	$200
2	250	10	150
3	3,500	200	1,950

Segment	Total Revenue	Operating Profit	Identifiable Assets
4	1,500	100	900
	$5,750	$360	$3,200

The revenue test is 10% × $5,750 = $575. Segments 3 and 4 satisfy this test. The operating profit (loss) test is 10% × $360 = $36. Segments 1, 3, and 4 satisfy this test. The identifiable assets test is 10% × $3,200 = $320. Segments 3 and 4 satisfy this test. Therefore, the reportable segments are 1, 3, and 4.

EXAMPLE

A company has six industry segments with operating profits and losses as follows:

Industry Segment		Operating Profit (Loss)
1	$400,000	
2	100,000	
3	800,000	Total $1,300,000
4	(200,000)	
5	(80,000)	
6	(1,000,000)	Total ($1,280,000)

The absolute amount of the combined operating profits of all profitable industry segments is $1,300,000, and the absolute amount of the combined operating losses of all industry segments with losses is $1,280,000. The greater of these two absolute amounts is $1,300,000. Thus, all industry segments with operating profits or losses having an absolute amount equal to or greater than $130,000 (10% × $1,300,000) satisfy the operating profit or loss test. Therefore, industry segments 1, 3, 4, and 6 are reportable.

If a segment failed the 10% test this year but was significant in previous years and is expected to be significant in the future, it should still be reported on in the current year. On the other hand, a segment may not be reported this year even though it satisfies the 10% test because of abnormal profits, if it was not reportable in previous years and is not expected to be reportable in the future. In other words, if a segment passes the 10% test in the current year because of some unusual or rare occurrence, it should be excluded from reporting in the current year.

In applying the 10% rule, the following should be noted:

☐ *Revenue* Revenue to unaffiliated customers and revenue to other businesses should be separated. Transfer prices are set for intersegment transfers. However, intersegment sales should not include the cost of joint facilities or other joint costs. Interest income on intersegment receivables is includable in intersegment sales, as long as the receivables are part of identifiable assets. However, interest earned on advances or loans to industry segments is excluded from intersegment revenues. Disclosure should be made of the accounting bases used.

☐ *Operating Profit or Loss* Operating earnings excludes general (nonallo-cable) corporate income and expenses, interest expense (unless its a financial segment), income taxes, extraordinary gain or loss, cumulative effect of a change in accounting principle, minority interest, and income from unconsolidated subsidiaries or investees. Directly traceable and allocable costs should be charged to segments. Examples of allocation bases for common costs are sales, operating income before common costs, or total assets.

☐ *Identifiable Assets* Segmental assets include those directly in the segment and reasonably allocable general corporate assets. Allocation methods should be used consistently. Excluded from identifiable assets are advances or loans to other segments, except for income derived therefrom that is used to compute operating results.

Segments shall represent a significant portion (75% or more) of the entity's total revenue of all operating segments. The 75% test is applied separately each year.

In deriving 75%, no more than 10 segments should be presented because to do otherwise would result in too cumbersome and detailed reporting. If more than 10 are identified, similar segments may be combined. If, on the other hand, the reportable segments identified by the materiality tests account for only 75% of all industry segment revenue from unaffiliated customers, one or more additional industry segments must be included among reportable segments so that at least 75% of all industry segment revenue is accounted for by the reported segments.

Disclosures are not mandated for 90% enterprises (a company obtaining 90% or more of its revenues, operating earnings, and total assets from one segment). In essence, the segment is the business. Dominant industry segments should be identified.

The source of segmental revenue should be disclosed with the percent so derived when:

☐ Ten percent or more of revenue is generated from either a foreign government contract or domestic contract.

☐ Ten percent or more of sales is made to one customer. A group of customers under common control (e.g., subsidiaries of a parent, federal or local government) is deemed as one customer. **Note:** Departments or agencies within governments are not considered a single customer. The identity of the customer need not be disclosed.

☐ Ten percent or more of revenue or assets are in a particular foreign country or similar group of countries. Similarity might be indicated by proximity, business environment, interrelationships, and economic or political ties. If foreign activities are in more than one geographic area, required disclosures should be made for both—each *significant* individual foreign area and in total for *other insignificant* areas. For revenues from foreign operations, the amount of sales to unaffiliated customers and the amount of intracompany sales between geographic areas should be disclosed. The geographic areas that have been disaggregated should be identified along with the percentages derived.

Information about foreign geographic areas and customers is required even if this information is not used by the business in formulating operating decisions.

Under ASC 280-10-50-13, *Segment Reporting: Overall*, operating segments not satisfying the quantitative thresholds can be aggregated into a reportable segment if aggregation is consistent with the objective and basic principles of ASC 280-10, *Segment Reporting: Overall*; the segments have similar economic characteristics; and the segments share a majority of the other aggregation criteria.

In some cases, prior-period segmental financial information, such as for industry segments, foreign operations, and major customers, needs to be restated for comparative purposes when:

- ☐ There has been a change in the grouping of products, services, or geographic areas for segment determination and presentation.
- ☐ There has been a change in the grouping of foreign activities.
- ☐ There has been a change in accounting principle or reporting entity.
- ☐ Financial statements of the entire company have been restated.

There should be disclosure of the nature and effect of restatement.

A company does not have to use the same accounting principles for segmental purposes as that used to prepare the consolidated financial statements. There must be a reconciliation between segmental financial data and general-purpose financial statements. The reconciliation is for revenue, operating profit or loss, and assets. Any differences in measurement approaches between the company as a whole and its segments should be explained. If measurement practices have changed over the years regarding the operating segments, that fact should be disclosed and explained. The business must describe its reasoning and methods in deriving the composition of its operating segments.

RELATED PARTIES

ASC 850-10-05-3, *Related Party Disclosures: Overall*, covers the accounting for and disclosing of related-party transactions.[*] Related-party transactions take place when a transacting party has the ability to influence significantly or exercise control of another transacting party due to a financial, common ownership, or familial relationship with that party. Related-party transactions may also occur when a nontransacting party can substantially affect the policies of two other transacting parties. Related-party transactions include those involving:

- ☐ Activities between a parent and its subsidiaries.
- ☐ Activities between affiliates of the same parent company.
- ☐ Joint ventures.

---

[*] This section is partly based on the authors' article: Marc Levine, Adrian Fitzsimons, and Joel Siegel, "Auditing Related Party Transaction," *CPA Journal*, March 1997, pp. 46–50.

☐ Relationships between the company and its major owners, management, or their immediate families.

☐ Company and employee trusts established and managed by the company, such as a profit sharing or pension plan.

ASC 850-10-05-4 notes that related-party transactions often take place in the ordinary course of business and may include such activities as sales, purchases, services performed or received, property transfers, rentals, filing consolidated tax returns, guarantees, granting loans or incurring debt, compensating balance requirements, and allocating common costs as the basis for billings.

The pronouncement also indicates that related-party transactions are assumed not to be at arm's length. That is, they are not derived under conditions of competitive, free-market dealings. Because of this, GAAP requires that material related-party transactions be disclosed in the financial statements. Exceptions include compensation arrangements, expense allowances, and similar items in the normal course of business.

ASC 275-10-50-18, *Risks and Uncertainties: Overall*, requires disclosure of concentrations in the volume of transactions with a particular customer if loss of that customer could result in a significant negative impact on the business.

A transaction between related parties may not have occurred or may have been on different terms if the entities were autonomous and conducted their own best interests, as when:

☐ A lease of property from the parent to a subsidiary occurs at a significantly different price than if a related-party relationship existed.

☐ A loan is made at an unusually low interest rate because a bank is associated with the borrower.

☐ A *shell corporation* (with no economic substance) buys goods at inflated prices.

☐ A company pays consulting fees for the year ending December 31, 2002 in the amount of $400,000 to an individual who is a director and stockholder of the company.

Examples of events that suggest that undisclosed related-party transactions may be occurring include:

☐ Unusual guarantees or pledging of personal assets.

☐ Low-cost leases.

☐ Sales with a commitment to repurchase that, if known, would preclude recognition of all or part of revenue.

☐ Sales at below market rates.

☐ Interest revenue at above market rates on loans.

☐ Borrowing at below market rates of interest.

☐ Loans to parties that do not possess the ability to repay.

☐ Purchases of assets at prices in excess of fair market value.

☐ Payments for services at inflated prices.

☐ Sales without substance, such as funding the other party to the transaction so that the sales price is fully remitted.

Related-party disclosures usually include the following:

☐ Terms and settlements.

☐ Nature and substance of relationship.

☐ Description of the transactions, whether or not dollar amounts are involved.

☐ Dollar figures for the applicable transactions.

☐ Balances due from or owed to the related parties at year-end, including payment terms.

☐ Nature of the control relationship between entities under common ownership or management control.

☐ Significant customers or leases.

Although related-party transactions are not inherently bad, they have proven to be an easy and effective means to perpetrate a misstatement of economic substance and reality of financial transactions. There are inherent measuring problems with related-party dealings that, by their nature, may not be comparable to what would have occurred had the transactions taken place between unrelated third parties.

DISCLOSURE OF CONTINGENCIES AND COMMITMENTS

Footnote disclosure is required for reasonably possible losses arising from contingencies. The disclosure includes the type of contingency and estimate of probable loss or range of loss. If the loss cannot be estimated, that fact should be stated. Examples of items to be disclosed are guarantees, renegotiation proceedings on government contracts, tax disputes, and environmental risks. Gain contingencies, such as a possible award from a lawsuit, are also disclosed.

DISCLOSURE OF LONG-TERM PURCHASE CONTRACT OBLIGATIONS

ASC 440-10-50-2, *Exit or Disposal Cost Obligations: Overall*, covers the disclosure of long-term obligations. An unconditional purchase obligation is any obligation to provide funds from products and services at a specified price at a later date. An example is a take-or-pay contract in which the purchaser must make periodic specified payments for goods or services even if it did not receive them. Another example is a through-put contract in which the shipper contracts to pay another party stipulated sums to deliver or process the product even if it does not provide the minimum amount of goods for transporting or processing.

Unconditional purchase obligations with a term less than one year do not require disclosure. Unconditional purchase obligations must be disclosed in the footnotes if the following criteria exist:

☐ The term is one year or more.

☐ The obligation is noncancelable. However, it may be cancelable only because of a remote contingency, with the other party's consent, such as a replacement agreement mutually agreed to or a mutual agreement to pay a penalty.

Disclosure is optional for the amount of imputed interest required to reduce the unconditional purchase obligation to present value.

For unrecorded unconditional purchase obligations, disclosure should be made of the fixed and variable amounts, description of variable portions, total amount for the current year and for the next five years, total amount due after five years (labeled "subsequent years"), nature and term, and purchases for each year presented.

When unconditional purchase obligations are recorded in the balance sheet, disclosure should be made of any payments made, maturity dates, sinking fund provisions, and redemptions of capital stock at determinable prices. Disclosure must be made of the payments to be made under the obligation for each of the next five years.

Certain types of leases require disclosure if the leases are noncancelable, involve financing facilities to provide merchandise or services, and have a time period of more than one year.

An example of a typical disclosure required under ASC 440-10-50-2 follows:

ABC Company signed a long-term agreement to buy product XYZ from vendor DEF. The contract is for a 10-year period. ABC Company is obligated to make minimum annual payments to DEF regardless of whether ABC is able to accept delivery of the product XYZ. The minimum total payments of each of the five and later years after December 31, 20XI follows:

Year	Total Payments (in thousands)
20X2	$5,000
20X3	10,000
20X4	12,000
20X5	14,000
20X6	13,000
Later years	20,000
Total	$74,000
Less: imputed interest	28,000
Present value of payments	$46,000

GUARANTEES

As per ASC 460-10-50, *Guarantees: Overall*, the guarantor must record an initial liability at fair value at the inception of a guarantee or indemnification agreement even if it is *not* probable that future payments will be required. When the liability is recognized because of the issuance of the guarantee, the offsetting debit is based on the nature of the original transaction giving rise to the guarantee. If the guarantee is to an unrelated party *without* consideration, an expense is recorded; however, if consideration exists, the debit is to cash or a receivable. If the guarantee applies to starting a partially owned business or joint venture, the investment account is debited. If the lessee guarantees the salvage value of property in an operating lease, prepaid rent is debited. If the guarantee relates to a part of the sale of assets, a business, or product, the consideration received from the sale is allocated between the guarantee and the assets, business, or product sold.

In the case of product warranties, the guarantor must disclose its accounting policy and method to compute the liability under warranty instead of disclosing the maximum potential amount for future payments. Further, a tabular reconciliation of the changes in the guarantor's product warranty liability for the year is mandated.

The guarantor must disclose the following:

- ☐ Nature of the guarantee.
- ☐ Time period covered by the guarantee.
- ☐ Reasons and circumstances surrounding the guarantee.
- ☐ Recourse provisions.
- ☐ Occurrence that would obligate the guarantor.
- ☐ Maximum exposure in future payments to satisfy the guarantee.
- ☐ The carrying value of the liability, if any, on the part of the guarantor.
- ☐ Collateral under the agreement to enable the guarantor to be reimbursed for any amounts paid because of the guarantee.
- ☐ Obligations under product warranties.

ASC 460-10-30-2, *Guarantees: Overall*, requires the recognition and disclosure of the fair value of an obligation undertaken for a minimum revenue guarantee granted to a business or its owners that the revenue of the business, for a specified period of time, will be a certain minimum amount.

DEVELOPMENT STAGE COMPANIES

ASC 915-10-05, *Development Stage Entities: Overall*, deal with the accounting, reporting, and disclosure for development stage enterprises. A development stage company is one starting a new business in which either operations have not begun or operations have begun but no significant revenue has been obtained. After the business starts its principal activities and generates substantial revenues, it is no longer in the development stage.

A development stage enterprise usually is involved with such activities as hiring and training workers, obtaining initial financing, beginning production, budgeting and planning, engaging in research, entering markets, testing products, fostering relationships with vendors, and buying operating assets such as machinery.

A development stage company must use the same GAAP and prepare the same required financial statements as an established company. However, the following reporting is required for development stage enterprises:

☐ In the balance sheet, retained earnings will typically show a deficit. A descriptive caption would be "deficit accumulated in the development stage." For each equity security, the number of shares issued and dollar figures per share must be shown from inception. The dates of issue must also be presented. Besides common stock or preferred stock, the company must provide similar information for stock warrants, stock rights, or other equities. If noncash consideration is received, such consideration must be specified along with the basis of deriving its value.

☐ In the income statement, the total revenue and expenses from the beginning of the business must be disclosed separately.

☐ In the statement of cash flows, cumulative cash flows from operating, investing, and financing activities from inception, in addition to current-year amounts, must be shown.

The financial statements must be headed "Development Stage Enterprise." Footnote disclosure is required of the development stage activities and the proposed lines of business. In the first year the company is no longer in the development stage, it must disclose that in prior years it was.

If comparative financial statements are issued, the company must disclose that in previous years it was in the development stage.

REPORTING ON THE COSTS OF START-UP ACTIVITIES

ASC 720-15-15-3 and 25-1, *Other Expenses: Start-Up Costs*, requires that start-up costs be expensed as incurred. Start-up costs are commonly referred to as preopening expenditures. They are those one-time costs that are incurred, for example, when opening a new facility, introducing a new product or service, conducting business in a new territory, conducting business with a new class of customer, or beginning some new operation. In some industries, it was common to defer some of those costs if it could be shown that future net operating results would be sufficient to recover these costs. They would then be expensed when the business opened or over a period not to exceed one year. All start-up costs, including organization costs, are to be expensed as incurred.

INFLATION INFORMATION

ASC 225-10-50-6, *Income Statement: Overall*, allows a company to disclose voluntarily, in its annual report, inflation data so management and financial statement readers can better assess the effect of inflation on the company. The pronouncement recommends that businesses present selected summarized financial data based on current costs and adjusted for inflation (in constant purchasing power) for a five-year period. The Consumer Price Index for All Urban Consumers may be used. Inflation information to be disclosed includes sales and operating revenue expressed in constant purchasing power, income from continuing operations (including per share amounts) on a current cost basis, cash dividends per share in constant purchasing power, market price per share restated in constant purchasing power, purchasing power gain or loss on net monetary items, inflation-adjusted inventory, restated fixed assets, foreign currency translation based on current cost, net assets based on current cost, and the Consumer Price Index used.

COLLABORATIVE ARRANGEMENTS

As per ASC 808-10-10, *Collaborative Arrangements: Overall*, a collaborative arrangement is a contractual agreement in which the parties are active participants and have significant risks and rewards that depend on the eventual commercial success of the endeavor. Many collaborative arrangements apply to developing and commercializing intellectual property. A collaborative arrangement can start at any point in the endeavor's life cycle.

According to ASC 808-10-15-2, transactions with third parties (i.e., revenue generated and cost incurred by participants from transactions with parties outside of a collaborative arrangement) should be shown gross or net on the appropriate line item in each participant's respective financial statements. For example, a participant in a collaborative arrangement that is considered to be the principal for a given transaction should record that transaction on a gross basis in its financial statements. Further, the equity method should not be applied to an arrangement that is performed by the participants without creating a separate legal entity for the arrangement.

If one party to an arrangement must make a payment to the other party to reimburse a part of that party's research and development (R&D) cost, that portion of the net payment may be an R&D expense in the payor's financial statements.

A participant in a collaborative arrangement should disclose the following:

☐ Amounts owed to or due from other participants.

☐ Accounting policy for collaborative arrangements.

☐ Rights and obligations under collaborative arrangements.

☐ Nature and purpose of arrangement.

☐ Life cycle stage.

☐ Classification in the income statement and amounts attributable to transactions between participants.

DISCLOSURES FOR DERIVATIVES

ASC 815-10-50-5, *Derivatives and Hedging: Overall*, requires both qualitative and quantitative disclosures related to derivatives. Qualitative disclosures include the business purpose behind holding or issuing derivatives for both trading and hedging purposes. Qualitative disclosures should be aligned with a discussion of the reporting unit's risk management strategy. ASC 815-10-50-4A and 50-5 requires quantitative disclosure of amounts recognized in the financial statements for derivatives used for trading purposes, as well as for derivatives used for hedging purposes. The company must differentiate between fair value and cash flow hedges and relate these hedges to their intended purposes, such as reduction of risk on firm commitments and hedging of forecasted transactions. Chapter 17, "Derivatives, Repurchase Agreements, and Disclosures of Credit

Risk and Fair Values: Accounting, Reporting, and Disclosures," provides a full discussion of derivative instruments, hedging, and disclosure requirements.

DISCLOSURES FOR BUSINESS COMBINATIONS

For each acquisition that occurs during the reporting period, or after the reporting period but before financial statements are issued, the acquirer must identify the acquiree and disclose the acquisition date, percentage of voting interest acquired, rationale for the business combination as well as information supporting fair values, contingent consideration, acquisition-related costs, goodwill expected to be deductible for tax purposes, and other supplemental information, as discussed in Chapter 11, "Business Combinations."

SUBSEQUENT EVENTS

The purpose of ASC 855, *Subsequent Events*, is to set forth standards for accounting and disclosure for events taking place between the balance sheet date and the date the financial statements are issued or available to be issued.

The Statement provides for the following information:

1. The period subsequent to the date of the financial statements during which management should appraise events or transactions that may occur for possible recognition or disclosure in the financial statements.

2. The circumstances that a company should recognize events or transactions taking place after the balance sheet date.

3. The disclosures that should be made for subsequent events or transactions.

The effective date of the pronouncement is June 15, 2009. It applies to interim and annual financial periods.

Subsequent events are events or transactions that take place after the balance sheet date but before the financial statements are issued or available to be issued. The two types of subsequent events are:

1. Event or transaction that provides additional evidence about conditions that existed at the balance sheet date, including the estimates inherent in the process of preparing financial statements.

2. Event providing evidence about conditions that did not exist at the balance sheet date but arose after that date. This is a nonrecognized subsequent event.

A company shall recognize in the financial statements the effect of a subsequent event that provides additional evidence about conditions existing at the balance sheet date. Recognized subsequent events include a settlement amount in a lawsuit different from that estimated at the balance sheet date and a customer's bankruptcy filing after year-end but before the issue date of the financial statements.

A company should not recognize subsequent events providing evidence about conditions that did not exist at the balance sheet date but arose after the balance sheet date but before the financial statements are issued. Examples are the sale of stocks or bonds after the balance sheet date but before the financial statements are issued, a business combination taking place after the balance sheet date, fire loss on fixed assets and inventory after the balance sheet date, and issuing significant guarantees after the balance sheet date but before the statements are issued.

Disclosure should be made of the date through which subsequent events have been appraised, and whether that date is the date the financial statements were issued or available to be issued.

Some nonrecognized subsequent events may be of such a nature that they must be disclosed to keep the financial statements from being misleading. For this type of event, the company should disclose the nature of the event, and an estimate of its financial effect, or a statement that such an estimate cannot be made.

A company should consider supplementing the historical financial statements with pro forma financial information. In some cases, a nonrecognized subsequent event may be so material that disclosure can best be made by way of pro forma financial data. Such data shall give effect to the event as if it had taken place on the balance sheet date.

According to Accounting Standards Update (ASU) No. 2010-09 (February 2010) (ASC 855, *Subsequent Events*), *Amendments to Certain Recognition and Disclosure Requirements*, a company must appraise subsequent events up to the time of issuance of the balance sheet and income statement. A revised financial statement includes one resulting from an error correction or restatement of previous years because of the adoption of a new accounting method. This amendment is effective for periods ending subsequent to June 15, 2010 (ASC 855-10; 855-10-25-1A; 855-10-65-1).

In addition, as per ASC 855, *Subsequent Events*, a company must appraise subsequent events or transactions through the date the financial statements are issued or available to be issued, depending on the firm's expectation of the distribution of the financial statements. A company must show in the financial statements the impact of all subsequent events that provide additional information about the conditions that existed on the balance sheet date including relevant estimates. The business entity must disclose the last date through which subsequent events were appraised.

ANNUAL REPORT REFERENCES

Microsoft
2011 Annual Report

NOTE 17—CONTINGENCIES

Government Competition Law Matters

Since 2001, we have been subject to a Consent Decree and Final Judgment ("Final Judgments") that resolved lawsuits brought by the U.S. Department of Justice, 18 states, and the District of Columbia in two separate actions. The Final Judgments imposed various constraints on our Windows operating system businesses. The Final Judgments expired in May 2011.

In other ongoing investigations, various foreign governments and several state attorneys general have requested information from us concerning competition, privacy, and security issues.

Antitrust, Unfair Competition, and Overcharge Class Actions

A large number of antitrust and unfair competition class action lawsuits were filed against us in various state, federal, and Canadian courts on behalf of various classes of direct and indirect purchasers of our PC operating system and certain other software products. We obtained dismissals of damages claims of indirect purchasers under federal law and in 15 states. Courts refused to certify classes in two additional states. We have reached agreements to settle all claims that have been made to date in 19 states and the District of Columbia.

The settlements in all states have received final court approval. Under the settlements, generally class members can obtain vouchers that entitle them to be reimbursed for purchases of a wide variety of platform-neutral computer hardware and software. The total value of vouchers that we may issue varies by state. We will make available to certain schools a percentage of those vouchers that are not issued or claimed (one-half to two-thirds depending on the state). The total value of vouchers we ultimately issue will depend on the number of class members who make claims and are issued vouchers. The maximum value of vouchers to be issued is approximately $2.7 billion. The actual costs of these settlements will be less than that maximum amount, depending on the number of class members and schools that are issued and redeem vouchers. We estimate the total cost to resolve all of the state overcharge class action cases will range between $1.9 billion and $2.0 billion. At June 30, 2011, we have recorded a liability related to these claims of approximately $568 million, which reflects our estimated exposure of $1.9 billion less payments made to date of approximately $1.3 billion mostly for vouchers, legal fees, and administrative expenses.

The three cases pending in British Columbia, Ontario, and Quebec, Canada have not been settled. In March 2010, the court in the British Columbia case certified it as a class action. On April 15, 2011, the British Columbia Court of Appeal reversed the class certification ruling and dismissed the case, holding that indirect purchasers do not have a claim. The plaintiffs have sought review by the Canadian Supreme Court. The other two actions have been stayed.

Other Antitrust Litigation and Claims

In November 2004, Novell, Inc. ("Novell") filed a complaint in U.S. District Court for the District of Utah (later transferred to federal court in Maryland), asserting antitrust and unfair competition claims against us related to Novell's ownership of WordPerfect and other productivity applications during the period between June 1994 and March 1996. In June 2005, the trial court granted our motion to dismiss four of six claims of the complaint. In March 2010 the trial court granted summary judgment in favor of Microsoft as to all remaining claims. The court of appeals has reversed that ruling, and the case is scheduled for trial in Utah in October 2011.

Patent and Intellectual Property Claims

In 2003, we filed an action in U.S. District Court in California seeking a declaratory judgment that we do not infringe certain Alcatel-Lucent patents (although this action began before the merger of Alcatel and Lucent in 2006, for simplicity we refer to the post-merger entity of Alcatel-Lucent). In April 2008, a jury returned a verdict in Alcatel-Lucent's favor in a trial on a consolidated group of one video and three user interface patents. The jury concluded that we had infringed two user interface patents and awarded $367 million in damages. In June 2008, the trial judge increased the amount of damages to $512 million to include $145 million of interest. We appealed that award. In December 2008, we entered into a settlement agreement resolving all other litigation pending between Microsoft and Alcatel-Lucent, leaving approximately $500 million remaining in dispute. In September 2009, the court of appeals affirmed the liability award but vacated the verdict and remanded the case to the trial court for a retrial of the damages ruling, indicating the damages previously awarded were too high. Trial on the remanded damages claim was held in July 2011.

In October 2003, Uniloc USA Inc. ("Uniloc"), a subsidiary of a Singapore-based company, filed a patent infringement suit in U.S. District Court in Rhode Island, claiming that product activation technology supporting Windows XP and certain other Microsoft programs violated a Uniloc patent. After we obtained a favorable summary judgment that we did not infringe any of the claims of this patent, the court of appeals vacated the trial court decision and remanded the case for trial. In April 2009, the jury returned a $388 million verdict against us, including a finding of willful infringement. In September 2009, the district court judge overturned the jury verdict, ruling that the evidence did not support the jury's findings either that Microsoft infringed the patent or was willful. Uniloc appealed, and in January 2011 the court of appeals reversed the district court's finding of non-infringement (thus reinstating the jury verdict of infringement) but affirmed the district court's ruling that Microsoft was not willful and affirmed the district court's grant of a new trial on damages. Uniloc's petition for rehearing of the court of appeals' decision as to damages was denied. A new trial on damages has been set for January 2012.

In March 2007, i4i Limited Partnership ("i4i") sued Microsoft in U.S. District Court in Texas claiming that certain custom XML technology in Word 2003 and 2007 infringed i4i's patent. In May 2009, a jury returned a verdict against us, finding damages of $200 million and that we willfully infringed the patent. In August 2009, the court denied our post-trial motions and awarded enhanced damages of $40 million and prejudgment interest of $37 million. The court also issued a permanent injunction prohibiting additional distribution of the allegedly infringing technology. We appealed and the appellate court stayed the injunction pending our appeal. In December 2009, the court of appeals rejected our appeal and affirmed the trial court's judgment and injunction, except that the court of appeals modified the effective date of the injunction to January 11, 2010. We appealed to the U.S. Supreme Court, and in June 2011 the court affirmed the judgment of the court of appeals.

In October 2010, we filed suit against Motorola with the International Trade Commission ("ITC") and in U.S. District Court in Washington for infringement of nine Microsoft patents by Motorola's Android-based devices. Since then, Microsoft and Motorola have filed additional actions against each other in the ITC and federal courts in Washington, Wisconsin, Florida, and California. Microsoft asserts Motorola's Android-based devices violate 23 of its patents, and Motorola asserts various Microsoft products (including Windows, Windows Phone 7, Windows Mobile 6.5, Xbox, Bing Maps, Hotmail, Messenger, and Exchange Server) violate 21 Motorola patents. Microsoft also claims Motorola has breached its contractual commitments to the Institute of Electrical and Electronics Engineers ("IEEE") and International Telecommunications Union ("ITU") to license identified patents related to wireless and video coding technologies under reasonable and non-discriminatory ("RAND") terms and conditions. Motorola asserts that Microsoft breached contractual commitments to the SD Card Association to license two patents under RAND terms and conditions, and asserts federal antitrust and state unfair business practice claims. Trial in our ITC case is set for August 2011, trial in Motorola's ITC case is set for October 2011, and trial of both parties' patent infringement claims in Florida also is set for October 2011.

In addition to these cases, there are approximately 55 other patent infringement cases pending against Microsoft.

Other

We also are subject to a variety of other claims and suits that arise from time to time in the ordinary course of our business. Although management currently believes that resolving claims against us, individually or in aggregate, will not have a material adverse impact on our financial statements, these matters are subject to inherent uncertainties and management's view of these matters may change in the future.

As of June 30, 2011, we had accrued aggregate liabilities of $693 million in other current liabilities and $276 million in other long-term liabilities for all of the contingent matters described in this note. While we intend to vigorously defend these matters, there exists the possibility of adverse outcomes that we estimate could reach approximately $800 million in aggregate beyond recorded amounts. Were unfavorable final outcomes to occur, there exists the possibility of a material adverse impact on our financial statements for the period in which the effects become reasonably estimable.

Texas Instruments
2011 Annual Report

14. Commitments and contingencies

Operating leases

We conduct certain operations in leased facilities and also lease a portion of our data processing and other equipment. In addition, certain long-term supply agreements to purchase industrial gases are accounted for as operating leases. Lease agreements frequently include purchase and renewal provisions and require us to pay taxes, insurance and maintenance costs. Rental and lease expense incurred was $109 million, $100 million and $114 million in 2011, 2010 and 2009, respectively.

Capitalized software licenses

We have licenses for certain internal-use electronic design automation software that we account for as capital leases. The related liabilities are apportioned between Accounts payable and Deferred credits and other liabilities on our Consolidated balance sheets, depending on the contractual timing of the payment.

Purchase commitments

Some of our purchase commitments entered in the ordinary course of business provide for minimum payments. At December 31, 2011, we had committed to make the following minimum payments under our non-cancellable operating leases, capitalized software licenses and purchase commitments:

	Operating Leases	Capitalized Software Licenses	Purchase Commitments
2012	$ 102	$ 73	$ 215
2013	77	35	97
2014	55	31	20
2015	48	12	4
2016	36	–	2
Thereafter	118	–	10

Indemnification guarantees

We routinely sell products with an intellectual property indemnification included in the terms of sale. Historically, we have had only minimal, infrequent losses associated with these indemnities. Consequently, we cannot reasonably estimate or accrue for any future liabilities that may result.

Warranty costs/product liabilities

We accrue for known product-related claims if a loss is probable and can be reasonably estimated. During the periods presented, there have been no material accruals or payments regarding product warranty or product liability. Historically, we have experienced a low rate of payments on product claims. Although we cannot predict the likelihood or amount of any future claims, we do not believe they will have a material adverse effect on our financial condition, results of operations or liquidity. Consistent with general industry practice, we enter into formal contracts with certain customers that include negotiated warranty remedies. Typically, under these agreements our warranty for semiconductor products includes: three years coverage; an obligation to repair, replace or refund; and a maximum payment obligation tied to the price paid for our products. In some cases, product claims may exceed the price of our products.

General

We are subject to various legal and administrative proceedings. Although it is not possible to predict the outcome of these matters, we believe that the results of these proceedings will not have a material adverse effect on our financial condition, results of operations or liquidity. From time to time, we also negotiate contingent consideration payment arrangements associated with certain acquisitions, which are recorded at fair value.

Discontinued operations indemnity

In connection with the 2006 sale of the former Sensors & Controls (S&C) business, we have agreed to indemnify Sensata Technologies, Inc., for specified litigation matters and certain liabilities, including environmental liabilities. In a settlement with a third party, we have agreed to indemnify that party for certain events relating to S&C products, which events we consider remote. We believe our total remaining potential exposure from both of these indemnities will not exceed $200 million. As of December 31, 2011, we believe future payments related to these indemnity obligations will not have a material effect on our financial condition, results of operations or liquidity.

ConAgra Foods
2010 Annual Report

18. Contingencies

In fiscal 1991, we acquired Beatrice Company ("Beatrice"). As a result of the acquisition and the significant pre-acquisition contingencies of the Beatrice businesses and its former subsidiaries, our consolidated post-acquisition financial statements reflect liabilities associated with the estimated resolution of these contingencies. These include various litigation and environmental proceedings related to businesses divested by Beatrice prior to its acquisition by us. The litigation includes suits against a number of lead paint and pigment manufacturers, including ConAgra Grocery Products and the Company as alleged successors to W. P. Fuller Co., a lead paint and pigment manufacturer owned and operated by Beatrice until 1967. Although decisions favorable to us have been rendered in Rhode Island, New Jersey, Wisconsin, and Ohio, we remain a defendant in active suits in Illinois and California. The Illinois suit seeks class-wide relief in the form of medical monitoring for elevated levels of lead in blood. In California, a number of cities and counties have joined in a consolidated action seeking abatement of the alleged public nuisance.

The environmental proceedings include litigation and administrative proceedings involving Beatrice's status as a potentially responsible party at 36 Superfund, proposed Superfund, or state-equivalent sites; these sites involve locations previously owned or operated by predecessors of Beatrice that used or produced petroleum, pesticides, fertilizers, dyes, inks, solvents, PCBs, acids, lead, sulfur, tannery wastes, and/or other contaminants. Beatrice has paid or is in the process of paying its liability share at 33 of these sites. Reserves for these matters have been established based on our best estimate of the undiscounted remediation liabilities, which estimates include evaluation of investigatory studies, extent of required clean-up, the known volumetric contribution of Beatrice and other potentially responsible parties, and its experience in remediating sites. The reserves for Beatrice-related environmental matters totaled $69.6 million as of

May 30, 2010, a majority of which relates to the Superfund and state-equivalent sites referenced above. The reserve for Beatrice-related environmental matters reflects a reduction in pre-tax expense of $15.4 million made in the third quarter of fiscal 2010 due to favorable regulatory developments at one of the sites. We expect expenditures for Beatrice-related environmental matters to continue for up to 20 years.

In limited situations, we will guarantee an obligation of an unconsolidated entity. At the time in which we initially provide such a guarantee, we assess the risk of financial exposure to us under these agreements. We consider the credit-worthiness of the guaranteed party, the value of any collateral pledged against the related obligation, and any other factors that may mitigate our risk (e.g., letters of credit from a financial institution). We actively monitor market and entity-specific conditions that may result in a change of our assessment of the risk of loss under these agreements.

We guarantee certain leases and other commercial obligations resulting from the 2002 divestiture of our fresh beef and pork operations. The remaining terms of these arrangements do not exceed six years and the maximum amount of future payments we have guaranteed was $16.0 million as of May 30, 2010.

We have also guaranteed the performance of the divested fresh beef and pork business with respect to a hog purchase contract. The hog purchase contract requires the divested business to purchase a minimum of approximately 1.2 million hogs annually through 2014. The contract stipulates minimum price commitments, based in part on market prices, and, in certain circumstances, also includes price adjustments based on certain inputs. We have not established a liability for any of the fresh beef and pork divestiture-related guarantees, as we have determined that the likelihood of our required performance under the guarantees is remote.

We are a party to various potato supply agreements. Under the terms of certain such potato supply agreements, we have guaranteed repayment of short-term bank loans of the potato suppliers, under certain conditions. At May 30, 2010, the amount of supplier loans we have effectively guaranteed was $29.0 million. We have not established a liability for these guarantees, as we have determined that the likelihood of our required performance under the guarantees is remote.

We are a party to a supply agreement with an onion processing company. We have guaranteed repayment of a loan of this supplier, under certain conditions. At May 30, 2010, the term of the loan is 14 years. The amount of our guaranty was $25 million as of May 30, 2010. In the event of default on this loan by the supplier, we have the contractual right to purchase the loan from the lender, thereby giving us the rights to the underlying collateral. We have not established a liability in connection with this guaranty, as we believe the likelihood of financial exposure to us under this agreement is remote.

Federal income tax credits were generated related to our sweet potato production facility currently under construction in Delhi, Louisiana. Third parties invested in certain of these income tax credits. We have guaranteed these third parties the face value of these income tax credits over their statutory lives, a period of seven years, in the event that the income tax credits are recaptured or reduced. The face value of the income tax credits was $21 million as of May 30, 2010. We believe the likelihood of the recapture or reduction of the income tax credits is remote, and therefore we have not established a liability in connection with this guarantee.

We are a party to a number of lawsuits and claims arising out of the operation of our business, including lawsuits and claims related to the February 2007 recall of our peanut butter products and litigation we initiated against an insurance carrier to recover our settlement expenditures and defense costs. We recognized a charge of $24.8 million during the third quarter of fiscal 2009 in connection with the disputed coverage with this insurance carrier. During the second quarter of fiscal 2010, a Delaware state court rendered a decision on certain matters in our claim for the disputed coverage favorable to the insurance carrier. We intend to appeal this decision and continue to pursue this matter vigorously.

In June 2009, an accidental explosion occurred at our manufacturing facility in Garner, North Carolina. See Note 5 for information related to this matter.

An investigation by the Division of Enforcement of the U.S. Commodity Futures Trading Commission ("CFTC") of certain commodity futures transactions of a former Company subsidiary has led to an investigation of us by the CFTC. The investigation may result in litigation by the CFTC against us. The former subsidiary was sold on June 23, 2008, as part of the divestiture of our trading and merchandising operations. The CFTC's Division of Enforcement has advised us that it questions whether certain trading activities of the former subsidiary violated the Commodity Exchange Act and that the CFTC has been evaluating whether we should be implicated in the matter based on the existence of the parent-subsidiary relationship between the two entities at the time of the trades. Based on information we have learned to date, we believe that both we and the former subsidiary have meritorious defenses. There have been discussions with the CFTC concerning resolution of this matter. We also believe the sale contract with the purchaser of the business provides us indemnification rights. Accordingly, we do not believe any decision by the CFTC to pursue this matter will have a material adverse effect on our financial condition or results of operations. If litigation ensues, we intend to defend this matter vigorously.

We are a party to several lawsuits concerning the use of diacetyl, a butter flavoring ingredient that was added to our microwave popcorn until late 2007. The cases are primarily consumer personal injury suits claiming respiratory illness allegedly due to exposures to vapors from microwaving popcorn. Another was brought by an ex-employee alleging that we fraudulently concealed the risks of diacetyl and therefore his recovery should not be limited to the otherwise exclusive remedy of workers compensation benefits. The final case is a putative class action contending that our packaging information with respect to diacetyl is false and misleading. We do not believe these cases possess merit and are vigorously defending them.

After taking into account liabilities recognized for all of the foregoing matters, management believes the ultimate resolution of such matters should not have a material adverse effect on our financial condition, results of operations, or liquidity. It is reasonably possible that a change in one of the estimates of the foregoing matters may occur in the future. Costs of legal services are recognized in earnings as services are provided.

Energizer Holdings
2010 Annual Report

14. Environmental and Legal Matters

Government Regulation and Environmental Matters—The operations of the Company, like those of other companies engaged in the Household Products and Personal Care businesses, are subject to various federal, state, foreign and local laws and regulations intended to protect the public health and the environment. These regulations relate primarily to worker safety, air and water quality, underground fuel storage tanks and waste handling and disposal. The Company has received notices from the U.S. Environmental Protection Agency, state agencies and/or private parties seeking contribution, that it has been identified as a "potentially responsible party" (PRP) under the Comprehensive Environmental Response, Compensation and Liability Act, and may be required to share in the cost of cleanup with respect to eight federal "Superfund" sites. It may also be required to share in the cost of cleanup with respect to state-designated sites or other sites outside of the U.S.

Accrued environmental costs at September 30, 2010 were $10.2, of which $2.8 is expected to be spent in fiscal 2011. This accrual is not measured on a discounted basis. It is difficult to quantify with certainty the cost of environmental matters, particularly remediation and future capital expenditures for environmental control equipment. Nevertheless, based on information currently available, the Company believes the possibility of material environmental costs in excess of the accrued amount is remote.

Certain of the Company's products are subject to regulation by the United States Food and Drug Administration (FDA), including tampons and sun care products.

Legal Proceedings—The Company and its subsidiaries are parties to a number of legal proceedings in various jurisdictions arising out of the operations of the Energizer business. Many of these legal matters are in preliminary stages and involve complex issues of law and fact, and may proceed for protracted periods of time. The amount of liability, if any, from these proceedings cannot be determined with certainty. However, based upon present information, the Company believes that its ultimate liability, if any, arising from pending legal proceedings, asserted legal claims and known potential legal claims which are likely to be asserted, are not reasonably likely to be material to the Company's financial position, results of operations, or cash flows, taking into account established accruals for estimated liabilities.

Texas Instruments
2010 Annual Report

12. Commitments and contingencies

Operating leases: We conduct certain operations in leased facilities and also lease a portion of our data processing and other equipment. In addition, certain long-term supply agreements to purchase industrial gases are accounted for as operating leases. Lease agreements frequently include purchase and renewal provisions and require us to pay taxes, insurance and maintenance costs. Rental and lease expense incurred was $100 million, $114 million and $124 million in 2010, 2009 and 2008.

Capitalized software licenses: We have licenses for certain internal-use electronic design automation software that we account for as capital leases. The related liabilities are apportioned between Accounts payable and Deferred credits and other liabilities on our balance sheets, depending on the contractual timing of the payment.

Purchase commitments: Some of our purchase commitments entered in the ordinary course of business provide for minimum payments.

Summary: At December 31, 2010, we had committed to make the following minimum payments under our non-cancellable operating leases, capitalized software licenses and purchase commitments:

	Operating Leases	Capitalized Software Licenses	Purchase Commitments
2011	$ 80	$ 67	$ 221
2012	65	54	105
2013	50	7	38
2014	45	6	8
2015	39	–	2
Thereafter	80	–	1

Indemnification guarantees: We routinely sell products with an intellectual property indemnification included in the terms of sale. Historically, we have had only minimal, infrequent losses associated with these indemnities. Consequently, we cannot reasonably estimate or accrue for any future liabilities that may result.

Warranty costs/product liabilities: We accrue for known product-related claims if a loss is probable and can be reasonably estimated. During the periods presented, there have been no material accruals or payments regarding product warranty or product liability. Historically, we have experienced a low rate of payments on product claims. Although we cannot predict the likelihood or amount of any future claims, we do not believe they will have a material adverse effect on our financial condition, results of operations or liquidity. Consistent with general industry practice, we enter into formal contracts with certain customers that include negotiated warranty remedies. Typically, under these agreements our warranty for semiconductor products includes: three years coverage; an obligation to repair, replace or refund; and a maximum payment obligation tied to the price paid for our products. In some cases, product claims may exceed the price of our products.

General: We are subject to various legal and administrative proceedings. Although it is not possible to predict the outcome of these matters, we believe that the results of these proceedings will not have a material adverse effect on our financial condition, results of operations or liquidity. From time to time, we also negotiate contingent consideration payment arrangements associated with certain acquisitions, which are recorded at fair value.

Discontinued operations indemnity: In connection with the 2006 sale of the former Sensors & Controls business, we have agreed to indemnify Sensata Technologies, Inc., for specified litigation matters and certain liabilities, including environmental liabilities. Our indemnification obligations with respect to breaches of representations and warranties and the specified litigation matters are generally subject to a total deductible of $30 million and our maximum potential exposure is limited to $300 million. We have not made any indemnity payments related to this matter and do not expect that any potential payments related to this indemnity obligation would have a material adverse effect on our financial condition, results of operations or liquidity in future periods.

Tyco International
2010 Annual Report

10. Related Party Transactions

The Company has amounts due related to loans and advances issued to employees in prior years under the Company's Key Employee Loan Program, relocation programs and other advances made to executives. Loans were provided to employees under the Company's Key Employee Loan Program, which is now discontinued, except for outstanding loans for the payment of taxes upon the vesting of shares granted under our Restricted Share Ownership Plans. During the fourth quarter of 2002, the Board of Directors and new senior management adopted a policy under which no new loans are allowed to be granted to any officers of the Company and existing loans are not allowed to be extended or modified. There have been no loans made to any of the Company's current executives. The outstanding loans are not collateralized and bear interest, payable annually, at a rate based on the six-month LIBOR, calculated annually as the average of the rates in effect on the first day of each of the preceding 12 months. Loans are generally repayable in ten years; however, earlier payments are required under certain circumstances, such as when an employee is terminated. In addition, the Company made mortgage loans to certain employees under employee relocation programs. These loans are generally payable in 15 years and are collateralized by the underlying property. During 2010 and 2009, the maximum amount outstanding under these programs was $21 million and $22 million, respectively. Loans receivable under these programs, as well as other unsecured advances outstanding, were $21 million and $22 million as of September 24, 2010 and September 25, 2009, respectively. The total outstanding loans receivable includes loans to L. Dennis Kozlowski, the Company's former chairman and chief executive officer (until June 2002). The amount outstanding under these loans, plus accrued interest, was $28 million and $27 million as of September 24, 2010 and September 25, 2009, respectively, and the rate of interest charged on such loans was 0.5% and 1.9% for 2010 and 2009, respectively. Interest income on these interest bearing loans totaled nil in both 2010 and 2009 and $1 million in 2008. Certain of the above loans totaling $1 million as of both September 24, 2010 and September 25, 2009 are non-interest bearing.

The Company filed civil complaints against Messrs. Kozlowski and its former chief financial officer, Mark Swartz, for breach of fiduciary duty and other wrongful conduct relating to alleged abuses of our Key Employee Loan Program and relocation program, unauthorized bonuses, unauthorized payments, self-dealing transactions and other improper conduct.

In June 2002, the Company filed a civil complaint against Frank E. Walsh, Jr., a former director, for breach of fiduciary duty, inducing breaches of fiduciary duty and related wrongful conduct involving a $20 million payment by Tyco, $10 million of which was paid to Mr. Walsh with the balance paid to a charity of which Mr. Walsh is trustee. The payment was purportedly made for Mr. Walsh's assistance in arranging our acquisition of The CIT Group, Inc. On December 17, 2002, Mr. Walsh pleaded guilty to a felony violation of New York law in the Supreme Court of the State of New York, (New York County) and settled a civil action for violation of federal securities laws brought by the SEC in United States District Court for the Southern District of New York. Both the felony charge and the civil action were brought against Mr. Walsh based on such payment. The felony charge accused Mr. Walsh of intentionally concealing information concerning the payment from Tyco's directors and shareholders while engaged in the sale of Tyco securities in the State of New York. The SEC action alleged that Mr. Walsh knew that the registration statement covering the sale of Tyco securities as part of the CIT Group acquisition contained a material misrepresentation concerning fees payable in connection with the acquisition. Pursuant to the plea and settlement, Mr. Walsh paid $20 million in restitution to Tyco on December 17, 2002. In connection with the Company's civil complaint against Mr. Walsh, in October 2010, the United States District Court for the Southern District of New York ruled that while Mr. Walsh breached his fiduciary duties to the Company, the Company's Board of Directors implicitly ratified the payment to Mr. Walsh in the weeks immediately following the revelation of the payment to the Board of Directors in early 2002. As a result, the Court ruled that the Company is not entitled to damages from Mr. Walsh. The Company believes, based on the facts and the law, that this determination by the Court is incorrect. The Company is in the process of appealing the Court's ruling.

During 2010, 2009 and 2008, the Company engaged in commercial transactions in the normal course of business with companies where the Company's Directors were employed and served as officers. Purchases from these companies during each year aggregated less than 1 percent of consolidated net revenue.

Brown-Forman
2009 Annual Report

5. Commitments

We have contracted with various growers and wineries to supply some of our future grape and bulk wine requirements. Many of these contracts call for prices to be adjusted annually up or down, according to market conditions. Some contracts set a fixed purchase price that might be higher or lower than prevailing market price. We have total purchase obligations related to both types of contracts of $29 in 2010, $24 in 2011, $16 in 2012, $11 in 2013, $8 in 2014, and $15 after 2014.

We also have contracts for the purchase of agave, which is used to produce tequila. These contracts provide for prices to be determined based on market conditions at the time of harvest, which, although not specified, is expected to occur over the next 10 years. As of April 30, 2009, based on current market prices, obligations under these contracts totaled $10.

We made rental payments for real estate, vehicles, and office, computer, and manufacturing equipment under operating leases of $19 in 2007, $19 in 2008, and $21 in 2009. We have commitments related to minimum lease payments of $16 in 2010, $13 in 2011, $8 in 2012, $5 in 2013, $3 in 2014, and $3 after 2014.

Carnival
2009 Annual Report

Note 6—Commitments

Ship Commitments

At November 30, 2009, we had 13 ships under contract for construction with an aggregate passenger capacity of 30,442. The estimated total cost of these ships is approximately $8.2 billion, which includes the contract price with the shipyard, design and engineering fees, capitalized interest, construction oversight costs and various owner supplied items. We have paid $770 million through November 30, 2009 and anticipate paying the remaining estimated total costs as follows: $3.4 billion, $2.2 billion and $1.8 billion in fiscal 2010, 2011 and 2012, respectively.

Operating Leases, Port Facilities and Other Commitments

Rent expense under our operating leases, primarily for office and warehouse space, was $54 million, $52 million and $46 million in fiscal 2009, 2008 and 2007, respectively. At November 30, 2009, minimum amounts payable for our operating leases, with initial or remaining terms in excess of one year, and for the annual usage of port facilities and other contractual commitments with remaining terms in excess of one year, were as follows (in millions):

Fiscal Year	Operating Leases	Port Facilities and Other
2010	$49	$146
2011	43	112
2012	37	87
2013	33	77
2014	24	50
Thereafter	115	490
Total	$301	$962

Note 7—Contingencies

Litigation

In the normal course of our business, various claims and lawsuits have been filed or are pending against us. Most of these claims and lawsuits are covered by insurance and, accordingly, the maximum amount of our liability, net of any insurance recoverables, is typically limited to our self-insurance retention levels. However, the ultimate outcome of these claims and lawsuits which are not covered by insurance cannot be determined at this time.

Contingent Obligations—Lease Out and Lease Back Type ("LILO") Transactions

At November 30, 2009, Carnival Corporation had estimated contingent obligations totaling $585 million, excluding termination payments as discussed below, to participants in LILO transactions for two of its ships. At the inception of these leases, the aggregate of the net present value of these obligations was paid by Carnival Corporation to a group of major financial institutions, one of which includes American International Group Inc. ("AIG"), who agreed to act as payment undertakers and directly pay these obligations. Accordingly, these contingent obligations are considered extinguished, and neither the funds nor the contingent obligations have been included in our accompanying Consolidated Balance Sheets.

In the event that Carnival Corporation were to default on its contingent obligations and assuming performance by all other participants, we estimate that we would, as of November 30, 2009, be responsible for a termination payment of approximately $95 million. In 2017 we have the right to exercise options that would terminate these two LILO transactions at no cost to us.

In certain cases, if the credit ratings of the financial institutions who are directly paying the contingent obligations fall below AA-, then Carnival Corporation will be required to replace these financial institutions with other financial institutions whose credit ratings are at least AA or meet other specified credit requirements. In such circumstances we would incur additional costs, although we estimate that they will be immaterial to our financial statements. All of the financial institution payment undertakers subject to this AA- credit rating threshold have credit ratings of AAA. If Carnival Corporation's credit rating, which is

BBB+, falls below BBB, it will be required to provide a standby letter of credit for $67 million, or, alternatively, provide mortgages for this aggregate amount on these two ships.

In September 2008, the credit ratings of AIG and its subsidiaries involved in one of the above LILO transactions were downgraded from AA- to A-. As a result of this downgrade, AIG pledged collateral to support its obligations as a payment undertaker under the terms of this LILO transaction and, accordingly, AIG is no longer subject to the AA- credit rating threshold discussed above.

Carnival Corporation and AIG were also parties to a third LILO transaction. In September 2008, we replaced AIG as the payment undertaker under this third LILO transaction by purchasing $80 million of U.S. Treasury strip securities using funds substantially all of which were provided by AIG. In February 2009, Carnival and the remaining participants voluntarily unwound this LILO transaction. Accordingly, the $80 million of long-term U.S. Treasury strip securities that we held as collateral for our recorded LILO obligation were released to extinguish this obligation. As a result of the unwinding of this third LILO transaction, we recorded a $15 million nonoperating gain in February 2009, which had originally been deferred at the inception of the LILO transaction and was being amortized over its term.

Contingent Obligations—Indemnifications

Some of the debt agreements that we enter into include indemnification provisions that obligate us to make payments to the counterparty if certain events occur. These contingencies generally relate to changes in taxes and changes in laws that increase lender capital costs and other similar costs. The indemnification clauses are often standard contractual terms and were entered into in the normal course of business. There are no stated or notional amounts included in the indemnification clauses and we are not able to estimate the maximum potential amount of future payments, if any, under these indemnification clauses. We have not been required to make any material payments under such indemnification clauses in the past and, under current circumstances, we do not believe a request for material future indemnification payments is probable.

Sonic Foundry
2009 Annual Report

10. Related-Party Transactions

The Company incurred fees of $255 and $249 thousand during the years ended September 30, 2009 and 2008, respectively, to a law firm whose partner is a director and stockholder of the Company. The Company had accrued liabilities for unbilled services of $19 thousand at September 30, 2009 to the same law firm. There were no unbilled services at September 30, 2008.

The Company recorded Mediasite product and customer support revenue related to $600 and $580 thousand of billings during the years ended September 30, 2009 and 2008 to Mediasite KK, a Japanese reseller in which the Company has an equity interest. Mediasite KK owed the Company $128 and $108 thousand on such billings at September 30, 2009 and 2008, respectively. The Company accounts for its investment in Mediasite KK under the equity method. The recorded value as of September 30, 2009 and 2008 is zero.

During the years ended September 30, 2009 and 2008, the Company had a loan outstanding to an executive totaling $26 thousand. The loan is collateralized by company stock.

Texas Instruments
2009 Annual Report

11. Commitments and contingencies

Operating leases: We conduct certain operations in leased facilities and also lease a portion of our data processing and other equipment. In addition, certain long-term supply agreements to purchase industrial gases are accounted for as operating leases. Lease agreements frequently include purchase and renewal provisions and require us to pay taxes, insurance and maintenance costs. Rental and lease expense incurred was $114 million, $124 million and $123 million in 2009, 2008 and 2007.

Capitalized software licenses: We have licenses for certain internal use electronic design automation software that we account for as capital leases. The related liabilities are apportioned between Accounts payable and Deferred credits and other liabilities on our balance sheets, depending on the contractual timing of the payment.

Purchase commitments: Some of our purchase commitments entered in the ordinary course of business provide for minimum payments.

Summary: At December 31, 2009, we had committed to make the following minimum payments under our non-cancellable operating leases, capitalized software licenses and purchase commitments:

	Operating Leases	Capitalized Software Licenses	Purchase Commitments
2010	$ 86	$ 83	$159
2011	75	63	72
2012	56	50	72
2013	47	8	25
2014	43	8	14
Thereafter	130	–	27

Indemnification guarantees: We routinely sell products with an intellectual property indemnification included in the terms of sale. Historically, we have had only minimal, infrequent losses associated with these indemnities. Consequently, we cannot reasonably estimate or accrue for any future liabilities that may result.

Warranty costs/product liabilities: We accrue for known product-related claims if a loss is probable and can be reasonably estimated. During the periods presented, there have been no material accruals or payments regarding product warranty or product liability. Historically, we have experienced a low rate of payments on product claims. Although we cannot predict the likelihood or amount of any future claims, we do not believe they will have a material adverse effect on our financial condition, results of operations or liquidity.

Consistent with general industry practice, we enter into formal contracts with certain customers that include negotiated warranty remedies. Typically, under these agreements our warranty for semiconductor products includes: three years coverage; an obligation to repair, replace or refund; and a maximum payment obligation tied to the price paid for our products. In some cases, product claims may exceed the price of our products.

General: We are subject to various legal and administrative proceedings. Although it is not possible to predict the outcome of these matters, we believe that the results of these proceedings will not have a material adverse effect on our financial condition, results of operations or liquidity.

Discontinued operations indemnity: In connection with the sale of the former Sensors & Controls business in 2006, we have agreed to indemnify Sensata for specified litigation matters and certain liabilities, including environmental liabilities. Our indemnification obligations with respect to breaches of representations and warranties and the specified litigation matters are generally subject to a total deductible of $30 million and our maximum potential exposure is limited to $300 million. We have not made any indemnity payments related to this matter and do not expect that any potential payments related to this indemnity obligation would have a material adverse effect on our financial position, results of operations or liquidity in future periods.

14. Segment and Geographic Area Data

Our financial reporting structure comprises three reportable segments. These reportable segments, which are established along major product lines having unique design and development requirements, are as follows:

Analog—Analog semiconductors change real-world signals—such as sound, temperature, pressure or images—by conditioning them, amplifying them and often converting them to a stream of digital data that can be processed by other semiconductors, such as DSPs. Analog semiconductors are also used to manage power distribution and consumption. Analog includes high-performance analog, high-volume analog & logic and power management products.

Embedded Processing—Our Embedded Processing products include our DSPs (other than DSPs specific to our Wireless segment) and microcontrollers. DSPs perform mathematical computations almost instantaneously to process or improve digital data. Microcontrollers are designed to control a set of specific tasks for electronic equipment. We make and sell standard, or catalog, Embedded Processing products used in many different applications and custom Embedded Processing products used in specific applications, such as communications infrastructure equipment and automotive.

Wireless—Cell phones require a modem or "baseband" to connect to the wireless carrier's network. Many of today's advanced cell phones, which contain email, media, games and computing capability, also require an applications processor to run the phone's software and services, and semiconductors to enable connectivity to Bluetooth® devices, WiFi networks or GPS location services. We design, make and sell products to satisfy each of these requirements. Our Wireless portfolio includes both standard products and custom products.

We also have Other, which includes other operating segments that neither meet the quantitative thresholds for individually reportable segments nor are they aggregated with other operating segments. These operating segments primarily include our smaller semiconductor product lines such as DLP® products (primarily used in projectors to create high-definition images); RISC microprocessors (designed to provide very fast computing and are often implemented in servers); and, custom semiconductors known as ASICs. Other also includes handheld graphing and scientific calculators and royalties received for our patented technology that we license to other electronics companies.

Other may also include certain unallocated income and expenses such as gains and losses on sales of assets; sales tax refunds; and certain litigation costs, settlements or reserves. Except for the few unallocated items just mentioned, we allocate all of our expenses associated with corporate activities to our operating segments based on specific methodologies, such as percentage of operating expenses or headcount.

With the exception of goodwill, we do not identify or allocate assets by operating segment, nor does the chief operating decision maker evaluate operating segments using discrete asset information. There was no significant intersegment revenue. The accounting policies of the segments are the same as those described in the summary of significant accounting policies.

Segment Information

	Analog	Embedded Processing	Wireless	Other	Total
Revenue					
2009	**$4,270**	**$1,471**	**$2,558**	**$2,128**	**$10,427**
2008	4,857	1,631	3,383	2,630	12,501
2007	4,927	1,588	4,195	3,125	13,835
Operating profit					
2009	**$ 753**	**$ 194**	**$ 332**	**$ 712**	**$ 1,991**
2008	1,050	268	347	772	2,437
2007	1,548	290	763	896	3,497

See Note 2 for restructuring expenses impacting segment results.

The following geographic area data includes revenue, based on product shipment destination and royalty payor location, and property, plant and equipment based on physical location:

Geographic Area Information

	U.S.	Asia	Europe	Japan	Rest of World	Total
Revenue						
2009	**$1,140**	**$6,575**	**$1,408**	**$976**	**$328**	**$10,427**
2008	1,551	7,387	1,875	1,268	420	12,501
2007	1,758	8,013	2,258	1,423	383	13,835
Property, plant and equipment, net						
2009	**$1,727**	**$1,013**	**$161**	**$244**	**$13**	**$3,158**
2008	1,785	988	200	314	17	3,304
2007	2,188	965	190	252	14	3,609

Major Customer

Direct sales to the Nokia group of companies were 21 percent of our revenue in 2009, 18 percent of our revenue in 2008 and 16 percent of our revenue in 2007; if indirect sales such as to contract manufacturers are included, Nokia accounted for 21 percent, 20 percent and 19 percent of our 2009, 2008 and 2007 revenue. Revenue from sales to Nokia is reflected primarily in our Wireless segment.

Tyco Electronics
2009 Annual reports

24. Segment and Geographic Data

The Company operates through four reporting segments: Electronic Components, Network Solutions, Specialty Products, and Undersea Telecommunications. See Note 1 for a description of the segments in which the Company operates. The Company aggregates its operating segments into reportable segments based upon the Company's internal business structure. Segment information has been revised to reflect the Company's current segment reporting structure. Prior period segment results have been reclassified to conform to the current presentation.

The Company sold its Wireless Systems business in May 2009. This business has been reclassified as discontinued operations on the Consolidated and Combined Financial Statements. See Note 5 for additional information regarding discontinued operations and the divestiture of the Wireless Systems business. Prior to reclassification to held for sale and discontinued operations, this business was reported as the Company's former Wireless Systems segment.

Effective January 1, 2009, the Company established the Specialty Products Group from its existing businesses. The results of this new organization are reported as a separate reporting segment on the Consolidated and Combined Financial Statements. This new segment is comprised of the Aerospace, Defense, and Marine; Touch Systems; Medical; and Circuit Protection businesses which were formerly reported in the Electronic Components segment.

Segment performance is evaluated based on net sales and operating income. Generally, the Company considers all expenses to be of an operating nature, and, accordingly, allocates them to each reportable segment. Costs specific to a segment are charged to the segment. Corporate expenses, such as headquarters administrative costs, are allocated to the segments based on segment operating income. Pre-Separation litigation charges and separation costs were not allocated to the segments. Intersegment sales are not material and are recorded at selling prices that approximate market prices. Corporate assets are allocated to the segments based on segment assets.

Net sales and operating income (loss) by business segment are presented in the following table for fiscal 2009, 2008, and 2007:

| | Net Sales | | | Operating Income (Loss) | | |
| | Fiscal | | | Fiscal | | |
(in millions)	*2009*	*2008*	*2007*	*2009*	*2008*	*2007*
Electronic Components	$5,961	$9,277	$8,531	$(3,716)[1]	$978[2]	$1,063
Network Solutions	1,719	2,162	1,897	133	251	229
Specialty Products	1,415	1,769	1,581	34[1]	296	258
Undersea Telecommunications	1,161	1,165	565	219	160	36
Pre-Separation litigation charges, net and separation costs	–	–	–	(144)	(22)	(931)
Total	$10,256	$14,373	$12,574	$(3,474)	$1,663	$655

[1] The Electronic Components and Specialty Products segments recorded charges of $3,435 million and $112 million, respectively, related to the impairment of goodwill in fiscal 2009. See Note 8 for additional information regarding the impairment of goodwill.
[2] Includes goodwill impairment of $103 million in fiscal 2008. See Note 8 for additional information regarding the impairment of goodwill.

No single customer accounted for more than 10% of net sales in fiscal 2009, 2008, or 2007.

As the Company is not organized by product or service, it is not practicable to disclose net sales by product or service.

Depreciation and amortization and capital expenditures for fiscal 2009, 2008, and 2007 were as follows:

| | Depreciation and Amortization | | | Capital Expenditures | | |
| | Fiscal | | | Fiscal | | |
(in millions)	*2009*	*2008*	*2007*	*2009*	*2008*	*2007*
Electronic Components	$417	$438	$419	$257	$479	$472
Network Solutions	48	48	33	31	66	52
Specialty Products	23	28	22	29	51	51

(in millions)	Depreciation and Amortization			Capital Expenditures		
	Fiscal			Fiscal		
	2009	2008	2007	2009	2008	2007
Undersea Telecommunications	27	25	22	11	14	288[1]
Total	$515	$539	$496	$328	$610	$863

[1] Includes $280 million related to the Company's exercise of its option to buy five cable-laying sea vessels in fiscal 2007.

Segment assets and a reconciliation of segment assets to total assets at fiscal year end 2009, 2008, and 2007 were as follows:

(in millions)	Segment Assets		
	Fiscal		
	2009	2008	2007
Electronic Components	$4,430	$5,578	$5,438
Network Solutions	929	1,139	1,027
Specialty Products	624	786	688
Undersea Telecommunications	628	654	511
Total segment assets[1]	6,521	8,157	7,664
Other current assets	2,169	2,820	6,112
Non-current assets	7,530	10,623	9,912
Total assets	$16,220	$21,600	$23,688

[1] The Electronic Components and Specialty Products segments recorded charges of $3,435 million and $112 million, respectively, related to the impairment of goodwill in fiscal 2009. See Note 8 for additional information regarding the impairment of goodwill.

Net sales by geographic region for fiscal 2009, 2008, and 2007 and net property, plant, and equipment by geographic area at fiscal year end 2009, 2008, and 2007 were as follows:

(in millions)	Net Sales[1]			Property, Plant, and Equipment, Net		
	Fiscal			Fiscal		
	2009	2008	2007	2009	2008	2007
Americas:						
United States	$3,373	$4,208	$3,604	$842	$923	$934
Other Americas	421	592	475	48	45	51
Total Americas	3,794	4,800	4,079	890	968	985
Europe/Middle East/ Africa:						
Switzerland	2,651	4,197	3,538	78	87	86

	Net Sales[1]			Property, Plant, and Equipment, Net		
	Fiscal			Fiscal		
(in millions)	2009	2008	2007	2009	2008	2007
Germany	334	488	440	451	458	443
Other Europe/Middle East/Africa	543	830	838	759	856	791
Total Europe/Middle East/Africa	3,528	5,515	4,816	1,288	1,401	1,320
Asia Pacific:						
China	1,407	1,815	1,604	356	388	343
Other Asia-Pacific	1,527	2,243	2,075	577	585	583
Total Asia-Pacific	2,934	4,058	3,679	933	973	926
Total	$10,256	$14,373	$12,574	$3,111	$3,342	$3,231

[1] Net sales from external customers are attributed to individual countries based on the legal entity that records the sale.

Corning
2008 Annual Report

13. Commitments, Contingencies, and Guarantees

The amount of our obligations follow (in millions):

		Amount of commitment and contingency expiration per period				
	Total	Less than 1 year	1 to 2 years	2 to 3 years	3 to 4 years	5 years and thereafter
Performance bonds and guarantees	$ 63	$ 35	$ 4	$ 4	$ 2	$ 18
Credit facilities for equity companies	150	25	25	25	25	50
Stand-by letters of credit[1]	68	68				
Loan guarantees	11					11
Subtotal of commitment expirations per period	$ 292	$128	$ 29	$ 29	$ 27	$ 79
Purchase obligations	$ 126	$ 77	$ 41	$ 6	$ 1	$ 1
Capital expenditure obligations[2]	525	525				
Total debt[3]	1,444	77	81	23	23	1,240
Minimum rental commitments	203	45	35	27	22	74
Capital leases[4]	113	6	6	34	3	64

The amount of our obligations follow (in millions):

	Total	Less than 1 year	1 to 2 years	2 to 3 years	3 to 4 years	5 years and thereafter
			Amount of commitment and contingency expiration per period			
Interest on long-term debt[5]	1,146	90	88	84	83	801
Uncertain tax positions[6]	11	4	2	3	2	
Subtotal of contractual obligation payments due by period	3,568	824	253	177	134	2,180
Total commitments and contingencies	$3,860	$952	$282	$206	$161	$2,259

[1] At December 31, 2008, $38 million of the $68 million was included in other accrued liabilities on our consolidated balance sheets.

[2] Capital expenditure obligations, primarily related to our Display Technologies segment expansions, are included on our balance sheet.

[3] At December 31, 2008, $1,605 million was included on our balance sheet. Amounts above are stated at their maturity value.

[4] At December 31, 2008, $25 million of the $113 million represents imputed interest.

[5] The estimate of interest payments assumes interest is paid through the date of maturity or expiration of the related debt, based upon stated rates in the respective debt instruments.

[6] At December 31, 2008, $19 million was included on our balance sheet related to uncertain tax positions. Of this amount, we are unable to estimate when $8 million of that amount will become payable.

FASB Interpretation No. 45, "Guarantor's Accounting and Disclosure Requirements for Guarantees, Including Indirect Guarantees of Indebtedness of Others" (FIN 45), requires a company, at the time a guarantee is issued, to recognize a liability for the fair value or market value of the obligation it assumes. In the normal course of our business, we do not routinely provide significant third-party guarantees. Generally, third-party guarantees provided by Corning are limited to certain financial guarantees, including stand-by letters of credit and performance bonds, and the incurrence of contingent liabilities in the form of purchase price adjustments related to attainment of milestones. These guarantees have various terms, and none of these guarantees are individually significant.

We have agreed to provide a credit facility related to Dow Corning. The funding of the Dow Corning credit facility will be required only if Dow Corning is not otherwise able to meet its scheduled funding obligations in its confirmed Bankruptcy Plan. The purchase obligations primarily represent raw material and energy-related take-or-pay contracts. We believe a significant majority of these guarantees and contingent liabilities will expire without being funded.

Minimum rental commitments under leases outstanding at December 31, 2008 follow (in millions):

2009	2010	2011	2012	2013	2014 and thereafter
$45	$35	$27	$22	$21	$53

Total rental expense was $59 million for 2008, $69 million for 2007 and $65 million for 2006.

A reconciliation of the changes in the product warranty liability for the year ended December 31 follows (in millions):

	2008	2007
Balance at January 1	$19	$26
Adjustments for warranties issued for current year sales	$7	$7
Adjustments for warranties related to prior year sales	$(7)	$(13)
Settlements made during the current year	$(1)	$(1)
Balance at December 31	$18	$19

Corning is a defendant in various lawsuits, including environmental, product-related suits, the Dow Corning and PCC matters discussed in Note 7 (Investments), and is subject to various claims which arise in the normal course of business. In the opinion of management, the ultimate disposition of these matters will not have a material adverse effect on Corning's consolidated financial position, liquidity, or results of operations. Other than certain asbestos related claims, there are no other material loss contingencies related to litigation.

We have been named by the Environmental Protection Agency under the Superfund Act, or by state governments under similar state laws, as a potentially responsible party for 19 active hazardous waste sites. Under the Superfund Act, all parties who may have contributed any waste to a hazardous waste site, identified by such Agency, are jointly and severally liable for the cost of cleanup unless the Agency agrees otherwise. It is our policy to accrue for the estimated liability related to Superfund sites and other environmental liabilities related to property owned and operated by us based on expert analysis and continual monitoring by both internal and external consultants. At December 31, 2008 and 2007, we had accrued approximately $21 million (undiscounted) and $19 million (undiscounted), respectively, for the estimated liability for environmental cleanup and related litigation. Based upon the information developed to date, we believe that the accrued amount is a reasonable estimate of our liability and that the risk of an additional loss in an amount materially higher than that accrued is remote.

The ability of certain subsidiaries and affiliated companies to transfer funds is limited by provisions of foreign government regulations, affiliate agreements and certain loan agreements. At December 31, 2008, the amount of equity subject to such restrictions for consolidated subsidiaries totaled $1.1 billion. While this amount is legally restricted, it does not result in operational difficulties since we have generally permitted subsidiaries to retain a majority of equity to support their growth programs.

Parker Drilling
2008 Annual Report

Note 13—Commitments and Contingencies

At December 31, 2008, the Company had an $80.0 million revolving credit facility available for general corporate purposes and to support letters of credit. As of December 31, 2008, $12.8 million of availability has been reserved to support letters of credit that have been issued and $58.0 million of loans outstanding under the facility.

The Company has various lease agreements for office space, equipment, vehicles and personal property. These obligations extend through 2012 and are typically non-cancelable. Most leases contain renewal options and certain of the leases contain escalation clauses. Future minimum lease payments at December 31, 2008, under operating leases with non-cancelable terms are as follows (dollars in thousands):

2009	$4,689
2010	1,739
2011	1,125
2012	831
2013	262
Total	$8,646

Total rent expense for all operating leases amounted to $13.7 million for 2008, $10.1 million for 2007 and $9.0 million for 2006.

The Company is self-insured for certain losses relating to workers' compensation, employers' liability, general liability (for onshore liability), protection and indemnity (for offshore liability) and property damage. The Company's exposure (that is, the retention or deductible) per occurrence is $250,000 for worker's compensation, employer's liability, general liability, protection and indemnity and maritime employers' liability (Jones Act). In addition, the Company assumes a $750,000 annual aggregate deductible for protection and indemnity and maritime employers' liability claims. The annual aggregate deductible is eroded by every dollar that exceeds the $250,000 per occurrence retention. The Company continues to assume a straight $250,000 retention for workers' compensation, employers' liability, and general liability losses. The self insurance for automobile liability applies to historic claims only as the Company is currently on a first dollar policy, with those reserves being minimal. For all primary insurances mentioned above, the Company has excess coverage for those claims that exceed the retention and annual aggregate deductible. The Company maintains actuarially-determined accruals in its consolidated balance sheets to cover the self-insurance retentions.

The Company has self-insured retentions for certain other losses relating to rig, equipment, property, business interruption and political, war, and terrorism risks which vary according to the type of rig and line of coverage. Political risk insurance is procured for international operations. This coverage may not adequately protect the Company against liability from all potential consequences.

As of December 31, 2008, the Company's gross self-insurance accruals for workers' compensation, employers' liability, general liability, protection and indemnity and maritime employers' liability totaled $8.1 million and the related insurance recoveries/receivables were $2.5 million.

The Company has entered into employment agreements with terms of one to three years with certain members of management with automatic one or two year renewal periods at expiration dates. The agreements provide for, among other things, compensation, benefits and severance payments. They also provide for lump sum compensation and benefits in the event of a change in control of the Company.

The Company is a party to various lawsuits and claims arising out of the ordinary course of business. Management, after review and consultation with legal counsel, does not anticipate that any liability resulting from these matters would materially affect the results of operations, the financial position or the net cash flows of the Company, but there can be no assurance that an adverse ruling not anticipated by the Company will not have a material adverse effect on the results of operations or the financial position of the Company.

Kazakhstan Tax Claims

On October 12, 2005, the Kazakhstan Branch ("PKD Kazakhstan") of Parker Drilling's subsidiary, Parker Drilling Company International Limited ("PDCIL"), received an Act of Tax Audit from the Ministry of Finance of Kazakhstan ("MinFin") assessing PKD Kazakhstan an amount of KZT (Kazakhstan Tenge) 14.9 billion (approximately $125.8 million). Approximately KZT7.5 billion or $63.3 million was assessed for import Value Added Tax ("VAT"), administrative fines and interest on equipment imported to perform the drilling contracts (the "VAT Assessment") and approximately KZT7.4 billion or $62.5 million for corporate income tax, individual income tax and social tax, administrative fines and interest in connection with the reimbursements received by PDCIL from a client for the upgrade of Barge Rig 257 and other issues related to PKD Kazakhstan's operations in the Republic of Kazakhstan (the "Income Tax Assessment").

On May 24, 2006, the Supreme Court of the Republic of Kazakhstan ("SCK") issued a decision upholding the VAT Assessment. Consistent with its contractual obligations, on November 20, 2006, the client advanced the actual amount of the VAT Assessment and this amount has been remitted to MinFin. The administrative fines related to the VAT Assessment are being appealed by the client who is contractually responsible to reimburse PKD Kazakhstan for any administrative fines ultimately assessed. The client has also contractually agreed to reimburse PKD Kazakhstan for any incremental income taxes that PKD Kazakhstan incurs from the reimbursement of this VAT Assessment.

After multiple appeals to the SCK and two meetings of the U.S. Competent Authorities under the Mutual Agreement Procedure of the U.S.-Kazakhstan Tax Treaty, the SCK ultimately upheld the Income Tax Assessment and on December 12, 2007, PKD Kazakhstan paid the principal tax portion of the Income Tax Assessment, net of estimated taxes previously paid. After a further appeal against the interest portion of the notice of assessment, on February 25, 2008, the Atyrau Economic Court issued a ruling that interest on the income tax assessed should accrue from the October 12, 2005 assessment date as opposed to the original assessment in 2001, which resulted in a revised interest assessment by the Atyrau Tax Committee of approximately US$13 million, which was paid by PKD Kazakhstan on March 14, 2008, in final resolution of this matter. Income tax for the year ended December 31, 2008 includes a benefit of $13.4 million of FIN 48 interest and foreign currency exchange rate fluctuations related to this final resolution.

Bangladesh Claim

In September 2005, a subsidiary of the Company was served with a lawsuit filed in the 152nd District Court of Harris County State of Texas on behalf of numerous citizens of Bangladesh claiming $250 million in damages due to various types of property damage and personal injuries (none involving loss of life) arising as a result of two blowouts that occurred in Bangladesh in January and June 2005, although only the June 2005 blowout involved the Company. The court dismissed the case on the basis that Houston, Texas, is not the appropriate location for this suit to be filed. The plaintiffs have appealed this dismissal; however, the Company believes the plaintiffs' prospects of being successful on appeal are remote. No amounts were accrued at December 31, 2008.

Asbestos-Related Claims

In August 2004, the Company was notified that certain of its subsidiaries have been named, along with other defendants, in several complaints that have been filed in the Circuit Courts of the State of Mississippi by several hundred persons that allege that they were employed by some of the named defendants between approximately 1965 and 1986. The complaints name as defendants numerous other companies that are not affiliated with the Company, including companies that allegedly manufactured drilling- related products containing asbestos that are the subject of the complaints.

The complaints allege that the Company's subsidiaries and other drilling contractors used asbestos containing products in offshore drilling operations, land-based drilling operations and in drilling structures, drilling rigs, vessels and other equipment and assert claims based on, among other things, negligence and strict liability and claims under the Jones Act and that the plaintiffs are entitled to monetary damages. Based on the report of the special master, these complaints have been severed and venue of the claims transferred to the county in which the plaintiff resides or the county in which the cause of action allegedly accrued. Subsequent to the filing of amended complaints, Parker Drilling has joined with other co-defendants in filing motions to compel discovery to determine what plaintiffs have an employment relationship with which defendant, including whether or not any plaintiffs have an employment relationship with subsidiaries of Parker Drilling. Out of 668 amended single-plaintiff complaints filed to date, sixteen (16) plaintiffs have identified Parker Drilling or one of its affiliates as a defendant. Discovery is proceeding in groups of 60 and none of the plaintiff complaints naming Parker are included in the first 60 (Group I). The initial discovery of Group I resulted in certain dismissals with prejudice, two dismissals without prejudice and two withdraws from Group I, leaving only 40 plaintiffs remaining in Group I. Selection of Discovery Group II was completed on April 21, 2008. Out of the 60 plaintiffs selected, Parker Drilling was named in one suit in which the plaintiff claims that during 1973 he earned $587.40 while working for a former subsidiary of a company Parker Drilling acquired in 1996.

The subsidiaries named in these asbestos-related lawsuits intend to defend themselves vigorously and, based on the information available to the Company at this time, the Company does not expect the outcome to have a material adverse effect on its financial condition, results of operations or cash flows; however, the Company is unable to predict the ultimate outcome of these lawsuits. No amounts were accrued at December 31, 2008.

Gulfco Site

Several years ago the Company received an information request under the Comprehensive Environmental Response, Compensation and Liability Act ("CERCLA") designating Parker Drilling Offshore Corporation, a subsidiary of Parker Drilling as a potentially responsible party with respect to the Gulfco Marine Maintenance, Inc. Superfund Site in Freeport, Texas (EPA No. TX 055144539). The subsidiary responded to this request in 2003 with documents. In January, 2008 the subsidiary received an administrative order to participate in an investigation of the site and a study of the remediation needs and alternatives. The EPA alleges that the subsidiary is successor to a party who owned the Gulfco site during the time when chemical releases took place there. Two other parties have been performing that work since mid-2005 under an earlier version of the same order. The subsidiary believes that it has a sufficient cause to decline participation under the order and has notified the EPA of that decision. Non-compliance with an EPA order absent sufficient cause for doing so can result in substantial penalties under CERCLA. The subsidiary is continuing to evaluate its relationship to the site and has conferred with the EPA and the other parties in an effort to resolve the matter. The Company has not yet estimated the amount or impact on our operations, financial position or cash flows of any costs related to the site. To date, the EPA and the other two parties have spent over $2.7 million studying and conducting initial remediation of the site. It is anticipated that an additional $1.3 million will be required to complete the remediation. Other costs (not yet quantified) such as interest and administrative overhead could be added to any action against the Company. Although we can provide no assurance as to the total amount necessary to finally resolve this matter, we currently anticipate that the total claim will not exceed $5 million and will be shared by all responsible parties. The Company does not believe it has any obligation with respect to the remediation of the property, and accordingly no accrual was made as of December 31, 2008.

Customs Agent Investigation

As previously disclosed, the Company received requests from the United States Department of Justice ("DOJ") in July 2007 and the United States Securities and Exchange Commission ("SEC") in January 2008 relating to the Company's utilization of the services of a customs agent. In response to those requests, the Company is conducting an internal investigation. The DOJ and the SEC are conducting parallel investigations into possible violations of U.S. law by the Company, including the Foreign Corrupt Practices Act (the "FCPA"). In particular, the DOJ and the SEC are investigating the Company's use of customs agents in certain countries in which the Company currently operates or formerly operated, including Kazakhstan and Nigeria. The Company is fully cooperating with the DOJ and SEC investigations. At this point, we are unable to predict the duration, scope or result of the DOJ or the SEC investigation or whether either agency will commence any legal action. If we are not in compliance with the FCPA and other laws governing the conduct of business with foreign government entities (including other United States laws and regulations as well as local laws), we may be subject to criminal and civil penalties and other remedial measures, which could have an adverse impact on our business, results of operations, financial condition and liquidity.

Economic Sanctions Compliance

Our international operations are subject to laws and regulations restricting our international operations including activities involving restricted countries, organizations, entities and persons that have been identified as unlawful actors or that are subject to U.S. economic sanctions. Pursuant to an internal review, we have identified certain shipments of equipment and supplies that were routed through Iran as well as other activities that may have violated applicable U.S. laws and regulations. In addition, we have engaged in drilling wells in the Korpedje Field in Turkmenistan, from where natural gas may be exported by pipeline to Iran. We are currently reviewing these shipments, transactions and drilling activities to determine whether the timing, nature and extent of such activities or other conduct may have given rise to violations of these laws and regulations. Although we are unable to predict the scope or result of this internal review or its ultimate outcome, we have initiated voluntary disclosure of these potential compliance issues to the appropriate U.S. government agency. If we are not in compliance with export restrictions, U.S. economic sanctions or other laws and regulations that apply to our international operations, we may be subject to civil or criminal penalties and other remedial measures, which could have an adverse impact on our business, results of operations, financial condition and liquidity.

Sonic Foundry
2008 Annual Report

9. Related-Party Transactions

The Company incurred fees of $249, $241 and $153 thousand during the years ended September 30, 2008, 2007 and 2006, respectively, to a law firm whose partner is a director and stockholder of the Company. The Company had accrued liabilities for unbilled services of $86 thousand at September 30, 2007 to the same law firm. There were no unbilled services at September 30, 2008.

The Company recorded Mediasite product and customer support revenue related to $580, $583 and $602 thousand of billings during the years ended September 30, 2008, 2007 and 2006 to Mediasite KK, a Japanese reseller in which the Company has an equity interest. Mediasite KK owed the Company $108 and $132 thousand on such billings at September 30, 2008 and 2007, respectively.

During 2007, the Company entered into two transactions with an entity in which a member of the Company's Board of Directors is a significant share-holder. The transactions included billings of $236 thousand for the Company's products and services in exchange for advertising services. The Company recognized $137 thousand of revenue during the year ended September 30, 2007 and deferred $99 thousand of revenue at September 30, 2007. The deferral was recognized in full in 2008. No sales were recorded during the years ended September 30, 2008 and 2006.

During the years ended September 30, 2008, 2007 and 2006, the Company had a loan outstanding to an executive totaling $26. The loan is collateralized by company stock.

Johnson & Johnson
2008 Annual Report

11. Segments of Business[1] and Geographic Areas

| (Dollars in millions) | Sales to Customers[2] | | |
	2008	2007	2006
Consumer—			
United States	$ 6,937	6,408	4,573
International	9,117	8,085	5,201
Total	16,054	14,493	9,774
Pharmaceutical—			
United States	14,831	15,603	15,092
International	9,736	9,263	8,175
Total	24,567	24,866	23,267
Medical Devices and Diagnostics—			
United States	10,541	10,433	10,110
International	12,585	11,303	10,173
Total	23,126	21,736	20,283

(Dollars in millions)	Sales to Customers[2]		
	2008	2007	2006
Worldwide total	$63,747	61,095	53,324

[1] See Note 1 for a description of the segments in which the Company operates.
[2] Export sales are not significant. In 2008, 2007 and 2006, the Company did not have a customer that represented 10% of total revenues.

(Dollars in millions)	Operating Profit			Identifiable Assets		
	2008[5]	2007[6]	2006[7]	2008	2007	2006
Consumer	$2,674	2,277	1,374	$23,765	26,550	25,380
Pharmaceutical	7,605	6,540	6,894	19,544	19,780	18,799
Medical Devices and Diagnostics	7,223	4,846	6,126	20,779	19,978	18,601
Total	17,502	13,663	14,394	64,088	66,308	62,780
Less: (Income) Expense not allocated to segments[3]	573	380	(193)			
General Corporate[4]				20,824	14,646	7,776
Worldwide total	$16,929	13,283	14,587	$84,912	80,954	70,556

[3] Amounts not allocated to segments include interest (income) expense, minority interest and general corporate (income) expense.
[4] General corporate includes cash and marketable securities.
[5] Includes $7 million and $174 million of In-Process Research and Development (IPR&D) for the Consumer and Medical Devices and Diagnostics segments, respectively. Includes $379 million of fourth quarter net litigation gain, comprised of a $50 million expense in the Consumer segment and a gain of $429 million in the Medical Devices and Diagnostics segment. The Medical Devices and Diagnostics segment also includes $536 million gain on the divestiture of the Professional Wound Care business of Ethicon, Inc.
[6] Includes $745 million of restructuring expense, comprised of $15 million, $429 million, and $301 million for the Consumer, Pharmaceutical, and Medical Devices and Diagnostics segments, respectively. The Medical Devices and Diagnostics segment includes $807 million of IPR&D. The Pharmaceutical segment also includes $678 million for the write-down of the NATRECOR® intangible asset.
[7] Includes $320 million and $239 million of IPR&D for the Consumer and Medical Devices and Diagnostics segments, respectively. The Medical Devices and Diagnostics segment also includes the Guidant acquisition agreement termination fee, less associated expenses, of $622 million.

(Dollars in millions)	Additions to Property, Plant & Equipment			Depreciation and Amortization		
	2008	2007	2006	2008	2007	2006
Consumer	$499	504	344	$489	472	255
Pharmaceutical	920	1,137	1,246	986	1,033	929
Medical Devices and Diagnostics	1,251	919	823	1,146	1,080	861
Segments total	2,670	2,560	2,413	2,621	2,585	2,045

(Dollars in millions)	Additions to Property, Plant & Equipment			Depreciation and Amortization		
	2008	2007	2006	2008	2007	2006
General corporate	396	382	253	211	192	132
Worldwide total	$3,066	2,942	2,666	$2,832	2,777	2,177

(Dollars in millions)	Sales to Customers[2]			Long-Lived Assets[8]		
	2008	2007	2006	2008	2007	2006
United States	$32,309	32,444	29,775	$21,674	21,685	22,432
Europe	16,782	15,644	12,786	14,375	15,578	14,443
Western Hemisphere excluding U.S.	5,173	4,681	3,542	3,328	3,722	3,108
Asia-Pacific, Africa	9,483	8,326	7,221	1,898	1,261	1,206
Segments total	63,747	61,095	53,324	41,275	42,246	41,189
General corporate				785	702	543
Other non long-lived assets				42,852	38,006	28,824
Worldwide total	$63,747	61,095	53,324	$84,912	80,954	70,556

[2] Export sales are not significant. In 2008, 2007 and 2006, the Company did not have a customer that represented 10% of total revenues.

[8] Long-lived assets include property, plant and equipment, net for 2008, 2007 and 2006 of $14,365, $14,185 and $13,044, respectively, and intangible assets and goodwill, net for 2008, 2007 and 2006 of $27,695, $28,763 and $28,688, respectively.

Whirlpool
2007 Annual Report

(1) Summary of Principal Accounting Policies

General Information

Whirlpool Corporation, a Delaware corporation, is the world's leading manufacturer and marketer of major home appliances. We manufacture appliances in 12 countries under 13 principal brand names in 4 geographic segments and market products in nearly every country around the world. Our Consolidated Financial Statements include all majority-owned subsidiaries. All intercompany transactions have been eliminated upon consolidation.

Use of Estimates

We are required to make estimates and assumptions that affect the amounts reported in the Consolidated Financial Statements and accompanying notes. Actual results could differ materially from those estimates.

Revenue Recognition

Sales are recorded when title passes to the customer. The point at which title passes is determined by the shipping terms. For the majority of our sales, title is transferred to the customer as soon as products are shipped. For a portion of our sales, title is transferred to the customer upon receipt of products at the customer's location. Allowances for estimated returns are made on sales of certain products based on historical return rates for the products involved.

Accounts Receivable and Allowance for Doubtful Accounts

We carry accounts receivable at sales value less an allowance for doubtful accounts. On a periodic basis, we evaluate accounts receivable and establish an allowance for doubtful accounts based on a combination of specific customer circumstances, credit conditions and the history of write-offs and collections. We evaluate items on an individual basis when determining accounts receivable write-offs. Our policy is not to charge interest on trade receivables after the invoice becomes past due. A receivable is considered past due if payments have not been received within agreed upon invoice terms.

Freight and Warehousing Costs

We apply Emerging Issues Task Force ("EITF") No. 00-10, "Accounting for Shipping and Handling Fees and Costs". This EITF requires the classification of such costs within cost of products sold, or if classified elsewhere, to be disclosed. Effective January 1, 2006, we reclassified freight and warehousing costs from selling, general and administrative expense to the cost of products sold in the Consolidated Statements of Income. This change was adopted to better reflect these costs being directly tied to product sales. The amounts reclassified from the selling, general and administrative expense to the cost of products sold were $854 million in 2005. There was no change to net earnings as a result of this reclassification.

Cash and Equivalents

All highly liquid debt instruments purchased with an initial maturity of three months or less are considered cash equivalents.

Inventories

Inventories are stated at first-in, first-out ("FIFO") cost, except U.S. production inventories, which are stated at last-in, first-out ("LIFO") cost, and Brazilian inventories, which are stated at average cost. Costs do not exceed realizable values. See Note 6 for additional information about inventories.

Goodwill and Other Intangibles

Goodwill and other intangible assets are accounted for in accordance with Statement of Financial Accounting Standards ("SFAS") No. 142, "Goodwill and Other Intangible Assets" which requires that we evaluate goodwill and other indefinite lived intangible assets for impairment on an annual basis (or whenever events occur which may indicate possible impairment). Goodwill impairment is determined by comparing the fair value of a reporting unit to its carrying amount. If the fair value of the reporting unit exceeds its carrying amount, goodwill of the reporting unit is not considered impaired.

Definite lived intangible assets are amortized over the estimated useful life ranging from 1 to 18 years. See Note 4 for additional information about goodwill and intangible assets.

Property, Plant and Equipment

Property, plant and equipment are stated at cost. Depreciation of property, plant and equipment is computed using the straight-line method based on the estimated useful lives of the assets. Useful lives for buildings range from 25 to 50 years, machinery and equipment range from 3 to 10 years, and computer/software range from 1 to 8 years. Depreciation expense for property, plant and equipment was $562 million, $520 million and $440 million in 2007, 2006 and 2005, respectively.

Accounts Payable Outsourcing

We offer our suppliers access to a payables presentment and settlement service (PPS) provided by a third party processor. This service allows our suppliers to view scheduled Whirlpool payments online, enabling them to better manage their cash flow and reduce payment processing costs. Independent of Whirlpool, the PPS provider also allows suppliers to sell their receivables to financial institutions at the sole discretion of both the supplier and the financial institution. We have no economic interest in the sale of these receivables and no direct relationship with financial institutions concerning this service. All of our obligations, including amounts due, remain to our suppliers as stated in our supplier agreements. As of December 31, 2007 approximately $13 million of our total accounts payable is available for this purpose and approximately $6 million has been sold by suppliers to participating financial institutions.

Research and Development Costs

Research and development costs are charged to expense as incurred. Such costs were $421 million, $375 million and $339 million in 2007, 2006 and 2005, respectively.

Advertising Costs

Advertising costs are charged to expense when the advertisement is first communicated. Such costs were $321 million, $316 million and $239 million in 2007, 2006 and 2005, respectively.

Discontinued Operations

We present the results of operations, financial position and cash flows of operations that have either been sold or that meet the "held for sale accounting" and certain other criteria as discontinued operations. See Note 3 for additional information about discontinued operations.

Foreign Currency Translation

The functional currency for our international subsidiaries and affiliates is typically the local currency. Certain international subsidiaries primarily utilize the U.S. dollar and Euro as the functional currency.

Derivative Financial Instruments

We use derivative instruments designated as cash flow and fair value hedges to manage our exposure to the volatility in material costs, foreign currency and interest rates on certain debt instruments. Derivative instruments are accounted for in accordance with SFAS No. 133, "Accounting for Derivative Instruments and Hedging Activities," as amended, which requires us to fair value our derivative instruments periodically. Changes in the fair value of derivative assets or liabilities (i.e., gains or losses) are recognized depending upon the type of hedging relationship and whether a hedge has been designated. For those derivative instruments that qualify for hedge accounting, we designate the hedging instrument, based upon the exposure being hedged, as a cash flow hedge, fair value hedge, or a hedge of a net investment in a foreign operation. Changes in fair value of derivative instruments that do not qualify for hedge accounting are recognized immediately in current earnings. See Note 9 for additional information about hedges and derivative financial instruments.

Income Taxes

We account for income taxes in accordance with SFAS No. 109, "Accounting for Income Taxes." Under SFAS No. 109, deferred tax assets and liabilities are determined based on the difference between the financial statement and tax basis of the respective assets and liabilities, using enacted tax rates in effect for the year in which the differences are expected to reverse. Judgment is required in determining and evaluating our income tax provisions. We establish provisions for income taxes when, based on the technical merits of the uncertain tax position, it is not more likely than not to be substantiated on a review by tax authorities. We evaluate and adjust these accruals in light of changing facts and circumstances. For additional information about income taxes, see Note 13.

Stock Based Compensation

Effective January 1, 2006, we adopted the fair value recognition provisions of SFAS No. 123(R), "Share-Based Payments", using the modified-prospective-transition method. Under that transition method, compensation cost includes: (1) compensation cost for all share-based payments granted prior to, but not yet vested as of, January 1, 2006, based on the grant date fair value estimated in accordance with the original provisions of SFAS No. 123, and (2) compensation cost for all share-based payments granted subsequent to January 1, 2006, based on the grant date fair value estimated in accordance with the provisions of SFAS No. 123(R). Prior to the adoption of SFAS No. 123(R), we accounted for share based compensation in accordance with Accounting Principles Board No. 25 Accounting for Stock Issued to Employees. Accordingly, we recognized no compensation expense for share based compensation if the exercise price was equal to or more than the fair value of the shares at the date of the grant.

The following table illustrates the effect on net earnings and earnings per share for the year ended December 31, 2005 if we had applied the fair value recognition provisions of SFAS No. 123 to options granted under our stock option plans. For purposes of this pro forma disclosure, the value of the options is estimated using a Black-Scholes option-pricing model with share-based awards amortized over the vesting periods.

millions of dollars, except per share data	*Year Ended* *December 31, 2005*
Net earnings as reported	$422
Add: Share-based employee compensation expense included in reported net earnings, net of related tax effects	15
Deduct: Total share-based employee compensation expense determined under the fair value based method for all awards, net of related tax effects	(19)
Pro forma net earnings	$418
Earnings per share:	
Basic—as reported	$6.30
Basic—pro forma	$6.23
Diluted—as reported	$6.19
Diluted—pro forma	$6.13

Reclassifications

We adopted SFAS No. 158, "Employers Accounting for Defined Benefit Pensions and Other Postretirement Plans, an amendment of SFAS No. 87, 88, 106 and 132(R)" and reflected the under-funded liability with a corresponding offset in accumulated other comprehensive income on our Consolidated Balance Sheet at December 31, 2006. During adoption, we recorded a long-term deferred tax asset in other long term assets in the amount of $160 million which has been reclassified in the prior year to net with other long term liabilities to conform to current year presentation.

During the first quarter of 2007, we adopted changes to our segment reporting consistent with the methodology the chief operating decision maker now uses to evaluate each segment's operating and financial results. We previously included the financial results for our Caribbean operations and exports of certain portable appliances to Europe within our North America business segment. The results for these businesses are now being reported within the Latin America and Europe segments, respectively. In addition, we have reallocated certain costs previously included within corporate administrative expense to each of the respective regions. Regional results for 2006 and 2005 have been reclassified to reflect these changes to conform to the 2007 presentation.

We reclassified certain other prior period amounts in our Consolidated Financial Statements to be consistent with current period presentation. The effect of these reclassifications is not material.

New Accounting Standards

In December 2007, the FASB issued SFAS No. 141(R), "Business Combinations." SFAS No. 141(R) requires us to continue to follow the guidance in SFAS No. 141 for certain aspects of business combinations, with additional guidance provided defining the acquirer, recognizing and measuring the identifiable assets acquired, the liabilities assumed, and any noncontrolling interest in the acquiree, assets and liabilities arising from contingencies, defining a bargain purchase and recognizing and measuring goodwill or a gain from a bargain purchase. This statement is effective for all business combinations for which the acquisition date is on or after the beginning of an entity's first fiscal year that begins after December 15, 2008. We will implement SFAS No. 141(R) for any business combinations occurring at or subsequent to January 1, 2009.

In December 2007, the FASB issued SFAS No. 160, "Noncontrolling Interests in Consolidated Financial Statements," an Amendment of ARB No. 51, "Consolidated Financial Statements." SFAS No. 160 establishes accounting and reporting standards for the noncontrolling interest in a subsidiary and for the deconsolidation of a subsidiary. It clarifies that a noncontrolling interest in a subsidiary is an ownership interest in the consolidated entity that should be reported as equity in the consolidated financial statements. This statement is effective as of the beginning of an entity's first fiscal year that begins after December 15, 2008 with retrospective application. We will implement SFAS No. 160 beginning January 1, 2009 and are currently evaluating the potential impact on our financial statements when implemented.

In September 2006, the FASB issued SFAS No. 157, "Fair Value Measurements", which defines fair value, establishes a framework for measuring fair value in generally accepted accounting principles (GAAP) and expands disclosures about fair value measurements. The expanded disclosures in this statement about the use of fair value to measure assets and liabilities should provide users of financial statements with better information about the extent to which fair value is used to measure recognized assets and liabilities, the inputs used to develop the measurements, and the effect of certain of the measurements on earnings (or changes in net assets) for the period. SFAS No. 157 is effective for financial statements issued for fiscal years beginning after November 15, 2007, and interim periods within those fiscal years. We implemented SFAS No. 157 beginning January 1, 2008. SFAS No. 157 will not impact our financial statements, but will provide expanded disclosure on our fair value measurements.

(2) Maytag Acquisition

On March 31, 2006, we completed the acquisition of Maytag. The results of Maytag's operations have been included in our Consolidated Financial Statements beginning April 1, 2006.

The purchase price for Maytag was approximately $1.9 billion, including approximately $848 million of cash and approximately 9.7 million shares of Whirlpool common stock. The purchase price also included the exchange of fully-vested Whirlpool options for fully-vested Maytag options to become exercisable, in aggregate, for an additional 1.8 million shares of Whirlpool common stock and the settlement of Maytag restricted stock and performance units for cash. The combined value of the above share-based consideration was approximately $920 million. The value of the approximately 9.7 million shares of Whirlpool common stock was determined using the average market price of the common shares for the two days prior to, through the two days after, March 29, 2006.

We assumed Maytag's existing debt of approximately $966 million and incurred approximately $102 million in acquisition-related expenses, which are included in the purchase price. Initially, we borrowed amounts required to fund the cash portion of the purchase price through issuances in the U.S. commercial paper market and in June 2006 refinanced a portion of this commercial paper through the issuance of long-term bonds.

We finalized the purchase price allocation to individual assets acquired and liabilities assumed on March 31, 2007. The final purchase price allocation is based on management and independent appraisers' best estimates.

The following table presents the final purchase price allocation as of March 31, 2006:

millions of dollars	
Current assets	$1,352
Assets of discontinued operations	442
Property, plant and equipment	487
Goodwill	1,585
Intangible assets	1,845
Other non-current assets	19
Total assets acquired	5,730
Current liabilities	1,657
Liabilities of discontinued operations	168
Non-current liabilities	2,035
Total liabilities assumed	3,860
Net assets acquired	$1,870

Goodwill, which is not deductible for tax purposes, has been allocated to the North America operating segment on the basis that the cost efficiencies identified will primarily benefit this segment of the business.

We estimate the fair value of Maytag's identifiable intangible assets is $1,845 million. The allocation of identifiable intangible assets is as follows:

millions of dollars	Estimated Fair Value	Estimated Useful Life
Trademarks	$1,463	Indefinite life
Customer relationships	288	18 years
Patents and non-compete agreements	94	1 to 7 years
Total intangible assets acquired	$1,845	

Identifiable intangible assets consist of trademarks, customer relationships, patents and noncompete agreements. These intangible assets, excluding trademarks, are definite lived intangible assets and are amortized over their estimated economic lives based on a number of assumptions including customer attrition rates and the life of technology and associated products.

We have also completed the analysis of integration plans, pursuant to incurred costs associated with the elimination of duplicative manufacturing facilities and selling, general and administrative overlap. Certain reserves in the amount of $239 million were established for severance and exit costs relating to the closure of Maytag facilities including manufacturing plants, the former headquarters location and other administrative offices. Costs associated with these actions have not impacted earnings and have been recognized as a component of purchase accounting, resulting in a corresponding increase to recorded goodwill. These reserves are related to closed Maytag facilities in Galesburg, Illinois and Florence, South Carolina, along with the closure of the Maytag facilities mentioned above.

The following table provides pro forma results of operations for the years ended December 31, 2006 and 2005 as if Maytag had been acquired as of the beginning of each period presented. The pro forma results include certain purchase accounting adjustments such as the estimated changes in depreciation and amortization expense on acquired tangible and intangible assets as well as interest expense on borrowings used to finance the integration. However, pro forma results do not include any anticipated cost savings or other effects of the planned integration of Maytag. Accordingly, such amounts are not necessarily indicative of the results that would have occurred if the acquisition had occurred on the dates indicated or that may result in the future.

	Year Ended December 31,	
	2006	2005
Net sales	$19,097	$18,430
Earnings from continuing operations	474	307
Net earnings	421	267
Diluted net earnings per share:		
Earnings from continuing operations	$5.96	$3.93
Loss from discontinued operations	(0.67)	(0.51)
Net earnings	$5.29	$3.42

Certain non-recurring acquisition charges of $52 million recorded by Maytag prior to March 31, 2006, directly related to the acquisition, including $27 million of accelerated stock compensation expense triggered by certain change in control provisions and approximately $25 million of direct transaction costs are not included in the pro forma information presented above.

Crane
2007 Annual Report

Note 10—Commitments and Contingencies

Leases

The Company leases certain facilities, vehicles and equipment. Future minimum payments, by year and in the aggregate, under leases with initial or remaining terms of one year or more consisted of the following at December 31, 2007:

(in thousands)	Operating Leases	Minimum Sublease Income	Net
2008	$14,503	$58	$14,445
2009	12,021	79	11,942
2010	8,434	–	8,434
2011	4,194	–	4,194
2012	2,754	–	2,754
Thereafter	6,685	–	6,685
Total minimum lease payments	$48,591	$137	$48,454

Rental expense was $25.5 million, $20.9 million and $19.3 million for 2007, 2006 and 2005, respectively.

Asbestos Liability

Information Regarding Claims and Costs in the Tort System

As of December 31, 2007, the Company was a defendant in cases filed in various state and federal courts alleging injury or death as a result of exposure to asbestos. Activity related to asbestos claims during the periods indicated was as follows:

(in millions)	Year Ended December 31,		
	2007	2006	2005
Beginning claims	$85,941	$89,017	$84,977
New claims	3,417	4,853	7,986
Settlements	(1,441)	(1,043)	(1,829)
Dismissals	(6,918)	(6,886)	(2,117)
Ending claims*	$80,999	$85,941	$89,017

* Does not include 36,332 maritime actions that were filed in the United States District Court for the Northern District of Ohio and transferred to the Eastern District of Pennsylvania pursuant to an order by the Federal Judicial Panel on Multi-District Litigation ("MDL"). These claims have been placed on the inactive docket of cases that are administratively dismissed without prejudice in the MDL.

Of the 80,999 pending claims as of December 31, 2007, approximately 25,000 claims were pending in New York, approximately 24,000 claims were pending in Mississippi, approximately 9,000 claims were pending in Texas and approximately 4,000 claims were pending in Ohio, all jurisdictions in which legislation or judicial orders restrict the types of claims that can proceed to trial on the merits.

Since the termination of the comprehensive master settlement agreement ("MSA") on January 24, 2005, the Company has been resolving claims filed against it in the tort system. The Company has not re-engaged in discussions with representatives of current or future asbestos claimants with respect to such a comprehensive settlement. While the Company believes that federal legislation to establish a trust fund to compensate asbestos claimants is the most appropriate solution to the asbestos litigation problem, there is substantial uncertainty regarding whether this will occur and, if so, when and on what terms. The Company remains committed to exploring all feasible alternatives available to resolve its asbestos liability in a manner consistent with the best interests of the Company's shareholders.

Substantially all of the claims the Company resolves are concluded through settlements. The Company recently tried the Joseph Norris asbestos claim (the "Norris Claim") to verdict in California, however, and received an adverse jury verdict on September 15, 2006. On October 10, 2006 the court entered judgment on this verdict against the Company in the amount of $2.15 million, together with interest thereon at the rate of 10% per annum until paid. The Company does not believe that the verdict was supported by the evidence. In addition, the Company believes that procedural irregularities prevented an appropriate determination of the Company's alleged responsibility for plaintiffs' injuries. The Company's post-trial motions were denied by order dated December 15, 2006. On January 3, 2007, the Company appealed the judgment; the appeal is pending.

The gross settlement and defense costs incurred (before insurance and tax effects) for the Company in the years ended December 31, 2007, 2006 and 2005 totaled $87.5 million, $69.1 million and $45.1 million, respectively. In contrast to the recognition of settlement and defense costs that reflect the current level of activity in the tort system, cash payments and receipts generally lag the tort system activity by several months or more. Cash payments of settlement amounts are not made until all releases and other required documentation are received by the Company. The Company's pre-tax cash payments for settlement and defense costs, including payments from insurers, in the years ended December 31, 2007, 2006 and 2005 totaled a $10.2 million net payment in 2007 (reflecting the receipt of $31.5 million in previously escrowed funds from Equitas Limited ("Equitas") in January 2007 and the receipt of $10.0 million for a full policy buyout from Employers Reinsurance Company ("ERC") in April 2007), a $40.6 million net payment in 2006 and a $45.3 million net payment in 2005, respectively. Detailed below are the comparable amounts for the periods indicated.

(in millions)	Year Ended December 31,			Cumulative to Date through Dec. 31, 2007
	2007	2006	2005	
Settlement costs incurred[1]	$41.6	$26.3	$17.4	$124.1
Defense cost incurred[1]	45.9	42.8	27.7	162.4
Total costs incurred	$87.5	$69.1	$45.1	$286.5
Pre-tax cash payments (receipts)[2]	$10.2	$40.6	$ 45.3	$135.9
(Refund) associated with terminated MSA			$(9.9)	$ 0.1

[1] Before insurance recoveries and tax effects.

[2] Net of payments received from insurers, including a $31.5 million payment from Equitas in January 2007 and a $10.0 million payment from ERC in April 2007. The cumulative amounts include certain legal fees and expenses related to the terminated MSA.

The amounts shown for settlement and defense costs incurred, and cash payments, are not necessarily indicative of future period amounts, which may be higher or lower than those reported.

Effects on the Consolidated Financial Statements

The Company has retained the firm of Hamilton, Rabinovitz & Associates, Inc. ("HR&A"), a nationally recognized expert in the field, to assist management in estimating the Company's asbestos liability in the tort system. HR&A reviews information provided by the Company concerning claims filed, settled and dismissed, amounts paid in settlements and relevant claim information such as the nature of the asbestos-related disease asserted by the claimant, the jurisdiction where filed and the time lag from filing to disposition of the claim. The methodology used by HR&A to project future asbestos costs is based largely on the Company's experience during the two full preceding calendar years (and additional quarterly periods to the estimate date) for claims filed, settled and dismissed. The Company's experience is then compared to the results of previously conducted epidemiological studies estimating the number of individuals likely to develop asbestos-related diseases. Those studies were undertaken in connection with national analyses of the population of workers believed to have been exposed to asbestos. Using that information, HR&A estimates the number of future claims that would be filed against the Company, as well as the related settlement or indemnity costs that would be incurred to resolve those claims. This methodology has been accepted by numerous courts. After discussions with the Company, HR&A augments its liability estimate for the costs of defending asbestos claims in the tort system using a forecast from the Company which is based upon discussions with its defense counsel. Based on this information, HR&A compiles an estimate of the Company's asbestos liability for pending and future claims, based on claim experience over the past two years and covering claims expected to be filed through the indicated period. Although the methodology used by HR&A will also show claims and costs for subsequent periods (up to and including the endpoint of the asbestos studies referred to above), management believes that the level of uncertainty is too great to provide for reasonable estimation of the number of future claims, the nature of such claims or the cost to resolve them for years beyond the indicated estimate.

In the Company's view, the forecast period used to provide the best estimate for asbestos claims and related liabilities and costs is a judgment based upon a number of trend factors, including the number and type of claims being filed each year, the jurisdictions where such claims are filed and the effect of any legislation or judicial orders in such jurisdictions restricting the types of claims that can proceed to trial on the merits and the likelihood of any comprehensive asbestos legislation at the federal level. In addition, the dynamics of asbestos litigation in the tort system have been significantly affected over the past five to ten years by the substantial number of companies that have filed for bankruptcy protection, thereby staying any asbestos claims against them until the conclusion of such proceedings, and the establishment of a number of post-bankruptcy trusts for asbestos claimants, which are estimated to hold $25 billion for payments to current and future claimants. These trend factors have both positive and negative effects on the dynamics of asbestos litigation in the tort system and the related best estimate of the Company's asbestos liability, and these effects do not move in a linear fashion but rather change over multi-year periods. Accordingly, the Company's management monitors these trend factors over time and periodically assesses whether an alternative forecast period is appropriate.

Liability Estimate

With the assistance of HR&A, effective as of September 30, 2007 the Company updated and extended its estimate of the asbestos liability, including the costs of settlement or indemnity payments and defense costs relating to currently pending claims and future claims projected to be filed against the Company through 2017. The Company's previous estimate was for asbestos claims filed through 2011. As a result of this updated estimate, the Company recorded an additional liability of $586 million as of September 30, 2007. The Company's decision to take this action at such date was based on several factors. First, the number of asbestos claims being filed against the Company has moderated substantially over the past several years, and in the Company's opinion, the outlook for asbestos claims expected to be filed and resolved in the forecast period should be reasonably stable. Second, the stable outlook for future claims is particularly true for mesothelioma claims, which although constituting only 11% of the Company's asbestos claims account for approximately 85% of the Company's aggregate settlement and defense costs over the past five years. Third, federal legislation that would significantly change the nature of asbestos litigation failed to pass in 2006, and in the Company's opinion, the prospects for such legislation at the federal level are remote. Fourth, there have been significant actions taken by certain state legislatures and courts over the past several years that have reduced the number and types of claims that can proceed to trial, which has been a significant factor in stabilizing the asbestos claim activity. Fifth, the Company has now entered into coverage-in-place agreements with a majority of its excess insurers, which enables the Company to project a more stable relationship between settlement and defense costs paid by the Company and reimbursements from its insurers. Taking all of these factors into account, the Company believes that it can reasonably estimate the asbestos liability for pending claims and future claims to be filed through 2017. While it is probable that the Company will incur additional charges for asbestos liabilities and defense costs in excess of the amounts currently provided, the Company does not believe that any such amount can be reasonably estimated beyond 2017. Accordingly, no accrual has been recorded for any costs which may be incurred for claims made subsequent to 2017.

Management has made its best estimate of the costs through 2017 based on the analysis by HR&A completed in October 2007. A liability of $1,055 million was recorded as of September 30, 2007 to cover the estimated cost of asbestos claims now pending or subsequently asserted through 2017, of which approximately 68% is attributable to settlement and defense costs for future claims projected to be filed through 2017. The liability is reduced when cash payments are made in respect of settled claims and defense costs. The liability was $1,027 million as of December 31, 2007. It is not possible to forecast when cash payments related to the asbestos liability will be fully expended; however, it is expected such cash payments will continue for a number of years past 2017, due to the significant proportion of future claims included in the estimated asbestos liability and the lag time between the date a claim is filed and when it is resolved.

Estimation of the Company's ultimate exposure for asbestos-related claims is subject to significant uncertainties, as there are multiple variables that can affect the timing, severity and quantity of claims. The Company cautions that its estimated liability is based on assumptions with respect to future claims, settlement and defense costs based on recent experience during the last few years that may not prove reliable as predictors. A significant upward or downward trend in the number of claims filed, depending on the nature of the alleged injury, the jurisdiction where filed and the quality of the product identification, or a significant upward or downward trend in the costs of defending claims, could change the estimated liability, as would any substantial adverse verdict at trial. A legislative solution or a revised structured settlement transaction could also change the estimated liability.

Insurance Coverage and Receivables

Prior to 2005, a significant portion of the Company's settlement and defense costs were paid by its primary insurers. With the exhaustion of that primary coverage, the Company began negotiations with its excess insurers to reimburse the Company for a portion of its settlement and defense costs as incurred. To date, the Company has entered into agreements providing for such reimbursements, known as "coverage-in-place", with eight of its excess insurer groups. With three of its excess insurer groups, the Company entered into policy buyout agreements, settling all asbestos and other coverage obligations for an agreed sum, totaling $46.8 million in aggregate. The Company is in discussions with or expects to enter into additional coverage-in-place agreements with other of its excess insurers whose policies are expected to respond to the aggregate costs included in the updated liability estimate. Under such coverage-in-place agreements, an insurer's policies remain in force and the insurer undertakes to provide coverage for the Company's present and future asbestos claims on specified terms and conditions that address, among other things, the share of asbestos claims costs to be paid by the insurer, payment terms, claims handling procedures and the expiration of the insurer's obligations. Reimbursements from such insurers for past and ongoing settlement and defense costs allocable to their policies have been made as coverage-in-place and other agreements are reached with such insurers. All of these agreements include provisions for mutual releases, indemnification of the insurer and, for coverage-in-place, claims handling procedures.

The same factors that affect developing estimates of probable settlement and defense costs for asbestos-related liabilities also affect estimates of the probable insurance payments, as do a number of additional factors. These additional factors include the financial viability of the insurance companies, the method by which losses will be allocated to the various insurance policies and the years covered by those policies, how settlement and defense costs will be covered by the insurance policies and interpretation of the effect on coverage of various policy terms and limits and their interrelationships. In addition, the timing and amount of reimbursements will vary because the Company's insurance coverage for asbestos claims involves multiple insurers, with different policy terms and certain gaps in coverage. In addition to consulting with legal counsel on these insurance matters, the Company retained insurance consultants to assist management in the estimation of probable insurance recoveries based upon the aggregate liability estimate described above and assuming the continued viability of all solvent insurance carriers. After considering the foregoing factors and consulting with legal counsel and such insurance consultants, the Company determined its probable insurance reimbursement rate for the aggregate liability recorded as of September 30, 2007 to be 33%. An asset of $351 million was recorded as of September 30, 2007 representing the probable insurance reimbursement for such claims. The asset is reduced as reimbursements and other payments from insurers are received. The asset was $340 million as of December 31, 2007.

Uncertainties

Many uncertainties exist surrounding asbestos litigation, and the Company will continue to evaluate its estimated asbestos-related liability and corresponding estimated insurance reimbursement as well as the underlying assumptions and process used to derive these amounts. These uncertainties may result in the Company incurring future charges or increases to income to adjust the carrying value of recorded liabilities and assets, particularly if the number of claims and settlement and defense costs change significantly or if legislation or another alternative solution is implemented; however, the Company is currently unable to estimate such future changes. Although the resolution of these claims may take many years, the effect on results of operations, financial position and cash flow in any given period from a revision to these estimates could be material.

Other Contingencies

Environmental Matters

For environmental matters, the Company records a liability for estimated remediation costs when it is probable that the Company will be responsible for such costs and they can be reasonably estimated. Generally, third party specialists assist in the estimation of remediation costs. The environmental remediation liability at December 31, 2007 is substantially all for the former manufacturing site in Goodyear, Arizona (the "Site") discussed below.

The Site was operated by UniDynamics/Phoenix, Inc. ("UPI"), which became an indirect subsidiary of the Company in 1985 when the Company acquired UPI's parent company, UniDynamics Corporation. UPI manufactured explosive and pyrotechnic compounds, including components for critical military programs, for the U.S. government at the Site from 1962 to 1993, under contracts with the Department of Defense and other government agencies and certain of their prime contractors. No manufacturing operations have been conducted at the Site since 1994. The Site was placed on the National Priorities List in 1983, and is now part of the Phoenix-Goodyear Airport North Superfund site. In 1990, the U.S. Environmental Protection Agency ("EPA") issued administrative orders requiring UPI to design and carry out certain remedial actions, which UPI has done. Groundwater extraction and treatment systems have been in operation at the Site since 1994. A soil vapor extraction system was in operation from 1994 to 1998, was restarted in 2004, and is currently in operation. On July 26, 2006, the Company entered into a consent decree with the EPA with respect to the Site providing for, among other things, a work plan for further investigation and remediation activities at the Site. The Company recorded a liability in 2004 for estimated costs through 2014 after reaching substantial agreement on the scope of work with the EPA. At the end of September 2007, the liability totaled $15.4 million. During the fourth quarter 2007, the Company and its technical advisors determined that changing groundwater flow rates and contaminant plume direction at the Site required additional extraction systems as well as modifications and upgrades of the existing systems. In consultation with its technical advisors, the Company prepared a forecast of the expenditures required for these new and upgraded systems as well as the costs of operation over the forecast period through 2014. Taking these additional costs into consideration, the Company's estimated liability for the costs of such activities through 2014 was $41.5 million as of December 31, 2007, which is included in accrued liabilities and other liabilities in the Company's consolidated balance sheet.

On July 31, 2006, the Company entered into a consent decree with the U.S. Department of Justice ("DOJ") on behalf of the Department of Defense and the Department of Energy pursuant to which, among other things, the U.S. Government reimburses the Company for 21 percent of qualifying costs of investigation and remediation activities at the Site. As of December 31, 2007 the Company has recorded a receivable of $7.8 million for the expected reimbursements from the U.S. Government in respect of the aggregate liability as at that date.

The EPA and the DOJ have alleged that one of the Company's subsidiaries (Crane Composites, Inc.) is in violation of certain Clean Air Act regulations and a Clean Air Act operating permit at a manufacturing facility located in Channahon, Illinois. The allegations originated from a neighbor's complaint in late 2003 about an odor emanating from the facility. The Company has cooperated with EPA's investigation, and it is in the late stage of discussions with the EPA and the DOJ in an effort to resolve the dispute regarding emission, as well as their claim for a civil penalty relative to the alleged violations. The DOJ has demanded a civil penalty in the amount of $1.2 million. While the Company believes that it has not violated its Clean Air Act operating permit or the regulations in question, it recognizes that the cost and risk associated with a protracted litigation with the U.S. Government could be avoided through a reasonable settlement. The Company intends to continue discussions with the DOJ and EPA in an effort to find a mutually acceptable resolution.

False Claims Proceeding

The Company engaged in discussions with attorneys from the Civil Division of the DOJ for over a year regarding allegations that certain valves sold by the Company's Crane Valves North America unit ("CVNA") to private customers that ultimately were delivered to U.S. military agencies did not conform to contractual specifications relating to the place of manufacture and the origin of component parts. The DOJ's allegations originated with a *qui tam* complaint filed under seal by a former CVNA employee. The DOJ ultimately intervened in that case, and on March 31, 2007, filed a complaint against the Company in the United States District Court for the Southern District of Texas seeking unspecified damages for violations of the False Claims Act, and other common law claims. The complaint alleged that CVNA failed to notify the correct U.S. military agency when its manufacturing location for Mil-Spec valves listed on the Qualified Products List was moved from Long Beach, California to Conroe, Texas in 2003. As a result, the complaint alleged that the valves manufactured in Texas were not properly listed on the Qualified Product List as required by the contract specifications.

The Company received a letter from the Department of the Navy on February 14, 2007, conveying the Navy's concerns about the Qualified Products List allegations raised by the DOJ. The Department of the Navy advised the Company that, if true, these allegations could potentially result in the Company and its subsidiaries and affiliates being suspended and/or debarred from doing business with the U.S. Government.

The Company cooperated with the Government's investigation of these matters and negotiated a settlement agreement with the DOJ providing for, among other things, the payment of $7.5 million to the United States and $125,000 to pay the legal fees of the former employee who filed the *qui tam* complaint. In addition, the Company negotiated an administrative agreement with the Department of the Navy for a term of three years pursuant to which the Company will implement certain changes to its compliance programs and report to the Navy on a quarterly basis. These agreements were executed and became effective on July 27, 2007. The Company acknowledged the failure to notify the Navy and update the Qualified Products List but denies that this omission violated the False Claims Act. The failure to notify the Navy was unintentional and there was no misconduct by Company personnel. The Company determined to settle this matter to avoid the risks of costly and protracted legal proceedings.

Other Proceedings

The Company is defending two separate lawsuits brought by customers alleging failure of the Company's fiberglass-reinforced plastic material in recreational vehicle sidewalls manufactured by such customers. The aggregate damages sought in these two lawsuits are approximately $13 million in direct costs allegedly incurred by the plaintiffs, as well as other consequential losses allegedly suffered. One of these lawsuits is currently in trial, and is expected to conclude by the end of February, 2008. The other is nearing completion of fact and expert discovery and a trial on that lawsuit is expected to take place in late 2008. The Company continues to believe that it has valid defenses to the claims raised in both of these lawsuits.

The Company has given notice of these lawsuits to its insurance carriers and will seek coverage for any liability in accordance with the applicable policies.

The Company is also defending a series of five separate lawsuits, which have now been consolidated, revolving around a fire that occurred in May, 2003 at a chicken processing plant located near Atlanta, Georgia that destroyed the plant. The aggregate damages demanded by the plaintiff are in excess of $50 million. These lawsuits contend that certain fiberglass-reinforced plastic material manufactured by the Company that was installed inside the plant was unsafe in that it acted as an accelerant, causing the fire to spread rapidly, resulting in the total loss of the plant and property. The suits are in the early stages of pre-trial discovery and the Company believes that it has valid defenses to the underlying claims raised in these lawsuits. The Company has given notice of these lawsuits to its insurance carriers, and will seek coverage for any resulting losses. Based on a review of its coverage, however, the Company has determined that it is facing a potential $25 million gap in insurance coverage, for the layer of insurance which would have provided protection for losses above $25 million but below $50 million. The Company has initiated certain actions aimed at closing the gap in insurance coverage. If the plaintiffs in these lawsuits were to prevail at trial and be awarded the full extent of their claimed damages, and the gap in coverage was not closed, the resulting liability could have a material adverse effect on the Company's results of operations and cash flows in the periods affected.

A number of other lawsuits, claims and proceedings have been or may be asserted against the Company relating to the conduct of its business, including those pertaining to product liability, patent infringement, commercial, employment, employee benefits, environmental and stockholder matters. While the outcome of litigation cannot be predicted with certainty, and some of these other lawsuits, claims or proceedings may be determined adversely to the Company, the Company does not believe that the disposition of any such other pending matters is likely to have a material adverse effect on its financial condition or liquidity, although the resolution in any reporting period of one or more of these matters could have a material adverse effect on the Company's results of operations for that period.

Olin
2007 Annual Report

Restructuring Charges

On February 1, 2006, we announced that, in connection with the ongoing cost reduction efforts of the Metals business, we decided to close our Waterbury facility and consolidate those production activities into our East Alton, IL mill. In addition, on March 14, 2006, we decided to reduce the utilization of one of the Metals service center facilities by consolidating certain activities into another service center facility, and make overhead reductions in the Metals business affecting approximately 20 employees. We based our decision on our evaluation of the size, location, and capability of the facilities and staffing in light of anticipated business needs. We substantially completed these activities by September 30, 2006. As a result of these cost reduction efforts, we recorded a pretax restructuring charge of $15.7 in the first quarter of 2006, which was included in income from discontinued operations. In the fourth quarter of 2006 and the second quarter of 2007, primarily as a result of realizing more proceeds from equipment sales than expected, we reduced our previously established restructuring reserve related to the Waterbury facility by $1.6 and $1.5, respectively, which were included in income from discontinued operations. The net restructuring charge of $12.6 primarily included lease and other contract termination costs ($6.9), write-off of equipment and facility costs ($2.6), and employee severance and related benefit costs ($3.1). We expected to incur cash expenditures of $8.7 related to this restructuring charge, of which $8.4 has been paid as of December 31, 2007. The impact of this restructuring charge was substantially offset by a LIFO inventory liquidation gain of $13.5 realized in 2006 related to the closure of our Waterbury facility. This action was included in income from discontinued operations. Under the terms of the Metals sale agreement, we retained the liability associated with this restructuring and the ownership of the related facility and equipment.

On November 27, 2006, we announced that, in connection with the ongoing cost reduction efforts of the Metals business, we decided to close our Seymour facility and consolidate some of those production activities into other Olin locations. We substantially completed the closing of the Seymour facility during the first quarter of 2007. We based our decision on our evaluation of the size, location, and capability of the facilities and staffing in light of anticipated business needs. We recorded a one-time pretax restructuring charge of $3.5 in 2006, which was included in income from discontinued operations. This restructuring charge included write-off of equipment and facility costs ($2.4), employee severance and related benefit costs ($0.9), and contract termination costs ($0.2). We expected to incur cash expenditures of $1.6 related to this restructuring, of which $1.2 has been paid as of December 31, 2007. The impact of this restructuring charge was more than offset by a LIFO inventory liquidation gain of $10.4 realized in 2006 related to the closure of our Seymour facility. This action was included in income from discontinued operations. Under the terms of the Metals sale agreement, we retained the liability associated with this restructuring and the ownership of the related facility and equipment.

The following table summarizes the major components of the 2006 charges and the remaining balances as of December 31, 2007:

	December 31, 2006 Accrued Costs	Amounts Utilized	Adjustments	December 31, 2007 Accrued Costs
Lease and other contract termination costs	$7.5	$(6.4)	$(1.1)	–
Employee severance and job related benefits	2.5	(1.8)	(0.3)	0.4
Write-off of equipment and facilities	1.4	(1.3)	(0.1)	–
	$11.4	$(9.5)	$(1.5)	$0.4

The majority of the remaining balance of the 2006 restructuring charges are expected to be paid in 2008.

Environmental

In the United States, the establishment and implementation of federal, state and local standards to regulate air, water and land quality affect substantially all of our manufacturing locations. Federal legislation providing for regulation of the manufacture, transportation, use and disposal of hazardous and toxic substances, and remediation of contaminated sites, has imposed additional regulatory requirements on industry, particularly the chemicals industry. In addition, implementation of environmental laws, such as the Resource Conservation and Recovery Act and the Clean Air Act, has required and will continue to require new capital expenditures and will increase plant operating costs. Our Canadian facilities are governed by federal environmental laws administered by Environment Canada and by provincial environmental laws enforced by administrative agencies. Many of these laws are comparable to the U.S. laws described above. We employ waste minimization and pollution prevention programs at our manufacturing sites.

We are party to various governmental and private environmental actions associated with past manufacturing facilities and former waste disposal sites. Associated costs of investigatory and remedial activities are provided for in accordance with generally accepted accounting principles governing probability and the ability to reasonably estimate future costs. Our ability to estimate future costs depends on whether our investigatory and remedial activities are in preliminary or advanced stages. With respect to unasserted claims, we accrue liabilities for costs that, in our experience, we may incur to protect our interests against those unasserted claims. Our accrued liabilities for unasserted claims amounted to $6.7 at December 31, 2007. With respect to asserted claims, we accrue liabilities based on remedial investigation, feasibility study, remedial action and OM&M expenses that, in our experience, we may incur in connection with the asserted claims. Required site OM&M expenses are estimated and accrued in their entirety for required periods not exceeding 30 years, which reasonably approximates the typical duration of long-term site OM&M.

Our liabilities for future environmental expenditures were as follows:

	December 31,	
	2007	2006
Beginning balance	$90.8	$102.9
Charges to income	37.9	23.8
Remedial and investigatory spending	(29.4)	(35.9)
Pioneer acquired liabilities	55.4	–
Currency translation adjustments	0.9	–
Ending balance	$155.6	$90.8

At December 31, 2007 and 2006, our Consolidated Balance Sheets included environmental liabilities of $120.6 and $55.8, respectively, which were classified as other noncurrent liabilities. As part of the acquisition of Pioneer, we assumed $55.4 of environmental liabilities associated with their current and past manufacturing operations and former waste disposal sites. Our environmental liability amounts did not take into account any discounting of future expenditures or any consideration of insurance recoveries or advances in technology. These liabilities are reassessed periodically to determine if environmental circumstances have changed and/or remediation efforts and our estimate of related costs have changed. As a result of these reassessments, future charges to income may be made for additional liabilities. Of the $155.6 included on our consolidated balance sheet at December 31, 2007 for future environmental expenditures, we currently expect to utilize $95.7 of the reserve for future environmental expenditures over the next 5 years, $28.9 for expenditures 6 to 10 years in the future, and $31.0 for expenditures beyond 10 years in the future.

In conjunction with the acquisition of Pioneer, we assumed their environmental liabilities, which are currently attributable to nine sites. Our estimated environmental liability at the end of 2007, including the Pioneer sites, was attributable to 74 sites, 19 of which were USEPA NPL sites. Eleven sites accounted for 77% of such liability and, of the remaining 63 sites, no one site accounted for more than 2% of our environmental liability. At two of these eleven sites a remedial action plan is being implemented. At four of the eleven sites, part of the site is subject to a remedial investigation and another part is in the long-term OM&M stage. At one of these eleven sites, part of the site is subject to a remedial investigation, part to a remedial action plan, and another part is in the long-term OM&M stage. At one site, part of the site is subject to a remedial action plan and part of the site to long-term OM&M. The three remaining sites are in long-term OM&M. All eleven sites are either associated with past manufacturing operations or former waste disposal sites. None of the eleven largest sites represents more than 20% of the liabilities reserved on our consolidated balance sheet at December 31, 2007 for future environmental expenditures.

Charges or credits to income for investigatory and remedial efforts were material to operating results in 2007, 2006, and 2005 and may be material to net income in future years.

Environmental provisions (credits) charged (credited) to income were as follows:

	2007	2006	2005
Charges to income	$37.9	$23.8	$22.7
Recoveries from third parties of costs incurred and expensed in prior periods	–	(1.2)	(38.5)
Total provision (credit)	$37.9	$22.6	$(15.8)

These charges relate primarily to remedial and investigatory activities associated with past manufacturing operations and former waste disposal sites.

Annual environmental-related cash outlays for site investigation and remediation are expected to range between approximately $20 to $40 over the next several years, which are expected to be charged against reserves recorded on our balance sheet. While we do not anticipate a material increase in the projected annual level of our environmental-related cash outlays, there is always the possibility that such an increase may occur in the future in view of the uncertainties associated with environmental exposures. Environmental exposures are difficult to assess for numerous reasons, including the identification of new sites, developments at sites resulting from investigatory studies, advances in technology, changes in environmental laws and regulations and their application, changes in regulatory authorities, the scarcity of reliable data pertaining to identified sites, the difficulty in assessing the involvement and financial capability of other PRPs and our ability to obtain contributions from other parties and the lengthy time periods over which site remediation occurs. It is possible that some of these matters (the outcomes of which are subject to various uncertainties) may be resolved unfavorably to us, which could materially adversely affect our financial position or results of operations. At December 31, 2007, we estimate we may have additional contingent environmental liabilities of $50.0 in addition to the amounts for which we have already recorded as a reserve.

Commitments and Contingencies

We lease certain properties, such as railroad cars; distribution, warehousing and office space; and data processing and office equipment. Virtually none of our lease agreements contain escalation clauses or step rent provisions. Total rent expense charged to operations amounted to $33.3, $25.1, and $22.6 in 2007, 2006, and 2005, respectively (sublease income is not significant). Future minimum rent payments under operating leases having initial or remaining non-cancelable lease terms in excess of one year at December 31, 2007 are as follows: $40.9 in 2008, $35.2 in 2009, $31.8 in 2010, $27.1 in 2011, $21.6 in 2012, and a total of $76.1 thereafter.

On December 31, 1997, we entered into a long-term, sulfur dioxide supply agreement with Alliance, formerly known as RFC SO2, Inc. Alliance has the obligation to deliver annually 36,000 tons of sulfur dioxide. Alliance owns the sulfur dioxide plant, which is located at our Charleston, TN facility and is operated by us. The price for the sulfur dioxide is fixed over the life of the contract, and under the terms of the contract, we are obligated to make a monthly payment of $0.2 regardless of the sulfur dioxide purchased. Commitments related to this agreement are $2.4 per year for 2008 through 2011 and $0.6 in 2012. This supply agreement expires in 2012.

We and our subsidiaries are defendants in various legal actions (including proceedings based on alleged exposures to asbestos) incidental to our past and current business activities. While we believe that none of these legal actions will materially adversely affect our financial position, in light of the inherent uncertainties of litigation, we cannot at this time determine whether the financial impact, if any, of these matters will be material to our results of operations.

During the ordinary course of our business, contingencies arise resulting from an existing condition, situation, or set of circumstances involving an uncertainty as to the realization of a possible gain contingency. In certain instances such as environmental projects, we are responsible for managing the clean-up and remediation of an environmental site. There exists the possibility of recovering a portion of these costs from other parties. We account for gain contingencies in accordance with the provisions of SFAS No. 5, and therefore do not record gain contingencies and recognize income until it is earned and realizable.

Sunoco
2007 Annual Report

14. Commitments and Contingent Liabilities

Leases and Other Commitments

Sunoco, as lessee, has noncancelable operating leases for marine transportation vessels, service stations, office space and other property and equipment. Total rental expense for such leases for the years 2007, 2006 and 2005 amounted to $199, $199 and $198 million, respectively, which include contingent rentals totaling $15, $13 and $12 million, respectively. Approximately 6 percent of total rental expense was recovered through related sub-lease rental income during 2007.

The aggregate amount of future minimum annual rentals applicable to noncancelable operating leases, including amounts pertaining to lease extension options which are assumed to be exercised, are as follows:

(millions of dollars)	Current Lease Term	Lease Extension Options	Total
Year ending December 31:			
2008	$155	$–	$155
2009	127	1	128
2010	109	3	112
2011	67	6	73
2012	53	8	61
Thereafter	273	214	487

(millions of dollars)	Current Lease Term	Lease Extension Options	Total
Future minimum lease payments	$784	$232	1,016
Less: Sub-lease rental income			(24)
Net minimum lease payments			$992

Approximately 26 percent of the aggregate amount of future minimum annual rentals applicable to noncancelable operating leases relates to time charters for marine transportation vessels. Most of these time charters contain terms of between three to seven years with renewal and sublease options. The time charter leases typically require a fixed-price payment or a fixed-price minimum and a variable component based on spot-market rates. In the table above, the variable component of the lease payments has been estimated utilizing the average spot-market prices for the year 2007. The actual variable component of the lease payments attributable to these time charters could vary significantly from the estimates included in the table.

Over the years, Sunoco has sold thousands of retail gasoline outlets as well as refineries, terminals, coal mines, oil and gas properties and various other assets. In connection with these sales, the Company has indemnified the purchasers for potential environmental and other contingent liabilities related to the period prior to the transaction dates. In most cases, the effect of these arrangements was to afford protection for the purchasers with respect to obligations for which the Company was already primarily liable. While some of these indemnities have spending thresholds which must be exceeded before they become operative, or limits on Sunoco's maximum exposure, they generally are not limited. The Company recognizes the fair value of the obligations undertaken for all guarantees entered into or modified after January 1, 2003. In addition, the Company accrues for any obligations under these agreements when a loss is probable and reasonably estimable. The Company cannot reasonably estimate the maximum potential amount of future payments under these agreements.

Sunoco is a party under agreements which provide for future payments to secure wastewater treatment services at its Toledo refinery and coal handling services at its Indiana Harbor cokemaking facility.

The fixed and determinable amounts of the obligations under these agreements are as follows:

(millions of dollars)	
Year ending December 31:	
2008	$ 8
2009	8
2010	8
2011	8
2012	8
2013 through 2018	22

(millions of dollars)	
Total	62
Less: Amount representing interest	(15)
Total at present value	$ 47

Payments under these agreements, including variable components, totaled $21, $21 and $20 million for the years 2007, 2006 and 2005, respectively.

Environmental Remediation Activities

Sunoco is subject to extensive and frequently changing federal, state and local laws and regulations, including, but not limited to, those relating to the discharge of materials into the environment or that otherwise relate to the protection of the environment, waste management and the characteristics and composition of fuels. As with the industry generally, compliance with existing and anticipated laws and regulations increases the overall cost of operating Sunoco's businesses, including remediation, operating costs and capital costs to construct, maintain and upgrade equipment and facilities.

Existing laws and regulations result in liabilities and loss contingencies for remediation at Sunoco's facilities and at formerly owned or third-party sites. The accrued liability for environmental remediation is classified in the consolidated balance sheets as follows:

	December 31	
(millions in dollars)	2007	2006
Accrued liabilities	$ 39	$ 36
Other deferred credits and liabilities	83	85
	$122	$121

The following table summarizes the changes in the accrued liability for environmental remediation activities by category:

(millions of dollars)	Refineries	Retail Sites	Chemicals Facilities	Pipelines and Terminals	Hazardous Waste Sites	Other	Total
At December 31, 2004	$48	$74	$5	$15	$4	$2	$148
Accruals	2	22	1	6	1	–	32
Payments	(14)	(25)	(2)	(7)	(2)	–	(50)
Other	–	7	(1)	1	–	–	7
At December 31, 2005	$36	$78	$3	$15	$3	$2	$137
Accruals	6	19	1	2	1	–	29
Payments	(9)	(24)	(1)	(5)	(2)	(1)	(42)
Other	1	(4)	–	–	–	–	(3)

(millions of dollars)	Refineries	Retail Sites	Chemicals Facilities	Pipelines and Terminals	Hazardous Waste Sites	Other	Total
At December 31, 2006	$34	$69	$3	$12	$2	$1	$121
Accruals	13	19	2	5	2	–	41
Payments	(12)	(21)	(1)	(5)	(2)	–	(41)
Other	–	–	–	–	1	–	1
At December 31, 2007	$35	$67	$4	$12	$3	$1	$122

Sunoco's accruals for environmental remediation activities reflect management's estimates of the most likely costs that will be incurred over an extended period to remediate identified conditions for which the costs are both probable and reasonably estimable. Engineering studies, historical experience and other factors are used to identify and evaluate remediation alternatives and their related costs in determining the estimated accruals for environmental remediation activities. Losses attributable to unasserted claims are also reflected in the accruals to the extent they are probable of occurrence and reasonably estimable.

Total future costs for the environmental remediation activities identified above will depend upon, among other things, the identification of any additional sites, the determination of the extent of the contamination at each site, the timing and nature of required remedial actions, the nature of operations at each site, the technology available and needed to meet the various existing legal requirements, the nature and terms of cost-sharing arrangements with other potentially responsible parties, the availability of insurance coverage, the nature and extent of future environmental laws and regulations, inflation rates and the determination of Sunoco's liability at the sites, if any, in light of the number, participation level and financial viability of the other parties. Management believes it is reasonably possible (i.e., less than probable but greater than remote) that additional environmental remediation losses will be incurred. At December 31, 2007, the aggregate of the estimated maximum additional reasonably possible losses, which relate to numerous individual sites, totaled approximately $100 million. However, the Company believes it is very unlikely that it will realize the maximum reasonably possible loss at every site. Furthermore, the recognition of additional losses, if and when they were to occur, would likely extend over many years and, therefore, likely would not have a material impact on the Company's financial position.

Under various environmental laws, including the Resource Conservation and Recovery Act ("RCRA") (which relates to solid and hazardous waste treatment, storage and disposal), Sunoco has initiated corrective remedial action at its facilities, formerly owned facilities and third-party sites. At the Company's major manufacturing facilities, Sunoco has consistently assumed continued industrial use and a containment/remediation strategy focused on eliminating unacceptable risks to human health or the environment. The remediation accruals for these sites reflect that strategy. Accruals include amounts to prevent off-site migration and to contain the impact on the facility property, as well as to address known, discrete areas requiring remediation within the plants. Activities include closure of RCRA solid waste management units, recovery of hydrocarbons, handling of impacted soil, mitigation of surface water impacts and prevention of off-site migration.

Many of Sunoco's current terminals are being addressed with the above containment/remediation strategy. At some smaller or less impacted facilities and some previously divested terminals, the focus is on remediating discrete interior areas to attain regulatory closure.

Sunoco owns or operates certain retail gasoline outlets where releases of petroleum products have occurred. Federal and state laws and regulations require that contamination caused by such releases at these sites and at formerly owned sites be assessed and remediated to meet the applicable standards. The obligation for Sunoco to remediate this type of contamination varies, depending on the extent of the release and the applicable laws and regulations. A portion of the remediation costs may be recoverable from the reimbursement fund of the applicable state, after any deductible has been met.

Future costs for environmental remediation activities at the Company's retail marketing sites will also be influenced by the extent of MTBE contamination of groundwater, the cleanup of which will be driven by thresholds based on drinking water protection. Though not all groundwater is used for drinking, several states have initiated or proposed more stringent MTBE cleanup requirements. Cost increases result directly from extended remedial operations and maintenance on sites that, under prior standards, could otherwise have been completed. Cost increases will also result from installation of additional remedial or monitoring wells and purchase of more expensive equipment because of the presence of MTBE. While actual cleanup costs for specific sites are variable and depend on many of the factors discussed above, expansion of similar MTBE remediation thresholds to additional states or adoption of even more stringent requirements for MTBE remediation would result in further cost increases. Sunoco does not currently, nor does it intend to, manufacture or sell gasoline containing MTBE.

The accrued liability for hazardous waste sites is attributable to potential obligations to remove or mitigate the environmental effects of the disposal or release of certain pollutants at third-party sites pursuant to the Comprehensive Environmental Response Compensation and Liability Act ("CERCLA") (which relates to releases and remediation of hazardous substances) and similar state laws. Under CERCLA, Sunoco is potentially subject to joint and several liability for the costs of remediation at sites at which it has been identified as a "potentially responsible party" ("PRP"). As of December 31, 2007, Sunoco had been named as a PRP at 33 sites identified or potentially identifiable as "Superfund" sites under federal and state law. The Company is usually one of a number of companies identified as a PRP at a site. Sunoco has reviewed the nature and extent of its involvement at each site and other relevant circumstances and, based upon the other parties involved or Sunoco's level of participation therein, believes that its potential liability associated with such sites will not be significant.

Management believes that none of the current remediation locations, which are in various stages of ongoing remediation, is individually material to Sunoco as its largest accrual for any one Superfund site, operable unit or remediation area was less than $8 million at December 31, 2007. As a result, Sunoco's exposure to adverse developments with respect to any individual site is not expected to be material. However, if changes in environmental laws or regulations occur, such changes could impact multiple Sunoco facilities, formerly owned facilities and third-party sites at the same time. As a result, from time to time, significant charges against income for environmental remediation may occur.

The Company maintains insurance programs that cover certain of its existing or potential environmental liabilities, which programs vary by year, type and extent of coverage. For underground storage tank remediations, the Company can also seek reimbursement through various state funds of certain remediation costs above a deductible amount. For certain acquired properties, the Company has entered into arrangements with the sellers or others that allocate environmental liabilities and provide indemnities to the Company for remediating contamination that occurred prior to the acquisition dates. Some of these environmental indemnifications are subject to caps and limits. No accruals have been recorded for any potential contingent liabilities that will be funded by the prior owners as management does not believe, based on current information, that it is likely that any of the former owners will not perform under any of these agreements. Other than the preceding arrangements, the Company has not entered into any arrangements with third parties to mitigate its exposure to loss from environmental contamination. Claims for recovery of environmental liabilities that are probable of realization totaled $14 million at December 31, 2007 and are included principally in deferred charges and other assets in the consolidated balance sheets.

MTBE Litigation

Sunoco, along with other refiners, manufacturers and sellers of gasoline are defendants in approximately 77 lawsuits in 18 states and the Commonwealth of Puerto Rico, which allege MTBE contamination in groundwater. Plaintiffs, who include water purveyors and municipalities responsible for supplying drinking water and private well owners, allege that refiners and suppliers of gasoline containing MTBE are responsible for manufacturing and distributing a defective product that contaminates groundwater. Plaintiffs are asserting primarily product liability claims and additional claims including nuisance, trespass, negligence, violation of environmental laws and deceptive business practices. In addition, several actions commenced by state authorities allege natural resource damages. Plaintiffs are seeking to rely on a "joint liability of industry" theory at trial, although there has been no ruling as to whether the plaintiffs will be permitted to pursue this theory. Plaintiffs are seeking compensatory damages, and in some cases injunctive relief, punitive damages and attorneys' fees.

The majority of MTBE cases have been removed to federal court and consolidated for pretrial purposes in the U.S. District Court for the Southern District of New York (MDL 1358) ("MDL Litigation"). Discovery is proceeding in four focus cases. Sunoco is a defendant in three of those cases. In one of the four cases, the *Suffolk County Water Authority* case, the court has set a trial date in September 2008. In addition, several private well owner cases are moving forward. Sunoco is a defendant in two of those cases. The Second Circuit Court of Appeals ("Second Circuit") recently rendered a decision in two MTBE cases that are part of the MDL Litigation in which it held that there was no federal jurisdiction for the removal of these cases to federal court and consequently ordered that the cases be remanded back to the state courts from which they originated. The parties and the judge in the MDL Litigation are evaluating the impact of the Second Circuit's decision on the remaining cases that are part of the MDL Litigation and a number of additional cases have been remanded back to the state court.

In December 2007, Sunoco, along with other refiners, entered into a settlement in principle pertaining to certain MTBE cases. This settlement will cover 53 of the cases referred to above, including the *Suffolk County Water Authority* case. The settlement for these cases will require a cash payment by the group of settling refiner defendants of approximately $424 million (which includes attorneys' fees) plus an agreement in the future to fund costs of treating existing wells as to which MTBE has not currently been detected which later is detected, over four consecutive quarters, above certain concentration levels. As MTBE is no longer used, and based on a generally declining trend in MTBE contamination, the Company does not anticipate substantial costs associated with the future treatment of existing wells. Under the settlement, Sunoco was assigned an allocation percentage and will be required to make a cash payment of approximately $28 million. In addition to the cash payment, Sunoco will participate on the same basis in any costs of future treatment of existing wells. Sunoco is attempting to recover the amount it is required to pay in settlement from its insurance carriers. In connection with the settlement, the Company established a $28 million accrual ($17 million after tax) in 2007 (Note 2).

For the group of MTBE cases that are not covered by the settlement, there has been insufficient information developed about the plaintiffs' legal theories or the facts that would be relevant to an analysis of the ultimate liability to Sunoco. Based on the current law and facts available at this time, no accrual has been established for any potential damages at December 31, 2007 and Sunoco believes that these cases will not have a material adverse effect on its consolidated financial position.

Conclusion

Many other legal and administrative proceedings are pending or may be brought against Sunoco arising out of its current and past operations, including matters related to commercial and tax disputes, product liability, antitrust, employment claims, leaks from pipelines and underground storage tanks, natural resource damage claims, premises-liability claims, allegations of exposures of third parties to toxic substances (such as benzene or asbestos) and general environmental claims. Although the ultimate outcome of these proceedings and other matters identified above cannot be ascertained at this time, it is reasonably possible that some of these matters could be resolved unfavorably to Sunoco. Management believes that these matters could have a significant impact on results of operations for any future quarter or year. However, management does not believe that any additional liabilities which may arise pertaining to such matters would be material in relation to the consolidated financial position of Sunoco at December 31, 2007.

15. Minority Interests

Cokemaking Operations

Sunoco received a total of $309 million in exchange for interests in its Jewell cokemaking operations in two separate transactions in 1995 and 2000. Sunoco also received a total of $415 million in exchange for interests in its Indiana Harbor cokemaking operations in two separate transactions in 1998 and 2002. Sunoco did not recognize any gain as of the dates of these transactions because the third-party investors were entitled to a preferential return on their respective investments. In December 2006, Sunoco acquired the limited partnership interest of the third-party investor in the Jewell cokemaking operation for $155 million and recognized a $3 million after-tax loss in other income (loss), net, in the 2006 consolidated statement of income in connection with this transaction. As a result, such third-party investor is no longer entitled to any preferential or residual return in this operation.

The returns of the investors in the Indiana Harbor cokemaking operations were equal to 98 percent of the cash flows and tax benefits from such cokemaking operations during the preferential return period, which continued until the fourth quarter of 2007 at which time the investor entitled to the preferential return recovered its investment and achieved a cumulative annual after-tax return of approximately 10 percent. After payment of the preferential return, the investors in the Indiana Harbor operations are now entitled to a minority interest in the related net income amounting to 34 percent which declines to 10 percent by 2038.

The Company indemnifies the third-party investors (including the former investor in the Jewell cokemaking operations) for certain tax benefits that were available to them during the preferential return period in the event the Internal Revenue Service disallows the tax deductions and benefits allocated to the third parties or if there is a change in the tax laws that reduces the amount of nonconventional fuel tax credits. These tax indemnifications are in effect until the applicable tax returns are no longer subject to Internal Revenue Service review. Although the Company believes the possibility is remote that it will be required to do so, at December 31, 2007, the maximum potential payment under these tax indemnifications would have been approximately $265 million.

The following table sets forth the minority interest balances and the changes in these balances attributable to the third-party investors' interests in cokemaking operations:

(millions of dollars)	2007	2006	2005
Balance at beginning of year	$102	$234	$287
Nonconventional fuel credit and other tax benefits*	(3)	(45)	(57)
Preferential return*	20	48	42
Cash distributions to third-party investors	(36)	(43)	(38)
Acquisition of third-party investor's interest in Jewell cokemaking operations (Note 2)	–	(92)	–
Balance at end of year	$ 83	$102	$234

* The nonconventional fuel credit and other tax benefits and the preferential return are included in other income (loss), net, in the consolidated statements of income (Notes 1 and 3). The preferential return for 2006 includes an $11 million increase ($7 million after tax) attributable to a correction of an error in the computation of the preferential return relating to prior years. Prior-period amounts have not been restated as this adjustment was not deemed to be material.

Logistics Operations

During the 2005-2006 period, Sunoco Logistics Partners L.P. issued a total of 7.1 million limited partnership units in a series of public offerings, generating $270 million of net proceeds. Coincident with certain of these offerings, the Partnership redeemed 2.8 million limited partnership units owned by Sunoco for $99 million. Upon completion of these transactions, Sunoco's interest in the Partnership, including its 2 percent general partnership interest, decreased to 43 percent. The accounts of the Partnership continue to be included in Sunoco's consolidated financial statements.

As of December 31, 2007 and 2006, Sunoco owned 12.06 million limited partnership units. At December 31, 2006, this ownership interest consisted of 6.37 million common units and 5.69 million subordinated units. Distributions on Sunoco's subordinated units were payable only after the minimum quarterly distributions of $.45 per unit for the common units held by the public and Sunoco, including any arrearages, had been made. The subordinated units were convertible to common units if certain financial tests related to earning and paying the minimum quarterly distribution for the preceding three consecutive one-year periods had been met. In February 2007, 2006 and 2005, when the quarterly cash distributions pertaining to the fourth quarters of 2006, 2005 and 2004 were paid, all three three-year requirements were satisfied. As a result, all of Sunoco's subordinated units have been converted to common units, 5.69 million in February 2007 and 2.85 million each in February 2006 and February 2005.

The Partnership's prior issuance of common units to the public resulted in an increase in the value of Sunoco's proportionate share of the Partnership's equity as the issuance price per unit exceeded Sunoco's carrying amount per unit at the time of issuance. Prior to February 2007, the resultant gain to Sunoco on these transactions had been deferred as a component of minority interest in the Company's consolidated balance sheets as the common units issued did not represent residual interests in the Partnership due to Sunoco's ownership of the subordinated units. The deferred gain, which amounted to $151 million ($90 million after tax), was recognized in income in the first quarter of 2007 when Sunoco's remaining subordinated units converted to common units at which time the common units became the residual interests.

Sunoco is a party to various agreements with the Partnership which require Sunoco to pay for minimum storage and throughput usage of certain Partnership assets. Sunoco also has agreements with the Partnership which establish fees for administrative services provided by Sunoco and provide indemnifications by Sunoco for certain environmental, toxic tort and other liabilities related to operation of the Partnership's assets prior to its initial public offering in February 2002.

The following table sets forth the minority interest balance and the changes to this balance attributable to the third-party investors' interests in Sunoco Logistics Partners L.P.:

(millions of dollars)	2007	2006	2005
Balance at beginning of year	$503	$397	$232
Gain recognized in income related to prior issuance of the Partnership's limited partnership units	(151)	–	–
Net proceeds from public equity offerings	–	110	160
Minority interest share of income*	56	42	28
Increase attributable to Partnership management incentive plan	3	2	5
Cash distributions to third-party investors**	(55)	(48)	(28)
Balance at end of year	$356	$503	$397

* Included in selling, general and administrative expenses in the consolidated statements of income.
** During the 2005-2007 period, the Partnership increased its quarterly cash distribution per unit from $.625 to $.87.

Epsilon Joint Venture Operations

Sunoco and a third party were owners of Epsilon Products Company, LLC ("Epsilon"), a joint venture that consists of polymer-grade propylene operations at Sunoco's Marcus Hook, PA refinery and an adjacent polypropylene plant. The joint venture was a variable interest entity for which the Company was the primary beneficiary. As such, the accounts of Epsilon were included in Sunoco's consolidated financial statements. In December 2007, in connection with mediation concerning litigation among Sunoco, Inc., Epsilon and the Epsilon joint-venture partners related to Sunoco, Inc.'s repayment under a debt guarantee of $151 million of Epsilon's debt in 2006, Sunoco agreed to purchase the joint-venture partner's interest in Epsilon for $18 million. All litigation concerning this matter is now settled.

The following table sets forth the minority interest balance and the changes to this balance attributable to the third-party investor's interest in Epsilon:

(millions of dollars)	2007	2006	2005
Balance at beginning of year	$13	$16	$11
Minority interest share of income (loss)*	(6)	(3)	5
Acquisition of third-party investor's interest in Epsilon	(7)	–	–
Balance at end of year	–	$13	$16

* Included in selling, general and administrative expenses in the consolidated statements of income.

16. Shareholders' Equity

Each share of Company common stock is entitled to one full vote. The $7 million of outstanding $6^3/4$ percent subordinated debentures are convertible into shares of Sunoco common stock at any time prior to maturity at a conversion price of $20.41 per share and are redeemable at the option of the Company. At December 31, 2007, there were 355,561 shares of common stock reserved for this potential conversion (Note 12).

On July 7, 2005, the Company's Board of Directors ("Board") approved a two-for-one split of Sunoco's common stock to be effected in the form of a stock dividend. The shares were distributed on August 1, 2005 to shareholders of record as of July 18, 2005. In connection with the common stock split, the number of authorized shares of common stock was increased from 200 million to 400 million, and the shares of common stock reserved for issuance pertaining to Sunoco's $6^3/4$ percent convertible debentures and various employee benefit plans were proportionally increased in accordance with the terms of those respective agreements and plans.

The Company increased the quarterly cash dividend paid on common stock from $.20 per share ($.80 per year) beginning with the second quarter of 2005, to $.25 per share ($1.00 per year) beginning with the second quarter of 2006, to $.275 per share ($1.10 per year) beginning with the second quarter of 2007 and to $.30 per share ($1.20 per year) beginning with the second quarter of 2008.

The Company repurchased in 2007, 2006 and 2005, 4.0, 12.2 and 6.7 million shares, respectively, of its common stock for $300, $871 and $435 million, respectively. In 2006, the Company announced that its Board had approved additional share repurchase authorizations totaling $1.5 billion. At December 31, 2007, the Company had a remaining authorization from its Board to repurchase up to $649 million of Company common stock from time to time depending on prevailing market conditions and available cash.

The Company's Articles of Incorporation authorize the issuance of up to 15 million shares of preference stock without par value, subject to approval by the Board. The Board also has authority to fix the number, designation, rights, preferences and limitations of these shares, subject to applicable laws and the provisions of the Articles of Incorporation. At December 31, 2007, no such shares had been issued.

The following table sets forth the components (net of related income taxes) of the accumulated other comprehensive loss balances in shareholders' equity:

	December 31	
(millions of dollars)	2007	2006
Retirement benefit plan funded status adjustment (Notes 1 and 9)	$(185)	$(223)
Hedging activities (Note 18)	(13)	38
Available-for-sale securities	5	9
	$(193)	$(176)

Amgen
2007 Annual Report

4. Related Party Transactions

We own a 50% interest in KA, a corporation formed in 1984 with Kirin Holdings Company, Limited ("Kirin") (formerly named Kirin Brewery Company, Limited) for the development and commercialization of certain products based on advanced biotechnology. We account for our interest in KA under the equity method and include our share of KA's profits or losses in "Selling, general and administrative" in the Consolidated Statements of Income. For the years ended December 31, 2007, 2006 and 2005, our share of KA's profits were $51 million, $61 million and $58 million, respectively. At December 31, 2007 and 2006, the carrying value of our equity method investment in KA was $292 million and $241 million, respectively, and is included in non-current "Other assets" in the Consolidated Balance Sheets. KA's revenues consist of royalty income related to its licensed product rights. All of our rights to manufacture and market certain products including darbepoetin alfa, pegfilgrastim, granulocyte colony-stimulating factor ("G-CSF") and recombinant human erythropoietin are pursuant to exclusive licenses from KA. We currently market certain of these products under the brand names Aranesp®, Neulasta®, NEUPOGEN® and EPOGEN®, respectively. KA receives royalty income from us, as well as Kirin, J&J and F. Hoffman-La Roche Ltd. ("Roche") under separate product license agreements for certain geographic areas outside of the United States. During the years ended December 31, 2007, 2006 and 2005, KA earned royalties from us of $336 million, $324 million and $288 million, respectively. These amounts are included in "Cost of sales (excludes amortization of acquired intangible assets)" in the Consolidated Statements of Income. At December 31, 2007 and 2006, we owed KA $91 million and $78 million, respectively, which were included in "Accrued liabilities" in the Consolidated Balance Sheets.

KA's expenses primarily consist of costs related to R&D activities conducted on its behalf by Amgen and Kirin. KA pays Amgen and Kirin for such services at negotiated rates. During the years ended December 31, 2007, 2006 and 2005, we earned revenues from KA of $180 million, $131 million and $113 million, respectively, for certain R&D activities performed on KA's behalf. These amounts are included in "Other revenues" in the Consolidated Statements of Income. In addition, included in "Other revenues" in the Consolidated Statements of Income for the year ended December 31, 2007 is $45 million received from KA with respect to achieving certain regulatory filing milestones.

Frontier Oil
2007 Annual Report

11. Price Risk Management Activities

The Company, at times, enters into commodity derivative contracts to manage its price exposure to its inventory positions, purchases of foreign crude oil and consumption of natural gas in the refining process or to fix margins on certain future production. The commodity derivative contracts used by the Company may take the form of futures contracts, collars or price swaps and are entered into with creditworthy counterparties. The Company believes that there is minimal credit risk with respect to its counterparties. The Company accounts for its commodity derivative contracts under the hedge (or deferral) method of accounting when the derivative contracts are designated as hedges for accounting purposes, or mark-to-market accounting if the Company elects not to designate derivative contracts as accounting hedges or if such derivative contracts do not qualify for hedge accounting under FAS No. 133, "Accounting for Derivative Instruments and Hedging Activities." As such, gains or losses on commodity derivative contracts accounted for as fair value hedges are recognized in the related inventory in "Inventory of crude oil, products and other" on the Consolidated Balance Sheets and ultimately, when the inventory is charged or sold, in "Raw material, freight and other costs" on the Consolidated Statements of Income. Gains and losses on transactions accounted for using mark-to-market accounting are reflected in "Other revenues" at each period end. The Company has derivative contracts which it holds directly and also derivative contracts held on Frontier's behalf by Utexam, in connection with the Master Crude Oil Purchase and Sale Contract (see Note 9 "Lease and Other Commitments"). The market value of open derivative contracts is included on the Consolidated Balance Sheets in "Accrued liabilities and other" when the unrealized value is a loss ($15.1 million at December 31, 2007), or in "Other current assets" when the unrealized value is a gain ($2.5 million at December 31, 2006).

Stride Rite
2004 Annual Report

1. Summary of Significant Accounting Policies

Nature of Operations—The Stride Rite Corporation (the "Company") designs, sources, markets, and distributes footwear primarily under the Stride Rite, Keds, PRO-Keds, Sperry Top-Sider, Sperry, Mainsail, Tommy Hilfiger, Grasshoppers, Munchkin, BabySmart, and Born brands. The Company is predominantly a wholesaler of footwear, selling its products throughout the United States and Canada in a wide variety of retail formats including premier department stores, independent show stores, value retailers, e-commerce sites, and specialty stores. The Company also markets its products directly to consumers in the United

States by selling children's footwear thought its Stride Rite children's shoe stores and footwear for all of its brands through its outlet stores. The Company's products are marketed in countries outside the United States and Canada through independent distributors and licensees.

Principles of Consolidation—The consolidated Financial statements of the Company include the accounts of the Company and all its wholly-owned subsidiaries. Intercompany transactions between the Company and its consolidated subsidiaries have eliminated.

Fiscal Year—The Company's Fiscal year ends on the Friday closest to November 30 in each year. Fiscal years 2004, 2003, and 2002 ended on December 3, 2004, November 28, 2003, and November 29, 2002, respectively. The 2004 fiscal year contained 53 weeks. The 2003 and 2002 fiscal years contained 52 weeks each.

Revenue Recognition—Revenues consist of sales to customers and royalty income. Wholesale revenues are recognized when title passes and the risks and rewards of ownership have transferred to the customer, based on the shipping terms. Retail store revenues are recognized at the time of sale. Revenue from gift certificates is deferred until redemption. The Company permits merchandise returns from its customer under certain circumstances. The Company also engages in buy-down programs with certain retailers, principally in the form of product markdown allowances for obsolete and slow moving products that are in the retailer's inventory. The Company has established an allowance for merchandise returns and markdowns based on historical experience, products sell-through performance by product and customer, current and historical trends in the footwear industry and changes in demand for our products, in accordance with Statement of Financial Accounting Standards (SFAS) No. 48, "Revenues When Right of Return Exists." The returns allowance is recorded as a reduction to revenues for the estimated sales cause of the projected merchandise returns and as a reduction in cost recorded at the time that revenue is recognized. From time to time actual results will vary from the estimates that were preciously established. Due to the existence of good monitoring systems, the Company's visibility into its customers' inventory levels and ongoing communication with its customers, the Company is able to identify and reflect in its financial statements in a timely manner variances from estimates previously established. Royalty income which accounted for approximately $7.9 million, $6.4 million and $6.2 million in fiscal years 2004, 2003, and 2002, respectively, is recognized when earned.

Co-operative Advertising—The Company engages in co-op advertising programs and buy-down programs with retailers. Co-op advertising funds are available to all retailers in good standing. Retailers receive reimbursement under this program if they meet established advertising guidelines and trademark requirements. Costs are accrued on the basis of sales to qualifying customers and accounted for as an operation expense. The Company engages in buy-down programs with certain retailers. These buy-down programs are accounted for as a reduction in revenues. The Company has historically adhered to EITF 01-09 "Accounting for Consideration Given by vendor to a Customer or a Reseller of the Vendor's Products" in accounting for co-op advertising and buy-down programs, and therefore, its adoption did not affect its financial statements.

Shipping and Handling—Products are sold FOB shipping point and shipping costs are paid by the Company's customers. The Company not bill for products handling costs, which are included in selling and administrative expenses.

Cash Equivalents and Marketable Securities—Cash equivalents represent highly liquid investments, with a maturity of three months or less at the time of purchase. Marketable securities, representing funds invested in fixed income instruments with maturities greater than one year, are stated at fair value and are considered trading securities.

Financial Instruments—Financial instruments consist principally of cash, investments, trade receivables and payables. The Company places its investments with highly rated financial institutions and in investment grade, short-term financial instruments, which limits the amount of credit exposure. The Company sells footwear to numerous retailers. Historically, the Company has not experienced significant losses related to investments or trade receivables. The Company's exposure to foreign exchange risk is limited through U.S. dollar denominated transactions. The Company had not entered into derivative financial instruments such as futures, forward or option contracts. The Company calculates the fair value of all financial instruments and includes this additional information in the consolidated financial statements when the fair value is different from book value. The Company uses quoted market prices, when available, to calculate these fair values.

Foreign Currency—For international subsidiaries, the local currency is the functional currency. Assets and liabilities of the Company's international subsidiaries are translated at the rate of exchange existing at year-end. Income statement amounts are translated at the average monthly exchange rates for the period. The cumulative translation adjustments resulting from changes in exchange are included in the consolidated balance sheet as a separate component of stockholders' equity, "accumulated Other Comprehensive Loss." Transaction gains and losses are included in the consolidated statement of income and are not significant.

Hedging Policy—The Company adopted SFAS No. 133, "Accounting for Derivative Instruments and Hedging Activities," as amended in the first quarter of Fiscal 2001. SFAS 133 requites an entity to recognize all derivatives as either assets or liabilities in the consolidated balance sheet and to measure those instruments at fair value. The Company evaluates its exposure to volatility in foreign currency rates and interest rates and may enter in derivative transactions, as it deems necessary. The Company did not enter into any derivative transactions in fiscal years 2004, 2003, and 2002 and accordingly, the adoption of SFAS No. 133 did not have any effect on the Company's net earnings or financial position.

Inventory Valuation—Inventories are stated at the lower of cost or market. The cost of inventories is determined on the last-in, first-out (LIFO) basis. The Company performs regular detailed product sell-through analysis to determine excess and closeout inventory and makes adjustments to provisions for obsolete products as they become known.

Property and Equipment—Property and equipment are stated at cost. The cost of equipment includes the capitalization of certain associated computer software costs. Depreciation, which is calculated on the straight-line method, is provided by periodic charges to expense over the estimated useful lives of the assets. Leaseholds and whichever is shorter, using the straight-line method.

Impairment of Long-Lived Assets—Effective November 30, 2002, the Company adopted SFAS No. 144, "Accounting for the Impairment or Disposal of Long-Lived Assets" (SFAS 144). This statement superseded SFAS No. 121, "Accounting for the Impairment of Long-Lived Assets and for Long-Lived Assets to be Disposed Of" (SFAS 121), and amends Accounting Principles Board Opinion No. 30, "Reporting Effects of Disposal of a Segment of a Business, and Extraordinary, Unusual and Infrequently Occurring Events and Transactions" (APB30). SFAS 144 requires that long-lived assets that are to be disposed of by sale be measured at the lower of book value or fair value less costs to sell. SFAS 144 retains the fundamental provisions of SFAS 121 for (a) recognition and measurement of the impairment of long-lived assets to be held and used and (b) measurement of long-lived assets to be disposed of by sale. This statement also retains APB 30's requirement that companies report discontinued operations separately from continuing operations. The Company reviews long-lived assets for impairment whenever events or changes in business circumstances indicate that the carrying amount of an asset may not recoverable. Each impairment test is based on a comparison of the carrying amount of the assets to the future net cash flows expected to be generated by the assets. If such assets are considered to be impaired, the impairment to be recognized is measured by the amount by which the carrying amount of the assets exceeds the fair value of the assets.

Goodwill, Trademarks, and Other Intangible Assets—The Company adopted SGAS 142, "Goodwill and Other Intangible Assets" (SFAS 142) effective with the beginning of the 2003 fiscal year. SFAS 142 requires that goodwill and intangible assets with indefinite lives no longer be amortized but instead be measured for impairment at least annually, or when events indicate that an impairment exists. As of the adoption date, amortization of outstanding goodwill and other indefinite- lived intangible assets have ceased. As requited by SFAS 142, the Company performs impairment tests annually and whenever events or circumstances indicate that the value of goodwill or other indefinite-lived intangible assets might be impaired. In connection with the SFAS 142 indefinite-lived intangible asset impairment test, the Company utilizes the required one-step method to determine whether impairment exists as of the adoption date. In connection with the SFAS 142 transitional goodwill impairment test, the Company utilized the required two-step method for determining goodwill impairment as of the adoption date. See Note 4 for discussion of the company's adoption of SFAS 142.

Income Taxes—Deferred income taxes are provided for temporary differences between financial and taxable income.

Retail Store Construction Allowances and Pre-Operating Costs—Commencing in fiscal 2004 construction allowances and other considerations received upon entering into certain store leases are recognized on a straight-line basis as a reduction to rent expense over the lease term. Prior years have not been restated due to its immateriality. The Company expenses all of the costs that are incurred prior to the opening of new retail stores as they occur.

Advertising—In accordance with Statement of Position 93-7, "Reporting on Advertising Costs," the Company expenses advertising costs as incurred. Total advertising expense amounted to $26,399,000, $26,624,000, and $22,791,000 for fiscal years 2004, 2003 and 2002, respectively.

Estimates Included in Financial Statements—The preparation of financial statements in conformity with generally accepted accounting principles requires management to make estimates and assumptions that affect the reported amounts of assets and liabilities and disclosure of contingent assets and liabilities at the date of the financial statements and the reported amounts of revenues and expenses during the reporting period. The most significant estimates included in these financial statements include valuation allowances and reserves for accounts receivable, markdowns (which reduce revenues), inventory and income taxes; assumptions related to the defined benefit pension plan; and estimates of future undiscounted cash flows on property and equipment that may be impaired. Actual results could differ from those estimates.

Comprehensive Income—Comprehensive income represents net earnings and any revenues, expenses, gains and losses that, under accounting principles generally accepted in the United States, are excluded from net earnings and recognized directly as a component of stockholders' equity.

The Components of accumulated other comprehensive loss as of Decemeber 3, 2004 and November 28, 2003 are as follows:

	2004	2003
	(In thousands)	
Foreign currency translation adjustments	$(165)	$(217)
Minimum pension liability adjustments, net of taxes	(9233)	(7581)
Accumulated other comprehensive loss	(9398)	(7798)

Reclassifications—Certain reclassification have been made to the fiscal 2003 and 2002 balances to conform to the current year presentation.

Net Income per Common Share—Basic earnings per common share is calculated by dividing net income by the weighted aver number of common shares out-standing during the period. Diluted earnings per share is calculated by dividing net income by the sum of the weighted average number of shares plus additional common shares that would have been outstanding if potential dilutive common shares had been issued for stock options granted. The following table reconciles the number of shares for the basic and dilutive computations for the fiscal years presented in the consolidated statements of income:

	2004	2003	2002
	(In thousands, except for per share date)		
Net income	$25644	$25488	$24117
Weighted average common shares outstanding (basic)	37,976	39,389	41,315
Dilutive effext of stock options	777	674	398
Weighted average common share outstanding (diluted)	38,753	40,063	41,713
Earning per common share:			
Basic	$ .68	$ .65	$ .58
Diluted	$ .66	$ .64	$ .58

The following options were not included in the computation of diluted earnings per share because the options' exercise prices were greater than the average market price of the common shares:

	2004	2003	2002
	(In thousands)		
Options to purchase shares of common stock	1,041	551	1,323

Accounting for Stock-Based Compensation—During the first quarter of fiscal 2003, the Company adopted the disclosure provisions of SFAS No. 148, "Accounting for Stock Based Compensating—Transition and Disclosure" (SFAS 148). SFAS 148 amended SFAS No. 123, "Accounting for Stock-Based Compensation" (SFAS 123) to provide two additional alternative transition methods if a company voluntarily decided to change its method of accounting for stock-based employee compensation to the fair-value method. SFAS 148 also amends the disclosure requirements of SFAS 123 by requiring that companies make quarterly disclosures regarding the pro forma effects of using the fair-value method of accounting for stock-based compensation, effective for interim periods beginning after December 15, 2002.

The Company has elected to continue to account for stock options in accordance with APB No. 25, "Accounting for Stock Issued to Employees" (APB 25) and related interpretations. Accordingly, no compensation expense has been recorded in connection with fair market value stock option grants under the Company's stock option plans and its employee stock purchases plan.

Pro forma net income and earnings per share information, included in the table below, has been calculated as if the Company had accounted for stock options and other stock-based compensation under the fair value method. The fair value was estimated as of the date of grant using the Black-Scholes option pricing model with the following weighted average assumptions:

Employee Stock Options	2004	2003	2002
Risk-free interest rate	3.17%	2.95%	4.30%
Dividend yield	2.1%	2.5%	2.6%
Volatility factor	39%	41%	40%
Weighted average expected life of options (years)	4.5	4.5	4.5
Employees Stock Purchases Plan	2004	2003	2002
Risk-free interest rate	1.29%	1.09%	1.68%
Dividend yield	2.3%	2.5%	2.6%
Volatility factor	39%	41%	40%
Weighted average expected life of options (years)	0.5	0.5	0.5

Accordingly, the weighted average grant date fair values of stock options granted during 2004, 2003, and 2002 were estimated at $3.41, $2.59, and $2.19, respectively. The weighted average grant date fair values of shares issued under the employee stock purchase plan during 2004, 2003, and 2002 were estimated at $0.93, $0.82, and $0.75, respectively. For purposes of pro forma disclosure, the estimated fair value is amortized to expense on a straight-line basis over the options vesting periods. A comparison of reported and pro forma earnings is as follows for the three years in the period ended December 3, 2004:

	2004	2003	2002
	(In thousands, except for per share date)		
Net income, as reported	$25,654	$25,488	$24,117
Add: Stock based employee compensation expense included in net income, net of related tax effects	13	40	60
Deduct: Total stock based employee compensation expense determined under fair value based method for all awards, net of related tax effects	(1876)	(1678)	(1376)
Pro forma net income	$23,791	$2,3850	$22,801
Earnings per share:			
Basic—as reported	$ .68	$ .65	$ .58
Basic—pro forma	$ .63	$ .61	$ .55
Diluted—as reported	$ .66	$ .64	$ .58
Diluted—pro forma	$ .61	$ .60	$ .55

The Black-Scholes option pricing model was developed for use in estimating the fair value of traded options that have no vesting restrictions and are fully transferable. In addition, option pricing models require the use of highly subjective assumptions, including the expected stock price volatility. As the Company's employee stock options have characteristics significantly different from those of traded options, and because changes in the subjective assumptions can materially affect the fair value estimates, in management's opinion, the existing model do not necessarily provide a reliable single measure of the fair value of its employee stock options and other stock-based compensation.

United Technologies
2004 Annual Report

Note 1—Summary of Accounting Principles

The preparation of financial statements requires management to make estimates and assumptions that affect the reported amounts of assets, liabilities, revenues, and expenses. Actual results could differ from those estimates.

Certain reclassifications have been made to prior year amounts to conform to the current year presentation.

Consolidation. The consolidated financial statements include the accounts of UTC and its controlled subsidiaries. Intercompany transactions have been eliminated.

Cash and Cash Equivalents. Cash and cash equivalents includes cash on hand, demand deposits and short-term cash investments which are highly liquid in nature and have original maturities of three months or less.

Accounts Receivable. Current and long-term accounts receivable include:

(in millions of dollar)	2004	2003
Retainage	$ 67	$ 53
Unbilled receivables	$454	$199

Retainage represents amounts which, pursuant to the contract, are not due until project completion and acceptance by the customer. Unbilled receivables represents revenues that are not currently billable to the customer under the terms of the contract. These items are expected to be collected in the normal course of business. Long-term accounts receivable are included in Other assets in the Consolidated Balance Sheet.

Marketable Equity Securities. Equity securities that have a readily determinable fair value and management does not intend to hold are classified as available for sale and carried at fair value. Unrealized holding gains and losses are recorded as a separate component of shareowners' equity, net of deferred income taxes.

Inventories and Contracts in Progress. Inventories and contracts in progress are stated at the lower of cost or estimated realizable value and are primarily based on first-in, first-out ("FIFO") or average cost methods; however, certain subsidiaries use the last-in, first-out ("LIFO") method.

Costs accumulated against specific contracts or orders are at actual cost. Materials in excess of requirements for contracts and current or anticipated orders have been reserved and written-off as appropriate.

Manufacturing costs are allocated to current production and firm contracts.

Fixed Assets. Fixed assets are stated at cost. Depreciation is computed over the assets' useful lives generally using the straight-line method, except for aerospace assets acquired prior to January 1, 1999, which are depreciated using accelerated methods.

Goodwill and Other Intangible Assets. Goodwill represents costs in excess of fair values assigned to the underlying net assets of acquired businesses. Goodwill and intangible assets deemed to have indefinite lives are not amortized. All other intangible assets are amortized over their estimated useful lives. Goodwill and indefinite-lived intangible assets are subject to annual impairment testing using the guidance and criteria described in Statement of Financial Accounting Standard No. 142, "Goodwill and Other Intangible Assets." This testing compares carrying values to fair values and, when appropriate, the carrying value of these assets is reduced to fair value. During 2004, UTC was not required to record any impairment on goodwill or indefinite-lived intangibles.

Other Long-Lived Assets. UTC evaluates the potential impairments of other long-lived assets when appropriate. If the carrying value of assets exceeds the sum of the undiscounted expected future cash flows, the carrying value of the asset is written down to fair value.

Income Taxes. UTC has exposures related to tax filings in the ordinary course of business. UTC periodically assesses its liabilities and contingencies for all tax years under audit based upon the latest information available. For these matters where it is probable that an adjustment will be asserted, UTC has recorded its best estimate of tax liability, including related interest charges, in its Consolidated Financial Statements.

Revenue Recognition. Sales under government and commercial fixed-price contracts and government fixed-price-incentive contracts are recorded at the time deliveries are made or, in some cases, on a percentage-of-completion basis. Sales under cost reimbursement contracts are recorded as work is performed.

Sales under elevator and escalator installation and modernization contracts are accounted for under the percentage-of-completion method.

Losses, if any, on contracts are provided for when anticipated. Loss provisions on original equipment contracts are recognized to the extent that estimated inventoriable manufacturing, engineering, estimated product warranty and product performance guarantee costs exceed the projected revenue from the products contemplated under the contractual arrangement. Products contemplated under the contractual arrangement include products purchased under the contract and, in the aerospace business, required replacement parts that are purchased separately and subsequently for incorporation into the original equipment. Revenue projections used in determining contract loss provisions are based upon estimates of the quantity, pricing and timing of future product deliveries. Losses are recognized on shipment to the extent that inventoriable manufacturing costs, estimated warranty costs and product performance guarantee costs exceed revenue realized. Contract accounting requires estimates of future costs over the performance period of the contract as well as estimates of award fees and other sources or revenue. These estimates are subject to change and result in adjustments to margins on contracts in progress. The extent of progress toward completion on UTC's long-term commercial aerospace equipment and helicopter contracts is measured using units of delivery. In addition, UTC uses the cost-to-cost method for development contracts in the aerospace businesses and for elevator and escalator installation and modernization contracts. For long-term aftermarket contracts revenue is recognized over the contract period in proportion to the costs expected to be incurred in performing services under the contract. UTC reviews its cost estimates on significant contracts on a quarterly basis, and for others, no less frequently than annually, or when circumstances change and warrant a modification to a previous estimate. Adjustments to contract loss provisions are recorded in earnings upon identification.

Service sales, representing aftermarket repair and maintenance activities, are recognized over the contractual period or as services are performed.

Revenues from engine programs under collaboration agreements are recorded as earned and the collaborator share of revenue is recorded as a reduction of revenue at that time. The collaborator share of revenues under Pratt and Whitney's engine programs was approximately $583 million, $542 million, and $595 million for 2004, 2003, and 2002, respectively. Costs associated with engine programs under collaboration agreements are expensed as incurred. The collaborator share of program costs is recorded as a reduction of the related expense item at that time.

Research and Development. Research and development costs not specifically covered by contracts and those related to UTC-sponsored share of research and development activity in connection with cost-sharing arrangements are charged to expense as incurred.

Research and development costs incurred under contracts with customers are expensed as incurred and are reported as a component of cost of products sold. Revenue from such contracts is recognized as product sales when earned.

Hedging Activity. UTC uses derivative instruments, including swaps, forward contracts and options, to manage certain foreign currency, interest rate, and commodity price exposures. Derivative instruments are viewed as risk management tools by UTC and are not used for trading or speculative purposes. Derivatives used for hedging purposes must be designated and effective as a hedge of the identified risk exposure and the inception of the contract. Accordingly, changes in fair value of the derivative contract must be highly correlated with changes in the fair value of the underlying hedged item at inception of the hedge and over the life of the hedge contract.

All derivative instruments are recorded on the balance sheet at fair value. Derivatives used to hedge foreign-currency denominated balance sheet items are reported directly in earnings along with offsetting transaction gains and losses on the items being hedged. Derivatives used to hedge forecasted cash flows associated with foreign currency commitments or forecasted commodity purchases are accounted for as cash flow hedges. Gains and losses on derivatives designated as cash flow hedges are recorded in other comprehensive income and reclassified to earnings in a manner that matches the timing of the earnings impact of the hedged transactions. The ineffective portion of all hedges, if any, is recognized currently in earnings.

Environmental. Environmental investigatory, remediation, operating, and maintenance costs are accrued when it is probably that a liability has been incurred and the amount can be reasonably estimated. The most likely cost to be incurred is accrued based on an evaluation of currently available facts with respect to each individual site, including existing technology, current laws and regulations and prior remediation experience. Where no amount within a range of estimates is more likely, the minimum is accrued. For sites with multiple responsible parties, UTC considers its likely proportionate share of the anticipated remediation costs and the ability of the other parties to fulfill their obligations in establishing a provision for those costs. Liabilities with fixed or reliably determinable future cash payments are discounted. Accrued environmental liabilities are not reduced by potential insurance reimbursements.

Stock-Based Compensation. As more fully described in Note 10, UTC has long-term incentive plans authorizing various types of market and performance based incentive awards that may be granted to officers and employees. UTC applies APB Opinion 25, "Accounting for Stock Issued to Employees," and related interpretations in accounting for its long-term incentive plans. The exercise price of stock options is set on the grant date and may not be less than the fair market value per share on that date. Stock options have a term of ten years and generally vest after three years.

The following table illustrates the effect on net income and earnings per share as if the Black-Scholes fair value method described in SFAS No. 123, "Accounting for Stock-Based Compensation" had been applied to UTC's long-term incentive plans:

	Year Ended December 31		
(in millions of dollars, except per share amounts)	*2004*	*2003*	*2002*
Net income, as reported	**$2,788**	$2,361	$2,236
Add: Stock based employee compensation expense included in net income, net of related tax effects.	**4**	8	3
Less: Total stock-based employee compensation expense determined under Black-Scholes option pricing model, net of related tax effects	**(119)**	(133)	(121)
Pro forma net income	**$2,673**	$2,236	$2,118
Earnings per share:			
Basic—as reported	**$ 5.62**	$ 4.93	$ 4.67
Basic—pro forma	**$ 5.39**	$ 4.67	$ 4.42
Diluted—as reported	**$ 5.52**	$ 4.69	$ 4.42
Diluted—pro forma	**$ 5.29**	$ 4.44	$ 4.19

Genuine Parts
2004 Annual Report

1. Summary of Significant Accounting Policies Business

Genuine Parts Company and all of its majority-owned subsidiaries (the Company) is a distributor of automotive replacement parts, industrial replacement parts, office products and electrical/electronic materials. The Company serves a diverse customer base through more than 1,900 locations in North America and, therefore, has limited exposure from credit losses to any particular customer or industry segment. The Company performs periodic credit evaluations of its customers' financial condition and generally does not require collateral.

Principles of Consolidation

The consolidated financial statements include all of the accounts of the Company. Income applicable to minority interests is included in selling, administrative and other expenses. Significant intercompany accounts and transactions have been eliminated in consolidation.

Use of Estimates

The preparation of the consolidated financial statements in conformity with accounting principles generally accepted in the United States requires management to make estimates and assumptions that affect the amounts reported in the consolidated financial statements and accompanying notes. Actual results may differ from those estimates and the differences could be material.

Revenue Recognition

The Company recognizes revenues from product sales upon shipment to its customers.

Foreign Currency Translation

The consolidated balance sheets and statements of income of the Company's foreign subsidiaries have been translated into U.S. dollars at the current and average exchange rates, respectively. The foreign currency translation adjustment is included as a component of accumulated other comprehensive income (loss).

Cash and Cash Equivalents

The Company considers all highly liquid investments with maturities of three months or less when purchased to be cash and cash equivalents.

Trade Accounts Receivable and the Allowance for Doubtful Accounts

The Company evaluates the collectibility of trade accounts receivable based on a combination of factors. Initially, the Company estimates an allowance for doubtful accounts as a percentage of net sales based on historical bad debt experience. This initial estimate is periodically adjusted when the Company becomes aware of a specific customer's inability to meet its financial obligations (e.g., bankruptcy filing) or as a result of changes in the overall aging of accounts receivable. While the company has a large customer base that is geographically dispersed, a general economic downturn in any of the industry segments in which the Company operates could result in higher than expected defaults, and, therefore, the need to revise estimates for bad debts. For the years ended December 31, 2004, 2003, and 2002, the Company recorded provisions for bad debts of approximately $20,697,000, $23,800,000, and $20,900,000, respectively.

Merchandise Inventories, including Consideration Received from Vendors Merchandise inventories are valued at the lower of cost or market. Cost is determined by the last-in, first-out (LIFO) method for a majority of automotive parts, electrical/electronic materials and industrial parts, and by the first-in, first-out (FIFO) method for office products and certain other inventories. If the FIFO method had been used for all inventories, cost would have been approximately $226,914,000 and $187,444,000 higher than reported at December 31, 2004 and 2003, respectively.

The Company identifies slow moving or obsolete inventories and estimates appropriate provisions related thereto. Historically, these losses have not been significant as the vast majority of the Company's inventories are not highly susceptible to obsolescence and are eligible for return under various vendor return programs. While the Company has no reason to believe its inventory return privileges will be discontinued in the future, its risk of loss associated with obsolete or slow moving inventories would increase if such were to occur.

The Company enters into agreements at the beginning of each year with many of its vendors providing for inventory purchase incentives and advertising allowances. Generally, the Company earns inventory purchase incentives and advertising allowances upon achieving specified volume purchasing levels or other criteria. The Company accrues for the receipt of inventory purchase incentives and advertising allowances as part of its inventory cost based on cumulative purchases of inventory to date and projected inventory purchases through the end of the year or, in the case of specific advertising allowances, upon completion of the Company's obligations related thereto. While management believes the Company will continue to receive consideration from vendors in 2005 and beyond, there can be no assurance that vendors will continue to provide comparable amounts of incentives and allowances in the future.

Prepaid Expenses and Other Current Assets

Prepaid expenses and other current assets consist primarily of prepaid expenses and amounts due from vendors.

Goodwill and Other Intangible Assets

Goodwill and other intangible assets primarily represent the excess of the purchase price paid over the fair value of the net assets acquired in connection with business acquisitions.

Effective January 1, 2002, the Company adopted Statement of Financial Accounting Standards No. 142, Goodwill and Other Intangible Assets (SFAS No. 142). SFAS No. 142 requires that entities assess the fair value of the net assets underlying all acquisition-related goodwill on a reporting unit basis effective beginning in 2002. When the fair value is less than the related carrying value, entities are required to reduce the amount of goodwill. The approach to evaluating the recoverability of goodwill as outlined in SFAS No. 142 requires the use of valuation techniques utilizing estimates and assumptions about projected future operating results and other variables. The impairment only approach required by SFAS No. 142 may have the effect of increasing the volatility of the Company's earnings if additional goodwill impairment occurs at a future date. SFAS No. 142 also requires that entities discontinue amortization of all purchased goodwill, including amortization of goodwill recorded in past business combinations. Accordingly, the Company no longer amortizes goodwill beginning in 2002.

Other Assets

Other assets consist primarily of a prepaid pension asset, an investment accounted for under the cost method and the cash surrender value of certain life insurance policies. The investment accounted for under the cost method was $21,400,000 at both December 31, 2004 and 2003, respectively.

Property, Plant, and Equipment

Property, plant and equipment are stated at cost. Land and buildings include certain leases capitalized at December 31, 2004. Depreciation and amortization is primarily determined on a straight-line basis over the following estimated useful life of each asset: buildings and improvements, 10 to 40 years; machinery and equipment, 5 to 15 years.

Long-Lived Assets Other Than Goodwill

The Company assesses its long-lived assets other than goodwill form impairment annually or whenever facts and circumstances indicate that the carrying amount may not be fully recoverable. To analyze recoverability, the Company projects undiscounted net future cash flows over the remaining life of such assets. If these projected cash flows are less than the carrying amount, an impairment would be recognized, resulting in a write-down of assets with a corresponding charge to earnings. Impairment losses, if any, are measured based upon the difference between the carrying amount and the fair value of the assets.

Other Long-Term Liabilities

Other long-term liabilities consist primarily of certain benefit and workers' compensation liabilities, the fair value of an interest rate swap agreement and obligations under capital leases.

Accumulated Other Comprehensive Income

Accumulated other comprehensive income is comprised of the following:

(in thousands) December 31	2004	2003
Foreign currency translation	$38,813	$11,611
Net unrealized loss on derivative instruments, net of taxes	(3,990)	(6,776)
Minimum pension liability, net of taxes	(8,345)	–
Total accumulated other comprehensive income	$26,478	$ 4,835

Fair Value of Financial Instruments

The carrying amount reflected in the consolidated balance sheets for cash and cash equivalents, trade accounts receivable and trade accounts payable approximate their respective fair values based on the short-term nature of these instruments. The fair value of interest rate swap agreements, included in other long-term liabilities in the consolidated balance sheets, was approximately $5,592,000 and $11,586,000 at December 31, 2004 and 2003, respectively. The fair value of derivative financial instruments has been determined based on quoted market prices. At December 31, 2004 and 2003, the carrying amount for variable rate long-term debt approximates fair market value since the interest rates on these instruments are reset periodically to current market rates. At December 31, 2004 and 2003, the fair market value of fixed rate long-term debt was approximately $534,000,000 and $543,000,000, respectively, based primarily on quoted prices for these or similar instruments. The fair value of fixed rate long-term debt was estimated by calculating the present value of anticipated cash flows. The discount rate used was an estimated borrowing rate for similar debt instruments with like maturities.

Derivative Instruments and Hedging Activities

From time to time, the Company uses interest rate swap agreements to synthetically manage the interest rate characteristics of a portion of its outstanding debt and to limit the Company's exposure to rising interest rates. The Company designates at inception that interest rate swap agreements hedge risks associated with future variable interest payments and monitors each swap agreement to determine if it remains an effective hedge. The effectiveness of the derivative as a hedge is based on a high correlation between changes in the value of the underlying hedged item. Ineffectiveness related to the Company's derivative transactions is not material. The Company records amounts to be received or paid as a result of interest rate swap agreements as an adjustment to interest expense. All of the Company's interest rate swaps are designated as cash flow hedges. Gains or losses on terminations or redesignation of interest rate swap agreements are deferred and amortized as an adjustment to interest expense of the related debt instrument over the remaining term of the original contract life of the agreements. The Company does not enter into derivatives for speculative or trading purposes.

Shipping and Handling Costs

Shipping and handling costs are classified as selling, administrative and other expenses in the accompanying consolidated statements of income and totaled approximately $216,000,000, $202,000,000, and $200,000,000 in the years ended December 31, 2004, 2003, and 2002, respectively.

Stock Compensation

Effective January 1, 2003, the Company prospectively adopted the fair value method of accounting for stock compensation. The adoption of SFAS No. 123, Accounting for Stock-Based Compensation (SFAS 123), had no significant impact on the Company's consolidated financial statements for the years ended December 31, 2004 and 2003. Until January 1, 2003, the Company had elected to follow Accounting Principles Board Opinion No. 25, Accounting for Stock Issued to Employees (APB 25), and related Interpretations in accounting for stock compensation. Under APB 25, no compensation expense is recognized if the exercise price of stock options equals the market price of the underlying stock on the date of grant. Note 7 contains a tabular presentation as if the Company had applied the alternative fair value accounting provided for under SFAS 123, to all stock options.

Net Income (Loss) Per Common Share

Basic net income (loss) per common share is computed by dividing net income (loss) by the weighted average number of common shares outstanding during the year. The computation of diluted net income (loss) per common share includes the dilutive effect of stock options and non-vested restricted stock awards. Options to purchase 5,219,000 and 679,000, shares of common stock at prices ranging from $32 to $38 per share were outstanding at December 31, 2003 and 2002, respectively, but were not included in the computation of diluted net income (loss) per common share in those years because the options' exercise price was greater than the average market price of the common shares at the time. At December 31, 2004, 2003, and 2002, the dilutive effect of options to purchase approximately 12,000, 39,000 and 56,000 shares of common stock, respectively, at an average exercise price of approximately $18 per share issued in connection with a 1998 acquisition have been included in the computation of diluted net income (loss) per common share since the date of the 296 acquisition.

Reclassifications

Certain reclassifications have been made to prior year amounts to conform to current year presentation.

Recently Issued Accounting Pronouncements

In January 2003, the FASB issued Interpretation No. 46 (FIN 46), Consolidation of Variable Interest Entities, an Interpretation of ARB No. 51. FIN 46, as revised in December 2003, requires certain variable interest entities to be consolidated by the primary beneficiary of the entity if the equity investors in the entity do not have the characteristics of a controlling financial interest or do not have sufficient equity at risk for the entity to finance its activities without additional subordinated financial support from other parties. FIN 46 is effective for all new variable interest entities created or acquired after January 31, 2003. For variable interest entities created or acquired prior to February 1, 2003, the provisions of FIN 46 must be applied no later than December 31, 2003 for entities meeting the definition of special-purpose entities, and no later than fiscal periods ending after March 15, 2004 for all other entities under consideration.

In connection with the adoption of FIN 46, in June 2003, the Company's construction and lease facility was amended. Subject to the amendment, FIN 46 did not change the Company's accounting for the construction and lease facility. This construction and lease facility, expiring in 2008, contains residual value guarantee provisions and other guarantees which would become due in the event of a default under the operating lease agreement or at the expiration of the operating lease agreement if the fair value of the leased properties is less that the guaranteed residual value. The maximum amount of the Company's potential guarantee obligation at December 31, 2004 is approximately $83,880,000. The Company believes the like likelihood of funding the guarantee obligation under any provision of the operating lease agreement is remote.

In addition to the construction and lease facility, the Company has relationships with entities that are required to be considered for consolidation under FIN 46. Specifically, the Company guarantees the borrowings of certain independently controlled automotive parts stores (independents) and certain other affiliates in which the Company has a minority equity ownership interest (affiliates). Presently, the independents are generally consolidated by an unaffiliated enterprise that has a controlling financial interest through ownership of a majority voting interest in the entity. The Company has no voting interest or other equity conversion rights in any of the independents. The Company does not control the independents or the affiliates, but receives a fee for the guarantee. The Company has concluded that it is not the primary beneficiary with respect to any of the independents and that the affiliates are not variable interest entities. The Company's maximum exposure to loss as a result of its involvement with these independents and affiliates is equal to the total borrowings subject to the Company's guarantee. At December 31, 2004, the total borrowings of the independents and affiliates subject to guarantee by the Company were approximately $169,000,000. These loans generally mature over periods from one to ten years. In the event that the Company is required to make payments in connection with guaranteed obligations of the independents or the affiliates, the Company would obtain and liquidate certain collateral (e.g., accounts receivable and inventory) to recover all or a portion of the amounts paid under the guarantee. To date, the Company has had no significant losses in connection with guarantees of independents' and affiliates' borrowings.

In January 2003, the Emerging Issues Task Force (EITF) of the FASB issued EITF Issue No. 02-16, Accounting by a Customer (Including Reseller) for Certain Consideration Received from a Vendor (EITF 02-16). EITF 02-16 addresses accounting and reporting issues related to how a reseller should account for certain consideration received from vendors. Generally, certain consideration received from vendors is presumed to be a reduction of prices of the vendor's products or services and should, therefore, be characterized as a reduction of cost of sales when recognized in the customer's income statement. However, under certain circumstances, this presumption may be overcome and recognition as revenue or as a reduction of other costs in the income statement may be appropriate. The Company, in certain circumstances, previously included funds of this type in selling, administrative and other expenses. Under the new method, vendor allowances for advertising and catalog related programs are generally considered a reduction of cost of goods sold. On January 1, 2003, the Company adopted EITF 02-16 and recorded a non-cash charge of $19.5 million ($.11 and $.12 per basic and diluted share, respectively), net of a tax benefit of $13.6 million, related to the capitalization of certain vendor consideration as part of inventory cost. Had the Company accounted for vendor considerations in accordance with EITF 02-16 in prior years, the capitalization of these vendor considerations would not have a significant impact on the consolidated statements of income for the year ended December 31, 2002. In addition, as a result of the January 1, 2003 adoption of EITF 02-16, approximately $111 million and $102 million were reclassified from selling, administrative and other expenses to cost of goods sold in the consolidated statement of income for the years ended December 31, 2004 and 2003, respectively. In accordance with EITF 02-16, the income statement presentations for periods prior to January 1, 2003 have not been reclassified. Had the Company accounted for consideration received from vendors in accordance with EITF 02-16 in prior years, approximately $90 million would have been reclassified from selling, administrative and other expenses to cost of goods sold in the consolidated statement of income for the year ended December 31, 2002.

FASB Staff Position (FSP) No. 109-2, Accounting and Disclosure Guidance for the Foreign Earnings Repatriation Provision within the American Jobs Creation Act of 2004 (FSP 109-2), provides guidance under FASB Statement No. 109, Accounting for Income Taxes, with respect to recording the potential impact of the repatriation provisions of the American Jobs Creation Act of 2004 (the Jobs Act) on enterprises' income tax expense and deferred tax liability. The Jobs Act was enacted on October 22, 2004. FSP 109-2 states that an enterprise is allowed time beyond the financial reporting period of enactment to evaluate the effect of the Jobs Act on its plan for reinvestment or repatriation of foreign earnings for purposes of applying FASB Statement No. 109. The Company has not yet completed evaluating the impact of the repatriation 109-2, the Company has not adjusted its tax expense or deferred tax liability to reflect the repatriation provisions of the Jobs Act. On December 16, 2004, the Financial Accounting Standards Board (FASB) issued FASB Statement No. 123 (revised 2004), Share-Based Payment, which is a revision of FASB Statement No. 123, Accounting for Stock-Based Compensation. Statement 123(R) supersedes APB Opinion No. 25, Accounting for Stock Issued to Employees, and amends FASB Statement No. 95, Statement of Cash Flows. Generally, the approach in Statement 123(R) is similar to the approach described in Statement 123. However, to employees, including grants of employee stock options, to be recognized in the income statement based on their fair values. Pro forma disclosure is no longer an alternative. We expect to adopt Statement 123(R) on July 1, 2005.

Statement 123(R) permits public companies to adopt its requirements using one of two methods:

1. A "modified prospective" method in which compensation cost is recognized beginning with the effective date (a) based on the requirements of Statement 123(R) for all share-based payments granted after the effective date and (b) based on the requirements of Statement 123 for all awards granted to employees prior to the effective date of Statement 123(R) that remain unvested on the effective date.

2. A "modified retrospective" method which includes the requirements of the modified prospective method described above, but also permits entities to restate based on the amounts previously recognized under Statement 123 for purposes of pro forma disclosures either (a) all prior periods presented or (b) prior interim periods of the year of adoption.

The Company adopted the fair-value-based method of accounting for share-based payments effective January 1, 2003 using the prospective method described in FASB Statement No. 148, Accounting for Stock-Based Compensation— Transition and Disclosure. Currently, the Company uses the Black-Scholes formula to estimate the value of stock options granted to employees and expects to continue to use this acceptable option valuation model upon the required adoption of Statement 123(R) on July 1, 2005. Because Statement 123(R) must be applied not only to new awards but to previously granted awards that are not fully vested on the effective date, and because the Company adopted Statement 123 using the prospective transition method (which applied only to awards granted, modified or settled after the adoption date), compensation cost for some previously granted awards that were not recognized under Statement 123 will be recognized under Statement 123(R). However, had we adopted Statement 123(R) in prior periods, the impact of that standard would have approximated the impact of Statement 123 as described in the disclosure of pro forma net income and earnings per share in Note 7 to our consolidated financial statements. Statement 123(R) also requires the benefits of tax deductions in excess of recognized compensation cost to be reported as a financing cash flow, rather than as an operating cash flow as required under current literature. This requirement will reduce net operating cash flows and increase net financing cash flows in periods after adoption. While the Company cannot estimate what those amounts will be in the future (because they depend on, among other things, when employees exercise stock options), the amount of operating cash flows recognized in prior periods for such excess tax deductions were $6,072,000, $1,254,000, and $4,468,000 in 2004, 2003, and 2002, respectively.

Novell
2004 Annual Report

B. Summary of Significant Accounting Policies

The accompanying consolidated financial statements reflect the application of significant accounting policies as described in this note and elsewhere in the accompanying consolidated financial statements.

Principles of Consolidation

The accompanying consolidated financial statements include the accounts of Novell, Inc., its subsidiaries and majority-owned joint ventures. All material inter-company accounts and transactions have been eliminated in consolidation.

Management's Estimates and Uncertainties

The preparation of financial statements in conformity with accounting principles generally accepted in the United States requires management to make estimates and assumptions that affect the amounts reported in the financial statements and accompanying notes. Actual results could differ materially from those estimates.

Reclassifications

Certain amounts reported in prior years have been reclassified from what was previously reported to conform to the current year's presentation.

Foreign Currency Translation

Due to increased activity in non-U.S. dollar currencies, beginning November 1, 2002, we determined the functional currency of all of our international subsidiaries, except for our Irish subsidiaries and a German holding company, to be the local currency. In our Irish subsidiary and German holding company, the functional currency is the U.S. dollar. These subsidiaries generate and expend cash primarily in their respective local currencies. Assets and liabilities of these subsidiaries are translated at current month-end exchange rates. Revenue and expenses are translated monthly at the average monthly exchange rate. Translation adjustments are recorded in accumulated other comprehensive income. Previously, the functional currency of our international subsidiaries, except Novell Japan, Novell India, and the international subsidiaries of Cambridge Technology Partners ("Cambridge") and Silver Stream Software, Inc. ("Silver Stream"), was the U.S. dollar. All transaction gains and losses are reported in other income (expense). Foreign exchange resulted in a loss of $5.0 million and $3.0 million, respectively, during fiscal 2004 and 2003, and a gain of $0.3 million in Fiscal 2002.

Cash, Cash Equivalents, and Short-Term Investments

We consider all investments purchased with an initial term to maturity of three months or less to be cash equivalents. All auction market securities are classified as short-term investments. Short-term investments are diversified, primarily consisting of investment grade securities that either mature within the next 12 months or have other characteristics of short-term investments. All of our auction market securities have auction dates within at least 6 months of the prior auction date. Our fixed income securities have maturities, puts, announced calls, auctions, or resets ranging from zero to seven years. These securities are available to be used for current operations and thus are classified as short-term investments, even though some maturities may extend beyond one year.

All marketable debt and equity securities that are included in cash and short-term investments are considered available-for-sale and are carried at fair value. The unrealized gains and losses related to these securities are included in accumulated other comprehensive income, net of tax, after any applicable tax valuation allowances (see Note U). Fair values are based on quoted market prices where available. If quoted market prices are not available, as in the case of municipal debt securities, we use third-party pricing services to assist in determining fair value. In many instances, these services examine the pricing of similar instruments to estimate fair value. When securities are sold, their cost is determined based on the specific identification method.

Concentrations of Credit Risk

Financial instruments that subject us to credit risk primarily consist of cash and cash equivalents, short term investments, accounts receivable, notes receivable, and amounts due under subleases. Our credit risk is managed by investing cash and cash equivalents in high-quality money market instruments and securities of the U.S. government and its agencies. Accounts receivable include amounts owed by geographically dispersed end users, distributors, resellers, and original equipment manufacturer ("OEM") customers. No collateral is required. We provide a standard right of return of 30 days. Provisions are made for sales returns and bad debts and are based on historical experience and on specific customer situations. Accounts receivable are not sold or factored. There were no customers with outstanding receivable balances greater than 10% of total accounts receivable at October 31, 2004 or 2003. We generally have not experienced any material losses related to receivables from individual customers or groups of customers. Due to these factors, no significant additional credit risk, beyond amounts provided for, is believed by management to be inherent in our accounts receivable. Our long term notes receivable in the amount of $9.8 million is secured by collateral. Our subleases are with many different parties and thus no concentration of credit risk exists at October 31, 2004.

During the years ended October 31, 2004, 2003 and 2002 there were no customers who accounted for more than 10% of total net revenue.

Property, Plant, and Equipment

Property, plant and equipment are carried at cost less accumulated depreciation and amortization. Depreciation and amortization is computed on the straight-line method over the estimated useful lives of the assets, or lease term, if shorter. Such lives are as follows:

Asset classification	Useful Lives
Buildings	30 years
Furniture and equipment	2-7 years
Leasehold improvements and other	3-10 years

Goodwill and Intangible Assets

In accordance with SFAS No. 142, "Goodwill and Other Intangible Assets," we do not amortize goodwill or intangibles with indefinite lives resulting from acquisitions. We review these assets periodically for potential impairment issues. Separable intangible assets that are not deemed to have an indefinite life are amortized over their estimated useful lives.

Disclosure of Fair Value of Financial Instruments

Our financial instruments mainly consist of cash and cash equivalents, short-term investments, accounts receivable, notes receivable, long-term investments, accounts payable, and senior convertible debentures. The carrying amounts of our cash equivalents and short-term investments, accounts receivable and accounts payable approximate fair value due to the short term nature of these instruments. Long-term investments are accounted for initially at cost. The Company periodically reviews the realizability of each long-term investment when impairment indicators exist with respect to the investment. If another-than temporary impairment of the value of the investments is deemed to exist, the carrying value of the investment is written down to its estimated fair value. We consider an impairment to be other than temporary when market evidence or issuer-specific knowledge does not reflect long-term growth to support current carrying values. As of October 31, 2004 and 2003, we did not hold any publicly-traded long-term equity securities. Our long-term notes receivable and senior convertible debentures have interest rates that approximate current market rates; therefore the carrying value of the both approximate fair value.

Revenue

Our revenue is derived primarily from the sale of software licenses and maintenance, technical support, training, and consulting services. Revenue is recognized in accordance with the requirements of Statement of Position ("SOP") 97-2, "Software Revenue Recognition." Under SOP 97-2, when an arrangement does not require significant production, modification or customization of the software, revenue is recognized when the following four criteria are met

☐ Persuasive evidence of an arrangement exists—We require evidence of an agreement with a customer specifying the terms and conditions of the products or services to be delivered.

☐ Delivery has occurred—For software licenses, delivery takes place when the customer is given access to the software programs. For services, delivery takes place as the services are provided.

☐ The fee is fixed or determinable—Fees are fixed or determinable if they are not subject to a refund or cancellation and do not have payment terms that exceed our standard terms.

☐ Collectibility is probable. We perform a credit review of all customers with significant transactions to determine whether a customer is credit-worthy and collectibility is probable.

Revenue from software license fees is generally recognized upon delivery of the software. If the fee due from the customer is not fixed or determinable, revenue is recognized as payments become due from the customer. If collection is not considered probable, revenue is recognized when the fee is collected. Allowances for estimated sales returns and allowances are recorded in the same period as the related revenue. We recognize revenue on the sale of shrink-wrapped box products through our distributor channel on a sell-through basis.

Revenue from maintenance contracts, subscription agreements, support, and other similar services, is recognized as services are performed over the term of the performance period. Certain sales require continuing service, support, and performance by us, and accordingly, a portion of the revenue is deferred until the future service, support, and performance are provided.

Consulting project contracts are either time-and-materials or fixed-price contracts. Revenue from consulting projects is recognized only if a signed contract exists, the fee is Fixed or determinable, and collection of the resulting receivable is probable. Revenue from time-and-materials contracts is recognized as the services are performed. Revenue from Fixed-price contracts is recognized using the proportional performance method, using the estimated time-to-completion to measure the percent complete. The cumulative impact of any revision in estimates of the percent complete or recognition of losses on contracts is reflected in the period in which the changes or losses become known.

Many of our software arrangements include multiple elements, such as product upgrade protection, software support services, consulting, and training, in addition to software licenses and maintenance. These multiple element arrangements are accounted for using a proportional method of accounting in which we allocate revenue to each element of the transaction based upon the relative fair values of the elements, which may include software products, product upgrade protection, software support services, consulting, and training. Fair value is determined by Novell-specific objective evidence of the price charged to other customers when each element is sold separately. We have established sufficient Novell specific objective evidence of the fair value of all elements of a multiple element arrangement.

Services revenue includes reimbursable expenses charged to our clients.

We record provisions against revenue for estimated sales returns and allowances on product and service related sales in the same period as the related revenue is recorded. We also record a provision to operating expenses for bad debts resulting from customers' inability to pay for the products or services they have received, due to such factors as bankruptcy. These estimates are based on historical sales returns and bad debt expense, analyses of credit memo data, and other known factors.

Cost of Revenue

Amortization charges for product and services related intangible assets are recorded as a cost of revenue in the statements of operations.

Expenses

Product development costs are expensed as incurred. Due to the use of the working model approach, capitalized development costs have not been material.

Advertising costs are expensed as incurred. Advertising expenses totaled $10.6 million, $37.5 million, and $19.5 million, in fiscal 2004, 2003, and 2002, respectively.

Stock-Based Compensation

We account for our stock-based compensation plans under the intrinsic value method of accounting as defined by Accounting Principles Board ("APB") Opinion No. 25, "Accounting for Stock Issued to Employees" and related interpretations. We apply the disclosure provisions of SFAS No. 123, "Accounting for Stock-Based Compensation," as amended by SFAS No. 148, "Accounting for Stock-Based Compensation I Transition and Disclosure." We account for stock based awards issued to no employees using the fair value model as defined by SFAS No. 123.

At October 31, 2004, we had authorized several stock-based compensation plans which are more fully described in Note R. Under these plans, options to purchase shares of our common stock could be granted to employees, consultants, and outside directors. Under the intrinsic value method, compensation expense is calculated based on the difference between the fair value of our common stock and the option exercise price at the date of grant. We generally grant employee stock options with an exercise price equal to the fair value of our common stock. If compensation expense for our stock-based compensation had been determined based on the fair value of the stock grants, our net income (loss) and net income (loss) per share would have been the pro forma amounts indicated below:

	Fiscal Year Ended		
	October 31, 2004	October 31, 2003	October 31, 2002
	(Amounts in thousands, except per share amounts)		
Net income (loss) available to common stockholders:			
As reported	$ 31,092	$(161,904)	$(246,823)
Less: total stock-based compensation expense determined under fair value-based method for all awards, net of related tax effects	(51,436)	(28,753)	(63,086)
Add: total stock-based compensation expense recorded in the statement of operations	4,940	3,445	7,534
Pro forma	$(15,404)	$(187,212)	$(302,375)
Net income (loss) per common share:			
As reported basic and diluted	$ 0.08	$ (0.44)	$ (0.68)
Pro forma basic and diluted	$ (0.04)	$ (0.51)	$ (0.83)

For the purpose of the above table, the fair value of each option grant is estimated as of the date of grant using the Black-Scholes option-pricing model with the following weighted-average assumptions used for grants in Fiscal 2004, 2003, and 2002: a risk-free interest rate of approximately 2.8% for Fiscal 2004, 2.8% for Fiscal 2003, and 3.6% for Fiscal 2002; a dividend yield of 0.0% for all years; a weighted-average expected life of 3.75 years for Fiscal 2004 and five years for Fiscal 2003 and 2002; and a volatility factor of the expected market price of our common stock of 0.77 for Fiscal 2004, 0.85 for Fiscal 2003, and 0.87 for Fiscal 2002. The weighted-average fair value of options granted in Fiscal 2004, 2003, and 2002 was $5.63, $2.38, and $1.70, respectively.

We do not recognize compensation expense related to employee purchase rights under the Novell, Inc. 1989 Employee Stock Purchase Plan. Pro forma compensation expense is estimated for the fair value of the employees' purchase rights using the Black-Scholes model with the following assumptions for the rights granted in Fiscal 2004, 2003, and 2002: a dividend yield of 0.0% for all years; an expected life of six months for all years; an expected volatility factor of 0.77 for Fiscal 2004, 0.85 for Fiscal 2003, and 0.87 for Fiscal 2002; and a risk-free interest rate of approximately 1.2% for Fiscal 2004, 1.1% for Fiscal 2003, and 1.5% for Fiscal 2002. The weighted-average fair value of the purchase rights granted on April 19, 2004, October 20, 2003, May 7, 2003, October 21, 2002, April 22, 2002, and October 22, 2001, was $4.19, $2.19, $1.07, $0.93, $1.50, and $1.52, respectively.

Net Income (Loss) Per Share

Basic and diluted net income (loss) per share available to common stockholders is presented in conformity with SFAS No. 128, "Earnings per Share." Basic net income (loss) per share attributable to common stockholders is computed by dividing net income (loss) by the weighted-average number of common shares outstanding during the period and excludes the dilutive effects of common stock equivalents. Common stock equivalents include stock options and, in certain circumstances, convertible securities such as our senior convertible debentures and convertible Series B preferred stock. Diluted earnings per share includes the dilutive effect of common stock equivalents.

In March 2004, the EITF reached a Final consensus on Issue 03-6, "Participating Securities and the Two-Class Method under FASB Statement 128." Issue 03-6 requires the two-class method of calculating earnings per share for companies that have issued securities other than common stock that contractually entitle the holder to participate in dividends of the company. Because the Series B preferred stock participates in dividends, we are required to use the two-class method of calculating earnings per share, effective in Fiscal 2004 and retroactively for all prior periods. This change in computational methods had no impact on earnings per share for any period in Fiscal 2004 or any prior period.

Derivative Instruments

A large portion of our revenue, expense, and capital purchasing activities are transacted in U.S. dollars. However, we do enter into transactions in other currencies, primarily the Euro, Japanese Yen, and certain other European, Latin American and Asian currencies. To protect against reductions in value caused by changes in foreign exchange rates, we have established balance sheet and inter-company hedging programs. We hedge currency risks of some assets and liabilities denominated in foreign currencies through the use of one-month foreign currency forward contracts. We do not currently hedge currency risks related to revenue or expenses denominated in foreign currencies.

We enter into these one-month hedging contracts two business days before the end of each month and settle them at the end of the following month. Due to the short period of time between entering into the forward contracts and the year-end, the fair value of the derivatives as of October 31, 2004 is insignificant.

Gains and losses recognized during the year on these foreign currency contracts are recorded as other income or expense and would generally be offset by corresponding losses or gains on the related hedged items, resulting in negligible net exposure to our Financial statements.

Recent Pronouncements

In November 2004, the EITF reached a Final conclusion on Issue 04-8, "Accounting Issues Related to Certain Features of Contingently Convertible Debt and the Effect on Diluted Earnings per Share." This issue addresses when the dilutive effect of contingently convertible debt with a market price trigger should be included in diluted earnings per share calculations. The EITF's conclusion is that the market price trigger should be ignored and that these securities should be treated as convertible securities and included in diluted earnings per share regardless of whether the conversion contingencies have been met. The effect of Issue 04-8 is discussed in Note T.

In December 2004, the FASB issued its final standard on accounting for employee stock options, SFAS No. 123(R), "Share-Based Payment," which replaces SFAS Nos. 123 and supercedes Accounting Principles Board Opinion 25, "Accounting for Stock Issued to Employees." SFAS No. 123(R) requires all companies to measure compensation costs for all share-based payments, including stock options, at fair value and expense such payments to the statement of operations over the service period. SFAS No. 123(R) is effective beginning for interim or annual periods beginning after June 15, 2005, which would be our fourth fiscal quarter of Fiscal 2005. We are in the process of determining the impact SFAS No. 123(R) will have on our consolidated financial statements.

BJ Services
2005 Annual Report

8. Segment Information

The Company currently has thirteen operating segments for which separate financial information is available and that have separate management teams that are engaged in oilfield services. The results for these operating segments are evaluated regularly by the chief operating decision maker in deciding how to allocate resources and assessing performance. The operating segments have been aggregated into three reportable segments: U.S./Mexico Pressure Pumping, International Pressure Pumping and Other oilfield Services.

The U.S./Mexico Pressure Pumping has two operating segments and includes cementing services and stimulation services (consisting of fracturing, acidizing, sand control, nitrogen, coiled tubing and service tool services) provided throughout the United States and Mexico. These two operating segments have been aggregated into one reportable segment because they offer the same type of services, have similar economic characteristics, have similar production processes and use the same methods to provide their services.

The International Pressure Pumping segment has six operating segments. Similar to U.S./Mexico Pressure Pumping, it includes cementing and stimulation services (consisting of fracturing, acidizing, sand control, nitrogen, coiled tubing and service tool services). These services are provided to customers in more than 48 countries in the major international oil and natural gas producing areas of Canada, Latin America, Europe and Africa, Asia Pacific, Russia and the Middle East. The operating segments have been aggregated into one reportable segment because they have similar economic characteristics, offer the same type of services, have similar production processes and use the same methods to provide their services. They also serve the same or similar customers, which include major multi-national, independent and national or state-owned oil companies.

The Other Oilfield Services segment has five operating segments. These operating segments provide other oilfield services such as production chemicals, casing and tubular services, process and pipeline services, completion tools and completion fluids services in the U.S. and in select markets internationally. The operating segments have been aggregated into one reportable segment as they all provide other oilfield services, serve same or similar customers and some of the operating segments share resources.

The accounting policies of the segments are the same as those described in the summary of significant accounting policies. The Company evaluates the performance of its segments based on operating income. Intersegment sales and transfers are not material.

Summarized financial information concerning the Company's segments for each of the three years ended September 30, 2005 is shown in the following tables. The "Corporate" column includes corporate expenses not allocated to the operating segments. Revenue by geographic location is determined based on the location in which services are rendered or products are sold. For the years ended September 30, 2005, 2004 and 2003, the Company provided services to several thousand customers, none of which accounted for more than 5% of consolidated revenue.

Business Segments (in thousands)	U.S./Mexico Pressure Pumping	International Pressure Pumping	Other Oilfield Services	Corporate	Total
2005					
Revenue	$1,683,202	$1,041,910	$517,659	$ 424	$3,243,186
Operating income (loss)	524,893	135,838	67,626	(91,298)	637,059
Total assets	1,049,019	1,195,455	592,861	559,163	3,396,498
Capital expenditures	149,986	115,357	34,906	23,514	323,763
Depreciation	51,990	60,727	20,206	3,938	136,861
2004					
Revenue	$1,269,786	$ 891,427	$438,788	$ 985	$2,600,986
Operating income (loss)	337,030	91,409	54,030	(44,084)	438,385
Total assets	901,272	1,056,728	549,051	783,646	3,290,697
Capital expenditures	92,080	62,688	31,704	14,105	200,577
Depreciation	45,699	56,414	19,492	4,063	125,668
2003					
Revenue	$ 982,630	$ 801,746	$358,479	$ 22	$2,142,877
Operating income (loss)	190,301	90,662	49,950	(37,672)	293,241
Total assets	832,736	1,044,811	482,193	429,762	2,789,502
Capital expenditures	72,827	60,380	19,557	14,419	167,183
Depreciation	44,491	55,110	16,132	4,480	120,213

Geographic Information	Revenue	Long-lived Assets
2005		
United States	$1,820,191	$1,519,193
Canada	392,380	172,609
Other countries	1,030,615	346,085
Consolidated total	$3,243,186	$2,037,887

Geographic Information	Revenue	Long-lived Assets
2004		
United States	$1,357,139	$1,385,343
Canada	331,521	114,642
Other countries	912,326	342,505
Consolidated total	$2,600,986	$1,842,490
2003		
United States	$1,068,465	$1,322,962
Canada	253,851	111,618
Other countries	820,561	342,792
Consolidated total	$2,142,877	$1,777,372

Revenue by Product Line	2005	2004	2003
Cementing	$ 822,447	$ 745,929	$ 594,743
Stimulation	1,835,560	1,361,273	$1,139,607
Other	585,179	493,784	408,527
Total revenue	$3,243,186	$2,600,986	$2,142,877

A reconciliation from the segment information to consolidated income before income taxes for each of the three years ended September 30, 2005 is set forth below:

(in thousands)	2005	2004	2003
Total operating profit for reportable segments	$637,059	$483,385	$293,241
Interest expense	(10,951)	(16,389)	(15,948)
Interest income	11,281	6,073	2,141
Other (expense) income, net	15,958	92,668	(3,762)
Income before income taxes	$653,347	520,737	$275,672

Black & Decker
2002 Annual Report

Note 15: Business Segments and Geographic Information

The Corporation has elected to organize its businesses based principally upon products and services. In certain instances where a business does not have a local presence in a particular country or geographic region, however, the Corporation has assigned responsibility for sales of that business's products to one of its other business with a presence in that country or region.

The Corporation operates in three reportable business segments: Power Tools and Accessories, Hardware and Home Improvement, and Fastening and

Assembly Systems. The Power Tools and Accessories segment has worldwide responsibility for the manufacture and sale of consumer and professional power tools and accessories, electric cleaning and lighting products, and electric lawn and garden tools, as well as for product service. In addition, the Power Tools and Accessories segment has responsibility for the sale of security hardware to customers in Mexico, Central America, the Caribbean, and South America; for the sale of plumbing products to customers outside the United States and Canada; and for sales of household products. The Hardware and Home Improvement segment has worldwide responsibility for the manufacture and sale of security hardware (except for the sale of security hardware in Mexico, Central America, the Caribbean, and South America). It also has responsibility for the manufacture of plumbing products and for the sale of plumbing products to customers in the United States and Canada. The Fastening and Assembly Systems segment has worldwide responsibility for the manufacture and sale of fastening and assembly systems.

Business Segments
(Millions of Dollars)
(Table on Next page)

The Corporation assesses the performance of its reportable business segments based upon a number of factors, including segment profit. In general, segments follow the same accounting policies as those described in Note 1, except with respect to foreign currency translation and except as further indicated below. The financial statements of a segment's operating units located outside of the United States, except those units operating in highly inflationary economies, are generally measured using the local currency as the functional currency. For these units located outside of the United States, segment assets and elements of segment profit are translated using budgeted rates of exchange. Budgeted rates of exchange are established annually and, once established, all prior period segment data is restated to reflect the current year's budgeted rates of exchange. The amounts included in the preceding table under the captions "Reportable Business Segments," and "Corporate, Adjustments, & Eliminations" are reflected at the Corporation's budgeted rates of exchange for 2002. The amounts included in the preceding table under the caption "Currency Translation Adjustments" represent the difference between consolidated amounts determined using those budgeted rates of exchange and those determined based upon the rates of exchange applicable under accounting principles generally accepted in the United States.

| | Reportable Business Segments | | | | | Corporate Adjustments and | |
	Power Tools & Accessories	Hardware & Home Improvement	Fastening & Assembly Systems	Total	Currency Translation Adjustments	Eliminations	Consolidated
Year Ended December 31, 2002							
Sales to unaffiliated customers	$3,108.3	$758.0	$502.4	$4,368.7	$25.3	$ —	$4,394.0
Segment profit (loss)(for Consolidated, operating income before restructuring and exit costs)	352.1	53.0	72.1	477.2	1.2	(57.6)	420.8
Depreciation and amortization	78.8	30.7	13.8	123.3	1.2	3.3	127.8
Income from equity method investees	20.8	—	—	20.8	—	3.0	
Capital expenditures	69.5	11.2	13.6	94.3	1.5	.8	96.6
Segment assets (for Consolidated, total assets)	1,570.4	416.2	311.0	2,297.6	82.4	1,750.5	4,130.5
Investment in equity method investees	25.4	—	1	25.5	—	(1.7)	23.8
Year Ended December 31, 2001							
Sales to unaffiliated customers	$3,008.9	$766.2	$478.4	$4,253.5	$(7.9)	$ —	$4,245.6
Segment profit (loss) (for Consolidated, operating income before restructuring and exit costs)	250.0	59.1	68.4	377.5	.4	(30.3)	347.6
Depreciation and amortization	85.2	33.7	14.3	133.2	.425	.8	159.4
Income from equity method investees	13.2	—	—	13.2	—	2.1	15.3
Capital expenditures	85.1	33.1	15.4	133.6	.4	.8	134.8
Segment assets (for Consolidated, total assets)	1,577.2	517.6	296.5	2,391.3	(18.1)	1,641.0	4,014.2
Investment in equity method investees	36.9	—	1.1	37.0	(.4)	(2.7)	33.9
Year Ended December 31, 2000							
Sales to unaffiliated customers	$3,072.4	$831.5	$489.3	$4,393.2	$81.7	$ —	$4,474.9

Year Ended December 31, 2002	Power Tools & Accessories	Hardware & Home Improvement	Reportable Business Segments Fastening & Assembly Systems	Total	Currency Translation Adjustments	Corporate Adjustments and Eliminations	Consolidated
Segment profit (loss) (for Consolidated, operating income before restructuring and exit costs and gain on sale of business)	349.4	113.5	80.4	543.3	8.4	(29.4)	522.3
Depreciation and amortization	83.4	34.3	15.9	133.6	3.4	26.4	163.4
Income from equity method investees	15.6	–	–	15.6	–	(.1)	15.5
Capital expenditures	138.6	30.8	25.6	195.0	4.4	.8	200.2
Segment assets (for Consolidated, total assets)	1,771.2	537.5	266.5	2,575.2	16.5	1,498.0	4,089.7
Investment in equity method investees	25.6	–	.1	25.7	.1	(1.7)	24.1

Segment profit excludes interest income and expense, non-operating income and expense, adjustments to eliminate intercompany profit in inventory, income tax expense, and, for 2001 and 2000, goodwill amortization (except for the amortization of goodwill associated with certain acquisitions made by the Power Tools and Accessories and Fastening and Assembly Systems segments). In addition, segment profit excludes restructuring and exit costs and the gain on sale of business. In determining segment profit, expenses relating to pension and other postretirement benefits are based solely upon estimated service costs. Corporate expenses, as well as certain centrally managed expenses, are allocated to each reportable segment based upon budgeted amounts. While sales and transfers between segments are accounted for at cost plus a reasonable profit, the effects of intersegment sales are excluded from the computation of segment profit. Intercompany profit in inventory is excluded from segment assets and is recognized as a reduction of cost of goods sold by the selling segment when the related inventory is sold to an unaffiliated customer. Because the Corporation compensates the management of its various businesses on, among other factors, segment profit, the Corporation may elect to record certain segment-related expense items of an unusual or non-recurring nature in consolidation rather than reflect such items in segment profit. In addition, certain segment-related items of income or expense may be recorded in consolidation in one period and transferred to the various segments in a later period.

Segment assets exclude pension and tax assets, intercompany profit in inventory, intercompany receivables, and, for 2001 and 2000, goodwill (except for the goodwill associated with certain acquisitions made by the Power Tools and Accessories and Fastening and Assembly Systems segments).

Amounts in the preceding table under the caption "Corporate, Adjustments & Eliminations" on the lines entitled "Depreciation and amortization" represent depreciation of Corporate property and, for 2001 and 2000, goodwill amortization (except for the amortization of goodwill associated with certain acquisitions made by the Power Tools and Accessories and Fastening and Assembly Systems segments). The reconciliation of segment profit to consolidated earnings before income taxes for each year, in millions of dollars, is as follows:

	2002	2001	2000
Segment profit for total reportable business segments	**$477.2**	$377.5	$543.3
Items excluded from segment profit:			
Adjustment of budgeted foreign exchange rates to actual rates	**1.2**	4	8.4
Depreciation of Corporate property and amortization of certain goodwill	**(1.3)**	(25.8)	(26.4)
Adjustment to businesses' postretirement benefit expenses booked in consolidation	**37.6**	41.3	36.4
Other adjustments booked in consolidation directly related to reportable business segments	**(8.6)**	(.6)	(14.1)

	2002	2001	2000
Amounts allocated to businesses in arriving at segment profit in excess of (less than) Corporate center operating expenses, eliminations, and other amounts identified above	**(85.3)**	(45.2)	(25.3)
Operating income before restructuring and exit costs, and gain on sale of business	**420.8**	347.6	522.3
Restructuring and exit costs	**50.7**	99.8	39.1
Gain on sale of business	**–**	–	20.1
Operating income	**370.1**	247.8	503.3
Interest expense, net of interest income	**57.8**	84.3	104.2
Other expense (income)	**4.9**	8.2	(5.5)
Earnings before income taxes	**$307.4**	$155.3	$404.6

The reconciliation of segment assets to the consolidated total assets at the end of each year, in millions of dollars, is as follows:

	2002	2001	2000
Segment assets for total reportable business segments	$2,297.6	$2,391.3	$2,575.2
Items excluded from segment assets:			
Adjustment of budgeted foreign exchange rates to actual rates	82.4	(18.1)	16.5
Goodwill	673.0	656.2	690.2
Pension assets	36.7	406.2	380.0
Other Corporate assets	1,040.8	578.6	427.8
	$4,130.5	$4,014.2	$4,089.7

Other Corporate assets principally consist of cash and cash equivalents, tax assets, property, and other assets.

Sales to The Home Depot, a customer of the Power Tools and Accessories and Hardware and Home Improvement segments, accounted for $857.9 million, $841.6 million, and $851.9 million of the Corporation's consolidated sales for the years ended December 31, 2002, 2001, and 2000, respectively. Sales to Lowe's Home Improvement Warehouse (Lowe's), a customer of the Power Tools and Accessories and Hardware and Home Improvement segments, accounted for $467.5 million of the Corporation's consolidated sales for the year ended December 31, 2002. Sales to Lowe's for the years ended December 31, 2001 and 2000, did not exceed 10% of the Corporation's consolidated sales in either of those years.

The composition of the Corporation's sales by product group for each year, in millions of dollars, is set forth below:

	2002	2001	2000
Consumer and professional power tools and product service	$2,308.4	$2,227.2	$2,304.1
Consumer and professional accessories	317.8	311.1	337.9
Electric lawn and garden products	285.4	279.3	300.1
Electric cleaning and lighting products	157.6	122.8	124.5
Household products	36.8	45.1	47.7
Security hardware	563.2	531.3	573.2
Plumbing products	221.6	252.3	281.4
Fastening and assembly systems	503.2	476.5	506.0
	$4,394.0	$4,245.6	$4,474.9

The Corporation markets its products and services in over 100 countries and has manufacturing sites in 11 countries. Other than in the United States, the Corporation does not conduct business in any country in which its sales in that country exceed 10% of consolidated sales. Sales are attributed to countries based on the location of customers. The composition of the Corporation's sales to unaffiliated customers between those in the United States and those in other locations for each year, in millions of dollars, is set forth below:

	2002	2001	2000
United States	$2,824.0	$2,715.6	$2,843.1
Canada	138.6	136.5	146.1
North America	2,962.6	2,852.1	2,989.2
Europe	1,089.0	1,055.9	1,136.7
Other	342.4	337.6	349.0
	$4,394.0	$4,245.6	$4,474.9

The composition of the Corporation's property, plant, and equipment between those in the United States and those in other countries as of the end of each year, in millions of dollars, is set forth below:

	2002	2001	2000
United States	$384.1	$425.2	$466.4
United Kingdom	72.2	72.1	100.5
Other countries	199.6	190.2	181.2
	$655.9	$687.5	$748.1

John Deere
2004 Annual Report

27. Segment and Geographic Area Data for the Years Ended October 31, 2004, 2003, and 2002

The company's operations are organized and reported in four major business segments described as follows:

The agricultural equipment segment manufactures and distributes a full line of farm equipment and related service parts—including tractors; combine, cotton and sugarcane harvesters; tillage, seeding and soil preparation machinery; sprayers; hay and forage equipment; material handling equipment; and integrated agricultural management systems technology. In 2004, the special technologies group's results were transferred from the "Other" segment to the agricultural equipment segment due to changes in internal reporting. The following information for the agricultural segment has been restated for this change in 2003 and 2002.

The commercial and consumer equipment segment manufactures and distributes equipment, products and service parts for commercial and residential uses—including small tractors for lawn, garden, commercial and utility purposes; walk-behind mowers; golf course equipment; utility vehicles (including those commonly referred to as all-terrain vehicles, or "ATVs"); landscape products and irrigation equipment; and other outdoor power products. The construction and forestry segment manufactures, distributes to dealers and sells at retail a broad range of machines and service parts used in construction, earthmoving, material handling and timber harvesting—including backhoe loaders; crawler dozers and loaders; four-wheel-drive loaders; excavators; motor graders; articulated dump trucks; landscape loaders; skid-steer loaders; and log skidders, feller bunchers, log loaders, log forwarders, log harvesters and related attachments.

The products and services produced by the equipment segments are marketed primarily through independent retail dealer networks and major retail outlets.

The credit segment primarily finances sales and leases by John Deere dealers of new and used agricultural, commercial and consumer, and construction and forestry equipment. In addition, it provides wholesale financing to dealers of the foregoing equipment, provides operating loans, finances retail revolving charge accounts and plans to offer certain crop risk mitigation products.

Certain operations do not meet the materiality threshold of FASB Statement No. 131, Disclosures about Segments of an Enterprise and Related Information, and have been grouped together as an "Other" segment. In 2004, the special technologies group's results, which were previously included in the "Other" segment, were transferred to the agricultural equipment segment due to changes in internal reporting. The information for the "Other" segment was restated for this change in 2003 and 2002 and, as a result, consists of only the health care operations in those years. In 2004, the "Other" segment information primarily consists of the health care operations, as well as certain miscellaneous service operations added in 2004.

Corporate assets are primarily the Equipment Operations' prepaid pension costs, deferred income tax assets, other receivables and cash and cash equivalents as disclosed in Note 29, net of certain intercompany eliminations.

Because of integrated manufacturing operations and common administrative and marketing support, a substantial number of allocations must be made to determine operating segment and geographic area data. Intersegment sales and revenues represent sales of components and finance charges which are generally based on market prices.

Information relating to operations by operating segment in millions of dollars follows. In addition to the following unaffiliated sales and revenues by segment, intersegment sales and revenues in 2004, 2003 and 2002 were as follows: Agricultural equipment net sales of $88 million, $61 million and $54 million, construction and forestry net sales of $11 million, $9 million and none, and credit revenues of $216 million, $209 million and $167 million, respectively.

OPERATING SEGMENTS	2004	2003	2002
Net sales and revenues			
Unaffiliated customers:			
Agricultural equipment net sales	$ 9,717	$ 7,390	$ 6,792
Commercial and consumer equipment net sales	3,742	3,231	2,712
Construction and forestry net sales	4,214	2,728	2,199
Total net sales	17,673	13,349	11,703
Credit revenues	1,276	1,347	1,426
Other revenues	1,037	839	818
Total	$19,986	$15,535	$13,947
Operating profit (loss)*			
Agricultural equipment	$1,072	$329**	$397**
Commercial and consumer equipment	246	227	79
Construction and forestry	587	152	(75)
Credit***	466	474	386
Other***	5	30**	30**
Total operating profit	2,376	1,212	817
Interest income	64	59	66
Interest expense	(205)	(217)	(223)
Foreign exchange loss from equipment operations' financing activities	(10)	(12)	(17)
Corporate expenses—net	(111)	(62)	(66)
Income taxes	(708)	(337)	(258)

OPERATING SEGMENTS	2004	2003	2002
Total	(970)	(569)	(498)
Net income	$1,406	$ 643	$ 319

* In 2004 and 2003, there was no goodwill amortization and the costs or income for special items were not material. In 2002, the operating profit (loss) of the agricultural equipment, commercial and consumer equipment and construction and forestry segments included pretax goodwill amortization of $27 million, $14 million, and $17 million, respectively, for a total of $58 million. In 2002, operating profit (loss) of the agricultural equipment, commercial and consumer equipment and construction and forestry segments included expense for special items of $21 million, $24 million, and $27 million, respectively, for a total of $72 million (see Note 2).

** Years 2003 and 2002 were restated for sales of $41 million and $54 million, operating losses of $8 million and $42 million and identifiable assets of $67 million and $73 million, respectively, for the transfer of the special technologies group's results from the "Other" segment to the agricultural equipment segment. Other insignificant restatements of the agricultural equipment segment information related to this transfer were also made.

*** Operating profit of the credit business segment includes the effect of interest expense, which is the largest element of its operating costs, and foreign exchange gains or losses. Operating profit of the "Other" segment includes health care investment income.

OPERATING SEGMENTS	2004	2003	2002
Interest income*			
Agricultural equipment	$ 6	$ 6	$ 7
Commercial and consumer equipment	5	4	5
Construction and forestry	8	8	7
Credit**	992	1,000	948
Corporate	64	59	66
Intercompany**	(241)	(226)	(187)
Total	$834	$851	$846

* Does not include finance rental income for equipment on operating leases.
** Includes interest income from Equipment Operations for financing trade receivables.

Interest expense			
Agricultural equipment*	$127	$133	$ 94
Commercial and consumer equipment*	54	48	46
Construction and forestry*	24	19	18
Credit	423	437	443
Corporate	205	218	223
Intercompany*	(241)	(226)	(187)
Total	$592	$629	$637

* Includes interest compensation to credit operations for financing trade receivables.

Depreciation* and amortization expense			
Agricultural equipment	$225	$213	$232
Commercial and consumer equipment	73	69	81
Construction and forestry	65	60	82
Credit	250	281	322

8116 Part I: Financial Statements

Other	8	8	8
Total	$621	$631	$725

* Includes depreciation for equipment on operating leases.

Equity in income (loss) of unconsolidated affiliates

Agricultural equipment	$2	$(2)	$(10)
Commercial and consumer equipment	(2)	(1)	
Construction and forestry		12	(11)
Credit	1		(4)
Total	$1	$ 9	$(25)

Identifiable operating assets

Agricultural equipment	$ 3,145	$2,778**	$2,948**
Commercial and consumer equipment	1,330	1,295	1,324
Construction and forestry	1,970	1,461	1,423
Credit	15,937	14,714	13,671
Other	368	321**	283**
Corporate	6,004	5,689	4,119
Total	$28,754	$26,258	$23,768

** See previous ** note in the operating profit information.

OPERATING SEGMENTS	2004	2003	2002
Capital additions			
Agricultural equipment	$246	$205	$233
Commercial and consumer equipment	64	71	62
Construction and forestry	37	38	59
Credit	4	4	3
Other	14	2	1
Total	$365	$320	$358
Investment in unconsolidated affiliates			
Agricultural equipment	$ 18	$ 19	$ 22
Commercial and consumer equipment	4	6	6
Construction and forestry	81	167	145
Credit	4	3	7
Other		1	1
Total	$107	$196	$181

The company views and has historically disclosed its operations as consisting of two geographic areas, the U.S. and Canada, and outside the U.S. and Canada, shown below in millions of dollars. Operating income for these areas has been disclosed in addition to the requirements under FASB Statement No. 131. No individual foreign country's net sales and revenues were material for disclosure purposes.

GEOGRAPHIC AREAS	2004	2003	2002
Net sales and revenues			
Unaffiliated customers:			
U.S. and Canada:			
Equipment Operations net sales (91%)*	$12,332	$ 9,249	$ 8,199
Financial Services revenues (88%)*	1,845	1,861	1,950
Total	11,110	10,149	
Outside U.S. and Canada:			
Equipment Operations net sales	5,340	4,100	3,504
Financial Services revenues	214	165	127
Total	5,554	4,265	3,631
Other revenues	255	160	167
Total	$19,986	$15,535	$13,947

* The percentages indicate the approximate proportion of each amount that relates to the U.S. only and are based upon a three-year average for 2004, 2003, and 2002.

	2004	2003	2002
Operating profit			
U.S. and Canada:			
Equipment Operations	$1,284	$ 386	$170
Financial Services	418	469	410
Total	1,702	855	580
Outside U.S. and Canada:			
Equipment Operations	621	322	231
Financial Services	53	35	6
Total	674	357	237
Total	$2,376	$1,212	$817

GEOGRAPHIC AREAS	2004	2003	2002
Property and equipment			
U.S.	$1,328	$1,297	$1,285
Germany	276	241	192
Mexico	200	215	217
Other countries	358	323	304
Total	$2,162	$2,076	$1,998

A.O. Smith
2004 Annual Report

13. Operations by Segment

The company has two reportable segments: Electrical Products and Water Systems. The Electrical Products segment manufactures fractional horsepower alternating current (A/C) and direct current (D/C) and integral horsepower motors used in fans and blowers in furnaces, air conditioners and ventilating systems; industrial applications such as material handling; as well as in other consumer products such as home appliances and pumps, swimming pools, hot tubs and spas. In addition, the Electrical Products segment manufactures hermetic motors which are sold worldwide to manufacturers of compressors used in air conditioning and refrigeration systems. The Water Systems segment manufactures residential gas and electric water heaters as well as commercial water heating equipment used in a wide range of applications including hotels, laundries, car washes, factories and large institutions. In addition, the Water Systems segment manufactures copper tube boilers used in large-volume hot water and hydronic heating applications.

The accounting policies of the reportable segments are the same as those described in the "Summary of Significant Accounting Policies" outlined in Note 1. Intersegment sales have been excluded from segment revenues and are immaterial. Operating earnings, defined by the company as earnings before interest, taxes, general corporate and corporate research and development expenses, is used to measure the performance of the segments and allocate resources.

Years ended December 31 (dollars in millions)	Net Earnings			Net Sales		
	2004	2003	2002	2004	2003	2002
Electrical Products	$51.5	$54.2	$57.6	$ 860.7	$ 824.6	$ 790.4
Water Systems	36.8	57.2	58.4	792.4	706.1	678.7
Total segments— operating earnings	88.3	111.4	116.0	$1,653.1	$1,530.7	$1,469.1
General corporate and research and development expenses	(27.3)	(20.2)	(23.7)			
Interest expense	(13.5)	(12.2)	(13.9)			
Earnings before income taxes	47.5	79.0	78.4			
Provision for income taxes	(12.1)	(26.8)	(27.1)			
Net earnings	$35.4	$52.2	$51.3			

There were no sales to customers exceeding 10% of consolidated net sales in 2004. Net sales of the Electrical Products segment include sales to York International Corporation of $157.3 and $173.3 million in 2003 and 2002, respectively.

Assets, depreciation and capital expenditures by segment

(dollars in millions)	Total Assets (December 31)			Depreciation and Amortization (Years Ended December 31)			Capital Expenditures (Years Ended December 31)		
	2004	2003	2002	2004	2003	2002	2004	2003	2002
Electrical Products	$738.4	$732.1	$697.4	$33.3	$33.7	$33.1	$27.9	$27.3	$27.0
Water Systems	488.5	466.8	434.7	19.8	17.6	16.9	19.9	20.8	18.6
Total segments	1,226.9	1,199	1,132.1	53.1	51.3	50.0	47.8	48.1	45.6
Corporate assets	85.9	81.0	92.8	0.8	0.8	0.7	0.7	0.5	0.7
Total	$1,313	1,280	$1,224.9	$53.9	$52.1	$50.7	$48.5	$48.6	$46.3

Corporate assets consist primarily of cash and cash equivalents, deferred income taxes, and derivative assets.

Net sales and long-lived assets by geographic location

The following data by geographic area includes net sales based on product shipment destination and long-lived assets based on physical location. Long-lived assets include net property, plant and equipment and other long-term assets and exclude prepaid pension, other intangibles and long-lived assets of discontinued operations.

(dollars in millions)	Long-lived Assets				Net Sales		
	2004	2003	2002		2004	2003	2002
United States	$254.5	$267.1	$283.0	United States	$1,384.8	$1,295.9	$1,282.9
Mexico	111.0	110.3	102.7	Foreign	268.3	234.8	186.2
China	36.6	32.5	26.6	Total	$1,653.1	$1,530.7	$1,469.1
Other Foreign	12.5	11.4	9.8				
Total	$414.6	$421.3	$422.1				

Applied Materials
2004 Annual Report

Note 10—Industry Segment and Foreign Operations

Applied operates in one segment for the manufacture, marketing and servicing of integrated circuit fabrication equipment. In accordance with SFAS No. 131 (SFAS 131), "Disclosures About Segments of an Enterprise and Related Information," Applied's chief operating decision-maker has been identified as he President and CEO, who reviews operating results to make decisions about allocating resources and assessing performance for the entries company. All material operating units qualify for aggregation under SFAS 131 due to their identical customer base and similarities in: economic characteristics; nature of products and services; and procurement, manufacturing and distribution processes. Since Applied operates in one segment and in one group of similar products and services all financial segment and product line information required by SFAS 131 can be found in the consolidated financial statements.

For geographical reporting, revenues are attributed to the geographic location in which the customers' facilities are located. Long-lived assets consist primarily of property, plant and equipment, and are attributed to the geographic location in which they are located. Net sales and long-lived assets by geographic region were as follows:

	Net Sales	Long-lived Assets
	(In thousands)	
2002:		
North America (1)	$1,327,886	$1,497,247
Taiwan	1,238,504	41,497
Japan	756,700	107,424
Europe	660,042	119,105
Korea	443,099	21,298
Asia-Pacific (2)	636,081	33,981
	$5,062,312	$1,820,522
2003:		
North America (1)	$1,179,131	$1,341,485
Taiwan	583,439	41,064
Japan	827,193	92,830
Europe	695,085	95,218
Korea	665,502	20,125
Asia-Pacific (2)	526,942	33,494
	$4,477,291	$1,624,816
2004:		
North America (1)	$1,337,050	$1,172,298
Taiwan	2,006,402	21,869
Japan	1,416,639	87,784
Europe	794,026	93,543
Korea	879,333	19,300
Asia-Pacific (2)	1,579,603	30,988
	$8,013,053	$1,425,782

(1) Primarily the United States.
(2) Includes China.

Net sales to Intel Corporation represented 10 percent of Applied's fiscal 2002 net sales. During fiscal 2003, two customers individually accounted for more than 10-percent of net sales: net sales to Intel Corporation represented 13 percent of Applied's net sales; and net sales to Samsung America, Inc. represented 12 percent of Applied's net sales. During fiscal 2004, no individual customer accounted for more than 10 percent of Applied's net sales.

Del Monte Foods
2005 Annual Report

Note 12. Related-Party Transactions

Transactions with Texas Pacific Group. Through affiliated entities, Texas Pacific Group ("TPG"), a private investment group, was a majority stockholder of DMFC common stock prior to the Merger. During the year ended May 2, 2004, these affiliated entities, TPG Partners, L.P. and TPG Parallel I, L.P., exercised their right pursuant to the Stockholder Rights Agreement ("Stockholder Rights Agreement"), dated as of June 12, 2002, to request the filing of a shelf registration of DMFC common stock. Under the terms of the Stockholder Rights Agreement, TPG had the right, subject to certain restrictions, to demand that the Company file up to two registration statements to register the resale of DMFC common stock owned by them. On September 9, 2003, the Company filed a shelf registration statement on Form S-3 in accordance with the TPG request, covering 24,341,385 shares of our common stock held by TPG Partners, L.P. and TPG Parallel I, L.P. On November 21, 2003, the Company filed an amendment to the shelf registration statement on Form S-3, which incorporated our quarterly report on Form 10-Q for the quarter ended July 27, 2003. On November 25, 2003, the shelf registration statement was declared effective by the Securities and Exchange Commission. On January 14, 2004, Del Monte, TPG Partners, L.P., TPG Parallel I, L.P. and Goldman, Sachs & Co. entered into an Underwriting Agreement in connection with the sale by TPG Partners, L.P. and TPG Parallel I, L.P. of 12,000,000 shares of the Company's common stock covered by the shelf registration statement for $10.08 per share. The Company did not receive any proceeds from the sale. On September 10, 2004, Del Monte, TPG Partners, L.P., TPG Parallel I, L.P. and Lehman Brothers Inc. entered into an Underwriting Agreement in connection with the sale by TPG Partners, L.P. and TPG Parallel I, L.P. of the remaining 12,341,385 shares of the Company's common stock covered by the shelf registration statement for $132.1 in aggregate. The Company did not receive any proceeds from the sale. The Company has incurred expenses of approximately $0.3 in connection with performing its obligations under the Stockholder Rights Agreement.

Compensation earned by Mr. William Price as a member of the Board of Directors of DMFC, excluding options, was paid to TPG Partners, L.P. Mr. Price is an officer of TPG. On September 30, 2004, Mr. Price ceased being a member of the Company's Board of Directors. In fiscal 2005 Mr. Price earned $0.02 as well as 1,666 shares of Del Monte Foods Company common stock.

Transactions with Management. In 1998, the Company sold shares of Del Monte Foods Company common stock to certain key employees, including the then executive officers of the Company, under the Del Monte Employee Stock Purchase Plan. The Chief Executive Officer and Chief Operating Officer each paid $0.2 in cash and borrowed an additional equal amount from the Company, under individual secured Promissory Notes, to acquire the stock purchased by each of them under the plan. On November 11, 2003, the Chief Executive Officer and Chief Operating Officer each repaid their loans to the Company in full, including interest thereon in accordance with the terms thereof. Other than the aforementioned loans, there were no outstanding Company loans or advances to any of the Company's directors or executive officers or members of their immediate families, during fiscal 2004 or fiscal 2005.

Note 15. Segment Information

During the second quarter of fiscal 2005, the Company made changes to one of the Company's operating segments due to changes in its management and reporting of certain product groupings. The StarKist Brands operating segment has been divided into two separate operating segments: StarKist Seafood and Private Label Soup. The Company concluded that these two operating segments, together with the Del Monte Brands operating segment, continue to have similar economic characteristics, production processes, customers and distribution methods. Therefore, in accordance with the aggregation criteria of FASB Statement No. 131, *"Disclosures about Segments of an Enterprise and Related Information"* ("SFAS 131") the Company will continue to combine these three operating segments into the Consumer Products reportable segment. Accordingly, this operating segment change did not affect the Company's reportable segments.

The Company has the following reportable segments:

- The Consumer Products reportable segment includes the Del Monte Brands, StarKist Seafood and Private Label Soup operating segments, which manufacture, market and sell shelf-stable products, including fruit, vegetable, tomato, broth, infant feeding, tuna and soup products.

- The Pet Products reportable segment includes the Pet Products operating segment, which manufactures, markets and sells dry and wet pet food and pet snacks.

The Company's chief operating decision-maker, its Chief Executive Officer, reviews financial information presented on a consolidated basis accompanied by disaggregated information on net sales and operating income, by operating segment, for purposes of making decisions and assessing financial performance. The chief operating decision-maker reviews assets of the Company on a consolidated basis only. The accounting policies of the individual operating segments are the same as those of the Company.

The following table presents financial information about the Company's reportable segments:

| | Fiscal Year | | |
	2005	2004	2003
Net Sales:			
Consumer Products	$2,314.0	$2,340.6	$1,333.8
Pet Products	839.9	789.3	758.5
Total company	$3180.9	$3,129.9	758.5
Operating Income:			
Consumer Products	$ 238.4	$ 252.9	$ 111.8
Pet Products	129.7	159.7	147.8
Corporate(a)	(44.2)	(34.1)	(14.5)
Total company	$ 323.9	$ 378.5	$ 245.1

(a) Corporate represents expenses not directly attributable to reportable segments.

As of May 1, 2005, the Company's goodwill was comprised of $213.4 related to the Consumer Products reportable segment and $555.7 related to the Pet Products reportable segment. As of May 2, 2004, the Company's goodwill was comprised of $215.4 related to the Consumer Products reportable segment and $555.5 related to the Pet Products reportable segment. *See Note 10 for accrued termination and severance costs detailed by reportable segment.*

Revenues from foreign countries

The following table presents domestic and foreign and export sales:

| | Fiscal Year | | |
	2005	2004	2003
Net sales—United States	$3,075.3	$3,034.0	$2,040.1
Net sales—foreign and export . .	105.6	95.9	52.2
Total net sales	$3,180.9	$3,129.9	$2,092.3
Percentage of sales:			
United States	96.7%	96.9%	97.5%
Foreign and export	3.3%	3.1%	2.5%

Monsanto
2002 Annual Report

Note 25—Related-Party Transactions

On Sept. 1, 2000, Monsanto entered into a master transition services agreement with Pharmacia, its then majority shareowner. Some terms under this master agreement expired on Dec. 31, 2001. New terms were negotiated in 2002, which do not differ materially from previously agreed terms. Under these agreements, Monsanto provides certain administrative support services to Pharmacia, and Pharmacia primarily provides information technology and human resources support for Monsanto. These agreements continue to be effective after

Pharmacia's Aug. 13, 2002, spinoff of Monsanto. During the period from Jan. 1, 2002, to Aug. 13, 2002, Monsanto recognized expenses of $22 million, and recorded a reimbursement of $27 million, for costs it incurred on behalf of Pharmacia. During 2001, Monsanto recognized expenses of $70 million and recorded a reimbursement of $48 million for costs incurred on behalf of Pharmacia. During the last four months of 2000, Monsanto recognized expenses of $25 million and recorded a reimbursement of $24 million for costs it incurred on behalf of Pharmacia. As of Dec. 31, 2002, the company had a net receivable balance of $2 million with Pharmacia. As of Dec. 31, 2001, the company had a net payable balance (excluding dividends payable) of $43 million with Pharmacia. Transition services, employee benefits, capital project costs, and information technology costs comprised both balances.

From the IPO closing date until November 2002, Pharmacia provided loan and deposit management services to Monsanto's ex-U.S. subsidiaries. Since November 2002, Monsanto has maintained its cash-management strategy by working with third-party banks. Until Aug. 13, 2002, Pharmacia was also the counterparty for some of Monsanto's foreign-currency exchange contracts. Subsequent to Aug. 13, 2002, Monsanto has maintained its foreign-currency exchange strategies by working with third-party banks. As of Dec. 31, 2001, the fair value of the company's outstanding foreign-currency exchange contracts with Pharmacia was a loss of $7 million. In addition, Monsanto pays a fee to Pharmacia because Pharmacia is the named party on a guarantee of debt of a Monsanto subsidiary, which was issued prior to Monsanto's separation from Pharmacia on Sept. 1, 2000. Fees for these services are comparable to those that Monsanto would have incurred with a third party.

On Aug. 13, 2002, Monsanto repaid its outstanding short-term debt to Pharmacia and entered into a new short-term debt arrangement with Pharmacia for $150 million. This new short-term debt was repaid in August with a portion of the proceeds received from Monsanto's issuance of senior notes. As of Dec. 31, 2001, Monsanto was in a net borrowing position of $224 million with Pharmacia. Interest rates were comparable to those that Monsanto would have incurred with a third party.

Monsanto and Pharmacia entered into an agreement whereby Pharmacia paid Monsanto approximately $40 million, as payment for certain expenses incurred by Monsanto relating to the spinoff of Monsanto by Pharmacia effective Aug. 13, 2002. Monsanto expects to use these funds to pay for the separation of the Monsanto and Pharmacia research and development organizations, legal activities required to definitively separate the ownership of certain intellectual property, and other types of activities that arose directly as a result of the spinoff from pharmacia. Remaining funds to be spent as of Dec. 31, 2002, are recorded in short-term accruals and the company expects to fully utilize these funds for their designated purposes by June 2003.

Skyworks Solutions
2002 Annual Report

Note 12—Related Party Transactions

Historically, a significant portion of Conexant's semiconductor product assembly and test function has been performed by the Mexicali Operations. In addition, Conexant has purchased certain semiconductor products from the Newbury Park wafer fabrication facility included in Conexant's wireless business. Revenues and related costs of goods sold for products manufactured in the Newbury Park wafer fabrication facility and assembled and tested by the Mexicali Operations for Conexant have been separately presented in the combined statements of operations.

The Company has entered into various agreements with Conexant providing for the supply of gallium arsenide wafer fabrication and assembly and test services to Conexant, initially at substantially the same volumes as historically obtained by Conexant from Washington/Mexicali. The Company has also entered into agreements with Conexant providing for the supply to the Company of transition services by Conexant and silicon-based wafer fabrication services by Jazz Semiconductor, Inc., the Newport Beach, California foundry joint venture between Conexant and The Carlyle Group to which Conexant contributed its Newport Beach wafer fabrication facility. Historically, Washington/Mexicali has obtained a portion of its silicon-based semiconductors from the Newport Beach wafer fabrication facility. Pursuant to the supply agreement with Conexant, the Company is initially obligated to obtain certain minimum volume levels from Jazz Semiconductor based on a contractual agreement between Conexant and Jazz Semiconductor. The Company estimates that its minimum purchase obligation under this agreement will result in excess costs of approximately $5.1 million and has recorded this liability and charged cost of sales in fiscal 2002.

Under transition services agreements with Conexant entered into in connection with the Merger, Conexant will continue to perform various research and development services for the Company at actual cost generally until December 31, 2002, unless the parties otherwise agree. To the extent the Company uses these services subsequent to the expiration of the specified term, the pricing is subject to negotiation.

Eli Lilly
2002 Annual Report

Note 13: Contingencies

In February 2001, we were notified that Zenith Goldline Pharmaceuticals, Inc. (Zenith), had submitted an abbreviated new drug application (ANDA) seeking permission to market a generic version of Zyprexa in various dosage forms several years prior to the expiration of our U.S. patents for the product. Zenith alleges that our patents are invalid or not infringed. On April 2, 2001, we filed suit against Zenith in federal district court in Indianapolis seeking a ruling that Zenith's challenge to the U.S. compound patent (expiring in 2011) is without merit. In May 2001, we were notified that Dr. Reddy's Laboratories, Ltd. (Reddy), had also filed an ANDA covering two dosage forms, alleging that the patents are invalid or not infringed. On June 26, 2001, we filed a similar patent infringement suit against Reddy in federal district court in Indianapolis. Thereafter, we were notified that Reddy had filed an ANDA for additional dosage forms and in February 2002, we filed an infringement suit in the same court based on Reddy's additional ANDA. We received notice in August 2002 of a similar ANDA filing by Teva Pharmaceuticals, and in September 2002, we filed suit against Teva in the same court. The cases have been consolidated and are in the discovery stage. We currently expect a trial date to be scheduled for the fourth quarter of 2003. We believe that the generic manufacturers' patent claims are without merit and we expect to prevail in this litigation. However, it is not possible to predict or determine the outcome of this litigation and, accordingly, we can provide no assurance that we will prevail. An unfavorable outcome could have a material adverse impact on our consolidated results of operations, liquidity, and financial position.

In October 2002, we were notified that Barr Laboratories, Inc. (Barr), had submitted an ANDA with the U.S. FDA seeking permission to market a generic version of Evista several years prior to the expiration of our U.S. patents covering the product, alleging that the patents are invalid or not infringed. On November 26, 200, we filed suit against Barr in federal district court in Indianapolis seeking a ruling that Barr's challenges to our patents claiming the method of use and pharmaceutical form (expiring from 2012 to 2017) are without merit. While we believe that Barr's claims are without merit and expect to prevail, it is not possible to predict or determine the outcome of the litigation. Therefore we can provide no assurance that we will prevail. An unfavorable outcome could have a material adverse impact on our consolidated results of operations, liquidity, and financial position.

We have been named as a defendant in numerous product liability lawsuits, involving primarily diethylstilbestrol (DES) and thimerosal. We have accrued for our estimated exposure with respect to all current product liability claims. In addition, we have accrued for certain product liability claims incurred, but not filed, to the extent we can formulate a reasonable estimate of their costs. We estimate these expenses based primarily on historical claims experience and data regarding product usage. We expect the cash amounts related to the accruals to be paid out over the next several years. A portion of the costs associated with defending and disposing of these suits is covered by insurance. We estimate insurance recoverables based on existing deductibles, coverage limits, and the existing and projected future level of insolvencies among the insurance carriers.

Under the Comprehensive Environmental Response, Compensation, and Liability Act, commonly known as Superfund, we have been designated as one of several potentially responsible parties with respect to fewer than 10 sites. Under Superfund, each responsible party may be jointly and severally liable for the entire amount of the cleanup. We also continue remediation of certain of our own sites. We have accrued for estimated Superfund cleanup costs, remediation, and certain other environmental matters, taking into account, as applicable, available information regarding site conditions, potential cleanup methods, esti-mated costs, and the extent to which other parties can be expected to contribute to payment of those costs. We have reached a settlement with our primary liability insurance carrier and certain excess carriers providing for coverage for certain environmental liabilities. Litigation seeking coverage from certain other excess carriers is ongoing.

The environmental liabilities and litigation accruals have been reflected in our consolidated balance sheet at the gross amount of approximately $267.4 million at December 31, 2002. Estimated insurance recoverables of approximately $111.7 million at December 31, 2002, have been reflected as assets in the consoli-dated balance sheet.

While it is not possible to predict or determine the outcome of the patent, product liability, or other legal actions brought against us or the ultimate cost of environmental matters, we believe that, except as noted above with respect to the Zyprexa and Evista patent litigation, the costs associated with all such matters will not have a material adverse effect on our consolidated financial position or liquidity but could possibly be material to the consolidated results of our operations in any one accounting period.

Schering-Plough
2002 Annual Report

Legal, Environmental and Regulatory Matters

Background   The Company has responsibilities for environmental cleanup under various state, local and federal laws, including the Comprehensive Envi-ronmental Response, Compensation and Liability Act, commonly known as Superfund. At several Superfund sites (or equivalent sites under state law), the Company is alleged to be a potentially responsible party (PRP). The Company estimates its obligations for cleanup costs for Superfund sites based on informa-tion obtained from the federal Environmental Protection Agency, an equivalent state agency and/or studies prepared by independent engineers, and on the probable costs to be paid by other PRPs. The Company records a liability for environmental assessments and/or cleanup when it is probable a loss has been incurred and the amount can be reasonably estimated.

The Company is also involved in various other claims and legal proceedings of a nature considered normal to its business, including product liability cases. The Company adjusts its accrued liabilities to reflect the current best estimate of its probable loss exposure. Where no best estimate is determinable, the Company accrues the minimum amount within the most probable range of its liability.

The recorded liabilities for the above matters at December 31, 2002, and the related expenses incurred during the year ended December 31, 2002, were not material. Expected insurance recoveries have not been considered in determining the costs for environmental-related liabilities. Management believes that, except for the matters discussed in the remainder of this section, it is remote that any material liability in excess of the amounts accrued will be incurred. With respect to the matters discussed in the remainder of this section, except where noted, it is not practicable to estimate a range of reasonably possible loss; where it has, a reserve has been included in the financial statements. Resolution of any or all of the matters discussed in the remainder of this section, individually or in the aggregate, could have a material adverse effect on the Company's results of operations or financial condition. Management reviews the status of these matters on an ongoing basis and from time to time may settle or otherwise resolve them on such terms and conditions as management believes are in the best interests of the Company. The Company is aware that settlements of matters of the types set forth in the remainder of this section, and in particular under "Investigations," frequently involve fines and/or penalties that are material to the financial condition and the results of operations of the entity entering into the settlement. There are no assurances that the Company will prevail in any of these matters, that settlements can be reached on acceptable terms or in amounts that do not exceed the amounts reserved, and outcomes cannot be predicted.

Environmental   Residents in the vicinity of a publicly owned waste-water treatment plant in Barceloneta, Puerto Rico, have filed two lawsuits against the plant owner and operator, and numerous companies that discharge into the plant, including a subsidiary of the Company, for damages and injunctive relief relating to odors allegedly coming from the plant and connecting sewers. One of these lawsuits is a class action claiming damages of $600. Discovery is ongoing in both lawsuits.

Patent Matters   In February 1998, Geneva Pharmaceuticals, Inc. (Geneva) submitted an Abbreviated New Drug Application (ANDA) to the U.S. FDA seeking to market generic CLARITIN tablets before the expiration in 2004 of the Company's desloratadine compound patent, which the Company believes protects CLARITIN. Geneva alleged that the desloratadine compound patent is invalid. This patent is material to the Company's business. In March 1998, the Company filed suit in federal court seeking a ruling that Geneva's ANDA submission constitutes infringement of the Company's desloratadine compound patent and that its challenge to this patent is without merit. In addition to Geneva, from 1998 through 2002, the following companies made similar ANDA submissions for generic CLARITIN tablets: Zenith Goldline Pharmaceuticals, Mylan Pharmaceuticals Inc., Teva Pharmaceuticals USA, Inc. (Teva), Ranbaxy Pharmaceuticals, Inc., Genpharm Incorporated, and L. Perrigo Company (Perrigo). The following companies made similar ANDA submissions for generic CLARITIN syrup: Teva, Copley Pharmaceuticals, Inc., Novex Pharma, Alpharma USPD Inc., Taro Pharmaceuticals USA, Inc., Morton Grove Pharmaceuticals, Inc., and Perrigo. Andrx Pharmaceuticals, L.L.C. (Andrx) and Impax Laboratories Inc. (Impax) made similar ANDA submission for a generic CLARITIN-D 12 Hour and CLARITIN-D 24 Hour formulations. ESI Lederle, Inc. (Lederle), a subsidiary of Wyeth, made a similar ANDA submission for a generic CLARITIN REDITAB formulation. The following companies submitted "paper" New Drug Applications ("paper" NDAs) under Section 505 (b) (2) of the Federal Food, Drug and Cosmetic Act seeking to market a generic OTC form of CLARITIN prior to the expiration of the Company's desloratadine compound patent: White-hall-Robins Healthcare, a division of Wyeth (for an OTC REDITAB formulation), McNeil Consumer Healthcare (McNeil) (for OTC tablets), and Perrigo (for OTC tablets).

In each case, the Company filed suit in federal court seeking a ruling that the applicable ANDA or "paper" NDA submission and proposed marketing of a generic prescription or OTC product constitutes infringement of the Company's desloratadine compound patent, and that the challenge to the patent is without merit. On August 8, 2002, a federal district court in New Jersey ruled on motions for summary judgment, finding that certain claims of the desloratadine compound patent were anticipated by a prior patent and, thus, were not valid. On September 18, 2002, the district court denied a request for reconsideration. The Company has appealed the rulings. The appeal is scheduled to be argued on April 8, 2003. The Company anticipates that the appeal will be decided in the second half of 2003 or early 2004. With these rulings, actions against the defendants for infringement of the desloratadine compound patent will not proceed unless the Company's appeal is successful. The Company has also asserted that Impax's and Andrx's ANDAs for their generic CLARITIN-D 24 Hour formulations infringe the Company's patent covering its CLARITIN-D 24 Hour formulation. This issue has not yet been resolved by the district court.

In August 2001, Geneva Pharmaceuticals Technology Corp. (Geneva Pharmaceuticals) and Three Rivers Pharmaceuticals, L.L.C. (Three Rivers), and in January 2002, Teva, submitted separate ANDAs with the FDA seeking to market generic forms of 200 mg REBETOL (ribavirin) Capsules in the United States before the expiration of the Company's patents covering ribavirin formulations. Geneva Pharmaceuticals, Three Rivers and Teva have asserted that they do not infringe the Company's REBETOL patents and/or the patents are invalid. The REBETOL patents are material to the Company's business. In September 2001, October 2001 and March 2002, the Company filed suits in federal court seeking rulings that the ANDA submissions by Geneva Pharmaceuticals, Three Rivers and Teva, respectively, constitute infringement of the Company's patents and that the challenges to the Company's patents are without merit. In February 2003, the Company entered into a licensing agreement with Three Rivers that will settle all patent litigation between the Company and Three Rivers. Under the terms of the agreement, the Company will grant Three Rivers a non-exclusive, non-sublicensable license to the Company's U.S. ribavirin patents. Three Rivers will pay the Company a royalty on its ribavirin sales. The agreement does not affect Three Rivers' reported patent litigation with Ribapharm, Inc. The agreement is subject to the dismissal of the relevant lawsuits in court. The patent litigation with Geneva and Teva has been temporarily stayed while the parties seek to reach a settlement.

In January 2000, a jury found that the Company's PRIME PAC PRRS (Porcine Respiratory and Reproductive Syndrome) vaccine infringed a patent owned by Boehringer Ingelheim Vetmedica, Inc. An injunction was issued in August 2000 barring further sales of the Company's vaccine. The Company's post-trial motions for either a reversal of the jury's verdict or a new trial were denied in September 2001. The Company appealed, and the verdict was affirmed by the appellate court in February 2003. Discovery in the damages phase of the case is ongoing.

Investigations   In October 1999, the Company received a subpoena from the U.S. Attorney's Office for the Eastern District of Pennsylvania, pursuant to the Health Insurance Portability and Accountability Act of 1996, concerning the Company's contracts with pharmacy benefit managers (PBMs) and managed care organizations to provide disease management services in connection with the marketing of its pharmaceutical products. It appears that the subpoena was one of a number addressed to industry participants as part of an inquiry into, among other things, pharmaceutical marketing practices. The government's inquiry has focused on, among other things, whether the Company's disease management and other marketing programs and arrangements comply with federal health care laws and whether the value of its disease management programs and other marketing programs and arrangements should have been included in the calculation of rebates to the government. The Company has been cooperating with the investigation. In March 2002, the U.S. Attorney's Office began issuing grand jury subpoenas. The grand jury investigation appears to be focused on one or more transactions with managed care organizations where the government believes the Company offered or provided deeply discounted pharmaceutical products (known as "nominally priced" products, which are generally excluded from Medicaid rebate calculations), free or discounted disease management services, and other marketing programs and arrangements that delivered value, in order to place or retain one or more of the Company's major pharmaceutical products on the managed care organization's formulary. The grand jury appears to be investigating, among other things, (i) whether the transactions described above and conduct relating thereto violated federal anti-kickback statutes; and (ii) whether the value of the items and services described above should have been included in the Company's calculation of Medicaid rebates. The outcome of the investigations could include the commencement of civil and/or criminal proceedings involving substantial fines, penalties and injunctive or administrative remedies, including exclusion from government reimbursement programs, and the Company cannot predict whether the investigations will affect its marketing practices or sales. In February 2003, the Company increased its litigation reserves related to this investigation and the investigations described below by the U.S. Attorney's Office for the District of Massachusetts, by $150. The increased litigation reserves reflect an adjustment to the Company's estimate of its minimum liability relating to those investigations, in compliance with generally accepted accounting principles (GAAP). Under GAAP, companies are required to estimate and recognize a minimum liability when a loss is probable but no better estimate of the loss can be made. Also, under GAAP, the Company is required to recognize this liability in 2002. The Company notes that its total reserves reflect an estimate and that any final settlement or adjudication of any of these matters could possibly be less than or could materially exceed the aggregate liability accrued by the Company and could have a materially adverse effect on the operations or financial condition of the Company. This adjustment is consistent with the Company's policy of reviewing regularly the status of pending actions and investigations and making adjustments as appropriate.

The Company is responding to investigations by the Department of Health and Human Services, the Department of Justice and certain states into certain industry and Company practices regarding average wholesale price (AWP). These investigations include a Department of Justice review of the merits of a federal action filed by a private entity on behalf of the United States in the U.S. District Court for the Southern District of Florida, as well as an investigation by the U.S. Attorney's Office for the District of Massachusetts, regarding, inter alia, whether the AWP set by pharmaceutical companies for certain drugs improperly exceeds the average prices paid by dispensers and, as a consequence, results in unlawful inflation of certain government drug reimbursements that are based on AWP. In March 2001, the Company received a subpoena from the Massachusetts Attorney General's office seeking documents concerning the use of AWP and other pricing and/or marketing practices. The Company is cooperating with these investigations. The outcome of these investigations could include the imposition of substantial fines, penalties and injunctive or administrative remedies.

The U.S. Attorney's Office for the District of Massachusetts is also investigating whether the Company's sales of a product that was repackaged for sale by a managed care organization should have been included in the Company's Medicaid best price calculations. In early November 2002, the Company was served with two additional grand jury subpoenas by the U.S. Attorney for the District of Massachusetts. Among other information, the subpoenas seek a broad range of information concerning the Company's sales, marketing and clinical trial practices and programs with respect to INTRON A, REBETRON and TEMODAR; the Company's sales and marketing contacts with managed care organizations and doctors; and the Company's offering or provision of grants, honorariums or other items or services of value to managed care organizations, physician groups, doctors and educational institutions. The Company understands that this investigation is focused on whether certain sales, marketing and clinical trial practices and conduct related thereto, which in certain instances relate to the use of one or more of the above-mentioned products for indications for which FDA approval had not been obtained-so-called "off-label" uses—were in violation of federal laws and regulations with respect to off-label promotional activities. The investigation also appears to focus on whether drug samples, clinical trial grants and other items or services of value were given to providers to incentivize them to prescribe one or more of the above-mentioned products, including for "off-label" uses, in violation of the federal health care antikickback laws. The Company has implemented certain changes to its sales, marketing and clinical trial practices and is continuing to review those practices to ensure compliance with relevant laws and regulations. The Company is cooperating with these investigations. Future sales of INTRON A, REBETRON and TEMODAR may be adversely affected, but the Company cannot at this time predict the ultimate impact, if any, on such sales. The outcome of these investigations could include the commencement of civil and/or criminal proceedings involving the imposition of substantial fines, penalties and injunctive or administrative remedies, including exclusion from government reimbursement programs. In February 2003, the Company increased its litigation reserves related to the investigations by the U.S. Attorney's Office for the District of Massachusetts described in this paragraph and the paragraph immediately preceding it and the investigation described above by the U.S. Attorney's Office for the Eastern District of Pennsylvania, by $150. The increased litigation reserves reflect an adjustment to the Company's estimate of its minimum liability relating to those investigations, in compliance with GAAP. Under GAAP, companies are required to estimate and recognize a minimum liability when a loss is probable but no better estimate of the loss can be made. Also, under GAAP, the Company is required to recognize this liability in 2002. The Company notes that its total reserves reflect an estimate and that any final settlement or adjudication of any of these matters could possibly be less than or could materially exceed the aggregate liability accrued by the Company and could have a materially adverse effect on the operations or financial condition of the Company. This adjustment is consistent with the Company's policy of reviewing regularly the status of pending actions and investigations and making adjustments as appropriate.

The U.S. Attorney's Office in New Jersey along with the FDA's Office of Criminal Investigation is conducting an investigation which may focus on one or more Company products, including ribavirin, manufactured in Puerto Rico. The Company is cooperating with the government in the investigation.

The U.S. Department of Justice, Antitrust Division is investigating whether the Company's Consumer Products Division entered into an agreement with another company to lower the commission rate of a consumer products broker. In February 2003, the Antitrust Division served a grand jury subpoena on the Company seeking documents for the first time. The Company is cooperating with the investigation.

Securities and Class Action Litigation   On February 15, 2001, the Company stated in a press release that the FDA had been conducting inspections of the Company's manufacturing facilities in New Jersey and Puerto Rico and had issued reports citing deficiencies concerning compliance with current Good Manufacturing Practices, primarily relating to production processes, controls and procedures. The next day, February 16, 2001, a lawsuit was filed in the U.S. District Court for the District of New Jersey against the Company and certain named officers alleging violations of Sections 10(b) and 20(a) of the Securities Exchange Act of 1934 and Rule 10b-5 promulgated thereunder. Additional lawsuits of the same tenor followed. The plaintiffs in the suits purport to represent classes of shareholders who purchased shares of Company stock between dates as early as March 2, 2000, and February 15, 2001, the date of the press release. In April 2001, a lawsuit was filed in the U.S. District Court for the District of New Jersey against the Company and certain named officers alleging substantially the same violations of the Securities Exchange Act of 1934 as alleged in the putative class actions described above in this paragraph, as well as alleging violations of Section 11 of the Securities Act of 1933 and failure to disclose information which is the subject matter of the Federal Trade Commission (FTC) administrative proceeding described below and purporting to represent a class of shareholders who purchased shares of Company stock between July 25, 2000, and March 30, 2001, the last business day before the Company issued a press release relating to the FTC administrative proceeding. This complaint and all of the previously filed complaints were consolidated into one action in the U.S. District Court for the District of New Jersey, and a lead plaintiff, the Florida State Board of Administration, was appointed by the court on July 2, 2001. On October 11, 2001, a consolidated amended complaint was filed, alleging the same violations described in the second sentence of this paragraph (but not a Section 11 claim) and purporting to represent a class of shareholders who purchased shares of Company stock from May 9, 2000, through February 15, 2001. The Company's motion to dismiss the consolidated amended complaint was denied on May 24, 2002. Discovery is ongoing.

In addition to the lawsuits described in the immediately preceding paragraph, two lawsuits were filed in the U.S. District Court for the District of New Jersey, and two lawsuits were filed in New Jersey state court against the Company (as a nominal defendant) and certain officers, directors and a former director seeking damages on behalf of the Company, including disgorgement of trading profits made by defendants allegedly obtained on the basis of material non-public information. The complaints in each of those four lawsuits relate to the issues described in the Company's February 15, 2001, press release, and allege a failure to disclose material information and breach of fiduciary duty by the directors. One of the federal court lawsuits also includes allegations related to the investigations by the U.S. Attorney's Offices for the Eastern District of Pennsylvania and the District of Massachusetts, the FTC's administrative proceeding against the Company, and the lawsuit by the state of Texas against Warrick Pharmaceuticals (Warrick), the Company's generics subsidiary, all of which are described herein. Each of these lawsuits is a shareholder derivative action that purports to assert claims on behalf of the Company, but as to which no demand was made on the Board of Directors and no decision has been made on whether the Company can or should pursue such claims. In August 2001, the plaintiffs in each of the New Jersey state court shareholder derivative actions moved to dismiss voluntarily the complaints in those actions, which motions were granted. The two shareholder derivative actions pending in the U.S. District Court for the District of New Jersey have been consolidated into one action, which is in its very early stages. This consolidated action is being coordinated for most pre-trial purposes with the consolidated action described in the immediately preceding paragraph. On January 2, 2002, the Company received a demand letter dated December 26, 2001, from a law firm not involved in the derivative actions described above, on behalf of a shareholder who also is not involved in the derivative actions, demanding that the Board of Directors bring claims on behalf of the Company based on allegations substantially similar to those alleged in the derivative actions. On January 22, 2002, the Board of Directors adopted a Board resolution establishing an Evaluation Committee, consisting of three directors, to investigate, review and analyze the facts and circumstances surrounding the allegations made in the demand letter and the consolidated amended derivative action complaint described above, but reserving to the full Board authority and discretion to exercise its business judgment in respect of the proper disposition of the demand. The Committee engaged independent outside counsel to advise it and issued a report on the findings of its investigation to the independent directors of the Board in late October 2002. That report determined that the shareholder demand should be refused, and finding no liability on the part of any officers or directors. In November 2002, the full Board adopted the recommendation of the Evaluation Committee.

On August 9, 2001, the Prescription Access Litigation (PAL) project, a Bostonbased group formed in 2001 to litigate against drug companies, issued a press release stating that PAL members filed a lawsuit in New Jersey state court against the Company. In December 2001, the Company was served with an amended complaint in the case. The suit, which PAL purports to be a class action, alleges, among other things, that the Company's direct-to-consumer advertising falsely depicts the benefits of CLARITIN in violation of the New Jersey Consumer Fraud Act. In February 2002, the Company filed a motion to dismiss this case. In May 2002, the court dismissed the complaint in its entirety for failure to state a claim. The plaintiffs have appealed.

In December 2001, PAL filed a class action suit in federal court in Massachusetts against the Company. In September 2002, a consolidated complaint was filed in this court as a result of the coordination by the Multi-District Litigation Panel of all federal court AWP cases from throughout the country. The consolidated complaint alleges that the Company and Warrick conspired with providers to defraud consumers by reporting fraudulently high AWPs for prescription medications reimbursed by Medicare or third-party payers. The complaint seeks a declaratory judgment and unspecified damages, including treble damages.

The Company is a defendant in a number of purported nationwide or state class action lawsuits in which plaintiffs seek a refund of the purchase price of laxatives or phenylpropanolamine-containing cough/cold remedies they purchased. Other pharmaceutical manufacturers are co-defendants in some of these lawsuits. In general, plaintiffs claim that they would not have purchased or would have paid less for these products had they known of certain defects or medical risks attendant with their use. All of these lawsuits are in the early stages of discovery; plaintiffs' theories for recovery have yet to be legally tested, and the courts have not yet agreed that these cases should go forward as class actions. A number of lawsuits involving these products, as well as recalled albuterol/VANCERIL/VANCENASE inhalers, have also been filed against the Company seeking recovery for personal injuries or death. In several of these lawsuits punitive damages are claimed. The Company settled a California state court class action seeking refund of the purchase price of inhalers through a program of issuing 4.5 million vouchers for free inhalers plus payment of attorneys' fees. The court gave final approval to the settlement in October 2002.

Royalties/Contract Matters   The Company was a party to arbitration proceedings by Biogen, Inc. relating to, among other things, royalty payments. These arbitrations have been settled.

In October 2001, ICN Pharmaceuticals, Inc. notified the Company of its intention to begin an alternative resolution dispute proceeding against the Company seeking the payment of royalties on REBETOL provided by the Company without charge or at a reduced charge to indigent patients participating in SCHERING'S COMMITMENT TO CARE program.

Antitrust and FTC Matters   The Company is a defendant in numerous antitrust actions commenced (starting in 1993) in state and federal courts by independent retail pharmacies, chain retail pharmacies and consumers. The plaintiffs allege price discrimination and/or conspiracy between the Company and other defendants to restrain trade by jointly refusing to sell prescription drugs at discounted prices to the plaintiffs. The Company, in February 1996, agreed to settle a federal class action on behalf of approximately two-thirds of all retail pharmacies in the United States for a total of $22, which has been paid in full. The U.S. District Court in Illinois approved the settlement of the federal class action in 1996. In 1997, the Seventh Circuit Court of Appeals dismissed all appeals from that settlement, and it is not subject to further review.

In April 1997, certain of the plaintiffs in the federal class action commenced another purported class action in the U.S. District Court in Illinois against the Company and the other defendants who settled the previous federal class action. The complaint alleges that the defendants conspired not to implement the settlement commitments following the settlement discussed above. The District Court has denied the plaintiffs' motion for a preliminary injunction hearing.

The Company has either settled or had dismissed on motion all the state court retailer and consumer actions. The settlement amounts were not material to the Company.

The Federal Court in Illinois remanded the conspiracy portion of the cases of those retailers that opted out of the class action back to the district courts where they were filed. The Federal Court in Illinois has jurisdiction over the Robinson-Patman portion of these cases.

Plaintiffs in these antitrust actions generally seek treble damages in an unspecified amount and an injunction against the allegedly unlawful conduct.

On April 2, 2001, the FTC started an administrative proceeding against the Company, Upsher-Smith, Inc. (Upsher-Smith) and Lederle. The complaint alleges anti-competitive effects from the settlement of patent lawsuits between the Company and Lederle, and the Company and Upsher-Smith. The lawsuits that were settled related to generic versions of K-DUR, the Company's long-acting potassium chloride product, which was the subject of ANDAs filed by Lederle and Upsher-Smith. In June 2002, the administrative law judge overseeing the case issued a decision that the patent litigation settlements complied with the law in all respects and dismissed all claims against the Company. An appeal of this decision to the full Commission filed by the FTC staff is currently pending. The outcome of the proceeding could result in the imposition of injunctive or administrative remedies.

Following the commencement of the FTC administrative proceeding, alleged class action suits were filed on behalf of direct and indirect purchasers of K-DUR against the Company, Upsher-Smith and Lederle in federal and state courts. These suits all allege essentially the same facts and claim violations of federal and state antitrust laws, as well as other state statutory and/or common law causes of action.

Pricing Matters   During the third quarter of 2000, Warrick was sued by the state of Texas. In June 2002, the Company and its subsidiary, Schering Corporation, were added as defendants. The lawsuit alleges that Warrick supplied the state with false reports of wholesale prices, which caused the state to pay Medicaid claims on prescriptions of Warrick's albuterol sulfate solution and inhaler at a higher-than-justified level. The state seeks damages of approximately $106 against Warrick, including treble damages and penalties. The outcome of the litigation could result in the imposition of fines, penalties and injunctive remedies.

The Company and Warrick are defendants in numerous lawsuits brought in state and federal courts, which allege that the Company and Warrick reported inflated AWPs for prescription pharmaceuticals and thereby caused third-party payers to make excess reimbursements to providers. Some of these actions also allege that the Company and Warrick failed to report accurate prices under the Medicaid Rebate Program and thereby underpaid rebates to some states. These actions, which began in October 2001, have been brought by state Attorneys General, private plaintiffs, nonprofit organizations and employee benefit funds. They allege violations of federal and state law, including fraud, antitrust, Racketeer Influenced Corrupt Organizations Act (RICO) and other claims. The actions seek unspecified damages, including treble and punitive damages.

SEC Inquiry and Related Litigation   The Company is providing information to the SEC in connection with the Commission's inquiry relating to the Company's meetings with investors and other communications. The Company believes that it has complied with all applicable securities laws in this matter.

The Company has been served with several purported federal class action lawsuits alleging violations of Sections 10(b) and 20(a) of the Securities Exchange Act of 1934, as well as SEC Regulation Fair Disclosure (FD) relating to the alleged disclosures made during meetings with investors referred to in the preceding paragraph.

Tax Matters   In October 2001, IRS auditors have asserted, in reports, that the Company is liable for additional tax for the 1990 through 1992 tax years. The reports allege that two interest rate swaps that the Company entered into with an unrelated party should be recharacterized as loans from affiliated companies, resulting in additional tax on income. The tax sought by the IRS auditors relating to recharacterization is approximately $195, plus interest. The Company has not accrued the $195 because the Company and its tax advisers do not believe it is probable that the IRS will prevail in this matter.

Coca Cola
2002 Annual Report

Note 19: Subsequent Events

During the first quarter of 2003, the Company initiated steps to streamline and simplify its operations, primarily in North America and Germany.

In North America, the Company is integrating the operations of our three separate North American business units—Coca-Cola North America (including our interest in CCDA), The Minute Maid Company (including our Odwalla business) and Fountain. The integration is expected to result in a headcount reduction of approximately 1,000 people, with the identification of the individuals expected to be completed by the end of the first quarter of 2003.

In Germany, CCEAG has taken steps to improve efficiency in sales and distribution, including the closure of three bottling plants in 2003. The streamlining initiative is expected to affect approximately 900 employees in Germany.

IBM
2002 Annual Report

Y Subsequent Events

On January 21, 2003, the company filed with the Securities and Exchange Commission a shelf registration to periodically sell up to $20 billion in debt securities, preferred and capital stock, depositary shares and warrants. The company may sell securities in one or more separate offerings with the size, price and terms to be determined at the time of sale. The net proceeds from the sale of the securities will be used for general corporate purposes, which may include debt repayment, investments in or extensions of credit to its subsidiaries, redemption of any preferred stock the company may issue, or financing of possible acquisitions or business expansion. The net proceeds may be invested temporarily or applied to repay shortterm debt until they are used for their stated purpose.

Consistent with the company's strategy to concentrate borrowing at the IBM level, this shelf registration eliminates the need for a shelf registration associated with its U.S. financing subsidiary, IBM Credit Corporation (ICC). The ICC shelf will be terminated shortly after the effective date of the new IBM shelf.

On February 21, 2003, the company purchased the outstanding stock of Rational Software Corp. (Rational) for approximately $2.1 billion in cash. Rational provides open, industry standard tools, best practices and services for developing business applications and building software products and systems. The Rational acquisition provides the company with the ability to offer a complete software development environment for customers. The company intends to merge Rational's business operations and employees into the IBM Software Group as a new division and brand. The results of operations of Rational will be included in the company's Consolidated Financial Statements as of February 21, 2003. The company has not completed the allocation of the purchase price related to the Rational acquisition as it is in the process of identifying and determining the fair value of all assets acquired and liabilities assumed.

Textron
2002 Annual Report

Note 16—Joint Ventures

In the normal course of business, Textron has entered into various joint venture agreements. At December 28, 2002 and December 29, 2001, other assets includes

$35 million and $37 million, respectively, attributable to investments in unconsolidated joint ventures. Textron accounts for its interest in these ventures under the equity method of accounting. Since Textron's equity in income (loss) from joint ventures is not material, this amount is reported in cost of sales rather than as a separate line item. Textron's loss from unconsolidated joint ventures totaled $10 million each year for 2002 and 2001, and $2 million in 2000.

Textron has entered into an agreement with Agusta to share certain costs and profits for the joint design, development, manufacture, marketing, sale, customer training and product support of Bell Agusta Aerospace's BA609 and AB139. These programs are currently in the development stage, and only certain marketing costs are being charged to the venture. Bell Helicopter's share of the development costs are being charged to earnings as a period expense. Bell Helicopter has also partnered with The Boeing Company in the development and production of the V-22 tiltrotor aircraft.

Textron has also entered into a joint venture with TAG Aviation USA, Inc. to sell fractional share interests in small business jets. During 2002, 2001 and 2000, Textron recorded revenue of $101 million, $38 million and $26 million, respectively, for the sale of aircraft to this venture through arm's length transactions. Profit on these sales is initially deferred then recognized on a pro-rata basis as fractional share interests are sold to third parties. Textron has guaranteed one-half of the venture's debt and lease obligations up to a maximum of $70 million. At December 28, 2002, Textron's portion of the outstanding debt and operating lease commitments covered by this guarantee totaled $30 million. Textron would be required to make payments under these guarantees if the joint venture defaults under the related debt agreements.

Part II
MAJOR ACCOUNTING AREAS AND REPORTING

Chapter 9
Accounting Changes and Error Corrections

CONTENTS

This chapter covers the accounting, reporting, and disclosures associated with changes in accounting principles (method), estimates, and reporting entities as stipulated in ASC 250-10-05, *Accounting Changes and Error Corrections: Overall*. If an accounting change is immaterial in the current year but is expected to be significant in future years, it should be completely disclosed in the year of change. This chapter also discusses how to present and disclose corrections of errors made in a prior year.

CHANGE IN ACCOUNTING PRINCIPLE (METHOD)

There is an underlying presumption that an accounting principle, once adopted, should not be changed for similar events and transactions. A change in principle may be caused by new events, changing conditions, or additional information or experience.

As per ASC 250-10-55-1, *Accounting Changes and Error Corrections: Overall*, a change in the composition of the cost factors in valuing inventory represents an accounting change in principle and must be footnoted as to why it is preferred.

ASC 250-10-05-1 through 05-3 requires retrospective application (i.e., the application of a different accounting method to previous years as if that new method had always been used) to prior years' financial statements of changes in accounting principle, unless it is impractical to ascertain either the period-specific impact or the cumulative effect of the change. If it is impractical to do so, the newly adopted accounting principle must be applied to the beginning balances of assets or liabilities of the earliest period for practical retrospective application. Further, a corresponding adjustment must be made to the beginning balance of retained earnings (or other appropriate equity components or net assets) for that period (it is not to be reported in the income statement). If the cumulative dollar effect of applying an accounting principle change to prior periods is impractical, the new accounting principle must be applied as if it were adopted prospectively from the earliest practical date.

It is considered impractical to apply the impact of a change in method retrospectively only if any of the following three conditions is present:

1. Retrospective application requires presumptions of management's intent in a previous year that cannot be verified.

2. After making a good faith effort, the company is not able to apply the pronouncement's requirement.

3. It is impossible to objectively estimate amounts needed that (a) would have been available in the prior year and (b) provide proof of circumstances that existed on the date or dates at which the amounts would be recognized, measured, or disclosed under retrospective application.

Reminder: If any of these three conditions exists, it is impracticable to apply the retrospective approach. In this case, the new accounting principle is applied prospectively as of the earliest date it is practical to do so.

An example of an impractical condition is the change to the LIFO method. In this case, the base-year inventory for all subsequent LIFO computations is the beginning inventory in the year the method is adopted. It is impractical to restate previous years' income. A restatement to LIFO involves assumptions as to the different years the layers occurred, and these assumptions would typically result in the calculation of a number of different earnings figures. The only adjustment required may be to restate the opening inventory to a cost basis from a lower-of-cost-or-market-value approach.

Disclosure is thus limited to showing the impact of the change on the results of operations in the year of change.

ASC 250-10-05 mandates retrospective application to a change in accounting method be restricted to the *direct* effects of the change (net of tax). An example of a change in principle is switching from the average cost inventory method to the FIFO method. *Indirect* effects of a change in method are recognized in the year of change. Examples are altering profit-sharing or royalty payments arising from an accounting change.

A change in depreciation, depletion, or amortization must be accounted for as a change in estimate effected by a change in principle.

The Retained Earnings Statement after a retroactive change for a change in accounting principle follows:

Retained earnings—1/1, as previously reported

Add: adjustment for the cumulative effect on previous years of applying retrospectively the new accounting method for long-term construction contracts

Retained earnings—1/1, as adjusted

An example of the retrospective accounting change approach when prior years are presented appears below.

EXAMPLE

XYZ Construction Company has in previous years used the completed contract method for construction contracts. In 20X6, the company switched to the percentage-of-completion method. The tax rate is 30%. The following information is provided:

Before-Tax Income from

Year	Percentage of Completion	Completed Contract
Before 20X6	$300,000	$200,000
In 20X6	90,000	80,000
Total at beginning of 20X6	$390,000	$280,000
Total in 20X6	100,000	95,000

The basis for the journal entry to record the change in 20X6 is:

	Difference	Tax (30%)	Net of Tax
Before 20X6	$100,000	$30,000	$70,000
In 20X6	10,000	3,000	7,000
Total at beginning of 20X6	$110,000	$33,000	$77,000
Total in 20X6	5,000	1,500	3,500

The journal entry to record the change in 20X6 is:

Construction in progress	110,000	
Deferred tax liability		33,000
Retained earnings		77,000

EXAMPLE

In 20X5, D Corporation decided to change from the FIFO method of inventory valuation to the weighted-average method. Inventory balances under each of the methods were as follows:

	FIFO	Weighted Average
January 1, 20X5	$171,000	$177,000
December 31, 20X5	179,000	183,000

D's income tax rate is 40%.

In its 20X5 financial statements, what amount should D report as the cumulative effect of this accounting change?

The required computation is as follows:

Weighted-average method as of January 1, 20X5, the year in which the change is adopted	$177,000
Less: FIFO method	171,000
Cumulative effect of the change before taxes	6,000
Cumulative effect, net of taxes:	
$6,000 \times (1 - 40\%)$	$ 3,600

Footnote disclosure should be made if an accounting change in principle is considered immaterial in the current year but is expected to be material in a later year.

The following is *not* considered a change in principle:

☐ A principle adopted for the first time on new (e.g., different depreciation method for a new fixed asset) or previously insignificant events or transactions. (**Note:** A change in principle occurs when a new principle is used for a pre-existing asset.)

☐ A principle adopted or changed because of significantly different occurrences or transactions. However, footnote disclosure should be made of the change in policy.

Changes in classification are not a change in principle but should be disclosed.

Footnote disclosure should be made of the nature and justification for a change in principle, including the reason why the new principle is preferred. Justifiable reasons for a change in principle include the issuance of a new authoritative pronouncement (e.g., FASB statement), a change in tax law, a new AICPA recommended policy (e.g., AICPA statement of position), a change in circumstances of the company, and a change in principle that better conforms to industry practice. However, note that a change in principle solely for income tax purposes is not a change in principle for financial reporting purposes.

Other footnote disclosures for a change in accounting principle follow:

☐ The new method used.

☐ Description of prior-year data that were retrospectively adjusted.

☐ The effect of the change on income from continuing operations, net income, and any other affected financial statement line item.

☐ Per-share amounts for the current year and for the previous years retrospectively adjusted.

☐ The cumulative effect of the change on retained earnings as of the beginning of the earliest period presented.

☐ When it is impractical to derive retrospective application to prior years, the reasons it is such and a description of the alternative method used to report the change.

☐ In the case of indirect effects of a change in accounting principle, a description of such indirect effects, including the amounts that have been recognized in the current year and the related per-share amounts. Disclosure should also be made of the amount of the total recognized indirect effects and the related per-share amounts for each prior year presented.

A change in accounting principle should be recognized by a retroactive adjustment of previous year's financial statements recast with the newly adopted principle. Any cumulative effect of the change for years prior to those presented is recorded as an adjustment to beginning retained earnings of the earliest year presented. Therefore, under the required retrospective approach, the previous years' income numbers are restated under the newly adopted principle in the current year. As a result, comparability exists over the years.

CHANGE IN ACCOUNTING ESTIMATE

A change in estimate arises from new events or occurs from additional information or experience. A change in estimate is accounted for only over current and future years. Prior years are not adjusted. Examples of a change in estimate are changing the life or salvage value of a fixed asset, the life of an intangible, and the estimated percent of bad debts or warranties.

Footnote disclosure should be made of the nature and reasons for the change unless it involves changes in the ordinary course of business (e.g., modifying a bad debt percentage). The impact of the change in estimate on net income and per share earnings should be disclosed if the change will affect future-year results.

When a change in estimate is coupled with a change in principle and the effects cannot be distinguished, the change should be accounted for as a change in estimate. An example is a change from deferring and amortizing cost to expensing it as incurred because of doubtful future benefit.

A permanent loss on an asset is not a change in accounting estimate but rather a current-period loss.

EXAMPLE: In 20X3, ABC Company changed its bad debt estimate based on an aging of accounts receivable, resulting in recording bad debts of $60,000, which is $3,000 less than if a revised estimate was not made. The journal entry is:

Bad debts	60,000	
Allowance for bad debts		60,000

The related footnote would state that ABC Company modified its estimate of uncollectible accounts to reflect better the net realizable value of accounts receivable. The impact of the change in estimate was to increase 20X3 net income by $3,000.

EXAMPLE

On January 1, 19X9, a fixed asset was purchased costing $50,000 and having an estimated life of 20 years with a salvage value of $2,000. On January 1, 20X2, the estimated life was revised to 14 remaining years with a new salvage value of $2,200. Assuming that the straight-line depreciation method is used, the journal entry on December 31, 20X2, for depreciation expense follows:

Depreciation expense	2,900	
Accumulated depreciation		2,900
Computation:		
Book value on 1/1/20X2:		
Initial cost		$50,000
Less: accumulated depreciation		
($50,000 − $2,000)/20 years = $2,400		
$2,400 × 3 years		
depreciated = $7,200		(7,200)
Book value		$42,800

Depreciation for 20X2:

Book value	42,800
Less: new salvage value	2,200
Balance	$40,600

$$\frac{\text{Depreciable cost}}{\text{New life}} = \frac{\$40,600}{14 \text{ years}} = \$2,900$$

CHANGE IN REPORTING ENTITY

A change in reporting entity refers to preparing financial statements for an entity different from the one reported in previous years. Examples of a change in reporting entity are:

☐ A change in the subsidiaries making up consolidated financial statements.

☐ Presentation of consolidated or combined statements rather than individual company statements.

A change in reporting entity requires the restatement of previous years' financial statements as if both of the previously separate companies were always combined. No more than five years are restated. The restatement is needed for comparative financial purposes and for meaningful historical trends.

The impact of the change in reporting entity on income before extraordinary items, net income, and earnings per share is presented for all years.

A change in the legal structure of a business is not considered a change in reporting entity. An example is a sole proprietorship becoming a corporation. Further, the purchase or sale of an investee is not a change in reporting entity.

A footnote is required on the nature of and reason for the change in reporting entity in the year it is made.

ERROR CORRECTIONS

ASC 250-10-05-4 covers correction of errors made in a previous year. They are treated for accounting purposes as prior-period adjustments. Prior-period adjustments adjust the beginning balance of retained earnings for the net of tax effect of the error as follows:

Retained earnings—1/1 unadjusted

Prior-period adjustments (net of tax)

Retained earnings—1/1 adjusted

Add: net income

Less: dividends

Retained earnings—12/31

Errors may arise because of mathematical mistakes, erroneous application of GAAP, or misuse of information existing at the time the financial statements were prepared. Additionally, changing a principle that is not GAAP to one that is GAAP represents an error correction.

In ascertaining whether an error is material and therefore reportable, consideration should be given to the significance of each correction on an individual basis and to the aggregate effect of all corrections. An error must be corrected immediately when uncovered.

If comparative financial statements are presented, there should be a retroactive adjustment for the error as it impacts previous years. The retroactive adjustment is presented via disclosure of the impact of the adjustment on prior years' earnings and components of net income.

Footnote disclosure for error corrections in the year found include the nature and description of the error, financial effect on income before extraordinary items, net income, and related earnings per share amounts.

EXAMPLE

At year-end 20X1, a company omitted the accrual of utilities expense of $3,000, which was paid on January 4, 20X2. The correcting entry on December 31, 20X2 is:

Retained earnings	3,000	
Utilities expense		3,000

EXAMPLE

Drake Company bought Travis Company on January 1, 20X1, recording patents of $80,000. Patents has not been amortized. Amortization is over 20 years. The correcting entry on December 31, 20X3 is:

Amortization expense		
($80,000/20 years = $4,000 × 1 year for 20X3)	4,000	
Retained earnings	8,000	
($4,000 × 2 years for 20X1 and 20X2)		
Patents		12,000

EXAMPLE

At the beginning of 19X7, a company purchased machinery for $500,000 with a salvage value of $50,000 and an expected life of 20 years. Straight-line depreciation is used. By mistake, salvage value was not subtracted in arriving at depreciation. The calculations on December 31, 20X0 are:

	19X7–19X9
Depreciation taken (incorrect):	
$500,000/20 years × 3	$75,000

Depreciation (correct):

($500,000 − $50,000)/20 years × 3		67,500
Difference		$ 7,500

The correcting journal entries on December 31, 20X0 are

Accumulated depreciation	7,500	
Retained earnings		7,500
To correct for error.		
Depreciation expense	22,500	
Accumulated depreciation		22,500
To record depreciation for 20X0.		

EXAMPLE

Mills Corporation purchased equipment on January 1, 19X9 for $40,000 with a $5,000 salvage value and a 10-year life. Maintenance expense was charged by mistake. On December 31, 20X2, the error was uncovered before the books were closed. The calculations and correcting entry follow:

Depreciation expense equals:

($40,000 − $5,000)/10 years = $3,500 per year

Depreciation expense	3,500	
Equipment	40,000	
Accumulated depreciation		
($3,500 × 4 years)		14,000
Retained earnings		
($40,000 − $10,500)*		29,500

* 3,500 × 3 years (19X9 − 20X1) = $10,500.

EXAMPLE

On January 1, 20X1, a six-year advance of $120,000 was received. In error, revenue was recorded for the entire amount. The error was found on December 31, 20X2 before the books were closed. The correcting entry is:

Retained earnings ($120,000 − $20,000) 100,000		
Revenue (for current year)		20,000
Deferred revenue ($20,000 × 4 years)		80,000

EXAMPLE

If an enterprise changes from the recognition of vacation pay expense from the cash basis to the accrual basis, how should the change be accounted for?

In general, a change from an accounting principle that is not generally accepted (accounting for vacation pay expense on the cash basis) to one that is generally accepted (accounting for it on the accrual basis) should be presented as a correction of an error. The following procedures should be followed in this circumstance:

☐ The correction should be accounted for as a prior-period adjustment (i.e., an adjustment as of the beginning balance of retained earnings, net of taxes) for the earliest year presented.

☐ There should be a restatement of all comparative prior financial statements presented so that they now reflect the accounting for vacation pay expense on the accrual basis instead of the cash basis.

☐ Footnote disclosure should be made in the financial statements regarding the prior-period adjustment correcting the error, the restatement of the financial statements presented, and the effect of the correction on net income.

EXAMPLE

If an entity changes from the cash basis of accounting for service contracts to the accrual method, how should the change be treated in the financial statements?

This represents another example of a change from an accounting principle that is not generally accepted to one that is generally accepted. It therefore should be accounted for as a correction of an error. As in the previous example, the correction should be handled as a prior-period adjustment, net of taxes, for the earliest year presented of the beginning balance of retained earnings. Restatement of all comparative financial statements presented should also be made as well as proper footnote disclosure of the changes and their effects.

EXAMPLE

Tessie Company had a retained earnings balance of $800,000 at December 31, 20X1. In September 20X2, Tessie ascertained that insurance premiums of $120,000 covering a four-year period beginning January 1, 20X1, had been fully paid and fully expensed in 20X1. Tessie has a 40% tax rate. What amount should Tessie report as adjusted beginning retained earnings in its 20X2 statement of retained earnings?

The $120,000 of insurance premiums for the four-year period beginning January 1, 20X1, which had been fully paid and expensed, clearly should not have been expensed in total. Because the premiums represented coverage for a four-year period and only one (20X1) had transpired, net income and retained earnings in 20X1 was understated by $3/4$ of $120,000 ($90,000), net of taxes. This amount, $90,000, should have been accounted for as an insurance prepayment at the end of 20X1. Thus, a correction (an addition) of $90,000 × (100% 40%), or $54,000, is needed to correct the beginning balance of retained earnings in 20X2. Tessie should report $854,000 ($800,000 + $54,000) as its adjusted beginning retained earnings balance in its 20X2 statement of retained earnings.

Classification errors usually do not affect net income. However, prior years' financial statements issued for comparative purposes should be corrected to present the appropriate classification.

ANNUAL REPORT REFERENCES

IBM
2008 Annual Report

Note B. Accounting Changes

New Standards to Be Implemented

In December 2008, the FASB issued FASB Staff Position (FSP) financial Accounting Standard (FAS) 132(R)-1 "Employers' Disclosures about Postretirement Benefit Plan Assets". This FSP amends SFAS No. 132(R), "Employers' Disclosures about Pensions and Other Postretirement Benefits" to require more detailed disclosures about the fair value measurements of employers' plan assets including (a) investment policies and strategies; (b) major categories of plan assets; (c) information about valuation techniques and inputs to those techniques, including the fair value hierarchy classifications (as defined by SFAS No. 157) of the major categories of plan assets; (d) the effects of fair value measurements using significant unobservable inputs (Level 3) on changes in plan assets; and (e) significant concentrations of risk within plan assets. The disclosures required by the FSP will be made in the December 31, 2009 Consolidated Financial Statements. This Statement does not impact the consolidated financial results as it is disclosure-only in nature.

In November 2008, the FASB ratified the Emerging Issues Task force (EITF) Issue 08-7, "Accounting for Defensive Intangible Assets". A defensive intangible asset is an asset acquired in a business combination or in an asset acquisition that an entity does not intend to actively use. According to the guidance, defensive intangible assets are considered to be a separate unit of account and valued based on their highest and best use from the perspective of an external market participant. EITF 08-7 is effective January 1, 2009. The adoption of this EITF issue is not expected to have an impact on the Consolidated Financial Statements.

In June 2008, the FASB issued FSP EITF 03-6-1, "Determining Whether Instruments Granted in Share-Based Payment Transactions Are Participating Securities," which will become effective in 2009 via retrospective application. Under the FSP, unvested share-based payment awards that contain non-forfeitable rights to dividends or dividend equivalents are participating securities and, therefore, are included in computing earnings per share (EPS) pursuant to the two-class method. The two-class method determines earnings per share for each class of common stock and participating securities according to dividends or dividend equivalents and their respective participation rights in undistributed earnings. Restricted Stock Units (RSUs) granted to employees prior to December 31, 2007 are considered participating securities as they receive non-forfeitable dividend equivalents at the same rate as common stock. RSUs granted after December 31, 2007 do not receive dividend equivalents and are not considered participating securities. The company will adopt the FSP in fiscal year 2009. The implementation of the FSP is expected to decrease diluted EPS by $0.04 and $0.03 for the years ended December 31, 2008 and December 31, 2007, respectively.

Basic EPS is expected to decrease by $0.05 in each of the years ended December 31, 2008 and 2007.

In March 2008, the FASB issued SFAS No. 161, "Disclosures about Derivative Instruments and Hedging Activities—an amendment of FASB Statement No. 133." SFAS No. 161 expands the current disclosure requirements of SFAS No. 133, "Accounting for Derivative Instruments and Hedging Activities," such that entities must now provide enhanced disclosures on a quarterly basis regarding how and why the entity uses derivatives; how derivatives and related hedged items are accounted for under SFAS No. 133 and how derivatives and related hedged items affect the entity's financial position, financial results and cash flow. Pursuant to the transition provisions of the Statement, the company will adopt SFAS No. 161 in fiscal year 2009 and will present the required disclosures in the prescribed format on a prospective basis. This Statement does not impact the consolidated financial results as it is disclosure-only in nature.

In February 2008, the FASB issued FSP FAS 157-2, "Effective Date of FASB Statement No. 157." FSP FAS 157-2 delayed the effective date of SFAS No. 157 "fair Value measurements" from 2008 to 2009 for all nonfinancial assets and nonfinancial liabilities, except those that are recognized or disclosed at fair value in the financial statements on a recurring basis (at least annually). The adoption of the provisions of SFAS No. 157 related to nonfinancial assets and nonfinancial liabilities is not expected to have a material impact on the Consolidated Financial Statements. See the "Standards Implemented" section of this note for a further discussion of SFAS No. 157.

In December 2007, the FASB issued SFAS No. 160, "Noncontrolling Interests in Consolidated Financial Statements—an amendment of ARB No. 51." This Statement requires that the noncontrolling interest in the equity of a subsidiary be accounted for and reported as equity, provides revised guidance on the treatment of net income and losses attributable to the noncontrolling interest and changes in ownership interests in a subsidiary and requires additional disclosures that identify and distinguish between the interests of the controlling and noncontrolling owners. Pursuant to the transition provisions of SFAS No. 160, the company will adopt the Statement on January 1, 2009 via retrospective application of the presentation and disclosure requirements. The company does not expect the adoption of this Statement to have a material effect on the Consolidated Financial Statements.

In December 2007, the FASB issued SFAS No. 141(R), "Business Combinations," which will become effective in 2009 via prospective application to business combinations. This Statement requires that the acquisition method of accounting be applied to a broader set of business combinations, amends the definition of a business combination, provides a definition of a business, requires an acquirer to recognize an acquired business at its fair value at the acquisition date and requires the assets and liabilities assumed in a business combination to be measured and recognized at their fair values as of the acquisition date (with limited exceptions). The company will adopt this Statement in fiscal year 2009 and its effects on future periods will depend on the nature and significance of business combinations subject to this statement.

Standards Implemented

In September 2006, the FASB finalized SFAS No. 157 which became effective January 1, 2008 except as amended by FSP FAS 157-2 as previously described and FSP FAS 157-1 and FSP FAS 157-3 as discussed below. This Statement defines fair value, establishes a framework for measuring fair value and expands disclosures about fair value measurements; however, it does not require any new fair value measurements. On January 1, 2008, the provisions of this Statement were applied prospectively to fair value measurements and disclosures of (a) financial assets and financial liabilities and (b) nonfinancial assets and nonfinancial liabilities which are recognized or disclosed at fair value in the financial statements on a recurring basis (at least annually). The adoption of this Statement did not have a material effect on the Consolidated Financial Statements for fair value measurements made for the year ended December 31, 2008. See note D, "fair Value," on page 84 for additional information.

In February 2008, the FASB issued FSP FAS 157-1, "Application of FASB Statement No. 157 to FASB Statement No. 13 and Other Accounting Pronouncements That Address fair Value Measurements for Purposes of Lease Classification or Measurement under Statement 13". FSP FAS 157-1 removed leasing from the scope of SFAS No. 157. In October 2008, the FASB issued FSP FAS 157-3, "Determining the fair Value of a financial Asset When the Market for That Asset is Not Active". FSP FAS 157-3 clarified the application of SFAS 157 in a market that is not active and provided an example to illustrate key considerations in determining the fair value of a financial asset when the market for that financial asset is not active. FSP FAS 157-3 became effective immediately upon issuance, and its adoption did not have an effect on the Consolidated Financial Statements.

In February 2007, the FASB issued SFAS No. 159, "The fair Value Option for financial Assets and financial Liabilities, Including an amendment of FASB Statement No. 115," which became effective January 1, 2008. SFAS No. 159 permits entities to measure eligible financial assets, financial liabilities and firm commitments at fair value, on an instrument-by-instrument basis, that are otherwise not permitted to be accounted for at fair value under other generally accepted accounting principles. The fair value measurement election is irrevocable and subsequent changes in fair value must be recorded in earnings. The company adopted this Statement as of January 1, 2008 but has not applied the fair value option to any eligible assets or liabilities. Thus, the adoption of this Statement did not affect the Consolidated Financial Statements.

In the first quarter of 2007, the company adopted SFAS No. 156, "Accounting for Servicing of financial Assets—an amendment of FASB Statement No. 140," that provides guidance on accounting for separately recognized servicing assets and servicing liabilities. In accordance with the provisions of SFAS No. 156, separately recognized servicing assets and servicing liabilities must be initially measured at fair value, if practicable. Subsequent to initial recognition, the company may use either the amortization method or the fair value measurement method to account for servicing assets and servicing liabilities within the scope of this Statement. The adoption of this Statement did not have a material effect on the Consolidated Financial Statements.

On January 1, 2007, the company adopted SFAS No. 155, "Accounting for Certain Hybrid financial Instruments—an amendment of FASB Statements No. 133 and 140," which permits fair value remeasurement for any hybrid financial instrument that contains an embedded derivative that otherwise would require bifurcation in accordance with the provisions of SFAS No. 133, "Accounting for Derivative Instruments and Hedging Activities." The adoption of this Statement did not have a material effect on the Consolidated Financial Statements.

The company adopted FASB Interpretation No. 48, "Accounting for Uncertainty in Income Taxes—an Interpretation of FASB Statement No. 109" (FIN 48) on January 1, 2007. FIN 48 clarifies the accounting and reporting for uncertainties in income tax law. This Interpretation prescribes a comprehensive model for the financial statement recognition, measurement, presentation and disclosure of uncertain tax positions taken or expected to be taken in income tax returns. The cumulative effect of adopting FIN 48 was a decrease in tax reserves and an increase of $117 million to the January 1, 2007 retained earnings balance.

Effective December 31, 2006, the company adopted SFAS No. 158, "Employer's Accounting for Defined Benefit Pension and Other Postretirement Plans, an Amendment of FASB Statements No. 87, 88, 106 and 132(R)," which requires the recognition of the funded status of the retirement-related benefit plans in the Consolidated Statement of financial Position and the recognition of the changes in that funded status in the year in which the changes occur through gains and (losses) not affecting retained earnings, net of applicable tax effects. The provisions of SFAS No. 158 were adopted pursuant to the transition provisions therein. The company measures defined benefit plan assets and obligations as of December 31 and SFAS No. 158 did not affect the company's existing valuation practices. The adoption of SFAS No. 158 had a significant non-cash impact on the company's 2006 reported financial position and stockholders' equity, reducing equity by $9.5 billion, net of tax. The adoption of SFAS No. 158 had no impact on the company's existing debt covenants, credit ratings or financial flexibility.

In September 2006, the Securities and Exchange Commission (SEC) issued Staff Accounting Bulletin (SAB) No. 108, codified as SAB Topic 1.N, "Considering the Effects of Prior Year Misstatements when Quantifying Misstatements in Current Year Financial Statements." SAB No. 108 describes the approach that should be used to quantify the materiality of a misstatement and provides guidance for correcting prior-year errors. The company early adopted SAB No. 108 in the third quarter of 2006 and accordingly, follows SAB No. 108 requirements when quantifying financial statement misstatements. The adoption of SAB No. 108 did not require any changes to the Consolidated Financial Statements.

In the third quarter of 2006, the company adopted FSP Fin 46(R)-6, "Determining the Variability to Be Considered in Applying FASB Interpretation No. 46(R)." FSP FIN No. 46(R)-6 clarifies that the variability to be considered in applying FASB Interpretation 46(R) shall be based on an analysis of the design of the variable interest entity. The adoption of this FSP did not have a material effect on the Consolidated Financial Statements.

In the first quarter of 2006, the company adopted SFAS No. 154, "Accounting Changes and Error Corrections—a replacement of APB Opinion No. 20 and FASB

Statement No. 3." SFAS No. 154 changed the requirements for the accounting for and reporting of a voluntary change in accounting principle. The adoption of this statement did not affect the Consolidated Financial Statements.

Beginning January 2006, the company adopted SFAS No. 151, "Inventory Costs—an amendment of ARB No. 43, Chapter 4." SFAS No. 151 requires certain abnormal expenditures to be recognized as expenses in the current period versus being capitalized in inventory. It also requires that the amount of fixed production overhead allocated to inventory be based on the normal capacity of the production facilities. The adoption of this statement did not have a material effect on the Consolidated Financial Statements.

Tyco International
2008 Annual Report

7. Cumulative Effect of Accounting Change

During 2006, the Company adopted FIN No. 47, "Accounting for Conditional Asset Retirement Obligations—an Interpretation of FASB Statement No. 143." FIN No. 47 clarifies the timing of liability recognition for legal obligations associated with an asset retirement when the timing and (or) method of settling the obligation are conditional on a future event that may or may not be within the control of the entity and clarifies when an entity would have sufficient information to reasonably estimate the fair value of an asset retirement obligation. FIN No. 47 requires that conditional asset retirement obligations, along with the associated capitalized asset retirement costs, be initially reported at their fair values. Upon adoption, the Company recognized a liability of $32 million for asset retirement obligations and an increase of $10 million in the carrying amount of the related assets, of which $19 million and $5 million are reflected in liabilities and assets of discontinued operations, respectively. The initial recognition resulted in a cumulative effect of accounting change of $14 million after-tax loss ($22 million pre-tax), reflecting the accumulated depreciation and accretion that would have been recognized in prior periods had the provisions of FIN No. 47 been in effect at the time.

IBM
2007 Annual Report

Note B. Accounting Changes

New Standards to Be Implemented

In February 2008, the FASB issued FASB Staff Position (FSP) Financial Accounting Standard (FAS) 157-1, "Application of FASB Statement No. 157 to FASB Statement No. 13 and Its Related Interpretive Accounting Pronouncements That Address Leasing Transactions," and FSP FAS 157-2, "Effective Date of FASB Statement No. 157." FSP FAS 157-1 removes leasing from the scope of SFAS No. 157, "Fair Value Measurements." FSP FAS 157-2 delays the effective date of SFAS No. 157 from 2008 to 2009 for all nonfinancial assets and nonfinancial liabilities, except those that are recognized or disclosed at fair value in the financial statements on a recurring basis (at least annually). See SFAS No. 157 discussion on page 74.

In December 2007, the FASB issued SFAS No. 141(R), "Business Combinations," which will become effective in 2009 via prospective application to new business combinations. This Statement requires that the acquisition method of accounting be applied to a broader set of business combinations, amends the definition of a business combination, provides a definition of a business, requires an acquirer to recognize an acquired business at its fair value at the acquisition date and requires the assets and liabilities assumed in a business combination to be measured and recognized at their fair values as of the acquisition date (with limited exceptions). The company will adopt this Statement in fiscal year 2009 and its effects on future periods will depend on the nature and significance of any acquisitions subject to this Statement.

In December 2007, the FASB issued SFAS No. 160, "Noncontrolling Interests in Consolidated Financial Statements—an amendment of ARB No. 51." This Statement requires that the noncontrolling interest in the equity of a subsidiary be accounted for and reported as equity, provides revised guidance on the treatment of net income and losses attributable to the noncontrolling interest and changes in ownership interests in a subsidiary and requires additional disclosures that identify and distinguish between the interests of the controlling and noncontrolling owners. Pursuant to the transition provisions of SFAS No. 160, the company will adopt the Statement in fiscal year 2009 via retrospective application of the presentation and disclosure requirements. The company does not expect the adoption of this Statement to have a material effect on the Consolidated Financial Statements.

In February 2007, the FASB issued SFAS No. 159, "The Fair Value Option for Financial Assets and Financial Liabilities, Including an amendment of FASB Statement No. 115," which will become effective in 2008. SFAS No. 159 permits entities to measure eligible financial assets, financial liabilities and firm commitments at fair value, on an instrument-by-instrument basis, that are otherwise not permitted to be accounted for at fair value under other generally accepted accounting principles. The fair value measurement election is irrevocable and subsequent changes in fair value must be recorded in earnings. The company will adopt this Statement in fiscal year 2008 and does not expect the adoption of this Statement to have a material effect on the Consolidated Financial Statements.

In September 2006, the FASB finalized SFAS No. 157 which will become effective in 2008 except as amended by FSP FAS 157-1 and FSP FAS 157-2 as previously described. This Statement defines fair value, establishes a framework for measuring fair value and expands disclosures about fair value measurements; however, it does not require any new fair value measurements. The provisions of SFAS No. 157 will be applied prospectively to fair value measurements and disclosures for financial assets and financial liabilities and nonfinancial assets and nonfinancial liabilities recognized or disclosed at fair value in the financial statements on at least an annual basis beginning in the first quarter of 2008. While the company does not expect the adoption of this Statement to have a material impact on its Consolidated Financial Statements at this time, the company will monitor any additional implementation guidance that is issued that addresses the fair value measurements for certain financial assets, such as private market pension plan assets, and nonfinancial assets and nonfinancial liabilities not disclosed at fair value in the financial statements on at least an annual basis.

Standards Implemented

In the first quarter of 2007, the company adopted SFAS No. 156, "Accounting for Servicing of Financial Assets—an amendment of FASB Statement No. 140," that provides guidance on accounting for separately recognized servicing assets and servicing liabilities. In accordance with the provisions of SFAS No. 156, separately recognized servicing assets and servicing liabilities must be initially measured at fair value, if practicable. Subsequent to initial recognition, the company may use either the amortization method or the fair value measurement method to account for servicing assets and servicing liabilities within the scope of this Statement. The adoption of this Statement did not have a material effect on the Consolidated Financial Statements.

In the first quarter of 2007, the company adopted SFAS No. 155, "Accounting for Certain Hybrid Financial Instruments—an amendment of FASB Statements No. 133 and 140," which permits fair value remeasurement for any hybrid financial instrument that contains an embedded derivative that otherwise would require bifurcation in accordance with the provisions of SFAS No. 133, "Accounting for Derivative Instruments and Hedging Activities." The adoption of this Statement did not have a material effect on the Consolidated Financial Statements.

The company adopted FASB Interpretation No. 48, "Accounting for Uncertainty in Income Taxes—an Interpretation of FASB Statement No. 109" (FIN 48) on January 1, 2007. FIN 48 clarifies the accounting and reporting for uncertainties in income tax law. This Interpretation prescribes a comprehensive model for the financial statement recognition, measurement, presentation and disclosure of uncertain tax positions taken or expected to be taken in income tax returns. See note O, "Taxes," on pages 97 to 99 for additional information, including the effects of adoption on the Consolidated Statement of Financial Position.

Effective December 31, 2006, the company adopted SFAS No. 158, "Employer's Accounting for Defined Benefit Pension and Other Postretirement Plans, an Amendment of FASB Statements No. 87, 88, 106 and 132(R)," which requires the recognition of the funded status of the retirement-related benefit plans in the Consolidated Statement of Financial Position and the recognition of the changes in that funded status in the year in which the changes occur through Gains and (losses) not affecting retained earnings, net of applicable tax effects. The provisions of SFAS No. 158 were adopted pursuant to the transition provisions therein. The company measures defined benefit plan assets and obligations as of December 31 and SFAS No. 158 did not affect the company's existing valuation practices. The adoption of SFAS No. 158 had no impact on the company's existing debt covenants, credit ratings or financial flexibility. See note U, "Retirement-Related Benefits," on pages 105 to 116 for additional information, including the incremental effect of adoption on the Consolidated Statement of Financial Position.

In September 2006, the Securities and Exchange Commission (SEC) issued Staff Accounting Bulletin (SAB) No. 108, codified as SAB Topic 1.N, "Considering the Effects of Prior Year Misstatements when Quantifying Misstatements in Current Year Financial Statements." SAB No. 108 describes the approach that should be used to quantify the materiality of a misstatement and provides guidance for correcting prior-year errors. The company early adopted SAB No. 108 in the third quarter of 2006 and accordingly, follows SAB No. 108 requirements when quantifying financial statement misstatements. The adoption of SAB No. 108 did not require any changes to the Consolidated Financial Statements.

In the third quarter of 2006, the company adopted FSP FIN 46(R)-6, "Determining the Variability to Be Considered in Applying FASB Interpretation No. 46(R)." FSP FIN No. 46(R)-6 clarifies that the variability to be considered in applying FASB Interpretation 46(R) shall be based on an analysis of the design of the variable interest entity. The adoption of this FSP did not have a material effect on the Consolidated Financial Statements.

In the first quarter of 2006, the company adopted SFAS No. 154, "Accounting Changes and Error Corrections—a replacement of APB Opinion No. 20 and FASB Statement No. 3." SFAS No. 154 changed the requirements for the accounting for and reporting of a voluntary change in accounting principle. The adoption of this statement did not affect the Consolidated Financial Statements in fiscal years 2007 and 2006. Its effects on future periods will depend on the nature and significance of any future accounting changes subject to this Statement.

Beginning January 2006, the company adopted SFAS No. 151, "Inventory Costs—an amendment of ARB No. 43, Chapter 4." SFAS No. 151 requires certain abnormal expenditures to be recognized as expenses in the current period versus being capitalized in inventory. It also requires that the amount of fixed production overhead allocated to inventory be based on the normal capacity of the production facilities. The adoption of this Statement did not have a material effect on the Consolidated Financial Statements.

Effective January 1, 2005, the company adopted the provisions of SFAS No. 123(R), "Share-Based Payment." The company elected to adopt the modified retrospective application method provided by SFAS No. 123(R) and accordingly, financial statement amounts for the periods presented herein reflect results as if the fair value method of expensing had been applied from the original effective date of SFAS No. 123. See note A, "Significant Accounting Policies," on page 70 and note T, "Stock-Based Compensation," on pages 102 to 105 for additional information.

In March 2005, the FASB issued FASB Interpretation No. 47, "Accounting for Conditional Asset Retirement Obligations, an interpretation of FASB Statement No. 143" (FIN 47). FIN 47 clarifies that conditional AROs meet the definition of liabilities and should be recognized when incurred if their fair values can be reasonably estimated. The company implemented FIN 47 at December 31, 2005 and recorded conditional AROs of approximately $85 million. These conditional AROs relate to the company's contractual obligations to remove leasehold improvements in certain non-U.S. locations thereby restoring leased space to its original condition. Upon implementation of FIN 47, the company recorded a $36 million charge (net of income tax benefit of $21 million) which was reported as a cumulative effect of a change in accounting principle in the 2005 Consolidated Statement of Earnings. The company's accounting policy for AROs is described in note A, "Significant Accounting Policies," on page 69. The pro forma effect of retroactively applying FIN 47 for the year 2005 was:

($ in millions except per share amounts) FOR THE YEAR ENDED DECEMBER 31:	*2005*
Pro forma amounts assuming accounting change is applied retroactively:	
Pro forma net income	$7,964
Pro forma earnings per share of common stock—assuming dilution	$ 4.89
Pro forma earnings per share of common stock—basic	$ 4.98
ARO liabilities at December 31, 2005	$ 85

As of December 31, 2005, the company was unable to estimate the range of settlement dates and the related probabilities for certain asbestos remediation AROs. These conditional AROs are primarily related to the encapsulated structural fireproofing that is not subject to abatement unless the buildings are demolished and non-encapsulated asbestos that the company would remediate only if it performed major renovations of certain existing buildings. Because these conditional obligations have indeterminate settlement dates, the company could not develop a reasonable estimate of their fair values. The company will continue to assess its ability to estimate fair values at each future reporting date. The related liability will be recognized once sufficient additional information becomes available.

In June 2005, the FASB issued FSP No. FAS 143-1, "Accounting for Electronic Equipment Waste Obligations," (FSP FAS 143-1) that provides guidance on how commercial users and producers of electronic equipment should recognize and measure asset retirement obligations associated with the European Directive 2002/96/EC on Waste Electrical and Electronic Equipment (the "Directive"). In 2005, the company adopted FSP FAS 143-1 in those European Union (EU) member countries that transposed the Directive into country-specific laws. Its adoption did not have a material effect on the Consolidated Financial Statements. The effect of applying FSP FAS 143-1 in the remaining countries in future periods is not expected to have a material effect on the Consolidated Financial Statements.

In the third quarter of 2005, the company adopted SFAS No. 153, "Exchanges of Nonmonetary Assets, an amendment of APB Opinion No. 29." SFAS No. 153 requires that exchanges of productive assets be accounted for at fair value unless fair value cannot be reasonably determined or the transaction lacks commercial substance. The adoption of SFAS No. 153 did not have a material effect on the Consolidated Financial Statements.

Note C. Acquisitions/Divestitures

Acquisitions

In 2007, the company completed 12 acquisitions at an aggregate cost of $1,144 million.

The Software segment completed six acquisitions: in the first quarter, Consul Risk Management International BV and Vallent Corporation, both privately held companies. Four acquisitions were completed in the third quarter: Watchfire Corporation, WebDialogs Inc. and Princeton Softech Inc., all privately held companies, and DataMirror Corporation, a publicly held company. Each acquisition further complemented and enhanced the software product portfolio.

Global Technology Services completed four acquisitions: in the first quarter, Softek Storage Solutions Corporation (Softek) and DM Information Systems, Ltd. (DMIS), both privately held companies. Two acquisitions were completed in the fourth quarter: Novus Consulting Group, Inc. and Serbian Business Systems, both privately held companies. Softek augments the company's unified data mobility offerings and worldwide delivery expertise for managing data in storage array, host and virtualized IT environments. DMIS will enhance and complement the Technology Service offerings. Novus CG, a storage solution company, will provide improved access to business information, enable stronger regulatory and corporate compliance and improve overall information technology performance. Serbian Business Systems establishes the company's maintenance and technical support services business in Serbia.

Global Business Services completed one acquisition in the fourth quarter: IT Gruppen AS, which will add to the company's presence in the retail and media sectors.

Systems and Technology completed one acquisition in the fourth quarter: XIV, Ltd., a privately held company focused on storage systems technology.

Purchase price consideration was paid in cash. These acquisitions are reported in the Consolidated Statement of Cash Flows net of acquired cash and cash equivalents.

The table on page 77 reflects the purchase price related to these acquisitions and the resulting purchase price allocations as of December 31, 2007.

During the fourth quarter of 2007, the company entered into a definitive agreement to acquire Cognos, Inc. The acquisition of Cognos, Inc., a publicly held company, was completed in January 2008. The acquisition of Cognos, Inc. supports the Information on Demand strategy and will provide the company with a strong entry in the Business Intelligence market.

The closing of the Telelogic AB acquisition, announced in the second quarter of 2007, is conditioned upon satisfactory completion of regulatory reviews in the European Union. Regulatory reviews in the U.S. have been completed.

Unisys 2002 Annual Report

3 Accounting Changes

Effective January 1, 2002, the company adopted SFAS No. 142, "Goodwill and Other Intangible Assets." SFAS No. 142 no longer permits the amortization of goodwill and indefinite-lived intangible assets. Instead, these assets must be reviewed annually for impairment in accordance with this statement. SFAS No. 142 required the company to perform a transitional impairment test of its goodwill as of January 1, 2002, as well as perform impairment tests on an annual basis and whenever events or circumstances occur indicating that the goodwill may be impaired. During 2002, the company performed its transitional and annual impairment tests, which indicated that the company's goodwill was not impaired.

The changes in the carrying amount of goodwill by segment for the year ended December 31, 2002, were as follows:

(Millions)	Total	Services	Technology
Balance at December 31, 2001	$159.0	$41.9	$117.1
Acquisition	3.0	3.0	
Foreign currency translation adjustments	(1.4)	(2.4)	1.0
Balance at December 31, 2002	$160.6	$42.5	$118.1

The company's net income and earnings per share adjusted to exclude goodwill amortization was as follows:

Year Ended December 31, (Millions, except per share data)	2002	2001	2000
Reported income (loss) before extraordinary items	$223.0	$(49.9)	$244.8
Add back goodwill amortization, net of tax		14.1	20.1
Adjusted income (loss) before extraordinary items	$223.0	$(35.8)	$264.9
Reported net income (loss)	$223.0	$(67.1)	$225.0
Add back goodwill amortization, net of tax		14.1	20.1
Adjusted net income (loss)	$223.0	$(53.0)	$245.1
Earnings (loss) per share before extraordinary items			
Basic			
As reported	$ .69	$ (.16)	$ .78
Goodwill amortization	$ .69	.04	.06
As adjusted	$ .69	$ (.12)	$ .84
Diluted			
As reported	$ .69	$ (.16)	$ .77
Goodwill amortization	$ .69	.04	.06
As adjusted	$ .69	$ (.12)	$ .83
Earnings (loss) per share			
Basic			
As reported	$ .69	$ (.21)	$ .72
Goodwill amortization	$ .69	.04	.06

Year Ended December 31, (Millions, except per share data)	2002	2001	2000
As adjusted	$ **.69**	$ (.17)	$ .78
Diluted			
As reported	$ **.69**	$ (.21)	$ .71
Goodwill amortization	$ **.69**	.04	.06
As adjusted	$ **.69**	$ (.17)	$ .77

Effective January 1, 2002, the company adopted SFAS No. 143, "Accounting for Asset Retirement Obligations." This statement addresses financial accounting and reporting for legal obligations associated with the retirement of tangible long-lived assets that result from the acquisition, construction, development and normal operation of a long-lived asset. SFAS No. 143 requires that the fair value of a liability for an asset retirement obligation be recognized in the period in which it is incurred if a reasonable estimate of fair value can be made. The associated asset retirement costs are capitalized as part of the carrying amount of the long-lived asset and subsequently allocated to expense over the asset's useful life. Adoption of SFAS No. 143 had no effect on the company's consolidated financial position, consolidated results of operations, or liquidity.

Effective January 1, 2002, the company adopted SFAS No. 144, "Accounting for the Impairment or Disposal of Long-Lived Assets." This statement addresses financial accounting and reporting for the impairment or disposal of long-lived assets. SFAS No. 144 requires an impairment loss to be recognized only if the carrying amounts of long-lived assets to be held and used are not recoverable from their expected undiscounted future cash flows. Adoption of SFAS No. 144 had no effect on the company's consolidated financial position, consolidated results of operations, or liquidity.

In April 2002, the Financial Accounting Standards Board ("FASB") issued SFAS No. 145, "Rescission of FASB Statements No. 4, 44 and 64, Amendment of FASB Statement No. 13, and Technical Corrections." SFAS No. 145 rescinds SFAS No. 4, which required that all gains and losses from extinguishment of debt be reported as an extraordinary item. The provisions of SFAS No. 145 related to the rescission of SFAS No. 4 must be applied in fiscal years beginning after May 15, 2002. The company will adopt this statement effective January 1, 2003. Previously recorded losses on the early extinguishment of debts that were classified as an extraordinary item in prior periods will be reclassified to other income (expense), net. Adoption of SFAS No. 145 will have no effect on the company's consolidated financial position, consolidated results of operations, or liquidity.

In June 2002, the FASB issued SFAS No. 146, "Accounting for Costs Associated with Exit or Disposal Activities." SFAS No. 146 requires companies to recognize costs associated with exit or disposal activities when they are incurred rather than at the date of a commitment to an exit or disposal plan. SFAS No. 146 replaces previous accounting guidance provided by EITF Issue No. 94-3, "Liability Recognition for Certain Employee Termination Benefits and Other Costs to Exit an Activity (including Certain Costs Incurred in a Restructuring)" and will be effective for the company for exit or disposal activities initiated after December 31, 2002. The company does not believe that adoption of this statement will have a material impact on its consolidated financial position, consolidated results of operations, or liquidity.

In November 2002, the FASB issued EITF Issue No. 00-21, "Accounting for Revenue Arrangements with Multiple Deliverables." This issue addresses how to account for arrangements that may involve the delivery or performance of multiple products, services, and/or rights to use assets. The final consensus of this issue is applicable to agreements entered into in fiscal periods beginning after June 15, 2003. Additionally, companies will be permitted to apply the guidance in this issue to all existing arrangements as the cumulative effect of a change in accounting principle in accordance with APB Opinion No. 20, "Accounting Changes." The company does not believe that adoption of this issue will have a material impact on its consolidated financial position, consolidated results of operations, or liquidity.

In November 2002, the FASB issued Interpretation No. 45, "Guarantor's Accounting and Disclosure Requirements for Guarantees, Including Indirect Guarantees of Indebtedness of Others, an Interpretation of FASB Statements No. 5, 57, and 107 and Rescission of FASB Interpretation No. 34" ("FIN No. 45"). The interpretation requires that upon issuance of a guarantee, the entity must recognize a liability for the fair value of the obligation it assumes under that obligation. This interpretation is intended to improve the comparability of financial reporting by requiring identical accounting for guarantees issued with separately identified consideration and guarantees issued without separately identified consideration. For the company, the initial recognition, measurement provision and disclosure requirements of FIN No. 45 are applicable to guarantees issued or modified after December 31, 2002. The company is currently evaluating what impact, if any, adoption of FIN No. 45 will have on its consolidated financial position, consolidated results of operations, or liquidity.

In January 2003, the FASB issued Interpretation No. 46, "Consolidation of Variable Interest Entities" ("FIN No. 46"). This interpretation clarifies the application of Accounting Research Bulletin No. 51, "Consolidated Financial Statements," to certain entities in which equity investors do not have the characteristics of a controlling financial interest or do not have sufficient equity at risk for the entity to finance its activities without additional subordinated financial support from other parties. FIN No. 46 applies immediately to variable interest entities created after January 31, 2003, and to variable interest entities in which an enterprise obtains an interest after that date. For the company's synthetic lease, as described in Note 12, FIN No. 46 is effective for the period beginning July 1, 2003.

Microsoft
2003 Annual Report

Note 3—Accounting Changes

Effective July 1, 2000, we adopted SFAS 133 which establishes accounting and reporting standards for derivative instruments, including certain derivative instruments embedded in other contracts and for hedging activities. The adoption of SFAS 133 on July 1, 2000, resulted in a cumulative pre-tax reduction to income of $560 million ($375 million after-tax) and a cumulative pre-tax reduction to OCI of $112 million ($75 million after-tax). The reduction to income was mostly attributable to a loss of approximately $300 million reclassified from OCI for the time value of options and a loss of approximately $250 million reclassified from OCI for derivatives not designated as hedging instruments. The reduction to OCI was mostly attributable to losses of approximately $670 million on cash flow hedges offset by reclassifications out of OCI of the approximately $300 million loss for the time value of options and the approximately $250 million loss for derivative instruments not designated as hedging instruments. The net derivative losses included in OCI as of July 1, 2000 were reclassified into earnings during the twelve months ended June 30, 2001. The change in accounting from the adoption of SFAS 133 did not materially affect net income in 2001.

Effective July 1, 2001, we adopted SFAS 141, *Business Combinations*, and SFAS 142. SFAS 141 requires business combinations initiated after June 30, 2001 to be accounted for using the purchase method of accounting. It also specifies the types of acquired intangible assets that are required to be recognized and reported separate from goodwill. SFAS 142 requires that goodwill and certain intangibles no longer be amortized, but instead tested for impairment at least annually. There was no impairment of goodwill upon adoption of SFAS 142.

Net income and earnings per share for fiscal 2001 adjusted to exclude amortization expense (net of taxes) is as follows:

(In millions, except earnings per share)

Year Ended June 30	2001
Net income:	
Reported net income	$7,346
Goodwill amortization	252
Equity method goodwill amortization	26
Adjusted net income	$7,624
Basic earnings per share:	
Reported basic earnings per share	$ 0.69
Goodwill amortization	0.02
Equity method goodwill amortization	–
Adjusted basic earnings per share	$ 0.71
Diluted earnings per share:	
Reported diluted earnings per share	$ 0.66

(In millions, except earnings per share)	
Goodwill amortization	0.02
Equity method goodwill amortization	–
Adjusted diluted earnings per share	$ 0.68

Smucker's
2003 Annual Report

Note B: Changes in Accounting Principle

Effective May 1, 2002, the Company adopted Statement of Financial Accounting Standards No. 142, *Goodwill and Other Intangible Assets* (SFAS 142). In accordance with SFAS 142, goodwill and indefinite-lived intangible assets are no longer amortized but are reviewed at least annually for impairment. Prior to the adoption of SFAS 142, amortization expense was recorded for goodwill and other intangible assets.

The following table sets forth a reconciliation of net income and earnings per share information adjusted for the nonamortization provisions of SFAS 142.

(Dollars in thousands, except per share data)	Year Ended April 30,		
	2003	2002	2001
Net income, as reported	$96,342	$30,851	$27,206
Goodwill and indefinite-lived intangible asset amortization, net of tax benefit	–	2,177	2,347
Net income, as adjusted	$96,342	$33,028	$29,553
Earnings per common share:			
Net income, as reported	$ 2.04	$ 1.33	$ 1.13
Goodwill and indefinite-lived intangible asset amortization, net of tax benefit	–	0.10	0.10
Net income, as adjusted	$ 2.04	$ 1.43	$ 1.23
Net income, as reported-assuming dilution	$ 2.02	$ 1.31	$ 1.12
Goodwill and indefinite-lived intangible asset amortization, net of tax benefit-assuming dilution	–	0.10	0.10
Net income, as adjusted-assuming dilution	$ 2.02	$ 1.41	$ 1.22

In fiscal 2003, the Company completed its initial and annual impairment tests for goodwill, under SFAS 142. These tests confirmed that the fair value of the Company's reporting units exceeds their carrying values, and that no impairment loss needed to be recognized for goodwill during fiscal 2003.

Chapter 10
Investments in Equity and Debt Securities

CONTENTS

INVESTMENTS IN DEBT AND EQUITY SECURITIES

ASC 320-10-05-1 and 05-2, *Investments—Debt and Equity Securities: Overall*, set forth the accounting and financial reporting requirements for investments in equity securities with determinable fair market value and for all investments in debt securities. ASC 320-10-05-1 and 05-2 applies to preferred stock and common stock (if ownership is less than 20%, or if ownership exceeds 20% but effective control [significant influence] is lacking). As per ASC 323-10-15-10, *Investments—Equity Method and Joint Ventures Overall*, the following circumstances may imply that the investor is *not* able to exercise effective control:

☐ The investor is not included on the investee's board of directors.

☐ The investor is unable to gather the financial data required to account under the equity method.

☐ The investee is opposed to the investment, such as by instituting a lawsuit against it or filing a complaint with the Securities and Exchange Commission (SEC).

☐ A written agreement between the parties specifies that there is no effective control.

☐ Significant influence exists by a small group of stockholders, excluding the investor constituting majority ownership of the investee.

ASC 320-10-05-1 and 05-2 are not applicable to investments under the equity method, consolidated subsidiaries, such specialized industries as brokers and dealers, or not-for-profits. Nonprofit entities are governed by ASC 958-320-05-2, *Not-for-Profit Entities: Investments—Debt and Equity Securities*, which requires fair value reporting for all investment categories, including held-to-maturity. ASC 323-10-15-8, *Investments—Equity Method and Joint Ventures: Overall*, provides the accounting, reporting, and disclosure requirements under the equity method. The equity method generally applies if the investor owns between 20% and 50% of the voting common stock of the investee. The equity method may also apply if ownership is less than 20% but effective control exists.

MARKET VALUE METHOD AND AMORTIZED COST METHOD PER ASC 320

Equity securities represent an ownership interest either in common stock or preferred stock, or in rights to buy or sell interests, such as warrants, rights, or calls and put options. Redeemable preferred stock, however, is not treated as equity securities.

Debt securities are financial instruments evidencing a creditor relationship with a company or government. Examples are redeemable preferred stock, corporate bonds, municipal bonds, U.S. government obligations, convertible debt, collateralized mortgage obligations, strips, and commercial paper. Debt securities do not include futures contracts and option contracts.

Equity and debt securities are broken down into the following categories:

☐ Trading securities.

☐ Available-for-sale securities.

☐ Held-to-maturity securities.

Classification of the securities will be based on such factors as management intent considering past history of investments, subsequent events after the balance sheet date, and the nature and objective of the investment.

Trading Securities

Trading securities may include equity and debt securities. Mortgage-backed securities held for sale related to mortgage banking activities are included in trading securities. Trading securities are purchased and held mainly to sell them in the short term (usually three months or less). There is active buying and selling of the securities to earn short-term profits from price appreciation.

Trading securities are recorded in the balance sheet under *current assets at fair market value.* Fair market value is based on stock or bond quotations on listed exchanges or in the over-the-counter market. However, restricted stock (stock restricted by governmental or contractual provisions) does not have a readily available fair value because it is not traded. Foreign securities are based on the market price of the foreign exchange if comparable to U.S. markets. Fair value of investments in a mutual fund is based on the published fair value per share. To determine the fair value of debt securities in which market price is unavailable, other valuation methods may be used, including present value of future cash flows, fundamental analysis, matrix pricing, and option-adjusted spread models. Market value is compared to cost on a total portfolio basis.

The valuation allowance (adjustment) account is a contra (offset) account to trading securities in the balance sheet to present market value. Balance sheet presentation follows:

Trading securities (cost)
Add (Less): Valuation allowance
Net (market value)

Unrealized (holding) gains and losses on trading securities are presented separately in the income statement.

Disclosure should be made of the method on which cost was determined in computing realized gain or loss on sale (e.g., specific identification, first- in, first-out [FIFO], and average cost).

EXAMPLE

On December 31, 20X1, a company had a portfolio of trading securities having a total cost of $200,000 and a total market value of $225,000. The entry is:

Valuation allowance	25,000	
Unrealized gain		25,000

The unrealized gain on trading securities is shown as a separate item in the income statement. Also, the valuation allowance account is a contra account to trading securities in the balance sheet. Therefore, the following is presented in the financial statements:

Income Statement
For the year Ended December 31, 20X1

Unrealized gain on trading securities	$25,000

Balance Sheet
December 31, 20X1

Current assets	
Trading securities (cost)	$200,000

Add: valuation allowance		25,000
Net (market value)		$225,000

On February 5, 20X2, trading securities costing $60,000 were bought. The entry is:

Trading securities	60,000	
Cash		60,000

On July 1, 20X2, a cash dividend of $15,000 is received. The entry is:

Cash	15,000	
Dividend revenue		15,000

On October 8, 20X2, trading securities costing $50,000 were sold for $49,000. The entry is:

Cash	49,000	
Realized loss on scale	1,000	
Trading securities		50,000

On December 31, 20X2, the total cost of trading securities remaining equaled $210,000 ($200,000 + $60,000 – $50,000). The total market value of the portfolio is assumed to be $206,000. Before showing the journal entry at year-end, it is easier to understand by presenting the current asset section of the balance sheet on 12/31/20X2:

CURRENT ASSETS

Trading securities cost	$210,000
Less: valuation allowance	4,000
Net (market value)	$206,000

The valuation allowance account appears as follows:

Valuation Allowance

12/31/20X1	25,000	Entry	29,000
		12/31/20X2	4,000

This requires a credit for the year to the valuation allowance of $29,000 to balance. Therefore, the journal entry to do this follows:

12/31/20X2 Unrealized loss	29,000	
Valuation allowance		29,000

The following is presented in the income statement for the year ended December 31, 20X2:

Dividend revenue	$15,000
Realized loss on sale of trading securities	1,000
Unrealized loss on trading securities	29,000

In the case of trading securities, a change in market value of a forward contract or option contract is recognized in the income statement in the year it accrues. Trading securities bought under a forward contract or by exercising an option are recognized at fair value on the settlement date.

Available-for-Sale Securities

Available-for-sale securities may include equity and debt securities. Available- for-sale securities are not held for short-term profits, nor are they to be held to maturity. Therefore, they are in between trading and held-to-maturity classifications. Available-for-sale securities are presented in the balance sheet as either current assets or noncurrent assets at *fair market value*. They are *often* listed as *noncurrent assets*. However, if the intent is to hold for less than one year, they are current assets. Further, available-for-sale securities available for use in current operations should be listed as current assets. For example, if cash is used to buy equity securities for a contingency fund to be used as needed, the securities are classified as current.

Available-for-sale securities bought when exercising an option are recorded at the option strike price plus the fair value of the option at the exercise date. If the option is worthless and the same security is bought in the market, the security is recorded at the market value plus the remaining carrying amount of the option premium.

Market value is compared to cost on a total portfolio basis. Cumulative unrealized (holding) gains and losses are presented as a separate item in the stockholders' equity section and identified as "accumulated other comprehensive loss or gain." In addition, the holding loss or gain arising during the period is presented in the Statement of Comprehensive Income as Other Comprehensive Income, per ASC 220-10-15, *Comprehensive Income: Overall.*

The valuation allowance (adjustment) account is a contra (offset) account to available-for-sale securities in the balance sheet to present market value. Balance sheet presentation follows:

> Available-for-sale securities (cost)
> Add (Less): valuation allowance
> Net (market value)

EXAMPLE

On April 1, 20X3, the following three available-for-sale securities were bought:

Stock	Shares	Cost per Share	Total Cost
A	1,000	$60	$ 60,000
B	2,000	40	80,000
C	500	90	45,000
			$185,000

The entry is:

4/1/20X3	Available-for-sale securities	185,000	
	Cash		185,000

On September 1, 20X3, a cash dividend of $20,000 is received.

The entry is:

9/1/20X3	Cash	20,000	
	Dividend revenue		20,000

On December 31, 20X3, the market prices per share of the securities are stock A $55, stock B $42, and stock C $83.

An analysis of the year-end portfolio is now possible.

Portfolio of Available-for-Sale Securities
12/31/20X3

Stock	Cost	Market Value	
A	$ 60,000	$ 55,000	(1,000 × $55)
B	80,000	84,000	(2,000 × $42)
C	45,000	41,500	(500 × $83)
Total	$185,000	$180,500	
Unrealized Loss		$ 4,500	

The entry is:

12/31/20X3	Unrealized loss	4,500	
	Valuation allowance		4,500

As mentioned previously, the unrealized loss on available- for-sale securities for the period is disclosed in the statement of comprehensive income and transferred to the "accumulated other comprehensive loss or gain" section of stockholders' equity on the balance sheet. In addition, the valuation allowance account is a contra account to available-for-sale securities in the balance sheet. As such, the following is presented in the financial statements:

Combined Statement of Comprehensive Income (Select Items)
For the year ended 12/31/20X3

Dividend revenue	$20,000
Unrealized holding loss (other comprehensive income)	(4,500)

Balance Sheet
12/31/20X3

Noncurrent assets	
Available-for-sale securities (cost)	$185,000
Less: valuation allowance	4,500
Net (market value)	$180,500
Stockholders' equity:	
Accumulated other comprehensive loss	$ 4,500

On July 8, 20X4, the company sells all of stock A for $62 per share. The journal entry is:

7/8/20X4	Cash	62,000	
	Available-for-sale securities		60,000
	Realized gain on sale		2,000

The computation of the gain follows:

Net proceeds from sale	$62,000
Cost basis	60,000
Gain on sale of stock	$ 2,000

The realized gain on sale is presented separately in the income statement.

On September 5, 20X4, 4,000 shares of stock D are bought at $10 per share. The entry is:

9/5/20X4	Available-for-sale securities	40,000	
	Cash		40,000

On December 31, 20X4, the market prices per share of the securities remaining in the portfolio are stock B $36, stock C $78, and stock D $11.

An analysis of the year-end portfolio is now possible.

Portfolio of Available-for-Sale Securities
12/31/20X4

Stock	Cost	Market Value	
B	$ 80,000	$ 72,000	(2,000 × $36)
C	45,000	39,000	(500 × $78)
D	40,000	44,000	(4,000 × $11)
Total	$165,000	$155,000	

Before showing the journal entry needed at year-end, it is easier to under-stand by presenting the asset section of the balance sheet on December 31, 20X4:

NONCURRENT ASSETS

Available-for-sale securities (cost)	$165,000
Less: valuation allowance	10,000
Net (market value)	$155,000

The valuation allowance account appears as follows:

Valuation Allowance

	12/31/20X3	4,500
	Entry	5,500
	12/31/20X4	10,000

This requires an additional credit for the year to the valuation allowance of $5,500 to balance. Therefore, the journal entry to do this follows:

12/31/20X4	Unrealized loss	5,500	
	Valuation allowance		5,500

The unrealized loss to be presented in the December 31, 20X4 stockholders' equity section of the balance sheet is a cumulative $10,000. This is because as a balance sheet account the unrealized loss is cumulatively carried forward. In the statement of comprehensive income for the year ended December 31, 20X4, the holding loss arising during the year of $5,500 would be reported as part of comprehensive income as another comprehensive loss item.

EXAMPLE

The same information as in the preceding example is assumed, except that the December 31, 20X4 total market value of the portfolio is $163,000 instead of $155,000. In that case, the asset section of the December 31, 20X4, balance sheet would be:

Available-for-sale securities (cost)	$165,000
Less: valuation allowance	2,000
Net (market value)	$163,000

The valuation allowance account appears as follows:

Valuation Allowance

Entry	2,500		12/31/20X3	4,500
			12/31/20X4	2,000

This requires a debit of $2,500 to the valuation allowance account to balance. Therefore, the journal entry to do this follows:

12/31/20X4	Valuation allowance	2,500	
	Unrealized gain		2,500

The net unrealized cumulative loss to be presented in the December 31, 20X4 stockholders' equity section (as accumulated other comprehensive income) of the balance sheet is a net $2,000 ($4,500 − $2,500). However, the unrealized gain of $2,500 would be reported as part of comprehensive income as a $2,500 gain item of other comprehensive income.

EXAMPLE

The same information is again assumed, except that the December 31, 20X4 total market value of the portfolio is $170,000. In that case, the asset section of the December 31, 20X4 balance sheet would be:

Available-for-sale securities (cost)	$165,000
Add: valuation allowance	5,000
Net (market value)	$170,000

The valuation allowance account would appear as follows:

Valuation Allowance

Entry	9,500	12/31/20X3	4,500
12/31/20X4	5,000		

This requires a debit of $9,500 to the valuation allowance account to balance. Therefore, the journal entry to do this follows:

12/31/20X4	Valuation allowance	9,500	
	Unrealized gain		9,500

The net unrealized cumulative gain to be presented in the December 31, 20X4 stockholders' equity section of the balance sheet is a net $5,000 ($9,500 – $4,500). In addition, the unrealized gain is disclosed as other comprehensive income in the comprehensive income statement.

Held-to-Maturity Securities

Held-to-maturity securities can only be debt securities (principally bonds) because they have maturity dates and the intent is to hold to maturity. (Because equity securities do not have a maturity date, they are not in this category.) It is presumed that the company can, and does, hold the securities to maturity. If the company is not financially able to do so, then held-to-maturity classification is not possible. Held-to-maturity securities still may be classified as such even if they are pledged as collateral for a loan.

Debt securities should not be classified as held to maturity if they may be sold to respond to changing market conditions (e.g., prepayment risk, interest rate risk, foreign currency risk, liquidity requirements), changing fund sources and terms, changing availability and yield on alternative investments, or other asset-liability management reasons. If contractual provisions allow a debt security to be paid off in advance or settled in some other manner before maturity, held-to-maturity classification may not be appropriate. However, certain circumstances of an unusual and nonrecurring nature, which were not expected initially, may force a company to alter its intent to hold the security to the maturity date. In such case, no intent to deceive was present. For example, selling a security classified as held to maturity would not indicate initial incorrect classification if the sale decision was due to such reasons as change in tax law (e.g., interest on the security is no longer tax free) or governmental rules (e.g., SEC requirements), deteriorating financial condition of the issuer, change in credit risk policy resulting from a business combination, change in regulatory policy concerning the issuer's capital balances, or change in statutory requirements amending what qualifies as an allowable or dollar amount of investment in certain types of securities.

The sale of a debt security classified as held to maturity is deemed to be at maturity if the sale takes place just prior to the maturity date (usually within three months) and as such the security's fair value is not affected (or minimally affected) by changing market interest rates. The sale of a debt security classified as held to maturity is also considered at maturity if the company has already received 85% or more of the principal from the investment.

Held-to-maturity securities in the balance sheet are presented under *noncurrent assets at amortized cost*. However, those held-to-maturity securities maturing within one year are presented under current assets. An example is a 30-year bond that is maturing next year (its thirtieth year). **Warning:** If a held-to-maturity security is sold before its maturity date, this may raise questions as to management's "real intent" and may result in reporting problems, such as reclassification.

Note: Under ASC 825-10-35-4, *Financial Instruments: Overall*, a company has the option to measure held-to-maturity securities at fair market value. If this fair value option is selected, unrealized (holding) gains and losses will be presented separately in the income statement.

According to ASC 320, an investment is impaired if the fair value is less than the amortized cost. This accounting standard applies to debt securities classified as available-for-sale and held-to-maturity that are subject to other-than-temporary impairment guidance.

If the fair value of a debt security is less than amortized cost at year-end, the company shall assess if impairment is other than temporary. If a company intends to sell the debt security, an other-than-temporary impairment has taken place. If a company is more likely than not to be required to sell the security before there is a recovery in its amortized cost, an other-than-temporary impairment has occurred.

If the company does not anticipate to recover the full amortized cost of the security, the company would be unable to assert it will recover its amortized cost. In this case, an other-than-temporary impairment has occurred. If the present value of cash flows expected to be collected is less than amortized cost, credit loss still exists, and an other-than-temporary impairment has occurred. To determine whether a credit loss exists consider such factors as the time period and degree to which fair value has been less than amortized cost.

If a company intends to sell the debt security or more likely than not will be required to sell the security before recovery of its amortized cost basis less any current period credit loss, the other-than-temporary impairment shall be recognized in earnings equal to the difference between the investment's amortized cost basis and its fair value on the balance sheet date. If the entity does not intend to sell the security, the other-than-temporary impairment shall be separated into (1) the credit loss and (2) amount related to other factors. The amount of impairment related to the credit loss is recognized in earnings while the impairment related to other factors is recognized in other comprehensive income.

Held-to-maturity securities pledged as collateral may still be classified as such if the company intends and expects to be able to repay the borrowing and recover access to its collateral.

Amortization of bond discount or premium is either based on the effective interest method (preferred) or the straight-line method. The effective interest method of amortization results in the following journal entry:

Interest receivable (nominal interest rate × face value of bond)
    Held-to-maturity securities (for discount amortization) – for difference
        Interest revenue (yield × carrying value of bond)
        Held-to-maturity securities (for premium amortization) – for difference

Under the effective interest method, yield is based on the yield to maturity formula (not the simple yield formula). Yield to maturity equals:

$$\frac{\text{Nominal interest} + \text{Discount/Years or } (-\text{ Premium/Years})}{(\text{Purchase price} + \text{Maturity value})/2}$$

EXAMPLE

A $10,000, 8% bond is bought at $9,500 having a 10-year life. The yield equals:

$$\frac{\$800 + \$500/10}{(\$9,500 + \$10,000)/2} = \frac{\$850}{\$9,750} = 8.7\%$$

The effective interest method results in a constant rate but different dollar amount of amortization each period. The straight-line method of amortization for discount or premium per period equals:

Discount or (– Premium)/Number of periods

EXAMPLE

A $10,000, 10% bond bought at $9,000 and having a 10-year life would have an annual amortization of:

$1,000/10 years = $100

The straight-line method results in the following journal entry:

Interest receivable (nominal interest × face value of bond)
Held-to-maturity securities (for discount amortization)
   Held-to-maturity securities (for premium amortization)
   Interest revenue (for difference)

The straight-line method results in a constant dollar amount of amortization each period but at a different rate.

EXAMPLE

On January 1, 20X1, ABC Company buys $100,000, 10%, five-year bonds of XYZ Company at 98%. Interest is payable annually on January 1. The effective interest method of amortization is used. The yield to maturity (effective interest rate) equals:

Nominal (coupon) interest = $100,000 × 10% = $10,000

Purchase price = $100,000 × 98% = $98,000

Discount = $100,000 – 98,000 = $2,000

Yield to maturity equals:

$$\text{Nominal Interest} + \text{Discount/Years} = \frac{\$10,000 + \$2,000/5}{(\$98,000 + \$100,000)/2}$$

$$\text{(Purchasing price + Maturity value)/2} = \frac{\$10,400}{\$99,000} = 10.505\%$$

The yield (10.505%) exceeds the nominal interest rate (10%) because the bond was bought at a discount (below face value). The investor earns the $2,000 discount between the purchase date and maturity date so as to increase the effective rate of return.

The entry for the purchase of the bond is:

1/1/20X1	Held-to-maturity securities	98,000	
	Cash		98,000

The following table is used to compute the cash interest received, interest revenue, amortization of bond discount, and carrying value of the bond:

10% Bond Bought to Yield 10.505%

Date	Cash Interest Received 10% × $100,000	Interest Revenue 10.505% × Carrying Value	Amortization of Bond Discount	Carrying Value of Bond
1/1/20X1				$98,000
1/1/20X2	$10,000	$10,295	$ 295	98,295
1/1/20X3	10,000	10,326	326	98,621
1/1/20X4	10,000	10,360	360	98,981
1/1/20X5	10,000	10,398	398	99,379
1/1/20X6	10,000	10,440	440	99,819*
Total	$50,000	$51,819	1,819	

* Difference between $99,819 and $100,000 maturity value is due to the inaccuracy of the approximation technique above. Actual interest rate = 10.535%

Note: The carrying value of the bond increases from $98,000 to $100,000 because it was bought at a discount (below face value). At maturity, the bond is worth its face value. Interest revenue increases because the carrying value of the bond increases. Amortization of bond discount increases because of the increasing interest revenue.

Based on this table, journal entries are prepared for 20X1 and 20X2.

12/31/20X1	Interest receivable	10,000	
	Held-to-maturity securities	295	
	Interest revenue		10,295
1/1/20X2	Cash	10,000	
	Interest receivable		10,000
12/31/20X2	Interest receivable	10,000	
	Held-to-maturity securities	326	
	Interest revenue		10,326

At the end of 20X1 and 20X2, respectively, the following are presented in the balance sheet and income statement:

Balance Sheet

	20X1	20X2
Current assets		
Interest receivable	$10,000	$10,000
Noncurrent assets		
Held-to-maturity securities (amortized cost)	98,295	98,621

Income Statement

	20X1	20X2
Other revenue		
Interest revenue	$10,295	$10,326

EXAMPLE

The facts from the previous example are again assumed, except that instead of using the effective interest method of amortization (the preferred method), the straight-line amortization method is used (less preferable under GAAP but accepted). The straight-line amortization per year equals:

Discount/Years = $2,000/5 = $400

The entry on January 1, 20X1, for the purchase of the bond is still the same. However, the other journal entries would be different because the amount of amortization per year is different. The entries would be:

12/31/20X1	Interest receivable	10,000	
	Held-to-maturity securities	400	
	Interest revenue		10,400
1/1/20X2	Cash	10,000	
	Interest receivable		10,000
12/31/20X2	Interest receivable	10,000	
	Held-to-maturity securities	400	
	Interest revenue		10,400

At the end of 20X1 and 20X2, respectively, the following are presented in the balance sheet and income statement:

Balance Sheet

	20X1	20X2
Current assets		
Interest receivable	$10,000	$10,000
Noncurrent assets		
Held-to-maturity securities (amortized cost)	$98,400	$98,800

Income Statement

	20X1	20X2
Other revenue		
Interest revenue	$10,400	$10,400

With regard to held-to-maturity securities, a change in market price of a forward contract or purchased option should be recognized if there has been a *permanent decline* in value. The permanent loss is presented in the current year's income statement.

FAIR VALUE ALTERNATIVE FOR AVAILABLE-FOR-SALE AND HELD-TO-MATURITY SECURITIES

ASC 825-10-10-1, *Financial Instruments: Overall*, provides an entity with an option to improve its financial reporting by disclosing more relevant and understandable information relating to its financial assets and liabilities in the form of fair value. According to the FASB, fair value would improve users' assessment of an entity's current financial position because fair value better reflects the current cash equivalent of both the entity's financial assets and liabilities. In addition, this would be preferable to the use of historical prices, which would become irrelevant with the passage of time.

ASC 825-10-35-4, *Financial Instruments: Overall*, provides an entity with an irrevocable fair value reporting option for its available-for-sale and held-to-maturity securities held at the effective date currently accounted for under ASC 320-10-05, *Investments—Debt and Equity Securities: Overall*. Under this option, the entity may choose to report all unrealized holding gains and losses in earnings for which this election has been chosen. Essentially, this accounting is the same as that which currently exists for trading securities under ASC 320-10-05. This topic is more fully discussed in Chapter 4, "Balance Sheet Presentation and Disclosures: Liabilities."

IMPAIRMENT GUIDANCE

ASC 325-40-65-1 deals with whether a company's investments should be considered "other-than-temporarily" impaired. This applies when a company holds corporate debt, equities, or structural investment securities (CDOs, mortgage-backed and other asset-backed securities). Companies must make a subjective evaluation in ascertaining when impairment is "other than temporary," and if such is the case, to write down the impaired asset to its fair value recognizing a loss. After the realized loss is recognized, a new cost basis is established for the security. A later recovery in fair value cannot be recognized unless the security is later sold.

The EITF provides disclosure requirements for securities with fair values below recorded cost. Companies must disclose in tabular form the amount of unrealized losses and the total fair value of investments with unrealized losses in investment securities having a fair value below book value and for which an other-than-temporary impairment charge has not been taken. The rationale for considering impairment as temporary should be presented. Disclosure should be made of the amounts of unrealized losses and the aggregated fair value of investments with unrealized losses. Companies must disclose in narrative form their rationale for considering existing impairment temporary including the following:

☐ Reasons for the impairment.

☐ Length and severity of the impairment.

☐ Nature of the investments.

☐ Number of investment positions that are considered unrealized.

☐ Other evidence in concluding the investment is not other-than-temporarily impaired.

Factors indicating an other-than-temporary impairment of a security's value has taken place include:

☐ Issuer's financial health.

☐ Investee's cash position.

☐ Credit rating of the security and any credit downgrading.

☐ How long and degree to which the market value has been below cost.

☐ Issuer's short-term prospects.

☐ Failure to make required interest payments.

☐ If the decline in fair value is applicable to negative conditions specifically related to, for example, the security, geographic locality, industry, overall economy, politics.

☐ Dividend reduction or elimination.

☐ Information about collectibility of the security such as present conditions, reasonable forecasts, prior events, and estimates of future cash flows.

If there is default by the issuer on principal and/or interest payments on debt, it is very probable that there is an other-then-temporary impairment. If the investor does not plan or is unable to hold the security long enough to realize the recorded amount, an impairment charge should be made.

The following is suggested:

☐ Document the factors for each security evaluated.

☐ Examine the inability to hold a security to maturity.

☐ Quarterly appraise impairment.

☐ Look at credit-related issues.

☐ Apply methodology consistently.

☐ Look at the nature of collateral including kind of assets and date of origination.

☐ Consider illiquidity.

STRUCTURED NOTES

Structured notes are debt instruments whose cash flows are tied to the change in some index (e.g., Consumer Price Index, or CPI), foreign exchange rate, interest rate (e.g., prime interest rate), or price of some item (e.g., commodity). The notes usually include a nondetachable forward or option component (e.g., calls, caps). The cash flow associated with the payment of interest and/or principal will change in timing and amount over time, depending on the linked index, interest rate, or other market factor.

Income on structured notes classified as held to maturity or available for sale should be accounted for under the *retrospective interest method*, as long as at least one or more of the following criteria exist:

☐ The maturity date of the note depends on a particular index or happening of a given event not within the control of the participants to the transaction. An example is the maturity date tied to the prime interest rate or price of wheat.

☐ The interest on the note varies over its life such as an inverse floating- rate note.

☐ The maturity value of the note may change, such as when the principal at the maturity date is tied to the S&P 100 index.

When the retrospective interest method is used, the interest income for the year equals the difference between the amortized cost of the security at year-end versus at the beginning of the year, plus the cash received for the year on the note. Amortized cost is based on the discounted value of projected future cash flows using the effective yield. If a permanent decline in value occurs, a write-down of the amortized cost is required. The loss is reported in the income statement.

BOND QUOTES

A basis point is one one-hundredth of one percentage point, usually used in quoting of spreads between interest rates or describing changes in yields of securities. Quotes for notes and bonds are expressed in thirty-seconds. However, quotes may be in sixty-fourths by using pluses. For example, a trade at 100 : 08 bid means a bid of 100 and 8 thirty-seconds. A quote of 103 : 12 + bid means a bid of 103 and $12^1/_2$ thirty-seconds, or 103 25/64. Refer to the "bid" column in a financial newspaper for the current average price for a note or bond.

STATEMENT OF CASH FLOWS

In the statement of cash flows, cash flows from buying or selling trading securities are presented in the operating activities section. However, cash flows from buying, selling, or maturing available-for-sale or held-to-maturity securities are shown in the investing activities section. Realized gains or losses, dividend income, or interest income are included in the operating section because they affect earnings.

GENERAL ACCOUNTING FOR INVESTMENTS

Dividend and interest income (revenue) are included in "Other (Financial) Income" as earned and as an element of net income.

EXAMPLE

An investor owns 1,000 shares of a stock. The company declares a $.30 dividend per share. The entry is:

Dividend receivable	300	
Dividend revenue		300

EXAMPLE

An investor owns a $20,000 face value bond having a coupon interest rate of 10% paid annually. The entry is:

Cash	2,000	
Interest income		2,000

Interest income is shown net of the amortization of discount or premium for held-to-maturity securities.

Realized gains and losses on the sale of securities for all three types (trading, available-for-sale, and held-to-maturity securities) are included as a separate item in the income statement in the year of sale. The gain or loss equals the difference between the net proceeds and the adjusted cost basis. The net proceeds equal the selling price less brokerage commissions less service fees less any transfer taxes. The adjusted cost basis equals the purchase price plus brokerage commissions plus service fees plus taxes.

EXAMPLE

An investor buys 100 shares of ABC stock having a market price of $20. The brokerage fee is $50. The investor later sells the shares at a market price of $25. The brokerage commission upon sale is $75. The net gain or loss equals:

Net sales proceeds (100 shares × $25) – $75	$2,425
Less: adjusted cost basis (100 shares × $20) + $50	2,050
Capital gain	$ 375

Gains and losses on financial instruments used to hedge trading securities should be included in the income statement. However, gains and losses on instruments that hedge available-for-sale securities should initially be presented as a separate item in the stockholders' equity section and then amortized as an adjustment to yield.

Permanent losses (e.g., due to bankruptcy, liquidity crisis) on either available-for-sale or held-to-maturity securities are considered a realized loss and included in earnings. The carrying amount of the investment is similarly reduced. When the security is written down, fair value at that date becomes the new cost basis. For the purposes of determining permanent losses, declines are measured by individual security. Permanent losses in value of one security cannot be offset by gains in another. Factors in considering whether a permanent impairment in value has occurred include an adverse event or condition, how long and how much market value has been less than cost, financial status of issuing company, poor economic conditions, industry problems, reduction or cessation in dividends, missing interest payments, and investor's ability to wait for a possible recovery in value. A subsequent recovery (gain) in the fair value of available-for-sale securities which had been written down because of a permanent loss should be added to the investment account and included as a separate component in the stockholders' equity section of the balance sheet. The journal entry for a recovery in fair value is:

Available-for-sale securities
  Unrealized gain

Note: Even though a permanent loss on available-for-sale securities is presented in the income statement, recovery in fair value is reported in the stockholders' equity section and in the comprehensive income statement (other comprehensive income).

If held-to-maturity securities are similarly permanently written down as a loss, the fair value increase will not be reported in the balance sheet, though disclosure will usually be made in the footnotes.

EXAMPLE

A company held available-for-sale debt securities having an amortized cost of $250,000. The fair market value of the securities is $200,000. The unrealized loss on these securities presented in the comprehensive income statement (other comprehensive items) and as a reduction of stockholders' equity is $50,000. It is now determined that a permanent loss exists because the investor will not be able to collect all amounts due. Therefore, the unrealized loss of $50,000 is now considered a permanent loss to be included in earnings. The entry is:

Permanent loss	50,000	
Valuation allowance	50,000	
Unrealized loss		50,000
Available-for-sale securities		50,000

The new cost basis of the debt securities is $200,000. Any later change in fair market value of the impaired securities is included in the stockholders' equity section and in the comprehensive income statement (other comprehensive income).

EXAMPLE

Available-for-sale securities were written down because of a permanent loss by $18,000. A subsequent recovery of such loss was $7,000. The appropriate journal entry for the recovery is:

Available-for-sale securities	7,000	
Unrealized gain		7,000

Unrealized (holding) gains and losses on trading securities and available-for-sale securities are not recognized for tax purposes until realized by sale. Therefore, differences between the tax basis and financial reporting basis of trading securities (shown in the income statement) and available-for-sale securities (presented in the stockholders' equity section) are temporary differences. A deferred tax liability (asset) is recognized for unrealized gains (losses).

Note: Permanent declines in value of available-for-sale and held-to-maturity securities also result in temporary differences because the loss is not deductible on the tax return until the securities are sold.

Deferred tax liabilities and deferred tax assets are reported in the balance sheet. The corresponding tax provisions will be presented in the income statement for trading securities or in the stockholders' equity section for available-for-sale securities. **Note:** No deferred taxes exist for temporary declines in price of held-to-maturity securities because no recognition is given for such a decline.

EXAMPLE

A trading security was bought at a cost of $200,000. At year-end, the fair market value of the security was $150,000, resulting in a temporary decline. The tax rate is 40%. The journal entries to record the fair value adjustment and the tax effect follow:

Unrealized loss	50,000	
Valuation allowance		50,000
Deferred tax asset	20,000	
Tax provision		20,000

If the security was available for sale instead of trading, the credit for $20,000 would go to unrealized loss (presented in the stockholders' equity section). If the security was held to maturity, no entry is made for temporary declines in price. However, if a permanent loss were incurred, deferred taxes would be recognized. In such a case, the entries would be:

Realized loss	50,000	
Held-to-maturity securities		50,000
Deferred tax asset	20,000	
Tax provision		20,000

The tax provision would be presented in the income statement for held-to-maturity securities.

In an unclassified balance sheet, the portfolio is considered noncurrent.

Equity securities acquired by exchanging noncash consideration (property or services) are recorded at either the fair market value of the consideration given or received, whichever is more clearly evident. Fair market value may be based on appraisal.

Exhibit 10-1 presents the accounting and reporting for trading, available-for-sale, and held-to-maturity securities.

Exhibit 10-1: Accounting and Reporting for Investments in Equity and Debt Securities

	Trading	Available for Sale	Held to Maturity
Valuation	Fair value	Fair value	Amortized cost
Unrealized (holding) gain or loss	Income statement	Comprehensive income statement (other comprehensive income) stockholders' equity	Not reported
Realized gain or loss	Income statement	Income statement	Income statement
Classification in balance sheet	Current assets	Current or noncurrent assets	Noncurrent assets
Type of security	Equity or debt	Equity or debt	Debt only
Periodic income	Dividend or interest revenue	Dividend or interest revenue	Interest revenue

Blocks of Stock

A company's stock may be bought on different dates and then later sold. The sale can be based on specific identification (preferred), FIFO, or average cost. FIFO is the method typically used in practice. The realized gain or loss on sale is presented in the income statement.

EXAMPLE

On January 1, 20X3 an investor bought 100 shares of L Company Stock at $9 per share. On February 3, 20X3, another 200 shares were purchased at $10 per share. On March 6, 20X3, the investor sold 50 shares at $11 per share. The FIFO method is used. The journal entry is:

Cash (50 × $11)	550	
Investment in L Company (50 × $9)		450
Gain on sale		100

The T-account looks as follows:

L Company

1/1/20X3	100 @ $9	900		3/6/20X3	50 @ $9	450
2/3/20X3	200 @ $10	2,000				
	300	2,900				
Balance	250	2,450				

Lump-Sum Purchase

If two or more stocks are bought for one price, the cost is allocated to the securities proportionately, based on their market values.

EXAMPLE

An investor pays $5,800 for 100 shares of stock A, having a market price per share of $40, and 200 shares of stock B, having a market price of $10 per share. The cost allocation follows:

Stock	Market Value	Allocated Cost
A 100 shares × $40	$4,000	$3,867[a]
B 200 shares × $10	2,000	1,933[b]
Total	$6,000	$5,800

[a] $4,000/$6,000 × $5,800 = $3,867
[b] $2,000/$6,000 × $5,800 = $1,933

The journal entry is:

Investment—stock A	3,867	
Investment—stock B	1,933	
Cash		5,800

If market value is available for one security but not the other, the incremental method must be used. Under this method, cost is first assigned to the market value of the security for which it is known, with the balance assigned to the other security.

EXAMPLE

An investor pays $50,000 for 1,000 shares of stock X with a market price of $30 and 300 shares of stock Y, which does not have a market price because it is a closely held company. The cost allocation follows:

	Stock	Allocated Cost
Stock X	1,000 shares @ $30	$30,000
Stock Y	Balancing figure	$20,000 ($50,000 − $30,000)
Total		$50,000

Exchange (Conversion) of Securities

A conversion of securities may include exchanging preferred stock or bonds for common stock. The security received is recorded at its market value. The difference between the market value of the security received and the cost basis of the security given up represents a gain or loss on conversion. The gain or loss is reported in the income statement.

EXAMPLE

An investor owns preferred stock costing $10,000, which he or she converts into 1,000 shares of common stock having a market price of $15 per share. The journal entry is:

Investment in common stock	15,000	
Investment in preferred stock		10,000
Gain—conversion of stock investment		5,000

Stock Dividends

A stock dividend increases the number of shares held without increasing the cost. Because total cost remains the same, the cost per share after the stock dividend is received decreases. A stock dividend involves only a memo entry.

EXAMPLE

An investor owns 100 shares of DEF Company at a total cost of $1,000. Therefore, the cost per share is $10. A 20% stock dividend is received, so the shares owned now are 120. It costs the investor nothing to get those shares. Because total cost remains at $1,000, the cost per share decreases to $8.33 ($1,000/120). The T-account looks as follows:

Investment in DEF

100	$10	$1,000	I
20		0	I
120	$8.33	$1,000	I

EXAMPLE

On April 3, 20X3, Robert Company bought 1,000 shares of DEF common stock at $82 per share. On October 15, 20X3, Robert received 1,000 stock rights to buy an additional 1,000 shares at $95 per share. On October 30, 20X3, DEF common stock had a market value, rights on, of $100 per share, and the stock rights had a market value of $6 each. At October 30, 20X3, the investment in stock rights has a carrying value equal to $4,920, computed as follows:

Original cost of stock	$ 82,000
Ratio of value of stock rights to value of stock	× $6/$100
Investment in stock rights	$ 4,920

Preferred Stock Received for Common Stock Dividend

Instead of cash, a company may receive shares of preferred stock as its common stock dividend. The nonmonetary asset received (investment in preferred stock) should be recorded at the fair value of the asset received. Thus, the investment and related dividend income should be recorded at the fair market value of the preferred stock at the date of the transaction, as follows:

Investment in preferred stock
    Dividend income on common stock

Stock Splits

A stock split increases the number of shares held without increasing the cost. After a stock split, the cost per share is proportionately reduced. A stock split involves only a memo entry.

EXAMPLE

An investor owns 500 shares of PQ Company at a total cost of $10,000. Therefore, the cost per share is $20. A 2-for-1 stock split is issued. As a result, the investor will now have 1,000 shares. Because total cost remains the same ($10,000), the cost per share is proportionately reduced to $10. The T-account looks as follows:

Investment in PQ Company

500	$20	$10,000	I
1,000	$10	$10,000	I

RECLASSIFICATION ADJUSTMENTS RELATING TO INVESTMENTS

As indicated in previous discussions, any unrealized holding gains or losses relating to the available-for-sale portfolio are reported in an enterprise's comprehensive income statement as part of other comprehensive income. These gains or losses are then closed to the accumulated other comprehensive income section of stockholders' equity. However, when securities from this portfolio are actually sold, double counting may occur. This is due to the recognition of realized gains and losses from the sale of available-for-sale securities in the income statement (and comprehensive income statement) as well as their disclosure in comprehensive income from the current or prior periods. The latter may have occurred as part of the recognition of unrealized holding gains or losses derived from the mark-to-market entry made on the available-for-sale portfolio at the end of the current or prior periods. To ensure that such double counting does not occur when the sale of available-for-sale securities occurs, it is necessary to ascertain the extent of the duplication and record a reclassification adjustment in the comprehensive income statement. This adjustment may either be shown on the face of the financial statement in which comprehensive income is shown or be disclosed in the notes to the financial statements.

EXAMPLE

X Company has the following securities in its available-for-sale portfolio at December 31, 20X1 (this was the company's first year of operations):

	Cost	Fair Value	Unrealized Gain (Loss)
Y Company stock	$ 60,000	$40,000	$(20,000)
Z Company stock	50,000	20,000	(30,000)
	$110,000	$60,000	$(50,000)

In its comprehensive income statement for the year, 20X1, the unrealized holding losses of $50,000 will be included in other comprehensive income, as follows:

X Company
Statement of Comprehensive Income
For the Year Ended December 31, 20X1

Net income	$ XX,XXX
Other comprehensive income	
Unrealized holding losses on available for-sale securities	$(50,000)
Comprehensive income	$ XX,XXX

At the beginning of the next year, 20X2, X Company sells its Y Company stock and incurs a realized loss of $20,000 on the sale. At December 31, 20X2, the fair value of Z Company stock (the remaining security in its available-for-sale portfolio) dropped to $10,000 (from $20,000). This represented an additional $10,000 unrealized holding loss in the year 20X2 and is disclosed in X Company's statement of comprehensive income (as part of other comprehensive income). It is also assumed that X Company had net income of $150,000 for the year 2002, which included the realized loss of $20,000 from the sale of Y Company stock. The X Company comprehensive income statement for the year 20X2 appears as follows:

X Company
Statement of Comprehensive Income
for the Year Ended December 31, 20X2

Net income	$150,000
Other comprehensive income	
Less: unrealized holding losses on available for-sale securities	$10,000

Add: reclassification adjustment for losses included in net income	20,000	10,000
Comprehensive income		$160,000

In the year 20X1, the unrealized loss of $20,000 was included in the X Company's comprehensive income statement. The next year, 20X2, the company sold its Y Company stock and incurred a realized loss of $20,000, which decreased its net income and comprehensive income for the period. A reclassification adjustment (shown in the preceding statement of comprehensive income) is required, causing an unrealized gain of $10,000 to avoid double counting.

TRANSFERS OF SECURITIES BETWEEN CATEGORIES

The reasonableness of a security's classification should be reevaluated at each reporting date. For example, there may have been a change in circumstances, such as a change in financial condition (e.g., cash flow, liquidity, profitability).

All types of transfers between categories should be accounted for at fair market value on the transfer date. This requirement ensures that a company cannot avoid fair value recognition by transferring a security from one category to another. If, for example, a security is transferred from the trading to the available-for-sale portfolio, it is recorded in the available-for-sale portfolio at fair value (at the date of transfer), and any unrealized holding gain or loss (due to the difference between fair value and cost) is recorded as part of net income and closed to retained earnings in stockholders' equity. Fair value at the date of transfer becomes the new cost basis of the security. At the next reporting date, an adjusting entry is made to record any new changes in the fair value of the available-for-sale portfolio. ASC 320-10-55 notes, however, that transfers of this nature should, in fact, be rare. The same parameters apply to the transfer of a security from the available-for-sale to the trading portfolio. For a debt security transferred from the held-to-maturity to the available-for-sale portfolio, any unrealized holding gain or loss (due to the difference between cost and fair value increases and decreases) is disclosed in the comprehensive income statement as other comprehensive income and is ultimately transferred to the accumulated other comprehensive income section of stockholders' equity (as a separate component of stockholders' equity). A securities valuation account is also used in this transfer because its balance must always equal the balance in the unrealized holding gain or loss account (unlike the prior types of transfers, where net income was changed). Net income in this situation is not affected. The same guidelines apply to the transfer of a debt security from the available-for-sale to the held-to-maturity portfolio except that any unrealized gain or loss at the date of transfer represents a component of stockholders' equity and is amortized over the remaining life of the debt security. A securities valuation account (held to maturity) is also used in this transfer. Both the unrealized holding gain or loss account and its equivalent securities valuation account (held to maturity) are amortized over the remaining life of the debt securities. The results of these calculations are netted against each other so there is no effect on net income. In addition, if the debt security was originally purchased at a discount or premium, the discount or premium should be amortized over the life of the debt security as well. All of the aforementioned guidelines presume that end-of-period adjusting entries to report portfolio changes in fair value were not yet recorded.

Exhibit 10-2 presents the accounting for the transfers between categories.

Exhibit 10-2: Transfer Between Classifications

Nature of Transfer	How Measured	Effect on Income	Effect on Stockholders' Equity
1. Trading to available for sale	Transfer at market value, which becomes new cost basis at the date of transfer	Unrealized gain or loss is recognized as part of income	Unrealized gain or loss is recognized as part of stockholders' equity
2. Available for sale to trading	Same as above	Same as above	Same as above
3. Held to maturity to available for sale	Transfer security at market value on transfer date	None	The separate component of stockholders' equity is increased or decreased by the unrealized gain or loss at the date of transfer
4. Available for sale to held to maturity	Same as above	None	Amortize balance of unrealized gain or loss as part of stockholders' equity over the remaining life of the security

EXAMPLE

On December 31, 20X2, a company elects to transfer from trading to available for sale one stock of many stocks. On the transfer date, the stock's cost is $100,000 and its market value is $120,000. The transfer will be made at fair market value, which becomes the new cost basis. Assuming that the adjusting entry to record any change of fair value for the current period has not been made, the entry is:

Available-for-sale securities	120,000	
Trading securities		100,000
Unrealized holding gain—net income		20,000

The unrealized holding gain increases net income for the period.

EXAMPLE

A company elects to transfer from available for sale to trading one stock in its portfolio. On the transfer date, cost equals $100,000 and market value equals $90,000 of that stock. Assuming that the adjusting entry to record any change of fair value for the current period has not been made, the entry is:

Trading securities	90,000	
Unrealized holding loss—net income	10,000	
Available-for-sale securities		100,000

The unrealized loss will decrease net income for the period.

EXAMPLE

A company decides to transfer one of its corporate bonds in its portfolio from held to maturity to available for sale. The amortized cost is $40,000 and the fair market value is $55,000. The transfer is made at fair market value. Assuming that the adjusting entry to record any change of fair value for the current period has not been made, the entry is:

Valuation adjustment (available for sale)	15,000	
Available-for-sale securities	40,000	
Unrealized holding gain—stockholders' equity		15,000
Held-to-maturity securities		40,000

Note that the unrealized gain of $15,000 will be reflected in the other comprehensive income section of comprehensive income as well as stockholders' equity.

DISCLOSURES

The following information should be disclosed about investments in equity and debt securities:

☐ Valuation basis used.

☐ Total portfolio market value.

☐ Method used to determine cost (e.g., FIFO, average cost, specific identification) in computing the realized gain or loss on sale of securities.

☐ Unrealized (holding) gains and losses for trading and available-for-sale securities.

☐ Reasons for selling or transferring securities.

☐ Gains and losses from transferring available-for-sale securities to trading included in the income statement.

☐ Market value and cost by major equity security.

☐ Fair value and amortized cost basis by major debt security type.

☐ Proceeds from selling available-for-sale securities, with associated realized gains and losses.

☐ Subsequent event disclosure in the form of significant changes in market value taking place after year-end but before the issuance of the financial statements.

☐ Name of companies owned when ownership is significant.

Disclosure for debt securities classified as available for sale or held to maturity should include contractual maturity dates.

Financial institutions should disclose their holdings in equity securities, corporate debt securities, mortgage-backed securities, U.S. government securities, foreign government securities, and other debt securities. Financial institutions should disclose fair value and amortized cost of debt securities in maturity groupings, including within one year, in 1 to 5 years, after 5 to 10 years, and after 10 years.

FINANCIAL STATEMENT ANALYSIS

Held-to-maturity securities for analytical purposes should be valued at market value rather than amortized cost to reflect current prices. However, this is not GAAP. Exhibit 10-3 shows a comprehensive example of the accounting and reporting of trading, available-for-sale, and held-to-maturity securities.

Exhibit 10-3: Comprehensive Example of ASC 320

The GI Corporation Makes the Following Debt and Equity Investments:

Bonds	Par value:	$200,000
	Nominal interest rate:	8%
	Market interest rate:	10%
	Years to maturity:	5
	Interest paid:	Annually
Stocks	Number of shares:	4,000
	Par value stock:	$ 20.00
	Purchase price:	$ 25.00

Purchase price of investments is calculated as follows:

Bonds	Present value of amount due at maturity	$124,184	
	Present value of interest payments	$ 60,653	
	Purchase priced of bonds		$184,837
Stocks	Purchase price of stocks [4,000 shares at $25 each]		$100,000
	Total purchase price of investments (Bonds & stocks):		$284,837

The bond discount will be amortized using the effective interest method over a period of five years as follows:

Year	(I) Interest Income	(II) Cash Received	(III) Discount Amortization	(IV) Discount Remaining	(V) Carrying Amount
1/1/X1				15,163	184,837
12/31/X1	18,484	16,000	2,484	12,679	187,321
12/31/X2	18,732	16,000	2,732	9,947	190,053
12/31/X3	19,005	16,000	3,005	6,942	193,058
12/31/X4	19,306	16,000	3,306	3,636	196,364
12/31/X5	19,636	16,000	3,636	–	200,000

[I] Interest income is calculated by multiplying previous year's carrying amount (V) by the market interest rate of 10%.
[II] Cash received is calculated by multiplying the par value of bonds by the nominal interest rate: $200,000 \times 8\%$.
[III] Discount amortization is (I)–(II).
[IV] Discount remaining is prior year's carrying amount (V) minus current year's discount (III).
[V] Carrying amount is par value of bonds, $200,000, minus the discount remaining (IV).

Market values for the investments are as follows:

	12/31/X1	12/31/X2
Bonds	180,000	170,000
Stocks	150,000	125,000
Total investments	330,000	295,000

Dividend is paid on Common Stock as follows:

8/31/X1	10.00 dollars per share
8/31/X2	5.00 dollars per share

Trading Securities

It is assumed that these investments are classified as trading securities.

1/1/X1	Investments—trading	$184,837	
	Cash		$184,837
	Purchase of bonds classified as trading		
1/1/X1	Investments—trading	$100,000	
	Cash		$100,000
	Purchase of common stocks classified as trading		
8/31/X1	Cash	$ 40,000	
	Dividend income		$ 40,000
	Dividends received on common stocks		
12/31/X1	Investments—trading	$ 2,484	
	Cash	$ 16,000	
	Interest income		$ 18,484

Interest received and amortization of bond discount

12/31/X1	Investments—trading*	$ 42,679	
	Unrealized gain on Investments*		$ 42,679

*The unrealized GAIN is calculated as follows:

Market value of bonds and stocks at 12/31/X1 [180,000 + 150,000]	330,000
Carrying value of bonds and stocks at 12/31/X1 [187,321 + 100,000]	287,321
Unrealized gain	$42,679

In the second year, the journal entries will be as follows:

8/31/X2	Cash	$ 20,000	
	Dividend income		$ 20,000
	Dividends received on common stocks		
12/31/X2	Investments—trading	$ 2,732	
	Cash	$ 16,000	
	Interest income		$ 18,732
12/31/X2	Unrealized loss on investments**	$ 37,732	
	Investments—trading**		$ 37,732
	Adjustment to market value for trading investments		

**The unrealized loss is calculated as follows:

Market value of bonds and stocks at 12/31/X2 [170,000 + 125,000]	295,000
Carrying value of bonds# and stocks at 12/31/X2 [182,732 + 150,000]	332,732
Unrealized Loss	(37,732)

#The carrying value of bonds on 12/31/X2 is calculated as follows:

Market value of bonds at 12/31/X1:	180,000
Plus: bond discount amortization for year 2:	2,732
	182,732

The trading investments will be presented in the financial statements as follows:

	Year 1	Year 2
INCOME STATEMENT:		
Interest income	18,484	18,732
Dividend income	40,000	20,000
Unrealized gain (loss) on investments	42,679	(37,732)
BALANCE SHEET:		
Current Assets:		
Investments—trading	330,000	295,000
STATEMENT OF CASH FLOWS:		
Operating Activities:		
Interest	16,000	16,000

	Year 1	Year 2
Dividends	40,000	20,000
Investment purchases	284,837	–

Securities Available for Sale

It is assumed that these investments are now classified as available for sale.

When securities are available for sale, the unrealized gain or loss is presented as part of "other comprehensive income" in the income statement.

The journal entries to record the unrealized gain or loss are:

12/31/X1	Investments—available for sale	$ 42,679	
	Unrealized gain on investments		$ 42,679
	Adjustment to market value for available-for-sale investments		
12/31/X2	Unrealized loss on investments	$ 37,732	
	Investments—available for sale		$ 37,732
	Adjustments to market value for available-for-sale investments		

The available-for-sale investments will be presented in the financial statements as follows:

	Year 1	Year 2
INCOME STATEMENT:		
Interest income	18,484	18,732
Dividend income	40,000	20,000
OTHER COMPREHENSIVE INCOME:		
Unrealized gain or (loss) on investments available for sale	42,679	(37,732)
BALANCE SHEET:		
Asset (current or long-term based upon intent):		
Investments—available for sale	330,000	295,000
STATEMENT OF CASH FLOWS:		
Operating Activities:		
Interest	16,000	16,000
Dividends	40,000	20,000
INVESTMENT ACTIVITIES:		
Investment Purchases	284,837	–

Securities Held to Maturity

It is assumed that the bonds are now classified as investments held to maturity. Recall that common stocks do not have a maturity date and are therefore not included in this example.

Journal entries for discount amortization and cash received are the same as entries for trading securities. However, no journal entries are required at the end of the year to record unrealized gain or loss.

The financial statement presentation for securities held to maturity is as follows:

For Bonds Only

	Year 1	Year 2
INCOME STATEMENT:		
Interest income	18,484	18,732
BALANCE SHEET:		
Asset:		
Investments—held to maturity	187,321	190,053
STATEMENT OF CASH FLOWS:		
Operating Activities:		
Interest	16,000	16,000
INVESTMENT ACTIVITIES:		
Investment purchases	184,837	–

EQUITY METHOD

ASC 323-10-15-8 covers the accounting, reporting, and disclosures under the equity method to account for investments in other companies. The investor is the owner and the investee is the company owned. The equity method is used if:

☐ An investor owns between 20% *and* 50% of the investee's voting common stock.

☐ The investor owns less than 20% of the investee's voting common stock but has effective control (significant influence). Significant influence may be indicated by a number of factors, including substantial intercompany transactions, exchanges of executives between investor and investee, investor's significant input in the investee's decision-making process, investor's representation on the investee's board of directors, investee's dependence on investor (e.g., operational, technological, or financial support), and substantial ownership of the investee by investor relative to other widely disbursed shareholder interests. The factors indicating that significant influence may not exist, thereby precluding the equity method, are that significant influence exists by a small group of stockholders excluding the investor representing majority ownership of investee, the investee sues the investor, the investee makes a formal complaint to governmental bodies regarding the investor, and the investor is unable to obtain needed financial data from the investee to use the equity method. Under ASC 323-10-15-10, if there is a standstill agreement stipulating that either the investor has relinquished major rights as a stockholder or that significant influence does not exist, it may indicate that the equity method is not appropriate. ASC 323-10-15-10 also may preclude the equity method if the investor attempts unsuccessfully in obtaining representation on the investee's board of directors. ASC 323-10-15-3, *Investments— Equity Method and Joint Ventures: Overall*, states that when an investor has the ability to exercise significant influence over the operating and financial policies of an investee, the equity method of accounting should be applied only when the investor has an investment in common stock and/ or an investment that is in-substance common stock.

☐ The investor owns in excess of 50% of the investee's voting common stock, but a negating factor exists, preventing consolidation. According to ASC 840-10-45, *Leases: Overall*, negating factors prohibiting consolidation might be temporary control, noncontrol, and foreign exchange restrictions. However, under ASC 840-10-45, the equity method is used to account for nonconsolidated majority-owned subsidiaries.

☐ There is a joint venture. A joint venture is an entity that is owned, operated, and jointly managed by a common group of investors.

The accounting under the equity method is illustrated in selected T-account form:

Investment in Investee

Cost	Ordinary loss
Ordinary profit	Extraordinary loss
Extraordinary gain	Dividends
	Permanent decline in market price
	Depreciation on excess of fair market value less book value of specific assets

Equity in Earnings of Investee

Depreciation expense on excess value	Ordinary profit
Ordinary loss	

Extraordinary Gain

	Extraordinary Gain

The accounting process as explained by these T-accounts involves the following:

☐ The cost of the investment includes brokerage charges. The investor recognizes its percentage ownership interest in the investee's ordinary earnings by debiting investment in investee and crediting equity in earnings of investee. The latter is like a revenue account.

☐ The investor's share in the investee's profits is determined after subtracting cumulative preferred dividends, whether or not declared. **Note:** The investor's share of investee earnings in excess of dividends paid is referred to as undistributed investee earnings. The investor's share is based on the investee's most recent income statement, provided the time lag in reporting each year is consistent. In other words, if the investor and investee have different year-ends, the investor may compute its share of investee's profits or losses based on the investee's financial statements for its fiscal year-end.

☐ Extraordinary gains or losses and prior-period adjustments are recognized by the investor exactly as presented on the investee's financial statements. Such items are separately reported if material.

☐ The investor's share of the investee's dividends reduces the carrying value of the investment in investee account. **Note:** The final financial effect on the investor's financial statements is identical whether the equity method or full consolidation is used. The only difference lies in the detail within the financial statements.

☐ The excess paid by the investor for the investee's net assets is first assigned to the specific assets and liabilities and is depreciated. The unidentifiable part of the excess is goodwill. The investment in investee account is credited, and the equity in earnings account is debited for the depreciation on excess of fair market value less book value of specific assets acquired.

☐ Although the equity method makes no adjustment for temporary declines in market price of the investment, permanent declines in value are recognized by debiting loss and crediting investment in investee.

EXAMPLE

Mavis Company acquires 30% of Blake Company's stock under the equity method for $500,000. Blake's net income and dividends for the year are $100,000 and $20,000, respectively. The carrying value of the investment at year-end equals:

Initial cost	$500,000
Add: share of net income $100,000 × 30%	30,000
Less: share of dividends $20,000 × 30%	(6,000)
Carrying value—year-end	$524,000

If, at the beginning of the next year, Mavis sells 50% of its interest in Blake for $275,000, the journal entry for the sale would be:

Cash	275,000	
Investment in Blake (50% × $524,000)		262,000
Gain on sale of investment		13,000

Other accounting aspects exist. If the investor's share of the investee's losses exceeds the carrying value of the investment account, the equity method should be discontinued at the zero amount. Thereafter, the investor should not record additional losses unless it has guaranteed the investee's debts, is otherwise committed to provide additional financial support to the investee, or immediate profitability is forthcoming. If the investee later shows net income, the investor can reinstate using the equity method only after its share of profit equals the share of unrecorded losses when the equity method was suspended. If the investor sells the investee's stock, a realized gain or loss is recognized for the difference between the selling price and carrying value of the investment in investee account at the time of sale. The realized gain or loss appears in the investor's income statement.

ASC 323-10-35-37 and 35-39, *Investments—Equity Method and Joint Ventures: Overall*, provides that when an investor loses significant influence, the investor must offset its proportionate share of the investee's equity adjustments of other comprehensive income against the book value of the investment. If the offset reduces the book value to below zero, the investor should reduce the carrying value to zero with the remaining amount recognized as income.

The equity method basically uses the consolidation approach by eliminating intercompany profits and losses. Such profits and losses are eliminated by reducing the investment balance and the equity earnings in investee for the investor's share of the unrealized intercompany profits and losses. Investee capital transactions affecting the investor are treated as in consolidation. The investee is treated as if it were a consolidated subsidiary. For example, the purchase or sale by the investee of its treasury stock, which changes the investor's ownership interest, is accounted for by the investor as if the investee were a consolidated subsidiary. Use of the equity method generally results in the investor's stockholders' equity and net earnings being the same as if the investor and investee were consolidated. For example, if the investee issues its common stock to third parties at a price above book value, the investment value increases, with a related increase in the investor's paid-in-capital. Similar results occur when holders of options or convertible securities exchange them for investee's common stock.

EXAMPLE

An investor sells merchandise "downstream" to an investee. At year- end, $100,000 of profit resides in inventory from intercompany sales. The investor owns 30% of the investee. The tax rate is 25%. The elimination entry for intercompany profits is:

Equity in earnings of investee ($100,000 × 30%)	30,000	
Deferred tax asset ($30,000 × 25%)	7,500	
Investment in investee		30,000
Income tax expense		7,500

Assuming that the intercompany sales were "upstream" (investee to investor), the elimination entry would be:

Equity in earnings of investee ($30,000 × 1 − .25)	22,500	
Deferred tax asset	7,500	
Inventory		30,000

EXAMPLE

On January 3, 20X2, Klemer Corporation buys a 25% interest (4,000 shares) in Jones Company's outstanding stock for $160,000. The cost equals both the book and fair values of Klemer's interest in Jones's underlying net assets. On January 14, 20X2, Jones purchases 2,000 shares of its stock from other shareholders for $100,000. Because the price paid ($50 per share) is more than Klemer's per share carrying value of its interest of $40 per share, Klemer's has experienced a loss by the transaction. Further, Klemer's percentage interest in Jones has increased because the shares held by third parties have been reduced.

Klemer's new interest in Jones's net assets follows:

$$\frac{4{,}000 \text{ shares owned by Klemer}}{14{,}000 \text{ shares outstanding in total}} \times \text{Jones's net assets}$$

$$.2857 \times (\$640{,}000 - \$100{,}000) = \$154{,}278$$

Klemer's interest has been decreased by $160,000 − $154,278, or $5,722. In consequence, the following entry is required:

Paid-in-capital (or retained earnings)	5,722	
Investment in Jones		5,722

Paid-in-capital is charged for the loss if such an account arose from previous similar transactions. If not, retained earnings is charged. If a gain arose, paid-in-capital would be credited.

A temporary tax difference arises under the equity method because the investor recognizes the investee's earnings for financial reporting purposes but recognizes dividend income on the tax return. This will cause a deferred tax liability.

If ownership falls below 20%, or if the investor loses effective control over the investee, the investor should stop recording the investee's earnings. The equity method is discontinued, but the balance in the investment account is retained. The market value method (under ASC 320-10-30-4) will then be applied in the future.

If the investor increases its ownership in the investee to 20% or more (e.g., 30%), the equity method should be used for current and future years. The effect of using the equity method instead of the market value method on previous years at the old percentage (e.g., 10%) should be recognized as a retroactive adjustment to retained earnings and other affected accounts (e.g., investment in investee). The retroactive adjustment on the investment, earnings, and retained earnings should be applied in a similar way as a step-by-step acquisition of a subsidiary.

The investor must disclose the following information in the footnotes, in separate schedules, or parenthetically:

☐ A statement that the equity method is being used.

☐ Identification of investee along with percent owned.

☐ Quoted market price of investee's stock.

☐ Investor's accounting policies.

☐ Significant subsequent events between the date and issuance of the financial statements.

☐ The reason for not using the equity method even though the investor owned 20% or more of the investee's common stock.

☐ The reason that the equity method was used even though the investor owned less than 20% of the investee's common stock.

☐ Summarized financial information as to assets, liabilities, and earnings of significant investments in unconsolidated subsidiaries.

☐ Significant realized and unrealized gains and losses applying to the subsidiary's portfolio taking place between the dates of the financial statements of the parent and subsidiary.

☐ Restatement of prior periods because of a change to the equity method.

☐ Significant effects of possible conversion and exercises of investee common stock.

☐ A statement when income taxes have not been provided for on a foreign subsidiary's undistributed profits and the reasons therefore. (The cumulative amount of undistributed earnings must be specified.)

EXAMPLE

On January 1, 20X2, ABC Company purchased 40,000 shares for a 30% interest in the common stock of XYZ Company at $35 per share. Brokerage fees were $7,000. During the year, XYZ's net income was $200,000 and dividends were $50,000. On January 1, 20X3, ABC received 20,000 shares of common stock because of a stock split by XYZ. On January 6, 20X3, ABC sold 4,000 shares at $25 per share of XYZ stock. The journal entries are:

1/1/20X2		
Investment in investee	1,400,000	
Cash		1,400,000
12/31/20X2		
Investment in investee	60,000	
Equity in earnings of investee		60,000
30% × $200,000 = $60,000		
Cash	15,000	
Investment in investee		
30% × $50,000 = $15,000		15,000
1/1/20X3 memo for stock split of 20,000 additional shares		
1/6/20X3		
Cash (4,000 × $25)	100,000	
Investment in investee*		96,320
Gain on sale of investment		3,680

---

* $1,445,000 balance ÷ 60,000 shares = $24.08; 4,000 shares × $24.08 =$96,320.

Investment in Investee

1/1/20X2	1,400,000	12/31/20X2	15,000
12/31/20X2	60,000		
	1,460,000		
Balance	1,445,000		

EXAMPLE

On January 1, 20X2, Gonzalez Corporation bought 200,000 shares of Richardson Corporation's 800,000 shares outstanding for $5,000,000. The book value of net assets acquired was $4,000,000. Of the $1,000,000 excess paid over book value, all of it is applicable to undervalued tangible assets. The depreciation period is 10 years. In 20X2, the investee's net income was $150,000, including an extraordinary loss of $10,000. Dividends of the investee paid on August 1, 20X2, were $80,000. The required journal entries for these events follow:

1/1/20X2		
Investment in investee	5,000,000	
Cash		5,000,000
8/1/20X2		
Cash	20,000	
Investment in investee		20,000
25% × $80,000 = $20,000		
12/31/20X2		
Investment in investee	40,000	
Equity in earnings of investee		40,000
$160,000 × 25% = $40,000		
Extraordinary loss	2,500	
Investment in investee		2,500
$10,000 × 25% = $2,500		
Equity in earnings of investee	100,000	
Investment in investee		100,000
Computations follow:		
Depreciation on undervalued depreciable assets		
$1,000,000/10 years		$ 100,000

EXAMPLE

An investor purchases 500,000 shares of an investee at an average cost per share of $5, or $2,500,000. The investee's total shares outstanding are 2,000,000. Therefore, the investor's percentage ownership interest is 25% (500,000/2,000,000). The *overall value* of the investee equals $10,000,000, computed as follows:

Actual cost/Percentage ownership

$2,500,000/25% = $10,000,000

If the book value of the net assets of the investee is $7,000,000, the excess of fair market value over book value is $3,000,000 ($10,000,000 – $7,000,000). The excesses of fair value over book value attributable to land and building are $500,000 and $1,000,000, respectively. This $3,000,000 excess is assigned to the investee's net assets as follows:

Excess		$3,000,000
Excess of fair market value over book value attributable to		
Land	$500,000	
Fixed assets	1,000,000	
Less: deferred income taxes		
30% × $1,500,000	(450,000)	1,050,000
Total goodwill of investee company		$1,950,000

The investor's share of the total goodwill of the investee company would be $487,500 ($1,950,000 × 25%). **Note:** Deferred income taxes are based on the investee's effective tax rate of 30% applicable to the excess of fair value over book value of investee's net assets.

Note: Under ASC 825-10-15-4 and 15-5 and 825-10-35-4, *Financial Instruments: Overall*, a company using the equity method can elect to use the fair value option. If that option is selected, the Investment in Investee account will reflect temporary changes in market value of the investee. The resulting unrealized (holding) loss or gain will be presented as a separate item in the income statement. For example, if the fair market value of the investee decreases, the investor will debit unrealized loss and credit the Investment in Investee account (or a Valuation Allowance account) for the decrease in value. On the other hand, if there is an increase in fair market value, the Investment in Investee account (or Valuation Allowance account) would be debited and unrealized gain would be credited for the increase in fair market value.

According to Accounting Standards Update (ASU) No. 2009-09 (September 2009) (ASC 505, *Equity*) (ASC 323, *Investments—Equity Method and Joint Ventures*), *Accounting for Investments—Equity Method and Joint Ventures and Accounting for Equity-Based Payments to Non-Employees*, companies should classify any income or expense in the same income statement caption as equity in earnings of investee for investor stock-based compensation based on the investor's stock granted to employees of an equity method investee (ASC 323-10-25-3).

SEC registrants can anticipate the SEC to challenge accounting by the grantee or grantor in transactions involving equity instruments granted to other than employees if their accounting does not reflect the same commitment date or similar values (ASC 505-50-25-2).

INVESTMENTS BY BANKS IN DEBT SECURITIES

Banks can only invest in debt securities that satisfy their suitability criteria. Banks may buy:

☐ *Revenue Anticipation Notes (RANs)*. These are short-term debt securities pledged with specific source revenues, such as sales taxes.

☐ *Tax Anticipation Notes (TANs)*. These are short-term debt securities used to finance expenditures pending the pledged receipt of anticipated real estate taxes.

☐ *Bond Anticipation Notes (BANs)*. These are a community's short-term debt securities repaid from amounts received from permanent financing.

Banks may invest in all federal government securities without limitation except for those of the Tennessee Valley Authority, which is limited to 10% of capital and surplus. Banks may invest in state and municipal bonds as follows:

☐ General obligation municipals may be bought by banks in unlimited amounts.

☐ Revenue bonds issued by municipals may be bought by banks only up to 10% of capital and surplus.

Banks may invest in corporate debt securities with the following restrictions:

☐ Banks are not legally allowed to invest in junk bonds because of the high risk.

☐ National banks cannot invest in privately placed corporate debt because of limited marketability due to the number and type of potential investors. However, a national bank may buy privately placed corporate securities and consider them loans.

The yield on government agency investments exceed the yield on U.S. Treasury investments. The reasons for the higher yield are that there is less liquidity and more risk with agency issues, the interest income is often taxable, and many agencies' debts are not guaranteed by the U.S. government.

Banks can deduct for tax purposes 80% of the interest expense on deposits used to buy obligations of "small issuer" municipalities (those in which debt obligations do not exceed $10 million per year).

Amortization of discount or premium is based on the effective interest method. Amortization is from the date of purchase to the maturity date. However, if it is probable that the security will be redeemed before maturity, amortization will be from the purchase date to the call date.

Gains and losses on sale of securities are reported at the trade date. However, if immaterial, the settlement date may be used.

INVESTMENT IN CERTAIN ENTITIES THAT CALCULATE NET ASSET VALUE PER SHARE (OR ITS EQUIVALENT)

An investor may invest in entities (investees) that allow the investor to redeem its investments directly with the investee. Many of these investments do not have readily determinable fair values. Examples of these investees (also called alternative investments) are hedge funds, private equity funds, real estate funds, and venture capital funds. Many of these investees provide their investors with a net asset value per share (or its equivalent).

The net asset value per share (or its equivalent) provided by the investee may not represent fair value of the investor's investment in all cases. Certain aspects of the investment (such as restrictions on redemption at the measurement date) and transaction prices from principal-to-principal or brokered transactions my require adjustments to net asset value per share to estimate fair value of the investment.

Disclosure should be made of any restrictions on the investor's ability to redeem its investment on the measurement date. Disclosure is required of unfunded commitments and the investment strategies of investees. An example of an unfunded commitment is a contract by the investor to invest additional capital at a later date to fund investments that the investee will make.

The amendment to this update improves financial reporting by allowing use of a practical expedient, with appropriate disclosures, when measuring the fair value of an alternative investment that does not have a readily determinable fair value.

The amendments to this update apply to all reporting entities holding an investment required or allowed to be measured or disclosed at fair value on a recurring or nonrecurring basis and, as of the reporting entity's measurement date, if the investment satisfies both of the following conditions:

1. The investment does not have a readily determinable fair value.

2. The investment is in an entity that has all of the attributes specified in ASC 946-10-15-2 or, if one or more of the attributes specified in that paragraph are not present, is in an entity for which industry practice is to issue financial statements using the measurement principles in ASC 946. An example is certain investments in real estate funds that measure investment assets at fair value on a recurring basis. ASC 946-10-15-2 limits the scope of ASC 946 to investment companies having the following attributes:

   a. Unit of ownership is in the form of units of investments, such as shares of stock.

   b. Pooling of funds exist.

   c. Reporting entity is the primary one.

   d. Investment activity is primarily investment in assets, usually in securities of other entities not under common management.

The amendments to the update are effective for periods ending after December 15, 2009 (ASC 820, *Fair Value Measurements and Disclosures*) (ASC 820-10) (ASC 946, *Financial Services—Investment Companies*) (ASC 946-10-15-2).

ANNUAL REPORT REFERENCES

Corning
2008 Annual Report

3. Short-term Investments

The following is a summary of the fair value of available-for-sale securities (in millions):

	December 31,	
	2008	*2007*
Bonds, notes and other securities		
U.S. government and agencies	$737	$ 179
States and municipalities		46
Asset-backed securities	5	301
Commercial paper		239
Other debt securities	201	535
Total short-term investments	$943	$1,300

Gross realized gains and losses in 2008 were $6 million and $59 million, respectively. Realized losses in 2008 included other-than temporary impairments of $37 million for financial industry securities and $22 million of losses from the sale of asset-back debt securities and debt securities of financial institutions as Corning reduced its exposure to these sectors. Gross realized gains and losses in 2007 and 2006 were not significant.

Gross unrealized gains and losses at December 31, 2008 were $2 million and $58 million, respectively, and were included in accumulated other comprehensive income. Unrealized losses included temporary impairments of asset-backed securities with a fair value of $40 million at December 31, 2008. Because we believe the $87 million cost-basis of these asset-backed securities, which are collateralized by mortgages, is recoverable in the long-term we have classified these securities as long-term assets. It is possible that a significant degradation in the delinquency or foreclosure rates in the underlying mortgages could cause further temporary or other-than-temporary impairments in the future. Gross unrealized gains and losses at December 31, 2007 were $4 million and $14 million, respectively.

The following table summarizes the contractual maturities of available-for-sale securities at December 31, 2008 (in millions):

Less than one year	$ 732
Due in 1–5 years	196
Due in 5–10 years	
Due after 10 years	15
Total	$ 943

Proceeds from sales and maturities of short-term investments totaled $2.1 billion, $2.9 billion and $2.0 billion in 2008, 2007 and 2006, respectively.

Schlumberger
2008 Annual Report

5. Investments in Affiliated Companies

The MI-SWACO drilling fluids joint venture is owned 40% by Schlumberger and 60% by Smith International, Inc. Schlumberger records income relating to this venture using the equity method of accounting. Schlumberger's investment in the joint venture on December 31, 2008 and 2007 was $1.3 billion and $1.2 billion, respectively. Schlumberger's equity income from this joint venture in 2008 was $210 million, $174 million in 2007 and $135 million in 2006. Schlumberger received cash distributions from the joint venture of $57 million in 2008 and $40 million in 2007. There were no such distributions in 2006.

Schlumberger's joint venture agreement with Smith International, Inc. contains a provision under which either party to the joint venture may offer to sell its entire interest in the venture to the other party at a cash purchase price per percentage interest specified in an offer notice. If the offer to sell is not accepted, the offering party will be obligated to purchase the entire interest of the other party at the same price per percentage interest as the prices specified in the offer notice.

Caterpillar
2008 Annual Report

11. Investments in Unconsolidated Affiliated Companies

Our investments in affiliated companies accounted for by the equity method have historically consisted primarily of a 50 percent interest in Shin Caterpillar Mitsubishi Ltd. (SCM) located in Japan. On August 1, 2008, SCM redeemed half of Mitsubishi Heavy Industries Ltd.'s (MHI's) shares in SCM. As a result, Caterpillar now owns 67 percent of the renamed entity, Caterpillar Japan Ltd. (Cat Japan). Because Cat Japan is accounted for on a lag, Cat Japan's August 1, 2008 financial position was consolidated on September 30, 2008. Cat Japan's results of operations were consolidated in the fourth quarter. See Note 25 for details on this share redemption. In February 2008, we sold our 23 percent equity investment in A.S.V. Inc. (ASV) resulting in a $60 million pretax gain. Accordingly, the December 31, 2008 financial position and equity investment amounts noted below do not include ASV or Cat Japan.

Combined financial information of the unconsolidated affiliated companies accounted for by the equity method (generally on a lag of 3 months or less) was as follows:

Results of Operations of unconsolidated affiliated companies:

(Millions of dollars)	Years ended December 31,		
	2008	2007	2006
Results of Operations:			
Sales	$3,727	$4,007	$4,420
Cost of sales	3,082	3,210	3,526
Gross profit	$ 645	$ 797	$ 894
Profit (loss)	$ 55	$ 157	$ 187
Caterpillar's profit (loss)	$ 37	$ 73	$ 81

Sales from SCM, while an unconsolidated affiliate, to Caterpillar of approximately $1.67 billion, $1.67 billion and $1.81 billion in 2008, 2007 and 2006, respectively, are included in the affiliated company sales. In addition, SCM purchases of Caterpillar product, while an unconsolidated affiliate, were $353 million, $268 million and $273 million in 2008, 2007 and 2006, respectively.

Financial Position of unconsolidated affiliated companies:

(Millions of dollars)	December 31,		
	2008	2007	2006
Financial Position:			
Assets:			
Current assets	$209	$2,062	$1,807
Property, plant and equipment—net	227	1,286	1,119
Other assets	26	173	176
	462	3,521	3,102
Liabilities:			
Current liabilities	173	1,546	1,394
Long-term debt due after one year	110	269	309
Other liabilities	35	393	145
	318	2,208	1,848
Ownership	$144	$1,313	$1,254

Caterpillar's investments in unconsolidated affiliated companies:

(Millions of dollars)	December 31,		
	2008	2007	2006
Investments in equity method companies	$66	$582	$542
Plus: Investments in cost method companies	28	16	20
Total investments in unconsolidated affiliated companies	$94	$598	$562

At December 31, 2008, consolidated "Profit employed in the business" in Statement 2 included $10 million representing undistributed profit of the unconsolidated affiliated companies.

Goodyear Tire & Rubber
2007 Annual Report

Note 8. Investments

Investments and Acquisitions

We have funded approximately 33% of the obligations under our Supplemental Pension Plan as of December 31, 2007 (approximately 37% at December 31, 2006) using a trust. The trust invests in debt and equity securities and funds current benefit payments under the Supplemental Pension Plan. No contributions were made to the trust in 2007 or 2006. The debt securities have maturities ranging from March 20, 2008 through September 1, 2036. The fair value of the trust assets was $21 million and $25 million at December 31, 2007 and 2006, respectively, and was included in Other Assets and Prepaid Pension Assets on the Consolidated Balance Sheets. We have classified the trust assets as available-for-sale, as provided in SFAS No. 115, "Accounting for Certain Investments in Debt and Equity Securities" ("SFAS No. 115"). Accordingly, gains and losses resulting from changes in the fair value of the trust assets are deferred and reported in AOCL on the Consolidated Balance Sheets. At December 31, 2007 and 2006, AOCL included a gross unrealized holding gain on the trust assets of $4 million ($2 million after tax) and $5 million ($2 million after-tax), respectively.

We owned 3,421,306 shares of Sumitomo Rubber Industries, Ltd. ("SRI") at December 31, 2007 and 2006 (the "Sumitomo Investment"). The fair value of the Sumitomo Investment was $31 million and $44 million at December 31, 2007 and 2006, respectively, and was included in Other Assets and Prepaid Pension Assets on the Consolidated Balance Sheets. We have classified the Sumitomo Investment as available-for-sale, as provided in SFAS No. 115. At December 31, 2007, AOCL included gross unrealized holding gains on the Sumitomo Investment of $14 million ($15 million after-tax), compared to $28 million ($29 million after-tax) at December 31, 2006.

In January 2006, we acquired the remaining 50% ownership interest in our South Pacific Tyres ("SPT") joint venture. In connection with the acquisition we paid approximately $40 million and repaid approximately $50 million of outstanding loans. As a result of the acquisition, we recorded goodwill of approximately $12 million and indefinite lived intangible assets of $10 million. The purchase price was allocated based on 50% of the assets acquired and liabilities assumed.

Dividends received from our consolidated subsidiaries were $562 million, $247 million and $290 million in 2007, 2006 and 2005, respectively, which included stock dividends of $16 million in 2005. Dividends received from our affiliates accounted for using the equity method were $3 million, $5 million and $7 million in 2007, 2006 and 2005, respectively.

Boeing
2007 Annual Report

Note 10—Cash, Cash Equivalents, and Investments

Our investments, which are recorded in either Cash and cash equivalents, Short-term investments or Investments, consisted of the following at December 31:

	2007	2006
Cash and cash equivalents		
Cash and time deposits	$ 5,406	$ 5,710
Available-for-sale investments	134	118
Held-to-maturity investments	1,502	290
Total cash and cash equivalents	7,042	6,118
Short-term Investments		
Time deposits	1,025	
Available-for-sale investments	442	268
Held-to-maturity investments	799	
Total short-term investments	2,266	268
Investments		
Available-for-sale investments	2,982	3,076
Equity method investments	1,085	964
Other investments	44	45
Total investments	4,111	4,085
Total cash, cash equivalents, and investments	$13,419	$10,471

Available-for-Sale Investments

Our investments in available-for-sale debt and equity securities consisted of the following at December 31:

		2007		
	Cost	Gross Unrealized Gain	Gross Unrealized Loss	Estimated Fair Value
Debt:[1]				
Marketable Securities[2]	$3,385	$29	$(11)	$3,403
ETCs/EETCs	145		(2)	143

	Cost	Gross Unrealized Gain	Gross Unrealized Loss	Estimated Fair Value
		2007		
Equity	2	10		12
	$3,532	$39	$(13)	$3,558

	Cost	Gross Unrealized Gain	Gross Unrealized Loss	Estimated Fair Value
		2006		
Debt:[1]				
Marketable Securities[2]	$3,319	$ 4	$(25)	$3,298
ETCs/EETCs	145	7		152
Equity	4	8		12
	$3,468	$19	$(25)	$3,462

[1] At December 31, 2007, debt securities with estimated fair values of $574 and cost of $580 have been in a continuous unrealized loss position for 12 months or longer.

[2] The portfolio is diversified and highly liquid and primarily consists of investment grade fixed income instruments such as U.S. dollar debt obligations of the United States Treasury, other government agencies, corporations, mortgage-backed and asset-backed securities. We believe that the unrealized losses are not other-than-temporary. We do not have a foreseeable need to liquidate the portfolio and anticipate recovering the full value of the securities either as market conditions improve, or as the securities mature.

The contractual maturities of available-for-sale debt securities at December 31, 2007, were as follows:

	Cost	Estimated Fair Value
Due in 1 year or less	$ 578	$ 576
Due from 1 to 5 years	1,575	1,591
Due from 5 to 10 years	99	100
Due after 10 years	1,278	1,279
	$3,530	$3,546

Supplemental information about gross realized gains and losses on available-for-sale investment securities for the years ended December 31, are as follows:

	2007	2006	2005
Gains	$ 5	$56	
Losses, including impairments	(11)	(11)	$(64)
Net	$ (6)	$45	$(64)

Held-to-maturity investments. Our investments in held-to-maturity securities consist of commercial paper with maturities of less than one year. The held-to-maturity securities are recorded at their amortized cost of $2,301 and $290 as of December 31, 2007 and 2006, which approximates their fair value.

Equity Method and Other Investments

Equity method investments. Our effective ownership percentages and balances of equity method investments consisted of the following as of December 31:

	Segment	Ownership Percentages	Investment Balance	
			2007	2006
United Launch Alliance	N&SS	50%	$1,019	$960
United Space Alliance	N&SS	50%	(70)[1]	(92)[1]
HRL Laboratories	PE&MS	50%	35	34
APB Winglets	Commercial Airplanes	45%	31	12
Other	Primarily Commercial Airplanes and Support Systems		70	50
			$1,085	$964

[1] Credit balances are a result of our proportionate share of the joint venture's pension and postretirement related adjustments which reduce the carrying value of the investment.

On December 1, 2006, we entered into a transaction with Lockheed Martin Corporation (Lockheed) to create a 50/50 joint venture named United Launch Alliance L.L.C. (ULA). ULA combines the production, engineering, test and launch operations associated with U.S. government launches of Boeing Delta and Lockheed Atlas rockets. ULA conducted 13 and one successful launches for the years ended December 31, 2007 and 2006. We and Lockheed each have agreed to provide ULA with initial cash contributions of up to $25, and we each have agreed to extend a line of credit to ULA of up to $200 to support its working capital requirements. See Note 21.

On July 24, 2007, we and Lockheed reached an agreement with respect to resolution of the final working capital and the value of the launch vehicle support contracts that each party contributed to form ULA. Effective August 15, 2007, the parties received all necessary approvals pursuant to the terms of the Consent Order with the U.S. Federal Trade Commission and the terms of the agreement, which resulted in additional contributions from both parties with Boeing agreeing to contribute an additional $97. Our additional contribution liability will be offset by future payments from ULA under the Inventory Supply Agreement.

The Sea Launch venture, in which we are a 40% partner with RSC Energia of Russia (25%), Aker ASA of Norway (20%), PO Yuzhmash (10%) and SDO Yuzhnoye (5%) of the Ukraine, provides ocean-based launch services to commercial satellite customers. The venture conducted zero, five and four successful launches for the years ended December 31, 2007, 2006 and 2005, respectively. A

Sea Launch Zenit-3SL vehicle, carrying a Boeing-built NSS-8 satellite, experienced an anomaly during launch on January 30, 2007. The launch platform has been repaired and resumed flight operations on January 15, 2008, successfully launching a Boeing-built satellite. We have financial exposure with respect to the venture, which relates to guarantees provided by us to certain Sea Launch creditors, performance guarantees provided by us to a Sea Launch customer, and financial exposure related to advances and other assets reflected in the consolidated financial statements.

We suspended recording equity losses after writing our investment in and direct loans to Sea Launch down to zero in 2001 and accruing our obligation for third-party guarantees on Sea Launch indebtedness. We are not obligated to provide any further financial support to the Sea Launch venture. However, in the event that we do extend additional financial support to Sea Launch in the future, we will recognize suspended losses as appropriate. In addition, we continue to look at alternative capital structures for the venture.

Other investments. During 2005, we recorded an asset impairment charge of $42 in Other income related to the sale of certain investments in technology related funds for proceeds of $24.

Qualcomm
2004 Annual Report

Note 2. Marketable Securities

Marketable securities were comprised as follows (in millions):

	Current September 30,		Noncurrent September 30,	
	2004	*2003*	*2004*	*2003*
Held-to-maturity				
Certificates of deposit	$–	$5	$–	$–
U.S. Treasury and federal agency securities	–	1	70	130
Corporate bonds and notes	10	161	60	70
	10	167	130	200
Available-for-sale:				
U.S. Treasury and federal agency securities	520	696	–	–
Foreign government bonds	8	–	–	–
Corporate bonds	2062	1118	3	22
Mortgage and asset-backed securities	2056	486	–	–
Non-investment grade debt securities	–	39	571	459
Equity mutual funds	–	–	296	–
Equity securities	112	10	653	130

	Current September 30,		Noncurrent September 30,	
	2004	2003	2004	2003
	4758	2349	1523	611
	4768	2516	1653	811

As of September 30, 2004, the contractual maturities of debt securities were as follows (in millions):

	Years to Maturity					
	Less than One Year	One to Five Years	Five to Ten Years	Greater than Ten Years	No Single Maturity Date	Total
Held-to-maturity	$ 10	$ 130	$ –	$ –	$ –	$ 140
Available-for-sale	826	1,820	495	25	2,054	5,220
	$836	$1,950	$495	$25	$2,054	$5,360

Securities with no single maturity date include mortgage-and asset-backed securities.

Available-for-sale securities were comprised as follows at September 30 (in millions):

	Cost	Unrealized Gains	Unrealized Losses	Fair Value
2004				
Equity securities	$1,003	77	$(19)	$1,061
Debt securities	5,208	27	(15)	5,220
Total	$6,211	$104	$(34)	$6,281
2003				
Equity securities	$ 104	$ 37	$ (1)	$ 140
Debt securities	2,758	69	(7)	2,820
Total	$2,862	$106	$ (8)	$2,960

The fair values of held-to-maturity debt securities at September 30, 2004 and 2003 approximate cost.

For the years ended September 30, 2004, 2003, and 2002, the Company recorded realized gains and losses on sales of available-for-sale marketable securities as follows (in millions):

	Gross Realized Gains	Gross Realized Losses	Net realized Gains
2004	$105	$(17)	$88
2003	82	(13)	69
2002	23	(11)	12

The following table shows the gross unrealized losses and fair values of the Company's investments in individual securities that have been in a continuous unrealized loss position deemed to be temporary for less than 12 months, aggregated by category, at September 30, 2004 (in millions):

Fair	Fair Value	Unrealized Losses
U.S. Treasury and federal agency securities	$ 309	$(1)
Corporate bonds and notes	1,261	(4)
Mortgage and asset-backed securities	559	(2)
Non-investment grade debt securities	108	(7)
Equity mutual funds	296	(7)
Equity securities	196	(13)
	$2,729	$(34)

At September 30, 2004, the Company did not have any investments in individual securities that have been in a continuous loss position to be temporary for more than 12 months.

Investment Grade Debt Securities. The Company's investments in investment grade debt securities consist primarily of investments in certificates of deposit, U.S. Treasury and federal agency securities, foreign government bonds, mortgage and asset-backed securities, and corporate bonds and notes. The unrealized losses on the Company's investments in investment grade debt securities were caused by interest rate increases. Due to the fact that the decline in market value is attributable to changes in interest rates and not credit quality, and because the severity and duration of the unrealized losses were not significant, the Company considered these unrealized losses to be temporary at September 30, 2004.

Non-Investment Grade Debt Securities. The Company's investments in non-investment grade debt securities consist primarily of investments in corporate bonds. The unrealized losses on the Company's investment in non-investment grade debt securities were caused by credit quality and industry or company specific events. Because the severity and duration of the unrealized losses were not significant, the Company considered these unrealized losses to be temporary at September 30, 2004.

Marketable Equity Securities. The Company's investments in marketable equity securities consist primarily of investments in common stock of large companies and equity mutual funds. The unrealized losses on the Company's investment in marketable equity securities were caused by overall equity market volatility and industry specific events. The duration and severity of the unrealized losses in relation to the carrying amounts of the individual investments were consistent with typical equity market volatility. Current market forecasts support a recovery of fair value up to (or beyond) the cost of the investment within a reasonable period of time. Accordingly, the Company considered these losses to be temporary at September 30, 2004.

Oracle
2003 Annual Report

6. Investments in Equity Securities

In accordance with Statement 115 and based on our intentions regarding these instruments, we classify all marketable equity securities as available-for-sale. Marketable equity securities are included in intangible and other assets in the accompanying consolidated balance sheets and all unrealized holding gains (losses) are reflected net of tax in stockholders' equity. If we determine that an investment has an other than temporary decline in fair value, generally defined as when our cost basis exceeds the fair value for approximately six months, we recognize the investment loss in other income, net. We periodically evaluate our investments to determine if impairment charges are required.

The following table shows the net carrying value of our equity securities as of May 31, 2003, 2002 and 2001 and unrealized gains (losses), net of tax, for fiscal 2003, 2002 and 2001:

(Dollars in millions)	Fair Value Basis	Unrealized Gains (Losses) in Stockholders' Equity, net of tax
May 31, 2003		
Liberate Technologies	$ 90	$ 25
Other investments	65	1
Total	$155	$ 26
May 31, 2002		
Liberate Technologies	$135	$ 27
Other investments	86	(4)
Total	$221	$ 23
May 31, 2001		
Liberate Technologies	$282	$(27)
Other investments	133	(42)
Total	$415	$(69)

In the fourth quarter of 2002, we recognized a $173.5 million impairment charge relating to an other than temporary decline in the fair value of our investment in Liberate Technologies. We concluded that our investment was other than temporarily impaired because our cost basis exceeded the publicly traded market value of the Liberate Technologies common stock for approximately six months. Due to further declines in the market value of Liberate Technologies, we recognized additional impairment charges of $87.2 million in the first six months of fiscal 2003. During the second half of fiscal 2003, the market value of our investment in Liberate Technologies increased by $41.7 million, which is reflected within stockholders' equity as an unrealized gain on equity securities, net of taxes. The carrying value of our remaining investment in Liberate Technologies as of May 31, 2003 was $89.8 million, which includes the unrealized gain of $41.7 million.

Prior to January 2001, we recorded our investment in Liberate Technologies using the equity method. In January 2001, we created an irrevocable trust (the "Liberate Trust") to hold all of our shares (the "Liberate Shares") of Liberate Technologies. The trustees of the Liberate Trust must vote the Liberate Shares in the same proportion as all the other stockholders of Liberate Technologies (determined as of the last business day prior to a Liberate Technologies Stockholders' Meeting or the earliest time thereafter that the voting results are provided to the Trustee). We control the timing of the sales of the Liberate Shares, subject to a standstill agreement with Liberate Technologies and the trustee of the Liberate Trust, and receive the proceeds of any such sales. The Liberate Trust terminates only after all shares have been sold. The standstill agreement prohibits us from acquiring any common shares or voting shares of Liberate Technologies or other securities or rights convertible or exchangeable for such shares and limits our ability to sell the Liberate Shares to: (1) sales in compliance with the volume and manner of sale limitations of Rule 144 under the Securities Act; (2) sales pursuant to a firm commitment, underwritten distribution to the public; (3) sales to a person who will own 10% or less of the total voting power of Liberate Technologies after such sale; (4) sales pursuant to a tender or exchange offer to the Liberate Technologies stockholders that is not opposed by Liberate Technologies Board of Directors; or (5) sales pursuant to the written consent of Liberate Technologies. The standstill agreement terminates two years after the termination of the Liberate Trust or sooner if Liberate Technologies is dissolved, liquidated or wound up, substantially all Liberate Technologies assets are sold or another entity acquires Liberate Technologies by merger or consolidation. Accordingly, effective February 1, 2001, we began to account for our ownership interest in Liberate Technologies as available for sale securities under Statement 115. As of May 31, 2003, our ownership interest in Liberate Technologies was approximately 32.1%.

In fiscal 2003, 2002 and 2001 we recognized $23.9 million, $70.0 million and $17.1 million, respectively, of impairment losses related to our other investments, which include investments in privately held companies, venture funds and publicly traded companies. We determined that the decreases in the fair value of these investments were other than temporary based upon the financial condition and near term prospects of the underlying investees, changes in the market demand for technology being sold or developed by the underlying investees and our intent regarding providing future funding to the underlying investees. The carrying value of our remaining other investments as of May 31, 2003 and 2002 was $64.8 million and $85.7 million, respectively.

Abbott Laboratories
2003 Annual Report

Note 3—Investment Securities

(dollars in thousands)

The following is a summary of investment securities at December 31:

Current Investment Securities	2003	2002	2001
Time deposits and certificates of deposit	$291,297	$120,000	$20,000
Other, primarily debt obligations issued or guaranteed by various governments or government agencies	–	141,677	36,162
Total	$291,297	$261,677	$56,162

Long-term Investment Securities	2003	2002	2001
Equity securities	$381,053	$222,667	$343,115
Time deposits and certificates of deposit	9,729	–	100,000
Corporate debt obligations	–	–	70,000
Debt obligations issued or guaranteed by various governments or government agencies	15,575	28,112	134,099
Total	$406,357	$250,779	$647,214

Of the investment securities listed above, $15,575, $247,998, and $323,974 were held at December 31, 2003, 2002, and 2001, respectively, by subsidiaries operating in Puerto Rico under tax incentive grants expiring in 2015 and 2020.

Abbott reviews the carrying value of investments in equity securities each quarter to determine whether an other than temporary decline in market value exists. Abbott considers factors affecting the investee, factors affecting the industry the investee operates in, and general equity market trends. Abbott considers the length of time an investment's market value has been below carrying value and the near-term prospects for recovery to carrying value. When Abbott determines that an other than temporary decline has occurred, the investment is written down with a charge to Other (income) expense, net.

Gross unrealized holding gains (losses) on current and long-term held-to-maturity investment securities totaled $1,400 and $(2,200), respectively, at December 31, 2003; $1,500 and $(8,500), respectively, at December 31, 2002; and $2,000 and $(17,200), respectively, at December 31, 2001. Gross unrealized holding gains (losses) on available-for-sale equity securities totaled $162,700 and $(4,000), respectively, at December 31, 2003; $24,400 and $(9,200), respectively, at December 31, 2002; and $57,000 and $(1,800), respectively, at December 31, 2001. For current and long-term held-to-maturity securities and available-for-sale equity securities, the adjusted cost basis of the investments have been above the market value for less than one year as of December 31, 2003.

Caterpillar
2004 Annual Report

13. Available-for-Sale Securities

Cat Insurance and Caterpillar Investment Management Ltd. Had investments in certain debt and equity securities at December 31, 2004, 2003 and 2002, that have been classified as available-for-sale in accordance with SFAS 115 and recorded at fair value based upon quoted market prices. These fair values are included in "Other assets" in Statement 3. Gains and losses arising from the revaluation of available-for-sale securities are included, net of applicable deferred income taxes, in equity ("Accumulated other comprehensive income" in Statement 3). Realized gains and losses on sales of investments are generally determined using the specific identification method for debt instruments and the FIFO method for equity securities. Realized gains and losses are included in "Other income (expense)" in Statement 1.

(Millions of dollars)	Cost Basis	December 31, 2004 Unrealized Pre-Tax Net Gains (Losses)	Fair Value
Government debt	$239	$(1)	$238
Corporate bonds	342	–	342
Equity securities	203	21	224
	$784	$ 20	$804

(Millions of dollars)	Cost Basis	December 31, 2003 Unrealized Pre-Tax Net Gains (Losses)	Fair Value
Government debt	$102	$ –	$102
Corporate bonds	288	3	291
Equity securities	191	21	212
	$581	$24	$605

(Millions of dollars)	Cost Basis	December 31, 2003 Unrealized Pre-Tax Net Gains (Losses)	Fair Value
Government debt	$ 89	$ –	$ 89
Corporate bonds	208	1	209
Equity securities	220	(51)	169
	$517	$(50)	$467

Investments in an unrealized loss position that are not other-than-temporarily impaired

(Millions of dollars)	Less than 12 months*		More than 12 months*		Total*	
	Fair Value	Unrealized Losses	Fair Value	Unrealized Losses	Fair Value	Unrealized Losses
Government debt	166	1	9	–	175	1
Corporate bonds	156	2	35	1	191	3
Equity securities	46	1	2	–	48	1
Total	369	4	46	1	414	5

December 31, 2004

* Indicates length of time that individual securities have been in a continuous unrealized loss position.

The fair value of available-for-sale debt securities at December 31, 2004, by contractual maturity, is shown below. Expected maturities will differ from contractual maturities because borrowers may have the right to prepay and creditors may have the right to call obligations.

(Millions of dollars)	Fair Value
Due in one year or less	$ 30
Due after one year through five years	$273
Due after five years through ten years	$ 50
Due after ten years	$227

Proceeds from sales of investments in debt and equity securities during 2004, 2003, and 2002 were $408 million, $329 million, and $288 million, respectively. Gross gains of $8 million, $3 million, and $9 million and gross losses of $6 million, $2 million, and $2 million have been included in current earnings as a result of these sales for 2004, 2003, and 2002, respectively.

During 2003 and 2002, we recognized pretax charges in accordance with the application of SFAS 115 for "other than temporary" declines in the market value of securities in the Cat Insurance and Caterpillar Investment Management Ltd. investment port-folios of $33 million and $41 million, respectively. During 2004, there were no pretax charges for "other than temporary" declines in the market value of securities.

Schering-Plough
2003 Annual Report

Equity Income from Cholesterol Joint Venture. The Company and Merck & Co., Inc. (Merck) have agreements to jointly develop and market ZETIA (ezetimibe) as a once-daily monotherapy, as co-administration of ZETIA with statins, and ezetimibe as a once-daily fixed-combination tablet with simvastatin (*Zocor*), Merck's cholesterol-modifying medicine. The agreements also involve the development and marketing of a once-daily, fixed-combination tablet containing CLARITIN and *Singulair.Singulair* is Merck's once-daily leukotriene receptor antagonist for the treatment of asthma and seasonal allergic rhinitis. In January 2002, Schering-

Plough/Merck Pharmaceuticals reported on results of Phase III clinical trials of a fixed-combination tablet containing CLARITIN and *Singulair*, which did not demonstrate sufficient added benefits in the treatment of seasonal allergic rhinitis.

The agreements generally provide for equal sharing of development costs and for co-promotion of approved products by each company in the United States and in most other countries of the world, except Japan. In Japan, no agreement exists. In general, co-promotion provides that each company will provide equal physician marketing efforts and that each company will bear the cost of its own sales force in marketing the products. In general, the agreement provides that the venture will operate in a "virtual" mode to the maximum degree possible by relying on the respective infrastructures of the two companies. However, the companies have agreed to share certain costs, but these costs are limited to a portion of the costs of manufacturing, the cost of a specialty sales force and certain specially identified promotion costs. It should be noted that the Company incurs substantial costs, such as selling costs, that are not reflected in Equity income from cholesterol joint venture and are borne entirely by the Company. The agreements do not provide for any jointly owned facilities and, as such, products resulting from the collaboration will be manufactured in facilities owned by either Merck or the Company.

During 2003, the Company earned a milestone of $20 that relates to certain European approvals of ZETIA. Under certain other conditions, Merck could pay additional milestones to the Company totaling $132.

Prior to 2003, the venture was in the research and development phase and the Company's share of research and development expense in 2002 and 2001 of $69 and $86, respectively, was reported in "Research and development" in the Statements of Consolidated Operations. The venture has now moved beyond the research and development phase. ZETIA was launched in late 2002, and a U.S. marketing application for the combination of ezetimibe/simvastatin was submitted to the FDA in September 2003. To reflect the venture's first full year of commercial operations, the Company adopted the equity method of accounting effective as of the beginning of 2003. Under that method, the Company records its share of the operating profits less its share of the research and development costs in "Equity income from cholesterol joint venture" in the Statements of Consolidated Operations. Prior year amounts have not been affected.

Equity income from cholesterol joint venture for the year ended December 31, 2003 was $54. Included in this amount are the Company's share of operating profits of $113, the $20 milestone receipt, less its share of research and development costs of $79.

Occidental Petroleum
2003 Annual Report

Note 14 Investments and Related-Party Transactions
Equity Investments

At December 31, 2003, Occidental's equity investments consisted of a 22-percent interest in Lyondell acquired in August 2002, a 24.5-percent interest in the entity that will own the pipeline being constructed by Dolphin Energy, the operator of the Dolphin Project, and other various partnerships and joint ventures, discussed below. Equity investments paid dividends of $81 million, $22 million and $27 million to Occidental in 2003, 2002 and 2001, respectively. Cumulative undistributed earnings since acquisition, in the amount of $55 million, of 50-percent-or-less-owned companies have been accounted for by Occidental under the equity method. At December 31, 2003, Occidental's investments in unconsolidated entities exceeded the underlying equity in net assets by $471 million, of which $356 million represents goodwill that will not be amortized and $115 million represents intangible assets, which will be amortized over the life of the underlying lease of the assets, when placed into service.

In October 2003, Occidental purchased an additional 2.7 million shares of Lyondell common stock for $12.40 a share, totaling approximately $33 million. At December 31, 2003, Occidental owned 22 percent (39.5 million shares) of Lyondell stock.

The following table presents Occidental's percentage interest in the summarized financial information of its equity method investments:

For the years ended December 31, (in millions)	2003	2002	2001
Revenues	$1,179	$1,782	$2,223
Costs and expenses	1,188	2,043	2,315
Net loss	$ (9)	$(261)	$ (92)

Balance at December 31,	2003	2002
Current assets	$ 349	$ 421
Non-current assets	$1,691	$1,946
Current liabilities	$ 407	$ 225
Long-term debt	$ 960	$1,458
Other non-current liabilities	$ 377	$ 404
Stockholders' equity	$ 365	$ 280

In Ecuador, Occidental has a 14-percent interest in the Oleoducto de Crudos Pesados (OCP) Ltd. oil export pipeline. Occidental made capital contributions of $64 million in 2003 and as of December 31, 2003, has contributed a total of $73 million to the project. Occidental reports this investment in its consolidated statements using the equity method of accounting.

The project was funded in part by senior project debt. The senior project debt is to be repaid with the proceeds of ship-or-pay tariffs of certain upstream producers in Ecuador, including Occidental. Under their ship-or-pay commitments, Occidental and the other upstream producers have each assumed their respective share of project-specific risks, including operating risk and force-majeure risk. Occidental would be required to make an advance tariff payment in the event of prolonged force majeure, upstream expropriation events, bankruptcy of the pipeline company or its parent company, abandonment of the project, termination of an investment guarantee agreement with Ecuador, or certain defaults by Occidental. This advance tariff would be used by the pipeline company to service or prepay project debt. Occidental's obligation relating to the pipeline company's senior project debt totaled $108 million, and Occidental's obligations relating to performance bonds totaled $14 million at December 31, 2003. As Occidental ships product using the pipeline, its overall obligations will decrease with the reduction of the pipeline company's senior project debt.

Occidental has a 50-percent interest in Elk Hills Power LLC (EHP), a limited liability company that operates a gas-fired, power-generation plant in California. EHP is a VIE under the provisions of FIN 46. Occidental has concluded it is not the primary beneficiary of EHP and, therefore, accounts for this investment using the equity method. In January 2002, EHP entered into a $400 million construction loan facility, which was amended in May 2003 to increase the facility to $425 million. Upon construction completion on July 17, 2003, the facility converted to a $415 million term loan, 50 percent of which is guaranteed by Occidental.

Available-for-Sale Securities

Investments in unconsolidated entities also include Occidental's investment in Premcor, Inc., which became a publicly traded company in April 2002. Occidental accounts for its investment in Premcor as available for sale and this investment is carried at fair valie. Prior to becoming public, Occidental carried its investment in Premcor at cost. As of December 31, 2003 and 2002, the fair value of the investment in Premcor was $235 million and $172 million, respectively, with cumulative unrealized after-tax gains of $89 million and $65 million, respectively, in OCI.

Related-Party Transactions

During 2003, 2002 and 2001, Occidental entered into the following transactions and amounts due from/to with its related parties and had the following amounts outstanding:

For the years ended December 31, (in millions)	2003	2002	2001
Purchases	$707	$604	$660
Sales	502	284	252
Services	1	7	7
Amounts due from	34	43	14
Amounts due to	21	70	35

Boeing
2003 Annual Report

Note 11—Investments

Joint ventures and other investments

All investments are recorded in other assets. As of December 31, 2003 and 2002, other assets included $98 and $124 attributable to investments in joint ventures.

We also held other non-marketable securities of $63 and $103 at December 31, 2003 and 2002.

The principal joint venture arrangements are United Space Alliance; HRL Laboratories, LLC; APB Winglets Company, LLC; BATA Leasing, LLC (BATA); and Sea Launch. We have a 50% partnership with Lockheed Martin in United Space Alliance, which is responsible for all ground processing of the Space Shuttle fleet and for space-related operations with the USAF. United Space Alliance also performs modifications, testing and checkout operations that are required to ready the Space Shuttle for launch. We are entitled to 33% of the earnings from HRL Laboratories, LLC, which conducts applied research in the electronics and information sciences; and creates new products and services for space, telecommunications, defense and automotive applications. We have a 45% ownership of APB Winglets Company, LLC, which was established for the purposes of designing, developing, manufacturing, installing, certifying, retrofitting, marketing, selling, and providing after-sales support with respect to winglets for retrofit aircraft.

We have a 50% partnership with ATA in BATA, which was established to acquire aircraft and market and lease the aircraft to third-parties. As of December 31, 2002, the carrying value was $19. During 2003, we finalized an amendment to the partnership, which gave us majority control in the management of the business and affairs of BATA. As a result, BATA is now consolidated in our financial statements.

The Sea Launch venture, in which we are a 40% partner with RSC Energia (25%) of Russia, Kvaerner ASA (20%) of Norway, and KB Yuzhnoye/PO Yuzhmash (15%) of Ukraine, provides ocean-based launch services to commercial satellite customers. The venture had three successful launches in 2003. Our investment in this venture as of December 31, 2003 and 2002, is reported at zero, which reflects the recognition of losses reported by Sea Launch in prior years. The venture incurred losses in 2003, 2002 and 2001, due to the relatively low volume of launches, reflecting a depressed commercial satellite market. We have financial exposure with respect to the venture, which relates to guarantees by us provided to certain Sea Launch creditors, performance guarantees provided by us to a Sea Launch customer and financial exposure related to advances and other assets reflected in the consolidated financial statements.

During 2003, we recorded a charge of $55 related to Resource 21, a partnership entered into with another party several years ago to develop commercial remote sensing and ground monitoring. The charge resulted from a decision by NASA to not award an imagery contract to Resource 21. During 2003, we also recorded adjustments to equity investments in Ellipso, SkyBridge and Teledesic resulting in the net write down of $27.

During 2002, a $100 impairment charge was recorded to write off a cost-method investment in Teledesic, LLC, which stopped work on its satellite constellation and announced its intent to reduce staff. In addition, we recorded a $48 impairment charge related to our BATA Leasing, LLC, joint venture investment. This charge was our share of the adjustment to estimated fair market value for the joint venture's 727 aircraft.

Investments in debt and equity securities

Investments consisted of the following at December 31:

| | 2003 | | | | 2002 | | | |
	Cost	Gross Unrealized Gain	Gross Unrealized (Losses)	Estimated Fair Value	Cost	Gross Unrealized Gain	Gross Unrealized (Losses)	Estimated Fair Value
Available for Sale								
Equity	$ 4	$7		$ 11	$ 5	$4		$ 9
Debt	20	1		21	4			4
Held-to-Maturity[1]								
Debt[2]	453		$57	396	490		$239	251
	$477	$8	$57	$428	$499	$4	$239	$264

[1] The unrealized gain/losses of held-to-maturity securities are not recorded in the consolidated financial statements.

[2] These debt securities have been in a continuous unrealized loss position for 12 months or longer.

Included in held-to-maturity investments carried at amortized cost as of December 31, 2003 and 2002, were $412 and $455 of Enhanced Equipment Trust Certificates (EETCs). EETCs are secured by aircraft on lease to commercial airlines. EETCs provide investors with tranched rights to cash flows from a financial instrument, as well as a collateral position in the related asset. While the underlying classes of equipment notes vary by maturity and/or coupon depending upon tenor or level of subordination of the specific equipment notes and their corresponding claim on the aircraft, the basic function of an EETC remains to passively hold separate debt investments to enhance liquidity for investors, whom in turn pass this liquidity benefit directly to the airline in the form of lower coupon and/or greater debt capacity. BCC participates in several EETCs as an investor. Our EETC investments are related to customers we believe have less than investment-grade credit.

Due to the commercial aviation market downturn, these EETC investments have been in a continuous unrealized loss position for twelve months or longer. Despite the unrealized loss position of these securities, we have concluded that these investments are not other-than-temporarily impaired. This assessment was based on the strength of the underlying collateral to the securities, the duration of the maturity, and both internal and third-party credit reviews and analyses of the counterparties, principally major domestic airlines. Accordingly, we have concluded that it is probable that we will be able to collect all amounts due according to the contractual terms of these debt securities.

Also included in held-to-maturity investments carried at amortized cost as of December 31, 2003 and 2002, were $41 and $35 of investments in preferred stock that have been in a continuous unrealized loss position for approximately three years. Despite the unrealized loss position of these securities, we have concluded that these investments are not other-than-temporarily impaired. This assessment was based on the duration of the maturity, and both internal and third-party credit reviews and analyses of the counterparty, a major domestic airline. Accordingly, we have concluded that it is probable that we will be able to collect all amounts due according to the contractual terms of the debt securities.

During 2002, we recorded an impairment of $79 related to one of BCC's long- held investments in equipment trust certificates (ETCs) secured by aircraft on lease to United, which is recorded in cost of products and services. This debt investment was classified as held-to-maturity and had declined in value for a period that was determined to be other-than-temporary.

Maturities of debt securities at December 31, 2003, were as follows:

	Available-for-Sale		Held-to-Maturity	
	Amortized Cost	Estimated Fair Value	Amortized Cost	Estimated Fair Value
Due in 1 year or less				
Due from 1 to 5 years	$20	$21	$324	$284
Due from 5 to 10 years			60	51
Due after 10 years			69	61
	$20	$21	$453	$396

As of December 31, 2003 and 2002, $14 and $13 of unrealized loss was recorded in accumulated other comprehensive income related to debt securities that were reclassified from available-for-sale to held-to-maturity at their fair values. The unrealized loss will be amortized to earnings over the remaining life of each security.

During 2002, $40 ($25 net of tax) of unrealized loss was re-classified from accumulated other comprehensive income to other income due to other than temporary impairments of available-for-sale investments. There were no other than temporary impairments recognized in 2003.

General Mills
2003 Annual Report

4. Investments in Joint Ventures

We have a 50 percent equity interest in Cereal Partners Worldwide (CPW), a joint venture with Nestlé that manufactures and markets ready-to-eat cereals outside the United States and Canada. We have a 40.5 percent equity interest in Snack Ventures Europe (SVE), a joint venture with PepsiCo that manufactures and markets snack foods in continental Europe. We have a 50 percent equity interest in 8th Continent, LLC, a domestic joint venture formed in fiscal 2001 with DuPont to develop and market soy foods and beverages. As a result of the Pillsbury acquisition, we have 50 percent interests in the following joint ventures for the manufacture, distribution and marketing of Häagen-Dazs frozen ice cream products and novelties: Häagen-Dazs Japan K.K., Häagen-Dazs Korea

Company Limited, Häagen-Dazs Taiwan Limited, Häagen-Dazs Distributors (Thailand) Company Limited, and Häagen- Dazs Marketing & Distribution (Philippines) Inc. We also have a 50 percent interest in Seretram, a joint venture with Co-op de Pau for the production of *Green Giant* canned corn in France. In July 2003, we purchased the remaining 50 percent interest in the Taiwan venture.

The joint ventures are reflected in our financial statements on an equity accounting basis. We record our share of the earnings or losses of these joint ventures. (The table that follows reflects the joint ventures on a 100 percent basis.) We also receive royalty income from certain joint ventures, incur various expenses (primarily research and development) and record the tax impact of certain joint venture operations that are structured as partnerships.

Our cumulative investment in these joint ventures (including our share of earnings and losses) was $372 million, $326 million, and $218 million at the end of fiscal 2003, 2002, and 2001, respectively. We made aggregate investments in the joint ventures of $17 million, $38 million, and $25 million in fiscal 2003, 2002 and 2001, respectively. We received aggregate dividends from the joint ventures of $95 million, $17 million, and $3 million in fiscal 2003, 2002 and 2001, respectively.

Summary combined financial information for the joint ventures on a 100 percent basis follows. Since we record our share of CPW results on a two-month lag, CPW information is included as of and for the 12 months ended March 31. The Häagen-Dazs and Seretram joint ventures are reported as of and for the 12 months ended April 30, 2003 and for the six months ended April 30, 2002. The SVE and 8th Continent information is consistent with our May year-end.

Combined Financial Information—Joint Ventures—100 Percent Basis

IN MILLIONS, FISCAL YEAR	2003	2002	2001
Net Sales	$2,159	$1,693	$1,468
Gross Profit	952	755	664
Earnings before Taxes	178	94	61
Earnings after Taxes	125	78	48

IN MILLIONS, FISCAL YEAR ENDED	2003	2002
Current Assets	$681	$587
Noncurrent Assets	868	712
Current Liabilities	679	630
Noncurrent Liabilities	9	9

Our proportionate share of joint venture net sales was $997 million, $777 million, and $666 million for fiscal 2003, 2002, and 2001, respectively.

Merck
2003 Annual Report

4. Joint Ventures and Other Equity Method Affiliates

In 1982, Merck entered into an agreement with Astra AB (Astra) to develop and market Astra's products under a royalty-bearing license. In 1993, the Company's total sales of Astra products reached a level that triggered the first step in the establishment of a joint venture business carried on by Astra Merck Inc. (AMI), in which Merck and Astra each owned a 50% share. This joint venture, formed in 1994, developed and marketed most of Astra's new prescription medicines in the United States including *Prilosec*, the first of a class of medications known as proton pump inhibitors, which slows the production of acid from the cells of the stomach lining.

In 1998, Merck and Astra completed the restructuring of the ownership and operations of the joint venture whereby the Company acquired Astra's interest in AMI, renamed KBI Inc. (KBI), and contributed KBI's operating assets to a new U.S. limited partnership, Astra Pharmaceuticals L.P. (the Partnership), in exchange for a 1% limited partner interest. Astra contributed the net assets of its wholly owned subsidiary, Astra USA, Inc., to the Partnership in exchange for a 99% general partner interest. The Partnership, renamed AstraZeneca LP (AZLP) upon Astra's 1999 merger with Zeneca Group Plc (the AstraZeneca merger), became the exclusive distributor of the products for which KBI retained rights.

While maintaining a 1% limited partner interest in AZLP, Merck has consent and protective rights intended to preserve its business and economic interests, including restrictions on the power of the general partner to make certain distributions or dispositions. Furthermore, in limited events of default, additional rights will be granted to the Company, including powers to direct the actions of, or remove and replace, the Partnership's chief executive officer and chief financial officer. Merck earns ongoing revenue based on sales of current and future KBI products and such revenue was $1.9 billion, $1.5 billion, and $1.9 billion in 2003, 2002, and 2001, respectively, primarily relating to sales of *Nexium* and *Prilosec*. In addition, Merck earns certain Partnership returns, which are recorded in Equity income from affiliates. Such returns include a priority return provided for in the Partnership Agreement, variable returns based, in part, upon sales of certain former Astra USA, Inc. products, and a preferential return representing Merck's share of undistributed AZLP GAAP earnings. These returns aggregated $391.5 million, $640.2 million, and $642.8 million in 2003, 2002, and 2001, respectively. The decrease in 2003 is attributable to a reduction in the preferential return, primarily resulting from the impact of generic competition for *Prilosec*. The AstraZeneca merger triggers a partial redemption of Merck's limited partnership interest in 2008. Upon this redemption, AZLP will distribute to KBI an amount based primarily on a multiple of Merck's average annual variable returns derived from sales of the former Astra USA, Inc. products for the three years prior to the redemption (the Limited Partner Share of Agreed Value).

In conjunction with the 1998 restructuring, for a payment of $443.0 million, which was deferred, Astra purchased an option (the Asset Option) to buy

Merck's interest in the KBI products, excluding the gastrointestinal medicines *Nexium* and *Prilosec*. The Asset Option is exercisable in 2010 at an exercise price equal to the net present value as of March 31, 2008 of projected future pretax revenue to be received by the Company from the KBI products (the Appraised Value). Merck also has the right to require Astra to purchase such interest in 2008 at the Appraised Value. In addition, the Company granted Astra an option to buy Merck's common stock interest in KBI at an exercise price based on the net present value of estimated future net sales of *Nexium* and *Prilosec*. This option is exercisable two years after Astra's purchase of Merck's interest in the KBI products.

The 1999 AstraZeneca merger constituted a Trigger Event under the KBI restructuring agreements. As a result of the merger, in exchange for Merck's relinquishment of rights to future Astra products with no existing or pending U.S. patents at the time of the merger, Astra paid $967.4 million (the Advance Payment), which is subject to a true-up calculation in 2008 that may require repayment of all or a portion of this amount. The True-Up Amount is directly dependent on the fair market value in 2008 of the Astra product rights retained by the Company. Accordingly, recognition of this contingent income has been deferred until the realizable amount, if any, is determinable, which is not anticipated prior to 2008.

Under the provisions of the KBI restructuring agreements, because a Trigger Event has occurred, the sum of the Limited Partner Share of Agreed Value, the Appraised Value and the True-Up Amount is guaranteed to be a minimum of $4.7 billion. Distribution of the Limited Partner Share of Agreed Value and payment of the True-Up Amount will occur in 2008. AstraZeneca's purchase of Merck's interest in the KBI products is contingent upon the exercise of either Merck's option in 2008 or AstraZeneca's option in 2010 and, therefore, payment of the Appraised Value may or may not occur.

In 1989, Merck formed a joint venture with Johnson & Johnson to develop and market a broad range of nonprescription medicines for U.S. consumers. This 50% owned venture was expanded into Europe in 1993, and into Canada in 1996. Sales of product marketed by the joint venture were $445.8 million for 2003, $413.0 million for 2002, and $395.0 million for 2001.

In 1994, Merck and Pasteur Mérieux Connaught (now Aventis Pasteur) established an equally-owned joint venture to market vaccines in Europe and to collaborate in the development of combination vaccines for distribution in Europe. Joint venture vaccine sales were $669.0 million for 2003, $546.4 million for 2002, and $499.6 million for 2001.

In 1997, Merck and Rhône-Poulenc (now Aventis) combined their animal health and poultry genetics businesses to form Merial Limited (Merial), a fully integrated animal health company, which is a stand-alone joint venture, equally owned by each party. Merial provides a comprehensive range of pharmaceuticals and vaccines to enhance the health, well-being and performance of a wide range of animal species. Merial sales were $1.8 billion for 2003, $1.7 billion for 2002, and $1.6 billion for 2001.

In 2000, the Company and Schering-Plough Corporation (Schering-Plough) entered into agreements to create separate equally-owned partnerships to develop and market in the United States new prescription medicines in the cholesterol-management and respiratory therapeutic areas. In 2001, the cholesterol-management partnership agreements were expanded to include all the countries of the world, excluding Japan. In October 2002, ezetimibe, the first in a new class of cholesterol-lowering agents, was approved in the United States as *Zetia* and in Germany as *Ezetrol*. *Zetia* was launched in the United States in November 2002. In 2003, following the successful completion of the European Union Mutual Recognition Procedure, *Ezetrol* had been launched in five European countries— Germany, the United Kingdom, Switzerland, Sweden and the Netherlands. Sales totaled $469.4 million in 2003 and $25.3 million in 2002. In September 2003, Merck/Schering-Plough Pharmaceuticals submitted a New Drug Application to the U.S. Food and Drug Administration (FDA) for *Vytorin*, which contains the active ingredients of both *Zetia* and *Zocor*. In November 2003, the filing was accepted by the FDA for standard review. Similar applications have been filed in other countries outside the United States.

In January 2002, the Merck/Schering-Plough respiratory partnership reported on results of Phase III clinical trials of a fixed combination tablet containing *Singulair* and *Claritin*, Schering-Plough's nonsedating antihistamine, which did not demonstrate sufficient added benefits in the treatment of seasonal allergic rhinitis.

Investments in affiliates accounted for using the equity method, including the above joint ventures, totaled $2.2 billion at December 31, 2003 and 2002, respectively. These amounts are reported in Other assets. Dividends and distributions received from these affiliates were $553.4 million in 2003, $488.6 million in 2002, and $572.2 million in 2001.

Archer Daniels Midland
2005 Annual Report

Note 4—Investments in and Advances to Affiliates

The Company has ownership interests in non-majority-owned affiliates accounted for under the equity method. The Company had 83 and 85 unconsolidated affiliates as of June 30, 2005 and 2004, respectively, located in North and South America, Africa, Europe and Asia. During fiscal 2005, the Company acquired controlling interests in 3 previously unconsolidated affiliates, made initial investments in 7 unconsolidated affiliates and disposed of its investments in 6 affiliates. The following table summarizes the combined balance sheets and the combined statements of earnings of the Company's unconsolidated affiliates as of and for each of the three years ended June 30, 2005, 2004, and 2003.

	2005	2004 (in thousands)	2003
Currents assets	$ 6,240,670	$ 5,159,660	
Non-current assets	7,384,141	8,305,256	

	2005	2004 *(in thousands)*	2003
Current liabilities	4,746,450	3,983,022	
Non-current liabilities	1,912,285	1,939,453	
Minority interests	430,530	369,991	
Net assets	$ 6,535,546	$ 7,172,450	
Net sales	$20,214,914	$17,744,217	$17,181,800
Gross profit	2,310,413	1,991,947	2,037,875
Net income (loss)	757,539	819,201	(62,707)

Undistributed earnings of the Company's unconsolidated affiliates as of June 30, 2005, is $436 million.

Two foreign affiliates for which the Company has a carrying value of $406 million have a market value of $384 million based on quoted market prices and exchange rates at June 30, 2005.

Oshkosh Truck
2006 Annual Report

6. Investments in Unconsolidated Affiliates

The Company records its investments in, and share of earnings of, OMFSP and Mezcladores under the equity method of accounting. Earnings, net of related income taxes, are reflected in Equity in Earnings of Unconsolidated Affiliates. The Company received cash distributions from OMFSP of $6,968, $8,024 and $6,407 in fiscal 2006, 2005 and 2004, respectively, and dividends of $490 from Mezcladores in fiscal 2004. The Company's investment in OMFSP was $16,923 and $18,466 at September 30, 2006 and 2005, respectively. The Company's investment in Mezcladores was $2,350 and $1,814 at September 30, 2006 and 2005, respectively.

On February 26, 1998, concurrent with the Company's acquisition of McNeilus, the Company and an unaffiliated third party, BA Leasing & Capital Corporation ("BALCAP"), formed OMFSP, a general partnership, for the purpose of offering lease financing to certain customers of the Company. Each partner contributed existing lease assets (and, in the case of the Company, related notes payable to third party lenders which were secured by such leases) to capitalize the partnership. Leases and related notes payable contributed by the Company were originally acquired in connection with the McNeilus acquisition.

OMFSP manages the contributed assets and liabilities and engages in new vendor lease business providing financing to certain customers of the Company. The Company sells vehicles, vehicle bodies and concrete batch plants to OMFSP for lease to user-customers. Company sales to OMFSP were $72,867, $72,994 and $58,182 in fiscal 2006, 2005 and 2004, respectively. Banks and other financial institutions lend to OMFSP a portion of the purchase price, with recourse solely to OMFSP, secured by a pledge of lease payments due from the user-lessees.

Each partner funds one-half of the equity portion of the cost of the new vehicle and batch plant purchases, and each partner is allocated its proportionate share of OMFSP cash flow and taxable income in accordance with the partnership agreement. Indebtedness of OMFSP is secured by the underlying leases and assets of, and is with recourse to, OMFSP. However, all OMFSP indebtedness is non-recourse to the Company or BALCAP.

Summarized financial information of OMFSP as of September 30, 2006 and 2005 and for the fiscal years ended September 30, 2006, 2005 and 2004 was as follows:

	September 30	
	2006	2005
Cash and cash equivalents	$ 3,546	$ 3,774
Lease assets, net	198,887	189,268
Other assets	603	606
	$203,036	$193,648
Notes payable	165,359	$154,820
Other liabilities	4,672	3605
Partners' equity	33,005	35,223
	$203,036	$193,648

	Fiscal Year Ended September 30		
	2006	2005	2004
Interest income	$ 11,301	$ 11,143	$ 12,808
Net interest income	2,955	3,347	3,885
Excess of revenues over expenses	3,457	4,433	3,589

Chapter 11
Business Combinations[*]

CONTENTS

Business combinations in the form of mergers and acquisitions of business entities occur when companies choose to combine (rather than grow internally) to take advantage of cost efficiencies or transform their businesses to the next level. The result of a business combination is that the combined company may have additional product offerings, greater geographic presence, increased market share, as well as control over all sources of production and product distribution (vertical integration). The accountant is frequently called upon to advise management of the impact of proposed combinations, as well as to prepare consolidated financial statements for completed transactions. Knowledge of the emerging accounting rules in this area is critical in supporting both functions.

With the exception of the elimination of pooling of interests for new acquisitions (in 2001) and the required consolidation of variable interest entities (revised in 2003), the accounting rules for business combinations and consolidations remained largely unchanged for over 50 years until December 2007, when the Financial Accounting Standards Board (FASB), after many years of deliberation, simultaneously issued two new standards reflected in the Codification as ASC 805, *Business Combinations*, and ASC 810, *Consolidation*. These statements, which require prospective treatment for new business combinations having fiscal years beginning after December 15, 2008, mandate what is referred to as the acquisition

---

[*] This chapter was co-authored by Jeffrey Satenstein, MS, CPA, Managing Director (retired), JPMorgan Chase Investment Bank, Lecturer, Accounting & Information Systems, Queens College, CUNY.

method. Moreover, the purchase method of accounting will no longer be permitted for acquisitions closed after the effective date of the new rules.

A critical distinction is that the new rules abandon the historical cost-based structure of accounting for acquisitions at the price paid and require that consolidation of the acquiree is at "business fair value." As retroactive adoption of the new standards is not permitted, mergers completed before the effective date must continue to be treated in accordance with the accounting standards that were in effect at the date of the original business combination. Therefore, there will continue to be many mergers that will be "grandfathered" under the accounting rules in existence at the dates they were completed (i.e., purchase method and pooling of interests method).

This chapter and Chapter 12, "Consolidations," emphasize both the theory and practice relating the new standards (i.e., the acquisition method). However, since preexisting accounting methods (e.g., poolings and purchase method) will continue to be used for transactions closed before the effective dates of ASC 805 and ASC 810, a comparison of old and new rules prepare practitioners for dealing with the variety of practices they will encounter at their clients or employers.

TERMINOLOGY

The following definitions of key terminology can be referred to throughout this chapter and Chapter 12, "Consolidation":

- ☐ *Acquisition.* Acquirer purchases a controlling financial interest in an acquiree and agrees to operate it as a majority owned or wholly owned subsidiary.

- ☐ *Acquisition method.* Required by ASC 805 and ASC 810 for consolidation of companies controlled by an acquirer; focuses on business fair value, not historical price paid to acquire a company.

- ☐ *Bargain purchase.* Under the acquisition method, when business fair value is less than the fair value of net assets received; under the purchase method, when purchase price is less than the fair value of net assets acquired.

- ☐ *Book value.* Amount recorded on the accounting records, also referred to as "carrying value."

- ☐ *Business combinations (mergers and acquisitions).* Legal joining of two or more companies into one economic entity.

- ☐ *Business fair value.* The sum of the fair value of the controlling interest and the fair value of the noncontrolling (minority) interest.

- ☐ *Contingent consideration.* Amounts that may be paid at a future date by the acquirer based on whether certain conditions are met (e.g., earnings, stock price, or employee retention).

- ☐ *Control.* The ability (whether used or not) of the acquirer to make decisions about the manner in which the acquiree conducts business (e.g., pricing of products, dividends, use of technology, or interchange of management personnel).

☐ *Control premium.* Additional amount paid by the acquirer to gain a controlling financial interest in the acquiree.

☐ *Cost, equity, and partial equity methods.* Alternative accounting methods used by a parent to account for its investment in its consolidated subsidiary on the parent's books.

☐ *Direct acquisition costs.* Costs incurred to complete the business combination (e.g., lawyer's and accountant's fees).

☐ *Economic unit method for consolidation of noncontrolling interests.* Required by ASC 810 for consolidation of noncontrolling interests arising from acquisitions completed by acquirers having a fiscal year beginning after December 15, 2008.

☐ *Fair value.* A price at which a willing buyer and a willing seller will exchange goods or services, with both parties under no duress to complete the transaction.

☐ *Goodwill.* Future economic benefits, obtained in a business combination, that are not attributable to separately recognized assets and liabilities of the acquiree. Under the acquisition method, computed as business fair value minus 100% of the fair value of net assets acquired.

☐ *Implied value.* Price paid to acquire a company divided by ownership percentage; used for the goodwill impairment test and the economic unit (acquisition) method of consolidating noncontrolling interests.

☐ *In process research and development costs.* Amounts expended by the acquiree for research and development costs prior to the date of acquisition, regardless of whether they are treated as an asset or expense on the acquiree books.

☐ *Intangible assets.* Gives the owner rights transferred by contract or other means.

☐ *Intercompany transactions.* Transactions that take place within the same economic entity, typically between a parent and a subsidiary, or between two subsidiaries of the same parent.

☐ *Net assets.* Total assets minus total liabilities.

☐ *Noncontrolling interests (alternatively referred to as minority interests).* Ownership associated with holders of less than 50% of the voting common shares of the acquiree.

☐ *Parent company.* Acquirer, when the acquiree is operated as a subsidiary.

☐ *Parent company method for consolidation of noncontrolling interests.* Most prevalent method for consolidation of noncontrolling interests prior to FASB adoption of the acquisition method—acquiree balance sheet accounts consolidated at 100% of book value + (ownership percentage × [fair value – book value]); this method was viewed as a "hybrid method" between the economic unit (acquisition) method and the proportionate method.

☐ *Pooling of interests method.* Accounting method that is intended to reflect a "merger of equals"; acquiree book values (not fair values) are recorded in consolidation; there is no goodwill in a pooling (no longer available to acquisitions closed after June 30, 2001).

☐ *Preacquisition contingencies.* Uncertainties arising prior to the date of the acquisition (e.g., lawsuits) that will be resolved after the acquisition closing date.

☐ *Proportionate method for consolidation of noncontrolling interests.* Acquiree assets and liabilities consolidated at fair value multiplied by the percentage of ownership; this method is no longer permissible for acquisitions completed after December 15, 2008, which are all subject to ASC 810.

☐ *Purchase method*   Accounting method that focuses on the historical cost of the acquisition (e.g., price paid by the parent); acquiree assets and liabilities are recorded in consolidation at fair value (no longer available to acquisitions closed after December 15, 2008, where the acquirer's fiscal year-end begins on or after that date).

☐ *Statutory consolidation.* Both companies agree to merge with a newly formed company replacing the two previous companies.

☐ *Statutory merger.* Acquirer purchases net assets or stock of acquiree and dissolves the acquiree, bringing the net assets on to the acquirer books at fair value (acquisition method).

☐ *Stock issuance costs.* Costs to register securities issued in conjunction with a business combination (e.g., exchange fees, printing costs [prospectus]).

☐ *Subsidiary company.* Acquiree, when it is operated as a subsidiary of the parent.

☐ *Variable interest entity.* Entity where the primary beneficiary (generally, the sponsor) does not own shares but nonetheless maintains control through contractual agreement (sometimes referred to as a special purpose vehicle or special purpose entity).

RELEVANT ACCOUNTING PRONOUNCEMENTS

Business combinations are accounted for in accordance with ASC 805, *Business Combinations*, ASC 350, *Intangibles—Goodwill and Other*, and ASC 810, *Consolidation*. Applicable Emerging Issues Task Force bulletins have been incorporated in the above Codification sections.

FORMS OF BUSINESS COMBINATIONS

In practice, there generally are three forms of business combinations. Deciding on the appropriate form to use is driven by a combination of legal, tax, regulatory, marketing, and operational issues. These business combinations are as follows:

1. *Statutory merger* The acquirer purchases either the net assets of the target company or acquires the stock of the target (acquiree) company; in either case, the acquiree company is dissolved, as the acquirer brings the assets

and liabilities of the acquiree on its books and cancels the stock of the acquiree.

2. *Statutory consolidation* A new company is formed by the combination of two or more companies; the previous companies no longer exist but may become operating divisions of the new company.

3. *Acquisition* The acquirer purchases the stock or net assets of the acquiree and operates it as a direct (wholly or majority owned) subsidiary of the acquirer (the parent). Unlike a statutory merger and statutory consolidation, there is a need to combine the accounts of the parent and subsidiary into a consolidated economic entity. Effective with ASC 805 and ASC 810, the acquisition method is the required method to account for business combinations having a closing date in fiscal periods beginning after December 15, 2008.

THE ACQUISITION METHOD

The acquisition method requires that the acquired company be reported in consolidation at business fair value. Acquiree assets and liabilities along with the fair value of unrecorded acquiree intangible assets will be reported in consolidation at fair value. The acquiree accounting records will continue to maintain the carrying values using the basis of accounting that was in existence prior to the acquisition. Fair value consolidation adjustments will be prepared on a worksheet used to effect the business combination and generally will not be posted to either the parent or subsidiary accounting records (for exceptions, see the discussion of push down accounting). Goodwill is recorded where the fair value of consideration transferred plus any fair value of any noncontrolling interest in the acquiree exceeds 100% of the fair value of net assets acquired.

When the fair value of consideration transferred plus any fair value of the noncontrolling interest in the acquiree is less than the fair value of net assets acquired, a gain from bargain purchase is recorded on the consolidated income statement in the accounting period that the acquisition takes place.

ACCOUNTING AND REPORTING UNDER THE ACQUISITION METHOD

Accounting for the three forms of business combinations (i.e., statutory merger, statutory consolidation, and acquisition) under the new accounting rules (ASC 805 and ASC 810) is discussed below, followed by a comparison of the new accounting rules with the "grandfathered" previous accounting rules and ASC 810-10-10). The "grandfathered" rules do not appear in the FASB Codification, but continue to be applicable to acquisitions completed on or before December 15, 2008.

Statutory Merger

Statutory mergers can be structured in one of two ways:

1. The acquirer purchases the assets and liabilities of the acquiree and dissolves the acquiree:

    a. The assets and liabilities, as well as any unrecorded intangibles of the acquiree are recorded at fair value directly on the acquirer books.

    b. Any excess of fair value of consideration transferred (generally the purchase price) over the fair values of the net assets (and intangibles) acquired is recorded as goodwill (where there is a purchase of 100% of acquiree stock).

    c. If acquiree fair values are greater than the consideration transferred, a gain on bargain purchase occurs.

    d. None of acquiree equity will appear on the consolidated financial statements.

2. The acquirer purchases the stock of the acquiree (Debit investment in acquiree, credit cash, debt, or stock of the acquirer) and dissolves the acquiree:

    a. Records the net assets on the books of the acquirer at fair value as in 1 above.

EXAMPLE

ABC Corporation pays $10 million to acquire 100% ownership of XYZ Corporation in a transaction that will be treated as a statutory merger. The purchase price equals business fair value. The fair value of XYZ assets is $15 million and the fair value of XYZ liabilities is $5 million. The accounting entries on ABC Corporation are as follows:

1. Dr. Investment in XYZ Corporation	$10 million	
Cr. Cash or other form of payment		$10 million
2. Dr. Assets (from XYZ)	$15 million	
Cr. Liabilities (from XYZ)		$ 5 million
Cr. Investment in XYZ Corp		$10 million

3. XYZ Corporation will then liquidate (debit liabilities and equity, credit assets) and cease to exist.

Statutory Consolidation

In this transaction, the acquirer and acquiree company merge to form a new company. Under the acquisition method, the new company records the assets, liabilities, and previously unrecorded intangibles of the acquirer and acquiree at fair value. The new company then cancels the common stock of the predecessor companies, which go out of existence.

EXAMPLE

Rim Company and Boyce Company agree to combine in a statutory consolidation. It is agreed that a new company, Weston Incorporated, will be the successor company and receive the net assets of Rim and Boyce. Under the acquisition method, Weston will record, at fair value, the net assets of Rim and Boyce. Any excess of consideration transferred to the owners of Rim and Boyce over the fair value of net assets acquired will be reported as goodwill by Weston.

Acquisition

The acquiree will be operated as a subsidiary of the acquirer. The assets, liabilities, and stockholders' equity of both companies will continue to be recorded using the same basis of accounting that was used previously. Consolidated financial statements will be prepared using the worksheet techniques described more fully in Chapter 12, "Consolidation." Briefly, the carrying amounts (book values) from the parent and subsidiary will be subtotaled and the appropriate elimination entries for intercompany transactions will be posted to the worksheet along with the acquiree fair value adjustments and elimination of subsidiary capital accounts and previously calculated acquiree goodwill. These are illustrated in Chapter 12, "Consolidation." Acquiree intangible assets and goodwill are treated identically for each of the three business combinations (i.e., statutory merger, statutory consolidation, and acquisition), as discussed below.

Treatment of Intangible Assets

Acquiree intangible assets are recorded in the consolidated financial statements at fair value as of the date of acquisition, even if not previously recorded on the acquiree books. A common example is the fair value of customer lists that must be appraised based on the size, profitability, and expected longevity of the customer relationship. Other purchased intangibles are included in investment cost only if contractual in nature (e.g., patents, copyrights, trademarks) or separable (i.e., are capable of alternative future use).

Definition of Goodwill under the Acquisition Method

Goodwill is defined as: (the fair value of consideration transferred + the fair value of any noncontrolling interest in the acquiree + the fair value of any previously held equity interest in the acquiree)—100% of the fair value of net assets acquired.

EXAMPLE 1

On July 1, 201X, Jeffries Incorporated issues 40,000 shares of its common stock in exchange for an initial acquisition of 80% of Bromard's outstanding shares. The aggregate fair value of the shares issued is $4,000,000 ($100 per share). It is determined by independent appraisal that the remaining 20% of Bromard has a fair value of $800,000. It is also determined that the fair value of 100% of the Bromard's net assets at date of acquisition is $4,200,000. What is the goodwill?

Solution

Goodwill = Fair value of consideration transferred ($4,000,000) + fair value of noncontrolling interest ($800,000) + fair value of previously held equity interest (0) – fair value of net assets acquired ($4,200,000) = $600,000

EXAMPLE 2

Same facts as above, but the fair value of Bromard's net assets at date of acquisition is $5,000,000.

Solution

In this second example, there is a $200,000 excess of fair value of net assets acquired over fair value of consideration transferred + the fair value of the noncontrolling interest. The result is a $200,000 gain on the bargain purchase that is recognized in the consolidated income statement in the period of acquisition.

Treatment of Goodwill

Goodwill recorded in consolidation is subject to an annual impairment test. This two-part test is applied to the reporting units within the consolidated entity. Reporting units may consist of legal entities, such as branches and subsidiaries, or business segments of the consolidated entity.

In the first part of the goodwill impairment test, the fair value of the reporting unit is compared to its carrying (book) value, including any allocated goodwill. Due to the complexity, subjectivity, and cost to some companies of determining fair value of a reporting unit, in Accounting Standards Update 2011-08, the FASB now permits companies to use a qualitative approach in determining if it necessary to apply the two-part impairment test. If, after assessing the relevant qualitative factors (discussed below) it is considered NOT "more likely than not" that the fair value of the reporting unit is less than its carrying value (including allocated goodwill), performing the two-step process is unnecessary and no impairment is recorded. "More likely than not" is defined as a probability of greater than 50%. As described in ASC 350-20-5-3C, these qualitative factors include, but are not limited to:

- Macroeconomic factors such as general economic conditions, availability of capital to fund expansion, fluctuations in interest rates, commodity prices, and/or foreign exchange rates that impact the reporting entity.

- Specific industry or market considerations affecting the reporting unit, such as competition, changes in the entities products, services, or distribution model.

- Cost factors including increases in raw material or labor costs having a detrimental impact on earnings and cash flows.

- Declining earnings or cash flows over several periods.

- Changes in management, key personnel, or unresolved legal matters.

- Management's plans to dispose of a significant segment of the business.

- A sustained decline in the price of the company's publicly traded shares or decline in earnings multiples at which the stock trades.

If it is considered more likely than not that the fair value of the reporting unit is less than its carrying value, the first step of the goodwill impairment test must be completed. Management has the option to forego the qualitative test and choose to proceed directly to the first step of the goodwill impairment test. This could occur when management believes that evaluation of all the qualitative factors would be more complex than determining the fair value of the acquired business.

While the determination whether it is more likely than not that the fair value of the reporting unit is less than its carrying value is judgmental in nature, the following examples are intended to provide guidance as to interpretation of the above qualitative circumstances:

- *Example 1:* Sands Company has $3,000,000 of goodwill recorded from an acquisition done in 2010. In the goodwill impairment test completed in 2011, Sands determined that the fair value of the company it acquired was $10,000,000 and the book value inclusive of goodwill of the acquired company was $6,000,000. Therefore, as step 1 of the goodwill test was passed, no goodwill was recorded. It is now 2012 and Sands has unexpectedly lost a customer that provided 30% of the acquiree revenues and 40% of its net income. Conclusion: Due to the reliance Sands had on this significant customer, it is necessary for Sands to perform the two-part impairment test.

- *Example 2:* Baxter Company has $5,000,000 of goodwill from an acquisition done in 2008. In the goodwill impairment test completed in 2011, Baxter determined that the fair value of the company it acquired was $25,000,000 and that the book value of the acquired company, including goodwill, was $9,000,000. The acquiree company has operations in Europe that have contributed 20% of earnings. Baxter's European entities have substantial foreign exchange risk and interest rate risk. Baxter has effectively hedged 95% of this risk using options, futures, and forward contracts. In addition, while the cost of raw materials has increased substantially, Baxter has demonstrated its ability to pass these costs along to its customers. Conclusion: In this case, Baxter can conclude it is not necessary to perform the two-part impairment test, as there was a sufficient margin of safety from the prior-year valuation and it appears to be successfully managing its market risks and pricing. Note that Baxter may not solely rely on the prior year's fair value determination in reaching this conclusion.

- *Example 3:* Peters Company has $7,000,000 of goodwill from an acquisition done in 2005. In the goodwill impairment test completed in 2011, Peters determined that the fair value of the company it acquired was $15,000,000 and that the book value of the acquired company, including goodwill, was $12,000,000. In the past six months, Peters has been sued for $4,000,000 by a major supplier over a purchase contract dispute. Peters believes the lawsuit does not have merit. In addition, the CEO of the acquiree company has recently resigned and gone to work for a competitor. Finally the acquired company has recently begun to experience a $2,000,000 annualized negative cash flow from operations, which has to be covered by additional long-term borrowings. Conclusion: Due to the number of factors having a potential bearing on the market value of the acquired company, Peters will need to apply the two-part impairment test.

The following describes the two steps in performing the goodwill impairment test:

1. *Step 1:* If the fair value of the reporting unit is less than the carrying value, including any allocated goodwill, proceed to step 2. If the carrying value of the reporting unit is zero or negative, it will still be necessary to perform step 2 of the goodwill impairment test if there are adverse qualitative factors indicating impairment may exist. Such factors may include an adverse change in legal factors or business climate, an adverse action or assessment by a regulator, unanticipated competition, a loss of key personnel, a more likely than not expectation that a reporting unit (or significant portion) will be sold or disposed of, impairment of a long lived asset within the reporting unit or recognition of an impairment loss in a subsidiary that is a component of the reporting unit. It is particularly targeted at companies with a single (or very few) business segments that were previously able to avoid performing step 2, below of the impairment test. (ASC 350-20-35-8A)

2. *Step 2:* If the implied value of goodwill of the business segment is greater than the carrying value of goodwill, goodwill impairment is recognized equal to the shortfall (Dr. Goodwill Impairment Loss Cr. Goodwill). If it is not, there is no goodwill impairment. Calculation of implied value involves estimating the fair value of the reporting unit being evaluated. Accepted methods to value a business include using discounted cash flows, discounted dividends ,or discounted residual earnings with the discount rate being either the weighted average cost of capital (cash flow and dividend discount model) or the cost of equity capital (residual earnings model).

The following example illustrates this test:

EXAMPLE

Adams Company has $70,000,000 in goodwill associated with its acquisition one year ago of Baker Company. Adams is required to test for impairment using the following steps:

1. At date of acquisition, goodwill is assigned to each of Adam's business segments; in this example, Adams has three divisions comprising its business segments, with book values excluding goodwill of: Division A—$60 million, Division B—$220 million, Division C—$180 million. The goodwill assigned to the three divisions is $20 million, $30 million and $20 million, respectively.

2. The book value (net assets) of each division inclusive of the allocated goodwill (from step 1) is compared to the fair value of each division; that is, the theoretical price at which the division could be sold. The fair values of the three divisions are $90 million, $200 million, and $300

million, respectively. (Note that these amounts may be determined by consultation with an expert in the field of mergers and acquisitions.)

3. If the fair value of each division is greater than the book value inclusive of goodwill, no further testing is required and there is no goodwill impairment. If the fair value of any division is less than the book value inclusive of goodwill, proceed to step 4 for that division. In this problem, the fair value of the individual net assets of Division B is given at $180 million.

4. Compute the implied value of goodwill. This is equal to the fair value of the division (price at which it could be sold) minus the fair value of the specific net assets of the division. If the implied value of goodwill is less than the book value of goodwill, the difference must be written off as an impairment loss on goodwill. If the implied value of goodwill is greater than the book value of goodwill, no impairment has taken place.

Solution

($ millions)

Book Value (without Goodwill)		*Goodwill*	*Book Value (with Goodwill)*	*Fair Value*	*Further Testing*
Division A	60	20	80	90	No
Division B	220	30	250	200	Yes
Division C	180	20	200	300	No
Total	460	70	530	590	

Step 1: Following the above rules, Division B requires further testing, as its fair value is less than the book value of net assets inclusive of goodwill.

Step 2:

Fair value of Division B (per above)	200
Fair value of individual net assets of Division B	180
Implied value of goodwill	20
Book value of goodwill	30
Writedown of goodwill	10

Journal entry: Dr. Impairment Loss on Goodwill $10 million
Cr. Goodwill $10 million

Note that when a previously acquired subsidiary is sold, any remaining goodwill must be reduced to zero as part of the calculation of the gain or loss on sale. In addition, if a subsidiary is acquired that had preexisting goodwill on its books, such goodwill is not recognized in the consolidated financial statements unless the business fair value of the acquired company exceeds 100% of the fair value of net assets acquired.

Income Statement Reporting

Under the acquisition method, income and expenses of the acquiree are recognized prospectively beginning from the date of acquisition. Under the acquisition method, preacquisition income (income earned by the acquiree before the effective date of the transaction) is not reported on the consolidated financial statements. This represents a departure from the prior purchase method, where preacquisition earnings of the acquiree were deducted from full-year consolidated earnings on the income statement.

Direct Combination Costs and Stock Issuance Costs

Direct combination costs associated with completing the business combination (e.g., legal, accounting, consulting, appraisals, and finder's fees) are treated as an operating expense under the acquisition method. When the acquirer issues stock in conjunction with a business combination, any stock issuance costs, such as underwriter costs and exchange fees, are treated as a reduction (debit) to Additional Paid in Capital.

According to Accounting Standards Update (ASU) No. 2010-22 (August 2010), *Accounting for Various Topics*, fees to an investment banker for underwriting services related to a business combination or purchase of an asset should be allocated between acquisition-related services and debt issue costs based on fair value.

Restructuring Costs

It is common to find that shortly after the announcement of an acquisition, the acquirer will establish a provision for restructuring costs, as well as announce anticipated savings. The restructuring cost can be recognized as part of the Investment in Subsidiary if certain conditions are met. These conditions are similar to the criteria for recognition of a liability if no acquisition had taken place; that is, a formal plan of restructuring needs to have the approval of the Board of Directors of the acquirer. If these conditions are not met, restructuring costs will need to be expensed.

Preacquisition Contingencies

Under ASC 805, contractual preacquisition contingencies of the acquiree must always be measured at acquisition date fair value, resulting in either an increase or decrease to the debit to the acquirer's investment account. Noncontractual contingencies (example-outstanding acquiree litigation) are recorded at acquisition date fair value only when they meet the "more likely than not" criteria for definition of an asset or liability.

Contingent Consideration

This consideration relates to an additional amount paid by the acquirer to the shareholders of the acquiree if certain conditions are met. Most commonly, this relates to whether the acquiree is able to meet future earnings targets specified in the merger agreement. Under the acquisition method, such "earn-outs" or other forms of contingent consideration are recorded at fair value as part of the debit to the investment account at the acquisition date. Subsequent changes in the fair value of contingent consideration are recorded in earnings and not as an adjustment of investment cost. An exception is when the contingent consideration qualifies as equity, there is no subsequent adjustment to fair value.

Subsequent adjustments under the acquisition method will require revision of prior period previously issued financial statements.

Push Down Accounting

While the FASB has given extensive guidance on how consolidated financial statements should be prepared to reflect a business combination, less attention has been given to how an acquired subsidiary reflects assets and liabilities on its books. One view is that the subsidiary should maintain its previous basis of recording, be that historical cost, market value, or other basis of accounting. According to that view, all fair value adjustments to prepare consolidated financial statements would appear on a worksheet only, and not be posted to the subsidiary's general ledger.

Under the alternative view, the change in ownership resulting from the acquisition of the subsidiary results in a new measurement basis for that company. That measurement basis is fair value and the balances on the subsidiary's general ledger are adjusted to fair value. This eliminates the need for certain consolidation worksheet adjustments, as these are now made directly to the affected accounts on the subsidiary's books. This view is referred to as push down accounting.

The differences in the two views becomes important if the subsidiary issues separate GAAP financial statements, which could be required if the subsidiary issues stock or requires a loan. The Securities and Exchange Commission, which governs reporting by publicly held companies, has, in ASC 805, *Business Combinations: Related Issues* (ASC 805-50-S99), indicated that push down accounting should be used in separately issued financial statements of a subsidiary when that subsidiary is "substantially wholly owned" (i.e., generally, greater than 95% ownership). The rationale is that if the subsidiary were merged into the parent as a statutory merger, the accounting basis for acquired assets and liabilities would be fair value under the acquisition method and that the basis of accounting should not be different when the parent decides to maintain the existence of the subsidiary.

Contrast of Acquisition Method with Purchase and Pooling of Interest Methods

Prior to the effective dates of ASC 805 and ASC 810, previously completed business combinations were accounted for under the purchase method or the pooling of interest method. Since the new rules are grandfathered, those business combinations will continue to be accounted for under the rules that were in place at the time the transaction closed. A listing of the main points of each method is as follows:

☐ *Acquisition method (effective for new acquisitions by acquirers having fiscal years beginning after December 15, 2008):*

— Focus is on fair value of the acquired entity.

— Direct combination costs are expensed.

— Stock issuance costs are treated as a reduction of Additional Paid in Capital.

— Bargain purchase is treated as income to the acquirer.

— Fair value of contingent consideration at acquisition date is considered part of the fair value of the acquired entity.

— Subsequent resolution of contingent consideration at a value different from that recorded at acquisition date is run through the income statement.

— Acquiree in process research and development costs and other purchased intangibles are recorded at fair value at acquisition date.

— Preacquisition contingencies that are resolved after the acquisition closing date are expensed.

— Acquiree assets and liabilities are reported in the consolidated entity at fair value.

☐ *Purchase method (effective for acquisitions closed prior to December 15, 2008, that have been accounted for under the purchase method)*:

— Acquisitions continue to be accounted for under the purchase method.

— Focus is on historical cost of the acquisition (i.e., the price paid to acquire an entity).

— Direct combination costs are capitalized as part of the investment cost.

— Stock issuance costs are treated as a reduction of Additional Paid in Capital.

— Bargain purchase results in a proportional reduction of noncurrent assets of the acquiree with any excess treated as an extraordinary gain.

— Contingent consideration is not recorded as part of acquisition cost until it is subsequently resolved. (**Note**: If the resolution of the contingency requires an additional payment to be made by the acquirer, that payment will either increase goodwill or lessen the reduction to noncurrent assets in the case of a bargain purchase).

— Acquiree in process research and development costs is included in acquisition cost only where considered either technologically feasible or subject to alternative future use.

— Assets and liabilities of the acquiree are reported at fair value, subject to any reduction in acquiree noncurrent assets due to a bargain purchase.

☐ *Pooling of Interest method (effective for acquisitions completed prior to June 30, 2001, assuming they met all 12 of the specific criteria in existence at that time)*:

— Acquisitions will continue to be consolidated under this method, until the entities are sold, closed, or otherwise disposed of.

— Assets and liabilities are consolidated at their book values.

— There are no adjustments to either the balance sheet (fair value allocations) or the income statement (amortization of fair value adjustments).

— Income and expense of the acquiree are reported retrospectively; that is, they are retroactively restated for all periods presented.

The following table presents the main differences between the acquisition and purchase methods of accounting:

Acquisition Method vs. Purchase Method

	New Rules (Acquisition Method) ASC 805; ASC 810	Old Rules (Purchase Method) Not Covered in FASB Codification
Focus	Fair value of entity acquired, referred to as "business fair value"	Historical cost; that is, price paid to acquire the entity
Direct combination costs	Expensed	Treated as part of cost of acquisition
Bargain purchase	Recognize as income on transaction closing date	Reduce noncurrent assets proportionately; any excess is extraordinary gain
Stock issuance costs	Decrease (debit) to Additional Paid In Capital	Same
Contingent consideration	Recorded at fair value at transaction closing date; subsequent changes in fair value recorded in income statement	Not recorded as part of acquisition cost until contingency is resolved. This will result in additional goodwill or less reduction to noncurrent assets (bargain purchase)
In process research and development costs	Capitalize at fair value as intangible assets, subject to impairment testing or amortization	Expensed
Preacquisition contingencies	Contractual contingencies recorded at fair value; noncontractual contingencies recorded at fair value if they meet "more likely than not" criteria for definition of an asset or liability	Not recorded unless occurrence is both probable and reasonably estimable
Valuation of equity issued	Fair value at transaction closing date	Fair value at the date the acquisition is announced
Other intangible assets	Recorded at fair value	Recorded as part of investment cost if meeting contractual criteria (e.g., patents) or separability (e.g., technology)

Steps to Accounting under the Acquisition Method

The following steps are taken in accounting for a business combination under the acquisition method:

1. Assets and liabilities of the acquired business are recorded at fair market value as follows: Trading securities are at market value. Receivables are recorded at the discounted present value of amounts to be received using current interest rates, less allowance for bad debts and collection

costs. Raw materials are recorded at current replacement cost. Work in process is recorded at estimated net realizable value of finished goods less the costs to complete and the profit allowance. Finished goods are recorded at estimated net realizable value less a reasonable profit allowance (lower limit). Fixed assets to be used in the business are recorded at replacement cost. If the fixed assets are to be sold, they are recorded at estimated selling price less cost to sell. Intangibles and other assets are recognized at appraised values. Any duplicate assets that are to be disposed of are recorded at estimated net salvage value. If there is no net salvage value, a zero valuation is assigned. Liabilities are typically recorded at the discounted present value of amounts to be paid based on current interest rates.

2. The excess of the fair value of consideration transferred over the fair value of net assets acquired is assigned to goodwill, which is subject to an annual impairment test.

3. Goodwill previously recorded by the acquiree is not brought forward.

4. The excess of the fair value of net assets received over the fair value of consideration transferred is recorded as a gain on bargain purchases.

5. None of the stockholders' equity accounts of the acquired company is shown on the acquirer's books or in the consolidated financial statements.

6. Net income of the acquired business is recognized from the acquisition date to year-end.

7. Direct costs of the acquisition (e.g., legal, accounting, consulting, engineering evaluation, appraisal, and finders' fees) are expensed. Indirect and general costs (internal costs) are also expensed as incurred. If the acquirer pays fees to an investment banker for advice and assistance, such costs must be expensed. The costs of registering and issuing any debt or equity securities to effect the combination are accounted for as any other issue cost; that is, the issuance cost for debt is deferred and amortized over the term of the debt using the interest method, and the cost of issuing stock (e.g., underwriting fees) is a reduction of additional paid-in-capital. Liabilities and commitments for the costs of closing an acquired company's plant are considered direct costs of the acquisition and are expensed. However, the costs of closing a duplicate plant of the acquirer are not part of the acquisition cost.

According to ASC 805-20-55-51, termination or employee relocation costs arising because of a business combination should be accrued when the combination is consummated.

A purchase of stock appreciation rights (awards) or stock options by an acquired company related to a business combination should be accounted for as compensation expense rather than as an element of acquisition cost by the acquirer.

If debt securities are issued in the acquisition, they should be recorded at their fair value based on the present value of the debt payments discounted at the market interest rate. Any difference between face value and present value is recorded as discount or premium on the debt.

In determining the fair value of securities issued in a business combination, consideration should be given to the quantity issued, price variability, and issue costs.

There is a step-by-step acquisition process to be followed:

☐ If control is not achieved on the initial purchase, the subsidiary is not included in consolidation until control has been achieved.

☐ After the parent owns more than 50% of the subsidiary, a retroactive adjustment is required, including the subsidiary's profits in consolidated retained earnings, in a step-by-step manner starting with the original investment.

☐ The subsidiary's profits are included in ownership years at the applicable percentage owned.

EXAMPLE

On October 31, 20X8, Kravis Company bought for cash at $10 per share all 300,000 of Hartman's outstanding common stock. It is agreed that the purchase price equals business fair value. At October 31, 20X8, Hartman's balance sheet showed a book value of net assets of $2,500,000. At that date, the fair value of Hartman's fixed assets exceeded its book value by $300,000. In the October 31, 20X8 consolidated balance sheet, Kravis reports goodwill of $200,000, computed as follows:

Fair value of consideration transferred ($10×300,000 shares)	$3,000,000
Book value of net assets acquired	2,500,000
Excess of cost over book value	$ 500,000
Excess of fair value over book value of fixed assets	300,000
Goodwill	$ 200,000

EXAMPLE

ABC Co. purchases 100% interest in common stock of DEF Co. for $1,800,000.

The journal entry to reflect the initial investment is:

Investment in DEF Company	1,800,000	
Cash		1,800,000

EXAMPLE

Moses Company bought 100% of Rolo Company in a business combination on September 30, 20X2. During 20X2, Moses declared dividends of $20,000 per quarter, and Rolo declared quarterly dividends of $5,000. The dividends declared to be reported in December 31, 20X2, consolidated retained earnings under the acquisition method are $80,000 (those paid by Moses only). The dividends paid by Rolo go to Moses and are eliminated in consolidation.

EXAMPLE

On June 30, 20X2, Harris Company exchanged 300,000 shares of its $10 par value common stock for all of Blake Company's common stock. The fair market value of Harris Company's common stock issued equals the carrying value of Blake's net assets. Both entities will continue their separate businesses and operations. The following data are presented:

	Harris	Blake
Retained earnings—12/31/20X1	$3,000,000	$900,000
Dividends paid—4/1/20X2	700,000	
Net income—1/1/20X2 to 6/30/20X2	850,000	250,000

If the acquisition method was used, the balance in retained earnings to be presented by the Harris Company in its June 30, 20X2, consolidated balance sheet would be based on the parent's retained earnings as follows:

Balance, 12/31/20X1	$3,000,000
Net income—1/1/20X2–6/30/20X2	850,000
Dividends paid—4/1/20X2	(700,000)
Retained earnings—6/30/20X2	$3,150,000

Earnings of Blake Company prior to the acquisition date are not included in consolidated retained earnings.

If there is an exchange by a partly owned subsidiary of its common stock for the voting common stock of the parent company, this *downstream merger* transaction is treated as a purchase.

EXAMPLE

Business Combination Accounted for under the Acquisition Method

ABC Company issues 50,000 shares on December 1, 20X2, to acquire all of XYZ Company's outstanding shares. This transaction will be accounted for under the acquisition method, with XYZ Company becoming a 100%-owned subsidiary of ABC Company.

ABC Company		
Shares issued to acquire XYZ Company:		50,000
Par value:	$ 3	
Fair value:	$ 10	
XYZ Company		
Total shares outstanding:		10,000
Par value:	$ 10	

OUT-OF-POCKET COSTS OF BUSINESS COMBINATION

Legal fees related to business combination:	$35,000
SEC stock registration related costs:	$15,000
Total:	$50,000

ABC Company and XYZ Company
Separate Balance Sheets (prior to combination)
As of Dec. 31, 20X2

	ABC Company	XYZ Company
ASSETS		
Current assets	900,000	135,000
Property, plant, and equipment (net)	2,500,000	400,000
Other assets	–	35,000
Total Assets	3,400,000	570,000
LIABILITIES & EQUITY		
Current liabilities	500,000	120,000
Long-term liabilities	1,200,000	200,000
Common stock, ABC Company	900,000	
Common stock, XYZ Company		100,000
Paid-in-capital	300,000	50,000
Retained earnings	500,000	100,000
Total liabilities and equity	3,400,000	570,000

It is assumed that there were no intercompany transactions prior to the business combination. Moreover, there were no contingent considerations related to this combination. The effect of income taxes is disregarded in this example.

ABC will record its investment in XYZ as follows:

12/31/20X2	Investment in XYZ Company	500,000	
	Common stock		150,000
	Additional Paid-in-capital		350,000

To record issuance of ABC shares in exchange for all of XYZ shares in a purchase type business combination.

12/31/20X2	Operating expenses	35,000	
	Additional Paid-in-capital	15,000	
	Cash		50,000

To record direct combination costs and stock issuance costs.

The fair value for XYZ Company's assets and liabilities differs from the carrying amount at the date of acquisition as follows:

	Carrying Amount	Fair Value
Inventory (part of current assets)	100,000	125,000
Plant assets	400,000	550,000
Long-term liabilities	200,000	170,000

Thus, XYZ's assets and liabilities in terms of fair values are as follows:

ASSETS		
Current assets	160,000*	
Property, plant, and equipment (net)	550,000	
Other assets	35,000	
Total assets		745,000
LIABILITIES		
Current liabilities	120,000	
Long-term liabilities	170,000	
Total liabilities		290,000
Fair value of XYZ		455,000

*[135,000+(125,000−100,000)]

The Goodwill generated by the acquisition may be calculated as follows:

ABC's total investment in XYZ	500,000
Less: fair value of XYZ	455,000
Goodwill	45,000

ABC Company and Subsidiary
Consolidated Balance Sheet
As of Dec. 31, 20X2

	ABC Company	XYZ Company	Eliminations Increases (Decreases)	Consolidated
ASSETS				
Current assets	850,000	135,000	25,000	1,010,000
Investment in XYZ	500,000		(500,000)	–
Property, plant, and equipment (net)	2,500,000	400,000	150,000	3,050,000
Other assets		35,000	–	35,000
Goodwill			45,000	45,000
Total assets	3,850,000	570,000	(280,000)	4,140,000
LIABILITIES & EQUITY				
Current liabilities	500,000	120,000		620,000
Long-term liabilities	1,200,000	200,000	(30,000)	1,370,000

	ABC Company	XYZ Company	Eliminations Increases (Decreases)	Consolidated
Common stock, ABC Company	1,050,000			1,050,000
Common stock, XYZ Company		100,000	(100,000)	–
Additional Paid-in-capital	635,000	50,000	(50,000)	635,000
Retained earnings	465,000*	100,000	(100,000)	500,000
Total liabilities and equity	3,850,000	570,000	(280,000)	4,140,000

* 500,000–35,000 direct combination costs.

RESEARCH AND DEVELOPMENT COSTS ACQUIRED AS PART OF A BUSINESS COMBINATION

ASC 805-20-30 requires that research and development assets acquired in a business combination of a business be initially recognized and measured at fair value, even if those assets do not have alternative future use. Subsequent to initial recording, such research and development costs are subject to the annual impairment review prescribed under ASC 350. The scope of this accounting extends to all acquired or purchased tangible and intangible assets resulting from research and development activities, including patents, blueprints, formulas, and designs for new products and processes. It also includes materials and supplies, and equipment and facilities used by the acquiree in its research and development activities.

Income Taxes

For business combinations occurring after the effective date of this statement, the acquiring company shall recognize a deferred tax asset or liability associated with temporary differences between the assigned value on the books and the tax bases of net assets acquired, in accordance with ASC 805-740-05-1. The acquirer shall also account for potential tax effects of temporary differences, carryforwards, and any income tax uncertainties of the acquiree in accordance with ASC 740-10.

For business transactions occurring before the effective date of the Statement, the acquirer shall not adjust the accounting for prior business combinations for previously recognized changes in acquired tax uncertainties or previously recognized changes in the valuation allowance for acquired deferred tax assets.

Disclosures

For each acquisition that occurs during the reporting period or after the reporting period but before financial statements are issued, the acquirer must disclose:

1. Name and description of the acquiree.

2. Acquisition date.

3. Percentage of voting interest acquired.

4. Rationale for the business combination and how the acquirer obtained control of the acquiree.

5. Qualitative factors supporting any goodwill from the transaction (e.g., expected synergies from combined operations or description of intangible assets not qualifying for separate recognition).

6. Fair value of total consideration transferred, as well as fair value of each component.

7. Amount and description of any contingent consideration, as well as a discussion of the circumstances in which payment will be made; also included should be a range of possible outcomes or, if a range cannot be estimated, the reasons why.

8. Amounts recognized at the acquisition date for each major class of assets acquired and liabilities assumed.

9. Nature of recognized and unrecognized contingencies along with a range of possible outcomes.

10. Total goodwill expected to be deducted for tax purposes.

11. If acquirer is required to disclose segment information, the amount of goodwill by reportable segment (this information will be used in the goodwill impairment test).

12. Where acquirer and acquiree have previously had a business relationship, any amounts that are not part of the exchange in the business combination between the acquirer and acquiree should be identified.

13. Any acquisition-related costs and, where reported in the financial statements, that is, expense, reduction of paid in capital, or other category.

14. For any bargain purchase, the amount of the gain included in the consolidated income statement and the reason why the business combination resulted in a gain.

15. Fair value of any noncontrolling interest and valuation techniques used to measure fair value.

16. For step acquisitions, the fair value and valuation technique of any equity interest held immediately prior to the acquisition date and the amount of gain or loss recognized as a result of remeasuring to fair value.

17. For public companies, the amount of revenue and earnings subsequent to the acquisition date, reported in the consolidated income statement.

As clarified by Accounting Standards Update (ASU) No. 2010-29, in December 2010, supplemental pro forma information, showed revenue and earnings of the acquiree as though the business combination occurred as of the beginning of the comparable annual reporting period. For example, if a calendar year-end company completed a business combination in April 2012, disclosures would be provided as if the business combination occurred as of January 1, 2010. In addition, disclosure is required of any material nonrecurring transactions included in the pro forma adjustments.

ANNUAL REPORT REFERENCES

Jacobs Engineering
2011 Annual Report

3. Business Combinations

Acquisitions of TechTeam, Sula, DSWA, Magellan Consulting, Alpha Telecom, and CES

In October 2010, we acquired TechTeam Government Solutions, Inc. ("TechTeam"), formerly a wholly-owned subsidiary of TechTeam Global, Inc. TechTeam is a 500-person information technology ("IT") solutions company that provides support to U.S. federal, state and local government agencies, including the United States Department of Homeland Security, U.S. Army, and U.S. Army Corps of Engineers. The firm's core competencies include systems integration, enterprise application integration, ERP implementation support, IT infrastructure support, network operations management, and call center operations. The primary purpose for acquiring TechTeam was to expand the Company's IT, modeling, and simulation services capabilities with the U.S. federal government.

Also in October 2010, we acquired Sula Systems Ltd ("Sula"), a 70-person professional services firm headquartered in Gloucestershire, England. Founded in 1996, Sula provides systems engineering and technical services on large, complex programs and projects to clients in the United Kingdom's defense and aerospace markets. Sula is also involved in a number of major defense programs in areas such as armored vehicles, complex weapons, test and evaluation, submarine nuclear propulsion, and capability and network level systems engineering. Sula also provides services relating to civil airliners and space-based subsystems. The primary purpose for acquiring Sula was to expand the Company's position in the defense and aerospace markets. In December 2010, we acquired the assets of Damon S. Williams Associates, L.L.C. ("DSWA"). DSWA is a 50 person professional services firm headquartered in Phoenix, Arizona specializing in water and wastewater facilities, with expertise in planning, design, construction administration and operations services. The primary purpose for acquiring DSWA was to expand our water and wastewater capabilities to better serve our customers in the western United States.

Also in December 2010, we acquired the assets of two other, smaller niche firms: (i) Magellan Consulting which provides services to clients in the education market, and (ii) Alpha Telecom Services Company which provides services to clients in the telecommunications industry. In May 2011, we acquired an additional 55% interest in Consulting Engineering Services (India) Private Limited ("CES") bringing our ownership interest to 70%. CES is a leading power, infrastructure, and civil engineering company in India, headquartered in Delhi. CES employs approximately 2,000 people and provides a range of solutions in infrastructure, development, planning, engineering, and construction management. The acquisition of CES significantly expands the Company's resources and capabilities in India and expands our presence in other regions in Asia and the Middle East.

The results of operations of the acquired businesses have been included in the Company's consolidated results of operations commencing with the dates control of the acquired businesses were obtained.

The above acquisitions were not material to the Company's consolidated financial statements at September 30, 2011 and for the year then ended.

The Aker Solutions ASA Transactions

On February 1, 2011, we acquired certain operations within the process and construction business of Aker Solutions ASA, and in April 2011, we completed the acquisition of Aker Projects (Shanghai) Company Limited (Aker Solutions' onshore P&C operations in China) (the acquired operations are referred to herein as the "Aker Entities"). We believe this acquisition will significantly expand Jacobs' global presence in the mining and metals market; provide a new geographic region with South America; and strengthen Jacobs' presence in China and Australia. Jacobs' regional presence in Europe and North America will also be enhanced as a result of this acquisition.

The purchase price was $675.0 million plus approximately $234.6 million representing certain transactions specified in the share purchase agreement ("SPA") and a preliminary estimate of net cash and working capital acquired. At closing, the Company funded approximately $909.6 million pursuant to the SPA. The acquisition was financed through a combination of cash-on-hand and borrowings under a number of new, bilateral credit facilities with major U.S. and European banks. The results of operations of the Aker Entities have been included in the Company's consolidated results of operations commencing with the date control of the entities was obtained.

The following table presents the unaudited, pro forma consolidated results of operations for each of fiscal 2011 and 2010 as if the acquisition of the Aker Entities had occurred at the beginning of fiscal 2010. These pro forma results are not necessarily indicative of (i) the results of operations that would have occurred had the Aker Entities operations actually been acquired at the beginning of fiscal 2010; or (ii) future results of operations (in thousands):

	2011	*2010*
Revenues	$10,733,797	$10,633,975
Net earnings attributable to Jacobs	$ 339,437	$ 262,114

Due to the size of the Aker transaction and considering the number of geographies in which it operates, we have not completed the purchase price allocation. The following table presents the preliminary allocation of the purchase price to the net assets (excluding intangibles and goodwill) of the Aker Entities as of the dates of acquisition (in thousands):

Assets:	
Cash and cash equivalents	$ 329,689
Receivables and other current assets	145,049
Property and equipment, and other assets	115,911
Total assets	590,649
Liabilities:	
Current liabilities	195,910
Long-term liabilities	22,534
Total liabilities	218,444
Net assets acquired	$ 372,205

The Company expects to collect substantially all of the acquired receivables of $134.2 million.

The following table presents the Company's latest estimate of the values of the acquired intangible assets (in thousands):

Customer relationships/backlog	$ 136,000
Technology	23,000
	$ 159,000

The preliminary values of intangible assets subject to amortization are included in "Other Noncurrent Assets" in the accompanying Consolidated Balance Sheet at September 30, 2011, and are being amortized over lives that range from 1 year to 15 years (the weighted average life for all intangibles is 12.8 years). The preliminary amount of goodwill created as a result of this transaction is summarized as follows (in thousands):

Purchase price	$ 910,000
Amount assigned to net assets acquired	(372,000)
Estimated amount assigned to intangible assets	(159,000)
Deferred taxes related to intangible assets	55,000
Goodwill recognized, preliminary	$ 434,000

Some of the factors contributing to a purchase price that resulted in the recognition of goodwill include: (i) access to a large, highly-trained and stable workforce; (ii) the opportunity to expand our client base in the United States, the United Kingdom, Canada, Australia, and China; (iii) the opportunity to enter new geographic markets in South America; (iv) the opportunity to expand our presence in the mining and minerals market; and (v) the opportunity of achieving operating synergies.

We do not expect a material amount of the goodwill recognized during fiscal 2011 to be deductible for income tax purposes. Included in selling, general and administrative expense for fiscal 2011 is $15.2 million of acquisition-related costs pertaining to our acquisition activities.

Tyco International
2011 Annual Report

5. Acquisitions

Fiscal 2011

Acquisitions

During the year ended September 30, 2011, cash paid for acquisitions included in continuing operations totaled $656 million, net of cash acquired, which primarily related to the acquisitions of Oceania Capital Partners Limited's Signature Security Group ("Signature Security Group"), KEF Holdings Ltd. ("KEF"), and Chemguard Inc. ("Chemguard"). Signature Security Group is an electronic security company operating in Australia and New Zealand primarily in small business and residential markets. Cash paid for Signature Security Group totaled approximately $184 million, net of cash acquired of $2 million by the Company's Tyco Security Solutions segment on April 29, 2011. On June 29, 2011 (the "KEF closing date"), the Company's Tyco Flow Control segment acquired a 75% equity interest in privately-held KEF, a vertically integrated valve manufacturer in the Middle East for approximately $295 million, net of cash acquired of $1 million. In accordance with the terms and conditions of the KEF acquisition agreement, beginning the first full fiscal quarter following the third anniversary of the KEF closing date, the Company can exercise a call option and the noncontrolling interest stakeholder can exercise a put option, which would require the Company to purchase the remaining 25% equity interest for the greater of $100 million or a multiple of KEF's average earnings before income taxes, depreciation and amortization ("EBITDA") for the prior twelve consecutive fiscal quarters. As the put option is redeemable at the option of the noncontrolling interest stakeholder, the remaining 25% equity interest has been accounted for as a redeemable noncontrolling interest. See Note 20. On September 1, 2011, the Company's Fire Protection segment completed the acquisition of Chemguard for approximately $130 million in cash, net of cash acquired of $1 million. Chemguard is a provider of firefighting foam concentrates and equipment, foam systems, services and specialty chemicals.

On September 15, 2011, the Company agreed to acquire Visonic Ltd. ("Visonic"), a global developer and manufacturer of electronic security systems and components, for approximately $100 million in cash. The transaction is expected to close during the first quarter of fiscal 2012. Following the close of the transaction, the Company intends to combine Visonic with the Company's Tyco Security Solutions segment.

Acquisition and Integration Related Costs

Acquisition and integration related costs are expensed as incurred. During the year ended September 30, 2011, the Company incurred acquisition costs of $6 million, primarily in connection with its acquisitions of Signature Security Group, KEF, and Chemguard. Such costs are recorded in selling, general and administrative expenses in the Company's Consolidated Statements of Operations. During the year ended September 30, 2011, the Company incurred integration costs of $33 million, primarily in connection with the integration of Brink's Home Security Holdings, Inc ("BHS" or "Broadview Security") into the Tyco Security Solutions segment. Of these costs, $31 million is recorded within selling, general and administrative expenses and $2 million is recorded within cost of product sales within the Company's Consolidated Statements of Operations.

ADT Account Acquisitions

During the year ended September 30, 2011, the Company paid $614 million of cash to acquire approximately 565,000 customer contracts for electronic security services in the Tyco Security Solutions segment.

Fiscal 2010

Acquisitions

During the year ended September 24, 2010, cash paid for acquisitions included in continuing operations totaled $600 million net of cash acquired of $137 million which, primarily related to the acquisition of Broadview Security. Net cash paid for Broadview Security totaled $448 million by the Company's Tyco Security Solutions segment. During the year ended September 24, 2010, the Company's Flow Control segment acquired two Brazilian valve companies, including Hiter Industria e Comercio de Controle Termo-Hidraulico Ltda ("Hiter"), a valve manufacturer which serves a variety of industries including the oil and gas, chemical and petrochemical markets. Net cash paid for the Brazilian valve companies totaled $104 million. The Company's former Electrical and Metal Products segment acquired certain assets of a business for $39 million and its Fire Protection segment acquired a business for $9 million during 2010.

Acquisition and Integration Related Costs

The Company incurred approximately $17 million of costs directly related to the acquisition of Broadview Security during the year ended September 24, 2010. In addition, the Company recorded $18 million of integration costs during the year ended September 24, 2010. Both acquisition and integration costs have been recorded within selling, general and administrative expenses in the Company's Consolidated Statements of Operations for the year ended September 24, 2010. The Company's Tyco Security Solutions segment and Corporate and Other recorded $32 million and $3 million, respectively, of acquisition and integration costs for the year ended September 24, 2010. In addition, the Company's Tyco Security Solutions segment recorded $14 million of restructuring expenses, in conjunction with the acquisition of Broadview Security, which have been recorded within restructuring, asset impairments and divestiture (gains) charges, net in the Company's Consolidated Statements of Operations for the year ended September 24, 2010.

ADT Account Acquisitions

During the year ended September 24, 2010, the Company paid $559 million of cash to acquire approximately 501,000 customer contracts for electronic security services in the Tyco Security Solutions segment.

Acquisition of Broadview Security

On May 14, 2010, the Company's Tyco Security Solutions segment acquired all of the outstanding equity of Broadview Security, a publicly traded company that was formerly owned by The Brink's Company, in a cash-and-stock transaction valued at approximately $2.0 billion. Prior to its acquisition, Broadview Security's core business was to provide security alarm monitoring services for residential and commercial properties in North America. Under the terms of the transaction, each outstanding share of BHS common stock was converted into the right to receive: (1) $13.15 in cash and 0.7562 Tyco common shares, for those shareholders who made an all-cash election, (2) 1.0951 Tyco common shares, for those shareholders who made an all stock election or (3) $12.75 in cash and 0.7666 Tyco common shares, for those shareholders who made a mixed cash/stock election or who failed to make an election.

Fair Value Calculation of Consideration Transferred

The calculation of the consideration transferred to acquire BHS is as follows. Certain amounts below cannot be recalculated as the exact BHS common share amounts have not been presented. ($ and common share data in millions, except per share data):

Cash consideration	
All cash consideration	
Number of shares of BHS common shares outstanding as of May 14, 2010 electing all cash	37
Cash consideration per common share outstanding	$ 13.15
Total cash paid to BHS shareholders making all cash election	$ 490
Mixed cash/stock consideration	
Number of shares of BHS common shares outstanding as of May 14, 2010 electing mixed consideration or not making an election	7
Cash consideration per common share outstanding	$ 12.75
Total cash paid to BHS shareholders making a mixed election or not making an election	$ 95
Total cash consideration	$ 585
Stock consideration	
All cash consideration	
Number of shares of BHS common shares outstanding as of May 14, 2010 electing all cash	37
Exchange ratio	0.7562
Tyco shares issued to BHS shareholders making an all cash election	28
All stock consideration	
Number of shares of BHS common shares outstanding as of May 14, 2010 electing all stock	1

Exchange ratio	1.0951
Tyco shares issued to BHS shareholders making an all stock election	1
Mixed cash/stock consideration	
Number of shares of BHS common shares outstanding as of May 14, 2010 electing mixed consideration or not making an election	7
Exchange ratio	0.7666
Tyco shares issued to BHS shareholders making a mixed election or not making an election	6
Total Tyco common shares issued	35
Tyco's average common share price on May 14, 2010	$ 38.73
Total stock consideration	$ 1,362
Fair value of BHS stock option, restricted stock unit and deferred stock unit replacement awards[1]	$ 27
Total fair value of consideration transferred	$ 1,974

[1] Represents the fair value of BHS stock option, restricted stock unit and deferred stock unit replacement awards attributable to pre-combination service issued to holders of these awards in the acquisition. The fair value was determined using the Black-Scholes model for stock option awards and Tyco's closing stock price for the restricted and deferred stock unit awards. The fair value of outstanding BHS stock-based compensation awards that immediately vested at the effective time of the acquisition was attributed to pre-combination service and was included in the consideration transferred. In addition, there were certain BHS stock-based compensation awards that did not immediately vest upon completion of the acquisition. For those awards, the fair value of the awards attributed to pre-combination service was included as part of the consideration transferred and the fair value attributed to post-combination service is being recognized as compensation expense over the requisite service period in the post-combination financial statements of Tyco.

Fair Value Allocation of Consideration Transferred to Assets Acquired and Liabilities Assumed

The consideration transferred for BHS has been allocated to identifiable assets acquired and liabilities assumed as of the acquisition date. The following amounts represent the final determination of the fair value of the identifiable assets acquired and liabilities assumed ($ in millions):

Net current assets[1]	$ 78
Subscriber systems	624
Other property, plant and equipment	49
Total property, plant and equipment	673
Contracts and related customer relationships (10-year weighted-average useful life)	738
Other intangible assets (4-year weighted-average useful life)	12
Total intangible assets	750

Net non-current liabilities[2]	(459)
Net assets acquired	1,042
Goodwill[3]	932
Purchase price	$ 1,974

[1] As of the acquisition date, the fair value of accounts receivable approximated book value. Included in net current assets is $32 million of accounts receivable. The gross contractual amount receivable was approximately $35 million of which $3 million was not expected to be collected.

[2] Included in net non-current liabilities is approximately $456 million of deferred tax liabilities which are recorded in other liabilities in the Company's Consolidated Balance Sheet.

[3] The goodwill recognized is primarily related to expected synergies and other benefits that the Company believes will result from combining the operations of BHS with the operations of Tyco Security Solutions. All of the goodwill has been allocated to the Company's Tyco Security Solutions segment. None of the goodwill is expected to be deductible for tax purposes.

Actual BHS Financial Results

BHS actual results from the acquisition date, May 14, 2010, which are included in the Consolidated Statement of Operations for the year ended September 24, 2010 are as follows ($ in millions):

	For the Year Ended September 24, 2010
Net Revenue	$ 193
Loss from continuing operations attributable to Tyco common shareholders	$ (25)

Supplemental Pro Forma Financial Information (unaudited)

The supplemental pro forma financial information for the year ended September 24, 2010 and September 25, 2009 are as follows ($ in millions):

	For the Year Ended September 24, 2010	For the Year Ended September 25, 2009
Net revenue	$ 17,367	$ 17,415
Income (loss) from continuing operations attributable to Tyco common shareholders	1,149	(1,845)
Income (loss) from continuing operations per share:		
Basic earnings (loss) per share attributable to Tyco common shareholders	$ 2.21	$ (3.63)
Diluted earnings (loss) per share attributable to Tyco common shareholders	$ 2.20	$ (3.63)

The supplemental pro forma financial information is based on the historical financial information for Tyco and BHS. The supplemental pro forma financial information for the period ended September 24, 2010 utilized BHS' historical financial information for its fiscal fourth quarter ended December 31, 2009 and the pre-acquisition period from January 1, 2010 through the acquisition date. The supplemental pro forma financial information reflect primarily the following pro forma pre-tax adjustments:

- Elimination of BHS historical intangible asset amortization and property, plant and equipment depreciation expense;

- Elimination of BHS historical deferred acquisition costs amortization;

- Elimination of BHS historical deferred revenue amortization;

- Additional amortization and depreciation expense related to the fair value of identifiable intangible assets and property, plant and equipment acquired;

- Reduction of interest income on cash used to fund the acquisition and Tyco dividends assumed to be paid to BHS shareholders; and

- All of the above pro forma adjustments were tax effected using a statutory tax rate of 39%.

The supplemental pro forma financial information for the year ended September 24, 2010 reflect the following non-recurring adjustments:

- Direct acquisition costs primarily relating to advisory and legal fees and integration costs; and

- Restructuring charges primarily related to employee severance and one-time benefit arrangements

The supplemental pro forma financial information gives effect to the acquisition, but should not be considered indicative of the results that would have occurred in the periods presented above, nor are they indicative of future results. In addition, the supplemental pro forma financial information does not reflect the potential realization of cost savings relating to the integration of the two companies.

Fiscal 2009

Acquisitions

During the year ended September 25, 2009, cash paid for acquisitions included in continuing operations totaled $48 million, net of cash acquired of $2 million, which primarily related to the acquisition of Vue Technology, Inc., a provider of radio frequency identification technology, for $43 million by the Company's Tyco Security Solutions segment.

Acquisition and Integration Related Costs

During the year ended September 25, 2009, the Company did not incur any acquisition or integration related costs.

ADT Account Acquisitions

During the year ended September 25, 2009, the Company paid $543 million of cash to acquire approximately 512,000 customer contracts for electronic security services in its Tyco Security Solutions segment.

6. Other Expense, Net

Other expense, net of $16 million in 2011, primarily relates to our share of Atkore's net loss of $9 million, which is accounted for under the equity method of accounting, and a decrease in the receivables due from Covidien and TE Connectivity under the Tax Sharing Agreement of $7 million. See Note 7.

Other expense, net of $75 million in 2010, primarily related to a charge of $87 million as a loss on extinguishment of debt on the redemption of our 6.375% public notes due 2011, 7% notes due 2028 and 6.875% notes due 2029. See Note 12. This loss was partially offset by an $8 million gain recorded as a result of an increase in the receivables due from Covidien and TE Connectivity under the Tax Sharing Agreement.

Other expense, net of $7 million in 2009, primarily related to a $14 million charge recorded as a result of a decrease in the receivables due from Covidien and TE Connectivity under the Tax Sharing Agreement, which was partially offset by income of $5 million relating to a gain on derivative contracts used to economically hedge the foreign currency risk related to the Swiss franc denominated dividends.

Humana
2010 Annual Report

3. Acquisitions

On December 21, 2010, we acquired Concentra Inc., or Concentra, a health care company based in Addison, Texas, for cash consideration of $804.7 million. Through its affiliated clinicians, Concentra delivers occupational medicine, urgent care, physical therapy, and wellness services to workers and the general public through its operation of medical centers and worksite medical facilities. The Concentra acquisition provides entry into the primary care space on a national scale, offering additional means for achieving health and wellness solutions and providing an expandable platform for growth with a management team experienced in physician asset management and alternate site care. The preliminary fair values of Concentra's assets acquired and liabilities assumed at the date of the acquisition are summarized as follows:

(in thousands)	Concentra
Cash and cash equivalents	$ 21,317
Receivables	108,571
Other current assets	20,589
Property and equipment	131,837
Goodwill	531,372
Other intangible assets	188,000
Other long-term assets	12,935
Total assets acquired	1,014,621
Current liabilities	(100,091)
Other long-term liabilities	(109,811)
Total liabilities assumed	(209,902)
Net assets acquired	$ 804,719

The other intangible assets, which primarily consist of customer relationships and trade name, have a weighted average useful life of 13.7 years. Approximately $57.9 million of the acquired goodwill is deductible for tax purposes. The purchase price allocation is preliminary, subject to completion of valuation analyses, including, for example, refining assumptions used to calculate the fair value of other intangible assets. The purchase agreement contains provisions under which there may be future consideration paid or received related to the subsequent determination of working capital that existed at the acquisition date. Any payments or receipts for provisional amounts for working capital will be recorded as an adjustment to goodwill when paid or received.

The results of operations and financial condition of Concentra have been included in our consolidated statements of income and consolidated balance sheets from the acquisition date. In connection with the acquisition, we recognized approximately $14.9 million of acquisition-related costs, primarily banker and other professional fees, in selling, general and administrative expense. The proforma financial information assuming the acquisition had occurred as of January 1, 2009 was not material to our results of operations.

On October 31, 2008, we acquired PHP Companies, Inc. (d/b/a Cariten Healthcare), or Cariten, for cash consideration of approximately $291.0 million, including the payment of $34.9 million during 2010 to settle a purchase price contingency. The Cariten acquisition increased our commercial fully-insured and ASO presence as well as our Medicare HMO presence in eastern Tennessee. During 2009, we continued our review of the fair value estimate of certain other intangible and net tangible assets acquired. This review resulted in a decrease of $27.1 million in the fair value of other intangible assets, primarily related to the fair value assigned to the customer contracts acquired. There was a corresponding adjustment to goodwill and deferred income taxes. The total consideration paid exceeded our estimated fair value of the net tangible assets acquired by approximately $145.8 million of which we allocated $52.3 million to other intangible assets and $93.5 million to goodwill. The other intangible assets, which primarily consist of customer contracts, have a weighted-average useful life of 11.6 years. The acquired goodwill is not deductible for tax purposes.

On August 29, 2008, we acquired Metcare Health Plans, Inc., or Metcare, for cash consideration of approximately $14.9 million. The acquisition expanded our Medicare HMO membership in central Florida.

On May 22, 2008, we acquired OSF Health Plans, Inc., or OSF, a managed care company serving both Medicare and commercial members in central Illinois, for cash consideration of approximately $87.3 million, including the payment of $3.3 million during 2009 to settle a purchase price contingency. This acquisition expanded our presence in Illinois, broadening our ability to serve multi-location employers with a wider range of products including our specialty offerings. The total consideration paid exceeded our estimated fair value of the net tangible assets acquired by approximately $31.1 million of which we allocated $10.1

million to other intangible assets and $21.0 million to goodwill. The other intangible assets, which primarily consist of customer contracts, have a weighted-average useful life of 9.9 years. The acquired goodwill is not deductible for tax purposes.

On April 30, 2008, we acquired UnitedHealth Group's Las Vegas, Nevada individual SecureHorizons Medicare Advantage HMO business, or SecureHorizons, for cash consideration of approximately $185.3 million, plus subsidiary capital and surplus requirements of $40 million. The acquisition expanded our presence in the Las Vegas market. The total consideration paid exceeded our estimated fair value of the net tangible assets acquired by approximately $185.3 million of which we allocated $69.3 million to other intangible assets and $116.0 million to goodwill. The other intangible assets, which primarily consist of customer contracts, have a weighted-average useful life of 10.9 years. The acquired goodwill is not deductible for tax purposes.

The purchase agreements for certain of the acquisitions discussed above occurring prior to January 1, 2009 contain provisions under which there may be future contingent consideration paid or received primarily associated with balance sheet settlements. Any contingent consideration paid or received will be recorded as an adjustment to goodwill when the contingencies are resolved. We do not expect these adjustments to be material.

The results of operations and financial condition of Cariten, Metcare, OSF, and SecureHorizons have been included in our consolidated statements of income and consolidated balance sheets since the acquisition dates.

Johnson Controls
2010 Annual Report

2. Acquisitions

In July 2010, the Company acquired an additional 40% of a power solutions Korean joint venture. The acquisition increased the Company's ownership percentage to 90%. The remaining 10% was acquired by the local management team. The Company paid approximately $86 million (excluding cash acquired of $57 million) for the additional ownership percentage and incurred approximately $10 million of acquisition costs and related purchase accounting adjustments. As a result of the acquisition, the Company recorded a non-cash gain of $47 million within power solutions equity income to adjust the Company's existing equity investment in the Korean joint venture to fair value. Goodwill of $51 million was recorded as part of the transaction. The purchase price allocation may be subsequently adjusted to reflect final valuation studies.

Also during fiscal 2010, the Company completed three acquisitions for a combined purchase price of $35 million, of which $32 million was paid as of September 30, 2010. The acquisitions in the aggregate were not material to the Company's consolidated financial statements. In connection with the acquisitions, the Company recorded goodwill of $9 million. The purchase price allocation may be subsequently adjusted to reflect final valuation studies.

During fiscal 2009, the Company completed four acquisitions for a combined purchase price of $43 million, of which $38 million was paid in the twelve months ended September 30, 2009. None of the acquisitions were material to the Company's consolidated financial statements. In connection with these acquisitions, the Company recorded goodwill of $30 million, of which $26 million was recorded during fiscal 2009.

In July 2008, the Company formed a joint venture to acquire the interior product assets of Plastech Engineered Products, Inc. (Plastech). Plastech filed for bankruptcy in February 2008. The Company owns 70% of the newly formed entity and certain Plastech term lenders hold the remaining noncontrolling interest. The Company contributed cash and injection molding plants to the new entity with a fair value of $262 million. The lenders contributed their rights to receive Plastech's interiors business obtained in exchange for certain Plastech debt. The combined equity in the new entity was approximately $375 million. Goodwill of $199 million was recorded as part of the transaction. In the third quarter of fiscal 2009, the Company finalized valuations associated with the acquisition and recorded a $21 million increase to goodwill.

Also in fiscal 2008, the Company completed seven additional acquisitions for a combined purchase price of $108 million, none of which were material to the Company's consolidated financial statements. In connection with these acquisitions, the Company recorded goodwill of $66 million.

Schlumberger NV
2010 Annual Report

4. Acquisitions

Merger with Smith International, Inc.

On August 27, 2010, Schlumberger acquired all of the outstanding shares of Smith, a leading supplier of premium products and services to the oil and gas exploration and production industry. The merger brings together the complementary drilling and measurements technologies and expertise of Schlumberger and Smith in order to facilitate the engineering of complete drilling systems which optimize all of the components of the drill string. Such systems will enable Schlumberger's customers to achieve improved drilling efficiency, better well placement and increased wellbore assurance as they face increasingly more challenging environments. In addition, Schlumberger's geographic footprint will facilitate the extension of joint offerings on a worldwide basis.

Under the terms of the merger agreement, Smith became a wholly-owned subsidiary of Schlumberger. Each share of Smith common stock issued and outstanding immediately prior to the effective time of the merger was converted into the right to receive 0.6966 shares of Schlumberger common stock, with cash paid in lieu of fractional shares.

At the effective time of the merger, each outstanding option to purchase Smith common stock was converted pursuant to the merger agreement into a stock option to acquire shares of Schlumberger common stock on the same terms and conditions as were in effect immediately prior to the completion of the merger. The number of shares of Schlumberger common stock underlying each converted Smith stock option was determined by multiplying the number of Smith stock options by the 0.6966 exchange ratio, and rounding down to the nearest whole share. The exercise price per share of each converted Smith stock option was determined by dividing the per share exercise price of such stock option by the 0.6966 exchange ratio, and rounded up to the nearest whole cent. Smith stock options, whether or not then vested and exercisable, became fully vested and exercisable and assumed by Schlumberger at the effective date of the merger in accordance with preexisting change-in-control provisions. Smith stock options were converted into 0.6 million of Schlumberger stock options.

At the effective time of the merger, Smith restricted stock units, whether or not then vested, became fully vested (except for grants between the date of the merger agreement and closing, which were not significant and did not automatically vest) and were converted into shares of Schlumberger common stock in connection with the merger, determined by multiplying the number of shares of Smith common stock subject to each award by the 0.6966 exchange ratio, rounded to the nearest whole share (assuming, in the case of performance-based Smith restricted stock unit awards, the deemed attainment of the performance goals under the award at the target level).

Calculation of Consideration Transferred

The following details the fair value of the consideration transferred to effect the merger with Smith.

(stated in millions, except exchange ratio and per share amounts)

Number of shares of Smith common stock outstanding as of the acquisition date	248
Number of Smith unvested restricted stock units outstanding as of the acquisition date	4
	252
Multiplied by the exchange ratio	0.6966
Equivalent Schlumberger shares of common stock issued	176
Schlumberger closing stock price on August 27, 2010	$ 55.76
Common stock equity consideration	$ 9,812
Fair value of Schlumberger equivalent stock options issued	$ 16
Total fair value of the consideration transferred	$ 9,828

Certain amounts reflect rounding adjustments

Preliminary Allocation of Consideration Transferred to Net Assets Acquired

The following amounts represent the preliminary estimates of the fair value of identifiable assets acquired and liabilities assumed in the merger. The final determination of fair value for certain assets and liabilities will be completed as soon as the information necessary to complete the analysis is obtained. These amounts will be finalized as soon as possible, but no later than one year from the acquisition date.

(stated in millions)

Cash	$ 399
Accounts receivable	1,831
Inventory[1]	2,013
Fixed assets	2,017
Intangible assets:	
Tradenames (weighted-average life of 25 years)	1,560
Technology (weighted-average life of 16 years)	1,170
Customer relationships (weighted average life of 23 years)	1,360
Other assets	429
Accounts payable and accrued liabilities	(1,460)
Long-term debt[2]	(2,141)
Deferred taxes[3]	(1,936)
Other liabilities	(528)
sub-total	$ 4,714
Less:	
Investment in M-I SWACO[4]	(1,429)
Noncontrolling interests	(111)
Total identifiable net assets	$ 3,174
Gain on investment in M-I SWACO[4]	(1,238)
Goodwill[5]	7,892
Total consideration transferred	$ 9,828

[1] Schlumberger recorded an adjustment of approximately $155 million to write-up the acquired inventory to its estimated fair value. Schlumberger's cost of revenue reflected this increased valuation as this inventory was sold. Accordingly, Schlumberger's margins were temporarily reduced in the initial periods subsequent to the merger.

[2] In connection with the merger, Schlumberger assumed all of the debt obligations of Smith including its long-term fixed rate notes consisting of the following: $220 million 6.75% Senior Notes due 2011, $300 million 8.625% Senior Notes due 2014, $275 million 6.00% Senior Notes due 2016 and $700 million 9.75% Senior Notes due 2019. Schlumberger recorded a $417 million adjustment to increase the carrying amount of these notes to their estimated fair value. This adjustment will be amortized as a reduction of interest expense over the remaining term of the respective obligations.

[3] In connection with the acquisition accounting, Schlumberger provided deferred taxes related to, among other items, the estimated fair value adjustments for acquired inventory, intangible assets and assumed debt obligations. Included in the provisions for deferred taxes are amounts relating to the outside basis difference associated with shares in certain Smith non-US subsidiaries for which no taxes have previously been provided. Schlumberger expects to reverse the outside basis difference primarily through the reorganization of those subsidiaries as well as through repatriating earnings in lieu of permanently reinvesting them. In this regard, Schlumberger is in the process of assessing certain factors that impact the ultimate amount of deferred taxes to be recorded. The amount of deferred taxes recorded will likely be revised after this assessment is completed. Any revision to the amount of deferred taxes recorded will impact the amount of goodwill recorded.

(4) Prior to the completion of the merger, Smith and Schlumberger operated M-I SWACO, a drilling fluids joint venture that was 40% owned by Schlumberger and 60% owned by Smith. Effective at the closing of the merger, M-I SWACO is now owned 100% by Schlumberger. As a result of obtaining control of this joint venture, Schlumberger was required under generally accepted accounting principles to remeasure its previously held equity interest in the joint venture at its merger-date fair value and recognize the resulting pretax gain of $1.3 billion ($1.2 billion after-tax) in earnings. This gain is classified as *Gain on Investment in M-I SWACO* in the *Consolidated Statement of Income*.

Prior to acquiring Smith, Schlumberger recorded income relating to this venture using the equity method of accounting. The carrying value of Schlumberger's investment in the joint venture on December 31, 2009 was $1.4 billion, and was included within *Investments in Affiliated Companies* on the *Consolidated Balance Sheet*. Schlumberger's equity income from this joint venture was $78 million in 2010 (representing the period from January 1, 2010 to August 27, 2010), $131 million in 2009 and $210 million in 2008. Schlumberger received cash distributions from the joint venture of $50 million in 2010, $106 million in 2009 and $57 million in 2008.

(5) The goodwill recognized is primarily attributable to expected synergies that will result from combining the operations of Schlumberger and Smith as well as intangible assets that do not qualify for separate recognition. Approximately $0.2 billion of the goodwill is deductible for income tax purposes.

Acquisition of Geoservices

On April 23, 2010, Schlumberger completed the acquisition of Geoservices, a privately owned oilfield services company specializing in mud logging, slickline and production surveillance operations, for $915 million in cash.

The purchase price has been allocated to the net assets acquired upon their estimated fair values as follows:

(stated in millions)

Cash	$ 26
Other assets	184
Fixed assets	90
Goodwill	599
Intangible assets	377
Long-term debt	(145)
Deferred tax liabilities	(64)
Other liabilities	(152)
	$ 915

The long-term debt was repaid at the time of closing.

Intangible assets recorded in connection with this transaction, which primarily relate to customer relationships, will be amortized over a weighted average period of approximately 17 years. The amount allocated to goodwill represents the excess of the purchase price over the fair value of the net assets acquired and is not tax deductible for income tax purposes.

Other Acquisitions

Schlumberger has made other acquisitions and minority investments, none of which were significant on an individual basis, for cash payments, net of cash acquired, of $212 million during 2010, $514 million during 2009, and $345 million during 2008.

Supplemental Pro Forma Data

Smith's results of operations have been included in Schlumberger's financial statements for periods subsequent to the effective date of the merger. Smith contributed revenues of $3.3 billion and net income of $160 million (including the recurring effects of purchase accounting) to Schlumberger for the period from the closing of the merger through December 31, 2010. The following unaudited supplemental pro forma data ("pro forma data") presents consolidated information as if the merger with Smith and the acquisition of Geoservices had been completed on January 1, 2009:

(stated in millions, except per share data)	2010	2009
Revenue	$ 33,468	$ 31,182
Net income	$ 3,376	$ 3,271
Net income attributable to Schlumberger	$ 3,370	$ 3,244
Diluted earnings per share	$ 2.44	$ 2.34

The pro forma data was prepared based on the historical financial information of Schlumberger, Smith and Geoservices and has been adjusted to give effect to pro forma adjustments that are (i) directly attributable to the transactions, (ii) factually supportable and (iii) expected to have a continuing impact on the combined results. The pro forma data is not necessarily indicative of what Schlumberger's results of operations actually would have been had the transactions been completed on January 1, 2009. Additionally, the pro forma data does not purport to project the future results of operations of the combined company nor do they reflect the expected realization of synergies associated with the transactions. The pro forma data reflects the application of the following adjustments:

- Elimination of the gain resulting from Schlumberger's remeasurement of its previously held 40% equity interest in M-I SWACO, which is considered non-recurring.

- Additional depreciation and amortization expense associated with fair value adjustments to acquired identifiable intangible assets and property, plant and equipment.

- Elimination of charges incurred in 2010 related to the fair value adjustments to Smith's inventory that has been sold as they will not have a long-term continuing impact.

- Reductions in interest expense as a result of increasing the carrying value of acquired debt obligations to its estimated fair value.

- Elimination of transaction costs incurred in 2010 that are directly related to the transactions, and do not have a continuing impact on the combined company's operating results.

- The issuance of 176 million of shares of Schlumberger common stock.

Included in the 2010 and 2009 pro forma net income attributable to Schlumberger and diluted earnings per share presented above are the following significant charges and credits:

(stated in millions, except per share data)	2010 Net Income Impact	Diluted EPS Impact*	2009 Net Income Impact	Diluted EPS Impact
Severance and other[1]	$ 77	$ 0.06	$ 85	$ 0.06
Impairment relating to WesternGeco's first generation Q-Land acquisition system[1]	71	0.05	–	–
Other WesternGeco-related charges[1]	63	0.05	–	–
Impact of elimination of tax deduction related to Medicare Part D subsidy[1]	40	0.03	–	–
Mexico restructuring[1]	36	0.03	–	–
Venezuelan currency-related losses[2]	35	0.03	–	–
Repurchase of bonds[1]	37	0.03	–	–
Gain on remeasurement of investment in @Balance[2]	(18)	(0.01)	–	–
Postretirement benefits curtailment[1]	–	–	122	0.09
Employee severance[2]	–	–	32	0.02
	$ 341	$ 0.25	$ 239	$ 0.17

* Does not add due to rounding
[1] Relates to Schlumberger's historical operations and is more fully described in Note 3 - *Charges and Credits*.
[2] Relates to Smith's historical operations.

Carnival
2009 Annual Report

Note 15—Acquisition

In September 2007, we entered into an agreement with Orizonia Corporation, Spain's largest travel company, to operate Ibero, a Spanish cruise line, for an investment of $403 million, which we funded with $146 million of cash and $257 million in proceeds that Ibero borrowed under a portion of our principal revolver. Orizonia contributed $49 million of assets, principally trademarks and goodwill, for their 25% interest in the venture. Ibero operated two contemporary Spanish cruise ships in September 2007, the 834-passenger capacity Grand Voyager, and the 1,244-passenger capacity Grand Mistral, which were built in 2000 and 1999, respectively. For reporting purposes, we have included Ibero's results of operations within our consolidated financial results since September 1, 2007.

The pro forma impact of including Ibero in our results as if the acquisition took place on December 1, 2006 has not been presented due to its immaterial effect.

The 2007 acquisition was accounted for as a business purchase combination using the purchase method of accounting. The purchase price was allocated to tangible and identifiable intangible assets acquired based on their estimated fair values at the acquisition date. The $451 million purchase price was allocated as follows: $254 million to ships, $161 million to goodwill, $35 million to trademarks and $1 million to other. In July 2009, we purchased the remaining 25% interest in Ibero that we did not own for $33 million, which approximated this minority interests' carrying value.

Sherwin-Williams
2009 Annual Report

Note 2—Acquisitions

All acquisitions have been accounted for as purchases and their results of operations have been included in the consolidated financial statements since the date of acquisition. During the first quarter of 2009, the Company acquired Altax Sp. zo.o. (Altax). Headquartered in Poznan, Poland, Altax is a leading innovator of protective woodcare coatings and serves multiple channels, including industrial, professional and DIY. Included in the Consumer Group, the acquisition provides a platform for further growth in Central Europe. The aggregate consideration paid for Altax was $11,500, net of cash acquired, including the assumption of certain financial obligations. The acquisition resulted in the recognition of goodwill and intangible assets.

In December 2008, the Company acquired Euronavy-Tintas Maritimas e Industriais S.A. of Portugal (Euronavy). Headquartered in Lisbon, Portugal, Euronavy is a leading innovator of marine and protective coatings applied to ships, off shore platforms, storage tanks, steel, concrete and flooring. Included in the Global Finishes Group, the acquisition strengthens the Company's global platform of protective and marine coatings.

In September 2008, the Company purchased certain assets of the Wagman Primus Group, LP (Wagman). The acquired assets are related to imported raw materials of brushes and foreign manufactured applicators and allow greater flexibility and control in the importation of applicators and related products for the Consumer Group.

In July 2008, the Company acquired the liquid coatings subsidiaries of Inchem Holdings International Limited (Inchem). Headquartered in Singapore, Inchem produces coatings applied to wood and plastic products in Asia. These waterborne, solvent-based, and ultraviolet curable coatings are applied to furniture, cabinets, flooring and electronic products. The coatings are made and sold in China, Vietnam and Malaysia and distributed to 15 other Asian countries.

This acquisition strengthens the Global Finishes Group's product offering throughout Asia.

In February 2008, the Company acquired Becker Powder Coatings, Inc. (Becker), a subsidiary of Sweden-based AB Wilh. Headquartered in Columbus, Ohio, Becker produces powder coatings applied to appliances, metal furniture, fixtures, equipment and electronic products manufactured throughout North America. This acquisition strengthens Global Finishes Group's position in the powder coatings market.

The aggregate consideration paid for Euronavy, Inchem, Wagman and Becker was $64,103, net of cash acquired, including acquisition costs and the assumption of certain financial obligations. The acquisitions resulted in the recognition of intangible assets. The Euronavy, Inchem and Becker acquisitions also resulted in the recognition of goodwill.

In October 2007, an indirect wholly owned subsidiary of the Company acquired the remaining 75 percent interest in Life Shield Engineered Systems LLC (Life Shield) by acquiring all of the outstanding membership interests. In late December 2007, the Company acquired substantially all the assets and business of Flex Recubrimientos, S.A. de C.V. and related companies (Flex group). The aggregate consideration paid in cash for these acquisitions was $27,056 including costs of acquisition and the assumption of certain financial obligations. Life Shield is a start-up company that develops and manufactures blast and fragment mitigating systems and ballistic resistant systems that will expand the product offering in the Consumer Group. Flex group is a leading manufacturer and distributor of automotive after-market body fillers, putties, primers and other vehicle refinish products headquartered in Monterrey, Mexico. This acquisition will strengthen the Global Finishes Group's automotive refinish market position in Mexico. These acquisitions resulted in the recognition of goodwill. The acquisition of Flex group resulted in the recognition of identifiable intangible assets.

During the third quarter of 2007, the Company acquired substantially all of the stock of Pinturas Industriales S.A. (PISA), substantially all of the assets and business of Napko, S.A. de C.V. (Napko), the brand names, formulas and patents of the VHT® brand paint line (VHT), and 100 percent of the stock of Columbia Paint & Coatings Co. (Columbia) for an aggregate cash consideration of $105,850, net of cash acquired, including costs of acquisition and the assumption of certain financial obligations. The acquisitions of Napko and Columbia resulted in the recognition of goodwill and all four acquisitions resulted in the recognition of identifiable intangible assets. Columbia, included in the Paint Stores Group, is a leading manufacturer and distributor of paints and coatings in the central and northwestern United States. Columbia services the professional painting contractor, builder and do-it-yourself markets through company-operated stores. Columbia was acquired to contribute to the Company's domestic controlled-distribution growth strategy. VHT, included in the Consumer Group, is the market leader in High Temperature coatings and premium aerosol products. VHT was acquired to broaden the product offering in Consumer Group and add to its growth strategy. Napko, included in the Global Finishes Group, is a leading manufacturer and distributor of industrial maintenance coatings primarily for the government oil and power industries in Mexico primarily through company-operated branches. PISA, also included in the Global Finishes Group, provides industrial paint products in Uruguay to the wood protection and industrial maintenance market. Napko and PISA were acquired to support and broaden the Company's international growth strategy.

During the second quarter of 2007, the Company acquired substantially all of the assets and business of Nitco Paints Private Limited (Nitco) and 100 percent of the stock of M. A.

Bruder & Sons Incorporated (MAB) for an aggregate consideration in cash of $149,508, net of cash acquired, including costs of acquisition and the assumption of certain financial obligations.

Both acquisitions resulted in the recognition of goodwill and identifiable intangible assets. MAB, included in the Paint Stores Group, is a leading manufacturer and distributor of paints and coatings in the eastern and southeastern portions of the United States. MAB services the professional painting contractor, builder and do-it-yourself markets through its own company-operated stores. MAB was acquired as part of the Company's domestic controlled-distribution growth strategy. Nitco, included in the Global Finishes Group, is a leading manufacturer and distributor, especially in western India, of exterior paints and coatings used in the construction of office buildings, high rise apartments, shopping malls, hospitals and schools. Nitco was acquired to support the Company's growth strategy into new international markets.

The following unaudited pro-forma summary presents consolidated financial information as if Altax, Euronavy, Wagman, Inchem, Becker, Flex group, Life Shield, Columbia, VHT, Napko, PISA, MAB and Nitco had been acquired at the beginning of each period presented. The unaudited pro-forma consolidated financial information does not necessarily reflect the actual results that would have occurred had the acquisitions taken place on January 1, 2007 or the future results of operations of the combined companies under ownership and operation of the Company.

	2009	*2008*	*2007*
Net sales			
Net income	**$7,094,519**	$8,025,041	$8,213,512
Net income per common share:	**435,470**	478,278	622,289
Basic	**3.84**	4.09	4.89
Diluted	**3.77**	4.01	4.75

Baker Hughes
2008 Annual Report

Note 3. Acquisitions

In April 2008, we acquired two firms for our reservoir technology and consulting group—Gaffney, Cline & Associates ("GCA") and GeoMechanics International ("GMI")—for $72 million in cash, including $4 million of direct transaction costs and net of cash acquired of $5 million. These firms provide consulting services related to reservoir engineering, technical and managerial advisory services and reservoir geomechanics. As a result of these acquisitions, we recorded $43 million of goodwill and $19 million of intangibles. Under the terms of the purchase agreements, we may be required to make additional payments of up to approximately $46 million based on the performance of the businesses during 2008, 2009 and 2010. During 2008, we made several other acquisitions having an aggregate purchase price of $53 million, of which $48 million was paid in cash. As a result of these acquisitions, we recorded $2 million of goodwill and $26 million of intangible assets through December 31, 2008.

In January 2006, we acquired Nova Technology Corporation ("Nova") for $55 million, net of cash acquired of $3 million, plus assumed debt. Nova is a supplier of permanent monitoring, chemical injection systems, and multi-line services for deepwater and subsea oil and gas well applications. As a result of the acquisition, we recorded $30 million of goodwill, $24 million of intangible assets and assigned $2 million to inprocess research and development.

For each of these acquisitions, the purchase price was allocated based on the fair value of the assets acquired and liabilities assumed using a discounted cash flow approach. Amounts related to in-process research and development were written off at the date of acquisition and are included in research and engineering expenses. Pro forma results of operations have not been presented individually or in the aggregate for these acquisitions because the effects of these acquisitions were not material to our consolidated financial statements.

Johnson & Johnson
2008 Annual Report

17. Mergers, Acquisitions and Divestitures

Certain businesses were acquired for $1,214 million in cash and $114 million of liabilities assumed during 2008. These acquisitions were accounted for by the purchase method and, accordingly, results of operations have been included in the financial statements from their respective dates of acquisition.

The 2008 acquisitions included: Amic AB, a privately held Swedish developer of in vitro diagnostic technologies for use in point-of-care and near-patient settings; Beijing Dabao Cosmetics Co., Ltd., a company that sells personal care brands in China; SurgRx, Inc., a privately held developer of the advanced bipolar tissue sealing system used in the ENSEAL® family of devices; HealthMedia, Inc., a privately held company that creates webbased behavior change interventions; LGE Performance Systems, Inc., a privately held company known as Human Performance Institute™, which develops science-based training programs to improve employee engagement and productivity and Omrix Biopharmaceuticals, Inc., a fully integrated biopharmaceutical company that develops and markets biosurgical and immunotherapy products.

The excess of purchase price over the estimated fair value of tangible assets acquired amounted to $891 million and has been assigned to identifiable intangible assets, with any residual recorded to goodwill. Approximately $181 million has been identified as the value of IPR&D associated with the acquisitions of Omrix Biopharmaceuticals, Inc., Amic AB, SurgRx, Inc. and HealthMedia, Inc.

The IPR&D charge related to the acquisition of Omrix Biopharmaceuticals, Inc. was $127 million and is associated with stand-alone and combination biosurgical technologies used to achieve hemostasis. The value of the IPR&D was calculated using cash flow projections discounted for the risk inherent in such projects. Probability of success factors ranging from 60 –90% were used to reflect inherent clinical and regulatory risk. The discount rate applied was 14%. As of the end of the 2008 fiscal year, 97.8% of the outstanding shares of Common Stock of Omrix Biopharmaceuticals, Inc. had been tendered by stockholders. Excluding shares that were tendered subject to guaranteed delivery procedures, 90.2% of the outstanding shares of Common Stock had been tendered. On December 30, 2008 the Company completed the acquisition of Omrix Biopharmaceuticals, Inc.

The IPR&D charge related to the acquisition of Amic AB was $40 million and is associated with point-of-care device and 4CAST Chip technologies. The value of the IPR&D was calculated using cash flow projections discounted for the risk inherent in such projects. The discount rate applied was 20%.

The IPR&D charge related to the acquisition of SurgRx, Inc. was $7 million and is associated with vessel cutting and sealing surgical devices. The value of the IPR&D was calculated using cash flow projections discounted for the risk inherent in such projects. Probability of success factors ranging from 90 – 95% were used to reflect inherent clinical and regulatory risk. The discount rate applied was 18%.

The IPR&D charge related to the acquisition of HealthMedia, Inc. was $7 million and is associated primarily with process enhancements to software technology. The value of the IPR&D was calculated using cash flow projections discounted for the risk inherent in such projects. A probability of success factor of 90% was used to reflect inherent risk. The discount rate applied was 14%.

Certain businesses were acquired for $1,388 million in cash and $232 million of liabilities assumed during 2007. These acquisitions were accounted for by the purchase method and, accordingly, results of operations have been included in the financial statements from their respective dates of acquisition.

The 2007 acquisitions included: Conor Medsystems, Inc., a cardiovascular device company, with new drug delivery technology; Robert Reid, Inc., a Japanese orthopedic product distributor; and Maya's Mom, Inc., a social media company.

The excess of purchase price over the estimated fair value of tangible assets acquired amounted to $636 million and has been assigned to identifiable intangible assets, with any residual recorded to goodwill. Approximately $807 million has been identified as the value of IPR&D associated with the acquisition of Conor Medsystems, Inc.

The IPR&D charge related to the acquisition of Conor Medsystems, Inc. was $807 million and is associated with research related to the discovery and application of the stent technology. The value of the IPR&D was calculated using cash flow projections discounted for the risk inherent in such projects. The discount rate applied was 19%.

Certain businesses were acquired for $18.0 billion in cash and $1.3 billion of liabilities assumed during 2006. These acquisitions were accounted for by the purchase method and, accordingly, results of operations have been included in the financial statements from their respective dates of acquisition except as noted below.

On December 20, 2006, the Company completed the acquisition of the Consumer Healthcare business of Pfizer Inc. for a purchase price of $16.6 billion in cash. The operating results of the Consumer Healthcare business of Pfizer Inc. were reported in the Company's financial statements beginning in 2007, as 2006 results subsequent to the acquisition date were not significant. In order to obtain regulatory approval of the transaction, the Company agreed to divest certain overlapping businesses. The Company completed the divestiture of the ZANTAC® product on December 20, 2006 and the divestitures of KAOPECTATE®, UNISOM®, CORTIZONE®, BALMEX® and ACT® products on January 2, 2007.

The following table provides pro forma results of operations for the fiscal year ended December 31, 2006, as if the Consumer Healthcare business of Pfizer Inc. had been acquired as of the beginning of the period presented. The pro forma results include the effect of divestitures and certain purchase accounting adjustments such as the estimated changes in depreciation and amortization expense on the acquired tangible and intangible assets. However, pro forma results do not include any anticipated cost savings or other effects of the planned integration of the Consumer Healthcare business of Pfizer Inc. Accordingly, such amounts are not necessarily indicative of the results if the acquisition had occurred on the dates indicated or which may occur in the future.

(Unaudited)

(Shares in millions except per share data)	Pro forma results Year ended December 31, 2006
Net sales	$57,115
Net earnings	$10,770
Diluted net earnings per share	$ 3.64

The IPR&D charge related to the acquisition of the Consumer Healthcare business of Pfizer Inc. was $320 million on a pre-tax basis and $217 million on an after-tax basis and is primarily associated with rights obtained to the switch of ZYRTEC® from U.S. prescription to over-the-counter status. The switch was approved by the FDA effective November 2007. The value of the IPR&D was calculated using cash flow projections discounted for the risk inherent in such projects. A probability of success factor of 95% was used to reflect inherent regulatory risk as of the acquisition date and the discount rate applied was 11%.

The Company completed the analysis of integration plans, pursuant to which the Company is incurring costs primarily related to the elimination of certain duplicate selling, general and administrative functions between the two companies in areas such as global business services, corporate staff and go-to-market support, as well as excess manufacturing capacity.

In addition to the acquisition of the Consumer Healthcare business of Pfizer Inc., 2006 acquisitions included: Animas Corporation, a leading maker of insulin infusion pumps and related products; Hand Innovations LLC, a privately held manufacturer of fracture fixation products for the upper extremities; Future Medical Systems S.A., a privately held company that primarily develops, manufactures and markets arthroscopic fluid management systems; Vascular Control Systems, Inc., a privately held company focused on developing medical devices to treat fibroids and to control bleeding in obstetric and gynecologic applications; Groupe Vendôme S.A., a privately held French marketer of adult and baby skin care products; ColBar LifeScience Ltd., a privately held company specializing in reconstructive medicine and tissue engineering and Ensure Medical, Inc., a privately held company that develops devices for postcatheterization closure of the femoral artery.

Excluding the acquisition of the Consumer Healthcare business of Pfizer Inc., the excess of purchase price over the estimated fair value of tangible assets acquired in 2006 amounted to $1,209 million and has been assigned to identifiable intangible assets, with any residual recorded to goodwill. Approximately $239 million has been identified as the value of IPR&D primarily associated with the acquisitions of Hand Innovations LLC, Future Medical Systems S.A., Vascular Control Systems, Inc., ColBar LifeScience Ltd. and Ensure Medical, Inc.

The IPR&D charge related to the acquisition of Hand Innovations LLC was $22 million and is associated with fracture repair technologies. The value of the IPR&D was calculated using cash flow projections discounted for the risk inherent in such projects. Probability of success factors ranging from 38 – 95% were used to reflect inherent clinical and regulatory risk and the discount rate applied was 17%.

The IPR&D charge related to the acquisition of Future Medical Systems S.A. was $15 million and is associated with the NEXTRA and DUO PUMP product technologies. The value of the IPR&D was calculated using cash flow projections discounted for the risk inherent in such projects. A probability of success factor of 90% for both technologies was used to reflect inherent clinical and regulatory risk and the discount rate applied was 22%.

The IPR&D charge related to the acquisition of Vascular Control Systems, Inc. was $87 million and is associated with the FLOSTAT system technology. The value of the IPR&D was calculated using cash flow projections discounted for the risk inherent in such projects. A probability of success factor of 75% was used to reflect inherent clinical and regulatory risk and the discount rate applied was 21%.

The IPR&D charge related to the acquisition of ColBar LifeScience Ltd. was $49 million and is associated with the EVOLENCE® family of products, which are biodegradable dermal fillers. The value of the IPR&D was calculated using cash flow projections discounted for the risk inherent in such projects. Probability of success factors ranging from 70–80% were used to reflect inherent clinical and regulatory risk and the discount rate applied was 21%.

The IPR&D charge related to the acquisition of Ensure Medical, Inc. was $66 million and is associated with the femoral artery closure device. The value of the IPR&D was calculated using cash flow projections discounted for the risk inherent in such projects. A probability of success factor of 75% was used to reflect inherent clinical and regulatory risk and the discount rate applied was 22%.

With the exception of the Consumer Healthcare business of Pfizer Inc., supplemental pro forma information for 2008, 2007 and 2006 per SFAS No. 141, *Business Combinations,* and SFAS No. 142, *Goodwill and Other Intangible Assets,* is not provided, as the impact of the aforementioned acquisitions did not have a material effect on the Company's results of operations, cash flows or financial position.

With the exception of the divestiture of the Professional Wound Care business of Ethicon, Inc., which resulted in a gain of $536 million before tax, and is recorded in other (income) expense, net, in 2008, divestitures in 2008, 2007 and 2006 did not have a material effect on the Company's results of operations, cash flows or financial position.

Humana
2008 Annual Report

3. Acquisitions

On October 31, 2008 we acquired PHP Companies, Inc. (d/b/a Cariten Healthcare), or Cariten, for cash consideration of approximately $256.1 million. The Cariten acquisition increased our commercial fully-insured and ASO presence as well as our Medicare HMO presence in eastern Tennessee. The total consideration paid exceeded our estimated fair value of the net tangible assets acquired by approximately $113.5 million of which we allocated $79.4 million to other intangible assets and $34.1 million to goodwill. The other intangible assets, which primarily consist of customer contracts, have a weighted-average useful life of 9.7 years. The acquired goodwill is not deductible for tax purposes. The purchase price allocation is preliminary, subject to completion of valuation analyses including refining assumptions used to calculate the fair value of other intangible assets, fixed assets, and certain reserves.

On August 29, 2008, we acquired Metcare Health Plans, Inc., or Metcare, for cash consideration of approximately $14.9 million. The acquisition expanded our Medicare HMO membership in central Florida.

On May 22, 2008, we acquired OSF Health Plans, Inc., or OSF, a managed care company serving both Medicare and commercial members in central Illinois, for cash consideration of approximately $84.0 million. This acquisition expanded our presence in Illinois, broadening our ability to serve multi-location employers with a wider range of products including our specialty offerings. The total consideration paid exceeded our estimated fair value of the net tangible assets acquired by approximately $27.8 million of which we allocated $10.1 million to other intangible assets and $17.7 million to goodwill. The other intangible assets, which primarily consist of customer contracts, have a weighted-average useful life of 9.9 years. The acquired goodwill is not deductible for tax purposes.

On April 30, 2008, we acquired UnitedHealth Group's Las Vegas, Nevada individual SecureHorizons Medicare Advantage HMO business, or SecureHorizons, for cash consideration of approximately $185.3 million, plus subsidiary capital and surplus requirements of $40 million. The acquisition expanded our presence into the rapidly growing Las Vegas market. The total consideration paid exceeded our estimated fair value of the net tangible assets acquired by approximately $185.3 million of which we allocated $69.3 million to other intangible assets and $116.0 million to goodwill. The other intangible assets, which primarily consist of customer and provider contracts, have a weighted-average useful life of 10.9 years. The acquired goodwill is deductible for tax purposes.

The Cariten, OSF, and Metcare purchase agreements contain provisions under which there may be future contingent consideration paid or received, primarily related to balance sheet settlements associated with medical claims runout and Medicare reconciliations with CMS. Any contingent consideration will be recorded as an adjustment to goodwill when the contingencies are resolved.

The pro forma effects of the 2008 acquisitions, individually and in the aggregate, on the consolidated statements of income were not material.

On November 30, 2007, we acquired KMG America Corporation, or KMG, for cash consideration of $155.2 million plus the assumption of $36.1 million of long-term debt. KMG provides long-duration insurance benefits including supplemental health and life products. The acquisition expanded our commercial product offerings allowing for significant cross-selling opportunities with our medical insurance products. The total consideration paid exceeded our estimated fair value of the net tangible assets acquired by approximately $204.5 million of which we allocated $43.0 million to other intangible assets and $161.5 million to goodwill. The other intangible assets, which primarily consist of customer contracts, have a weighted-average useful life of 19.3 years. The acquired goodwill is not deductible for tax purposes.

On October 1, 2007, we acquired CompBenefits Corporation, or CompBenefits, for cash consideration of $369.6 million. CompBenefits provides dental and vision insurance benefits. The acquisition expanded our commercial product offerings allowing for significant cross-selling opportunities with our medical insurance products. The total consideration paid exceeded our estimated fair value of the net tangible assets acquired by approximately $354.9 million of which we allocated $54.1 million to other intangible assets and $300.8 million to goodwill. The other intangible assets, which primarily consist of customer and provider contracts, have a weighted-average useful life of 11.5 years. The acquired goodwill is not deductible for tax purposes.

During 2008, we revised the fair value estimate of certain other intangible assets and future policy benefit reserves associated with our fourth quarter 2007 acquisitions of CompBenefits and KMG. This resulted in an increase in goodwill of $125.7 million, primarily related to refining assumptions used to calculate the fair value assigned to the KMG future policy benefits payable and customer contracts acquired, net of related deferred income taxes.

On March 1, 2007, we acquired DefenseWeb Technologies, Inc., or DefenseWeb, a company responsible for delivering customized software solutions for the Department of Defense, for cash consideration of $27.5 million.

On May 1, 2006, we acquired CHA Service Company, or CHA Health, a health plan serving employer groups in Kentucky, for cash consideration of $67.5 million.

The results of operations and financial condition of Cariten, Metcare, OSF, SecureHorizons, KMG, CompBenefits, DefenseWeb, and CHA have been included in our consolidated statements of income since the acquisition dates.

WM. Wrigley Jr.
2007 Annual Report

10. Acquisitions

On January 31, 2007, the Company acquired an 80% interest in A. Korkunov, a privately held premium chocolate company in Russia. The acquisition provided an opportunity for the Company to enter the chocolate confectionery marketplace, a significant component of the broader confectionery market, with a well recognized brand in a growing region. The Company acquired the 80% interest in A. Korkunov for $318,590. The Company financed the acquisition through short-term debt and cash on hand. Included in this purchase price is $25,000 the Company expects to pay in 2008 to A. Korkunov's minority shareholders due to the entity exceeding certain performance targets in 2007; however, final resolution and payment remains subject to review and due diligence. The Company expects to acquire an additional 10% in 2008 and the final 10% in 2009. The purchase price allocation remains preliminary and the results of operations have been included since January 31, 2007.

The following table contains a tentative purchase price allocation summarizing the assets and liabilities acquired, including the restated basis for 80% of the fair value with the remaining basis carried at historical cost, as prescribed for step acquisitions, at the date of acquisition:

($ in millions)	
Current assets	$ 22,834
Net property, plant and equipment	54,024
Goodwill	207,987
Intangibles	64,488
Other noncurrent assets	2,025
Total assets	351,358
Current liabilities	18,705
Noncurrent liabilities	14,063
Net assets acquired	$318,590

The fair value of intangible assets includes $54,776 with indefinite lives and $9,712 with determinable lives. Goodwill recognized is included in the EMEAI segment. All goodwill recognized for income tax purposes is deductible.

On June 26, 2005, the Company completed a transaction with Kraft Foods Global, Inc. to acquire certain confectionery assets. The transaction included the purchase of the Life Savers, Altoids, Crème Savers and Sugus brands. In addition, the transaction included the purchase of certain production facilities in the United States and Europe. The purchase provided additional diversification in key categories of mints and hard and chewy candy, expanded the product offering to customers' worldwide, added scale and brand depth to the innovation pipeline and increased efficiency across the Company's supply chain. The results of operations for the businesses acquired have been included in the consolidated financial results of the Company since June 26, 2005.

Cash consideration, including direct acquisition costs, totaled $1,436,259, net of proceeds received from the sale of the Trolli brand and related assets. The acquisition was initially funded with $1,350,000 of commercial paper, negotiated in part for purposes of this transaction, with the remaining amount funded from the Company's available cash.

The purchase price was allocated to the underlying assets acquired and liabilities assumed based upon their fair values at the date of acquisition. The Company determined the fair values based on independent appraisals, discounted cash flow analyses, quoted market prices and estimates made by management. To the extent the purchase price exceeded the fair value of the net identifiable tangible and intangible assets acquired, such excess was recorded as goodwill.

The following table contains the final purchase price allocation, which summarizes the fair values of the assets acquired and liabilities incurred as a result of integration plans, at the date of acquisition.

Inventory	$ 47,365
Net property, plant and equipment	86,904
Other noncurrent assets	45,808
Goodwill	912,093
Intangibles	367,695
Total assets	1,459,865
Accrued liabilities	23,606
Net assets acquired	$1,436,259

The fair value of the intangible assets as of the acquisition date is primarily associated with brand names which are not subject to amortization.

Other noncurrent assets included $28,356 associated with Sugus operations in China, the final purchase of which did not close until April 17, 2006.

Goodwill of $912,093 was recognized in connection with the acquisition, with $890,902 and $21,191 included in the North America and EMEAI segments, respectively. All goodwill recognized for income tax purposes is deductible.

The Company closed the acquired facility in Bridgend, Wales as of April 18, 2006. The Company recognized severance and other cash closing costs of $23,606 as a result of the Bridgend and other facility closures as well as other asset transfers. The majority of the activities were significantly completed by the first quarter of 2007.

Acquisition—Pro Forma Financial Statements

Results of operations of the acquired Kraft Foods Global, Inc. confectionery assets are included in the Company's consolidated financial statements from June 26, 2005. The following table includes the unaudited pro forma combined net sales, earnings and earnings per share for 2005, as if the Company had completed the acquisitions of the Kraft Goods Global, Inc. confectionery assets as of January 1, 2005.

In determining the unaudited pro forma amounts, income taxes, interest expense and depreciation and amortization of assets have been adjusted to the accounting base recognized for each in recording the combinations.

	2005
Net sales	$4,372,864
Net earnings	$ 519,217
Net earnings per share:	
Basic	$ 1.85
Diluted	$ 1.84

The pro forma results are not necessarily indicative of what actually would have occurred if the acquisitions had been completed as of the beginning of 2005, nor are they necessarily indicative of future consolidated results.

Schlumberger
2007 Annual Report

Recently Issued Accounting Pronouncements

In December 2007, the Financial Accounting Standards Board ("FASB") issued SFAS 141 (revised 2007), Business Combinations ("SFAS 141(R)"). SFAS 141(R) establishes principles and requirements for how an acquirer in a business combination recognizes and measures the assets acquired, liabilities assumed, and any noncontrolling interest (previously referred to as minority interest) in the acquiree. The provisions of SFAS 141(R) are effective for business combinations occurring on or after January 1, 2009.

In December 2007, the FASB issued SFAS 160, Noncontrolling Interests in Consolidated Financial Statements, an Amendment of ARB No. 51 ("SFAS 160").

This statement amends ARB 51 to establish accounting and reporting standards for the noncontrolling interest in a subsidiary and for the loss of control of a subsidiary. Upon its adoption on January 1, 2009, noncontrolling interests will be classified as equity in the Schlumberger financial statements.

SFAS 160 also changes the way the consolidated income statement is presented by requiring net income to include the net income for both the parent and the noncontrolling interest, with disclosure of both amounts on the consolidated statement of income. The calculation of earnings per share will continue to be based on income amounts attributable to the parent. The provisions of this standard must be applied retrospectively upon adoption.

3. Charges and Credits

Schlumberger recorded the following Charges and Credits in 2007, 2006 and 2005:

2007

Fourth quarter of 2007:

☐ Schlumberger sold certain workover rigs for $32 million, resulting in a pretax gain of $25 million ($17 million after-tax) which is classified in Interest and other income in the Consolidated Statement of Income.

2006

Second quarter of 2006:

☐ As discussed in further detail in Note 4 Acquisitions, Schlumberger acquired the remaining 30% minority interest in WesternGeco held by Baker Hughes Incorporated for $2.4 billion in cash during the second quarter of 2006. In connection with this transaction, a pretax and after-tax charge of $21 million was recorded, representing the portion of the purchase price that was allocated to in-process research and development. Schlumberger recorded an additional $6 million of in-process research and development charges, primarily related to a small acquisition which was also completed in the second quarter of 2006. These amounts were determined by identifying research and development projects that had not yet reached technological feasibility at the time of the acquisition. These charges are classified in Research & engineering in the Consolidated Statement of Income.

☐ Schlumberger recorded a pretax and after-tax loss of $9 million relating to the liquidation of certain investments in connection with the funding of the previously mentioned WesternGeco transaction. These losses are classified in Interest and other income in the Consolidated Statement of Income.

☐ In connection with the settlement of the WesternGeco visa matter described in Note 17 Contingencies, a pretax charge of $10 million ($7 million after-tax and minority interest) was recorded in the second quarter of 2006 and is classified in Cost of goods sold and services in the Consolidated Statement of Income.

The following is a summary of 2006 Charges and Credits:

(Stated in millions)	Pretax	Tax	Minority Interest	Net
Charges & Credits				
WesternGeco in-process R&D charge	$21.3	–	–	$21.0
Loss on liquidation of investments to fund WesternGeco transaction	9.4	–	–	9.4
WesternGeco visa settlement	9.7	0.3	(3.2)	6.8
Other in-process R&D charges	5.6	–	–	5.6
Net Charges	**$45.7**	**$0.3**	**$3.2**	**$42.8**

2005

Fourth quarter of 2005:

Schlumberger sold its investment in Hanover Compressor Company common stock for net proceeds of $110 million, resulting in a pretax and after-tax gain of $21 million. The pretax gain is classified in Interest and other income in the Consolidated Statement of Income.

Third quarter of 2005:

Schlumberger recorded a pretax and after-tax gain of approximately $18 million relating to the resolution of a contingency associated with the March 2005 sale of its facility in Montrouge, France. This gain is classified in Interest and other income in the Consolidated Statement of Income.

First quarter of 2005:

In March 2005, Schlumberger sold its facility in Montrouge, France for $230 million, resulting in a pretax and after-tax gain of $146 million, which is classified in Interest and other income in the Consolidated Statement of Income. Schlumberger also recorded other real estate related pretax charges of $12 million ($11 million after-tax), which are classified in Cost of goods sold and services in the Consolidated Statement of Income.

The following is a summary of 2005 Charges and Credits:

(Stated in millions)	Pretax	Tax	Net
Charges & Credits			
Gain on sale of Hanover Compressor stock	($ 20.9)		($ 20.9)
Gain on sale of Montrouge facility	(163.4)		(163.4)
Other real estate related charges	12.1	(0.8)	11.3
Net Credits	**($172.2)**	**($0.8)**	**($173.0)**

4. Acquisitions

Acquisition of Eastern Echo Holding Plc

On December 10, 2007, Schlumberger completed the acquisition of Eastern Echo Holding Plc ("Eastern Echo") for $838 million in cash. Eastern Echo is a Dubai-based marine seismic company that does not currently have any operations, but has signed contracts for the construction of six seismic vessels. The first four vessels are scheduled to be delivered in January, March, May and July of 2009, while the remaining two are scheduled to be delivered January and March of 2010.

The purchase price has been allocated to the net assets acquired based upon their estimated fair values as follows:

(Stated in millions)	
Cash and short-term investments	$266
Other current assets	23
Fixed income investments, held to maturity	54
Vessels under construction	735
Accounts payable and accrued liabilities	(17)
Long-term debt	(182)
Deferred tax liability	(41)
Total purchase price	838

Acquisition of WesternGeco Minority Interest

On April 28, 2006, Schlumberger acquired the remaining 30% minority interest in WesternGeco from Baker Hughes Incorporated for $2.4 billion in cash. Schlumberger also incurred direct acquisition costs of $6 million in connection with this transaction. As a result of this transaction, Schlumberger owns 100% of WesternGeco.

The purchase price has been allocated to the proportionate share of net assets acquired based upon their estimated fair values as follows:

(Stated in millions)	
Book value of minority interest acquired	$ 460
Fair value adjustments:	
Technology (weighted average life of 15 years)	293
Customer relationships (life of 20 years)	153
Vessels (weighted average remaining life of 11 years)	84
Other fixed assets (weighted average remaining life of 3 years)	10
Multiclient seismic data (maximum life of 3 years)	41
Other identifiable intangible assets (life of 15 years)	49
In-process research and development (expensed immediately—see Note 3)	21
Deferred income taxes	(43)
Goodwill	1,338
Total purchase price	$2,406

The amount allocated to goodwill represents the excess of the purchase price over the fair value of the net assets acquired. Approximately $0.8 billion of the $1.3 billion of goodwill is estimated to be tax deductible. In addition, approximately $650 million of the goodwill created as a result of this transaction has been allocated to the Oilfield Services business segment in recognition of the estimated present value of future synergies paid for in this transaction that will directly benefit that segment.

Vessels and other fixed assets

In analyzing the fair value of the WesternGeco vessels, it was determined that the remaining estimated useful lives of these assets exceeded the remaining estimated life currently being used to calculate depreciation expense. Therefore, the estimated remaining useful lives of the vessels were extended an additional 4 years (on a weighted average basis) as of the date of the acquisition. The impact of the fair value adjustments for all fixed assets, combined with the change in estimate regarding the depreciable lives of the vessels, resulted in a net reduction in depreciation expense of approximately $2 million in 2006.

Multiclient seismic data

The carrying value of the multiclient library immediately after the acquisition increased to $243 million from $202 million, reflecting the impact of the $41 million fair value adjustment. These capitalized costs will be charged to Cost of goods sold and services based on the percentage of the total costs on the balance sheet to the estimated total revenue that Schlumberger expects to receive from the sales of such data. Schlumberger policy has been that under no circumstance will an individual survey carry a net book value greater than a 4-year straight-line amortized value. After consideration of the estimated number of future years that revenues are expected to be derived from the multiclient seismic data at the time of the acquisition, Schlumberger concluded that the remaining minimum amortization period should be 3 years for all surveys in the multiclient seismic library at the time of the transaction, effectively resetting the minimum amortization period. Therefore, the $243 million of capitalized multiclient seismic data costs will be charged to expense over a period no longer than the next 3 years from the date of the transaction. Surveys comprising the $202 million of multiclient seismic data costs prior to this transaction had a weighted average remaining life for purposes of computing the minimum amortization of approximately 1.8 years. Given the current emphasis on requiring multiclient projects to be significantly prefunded before the project commences, Schlumberger currently estimates that the majority of revenues to be derived from sales of new surveys will be achieved within a 4-year period. Therefore, Schlumberger will continue its policy that under no circumstance will an individual survey carry a net book value greater than a 4-year straight-line amortized value for all surveys added to the library after the date of this transaction.

The net impact of the $41 million fair value adjustment combined with the resetting of the minimum amortization period resulted in an approximate $28 million net reduction in multiclient amortization expense in 2006 as compared to what multiclient amortization expense would have been had this transaction not been consummated.

Acquisition of PetroAlliance Minority Interest

On December 9, 2003, Schlumberger announced that it had signed an agreement to acquire PetroAlliance Services Company Limited ("PetroAlliance Services") over a 3-year period based on a formula determined at that time. Schlumberger acquired 26% of PetroAlliance Services in the second quarter of 2004 for $12 million in cash and 843,740 shares of Schlumberger common stock valued at $24 million. During the second quarter of 2005, Schlumberger acquired an additional 25% of PetroAlliance Services for $40 million in cash and 2,300,646 shares of Schlumberger common stock valued at $79 million bringing its total ownership interest to 51%. During the second quarter of 2006, Schlumberger acquired the remaining 49% of PetroAlliance Services that it did not own for $165 million in cash and 4,730,960 shares of Schlumberger common stock valued at approximately $330 million. The aggregate purchase price paid for PetroAlliance Services over the 3-year period was $650 million.

Schlumberger began consolidating the results of PetroAlliance Services in the second quarter of 2005. This investment had previously been accounted under the equity method.

The $495 million purchase price paid in the second quarter of 2006 has been allocated to the proportionate share of net assets acquired based upon their estimated fair values as follows:

(Stated in millions)	
Book value of minority interest acquired	$ 33
Fair value adjustments:	
Customer relationships (life of 12 years)	69
Other identifiable intangible assets (life of 5 years)	7
Deferred income taxes	(18)
Goodwill	404
Total purchase price	$495

The amount allocated to goodwill represents the excess of the purchase price over the fair value of the net assets acquired. The goodwill is not tax deductible.

Other Acquisitions

Schlumberger has made other acquisitions and minority interest investments, none of which were significant on an individual basis, for cash payments of $306 million during 2007, $356 million during 2006, and $56 million during 2005.

Under the terms of certain past acquisitions, Schlumberger had obligations to pay additional consideration if specific conditions were met. Schlumberger made cash payments of $63 million during 2006 and $21 million during 2005, with respect to certain transactions that were consummated in prior years, which were recorded as additional goodwill.

Pro forma results pertaining to the above acquisitions, including the WesternGeco and PetroAlliance Services transactions, are not presented as the impact was not significant.

5. Investments in Affiliated Companies

The MI-SWACO drilling fluids joint venture is owned 40% by Schlumberger and 60% by Smith International, Inc. Schlumberger records income relating to this venture using the equity method of accounting. Schlumberger's investment in the joint venture on December 31, 2007 and 2006 was $1.2 billion and $970 million, respectively. Schlumberger's equity income from this joint venture in 2007 was $174 million, $135 million in 2006 and $83 million in 2005. Schlumberger received cash distributions from the joint venture of $40 million in 2007 and $28 million in 2005. There were no such distributions in 2006.

Schlumberger's joint venture agreement with Smith International, Inc. contains a provision under which either party to the joint venture may offer to sell its entire interest in the venture to the other party at a cash purchase price per percentage interest specified in an offer notice. If the offer to sell is not accepted, the offering party will be obligated to purchase the entire interest of the other party at the same price per percentage interest as the prices specified in the offer notice.

Walt Disney
2007 Annual Report

3. Significant Acquisitions and Dispositions and Restructuring and Impairment Charges

Acquisition of Pixar On May 5, 2006 (the Closing Date), the Company completed an all stock acquisition of Pixar, a digital animation studio (the Acquisition). Disney believes that the creation of high quality feature animation is a key driver of success across many of its businesses and provides content useful across a variety of traditional and new platforms throughout the world. The acquisition of Pixar is intended to support the Company's strategic priorities of creating the finest content, embracing leading-edge technologies, and strengthening its global presence. The results of Pixar's operations have been included in the Company's consolidated financial statements since the Closing Date.

To purchase Pixar, Disney exchanged 2.3 shares of its common stock for each share of Pixar common stock, resulting in the issuance of 279 million shares of Disney common stock, and converted previously issued vested and unvested Pixar equity-based awards into approximately 45 million Disney equity-based awards.

The Acquisition purchase price was $7.5 billion ($6.4 billion, net of Pixar's cash and investments of approximately $1.1 billion). The value of the stock issued was calculated based on the market value of the Company's common stock using the average stock price for the five-day period beginning two days before the acquisition announcement date on January 24, 2006. The fair value of the vested equity-based awards issued at the Closing Date was estimated using the Black-Scholes option pricing model, as the information required to use a binomial valuation model was not reasonably available.

In connection with the Acquisition, the Company recorded a non-cash, non-taxable gain from the deemed termination of the existing Pixar distribution agreement. Under our previously existing distribution agreement with Pixar, the Company earned a distribution fee that, based on current market rates at the Closing Date, was favorable to the Company. In accordance with EITF 04-1, *Accounting for Pre-Existing Relationships between the Parties to a Business Combination* (EITF 04-1), the Company recognized a $48 million gain, representing the net present value of the favorable portion of the distribution fee over the remaining life of the distribution agreement. In addition, the Company abandoned the Pixar sequel projects commenced by the Company prior to the acquisition and recorded a pre-tax impairment charge totaling $26 million, which represents the costs of these projects incurred through the abandonment date. These two items are classified in "Restructuring and impairment (charges) and other credits, net" in the Consolidated Statement of Income.

The Company allocated the purchase price to the tangible and identifiable intangible assets acquired and liabilities assumed based on their fair values, which were determined primarily through third-party appraisals. The goodwill that arose from the Acquisition reflected the value to Disney from:

☐ Acquiring a talented, assembled workforce, particularly the creative and technological talents of key senior management and film directors with a successful track record of producing high quality feature animation

☐ Securing all of the economic results of future films produced by Pixar

☐ Obtaining the benefits of leveraging future Pixar-created intellectual property across Disney's diversified revenue streams and portfolio of entertainment assets

☐ Improving the results of Disney feature animation films

The following table summarizes the allocation of the purchase price:

	Estimated Fair Value	Weighted Average Useful Lives (Years)
Cash and cash equivalents	$ 11	
Investments	1,073	
Prepaid and other assets	45	
Film costs	538	
Buildings and equipment	225	12
Intangibles	233	16
Goodwill	5,557	17
Total assets acquired	$7,682	
Liabilities	64	
Deferred income taxes	123	
Total liabilities assumed	$ 187	
Net assets acquired	$7,495	

The weighted average useful life determination for intangibles excludes $164 million of indefinite-lived Pixar trademarks and tradenames. Goodwill of $4.8 billion, $0.6 billion, and $0.2 billion was allocated to the Studio Entertainment,

Consumer Products, and Parks and Resorts operating segments, respectively. The goodwill is not amortizable for tax purposes.

The following table presents unaudited pro forma results of Disney for fiscal 2006 as though Pixar had been acquired as of the beginning of fiscal 2006. These pro forma results do not necessarily represent what would have occurred if the Acquisition had taken place as of the beginning of fiscal 2006 and do not represent the results that may occur in the future. The pro forma amounts represent the historical operating results of Disney and Pixar with adjustments for purchase accounting.

	Fiscal Year 2006 (unaudited)
Revenues	$34,299
Income before cumulative effect of accounting change	3,395
Net Income	3,395
Earnings per share:	
Diluted	$ 1.52
Basic	$ 1.56

Other Acquisitions On August 1, 2007, the Company acquired all of the outstanding shares of Club Penguin Entertainment, Inc. (CPE), a Canadian company that operates clubpenguin.com, an online virtual world for children. The purchase price included upfront cash consideration of approximately $350 million and additional consideration of up to $350 million that may be paid if CPE achieves predefined earnings targets for calendar years 2008 and 2009.

On February 1, 2007, the Company acquired all the outstanding shares of NASN Limited, an Irish company that operates cable television networks in Europe dedicated to North American sporting events and related programming, for consideration valued at $112 million consisting of cash and assumption of debt.

We are in the process of finalizing the valuation of the assets acquired and liabilities assumed for both acquisitions.

ABC Radio Transaction On June 12, 2007, the Company completed the spin-off of its wholly-owned subsidiary, ABC Radio Holdings, Inc., and its merger into a subsidiary of Citadel Broadcasting Corporation (Citadel). Prior to the spin-off, the Company consolidated its ABC Radio business, consisting of 22 large-market radio stations and the ABC Radio Network businesses, under ABC Radio Holdings, Inc. The transaction did not include the Company's ESPN Radio or Radio Disney network and station businesses.

As a result of the spin-off and merger, Company shareholders received approximately 0.0768 shares of Citadel common stock in exchange for each share of Disney common stock held as of June 6, 2007. Approximately 151.7 million shares of Citadel common stock were issued to Company shareholders in the merger. As part of the transaction, the Company retained $1.35 billion of cash, representing the proceeds from debt raised by ABC Radio Holdings, Inc. prior to the spin-off. This debt and the assets and other liabilities of the ABC Radio business were removed from the Company's balance sheet as a distribution at book value. Consequently, there was no gain or loss recorded and the negative net book value of $132 million was credited to retained earnings.

Fiscal 2007 results of the ABC Radio business through June 12, 2007 have been reported as discontinued operations. Previously reported results have been reclassified to reflect this presentation.

Summarized financial information for the discontinued ABC Radio business is as follows (in millions):

Income Statement Data:	2007	2006	2005
Revenues	$ 372	$ 538	$570
Income from discontinued operations before income taxes	45	123	176

Balance Sheet Data:	June 12, 2007	September 30, 2006
Assets		
Current assets	$ 132	$ 129
Property and equipment	56	60
FCC licenses	476	476
Goodwill	726	726
Other assets	7	4
	1,397	1,395
Liabilities		
Current liabilities	25	20
Borrowings	1,350	–
Long-term liabilities	154	149
Net assets of discontinued operations	$ (132)	$1,226

Dispositions On November 21, 2006, in connection with the execution of new long-term agreements for the provision of programming to cable service provider Comcast Corporation (Comcast), the Company sold its 39.5% interest in E! Entertainment Television (E!) to Comcast (which owned the remainder of the interest in E!) for $1.23 billion, which resulted in a pre-tax gain of $780 million ($487 million after-tax). On October 2, 2006, the Company sold its 50% stake in Us Weekly for $300 million, which resulted in a pre-tax gain of $272 million ($170 million after-tax). These gains are reported in "Gains on sales of equity investments and businesses" in the Consolidated Statements of Income.

The following disposals occurred during fiscal 2006 and fiscal 2005:

☐ A cable television equity investment in Spain was sold for $67 million on November 23, 2005, resulting in a pre-tax gain of $57 million.

☐ The Discover Magazine business was sold for $14 million on October 7, 2005, resulting in a pre-tax gain of $13 million.

☐ The Mighty Ducks of Anaheim was sold for $39 million on June 20, 2005, resulting in a pre-tax gain of $26 million.

These gains were reported in "Gains on sales of equity investments and businesses" in the Consolidated Statements of Income.

On November 21, 2004, the Company sold substantially all of The Disney Store chain in North America under a long-term licensing arrangement to a wholly-owned subsidiary of The Children's Place (TCP). The Company received $100 million for the working capital transferred to the buyer at the closing of the transaction. During fiscal 2005, the Company recorded a loss on the working capital that was transferred to the buyer and additional restructuring and impairment charges related to the sale (primarily for employee retention and severance and lease termination costs) totaling $32 million.

The changes in the carrying amount of goodwill for the years ended September 29, 2007 and September 30, 2006 are as follows:

	Media Networks	Parks and Resorts	Studio Entertainment	Consumer Products	Total
Balance at October 1, 2005	$16,895	$ 27	$ 23	$ 29	$16,974
Goodwill acquired during the year	23	146	4,790	613	5,572
Other, net	(19)	–	(22)	–	(41)
Balance at September 30, 2006	16,899	173	4,791	642	22,505
Goodwill acquired during the year	475	–	–	21	496
Goodwill disposed of during the year	(726)	–	–	–	(726)
Capital Cities/ABC, Inc. acquisition adjustment and other, net	(187)	–	(3)	–	(190)
Balance at September 29, 2007	$16,461	$173	$4,788	$663	$22,085

During the fourth quarter of fiscal 2007, certain preacquisition tax contingencies related to the Company's 1996 acquisition of Capital Cities/ABC, Inc. were reversed against goodwill.

4. Investments

Investments consist of the following:

	September 29, 2007	September 30, 2006
Investments, equity basis[1]	$706	$1,075
Investments, other	237	188
Investment in aircraft leveraged leases	52	52
	$995	$1,315

[1] Equity investments consist of investments in companies over which the Company has significant influence but not the majority of the equity or risks and rewards.

Investments, Equity Basis A summary of combined financial information for equity investments, which include cable investments such as A&E Television Networks (37.5% owned) and Lifetime Entertainment Services (50.0% owned), is as follows:

	2007	2006	2005
Results of Operations:			
Revenues	$4,351	$4,447	$4,317
Net Income	$1,137	$1,170	$1,275

	September 29, 2007	September 30, 2006
Balance Sheet:		
Current assets	$2,383	$2,620
Non-current assets	1,331	1,562
	$3,714	$4,182
Current liabilities	$1,113	$1,048
Non-current liabilities	1,060	1,154
Shareholders' equity	1,541	1,980
	$3,714	$4,182

During fiscal 2007, the Company sold its interests in E! and Us Weekly. See Note 3 for further discussion.

Investments, Other As of September 29, 2007 and September 30, 2006, the Company held $99 million and $82 million, respectively, of securities classified as available-for-sale. As of September 29, 2007 and September 30, 2006, the Company also held $138 million and $106 million, respectively, of non-publicly traded cost-method investments.

In 2007 and 2006, the Company had no realized gain or loss on sales of available-for-sale securities. In 2005, the Company recognized $14 million in net gains on sales of available for sale securities. Realized gains and losses are determined principally on an average cost basis.

In 2007, 2006 and 2005, the Company recorded non-cash charges of $18 million, $0 million and $42 million, respectively, to reflect other-than-temporary losses in value of certain investments.

Investment in Aircraft Leveraged Leases During the fourth quarter of 2005, the Company recorded a $101 million pre-tax charge, or $0.03 per share, to write-off its remaining investment in aircraft leveraged leases with Delta Air Lines, Inc. (Delta) resulting from Delta's bankruptcy filing in September 2005. This charge was reported in "Net interest expense" in the Consolidated Statements of Income. Our remaining aircraft leveraged lease investment of $52 million is with FedEx Corp.

5. Euro Disney and Hong Kong Disneyland

The Company has a 51% effective ownership interest in the operations of Euro Disney and a 43% ownership interest in the operations of Hong Kong Disneyland which are both consolidated under FIN 46R, *Consolidation of Variable Interest Entities.*

The following table presents a condensed consolidating balance sheet for the Company as of September 29, 2007, reflecting the impact of consolidating the balance sheets of Euro Disney and Hong Kong Disneyland.

	Before Euro Disney and Hong Kong Disneyland Consolidation	Euro Disney, Hong Kong Disneyland and Adjustments	Total
Cash and cash equivalents	$ 3,066	$ 604	$ 3,670
Other current assets	7,379	265	7,644
Total current assets	10,445	869	11,314
Investments	1,766	(771)	995
Fixed assets	12,597	4,836	17,433
Other assets	31,143	43	31,186
Total assets	$55,951	$4,977	$60,928
Current portion of borrowings	$ 2,910	$ 370	$ 3,280
Other current liabilities	7,437	674	8,111
Total current liabilities	10,347	1,044	11,391
Borrowings	8,679	3,213	11,892
Deferred income taxes and other long-term liabilities	5,423	174	5,597
Minority interests	749	546	1,295
Shareholders' equity	30,753	–	30,753
Total liabilities and shareholders' equity	$55,951	$4,977	$60,928

The following table presents a condensed consolidating income statement of the Company for the year ended September 29, 2007, reflecting the impact of consolidating the income statements of Euro Disney and Hong Kong Disneyland.

	Before Euro Disney and Hong Kong Disneyland Consolidation[1]	Euro Disney, Hong Kong Disneyland and Adjustments	Total
Revenues	$ 33,695	$ 1,815	$ 35,510
Cost and expenses	(26,857)	(1,872)	(28,729)
Gains on sales of equity investments and businesses	1,052	–	1,052
Net interest expense	(430)	(163)	(593)
Equity in the income of investees	390	95	485
Income (loss) from continuing operations before income taxes and minority interests	7,850	(125)	7,725
Income taxes	(2,849)	(25)	(2,874)
Minority interests	(327)	150	(177)
Income from continuing operations	4,674	–	4,674
Discontinued operations, net of tax	13	–	13
Income from continuing operations	$ 4,687	$ –	$ 4,687

[1] These amounts include Euro Disney and Hong Kong Disneyland under the equity method of accounting. As such, royalty and management fee income from these operations is included in Revenues and our share of their net income is included in Equity in the income of investees.

The following table presents a condensed consolidating cash flow statement of the Company for the year ended September 29, 2007, reflecting the impact of consolidating the cash flow statements of Euro Disney and Hong Kong Disneyland.

	Before Euro Disney and Hong Kong Disneyland Consolidation	Euro Disney, Hong Kong Disneyland and Adjustments	Total
Cash provided by continuing operations	$ 5,137	$ 261	$ 5,398
Investments in parks, resorts, and other property	(1,310)	(256)	(1,566)
Other investing activities	948	–	948
Cash used in continuing financing activities	(3,619)	–	(3,619)
Cash flows from discontinued operations	98	–	98
Increase in cash and cash equivalents	1,254	5	1,259
Cash and cash equivalents, beginning of year	1,812	599	2,411
Cash and cash equivalents, end of year	$ 3,066	$ 604	$ 3,670

Euro Disney Financial Restructuring Effective October 1, 2004, Euro Disney, the Company, and Euro Disney's lenders finalized a Memorandum of Agreement (MOA) related to the financial restructuring of Euro Disney (the 2005 Financial Restructuring). The MOA provided for new financing as well as the restructuring of Euro Disney's existing financing at that time. The transactions contemplated by the MOA were fully implemented on February 23, 2005 with the completion of a € 253 million equity rights offering. The MOA included the following provisions:

Royalties and Management Fees

☐ Royalties and management fees for fiscal 2005 through fiscal 2009, totaling € 25 million per year, payable to the Company are to be unconditionally deferred and converted into subordinated long-term borrowings

☐ Royalties and management fees for fiscal 2007 through fiscal 2014, of up to € 25 million per year, payable to the Company are subject to conditional deferrals and will be converted into subordinated long-term borrowings if operating results do not achieve specified levels. Based on operating results and subject to third-party confirmation, the Company does not expect royalties and management fees subject to conditional deferral for fiscal 2007 to be converted into subordinated long-term borrowings

New Financing

☐ € 253 million equity rights offering, of which the Company's share was € 100 million

☐ New ten-year € 150 million line of credit from the Company for liquidity needs, which reduces to € 100 million after five years. There were no borrowings under the new line of credit as of September 29, 2007

The MOA provided for a 2% interest rate increase for certain tranches of Euro Disney's debt, resulting in a substantial modification of a portion of this debt. Relevant accounting rules required that the substantially modified portion be accounted for as though it had been extinguished and replaced with new borrowings recorded at fair value, which resulted in a $61 million gain recorded in "Net interest expense" in the Consolidated Statement of Income during the year ended October 1, 2005.

Certain indirect, wholly-owned subsidiaries of The Walt Disney Company have liability as current or former general partners of Disney S.C.A. In addition to their equity interest in Disney S.C.A., certain of these subsidiaries of the Company have been capitalized with interest-bearing demand notes with an aggregate face value of € 200 million.

Black and Decker
2007 Annual Report

Note 2: Acquisition

Effective March 1, 2006, the Corporation acquired Vector Products, Inc. (Vector). The cash purchase price for the transaction was $158.5 million, net of cash acquired of $.1 million and including transaction costs of $.9 million. The addition of Vector to the Corporation's Power Tools and Accessories segment allows the Corporation to offer customers a broader range of products.

The transaction has been accounted for in accordance with SFAS No. 141, Business Combinations, and accordingly, the financial position and results of operations have been included in the Corporation's Balance Sheet and Statement of Earnings since the date of acquisition.

In early 2007, the Corporation completed the purchase price allocation of Vector. The purchase price allocation of the acquired business, based upon an independent appraisal and management's estimates at the date of acquisition, in millions of dollars, is as follows:

Accounts receivable	$ 18.8
Inventories	42.5
Property and equipment	2.6
Goodwill	80.0
Intangible assets	30.9
Other current and long-term assets	9.1
Total assets acquired	183.9
Accounts payable and accrued liabilities	16.6
Other liabilities	8.8
Total liabilities	25.4
Fair value of net assets acquired	$158.5

The Corporation does not believe that the goodwill and intangible assets recognized will be deductible for income tax purposes.

Prior to the date of the acquisition of Vector and during 2006, the Corporation identified opportunities to integrate the business into its existing Power Tools and Accessories segment. Subsequent to the acquisition, the Corporation approved integration actions relating to the acquired business in the amount of $1.3 million. These actions principally reflect severance costs associated with administrative and distribution functions of the acquired business as well as the cost of lease and other contractual obligations for which no future benefit will be realized. The Corporation completed these actions during 2007.

Procter & Gamble
2006 Annual Report

Note 2. Acquisitions

Gillette Acquisition

On October 1, 2005, we completed our acquisition of The Gillette Company. Pursuant to the acquisition agreement, which provided for the exchange of 0.975 shares of The Procter & Gamble Company common stock, on a tax-free basis, for each share of The Gillette Company, we issued 962 million shares of The Procter & Gamble Company common stock, net of shares exchanged for retained Gillette treasury shares. The value of these shares was determined using the average Company stock prices beginning two days before and ending two days after January 28, 2005, the date the acquisition was announced. We also issued 79 million stock options in exchange for Gillette's outstanding stock options. Under the purchase method of accounting, the total consideration was approximately $53.43 billion including common stock, the fair value of vested stock options and acquisition costs. This acquisition resulted in two new reportable segments: Blades and Razors, and Duracell and Braun. The Gillette oral care and personal care businesses were subsumed within the Health Care and Beauty reportable segments, respectively. The operating results of the Gillette businesses are reported in our financial statements beginning October 1, 2005.

The Gillette Company is a market leader in several global product categories including blades and razors, oral care and batteries. Total sales for Gillette during its most recent pre-acquisition year ended December 31, 2004 were $10.48 billion.

In order to obtain regulatory approval of the transaction, we were required to divest certain overlapping businesses. We completed the divestiture of the Spinbrush toothbrush business, Rembrandt (a Gillette oral care product line), Right Guard and other Gillette deodorant brands during the fiscal year ended June 30, 2006.

In connection with this acquisition, we also announced a share buyback plan under which we planned to acquire up to $22 billion of Company common shares through the open market or from private transactions. We completed this share buyback plan in July 2006 with cumulative purchases of $20.10 billion, of which $19.82 billion was acquired through June 30, 2006. The repurchases were financed by borrowings under a $24 billion three-year credit facility with a syndicate of banks. This credit facility carries a variable interest rate. Interest on the facility is managed within our overall interest rate management policies described in Note 6.

The following table provides pro forma results of operations for the years ended June 30, 2006, 2005 and 2004, as if Gillette had been acquired as of the beginning of each fiscal year presented. The pro forma results include certain purchase accounting adjustments such as the estimated changes in depreciation and amortization expense on acquired tangible and intangible assets. However, pro forma results do not include any anticipated cost savings or other effects of the planned integration of Gillette. Accordingly, such amounts are not necessarily indicative of the results if the acquisition had occurred on the dates indicated or that may result in the future.

Pro forma results; Years ended June 30	*2006*	*2005*	*2004*
Net Sales	**$71,005**	$67,920	$61,112
Net Earnings	**8,871**	8,522	7,504
Diluted Net Earnings per Common Share	**$ 2.51**	$ 2.29	$ 1.98

We are in the process of finalizing the allocation of the purchase price to the individual assets acquired and liabilities assumed. The preliminary allocation of the purchase price included in the current period balance sheet is based on the best estimates of management. To assist management in the allocation, we engaged valuation specialists to prepare independent appraisals. The completion of the purchase price allocation may result in adjustments to the carrying value of Gillette's recorded assets and liabilities, revisions of the useful lives of intangible assets and the determination of any residual amount that will be allocated to goodwill. The related depreciation and amortization expense from the acquired assets is also subject to revision based on the final allocation.

The following table presents the preliminary allocation of purchase price related to the Gillette business as of the date of the acquisition.

Current assets	5,553
Property, plant and equipment	3,673
Goodwill	34,943
Intangible assets	29,736
Other noncurrent assets	771
TOTAL ASSETS ACQUIRED	74,676
Current liabilities	5,009
Noncurrent liabilities	16,241
TOTAL LIABILITIES ASSUMED	21,250
NET ASSETS ACQUIRED	53,426

The Gillette acquisition resulted in $34.94 billion in goodwill, preliminarily allocated primarily to the segments comprising the Gillette businesses (Blades and Razors, Duracell and Braun, Health Care and Beauty). A portion of the goodwill has also been preliminarily allocated to the other segments on the basis that certain cost synergies will benefit these businesses. See Note 3 for the allocation of goodwill to the segments. Millions of dollars except per share amounts or otherwise specified. 50 The Procter & Gamble Company and Subsidiaries Notes to Consolidated Financial Statements The preliminary purchase price allocation to the identifiable intangible assets included in these financial statements is as follows:

		Weighted Average Life
INTANGIBLE ASSETS WITH DETERMINABLE LIVES		
Brands	$ 1,607	20
Patents and technology	2,716	17
Customer relationships	1,445	27
BRANDS WITH INDEFINITE LIVES	23,968	Indefinite
TOTAL INTANGIBLE ASSETS	29,736	

The majority of the intangible asset valuation relates to brands. Our preliminary assessment as to brands that have an indefinite life and those that have a determinable life was based on a number of factors, including the competitive environment, market share, brand history, product life cycles, operating plan and macroeconomic environment of the countries in which the brands are sold. The indefinite-lived brands include Gillette, Venus, Duracell, Oral-B and Braun. The determinable-lived brands include certain brand sub-names, such as MACH3 and Sensor in the Blades and Razors business, and other regional or local brands. The determinable-lived brands have asset lives ranging from 10 to 40 years. The patents and technology intangibles are concentrated in the Blades and Razors and Oral Care businesses and have asset lives ranging from 5 to 20 years. The estimated customer relationship intangible asset useful lives ranging from 20 to 30 years reflect the very low historical and projected customer attrition rates among Gillette's major retailer and distributor customers.

We are in the process of completing our analysis of integration plans, pursuant to which we will incur costs primarily related to the elimination of selling, general and administrative overlap between the two companies in areas like Global Business Services, corporate staff and go-to-market support, as well as redundant manufacturing capacity. Our preliminary estimate of Gillette exit costs that have been recognized as an assumed liability as of the acquisition date is $1.14 billion, including $819 in separations related to approximately 5,600 people, $57 in employee relocation costs and $264 in other exit costs. We expect such activities to be substantially complete by June 30, 2008.

Wella Acquisition

On September 2, 2003, we acquired a controlling interest in Wella. Through a stock purchase agreement with the majority shareholders of Wella and a tender offer made on the remaining shares, we initially acquired a total of 81% of Wella's outstanding shares, including 99% of Wella's outstanding voting class shares. In June 2004, the Company and Wella entered into a Domination and Profit Transfer Agreement (the Domination Agreement) pursuant to which we are entitled to exercise full operating control and receive 100% of the future earnings of Wella. As consideration for the Domination Agreement, we agreed to pay the holders of the remaining outstanding Wella shares a guaranteed perpetual annual dividend payment. Alternatively, the remaining Wella shareholders may elect to tender their shares to us for an agreed price. The fair value of the total guaranteed annual dividend payments was $1.11 billion, which approximated the cost if all remaining shares were tendered. Because the Domination Agreement transfers operational and economic control of the remaining outstanding shares to the Company, it has been accounted for as an acquisition of the remaining shares, with a liability recorded equal to the fair value of the guaranteed payments. Because of the tender feature, the remaining liability is recorded as a current liability in the accrued and other liabilities line of the Consolidated Balance Sheets. Payments made under the guaranteed annual dividend and tender provisions are allocated between interest expense and a reduction of the liability, as appropriate. The total purchase price for Wella, including acquisition costs, was $6.27 billion based on exchange rates at the acquisition dates. It was funded with a combination of cash, debt and the liability recorded under the Domination Agreement. During the year ended June 30, 2006, a portion of the remaining shares was tendered, resulting in a $944 reduction in our liability under the Domination Agreement. As a result of the tender, we now own 96.9% of all Wella outstanding shares.

The acquisition of Wella, with over $3 billion in annual net sales, gave us access to the professional hair care category plus greater scale and scope in hair care, hair colorants, cosmetics and fragrance products, while providing potential for significant synergies. The operating results of the Wella business are reported in Beauty beginning September 2, 2003.

China Venture

On June 18, 2004, we purchased the remaining 20% stake in our China venture from our partner, Hutchison Whampoa China Ltd. (Hutchison), giving us full ownership in our operations in China. The net purchase price was $1.85 billion, which is the purchase price of $2.00 billion net of minority interest and related obligations that were eliminated as a result of the transaction. The acquisition was funded by debt.

Other minor business purchases and intangible asset acquisitions totaled $395, $572 and $384 in 2006, 2005 and 2004, respectively.

Hormel Foods
2006 Annual Report

Note B. Acquisitions and Divestitures

On March 31, 2006, the company acquired Valley Fresh, Inc. (Valley Fresh) for the preliminary purchase price of $80.4 million in cash, including related costs. Valley Fresh has the leading market share in the canned ready-to-eat chicken category and distributes more than 50 convenient precooked chicken products on a national basis, primarily under the Valley Fresh brand. Valley Fresh was a privately held company and employs approximately 265 employees at its 90,000-square-foot manufacturing facility in Turlock, California. Valley Fresh products are expected to further strengthen the portfolio within the company's Grocery Products segment.

On September 6, 2006, the company announced that it entered into a definitive merger agreement, pursuant to which the company will acquire Provena Foods Inc. (Provena). Provena is a publicly traded company based in

Chino, California, and provides pepperoni and pasta to pizza makers and packaged food manufacturers. The proposed acquisition has been approved by the board of directors of each company and is subject to customary closing conditions, including the approval of the Provena shareholders. Shareholders holding approximately 46 percent of the outstanding shares of Provena common stock, as of September 6, 2006, had agreed to vote their shares in favor of the merger agreement and against any competing proposal. Assuming shareholder approval, the transaction is expected to close by the end of calendar year 2006 with an estimated value of $16.8 million.

On November 10, 2006, subsequent to the end of fiscal year 2006, the company acquired the assets of Saag's Products, Inc. (Saag's) for a preliminary purchase price of $12.0 million cash, plus the assumption of certain obligations. Saag's is based in San Leandro, California, and is a leading processor and marketer of branded, premium quality gourmet sausages and specialty smoked meats. The acquisition provides opportunities to expand the company's production capacity, and to enhance the product portfolio within the Refrigerated Foods segment.

On December 29, 2004, the company purchased all of the outstanding stock of Clougherty Packing Company (Clougherty) for $208.2 million in cash, including related costs. Clougherty was a privately held Southern California pork processor and is the maker of the *Farmer John* brand of pork products popular throughout the Southwestern United States. The acquisition strengthens the company's presence in that geographic area and complements many of the company's existing product families. Clougherty was reorganized into Clougherty Packing, LLC (d/b/a Farmer John) after acquisition. Farmer John's operating results are reported in the Refrigerated Foods segment. Allocation of the final purchase price, including related costs, is presented in the table below.

(In Thousands)	
Current assets	$ 66,260
Goodwill	7,628
Other intangibles	21,400
Other assets	50
Property, plant, and equipment	139,585
Current liabilities	(26,704)
Purchase price (including related costs)	$208,219

On January 31, 2005, the company acquired Arriba Foods, Inc. (a/k/a Mexican Accent) for $48.0 million in cash, including related costs. Based in New Berlin, Wisconsin, Mexican Accent manufactures and distributes a wide variety of premium Mexican flour tortillas, corn tortillas, salsas, seasonings, and tortilla chips for retail markets and the foodservice industry. These products are marketed under the *Manny's*, *Gringo Pete's*, and *Mexican Accent* brands, and strengthen the company's presence in the ethnic products category. Mexican Accent's operating results are reported in the Grocery Products segment.

On March 30, 2005, the company acquired privately held Mark-Lynn Foods Inc. (Mark-Lynn) of Bremen, Georgia, for $43.2 million in cash, including related costs. Mark-Lynn manufactures and distributes a wide array of food products including salt and pepper packets, ketchup, mustard, sauces and salad dressings, creamers, sugar packets, jellies, desserts, and drink mixes. Mark-Lynn is managed by the Diamond Crystal Brands business unit and enhances the company's foodservice focus within the Specialty Foods segment.

On April 4, 2005, the company completed the acquisition of Lloyd's Barbeque Company (Lloyd's) for $50.5 million in cash, including related costs. Lloyd's has manufacturing operations in St. Paul, Minnesota, and offers a full range of barbeque products including original shredded pork, chicken and beef tubs, honey hickory shredded pork and chicken, barbeque pork spareribs, beef backribs, and pork babyback ribs, all under the *Lloyd's* brand name. Lloyd's products complement the company's existing offerings within the Refrigerated Foods segment, and is expected to enhance market share, particularly in the retail refrigerated entrée category.

Effective June 30, 2004, the company completed the sale of Vista International Packaging, Inc., the company's food packaging subsidiary. The company recorded an $18.1 million pre-tax gain ($11.5 million after tax, or $.08 per share) in the third quarter of fiscal 2004 related to the sale.

On October 18, 2004, the company purchased the assets of Concept Foods, Inc. (Concept) for $17.1 million in cash. Concept, located in Alma, Kansas, was renamed Alma Foods upon acquisition. Alma Foods manufactures a wide variety of fully cooked entrees.

Operating results for each completed acquisition above are included in the company's consolidated statements of operations from the date of acquisition. Pro forma results of operations are not presented, as no acquisitions in 2006, 2005, or 2004 were considered material, individually or in the aggregate, to the consolidated company.

BJ Services
2006 Annual Report

3. Acquisitions of Businesses

On June 25, 2006, we acquired an additional 2% interest in our Algerian joint venture, Societe Algerienne de Stimulation de Puits Productures d'Hydrocarbures ("BJSP"), for $4.6 million, increasing our total ownership in BJSP to 51%. L'Enterprise de Services aux Puits ("ENSP"), an indirect subsidiary of Sonatrach, owns the remaining 49%. BJSP provides coiled tubing and cementing services to the Algerian market. Prior to obtaining controlling interest in BJSP, we accounted for the investment using the cost method, as we could not exercise significant influence over the entity. Following this transaction, which is being accounted for as a step-acquisition, we have control of BJSP and now consolidate the entity. In accordance with APB 18, *Equity Method of Accounting of Investments in Common Stock*, and ARB 51, *Consolidated Financial Statements*, we have retroactively adjusted beginning retained earnings to adopt the equity method of accounting for our ownership interest in previous periods. This adjustment resulted in a $8.3 million increase to beginning retained earnings as reflected in the consolidated statement of stockholders' equity and other comprehensive income. The statement of operations has not been restated as the impact of adopting the equity method was not material in any given period.

Following the transaction, the assets and liabilities and results of operations of BJSP are included in our consolidated results, in the International Pressure Pumping segment. The consolidation resulted in an increase of $42.4 million in total current assets (including approximately $14.1 million in cash), $12.1 million in total current liabilities, $19.3 million in minority interest and $0.2 million in goodwill. We are in the process of completing our purchase price allocation for this step acquisition. The pro forma financial information for this acquisition is not included as it is not material to our consolidated financial statements.

On August 15, 2006, we purchased substantially all of the operating assets of Dyna Coil of South Texas, Ltd., Dyna Coil Injection Systems, Inc. and Dynochem, Ltd. (collectively, "Dyna-Coil") for $61.7 million in cash. Dyna-Coil is focused on production optimization services, particularly the installation and service of capillary injection systems and associated products (production chemicals) mostly in the U.S. and Canada and is included in our production chemicals business in the Oilfield Services segment. The acquisition resulted in an increase of $8.2 million in total current assets, $3.4 million in property and equipment, $7.1 million of technology based intangibles and $42.9 million in goodwill. We are in the process of completing our purchase price allocation. The pro forma financial information for this acquisition is not included as it is not material to our consolidated financial statements.

The Shaw Group
2006 Annual Report

Note 4—Acquisitions

SFAS No. 141, "Business Combinations," requires that all acquisitions be recorded utilizing the purchase method of accounting which requires the cost of an acquired operation to be allocated to the assets acquired and liabilities assumed based on their estimated fair values. These estimates are revised during an allocation period as necessary when, and if, information becomes available to further define and quantify the value of the assets acquired and liabilities assumed. The allocation period generally does not exceed one year from the date of the acquisition. To the extent additional information to refine the original allocation becomes available during the allocation period, the allocation of the purchase price is adjusted and reflected as an adjustment to goodwill. Likewise, to the extent such information becomes available after the allocation period, such items are generally included in our operating results in the period that the settlement occurs or information is available to adjust the original allocation to a better estimate. These future adjustments, if any, may materially favorably or unfavorably impact our future consolidated financial position or results of operations.

In connection with potential acquisitions, we incur and capitalize certain transaction costs, which include legal, accounting, consulting and other direct costs. When an acquisition is completed, these costs are capitalized as part of the acquisition price. We routinely evaluate capitalized transaction costs and expense those costs related to acquisitions that are not likely to occur. Indirect acquisition costs, such as salaries, corporate overhead and other corporate services are expensed as incurred.

The operating results of the acquisitions accounted for as a purchase are included in our consolidated financial statements from the applicable date of the transaction.

The following is a description of the various acquisitions that have occurred during the past three fiscal years.

Energy Delivery Services, Inc.

Effective December 31, 2003, we acquired all of the common stock of Energy Delivery Services, Inc. (EDS) from Duke Energy Global Markets, Inc. for a total purchase price, including direct acquisition costs, of approximately $22.4 million of which $18.4 million was paid in cash and $4.0 million was paid through a transfer of the ownership of a portion of EDS's receivables to the seller. In connection with this acquisition, we also acquired equipment under capital leases of approximately $5.4 million which is reflected as a purchase price adjustment during the third quarter of fiscal 2004. EDS, renamed Shaw EDS, provides a full line of vertical services to utility companies seeking to upgrade, install and maintain their energy grids and is included in our Energy & Chemicals (E&C) segment. During the second quarter of fiscal 2005, we finalized our purchase price allocation. The total purchase price of $22.4 million was allocated as follows: $11.8 million of goodwill, $0.9 million in other intangibles including tradename and customer relationships, $11.8 million in accounts receivable, $9.6 million of equipment, $0.5 million in other assets, $0.5 million in cash, $5.4 million in capital lease obligations and $7.3 million of other liabilities.

Walt Disney
2006 Annual Report

Note 3. Significant Acquisitions and Dispositions and Restructuring and Impairment Charges

Acquisition of Pixar   On May 5, 2006 (the Closing Date), the Company completed an all stock acquisition of Pixar, a digital animation studio (the Acquisition). Disney believes that the creation of high quality feature animation is a key driver of success across many of its businesses and provides content useful across a variety of traditional and new platforms throughout the world. The acquisition of Pixar is intended to support the Company's strategic priorities of creating the finest content, embracing leading-edge technologies, and strengthening its global presence. The results of Pixar's operations have been included in the Company's consolidated financial statements since the Closing Date.

To purchase Pixar, Disney exchanged 2.3 shares of its common stock for each share of Pixar common stock, resulting in the issuance of 279 million shares of

Disney common stock, and converted previously issued vested and unvested Pixar equity-based awards into approximately 45 million Disney equity-based awards.

The Acquisition purchase price was $7.5 billion ($6.4 billion, net of Pixar's cash and investments of approximately $1.1 billion). The value of the stock issued was calculated based on the market value of the Company's common stock using the average stock price for the five-day period beginning two days before the acquisition announcement date on January 24, 2006. The fair value of the vested equity-based awards issued at the Closing Date was estimated using the Black-Scholes option pricing model, as the information required to use a binomial valuation model was not reasonably available.

In connection with the Acquisition, the Company recorded a non-cash, non-taxable gain from the deemed termination of the existing Pixar distribution agreement. Under our previously existing distribution agreement with Pixar, the Company earned a distribution fee that, based on current market rates at the Closing Date, was favorable to the Company. In accordance with EITF 04-1, *Accounting for Pre-Existing Relationships between the Parties to a Business Combination* (EITF 04-1), the Company recognized a $48 million gain, representing the net present value of the favorable portion of the distribution fee over the remaining life of the distribution agreement. In addition, the Company abandoned the Pixar sequel projects commenced by the Company prior to the acquisition and recorded a pre-tax impairment charge totaling $26 million, which represents the costs of these projects incurred through the abandonment date. These two items are classified in "Restructuring and impairment (charges) and other credits, net" in the Consolidated Statement of Income.

The Company allocated the purchase price to the tangible and identifiable intangible assets acquired and liabilities assumed based on their fair values, which were determined primarily through third-party appraisals. The excess of the purchase price over those fair values was recorded as goodwill, which is not amortizable for tax purposes. The fair values set forth below are subject to adjustment if additional information is obtained prior to the one-year anniversary of the Acquisition that would change the fair value allocation as of the acquisition date. The following table summarizes the allocation of the purchase price:

	Estimated Fair Value	Weighted Average Useful Lives (years)
Cash and cash equivalents	$ 11	
Cash and cash equivalents	1,073	
Prepaid and other assets	45	
Film costs	538	12
Buildings and equipment	225	16
Intangibles	233	17
Goodwill	5,557	
Total assets acquired	$7,682	
Liabilities	64	

	Estimated Fair Value	Weighted Average Useful Lives (years)
Deferred income taxes	123	
Total liabilities assumed	$ 187	
Net assets acquired	$7,495	

The weighted average useful life determination for intangibles excludes $164 million of indefinite-lived Pixar trademarks and tradenames. Goodwill of $4.8 billion, $0.6 billion, and $0.2 billion was allocated to the Studio Entertainment, Consumer Products, and Parks and Resorts operating segments, respectively.

The following table presents unaudited pro forma results of Disney as though Pixar had been acquired as of the beginning of the respective periods presented. These pro forma results do not necessarily represent what would have occurred if the Acquisition had taken place on the dates presented and does not represent the results that may occur in the future. The pro forma amounts represent the historical operating results of Disney and Pixar with adjustments for purchase accounting. The $48 million non-cash gain pursuant to EITF 04-1 has been included in net income in fiscal year 2006.

	Fiscal Year 2006 (unaudited)	Fiscal Year 2005 (unaudited)
Revenues	$34,299	$31,973
Income before cumulative effect of accounting change	3,395	2,682
Net Income	3,395	2,646
Earnings per share:		
Diluted	$ 1.52	$ 1.12
Basic	$ 1.56	$ 1.15

ABC Radio Transaction   On February 6, 2006, the Company and Citadel Broadcasting Corporation (Citadel) announced an agreement to merge the ABC Radio business, which consists of 22 of the Company's owned radio stations and the ABC Radio Network, with Citadel. The ESPN Radio and Radio Disney networks and station businesses are not included in the transaction. The merger is expected to occur after the ABC Radio business is distributed to Disney shareholders (the Distribution). The agreement was subsequently amended on November 19, 2006. Under the amended terms, (i) Disney's stockholders are expected to collectively hold approximately 57% of Citadel's common stock post-merger, and (ii) the Company would retain between $1.10 billion and $1.35 billion in cash, depending upon the market price of Citadel's common stock over a measurement period ending prior to the closing. This cash will be obtained from loan proceeds raised by ABC Radio from a third party lender prior to the Distribution. Based on Citadel's stock price on November 20, 2006, the Company estimates that the aggregate value of the retained cash and Citadel common stock to be received by Disney shareholders would be approximately $2.5 billion. The amended agreement provides that the closing will occur no earlier than May 31, 2007, subject to regulatory approvals, and that either party may terminate the agreement if the closing does not occur by June 15, 2007.

Other Dispositions   The following disposals occurred during fiscal 2006 and fiscal 2005:

- A cable television equity investment in Spain was sold on November 23, 2005, resulting in a pre-tax gain of $57 million
- The Discover Magazine business was sold on October 7, 2005, resulting in a pre-tax gain of $13 million
- The Mighty Ducks of Anaheim was sold on June 20, 2005, resulting in a pre-tax gain of $26 million.

These gains were reported in "Gains on sale of equity investment and businesses" in the Consolidated Statements of Income.

Effective November 21, 2004, the Company sold substantially all of The Disney Store chain in North America under a long-term licensing arrangement to a wholly-owned subsidiary of The Children's Place (TCP). The Company received $100 million for the working capital transferred to the buyer at the closing of the transaction. During fiscal 2005, the Company recorded a loss on the working capital that was transferred to the buyer and additional restructuring and impairment charges related to the sale (primarily for employee retention and severance and lease termination costs) totaling $32 million. Pursuant to the terms of sale, The Disney Store North America retained its lease obligations related to the stores transferred to the buyer and became a wholly owned subsidiary of TCP. TCP is required to pay the Company a royalty on substantially all of the physical retail store sales beginning on the second anniversary of the closing date of the sale.

During the year ended September 30, 2004, the Company recorded $64 million of restructuring and impairment charges related to The Disney Store. The bulk of these charges were impairments of the carrying value of fixed assets related to the stores to be sold.

Other Acquisitions   On February 17, 2004, the Company acquired the film library and intellectual property rights for the *Muppets* and *Bear in the Big Blue House* for $68 million. Substantially all of the purchase price was allocated to amortizable intangible assets.

Note 4. Investments

Investments consist of the following:

	September 30, 2006	October 1, 2005
Investments, equity basis[1]	**$1,075**	$1,062
Investments, other	**188**	112

	September 30, 2006	October 1, 2005
Investment in aircraft leveraged leases	52	52
	$1,315	$1,226

(1) Equity investments consist of investments in affiliated companies over which the Company has significant influence but not the majority of the equity or risks and rewards.

Investments, Equity Basis A summary of combined financial information for equity investments, which include cable investments such as A&E Television Networks (37.5% owned), Lifetime Entertainment Services (50.0% owned), and E! Entertainment Television (39.6% owned), is as follows:

	2006	2005	2004
Results of Operations:			
Revenues	**$4,447**	$4,317	$3,893
	$1,170	$1,275	$1,017
Net Income			

	September 30, 2006	October 1, 2005
Balance Sheet:		
Current assets	**$2,620**	$2,323
Non-current assets	**1,562**	1,399
	$4,182	$3,722
Current liabilities	**1,048**	929
Non-current liabilities	**1,154**	915
Shareholders' equity	**1,980**	1,878
	$4,182	$3,722

Investments, Other As of September 30, 2006 and October 1, 2005, the Company held $82 million and $62 million, respectively, of securities classified as available-for-sale. As of September 30, 2006 and October 1, 2005, the Company also held $106 million and $50 million, respectively, of non-publicly traded cost-method investments.

In 2006, the Company had no realized gain or loss on sales of securities. In 2005 and 2004, the Company recognized $14 million and $2 million, respectively, in net gains on sales of securities. Realized gains and losses are determined principally on an average cost basis.

In 2006, the Company had no charges for other-than-temporary losses in value of investments. In 2005 and 2004, the Company recorded non-cash charges of $42 million and $23 million, respectively, to reflect other-than-temporary losses in value of certain investments.

Investment in Aircraft Leveraged Leases During the fourth quarter of 2005, the Company recorded a $101 million pre-tax charge, or $0.03 per share, to write-off its remaining investment in aircraft leveraged leases with Delta Air Lines, Inc.

(Delta) resulting from Delta's bankruptcy filing in September 2005. During the fourth quarter of 2004, the Company recorded a $16 million pre-tax charge to write down its leveraged lease investment in Delta consistent with our agreement with Delta to reduce lease payments. These charges were reported in "Net interest expense" in the Consolidated Statements of Income. Based on Delta's bankruptcy filing, we believe it is unlikely that the Company will recover these investments. In the event of a material modification to the Delta aircraft leases or foreclosure of the remaining Delta aircraft by the debt holders, certain tax payments of up to $40 million, as of September 30, 2006, could be accelerated. The expected tax payments are currently reflected on our balance sheet as a deferred tax liability and are not expected to result in a further charge to earnings. Our remaining aircraft leveraged lease investment of $52 million is with FedEx Corp.

Monsanto
2005 Annual Report

Note 5. Business Combinations

In first quarter fiscal year 2005, Monsanto acquired the canola seed businesses of Advanta Seeds (Advanta) from Advanta B.V., including the Advanta Seeds brand in Canada and the Interstate seed brand in the United States, for $52 million in cash (net of cash acquired), inclusive of transaction costs of $2 million. The addition of these canola seed businesses reinforces Monsanto's commitment to the canola industry and is intended to strengthen Monsanto's ability to bring continued technology innovations to canola growers. The transaction was completed on Sept. 8, 2004, from which time the operating results of this acquisitions were included in the company's consolidated financial statements.

In first quarter fiscal year 2005, Monsanto formed American Seeds, Inc. (ASI), a holding company established to support regional seed businesses with capital, genetics and technology investments. In November 2004, ASI acquired Channel Bio Corp. for $104 million in cash (net of cash acquired) and $15 million in assumed liabilities paid in second quarter 2005. In third quarter 2005, ASI, through its Channel Bio subsidiary, acquired NC+ Hybrids, Inc. for $40 million in cash (net of cash acquired). In addition to these purchase amounts, ASI paid transaction costs of $4 million for these acquisitions. Channel Bio and NC+ Hybrids are U.S. seed companies that sell, market and distribute primarily corn and soybean seeds, Channel Bio is an independent operating company of ASI. As a result of the NC+ Hybrids acquisition, Channel Bio markets its products through four brands: Crow's, Midwest Seed Genetics, NC+ Hybrids and Wilson Seeds. The acquisitions of Channel Bio and NC+ Hybrids are expected to provide Monsanto with additional opportunity for growth by accelerating the delivery of technology advances through these companies' strong customer relationships, local brands and quality service. The Channel Bio transaction was completed on March 1, 2005, from which time the operating results of this acquisition were included in the company's consolidated financial statements.

In third quarter fiscal year 2005, Monsanto acquired Seminis, Inc. for $1.0 billion in cash (net of cash acquired), inclusive of transaction costs of $23 million, and paid $495 million for the repayment of its outstanding debt. The acquisition was completed on March 23, 2005, from which time the operating results of this acquisition were included in the company's consolidated financial statements. Marinet Investments, LLC, which prior to the closing was a holder of co-investment rights in Seminis, elected to reduce the cash payment to which it was entitled upon completion of the transaction by $0 million in exchange for a contingent payment of up to $125 million based on the achievement of certain cumulative net sales targets over the 36-month period ending Sept. 30, 2007, or certain other factors. The cash portion of the acquisition was funded with cash on hand plus commercial paper borrowings of $600 million issued in March 2005. Prior to the closing of the transaction, Seminis initiated a tender offer to redeem all of its outstanding 10 $1/4$% Senior Subordinated Notes. In April 2005, payments totalling $390 million were made to settle tender offers and were funded with commercial paper borrowings.

Seminis is the global leader in the vegetable and fruit seed industry, and its brands (including Seminis, Royal Sluis, Asgrow and Petoseed) are among the most recognized in the vegetable and fruit segment of the agricultural industry. Seminis supplies more than 3,500 seed varieties to commercial fruit and vegetable growers, dealers, distributors and wholesalers in more than 150 countries. The acquisition of Seminis is expected to provide Monsanto with an opportunity for growth in the vegetable and fruits seen industry. In order to enhance connections among Monsanto and Seminis employees, including the application of back-shop technology advancements across certain support functions, Monsanto is finalizing plans to integrate certain support services of Seminis with its other businesses. In connection with this integration, in September 2005, Monsanto and the chief executive officer of Seminis have agreed that he will assist in the integration and will resign by Dec. 31, 2005. Monsanto is assessing whether the termination of his employment will accelerate the timing of the contingent payment discussed above. Any such payment would be reflected as an increase in the purchase price of Seminis, which would increase goodwill, and would require a use of cash by Monsanto.

In third quarter fiscal year 2005, Monsanto acquired Emergent Genetics, Inc. and Emergent Genetics India Ltd. (collectively, "Emergent" or "the Emergent acquisition") for $306 million (net of cash acquired), inclusive of transaction costs of $8 million. With its Stoneville and Nexgen brands in the United States and Mahalazmi and Paras brands in India, Emergent is the third-largest cotton see business in the United States, has two strong cotton see brands in India and has a solid presence in several other smaller cotton-growing markets around the world. The addition of the Emergent brands completes a strategic cotton germplasm and traits platform, which was modeled on the company's leading corn and soybean strategy. This cotton platform is expected to provide Monsanto with opportunities to deliver breeding advances and biotechnology traits in the cotton seed market. The transaction was completed on April 5, 2005, from which time the operating results of this acquisition were included in the company's consolidated financial statements. The cash portion of the acquisition was funded with $284 million of commercial paper borrowing issued in April 2005. Debt of $16 million was also assumed in the transaction.

For all fiscal year 2005 acquisitions described above, the business operations and employees of the acquired entities were added into the Seeds and Genomics segment results upon acquisition. These acquisitions were accounted for as purchase transactions. Accordingly, the assets and liabilities of the acquired entities were recorded at their estimated fair values at the dates of the acquisitions. The purchase price allocations for all fiscal year 2005 acquisitions as of Aug. 31, 2005, are preliminary and are summarized in the following table. The purchase price allocations for Advanta, Channel Bio and NC+ Hybrids are summarized as "All Other Acquisitions" in the table.

(Dollars in millions)	Seminis	Emergent	All Other Acquisitions	Aggregate Acquisitions
Current Assets	$ 707	$ 74	$ 107	$ 888
Property, Plant and Equipment	305	17	7	329
Goodwill	194	160	163	517
Other Intangible Assets	664	92	53	809
Acquired In-process Research and Development	200	48	18	266
Other Assets	100	2	8	110
Total Assets Acquired	2,170	393	356	2,919
Current Liabilities	759	48	108	915
Other Liabilities	335	20	31	386
Total Liabilities Assumed	1,094	68	139	1,301
Net Assets Acquired	$1,076	$ 325	$ 217	$1,618
Supplemental Information:				
Net assets acquired	$1,076	$ 325	$ 217	$1,618
Cash acquired	(56)	(19)	(2)	(77)
Cash paid, net of cash acquired	$1,020	$ 306	$ 215	$1,541

The primary items that generated the goodwill were the premium paid by the company for the right to control the businesses acquired and for the direct-to-farmer and farmer-dealer distribution networks (specific to the ASI acquisitions), and the value of the acquired assembled workforces. None of the goodwill is deductible for tax purposes.

As of the acquisition dates, management began to assess and formulate plans to integrate or restructure the acquired entities. These activities are accounted for in accordance with EITF 95-3, Recognition of Liabilities in Connection with a Purchase Business Combination (EITF 95-3), and primarily include the potential closure of facilities, the abandonment or redeployment of equipment, and employee terminations or relocations. Estimated integration costs of $7 million have been recorded and are recognized as current liabilities in the purchase price allocations above. As of Aug. 31, 2005, $3 million has been charged against these liabilities, primarily related to payments for employee terminations and relocations. Management is finalizing plans to integrate or restructure certain activities of Seminis and the Emergent India business. The plans for Seminis and the Emergent India business include employee terminations and relocations, exiting certain product lines and facility closures. In first quarter 2006, the company expects to record additional liabilities of approximately $20 million related to Seminis and the Emergent India business, which will be considered part of the purchase price allocation of the acquired companies. As these plans had not been finalized, these liabilities were not recorded as of Aug. 31, 2005.

The following table presents details of the acquired identifiable intangible assets:

(Dollars in millions)	Weighted Average Life (Years)	Useful Life (Years)	Seminis	Emergent	All Other Acquisitions	Aggregate Acquisitions
Acquired Germplasm	30	20-30	$295	$16	$10	$321
Acquired Biotechnology Intellectual Property	6	4-10	116	56	31	203
Trademarks	29	4-30	91	12	5	108
Customer Relationships	14	8-15	162	8	6	176
Other	4	3-5	–	–	1	1
Other Intangible Assets			$664	$92	$53	$809

Charges of $266 million were recorded in research and development (R&D) expenses in fiscal year 2005, for the write-off of acquired in-process R&D (IPR&D). Management believed that the technological feasibility of the IPR&D was not established and that the research had no alternative future uses. Accordingly, in accordance with generally accepted accounting principles.

The following unaudited pro forma financial information presents the combined results of operations of the company and the company's significant acquisitions (Seminis and Emergent) as if these acquisitions had occurred at the beginning of the periods presented. The pro forma results are not necessarily indicative of what actually would have occurred had the acquisitions been in effect for the periods presented and should not be taken as representative of Monsanto's future consolidated results of operations. Pro forma results were as follows for fiscal years 2005 and 2004:

(Dollars in millions, except per share)	2005	Year ended Aug. 31 2004
Net Sales	$6,672	$6,021
Net Income	524	206
Net Income per Basic Share	$ 1.96	$ 0.78
Net Income per Diluted Share	1.92	0.77

The pro forma information contains the actual combined operating results of Monsanto, Seminis and Emergent, with the results prior to the acquisition date adjusted to include the amortization of the acquired intangible assets presented above. The pro forma results exclude the write-off of acquired IPR&D and the increase in cost of goods sold due to the revaluation of inventory related to the Seminis and Emergetn acquisitions.

The historical financial information for Seminis includes charges of $32 million in the 12 months ended Aug. 31, 2004, related to one-time legal and professional fees and other costs directly attributable to a prior acquisition transaction. The historical financial information for Seminis also includes non-recurring costs under the previous ownership structure of $8 million and $11 million for fiscal year 2005 and 2004 respectively. In addition, interest costs related to Seminis debt have not been removed from the historical Seminis results. However, as discussed above, Seminis debt of $495 million, with a weighted average interest rate of approximately 10%, was repaid subsequent to the acquisition date, while interest expense on commercial paper issued to fund repayments of the debt was at an interest rate of approximately 3%. In July 2005, Monsanto issued $400 million of $5^1/2$% Senior Notes, which allowed the company to pay down the commercial paper borrowings. See Note 13—Debt and Other Credit Arrangement—for further discussion of the 5 $1/2$% Senior Notes due July 15, 2035.

National Semiconductor
2005 Annual Report

Note 4: Acquisitions

We did not have any acquisitions in fiscal 2005 and 2004. During fiscal 2003, we completed the acquisition of DigitalQuake, Inc., a development stage enterprise engaged in the development of flat panel display products located in Campbell, California in August 2002. DigitalQuake capabilities and products, which include a fourth-generation scaling solution, a triple analog-to-digital converter and an advanced digital video interface with encryption/decryption technologies, were intended to enhance our offerings of system solutions for flat panel display applications.

The purchase was completed through a step-acquisition where during the six months prior to the closing we acquired approximately a 30 percent equity interest through investments totaling $6.4 million. In August 2002, the remaining equity interest was acquired for additional consideration of $14.8 million. Of this amount, we paid $12.7 million upon the closing of the transaction and recorded the remaining liability of $2.1 million to be paid in 2 installments over the following two years. We allocated $18.6 million of the total purchase price to developed technology, $1.9 million to net tangible assets, and $0.7 million to in-process research and development. The in-process research and development was expensed upon completion of the acquisition and is included as a component of other operating income, net in the consolidated statement of operations for fiscal 2003. No amounts were allocated to goodwill since this development stage enterprise was not considered a business. The developed technology is an intangible asset that is being amortized over its estimated useful life of six years.

Employees and former shareholders of DigitalQuake were to receive additional contingent consideration of up to $9.9 million if certain revenue targets were achieved over the 24 months following the acquisition. The contingent consideration was to be recognized when it was probable that the revenue targets would be achieved. Of the total contingent consideration, $5.7 million was also contingent on future employment and was to be treated as compensation expense. The remainder was to be treated as an additional part of the purchase price. Since the revenue targets were not achieved by August 2004, no such amounts have been recognized.

Pro forma results of operations related to this acquisition have not been presented since the results of its operations were immaterial in relation to National.

Coca Cola
2004 Annual Report

Note 18: Acquisitions and Investments

During 2004, our Company's acquisition and investment activity totaled approximately $267 million, primarily related to the purchase of trademarks, brands and related contractual rights in Latin America, none of which was individually significant.

During 2003, our Company's acquisition and investment activity totaled approximately $359 million. These acquisitions included purchases of trademarks, brands and related contractual rights of approximately $142 million, none of which was individually significant. Refer to Note 4. Other acquisition and investing activity totaled approximately $217 million, and with the exception of the acquisition of Truesdale, none was individually significant. In March 2003, our Company acquired a 100 percent ownership interest in Truesdale from CCE for cash consideration of approximately $58 million. Truesdale owns a non-carbonated beverage production facility. The purchase price was allocated primarily to property, plant and equipment acquired. No amount was allocated to intangible assets. Truesdale is included in our North America operating segment.

During 2002, our Company's acquisition and investment activity totaled approximately $1,144 million. Included in this $1,144 million, our Company paid $544 million in cash and recorded a note payable of approximately $600 million to finance the CCEAG acquisition described below. In November 2001, we entered into the Control and Profit and Loss Transfer Agreement ("CPL") with CCEAG. Under the terms of the CPL, our Company acquired management control of CCEAG. In November 2001, we also entered into a Pooling Agreement with certain shareowners of CCEAG that provided our Company with voting control of CCEAG. Both agreements became effective in February 2002, when our Company acquired control of CCEAG for a term ending no later than December 31, 2006. CCEAG is included in our Europe, Eurasia and Middle East operating segment. As a result of acquiring control of CCEAG, our Company is working to help focus its sales and marketing programs and assist in developing the business. This transaction was accounted for as a business combination, and the results of CCEAG's operations have been included in the Company's consolidated financial statements since February 2002. Prior to February 2002, our Company accounted for CCEAG under the equity method of accounting. As of December 31, 2002, our Company had approximately a 41 percent ownership interest in the outstanding shares of CCEAG. In return for control of CCEAG, pursuant to the CPL we guaranteed annual payments, in lieu of dividends by CCEAG, to all other CCEAG shareowners. These guaranteed annual payments equal 0.76 euro for each CCEAG share outstanding. Additionally, all other CCEAG shareowners entered into either a put or a put/call option agreement with the Company, exercisable at any time up to the December 31, 2006 expiration date. In 2003, one of the other shareowners exercised its put option which represented approximately 29 percent of the outstanding shares of CCEAG. All payments related to the exercise of the put options will be made in 2006. Our Company entered into either put or put/call agreements for shares representing approximately a 59 percent interest in CCEAG. The spread in the strike prices of the put and call options is approximately 3 percent.

As of the date of the transaction, the Company concluded that the exercise of the put and/or call agreements was a virtual certainty based on the minimal differences in the strike prices. We concluded that either the holder of the put option would require the Company to purchase the shares at the agreed-upon put strike price, or the Company would exercise its call option and require the shareowner to tender its shares at the agreed-upon call strike price. If these puts or calls are exercised, the actual transfer of shares would not occur until the end of the term of the CPL. Coupled with the guaranteed payments in lieu of dividends for the term of the CPL, these instruments represented the financing vehicle for the transaction. As such, the Company determined that the economic substance of the transaction resulted in the acquisition of the remaining outstanding shares of CCEAG and required the Company to account for the transaction as a business combination. Furthermore, the terms of the CPL transferred control and all of the economic risks and rewards of CCEAG to the Company immediately.

The present value of the total amount likely to be paid by our Company to all other CCEAG shareowners, including the put or put/call payments and the guaranteed annual payments in lieu of dividends, was approximately $1,041 million at December 31, 2004. This amount increased from the initial liability of approximately $600 million due to the accretion of the discounted value to the ultimate maturity of the liability, as well as approximately $350 million of translation adjustment related to this liability. This liability is included in the line item other liabilities. The accretion of the discounted value to its ultimate maturity value is recorded in the line item other income (loss)—net, and this amount was approximately $58 million, $51 million, and $38 million, respectively, for the years ended December 31, 2004, 2003, and 2002.

In July 2002, our Company and Danone Waters of North America, Inc. ("DWNA") formed a new limited liability company, CCDA Waters, L.L.C. ("CCDA"), for the production, marketing, and distribution of DWNA's bottled spring and source water business in the United States. In forming CCDA, DWNA contributed assets of its retail bottled spring and source water business in the United States. These assets included five production facilities, a license for the use of the Dannon and Sparkletts brands, as well as ownership of several value brands. Our Company made a cash payment to acquire a controlling 51 percent equity interest in CCDA and is also providing marketing, distribution, and management expertise. This transaction was accounted for as a business combination, and the consolidated results of CCDA's operations have been included in the Company's consolidated financial statements since July 2002. This business combination expanded our water brands to include a national offering in all sectors of the water category with purified, spring and source waters. CCDA is included in our North America operating segment.

In January 2002, our Company and Coca-Cola Bottlers Philippines, Inc. ("CCBPI") finalized the purchase of RFM Corp.'s ("RFM") approximate 83 percent interest in Cosmos Bottling Corporation ("CBC"), a publicly traded Philippine beverage company. CBC is an established carbonated soft-drink business in the Philippines and is included in our Asia operating segment. The original sale and purchase agreement with RFM was entered into in November 2001. As of the date of this sale and purchase agreement, the Company began supplying concentrate for this operation. The purchase of RFM's interest was finalized on January 3, 2002. In March 2002, a tender offer was completed with our Company and CCBPI acquiring all shares of the remaining minority share-owners except for shares representing a 1 percent interest in CBC. This transaction was accounted for as a business combination, and the results of CBC's operations were included in the Company's consolidated financial statements from January 2002 to March 2003.

The Company and CCBPI agreed to restructure the ownership of the operations of CBC, and this transaction was completed in April 2003. This transaction resulted in the Company acquiring all the trademarks of CBC, and CCBPI owning approximately 99 percent of the outstanding shares of CBC. Accordingly, CBC was deconsolidated by the Company. No gain or loss was recorded by our Company upon completion of the transaction, as the fair value of the assets exchanged was approximately equal. Additionally, there was no impact on our cash flows related to this transaction.

Our Company acquired controlling interests in CCDA and CBC for a total combined consideration of approximately $328 million. As of December 31, 2003, the Company allocated approximately $56 million of the purchase price for these acquisitions to goodwill and $208 million to other indefinite-lived intangible assets, primarily trademarks, brands and licenses. This goodwill is all related to the CCDA acquisition and is allocated to our North America operating segment.

The combined 2002 net operating revenues of CCEAG, CBC, and CCDA were approximately $1.3 billion.

The acquisitions and investments have been accounted for by the purchase method of accounting. Their results have been included in our consolidated financial statements from their respective dates of acquisition. Assuming the results of these businesses had been included in operations commencing with 2002, pro forma financial data would not be required due to immateriality.

Sherwin Williams
2004 Annual Report

Note 2—Acquisitions

During the second quarter of 2004, the Company acquired a majority interest in Kinlita for $6,982 paid in cash. Kinlita, included in the Automotive Finishes Segment, supplies coatings to original equipment truck and bus manufacturers in the Peoples Republic of China. The acquisition was accounted for as a purchase, with results of operations included in the consolidated financial statements beginning with the month of April 2004. The Kinlita acquisition resulted in the recognition of goodwill and was completed primarily to participate in the growing Chinese automotive coatings market. See Note 4 for discussion of goodwill acquired with the acquisition of Kinlita.

During the third quarter of 2004, the Company completed its acquisitions of 100% of the stock of Duron, Inc. (Duron) and Paint Sundry Brands Corporation (PSB) for an aggregate consideration of $640,625, and the assumption of certain financial obligations. Both acquisitions were financed through the use of cash, liquidated short-term investments and $350,000 in proceeds from the sale of commercial paper under the Company's existing commercial paper program. Both acquisitions were accounted for as purchases, with results of operations included in the consolidated financial statements beginning with the month of September 2004.

Duron, included in the Paint Stores Segment, is a leading coatings company in the eastern and southeastern portion of the United States servicing the professional painting contractor, builder and do-it-yourself markets through 229 company-operated stores. PSB, included in the Consumer Segment, provides high quality paint applicators to professional paint contractors and do-it-yourself users in the United States, Canada and the United Kingdom under the Purdy®, Bestt Liebco® and other brands. The Duron and PSB acquisitions resulted in the recognition of goodwill and were completed primarily to assist with the continued implementation of the Company's growth strategy of supplying high quality products and services to professional paint contractors and do-it-yourself users through various channels of distribution. See Note 4 for discussion of goodwill and intangible assets acquired with the acquisitions of Duron and PSB. The following unaudited pro-forma summary presents consolidated financial information as if Kinlita, Duron and PSB had been acquired at the beginning of each period presented. The pro-forma consolidated financial information does not necessarily reflect the actual results that would have occurred had the acquisitions taken place on January 1, 2002 or of future results of operations of the combined companies under ownership and operation of the Company.

	2004	*2003*	*2002*
Net sales	**$6,450,573**	$5,878,713	$5,632,754
Net income[1]	**379,597**	363,411	152,024
Net income per common share:			
Basic:[1]	**2.70**	2.51	1.01
Diluted[1]	**2.62**	2.47	1.00

[1] Included in the reported pro-forma net income for 2004 are material charges of $30,500 paid by Duron for settlement of certain compensation arrangements incurred prior to closing and $4,781 paid by PSB for loan origination fees written off prior to closing.

Rockwell Collins
2005 Annual Report

3. Acquisitions

During the years ended September 30, 2005, 2004 and 2003, the Company completed two acquisitions that are summarized as follows:

(dollars in millions)	FISCAL YEAR ACQUIRED	CASH PURCHASE PRICE	GOODWILL	INTANGIBLE ASSETS	
				FINITE-LIVED	WEIGHTED AVERAGE LIFE IN YEARS
TELDIX GmbH	2005	$ 19	$ 45	$15	11
NLX Holding Corporation	2004	$126	$102	$17	5

On March 31, 2005, the Company acquired 100% of the stock of TELDIX GmbH (TELDIX), a leading provider of military aviation electronics products and services, based in Heidelberg, Germany. TELDIX supplies a broad portfolio of complex military aircraft computer products, advanced mechanical space mechanisms and related support services primarily to major prime contractors throughout Europe. The acquisition of TELDIX broadens the Company's European presence and provides complementary product lines that will allow the Company to enhance its offerings to customers worldwide and should provide new channel-to-market opportunities for the Company's current products and services. The purchase price, net of cash acquired, was $19 million. Based on preliminary valuation reports, the excess purchase price over net assets acquired reflects the Company's view that there are opportunities to expand its market share in the European region. Approximately 18 percent of the goodwill resulting from this acquisition is tax deductible. Goodwill is included within the assets of the Government Systems segment.

In December 2003, the Company acquired 100% of NLX Holding Corporation (NLX), a provider of integrated training and simulation systems. This business is now called Rockwell Collins Simulation and Training Solutions and provides simulators ranging from full motion simulators to desktop simulators, training, upgrades, modifications, and engineering and technical services primarily to branches of the United States military. The acquisition of Rockwell Collins Simulation and Training Solutions extends the Company's capabilities in the areas of training and simulation and enables the Company to provide a more complete service offering to its customers. The excess purchase price over net assets acquired reflects the Company's view that there are significant opportunities to expand its market share in the areas of simulation and training. Approximately 20 percent of the goodwill resulting from this acquisition is tax deductible. Goodwill is included within the assets of the Government Systems segment.

The results of operations of these acquired businesses are included in the Statement of Operations since their respective dates of acquisition. Pro forma financial information is not presented as the effect of these acquisitions is not material to the Company's results of operations.

Honeywell
2004 Annual Report

Note 2—Acquisitions

We acquired businesses for an aggregate cost of $396, $199, and $520 million in 2004, 2003, and 2002, respectively. All of our acquisitions were accounted for under the purchase method of accounting, and accordingly, the assets and liabilities of the acquired businesses were recorded at their estimated fair values at the dates of acquisition. Significant acquisitions made in these years are discussed below.

In May 2003, Honeywell sold its Engineering Plastics business to BASF in exchange for BASF's nylon fiber business and $90 million in cash. BASF's nylon fiber business became part of Specialty Materials' nylon business. Since the cash consideration received from BASF was in excess of 25 percent of the fair value of this exchange, this transaction was viewed as "monetary" in accordance with Issue 8(a) of EITF 01-2, "Interpretations of APB Opinion No. 29." Accordingly, the pre-tax gain on the sale of our Engineering Plastics business of $38 million was based on the fair value of the consideration received from BASF less the sum of the net book value of our Engineering Plastics business and related transaction costs. We recorded the assets and liabilities acquired in the BASF business at fair market value based on a valuation performed by an independent appraisal firm at the acquisition date which corresponded to the value agreed upon in the asset purchase agreement for this transaction. Specialty Materials' Engineering Plastics business and BASF's nylon fiber business both had annual sales of approximately $400 million.

In October 2002 we acquired Invensys Sensor Systems (ISS) for approximately $416 million in cash with $115 million allocated to tangible net assets,

$206 million allocated to goodwill, and $95 million allocated to other intangible assets with determinable lives. ISS is a global supplier of sensors and controls used in the medical, office automation, aerospace, HVAC, automotive, off road vehicle, and consumer appliance industries. ISS is part of our Automation and Control Products business in our Automation and Control Solutions reportable segment. ISS had sales of approximately $253 million in 2002.

In connection with all acquisitions in 2004, 2003, and 2002, the amounts recorded for transaction costs and the costs of integrating the acquired businesses into Honeywell were not material. The results of operations of all acquired businesses have been included in the consolidated results of Honeywell from their respective acquisition dates. The pro forma results for 2004, 2003, and 2002, assuming these acquisitions had been made at the beginning of the year, would not be materially different from reported results.

On December 13, 2004, we announced that we had reached agreement with the board of directors of Novar plc (Novar) on the terms of recommended Offers for the entire issued and ordinary preference share capital of Novar. The aggregate value of the Offers is $2.4 billion (fully diluted for the exercise of all outstanding options), including the assumption of approximately $580 million of outstanding debt, net of cash. The Novar board has unanimously recommended the Offers. We expect to complete the transaction in the first quarter of 2005 and to fund the acquisition with existing cash resources.

Novar is a UK listed holding company which operates globally in the electrical, electronic and control products, the aluminum extrusion and the security printing businesses and had reported 2003 revenues of $2.7 billion. We do not intend to hold the aluminum extrusion and security printing businesses in the long-term and expect to pursue strategic alternatives for these units as soon as practical.

Archer Daniels Midland
2003 Annual Report

Note 1—Acquisitions

On September 6, 2002, the Company acquired all of the outstanding Class A units of Minnesota Corn Processors, LLC (MCP), an operator of corn wet-milling plants in Minnesota and Nebraska. These Class A units represented 70% of the outstanding equity of MCP. Prior to September 6, 2002, the Company owned non-voting Class B units, which represented the remaining 30% of the outstanding equity of MCP. The acquisition was structured as a cash-for-stock transaction whereby the Company paid MCP shareholders a price of $2.90 for each outstanding Class A unit. The Company paid $382 million for the outstanding Class A units and assumed $233 million of MCP long-term debt. At the date of the MCP acquisition, the Company recognized $36 million in liabilities for the costs of closing MCP's administrative offices and terminating MCP's corn sweetener marketing joint venture. As of June 30, 2003, the Company has paid substantially all of the costs related to these activities. The operating results of MCP are included in the Company's net earnings from September 6, 2002. Prior to

September 6, 2002, the Company accounted for its investment in MCP on the equity method of accounting.

On February 24, 2003, the Company acquired six wheat flour mills located in the United Kingdom from Associated British Foods plc (ABF). The Company acquired the assets and inventories of the ABF mills for cash of approximately $96 million and assumed no liabilities in connection with the acquisition. The operating results of the ABF mills are included in the Company's net earnings from February 24, 2003.

During February 2003, the Company tendered an offer to acquire all of the outstanding shares of Pura plc (Pura), a United Kingdom based company that processes and markets edible oil, for cash of approximately $1.78 per share. These shares represented 72% of the outstanding equity of Pura. Prior to the offer, the Company owned 28% of the outstanding equity of Pura. The Company purchased a sufficient number of shares to obtain majority ownership of Pura on April 7, 2003, and the results of Pura's operations are included in the Company's net earnings from April 7, 2003. As of June 30, 2003, the Company had acquired all of the outstanding shares of Pura plc for cash of $58 million.

These acquisitions were accounted for as purchases in accordance with Statement of Financial Accounting Standards Number 141, "Business Combinations." Accordingly, the tangible assets and liabilities have been adjusted to fair values with the remainder of the purchase price recorded as goodwill. The identifiable intangible assets acquired as part of these acquisitions are not material. The Company has completed the allocation of the purchase price for the MCP acquisition. The Company has recorded a preliminary allocation of the purchase price for the ABF mills and Pura acquisitions as of June 30, 2003, as the valuation of the long-lived assets acquired and certain other transaction costs have not been finalized.

The following table summarizes the estimated fair values of the assets acquired and liabilities assumed, pertaining to the acquisitions described above, as of the acquisition dates.

	(In thousands)
Current assets	$ 198,709
Property, plant and equipment	695,874
Goodwill	124,586
Investments in unconsolidated affiliates	47,879
Other assets	7,397
Total assets acquired	1,074,445
Current liabilities	121,639
Long-term debt	255,772
Deferred income taxes	34,773
Other liabilities	21,269
Total liabilities assumed	433,453
Net assets acquired	640,992

	(In thousands)
Less equity method investments in MCP and Pura (including goodwill of $16,867) at date of acquisition, net of deferred taxes	105,146
Total purchase price	$535,846

Acquired goodwill related to these acquisitions of $12 million, $74 million, and $39 million was assigned to the Oilseeds Processing, Corn Processing, and Wheat Processing segments, respectively. The Company estimates approximately $106 million of the acquired goodwill will be deductible for tax purposes.

Pfizer
2004 Annual Report

2. Acquisitions

A. Pharmacia Corporation

Description of Acquisition

On April 16, 2003, Pfizer acquired Pharmacia for a purchase price of approximately $56 billion. The fair value of Pfizer equity items was derived using an average market price per share of Pfizer common stock of $29.81, which was based on Pfizer's average stock price for the period two days before through two days after the terms of the acquisition were agreed to and announced on July 15, 2002.

Under the terms of the merger agreement, each outstanding share of Pharmacia common stock was exchanged for 1.4 shares of Pfizer common stock in a tax-free transaction. Each share of Pharmacia Series C convertible perpetual preferred stock was exchanged for a newly created class of Pfizer Series. A convertible perpetual preferred stock with rights substantially similar to the rights of the Pharmacia Series C convertible perpetual preferred stock.

Pharmacia's core business was the development, manufacture and sale of prescription pharmaceutical products as well as the production and distribution of consumer healthcare products and animal healthcare products.

The following table summarizes the components of the purchase price:

(MILLIONS OF DOLLARS)	FAIR VALUE
Pfizer common stock	$54,177
Pfizer Series A convertible perpetual preferred stock[a]	462
Pfizer stock options[b]	1,102
Pharmacia vested share awards[c]	130
Other transaction costs	101
Total estimated purchase price	$55,972

(a) The estimated fair value of shares of a newly created class of Series A convertible perpetual preferred stock (see Note 13B, Equity and Stock Plans: Preferred Stock) was based on the same exchange ratio as for the Pharmacia common stock and a Pfizer stock price of $29.81.

(b) The estimated fair value of Pfizer stock options issued as of April 16, 2003 in exchange for Pharmacia outstanding stock options was calculated using the Black-Scholes option pricing model, modified for dividends, with model assumptions estimated as of April 16, 2003, and a Pfizer stock price of $29.81.

(c) The estimated fair value of unissued shares of fully vested awards was based on the same exchange ratio as for the Pharmacia common stock and a Pfizer stock price of $29.81. Awards can be settled in cash or shares, at the election of the program participant.

Allocation of Pharmacia Purchase Price

The purchase price allocation, finalized in the early part of 2004, was based on an estimate of the fair value of assets acquired and liabilities assumed.

(MILLIONS OF DOLLARS)	AMOUNT
Book value of net assets acquired	$ 8,795
Less: Recorded goodwill and other intangible assets	1,559
Tangible book value of net assets acquired	7,236
Remaining allocation:	
Increase inventory to fair value	2,939
Increase long-term investments to fair value	40
Decrease property, plant and equipment to fair value	(317)
Record in-process research and development charge	5,052
Record identifiable intangible assets(a)	37,066
Increase long-term debt to fair value	(370)
Increase benefit plan liabilities to fair value	(1,471)
Decrease other net assets to fair value	(477)
Restructuring costs(b)	(2,182)
Tax adjustments(c)	(12,947)
Goodwill(a)	21,403
Purchase price	$55,972

(a) See Note 11, Goodwill and Other Intangible Assets.
(b) See Note 3, Merger-Related Costs.
(c) See Note 5, Taxes on Income.

Since our interim allocation in the fourth quarter of 2003, the significant revisions to our estimates relate primarily to fixed assets ($756 million decrease), identifiable intangible assets ($155 million decrease), and tax adjustments ($645 million decrease). In addition, in 2004, we recorded an additional $604 million in restructuring charges as a component of the purchase price allocation.

The more significant revisions to our estimates relating to our initial allocation of the purchase price in the second quarter of 2003 include inventory ($1,331 million increase), fixed assets ($1,128 million decrease), identifiable intangible assets ($560 million increase), and tax adjustments ($986 million decrease). In addition, we recorded an additional $1,415 million in restructuring charges.

Pro Forma Results of Pharmacia Acquisition

The following unaudited pro forma financial information presents the combined results of operations of Pfizer and Pharmacia as if the acquisition had occurred as of the beginning of the years presented. The unaudited pro forma financial information is not necessarily indicative of what our consolidated results of operations actually would have been had we completed the acquisition at the beginning of each year. In addition, the unaudited pro forma financial information does not attempt to project the future results of operations of the combined company.

(MILLIONS OF DOLLARS, EXCEPT PER COMMON SHARE DATA) (UNAUDITED)	2003	2002
Revenues	**$48,292**	**$44,412**
Income from continuing operations before cumulative effect of change in accounting principles	8,265	9,167
Net income	10,536	7,373
Per share amounts:		
Income from continuing operations before cumulative effect of change in accounting principles per common share—basic	1.06	1.15
Net income per common share—basic	1.36	.92
Income from continuing operations before cumulative effect of change in accounting principles per common share—diluted	1.05	1.13
Net income per common share—diluted	1.34	.91

The unaudited pro forma financial information above reflects the following:

☐ The elimination of transactions between Pfizer and Pharmacia, which upon completion of the merger would be considered intercompany. The majority of these transactions occurred under the Celebrex and Bextra marketing agreements. This reflects:

— The elimination of certain sales, alliance revenue and certain copromotion expenses

— The elimination of certain impacts of milestone payments made by Pfizer to Pharmacia

☐ A decrease in interest expense of $11 million in 2003 and $38 million in 2002 related to the estimated fair value adjustment of long-term debt from the purchase price allocation

☐ Additional amortization and depreciation expense of approximately $993 million in 2003 and $3,311 million in 2002 related to the estimated fair value of identifiable intangible assets and property, plant, and equipment from the purchase price allocation

The unaudited pro forma financial information above excludes the following material, non-recurring charges incurred in the year ended December 31, 2003:

☐ Purchase accounting adjustments related to a charge for IPR&D of $5,052 million and the incremental charge of $2,747 million reported in Cost of sales for the sale of acquired inventory that was written up to fair value

B. Other Acquisitions

On February 10, 2004, we completed the acquisition of all of the outstanding shares of Esperion Therapeutics, Inc. (Esperion), a biopharmaceutical company with no approved products, for $1.3 billion in cash (including transaction costs). The allocation of the purchase price includes IPR&D of $920 million, which was expensed and is included in merger-related in-process research and development charges, and goodwill of $240 million, which has been allocated to our Human Health segment. Neither of these items is deductible for tax purposes.

On September 30, 2004, we completed the acquisition of Campto (irinotecan), from Sanofi-Aventis for $550 million in cash. Additional payments of up to $70 million will be payable upon obtaining regulatory approvals for additional indications in certain European countries. In connection with the acquisition, we recorded an intangible asset for developed technology rights of $525 million.

In 2004, we also completed several other acquisitions. The total purchase price associated with these transactions was approximately $430 million. In connection with these transactions, we expensed $151 million of IPR&D, which was included in merger related in-process research and development charges, and recorded $206 million in intangible assets, primarily brands (indefinite-lived), and developed technology rights.

3. Merger-Related Costs

We incurred the following merger-related costs primarily in connection with our acquisition of Pharmacia which was completed on April 16, 2003:

(MILLIONS OF DOLLARS)	2004	2003	2002
Integration costs:			
Pharmacia	$ 475	$ 838	$ 98
Other[a]	21	33	345
Restructuring costs:			
Pharmacia	704	177	–
Other[a]	(7)	10	187
Total merger-related costs—expensed	$1,193	$1,058	$630
Total merger-related costs—capitalized	$ 581	$1,578	$ –

[a] Includes costs incurred in connection with our merger with Warner-Lambert Company (Warner Lambert) which was completed on June 19, 2000.

A. Integration Costs

Integration costs represent external, incremental costs directly related to an acquisition, including expenditures for consulting and systems integration.

B. Restructuring Costs—Pharmacia

In connection with the acquisition of Pharmacia, Pfizer management approved plans throughout 2003 and 2004 to restructure the operations of both legacy Pfizer and legacy Pharmacia to eliminate duplicative facilities and reduce costs. The restructuring of our operations as a result of our acquisition of Pharmacia is expected to continue through at least 2005 and is expected to include severance, costs of vacating duplicative facilities, contract termination, and other exit costs. Total merger-related expenditures (income statement and balance sheet) expected to be incurred during 2003-2005 to achieve these synergies are about $6.0 billion, on a pre-tax basis. The remaining costs expected to be incurred are primarily associated with asset impairments, exist costs and employee terminations.

Restructuring Costs Associated with Legacy Pharmacia—Capitalized

We recorded, through April 15, 2004, restructuring costs associated primarily with employee terminations and exiting certain activities of legacy Pharmacia. These costs were recognized as liabilities assumed in the purchase business combination. Accordingly, the restructuring costs incurred in the first year after the acquisition are considered part of the purchase price of Pharmacia and have been recorded as an increase to goodwill. These restructuring costs also include costs associated with relocation. Restructuring costs after April 15, 2004 that are associated with legacy Pharmacia are charged to the results of operations. Changes to previous estimates of restructuring costs included as part of the purchase price allocation of Pharmacia are recorded as a reduction to goodwill or as an expense to operations, as appropriate. The components of the restructuring costs capitalized as a cost of the acquisition of Pharmacia follow:

(MILLIONS OF DOLLARS)	COSTS INCURRED			UTILIZATION THROUGH DEC. 31,	RESERVE* DEC. 31,
	2004	2003	TOTAL	2004	2004
Employee termination costs	$246	$1,289	$1,535	$1,469	$ 66
Other	335	289	624	499	125
	$581	$1,578	$2,159	$1,968	$191

* Included in Other current liabilities.

Through December 31, 2004, Employee termination costs represent the approved reduction of the legacy Pharmacia work force by 12,820 employees, mainly in corporate, manufacturing, distribution, sales and research. We notified affected individuals and 12,248 employees were terminated as of December 31, 2004. Employee termination costs include accrued severance benefits and costs associated with change-in-control provisions of certain Pharmacia employment contracts.

Restructuring Costs Associated with Legacy Pfizer and Legacy Pharmacia—Expensed

We have recorded restructuring costs associated with exiting certain activities of legacy Pfizer and legacy Pharmacia (from April 16, 2004), including severance, costs of vacating duplicative facilities, contract termination and other exit costs. These costs have been recorded as a charge to the results of operations and are included in Merger-related costs. The components of the restructuring costs associated with the acquisition of Pharmacia, which were expensed, follow:

(MILLIONS OF DOLLARS)	PROVISIONS			UTILIZATION THROUGH DEC. 31,	RESERVE* DEC. 31,
	2004	*2003*	*TOTAL*	*2004*	*2004*
Employee termination costs	**$377**	$140	$517	**$343**	**$174**
Asset impairments	**269**	21	290	**290**	–
Other	**58**	16	74	**30**	44
	$704	$177	$881	**$663**	**$218**

* Included in Other current liabilities.

Through December 31, 2004, Employee termination costs represent the approved reduction of the legacy Pfizer and legacy Pharmacia (from April 16, 2004) work force by 3,830 employees, mainly in corporate, manufacturing, distribution, sales and research. We notified affected individuals and 3,118 employees were terminated as of December 31, 2004. Employee termination costs include accrued severance benefits and costs associated with change-in-control provisions of certain Pharmacia employment contracts. Asset impairments primarily include charges to write-down property, plant, and equipment. Other primarily includes costs to exit certain activities of legacy Pfizer and legacy Pharmacia (from April 16, 2004).

Emerson Electric
2005 Annual Report

(3) Acquisitions and Divestitures

The Company acquired Do+Able, a manufacturer of ready-to-assemble wood and steel home and garage organization and storage products, which is included in the Appliance and Tools segment, in the second quarter of 2005 and Numatics, a manufacturer of pneumatic and motion control products for industrial applications, which is included in the Industrial Automation segment, in the fourth quarter of 2005. In addition to Do+Able and Numatics, the Company acquired several smaller businesses during 2005, mainly in the Process Management and Appliance and Tools segments. Total cash paid (including assumed debt of approximately $100, which was repaid in October 2005) and annualized sales for these businesses were approximately $466 and $430, respectively. Goodwill of $236 ($58 of which is expected to be deductible for tax purposes) and identifiable intangible assets of $122, which are being amortized on a straight-line basis over a weighted-average useful life of ten years, were recognized from these transactions in 2005. Third-party valuations of assets are in-process; thus, the allocations of the purchase prices are subject to refinement.

In the fourth quarter of 2004, the Company acquired the outside plant and power systems business of Marconi Corporation PLC, a leading provider of DC power products and engineering and installation services to major telecommunication carriers throughout North America, which is included in the Network Power segment. Marconi (renamed Emerson Network Power Energy Systems— North America) and several smaller businesses acquired during 2004 for a total of $414 in cash (net of cash and equivalents acquired) had annualized sales of approximately $430. Goodwill of $224 (substantially all of which is expected to be deductible for tax purposes) and intangible assets of $120 (all of which is being amortized on a straight-line basis with a weighted-average life of 14 years) were recognized from these transactions.

Several small businesses were also acquired during 2003. Due to challenging market conditions, Emerson began evaluating strategies during 2003 to maximize the value of the Jordan business (renamed Emerson Telecommunication Products, Inc. (Jordan)) acquired in 2000. In May 2003, the Board of Directors approved a plan to restructure Jordan in which all but one of its businesses would be retained by Emerson (and will continue to do business as Emerson Telecommunication Products, LLC (ETP)), and the Dura-Line fiber-optic conduit business would be sold. In June 2003, after the restructuring, the Jordan stock, including its Dura-Line operations, was sold for $6, resulting in a pretax loss of $87, which is reported as discontinued operations. In addition, an appraisal of the retained ETP business was performed. All of the businesses in the Network Power segment, including ETP, were reviewed for impairment and a goodwill impairment charge of $54 was recorded in the third quarter of 2003, the majority of which related to the ETP business. The restructuring and sale resulted in income tax benefits of $238 as the tax basis in the stock of these businesses significantly exceeded the carrying value primarily due to a goodwill impairment of $647 in 2002. Approximately $164 of the benefits were received in cash in 2004 due to the carryback of the capital loss against prior capital gains and application to current year capital gains, with the remainder expected to be received in subsequent years as the capital loss carryforward is utilized against future capital gains. The income tax benefits were recognized in the third quarter of 2003: $170 was associated with discontinued operations and $68 was associated with the retained ETP business.

The tax benefits from the restructuring of the ETP business net of the impairment charge contributed $14 ($0.03 per share) to continuing operations in 2003. The net gain of $83 from the sale of Jordan (including income tax benefit of $170) is reported as discontinued operations in the Consolidated Statements of Earnings. The operating results of Dura-Line are also classified as discontinued operations for 2003. Sales were $41 and the net loss was $7 for the year ended September 30, 2003. Other businesses divested in 2003 represented total annual sales of approximately $80 in 2002.

The results of operations of these businesses have been included in the Company's consolidated results of operations since the respective dates of acquisition and prior to the respective dates of divestiture.

Arvin Meritor
2005 Annual Report

5. Acquisitions and Divestitures

On October 4, 2004, the company formed two joint ventures in France with AB Volvo to manufacture and distribute axles. The company acquired its 51-percent interest for a purchase price of € 19.3 million ($25 million). Accordingly, beginning in the first quarter of fiscal year 2005, the results of operations and financial position of these joint ventures are consolidated by the company. The company has an option to purchase the remaining 49-percent interest in one of the joint ventures beginning in the first quarter of fiscal year 2008 for € 15.7 million ($19 million) plus interest at EURIBOR rates, plus a margin. This option to purchase the minority interest is essentially a financing arrangement as the minority shareholder does not participate in any profits or losses of the joint venture. Therefore, this is recorded as a long-term obligation of the company which is included in other liabilities (see Note 14). Accordingly, no minority interest is recognized for the 49-percent interest in this joint venture. The company recorded $4 million of goodwill associated with the purchase price allocation. In September 2005, as part of the purchase agreement, the company purchased approximately $5 million of additional machinery and equipment from AB Volvo.

In December 2004, the company completed the divestiture of its LVS Columbus, Indiana automotive stamping and components manufacturing business and recognized a pre-tax gain on the sale of $4 million. This divestiture is part of the company's plan to rationalize its operations and focus on its core automotive businesses. This manufacturing operation had sales of $83 million in fiscal year 2004.

As part of the company's continuing strategy to divest non-core businesses, in the third quarter of fiscal 2004, the company completed the sale of its CVS trailer beam fabrication facility in Kenton, OH. The divestiture of this facility is in line with the company's strategy to be less vertically integrated and more focused on its core processes for the design and assembly of complete systems. This divestiture did not have a material impact on sales or net income. Net proceeds from this divestiture were approximately $14 million.

In the second quarter of fiscal year 2004, the company completed the sale of its 75-percent shareholdings in AP Amortiguadores, S.A. (APA), a LVS joint venture that manufactured ride control products. Net proceeds from the sale were $48 million, resulting in a pre-tax gain of $20 million.

In 1998, the company acquired a 49-percent interest in Zeuna Stärker, a German air and emissions systems company. In the second quarter of fiscal year 2003, the company purchased the remaining 51-percent interest in Zeuna Stärker for a net purchase price of $69 million. The company recorded $111 million of goodwill associated with the purchase price allocation. Incremental sales from Zeuna Stärker were $203 million and $550 million in fiscal years 2004 and 2003, respectively.

The company divested its LVS exhaust tube manufacturing facility during the fourth quarter of fiscal year 2003. This divestiture is part of the company's long-term strategy to be less vertically integrated and to focus on core competencies. The company received $67 million in cash, resulting in a pre-tax gain of $36 million. The company will continue to purchase exhaust tubing from the buyer under a supply agreement that expires in 2006. Management concluded that due to the supply agreement terms, a portion of the gain should be deferred and recognized as a reduction of cost of sales over the supply agreement term. During fiscal year 2003, $20 million ($14 million after-tax, or $0.21 per diluted share) of the gain was recognized as a gain on divestiture, with the remaining amount to be recognized in fiscal years 2004 through 2006. This transaction had no material impact on the consolidated sales of the company. In connection with this transaction, the company used $23 million of the proceeds to repay a portion of long term debt associated with this facility.

The company completed the sale of net assets related to the manufacturing and distribution of its CVS off-highway planetary axle products in the second quarter of fiscal year 2003 for $36 million and recorded a pre-tax loss of $5 million. The company did not consider these products core to its commercial vehicle systems business.

Chapter 12
Consolidated Financial Statements[*]

CONTENTS

Consolidated financial statements present the financial position, operating results, and cash flows of the single economic entity comprised of a parent and one or more subsidiaries or variable interest entities that they control. Consolidated financial statements are believed to be more useful to users of financial information than the financial statements of individual companies that are related by ownership. Traditionally, consolidation takes place when the parent controls greater than 50% of the voting common shares of its subsidiary; however, the Financial Accounting Standards Board (FASB) has acknowledged that where control is exercised through contractual arrangements (known as variable interest) rather than direct ownership, consolidation is also required. Conversely,

* This chapter was co-authored by Jeffrey Satenstein, MS, CPA, Managing Director (retired) JPMorgan Chase Investment Bank, Lecturer, Accounting & Information Systems, Queens College, CUNY.

there are limited exceptions when majority owned subsidiaries are not consolidated.

This chapter is not applicable to a statutory merger, where an acquirer liquidates an acquiree and combines the acquiree's operations with that of the acquirer; or a statutory consolidation, where both the acquirer and acquiree company are liquidated and a new company is formed. Both statutory mergers and statutory consolidations are covered in Chapter 11, "Business Combinations."

This chapter explains the worksheet techniques used to consolidate a parent with one or more of its subsidiaries to achieve consolidated financial statements presented in accordance with generally accepted accounting principles (GAAP). As discussed in Chapter 11, "Business Combinations," the acquisition method will be emphasized in the examples, with comments made as to the differences between the acquisition and the "grandfathered" purchase and pooling of interest methods of accounting. It should be assumed that the parent company accounts for its investment in its consolidated subsidiaries using the equity method of accounting. It is important to note that when the parent accounts for its investment in its subsidiaries using a method other than the equity method (such as initial value or partial equity method), the consolidated results will be identical. What will differ is the consolidation worksheet entries used to achieve the consolidated results as well as the balance in the parent's investment account. Under the initial value method, the parent will record dividend income to the extent of its ownership percentage, and will not reflect any portion of the income of the subsidiary or amortization of fair value adjustments in its investment account. The partial equity method is identical to the equity method with respect to treatment of subsidiary income and dividends. The only difference is that under the partial equity method the parent does not reflect amortization of fair value adjustments on its books.

RELEVANT AUTHORITATIVE PRONOUNCEMENTS

The major authoritative pronouncements governing consolidated financial statements are ASC 805 and ASC 810. Relevant FASB Emerging Issues Task Force conclusions have been incorporated into ASC 805 and 810. The following discussion incorporates the most recent guidance.

According to Accounting Standards Update (ASU) No. 2010-02 (January 2010) (ASC 810, *Consolidation*), *Accounting and Reporting for Decreases in Ownership of a Subsidiary—a Scope Clarification*, a deconsolidation of a subsidiary by a parent is appropriate when the parent no longer has a controlling financial interest. This can occur when a parent sells all or part of its ownership interest (bringing its remaining ownership percentage below 50%); when a contractual agreement expires that gave the parent control; when the subsidiary issues additional shares of common stock resulting in the parent no longer having control; or when the subsidiary comes under regulatory, government, court, or administrative control (e.g., bankruptcy). A gain or loss is recognized by the parent equal to the difference between:

1. The fair value of consideration received plus the fair value of any retained noncontrolling interest plus the carrying (book) value of any noncontrolling interest in the former subsidiary; and

2. The carrying amount of the former subsidiary's assets and liabilities.

A parent's ownership changes if it buys, sells, or reacquires shares in the subsidiary. (ASC 810-10-45-22) A deconsolidation should include disclosure of the nature of activities, any related-party transaction, valuation method to determine fair value, fair value inputs, and resulting gain or loss. (ASC 810-10-50-1B)

Alternatively, when a parent that has a controlling financial interest sells or transfers a portion of its interest to a third party, but still retains control (greater than 50% ownership), the reduction in the parent's ownership interest is treated as an equity transaction. As a result, a gain or loss is not recorded, but instead is treated as an increase or decrease to Additional Paid in Capital.

Disclosure for a business combination includes the date of purchase, identification and description of the acquiree, percentage of ownership bought, way in which control of the targeted company occurred, accounting treatment for the combination, reasons for the combination, transaction description, issuance costs, information if the combination occurred in stages, fair value measurements, acquisition costs, valuation method, acquiree's profit after the purchase date, and profit for the combined company for a comparable previous period. (ASC 805, *Business Combinations*) (ASC 805-10-50-2)

EXCEPTIONS TO CONSOLIDATION OF MAJORITY OWNED SUBSIDIARIES

The usual condition for consolidation is ownership of a controlling financial interest, which is generally evidenced by direct ownership of greater than 50% of the outstanding voting shares of another company. However, over the years many companies excluded from consolidation certain "nonhomogeneous" subsidiary operations that were different in character than the parent. Consolidation is required even where the business activities of the parent and subsidiary significantly differ. However, the FASB in that statement did not address the practice of not consolidating subsidiaries, where control is likely to be temporary, for instance, when a subsidiary is in a legal reorganization under bankruptcy laws. Therefore, not consolidating subsidiaries where control is considered to be temporary continues to be acceptable.

Additionally, if a subsidiary operates under foreign exchange restrictions that are so severe that they hamper the ability of the parent to control the timing of subsidiary dividends, then consolidation is not appropriate. If one of these exceptions to consolidations applies, the parent should account for its investment in its unconsolidated subsidiary by the equity method.

STEPS TO ACHIEVE CONSOLIDATION

Under the acquisition, purchase, and pooling of interests methods, a consolidation worksheet is used to make the appropriate adjustments (discussed below) to report combined results of the parent and its subsidiaries in consolidated financial statements in accordance with the accounting rules in effect at the date the acquisition was completed. The worksheet consists of columns for the book values of the parent and subsidiaries, a column for worksheet adjustments, and a final column for consolidated totals. Figures for the parent and subsidiaries come from the final U.S. GAAP financial statements and use the accounting basis appropriate for transactions recorded on their individual books (e.g., historical cost or fair value). The parent's figures will include the balance for its Investment in Subsidiaries account along with equity earnings (when the equity method is used) and dividends received.

Eleven types of worksheet entries that may be appropriate, depending on the circumstances, are illustrated and discussed below. Worksheet entries are *not* posted to the general ledgers of either the parent or subsidiary companies (with the limited exception of push down accounting). While the parent does have the choice of accounting for its investment using the equity, cost, or partial equity methods, the consolidated results will be identical. Therefore, subsidiary earnings will be included as part of consolidated retained earnings.

A critical consolidation principle is that intercompany transactions between a parent and its consolidated subsidiaries must be eliminated in consolidation. The reason is that such transactions are not considered "arms length" or subject to independent pricing because they take place within the same economic entity. The result is that intercompany loans and borrowings, as well as dividends and intercompany sales, purchases, and unrealized gains on inventory transfers between parent and subsidiary must be eliminated. These are illustrated in the consolidation entries discussed below.

CONSOLIDATION WORKSHEET ENTRIES AND EXAMPLES

Consolidated financial statements consist of combining parent and subsidiary accounts and eliminating intercompany balances and transactions. Thus, all gains and losses on transactions between the parent and subsidiaries, or between subsidiaries, must be eliminated.

Intercompany eliminations include those for intercompany payables and receivables, advances, investments, and profits. The existence of a noncontrolling (minority) interest in a subsidiary does not affect the amount of intercompany profit to be eliminated. That is, the entire intercompany profit should be eliminated, not just the portion related to the controlling interest. In the case of certain regulated companies, intercompany profits do not need elimination to the degree that the profit constitutes a reasonable return on investment. Subsidiary investment in the parent's shares is not considered outstanding stock in the consolidated balance sheet.

Intercompany sales and purchases require elimination because revenue and expenses are not realized for consolidated purposes until the inventory is sold to outsiders. The elimination of intercompany profits will result in inventory being valued at cost on the consolidated balance sheet and is accomplished as indicated in the following discussion.

Intercompany profits in ending inventory are eliminated by crediting inventory and debiting cost of sales or retained earnings (if books are closed). Further, cost of sales and beginning retained earnings must be adjusted for intercompany profit in beginning inventory resulting from intercompany transactions in the prior year. Unless intercompany profits in inventories are eliminated, consolidated net income and ending inventory will be misstated.

If merchandise, including an intercompany profit, is reduced from the intercompany transfer price to market value and the reduction equals or exceeds the intercompany inventory profit, there is no need for a deferral of profit entry in consolidation. For example, if merchandise costing one affiliate $15,000 is sold to another affiliate for $18,000, who reduces it to market value of $16,500, the consolidated workpaper adjustment for unrealized intercompany profits should be only $1,500.

Following is a description of the most common consolidation worksheet entries to properly present consolidated financial statements in accordance with GAAP. As noted previously, these entries are not posted to the individual books of the parent or subsidiary, with the limited exception of when push down accounting (discussed later) is applicable. These entries are subsequently used in the illustrative examples. The descriptions that follow assume consolidation subsequent to the year of acquisition and that the parent uses the equity method of accounting to record its investment in its consolidated subsidiary:

1. Elimination of subsidiary capital as of January 1 of the year of reporting against the parent's investment account balance.

   Dr. Common stock (subsidiary)

   Dr. Additional paid in capital (subsidiary)

   Dr. Retained earnings (subsidiary)

      Cr. Investment in subsidiary (parent)

2. Recording of unamortized fair value adjustments and goodwill as of January 1 of the year of reporting.

   Dr. Fixed assets

   Dr. Inventory

   Dr. Intangible assets

   Dr. Goodwill

      Cr. Investment in subsidiary

   (Assumes fair value of consideration transferred exceeds carrying value at date of acquisition; if fair value of consideration transferred is less than carrying value at date of acquisition, a credit to gain on bargain purchase is substituted for the debit to goodwill.)

3. Elimination of subsidiary net income against equity earnings recorded by the parent (assumes parent company accounts for its investment in its subsidiary using the equity method). This entry assumes that the subsidiary has positive net income. The entry would be reversed if the subsidiary had a net loss.

Dr. Equity income

   Cr. Investment in subsidiary

4. Elimination of dividends paid by the subsidiary to the parent (assumes parent uses the equity method). This is an intercompany transaction within the economic entity of the parent and its subsidiary.

Dr. Investment in subsidiary

   Cr. Dividends paid

5. Recording of excess amortization on the fair value adjustments (entry 2) as applicable (e.g., applies to excess of fair value over book value of depreciable fixed assets at date of acquisition). Note that this entry would be reversed if the fair value was less than the book value at the date of acquisition.

Dr. Amortization expense

   Cr. Accumulated amortization-fixed assets

6. Elimination of intercompany receivables and payables (intercompany debt).

Dr. Payable from sub/parent

   Cr. Receivable from sub/parent

7. Elimination of interest income and expense on intercompany debt.

Dr. Interest income

   Cr. Interest expense

8. Elimination of intercompany sales and purchases between the parent and subsidiary.

Dr. Sales

   Cr. Cost of goods sold (purchases)

9. Elimination of intercompany profit on sale of inventory between the parent and subsidiary (in year of intercompany sale to the extent the inventory has not been sold to third parties).

Dr. Cost of goods sold

   Cr. Ending inventory

10. Elimination of intercompany purchases and sales.

Dr. Sales

   Cr. Purchases

11. Elimination of intercompany profit on unsold inventory, subsequent to the year of sale, when the ending inventory of the prior period becomes the beginning inventory of the current period.

Dr. Beginning inventory

   Cr. Cost of goods sold

EXAMPLE

Information from the individual and consolidated income statements and balance sheets of Hand Inc. and its subsidiary, Foot Company, for the year ended December 31, 20X2, and as of the year then ended are as follows:

	Hand	Foot	Consolidated
INCOME STATEMENT ACCOUNTS			
Revenues	$200,000	$140,000	$308,000
Cost of goods sold	150,000	110,000	231,000
Gross profit	$ 50,000	$ 30,000	$ 77,000
BALANCE SHEET ACCOUNTS			
Accounts receivable	$ 26,000	$ 19,000	$ 39,000
Inventory	30,000	25,000	52,000

ADDITIONAL DATA

During 20X4, Hand sold goods to Foot at the same markup on cost that Hand uses for all of its sales.

The following questions relate to the aforementioned data:

☐ What was the amount of intercompany sales from Hand to Foot during 20X4?

☐ What was the amount of Foot's payable to Hand for intercompany sales?

☐ In Hand's consolidated worksheet, what amount of unrealized intercompany profit was eliminated?

GAAP requires that in the preparation of consolidated financial statements, all intercompany transactions must be eliminated so that only those transactions between the consolidated entity and its outside parties are included in the financial statements.

The amount of intercompany sales from Hand to Foot must be ascertained from Hand's revenue, Foot's revenue, and consolidated revenues. Hand's revenue, it should be noted, includes intercompany sales to Foot. That is, part of the Hand's $200,000 includes sales that were made to Foot. The $308,000 of consolidated revenues represents the amount that has already been reduced for intercompany sales. Therefore, the amount of intercompany sales may be computed as follows:

Total combined revenues of Hand and Foot ($200,000 + 140,000)	$340,000
Less: consolidated revenues	308,000
Intercompany sales for 20X2	$ 32,000

The worksheet entry to eliminate this in consolidation is:

Dr. Sales (revenues)	32,000	
Cr. Purchases (cost of goods sold)		32,000

In computing the amount of Foot's payable to Hand, the consolidated balance sheet should include only those amounts due to or from those outside the consolidated entity. The computation, therefore, of Foot's payable to Hand may be computed as follows:

Total combined accounts receivable of Hand and Foot ($26,000 + 19,000)	$45,000
Less: consolidated receivables	39,000
Foot's payable to Hand for intercompany sales	$ 6,000

Finally, with respect to the inventory purchased by one member of the consolidated group from another, from the perspective of consolidated entity, the inventory must be stated at historical cost. That is, the difference between the selling price of the inventory and its historical cost at the date of consolidated financial statements should be considered unrealized intercompany profit and eliminated in consolidation. Thus, the following computation must be made to determine the unrealized intercompany (gross) profit in inventory that was eliminated:

Total combined inventory of Hand and Foot ($30,000 + $25,000)	$55,000
Less: consolidated inventory	52,000
Unrealized intercompany (gross) profit in ending inventory that was eliminated	$ 3,000

This unrealized gain is eliminated by the following worksheet entry:

Dr. Cost of goods sold	3,000	
Cr. Ending inventory		3,000

Profits or losses on sales or purchases before an affiliation are not adjusted in consolidation.

EXAMPLE

Intercompany Sale of Inventory

Page Company purchased inventory from its wholly owned subsidiary, Sage Company, during year ended December 31, 201X, as follows:

	Selling Price	Cost	Gross Profit
Beginning inventory	400,000	320,000	80,000
Purchases	700,000	560,000	140,000
Ending inventory	300,000	240,000	60,000
Cost of goods sold	800,000	640,000	160,000

The worksheet entry to eliminate intercompany profits is as follows:

Dr. Retained earnings—Page	80,000	
Dr. Intercompany sales—Page	700,000	
Cr. Intercompany cost of goods sold—Page		560,000

Cr. Cost of goods sold—Page		160,000
Cr. Inventories—Sage		60,000

All intercompany receivables, payables, notes, and advances are eliminated for the purposes of consolidation. An illustrative entry is:

Dr. Accounts (notes) payable	xx	
Cr. Accounts (notes) receivable		xx

If the balance sheet includes discounted receivables from another affiliate, it must be eliminated by debiting discounted receivables and crediting receivables. As to notes receivable, where the holder of an intercompany note has discounted the instrument with an outsider, the contingent liability for notes receivable discounted is considered a primary liability.

When an intercompany sale/purchase of a fixed asset occurs, such assets remain within the consolidated group. Intercompany profits on the sale and/or acquisition of fixed assets between affiliates are eliminated in consolidation so as to reflect the carrying value of the fixed assets at cost to the consolidated group. A similar adjustment for intercompany profit is made for depreciable and nondepreciable long-lived assets. An adjustment must also be made for any depreciation recorded on the intercompany profit so that depreciation is adjusted based on cost of the asset to the consolidated entity. Illustrative entries follow:

In the year a fixed asset is sold at a gain, the worksheet elimination entry is:

Dr. Accumulated depreciation

Dr. Gain on sale

   Cr. Fixed asset

   Cr. Depreciation expense

In the years after sale, the elimination entry would be:

Dr. Retained earnings (beginning)

Dr. Accumulated depreciation

   Cr. Fixed asset

   Cr. Depreciation expense

This elimination is cumulative until the asset is fully depreciated.

EXAMPLE

Intercompany Sale of Equipment

A parent had equipment (original purchase price $60,000, accumulated depreciation of $30,000) with a five-year remaining life. The parent sold the equipment to its subsidiary for $40,000. The parent's journal entry for the sale was:

Dr. Cash	40,000	
Dr. Accumulated depreciation	30,000	
Cr. Equipment		60,000
Cr. Gain on sale of equipment		10,000

The subsidiary recorded its purchase as:

Dr. Equipment	40,000	
Cr. Cash		40,000

The subsidiary will record depreciation expense each year at $8,000 ($40,000/5 years).

The gain on sale of $10,000 must be eliminated along with the difference in depreciation of $2,000 ($8,000 – $6,000). The $6,000 in depreciation is based on a $30,000 carrying value.

The elimination entry is:

Dr. Gain on sale of equipment	10,000	
Dr. Accumulated depreciation	2,000	
Cr. Depreciation expense		2,000
Cr. Equipment		10,000

The depreciation adjustment will be required at each year-end over the life of the asset.

In subsequent years, the debit to gain on sale instead will be to retained earnings for an amount that is reduced by the accumulated excess amortization.

An affiliate experiencing an intercompany profit on the sale of a longlived asset to another affiliate may have to pay income taxes on that gain. In this instance, the intercompany profit on the sale should be reduced by the tax effect in making the consolidated adjusting entry.

"Intercompany bonds" (parent issues bonds to third parties and subsidiary purchases bonds in the open market) bought by an affiliate are considered as being retired in the year of purchase. In other words, intercompany bonds (along with any premium or discount) are eliminated and treated as if the bonds were retired in exchange for the investment. A resulting gain or loss is recognized in the consolidated income statement. The gain or loss is allocated between the consolidated (parent) interest and the noncontrolling (minority) interest in transactions where a parent holds bonds of a partially owned subsidiary or where one subsidiary holds bonds of another subsidiary.

An illustrative entry to eliminate an intercompany transaction in bonds follows:

Dr. Bonds payable	xx	
Dr. Discount on bonds	xx	
Dr. Loss on retirement of bonds	xx	
Cr. Investment in bonds		xx

EXAMPLE

A parent buys $40,000 face value 10% bonds from a 100%-owned subsidiary for $39,000. This amount equals the book value on the subsidiary's books. The following entry is recorded on the parent's investor's books:

Dr. Investment in bonds	39,000	
Cr. Cash		39,000

The subsidiary makes the following entry on issuance:

Dr. Cash	39,000	
Dr. Discount on bonds payable	1,000	
Cr. Bonds payable		40,000

The consolidation worksheet entry is:

Dr. Bonds payable	40,000	
Cr. Discount on bonds payable		1,000
Cr. Investment in bonds		39,000

An intercompany gain or loss on bonds does not occur if the acquisition price is the same as the book value of the bonds on the affiliated issuer's records (as in the above example).

In order for an affiliated investor to recognize a gain or loss on intercompany bondholdings, the following must exist:

☐ The bonds are sold outside of the affiliated group.

☐ The price paid differs from the carrying value of the affiliated issuer.

☐ The bonds are outstanding.

Intercompany dividends are eliminated in consolidation. Consolidated retained earnings should include the accumulated earnings of the consolidated group arising after acquisition that have not been distributed to stockholders of the parent company.

Comprehensive Consolidation Problem—Acquisition Method

An example of a comprehensive consolidation problem using the acquisition method is illustrated below involving Broad Company, the acquirer, and Romaro Company, the acquiree. A solution is included in the form of a consolidation worksheet.

EXAMPLE

Comprehensive Consolidation Problem

On January 1, 20X9, Broad Company purchases 100% of the voting common shares of Romaro Company. Broad uses the equity method to account for its investment in Romaro. At the acquisition date, $81,000 of the purchase price was attributed to land that had a fair value in excess of the carrying value on Romaro's books. In addition, $45,000 of the purchase price was attributed to equipment that had a fair value in excess of the carrying value on Romaro's books. At acquisition date, the equipment had a remaining useful life of 10 years. It is assumed that the consideration transferred by Broad to acquire Romaro was equal to the business fair value and that the business fair value exceeded the fair value of net assets acquired at the acquisition date by $54,000.

It is now December 31, 2X13, and consolidated financial statements need to be prepared. At the financial statement date, Romaro has borrowed $100,000 from Broad Company, without interest. This acquisition was completed subsequent to the effective date of ASC 805 and the acquisition method must be used.

The following are the applicable income statement and balance sheet accounts for Broad and Romaro at December 31, 2X13:

($ thousands)

	Broad	Romaro
Sales	1,057	324
Less: Cost of goods sold	495	81
Equity earnings—Romaro	121	–
Depreciation and amortization	155	117
Net income	528	126
Current assets	358	286
Investment in Romaro	895	–
Land	396	149
Equipment	274	377
Buildings	483	257
Due from Romaro	100	–
Goodwill	–	–
Total assets	2,506	1,069
Accounts payable	400	92
Due to parent		100
Other liabilities	356	139
Total liabilities	756	331
Common stock @ par	24	15
Additional paid in capital	200	138
Retained earnings	1,526	585
Total stockholders' equity	1,750	738
Total liabilities and stockholders' equity	2,506	1,069

Statement of Retained Earnings

	Broad	Romaro
Retained earnings, January 1, 2X13	1,275	558
Add net income	528	126
Less dividends paid	277	99
Retained earnings, December 31, 2X13	1,526	585

Required: Prepare a consolidation worksheet as of December 31, 2X13, with all appropriate elimination entries.

Analysis: In this problem, the original acquisition cost is not provided, but both the fair value adjustments and goodwill as of the acquisition date is provided. It is necessary to roll forward the fair value adjustments to obtain the unamortized fair value adjustments as of January 1 of the year of reporting (2X13). The only fair value adjustment that requires this calculation is equipment (a depreciable asset). The accumulated amortization of the fair value adjustment as of January 1, 2X13 (4 years after acquisition date), is $18,000 ($4,500 × 4). The $18,000 is deducted from the fair value adjustment at the acquisition date ($45,000) to arrive at the unamortized fair value adjustment at January 1, 2X13, of $27,000. The $27,000 is used in the second consolidation entry. The following consolidation entries follow the outline previously given of the required adjustments (All entries are in $ thousands):

1. Dr. Retained earnings—Romaro January 1, 2X13	558	
Dr. Common stock—Romaro	15	
Dr. Additional paid in capital	138	
Cr. Investment in Romaro		711

To eliminate the stockholders' equity of the subsidiary against the parent's investment account, to allow the amortized fair value of net assets to flow through in consolidation.

2. Dr. Goodwill	54	
Dr. Land	81	
Dr. Equipment	27	
Cr. Investment in Romaro		162

To recognize goodwill as of the date of acquisition (no subsequent impairment has taken place) and recognize the unamortized fair value adjustments as of January 1 of the year of reporting.

3. Dr. Equity earnings—Romaro	121	
Cr. Investment in Romaro		121

To reverse the equity income accrued by Broad to allow the revenue and expense of Romaro to flow through in consolidation. If this entry were not made, the earnings of Romaro would be double counted. The difference between the net income of Romaro and the equity earnings of Broad relates to the annual excess amortization recorded by Broad under the equity method.

4. Dr. Investment in Romaro	99	
Cr. Dividends paid		99

To eliminate the dividends paid by Romaro to its parent (Broad), an intercompany transaction within the same economic entity. This entry is the reverse of what was recorded by Broad when it received the dividend from Romaro, as Broad is using the equity method of accounting for its investment in its wholly owned subsidiary.

5. Dr. Amortization of fair value adjustment— equipment	5 (rounded)	
Cr. Accumulated amortization—equipment		5 (rounded)

To record current-year amortization of the fair value adjustment related to equipment:

6. Dr. Due to Broad	100	
Cr. Due from Romaro		100

To eliminate intercompany receivables and payables.

The above entries are posted to the consolidation worksheet.

Solution

Consolidation Worksheet December 31, 2X13
($ thousands)

	Broad	Romaro	Worksheet Entries (see note) Dr.	Cr.	Consolidated Totals
Sales	1,057 cr.	324 cr.			1,381 cr.
Less: Cost of goods sold	495 dr.	81 dr.			576 dr.
Equity earnings— Romaro	121 cr.		121(3)		
Depreciation/ amortization	155 dr.	117 dr.	5(5)		277 dr.
Net income	528 cr.	126 cr.	126 dr.		528 cr.
Current assets	358 dr.	286 dr.			644 dr.
Investment in Romaro	895 dr.		99(4)	162(2) 711(1) 121(3)	–
Land	396 dr.	149 dr.	81(2)		626 dr.
Equipment	274 dr.	377 dr.	27(2)	5(5)	673 dr.
Building	483 dr.	257 dr.			740 dr.
Due from Romaro	100 dr.			100(6)	–
Goodwill			54(2)		54 dr.
Total assets	2,506 dr.	1,069 dr.			2,737 dr.
Accounts payable	400 cr.	92 cr.			492 cr.
Due to parent		100 cr.	100(6)		–
Other liabilities	356 cr.	139 cr.			495 cr.
Total liabilities	756 cr.	331 cr.			987 cr.
Common stock @ par	24 cr.	15 cr.	15(1)		24 cr.
Additional paid in capital	200 cr.	138 cr.	138(1)		200 cr.
Retained earnings	1,526 cr.	585 cr.			1,526 cr.
Total stockholders' equity	1,750 cr.	646 cr.			1,750 cr.
Total liabilities and stockholders' equity	2,506 cr.	1,069 cr.			2,737 cr.
Retained earnings, January 1, 2X13	1,275 cr.	558 cr.	558(1)		1,275 cr.

Consolidation Worksheet December 31, 2X13
($ thousands)

	Broad	Romaro	Worksheet Entries (see note) Dr.	Cr.	Consolidated Totals
Add: Net income	528 cr.	126 cr.			528 cr.
Subtract: Dividends paid	277 dr.	99 dr.		99(4)	277 dr.
Retained earnings, December 31, 2X13	1,526 cr.	585 cr.			1,526 cr.

Note: Numbers in parenthesis in the worksheet entries columns correspond with the entries immediately preceding this page

CONSOLIDATION OF NONCONTROLLING (MINORITY) INTERESTS

Noncontrolling interest (also referred to as minority interest) represents the portion of a subsidiary's equity that is not owned directly or indirectly by the parent. Noncontrolling interest has three implications:

1. Noncontrolling shareholders have an interest in the equity (net assets) of the subsidiary, which must be clearly identified and presented within stockholders' equity in the consolidated financial statements, but separate from the parent's equity. Prior to the adoption of ASC 810, the interest of the minority shareholders was sometimes reflected in the "mezzanine" section of the balance sheet, between liabilities and stockholders' equity, which is no longer acceptable.

2. Noncontrolling shareholders have an interest in the net income of the subsidiary, which is separately reported on the face of the income statement apart from the earnings associated with the controlling interest (parent).

3. Noncontrolling shareholders have an interest in any dividends paid by the subsidiary.

The following example illustrates the application of these concepts.

EXAMPLE

On January 2, 20X4, Suz Company purchased 75% of the Levita Company's outstanding common stock. Selected balance sheet data at December 31, 20X4, follow:

	Suz	Levita
Total assets	$210,000	$90,000
Liabilities	$ 60,000	$30,000

	Suz	Levita
Common stock	50,000	25,000
Retained earnings	$100,000	$35,000
	$210,000	$90,000

During 20X4, Suz and Levita paid cash dividends of $12,500 and $2,500, respectively, to their shareholders. There were no other intercompany transactions.

The following questions relate to the data just presented:

☐ In Suz's December 31, 20X4, consolidated balance sheet, what amount should be reported as noncontrolling (minority) interests in net assets?

☐ What amount should Suz report as dividends paid on its December 31, 20X4, consolidated statements of retained earnings?

☐ In its December 31, 20X4, consolidated balance sheet, what amount should Suz report as common stock?

The noncontrolling (minority) interest represents the portion of total stockholders' equity owned by investors in a subsidiary who are not part of the controlling interest. That is, they are not part of the parent entity. The noncontrolling (minority) interest is computed by referring to the stockholders' equity accounts of the subsidiary standing alone. Any adjustments made for consolidated financial statements are ignored in this calculation. Examination of the data given in the illustration enumerated previously indicates that the noncontrolling (minority) interest in Levita's net assets at December 31, 20X4, is $15,000. This amount is computed by multiplying Levita's net assets ($60,000) by the portion of Levita's stock (25%) that is not owned by the parent company (Suz Company). The computation is as follows:

$$(\$25,000 + \$35,000) \times 25\% = \$15,000$$

When a business combination is accounted for under the acquisition method, any preacquisition dividends are not adjusted. Only those transactions of the subsidiary subsequent to the date of the purchase are presented in the consolidated financial statements. Thus, any dividends paid by the subsidiary to the parent should be eliminated in preparing the consolidated financial statements. In general, all dividends paid to minority shareholders of the subsidiary should be accounted for as a reduction of the minority interest in the subsidiary's net assets. In this illustration, Suz should report dividends as $12,500 in its December 31, 20X4, consolidated statement of retained earnings. This is the amount Suz paid to its shareholders that year.

In the preparation of Suz's consolidated balance sheet, the entire stockholders' equity of the subsidiary must be eliminated. Thus, Suz's December 31, 20X4, balance sheet should report common stock as $50,000.

When consolidated financial statements are presented, 100% of the assets, liabilities, revenue, and expenses and the revenue and expenses in the income statement of the subsidiary are shown. Therefore, a contra must be presented for the part of these financial statement items not belonging to the parent. In the balance sheet, the contra for the noncontrolling (minority) interest in consolidated net assets based on the minority's percentage ownership in the net assets of the subsidiary must be presented. If a debit balance for the noncontrolling (minority) interest arises, it may be shown as a deduction to stockholders' equity or a reduction to the parent's retained earnings.

There are acceptable alternative presentations to presenting noncontrolling (minority) interests in the balance sheet. Noncontrolling (minority) interest may be shown as a part of stockholders' equity but segregated from the equity of the controlling interest. This presentation is as follows:

STOCKHOLDERS' EQUITY	
Controlling interests:	
Common stock	$100,000
Retained earnings	800,000
Noncontrolling interests	70,000
Total	$970,000

In the consolidated income statement, noncontrolling (minority) interests are presented as a deduction (expense) if there is a consolidated profit. If there is a consolidated net loss, the noncontrolling (minority) interest will be an income item because the noncontrolling (minority) interest would decrease the consolidated loss. The noncontrolling (minority) interest is calculated by multiplying the subsidiary's profit (after elimination of intercompany profits) by the percentage of the subsidiary's stock held by the noncontrolling (minority) interest. The noncontrolling (minority) interest may be presented in the income statement as a separate item, if material, after consolidated net income.

This consolidated income statement presentation is illustrated below for a 30% noncontrolling interest in XYZ:

Revenues	$ 5,000,000
Expenses	(4,000,000)
Income from continuing operations, pretax	1,000,000
Income tax expense	(400,000)
Income from continuing operations, net of tax	600,000
Discontinued operations, net of tax	(100,000)
Net income	500,000
Less: Net income attributable to noncontrolling interest	(150,000)
Net income attributable to XYZ	350,000

Losses may be incurred by the subsidiary, with their concurrent negative financial effects on noncontrolling interest. If the noncontrolling interest in subsidiary net assets has been reduced to zero because of losses, the noncontrolling interest will continue to be charged for its share of additional losses, even if that results in a deficit balance in the noncontrolling interest account. This represents a change from prior practice and is mandated by ASC 810-10-65-10.

Noncontrolling (minority) interests do not affect the adjustment for unrealized intercompany profits in inventories. However, consolidated profit and noncontrolling (minority) interests in the net income of a subsidiary are affected by the adjustment because the change in beginning or ending inventory of a partly owned subsidiary does impact net income determination.

CONTRAST OF ACQUISITION AND PURCHASE METHODS FOR NONCONTROLLING INTERESTS

The following terminology is mentioned in ASC 805 and ASC 810 as it relates to various aspects of the treatment of noncontrolling interest:

☐ *Control Premium* Represents extra dollars paid to acquire control; remainder of shares sell at a lower price.

Business fair value = FV of Controlling Interests + FV of Noncontrolling Interest

Goodwill = Total business FV–FV of Net Assets Acquired

☐ *Control Premium* Not discussed. Report noncontrolling interest as a percentage of subsidiary net assets (parent company method).

☐ *Step Acquisition*

— If the parent held a noncontrolling interest prior to obtaining control, remeasure the noncontrolling interest at fair value and calculate the gain or loss that will appear on the income statement.

— If the parent had control prior to the acquisition of additional shares, remeasure the noncontrolling interest at fair value and treat the acquisition as an equity transaction (debit or credit to additional paid in capital).

☐ *Step Acquisition* Each step requires separate fair value allocations and amortization (cost accumulation), potentially resulting in several layers of goodwill.

☐ *Sale of Subsidiary Shares* Establish a cost basis of shares sold (first in, first out [FIFO], specific identification, and weighted average cost are acceptable cost flow assumptions).

— If control is maintained after the sale, treat the sale as a capital transaction (difference between proceeds received and cost of shares sold is a debit or credit to additional paid in capital).

— If control is not maintained after the sale, calculate the gain or loss reported in earnings.

☐ *Sale of Subsidiary Shares*

— Establish a cost basis of shares sold (FIFO, specific identification, and weighted average cost are acceptable cost flow assumptions).

— Gain or loss reported on the income statement; there is no distinction between whether control is maintained after the sale.

☐ *Preacquisition Income* Report revenue and expense subsequent to the date of acquisition (separately show 100% of postacquisition revenue and expense less the noncontrolling interest share of net income).

☐ *Preacquisition Income* For acquisitions after January 1, report full-year revenue and expense and deduct "preacquisition net income" for the months not owned.

☐ *Presentation of Noncontrolling Interest on Balance Sheet* This should be reported in stockholders' equity.

☐ *Presentation of Noncontrolling Interest on Balance Sheet* Prior rules did not mandate the presentation. Noncontrolling interest on the balance sheet was reported in liabilities, between liabilities and stockholders' equity (known as the "mezzanine section"), or in stockholders' equity.

The following chart contrasts the new acquisition method rules with the grandfathered old rules for the purchase and pooling of interests methods.

Noncontrolling Interests—New Rules vs. Old Rules

	ASC 805 and ASC 810 (Acquisition Method)	Old Rules (Purchase Method) (Not in Codification)
Control Premium	Represents extra dollars (above fair value of acquiree stock) to obtain control. Used in determining business fair value and goodwill.	Not discussed. Noncontrolling interest on balance sheet reported as percentage of book value of subsidiary net assets.
Step Acquisitions	There are two possible treatments for additional purchases (steps): 1. If the parent held noncontrolling interest (NCI) and now obtains control, remeasure NCI at fair value with gain or loss in earnings. 2. If the parent had control and acquires additional shares, treat as an equity transaction with an increase or decrease in additional paid in capital.	Each additional purchase (step) requires separate fair value allocations and amortization. This is referred to as the cost accumulation method and results in several layers of goodwill.

Noncontrolling Interests—New Rules vs. Old Rules

	ASC 805 and ASC 810 (Acquisition Method)	Old Rules (Purchase Method) (Not in Codification)
Sale of Subsidiary Shares	1. Establish a cost basis of shares sold (e.g., FIFO, specific identification, weighted average). 2. Determine if control is maintained after the sale: a. If control is maintained, treat the sale as an equity transaction (increase or decrease in additional paid in capital). b. If control is not maintained, calculate the gain or loss in earnings. As clarified in 2010 by a revision to ASC 810-10-65, (a) and (b) are applied as long as there is no other conflicting GAAP.	First establish the cost basis of shares sold (i.e., FIFO, specific identification, weighted average) and then calculate gain or loss on the sale to be reported in earnings. There is no distinction as to whether control is maintained after the sale.
Preacquisition Income (acquiree earnings prior to business combination)	Not reflected in consolidated financial statements.	In the year of the acquisition, show 100% of full-year acquiree income and expense and deduct preacquisition income for the months not owned.

SPIN-OFFS

A parent may transfer a wholly or partly owned subsidiary or an investee to the entity's stockholders. The accounting for a spin-off varies with the percentage of the company that is owned. If ownership is minor (e.g., 20%), the transfer is considered a dividend in kind (property dividend) and is accounted for at the fair value of the shares in the investee transferred. If the spin-off is for a majority or wholly owned subsidiary, the impact is to remove its operations from the former parent and to vest them with the parent's stockholders. This transaction is clearly a spin-off of substance. Such a spinoff is accounted for at the recorded book values of the net assets transferred. The profit of the subsidiary to be disposed should be included in the parent's earnings up to the actual date of spin-off.

CONSOLIDATION REPORTING—OTHER TOPICS

If a subsidiary holds shares in the parent, the shares should not be reported as outstanding stock in the consolidated balance sheet but rather treasury shares to be deducted from consolidated stockholders' equity.

If an investment in subsidiary is sold during the year, the parent should include in its income statement its percentage interest in the subsidiary's profits up to the disposal date and any gain or loss on sale.

Consolidation is still allowed without adjustments if the parent and subsidiary have fiscal year-ends of three months or less apart. The parent's fiscal year results are added to the subsidiary's fiscal year results. There should be footnote disclosure of significant occurrences during the intervening time period.

There are situations in which parent company statements are required in addition to consolidated statements so as to provide information to lenders, suppliers, and preferred stockholders. In such cases, dual columns are warranted: one column for the parent and the other for the subsidiary. Alternatively, separate "parent company only" financial statements may be presented.

TAXES

There is a deferral of income taxes on any intercompany profits if the asset remains within the consolidated group. If consolidated tax returns are prepared, no adjustment is required for deferred income taxes because the intercompany profits are eliminated in deriving the consolidated tax liability.

Consolidated income tax expense may be recorded on the parent's books or allocated among the affiliates so each affiliate will recognize its share of consolidated income tax expense on its own books. However, if affiliates issue their own separate financial statements in addition to consolidated statements being prepared, the income tax expense must be allocated to the affiliates.

If the parent and subsidiary prepare separate tax returns instead of a consolidated tax return, the parent or a subsidiary may include in its accounts income taxes paid on intercompany profits. In this case, the taxes should be deferred or the intercompany profits that have been eliminated in consolidation reduced.

EXAMPLE

A subsidiary sells inventory costing $200,000 to its parent and records a $50,000 profit on the transaction. All of this inventory remains with the parent through year-end. The subsidiary files a separate tax return from its parent and pays $15,000 in income taxes from the transaction. If consolidated financial statements were prepared, the following consolidating (worksheet) entries are required:

Dr. Sales	250,000	
Cr. Cost of goods sold (purchases)		250,000
To eliminate intercompany sales and purchases:		
Dr. Cost of goods sold	50,000	
Cr. Inventory		50,000
To eliminate profit on intercompany sale		
Deferred income tax asset	15,000	
Income tax expense		15,000

To defer tax expense on intercompany profits eliminated in consolidation.

ACCOUNTING FOR TRANSFERS OF FINANCIAL ASSETS (ASC 860)

This topic deals with appropriate accounting recognition by a transferor (seller) for transfers of financial assets. The principal issue is whether a sale or a collateralized borrowing is recognized by the transferor at the date of transfer. The answer is critical when a sale occurs, a gain or loss is recognized, and the assets in question are removed from the books of the transferor. Recognition of a sale and profit increases the return on assets (net income/average assets) ratio of the transferor and will reduce the leverage (debt/equity) ratio, which is generally considered a desired result. If the criteria for sales accounting are not met, no gain or loss is recognized and the assets stay on the transferor's balance sheet along with a borrowing. This will increase the leverage ratio, and potentially place the transferor in violation of debt covenants.

Accounting Treatment

As a general principle, when a transferor has no continuing involvement with both the transferred financial assets and the transferee, sales treatment with recognition of gain or loss on a sale, along with removing the assets from the transferor's balance sheet, is appropriate.

However, there are situations where the transferor will have some continuing involvement with the transferred financial assets and/or the transferee. Examples of situations include transferor servicing, recourse or guarantee arrangements, agreements to purchase or redeem the transferred financial assets, options written (sold) or held, pledges of collateral, and possible retained transferor beneficial interests in the transferred financial assets. Each of the above situations raises questions as to whether the transferor should account for the transfers as sales or as secured borrowings.

ASC 860 provides specific guidance on transactions that fall into the categories of securitizations, factoring, transfers of receivables with recourse, securities lending transactions, repurchase agreements, loan participations, and banker's acceptances. A brief description of the most common of these structures and a summary of accounting guidance follows.

Securitizations. Beneficial interests in a portfolio of financial assets, such as mortgage or auto loans, or trade or credit card receivables, are transferred (sold) by the transferor to a trust. The trust will securitize the pool of assets and pass through the interest and principal collected to investors, who have purchased a portion of the pool of assets. (Note that the transferor may have been the originator of these assets or acquired them from another entity.) There may be several classes of investors who are entitled to differing cash flows generated from these assets. In some instances, a "turbo provision" provides that cash received during the amortization period of the securitization is paid to one class of investors before any cash is available for repayment to other investors. The transferor may have the right, under certain conditions and with trustee approval, to withdraw receivables from the pool of securitized receivables.

Factoring. Factoring arrangements are discussed in sections 3.08 and 3.09.

Transfers of receivables with recourse. One or more entire receivables are transferred, where the transferor provides the transferee (buyer) with full or limited recourse. If there is a payment default by the obligor of the receivables, the transferor is required, as specified by the terms of the arrangement, to make full or limited payment to the transferee, or repurchase the receivables sold.

Repurchase agreements. Repurchase agreements are discussed in sections 17.28 and 17.29.

Participating interests. To be eligible for sale accounting (described in the next paragraph), GAAP requires that an entire financial asset cannot be divided into component parts (e.g., interest and principal on a receivable) unless it meets the definition of a *participating interest*. The definition of the term participating interest will be incorporated in ASC 860-10-40-6A and represents a proportionate (pro rata) ownership interest in an entire financial asset. Cash flows received from the entire financial asset are divided proportionately among participating interest holders. No participating interest holder's interest may be subordinated to the interest of another participating interest holder; and participating interest holders are not permitted to have recourse to the transferor.

Accounting. A transfer of an entire financial asset, a group of entire financial assets, or a participating interest in an entire financial asset in which the transferor surrenders control over those financial assets shall be accounted for as a sale if all of the following conditions are met (ASC 860-10-40-5):

1. The financial assets have been "isolated" (put out of reach) from the transferor and its creditors.

2. The transferee has the right to pledge or exchange the transferred financial assets with no conditions constraining the transferee (or third-party holder of its beneficial interest) from taking advantage of these rights.

3. The transferor or its consolidated affiliates does not maintain effective control of those financial assets. Effective control exists if (a) there is an agreement that obligates the transferor to repurchase or redeem the financial assets before their maturity or (b) there is an agreement that permits the transferee to require the transferor to repurchase the transferred assets at a price so favorable to the transferee that it is probable that the repurchase will take place.

4. Derecognition of a transferred financial asset (treatment as a sale by the transferor) is appropriate only where there is reasonable assurance that the transferred financial is beyond the reach of the bankruptcy trustee of the transferor.

The following are examples of the application of the above criteria.

1. If the transferor and transferee are related by majority ownership, treatment as a sale in the consolidated financial statements is not permitted (this is an intercompany transaction).

2. A transfer of receivables in their entirety with recourse shall be accounted for as a sale, with the proceeds of the sale reduced by the fair value of the recourse obligation (see Example 1, below).

3. If the transferor has the power to require the return of transferred financial assets from the transferee through a repurchase agreement or call option (option to purchase given by the transferee to the transferor), sales treatment is not permitted. However, "cash settled call options," where the receivable is not returned to the transferor, do not preclude sales treatment. Additionally, a call option embedded by the issuer of a callable bond would not result in the transferor maintaining effective control. A put option (option to sell) written (sold) to the transferee generally does not provide the transferor with effective control over the transferred financial asset and does not create issues as to recognition of sale by the transferor. An exception would be a put option written on a not-readily-obtainable asset that may benefit the transferor and constrain the transferee if the option is "deep in the money" when written, as it is probable that the transferee will exercise it.

4. If a transferor imposes restrictions on the ability of a transferee to pledge or exchange the transferred financial assets, where that restriction provides more than a trivial benefit to the transferor, the transaction cannot be treated by the transferor as a sale. On the other hand, a transferor's right of first refusal if the transferee chooses to sell the asset does not jeopardize sales accounting by the transferor, as it cannot compel the transferee to sell the asset. A right by the transferor to reclaim specific transferred financial assets by paying their fair value when reclaimed does not maintain effective control and thus sales treatment is appropriate assuming the other above conditions are met. Any retained beneficial interest in a transferred financial asset should initially be recognized at fair value.

5. In a loan participation, the lead bank (transferor) allows the participating bank to resell the asset, but the transferor may retain the right to call (purchase) the asset at any time from whoever holds it, and can enforce the call option by withholding the flow of interest at the call date. This transferor-imposed restriction provides more than a trivial benefit to the transferor, and sale accounting is not appropriate.

ASC 860 has eliminated the previous concept of "qualifying special purpose entities" and now requires that all SPEs be analyzed for consolidation using ASC 810. This is further discussed in Chapter 12, "Consolidated Financial Statements."

If the transferee is consolidated by the transferor, then even if the criteria under *Accounting* above are met, the transferred assets would not be treated as sold in the consolidated financial statements. However, the transferee may recognize the transferred assets in its separate entity financial statements and the transferor would recognize a sale in its separate entity financial statements.

Treatment as a sale or as collateralized financing is determined using the above guidance and is based on the facts and circumstances of the particular situation.

The following are the minimum disclosure requirements for transactions subject to these rules:

1. Explain the transferor's continuing involvement, if any, with the transferred financial asset.

2. Discuss the nature of any restriction on assets reported by an entity in its statement of financial position relating to a transferred financial asset.

3. Describe any servicing arrangements existing between the transferor or transferee, as well as the classification of servicing assets and servicing liabilities in the statement of condition.

4. For transfers treated as sales, indicate the impact on the entity's balance sheet, income statement, and statement of cash flows.

5. For transfers treated as secured borrowings, indicate the impact on the entity's balance sheet, income statement, and statement of cash flows.

6. Discuss any risks related to the transferred assets to which the transferor continues to be exposed after the transfer.

The above disclosures may be reported in aggregate form for similar transactions.

The effective date of ASC 860 is the beginning of each reporting entity's first annual reporting period beginning after November 15, 2009. A reporting entity is encouraged, but not required, to disclose comparative information for periods earlier than the effective date.

The following examples illustrate the principal requirements in this area.

EXAMPLE 1

ABC Corp., a financial institution, has originated $10,000,000 of fixed rate, interest-bearing auto loans in its program with a major car dealer. To raise money, ABC sells the entire auto loan portfolio to an unrelated securitization entity and receives proceeds of $10,800,000. ABC does not service the loans, nor does it restrict the ability of the securitization entity from pledging or selling the assets to investors or others. ABC does agree to provide a limited recourse obligation, meaning ABC agrees to repurchase delinquent loans up to 5% of the aggregate face amount. In addition, ABC agrees to provide a variable interest rate return to the securitization entity, in substance, making this a interest rate swap, that is, ABC receives the fixed rate on the auto loans and pays a variable interest rate to the securitization entity. Assume that on the reporting date, the fair value of this swap is $300,000.

Analysis: This transaction qualifies as a sale, because the transferred financial assets are out of the effective control of ABC. ABC records the recourse obligation and the fair value of the interest rate swap along with the gain on sale.

Net Proceeds:	
Cash received	10,800,000
Plus interest rate swap asset	300,000
Less: recourse obligation	(500,000)
Net proceeds	10,600,000
Gain on Sale	
Net proceeds	10,600,000

Less: Carrying amount of loans sold		10,000,000
Gain on Sale		600,000

Journal Entry:

Dr. Cash		10,800,000
Dr, Interest Rate Swap		300,000
Cr. Auto Loans	10,000,000	
Cr. Recourse Obligation	500,000	
Cr. Gain on Sale	600,000	

EXAMPLE 2

XYZ has $7,000,000 of accounts receivable arising from credit sales on its books. XYZ sells these assets to HIJ for $7,100,000, but retains the right to repurchase the assets at the face value of $7,000,000 at any date before the assets contractually mature.

Analysis: XYZ as transferor retains a call option on these receivables that provides "more than a trivial benefit" (the FASB's term) to them. Sale accounting is not permitted, as the transferred assets are not fully beyond the control of the transferor. The transaction is treated as a collateralized borrowing on the books of XYZ.

Journal Entry (XYZ):

Dr. Cash		7,100,000
Cr. Collateralized Borrowing	7,100,000	

VARIABLE INTEREST ENTITIES

Traditional criteria for consolidation have required the parent to have a controlling financial interest in its subsidiaries, typically in the form of voting common shares. In the 1990s, companies began to sponsor the formation of so-called special purpose entities to isolate certain assets and liabilities into separate legal entities so that investors and creditors of those entities could better understand the risks and require a lower return on those risks. Companies seeking to raise money for their operations may sponsor the creation of a special purpose entity (SPE) to which they sell assets for money. Companies often create SPEs for a single specific purpose, for example, to facilitate securitization of financial assets, support leasing activities or reduce risk through hedging, or for research and development, and reinsurance.

The SPE obtains money by issuing stock, borrowing, or selling assets to investors and passing through the proceeds to the sponsor company to pay for the assets purchased. The SPE is owned by shareholders unrelated to the sponsor and may use the assets as security for a collateralized borrowing. The principal question with these structures is the same as with ASC 860; that is, can the sponsor company record a sale of assets along with a gain or loss on a sale and remove the assets from its balance sheet or must the sponsor treat this structure as a collateralized borrowing?

The answer is that if the SPE structure meets the definition of a variable interest entity (VIE), a sponsor company that is a primary beneficiary must consolidate the VIE with its operations and thus cannot record a sale. However, if the SPE structure is not in the form of a VIE and if the transferor meets the requirements of ASC 860 and is not a primary beneficiary, sale accounting is appropriate. These accounting standards are meant to protect against the abusive practices of some companies, notably Enron, to not consolidate SPEs they controlled in substance, particularly when there was no substantial outside equity investors and when the sponsor guaranteed a minimum return to investors as well as agreeing to reimburse the SPE for any losses incurred.

The determination of whether a legal entity meets the definition of a VIE and whether the reporting unit meets the criteria of a primary beneficiary is made at the date that the reporting entity first becomes involved with the legal entity or later if events subsequent to the formation of the VIE now make the reporting unit a primary beneficiary.

In defining a VIE, the FASB clarified their replacement of a quantitative-based risks and rewards approach to a more qualitative approach. (ASC 810-10-05-8) This qualitative approach relates to SPE structures, where equity investors lack sufficient equity capital to be able to finance SPE operations without additional subordinated financial support, or if holders of the equity investment in the entity, in the aggregate, lack any one of the following three characteristics:

1. The power to direct activities of the legal entity that most significantly impact economic performance, even if that power is not used. This power may exist despite the fact that the entity that has this ability lacks significant voting rights through stock ownership. It is possible that the power is shared among multiple unrelated parties. The reporting entity is responsible for identifying the party that directs the activities with the most significant impact on the VIE's economic performance. (ASC 810-10-25-38E)

2. The obligation to absorb expected losses of the legal entity, which may occur when there is a minimum return on invested capital provided to investors based on the legal entity's governing document. This condition may also exist when the voting rights of some investors are not proportional to their obligations to absorb expected losses.

3. The right to receive residual returns of the legal entity, including if this right is capped by the legal entity's governing document.

When one or a combination of the above conditions exists, someone other than the equity holders in the SPE will be the primary beneficiary of the risks and rewards of ownership. This may be the sponsor company or another company on whose behalf the sponsor created the SPE. In such cases, a controlling financial interest is achieved through contractual arrangements that do not involve ownership of voting equity interests. In addition, some SPEs do not have an independent governing board and may have activities that are limited by the articles of incorporation, partnership, or trust agreement. The reporting entity, in substance, may implicitly accept all the activities that the SPE is permitted to engage. The reporting entity that has the variable interests is required to assess whether it has a controlling financial interest in the SPE based on its ability to direct activities of the SPE and have the obligation to absorb losses of the SPE or receive benefits from the SPE that can be considered significant to the SPE's financial performance. (ASC 810-10-25-38A)

The reporting entity must also consider if it holds an implicit variable interest in the SPE. (ASC 810-10-25-54) Implicit variable interests commonly occur in leasing transactions among related parties and in other types of arrangements, where the reporting entity receives the variability of return on the SPE, irrespective of whether there is a contractual relationship between the parties. When a variability of return is given to the reporting entity, a controlling financial interest will exist.

Fees that are paid to a legal entity's decision makers or service provider are not considered variable interests if the fees are compensation for services provided, have the same seniority as other payables of the SPE, are considered customary compensation, and are insignificant to the SPE's overall performance. (ASC 810-10-55-37)

If a controlling financial interest exists, the reporting entity is considered the primary beneficiary and the SPE meets the criteria of being a VIE that must be consolidated with the reporting entity's operations. Thus, the assets, liabilities, and noncontrolling (minority) interests are consolidated at fair value and results of operations of the VIE must be included in the consolidated financial statements of the primary beneficiary. These rules are applied to the entire VIE and not to divisions, departments, branches, or pools of assets within the VIE. An exception exists when the activities of the VIE primarily relate to securitizations and the assets of the VIE can only be used to settle the obligations of that entity. In that case, the assets and liabilities of the VIE may be measured at their unpaid principal balances (an alternative to fair value measurement). The primary beneficiary will still be required to recognize any other than temporary impairment in its investment, any needed allowance for credit losses, as well as accrued interest.

The requirement to determine the primary beneficiary is ongoing, although that assessment may change, depending on the facts and circumstances of how the VIE and the reporting entity treat their relationship. There are no longer any qualifying special purpose entities (QSPE) that are not subject to these standards. QSPE designation was removed in ASC 860 in December 2009.

The logic behind these rules is to prevent abuses, where some SPEs are designed to avoid having to report them in the consolidated financial statements of the primary beneficiary. Many VIEs do not have a governing board to make economic decisions on how these entities operate; instead, they rely on the direction of the primary beneficiary. Now all SPE structures that meet the definition of a VIE must be consolidated with the primary beneficiary's other operations.

SPEs are often created for a single specific purpose, for example, to facilitate securitization of financial assets and to support leasing activities, risk reduction through hedging, research and development, and reinsurance. Other entities having the same characteristics may also qualify as VIEs.

The initial measurement by a consolidating entity of the assets, liabilities, and noncontrolling interests of a VIE depend on whether the determination of their carrying value is practical. In this context, carrying value means the amounts that the assets, liabilities, and noncontrolling interests would be reported in the consolidated financial statements if the VIE rules described above had been in effect when the reporting entity first met the conditions of primary beneficiary. Under the acquisition method of accounting, this requires measurement at fair value as of the date the conditions of primary beneficiary are first met. However, if carrying values described above are not available and the activities of the VIE primarily relate to securitizations and the assets of the VIE can be used only to settle obligations of the entity, then the assets and liabilities of the VIE can be measured by the reporting entity at their unpaid principal balance.

The one significant exception is in regard to assets or liabilities transferred at inception by the primary beneficiary to the VIE. These are, in effect, intercompany transactions, which will be measured in the consolidated financial statements in the same manner as the intercompany transactions previously described (i.e., any intercompany profit on a transfer is eliminated in consolidation through a worksheet adjustment).

Any difference between the net amount added to the balance sheet of the consolidating entity and the book value of the VIE previously recognized by the reporting entity is treated as a cumulative effect adjustment to beginning retained earnings of the first year restated. (ASC 810-10-30-9) Once an entity has been designated as a VIE, that designation will not change unless there is a change in the underlying contractual relationship, a return of capital to other equity investors, a change in the nature of the activities of the VIE, or the consolidating entity loses its power to direct the activities of the VIE in a way that significantly impacts the entity's performance.

Note that in ASU 2010-10, issued in February 2010, the FASB has chosen to defer for investment companies only, the consolidation requirements from ASC 810 (as revised by FASB Statement No. 167). The reason for the deferral is to allow the International Accounting Standards Board (IASB) and FASB sufficient time to issue joint consistent guidance on principal and agent relationships as part of their joint consolidation project.

Fair Value Option Relating to VIEs

A reporting entity that is required to consolidate a VIE may elect to use the fair value option ASC 825-10 if the reporting entity elects that option for all financial assets and liabilities of the VIE.

Disclosure

Disclosure is extensive and depends on whether the reporting entity is a primary beneficiary or nonprimary beneficiary of the VIE. (ASC 810-10-50-5A) A primary beneficiary of a VIE or a reporting entity that holds a variable interest in a VIE must disclose the following:

1. Qualitative and quantitative information about the reporting entity's involvement in the VIE, including, but not limited to, the nature, purpose, size and activities of the VIE, including how the VIE is financed.

2. The carrying amount and classification of consolidated assets that are collateral for the VIE's obligations.

3. Lack of recourse if creditors (or beneficial interest holders) of a consolidated VIE have no recourse to the general credit of the primary beneficiary.

4. Methodology, including assumptions and judgments made, to determine whether the reporting entity is the primary beneficiary.

5. Whether the conclusion has changed as to need to consolidate the VIE in the periods presented in the most recent financial statements.

6. Whether the reporting entity has provided financial or other support to the VIE during the periods presented, and if so, the amount, type and primary reasons such support has been given.

Notes:

1. The above disclosures do not apply when the reporting entity holds both a majority of voting interests of a VIE (that is a business) and is also a primary beneficiary. Normal disclosure for consolidated entities applies.

2. In addition, the above disclosures are not required for VIEs created before December 31, 2003, where the reporting entity is unable to

   a. Determine whether a legal entity is a VIE.

   b. Determine whether the reporting entity is the VIE's primary beneficiary.

   c. Perform the accounting required to consolidate the VIE when it has been determined it is the primary beneficiary. (ASC 810-10-15-17) For VIEs created prior to December 31, 2003, meeting condition (2.) in the note above, the following disclosure is required:

For VIEs created prior to December 31, 2003, meeting condition (2.) in the note above, the following disclosure is required:

1. Number of legal entities to which this applies and why the information required to apply the guidance is not available.

2. Nature, purpose, size (if available), and activities of the legal entities and the nature of the reporting entity's involvement with the legal entities.

3. Reporting entity's maximum exposure to loss because of its involvement with the legal entities.

4. Amount of income, expense, purchases, sales, or other measure of activity between the reporting entity and legal entities.

In addition to the four disclosure items above, a nonprimary beneficiary holder of an interest in a VIE is required to disclose:

1. The carrying amounts and classification of assets and liabilities in the reporting entity's balance sheet that relate to the reporting entity's variable interest in the VIE.

2. The reporting entity's maximum exposure to loss as a result of its involvement with the VIE and how that maximum exposure is determined. A description of the nature of the sources of the reporting entity's exposure to loss should be discussed.

3. A table that compares the book value of the VIE's assets and liabilities to the maximum loss exposure and the qualitative and quantitative factors that could require the reporting entity to provide financial support to the VIE.

4. Any liquidity arrangements, guarantees, or other commitments that may affect the fair value or risk of the reporting entity's VIE.

5. A description of all factors used to conclude that the power to direct activities influencing VIE performance is shared with other entities.

The footnote disclosures required above may be provided in more than one note to the financial statements as long as there is a cross reference to the other notes that contain the remaining required disclosures.

The effective date with respect to the variable interest entity amendments of ASC 810 are to be applied to the reporting entity's first annual reporting period beginning after November 15, 2009, and to interim periods within that first annual period.

EFFECTIVE DATE

The accounting for noncontrolling interests (ASC 810-10-65-1A) is to be applied prospectively for fiscal years beginning on or after December 15, 2008. Earlier adoption is prohibited. The presentation and disclosure requirements must be applied prospectively.

DISCLOSURES

In addition to the presentation requirements previously discussed for noncontrolling interests on the face of the balance sheet and income statement, the following additional disclosures are required:

1. A reconciliation of total equity (net assets) attributable to the parent and noncontrolling interest. This reconciliation shall separately disclose, net income, transactions with owners, and each component of other comprehensive income.

2. In the notes to the consolidated financial statements, a separate schedule showing the impact of changes in the parent's ownership in a subsidiary.

3. For a subsidiary that is deconsolidated, the parent must disclose the gain or loss recognized at the time the subsidiary is no longer consolidated.

Disclosure is required on the financial statements or footnotes of the company's consolidation policy (e.g., composition of companies consolidated, intercompany transactions eliminated), on intervening events affecting financial position when the reporting periods of subsidiaries differ from that of the parent, on tax implications on the accounts, and on allocation methods (e.g., taxes among members of the consolidated group).

ASC 810-10-50-2 requires disclosure whenever a change is made to modify or eliminate the time lag (typically three months or less) used for recording results of consolidated entities or equity method investees having a different fiscal year-end.

COMBINED FINANCIAL STATEMENTS

Combined financial statements present the financial status and operating results of legally separate entities, related by common ownership, as if they were a single entity.

Consolidated financial statements are prepared when the parent has control over its affiliates. However, when control does not exist, combined financial statements are more suitable than consolidated statements. Examples of when combined statements should be prepared are when one stockholder owns a controlling interest in several related operating companies (brother-sister corporation), companies are under common management, subsidiaries are not consolidated when control does not exist, and combined statements are more meaningful than separate statements. For example, combined financial statements may be suitable for a combination of a partnership and a corporation that are commonly owned.

Combined financial statements are prepared in a similar manner as consolidated statements. In other words, intercompany transactions and profits are eliminated. There is similar accounting treatment for noncontrolling interests, foreign operations, income taxes, and differences in fiscal year-ends among the combined group.

The major difference between combined and consolidated financial statements is that in the former none of the combining companies has an ownership interest in any of the other combining companies. The equity accounts of the combining companies are added. The equity section of the combined balance sheet incorporates the paid-in-capital accounts of the combining entities. However, there is only a single combined retained earnings account. Combined statements are unlike consolidation, in which the equity accounts are eliminated in a consolidation worksheet against the investment in subsidiaries held by the parent company.

COMPREHENSIVE EXAMPLES AND APPLICATIONS— PURCHASE METHOD

Note: The following two problems are presented using the purchase method of accounting, which continues to be required for all acquisitions (not qualifying for poolings) completed prior to the effective dates of ASC 805 and ASC 810.

Problem 1 (Use Exhibit 12-1)

On December 31, 20X1, Popular Corporation issued 21,040 shares of its $1 par (current fair value $10) common stock for *all* the outstanding common stock of Sky Company in a statutory merger. The business combination is recorded under the purchase method.

Required: Using the information given in Exhibit 12-1, prepare Popular Corporation's journal entries on December 31, 20X1, (a) to record the stock exchange, (b) to record payment of the out-of-pocket costs incurred in merger with Sky Company, and (c) to record the merger with Sky Company.

Exhibit 12-1: Purchase Combinations

Out-of-pocket costs of the business combination paid in cash by popular on December 31, 20X1 were as follows:

Finder's and legal fees to business combination	$10,450
Costs associated with SEC registration statement	14,550
Total out-of-pocket costs of business combination	$25,000

Popular and Sky's modified balance sheets and current fair values (*prior* to the business combination) on December 31, 20X1 follow:

	Popular Carrying Amounts	Sky Carrying Amounts	Sky Current Fair Values	Excess of Current Fair Value Over Book Value
ASSETS				
Cash	$40,000	$20,000	$20,000	$0
Inventory	160,000	100,000	105,200	5,200
Other current assets	110,000	43,000	43,000	0
Plant assets (net)	*700,000*	*220,000*	*258,000*	*38,000*
Land	200,000	50,000	62,000	12,000
Building (economic life = 20 years)	260,000	120,000	136,000	16,000
Machinery (economic life = 5 years)	240,000	50,000	60,000	10,000
Patent (economic life = 6 years)	0	0	42,000	42,000
Goodwill (net)	20,000	0	?	?
Total assets	$1,030,000	$383,000		
LIABILITIES & STOCKHOLDERS' EQUITY				
Current liabilities	$ 20,000	$ 3,200	$ 3,200	$ 0
Long-term liabilities	490,000	186,000	222,000	36,000
Common stock, $1 par	200,000			
Common stock, $5 par		80,000		

	Popular Carrying Amounts	Sky Carrying Amounts	Sky Current Fair Values	Excess of Current Fair Value Over Book Value
Additional paid-in-capital		110,000	47,000	
Retained earnings	210,000	66,800		
Total liabilities & stockholders' equity	$1,030,000	$383,000		

Solution (Problem 1)

(a) 12/31/20X1

Investment in Sky's common stock	210,400	
Common stock		21,040
Additional paid-in-capital		189,360

(b) 12/31/20X1

Investment in Sky's common stock	10,450	
Additional paid-in-capital	14,550	
Cash		25,000

(c) 12/31/20X1

Cash	20,000	
Inventories	105,200	
Other current assets	43,000	
Plant assets (note 1)	238,951	
Patent (note 1)	38,899	
Current liabilities		3,200
Long-term debt		186,000
Premium on long-term debt		36,000
Investment in Sky's common stock		220,850

Under precodification standard FAS-141 purchase accounting, a bargain purchase occurs when the purchase price (debit to investment account) is less than the fair value of net assets acquired. The bargain amount is used to reduce noncurrent assets (plant assets and patent in this example) proportionately with any excess treated as an extraordinary gain. The following table derives the amounts used to consolidate plant assets and patents:

Noncurrent Asset	Fair Value	Percentage	Allocation of Bargain Purchase	Net Amount
Plant assets	258,000	86%	(19,049)	238,951
Patent	42,000	14%	(3,101)	38,899
Total	300,000		(22,150)	277,850
Purchase price (210,400 + 10,450)				220,850
Fair value of net assets acquired				(243,000)
Bargain purchase amount				(22,150)

Note: If this transaction was accounted for under the acquisition method (ASC 805 (FAS-141R)), the finder's and legal fees of $10,450 would be charged to acquisition expense. A gain on the bargain purchase would be recorded rather than the proportionate reduction of noncurrent assets.

Problem 2 (Use Exhibits 12-1 and 12-2)

On December 31, 20X1, Popular Corporation issued 22,800 shares of its $1 par (current fair value $10) common stock to stockholders of Sky Company in exchange for 15,200 of the 16,000 outstanding shares of Sky's $5 par common stock in a *purchase-type* business combination.

Required: Based on the information previously presented in Exhibit 12-1:

1. Prepare the elimination entries for the consolidated working paper on December 31, 20X1.

2. Prepare the journal entries Popular Corporation should make on its books (a) to record dividend declared by Sky Company on November 24, 20X2, (b) to record net income of Sky Company for the year ended December 31, 20X2, and (c) to amortize differences between current fair values and carrying amounts of Sky Company's identifiable net assets.

3. Prepare the elimination entries for the consolidated working paper on December 31, 20X2.

4. Complete the working paper for Consolidated Financial Statements (use Exhibit 12-2).

Exhibit 12-2: Consolidation

POPULAR CORPORATION AND SUBSIDIARY
Working Paper for Consolidated Financial Statements
For Year Ended December 31, 20X2

	Popular	Sky	Eliminations Dr.	Cr.	Consolidated
INCOME STATEMENT					
Revenue:					
Net sales	1,122,200	217,800			
Intercompany					

	Popular	Sky	Eliminations Dr.	Cr.	Consolidated
investment income	7,790				
Total revenue	1,129,990	217,800			
Costs and expenses:					
Cost of goods sold	785,000	140,000			
Operating expenses	111,390	25,800			
Interest and income taxes expense	142,000	34,000			
MI* in net income of subsidiary					
Total costs and expenses	1,038,390	199,800			
Net income	$91,600	$18,000			

STATEMENT OF RETAINED EARNINGS

Retained earnings, beginning of year	210,000	66,800			
Net income	91,600	18,000			
Subtotal	301,600	84,800			
Dividends declared	26,010	8,000			
Retained earnings, end of year	275,590	76,800			

BALANCE SHEET
ASSETS

Inventories	172,200	110,000			
Other current assets	133,000	52,000			
Investment in Sky common stock	238,450				
Plant assets (net)	720,000	230,000			
Patent (net)	0	0			
Goodwill (net)	19,500	0			
Total assets	1,283,150	392,000			

LIABILITIES AND STOCKHOLDERS' EQUITY

Liabilities	484,110	188,200			
Minority interest in net assets of subsidiary					
Common stock, $2 par	211,400				

	Popular	Sky	Eliminations Dr.	Cr.	Consolidated
Common stock, $10 par	0	80,000			
Additional paid-in-capital	312,050	47,000			
Retained earnings	275,590	76,800			
Total liabilities & stockholders' equity	1,283,150	392,000			

* MI = minority interest.

Solution (Problem 2)

(1) 12/31/20X1

Investment in Sky's common stock	228,000	
Common stock		22,800
Additional paid-in-capital		205,200
Investment in Sky's common stock	10,450	
Additional paid-in-capital	14,550	
Cash		25,000
Common stock—Sky	80,000	
Additional paid-in-capital—Sky	47,000	
Retained earnings—Sky	66,800	
Inventories—Sky	5,200	
Plant assets—Sky	38,000	
Patent—Sky	42,000	
Goodwill—Popular	7,600	
Investment in Sky's common stock—Popular		238,450
Minority interest in net assets of subsidiary		12,150
Premium on long-term debts—Sky		36,000

(2-a) 12/31/20X1

Cash (8,000×95%)	7,600	
Investment in Sky's common stock		7,600

(2-b)

Investment in Sky's common stock (18,000×95%)	17,100	
Intercompany investment income		17,100

(2-c)

Intercompany investment income	9,310	
Investment in Sky's common stock		9,310

(3) 12/31/20X2

Common stock—Sky	80,000	
Additional paid-in-capital—Sky	47,000	
Retained earnings—Sky	66,800	
Inventories—Sky	5,200	
Plant assets—Sky	35,200	

Patent—Sky	35,000	
Goodwill—Popular	7,410	
Intercompany investment income—Popular	7,790	
Operating expenses—Sky	9,800	
Minority interest in net income of subsidiary	410	
Investment in Sky's common stock—Popular		238,450
Minority interest in net assets of subsidiary		12,160
Dividends declared—Sky		8,000
Premium on long-term debts—Sky		36,000

POPULAR CORPORATION AND SUBSIDIARY
Working Paper for Consolidated Financial Statements
For Year Ended December 31, 20X2

	Popular	Sky	Eliminations Dr.	Eliminations Cr.	Consolidated
INCOME STATEMENT					
Revenue:					
Net sales	1,122,200	217,800			1,340,000
Intercompany investment income	7,790		7,790		
Total revenue	1,129,990	217,800	7,790		1,340,000
Costs and expenses:					
Cost of goods sold	785,000	140,000			925,000
Operating expenses	111,390	25,800	9,800		146,990
Interest and income taxes expense	142,000	34,000			176,000
Noncontrolling (minority) interest in net income of subsidiary			410		410
Total costs and expenses	1,038,390	199,800	10,210		1,248,400
Net income	91,600	$18,000	18,000		91,600
STATEMENT OF RETAINED EARNINGS					
Retained earnings, beginning of year	210,000	66,800	66,800		210,000
Net income	91,600	18,000	18,000		91,600
Subtotal	301,600	84,800	84,800		301,600
Dividends declared	26,010	8,000		8,000	26,010
Retained earnings, end of year	$275,590	$76,800	84,800	$8,000	$275,590

	Popular	Sky	Eliminations Dr.	Eliminations Cr.	Consolidated

	Popular	Sky	Dr.	Cr.	Consolidated
BALANCE SHEET					
ASSETS					
Inventories	172,200	110,000	5,200		287,400
Other current assets	133,000	52,000			185,000
Investment in Sky common stock	238,450			238,450	0
Plant assets (net)	720,000	230,000	35,200		985,200
Patent (net)	0	0	35,000		35,000
Goodwill (net)	19,500	0	7,410		26,910
Total assets	1,283,150	392,000	82,810	238,450	1,519,510
LIABILITIES AND STOCKHOLDERS' EQUITY					
Liabilities	484,110	188,200		36,000	708,310
Noncontrolling (minority) interest in net assets of subsidiary				12,160	12,160
Common stock, $2 par	211,400				211,400
Common stock, $10 par	0	80,000	80,000		0
Additional paid-in-capital	312,050	47,000	47,000		312,050
Retained earnings	275,590	76,800	76,800		275,590
Total liabilities & stockholders' equity	1,283,150	392,000	203,800	$48,160	1,519,520

Notes to Problem 2

1. Operating expenses worksheet adjustments totaling 9,800 consist of amortization of excess of fair value over book value (800 building; 2,000 machine; 7,000 patent).

2. Minority interest in net income of subsidiary is 5% (18,000 − 9,800) = 410. The 9,800 represents the amortization calculated in 1. above.

3. Amortization of difference between acquisition date fair values and carrying values is 9,800 × 95% = 9,310.

ANNUAL REPORT REFERENCES

Goodyear Tire and Rubber Company
2010 Annual Report

Note 21. Consolidating Financial Information

Certain of our subsidiaries have guaranteed our obligations under the $1.0 billion outstanding principal amount of 10.5% senior notes due 2016, the $1.0 billion outstanding principal amount of 8.25% senior notes due 2020, and the $282 million outstanding principal amount of 8.75% notes due 2020 (collectively, the "notes"). The following presents the condensed consolidating financial information separately for:

(i) The Parent Company, the issuer of the guaranteed obligations;

(ii) Guarantor subsidiaries, on a combined basis, as specified in the indentures related to Goodyear's obligations under the notes;

(iii) Non-guarantor subsidiaries, on a combined basis;

(iv) Consolidating entries and eliminations representing adjustments to (a) eliminate intercompany transactions between or among the Parent Company, the guarantor subsidiaries and the non-guarantor subsidiaries, (b) eliminate the investments in our subsidiaries, and (c) record consolidating entries; and

(v) The Goodyear Tire & Rubber Company and Subsidiaries on a consolidated basis.

Each guarantor subsidiary is 100% owned by the Parent Company at the date of each balance sheet presented. The notes are fully and unconditionally guaranteed on a joint and several basis by each guarantor subsidiary. Each entity in the consolidating financial information follows the same accounting policies as described in the consolidated financial statements, except for the use by the Parent Company and guarantor subsidiaries of the equity method of accounting to reflect ownership interests in subsidiaries which are eliminated upon consolidation. Intercompany cash advances and loans made primarily for the purpose of short-term operating needs are included in cash flows from operating activities. Intercompany transactions reported as investing or financing activities include the sale of the capital stock of various subsidiaries and other capital transactions between members of the consolidated group.

Beazer Homes
2009 Annual Report

(3) Investments in Unconsolidated Joint Ventures

As of September 30, 2009, we participated in land development joint ventures in which Beazer Homes had less than a controlling interest. The following table presents our investment in our unconsolidated joint ventures, the total equity and outstanding borrowings of these joint ventures and our guarantees of these borrowings as of September 30, 2009 and September 30, 2008:

(in thousands)	2009	2008
Beazer's investment in joint ventures	$ 30,124	$ 33,065
Total equity of joint ventures	328,875	340,374
Total outstanding borrowing of joint ventures	422,682	524,431
Beazer's estimate of its portions of loan-to-value maintenance guarantees	3,850	5,839

(in thousands)	2009	2008
Beazer's estimate of its portion of repayment guarantees	**15,789**	39,166

The reduction in our investment in unconsolidated joint ventures from September 30, 2008 to September 30, 2009 relates primarily to impairments totaling $14.8 million, distributions of earnings totaling $3.0 million, and return of capital in the form of cash and inventory assets totaling $15.9 million which were offset by $25.5 million of additional investments and $4.6 of accrued liabilities for guarantee payments and deferred income. During fiscal 2009, we also acquired our joint venture partner's interest in two joint ventures which are consolidated as of September 30, 2009. In connection with the acquisition of one of these joint ventures, we paid off the joint venture's debt of approximately $13.6 million.

For the fiscal year ended September 30, 2009, 2008 and 2007, the impairments of our investments in certain of our other unconsolidated joint ventures, totaling $14.8 million, $68.8 million and $28.6 million, respectively, were recorded in accordance with APB 18. In fiscal 2007, we also recorded $3.4 million in contractual obligation abandonments related to those ventures. Impairments totaling $13.8 million, $64.0 million and $28.6 million for fiscal 2009, 2008 and 2007, respectively, are included in equity in loss of unconsolidated joint ventures on the accompanying Consolidated Statements of Operations. The remaining impairments of $1.0 million and $4.8 million for fiscal 2009 and 2008 are included in loss from discontinued operations, net of taxes in the accompanying Consolidated Statements of Operations. Equity in loss of unconsolidated joint ventures related to our continuing operations totaled $13.3 million, $76.6 and $35.1 million for the fiscal years ended September 30, 2009, 2008 and 2007, respectively.

The aggregate debt of the unconsolidated joint ventures was $422.7 million and $524.4 million at September 30, 2009 and 2008, respectively. At September 30, 2009, total borrowings outstanding include $327.9 million related to one joint venture in which we are a 2.58% partner. The $101.7 million reduction in total outstanding joint venture debt during fiscal 2009 resulted primarily from the cancellation of $51.5 million of debt of four joint ventures and debt payments of $76.7 million in accordance with loan agreements and/or negotiated settlements offset by loan draws of $27.9 million to fund the development activities of the joint ventures.

During the fourth quarter of fiscal 2009, one of our unconsolidated joint ventures completed a modification of its loan agreement with its lender, which resulted in, among other things, an extension of its maturity, enhanced guarantees from our joint venture partner and the release of Beazer under all guarantees related to this joint venture. Beazer contributed $9.7 million as an additional investment in the joint venture as part of the loan modification. Also during the fourth quarter of fiscal 2009, the Company and its joint venture partners entered into agreements with a lender to repay the notes payable of one of its unconsolidated joint ventures at a discount. The Company contributed an additional $4.3 million as an investment which was used to reduce the loan balance of this joint venture. We also entered into an agreement with a lender and our joint venture partner to purchase the notes payable and our partner's interest in one of our unconsolidated joint ventures for a total of $13.6 million. This joint venture is consolidated in our financial statements as of September 30, 2009. In fiscal 2009, we also paid $3.0 million to settle our obligations under guarantees for three ventures which we had previously estimated at a maximum potential obligation of $16.6 million. As part of the settlement agreements, the lenders also cancelled $48.6 million of the outstanding debt of these three joint ventures. Subsequent to September 30, 2009, together with our joint venture partner, we reached agreement with a lender to another joint venture to pay down the outstanding debt by $7.6 million ($3.8 million per partner). In connection with this loan repayment, the lender has agreed to release the obligations under the related loan-to-value maintenance guarantee.

Three of our joint ventures are in default (or have received default notices) under their respective debt obligations. During fiscal 2008, the lender to the joint venture, in which we have a 2.58% investment, notified the joint venture partners that it believes the joint venture is in default of certain joint venture loan agreements as a result of certain of the Company's joint venture partners not complying with all aspects of the joint ventures' loan agreements. The joint venture partners are currently in discussions with the lender. In December 2008, the lender has filed individual lawsuits against some of the joint venture partners and certain of those partners' parent companies (including the Company), seeking to recover damages under completion guarantees, among other claims. We intend to vigorously defend against this legal action. The Company's share of the outstanding debt is approximately $14.5 million at September 30, 2009. Under the terms of the agreement, our repayment guarantee is estimated at $15.1 million, which is only triggered in the event of bankruptcy of the joint venture. Our equity interest at September 30, 2009 was $8.6 million in this joint venture. Given the inherent uncertainties in this litigation, as of September 30, 2009, no accrual has been recorded, as losses, if any, related to this matter are not both probable and reasonably estimable.

In addition, certain of our joint venture partners have curtailed their funding of their allocable joint venture obligations. Given the inherent uncertainties in these negotiations, as of September 30, 2009, no accrual has been recorded, as obligations to Beazer, if any, related to these matters were not both probable and reasonably estimable.

Our joint ventures typically obtain secured acquisition, development and construction financing. Generally Beazer and our joint venture partners provide varying levels of guarantees of debt and other obligations for our unconsolidated joint ventures. At September 30, 2009, these guarantees included, for certain joint ventures, construction completion guarantees, loan-to-value maintenance agreements, repayment guarantees and environmental indemnities.

In assessing the need to record a liability for the contingent aspect of these guarantees in accordance with FIN 45, *Guarantor's Accounting and Disclosure Requirements for Guarantees, Including Indirect Guarantees of Indebtedness of Others* (ASC 400), we consider our historical experience in being required to perform under the guarantees, the fair value of the collateral underlying these guarantees and the financial condition of the applicable unconsolidated joint ventures. In addition, we monitor the fair value of the collateral of these unconsolidated joint ventures to ensure that the related borrowings do not exceed the specified percentage of the value of the property securing the borrowings. We have not recorded a liability for the contingent aspects of any guarantees that we determined were reasonably possible but not probable.

Construction Completion Guarantees

We and our joint venture partners may be obligated to the project lenders to complete land development improvements and the construction of planned homes if the joint venture does not perform the required development. Provided the joint venture and the partners are not in default under any loan provisions, the project lenders typically are obligated to fund these improvements through any financing commitments available under the applicable loans. A majority of these construction completion guarantees are joint and several with our partners. In those cases, we generally have a reimbursement arrangement with our partner which provides that neither party is responsible for more than its proportionate share of the guarantee. However, if our joint venture partner does not have adequate financial resources to meet its obligations under such reimbursement arrangement, we may be liable for more than our proportionate share, up to our maximum exposure, which is the full amount covered by the relevant joint and several guarantee. The guarantees cover a specific scope of work, which may range from an individual development phase to the completion of the entire project. No accrual has been recorded, as losses, if any, related to construction completion guarantees are not both probable and reasonably estimable.

Loan-to-Value Maintenance Agreements

We and our joint venture partners may provide credit enhancements to acquisition, development and construction borrowings in the form of loan-to-value maintenance agreements, which can limit the amount of additional funding provided by the lenders or require repayment of the borrowings to the extent such borrowings plus construction completion costs exceed a specified percentage of the value of the property securing the borrowings. The agreements generally require periodic reappraisals of the underlying property value. To the extent that the underlying property gets reappraised, the amount of the exposure under the loan-to value-maintenance (LTV) guarantee would be adjusted accordingly and any such change could be significant. In certain cases, we may be required to make a re-balancing payment following a reappraisal in order to reduce the applicable loan-to-value ratio to the required level.

Our estimate of the Company's portion of LTV guarantees of the unconsolidated joint ventures was $3.9 million at September 30, 2009 and $5.8 million at September 30, 2008. Subsequent to September 30, 2009, the Company and its joint venture partner have reached an agreement with the lender of a joint venture to release the LTV guarantee and extend the related loan maturity up to two years in exchange for a loan repayment of $7.6 million. The Company and its joint venture partner have agreed to each invest an additional $3.8 million in the joint venture to facilitate this repayment.

Repayment Guarantees

We and our joint venture partners have repayment guarantees related to certain joint ventures' borrowings. These repayment guarantees require the repayment of all or a portion of the debt of the unconsolidated joint venture only in the event the joint venture defaults on its obligations under the borrowing or in some cases only in the event the joint venture files for bankruptcy.

Our estimate of Beazer's portion of repayment guarantees related to the outstanding debt of its unconsolidated joint ventures was $15.8 million and $39.2 million at September 30, 2009 and 2008, respectively. The reduction in the estimate of joint venture repayment guarantees was driven primarily by 1) the negotiated settlement with the lenders of two joint ventures for the cancellation of debt and the release of other loan obligations including $16.6 million in repayment guarantees for nominal consideration and 2) the negotiated loan modification and release of guarantees with the lender of one joint venture in return for the repayment of a portion of the outstanding debt. The Company contributed $9.7 million as an additional investment in this latter joint venture which was used to reduce the outstanding loan balance.

Environmental Indemnities

Additionally, we and our joint venture partners generally provide unsecured environmental indemnities to joint venture project lenders. In each case, we have performed due diligence on potential environmental risks. These indemnities obligate us to reimburse the project lenders for claims related to environmental matters for which they are held responsible. During the fiscal years ended September 30, 2009 and 2008, we were not required to make any payments related to environmental indemnities. No accrual has been recorded, as losses, if any, related to environmental indemnities are not both probable and reasonably estimable.

General Electric
2008 Annual Report

Note 26. Intercompany Transactions

Effects of transactions between related companies are eliminated and consist primarily of GECS dividend to GE; GE customer receivables sold to GECS; GECS services for trade receivables management and material procurement; buildings and equipment (including automobiles) leased by GE from GECS; information technology (IT) and other services sold to GECS by GE; aircraft engines manufactured by GE that are installed on aircraft purchased by GECS from third-party producers for lease to others; medical equipment manufactured by GE that is leased by GECS to others; and various investments, loans and allocations of GE corporate overhead costs.

These intercompany transactions are reported in the GE and GECS columns of our financial statements (and include customer receivables sold from GE to GECS), but are eliminated in deriving our Consolidated financial statements. The effects of these eliminations on our Consolidated cash flows from operating, investing and financing activities follow.

December 31 (In millions)	2008	2007	2006
OPERATING			
Sum of GE and GECS cash from operating activities—continuing operations	$ 50,290	$ 48,316	$ 45,351
Elimination of GECS dividend to GE	(2,351)	(7,291)	(9,847)
Net decrease (increase) in GE customer receivables sold to GECS	90	(255)	2,036
Other reclassifications and eliminations	(188)	(828)	(956)
Consolidated cash from operating activities—continuing operations	$ 47,841	$ 39,942	$ 35,512
INVESTING			
Sum of GE and GECS cash used for investing activities—continuing operations	$ (39,615)	$ (67,845)	$ (54,132)
Net increase (decrease) in GE customer receivables sold to GESC	(90)	255	2,036
Other reclassifications and eliminations	(320)	1,202	1,223
Consolidated cash used for investing activities—continuing operations	$ (40,025)	$ (66,388)	$ (50,873)
FINANCING			
Sum of GE and GECS cash used for investing activities—continuing operations	$ 22,760	$ 18,751	$ 16,772
Elimination of short-term intercompany borrowings	(787)	1,950	(2,732)
Elimination of GECS dividend to GE	2,351	7,291	9,847
Other reclassifications and eliminations	316	99	(48)
Consolidated cash from financing activities—continuing operations	$ 24,640	$ 28,091	$ 23,839

FMC
2007 Annual Report

Note 5. Investments in Joint Ventures

We are party to several joint venture investments throughout the world, which individually and in the aggregate are not significant to our financial results. Investment gains for the year ended December 31, 2005.

In November 2005, Astaris LLC (now known as Siratsa LLC), our 50%-owned joint venture with Solutia, completed the sale of substantially all of its assets, other than certain excluded assets used in the business of Astaris to certain subsidiaries of Israel Chemicals Limited ("ICL"). The buyers also assumed certain of the liabilities of Astaris. The final sales price was $263 million. In connection with this sale, we recorded a gain of $57.7 million, before tax. This gain is included in "Equity in (earnings) loss of affiliates" on our consolidated statements of income for the year ended December 31, 2005. We received cash totaling $99.4 million of which $69.1 million is a distribution and $30.3 million is the final payment of Astaris obligations due to us as well as payments for certain liabilities transferred from Astaris to us.

In the second quarter of 2005, we sold our 50 percent ownership investment in Sibelco Española SA ("Sibelco") for cash of $13.7 million. We accounted for Sibelco on the equity method. We recorded a gain of $9.3 million in conjunction with this sale which is included in "Investment gains" on our consolidated statements of income for the year ended December 31, 2005.

Note 6. In-Process Research and Development

Proprietary Fungicide Agreement

In the second quarter of 2006, our Agricultural Products segment entered into development agreements with a third-party company, whereby we were given the right to develop further one of the third party company's products in certain geographic markets. Under the agreements, we paid $2.0 million and have recorded this amount as a charge to "In-process research and development" in the consolidated statements of income for the year ended December 31, 2006.

In the first quarter of 2007, our Agricultural Products segment acquired further rights from this third-party company to develop their proprietary fungicide. In acquiring those further rights, we paid an additional $1.0 million and have recorded this amount as a charge to "In-process research and development" in the consolidated statements of income for the year ended December 31, 2007.

Collaboration and License Agreement

In the third quarter of 2007, our Agricultural Products segment entered into a collaboration and license agreement with another third-party company for the purpose of obtaining certain technology and intellectual property rights. We paid an initial $1.0 million upon entering into this agreement and have recorded the amount as a charge to "In-process research and development" in the consolidated statements of income for the year ended December 31, 2007.

Fluor
2007 Annual Report

Variable Interest Entities

National Roads Telecommunications Services ("NRTS") Project

In 2005, the company's Industrial & Infrastructure segment was awarded a $544 million project by a joint venture, GeneSYS Telecommunications Limited ("GeneSYS"), in which the company owns a 45 percent interest and HSBC Infrastructure Fund Management Limited owns a 55 percent interest. The project was entered into with the United Kingdom Secretary of State for Transport (the "Highways Agency") to design, build, maintain and finance a significant upgrade to the integrated transmission network throughout England's motorways. GeneSYS financed the engineering and construction ("E&C") of the upgraded telecommunications infrastructure with approximately $279 million of non-recourse debt (the "term loan facility") from a consortium of lenders (the "Banks") along with joint venture member equity contributions and subordinated debt which were financed during the construction period utilizing equity bridge loans from outside lenders. During September 2007, the joint venture members paid their required permanent financing commitments in the amount of $44 million and were issued Subordinated Notes by GeneSYS. These funds were used by GeneSYS to repay the temporary construction term financing including the company's equity bridge loan. In early October 2007, the newly constructed network achieved operational status and was fully accepted by the Highways Agency on December 20, 2007, thereby concluding the E&C phase and entering the operations and maintenance phase of the project.

Based on a qualitative analysis of the variable interests of all parties involved at the formation of GeneSYS, under the provisions of FIN 46-R, the company was initially determined to be the primary beneficiary of the joint venture. The company's consolidated financial statements included the accounts of GeneSYS, and, accordingly, the non-recourse debt provided by the Banks from the inception of the venture. Effective October 1, 2007, the company no longer consolidates the accounts of GeneSYS because it is no longer the primary beneficiary of the joint venture.

FIN 46-R requires that the initial determination of whether an entity is a variable interest entity ("VIE") shall be reconsidered under certain conditions. One of those conditions is when the entity's governing documents or contractual arrangements are changed in a manner that changes the characteristics or adequacy of the entity's equity investment at risk. Such an event occurred in September 2007 upon the infusion of capital by the joint venture members which resulted in permanent financing through issuance of Subordinated Notes by GeneSYS that replaced the temporary equity bridge loans that had been provided by outside lenders. This refinancing of temporary debt with permanent debt constituted a change in the governing documents of GeneSYS that required reconsideration of GeneSYS as a variable interest entity.

Based on the new capitalization structure of GeneSYS, the adequacy of the equity at risk in GeneSYS was evaluated and found to be inadequate to finance its operations without additional subordinated financial support. Accordingly, upon reconsideration, GeneSYS continues to be a variable interest entity. Because the company holds a variable interest in the entity through its equity and debt investments, a qualitative evaluation was undertaken to determine if it was the primary beneficiary. In this evaluation, the company considered all parties that have direct or implicit variable interests based on the contractual arrangements existing at the time of reconsideration. Based on this evaluation, the company has determined that it is no longer the primary beneficiary of GeneSYS. Accordingly, GeneSYS is not consolidated in the company's accounts at December 31, 2007 and is being accounted for on the equity method of accounting.

The company's maximum exposure to loss relating to its investment in GeneSYS is its aggregate $20 million equity and debt investment plus any unremitted earnings. The term loan is an obligation of GeneSYS and will never be a debt repayment obligation of the company because it is non-recourse to the joint venture members.

Interstate 495 Capital Beltway Project

In December 2007, the company was awarded the $1.3 billion Interstate 495 Capital Beltway high-occupancy toll ("HOT") lanes project in Virginia. The project is a public-private partnership between the Virginia Department of Transportation ("VDOT") and Capital Beltway Express LLC, a joint venture in which the company has a ten percent interest and Transurban (USA) Inc. has a 90 percent interest ("Fluor-Transurban"). Under the agreement, VDOT will own and oversee the addition of traffic lanes, interchange improvements and construction of HOT lanes on 14 miles of the I-495 Capital Beltway in northern Virginia. Fluor-Transurban, as concessionaire, will develop, design, finance, construct, maintain and operate the improvements and HOT lanes under an 80 year concession agreement. The construction will be financed through grant funding from VDOT, non-recourse borrowings from issuance of public tax-exempt bonds, a non-recourse loan from the Federal Transportation Infrastructure Finance Innovation Act (TIFIA) which is administered by the U.S. Department of Transportation and equity contributions from the joint venture members.

The construction of the improvements and HOT lanes will be performed by a construction joint venture in which the company has a 65 percent interest and Lane Construction has a 35 percent interest ("Fluor-Lane"). Transurban (USA) Inc. will perform the operations and maintenance upon completion of the improvements and commencement of operations of the toll lanes.

Fluor-Transurban has been determined to be a variable interest entity under the provisions of FIN 46-R. Pursuant to the requirements of the Interpretation, the company evaluated its interest in Fluor-Transurban including its project execution obligations and risks relating to its interest in Fluor-Lane and has determined based on a qualitative analysis that it is not the primary beneficiary of Fluor-Transurban. The company's maximum exposure to loss relating to its investment in Fluor-Transurban is its $35 million aggregate equity investment commitment, of which $9 million has been funded, plus any un-remitted earnings. The company will never have repayment obligations associated with any of the debt because it is non-recourse to the joint venture members. The company will account for its ownership interest in Fluor-Transurban on the equity method of accounting. The company will fully consolidate Fluor-Lane in its consolidated financial statements.

General Mills
2006 Annual Report

4. Investments in Joint Ventures

We have a 50 percent equity interest in Cereal Partners Worldwide (CPW), a joint venture with Nestlé S.A. that manufactures and markets cereal products outside the United States and Canada. We have guaranteed a portion of CPW's debt. See Note Fifteen. We have a 50 percent equity interest in 8th Continent, LLC, a domestic joint venture with DuPont to develop and market soy-based products. We have 50 percent equity interests in the following joint ventures for the manufacture, distribution and marketing of *Häagen-Dazs* frozen ice cream products and novelties: Häagen-Dazs Japan K.K.; Häagen-Dazs Korea Company Limited; and Häagen-Dazs Marketing & Distribution (Philippines) Inc. We have a 49 percent equity interest in Häagen-Dazs Distributors (Thailand) Company Limited. We also have a 50 percent equity interest in Seretram, a joint venture with Co-op de Pau for the production of *Green Giant* canned corn in France. In May 2006, we acquired a controlling financial interest in our Häagen-Dazs joint venture in the Philippines for less than $1 million.

Fiscal 2005 and fiscal 2004 results of operations include our share of the after-tax earnings of SVE through the date of its termination on February 28, 2005.

On July 14, 2006, CPW acquired the Uncle Tobys cereal business in Australia for approximately $385 million. This business had revenues of approximately $100 million for the fiscal year ended June 30, 2006. We funded our 50 percent share of the purchase price by making an additional equity contribution in CPW from cash generated from our international operations, including our international joint ventures.

In February 2006, CPW announced a restructuring of its manufacturing plants in the United Kingdom. Our after-tax earnings from joint ventures were reduced by $8 million for our share of the restructuring costs, primarily accelerated depreciation and severance, incurred in fiscal 2006.

Our cumulative investment in these joint ventures was $186 million at the end of fiscal 2006 and $211 million at the end of fiscal 2005. We made aggregate investments in the joint ventures of $7 million in fiscal 2006, $15 million in fiscal 2005 and $31 million in fiscal 2004. We received aggregate dividends from the joint ventures of $77 million in fiscal 2006, $83 million in fiscal 2005 and $60 million in fiscal 2004.

Results from our CPW joint venture are reported as of and for the twelve months ended March 31. The Häagen-Dazs and Seretram joint venture results are reported as of and for the twelve months ended April 30. 8th Continent's results are presented on the same basis as our fiscal year.

Summary combined financial information for the joint ventures (including SVE through the date of its termination on February 28, 2005) on a 100 percent basis follows:

In Millions, Fiscal Year Ended	2006	2005	2004
Net Sales	$1,796	$2,652	$2,625
Gross Margin	770	1,184	1,180
Earnings before Income Taxes	157	231	205
Earnings after Income Taxes	120	184	153

Gross margin is defined as net sales less cost of sales.

In Millions, At End of Fiscal Year	2006	2005
Current Assets	$634	$604
Noncurrent Assets	578	612
Current Liabilities	756	695
Noncurrent Liabilities	6	7

Ariba, Inc.
2005 Annual Report

Note 8—Minority Interests in Subsidiaries

In December 2000, the Company's consolidated subsidiary, Nihon Ariba, issued and sold 38,000 shares, or approximately 41% of its common stock, for cash consideration of approximately $40.0 million to Softbank pursuant to its strategic relationship with Softbank. In April 2001, Nihon Ariba issued and sold an additional 2% of its common stock for cash consideration of approximately $4.0 million to third parties. Prior to the transactions, the Company held 100% of the equity of Nihon Ariba in the form of common stock.

In April 2001, the Company's consolidated subsidiary, Ariba Korea, issued and sold 3,800 shares, or approximately 42% of its common stock, for each consideration of approximately $8.0 million to Softbank. Prior to the transaction, the Company held 100% of the equity of Ariba Korea in the form of common stock.

In October 2004, the Company purchased the 41% interest in Nihon Ariba and the 42% interest in Ariba Korea held by Softbank for $3.5 million. See Note 13 for a discussion of the Softbank settlement. The Company subsequently purchased an additional 2% interest in Nihon Ariba held by various sharehold-ers. These transactions resulted in a $19.5 million reduction to minority interests during the year ended September 30, 2005.

As of September 30, 2004, minority interests of $19.5 million are recorded on the consolidated balance sheet in order to reflect the share of the net assets of Nihon Ariba and Ariba Korea held by minority investors. For the years ended September 30, 2005 and 2003, the Company increased consolidated net loss by $17,000 and $3.5 million, which represented the minority interest' share of income of the two subsidiaries, respectively. For the year ended September 30, 2004, the Company reduced consolidated net loss by approximately $539,000, which represented the minority interest's share of losses of the two subsidiaries.

Sara Lee
2005 Annual Report

Note 10—Minority Interest in Subsidiaries

Minority interest in subsidiaries in 2005 consists of the equity interest of minority investors in consolidated subsidiaries of the corporation. In 2003, minority inter-est also included preferred equity securities issued by subsidiaries of the corpo-ration. The corporation's consolidated minority interest expense of $11 in 2005, $6 in 2004 and $20 in 2003 is recorded in "Selling, general and administrative expenses."

On the first day of 2004, the provisions of Statement of Financial Accounting Standards No. 150, "Accounting for Certain Financial Instruments with Characteristics of Both Liabilities and Equity" (SFAS No. 150) became effective for the corporation. Under the provisions of that standard, $295 of preferred equity securities were reclassified from "Minority interest in subsidiaries" to the "Current maturities of long-term debt" on the Consolidated Balance Sheet. These securities were outstanding in 2003 and included in "Minority interest in subsidiaries." These preferred equity securities were issued by a wholly owned foreign subsidiary of the corporation. The securities provided a rate of return based upon the Euribor interbank borrowing rate, which averaged 3.3% in 2003. The provisions of SFAS No. 150 prohibit the restatement of financial statements for periods prior to the effective date of the statement.

During 2003, the preferred equity securities issued by a domestic subsidiary were redeemed by the corporation for $250. The securities provided the holder a rate of return based upon the LIBOR interest rate plus 0.425%. The average LIBOR borrowing rates in 2003 were 2.0%.

No gain or loss was recognized as a result of the issuance of either of these preferred equity securities, and the corporation owned substantially all of the voting equity of the subsidiaries both before and after the transactions.

General Mills
2005 Annual Report

9. Minority Interests

In April 2002, the Company and certain of its wholly owned subsidiaries contributed assets with an aggregate fair market value of approximately $4 billion to another wholly owned subsidiary, General Mills Cereals, LLC (GMC), a limited liability company. GMC is a separate and distinct legal entity from the Company and its subsidiaries, and has separate assets, liabilities, businesses and operations. The contributed assets consist primarily of manufacturing assets and intellectual property associated with the production and retail sale of Big G ready-to-eat cereals, *Progresso* soups and *Old El Paso* products. In exchange for the contribution of these assets, GMC issued the managing membership interest and preferred membership interests to wholly owned subsidiaries of the Company. The managing member directs the business activities and operations of GMC and has fiduciary responsibilities to GMC and its members. Other than rights to vote on certain matters, holders of the preferred membership interests have no right to direct the management of GMC.

In May 2002, a wholly owned subsidiary of the Company sold 150,000 Class A preferred membership interests in GMC to an unrelated third-party investor in exchange for $150 million. On October 8, 2004, another wholly owned subsidiary of the Company sold 835,000 Series B-1 preferred membership interests in GMC in exchange for $835 million. In connection with the sale of the Series B-1 interests, GMC and its existing members entered into a Third Amended and Restated Limited Liability Company Agreement of GMC (the LLC Agreement), setting forth, among other things, the terms of the Series B-1 and Class A interests held by the third-party investors and the rights of those investors. Currently, all interests in GMC, other than the 835,000 Series B-1 interests and 150,000 Class A interests, but including all managing member interests, are held by wholly owned subsidiaries of the Company.

The Class A interests receive quarterly preferred distributions at a floating rate equal to (i) the sum of three-month LIBOR plus 90 basis points, divided by (ii) 0.965. The LLC Agreement requires that the rate of the distributions on the Class A interests be adjusted by agreement between the third-party investor holding the Class A interests and GMC every five years, beginning in June 2007. If GMC and the investor fail to mutually agree on a new rate of preferred distributions, GMC must remarket the Class A interests to set a new distribution rate. Upon a failed remarketing, the rate over LIBOR will be increased by 75 basis points until the next scheduled remarketing date. GMC, through its managing member, may elect to repurchase all of the Class A interests at any time for an amount equal to the holder's capital account, plus any applicable make-whole amount. Under certain circumstances, GMC also may be required to be dissolved and liquidated, including, without limitation, the bankruptcy of GMC or its subsidiaries, failure to deliver the preferred distributions, failure to comply with portfolio requirements, breaches of certain covenants, lowering of our senior debt rating below either Baa3 by Moody's or BBB by Standard & Poor's, and a failed attempt to remarket the Class A interests as a result of a breach of GMC's obligations to assist in such remarketing. In the event of a liquidation of GMC, each member of GMC would receive the amount of its then capital account balance. The managing member may avoid liquidation in most circumstances by exercising an option to purchase the Class A interests. An election to purchase the preferred membership interests could impact our liquidity by requiring us to refinance the purchase price.

The Series B-1 interests are entitled to receive quarterly preferred distributions at a fixed rate of 4.5% per year, which is scheduled to be reset to a new fixed rate through a remarketing in October 2007. Beginning in October 2007, the managing member of GMC may elect to repurchase the Series B-1 interests for an amount equal to the holder's then current capital account balance plus any applicable make-whole amount. GMC is not required to purchase the Series B-1 interests.

Upon the occurrence of certain exchange events (as described below), the Series B-1 interests will be exchanged for shares of perpetual preferred stock of the Company. An exchange will occur upon the senior unsecured debt rating of the Company falling below either Ba3 as rated by Moody's Investors Service, Inc. or BB-as rated by Standard & Poor's or Fitch, Inc., a bankruptcy or liquidation of the Company, a default on any senior indebtedness of the Company resulting in an acceleration of indebtedness having an outstanding principal balance in excess of $50 million, the Company failing to pay a dividend on its common stock in any fiscal quarter, or certain liquidating events as set forth in the LLC Agreement.

If GMC fails to make a required distribution to the holders of Series B-1 interests when due, we will be restricted from paying any dividend (other than dividends in the form of shares of common stock) or other distributions on shares of our common or preferred stock, and may not repurchase or redeem shares of our common or preferred stock, until all such accrued and undistributed distributions are paid to the holders of the Series B-1 interests. If the required distributions on the Series B-1 interests remain undistributed for six quarterly distribution periods, the managing member will form a nine-member board of directors to manage GMC. Under these circumstances, the holder of the Series B-1 interests will have the right to appoint one director. Upon the payment of the required distributions, the GMC board of directors will be dissolved. At May 29, 2005, we have made all required distributions to the Series B-1 interests. As discussed above, upon the occurrence of certain events the Series B-1 interests will be included in our computation of diluted earnings per share as a participating security.

For financial reporting purposes, the assets, liabilities, results of operations, and cash flows of GMC are included in our consolidated financial statements. The third-party investors' Class A and Series B-1 interests in GMC are reflected as minority interests on our consolidated balance sheet, and the return to the third party investors is reflected as interest, including minority interest, expense in the consolidated statements of earnings.

In fiscal 2003, General Mills Capital, Inc. (GM Capital), a wholly owned subsidiary, sold $150 million of its Series A preferred stock to an unrelated third-party investor. GM Capital regularly purchases our receivables. These receivables are included in the consolidated balance sheet and the $150 million purchase price for the Series A preferred stock is reflected as minority interest on the balance sheet. The proceeds from the issuance of the preferred stock were used to reduce short-term debt. The return to the third-party investor is reflected as interest, including minority interest, expense in the consolidated statements of earnings.

On September 24, 2003, we sold $500 million of 25/8% fixed-rate notes due October 24, 2006. Interest on these notes is payable semiannually on April 24 and October 24, beginning April 24, 2004. Concurrently, we entered into an interest rate swap for $500 million notional amount where we receive 25/8% fixed interest and pay LIBOR plus 11 basis points.

On August 11, 2003, we entered into a $75 million five-year term (callable after two years) bank borrowing agreement. The floating rate coupon is one month LIBOR plus 15 basis points and interest is payable on a monthly basis. On November 20, 2002, we sold $350 million of 37/8% fixed-rate notes and $135 million of 3.901% fixed-rate notes due November 30, 2007. Interest for these notes is payable semiannually on May 30 and November 30, beginning May 30, 2003.

On October 28, 2002, we completed a private placement of zero coupon convertible debentures with a face value of approximately $2.23 billion for gross proceeds of approximately $1.50 billion. The issue price of the debentures was $671.65 for each $1,000 in face value, which represents a yield to maturity of 2.00%. The debentures cannot be called by us for three years after issuance and will mature in 20 years. Holders of the debentures can require us to repurchase the notes on the third, fifth, tenth and fifteenth anniversaries of the issuance. We have the option to pay the repurchase price in cash or in stock. The notes are classified as current portion of long-term debt as the result of the associated put provisions. The debentures are convertible into our common stock at a rate of 13.0259 shares for each $1,000 debenture. This results in an initial conversion price of approximately $51.56 per share and represents a premium of 25 percent over the closing sale price of $41.25 per share on October 22, 2002. The conversion price will increase with the accretion of the original issue discount on the debentures. Generally, except upon the occurrence of specified events, holders of the debentures are not entitled to exercise their conversion rights until our stock price is greater than a specified percentage (beginning at 125 percent and declining by 0.25 percent each six months) of the accreted conversion price per share. At May 29, 2005, the conversion price was $54.29. The shares issuable upon conversion are included in diluted earnings per share. See Note Twelve—Earnings Per Share.

As of May 29, 2005, the amount recorded in Accumulated Other Comprehensive Income associated with our interest rate swaps ($119 million) will be reclassified to interest expense over the remaining lives of the hedged forecasted transaction, which mirrors the remaining life of swap contracts (ranging from one to eight years). The amount reclassified from Accumulated Other Comprehensive Income in fiscal 2005 was $161 million, of which $88 million was recorded as interest expense and $73 million was recorded as part of the debt repurchase costs described above. The amount expected to be reclassified from Accumulated Other Comprehensive Income to interest expense in fiscal 2006 is $34 million.

A summary of our long-term debt is as follows:

In millions	May 29, 2005	May 30, 2004
Zero coupon convertible debentures yield 2.0%, $2,233 due Oct. 28, 2022[1]	$ 1,579	$1,548
5 1/8% notes due Feb. 15, 2007	1,500	1,500
6% notes due Feb. 15, 2012	1,240	2,000
2.625% notes due Oct. 14, 2006	500	500
Medium-term notes, 4.8% to 9.1%, due 2005 to 2078	413	437
3 7/8% notes due Nov. 30, 2007	350	350
3.901% notes due Nov. 30, 2007	135	135
Zero coupon notes, yield 11.1%, $261 due Aug. 15, 2013	108	97
8.2% ESPO loan guaranty, due through June 30, 2007	6	11
Notes payable, reclassified	–	750
7.0% notes due Sept. 15, 2004	–	150
Zero coupon notes, yield 11.7%, $54 due Aug. 15, 2004	–	53
Other, primarily due July 11, 2008	62	112
	5,893	7,643

In millions	May 29, 2005	May 30, 2004
Less amounts due within one year[1]	(1,638)	(233)
Total Long-term Debt	$ 4,255	$7,410

[1] The zero coupon convertible debentures are included in the current portion of long-term debt as the result of put provisions described above.

See Note Seven—Financial Instruments and Risk Management Activities— for a description of related interest—rate derivative instruments.

We have guaranteed the debt of the Employee Stock Ownership Plan; therefore, the loan is reflected on our consolidated balance sheets as long-term debt with a related offset in Unearned Compensation in Stockholders' Equity.

The sinking fund and principal payments due on long-term debt based on stated contractual maturities are (in millions) $59, $2,037, $486, $172 and $15 in fiscal 2006, 2007, 2008, 2009 and 2010, respectively. The fiscal 2006 amount is exclusive of $1 million of interest yet to be accreted on zero coupon notes.

Schering-Plough 2004 Annual Report

3. Equity Income from Cholesterol Joint Venture

In May 2000, the Company and Merck entered into two separate agreements to jointly develop and market in the U.S. (1) two cholesterol lowering drugs and (2) an allergy/asthma drug. In December 2001, the cholesterol agreement was expanded to include all countries of the world except Japan. In general, the companies agreed that the collaborative activities under these agreements would operate in a virtual mode to the maximum degree possible by relying on the respective infrastructures of the two companies. These agreements generally provide for equal sharing of research and development costs and for co-promotion of approved products by each company.

The cholesterol agreements provide for the Company and Merck to jointly develop ezetimibe (marketed as ZETIA in the U.S. and Asia and EZETROL in Europe):

    i. as a once-daily monotherapy;

    ii. in co-administration with any statin drug, and;

    iii. as a once-daily fixed-combination tablet of ezetimibe and simvastatin (Zocor), Merck's cholesterol-modifying medicine. This combination medication (ezetimibe/simvastatin) is marketed as VYTORIN in the U.S. and as INEGY in many international countries.

ZETIA/EZETROL (ezetimibe) and VYTORIN/INEGY (the combination of ezetimibe/simvastatin) are approved for use in the U.S. and have been launched in several international markets.

The Company utilizes the equity method of accounting for the joint venture. The cholesterol agreements provide for the sharing of net income/(loss) based upon percentages that vary by product, sales level and country. In the U.S. market, Schering-Plough receives a greater share of profits on the first $300 of ZETIA sales. Above $300 of ZETIA sales, the companies share profits equally. Schering-Plough's allocation of joint venture income is increased by milestones earned. Further, either partner's share of the joint venture's net income/(loss) is subject to a reduction if the partner fails to perform a specified minimum number of physician details in a particular country. The partners agree annually to the minimum number of physician details by country.

The partners bear the costs of their own general sales forces and commercial overhead in marketing joint venture products around the world. In the U.S., Canada and Puerto Rico, the cholesterol agreements provide for a reimbursement to each partner for physician details that are set on an annual basis. This reimbursed amount is equal to each partner's physician details multiplied by a contractual fixed fee. Schering-Plough reports the receipt of this reimbursement as part of Equity income from cholesterol joint venture as under U.S. GAAP this amount does not represent a reimbursement of specific, incremental, identifiable costs for the Company's detailing of the cholesterol products in these markets. In addition, this reimbursement amount per physician detail is not reflective of Schering-Plough's joint venture sales force effort as Schering-Plough's sales force-related infrastructure costs per physician detail are generally estimated to be higher.

Costs of the joint venture that the partners contractually share are a portion of manufacturing costs, specifically identified promotion costs (including direct-to-consumer advertising and direct and identifiable out-of-pocket promotion) and other agreed upon costs for specific services such as market support, market research, market expansion, a specialty sales force, and physician education programs.

Certain specified research and development expenses are generally shared equally by the partners.

The following information provides a summary of the components of the Company's Equity income from cholesterol joint venture for the year ended December 31:

	2004	2003
	(Unaudited)	
Schering-Plough's share of net income/(loss) (including milestones of $7 and $20 in 2004 and 2003, respectively) .	$244	$(11)
Reimbursement to Schering-Plough for physician details . . .	121	68
Elimination of intercompany profit and other, net	(18)	(3)
Total equity income from cholesterol joint venture	$347	$ 54

During 2004 and 2003, the Company earned milestones of $7 and $20, respectively, relating to the approval of ezetimibe/simvastatin in Mexico in 2004 and certain European approvals of ezetimibe in 2003. Under certain other conditions, as specified in the agreements, Merck could pay additional milestones to the Company totaling $125.

Equity income from the joint venture excludes any profit arising from transactions between the Company and the joint venture until such time as there is an underlying profit realized by the joint venture in a transaction with a party other than the Company or Merck.

Due to the virtual nature of the joint venture, the Company incurs substantial costs, such as selling, general, and administrative costs, that are not reflected in Equity income from cholesterol joint venture . . . and are borne by the overall cost structure of the Company. These costs are reported on their respective line items in the Statements of Consolidated Operations. The cholesterol agreements do not provide for any jointly owned facilities and, as such, products resulting from the joint venture are manufactured in facilities owned by either Merck or the Company.

As discussed above, the Company accounts for the Merck/Schering-Plough Cholesterol Partnership under the equity method of accounting. As such, the Company's net sales do not include the sales of this joint venture. Prior to 2003, the joint venture was in the research and development phase and the Company's share of research and development expense in 2002 of $69 was reported in Research and development in the Statements of Consolidated Operations.

The allergy/asthma agreement provides for the development and marketing of a once-daily, fixed combination tablet containing CLARITIN and Singulair. Singulair is Merck's once-daily leukotriene receptor antagonist for the treatment of asthma and seasonal allergic rhinitis. In January 2002, the Merck/Schering-Plough respiratory joint venture reported on results of Phase III clinical trials of a fixed combination tablet containing CLARITIN and Singulair. This Phase III study did not demonstrate sufficient added benefits in the treatment of seasonal allergic rhinitis. The CLARITIN and Singulair combination tablet does not have approval in any country and remains in clinical development.

Applied Materials
2005 Annual Report

Note 14 Consolidation of Variable Interest Entities

In fiscal 2001, Applied formed Applied Materials Ventures I, L.P. (the Fund), to invest in privately-held, early-stage companies engaged in developing systems, components and devices relating to nanotechnology and/or communications technology for specific applications and products. The Fund was formed as a limited partnership, with Applied as the sole limited partner and an independent party as the general partner. During the fourth quarter of fiscal 2004, Applied exercised its right to limit capital contributions to the Fund to $25 million and to terminate the partnership. As a result, under the provisions of the partnership agreement, the activities of the partnership concluded and the partnership was dissolved in March 2005. Applied' cumulative capital contributions to the Fund through dissolution totaled approximately $24 million. The Fund's assets, which primarily consisted of shares of portfolio companies, were distributed between Applied and the general partner during fiscal 2005. Applied recorded its investment in the portfolio companies as other long-term assets on its consolidated balance sheet at October 30, 2005.

FASB Interpretation No. 46 (FIN 46), "Consolidation of Variable Interest Entities, an Interpretation of ARB No. 51," as amended, provides guidance on the identification, classification and accounting of variable interest entities. The Fund qualified for consolidation under FIN 46 and was consolidated in Applied's consolidated financial statements starting in the first quarter of fiscal 2004 until it was dissolved. The consolidation and dissolution of the Fund did have a material impact on Applied's consolidated financial condition or results of operations for the periods presented.

United States Steel
2005 Annual Report

1314B Partnership

In accordance with FIN 46R, U.S. Steel consolidated the 1314B Partnership as of January 1, 2004. The 1314B Partnership was previously accounted for under the equity method. U.S. Steel is the sole general partner and there are two unaffiliated limited partners. U.S. Steel is responsible for purchasing, operations and sales of coke and coke by-products. U.S. Steel has a commitment to fund operating cash shortfalls of the 1314B Partnership of up to $150 million. The partnership at times had operating cash shortfalls in 2004 and 2003 that were funded with loans from U.S. Steel. There were no outstanding loans with the partnership at December 31, 2005 and 2004. An unamortized deferred gain from the formation of the partnership of $150 million is included in deferred credits and other liabilities in the balance sheet. The gain will not be recognized in income as long as U.S. Steel has a commitment to fund cash shortfalls of the partnership. Additionally, U.S. Steel, under certain circumstances, is required to indemnify the limited partners if the partnership product sales fail to qualify for credits under Section 29 of the Internal Revenue Code. Furthermore, U.S. Steel, under certain circumstances, has indemnified the 1314B Partnership for environmental obligations. See Note 29 for further discussion of commitments related to the 1314B Partnership.

Upon the initial consolidation of the 1314B Partnership, $28 million of current assets, $8 million of net property, plant and equipment, no liabilities and a minority interest of $22 million were included on the balance sheet. A $14 million cumulative effect of change in accounting principle benefit, net of tax, was recorded in the first quarter of 2004.

Distributions to the limited partners totaled $33 million and $27 million in 2005 and 2004, respectively.

Blackbird Acquisition Inc. (Blackbird)

In accordance with FIN 46R, U.S. Steel consolidated Blackbird, an entity established during the third quarter of 2004 to facilitate the purchase and sale of certain property, plant and equipment.

U.S. Steel has no ownership interest in Blackbird Acquisition Inc. At December 31, 2005 and 2004, zero and $16 million of property, plant and equipment was consolidated through Blackbird.

Sale of Accounts Receivable

U.S. Steel has a Receivables Purchase Agreement to sell a revolving interest in eligible trade receivables generated by U.S. Steel and certain of its subsidiaries through a commercial paper conduit program with funding under the facility up to the lesser of eligible receivables or $500 million. The Receivables Purchase Agreement expires on November 28, 2006. Qualifying accounts receivables are sold, on a daily basis, without recourse, to U.S. Steel Receivables LLC (USSR), a consolidated wholly owned special purpose entity. USSR then sells an undivided interest in these receivables to certain conduits. The conduits issue commercial paper to finance the purchase of their interest in the receivables. U.S. Steel has agreed to continue servicing the sold receivables at market rates. Because U.S. Steel receives adequate compensation for these services, no servicing asset or liability has been recorded.

Sales of accounts receivable are reflected as a reduction of receivables in the balance sheet and the proceeds received are included in cash flows from operating activities in the statement of cash flows. Generally, the facility provides that as payments are collected from the sold accounts receivables, USSR may elect to have the conduits reinvest the proceeds in new eligible accounts receivable.

During 2005 and 2004, USSR did not sell any accounts receivable. During 2003, USSR sold to conduits and subsequently repurchased $190 million of revolving interest in accounts receivable.

As of December 31, 2005 and 2004, $500 million was available to be sold under this facility. The net book value of U.S. Steel's retained interest in the receivables represents the best estimate of the fair market value due to the short-term nature of the receivables.

USSR pays the conduits a discount based on the conduits' borrowing costs plus incremental fees. During 2005 and 2004, U.S. Steel incurred costs of $1 million and $2 million, respectively, relating to fees on the Receivables Purchase Agreement. These costs are included in net interest and other financial costs in the statement of operations.

The table below summarizes cash flows from and paid to USSR:

(In millions)	2005	2004
Proceeds from:		
Collections reinvested	**$10,283**	$10,129
Securitizations	–	–
Servicing fee	**10**	10

	December 31,	
(In millions)	*2005*	*2004*
Balance of accounts receivable-net, purchased by USSR	**$931**	$1,016
Revolving interest sold to conduits	–	–
Accounts receivable-net, included in the balance sheet of U.S. Steel	**$931**	$1,016

The facility would be terminated on the occurrence and failure to cure certain events, including, among others, certain defaults with respect to the Inventory Facility and other debt obligations, any failure of USSR to maintain certain ratios related to the collectability of the receivables, and failure to extend the commitments of the commercial paper conduits' liquidity providers which currently terminate on November 22, 2006.

Ford Motor
2002 Annual Report

Note 13. Variable Interest Entities

In January 2003, the Financial Accounting Standards Board (FASB) issued Interpretation No. 46 (FIN 46), Consolidation of Variable Interest Entities. Under FIN 46, we are required to consolidate variable interest entities for which we are deemed to be the primary beneficiary by the third quarter of 2003, and disclose information about those in which we have significant variable interests effective immediately.

The Automotive sector has invested in and contracted with several joint ventures to manufacture and/or assemble vehicles or components. The net investment in joint ventures that may be deemed variable interest entities was approximately $806 million at December 31, 2002.

Ford Credit has activities with a limited purpose trust owned by a Ford Credit subsidiary and outside investors. Activities are limited to the purchase of asset backed securities and the issuance of commercial paper. In its existing structure, it is likely that this trust would be consolidated. Ford Credit's equity investment and retained beneficial interest in this trust is approximately $1.7 billion. At December 31, 2002, this trust had gross assets of $12.2 billion and gross liabilities of $11.8 billion.

Ford Credit also participates in bank-sponsored asset-backed commercial paper conduits where pools of retail installment contracts are sold to committed issuers that are variable interest entities of the sponsoring banks. At December 31, 2002, about $5.9 billion of retail installment receivables originated by Ford Credit were held by these conduits. In general, the percentage of Ford Credit assets sold to these variable interest entities is less than 50% of the variable interest entities total assets.

We continue to analyze the impact of FIN 46 on our financial statements. Consolidation of the above variable interests could result in a material impact to the 2003 earnings and would be reported as a change in accounting principle. Because we are not required to perform on behalf of these entities if they do not fulfill their obligations, consolidation of any variable interest entities would not increase our exposure to risk or loss or increase our obligations related to these entities. We believe that the meaningful estimate of potential loss related to variable interest entities is equal to our investment and retained interests.

Chapter 13
Leases[*]

CONTENTS

The accounting, presentation, and disclosures for lease arrangements are provided in various authoritative pronouncements, including ASC 840-10-05, *Leases: Overall*; ASC 840-10-55-1 through 55-6, *Leases: Overall*; ASC 310-20-05-2, *Receivables: Nonrefundable Fees and Other Costs*; ASC 840, *Leases*; ASC 840-10-25-69, *Leases: Overall*; ASC 840-30-35-25, *Leases: Capital Leases*; ASC 958-840-55, *Not-for-*

---

[*] This chapter was co-authored by Robert Fonfeder, Ph.D., CPA, professor of accounting at Hofstra University.

Profit Entities: Leases; ASC 360-20-55-66, *Property, Plant, and Equipment: Real Estate Sales*; and ASC 210-20, *Balance Sheet: Offsetting*.

Leases are usually of a long-term noncancellable nature. *Noncancellable* means that (1) the lease cannot be terminated, (2) it is cancellable only upon the happening of a remote contingency, the lessor's approval, or entering into a new lease with the same lessor, or (3) the lease imposes a substantial penalty on the lessee for cancellation. The lessee pays the lessor (owner) a rental fee for the right to use property (tangible or intangible) for a specified time period. Although title is not transferred, the lease may in some cases transfer substantial risks and benefits of ownership. Theoretical substance comes before legality in accounting so that the lessee in a capital lease arrangement will have to record an asset and related liability. Other leases are simply a rental of property. A lessor's classification of a lease does not affect the accounting treatment for the lease by the lessee. Leases may be structured to derive certain tax benefits.

In certain situations, a lease may be transacted among related parties. This arises when one company has substantial influence over the operating and financial activities of the other businesses.

The inception date of a lease is the earlier date of the rental contract or commitment. A commitment must be in written form, it must be signed, and it must contain the major terms. If principal provisions are to be negotiated at a later date, no binding commitment is deemed to exist.

Leases may include contracts that are not referred to as leases as such but have the attributes of one, including the right to use property. An example is a contract requiring the rendering of services in order to operate equipment.

This chapter discusses the accounting, reporting, and disclosures of leases by lessees and lessors. It includes a discussion of sale-leasebacks, subleases, renewals and extensions, terminations, leveraged leases, and other issues.

LESSEE

Leasing has many advantages for the lessee, including:

☐ Immediate cash outlay is not required

☐ Typically, a purchase option exists, allowing the lessee to obtain the property at a bargain price at the expiration of the lease.

☐ The lessor's expert service is made available.

☐ There are usually fewer financing restrictions (e.g., limitations on dividends) placed on the lessee by the lessor than are imposed when obtaining a loan to buy the asset.

☐ The obligation for future rental payment does not have to be reported on the balance sheet in the case of an operating lease.

☐ Leasing allows the lessee under a capital lease, in effect, to depreciate land, which is not allowed if land is purchased.

☐ In bankruptcy or reorganization, the maximum claim of lessors against the company is three years of lease payments. In the case of debt, creditors have a claim for the total amount of the unpaid financing.

☐ The lessee may avoid having the obsolescence risk of the property if the lessor, in determining the lease payments, fails to estimate accurately the obsolescence of the asset.

There are several drawbacks to leasing, including:

☐ There is a higher cost in the long run than if the asset is purchased.

☐ The interest cost associated with leasing is typically higher than the interest cost on debt.

☐ If the property reverts to the lessor at termination of the lease, the lessee must either sign a new lease or buy the property at higher current prices. Also, the salvage value of the property is realized by the lessor.

☐ The lessee may have to retain property no longer needed (i.e., obsolete equipment).

☐ The lessee cannot make improvements to the leased property without the lessor's permission.

The lessee may account for a lease under either the operating method or capital lease method.

Operating Method

In an operating lease, there is a regular rental of property. In such a case, rent expense is charged as incurred under the accrual basis. The credit is either to payables or cash. Rent expense is usually reflected on a straight-line basis over the lease term even if the payments are not on a straight-line basis.

ASC 840-20-25-10 and 25-11, *Leases: Operating Leases*, stipulates that rental costs associated with operating leases should be (1) recognized as rental expense, (2) included in income from continuing operations, and (3) allocated over the lease term.

Note: According to ASC 840-20-25-2, *Leases: Operating Leases*, if a more suitable and rational method exists reflective of the time pattern that the leased property is used, it may be used, although this is a rare occurrence. Because the lessee is just engaged in a regular rental, no property is shown on the lessee's balance sheet.

EXAMPLE

This example shows rent expense on a straight-line basis even though the payments are not on such a basis. A lessee leases property for a 10-year period but, owing to an incentive, will not pay a rental in the first year. After the first year, the monthly rental is $400. Therefore, total rent under the rental agreement equals $43,200 ($400 × 108 months). The 108 months represents 9 years multiplied by 12 months in a year. As a result, the amount charged to rent expense each month will be $360 ($43,200/120 months). One hundred and twenty months represents 10 years multiplied by 12 months a year. In the first year, the journal entry each month would be to debit rent expense and credit an accrued liability since no cash payment is being made. After the first year, as payments are made the accrued liability will be reduced by the excess of the monthly payment over the monthly rent expense, amounting to $40 ($400–$360).

EXAMPLE

The lease may provide that the lessee will pay lower rentals in the early years and higher rentals in the later years of a lease. For example, in a six-year rental, the rentals per month are $250 for years 1 and 2, $375 for years 3 and 4, and $500 for years 5 and 6. The total rental over the six-year period equals $27,000 ($6,000 + $9,000 + 12,000), which must be amortized over the rental term on a straight-line basis. Hence, the monthly amortization for years 1 and 2 is $375 ($27,000/72 months) even though $250 is being paid.

As per ASC 840-10-55-39, *Leases: Overall*, a rental based on some factor or event not determinable at the inception of the lease (e.g., units sold, units produced, inflation rate, prime interest rate) is referred to as a contingent rental. However, a contingent rental does not apply to a variable that is dependent only on the passage of time. Further, a contingent rental does not include pass-through increases (escalation) in construction cost or the purchase cost of leased property. According to ASC 845-10-25-10, *Nonmonetary Transactions: Overall*, tax indemnification payments do not qualify as contingent rentals. A contingent rental payment is charged to rent expense as incurred.

ASC 840-20-25-6, *Leases: Operating Leases*, includes coverage of lease incentives in an operating lease. Lease incentives include giving a bonus payment to the lessee for signing the rental contract, reimbursing the lessee for certain costs (e.g., moving costs), and paying a third party an amount on behalf of the lessee (e.g., loan payment to the lessee's bank, payment for a leasehold improvement, assumption of a lessee's obligation under a preexisting lease). Lease incentive payments should be amortized by the lessee against rental expense over the rental time period. When a lease incentive is received, the lessee debits cash and credits a deferred rental incentive account. This latter account is amortized and reduces rent expense over the rental period using the straight-line method. (The lessor recognizes in a similar manner lease incentives given to the lessee by reducing rental income on a straight-line basis over the term of the new rental agreement.)

With regard to the costs or losses incurred by the lessee related to a lease incentive, the lessee will account for such costs or losses as usual. For example, moving costs will be expensed, and losses will be recognized on abandoned leasehold improvements. If the lessor incurs a loss because it provides the lessee with an incentive, the lessor will account for such loss as part of the new rental transaction.

EXAMPLE

A lessee receives a lease incentive of $25,000 to sign a 10-year lease requiring annual rentals of $75,000. The lessee's entry to record the incentive is to debit cash and credit deferred rental incentive for $25,000. The deferred rental incentive account will be amortized over the lease term using the straight-line method. The amortization each year will be $2,500 ($25,000/10 years). The journal entries each year to record the rental payment and the amortization of the incentive follow:

Rent expense	75,000	
Cash		75,000
Deferred rental incentive	2,500	
Rent expense		2,500

The net rental cost each year is $72,500 ($75,000 − $2,500).

A lease may stipulate escalated amounts that must be provided for in rent expense to the lessee. The escalated amounts are to be accounted for under the straight-line method over the rental period. If the contract gives the lessee control over additional property, the escalated rent applicable to the original leased property is charged to rent expense on a pro rata basis to the additional leased property in the years the lessee has control over the additional property. The lessor records the escalated amounts on the initial leased property as additional rental income. The rental expense of the lessee or rental income of the lessor should be on a pro rata basis dependent on the relative fair market value of the additional leased property as stipulated in the rental contract for the period the lessee controls such additional property.

An operating lease may contain a penalty clause. The lessee's payment of a penalty should be expensed as incurred. A penalty may be in the form of a cash payment, performance of services, liability incurrence, or significant extension of the lease term. A penalty should be so significant that the lessee will want to abide by contractual terms or reasonably ensure the lessee's renewal of the lease.

Any moving costs incurred by the lessee to move from one location to another are usually expensed as incurred.

The lessee can determine the periodic rental payments to be made under a lease by dividing the value of the leased property by the present value factor associated with the future rental payments.

EXAMPLE

Gonzalez Corporation enters into a lease for a $100,000 machine. It is to make equal annual payments at year-end. The interest rate is 14%.

The periodic payment equals $100,000/5.2161 = $19,171

Note: The present value of an ordinary annuity factor for $n = 10$, $i = 14\%$, is 5.2161.

Assuming the same information except that the annual payments are to be made at the beginning of each year, the periodic payment would equal $100,000/5.9464 = $16,817.

The interest rate associated with a lease agreement may also be computed. The value of the leased property is divided by the annual payment to obtain the factor, which is then used to find the interest rate using a present value of ordinary annuity table.

EXAMPLE

Coleman Company leased $300,000 of property and is to make equal annual payments at year-end of $40,000 for 11 years. The interest rate in the lease agreement is 7%. The factor equals $300,000/$40,000 = 7.5.

Going to the present value of an ordinary annuity table and looking across 11 years to a factor closest to 7.5 gives 7.4987 at a 7% interest rate. Therefore, the interest rate in the lease is 7%.

Capital Lease Method

A capital lease exists if any one of the following four criteria is met:

1. The lessee is to get property ownership at the end of the lease term. This criterion is still satisfied if ownership is transferred shortly after the end of the lease term.

2. A bargain purchase option exists in which the lessee can either buy the property at a minimal amount or renew the lease at very low rental payments relative to the "going rates."

3. The lease term is 75% or more of the life of the property.

4. The present value of minimum lease payments at the start of the lease equals or exceeds 90% of the fair market value of the property. Minimum lease payments do not include executory costs to be paid by the lessor, which are being reimbursed by the lessee. Examples of such costs are property taxes, insurance, and maintenance. Executory costs also include lessee payments to an unrelated third party to guarantee the residual value. When the lessor pays executory costs, any lessor's profit on such costs is construed the same as the executory costs.

If the lease term starts within the last 25% of the total life of the property (including earlier years of use), criteria 3 and 4 do not apply because the property has already been used for most of its life.

If criterion 1 or 2 is satisfied, the property is depreciated over its life. On the other hand, if criterion 3 or 4 is met, the lease term is the depreciation period.

The lease period cannot go past the date of exercisability of a bargain purchase option because it is presumed that the option will be exercised and the lease will terminate on that date.

The inception date of a lease is the date of agreement or commitment (if before) of the major provisions that are fixed in nature, with no major provisions yet to be settled.

The term of a lease may represent either a stated noncancellable period, a period covered by a bargain renewal option, the time period including a renewal term because of significant penalties that, in effect, ensure renewal, the time period including extensions or renewals at the lessor's option, and the time period including renewal options because of the lessee's guarantee of the lessor's debt that is related to the leased property.

If a lease has a noncancellable period followed by cancelable renewal periods (e.g., yearly, semiannually), only the noncancellable period should be taken into account when making a determination as to the classification of the lease.

In a capital lease, there is a transfer of substantial benefits and there are risks of property ownership to the lessee. A capital lease is treated for accounting purposes as if the lessee borrowed funds to buy the property.

In a capital lease, the asset and liability are presented at the inception date at the present (discounted) value of minimum lease payments plus the present (discounted) value of any bargain purchase option. It is anticipated that the lessee will take advantage of the nominal acquisition price. However, the asset cannot be recorded at more than its fair market value because that would violate conservatism. In other words, the asset would be recorded at the lower of the present value computation or the fair market value of the property. The liability is presented in the balance sheet at its current and noncurrent amounts.

In determining present value, the lessee uses as its discount rate the lower of the lessee's incremental borrowing rate if it was to buy the property outright at the inception of the lease or the lessor's desired (implicit) rate of return on the lease. According to FASB Technical Bulletin No. 79–12, *Interest Rate Used in Calculating the Present Value of Minimum Lease Payments* (Glossary-Incremental Borrowing Rate), the lessee may use its secured borrowing interest rate as its incremental borrowing rate as long as such rate is logical in the circumstances.

The lessee's minimum lease payments typically include:

☐ The lessee's penalty payment arising from not renewing or extending the lease upon expiration.

☐ Minimum lease payments over the rental period plus the lessee's guaranteed salvage value. The guarantee is the stated amount that the lessee agrees to pay the lessor for any deficiency below the stipulated amount in the lessor's realization of the residual value. ASC 840-30-35-25, *Leases: Capital Leases*, does not allow any upward adjustments of guaranteed residual values in lease agreements. Reference should also be made to ASC 840-20-30, *Leases: Operating Leases*. Besides executory costs, minimum lease payments exclude the lessee's guarantee of the lessor's debt and any contingent rentals.

The executory costs paid by the lessee are expensed as incurred. Therefore, unless paid directly with cash, executory costs will be accrued.

If during the lease term the recorded value of a leased asset exceeds its market value, it should be written down recognizing a loss.

Each minimum lease payment is debited to the liability account for the principal portion and is debited to interest expense for the interest portion. Interest expense is computed under the interest method (sometimes termed the effective interest method), which results in a constant periodic interest rate.

Interest expense equals the interest rate multiplied by the carrying (book) value of the liability at the beginning of the period.

The lessee will record depreciation expense on capitalized leased property. Depreciation expense equals the cost of the asset less the estimated residual value divided by the depreciable period.

ASC 840-30-35-16, *Leases: Capital Leases*, provides that if a lessee purchases a leased asset during the lease term that was originally capitalized, the transaction is deemed an extension rather than a termination of a capital lease. The difference between the purchase price and the book value of the lease obligation is treated as an adjustment of the carrying value of the asset. No loss recognition is required on an extension of a capital lease.

In general, under the capital lease method, the lessee's journal entries are as follows:

AT INCEPTION OF LEASE:

Asset (present value of future payments)

    Liability

AT THE END OF EACH YEAR, ASSUMING EACH PAYMENT IS MADE ON DECEMBER 31:

Interest expense (interest)

Liability (principal)

    Cash (interest and principal)

Depreciation

    Accumulated depreciation

Under the capital lease method, the lessee reports in its balance sheet the leased asset and the associated liability. In the income statement, the lessee presents interest expense and depreciation expense.

EXAMPLE

On January 1, 20X2, the lessee engages in a capital lease for property. The minimum lease payment is $30,000 per year for six years payable at year-end. The interest rate is 5%. The present value of an ordinary annuity factor for $n = 6$, $i = 5\%$ is 5.0757. The journal entries for the first two years follow:

1/1/20X2

Asset	152,271	
Liability		152,271

$30,000 \times 5.0757 = \$152,271$

12/31/20X2

Interest expense	7,614	
Liability	22,386	
Cash		30,000

$5\% \times \$152,271 = \$7,614$

Depreciation expense	25,379	

Accumulated depreciation			25,379
$152,271/6 years = $25,379			

The liability as of December 31, 20X2 is:

Liability

12/31/20X2	22,386	1/1/20X2		152,271
		12/31/20X2 Balance		129,885

12/31/20X3		
Interest expense	6,494	
Liability	23,506	
Cash		30,000
5% × $129,885 = $6,494		
Depreciation expense	25,379	
Accumulated depreciation		25,379

EXAMPLE

Levsee Corporation entered into a 10-year capital lease on a building on December 31, 20X2. Lease payments of $62,000, which include real estate taxes of $2,000, are due annually, beginning December 31, 20X3 and every December 31 thereafter for the lease term. Levsee does not know the interest implicit in the lease, but its (Levsee's) incremental borrowing rate is 10%. The rounded present value of an ordinary annuity for 10 years at 10% is 6.1. What amount should Levsee report as capitalized lease liability at December 31, 20X2?

The problem indicates that this lease is a capital lease. In addition, because payments are due at the end of the period (year), it is an ordinary annuity. The initial lease liability of the lessee must be calculated using the present value of the minimum lease payments discounted at the incremental borrowing rate because the implicit rate in the lease is not known. In general, we choose the lessee's incremental borrowing rate. However, the implicit rate in the lease is substituted if it is known and it is lower than the incremental rate.

Capitalized lease liability = minimum lease payments
× present value of an ordinary
annuity of 1 for ten years at 10%
= ($62,000–$2,000) × 6.1
= $60,000 × 6.1
= $366,000

Levsee Corporation, the lessee, should report the capitalized lease liability as $366,000.

EXAMPLE

Joel Company leased a machine for 10 years, its useful life, and agreed to pay $25,000 at the start of the lease term on December 31, 20X1. As part of the agreement, it was also required to continue such payments each December 31 for the next nine years. The present value on December 31, 20X1, of the 10 lease payments over the lease term, using the implicit rate of interest known to Joel Company of 8%, is $181,250. The present value of the lease payments using Joel's incremental borrowing rate of 10% is $169,000. Joel Company made a timely second lease payment. What amount should Joel report as its capital lease liability in its December 31, 20X2 balance sheet?

In this problem, it is stated that the lease is a capital lease. In addition, because all lease payments are being made at the beginning of the period by the lessee, the lease represents an annuity due. Also, because the implicit rate in the lease is known and it is lower than Joel's incremental rate (10%), the discount rate that should be used is the 8% rate. Therefore, Joel should originally record the capitalized lease (long-term asset and liability) at $181,250. This amount was derived in the following way:

Present value of minimum lease payments	= $25,000 × present value of 1 for 10 years at 8%
	= $25,000 × 7.25
	= $181,250

Present value of minimum lease payments at 12/31/20X1		$181,250
Less: payment at 12/31/20X1		25,000
Liability balance, 1/1/20X1-12/31/20X2		$156,250
Less: payment at 12/31/20X2	$25,000	
Less: portion of payment applicable to interest during 20X2, $156,200 × 8%	12,496	12,504
Capital lease at December 31, 20X2		$143,746

There are a number of considerations regarding residual value. A contractual clause mandating the lessee to pay for a deficiency in residual value applicable to unusual wear and tear, damage, or very significant usage is not deemed a lease guarantee in computing the discounted value of the minimum lease payments. This kind of guarantee is indeterminable at the lease inception date. As a result, it should be treated as a contingent rental. If a lessee receives a residual value guarantee from an unrelated third party to benefit the lessor, the guarantee should not be used to reduce the minimum lease payments unless the lessor releases the lessee from the obligation to make up all or part of the residual value deficiency. Any payments by a lessee to a third party to secure a guarantee are treated as executory costs. As such, they are not included in computing the minimum lease payments. According to ASC 360-10-25-2, *Property, Plant, and Equipment: Overall*, the purchase by a third party from a lessor of the unconditional right to own property at the end of the lease term should be accounted for as a purchase of an asset at the time the right is acquired.

ASC 840-10-15-16, *Leases: Overall*, requires Capital Lease treatment for arrangements containing an embedded lease, thereby conveying the right to control use of the property. The right is conveyed if the purchaser (lessee) obtains physical or operational control of the underlying property or takes substantially all of its output.

The capital lease is presented in the lessee's balance sheet under noncurrent assets as follows:

Asset under lease

Less: Accumulated depreciation

Book value

In the lessee's income statement, the capital lease shows interest expense and depreciation expense.

In the beginning years, expenses reported under a capital lease (interest expense and depreciation expense) exceed those under an operating lease (rent expense).

According to ASC 840-10-05-9A through 05-9C and 840-10-25-39B, *Leases: Overall*, under some equipment leases, a lessee is responsible for repair and maintenance of the leased asset for the lease term. In addition, certain lease arrangements require the lessee to make deposits to the lessor to financially protect the lessor if the lessee does not properly maintain the leased asset.

This applies to the lessee's accounting for maintenance deposits paid by a lessee under a lease that are refunded only if the lessee conducts specified maintenance activities.

Maintenance deposits are accounted for as a deposit asset.

When an amount on deposit is less than probable of being returned, it is recognized as additional expense. When the underlying maintenance is performed the maintenance costs shall be expensed or capitalized as per the lessee's maintenance accounting policy.

The lessee should make the following footnote disclosures:

☐ Assets under lease by category.

☐ Sublease rentals.

☐ Contingent rentals (rentals depending on something other than time such as sales). (Contingent rentals may increase or reduce rental payments.)

☐ Future minimum lease payments in the aggregate and for each of the next five years.

☐ Description of the rental arrangement, such as expiration date of lease, purchase options, escalation clauses, renewal term, and leasing restrictions (e.g., additional leasing activity, additional debt, dividend ceilings).

☐ Nature and degree of leasing activity with related parties.

LESSOR

There are three possible methods a lessor may use to account for leases as follows:

1. Operating method.
2. Direct financing method.
3. Sales-type method.

Operating Method

The operating method is a regular rental by the lessor, such as Hertz's leasing of automobiles to companies. With the operating method, the lessor recognizes rental income less applicable expenses (e.g., repairs, depreciation, insurance, taxes). Rental income is recognized as earned under the straight-line method over the lease period except if another method is more appropriate. Contingent rentals are accrued as earned. Therefore, the lessor's income statement under the operating method will show rental revenue less expenses. The balance sheet presents the asset under lease less accumulated depreciation to derive book value.

Initial direct costs are deferred and amortized proportionately over the lease term based on the rental revenue recognized. However, if initial direct costs are insignificant in amount, they may be immediately charged against earnings. Initial direct costs are those related to negotiating and closing a lease. Reference should be made to the FASB Implementation Guide (*Questions and Answers*) to ASC 310-20-05-2, *Receivables: Nonrefundable Fees and Other Costs*.

If the lessor makes incentive payments to the lessee to motivate the lessee to sign the contract, such payments should be amortized against rental revenue over the lease term. The payment is charged to a deferred lease incentive account (an asset) and credited to cash. The amortization of the deferred lease incentive account should be based on the straight-line method.

If the lessor assumes a lessee's preexisting lease with a third party, the lessor should treat any resulting loss as a rent incentive. The loss should be determined after taking into account the costs incurred less any anticipated benefits arising from a sublease or use of the property.

EXAMPLE

Dan Company leased office space from Ron Company for a five-year term beginning January 2, 20X2. Under the requirements of the operating lease, rent for the first year would be $9,000 and rent for the following year through year 5 (that is, year 2 through year 5) would be $12,000 per year. Ron Company offered Dan Company an inducement to enter the lease. The inducement consisted of waiving the rental payments for the first six months of the lease, making this period rent free for Dan. In its December 31, 20X2 income statement, what amount should Ron report as rental income?

The problem specifies that this is an operating lease. Under an operating lease, rental revenue should be recognized on a straight-line basis unless it is shown that some other systematic methodology is deemed to be more representative. Therefore, total rental revenue should be evenly recognized over all the years of the operating lease.

The following computation should be made. The total revenue over the life of the lease is:

1. $^1/_2 \times 9,000 = \$4,500$ for the first year (because the first six months are rent free) plus

2. $\$12,000 \times 4$ years $= \$48,000$ (years 2 through 5)

Therefore, total rental revenue over the life of the lease = $\$4,500 + \$48,000 = \$52,500$.

In its December 31, 20X2 income statement, Ron should record $\$52,500/5$ years = $\$10,500$.

EXAMPLE

On April 1, 20X2, XYZ Company manufactured equipment costing $600,000, which it leased out under the operating method. The lease is for 10 years, with equal monthly payments of $6,000 payable at the beginning of each month. The first payment was made on April 1, 20X2. The depreciation period is 12 years, with a salvage value of $40,000.

The lessor reports the following for 20X2 for the period 4/1 to 12/31:

Rental revenue ($6,000 × 9 months)	$54,000
Less: depreciation expense ($600,000/12 years × 9/12)	37,500
Income before tax	$16,500

The lessor determines the amount of rental based on its desired rate of return. The return the lessor will seek depends on such factors as the financial standing of the lessee, period of rental, and technological risk. The rental payment is often based on a present value computation.

EXAMPLE

The fair market value of leased equipment is $300,000 and the discounted (present) value of the residual (salvage) value is $20,000. There will be five beginning-of-year lease payments to yield a 10% return. The annual rental payments are computed as follows:

Fair market value of leased equipment	$300,000
Less: present value of residual value	20,000
Recoverable amount	$280,000

Annual rental equals

$$\text{Recoverable amount/present value factor for } n = 5, i = 10\%$$
$$\$280,000/4.16986 = \$67,149$$

Revenue applicable to maintenance services should be recognized into income as those services are performed using a proportional performance method based on what is most appropriate in the situation.

Direct Financing Method

The direct financing method meets one of the four criteria for a capital lease by the lessee plus both of the following two criteria for the lessor:

1. No significant uncertainties are present with respect to future costs to be incurred. However, a performance guarantee might present a significant uncertainty, negating this condition. Unusual and uncustomary warranties and commitments represent important uncertainties that violate this condition. **Note:** ASC 840-10-55-3, *Leases: Overall*, states that if the leased property has not been built or bought by the lessor at the lease date, this criterion is applied at the construction completion date or the date the property is bought.

2. There is assurance of lease payments being collected. This condition is met even if some uncollectibility is expected as long as payment can be reasonably estimated. However, if credit risks are substantial, this criterion is negated.

The lessor is not a manufacturer or dealer in the item. The lessor buys the property only to lease it out for a profit. The lease is treated as a financing arrangement. An example is an insurance company renting electronic equipment.

In a direct financing lease, the book value and fair value of the leased property are the same at the inception of the lease. In consequence, no gain or loss arises.

Note: Although in a direct financing arrangement, the fair value of the property is usually the same as its cost, market conditions need to be taken into account, particularly when there is a long time period between the time of lease and the purchase or construction of the property.

The lessor uses as the discount rate in determining the present value of future minimum lease payments its desired rate of return (implicit rate). The implicit rate is the rate that discounts the lease payments and the unguaranteed residual value to the property's fair value at the time of the lease.

Note: The lessor's minimum lease payments are identical to the lessee's except that the lessor includes a guarantee of the lease payments or residual value after the lease term by a third party as long as that party is financially healthy to meet its commitments.

Interest revenue is computed under the interest method. Interest revenue equals the interest rate multiplied by the carrying (book) value of the receivable at the beginning of the period. In effect, unearned interest revenue is amortized over the lease term, resulting in a constant interest rate. Contingent rentals are recognized as earned.

The lessor's minimum lease payments include:

☐ The minimum lease payments to be paid by the lessee.

☐ Any guarantee of residual value of the leased item or of rental payments after the lease term, made by an unrelated, financially sound third party.

If a change in the lease term occurs that would have meant an initially different lease classification, then the lease is deemed to be a new arrangement and should be classified and treated for accounting purposes under the new terms. However, exercising a renewal option is not considered an alteration of the lease. Further, a change in estimate does not mean a new lease.

An escalation clause related to the minimum lease payments during a construction or preacquisition period may be involved. The ensuing increase in minimum lease payments is used to determine the leased item's fair value at the time of the lease. Further, a change in residual value may also arise because of the escalation provision.

Initial direct costs are paid or accrued by the lessor to negotiate and finalize a lease. Examples are finders' commissions, attorney fees, credit appraisal, negotiating and processing fees, and an allocated portion of salesperson and employee compensation. In a direct financing lease, such costs are included in the gross receivable (investment). Initial direct costs do not include costs for failed lease opportunities, advertising and solicitation, and indirect costs (e.g., administrative, supervisory). The initial direct costs under a direct financing lease are amortized over the lease period using the interest method.

A portion of unearned income equal to the initial direct costs is recorded as income in the same accounting period.

If the leasing contract includes a penalty clause for not renewing and the penalty does not apply because of renewal or time extension, an adjustment must be made to the unearned interest income account for the difference between the present values of the original and revised agreements. The discounted value of future minimum lease payments under the new contract should be determined using the rate in the original lease.

Lease termination is accounted for by the lessor through eliminating the net investment and recording the leased property at the lower of cost or fair value. The net investment is then charged against earnings.

Contingent rentals are immediately recognized in earnings. They are not included in computing minimum lease payments.

Note: Contingent rentals do not include lessee reimbursement to the lessor of any tax savings because of a change in tax legislation.

ASC 310-20-05-2, *Receivables: Nonrefundable Fees and Other Costs*, provides for the accounting treatment of nonrefundable fees and expenses related to lending activities, including buying loans. The lessor's loan origination charges and associated costs are deferred and amortized over the loan period. Yield is adjusted accordingly.

In general, the journal entries under the direct financing method follow:

AT DATE OF LEASE

Gross receivable (total payments equal to principal + interest)

    Asset (principal)

    Unearned interest revenue (total interest)

Note: The difference between the gross receivable (investment) and the carrying value of the leased property (asset) equals unearned interest revenue.

AT EACH DATE OF RECEIPT OF RENTAL PAYMENT

Cash (amount of receipt including principal and interest portion)

Gross receivable

Unearned interest revenue

Interest revenue (interest earned for period)

On the balance sheet, the lessor reports as gross receivables (investment) the total minimum lease payments (net of any included executory costs and associated profits to be paid by the lessor) plus the unguaranteed residual value of the property belonging to the lessor at the end of the lease period. The unearned interest revenue account is deducted from gross receivables (investment) to obtain net receivables (investment). In summary, net receivables (investment) equals the gross receivables plus unamortized initial direct costs less the unearned interest income. The net receivables is classified as current or noncurrent, depending on whether collection will be made within one year from the balance sheet date. The presentation in the balance sheet follows:

Gross lease payments receivable (principal + interest)

Less: unearned interest revenue (interest)

Net lease payments receivable (principal)

In the income statement, the following is presented:

Interest revenue

Less: executory costs

Net Income

Note: The income statement may also include a loss associated with a permanent decline in the unguaranteed residual value requiring a writedown of the net receivable (investment) in the lease. However, the unguaranteed residual value should not be written up because to do so violates conservatism.

Sales-Type Method

A sales-type lease is sometimes entered into by the lessor in order to improve the marketability of a costly asset. A sales-type lease must meet the same criteria as must a direct financing lease. The only difference is that the former involves a lessor who is either the producer or dealer in the leased item. Therefore, a manufacturer or dealer profit arises. In a sales-type arrangement the book value of the leased property differs from its fair value (price the property may be exchanged for between unrelated parties in an arms-length agreement), resulting in a gain or loss to the lessor. Even though no legal sale has occurred, theoretical substance comes before legal form, and a sale is presumed to have occurred. An example of a sales-type lease is a manufacturer of a computer or photocopy system leasing it to a lessee with the option of the lessee purchasing it.

The differentiation between a sales-type lease and a direct financing lease is only of concern to the lessor. The lessee still uses the capital lease method, irrespective of which of the two methods the lessor uses.

In a sales-type lease, profit on the assumed sale of the property is recorded in the year of the lease and interest income is recorded over the lease term. The interest income calculation is based on the interest method. At inception of the lease, the cost and fair value (usually the normal selling Price) of the leased item are different. Therefore, under the sales-type method, there is both a profit and financial income component.

Each year the salvage value of the property should be evaluated. Such appraisal may require loss recognition with a reduction of the net receivable (investment).

Against the sales price is matched the cost of the leased item so as to obtain the assumed profit in the year of lease. Cost of sales equals the cost (or carrying value) of the leased property reduced by the discounted value of any unguaranteed residual value. In a sales-type lease, initial direct costs are immediately expensed.

Note: A lessor must recognize immediately in the current year's income statement a loss on selling peripheral equipment as a marketing strategy.

In general, under the sales-type method, the journal entries are:

AT DATE OF LEASE

Gross receivable (total payments equal to principal + interest)

    Sales (assumed selling price of leased item)

    Unearned interest revenue (total interest)

Cost of sales (cost of assumed item sold)

    Inventory

Note: The gross receivable (investment) in lease equals the total minimum lease payments to be received (net of executory costs and any associated profits to be paid by the lessor) plus the unguaranteed salvage (residual) value accruing to the lessor at the termination date of the lease. However, the estimated unguaranteed residual value may not be more than the amount of residual value estimated at lease inception. If the salvage value was guaranteed, it would be included in the minimum lease payments.

AT EACH DATE OF RENTAL RECEIPT

Cash (amount received equal to principal and interest)

    Gross receivable

Unearned interest revenue

    Interest revenue (interest earned)

Under the sales type method, the balance sheet is identical to that of the direct financing method, namely:

    Gross lease payments receivable (principal + interest)

    Less: unearned interest revenue (interest)

    Net lease payments receivable (principal)

Note: The lease payments receivable to be collected within one year should be classified as a current asset.

Under the sales-type method, the income statement in the first year only will show:

Interest revenue

Gross profit on leased item (sales less cost of sales)

Less: executory costs

Initial direct costs (e.g., attorney fees, commissions)

In the second year and thereafter, the income statement will show:

Interest revenue

Less: executory costs

The journal entries under the sales-type method are generally the same as those under the direct financing method, with the exception of the initial entry. This is illustrated in the following example.

EXAMPLE

On January 1, 20X3, the lessor leases property to the lessee. The lessee accounts for the lease under the capital lease method. The minimum lease payments are $30,000 per year for six years payable at year-end. The interest rate is 5%. The present value of an ordinary annuity factor for $n = 6$, $i = 5\%$ is 5.0757. The cost of the leased property is $120,000. (Note that this problem is identical to the one illustrated previously under the capital lease method used by the lessee. The calculations were provided in that example.) The lessor's accounting, assuming a direct financing lease and a sales-type lease, follows:

Direct Financing Lease		
1/1/20X3		
Gross receivable (6 × $30,000)	180,000	
Asset (5.0757 × $30,000)		152,271
Unearned interest revenue		27,729
12/31/20X3		
Cash	30,000	
Gross receivable		30,000
Unearned interest revenue	7,614	
Interest revenue (5% × $152,271)		7,614

The balance sheet as of December 31, 20X3 presents the following:

Gross Receivable	$150,000
Less: unearned interest revenue ($27,729 – $7614)	20,115
Net receivables	$129,885

The income statement for 20X3 presents interest revenue of $7,614.

12/31/20X4		
Cash	30,000	
Gross receivable		30,000

Unearned interest revenue	6,494	
Interest revenue (5% × $129,885*)		6,494

* $30,000 – $7,614 = $22,386. $152,271 – $22,386 = $129,885.

The balance sheet as of December 31, 20X4 shows:

Gross receivable	$120,000
Less: unearned interest revenue ($20,115 – $6,494)	13,621
Net Receivable	$106,379

The income statement for 20X4 presents interest revenue of $6,494.

Sales-Type Lease

1/1/20X3

Gross receivable	180,000	
Sales		152,271
Unearned interest revenue		27,729
Cost of sales	120,000	
Inventory		120,000

All other entries at year-end 20X3 and 20X4 are the same as that under the direct financing method in this set of facts.

The balance sheets at year-end 20X3 and 20X4 are also the same as that under the direct financing method. However, the income statement in the year of lease (20X3) will show not only the interest revenue of $7,614 but also the assumed gross profit on the sale of the item in the year of lease. In this example, the gross profit equals $32,271 (sales of $152,271 less cost of sales of $120,000). The income statement after 20X3 will be the same as that under the direct financing method based on the facts in this particular example.

EXAMPLE

On January 1, 20X2, Coleman Company leased equipment to a lessee under a sales-type lease. There will be 11 annual rentals of $10,000 beginning on January 1, 20X2. Further, the lessee will make an initial payment of $5,000 on the date of lease. The lessee will buy the property at the termination date of the lease for $5. The implicit interest rate is 10%. The book value of the leased property on Coleman Company's records is $45,000.

On January 1, 20X2, the gross receivable in the lease equals $115,000, calculated as follows:

Total lease payments ($10,000 × 11 payments)	$110,000
Down payment	5,000
Gross receivable (investment)	$115,000

The present (discounted) value of the gross receivable (investment) equals $76,450, computed as follows:

Present value of future payments ($10,000 × 6.145*)	$61,450

Payment made on 1/1/20X2 ($10,000 + $5,000)		15,000
Total		$76,450

* The present value factor for $n = 10$, $i = 10\%$ is 6.145

The journal entry on January 1, 20X2 follows:

Gross lease receivable	115,000	
Equipment		45,000
Unearned interest income		
($115,000 – $76,450)		38,550
Gain on sale of asset		31,450

EXAMPLE

On October 1, 20X2, Mavis Company leased machinery to Buyko Company. The lease is treated as a sales type by the lessor and as a capital lease by the lessee. The lease period is 10 years, with equal annual payments of $400,000 due on October 1 each period. The first payment was made on October 1, 20X2. The machinery cost Mavis $1,800,000. It has a life of 12 years with a salvage value of $200,000. The relevant interest rate is 10%.

Buyko, the lessee, will make the following calculations:

Present value of lease payments equals ($400,000 × 5.868*) = $2,347,200

* Present value of ordinary annuity factor.

    Therefore, the asset will be recorded at $2,347,200.

    Buyko presents the following in its income statement for 20X2:

Depreciation expense:	
[($2,347,200 – $200,000)/12 years × 3/12]	$44,733
Interest expense ($1,947,200* × 10% × 3/12)	$48,680

* Present value of lease payments	$2,347,200
Less: initial payment	400,000
Balance at beginning of lease	$1,947,200

Mavis, the lessor, presents the following in its income statement for 20X2:

Interest revenue		$ 48,680
Gross profit:		
Sales	$2,347,200	
Less: cost	1,800,000	547,200

EXAMPLE

Carol Company leased a truck to Queens Corporation on January 2, 20X2 for a seven-year period. Equal lease payments of $500,000 are due at the beginning of each year beginning January 2, 20X2. The carrying cost of the machine is $1,800,000. The lease expires January 2, 20X9. The lease is accounted for as a sales-type lease. The lessor's interest rate is 10%. What amount of profit on the sale should Carol report for the year ended December 31, 20X2?

The problem denotes that the lease is appropriately accounted for by the lessor (Carol) as a sales-type lease. The machine's sales price may be derived by calculating present value of the lease payments discounted at the lessor's interest rate (10%).

Sales price of the machine   = $500,000 × present value of an annuity due of 1
for 7 years discounted at 10
= $500,000 × 5.35526
= $2,677,630

The profit on the sale is the difference between the sales price of the machine and the lessor's carrying value of the asset sold. That is,

$2,677,630 − $1,800,000 = $877,630

EXAMPLE

Dauber Company, a dealer in equipment and machinery, leased equipment to Greene Inc. on July 1, 20X1. The lease is appropriately accounted for as a sale by Dauber and as a purchase by Greene. The lease is for a 10-year period (the useful life of the asset). The first of 10 equal annual payments of $500,000 was made on July 1, 20X1. Dauber had purchased the equipment for $2,675,000 on January 1, 20X1 and set a list selling price of $3,375,000 on the equipment. The present value at July 1, 20X1 of the minimum rental payments over the lease term discounted at 12% (the appropriate interest rate) was $3,165,000.

The entries for the lessor using the sales-type method follow:

TO RECORD THE SALE ON JULY 1, 20X1:

Lease payments receivable	5,000,000	
Sales		3,165,000
Unearned interest revenue		1,835,000
Cost of sales	2,675,000	
Equipment		2,675,000

TO RECORD THE PAYMENT ON JULY 1, 20X1:

Cash	500,000	
Lease payments receivable		500,000

TO RECORD INTEREST REVENUE ON DECEMBER 31, 20X1:

Unearned interest revenue	159,900	
Interest revenue		159,900*

* Sales price	$3,165,000
Payment, 7/1/20X1	500,000
Outstanding balance, 7/1/20X1	$2,665,000

Interest $2,665,000 × 12% × 6/12 = $159,900

The entries for the lessee follow:

TO RECORD THE PURCHASE ON JULY 1, 20X1:

Leased equipment	3,165,000	
Liability		3,165,000

TO RECORD THE PAYMENT ON JULY 1, 20X1:

Liability	500,000	
Cash		500,000

TO RECORD INTEREST EXPENSE AND DEPRECIATION ON DECEMBER 31, 20X1:

Interest expense ($2,665,000 × .12 × 6/12)	159,900	
Depreciation expense ($3,165,000/10 × 6/12)	158,250	
Accrued interest payable		159,900
Accumulated depreciation		158,250

Lessors should footnote the following:

☐ Major types of assets leased.

☐ Components of the net investment.

☐ Lease provisions, including interest rate, term, restrictions, renewal options, escalation clauses, and disposition of property when the lease expires.

☐ Executory costs.

☐ Initial direct costs.

☐ Unearned interest revenue.

☐ Contingent rentals.

☐ Future minimum lease payments in the aggregate and for each of the next five years.

☐ Lessee defaults and allowance for uncollectibles.

☐ Unguaranteed residual values accruing to the lessor's benefit.

☐ Nature and amount of third-party financing.

☐ Leasing activities with related parties.

☐ Tax treatment of the lease.

RESIDUAL VALUE CONSIDERATIONS

A leased asset's residual (salvage) value is how much it is worth at the end of the lease. In most cases residual value goes to the lessor's benefit. However, it occasionally may accrue to a nonlessor (e.g., lessee, lease broker).

Unguaranteed residual value is defined as the expected residual value of the leased property excluding any part guaranteed by the lessee, by a related party to the lessee, or by a third party. However, if the guarantor is associated with the lessor, the residual value is deemed unguaranteed.

A periodic review (at least yearly) should be made to ascertain whether there has been a permanent decline in the estimated unguaranteed residual values associated with direct financing or sales-type leases. If a permanent decline has occurred, the new estimated life should be used and any ensuing loss recognized in the year the change in estimate was made. However, no adjustment is made for a temporary decline. As noted before, an upward adjustment is prohibited either to unguaranteed or guaranteed residual values.

ASC 840-10-55-2, *Leases: Overall*, allows an increase in the estimated residual value taking place because of an escalation clause in the lease contract for leased property bought or built by the lessor. For example, when a lease was originally signed, the residual value was estimated at $50,000, and during the construction period the leased property increased in fair value by $5,000. The escalation provision allows for an increase in residual value to $55,000.

ASC 860-10-05-3, *Transfers and Servicing: Overall*, and ASC 360-10-25-2 through 25-4; 360-10-30-3 and 30-4; 360-10-25-35-13 and 35-14; 840-30-35-21 and 35-53, discuss the transfers of residual value. When there has been a purchase of interests in residual values of leased property by companies whose major business activity is not leasing or financing, such rights should be accounted for by the buyer at the fair value of the assets received. The purchaser may be buying either the right to own the leased property or the right to receive the sales proceeds of the leased property at the end of the lease period. If there has been an increase in value of the financial interest in the residual value after purchase but before the end of the lease period, it may be recorded for guaranteed residual values because they are financial assets. However, no accreditation in residual value is allowed for unguaranteed residual values. A permanent loss in residual value should be recognized immediately.

TRANSFER OF LEASE RECEIVABLE

The lessor may transfer a lease receivable. The gain on sale equals the cash received less both the portion of the gross investment sold applicable to the minimum lease payments and the unearned income related to the minimum lease payments.

EXAMPLE

A lessor has on its books a lease receivable with an unguaranteed residual value. The lessor sells an 80% interest in the minimum lease payments for $100,000. The lessor retains a 20% interest in the minimum lease payments and a 100% interest in the unguaranteed residual value. Other data follow:

Minimum lease payments	$110,000
Unearned income in minimum lease payments	75,000
Gross investment in minimum lease payments	$185,000

Unguaranteed residual value	$7,000	
Unguaranteed income in residual value	13,000	
Gross investment in residual value		20,000
Gross investment in lease receivable		$205,000

The journal entry for the sale of the lease receivable is:

Cash	100,000	
Unearned income ($75,000 × 80%)	60,000	
Lease receivable ($185,000 × 80%)		148,000
Gain on sale		12,000

SALE-LEASEBACK

As per ASC 840-40-25-2, *Leases: Sale-Leaseback Transactions*, a sale-leaseback takes place when the lessor sells the asset (e.g., equipment) and then leases all or some of it back. However, there is no physical transfer of the property. The seller is referred to as the seller-lessee, and the buyer is termed the buyer-lessor. Possible reasons for a sale-leaseback are to raise needed funds or to achieve a tax benefit.

The profit or loss on the sale is deferred and amortized proportionately as an adjustment to depreciation expense if a capital lease, or proportionately to rent expense if an operating lease. (The deferred gain is classified as a deferred credit if an operating lease or an asset valuation offset if a capital lease.) However, if the fair value of the equipment at the date of the sale-leaseback is less than its book value, a loss is immediately recognized for that difference. ASC 840-40-30-5 specifies that executory costs are excluded in computing the profit to be deferred on a sale-leaseback. ASC 840-40-55-26 applies to the deferred profit on a sale-leaseback transaction with lessee guarantee of residual value.

If the seller leases back just a minor part (discounted value of leaseback rentals is 10% or less of the fair market value of the property sold) of the remaining use of the property sold, the gain or loss is immediately recognized. However, part of the gain or loss must be deferred and amortized so as to adjust the rental to a reasonable figure if the rental amount differs from prevailing market conditions.

If the seller leases back more than a minor, but less than significantly all of the, use of the sold property, there is immediate recognition of part of the gain if it is more than the discounted value of the minimum lease payments, providing the leaseback is an operating lease or it is more than the amount capitalized when the leaseback is considered a capital lease. The excess amount in both cases is recognized immediately, with the balance being deferred and amortized.

The journal entries associated with a sale-leaseback arrangement are:

AT THE TIME OF SALE:

Cash (amount received)

  Asset (cost)

  Deferred gross profit (deferred profit)

AT YEAR-END, WHEN A RENTAL PAYMENT IS MADE ASSUMING AN OPERATING LEASE:

Rent expense (rental payment)

   Cash

Deferred gross profit (amortized profit for the period)

   Rent expense

EXAMPLE

On January 1, 20X3, an asset costing $200,000 was sold for $280,000. The property was then leased back under an operating lease. The deferred profit on the sale-leaseback is $80,000 ($280,000 − $200,000). Rental expense in 20X3 was $15,000 and total rentals are estimated at $120,000. The journal entries are:

1/1/20X3

Cash	280,000	
Asset		200,000
Deferred gross profit		80,000

12/31/20X3

Rent expense	15,000	
Cash		15,000
Deferred gross profit	10,000	
Rent expense		10,000

$80,000 × $15,000/$120,000 = $10,000

Rental expense is adjusted as follows:

Rental expense	$15,000
Less: amortization of deferred gross profit	10,000
Net rental expense	$ 5,000

EXAMPLE

X Company sold property and then leased it back as a capital lease for 20 years. The selling price was $1,000,000, the fair value of the property was $1,150,000, and the book value was $1,250,000. The transaction results in a loss of $250,000 (selling price of $1,000,000 less book value of $1,250,000). The loss recognized immediately is $100,000 (book value of $1,250,000 less fair market value of $1,150,000). The remaining loss of $150,000 ($250,000 less $100,000) is deferred and amortized over the useful life of the property. The journal entry for the sale-leaseback transaction follows:

Cash	1,000,000	
Deferred loss	150,000	
Recognized loss (sale-leaseback)	100,000	
Property		1,250,000

EXAMPLE

Travis Company sells a building and then leases part of it for 10 years. The selling price was $500,000 and the book value was $400,000 (cost of $450,000 less accumulated depreciation of $50,000). The discounted value of the minimum leaseback rental is $20,000.

The leaseback represents a minor part of the building because $20,000 is less than $50,000 ($500,000 × 10%). As such, the sale is a separate transaction. The journal entry is:

Cash	500,000	
Accumulated depreciation	50,000	
Building		450,000
Gain		100,000

The buyer-lessor must classify the lease as either an operating or direct financing one. It cannot treat it as a sales-type lease.

As per ASC 840-40-05, a partial sale transaction may preclude the use of sale-leaseback accounting if there is a continuing involvement of the seller-lessee in ownership of the property. Sale-leaseback accounting is also not appropriate when the seller-lessee requires a buyer-lessor to refinance the debt associated with the property and pass through any interest savings to the seller-lessee.

If a sale-leaseback arrangement does not qualify for sale-leaseback accounting and reporting, it should be handled under either the deposit method or the financing method, enumerated as follows:

☐ The deposit method involves crediting the down payment and collections on the note (principal and interest) to a deposit liability account. As rental payments are made, the liability is reduced.

☐ The financing method credits a liability for the down payment and collections on the note (principal and interest). Lease payments are allocated to interest expense and reducing the financing obligation. Interest expense is computed under the interest method, in which the effective interest rate is multiplied by the carrying value of the liability at the beginning of the period.

Even though the deposit method or financing method has been used, the seller-lessee should convert to sale-leaseback accounting when the conditions for sale-leaseback treatment are satisfied.

According to ASC 840-40-55-37 through 55-41, a sale-leaseback transaction is still recognized if a preexisting lease is modified in accordance with the terms of sale. An exercise of a renewal option or sublease clause in the preexisting lease does not affect the accounting for the transaction.

ASC 840-40-55-22 discusses the accounting for the sale and leaseback of an asset that is leased to another party.

ASC 840-40-S99-1 applies to sale-leaseback transactions with repurchase options.

ASC 840-40-25-15, *Leases: Operating Leases*, deals with an unsecured guarantee by a parent of its subsidiary's lease payments in a sale-leaseback transaction. Sale-leaseback accounting may still be used even if there is an unsecured guarantee of one member of the consolidated group for the lease payments of another member of that group.

ASC 840-40-25-14 considers the impact of an uncollateralized irrevocable letter of credit on a real estate sale-leaseback transaction.

Refer to ASC 605-15-05-6, *Revenue Recognition: Products*, for the treatment of revenue recognition on equipment sold and subsequently repurchased subject to an operating lease.

Footnote disclosure for a sale-leaseback includes the provisions of the agreement, such as the terms regarding future commitments, duties, and responsibilities of the parties.

SUBLEASES AND SIMILAR ARRANGEMENTS

A sublease occurs when the original lessee re-leases the leased property to a third party, called the *sublessee*. The original lessee is termed the *sublessor*. In most cases, the sublease contract does not impact the original lease agreement. The original lessee, who is now the sublessor, still has primary liability.

There are three kinds of subleases:

1. The new lease replaces and cancels the old one.
2. The new lease is substituted under the initial agreement. The original lessee may still be secondarily liable.
3. The original lessee rents the property to a third party. The lease contract of the original parties continues.

The original lessor continues its current accounting method if the initial lessee subleases or sells to a third party. If the original lease is substituted by a new arrangement with a new lessee, the lessor terminates the initial lease and accounts for the new lease in a separate transaction.

In accounting by the original lessee, if the original lessee is relieved of primary obligation by a transaction other than a sublease, the original lease should be terminated. The accounting procedure is as follows:

☐ If the original lease was a capital lease, remove the asset and liability and recognize a gain or loss for the difference, including any consideration paid or received. In addition, if a secondary liability exists, a loss contingency should be accrued.

☐ If the original lease was an operating lease and the initial lessee is secondarily responsible, a loss contingency should be accrued.

If the original lessee is not relieved of the primary obligation under a sublease, the initial lessee (now sublessor) accounts in the following way:

☐ If the original lease satisfied criterion 1 or 2 of a capital lease (see section titled "Capital Lease Method"), the new lease should be classified as per the lessor's normal classification criteria. If the sublease is a sales type or direct financing one, the unamortized asset balance becomes the cost of the leased property. Otherwise, it is an operating lease. The original lease obligation should continue to be accounted for as previously.

☐ If the original lease satisfied criterion 3 or 4 of a capital lease, the new lease should be classified using lessor criteria 1 and 2 (see section titled "Direct Financing Method"). It should be classified as a direct financing lease. The unamortized balance of the asset becomes the cost of the leased equipment. Otherwise, it is an operating lease. The original lease obligation should continue to be accounted for as previously.

If the original lease was an operating lease, the old and new leases should be accounted for as operating leases.

As per ASC 840-20-25-15, losses on subleases should be immediately recognized. The amount of loss is the excess of costs to be incurred over the expected revenue to be received over the term of the sublease.

If a lessee is secondarily liable for a lease, disclosure should be made of that contingency and any associated risks.

MODIFICATIONS AND TERMINATIONS

If the terms of a lease are changed and the revisions thereto would have caused a different classification if they existed when the lease was originally signed, the revised lease should be considered as a new agreement over its remaining life and classified accordingly. Accounts may need adjustment to what they would have been, assuming the revised terms had been in effect at the inception date of the lease.

With regard to the lessee, the revised terms are assumed to apply to what was accounted for as a capital lease. If the revised lease would have been an operating one rather than a capital lease, the asset and liability should be eliminated, with a gain or loss recorded for the difference. The modified lease would be accounted for as an operating one in future years. On the other hand, if the modification changes the remaining minimum lease payments but remains intact, the capital lease classification, the asset, and the lease liability should be revised to the discounted value of the remaining minimum lease payments. No gain or loss is recognized. If the modified provisions in an operating lease would have resulted in it being a capital lease at inception, the revised lease is considered a new contract. An asset and liability is recorded for the discounted value of the future minimum lease payments.

With regard to the lessor, if there is a revision to the terms of a direct financing lease or sales-type lease that would have resulted in it being considered an operating lease at inception, the following accounting adjustments are necessary: (1) writing off the net investment in the lease; (2) showing the leased asset at the lower of initial cost, current fair value, or current carrying value; (3) recognizing a loss for the difference between the net investment in the lease and the amount the asset is recorded at on the lessor's books (a gain will not occur since the asset cannot be presented at more than the net investment); and (4) accounting for the lease in later years as an operating one. If the modified terms to a direct financing lease or sales-type lease change only the remaining minimum lease payments and not the classification, the following adjustments are needed: (1) adjusting the gross investment in the lease to conform to the new minimum lease payments receivable and the revised salvage value (however, the residual value estimate cannot be more than the amount originally estimated), and (2) decreasing or increasing unearned income for the net adjustment. If modifications to an operating lease would have resulted in it being considered as a sales-type or direct financing one at inception, the revised lease should be considered as a new agreement.

ASC 840-20-25-4, *Leases: Operating Leases*, states that if a modification is made to future rental payments, the increase should be amortized over the remaining period of the revised lease. However, if the modification is considered a termination penalty, it should be recognized in the year of revision. The termination penalty is the amount by which the revised rentals exceed the original rentals that would have been made over the shortened lease period.

According to ASC 840-10-25-5, *Leases: Overall*, when a capital lease is terminated because the lessee buys the property from the lessor, the lessee eliminates the lease liability. The lessee records the difference between the acquisition cost and the obligation as an adjustment to the carrying value of the asset. The asset is then presented in the balance sheet and accounted for in a way similar to that of other owned assets. If a capital lease is terminated for a reason other than the lessee buying the property, the lessee must eliminate from its books the leased asset and related liability recognizing the difference as a gain or loss. The lessee should accrue a loss contingency if it is secondarily liable on the lease.

There is no accounting adjustment required by the lessee when an operating lease is terminated. However, the lessee should accrue a loss contingency if it is secondarily liable on the lease.

The lessor recognizes the effect on income of a termination of a lease in the period it occurs. The lessor eliminates the carrying value of the net investment in lease. The leased property is recorded as an asset based on the lower of its initial cost, current fair value, or current carrying amount. The difference between the net investment and the amount the asset is recorded on the lessor's records represents a loss in the year of termination.

ASC 840-30-40-1, *Leases: Capital Leases*, covers the situation when a lessee contracts for a new lease for replacement property before the end of a preexisting lease. If the preexisting lease is ended, costs related to that preexisting lease must be expensed if the leased property no longer benefits the lessee. Examples of such costs are moving costs, write-off of abandoned leasehold improvements, and termination charges. If the lease is not terminated and is not used by the lessee, the amount expensed, including any remaining costs and future rental payments, is reduced by any sublease income. If the preexisting lease is assumed by the new lessor, lessor incentives to the lessee are treated as incentives for accounting purposes. The incentives are amortized on a straight-line basis to rent expense or rent revenue over the life of the new lease. Moving costs are typically expensed.

RENEWALS AND EXTENSIONS

A renewal or extension to an existing lease contract impacts the accounting by both the lessor and lessee. A renewal or extension of a sales-type or direct financing lease shall be treated as a sales-type lease only if it satisfies the criteria for a sales-type lease and takes place at or near the end of the lease term (within the last few months). If a renewal or extension does not take place at or near the end of the lease period, such lease must be treated as a direct financing lease. When a renewal or extension is classified as a direct financing lease, the balances in the lease receivable and the estimated residual value accounts must be modified in accordance with the revised agreement. However, the estimated residual value may not be increased. The net adjustment increases or reduces an unearned income account. If the renewal or extension is treated as an operating lease, the balance in the new investment under the current direct financing or sales-type lease must be eliminated. The leased asset will be recorded at the lower of its original cost, current fair value, or current carrying amount. Any difference between the net investment and the amount of the leased asset is charged against income. The renewal or extension is then treated as an operating lease.

An occurrence that extends the lease term except to cancel a residual guarantee or a penalty for failing to renew the lease results in a new lease agreement that may need to be classified by different criteria.

If a penalty or guarantee no longer applies owing to a renewal or extension of the lease period, or if a new lease arises involving the rental of the same property by the lessee, the asset and liability from a capital lease must be adjusted for the difference in amount between the discounted values of future minimum lease payments between the original and revised lease contracts. The present value determinations for the original and revised lease agreements must be based on the original interest rate.

If a renewal or extension is classified as an operating lease, the current capital lease continues to be treated by the lessee as a capital lease until the expiration of its lease period. At the end of the lease term, the balances in the asset and liability accounts are eliminated, with any resulting gain or loss recognized for the difference. The renewal or extension is considered an operating lease.

If leased property accounted for as a capital lease is bought by the lessee, it is treated as a renewal or extension of a capital lease. The difference between the book value of the property and the acquisition price adjusts the property's carrying value.

A renewal or extension of an operating lease is accounted for as a new agreement.

LEVERAGED LEASES

A leveraged lease occurs when the lessor (equity participant) finances a minimal amount of the purchase but has total equity ownership. A third party (debt participant) finances the remainder. The property is leased to a lessee. Rental receivable is reduced by the difference between the amounts received from the lessee and payments made to the third-party creditor. The lessor maximizes its leveraged return by recognizing lease revenue and an income tax shelter (e.g., interest deduction, accelerated depreciation). A leveraged lease is structured so as to generate tax savings to the lessor without it being entirely at risk for lack of performance on the part of the lessee.

A leveraged lease must satisfy *all* of the following conditions:

☐ There are three participants: lessee, lessor, and long-term creditor. The creditor provides nonrecourse financing, with the lessor having substantial leverage (usually 60% or more of the lessor's cost of the property).

☐ The lessor's net receivable (investment) decreases in the early years of lease and then increases in later years.

☐ The lease meets the test for being a direct financing lease. A sales-type lease is not a leveraged lease. **Note:** Used assets of the lessor rarely qualify as direct financing leases and thus cannot be treated as leveraged leases.

ASC 840-10-25-43c, *Leases: Overall*, stipulates that the book value of an asset must be the same as its fair market value for the lease to qualify as a leveraged lease.

A lessee classifies and accounts for a leveraged lease in the same way as a nonleveraged lease. The lessee follows its normal leasing policy.

The lessor presents the investment in the leveraged lease net of the nonrecourse obligation. The net of the following balances constitutes the initial and continuing investment:

☐ Rentals receivable net of principal and interest associated with nonrecourse debt.

☐ Estimated salvage value.

☐ Unearned income.

The initial entry to record the leveraged lease follows:

 Lease receivable
 Salvage value of the asset
  Cash invested in asset
  Unearned income

The lessor's net investment in the leveraged lease for deriving net income is the investment in the leveraged lease less deferred income taxes.

Net income is computed as follows using the net investment in the leveraged lease:

☐ Compute annual cash flow equal to the following:

 Gross lease rental (add salvage value)
 Less: interest payments on debt
 Less: income tax charges
 Add: income tax credits

Less: principal reduction
Annual cash flow

The return rate on the net investment in the leveraged lease should be determined. It is the rate that when applied to the net investment will distribute cash flow.

The net investment will be:

☐ Positive in the early years but decline because of accelerated depreciation and interest expense.

☐ Negative in the middle years.

☐ Again positive in the later years owing to a declining tax shelter.

In the event that at any time expected net cash receipts over the remaining lease period are less than the lessor's investment in the lease, a loss must be recorded immediately.

ASC 840-30-55-14, *Leases: Capital Leases*, provides that recourse debt arising from a delayed equity investment may be treated as a leveraged lease if all other criteria except for the nonrecourse condition are met. The lessor's liability should be based on the discounted value of future payments.

ASC 840-30-35-41 requires the effect on a leveraged lease of a change in tax rate to be recognized as a gain or loss in the year in which the tax rate changes.

ASC 840-30-S99-2 also discusses the effect of a change in income tax law or rate on the accounting for leveraged leases.

A company must recompute its leveraged lease if there is an actual or projected change in the timing of cash flows related to income taxes generated by the lease. In the event that the projected timing of income tax cash flows is revised, the return rate and the allocation of income to positive investment years should be recomputed from the beginning of the lease.

The lessor must review the expected timing of income tax cash flows each year. There should be an update to any assumptions used to compute total periodic income. However, any interest or penalties assessed by a taxing authority should not be included in any recalculation of cash flows from a leveraged lease. Further, any actual cash flows of a leveraged lease should not include advance payments and deposits made to a taxing body. Instead those amounts should be included in the anticipated settlement amount. Accounts that comprise the net investment balance should be adjusted to conform to recomputed balances with the change in the net investment recorded as a gain or loss in the year that the assumption was modified.

If there is an investment tax credit retained by the lessor, it should be deferred and amortized to income over the lease term.

Disclosure for leveraged leases should be made of:

☐ Assumptions related to estimating the net income associated with the lease.

☐ Components of the net investment.

☐ Deferred taxes.

According to Accounting Standards Update (ASU) No. 2009-07 (September 2009) (ASC 845, *Nonmonetary Transactions*), *Accounting for Various Topics—Technical Corrections to SEC Paragraphs* (SEC Update), the amount of noninterest-bearing deposits and interest-bearing deposits should be disclosed separately. All components of a leveraged lease should be recalculated from lease inception based on revised after-tax cash flows arising from change in tax law, including revised tax rates. The difference between the amounts originally recorded and the recalculated amounts must be included in income of the year the tax law was enacted. (ASC 840-30-35 and 30-45)

RELATED PARTIES

A related party is one whom has substantial influence in financial or operating terms over another in a leasing arrangement, such as an owner, parent company, investor, creditor, or officer or director of the company. Substantial influence may be exercised through extending credit, owning debt or equity securities, or the guaranteeing indebtedness. In a related-party lease where significant influence is involved, the lease should be accounted for according to its economic substance, not its legal form. If substantial influence does not exist, the related-party lease should be classified and accounted for as if the participants were unrelated.

A parent is required to consolidate a subsidiary whose major business activity is leasing property from a parent or other affiliates.

According to ASC 958-840-55, *Not-for-Profit Entities: Leases*, a related-party lease arrangement involving substantial influence may require consolidation accounting for the lessor and lessee if all of the following criteria exist:

- ☐ Most of the lessor's activities relate to leasing assets to one particular lessee.
- ☐ The lessee incurs the risks and rewards associated with the rented property along with any related debt. This may arise if the lease contract gives the lessee control and management over the leased property, the lessee guarantees the lessor's debt or residual value of the leased item, and the lessee has the right to buy the property at a lower than fair value price.
- ☐ The lessor's owners do not have a significant residual equity capital investment that is at risk.

If the consolidation criteria are not satisfied, combined financial statements rather than consolidated financial statements may be appropriate.

ASC 850-10-05-3, *Related Party Disclosures: Overall*, requires disclosure of the nature and extent of leasing transactions between related parties.

MONEY-OVER-MONEY LEASE

ASC 840-30-55-19, *Leases: Capital Leases*, covers money-over-money lease transactions. This transaction occurs when an entity manufactures or buys an asset, leases it to the lessee, and receives nonrecourse financing exceeding the cost of the asset. The collateral for the borrowing is the leased asset and any future rentals derived therefrom. A money-over-money lease transaction is accounted for as the production or acquisition of an asset, the leasing is under one of the lessor's acceptable methods (operating, direct financing, or sales type), and the receipt of borrowed funds. The lessor is prohibited from offsetting the asset (in an operating lease) or the lease receivable (in other than an operating lease) and the nonrecourse obligation unless there is a legal right of set-off. In other words, the leasing and borrowing are considered separate transactions. If a sales-type lease is involved, the lessor may record a profit at the inception of the lease.

THIRD PARTIES

If a direct financing or sales-type lease is sold or assigned by a lessor to a third party, the original accounting policies are still retained; they should not be reversed. When the sale or assignment occurs, the profit or loss is recorded by the lessor except if the seller retains substantial risks. If the transfer qualifies as a sale, the transferor (seller) must record the proceeds received at fair value, credit the asset sold, and book the ensuing gain or loss. In the case where the seller is assuming significant risk of ownership (e.g., seller guarantees the buyer's investment, seller promises to repurchase the leased property if the lessee defaults), the transaction is accounted for as a secured borrowing rather than a sale.

If the lessor has an operating lease, the lessor (seller) records rental receipts as income even if the lessee pays the rentals to a third party. The rental payment includes imputed interest (charged to interest expense) and a reduction of the obligation. A sale or assignment of rentals received from lessees under an operating lease is treated for accounting purposes as a borrowing if the seller retains substantial risks of ownership in the leased property. The seller records the sales proceeds as an obligation on its books. The lessor (seller) records rent receipts as revenue and continues to keep the leased asset on its balance sheet. However, the asset is depreciated over a period not exceeding the period of the obligation.

If the lessee defaults or the rental terminates, the seller may buy the property or lease, substitute an existing lease, get a substitute lessee, or enter into a remarketing arrangement.

The accounting treatment just specified also applies even if the leased property is sold to a third party that intends to lease the property to another party.

WRAP LEASES

ASC 840, *Leases*, states that a wrap lease arrangement should be accounted for as a sale-leaseback transaction when: (1) the company buys an asset, (2) it leases the property to a lessee, (3) the company (now the lessor) receives nonrecourse financing in which the asset and rentals derived therefrom are used as collateral, (4) the lessor sells the asset and related nonrecourse debt to a third party (e.g., financial institution), and (5) the company leases the asset back while still being the principal (substantive) lessor under the initial lease (continuing to service the leased property). (Nonrecourse financing is a borrowing transaction in which the lender does not have general recourse against the borrower directly but instead has recourse against the collateralized property.) The company cannot offset the subleased asset and the related nonrecourse debt unless a legal right of offset exists.

In a wrap lease transaction, the lessor may or may not be responsible for leaseback payments in the case of lessee default or receive a fee to service the lease. The leaseback payments do not necessarily have to coincide with the collections under the note. Further, the leaseback provisions do not necessarily have to agree with the provisions of the initial lease.

In a sale-leaseback transaction, the sale portion is recognized by the seller-lessee as a sale. The seller-lessee eliminates from its balance sheet the asset sold and its associated liabilities. The lease portion of the sale-leaseback transaction is either treated as an operating or capital lease depending on the criteria met.

ASC 840-40-55-17, *Leases: Sale-Leaseback Transactions*, states that an original lessor should defer recognizing the revenue associated with future remarketing rights until such services are conducted. Further, the original lessor should present any retained interest in the salvage value of a leased asset in its balance sheet as an asset.

BUSINESS COMBINATIONS

Assets acquired and liabilities assumed in a business combination are required to be measured at fair value (see ASC 805-10, *Business Combinations: Overall*) regardless of whether those assets and liabilities are applicable to leases.

ASC 805-10-35-5, *Business Combinations: Overall*, states that a business combination by itself has no bearing on the classification of a lease.

The terms of a business combination may affect the classification, accounting, and reporting of a lease. A lease should be treated and accounted for as a new one if its provisions are modified and such revisions would have resulted in another classification at the inception date. In a transaction accounted for under the acquisition method, the acquirer may assign a new value to a capitalized lease because of the allocation of acquisition price to the net assets of the acquired company. However, as long as the lease terms are not revised, the lease should be accounted for using the initial terms and classification.

In the case of a leveraged lease when the purchase method is used in a business combination, the following guidelines are followed:

☐ The classification continues as a leveraged lease.

☐ The net investment in the leveraged lease should be recorded at fair market value, including tax effects. Fair market value is usually based on the discounted value of future cash flows.

☐ The three elements of the net investment are net rentals receivable (investment), expected salvage value, and unearned interest income.

☐ The usual accounting for a leveraged lease should be practiced.

DISPOSAL OF A BUSINESS SEGMENT

ASC 840-10-40, *Leases: Overall*, states that expected costs and expenses directly tied to a disposal of a business segment decision should include future rental payments less amounts to be received from subleases on those properties. The difference between the unamortized cost of the leased property and the discounted value of the minimum lease payments to be received from the sublease is recognized as a gain or loss. This gain or loss is includable in the overall gain or loss on disposing of the business segment.

CURRENT VALUE FINANCIAL STATEMENTS

ASC 840-10-45-2 covers the applicability of ASC 840, *Accounting for Losses*, to current value financial statements.

REAL ESTATE LEASES

A lessee will classify the lease as a capital lease if any of the following factors are present at the inception of the lease:

☐ *Ownership*. At the end of the lease term, the ownership of the property is transferred to the lessee.

☐ *Bargain*. The lease contains a bargain purchase option.

☐ *Life*. The lease term is for 75% or more of the estimated economic life of the property. This does not apply, however, to leases that begin in the last 25% of the original estimated economic life of the property.

☐ *Value*. The present value of minimum lease payments is equal to 90% or more of the fair value of the property. To determine the present value of minimum lease payments, one needs to consider the minimum lease payment, executory costs, and discount rate. Executory costs, such as insurance, maintenance, and taxes, should be excluded if they are to be paid by the lessor. This does not apply, however, to leases that begin in the last 25% of the original estimated economic life of the property.

Real estate leases are of four types:

☐ Land only.

☐ Land and building.

☐ Land, building, and equipment.

☐ Portion of a building.

Land Only

Lessee

Leases involving land only are classified by the lessee as a capital lease only if either the ownership or bargain criterion is met. The lease should be accounted for as an operating lease if both of these conditions are not met.

Lessor

The lessor classifies a lease involving land only as a sales-type lease if the transaction yields manufacturer's or dealer's profit or loss and the ownership criterion is met. Such a transaction is accounted for according to the provisions of ASC 976-10-15, *Real Estate—Retail Land: Overall*.

If the transaction does not yield manufacturer's or dealer's profit and the ownership criterion is met, the lease is classified as a direct financing lease or leveraged lease, as appropriate, as long as both the collectibility and no material uncertainties criteria are met.

If a lease satisfies both the collectibility and no material uncertainties criteria, and it contains a bargain purchase option, it should be accounted for as a direct financing, leveraged, or operating lease, as applicable. All other leases should be accounted for as operating leases.

Land and Building

There are three main categories of leases involving land and building:

1. Leases that satisfy the ownership or bargain criterion.
2. Leases in which the land is valued at less than 25%.
3. Leases in which the land is valued at 25% or more.

Lessee

If the lease agreement transfers the title (ownership) or the agreement contains a bargain purchase option, the lessee should separate the land and building components and capitalize each. The present value of the minimum lease payments (less executory costs to be paid by the lessor and any profits) should be allocated to the land and building components according to their fair values. The building component should be depreciated.

When a lease does not satisfy the ownership or bargain criterion, the fair value of the land must be determined.

☐ If the fair value of the land component is less than 25% of the total land and building lease, the land is considered immaterial. Thus, the lease should be accounted for as a single unit. The lease should be capitalized and depreciated over the economic life if either the life or value criterion is met.

☐ The land is considered material if the fair value of the land component is 25% or more of the total fair value of the lease, and each component should be accounted for separately. The minimum lease payment attributable to the land should be determined using the lessee's incremental borrowing rate and the fair value of the land. The remaining balance of the lease payment is attributable to the building component. The land component should *always* be accounted for as an operating lease. The building component of the lease should be capitalized and depreciated over the economic life if either the life or value criterion is met.

Lessor

If the lease satisfies the ownership criterion and results in dealer's profit or loss, the lessor is required to classify the lease as a sales-type lease. Such a lease should be accounted for as a single unit in a manner similar to a seller of the property.

If the lease satisfies the bargain criterion and results in dealer's/manufacturer's profit or loss, it should be classified as a sales-type lease. If the lease satisfies the bargain criterion but does *not* result in dealer's/manufacturer's profit or loss, it should be classified as direct financing or a leveraged lease, as appropriate. In both cases, if the lease does not satisfy either the ownership or the bargain criterion, the lessor should follow the same rules as the lessee in accounting for leases:

☐ If the fair value of the land is less than 25% of the total fair value of the leased property at the inception of the lease, and either the life or value criterion is met, and the lease gives rise to a dealer's or manufacturer's profit/loss, then the lease should be classified as a sales-type lease. Failing both criteria, it should be classified as an operating lease.

☐ If the fair value of the land is less than 25% of the total fair value of the leased property at the inception of the lease, and either the life or value criterion is met, but the lease does *not* give rise to a dealer's or manufacturer's profit/loss, then the lease should be classified as a direct financing or a leveraged lease, as appropriate, provided that the collection and no material uncertainties criteria are satisfied. Otherwise, the lease should be classified as an operating lease.

☐ If the fair value of the land is 25% or more of the total fair value of the leased property at the inception of the lease, and either the life or value criterion is met, and the lease gives rise to a dealer's or manufacturer's profit/loss, then the building portion of the lease should be classified as a sales-type lease. Otherwise, the building element should be classified as an operating lease. The land portion of the lease should always be accounted for as an operating lease.

☐ If the fair value of the land is 25% or more of the total fair value of the leased property at the inception of the lease, and either the life or value criterion is met, but the lease does *not* give rise to a dealer's or manufacturer's profit/loss, then the building portion of the lease should be classified as a direct financing or a leveraged lease, as appropriate, provided that the collection and no material uncertainties criteria are satisfied. Otherwise, the building portion of the lease should be classified as an operating lease. The land portion of the lease should always be accounted for as an operating lease.

Land, Building, and Equipment

When a lease involves land, building, and equipment, the equipment component, if material, should be estimated and accounted for separately. The capitalization requirements for equipment should be considered separately from the land and building components for both the lessee and lessor.

Portion of a Building

Frequently, a lease involves only a portion of a building. The classification of such leases depends on the ability of lessee and lessor to determine objectively the cost or fair value of the leased property.

Lessee

If the lessee can objectively determine the fair value of the property, the lease should be classified according to the criteria discussed for land and building leases in the previous sections. If the lessee cannot objectively determine the fair value of the property, only the life criterion should be used to determine the lease classification. If the lease is for a period greater than 75% of the economic life of the building, the lease is classified as a capital lease. In all other instances, it should be treated as an operating lease.

Lessor

If the lessor can objectively determine *both* the cost and fair value of the property, the lease should be classified according to the criteria discussed for land and building leases in the previous sections. If the lessor cannot objectively determine both the cost and fair value of the property, the lessor should classify the lease as an operating lease.

Sale-Leaseback Involving Real Estate

In a sale-leaseback, the seller-lessee sells property and then leases back from the purchaser-lessor all or part of the same property. Real estate is classified as a sales-type lease only if the title to the leased property is transferred to the lessee at or shortly after the end of the lease term.

Three conditions must exist for the seller-lessee to use sale-leaseback accounting. First, the leaseback should be a "normal leaseback." A lease-back is considered normal when the seller-lessee actively uses the leased-back property in a trade or business (up to 10% of the property may be subleased). Second, the buyer-lessor's initial and continuing investment in the property should be adequate. ASC 976-10-15, *Real Estate—Retail Land: Overall*, is used to determine the adequacy of the initial investment. Third, risk and reward are transferred to the buyer, the sale is complete, and the seller-lessee has no continuing involvement. The following factors indicate continuing involvement by the seller-lessee and preclude the use of sale-leaseback accounting:

☐ A specific residual value is guaranteed by the seller-lessee, whereby the seller-lessee will pay the buyer-lessor for a decline in fair value below estimated residual value, as long as the decline is not associated with excess wear and tear.

☐ Nonrecourse financing is provided by the seller-lessee to the buyer-lessor for any portion of the sales proceeds.

☐ Recourse financing is provided by the seller-lessee to the buyer-lessor where the only recourse is the leased property.

☐ Collateral, other than the property involved in the sale-leaseback transaction, is provided by the seller-lessee on behalf of the buyer-lessor.

☐ The seller-lessee is not relieved of the obligation under any existing debt related to the property, including secondary liability.

☐ The buyer-lessor's debt is guaranteed by the seller-lessee or a party related to the seller-lessee.

☐ Any appreciation on the property will be shared by the seller-lessee.

Subleases

Subleasing involves the original lessee leasing the property to a third party during the time period in which the original lease is in force. Sometimes a new lessee is substituted for the original lessee and the new lessee becomes primarily obligated. The original lease may be canceled and substituted with a new lessee. The accounting for such transactions depends on whether the original lessee is or is not relieved of primary liability.

ANNUAL REPORT REFERENCES

United States Steel
2011 Annual Report

23. Leases

Future minimum commitments for capital leases (including sale-leasebacks accounted for as financings) and for operating leases having initial non-cancelable lease terms in excess of one year are as follows:

(In millions)	Capital Leases	Operating Leases
2012	$ 22	$ 45
2013	–	31
2014	–	25
2015	–	21
2016	–	19
Later years	–	18
Sublease rentals	–	–
Total minimum lease payments	22	$ 159
Less imputed interest costs	1	
Present value of net minimum lease payments included in long-term debt *(see Note 16)*	$ 21	

Operating lease rental expense:

(In millions)	2011	2010	2009
Minimum rentals	$ 95	$ 93	$ 74
Contingent rentals	11	10	9
Sublease rentals	–	(5)	(5)
Net rental expense	$ 106	$ 98	$ 78

U.S. Steel leases a wide variety of facilities and equipment under operating leases, including land and building space, office equipment, production equipment and transportation equipment. Most long-term leases include renewal options and, in certain leases, purchase options. See the discussion of residual value guarantees under "other contingencies" in Note 24. Contingent rental payments are determined based on operating lease agreements that include floating rental charges that are directly associated to variable operating components.

Oshkosh
2010 Annual Report

10. Leases

Certain administrative and production facilities and equipment are leased under long-term agreements. Most leases contain renewal options for varying periods, and certain leases include options to purchase the leased property during or at the end of the lease term. Leases generally require the Company to pay for insurance, taxes and maintenance of the property. Leased capital assets included in net property, plant and equipment, which consist primarily of buildings and improvements, were $2.5 million and $2.8 million at September 30, 2010 and 2009, respectively.

Other facilities and equipment are leased under arrangements that are accounted for as noncancelable operating leases. Total rental expense for property, plant and equipment charged to continuing operations under noncancelable operating leases was $41.1 million, $34.8 million and $34.2 million in fiscal 2010, 2009 and 2008, respectively. In addition, included in cost of sales in fiscal 2010 were charges of $2.9 million related to the idling of a leased facility at JerrDan.

Future minimum operating and capital lease payments due under operating leases and the related present value of minimum capital lease payments at September 30, 2010 were as follows:

(in millions)	Capital Leases	Operating Leases	Total
2011	$ 0.7	$ 28.2	$ 28.9
2012	0.5	20.9	21.4
2013	0.4	15.4	15.8
2014	0.7	11.2	11.9
2015	–	9.4	9.4
Thereafter	–	21.2	21.2
Total minimum lease payments	2.3	$ 106.3	$ 108.6
Interest	(0.2)		
Present value of net minimum lease payments	$ 2.1		

Minimum rental payments include $1.2 million due annually under variable-rate leases.

Good Year Tire and Rubber Company
2009 Annual Report

Note 10. Leased Assets

Net rental expense comprised the following:

(In-millions)	2009	2008	2007
Gross rental expense	$382	$383	$372
Sublease rental income	(67)	(68)	(70)
	$315	$315	$302

We enter into leases primarily for our wholesale and retail distribution facilities, vehicles, and data processing equipment under varying terms and conditions. Many of the leases require us to pay taxes assessed against leased property and the cost of insurance and maintenance. A portion of our domestic retail distribution network is sublet to independent dealers.

While substantially all subleases and some operating leases are cancelable for periods beyond 2010, management expects that in the normal course of its business nearly all of its independent dealer distribution network will be actively operated. As leases and subleases for existing locations expire, we would normally expect to evaluate such leases and either renew the leases or substitute another more favorable retail location.

The following table presents minimum future lease payments:

(In millions)	2010	2011	2012	2013	2014	2015 and Beyond	Total
Capital Leases							
Minimum lease payments	$ 5	$ 5	$ 4	$ 9	$ –	$ –	$ 23
Imputed interest	(2)	(2)	(1)	–	–	–	(5)
Present value	$ 3	$ 3	$ 3	$ 9	$ –	$ –	$ 18
Operating Leases							
Minimum lease payments	$302	$254	$197	$152	$108	$ 348	$1,361
Minimum sublease rentals	(43)	(33)	(24)	(18)	(9)	(10)	(137)
	$259	$221	$173	$134	$ 99	$ 338	1,224
Imputed interest							(326)
Present value							$ 898

Matrix Service Company
2009 Annual Report

Note 8. Leases

Operating Leases

The Company is the lessee under operating leases covering real estate, office equipment and vehicles under non-cancelable operating lease agreements that expire at various times. Future minimum lease payments under non-cancelable operating leases that were in effect at May 31, 2009 total $13.8 million and are payable as follows: fiscal 2010—$2.9 million; fiscal 2011—$2.8 million; fiscal 2012—$2.4 million; fiscal 2013—$2.2 million; fiscal 2014 $1.6 million and thereafter—$1.9 million. Operating lease expense was $2.7 million, $1.9 million and $1.2 million for the years ended May 31, 2009, 2008 and 2007, respectively.

Capital Leases

The Company leases most of its copiers, printers, and passenger vehicles under various non-cancelable lease agreements. Minimum lease payments have been capitalized and the related assets and obligations recorded using various interest rates. The assets are depreciated on a straight line method over their estimated useful lives. Interest expense is recognized using the effective interest method.

The following table is a summary of future obligations under capital leases:

(In thousands)	Minimum Lease Payments
For the year ending May 31:	
2010	$1,049
2011	717
2012	219
2013	1
2014 and thereafter	–
Total Payments	1,986
Amounts representing interest	97
Total obligation	1,889
Current portion	1,039
Long-term capital lease obligation	$ 850

Assets with a cost of $4.6 million and $3.9 million have been capitalized under capital lease arrangements at May 31, 2009 and 2008. The net book value of these assets was $2.1 million at both dates.

Kellogg's
2008 Annual Report

Note 6. Leases and Other Commitments

The Company's leases are generally for equipment and warehouse space. Rent expense on all operating leases was (in millions): 2008-$145; 2007-$135; 2006-$123. The Company was subject to a residual value guarantee on one operating lease of approximately $13 million, which was scheduled to expire in July 2007. During the first quarter of 2007, the Company recognized a liability in connection with this guarantee of approximately $5 million, which was recorded in cost of goods sold within the Company's North America operating segment.

During the second quarter of 2007, the Company terminated the lease agreement and purchased the facility for approximately $16 million, which discharged the residual value guarantee obligation. During 2008, 2007 and 2006, the Company entered into approximately $3 million, $5 million and $2 million, respectively, in capital lease agreements to finance the purchase of equipment.

At January 3, 2009, future minimum annual lease commitments under noncancelable operating and capital leases were as follows:

(millions)	Operating leases	Capital leases
2009	$135	$1
2010	119	1
2011	99	1
2012	75	1
2013	56	0
2014 and beyond	143	2
Total minimum payments	$627	$6
Amount representing interest		(1)
Obligations under capital leases		5
Obligations due within one year		(1)
Long-term obligations under capital leases		$4

One of the Company's subsidiaries was guarantor on loans to independent contractors for the purchase of DSD route franchises. In July 2007, the Company exited these agreements. Refer to Note 3 for further information.

The Company has provided various standard indemnifications in agreements to sell and purchase business assets and lease facilities over the past several years, related primarily to pre-existing tax, environmental, and employee benefit obligations. Certain of these indemnifications are limited by agreement in either amount and/or term and others are unlimited. The Company has also provided various "hold harmless" provisions within certain service type agreements. Because the Company is not currently aware of any actual exposures associated with these indemnifications, management is unable to estimate the maximum potential future payments to be made. At January 3, 2009, the Company had not recorded any liability related to these indemnifications.

Goodyear Tire
2007 Annual Report

Note 10. Leased Assets

Net rental expense comprised the following:

(In-millions)	2007	2006	2005
Gross rental expense	$372	$361	$351
Sublease rental income	(70)	(75)	(76)
	$302	$286	$275

We enter into leases primarily for our wholesale and retail distribution facilities, vehicles, and data processing equipment under varying terms and conditions. Many of the leases require us to pay taxes assessed against leased property and the cost of insurance and maintenance. Aportion of our domestic retail distribution network is sublet to independent dealers.

While substantially all subleases and some operating leases are cancelable for periods beyond 2008, management expects that in the normal course of its business nearly all of its independent dealer distribution network will be actively operated. As leases and subleases for existing locations expire, we would normally expect to evaluate such leases and either renew the leases or substitute another more favorable retail location.

The following table presents minimum future lease payments:

(In millions)	2008	2009	2010	2011	2012	2013 and Beyond	Total
Capital Leases							
Minimum lease payments	$ 8	$ 8	$ 7	$ 7	$ 7	$ 16	$ 53
Imputed interest							(13)
Present value							$ 40
Operating Leases							
Minimum lease payments	$311	$244	$192	$144	$106	$406	$1,403
Minimum sublease rentals	(46)	(35)	(26)	(16)	(10)	(17)	(150)
	$265	$209	$166	$128	$ 96	$389	1,253
Imputed interest							(333)
Present value							$ 920

Sherwin-Williams
2007 Annual Report

Note 17—Operating Leases

The Company leases certain stores, warehouses, manufacturing facilities, office space and equipment. Renewal options are available on the majority of leases and, under certain conditions, options exist to purchase certain properties. Rental expense for operating leases, recognized on a straight-line basis over the lease term in accordance with FASB Technical Bulletin No. 85-3, "Accounting for Operating Leases with Scheduled Rent Increases," was $245,345, $217,567, and $197,362 for 2007, 2006 and 2005, respectively. Certain store leases require the payment of contingent rentals based on sales in excess of specified minimums. Contingent rentals included in rent expense were $30,704, $27,470, and $22,472 in

2007, 2006 and 2005, respectively. Rental income, as lessor, from real estate leasing activities and sublease rental income for all years presented was not significant.

Following is a schedule, by year and in the aggregate, of future minimum lease payments under noncancellable operating leases having initial or remaining terms in excess of one year at December 31, 2007:

2008	$207,393
2009	181,489
2010	148,953
2011	113,886
2012	81,802
Later years	175,973
Total minimum lease payments	$909,496

Note 15—Net Income Per common Share

	2007	*2006*	*2005*
Basic			
Average common shares outstanding	127,222,007	133,579,145	136,816,868
Net income	$ 615,578	$ 576,058	$ 463,258
Net income per common share	$ 4.84	$ 4.31	$ 3.39
Diluted			
Average common shares outstanding	127,222,007	133,579,145	136,816,868
Non-vested restricted stock grants	1,152,162	1,168,564	950,182
Stock options and other contingently issuable shares	2,550,521	2,594,399	3,311,882
Average common shares assuming dilution	130,924,690	137,342,108	141,078,932
Net income	$ 615,578	$ 576,058	$ 463,258
Net income per common share	$ 4.70	$ 4.19	$ 3.28

Note 16—Summary of Quarterly Results of Operations (Unaudited)

	2007				
	1st Quarter	*2nd Quarter*	*3rd Quarter*	*4th Quarter*	*Full Year*
Net sales	$1,756,178	$2,198,188	$2,197,042	$1,853,884	$8,005,292
Gross profit	791,367	986,570	988,388	832,002	3,598,327
Net income	111,802	202,607	200,349	100,820	615,578
Net income per common share— basic	0.85	1.56	1.59	0.82	4.84

	2007				
	1st Quarter	*2nd Quarter*	*3rd Quarter*	*4th Quarter*	*Full Year*
Net income per common share— diluted	0.83	1.52	1.55	0.8	4.7

Net income in the fourth quarter of 2007 was increased by $12,205 ($.09 per share) due primarily to physical inventory adjustments. Gross profit was increased by $12,396 primarily as a result of physical inventory adjustments of $14,492. Selling, general and administrative expenses decreased $7,383 primarily due to incentive compensation and benefit expense adjustments.

	2006				
	1st Quarter	*2nd Quarter*	*3rd Quarter*	*4th Quarter*	*Full Year*
Net sales	$1,768,528	$2,129,970	$2,116,711	$1,794,550	$7,809,759
Gross profit	771,411	936,588	935,778	770,863	3,414,640
Net income	113,671	184,592	179,112	98,683	576,058
Net income per common share— basic	0.84	1.37	1.34	0.75	4.31
Net income per common share— diluted	0.82	1.33	1.3	0.73	4.19

Sara Lee
2005 Annual Report

Note 13—Leases

The corporation leases certain facilities, equipment and vehicles under agreements that are classified as capital leases. The building leases have original terms that range from 10 to 15 years, while the equipment and vehicle leases have terms of generally less than seven years. The net book value of capital lease assets included in property at July 2, 2005, July 3, 2004 and June 28, 2003 was $79, $67 and $51, respectively.

Future minimum payments, by year and in the aggregate, under capital leases and noncancelable operating leases having an original term greater than one year at July 2, 2005 were as follows:

	Capital Leases	Operating Leases
2006	$28	$147
2007	21	126
2008	14	102
2009	7	86
2010	4	73

	Capital Leases	Operating Leases
Thereafter	11	200
Total minimum lease payment	85	$734
Amounts representing interest	(4)	
Present value of net minimum payments	81	
Current portion	26	
Noncurrent portion	$55	

Depreciation expense of capital lease assets was $35 in 2005, $22 in 2004 and $11 in 2003. Rental expense under operating leases was $210 in 2005, $198 in 2004 and $197 in 2003.

Contingent Lease Obligation The corporation is contingently liable for leases on property operated by others. At July 2, 2005, the maximum potential amount of future payments the corporation could be required to make, if all of the current operators default on the rental arrangements, is $213. The minimum annual rentals under these leases is $28 in 2006, $26 in 2007, $24 in 2008, $22 in 2009, $20 in 2010 and $93 thereafter. The largest single component of these amounts relate to a number of retail store leases operated by Coach, Inc., which is contractually obligated to provide the corporation, on an annual basis, with a standby letter of credit approximately equal to the next year's rental obligations. The letter of credit in place at the close of 2005 was $15. This obligation to provide a letter of credit expires when the corporation's contingent lease obligation is substantially extinguished. The corporation has not recognized a liability for the contingent obligation on the Coach, Inc. leases.

Winn-Dixie
2003 Annual Report

9. Leases

(a) **Lease Commitments:** The principal types of property leased by the Company are store facilities, manufacturing and warehouse buildings, equipment, and delivery vehicles. A majority of the leases in effect relate to store locations and other properties with remaining terms ranging from less than one year to 22 years. Certain lease agreements are classified as capital leases. Assets under capital lease are included in the consolidated balance sheets as follows:

	2003	2002
Store facilities	$36,508	36,948
Warehouses and manufacturing facilities	15,722	15,722
	52,230	52,670
Less: Accumulated amortization	38,060	36,287
	$14,170	16,383

Future minimum lease payments by year and in the aggregate under the aforementioned leases and other noncancellable operating leases on both closed and open stores having a remaining term in excess of one year at June 25, 2003 are as follows:

Future lease payments	Capital	Operating	Sublease	Net
Fiscal Year:				
2004	$ 6,433	414,270	(11,238)	409,465
2005	5,876	397,221	(9,262)	393,835
2006	5,556	364,361	(7,014)	362,903
2007	4,933	345,622	(4,666)	345,889
2008	4,345	328,419	(3,899)	328,865
Thereafter	12,205	2,618,249	(19,346)	2,611,108
Total minimum lease payments	39,348	4,468,142	(55,425)	4,452,065
Less: Amount representing estimated taxes, maintenance and insurance costs included in total minimum lease payments	658			
Net minimum lease payments	38,690			
Less: Amount representing interest	13,907			
Present value of net minimum lease	$24,783			

Rental expense and contingent rentals under operating leases were as follows:

	2003	2002	2001
Minimum rentals	$341,481	357,136	347,130
Contingent rentals	677	899	878
	$342,158	358,035	348,008

(b) Lease Liability on Closed Stores: The Company accrues for the obligation related to closed store locations based on the present value of expected future rental payment, net of estimated sub-lease income The following amounts are included in accrued rent and lease liability on closed stores, as of June 25, 2003:

Lease liability on closed stores	
Balance at June 26, 2002	$ 264,386
Additions/adjustments	34,216
Utilization	(82,576)
Balance at June 25, 2003	**$ 216,026**

The additions/adjustments amount includes the effect on earnings from the accretion of the present value of the expected future rental payments, additional leases added to the accrual and adjustments due to the settlement of certain existing leases. The utilization amount includes payments made for rent and related costs and the buyout of twenty leases. The lease liability on closed stores includes $111.4 million related to restructure and $58.1 million related to the discontinued operations. The additions/adjustments and the utilization for restructure were $11.7 million and $38.6 million, respectively for the year. The current portion of the accrued balance at June 25, 2003 totals $66.6 million and is included in accrued rent.

Genuine Parts
2003 Annual Report

6. Leased Properties

The Company leases land, buildings and equipment. Certain land and building leases have renewal options generally for periods ranging from two to ten years. In addition, certain properties occupied under operating leases contain normal purchase options. The Company also has an $85,000,000 construction and lease facility. Properties acquired by the lessor are constructed and/or then leased to the Company under operating lease agreements. The total amount advanced and outstanding under this facility at December 31, 2003 was approximately $80,057,000. Since the resulting leases are accounted for as operating leases, no debt obligation is recorded on the Company's balance sheet. Future minimum payments, by year and in the aggregate, under the noncancelable operating leases with initial or remaining terms of one year or more consisted of the following at December 31, 2003 (in thousands):

2004	$104,862
2005	80,027
2006	56,907
2007	41,801
2008	27,920
Subsequent to 2008	71,818
	$383,335

Rental expense for operating leases was approximately $119,595,000 in 2003, $114,352,000 in 2002 and $112,470,000 in 2001.

Safeway 2003 Annual Report

Note E: Lease Obligations

Approximately two-thirds of the premises that the Company occupies are leased. The Company had approximately 1,625 leases at year-end 2003, including approximately 225 that are capitalized for financial reporting purposes. Most leases have renewal options, some with terms and conditions similar to the original lease, others with reduced rental rates during the option periods. Certain of these leases contain options to purchase the property at amounts that approximate fair market value.

As of year-end 2003, future minimum rental payments applicable to non-cancelable capital and operating leases with remaining terms in excess of one year were as follows (in millions):

	Capital Leases	Operating Leases
2004	$ 118.0	$ 400.1
2005	104.6	394.6
2006	97.7	379.2
2007	94.2	358.4
2008	90.9	340.7
Thereafter	907.0	2,885.7
Total minimum lease payments	1,412.4	$4,758.7
Less amounts representing interest	(693.6)	
Present value of net minimum lease payments	718.8	
Less current obligations	(50.5)	
Long-term obligations	$ 668.3	

Future minimum lease payments under non-cancelable capital and operating lease agreements have not been reduced by minimum sublease rental income of $202.3 million.

Amortization expense for property under capital leases was $35.4 million in 2003, $42.4 million in 2002 and $38.9 million in 2001. Accumulated amortization of property under capital leases was $181.6 million at year-end 2003 and $151.6 million at year-end 2002.

The following schedule shows the composition of total rental expense for all operating leases (in millions). In general, contingent rentals are based on individual store sales.

	2003	2002	2001
Property leases:			
Minimum rentals	$411.4	$388.7	$369.0
Contingent rentals	25.6	17.0	16.5
Less rentals from subleases	(31.4)	(31.3)	(34.1)
	405.6	374.4	351.4
Equipment leases	25.2	25.6	31.0
	$430.8	$400.0	$382.4

Boise
2003 Annual Report

7. Leases

We capitalize lease obligations for which we assume substantially all property rights and risks of ownership. We did not have any material capital leases during any of the periods presented. We lease our retail store space as well as other property and equipment under operating leases. Some of our leases require percentage rentals on sales above specified minimums, contain escalation clauses and renewal options, and are noncancelable with aggregate minimum lease payment requirements. For the leases that contain predetermined fixed escalation clauses, we recognize the related rent expense on a straight-line basis over the life of the lease and record the difference between the amounts charged to operations and amounts paid to "Other long-term liabilities" in our Consolidated Balance Sheets. "Other long-term liabilities" included approximately $8.1 million and $5.7 million related to these future escalation clauses in 2003 and 2002.

The components of total rent expense for all operating leases is as follows:

| | Year Ended December 31 | | |
	2003	2002	2001
	(thousands)		
Minimum rentals	$77,038	$60,664	$60,660
Percentage rentals	3,222	2,890	2,754
Sublease rentals	(1,415)	(1,269)	(1,249)
	$78,845	$62,285	$62,165

For operating leases with remaining terms of more than one year, the minimum lease payment requirements are $387.1 million for 2004, $358.2 million for 2005, $324.8 million for 2006, $280.4 million for 2007, and $253.0 million for 2008, with total payments thereafter of $1,281.0 million. These minimum lease payments do not include contingent rental expenses that may be paid based on a percentage in excess of stipulated amounts. These future minimum lease payment requirements have not been reduced by $63.7 million of minimum sublease rentals due in the future under noncancelable subleases.

Cummins
2003 Annual Report

Note 18. Leases

We lease certain manufacturing equipment, facilities, warehouses, office space and equipment, aircraft and automobiles for varying periods under lease agreements. Most of the leases are non-cancelable operating leases with fixed rental payments, expire over the next ten years and contain renewal provisions. Rent expense under these leases approximated $88 million, $87 million and $75 million in 2003, 2002 and 2001, respectively. We have guaranteed residual values of $15 million under certain operating leases at December 31, 2003, excluding the Power Rent and Sale/Leaseback transactions discussed below.

Following is a summary of the future minimum lease payments under capital and operating leases with terms of more than one year at December 31, 2003 together with the net present value of the minimum payments under capital leases:

	Capital Leases	Operating Leases
	$ Millions	
2004	$11	$54
2005	10	35
2006	7	23
2007	1	19
2008	81	17
After 2008	3	72
Total minimum lease payments	33	220
Interest	(3)	
Present value of net minimum lease payments	$30	

In addition, we have subleased certain of the facilities under operating lease to third parties. The future minimum lease payments due from lessees under those arrangements are $1.1 million in 2004, $1.0 million in 2005, $1.1 million in 2006, $1.1 million in 2007, $1.1 million in 2008 and $1.5 million thereafter.

PowerRent Business

In 1999, our Power Generation Business entered into an ongoing leasing program in which it builds and sells power generation equipment inventory to a financial institution and leases the equipment and related components back under a three-month, noncancelable lease arrangement with subsequent renewals on a monthly basis up to a maximum of 36 months. The equipment is sold at cost and pursuant to lease accounting rules, the excess of the fair value of the equipment sold over its cost is recognized as prepaid rent and reflects the normal profit margin that would have been realized at the time of sale. The margins on the equipment sales are deferred and the leases recorded as operating leases. The prepaid rent is amortized ratably over the accounting lease term. Upon termination of the leases through a sale of the equipment to a third party, the previously deferred margins on the sale to the financial institution are recorded as income. We sublease the equipment to customers under short-term rental agreements with terms that vary based upon customer and geographic region.

During 2002 and 2003, we entered into new leases for portions of the equipment ($29 million in 2002 and $34 million in 2003) with a different lessor. The new leases had a minimum two-year non-cancellable lease term with monthly renewal options for the 2002 transaction and four six-month renewal options for the 2003 transaction. The deferred margin associated with the equipment that transferred to a new lessor remains unchanged, as there was not an ultimate sale to a third party.

At the end of the renewal terms, we may either negotiate a lease extension with the lessor, purchase the equipment based on rates derived from the equipment's expected residual value or arrange the sale of the equipment to an unrelated third party for fair market value. When the equipment is sold, we are obligated to pay the lessor the difference, if any, between the sales proceeds of the equipment and the lessor's unamortized value of the equipment up to the maximum amount of the residual guarantee. For one lessor, the residual guarantee is equal to 87% of the current unamortized balance. For the second lessor, the residual guarantee ranges from 64% to 78% of the equipment's original cost. The maximum amount of the guarantees at December 31, 2003, at the end of the respective minimum legal lease terms, was $106 million. Since the inception of the rental program, we have not incurred any losses on equipment sales under this program.

Future minimum lease payments during the legal lease term under each lease are included in the table above.

Sale and Leaseback Transactions

In June 2001, we entered into a bridge lease agreement whereby we sold and leased back certain heavy-duty engine manufacturing equipment. The lease was accounted for as an operating lease. Proceeds from the transaction were $119 million and were used to reduce debt and working capital and fund lease transaction costs. The net book value of the equipment was $104 million resulting in a $15 million pre-tax deferred gain.

The bridge lease contained a fixed purchase option that we exercised in December 2001. Under the option, we reacquired the equipment and refinanced the initial leaseback transaction by entering into a new sale-leaseback agreement with a grantor trust wholly-owned by a financial institution. The resulting lease was accounted for as an operating lease. Under the new lease, we received proceeds of $125 million, $6 million higher than the June proceeds, primarily as a result of an increase in the appraised value of the equipment during the interim period. We recorded a deferred gain of $23 million that was being amortized over the lease term net of a $9 million lease residual value guarantee. The lease term is 11.5 years, expiring June 28, 2013, and contains an early buyout purchase option on January 14, 2009. The early buyout option can be exercised for approximately $35 million, or 28 percent of the equipment's fair market value at the inception of the lease. If we do not exercise the early buyout option, we are obligated to purchase insurance that insures the residual value of the equipment. At the end of the lease term, we are obligated to pay the difference, if any, between the amount of the residual value guarantee and the fair market value of the equipment. Rent expense under the lease agreements approximated $12 million, $12 million and $6 million in 2003, 2002 and 2001, respectively.

The lease agreement includes certain default provisions requiring us to make timely rent payments, maintain, service, repair and insure the equipment, procure residual value insurance and maintain minimum debt ratings for our long-term senior unsecured debt obligations.

As of December 31, 2003, the grantor trust holding our lease was consolidated due to the adoption of FIN 46. See Note 2 for further details of the effect of this consolidation. Because the trust is now consolidated, the future minimum lease payments are no longer disclosed, but rather payments under the trust's debt obligations are included in Note 8. There will be no lease expense related to this lease going forward. Instead, we will report interest expense on the trust's debt obligations and depreciation expense on the equipment which is once again included in our balance sheet.

In September 2001, we entered into two sale-leaseback transactions with an aggregate value of $18 million, whereby we sold and leased back two aircraft. The leases were accounted for as operating leases. The transactions resulted in the recording of a pre-tax deferred gain of $8 million that is being amortized over the life of the leases as a reduction in rent expense. The base lease term for both leases is 124 months and provides for an early buyout option in January 2009 at expected fair market value or we may purchase the aircraft at the end of the lease term for its then fair market value. Rent expense under these leases approximated $0.9 million, $0.8 million and $0.2 million in 2003, 2002 and 2001, respectively. Future minimum lease payments under the leases are included in the table above.

United States Steel
2003 Annual Report

30. Leases

Future minimum commitments for capital leases (including sale-leasebacks accounted for as financings) and for operating leases having initial non-cancelable lease terms in excess of one year are as follows:

(In millions)	Capital Leases	Operating Leases
2004	$ 28	$132
2005	17	121
2006	23	86
2007	31	66
2008	23	29
Later years	90	152
Sublease rentals	–	(76)
Total minimum lease payments	212	$510
Less imputed interest costs	62	
Present value of net minimum lease payments included in long-term debt (see Note 20)	$150	

Operating lease rental expense:

(In millions)	2003	2002	2001
Minimum rental	**$148**	$109	$133
Contingent rental	**13**	12	18
Sublease rentals	**(23)**	(18)	(17)
Net rental expense	**$138**	$103	$134

U.S. Steel leases a wide variety of facilities and equipment under operating leases, including land and building space, office equipment, production facilities and transportation equipment. Most long-term leases include renewal options and, in certain leases, purchase options. See discussion of residual value guarantees in Note 31. Contingent rental payments are determined based on operating lease agreements that include floating rental charges that are directly associated to variable operating components.

Chapter 14
Pension Plans and Other Postretirement Benefit Plans

CONTENTS

The major types of pension plans are defined contribution and defined benefit. The reporting by a trustee for the plan is also presented, including the requirements surrounding pension plan financial statements. The accounting for settlements, curtailments, and terminations is presented. Postretirement benefit plans other than pensions are also discussed. Finally, the accounting and reporting for postemployment benefits are presented.

PENSION PLANS

Pension accounting is divided and treated separately between the employer's accounting and the accounting for the pension fund. The employer incurs the cost and makes contributions to the pension fund. The fund (plan) is the entity that receives the contributions, administers pension assets, and makes benefit payments to retirees. The assets and liabilities of a pension plan are not included in the employer's financial statements. The pension fund is a separate legal and accounting entity. It provides benefits to employees at retirement, death, disability, or some other covered event. Many pension plans allow for early retirement or termination of service.

Although a company is not required to have a pension plan, if it does it must follow financial accounting standards and government accounting and presentation dictates. Pension costs must be accounted for under the accrual basis. Pension expense is accrued as services are rendered. Reasonable estimates and averages may be used for future events in computing pension expense. Pension expense is presented in the income statement as a single amount. Pension expense is reflected in the service periods using a method that considers the benefit formula. The American Institute of CPAs (AICPA) has issued an *Industry Audit and Accounting Guide for Employee Benefit Plans*.

Pension expenses for administrative personnel are expensed, but those for factory workers are inventoriable.

The relationship among the parties in a pension plan is shown in Exhibit 14-1.

Exhibit 14-1: Relationship Among Parties in a Pension Plan

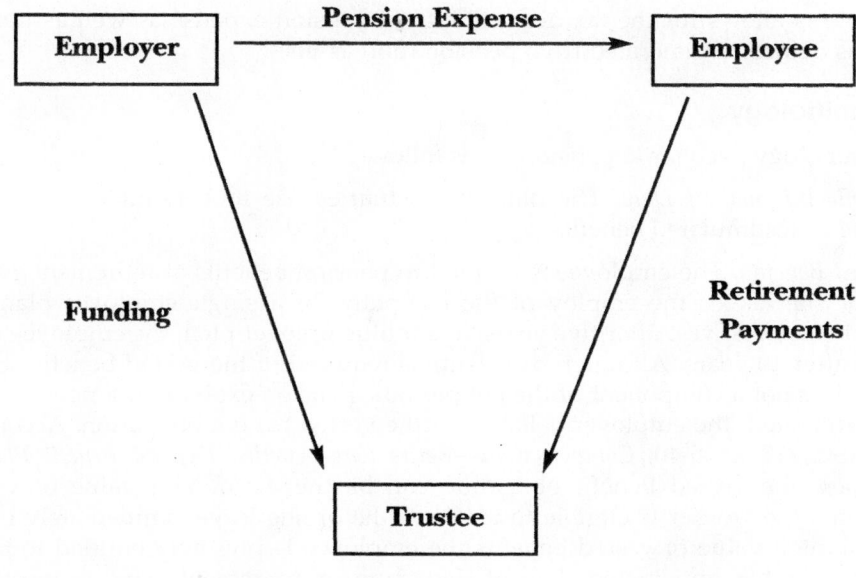

The purpose of pension accounting is to communicate the funded status of defined benefit postretirement plans in a clear and comprehensive way. Employers must incorporate future salary levels in measuring pension expense and the present obligation if the plan benefit includes them. The benefits/years-of-service actuarial method, which computes pension expense based on future compensation levels, should be used. The employer is required to fund at least the annual service cost computed under the plan.

Employers must incorporate future salary levels in measuring pension expense and the present obligation if the plan benefit includes them. FAS-158 adopts the benefits/years-of-service actuarial method, which computes pension expense based on future compensation levels. The employer is required to fund at least the annual service cost computed under the plan.

There are two kinds of pension plans: defined contribution and defined benefit. In *defined contribution plans*, the amount to be contributed each year by the employer is specified; the benefits to be paid at retirement are not specified or known. Defined contribution plan benefits equal the value of each participant's account balance. Examples of such plans include employee stock ownership, profit sharing, and money purchase. In *defined benefit plans*, the amount to be received by retirees is specified. The employer contributes amounts to fund the accumulation benefit. In most cases, annuity payments are made.

Note: The requirements of ASC 962-10-05 also apply to pension plans outside the United States, as long as they are similar to U.S. plans. In some countries, it may be the custom to pay employee benefits upon voluntary or involuntary termination of employees.

Employers usually design a pension plan so it qualifies under the federal tax law. This allows for the tax deductibility of pension expense as well as tax-free status of income generated from pension fund assets.

Terminology

Terminology peculiar to pension plans follows:

Benefit Information Date. The date that actuaries use to determine the present value of accumulated benefits.

Vested Benefits. The employee is entitled to pension benefits at retirement even if he or she leaves the employ of the company. In a single-employer plan, the employee must vest after five years; in a multiemployer plan, the employee must vest after 10 years. Although disclosure is required of the vested benefit obligation, it is not a component of the net periodic pension expense. If a pension plan is terminated, the employer is liable for the vested benefit obligation. According to ASC 715-30-35-40, *Compensation—Retirement Benefits: Defined Benefit Plans—Pension*, the vested benefit obligation can be the discounted value of vested benefits the worker is eligible to receive if he or she leaves immediately or the discounted value of vested benefits the employee is presently entitled to based on his or her anticipated date of departure or retirement. This is mostly of concern to foreign plans.

Net Assets Available for Pension Benefits. The excess of pension assets over pension liabilities. The pension liability does not include employees' accumulated benefits.

Actuarial Assumptions. Assumptions used by actuaries to compute pension expense and cash payment to the trustee. Examples of assumptions needed for mathematical computations are turnover rate, return rate, salary levels, retirement age, withdrawal, disablement, administrative costs, life expectancy, retirement age, and the length of time that benefits will be paid.

Actuarial Cost Method. The funding method actuaries use to calculate the employer's contribution so adequate funds will be available when workers retire. The method will determine the pension expense and associated liability.

Unrecognized Net Gain or Loss. The cumulative net gain or loss that has not been recognized as a component of pension expense.

Actuarial Present Value of Accumulated Plan Benefits. The discounted (time value) amount of money necessary to meet retirement obligations for current and retired employees. The calculation considers such factors as withdrawal, death, and disability.

Accumulated Benefit Obligation (ABO). The year-end pension obligation based on past and current salaries, not future compensation levels. It is the actuarial present value of vested and nonvested benefits attributable to the pension plan based on services rendered to date. It assumes that compensation to plan participants does not change. Attrition of current participants is considered, but no consideration is given to employees who will enter the plan in later years. If the pension plan is terminated, the amount of any unfunded accumulated benefit obligation continues as a liability of the employer.

Projected Benefit Obligation (PBO). The year-end pension obligation based on future projected salaries. It measures the deferred compensation amount and relates to the discounted value of benefits (whether vested or nonvested) earned to date. The employer does not record the projected benefit obligation on its books. It is only maintained on a worksheet record.

Examples of plans based on future salary levels are career average pay, pay related, and final pay. These plans take into account compensation increases and employee turnover rates. The projected benefit obligation equals the anticipated increase (progression) in salaries plus the accumulated benefit obligation. For example, if the accumulated benefit obligation is $150,000 and the expected progression in wages is $20,000, the projected benefit obligation will equal $170,000.

In the case of pension plans with flat-benefit or non-pay-related pension benefit formulas, the accumulated benefit obligation and the projected benefit obligation amounts will be the same.

The projected benefit obligation is used to calculate interest cost, prior service cost, and corridor amounts in the actuarial gains or losses computation.

Market-Related Asset Value. The fair market value of pension plan assets or a calculated value (e.g., moving average) that recognizes the changes in the actual fair value of pension assets over a period not exceeding five years. Market-related asset value is an average of fair values and is used because fair value may change significantly over the years, which would cause significant differences in pension expense each period. The valuation method must be used consistently. Market-related values may be assigned to different asset classes.

EXAMPLE

A calculated moving average value is to be used in measuring pension plan assets. The actual fair value of plan assets at the end of each of the last six years was $16,000, $20,000, $25,000, $28,000, $32,000, and $26,000. The net gain for the five years is $10,000 ($4,000 + $5,000 + $3,000 + $4,000 − $6,000). The five-year net gain is over a five-year period, or 20% (1/5). Therefore, only 20% of the $10,000 net gain, or $2,000, is included in deriving the calculated market-related value of the pension plan assets for the current period.

Note: The amount by which the actual fair value differs from the calculated market-related value is the net gain or loss from prior years that still has not been recognized in the calculated market-related value.

Contributory Plan. A plan in which employees must contribute their share to the pension and to its cost. The contribution rate is usually specified as a percentage. For example, a pension plan may require employees to contribute 5% of their annual salary while the employer contributes 10% of the salary. In some plans, employees have the option to contribute in order to receive increased benefits. In a noncontributory plan, employees do not contribute to the pension plan. The employer is the only one who funds the plan.

Measurement Date. The date in which pension plan assets and liabilities are measured. They should usually be measured at the employer's fiscal year-end.

Attribution. The procedure used to assign pension benefits or cost to the years of employee service. The attribution period usually starts when the employee is hired and ends when the employee becomes fully eligible under the plan. Each year of service is usually considered equal in application. However, a benefit formula may be used, attributing more or less benefits to later service years.

Full Eligibility. The date the employee achieves complete eligibility for pension benefits. The benefits may be received by either the employee or his or her beneficiaries in the case of death. Full eligibility may be based on reaching a predetermined number of service years, or age, or a combination of service and age.

Mortality Rate. The ratio of the number of deaths relative to the number of living persons in a particular group. This is one consideration used by actuaries in determining pension expense and related funding. Actuaries refer to mortality tables, which indicate the death rates by age.

Annuity Contract. An irrevocable agreement in which the insurer has the unconditional obligation to pay employees of the employer either specific periodic benefits or a lump-sum payment to another party. The employer pays the insurance company premiums over the life of the contract. In so doing, the employer transfers its risk to the insurer.

Defined Contribution Pension Plan

In a defined contribution plan, the employer and employees make contributions to a plan so as to provide pension benefits to employees when they retire. In this plan, only the employer's contribution is defined, so there is no assurance of the eventual benefits to be paid to retirees.

Under a defined contribution pension plan, pension expense is accrued each year based on services rendered. The amount funded (contributed) equals the pension expense for the period. The entry is to debit pension expense and credit cash. As a result, a deferred charge or deferred credit is not recorded.

In the event that the plan provides for contributions after retirement or termination, the associated expense should be accrued during the service years.

At retirement, the employee will receive pension benefits based on the amounts contributed to his or her account, income earned on investments, and forfeitures of amounts of other participants who leave employment before being vested.

The following should be footnoted:

☐ Cost recognized for the year.

☐ Method and basis in computing contributions.

☐ Description of the terms.

☐ Categorization of covered employees.

☐ Discussion of items affecting comparability over the years.

ASC 962-325-05, *Plan Accounting—Defined Contribution Pension Plans: Investments—Other*, discusses the reporting of investment contracts held by defined contribution pension plans.

ASC 715-70-55-4, *Compensation—Retirement Benefits: Defined Contribution Plans*, covers the measurement of excess contributions to a defined contribution plan or employee stock ownership plan.

According to Accounting Standards Update (ASU) No. 2010-25 (September 2010), *Plan Accounting—Defined Contribution Pension Plans (ASC 962), Reporting Loans to Participants*, participant loans should be presented as notes receivable and are to be segregated from plant investments and valued at their unpaid principal amount plus any accrued but unpaid interest.

AICPA Accounting Standards Executive Committee (AcSEC) Practice Bulletin No. 12 covers the reporting of separate investment fund option information of defined contribution pension plans.

Defined Benefit Pension Plan

Under a defined benefit plan, pension expense is charged to operations over the time period employees perform services. A benefit formula considers the pension benefits employees will receive upon retirement for their employment. The employer's contribution (cash funded) into the plan is based on the anticipated pension benefits employees will receive when they retire. When benefits are paid, plan assets are reduced. A cash balance plan should be considered a defined benefit plan.

In determining amounts, consideration is given to factors such as age, salary, and years of service. The employer has to provide plan contributions so that sufficient assets are accumulated to pay for the benefits when due.

Total Pension Expense

In a defined benefit plan, pension expense consists of the following components:

☐ Service cost (+).

☐ Amortization expense of any prior service cost included in "accumulated other comprehensive income" (+).

☐ Return on pension plan assets (–).

☐ Interest cost on projected benefit obligation (+).

☐ Actuarial loss (+) or gain (–).

Each of these pension elements is discussed in the following paragraphs.

Service cost. Pension cost assigned for services rendered in the current year is based on the actuarial-determined present value of future payments to be made using a benefit formula. It is charged in the current period. Service cost should take into account benefit changes per the pension agreement, such as cost increases arising from some inflation measure (e.g., Consumer Price Index). In other words, if the benefit formula includes benefits tied to expected future employee salaries, this must be considered in computing service cost for the current year. Future compensation levels should incorporate changes arising from such factors as productivity, promotion, seniority, and additional responsibilities.

Amortization expense on prior service cost. Pension expense is assigned for services performed prior to adopting or modifying a pension plan. The cost associated with granting retroactive benefits increases the projected benefit obligation at the amendment date. Prior service cost arising for an amendment to the plan is accounted for as a change in estimate. Prior service cost may be allocated over current and future years using the straight-line method in equal amounts, based on the average remaining service life of eligible active employees. However, if most of the pension plan participants are inactive, the prior service cost attributable to the benefits of the inactive participants is amortized over their remaining life expectancy.

A company may grant employees this privilege for one or more reasons, such as enhancing worker morale, reducing turnover rates, improving productivity, and controlling raises.

The amortization of prior service cost may take into account future service years, any change in the projected benefit obligation, the period employees will receive benefits, and any decrement in employees receiving benefits each year. Other comprehensive income is adjusted as a result of amortizing prior service cost.

A plan modification that retroactively increases benefits increases the projected benefit obligation. The cost of the benefit improvement is recognized as a charge to other comprehensive income at the amendment date. On the other hand, a plan amendment that retroactively reduces benefits decreases the projected benefit obligation. The reduction in benefits is recognized as a credit (prior service credit) to other comprehensive income that is used first to reduce any remaining prior service cost included in accumulated other comprehensive income. Any remaining credit is amortized as a component of pension cost on the same basis as the cost of a benefit increase.

The employer initially records the prior service cost as an adjustment to other comprehensive income. The employer then recognizes the prior service cost as a component of pension expense over the remaining service lives of employees covered by the plan. A years-of-service amortization method would consist of the following steps: (1) the total number of service years to be worked by all participating employees is computed; (2) the prior service cost is divided by the total number of service years to derive a cost per service year (unit cost); (3) the number of service years each year is multiplied by the cost per service year to compute the annual amortization charge. Employers may also use the straight line method of amortization in which prior service cost is amortized over the average remaining service life of employees.

EXAMPLE

On January 1, 20X3, a company amends its pension plan and grants $800,000 of prior service costs to employees. The employees are expected to provide 4,000 service years in the future with 500 service years in the year 20X3. The amortization of prior service cost for the year 20X3 is:

Cost per service year   =   prior service cost ÷ total service years = $800,000 ÷ 4,000 = $200

20X3 amortization   =   service years for current year × cost per service year
                                  =   500 × $200 = $100,000

EXAMPLE

A company has five employees who participate in the pension plan. Expected future service years from them at the beginning of 2X12 are as follows:

Employee	Future Service Years
A	3
B	4
C	5
D	6
E	6

On January 1, 2X12, the company amended its pension plan increasing the projected benefit obligation by $120,000.

Based on the aforementioned information, the cost per service year and the annual amortization of prior service cost can be computed.

			Computation of Service Years Employee			
Year	A	B	C	D	E	Total
2X12	1	1	1	1	1	5
2X13	1	1	1	1	1	5
2X14	1	1	1	1	1	5
2X15		1	1	1	1	4
2X16			1	1	1	3
2X17				1	1	2
Total	3	4	5	6	6	24

Cost per service year = $120,000 ÷ 24 = $5,000

	Computation of Annual Prior Service Cost Amortization			
Year	*Total Service Years*	*Cost per Service Year*	*Annual Amortization*	
2X12	5	$5,000	$25,000	
2X13	5	5,000	25,000	
2X14	5	5,000	25,000	
2X15	4	5,000	20,000	
2X16	3	5,000	15,000	
2X17	2	5,000	10,000	
Total			$120,000	

EXAMPLE

XYZ Company elects to amortize prior service cost using the years-of-service method. There are 600 workers. Prior service cost is $226,500. The grouping of employees based on expected retirement years are:

Grouping	Number of Workers	Expected Retirement on December 31
H	150	20X9
I	120	2X10
J	200	2X11
K	130	2X12
	600	

The calculation of the service hours per year and the total service years follows:

	Service Years				
Year	1	2	3	4	Total
20X9	150	120	200	130	600
2X10		120	200	130	450
2X11			200	130	330
2X12				130	130
Total	150	240	600	520	1,510

Because prior service cost is $160,000 and there is a total of 1,510 service years for all years, the cost per service year is $150 ($226,500 ÷1,510 service years). The annual amount of amortization based on a $150 cost per service year is computed below:

Year	Total Service Years	×	Cost per Service Year	=	Annual Amortization
20X9	600		$150		$ 90,000
2X10	450		150		67,500
2X11	330		150		49,500
2X12	130		150		19,500
Total	1,510				$116,500

EXAMPLE

On January 1, 20X3, XYZ adopted a pension plan giving a retroactive pension benefit for services rendered in the two years before adoption. The prior service cost amounted to $500,000. It is to be amortized over 10 years. Therefore, the amortization expense on prior service cost for 20X3 will be $50,000.

EXAMPLE

A company reported the following on January 1, 20X3:

Projected benefit obligation—1/1/20X3	$800,000
Fair market value of plan assets—1/1/20X3	600,000

The unamortized prior service cost on January 1, 20X3 equals:

Projected benefit obligation—1/1	$800,000
Fair market value of plan assets—1/1	600,000
Unamortized prior service cost—1/1	$200,000

If the amortization period is 20 years, the amortization expense on prior service cost for 20X3 would be $10,000 ($200,000/20 years), resulting in unamortized prior service cost on December 31, 20X3 of $190,000 ($200,000 – 10,000).

EXAMPLE

ABC Company modifies its pension formula from 3% to 4% of the last four years of pay multiplied by the service years on January 1, 20X1. This causes the projected benefit obligation to increase by $400,000. It is expected that employees will receive benefits over the next 10 years.

Total future service years equal:

$$\frac{n(n + 1) \times P}{2}$$

where:

n = service years to be made

p = annual population decrease

$$\frac{10(10 + 1) \times 9}{2} = 495$$

Amortization expense on prior service cost for 20X1 equals:

$$\frac{\$400,000109}{495} = \$72,727$$

Return on pension plan assets. Pension plan assets may include bank accounts, stocks, bonds, and real estate. The return on plan assets may be expressed in the form of expected or actual. The total expected return equals the long-term return rate multiplied by the market-related value of pension plan assets at the beginning of the year. The total expected return reduces pension expense. **Note:** It is possible for the return to be negative, such as in a stock market crash. In such a case, the negative return would increase pension expense.

The expected return is the anticipated increase in plan assets arising from investment activities. The FASB mandates that expected return on plan assets be included as a component of pension expense.

The actual return on pension plan assets equals the difference between the fair value of pension assets at the start and end of the year adjusted for employer contributions and benefit payments to retirees. In other words, the actual return results from realized and holding gains or losses on plan assets plus the periodic income earned (e.g., dividends, interest) on the plan assets. Actual return on plan assets increases the fund balance and reduces the employer's net cost of providing employees' pension benefits.

EXAMPLE

The fair values of plan assets at the beginning and end of the year were $2,800 and $3,086, respectively. The employer's contribution to the plan during the year was $290. Benefit payments to retirees were $320. The actual return is computed as follows:

Fair value of plan assets—1/1	$2,800
Plus: employer contributions	290
Plus: actual return	?
Less: benefit payments	(320)
Fair value of plan assets—12/31	$3,086

Solving for the unknown, the actual return equals $316.

Alternatively, the following formula may be used to derive the actual return:

Actual return = Fair value of assets (end of year) – fair value of assets (beginning of year) – employer contributions + benefit payments

Actual return = $3,086 – $2,800 – $290 + $320 = $316

EXAMPLE

The following data apply to a company's defined benefit pension plan for the year:

Fair market value of plan assets—1/1	$400,000
Fair market value of plan assets—12/31	570,000
Employer contributions	140,000
Benefits paid	100,000

The actual return on plan assets equals $ 130,000, computed as follows:

Fair market value of plan assets—12/31		$570,000
Fair market value of plan assets—1/1		400,000
Change in plan assets		$170,000
Adjusted for		
Employer contributions	$140,000	
Less: benefits paid	100,000	40,000
Actual return on plan assets		$130,000

EXAMPLE

Based on the following information, the actual return on pension plan assets will be computed as follows:

Benefit payments	$100,000	
Contribution	130,000	
Fair market value of plan assets:		
End of year		600,000
Beginning of year		400,000

The actual return equals $170,000, computed as follows:

Change in fair market value of plan assets		$200,000
Adjustments:		
Employer contribution	$130,000	
Benefit payments	100,000	30,000
Actual return on plan assets		$170,000

Interest on projected benefit obligation. This is computed by multiplying the interest (settlement discount) rate by the projected benefit obligation (discounted present value of employee benefits earned based on future salaries) at the beginning of the year. The interest (settlement) rate is usually based on the company's average borrowing cost. The settlement rate should be reviewed each year; it represents the time value of money. The assumed interest (discount) rate should reflect the rate companies can settle pension benefits. In ascertaining these settlement rates, return rates on high-quality fixed-income investments, whose cash flows match the amount and timing of the anticipated benefit payments, should be considered. The purpose is to derive a discount rate to measure an amount that, if invested in a high-quality debt portfolio, will generate required future cash flows to pay the pension benefits when due. The interest cost increases pension expense and the projected benefit obligation. The interest cost equals the increase in the projected benefit obligation (PBO) over time.

EXAMPLE

On January 1, 20X4, a company adopts a defined benefit pension plan. The expected return and interest rates are both 10%. The service cost for 20X4 and 20X5 is $100,000 and $120,000, respectively. The funding amount for 20X4 and 20X5 is $80,000 and $110,000, respectively.

The entry for 20X4 is:

Pension expense	100,000	
Cash		80,000
Pension liability		20,000

The entry for 20X5 is:

Pension expense	122,000	
Cash		110,000
Pension liability		12,000

Computation:

Service cost	$120,000
Interest on projected benefit obligation (10% × $100,000)	10,000
Expected return on plan assets (10% × $80,000)	(8,000)
Pension expense	$122,000

At December 31, 20X5:

Projected benefit obligation = $230,000 ($100,000 + $120,000 + $10,000)

Pension plan assets = $198,000 ($80,000 + $110,000 + $8,000)

Actuarial losses or gains. Actuarial losses or gains are the difference between actual experience and estimates. For example, an actuarial loss would arise if the actual interest rate earned was 6% when the anticipated interest rate was 8%. Actuarial losses or gains arise from the difference between the expected versus actual projected benefit obligation and/or fair value of plan assets at year-end. Actuarial gains or losses include unrealized and realized amounts. A change in actuarial assumptions will also result in actuarial gains or losses. Gains and losses that are not recognized immediately as a component of pension expense shall be recognized as increases or decreases in other comprehensive income as they arise.

Actuarial losses or gains are deferred and amortized as an adjustment to pension expense over future years. Recognition of actuarial gains or losses is based on the *corridor* method. This method lowers the amount of gain or loss to be reflected as an adjustment of pension cost. Under the corridor (materiality threshold) approach, recognition is given to certain gains or losses exceeding 10% of the greater of the beginning-of-year balances of the projected benefit obligation or the market-related value of plan assets. The excess over the corridor (test) is amortized over the average remaining service period for active employees expected to receive benefits in the plan. The amortization of actuarial losses increases pension expense; the amortization of actuarial gains reduces pension expense. If the balance of the unrecognized net gain or loss is below the corridor, no amortization occurs. The unrecognized net gain or loss balance is carried forward as is.

EXAMPLE

At the beginning of the year, the projected benefit obligation was $250,000 and the market-related value of plan assets was $325,000. The corridor equals $32,500 (10% × $325,000). Actuarial gain or loss is not recognized unless it exceeds $32,500. The excess over $32,500 (corridor) is amortized. Thus, if the actuarial gain were $40,000, $7,500 ($40,000 − $32,500) would be amortized as a reduction to pension expense over the average remaining service period for active employees in the plan. If the actuarial gain were $30,000, there would be no amortization because the corridor ($32,500) had not been exceeded.

However, actuarial losses or gains applicable to a single event unrelated to the pension plan and not in the ordinary course of business are immediately recognized in the current year's income statement. This may arise in the case of disposing of a business segment or closing a plant.

If the employer wishes to use an approach other than the minimum amortization of unrecognized gains and losses discussed previously, it can use an alternative amortization method, as long as it is logical, consistently applied to both gains and losses, disclosed, and reduces the unamortized balance by an amount more than that which would arise from the minimum amortization method.

ASC 715-30-35-90, *Compensation—Retirement Benefits: Defined Benefit Plans—Pension*, provides the accounting for pension benefits paid by employers after insurance companies fail to provide annuity benefits.

EXAMPLE

The following information is presented:

Service cost	$6,000
Return on plan assets	$ 700
Interest on projected benefit obligation	$1,000
Amortization of net loss	$ 200
Amortization of prior service cost	$2,000
Pension expense equals:	
Service cost	$6,000
Interest on projected benefit obligation	$1,000
Return on plan assets	$ (700)
Amortization of net loss	$ 200

Amortization of prior service cost	$2,000
Pension expense	$8,500

Note: If there was, in this example, an amortization of net gain (instead of amortization of net loss), then it would be a deduction.

EXAMPLE

The following information is presented of Harris Company's pension plan:

	1/1/20X4	12/31/20X4
Projected benefit obligation	$1,000	$1,040
Fair market value of plan assets	400	565
Accumulated OCI (G/L)—net gain	-0-	200

On January 1, 20X4, the Pension Liability is $600 ($1,000–$400).

Other information follows:

Service cost for 20X4	$140
Amortization of prior service cost for 20X4	$ 60
Contributions for 20X4	$125
Return rate on plan assets	10%
Interest rate on projected benefit obligation	10%

On January 1, 20X4, accumulated other comprehensive income (prior service cost) had a balance of $600. No benefit payments to retirees were made in 20X4.

Pension expense equals:

Service cost	$140
Interest on projected benefit obligation (10% × $1,000)	100
Expected return on plan assets (10% × $400)	(40)
Amortization of prior service cost	60
Pension expense	$260

The journal entry to record pension expense and the employer's contribution to the plan in 20X4 follow:

Pension expense	260	
Pension asset	125	
Other comprehensive income (prior service cost)		60
Other comprehensive income (gain/loss)		200
Cash		125

The December 31, 20X4, balance sheet will show a balance in pension liability of $475, computed as follows:

Projected benefit obligation—December 31, 20X4	$1,040
Less: Plan assets—December 31, 20X4	565
Plan liability	$ 475

The December 31, 20X4, presentation of stockholders' equity in the balance sheet will show:

Stockholders' equity:

Accumulated other comprehensive income (prior service cost) ($600–$60)	$540
Accumulated other comprehensive income (gain/loss)	$100

Actuarial Gains and Losses/Prior Service Costs

The gains and losses and prior service costs or credits that occur during the period are recognized as a component of other comprehensive income, net of tax, not as elements of net periodic benefit cost, as per either ASC 715-10-05, *Compensation—Retirement Benefits: Overall*. Amounts recognized in accumulated other comprehensive income, including the gains and losses and prior service costs or credits, are adjusted, as they are later recognized as components of net periodic benefit cost in accordance with the recognition and amortization provisions of ASC 715-10-05, *Compensation—Retirement Benefits: Overall*.

EXAMPLE

Paul Company provides the following information for the year 20X5:

Net income for 20X5	$150,000
Actuarial liability loss for 20X5	24,000
Prior service cost adjustment to provide additional benefits in December 20X5	6,000
Accumulated other comprehensive income—1/1/20X5	48,000

Looking more closely at prior service cost or credits, assume that none of the accumulated other comprehensive income—January 1, 20X5, should be amortized in 20X5. Therefore, accumulated other comprehensive income—January 1, 20X5, in this example, is not adjusted for actuarial gains and losses and prior service cost amortization that would change pension expense. However, these items will be amortized to pension expense in later years.

Both the actuarial liability loss and the prior service cost adjustment reduce the funded status of the plan on the balance sheet. However, neither the actuarial liability loss nor the prior service cost adjustment impacts pension expense in 20X5. However, in later years, these items will affect pension expense through amortization.

The computation of other comprehensive income for 20X5 equals:

Actuarial liability loss	$ 24,000
Prior service cost benefit adjustment	6,000
Other comprehensive loss	$ 30,000

Comprehensive income for 20X5 is presented as:

Net income	$150,000
Other comprehensive loss	(30,000)
Comprehensive income	$120,000

It is not a requirement to present earnings per share for comprehensive income.

The comprehensive income statement for the year ended December 31, 20X5, follows:

Net income		$150,000
Other comprehensive loss		
Actuarial liability loss	$24,000	
Prior service cost	6,000	30,000
Comprehensive loss		$120,000

The computation of accumulated other comprehensive income to be presented in the stockholders' equity section of the balance sheet on December 31, 20X5, follows:

Accumulated other comprehensive income—1/1/20X5	$ 48,000
Other comprehensive loss	30,000
Accumulated other comprehensive income—12/31/20X5	$ 18,000

Assume a company amends its defined benefit plan and gives additional service years to workers after plan initiation. This will increase the projected benefit obligation. ASC 715 requires that the prior service cost arising in the amendment year (which increases the projected benefit obligation) be reflected by an offsetting debit to other comprehensive income. This recognition is consistent with that applied to actuarial gains and losses.

EXAMPLE

Tudor Company presents the following data for the year 20X9:

Net income	$420,000
Actuarial liability loss for 20X9	126,000
Prior service cost adjustment during 20X9	31,500
Accumulated other comprehensive income	364,000

The actuarial liability loss and the prior service cost adjustment will reduce the funded status of the plan on the balance sheet because the projected benefit obligation increases. However, the actuarial liability loss and the prior service cost adjustment will not impact pension expense in 20X9. In later years, these two items usually affect pension expense through amortization.

Other comprehensive income for 20X9 equals:

Actuarial liability loss	$(126,000)
Prior service cost adjustment	(31.500)
Other comprehensive loss	$(157,500)

The computation of comprehensive income for 20X9 is:

Net income	$420,000

Other comprehensive loss	(157,500)
Comprehensive income	$262,500

The computation of accumulated other comprehensive income to be presented in the stockholders' equity section of the balance sheet at December 31, 20X9, follows:

Accumulated other comprehensive income—1/1/20X9	$364,000
Other comprehensive loss	(157,500)
Accumulated other comprehensive income—12/31/20X9	$206,500

Note: Assumed in this example is that accumulated other comprehensive income at January 1, 20X9, is not adjusted for any actuarial gains or losses and any prior service cost that would change pension expense. However, these items will be amortized into pension expense in future years.

Gain or Loss

Companies may encounter uncontrollable variability in pension expense due to (1) sudden and unanticipated changes in the fair market value of plan assets and (2) changes to actuarial assumptions affecting the projected benefit obligation (which can take place when actuaries change assumptions or when actual experience deviates from expected experience). The gain or loss is comprised of two elements: (1) the difference between actual return and expected return on plan assets and (2) the amortization of the net gain or loss from prior years. *Smoothing techniques* may be used to reduce the fluctuation in pension expense.

Smoothing Unexpected Gains and Losses on Plan Assets

Actual return on plan assets reduces pension expense. Because a very significant return rate can substantially impact pension expense, actuaries use an expected return rate as a component of pension expense. The expected return equals the expected rate of return multiplied by the market-related value of plan assets at the beginning of the period. Unexpected gain or loss is the difference between the expected return and actual return. This simply refers to asset gains and losses. If actual return is more (less) than expected return, there is an asset gain (loss). The employer records asset gains and losses in other comprehensive income, combining them with gains and losses accumulated in prior years. (This is treated in a similar way as prior service cost.) An unexpected asset loss is debited to other comprehensive income and credited to pension expense. An unexpected asset gain is debited to pension expense and credited to other comprehensive income.

Smoothing Unexpected Gains and Losses on the Pension Liability

Actuarial assumptions are used to estimate the projected benefit obligation (PBO). Any change in actuarial assumptions impacts the amount of the PBO. Actual experience is usually different from actuarial predictions. Liability gains and losses are the unexpected gains and losses arising from changes in the PBO.

An unexpected reduction in the PBO is a liability gain, whereas an unexpected increase in the PBO is a liability loss. Liability gains and losses are reported in other comprehensive income.

Note: Liability gains and losses as well as asset gains and losses are shown in the same other comprehensive income account. The employer accumulates the asset and liability gains and losses over the years that are not amortized in accumulated other comprehensive income, which is shown in the stockholders' equity section of the balance sheet.

An asset gain or loss occurs on plan assets when the expected return differs from the actual return.

$$\text{Asset gain} = \text{actual return} > \text{expected return}$$

$$\text{Asset loss} = \text{actual return} < \text{expected return}$$

A liability gain or loss arises when actuarial assumptions differ from actual experiences applicable to the computation of the projected benefit obligation.

$$\text{Liability gain} = \text{unexpected decrease in the PBO}$$
$$\text{Liability loss} = \text{unexpected increase in the PBO}$$

Asset gains and losses are combined with liability gains and losses to derive net gain or loss. Net gain or loss is the change in the fair market value of plan assets and the amount of change in the projected benefit obligation.

Corridor Amortization

Asset gains and losses and liability gains and losses can offset each other. The FASB has adopted the corridor method to amortize the accumulated other comprehensive income account balance when it becomes too large in amount. The FASB set a limit of 10% of the greater of the beginning balances of the market-related value of plan assets or the projected benefit obligation. Above the 10% limit, the accumulated other comprehensive income account related to gains and losses is too large and must be amortized.

EXAMPLE

Projected benefit obligation	$180,000
Market-related asset value	$150,000

Corridor = 10% × $180,000 = $18,000

Any amount exceeding $18,000 would be amortized; so if the accumulated other comprehensive income account balance was $25,000, the amount to be amortized would be $7,000 ($25,000–$18,000). However, if the balance of the accumulated net gain or loss account remains within the upper and lower limits of the corridor, no amortization is made. Thus, if the accumulated other comprehensive income account had a balance of $18,000 or below, no amortization is required.

If amortization is required, the minimum amortization is the excess ($7,000) divided by the average remaining service years of active employees that are to receive benefits. Assuming a service life of 10 years, the amortization for the year would be $700 ($7,000 ÷ 10 years).

The amortization of a loss increases pension expense, whereas the amortization of a gain reduces pension expense.

Note: A company can use any amortization method for gains and losses provided the gain or loss is greater than the minimum amount.

An employer can only include the amortization of net gain or loss as a component of pension expense if at the beginning of the year, the net gain or loss in accumulated other comprehensive income exceeds the corridor. The following example illustrates the amortization of net gains and losses.

EXAMPLE

In the years 2X12 and 2X13, a company has actuarial losses of $1,200 and $900, respectively, in other comprehensive income. The average remaining service life is 20 years. The beginning market-related asset values and projected benefit obligation for 2X12, 2X13, and 2X14 are:

	2X12	2X13	2X14
Market-related asset value	$7,800	$8,400	$8,100
Projected benefit obligation	6,300	7,800	8,700

The amortization schedule (Schedule 1) for the net gain or loss follows:

Schedule 1

Year	Plan Assets	PBO	Corridor	Accumulated OCI* (Gain/ Loss)—1/1	Amortization of Loss
2X12	$7,800	$6,800	$780	$ 0	$ 0
2X13	8,400	7,800	840	1,200	18[1]
2X14	8,100	8,700	870	2,082[2]	60.6[2]

* OCI = Other Comprehensive Income
[1] $1,200 − $840 = $360; $360/20 years = $18
[2] $1,200 − $18 + $900 = $2,082; $2,082 − $870 = $1,212; $1,212 ÷ 20 years = $60.6

Note: Employers determine the amortized net gain or loss by amortizing the accumulated other comprehensive income account related to net gain or loss at the beginning of the year subject to the corridor limitation. In other words, if the accumulated gain or loss exceeds the corridor, these net gains and losses are subject to amortization.

When the current year unexpected gain or loss is combined with the amortized net gain or loss, the current year gain or loss can be determined, resulting in the following:

☐ Current year unexpected gain or loss (current year actual return less current year expected return)

☐ Plus: Current year amortized net gain or loss (accumulated other comprehensive income (G/L) less corridor = Balance; Balance divided by average remaining service years)

☐ Total current year gain or loss

EXAMPLE

A company has a pension plan for its employees. On January 1, 20X5, the following information was presented:

Accumulated other comprehensive loss (prior service cost)	$37,500
Fair market value of plan assets	50,000
Projected benefit obligation	87,500

The average remaining service period for employees is 10 years. For the year 20X5, service cost was $13,000, actual return on plan assets was $2,750, and contributions were $16,250. No benefit payments were paid. On December 31, 20X5, the projected benefit obligation was $113,000 and the fair market value of plan assets was $69,000. The return rate on plan assets and the interest (settlement) rate on the projected benefit obligation were both 10%.

Pension expense for 20X5 equals:

Service cost	$13,000
Interest on projected benefit obligation (10% x $87,500)	8,750
Actual return on plan assets	(2,750)
Unexpected loss on plan assets	(2,250)*
Amortization of prior service cost ($37,500/10 years)	3,750
Pension expense	$ 20,500

$$* \text{ Unexpected loss on plan assets} = \text{expected return} - \text{actual return}$$
$$= \$5,000 - \$2,750 = \$2,250$$

$$\text{Expected return} = \text{rate of return} \times \text{plan assets (beginning of year)}$$
$$10\% \times \$50,000 = \$5,000$$

The journal entry for 20X5 is:

Pension expense	20,500	
Other comprehensive income (gain/loss)	6,000**	
Cash		16,250
Pension liability		6,500
Other comprehensive income (prior service cost)		3,750

** Other comprehensive income (gain/loss) is debited for $6,000 as computed below:

Asset loss:

Fair market value of plan assets—12/31/20X5		$69,000
Less: Fair market value of plan assets—		
1/1/20X5	$50,000	
Expected return	5,000	
Contributions	16,250	71,250
Asset loss		$ 2,250

Liability loss:

PBO—12/31/20X5		$113,000
Less: PBO—1/1/20X5	$87,500	
Interest	8,750	
Service cost	13,000	109,250
Liability loss		$ 3,750

Other comprehensive income (gain/loss):

Asset loss	$2,250
Liability loss	3,750
Net loss at 12/31/20X5	$6,000

The $6,000 net loss in the accumulated other comprehensive income (gain/loss) account becomes the beginning balance in 20X6.

The corridor at January 1, 20X6, is computed below:

Corridor = 10% of the greater of PBO—12/31/20X5 of $113,000 or fair market value of plan assets—12/31/20X5 of $69,000.

Corridor = 10% × $113,000 = $11,300

Because the corridor ($11,300) exceeds the accumulated other comprehensive income (gain/loss) account of $6,000, no gain or loss will be amortized in the year 20X6. **Note:** No amortization occurs in the year 20X5 because no balance existed in the accumulated other comprehensive income (gain/loss) account on January 1, 20X5.

Pension Plan Benefit Formula

When a pension plan benefit formula assigns all or a disproportionate share of total pension benefits to future years, the employee's total projected benefit is computed and used as the basis to assign total pension plan benefits. In this case, it is presumed that the employee's total projected benefit will accumulate proportionately based on the ratio of completed service years to date to the total completed service years ending when the benefit is fully vested.

Some benefit formulas are:

☐ *Career-average-pay formula.* This formula bases pension benefits on the worker's salary for his or her working career with the employer.

☐ *Final-pay formula.* Pension benefits are based on the employee's salary over a stipulated time period close to the retirement date or are based on the period of time in which the worker earns the most.

☐ *Flat-benefit formula.* Benefits are a constant dollar amount per year of service. An example is a retirement benefit of $30 of biweekly retirement income for each service year.

Plan Assets

Pension plan assets are typically maintained in a trust account. It is unusual for an employer to withdraw plan assets from the trust fund. However, a withdrawal may occur if the value of plan assets exceeds the pension obligation when the plan is ended. The plan contract may allow for employer withdrawal in this case, as long as all pension obligations have been met by the employer. Pension plan assets do not include those that are unrestricted for purposes other than paying pension benefits or those that are not segregated in a pension trust fund. Plan assets are increased from income thereon, such as capital gains, interest, and dividends. Plan assets are reduced by capital losses, administrative costs, and benefit payments to retirees.

Plan assets used to operate the pension plan are recorded at book value. These assets include office building, office equipment, and furniture and fixtures.

Pension plan assets held as investments so as to have sufficient funds to pay pension benefits to retirees are recorded at their fair market value.

Pension plan assets are recorded on the books of the pension plan. The employer keeps only worksheet records to track the cost and fair market value of those assets. Fair value of plan assets is measured in the following preferential order: market price, selling price of comparable investments, and present value of cash flows. Fair value is the price negotiated between a willing buyer and seller. It is not based on liquidation value.

Fair market value of plan assets at the end of the year equals the fair market value of plan assets at the beginning of the year plus employer contributions plus actual return on plan assets less benefit payments.

EXAMPLE

A company reports the following information regarding pension plan assets:

Fair market value of plan assets—1/1	$700,000
Employer contributions	100,000
Actual return on plan assets	50,000
Benefit payments to retirees	40,000

The fair market value of plan assets on December 31 equals $810,000, computed as follows:

Fair market value of plan assets—1/1	$700,000
Employer contributions	100,000
Actual return	50,000
Benefit payments	(40,000)
Fair market value of plan assets—12/31	$810,000

Underfunding or Overfunding

Pension expense will in most cases not equal the amount of cash funded into the plan by the employer. If pension expense is more than the cash funded (underfunded), a pension liability arises. On the other hand, if pension expense is less than the cash funded (over-funded), a pension asset arises.

The reporting of the funded position of the plan in the balance sheet arises because actuarial gains and losses and prior service costs are now recognized in other comprehensive income. Actuarial gains and losses and prior service costs will be reflected in the projected benefit obligation and plan assets, with corresponding entries in other comprehensive income. However, there will be no or little impact on pension expense because the amortization provisions for actuarial gains and losses and prior service costs remain intact as that required under ASC 962-10-05. In addition, the computation of other components of pension expense (e.g., service cost, interest on the projected benefit obligation) still conforms to the dictates of ASC 962-10-05.

The change in the projected benefit obligation equals:

Projected benefit obligation—beginning of year

Plus: Service cost

Plus: Interest cost

Plus: Amendments (prior service cost)

Plus: Actuarial loss

Minus: Benefits paid

Projected benefit obligation—end of year

An employer must recognize overfunded or underfunded status of a single-employer defined benefit postretirement plan in the balance sheet instead of the footnotes (which was previously done). Therefore, a reconciliation of funded status in the footnotes is eliminated. In addition, the pronouncement requires an employer to recognize all transactions and events impacting the overfunded or underfunded status of a defined benefit postretirement plan in comprehensive income in the year they take place. The employer must measure the funded status (assets and liabilities) of a plan at its fiscal year-end date used for financial reporting. However, the following two exceptions exist:

1. The plan is sponsored by a subsidiary that is consolidated using a fiscal year different from its parent, as permitted under ASC 810-10-45-10, *Consolidation: Overall.*

2. The sponsor of the plan is an investee accounted for using the equity method, using financial statements of the investee for a fiscal year different from the investor.

In the above two situations, the employer should measure the subsidiary's plan assets and benefit obligations as of the date used to consolidate the subsidiary's balance sheet and shall measure the investee's plan assets and benefit obligations as of the date of the investee's financial statements used to apply the equity method.

With regard to the net funded status of the defined-benefit pension plan, the employer is required to recognize, on its statement of financial position, the full underfunded or overfunded amount.

There should be an aggregation of the statuses of all overfunded plans and the amount should be recognized as an asset. The excess of the fair market value of plan assets over the projected benefit obligation is shown as a noncurrent asset. (**Note:** No part of pension assets is shown as a current asset.) The reasoning for the noncurrent classification is that the pension plan assets are restricted. Specifically, pension assets are used to fund the projected benefit obligation and, as a result, the noncurrent classification applies. There should be an aggregation of the statuses of all underfunded plans and the amount should be recorded as a liability. The liability for an underfunded plan may be classified as a current liability, noncurrent liability, or a combination of both. The current portion is the amount by which the actuarial present value of benefits included in the benefit obligation payable within the year or normal operating cycle of the business, if longer, exceeds the fair market value of plan assets.

All overfunded plans should be combined and presented as a pension plan asset; and all underfunded plans should be combined and presented as a pension plan liability. **Note:** It is prohibited to combine all plans and present a net amount as a single net asset or net liability.

EXAMPLE

Pension expense	800,000	
Cash		700,000
Pension liability		100,000
Pension expense	800,000	
Pension asset	100,000	
Cash		900,000

EXAMPLE

Daren Company has a projected benefit obligation of $600,000 and a fair market value of plan assets of $450,000. Thus, the pension plan is underfunded by $150,000 and must report a pension liability of $150,000.

EXAMPLE

Aaron Company has a fair market value of plan assets of $500,000 and a projected benefit obligation of $420,000. Therefore, the pension plan is overfunded by $80,000 and must report a pension asset of $80,000.

EXAMPLE

Jason Company has four pension plans as follows:

Plan	Fair Value of Plan Assets	Projected Benefit Obligation	Pension Asset/Liability
U	$600,000	$500,000	$100,000 Asset
V	700,000	740,000	40,000 Liability
W	200,000	170,000	30,000 Asset
X	900,000	980,000	80,000 Liability

Plan assets are reported as $130,000, whereas pension liabilities are separately reported as $120,000.

EXAMPLE

The following data relate to a company's defined benefit pension plan:

Pension asset—1/1	$ 4,000
Service cost	22,000
Interest cost	30,000
Actual return on plan assets	25,000
Amortization of prior service cost	43,000
Employer contribution	37,000

On December 31 the pension liability equals $29,000, computed as follows:

Pension expense:		
Service cost	$22,000	
Interest cost	30,000	
Actual return on plan assets	(25,000)	
Amortization of prior service cost	43,000	$70,000
Less: pension asset—1/1	$ 4,000	
Employer contributions	37,000	(41,000)
Pension liability—12/31		$29,000

EXAMPLE

The following data apply to a company's defined benefit pension plan:

Pension asset—beginning of year	$ 5,000
Employer contribution	60,000
Service cost	40,000
Interest on projected benefit obligation	25,000
Actual return on plan assets	30,000
Amortization of prior service costs	50,000

At December 31, the amount to be reported as pension liability is computed as follows:

Pension expense ($40,000 + $25,000 − $30,000 + $50,000)		$85,000
Less: pension asset—1/1	$5,000	
Employer contribution	60,000	65,000
Pension liability—12/31		$20,000

Retirement Benefit

A retirement benefit may be determined by considering such factors as salary and service years.

EXAMPLE

Mr. Paul has eight years before retirement. The expected salary at retirement is $60,000. The pension benefit is 4% of final salary for each service year payable at retirement. The retirement benefit is calculated as:

Final annual salary	$60,000
× Formula rate	× 4%
	$2,400
× Service years	× 8
Retirement benefit	$19,200

EXAMPLE

Coleman Company has a defined benefit plan for its 1,000 employees. On January 1, 20X3, the fair market value of pension plan assets is $500,000, and the projected benefit obligation is $650,000. It is expected that 10 workers eligible for pension benefits will leave each year over the next 10 years. Service cost for 19X6 is $90,000. On December 31, 20X3, the projected benefit obligation is $680,000, and the fair market value of pension plan assets is $510,000. The return on plan assets is 9% and the interest rate on debt is 10%. There are no actuarial gains or losses for the year. Cash funded to the trustee for the year is $120,000.

Pension expense equals:

Service cost	$ 90,000
Interest on projected benefit obligation (10% × $650,000)	65,000
Return on plan assets (9% × $500,000)	(45,000)
Amortization of actuarial gains or losses	−
Amortization of prior service cost	27,273
Pension expense	$137,273

Calculation of the amortization of prior service cost follows:

Projected benefit obligation—1/1	$650,000
Less: Fair value of pension plan assets—1/1	500,000
Initial net obligation—1/1	150,000

$$\text{Amortization} = \$150,000/5.5 \text{ years} = \$27,273$$

$$\frac{n(n+1)\,P}{2} = \frac{10(10+1)\times10}{2} = 55 \times 10 = 550$$

$$550/100 = 5.5 \text{ years}$$

$$P = \text{population decrement each year}$$

The journal entries at December 31, 20X3 are:

Pension expense	137,273	
Cash		120,000
Pension liability		17,273

Summary of Accounting for Pension Plans

Exhibit 14-2 presents a summary of the accounting for pension plans.

Exhibit 14-2: Pension Plan Accounting

Items	Journal Entry Account	Memo Account
Prior service cost (PSC) arising from plan amendment	Other comprehensive income (OCI)—prior service cost Dr.	Projected benefit obligation (PBO) Cr.
Service cost	Pension expense (PE) Dr.	PBO Cr.
Interest cost on PBO	Pension expense Dr.	PBO Cr.
Actual return	Pension expense Cr.	Plan assets (PA) Dr.
Amortization of PSC	PE Dr. and OCI (PSC) Cr.	
Contributions	Cash Cr.	Plan assets Dr.
Unexpected loss (expected return exceeds actual return on plan assets)	OCI (G/L) Dr. and PE Cr.	
Unexpected gain (actual return exceeds expected return on plan assets)	PE Dr. and OCI (G/L) Cr.	
Liability (PBO) increase	OCI (G/L) Dr.	PBO Cr.
Liability (PBO) decrease	OCI (G/L) Cr.	PBO Dr.
Amortization of excess loss over the corridor	PE Dr. and OCI (G/L) Cr.	
Amortization of excess gain over the corridor	OCI (G/L) Dr. and PE Cr.	

Application Examples

The application examples will make clearer the pension requirements.

EXAMPLE

Stevens Company provides the following data:

Fair market value of plan assets—1/1/20X1	$15,000
Projected benefit obligation—1/1/20X1	$15,000
Employer contributions	$ 1,200
Benefit payments to retirees	$ 1,050
Actual return on plan assets	$ 1,500
Service cost	$ 1,350
Interest rate	10%

The fair market value of plan assets and the projected benefit obligation are the same at January 1, 20X1, so there is a zero balance in the pension asset/liability account.

Interest cost = interest rate × PBO—1/1/20X1 = 10% × $15,000 = $1,500

Stevens Company Worksheet 1

	Journal Entries			Memo	
Items	Pension Expense	Cash	Pension Asset/ Liability	PBO	Plan Assets
Balance—1/1/20X1				15,000 Cr.	15,000 Dr.
Service cost	1,350 Dr.			1,350 Cr.	
Interest cost	1,500 Dr.			1,500 Cr.	
Actual return	1,500 Cr.				1,500 Dr.
Contributions		1,200 Cr.			1,200 Dr.
Benefit Payments				1,050 Dr.	1,050 Cr.
JE for year 20X1	1,350 Dr.	1,200 Cr.	150 Cr.		
Balance— 12/31/20X1			150 Cr.	16,800 Cr.	16,650 Dr.

Notes:

☐ Service cost and interest cost increase pension expense and the PBO.

☐ Actual return reduces pension expense and increases plan assets.

☐ Contributions reduce cash and increase plan assets.

☐ Benefit payments reduce plan assets and the PBO.

The journal entry on December 31, 20X1, is:

Pension expense	1,350	
Cash		1,200
Pension liability		150

A pension liability exists because the plan is underfunded (amount funded is less than pension expense). On the other hand, if the plan was overfunded, a pension asset would arise.

The pension liability of $150 can also be determined by comparing the PBO and plan assets, as indicated in the memo column of Worksheet 1 as follows:

Projected benefit obligation (credit)	$16,800
Fair market value of plan assets (debit)	16,650
Pension liability (credit)	$ 150

Note: If the fair market value of plan assets (debit) exceeded the projected benefit obligation (credit), there would be a pension asset (debit).

EXAMPLE

This continues the previous example for Stevens Company for the year 20X2. On January 1, 20X2, the company has a prior service cost of $12,000 due to modifying its pension plan. Amortization of prior service cost is assumed to be $4,080. Additional information follows:

Benefit payments to retirees	$ 1,200
Contributions	$ 3,000
Service cost	$ 1,425
Actual return on plan assets	$ 1,665
Accumulated other comprehensive income—12/31/20X1	- 0 -
Interest rate	10%

Stevens Company Worksheet 2

Items	Pension Expense	Cash	Other Compre-hensive Income (Prior Service Cost)	Pension Asset/Liability	PBO	Plan Assets
	Journal Entries				*Memo*	
Balance— 12/31/20X1				150 Cr.	16,800 Cr.	16,650 Dr.
Prior Service cost			12,000 Dr.		12,000 Cr.	
Balance— 1/1/20X2					28,800 Cr.	16,650 Dr.
Service cost	1,425 Dr.				1,425 Cr.	
Interest cost	2,880 Dr.				2,880 Cr.	
Actual return	1,665 Cr.					1,665 Dr.
Amortization of PSC	4,080 Dr.		4,080 Cr.			
Contributions		3,000 Cr.				3,000 Dr.
Benefit payments					1,200 Dr.	1,200 Cr.
JE for 20X2	6,720 Dr.	3,000 Cr.	7,920 Dr.	11,640 Cr.		
Accumulated OCI— 12/31/20X1			0			
Balance— 12/31/20X2			7,920 Dr.	11,790 Cr.	31,905 Cr.	20,115 Dr.

Notes:

☐ Interest cost = interest rate × PBO (beginning of year) = 10% × $28,800 = $2,880

☐ The granting of prior service cost increases the PBO and reduces OCI by $12,000.

☐ Amortization of prior service cost is debited to pension expense and credited to OCI for $4,080.

The journal entry on December 31, 20X2, is:

Pension expense	6,720	
Other comprehensive income (prior service cost)	7,920	
Cash		3,000
Pension liability		11,640

The balance in the pension liability presented in the balance sheet on December 31, 20X2, equals $11,790 ($150 + $11,640). The balance of the pension liability can also be derived as follows:

Projected benefit obligation (credit)	$31,905
Fair market value of plan assets (debit)	20,115
Pension liability (credit)	$11,790

EXAMPLE

This continues the previous example for Stevens Company for the year 20X3. The following data is presented for 20X3:

Service cost	$1,950
Amortization of prior service cost	$3,120
Actual return on plan assets	$1,800
Benefit payments to retirees	$1,575
Contributions	$3,600
Interest rate	10%
Expected return rate	10%

Changes in actuarial assumptions resulted in a year-end balance of the projected benefit obligation of $39,750.

Stevens Company Worksheet 3

	Journal Entries					Memo	
Items	Pension Expense	Cash	Other Comprehensive Income (Prior Service Cost)	(Gains/ Losses)	Pension Asset/ Liability	PBO	Plan Assets
Balance— 1/1/20X3					11,790 Cr.	31,905 Cr.	20,115 Dr.
Service cost	1,950 Dr.					1,950 Cr.	
Interest cost	3,191 Dr.					3,191 Cr.	
Actual return	1,800 Cr.						1,800 Dr.
Unexpected loss	212 Cr.			212 Dr.			
Amoritzation of PSC	3,120 Dr.		3,120 Cr.				
Contributions		3,600 Cr.					3,600 Dr.
Benefit payments						1,575 Dr.	1,575 Cr.

			Stevens Company Worksheet 3				
			Journal Entries			Memo	
			Other Comprehensive Income				
Items	Pension Expense	Cash	(Prior Service Cost)	(Gains/ Losses)	Pension Asset/ Liability	PBO	Plan Assets
Liability increase				7,845 Dr.		7,845 Cr.	
JE for 20X3	6,249 Dr.	3,600 Cr.	3,120 Cr.	8,057 Dr.	7,586 Cr.		
Accumulated OCI— 12/31/20X2			7,920 Dr.	0			
Balance— 12/31/20X3			4,800 Dr.	8,057 Dr.	19,376 Cr.	43,316 Cr.	23,940 Dr.

Notes:

☐ Interest cost = interest rate × PBO (beginning of year) = 10% × $31,905 = $3,191

☐ Unexpected loss = expected return − actual return = $2,012 $1,800 = $212

☐ Expected return = return rate × plan assets (beginning of year) = 10% × $20,115 = $2,012

☐ Stevens Company defers the unexpected loss of $212 by debiting OCI (G/L) and crediting pension expense. Because of this adjustment, the expected return on plan assets is the amount actually used to compute pension expense.

☐ Liability increase = PBO (end of year) (PBO (beginning of year)= $39,750 ($31,905 = $7,845

Entry 8 records the change in the PBO because of the change in actuarial assumptions. The actuary computed the ending balance of $39,750. The PBO balance at December 31, 20X3, is computed below:

PBO—12/31/20X2	$31,905
Service cost	1,950
Interest cost	3,191
Benefits paid	(1,575)
PBO—12/31/20X3 (before liability increase)	$35,471

The difference between the ending balance of $43,316 and the balance of the PBO (before liability increase) is $7,845 ($43,316 − ($35,471). The increase of $7,845 in the employer's liability is an unexpected loss.

The $19,376 balance in the pension liability at December 31, 20X3, equals the net of the balances in the memo accounts, as indicated below:

Projected benefit obligation (credit)	$43,316
Fair market value of plan assets (debit)	23,940
Pension liability (credit)	$19,376

The journal entry on December 31, 20X3, is:

Pension expense	6,249	
Other comprehensive income (G/L)	8,057	
Cash		3,600
Other comprehensive income (prior service cost)		3,120
Pension liability		7,586

EXAMPLE

This continues the previous example for Stevens Company for the year 20X4. The following information is given for 20X4:

Service cost	$2,400
Amortization of prior service cost	$2,640
Actual return on plan assets	$3,300
Benefit payments to retirees	$2,700
Contributions	$4,050
Interest rate	10%
Expected return rate	10%
Average service life of eligible workers	10 years

Stevens Company
Worksheet 4

	Journal Entries					Memo	
Items	Pension Expense	Cash	Other Comprehensive Income (Prior Service Cost)	(Gains/ Losses)	Pension Asset/ Liability	PBO	Plan Assets
Balance— 12/31/20X3					19,376 Cr.	43,316 Cr.	23,940 Dr.
Service cost	2,400 Dr.					2,400 Cr.	
Interest cost	4,332 Dr.					4,332 Cr.	
Actual return	3,300 Cr.						3,300 Dr.
Unexpected gain	906 Dr.			906 Cr.			
Amortization of PSC	2,640 Dr.		2,640 Cr.				
Contributions		4,050 Cr.					4,050 Dr.
Benefit payments						2,700 Dr.	2,700 Cr.
Amortization of loss	373 Dr.			373 Cr.			
JE for 20X4	7,351 Dr.	4,050 Cr.	2,640 Cr.	1,279 Cr.	618 Dr.		
Accumulated OCI— 12/31/20X3			4,800 Dr.	8,057 Dr.			
Balance— 12/31/20X4			2,160 Dr.	6,778 Dr.	18,758 Cr.	47,348 Cr.	28,590 Dr.

Notes:

☐ Interest cost = interest rate × PBO (beginning of year) = 10% × $43,316 = $4,332

☐ Unexpected gain = actual return − expected return = $3,300 − $2,394 = $906

☐ Expected return = return rate × plan assets (beginning of year) = 10% × $23,940 = $2,394

Stevens Company defers the unexpected gain of $906 by crediting OCI (G/L) and debiting pension expense. Because of this adjustment the expected return on plan assets is the amount actually used to compute pension expense. By netting the gain of $906 against the actual return of $3,300, pension expense is affected only by the expected return of $2,394.

Stevens Company begins the year 20X4 with a balance in the net loss account of $8,057. The corridor test is applied in 20X4 to determine if the balance is excessive and should be amortized. The corridor equals 10% of the greater of the beginning balances of plan assets ($23,940) or projected benefit obligation ($43,316). Therefore, the corridor equals $4,332 (10% × $43,316). Because the balance in the accumulated other comprehensive income account is a net loss of $8,057, the excess over the corridor equals $3,725 ($8,057 − $4,332). This excess ($3,725) is amortized over the average remaining service life of employees (10 years), so that the amortization for 20X4 is $373 ($3,725 ÷ 10 years). The company debits pension expense and credits other comprehensive income for $373.

A schedule for the 20X4 corridor test follows:

Net (gain) or loss at beginning of year in accumulated OCI	$8,057
10% of greater of plan assets or projected benefit obligation (10% × $43,316)	4,332
Amount to be amortized	3,725
Average service life	10 years
Amortization for 20X4 ($3,725 ÷ 10 years)	$ 373

The journal entry to record pension expense for 20X4 is:

Pension expense	7,351	
Pension asset/liability	618	
Cash		4,050
Other comprehensive income (G/L)		1,279
Other comprehensive income (prior service cost)		2,640

The balance on December 31, 20X4, of $18,758 in pension liability equals:

Projected benefit obligation (credit)	$47,348
Fair market value of plan assets (debit)	28,590
Pension liability (credit)	$18,758

Business Combinations

If a single-employer defined benefit pension plan is acquired as part of a acquisition method acquisition of another company, a liability must be recognized for the excess of the projected benefit obligation over the fair value of the pension plan assets. On the other hand, an asset would be recorded if the plan assets exceed the projected benefit obligation. The projected benefit obligation includes the impact of an anticipated curtailment or termination of the acquired pension plan. The asset or liability recognized at the purchase date will be adjusted for the differences between the acquiring company's net pension cost and the amounts contributed.

ASC 805-20-55-50, *Business Combinations: Identifiable Assets and Liabilities, and Any Noncontrolling Interest*, covers the recognition of liabilities for contractual termination benefits or changing benefit plan assumptions in anticipation of a business combination.

Discontinued Operations

If a disposal of a business segment occurs, any termination benefits must be recognized and reported as a component of discontinued operations in the income statement.

Employers Having More Than One Defined Benefit Plan

As per ASC 962-10-05, if an employer has more than one pension plan, it must make separate computations of pension expense, fair value of plan assets, and liabilities for each plan.

The employer may not offset assets or liabilities of different pension plans unless there is a legal right to use the assets on one plan to satisfy the debt or benefits of another plan.

Disclosures may be aggregated for all pension plans maintained by the employer except for U.S. pension plans, which may not be combined with foreign pension plans unless there are similar assumptions used for both.

Multiemployer Plans

A multiemployer plan typically includes participation of two or more unrelated employers and often ensues from a collective bargaining arrangement with the union. The plan is usually administered by a board of trustees. In this case, plan assets contributed by one employer may be used to pay employee benefits of another participating employer. Thus, the assets are aggregated for all employers and are available and unrestricted to pay benefits to all employees, regardless of whom they are employed by. In other words, there is no segregation of assets in a particular employer's account or any restrictions placed on that employer's assets. An example is a plan contributed to by all employers employing the members of a particular union, regardless of whom the employees are employed by. Retirees of different employers receive payment from the same pooled fund. The Teamster's Union is a case in point.

In a multiemployer plan, the employer's pension expense equals its contribution to the plan for the year. If a contribution is due but yet unpaid, the employer must recognize it as a liability.

If an employer withdraws from the multiemployer plan, it may incur a liability for its part of the unfunded benefit obligation of the plan. If an employer would probably incur a liability if it withdrew from the plan and the amount is reasonably determinable, a loss must be accrued with a concurrent liability. However, if the loss is reasonably possible, only footnote disclosure is required.

ASC 715-80-55-2, *Compensation—Retirement Benefits: Multiemployer Plans*, stipulates that an employer need not record a liability for an amount beyond that currently due.

The following must be disclosed by employers participating in a multiemployer plan:

☐ A description of the plan including workers covered.

☐ The benefits to be provided.

☐ Nature of matters impacting on the comparability of information for the years presented.

☐ Pension expense for the period.

In Accounting Standards Update (ASU) No. 2011-09 (September 2011), *Compensation–Retirement Benefits–Multiemployer Plans* (Topic 715-80), *Disclosures about an Employer's Participation in a Multiemployer Plan*, companies must give additional quantitative and qualitative disclosures for multiemployer pension plans and other postretirement benefit plans. The disclosures include identifying names and numbers, funded status, employer commitments and obligations, plan benefits, employer contributions, and surcharges on contributions.

Multiple-Employer Plans

These plans are similar to multiemployer plans. They also consist of two or more unrelated employers. However, multiple-employer plans are, in effect, aggregated single-employer plans that are combined so that assets of all may be totaled to lower administrative costs. The assets are also merged to improve the overall rate of return from investing them. In many cases, participating employers may use different benefit formulas for their respective pension contributions. Each employer in the plan accounts for its particular interest separately. An example of such an arrangement is when companies in an industry have their trade association handle the plans of all the companies. Each company retains its responsibilities only for its own workers. Multiple-employer plans are usually not associated with collective bargaining contracts.

Annuity (Allocated) Contracts

An employer may sign a valid and irrevocable insurance contract to pay benefit obligations arising from a defined benefit plan. Annuity contracts are used to transfer the risk of providing employee benefits from the employer to the insurance company.

If the annuity contracts are the basis for funding the pension plan and paying plan obligations thereto, the insurance premium paid by the employer is the pension expense for the period covering all currently earned benefits. In this case, the company and plan do not report plan assets, accumulated benefit obligation, or a projected benefit obligation. On the other hand, if the annuity contracts cover just part of the benefit obligation, the employer is liable for the uncovered obligation. Such uncovered obligation is accounted for as per the usual requirements under ASC 962-10-05 specified in this chapter for pension plans.

In a participating annuity contract, the insurer pays the employer part of the income earned from investing the insurance premiums. In most cases, income earned (e.g., dividends, interest) reduces pension cost. A drawback to the employer of a participating contract is that it costs more than one that is nonparticipating because of the participation right. This additional cost associated with the participation privilege should be recognized as a pension plan asset. Therefore, except for the cost of participation rights, pension plan assets exclude the cost of annuity contracts. In later years, fair value should be used in valuing the participation right included in plan assets. In the event that fair value may not be reasonably determined, the asset should be recorded at cost, with amortization based on the dividend period specified in the agreement. However, unamortized cost cannot exceed the net realizable value of the participation right.

Caution: If the terms of the participating annuity contract are such that the employer retains all or most of the risk related to the benefit obligation, the purchase of this contract does not represent a settlement of the employer's obligations under the pension plan.

Insurance contracts other than annuity contracts are considered investments. They are reported as pension plan assets and reported at fair value. Fair value may be in terms of conversion value, contract value, or cash surrender value, for example, depending on the circumstances.

In terms of accounting for pension plans, the definition of an annuity contract is not satisfied if one or both of the following exists:

☐ There is a captive insurance company, meaning that the insurance entity has as its major client the employer or any of its associated parties.

☐ There is uncertainty as to whether the insurance company will be able to pay its obligations because of financial problems.

ASC 715-30-35-90 and 35-91, *Compensation—Retirement Benefits: Defined Benefit Plans—Pension* (EITF Consensus Summary No. 91–7, *Accounting for Pension Benefits Paid by Employers after Insurance Companies Fail to Provide Annuity Benefits*), stipulates that the employer must record a loss when it assumes the obligation to pay retirees because the insurance company is financially unable to do so (e.g., bankruptcy). The loss is recorded at the lower of any gain associated with the original insurance contract or the amount of benefit obligation assumed. Any unrecognized additional loss should be treated as an amendment to the pension plan.

Disclosures

A single-employer pension plan requires the following footnote disclosures:

☐ Description of the plan, including categorization of workers covered, retirement age, funding policy, benefit formula, and benefits provided.

☐ Pension plan commitments, such as to increase benefits.

☐ Elements (components) of pension expense.

☐ Assumptions and changes therein used in determining pension expense and related funding, such as turnover rate, mortality rate, and interest rate.

☐ Prior service cost and a description of the amortization policy.

☐ Unrecognized net gain or loss.

☐ Annuity benefits due employees.

☐ Weighted-average assumed discount rate and the rate of compensation increases used in measuring the projected benefit obligation. (At each measurement date, the employer must ascertain the appropriate discount rate used to measure the pension liability, based on current interest rates.)

☐ Weighted-average long-term return rate on pension plan assets.

☐ Discounted value of vested and nonvested benefits.

☐ Fair value and type of pension plan assets.

☐ Amounts and type of securities included in pension plan assets. (Further, other pension plan assets should be identified.)

☐ Projected benefit obligation (included is the rate of compensation increase to measure the projected benefit obligation).

☐ Nonbenefit liabilities.

☐ Vested benefits.

☐ Liabilities of the pension plan other than those applicable for plan benefits. (Examples of these types of liabilities are unsecured borrowings and unsettled stock purchases.)

☐ Reconciling the plan's funded status with employer amounts recognized in the balance sheet (e.g., fair value of plan assets, projected benefit obligation).

☐ Specific investments representing 5% or more of pension plan assets.

☐ Insurance coverage for the pension plan, if any. (Reference to annuity contracts agreed to by the employer and insurer should be specified.)

☐ Related-party transactions.

☐ Nature and impact of matters bearing upon the ability to compare pension data over the years. (The amount of annual benefits to retirees covered by the annuity contracts should be indicated.)

☐ Modification in cost-sharing arrangements.

☐ Estimate of the expected contributions to be funded to the plan next year.

☐ Expected benefit payments to retirees for each of the next five years and in total for the five years thereafter.

☐ Rates used to measure benefit amounts such as discount rate, expected return rate on plan assets, and rate of compensation.

☐ Schedule presenting allocation of pension plan assets by category (e.g., equity securities, debt securities, real estate) and indicating the percentage of the fair value to total plan assets. The employer must also have a narrative discussion of investment policies, including any target allocation percentage.

☐ Reconciliation of how the fair market value of pension plan assets and the projected benefit obligation changed from the beginning to end of the year.

☐ Nature and amount of changes in pension plan assets and benefit obligations recognized in net income and in other comprehensive income.

☐ Effects on net periodic benefit cost for the next fiscal year that arises from delayed recognition of the gains and losses and prior service costs or credits.

☐ Amortization approach used for the excess of the accumulated other comprehensive income balance over the corridor amount.

☐ Amounts recognized in other comprehensive income in the income statement, showing separately the net gain or loss and net prior service cost or credit. Those amounts shall be separated into amounts arising during the year and reclassification adjustments of other comprehensive income as a result of being recognized as components of net periodic benefit cost for the year.

☐ Amount and timing of any plan assets expected to be returned to the company during the 12-month period or operating cycle, if longer.

☐ Amount of anticipated net actuarial gain or loss and prior service costs or credits that will be amortized from accumulated other comprehensive income into net income over the next fiscal year. This information aids in predicting the impact of deferred pension expense items on next year's income.

☐ Accumulated amount of changes in pension assets and benefit obligations that have been recognized in other comprehensive income and would be recycled into net profit in future years. This information indicates pension and related balances recognized in stockholders' equity, which will impact future income.

☐ Amount in accumulated other comprehensive income that has not yet been recognized as a component of net periodic benefit cost, showing separately the net gain or loss, net prior service cost or credit, and transition asset or obligation.

Optional disclosures for single-employer plans may also be provided, including the following:

☐ Categorization of pension plan assets by major type.

☐ Cash flow information with regard to employer funding and benefits paid during the period.

☐ Percentage of pension expense to total salaries.

☐ Change in the projected benefit obligation that would arise from a one-percentage change in the assumed discount rate and the assumed rate of compensation increase.

The preceding disclosures may be aggregated for all of the employer's pension plans or presented in groups. Disclosures associated with U.S. plans should be separate from those outside the United States unless the plans are similar and use the same assumptions.

Financial Statement Analysis

An analysis should be made of the components making up pension plan assets. Are there risky or speculative investments in the portfolio? Is there an excessive percentage of assets invested in a particular stock? If the company needs to be liquidated, how much of pension plan assets are protected to meet pension plan deficiencies?

Employee Retirement Income Security Act (ERISA)

This Act was passed in 1974. It enumerates law for pension plans so as to improve their financial viability and to safeguard employee interests. A Pension Benefit Guaranty Corporation (PBGC) was created to protect against employees losing their pension benefits. The PBGC guarantees that employees will receive a minimum amount of benefits based on their service years in the event of employer bankruptcy. To provide funds to pay employees, employers are required to pay insurance premiums to the PBGC. The Act requires certain employee participation in the pension plan. The PBGC has the authority to administer a terminated plan. The Act mandates that annual reports on the pension plan be provided, including plan assets and liabilities as well as a description of the plan. The Act generally provides for full vesting of pension benefits when an employee has been in the service of the employer for 15 years. Minimum funding levels for employers are specified. Past service costs must be funded over a period not exceeding 40 years. An employer's violation of the statute's provisions may result in penalties, liens on or seizure of assets, and the loss of tax deductions.

Life Insurance

ASC 715-60-05-13, *Compensation—Retirement Benefits: Defined Benefit Plans—Other Postretirement*, states that the employer should recognize a liability for future post-employment benefits based on the substantive employee agreement or collateral assignment arrangement.

SETTLEMENT, CURTAILMENT, AND TERMINATION

ASC 715-30, *Compensation—Retirement Benefits: Defined Benefit Plans—Pension*, amends ASC 715-60-05-12, *Compensation—Retirement Benefits: Defined Benefit Plans—Other Postretirement*. ASC 715-60-05-12 covers situations in which modifications are made to pension plans.

Settlement

A settlement of a pension plan is an action that discharges an employer from his or her primary responsibility for an entity's pension obligation and for the elimination of the risks associated with having sufficient assets available to satisfy this obligation. Examples of settlements include:

☐ Acquiring annuity contracts to cover participants' vested benefits.

☐ Making lump sum payments to pension plan participants in satisfaction of their right to receive pension benefits.

A settlement has to meet each of the following criteria:

☐ It must significantly reduce risk of the pension obligation.

☐ It must relieve pension benefit responsibility.

☐ It must be irrevocable.

After the settlement of a pension plan, the employer may choose to provide pension benefits in a new plan or continue the old plan.

In accounting for a settlement, the amount of the gain or loss is a function of the percentage of the projected benefit obligation (PBO) that has been reduced. That is, if only a portion of the PBO is settled, only a proportionate part of the maximum gain or loss is recognized. The maximum gain or loss that could be recognized is the unrecorded net gain or loss existing at the date of settlement and the unrecognized net asset or obligation that existed when ASC 962-10-05 was initially applied. If, for example, the PBO is reduced by 60%, then 60% of the gain or loss is recognized in the current year's income statement. Correspondingly, if the employer's PBO is completely discharged, the total gain or loss at the date of settlement is recognized. Settlement gains or losses do not, in most situations, meet the requirements of extraordinary items and therefore are considered ordinary. Full disclosure should always be made of the nature of the settlement.

EXAMPLE

1. On December 31, 20X2, X Company made a lump-sum payment to retirees to satisfy the benefits of all retired individuals.

2. On December 31, 20X2, the plan's projected benefit obligation consisted of the following two components:

Cost of settling retirees benefits	$100,000
Benefits owed to active employees—not settled	70,000
Total Projected Benefit Obligation	$170,000

3. On December 31, 20X2, the Company disclosed the following on its balance sheet related to pension disclosure:

Projected benefit obligation	$(170,000)
Plan assets	200,000
Funded status	30,000
Unrecognized prior service costs	24,000

Net loss	20,000
Net obligation at the time FAS-87 was adopted	(50,000)
Prepaid pension cost	24,000
MAXIMUM GAIN (LOSS) ON SETTLEMENT	
Unrecognized net loss prior to settlement	$(20,000)
Net Obligation at time FAS-87 was adopted	50,000
Maximum gain recognizable	$ 30,000

Settlement Reduction of the Projected Benefit Obligation:

$$\frac{\text{Projected benefit obligation settled}}{\text{Total project benefit obligation}} = \frac{\$100,000}{\$170,000} = 59\%$$

SETTLEMENT GAIN	
Maximum gain recognizable	$30,000
Reduction in projected benefit obligation	X59%
Settlement gain	$17,700

The same application would apply, for example, if an employer gives employees a lump-sum payment in exchange for their pension rights. The gain or loss on settlement is recognized in the current year's income statement. If there is a settlement of only part of the plan, only a proportionate share of the gain or loss, as before, is recognized.

Curtailment

A curtailment takes place when an occurrence materially reduces the future years of service of current employees or eliminates for most workers the accumulation of defined benefits for future services. An example is the closing of a plant, terminating employment.

The gain or loss arising from curtailment is recognized in the current year's income statement. The gain or loss is composed of the following components:

☐ Prior service cost for employee service no longer required.

☐ Change in the pension benefit obligation.

In a curtailment, some of the future pension benefits for employees currently employed are reduced, resulting in a gain (PBO decrease) or loss (PBO increase). For example, the PBO may be decreased by the amount of the pension benefits that the entity does not have to pay as a result of some employees being terminated. If, on the other hand, these employees (those who are terminated) are eligible for subsidized early retirement and benefits earlier than expected, an increase in the PBO occurs.

It is important to note that a pension plan curtailment may occur by itself or in conjunction with a settlement. If, for example, years of future service are cut back as a result of the discontinuance of a segment of a business, but the pension plan continues overall for the employees of the entity, a curtailment has occurred but a settlement has not. If, on the other hand, the employer totally terminates the entity's pension plan and then fully settles the pension obligation with employees, both a settlement and curtailment have occurred.

In accounting for curtailments, a curtailment gain is computed as the difference between the amount of the PBO decrease as a result of the curtailment less any related unrecognized net loss. A curtailment loss, on the other hand, is the difference between the amount of the PBO increase less any related unrecognized gain. In computing curtailment gains and losses, any unrecognized net asset or liability at transition is also considered part of the unrecognized gain or loss.

EXAMPLE

As a result of a termination of employees' services earlier than expected owing to the closing of a facility, the following occurred:

Increase in projected benefit obligation from curtailment	$600,000
Unrecognized net gain	(360,000)
Curtailment loss	$240,000

The same circumstances exist as in the prior situation; however, in this case:

Decrease in projected benefit obligation from curtailment	$(600,000)
Unrecognized net loss	360,000
Curtailment gain	$(240,000)

The amount of net periodic benefit cost should include the gain or loss recognized because of settlements or curtailments.

Termination

If early retirement benefits are offered by an employer, are accepted by employees, and the amount of the benefits can be reasonably estimated, an expense provision should be recorded by debiting expense, crediting cash (for the down payment), and crediting a liability (for future payments). The amount accrued equals the down payment plus the discounted value of future employer payments. In addition, there should be a footnote describing the particulars of the agreement.

Note: A gain or loss arising from a settlement or curtailment of a pension plan or termination benefits that are directly associated with disposing of a business segment is included in the gain or loss on the disposal of the segment.

EXAMPLE

ABC Company offers special termination benefits to employees that are accepted by the employees and can be reasonably estimated. The employees accept the offer on July 15, 20X3. The cost of the termination benefits includes a lump-sum payment of $2,500,000, and the present value of expected future payments amounts to $2,600,000. The entry that should be made for the accrual of termination benefits follows:

Retirement termination benefits expense	5,100,000	
Estimated liability for termination benefits		5,100,000

TRUSTEE REPORTING IN A DEFINED BENEFIT PENSION PLAN

ASC 960-205-10, *Plan Accounting—Defined Benefit Pension Plans: Presentation of Financial Statements*, specifies the accounting, reporting, and footnote disclosures required of the trustee of a defined benefit plan. The trustee reports for the plan as a separate accounting and legal entity for which books of record are kept. Accrual accounting must be followed. The trustee is not required to prepare financial statements for the plan. However, if issued, the financial statements must be prepared in accordance with certain rules. The major purpose of reporting is to allow one to evaluate the adequacy of the plan to pay employees' benefits after retirement.

In the balance sheet, pension assets are netted against pension liabilities. Operating assets are expressed at book value. Investments are reported at market value. One asset presented is "Contributions Receivable Due from Employer."

The pension plan liability presented by the employer excludes the employees' accumulated benefits because in reality plan participants are equity holders and not creditors of the plan.

The trustee must make the following footnote disclosure:

☐ Description of the plan, including changes therein.

☐ Accounting and funding policies.

☐ Net assets available for benefits and changes therein during the year, such as from capital appreciation of equity and debt securities. (Capital appreciation or depreciation by source must be given.)

☐ Actuarial present value of accumulated plan benefits separately presented for that attributable to current employees, retirees, and beneficiaries. (Changes in the discounted value of accumulated benefits should also be disclosed.)

There may be an annuity contract whereby an insurance company agrees to provide specified pension benefits based on premiums received.

POSTRETIREMENT BENEFIT PLANS OTHER THAN PENSIONS

The major differences between pension benefits and postretirement benefits (e.g., health care, welfare) are:

☐ Pension benefits are usually funded, whereas postretirement benefits are not.

☐ Pension benefits are well-defined within a level dollar amount, and postretirement benefits are typically uncapped and show significant fluctuation.

Health care benefits are generally considered the most important and largest postretirement benefits. The accrual basis of accounting requires that the employer's obligation regarding the payment of future postretirement benefits be measured and the resulting cost be accrued during the employees' service period. Measuring future payments for health care benefits is more difficult than for pension plans. The level of health care costs is difficult to measure because of constant changes in medical technology, increased longevity of retirees and their dependents and beneficiaries, as well as new and unexpected illnesses that surface and are expensive to cure. In addition, many postretirement plans do not limit the amount of health care benefits that can be utilized by retirees.

Accounting

As was noted, the accounting requirements for postretirement benefits other than pensions are similar to those of pension plans. However, there are several differences as well.

Postretirement benefits for current and future retirees represent deferred compensation. The time period the postretirement benefit cost accrues is referred to as the attribution period.

Accrual of postretirement benefits expense must be made of the benefits employees are entitled to receive based on services performed. In the case of a defined contribution plan, the cash funded for the year represents the postretirement benefits expense. However, in a defined benefit plan the amount funded and the expense will be different.

Postretirement benefits expense is based on actuarial calculations. The benefits are allocated over the employees' service years. The benefits must be completely accrued by the time the employee is fully vested (eligible) to receive them. Even if the employee resigns after the full eligibility date, he or she is entitled to those benefits.

The expected postretirement benefit obligation is the actuarial present value as of a particular date of the benefits expected to be paid to employees, beneficiaries, or covered dependents. It is used to calculate service cost.

In accounting for postretirement benefits, the health care and other postretirement benefits for current and future retirees are accrued over a period of time known as the attribution period. This period represents the period of service during which the employee earns the postretirement benefit. It begins when the employee is hired and terminates when the employee terminates performing services and therefore is not eligible to receive benefits. The employee becomes vested for postretirement benefits on this date and is eligible to receive benefits.

New terms for postretirement benefits accounting include:

☐ *Expected Postretirement Benefit Obligation (EPBO)* This is the total benefits expected to be paid after retirement to employees and their dependents. It is disclosed at its actuarial present value and is used in computing periodic postretirement expense.

☐ *Accumulated Postretirement Benefit Obligation (APBO)* This is the actuarial present value of future benefits related to employees' services rendered as of a particular date. The difference between the EPBO and APBO is that the APBO does not include active employees as yet ineligible for benefits. That is, before an employee achieves full eligibility, the APBO is only a portion of the EPBO. The APBO equals the EPBO for retirees and active employees who are fully eligible for benefits at the end of the attribution period.

Components

Net periodic postretirement benefit cost is made up of the following components:

- ☐ *Service cost.* Actuarial present value of benefits applicable to services performed during the year. This increases postretirement expense.

- ☐ *Interest cost.* Interest on the accumulated postretirement benefit obligation at the beginning of the period, adjusted for benefit payments during the year. The interest cost increases postretirement expense.

- ☐ *Actual return on plan assets.* Return based on the fair value of plan assets at the beginning and end of the year, adjusted for contributions and benefit payments. Actual return typically reduces postretirement expense.

- ☐ *Amortization expense on prior service cost.* Expense provision for the current year due to amortization of prior service cost arising from adoption or amendment to the plan. Prior service cost applies to credited services before adoption or amendment and is accounted for over current and future years. The usual amortization period, starting with the amendment date, is the remaining service years to the full eligibility date. There should be amortization of any prior service cost or credit included in accumulated other comprehensive income.

- ☐ *Gain or loss component.* Gains and losses apply to changes in the amount of either the accumulated postretirement benefit obligation or plan assets resulting from actual experience being different from the actuarial assumptions. The gains and losses may also apply to changes in actuarial assumptions. Gains and losses may be realized (i.e., sale of securities) or unrealized.

Gains and losses that are not recognized immediately as a component of net periodic postretirement benefit cost are recognized as increases or decreases in other comprehensive income as they occur.

EXAMPLE

On January 1, 2005, Barone Corporation adopts a health care benefit program and provides the following data:

Service cost	$540
Contributions	380
Benefit payments	250

The service cost of $540 increases postretirement expense and the accumulated postretirement benefit obligation (APBO). The contributions of $380 reduce cash and increase plan assets. The benefit payments to retirees of $250 reduce the APBO and plan assets.

Barone Corporation
Postretirement Schedule 1

| | Journal Entries (JE) | | | Memo | |
Items	Postretirement Expense	Cash	Postretirement Asset/Liability	APBO	Plan Assets
Balance— 1/1/20X5					
1. Service cost	540 Dr.			540 Cr.	
2. Contributions		380 Cr.			380 Dr.
3. Benefit payments				250 Dr.	250 Cr.
JE for 20X5	540 Dr.	380 Cr.	160 Cr.		
Balance— 12/31/20X5			160 Cr.	290 Cr.	130 Dr.

The journal entry for 12/31/20X5 is:

Postretirement expense	540	
Cash		380
Postretirement liability		160

The credit to postretirement liability can also be computed as:

Accumulated postretirement benefit obligation (credit)	$290
Fair market value of plan assets (debit)	130
Postretirement liability	$160

The postretirement liability shows the plan is underfunded by $160.

Plan Amendment

A plan amendment that retroactively increases benefits increases the accumulated postretirement benefit obligation. The cost of the benefit improvement is recognized as a charge to other comprehensive income at the amendment date. On the other hand, a plan modification that retroactively reduces the benefits decreases the accumulated postretirement benefit obligation. The reduction in benefits is recognized as a corresponding credit (prior service credit) to other comprehensive income that is first used to reduce any remaining prior service cost included in accumulated other comprehensive income, which reduces any transition obligation remaining in accumulated other comprehensive income. The excess, if any, must not immediately be recognized, but should be amortized as a component of net periodic postretirement benefit cost.

Corridor

As is the situation with pensions, employers amortize the gains and losses in accumulated other comprehensive income as an element of postretirement expense assuming, at the beginning of the year, the gains and losses exceed the corridor. In the case of postretirement plans, the corridor equals 10% of the greater of the accumulated postretirement benefit obligation or market-related value of plan assets.

The minimum amortization amount is the excess of the gains or losses over the corridor amount. The excess is amortized over the average remaining service life of active employees. The employer must recompute the amount of gains or losses in accumulated other comprehensive income each year and amortize the excess gains or losses.

EXAMPLE

This is a continuation of the previous example for Barone Corporation for the year 20X6. The following data is provided for 20X6:

Service cost	$140
Benefit payments	$ 50
Contributions	$180
Average remaining service period	25 years
Actual return on plan assets	$ 6
Expected return on plan assets	$ 8
Interest rate	12%
Increase in APBO due to change in actuarial assumptions	$600

Barone Corporation
Postretirement Schedule 2

	Journal Entries (JE)				Memo	
Items	Postretirement Expense	Cash	OCI* (G/L)	Postretirement Asset/ Liability	APBO	Plan Assets
Balance—1/1/20X6				160 Cr.	290 Cr.	130 Dr.
1. Service cost	140 Dr.				140 Cr.	
2. Interest cost	35 Dr.				35 Cr.	
3. Actual return	6 Cr.					6 Dr.
4. Unexpected loss	2 Cr.		2 Dr.			
5. Contributions		180 Cr.				180 Dr.
6. Benefit payments					50 Dr.	50 Cr.
7. Increase in APBO (loss)			600 Dr.		600 Cr.	
JE for 20X6	167 Dr.	180 Cr.	602 Dr.	589 Cr.		
Accumulated OCI—12/31/20X6			-0-			
Balance—12/31/20X6			602 Dr.	749 Cr.	1015 Cr.	266 Dr.

Notes:

2. Interest cost = interest rate × APBO (beginning of year) = 12% × $290 = <u>$35</u>

4. Unexpected loss = expected return (actual return = $8–$6 = <u>$2</u>

   The unexpected loss of $2 is deferred by debiting other comprehensive income (G/L) and crediting postretirement expense. Because of this adjustment, the expected return on plan assets is the amount actually used to compute postretirement expense.

The increase in the APBO because of a change in actuarial assumptions of $600 is an unexpected loss which is debited to other comprehensive income (G/L) and credited to APBO.

The journal entry for postretirement expense for 20X6 follows:

Postretirement expense	167	
Other comprehensive income (G/L)	602	
Cash		180
Postretirement liability		589

The postretirement liability at December 31, 2006, is $749. This balance may also be calculated as follows:

Accumulated postretirement benefit obligation (credit)	$1,015
Fair market value of plan assets (debit)	266
Postretirement liability	$ 749

The amortization of net gain or loss in the year 2007 follows based on the corridor method:

Accumulated other comprehensive income—beginning of year	$602
10% of the greater of the APBO or market-related value of plan assets (10% × $1,015)	102
Amount to be amortized	$500
Average remaining service period	25 years

Amortization of loss for 20X7 ($500 ÷25 years) = $20

Interim Periods

With respect to interim periods, unless a business entity remeasures both its plan assets and benefit obligations during the fiscal year, the funded status it reports in its interim balance sheet shall be the same asset or liability recognized in the prior year-end balance sheet adjusted for (1) subsequent accruals of net periodic postretirement benefit cost excluding the amortization of amounts previously recognized in other comprehensive income (e.g., subsequent accruals of service cost, interest, and return on plan assets) and (2) contributions to a funded plan, or benefit payments. Upon remeasurement, a business shall adjust its balance sheet in a later interim period to consider the underfunded or overfunded status of the plan consistent with that measurement date. **Note:** Sometimes a company remeasures both plan assets and benefit obligations during the fiscal year. An example is when a major event takes place such as a plan amendment, curtailment, or settlement.

Disclosures

Required footnote disclosures for postretirement benefits include:

☐ Description of the plan, including nature of benefits to be paid.

☐ Health care cost trend factors.

☐ Effect of a one-percentage-point increase in trend rates.

☐ Trend in compensation cost.

☐ Discount rate used to compute the accumulated postretirement benefit obligation. A company should consider return rates on high-quality fixed-income securities in deriving the discount rate. The assumed discount rate should be reevaluated at each measurement date. In the event that the general level of interest rates rises or declines, the assumed discount rate will change in a similar way.

☐ Funding policy and status.

☐ Cost of providing termination benefits recognized during the period.

☐ Components of postretirement expense.

☐ Accumulated postretirement benefit obligation showing separately the amount applicable to retirees, other eligible participants, and other active participants.

☐ Fair market value of plan assets.

☐ Return on plan assets on an after-tax basis.

ASC 715-60-05-14, *Compensation—Retirement Benefits: Defined Benefit Plans—Other Postretirement*, requires that arrangements providing employee benefits that extend to postretirement periods should be recognized as a liability and related compensation costs for the expected future benefits.

EMPLOYERS' DISCLOSURES ABOUT PENSION AND OTHER POSTRETIREMENT BENEFITS

ASC 715-20-05, *Compensation—Retirement Benefits: Defined Benefit Plans—General*, standardizes disclosures for retiree benefits. In general, it revises and improves the effectiveness of current note disclosure requirements for employers' pensions and other retiree benefits. Recognition or accounting measurement issues are not addressed. In addition, the statement eliminates certain disclosures that have been deemed to be no longer useful by the FASB and requires additional information to enhance financial analysis.

ASC 715-20-05 mandates additional disclosures to those in the original Statement No. 132 with respect to assets, obligations, cash flows, and net periodic benefit cost of defined benefit pension plans and other defined postretirement plans. The required data should be furnished separately for pension plans and for other postretirement benefit plans. The additional disclosures include investment policy, plan obligations, cash flows, measurement dates, and components of net periodic benefit cost recognized during *interim periods*. Information must be provided for each major category of plan assets that the percentage of the fair value of total plan assets held as of the measurement date used for each statement of financial position presented. There should be a narrative description of investment strategies, including target allocation percentages for each major category of plan assets presented on a weighted-average basis as of the measurement dates of the latest statement of financial position. Also disclosed to evaluate the investment approach are risk management practices, investment objectives, and unallowable investments in the pension plan such as certain derivatives. The overall expected long-term rate-of-return-on-assets assumption should be disclosed. The benefits expected to be paid in each of the next five fiscal years, and in the total for the five fiscal years following, should be disclosed. Expected contributions to the plan should be noted. The rates of compensation increase should be presented.

ASC 715-60-05-8, *Compensation—Retirement Benefits: Defined Benefit Plans—Other Postretirement*, notes that sponsors of retiree health care benefits providing prescription drug benefits that are at least "actuarially equivalent" to those provided under Medicare Part D will be eligible for a federal subsidy. The subsidy should be included in measuring the cost of benefits attributable to current service benefits because it affects the sponsor's share of the plan's costs. The sponsor's service cost will be reduced by the subsidy. Because the subsidy is not taxable, there is *no* effect on temporary differences.

Plan sponsors should take Medicare into account when measuring a plan's APBO and net periodic postretirement benefit cost.

The following disclosures should be made:

☐ Amount by which APBO is reduced for the subsidy.

☐ Effect of subsidy in the measurement of net periodic postretirement benefit cost.

PENSION PLAN FINANCIAL STATEMENTS

ASC 960-10-15, *Plan Accounting—Defined Benefit Pension Plans: Overall*, provides authoritative guidance in accounting and reporting for defined benefit pension plans. Additional guidance is provided by ASC 960-325-35, *Plan Accounting—Defined Benefit Pension Plans: Investments—Other* (AICPA Accounting Standards Executive Committee (AcSEC) Practice Bulletin, Reporting Separate Investment Fund Option Information of Defined Benefit Pension Plans). Other related information is given by:

☐ AICPA Industry Audit and Accounting Guide, *Audits of Employee Benefit Plans.*

☐ ASC 962-325, *Plan Accounting—Defined Contribution Pension Plans: Investments.*

A defined benefit plan pays specified or determinable retirement benefits to participants either on retirement or on the occurrence of certain events, such as death, disability, or termination of employment. Benefits are paid based on such factors as the participant's age, salary, and length of service. The employers' contributions in defined benefit plans are calculated actuarially based on specified benefits and may be periodically adjusted.

A defined contribution plan, unlike a defined benefit plan, maintains separate accounts for each participant, and the employer deposits a specified amount in each participant's account on a periodic basis. Defined contribution plans include 401(k) and 403(b) plans, employee stock ownership plans, profit sharing plans, and money purchase plans. Participants' benefits in a defined contribution plan are simply equal to the amount accumulated in their respective accounts. (**Note:** The information in this section applies only to defined benefit plans and not to defined contribution plans.)

Defined benefit plans are not required by ASC 960-205-45-1, *Plan Accounting—Defined Benefit Pension Plans: Presentation of Financial Statements*, to present financial statements. However, if the plan chooses to present financial statements, ASC 960-205-45-1 requires the following information:

☐ Net assets available to pay benefits.

☐ Changes in net assets available to pay benefits.

☐ Actuarial present value of accumulated plan benefits.

☐ Factors affecting the change in actuarial present value of accumulated plan benefits.

This information may be disclosed either in the statement or otherwise. Certain disclosures about the plan and its accounting policies are also required.

The primary purpose of these financial statements is to provide information to assess the present and future ability of pension plans to pay promised benefits. The following information should be disclosed in the financial statements:

☐ Resources of the pension plan.

☐ Accumulated benefits.

☐ Transactions affecting the plan's resources and benefits.

☐ Additional information to clarify financial statement presentation and make it understandable.

Financial statements should be prepared as of the most recent year-end period. However, if the actuarial present value of accumulated plan benefits is unavailable or cannot be determined, beginning-of-period information may be presented. Use of an interim date is not allowed by GAAP. Approximations may be used to determine benefit information at the beginning or end of the fiscal year, if such information becomes available during the fiscal year, as long as the method used to estimate benefits produces results comparable to those required by ASC 960-205-45-1. Information about the actuarial present value of accumulated plan benefits and changes to the benefits may be presented as a separate statement or on the face of the statement of net assets or in notes to financial statements.

Comparative financial statements *must* be presented if the plan presents the actuarial present value of accumulated plan benefits as of the beginning of the plan period. Comparative financial statements are preferable even when they are not required. Information from several years may be more useful in assessing a plan's ability to pay benefits.

A statement of cash flows is not required of defined benefit plans. However, GAAP encourages its presentation when such information would be relevant in assessing a plan's ability to meet future obligations, such as when the assets lack liquidity or when financing is obtained for investments.

Net Assets Available for Benefits

The resources available to pay benefits to participants are identified in the statement of net assets. The statement of net assets (as shown in Exhibit 14-3) is prepared using accrual accounting and includes information about a plan's assets and liabilities.

Investments

Benefit plans own many types of investments, such as marketable securities, restricted or unregistered securities, real estate, mortgages, leases, interests in limited partnerships, repurchase agreements, futures and options, and contracts with insurance companies that do not subject the insurance company to risks arising from policyholders' mortality or morbidity. Such investments must be identified in reasonable detail and presented at fair value in the financial statements. Fair value is defined as the amount that the plan could reasonably expect to receive in an arm's-length sale between willing buyers and sellers when neither is compelled to buy or sell. In an active market, quoted market values may be used. If an active market does not exist, the fair value may be determined using another method, such as discounted cash flow or estimates from independent expert appraisers. The method used should be disclosed in the financial statements or its footnotes. Brokerage commissions and other selling costs, if significant, should be considered in determining the fair value.

Exhibit 14–3: Statement of Net Assets Available for Benefits

Statement of Net Assets Available for Benefits
For Year Ended December 31, 20X2

ASSETS
Investments (fair value):

Government securities	$ 1,000,000
Corporate debt securities	$ 1,500,000
Investment contracts	$ 2,300,000
Common stock	$ 4,500,000
Preferred stock	$ 1,700,000
Mortgages	$ (850,000)
Real estate	$ 1,200,000
	$13,050,000

Receivables

Employees' contributions	$ (235,000)
Employer's contributions	$ (354,000)
Accrued interest	$ (400,000)
Accrued dividends	$ 325,000
	$ 1,314,000
Cash	$ 1,600,000

Total assets	$15,964,000

LIABILITIES		
Accounts payable	$ 365,000	
Accrued expenses	$ 475,000	
Total liabilities		$ 840,000
NET ASSETS AVAILABLE FOR BENEFITS		$15,124,000

Contributions Receivable

Contributions receivable from participants, employers, and other sources should be recorded as of the reporting date and identified in the financial statements. All amounts that are formally committed to be paid to the plan as well as amounts that are legally or contractually due should be included in contributions receivable. Note, however, that an employer's accruing a liability to the pension plan does not, by itself, constitute sufficient basis for the plan to record a receivable. The following factors may provide evidence that the employer has formally committed to make a contribution to the plan:

☐ A formal approval, such as a resolution, by the employer's governing body to make a contribution.

☐ A consistent pattern of making payments after the pension plan's year-end in accordance with an established funding policy that attributes the payments to the preceding plan year.

☐ A federal income tax deduction, taken by the employer for periods ending on or before the reporting date for the pension plan.

Insurance Contracts

Insurance contracts generally have two characteristics. The purchaser of the insurance contract makes payments to the insurance company before the insured event. The insurance company generally does not know if, when, or how much will have to be paid on the insurance contract at the time the contract is made.

Insurance contracts are required by ASC 960-325-35-1, *Plan Accounting—Defined Benefit Pension Plans: Investments—Other*, to be presented in the same format as specified in annual reports filed with certain governmental agencies pursuant to Employee Retirement Income Security Act (ERISA). The contracts are presented either at fair value or at amounts determined by the insurance company. If an insurance plan is not subject to ERISA, it still presents its insurance contracts as if the plan was subject to the reporting requirements of ERISA. Insurance contracts that do not relate to policyholders' mortality or morbidity are investments, not insurance contracts. Mortality or morbidity risk exists if the insurance company is required to make payments or forgo required premiums contingent upon the death or disability (life insurance contracts) or continued survival of specific individuals or groups of individuals (annuity contracts). An investment contract, such as a guaranteed interest contract, generally provides for a set return on principal over a given time period.

Operating Assets

Operating assets, such as property, plant, equipment, and leasehold improvements, are reported at historical costs less accumulated depreciation/amortization. If such assets are held for investment rather than in operations, they should be a reported at fair value with other investments.

Liabilities

Liabilities for expenses related to investment purchases, trustee fees, and administrative fees should be accrued. Benefit obligations, however, should not be recorded by a defined benefit plan as a liability.

Statement of Changes in Net Assets Available for Benefits

Significant changes in net assets available for benefits should be identified in the statement of changes in net assets available for benefits (see Exhibit 14–4). Investment income, excluding realized or unrealized gains or losses, should be disclosed separately in reasonable detail. It is not necessary to report separately interest, dividends, etc. Realized and unrealized gains or losses on investments with quoted market values are reported separately from investments presented at otherwise determined fair value. The net change in fair value for each significant class of investments should be reported. Cash and noncash contributions from the employer, participants, and others should be reported separately at fair value. The nature of noncash contributions should be described in footnotes. Benefits paid to participants, as well as administrative or operating expenses, should be identified and reported separately. Payment for insurance contracts that are excluded from the plan's assets, such as allocated contracts, is reported separately. Dividend income from such contracts may be netted against the purchase price. Footnote disclosure should be made about the dividend income policy.

Actuarial Present Value of Plan Benefits

Certain information about the actuarial present value of accumulated plan benefits of participants must be disclosed. ASC 960-205-45-1 requires disclosure of vested and nonvested benefits. Vested benefits are not contingent upon future services by employees. The total actuarial present value of accumulated plan benefits may be divided into three categories:

1. Vested benefits of participants currently receiving payments, including benefits due and payable as of the benefit information date.

2. Vested benefits of other participants.

3. Nonvested benefits.

Exhibit 14-4: Statement of Changes in Net Assets Available for Benefits

Statement of Changes in Net Assets Available for Benefits
For Year Ended December 31, 20X2

Investment Income	
Interest	$ 325,000
Dividend	415,000
Rental income	225,000
Increases (decreases) in fair value of investments	575,000
Less: investment expenses	125,000
	1,415,000
Contributions	
Employees' contributions	685,000
Employer's contributions	1,200,000
	1,885,000
Benefits paid directly to participants	(877,000)
Annuity contracts purchased	(1,125,000)
Administrative expenses	(195,000)
	(2,197,000)
Net increase (decrease) in assets	1,103,000
Net assets available for benefits	
Beginning of year	18,357,000
End of year	$19,460,000

Exhibit 14-5: Statement of Accumulated Plan Benefits

Statement of Accumulated Plan Benefits
For Year Ended December 31, 20X2

Actuarial present value of vested benefits	
Participants currently receiving payments	$2,900,000
Other participants	1,700,000
	4,600,000
Actuarial present value of nonvested benefits	1,200,000
Total actuarial present value of accumulated plan benefits	$5,800,000

Benefit obligation information may be presented as a separate statement, such as that shown in Exhibit 14–3, on another statement, or in footnotes to financial statements. Benefit obligation information, however, is not a liability on the statement of net assets. It also should not be disclosed as supplementary information. It is preferable to present benefit obligation information as of year-end. If this is not feasible due to difficulties in making actuarial determinations, information may be presented as of the beginning of the plan's year. An interim date, however, may not be used.

ASC 960-205-45-1 assumes that the pension plan is a going concern and will continue to exist. Each actuarial assumption should be based on the plan's most likely expectations. The assumed rate of return should reflect the expected rate of return. It should be consistent with returns typically achieved on the types of assets held by the plan. The inflation rate assumed in determining the automatic cost-of-living adjustments should also be consistent with the assumed rates of return. Administrative expenses to be paid by the plan may be recognized using two methods. In the first method, the assumed rate of return may be adjusted to reflect administrative expenses (disclosure should be made about the adjustment). In the second, the administrative expenses may be assigned to the future and discounted to the benefit information date. The actuarial present value of accumulated plan benefits may alternatively be determined using the assumptions an insurance company would use if it were to issue a contract providing the same benefits to the same participants.

Pension plan benefits are usually based on years of service. Benefits can generally be determined through the provisions of the plan. However, if the benefits cannot be determined from the provisions, ASC 960-205-45-1 requires the use of the following formula to determine the benefits includable in vested benefits:

$$\text{Percentage of plan benefits accumulated} = \frac{\text{Number of years of service completed to the benefit information date}}{\text{Number of years service that will have been completed when the benefits will first be fully vested}}$$

For benefits not included in vested benefits, the following formula may be used:

$$\text{Percentage of plan benefits accumulated} = \frac{\text{Number of years of service completed to the benefit information date}}{\text{Number of years service upon anticipated separation from covered employment}}$$

Employees' history of earnings and service should be used to determine accumulated plan benefits. When benefits increase periodically, the employees' projected years of service should be used to determine death benefits, early retirement benefits, and disability benefits. Automatic benefit increases specified in the plan, even though subsequent to the benefit information date, should be recognized in determining accumulated plan benefits. Amendments adopted after the benefit information date do not affect the calculation of accumulated plan benefits. Benefits that will be provided by a contract should not be considered if the contract is excluded from the plan's financial statements. Social Security benefits may need to be determined in an integrated plan. It is assumed that the participant's pay will remain the same during his or her assumed service years. Scheduled or future changes in the wage base or benefit level are ignored under Social Security.

Changes in Actuarial Present Value of Plan Benefits

All factors affecting the actuarial present value of accumulated plan benefits should be identified, if significant either individually or in the aggregate, in the financial statements or the footnotes (see Exhibit 14–6). Such changes include amendments to the plan, changes in the nature of the plan (such as a merger with another plan or a spin-off of a plan), and changes in actuarial assumptions. Other factors, such as the amount of accumulated benefits, change in the discount period, and the amount of benefits paid, should be disclosed.

Exhibit 14-6: Statement of Changes Affecting Actuarial Present Value of Plan Benefits

Statement of Changes in Accumulated Plan Benefits
For Year Ended December 31, 20X2

Actuarial present value of accumulated plan benefits, beginning of year	$16,755,000
Amendments to plan	(425,000)
Changes in actuarial assumptions	385,000
Other factors	175,000
Actuarial present value of accumulated plan benefits, end of year	$16,890,000

Required Disclosures

GAAP requires defined benefit plans to make several disclosures. A plan should disclose its accounting policies, including assumptions and methods used to derive the fair value of investments and the reported value of insurance contracts. Disclosure should be made of significant assumptions and methods used to determine the actuarial present value of accumulated plan benefits, including the rates of return, the inflation rate, and the retirement age of participants. A description of the provisions of pension plan vesting and benefit provisions should be presented. If that information is available elsewhere, making a reference to that published source is also acceptable. Amendments adopted on or before the latest benefit information date, if significant, should be described. A disclosure, including the effect on present value of accumulated plan benefits, is required if significant amendments are adopted after the benefit information date but before the plan's year-end. Disclosure is required of the order of priority of participants' claims to plan assets upon termination. If benefits are guaranteed by the Pension Benefit Guaranty Corporation (PBGC), the disclosure should include this information and a description of the applicability of any PBGC guaranty to recent plan amendments.

If the employer is absorbing significant plan administration costs, this should be disclosed. Any changes in the plan's funding policy, including the method for determining participants' contributions, should be described. For plans subject to ERISA, whether the minimum funding requirements have been met or if a waiver has been granted or is pending must be discussed. Insurance contracts that are excluded from the plan's assets, as well as the plan's policy concerning these assets, should be disclosed. Disclosure should be made of whether or not a favorable determination letter has been obtained for federal income tax purposes, and the plan's federal income tax status. Disclosure is also required of all investments that represent 5% or more of a plan's net assets available for benefits. A disclosure should be made of any significant real estate or other transactions between the plan and the sponsor, employer, or the employee organization. Finally, disclosure is required of all unusual or infrequent events that occur after the latest benefit information date, but before the financial statements are issued, if these events are significant and have an effect on the plan's present and future ability to pay benefits.

EMPLOYERS' ACCOUNTING FOR POSTEMPLOYMENT BENEFITS

ASC 712-10-05-1 through 05-6, *Compensation—Nonretirement Postemployment Benefits: Overall*, provides authoritative guidance in accounting and reporting for postemployment benefits. It concerns benefits provided to former or inactive employees, their beneficiaries, and dependents after employment but before retirement. Former or inactive employees include individuals on disability and those that have been laid off. However, individuals on vacation or holiday or who are ill are not considered inactive.

Postemployment benefits differ from postretirement benefits. Post employment benefits may be in cash or in kind and include salary continuation benefits, supplemental unemployment benefits, severance benefits, disability-related benefits, job training and counseling benefits, life insurance benefits, and health care benefits.

Postemployment benefits that meet certain conditions require accrual. These conditions include the following:

☐ Benefits are related to services already performed.

☐ Benefit obligations vest or accumulate.

☐ Payment of benefits is probable.

☐ The amount of benefits can be reasonably estimated.

Postemployment benefits that do not meet the conditions of ASC 710-10-05-5 should be accounted for in accordance with ASC 450, *Contingencies*, if:

☐ It is probable that an asset has been impaired or liability incurred at the date of the financial statements based on information available prior to the issuance of financial statements.

☐ The amount of loss can be reasonably estimated.

If the amount cannot be estimated in accordance with ASC 710-10-05-5, the financial statements should disclose this information.

ASC 715-30-55-81, *Compensation—Retirement Benefits: Defined Benefit Plans— Pension*, applies to early retirement programs, which create incentives for employees, within a specific age group, to transition from full- or part-time employment to retirement before legal retirement age.

PROFIT SHARING PLANS

A profit sharing plan may be discretionary (contributions are at the discretion of the board of directors) or nondiscretionary (contributions are based on a predetermined formula and depend on attaining a specified level of profit). In a discretionary plan, an accrual of expense should be made when set by the board of directors. The entry is to debit profit sharing expense and credit accrued profit sharing liability. In a nondiscretionary plan, an accrual is made when required under the terms of the plan.

ANNUAL REPORT REFERENCES

Sara Lee
2011 Annual Report

Note 16. Defined Benefit Pension Plans

The corporation sponsors a number of U.S. and foreign pension plans to provide retirement benefits to certain employees. The benefits provided under these plans are based primarily on years of service and compensation levels.

Measurement Date and Assumptions A fiscal year end measurement date is utilized to value plan assets and obligations for all of the corporation's defined benefit pension plans. Prior to 2009 the corporation had utilized a measurement date of March 31.

The weighted average actuarial assumptions used in measuring the net periodic benefit cost and plan obligations of continuing operations were as follows:

	2011	2010	2009
U.S. Plans			
Net periodic benefit cost			
Discount rate	5.4 %	6.5 %	6.7 %
Long-term rate of return on plan assets	7.3	7.6	7.5
Rate of compensation increase	NA	3.5	3.8
Plan obligations			
Discount rate	5.6 %	5.4 %	6.5 %
Rate of compensation increase	NA	NA	3.5
International Plans			
Net periodic benefit cost			
Discount rate	5.2 %	6.4 %	6.1 %
Long-term rate of return on plan assets	6.7	6.6	6.7
Rate of compensation increase	3.3	3.3	3.3
Plan obligations			
Discount rate	5.6 %	5.2 %	6.4 %
Rate of compensation increase	3.1	3.3	3.3

The discount rate is determined by utilizing a yield curve based on high-quality fixed-income investments that have a AA bond rating to discount the expected future benefit payments to plan participants. Compensation increase assumptions are based upon historical experience and anticipated future management actions. Compensation changes for participants in the U.S. plans no longer have an impact on the benefit cost or plan obligations as the participants in the U.S. salaried plan will no longer accrue additional benefits. In determining the long-term rate of return on plan assets, the corporation assumes that the historical long-term compound growth rates of equity and fixed-income securities and other plan investments will predict the future returns of similar investments in the plan portfolio. Investment management and other fees paid out of plan assets are factored into the determination of asset return assumptions.

Net Periodic Benefit Cost and Funded Status The components of the net periodic benefit cost for continuing operations were as follows:

In millions	2011	2010	2009
U.S. Plans			
Components of defined benefit net periodic benefit cost			
Service cost	$7	$17	$21
Interest cost	73	74	69
Expected return on assets	(80)	(65)	(66)
Amortization of prior service cost	1	(2)	–
Net actuarial loss	12	33	(1)
Net periodic benefit cost	$13	$57	$23
International Plans			
Components of defined benefit net periodic benefit cost			
Service cost	$32	$31	$30
Interest cost	161	166	166
Expected return on assets	(198)	(176)	(180)
Amortization of prior service cost	5	7	8
Net actuarial loss	23	14	12
Net periodic benefit cost	$23	$42	$36

In the fourth quarter of 2011, certain modifications to the corporation's defined benefit plan in the Netherlands were approved. The modifications included changes to the method of benefit indexation and employee contribution and salary participation levels. The plan amendments resulted in a $24 million reduction in the projected benefit obligation with a corresponding offset to the unamortized prior service cost balance in Accumulated Other Comprehensive Income. The corporation also expects to make an additional € 60 million contribution to this plan in 2012 related to the agreed upon plan modifications.

In 2011, the corporation recognized a curtailment loss of $5 million associated with the fresh bakery businesses as a result of the expected decline in expected years of future service associated with the planned disposition of this business. This amount is being reported as part of the results of discontinued operations. See Note 5 – "Discontinued Operations" for additional information.

In March 2010, the corporation announced changes to its U.S. defined benefit pension plans for salaried employees whereby participants would no longer accrue benefits under these plans. All future retirement benefits will be provided through a defined contribution plan. The benefit plan changes resulted in the elimination of any expected years of future service associated with these plans. As a result, a pretax curtailment gain of $25 million was recognized, of which $20 million impacted continuing operations and $5 million impacted discontinued operations. The curtailment gain resulted from the recognition of $3 million of previously unamortized net prior service credits associated with these benefit plans as well as a $22 million reduction in the projected benefit obligation associated with one of the plans.

In 2010, the corporation also recognized a curtailment loss of $10 million associated with its household and body care businesses as a result of the expected decline in expected years of future service. This amount is being reported as part of the results of discontinued operations. See Note 5 – "Discontinued Operations" for additional information. The corporation also recognized a settlement loss of $2 million in 2009.

The net periodic benefit cost associated with the North American fresh bakery operations are recognized in discontinued operations as the buyer is expected to assume all of the pension liabilities associated with those businesses.

Although the results of the household and body care businesses are classified as discontinued operations, the corporation has retained a significant portion of the pension and postretirement medical obligations related to these businesses. However, the corporation will no longer incur service cost for the participants in these plans after these businesses are sold and this cost component is being recognized in discontinued operations, while the remainder of the net periodic benefit cost associated with these businesses is recognized in continuing operations. The net periodic benefit cost of the corporation's U.S. defined benefit pension plans in 2011 was $44 million lower than in 2010. The decrease was primarily due to an increase in expected return on assets due to an increase in plan assets resulting from improved assets returns as well as a $200 million contribution into the U.S. plans in the fourth quarter of 2010. The benefit costs were also favorably impacted by a reduction in service cost and amortization due to the freezing of the U.S salaried pension plan, which not only reduced the amount of actuarial loss to be amortized but also increased the period of time over which the amount is to being amortized.

The net periodic benefit cost of the corporation's U.S. defined benefit pension plans in 2010 was $34 million higher than in 2009. The increase was primarily due to a $34 million increase in amortization of net actuarial losses due to net actuarial losses in the prior year, which increased the amount subject to amortization; as well as the increase in interest expense due to the year-over-year change in projected benefit obligations.

The net periodic benefit cost of the corporation's international defined benefit pension plans in 2011 was $19 million lower than in 2010 due to a $22 million improvement in the expected return on assets partially offset by an increase in the amortization of actuarial losses resulting from actuarial losses in the prior year due to a decline in the discount rate. The 2010 expense was $6 million higher than the 2009 due to a decline in the expected return on assets.

The amount of prior service cost and net actuarial loss that is expected to be amortized from accumulated other comprehensive income and reported as a component of net periodic benefit cost in continuing operations during 2012 is $1 million and $2 million, respectively, for U.S. plans and $3 million and $9 million, respectively, for international plans. The funded status of defined benefit pension plans at the respective year-ends was as follows:

	U.S. Plans		International Plans	
In millions	2011	2010	2011	2010
Projected benefit obligation				
Beginning of year	$1,372	$1,172	$2,963	$2,689
Service cost	7	17	35	37
Interest cost	73	74	161	166
Plan amendments/other	8	–	(24)	–
Benefits paid	(63)	(63)	(151)	(143)
Participant contributions	–	–	2	3
Actuarial (gain) loss	(27)	207	(169)	500
Divestitures	–	–	(8)	–
Settlement/curtailment	–	(35)	(6)	(10)
Foreign exchange	–	–	310	(279)
End of year	$1,370	$1,372	$3,113	$2,963
Fair value of plan assets				
Beginning of year	$1,127	$857	$2,760	$2,652
Actual return on plan assets	179	177	241	397
Employer contributions	6	156	118	117
Participant contributions	–	–	2	3
Benefits paid	(63)	(63)	(151)	(143)
Divestitures	–	–	(5)	–
Settlement	–	–	–	(3)
Foreign exchange	–	–	307	(263)
End of year	1,249	1,127	3,272	2,760
Funded status	$(121)	(245)	$159	$(203)
Amounts recognized on the consolidated balance sheets				
Noncurrent asset	$7	–	$258	$7
Accrued liabilities	(6)	(5)	(3)	(1)
Pension obligation	(122)	(240)	(96)	(209)
Net asset (liability) recognized	$(121)	$(245)	$159	$(203)
Amounts recognized in accumulated other comprehensive income				
Unamortized prior service cost	$7	$4	$20	$45
Unamortized actuarial loss, net	215	353	500	679
Total	$222	$357	$520	$724

The underfunded status of the U.S. plans declined from $245 million in 2010 to $121 million in 2011, due to a $122 million increase in plan assets. The increase in plan assets was the result of the strong investment performance during the year.

The funded status of the international plans improved to an overfunded position of $159 million from a $203 million underfunded position in the prior year. The improvement was the result of actuarial gains, a strong investment performance and currency changes as a $512 million increase in plan assets was only partially offset by a $150 million increase in the projected benefit obligation.

The accumulated benefit obligation is the present value of pension benefits (whether vested or unvested) attributed to employee service rendered before the measurement date and based on employee service and compensation prior to that date. The accumulated benefit obligation differs from the projected benefit obligation in that it includes no assumption about future compensation levels. The accumulated benefit obligations of the corporation's pension plans as of the measurement dates in 2011 and 2010 were $1,370 million and $1,372 million, respectively, for the U.S. plans and $3,049 million and $2,875 million, respectively, for the international plans.

The projected benefit obligation, accumulated benefit obligation and fair value of plan assets for pension plans with accumulated benefit obligations in excess of plan assets were:

In millions	2011	2010
U.S. Plans		
Projected benefit obligation	$1,113	$1,372
Accumulated benefit obligation	1,113	1,372
Fair value of plan assets	987	1,127
International Plans		
Projected benefit obligation	$294	$1,466
Accumulated benefit obligation	283	1,439
Fair value of plan assets	206	1,268

Plan Assets, Expected Benefit Payments and Funding The fair value of pension plan assets as of July 2, 2011 for the combined U.S. and International plans was determined as follows:

In millions	Total Fair Value	Quoted Prices in Active Market for Identical Assets (Level 1)	Significant Other Observable Inputs (Level 2)
Equity securities			
Non-U.S. securities - pooled funds	$875	$875	–
Fixed income securities			
Government bonds	804	804	–
Corporate bonds	1,000	1,000	–
U.S. pooled funds	157	157	–
Non-U.S. pooled funds	1,247	665	582
Total fixed income securities	3,208	2,626	582
Real estate	93	93	–
Cash and equivalents	121	121	–
Derivatives	49	61	(12)
Other	175	175	–
Total fair value of assets	$4,521	$3,951	$570

Level 1 assets were valued using market prices based on daily net asset value (NAV) or prices available through a public stock exchange. Level 2 assets were valued primarily using market prices, derived from either an active market quoted price, which may require adjustments to account for the attributes of the asset, or an inactive market transaction. The corporation did not have any level 3 assets, which would include assets for which values are determined by non-observable inputs. See Note 15 – Financial Instruments for additional information as to the fair value hierarchy.

The percentage allocation of pension plan assets based on fair value as of the respective year-end measurement dates is as follows:

	2011	2010
U.S. Plans		
Asset category		
Equity securities	3 %	4 %
Debt securities	89	84
Real estate	2	2
Cash and other	6	10
Total	100 %	100 %
International Plans		
Asset category		
Equity securities	25 %	22 %
Debt securities	66	69
Real estate	2	3
Cash and other	7	6
Total	100 %	100 %

The overall investment objective is to manage the plan assets so that they are sufficient to meet the plan's future obligations while maintaining adequate liquidity to meet current benefit payments and operating expenses. The actual amount for which these obligations will be settled depends on future events and actuarial assumptions. These assumptions include the life expectancy of the plan participants and salary inflation. The resulting estimated future obligations are discounted using an interest rate curve that represents a return that would be required from high quality corporate bonds. The corporation has adopted a liability driven investment (LDI) strategy and it is in various stages of implementation of the strategy in each of its largest pension plans. This strategy consists of investing in a portfolio of assets whose performance is driven by the performance of the associated pension liability. This means that plan assets managed under an LDI strategy may underperform general market returns, but should provide for lower volatility of funded status as its return matches the pension liability movement. Over time, as pension obligations become better funded, the corporation will further de-risk its investments and increase the allocation to fixed income.

For plans outside the U.S., the investment strategy is also subject to local regulations. These specific circumstances result in a level of equity exposure that is typically higher than the U.S. plans. In aggregate, the asset allocation targets of the international plans are broadly categorized as a mix of 25% equity securities, 70% fixed-income securities and 5% of real estate and other investments.

As noted, the asset allocation varies by plan and, on an aggregate fair value basis, it is currently at 72% fixed income securities and 20% equity securities. On a notional value basis, the plan assets include investments in equity market futures which effectively moves the asset allocation to the established targets of 72% fixed income and 22% equity. Fixed income securities can include, but are not limited to, direct bond investments, pooled or indirect bond investments and cash. Other investments can include, but are not limited to, international and domestic equities, real estate, commodities and private equity. Derivative instruments may also be used in concert with either fixed income or equity investments to achieve desired exposure or to hedge certain risks. Derivative instruments can include, but are not limited to, futures, options, swaps or swaptions. The assets are managed by professional investment firms and performance is evaluated against specific benchmarks. The responsibility for the investment strategies typically lies with a committee and the composition of the committee depends on plan jurisdiction.

Pension assets at the 2011 and 2010 measurement dates do not include any direct investment in the corporation's debt or equity securities. Substantially all pension benefit payments are made from assets of the pension plans. Using foreign currency exchange rates as of July 2, 2011 and expected future service, it is anticipated that the future benefit payments for the combined U.S. and international plans will be as follows: $234 million in 2012, $222 million in 2013,

$228 million in 2014, $234 million in 2015, $243 million in 2016 and $1,344 million from 2017 to 2021.

As part of a previously announced capital plan, the corporation made a voluntary contribution of $200 million into its U.S. defined benefit pension plans in the fourth quarter of 2010. At the present time, the corporation expects to contribute approximately $200 million of cash to its pension plans in 2012, of which approximately $194 million is expected to be to its international plans.

During 2006, the corporation entered into an agreement with the plan trustee to fully fund certain U.K. pension obligations by the end of calendar 2015. The anticipated 2012 contributions reflect the amounts agreed upon with the trustees of these U.K. plans. Subsequent to 2015, the corporation has agreed to keep the U.K. plans fully funded in accordance with certain local funding standards. The exact amount of cash contributions made to pension plans in any year is dependent upon a number of factors including minimum funding requirements in the jurisdictions in which the company operates, the tax deductibility of amounts funded and arrangements made with the trustees of certain foreign plans.

Defined Contribution Plans The corporation sponsors defined contribution plans, which cover certain salaried and hourly employees. The corporation's cost is determined by the amount of contributions it makes to these plans. The amounts charged to expense for contributions made to these defined contribution plans related to continuing operations totaled $34 million in 2011, $31 million in 2010 and $29 million in 2009.

Multi-Employer Plans The corporation participates in multi-employer plans that provide defined benefits to certain employees covered by collective bargaining agreements. Such plans are usually administered by a board of trustees composed of the management of the participating companies and labor representatives. The net pension cost of these plans is equal to the annual contribution determined in accordance with the provisions of negotiated labor contracts. The contributions for plans related to continuing operations were $3 million in 2011, $4 million in 2010 and $5 million in 2009. Assets contributed to such plans are not segregated or otherwise restricted to provide benefits only to the employees of the corporation. The future cost of these plans is dependent on a number of factors including the funded status of the plans and the ability of the other participating companies to meet ongoing funding obligations.

In addition to regular contributions, the corporation could be obligated to pay additional contributions (known as complete or partial withdrawal liabilities) if a multi-employer pension plan (MEPP) has unfunded vested benefits. The corporation recognized a partial withdrawal liability of $22 million in 2010 related to one collective bargaining agreement and recognized a partial withdrawal liability of $31 million in 2009 as a result of the cessation of contributions to a MEPP with respect to one collective bargaining unit. The charges for both years were recognized in the results of discontinued operations in the Consolidated Statements of Income as they both related to the North American fresh bakery business.

Omnova Solutions
2011 Annual Report

Note O—Employee Benefit Plans

The Company maintains a number of defined benefit and defined contribution plans to provide retirement benefits for employees. These plans are maintained and contributions are made in accordance with the Employee Retirement Income Security Act of 1974 ("ERISA"), local statutory law or as determined by the Board of Directors. The plans generally provide benefits based upon years of service and compensation. Pension plans are funded except for a domestic non-qualified pension plan for certain key employees and certain foreign plans. The Company uses a November 30 measurement date for its plans.

Effective November 30, 2009, the Company adopted authoritative guidance issued by the Financial Accounting Standards Board ("FASB") related to measurement of pension and other post-retirement benefit plans, which requires the Company to measure the assets and obligations of its pension and other post-retirement benefit plans as of the balance sheet date. Accordingly, during 2009 the Company changed the measurement date of its pension and other post-retirement benefit plans from August 31 to November 30.

Defined Benefit Plans

The Company's defined benefits plans generally provide benefits based on years of service and compensation for salaried employees and under negotiated non-wage based formulas for union-represented employees. The plans are funded except for a domestic non-qualified pension plan for certain key employees and certain foreign plans.

Changes in benefit obligations and plan assets are as follows:

	2011	2010
	(Dollars in millions)	
Change in Benefit Obligation		
Benefit obligation at beginning of year	$244.6	$229.6
Service cost	1.7	1.6
Interest cost	14.2	13.4
Curtailment	–	2.9
Actuarial loss	6.9	11.2
Acquisitions	7.2	–
Benefits paid net of retiree contributions	(15.0)	(14.1)
Exchange rate changes	(.2)	–
Benefit Obligation at End of Year	$259.4	$ 244.6
Change in Plan Assets		
Fair value of plan assets at beginning of year	$171.1	$163.7
Actual return on assets	8.4	16.4
Employer contributions	3.1	5.1
Acquisitions	.2	–

	2011	2010
	(Dollars in millions)	
Benefits and expenses paid net of retiree contributions	(15.0)	(14.1)
Fair Value of Plan Assets at End of Year	$167.8	$ 171.1
Funded Status at November 30	$ (91.6)	$ (73.5)
Amounts Recognized in the Consolidated Balance Sheets		
Current liability	$ (.4)	$ (.1)
Non-current liability	(91.5)	(73.3)
Net Amount Recognized	$ (91.9)	$ (73.4)

As of November 30, 2011 and 2010, the amounts included in Accumulated Other Comprehensive Loss that have not yet been recognized in net periodic benefit cost consist of:

	2011	2010
	(Dollars in millions)	
Net actuarial (loss) gain	$(118.2)	$ (107.0)
Prior service (costs) credit	–	$ (.2)

The after-tax amount of unrecognized net actuarial loss at November 30, 2011 was $112.3 million. The estimated net loss for defined benefit plans that will be amortized from Accumulated Other Comprehensive Loss during 2012 is $3.1 million.

Net Periodic Benefit Cost

	2011	2010	2009
	(Dollars in millions)		
Net Periodic Benefit Cost			
Service costs for benefits earned	$ 1.7	$ 1.6	$ 2.8
Interest costs on benefit obligation	14.2	13.4	14.2
Amortization of prior service costs	.1	.6	.7
Assumed return on plan assets	(15.0)	(15.6)	(15.7)
Amortization of net loss	2.3	4.0	1.6
Curtailment loss (gain)	.1	4.2	(.8)
Total	$ 3.4	$ 8.2	$ 2.8

The Company made $3.1 million and $5.1 million in contributions to this plan during 2011 and 2010, respectively. The Company anticipates that it will be required to make a contribution to its pension plans of approximately $7.9 million in 2012. The Company anticipates pension expense to be approximately $4.1 million in 2012.

During the fourth quarter of 2011, for its Jeannette, Pennsylvania union-represented employees, the Company suspended the accrual of future service benefits under its U.S. Consolidated Pension Plan, effectively freezing future service benefits for all participants in the Company's U.S. Consolidated Pension Plan. As a result, during 2011, the Company recognized a curtailment loss of $0.1 million. The Company also recognized curtailment losses of $4.2 million in 2010 and curtailment gains of $0.8 million in 2009 related to prior actions which froze future service benefits for other participants in this plan.

All benefits earned by affected employees through the effective dates have become fully vested with the affected employees eligible to receive benefits upon retirement, as described in the Plan document.

Estimated future benefit payments to retirees from the Company's U.S. pension trust are as follows: 2012—$15.2 million, 2013—$15.5 million, 2014—$15.8 million, 2015—$16.1 million, 2016—$16.2 million, 2017—2021—$87.0 million.

Information regarding pension plans with accumulated benefit obligations in excess of plan assets is as follows:

	2011	2010
	(Dollars in millions)	
U.S. Pension Plans		
Projected benefit obligation	$250.3	$244.0
Accumulated benefit obligation	250.3	244.0
Fair value of plan assets	167.6	171.1
Non-U.S. Pension Plans		
Projected benefit obligation	$ 8.8	$ .5
Accumulated benefit obligation	7.1	.4
Fair value of plan assets	.2	–

Assumptions. Weighted average assumptions used to measure the benefit obligation for the Company's defined benefit plans as of November 30, 2011 and 2010 were as follows:

	Pension Plans	
	2011	2010
Weighted Average Assumptions		
Discount rate used for liability determination	5.52 %	5.83 %
Annual rates of salary increase (non-U.S. plans)	3.07 %	4.0 %
Measurement date	11/30	11/30

Weighted average assumptions used to measure the net periodic benefit cost for the Company's defined benefit plans as of November 30, 2011, 2010 and 2009 were as follows:

	Pension Plans		
	2011	2010	2009
Net Periodic Benefit Cost			
Service costs for benefits earned	5.8 %	6.05 %	7.24 %
Interest costs on benefit obligation	8.0 %	8.0 %	8.0 %
Amortization of prior service costs	2.37 %	4.0 %	4.0 %

The discount rate reflects the current rate at which the pension liabilities could be effectively settled at the end of the year. The discount rate used considers a yield derived from matching projected pension payments with maturities of a portfolio of available non-callable bonds that receive one of the two highest ratings given by a recognized investment ratings agency. The decrease in the discount rate in 2011 and 2010 is due to lower yields for these types of investments as a result of the economic environment. The assumed long-term rate of return on plan assets assumption is based on the weighted average expected return of the various asset classes in the plans' portfolio. The asset class return is developed using historical asset return performance as well as current market conditions such as inflation, interest rates and equity market performance. The rate of compensation increase is based on managements' estimates using historical experience and expected increases in rates.

Pension Plans Assets

The Company's defined benefit plans are funded primarily through asset trusts, insurance contracts or through general assets of the Company. The Company employs a total return on investments approach for its U.S. defined benefit pension plan assets. A mix of equity securities, fixed income securities and alternative investments are used to maximize the long-term rate of return on assets for the level of risk. Asset allocation at November 30, 2011, target allocation for 2011 and expected long-term rate of return by asset category are as follows:

	Target Allocation 2011	Percentage of Plan Assets at November 30,		Weighted-Average Expected Long-Term Rate Of Return
		2011	2010	
Equity securities	53 %	52 %	51 %	5.1 %
Fixed income securities	25 %	24 %	22 %	1.0 %
Real estate partnerships	5 %	4 %	4 %	.4 %
Other	17 %	20 %	23 %	1.5 %
Total	100 %	100 %	100 %	8.0 %

Included in Other are short-term money funds and hedge funds.

The following table sets forth, by level within the fair value hierarchy, the U.S. defined benefit plans' assets at November 30, 2011:

	Total	Level 1	Level 2	Level 3
		(Dollars in millions)		
Money market funds	$ .1	$ .1	–	–
Registered investment companies:				
Equity mutual funds	86.3	86.3	–	–
Fixed income mutual funds	40.9	40.9	–	–
Registered Investment companies	127.2	127.2	–	–
Collective trust funds:				
Private investment funds	9.4	–	–	9.4
Collateralized loan obligations	23.5	–	–	23.5
Collective trust funds	32.9	–	–	32.9
Real estate partnerships	7.3	–	–	7.3
	$ 167.5	$ 127.3	–	$ 40.2

Money market funds are valued at a net asset value (NAV) of $1.00 per share held by the plan at year end, which approximates fair value.

Registered investment companies are valued at quoted market prices representing the NAV of shares held by the Plan at year end.

The fair value of the participation units owned by the Plan in the collective trust funds are based on the NAV of participating units held by the Plan at year end.

Investments in real estate partnerships are valued at the fair value of the underlying assets based on comparable sales value for similar assets, discounted cash flow models, appraisals and other valuation techniques.

The preceding methods described may produce a fair value calculation that may not be indicative of net realizable value or reflective of future fair values. Furthermore, although the Company believes its valuation methods are appropriate and consistent with other market participants, the use of different methodologies or assumptions to determine the fair value of certain financial instruments could result in a different fair value measurement at the reporting date.

A reconciliation of beginning and ending Level 3 measurements is as follows:

	Total	Collective Trusts	Real Estate Partnerships
		(Dollars in millions)	
Beginning balance, December 1, 2009	$ 48.6	$ 39.3	$ 9.3
Settlements	(6.3)	(6.3)	–
Total gains or losses included in funded status	3.4	5.4	(2.0)

	Total	Collective Trusts	Real Estate Partnerships
		(Dollars in millions)	
Ending balance, November 30, 2010	$ 45.7	$ 38.4	$ 7.3
Settlements	(8.9)	(8.9)	–
Total gains or losses included in funded status	3.4	3.4	–
Ending balance, November 30, 2011	$ 40.2	$ 32.9	$ 7.3

The following table sets forth a summary of the Plan's investments with a reported NAV as of November 30, 2011 (dollars in millions).

	Fair Value
SEI Structured Credit Collective Fund[a]	$23.5
SEI Opportunity Collective Fund[b]	$ 9.4

[a] The SEI Structured Credit Collective Fund seeks to provide high general returns by investing in collateralized debt obligations ("CDO's") and other structured credit instruments. The SEI Structured Credit Collective Fund requires a two-year non-redemption period after which investments can be redeemed at any time, however a 90 day redemption notification period is required. The Plan has satisfied all funding obligations related to this investment and has surpassed the two-year non-redemption period.

[b] The SEI Opportunity Collective Fund seeks to provide returns that are less correlated with investments in traditional asset classes and that provide a return that falls somewhere between stocks and bonds while incurring bond-like risk. Investment in the SEI Opportunity Collective Fund can be redeemed at any time; however, a 90 day redemption notification period is required. The Plan has satisfied all funding obligations related to this investment.

Defined Contribution Plans

The Company also sponsors a defined contribution 401(k) plan. Participation in this plan is available to substantially all U.S. salaried employees and to certain groups of U.S. hourly employees. Company contributions to this plan are based on either a percentage of employee contributions or on a specified amount per hour based on the provisions of the applicable collective bargaining agreement. All Company contributions are made with Company stock. The Company suspended the Company match provisions of this plan for all salaried employees between November 7, 2008 and August 14, 2009. The non-cash cost of this plan for the Company was approximately $1.8 million in 2011, $1.7 million in 2010 and $1.0 million in 2009. The defined contribution 401(k) plan contained approximately 1.9 million shares at both November 30, 2011 and 2010 of the Company's common stock.

Health Care Plans

The Company provides retiree medical plans for certain active and retired U.S. employees of which there were 956 participants as of November 30, 2011. The plans generally provide for cost sharing in the form of retiree contributions, deductibles and coinsurance between the Company and its retirees, and a fixed cost cap on the amount the Company pays annually to provide future retiree medical coverage. These post-retirement benefits are unfunded and are accrued by the date the employee becomes eligible for the benefits. Retirees in certain other countries are provided similar benefits by plans sponsored by their governments.

Because the Company's retiree health care benefits are capped, assumed health care cost trend rates have a minimal effect on the amounts reported for the retiree health care plans. A one-percentage point increase/decrease in assumed health care cost trend rates would not significantly increase or decrease the benefit obligation at November 30, 2011 and would have no effect on the aggregate of the service and interest components of the net periodic cost. Changes in benefit obligations are as follows:

	2011	2010
	(Dollars in millions)	
Change in Benefit Obligation		
Benefit obligation at beginning of year	$ 8.7	$ 9.6
Service cost	–	.1
Interest cost	.4	.5
Curtailment	–	(.8)
Actuarial loss	.2	.4
Benefits paid net of retiree contributions	(.6)	(1.1)
Benefit Obligation at End of Year	$ 8.7	$ 8.7
Change in Plan Assets		
Fair value of plan assets at beginning of year	–	–
Employer contributions	.6	1.1
Benefits and expenses paid net of retiree contributions	(.6)	(1.1)
Fair Value of Plan Assets at End of Year	$ –	$ –
Funded Status at November 30	$ (8.7)	$ (8.7)
Amounts Recognized in the Consolidated Balance Sheets		
Current liability	$ (.9)	$ (1.0)
Non-current liability	(7.8)	(7.7)
Net Amount Recognized	$ (8.7)	$ (8.7)

As of November 30, 2011 and 2010, the amounts included in Accumulated Other Comprehensive Loss that have not yet been recognized in net periodic benefit cost consist of:

	2011	2010
	(Dollars in millions)	
Net actuarial gain	$19.6	$21.6
Prior service credit	$ .9	$ 1.2

Net Periodic Benefit Cost

	2011	2010	2009
	(Dollars in millions)		
Net Periodic Benefit Cost			
Service costs for benefits earned	$ .1	$ .1	$ .1
Interest costs on benefit obligation	.4	.5	.7
Amortization of prior service credits	(.3)	(.3)	(.3)
Amortization of net gain	(1.9)	(2.3)	(2.4)
Curtailment gain	–	(.8)	–
Total	$(1.7)	$(2.8)	$(1.9)

Estimated future benefit payments and Medicare Part D subsidies for the retiree health care plans are as follows:

	Benefit Payments	Medicare Part D Subsidy
	(Dollars in millions)	
2012	$ 1.0	$ .2
2013	$ 1.0	$ .2
2014	$ 1.0	$ .2
2015	$ 1.0	$ .2
2016	$ 1.0	$ .2
2017 — 2021	$ 4.3	$ .9

The Company expects to record non-cash retiree medical health care income of approximately $1.5 million in 2011.

The estimated net gain and prior service credit for retiree medical plans that will be amortized from Accumulated Other Comprehensive Loss during 2012 are $1.7 million and $0.3 million, respectively.

Assumptions

	2011	2010	2009
Weighted Average Assumptions			
Discount rate used for liability determination	5.18 %	4.90 5	6.05 %
Discount rate used for expense determination	4.9 %	6.05 %	7.36 %
Current trend rate for health care costs	8.0 %	8.2 %	8.4 %

	2011	*2010*	*2009*
Ultimate trend rate for health care costs	4.5 %	4.5 %	4.5 %
Year reached	2028	2028	2028
Measurement date	11/30	11/30	11/30

The discount rate reflects the current rate at which the retiree medical liabilities could be effectively settled at the end of the year. The discount rate used considers a yield derived from matching projected health care payments with maturities of a portfolio of available non-callable bonds that receive one of the two highest ratings given by a recognized investment ratings agency. The decrease in the discount rate in 2011 and 2010 is due to lower yields for these types of investments as a result of the economic environment.

Walt Disney
2011 Annual Report

11. Pension and Other Benefit Programs

The Company maintains pension and postretirement medical benefit plans covering most of its employees not covered by union or industry-wide plans. Employees generally hired after January 1, 1994 and employees generally hired after January 1, 1987 for certain of our media businesses are not eligible for postretirement medical benefits. With respect to its defined benefit pension plans, the Company's policy is to fund, at a minimum, the amount necessary on an actuarial basis to provide for benefits in accordance with the requirements of the Employee Retirement Income Security Act of 1974, as amended by the Pension Protection Act of 2006 (PPA). Pension benefits are generally based on years of service and/or compensation.

In fiscal 2011, the Company substantially amended its salaried employees pension plans with respect to benefits earned for service after December 31, 2011. The Company reduced the vesting requirement from five years of vesting service to three years of vesting service, revised the early retirement reduction factors and excluded employees hired after December 31, 2011 from plan participation. In addition, the percentage of average monthly compensation on which salary-related benefits are based was reduced while overtime, commissions and regular bonus amounts were added to the calculation of average monthly compensation received after December 31, 2011 to the extent those elements of compensation were not previously included. These amendments will reduce fiscal 2012 expense by approximately $75 million. The Company intends to provide benefits under new defined contribution plans for employees who begin service after December 31, 2011.

The following chart summarizes the benefit obligations, assets, funded status and balance sheet impacts associated with the pension and postretirement medical benefit plans based upon the actuarial valuations prepared as of October 1, 2011 and October 2, 2010.

	Pension Plans		Postretirement Medical Plans	
	October 1, 2011	October 2, 2010	October 1, 2011	October 2, 2010
Projected benefit obligations				
Beginning obligations	$(8,084)	$(6,992)	$(1,280)	$(1,227)
Service cost	(293)	(263)	(18)	(21)
Interest cost	(411)	(396)	(66)	(70)
Actuarial (loss) / gain	(919)	(641)	(242)	7
Plan amendments and other	8	16	–	–
Benefits paid	218	192	28	31
Ending obligations	$(9,481)	$(8,084)	$(1,578)	$(1,280)
Fair value of plans' assets				
Beginning fair value	$ 5,684	$ 4,833	$311	$ 297
Actual return on plan assets	188	649	11	34
Contributions	926	421	9	12
Benefits paid	(218)	(192)	(28)	(31)
Expenses	(29)	(27)	(1)	(1)
Ending fair value	$ 6,551	$ 5,684	$302	$ 311
Underfunded status of the plans	$(2,930)	$(2,400)	$(1,276)	$ (969)
Amounts recognized in the balance sheet				
Non-current assets	$ 50	$40	$ –	$ –
Current liabilities	(18)	(17)	(15)	(14)
Non-current liabilities	(2,962)	(2,423)	(1,261)	(955)
	$(2,930)	$(2,400)	$(1,276)	$(969)

The components of net periodic benefit cost and key assumptions are as follows:

	Pension Plans			Postretirement Medical Plans		
	2011	2010	2009	2011	2010	2009
Service costs	$293	$263	$164	$18	$21	$17
Interest costs	411	396	363	66	70	71
Expected return on plan assets	(440)	(415)	(370)	(24)	(26)	(26)
Amortization of prior year service costs	14	14	14	(1)	(2)	(2)
Recognized net actuarial (gain)/loss	230	154	(9)	9	7	(8)
Net periodic benefit cost	$508	$412	$162	$68	$70	$52

	Pension Plans			Postretirement Medical Plans		
	2011	2010	2009	**2011**	2010	2009
Assumptions:						
Discount rate	**4.75 %**	5.25 %	5.75 %	**4.75 %**	5.25 %	5.75 %
Rate of return on plan assets	**7.75 %**	7.75 %	7.75 %	**7.75 %**	7.75 %	7.75 %
Salary increases	**4.00 %**	4.00 %	4.50 %	**n/a**	n/a	n/a
Year 1 increase in cost of benefits	n/a	n/a	n/a	**8.00 %**	8.25 %	8.50 %
Rate of increase to which the cost of benefits is assumed to decline (the ultimate trend rate)	n/a	n/a	n/a	**4.50 %**	4.75 %	5.00 %
Year that the rate reaches the ultimate trend rate	n/a	n/a	n/a	**2025**	2022	2019

Net periodic benefit cost is based on assumptions determined at the prior-year end measurement date.

Accumulated other comprehensive loss, before tax, as of October 1, 2011 consists of the following amounts that have not yet been recognized in net periodic benefit cost:

	Pension Plans	Postretirement Medical Plans	Total
Unrecognized prior service (cost) / credit	$(46)	$7	$(39)
Unrecognized net actuarial loss	(3,749)	(405)	(4,154)
Total amounts included in accumulated other comprehensive loss	(3,795)	(398)	(4,193)
Prepaid / (accrued) pension cost	865	(878)	(13)
Net balance sheet liability	$(2,930)	$(1,276)	$(4,206)

Amounts included in accumulated other comprehensive loss, before tax, as of October 1, 2011 that are expected to be recognized as components of net periodic benefit cost during fiscal 2012 are:

	Pension Plans	Postretirement Medical Plans	Total
Prior service (cost) / credit	$(11)	$2	$(9)
Net actuarial loss	(308)	(31)	(339)
Total	$(319)	$(29)	$(348)

Plan Funded Status

The projected benefit obligation, accumulated benefit obligation and aggregate fair value of plan assets for pension plans with accumulated benefit obligations in excess of plan assets were $8.7 billion, $8.1 billion and $5.7 billion, respectively, as of October 1, 2011 and $7.3 billion, $6.8 billion and $4.9 billion as of October 2, 2010, respectively.

For pension plans with projected benefit obligations in excess of plan assets, the projected benefit obligation and aggregate fair value of plan assets were $8.7 billion and $5.7 billion, respectively, as of October 1, 2011 and $7.3 billion and $4.9 billion as of October 2, 2010, respectively.

The Company's total accumulated pension benefit obligations at October 1, 2011 and October 2, 2010 were $8.8 billion and $7.5 billion, respectively, of which 97% for both years was vested.

The accumulated postretirement medical benefit obligations and fair value of plan assets for postretirement medical plans with accumulated postretirement medical benefit obligations in excess of plan assets were $1.6 billion and $0.3 billion, respectively, at October 1, 2011 and $1.3 billion and $0.3 billion, respectively, at October 2, 2010.

Plan Assets

A significant portion of the assets of the Company's defined benefit plans are managed on a commingled basis in a third party master trust. The investment policy and allocation of the assets in the master trust were approved by the Company's Investment and Administrative Committee which has oversight responsibility for the Company's retirement plans. The investment policy ranges for the major asset classes are as follows:

Asset Class	Minimum	Maximum
Equity investments		
Small cap	0%	10%
Mid/Large cap	15%	30%
International	7%	27%
Total equity investments	36%	60%
Fixed income investments	20%	40%
Alternative investments		
Diversified	0%	10%
Distressed	0%	10%
Private equity/Venture capital	0%	12%
Real estate	0%	15%
Total alternative investments	15%	30%
Cash	0%	5%

The primary investment objective for the assets within the master trust is to prudently and cost effectively manage assets to fulfill benefit obligations to plan participants. Financial risks are managed through diversification of plan assets, selection of investment managers and through the investment guidelines incorporated into investment management agreements. Assets are monitored to ensure that investment returns are commensurate with risks taken.

The long-term asset allocation policy for the master trust was established taking into consideration a variety of factors that include, but are not limited to, the average age of participants, the number of retirees, the duration of liabilities and the expected payout ratio. Liquidity needs of the master trust are generally managed using cash generated by investments or by liquidating securities.

Assets are generally managed by external investment managers and we have investment management agreements with respect to securities in the master trust. These agreements include account guidelines that establish permitted securities and risk controls commensurate with the account's investment strategy. Some agreements permit the use of derivative securities (futures, options, interest rate swaps, credit default swaps) that enable investment managers to enhance returns and manage exposures within their accounts. Investment managers are prohibited from using derivatives to leverage returns.

The Company's defined benefit plans asset mix (including assets held outside of the master trust) at each fiscal year end is as follows:

Asset Class	2011	2010
Equities:		
Small cap	3%	5%
Mid cap	3%	4%
Large cap	14%	17%
International	21%	18%
Fixed income:		
Corporate bonds	10%	10%
Government and federal agency bonds, notes and mortgage-backed securities (MBS)	21%	20%
Mortgage and asset-backed securities	4%	3%
Alternatives investments:		
Diversified	8%	9%
Distressed	3%	3%
Private equity	7%	6%
Venture capital	1%	1%
Real estate	4%	3%
Cash	1%	1%
Total	100%	100%

(1) Large cap domestic equities include 2.8 million shares of Company common stock valued at $85 million (1% of total plan assets) and $93 million (2% of total plan assets) at 2011 and 2010, respectively.

Fair Value Measurements of Plan Assets

Fair value is defined as the amount that would be received for selling an asset or paid to transfer a liability in an orderly transaction between market participants.

The Company's defined benefit plan assets carried at fair value are classified in the following categories:

- Level 1 – Quoted prices for identical instruments in active markets
- Level 2 – Quoted prices for similar instruments in active markets; quoted prices for identical or similar instruments in markets that are not active; and model-derived valuations in which all significant inputs and significant value drivers are observable in active markets
- Level 3 – Valuations derived from valuation techniques in which one or more significant inputs or significant value drivers are unobservable

Following is a description of the valuation methodologies used for assets reported at fair value. There have been no changes in the methodologies used at October 1, 2011 and October 2, 2010.

Level 1 investments are valued based on observable market prices on the last trading day of the year. Investments in common and preferred stocks are valued based on the securities exchange-listed price or a broker's quote in an active market. Investments in U.S. Treasury securities are valued based on a broker's quote in an active market.

Level 2 investments are valued at estimated fair value at year-end. Investments in certain government and federal agency bonds, mortgage-backed and asset-backed securities, and corporate bonds are valued using a broker's quote in a non-active market or an evaluated price based on a compilation of observable market information, such as benchmark yield curves, credit spreads and estimated default rates. Derivative financial instruments are valued based on models that incorporate observable inputs for the underlying securities, such as interest rates. Shares in money market and mutual funds are valued at the net asset value of the shares held by the Plan at year-end based on the fair value of the underlying investments.

Level 3 investments primarily consist of investments in limited partnerships, which are valued based on the Master Trust's pro-rata share of partnership holdings as of year-end. The fair value of the underlying investments are estimated using significant unobservable inputs (e.g., discounted cash flow models or relative valuation methods that incorporate comparable market information such as earnings and cash flow multiples from similar publicly traded companies or real estate properties).

The Company's defined benefit plan assets are summarized in the following table by the categories described above.

	Fair Value Measurements at October 1, 2011			
Description	Level 1	Level 2	Level 3	Total
Equities:				
Small cap	$ 35	$ 196	$ –	$ 231
Mid cap	208	–	–	208
Large cap	707	267	–	974
International	1,162	260	–	1,422
Fixed income				
Corporate bonds	–	673	–	673
Government and federal agency bonds, notes and MBS	440	989	–	1,429
Mortgage and asset-backed securities	2	241	–	243
Alternative investments				
Diversified	63	298	171	532
Distressed	–	–	228	228
Private equity	–	–	492	492
Venture capital	–	–	75	75
Real estate	–	–	263	263
Derivatives and other	–	10	–	10
Cash	23	50	–	73
Total	$ 2,640	$2,984	$1,229	$ 6,853

	Fair Value Measurements at October 2, 2010			
Description	Level 1	Level 2	Level 3	Total
Equities:				
Small cap	$ 27	$ 242	$ –	$ 269
Mid cap	212	–	–	212
Large cap	730	304	–	1,034
International	906	160	–	1,066
Fixed income				
Corporate bonds	–	610	–	610
Government and federal agency bonds, notes and MBS	141	1,053	–	1,194
Mortgage and asset-backed securities	–	199	–	199
Alternative investments				
Diversified	73	257	166	496
Distressed	–	–	196	196
Private equity	–	–	377	377
Venture capital	–	–	59	59
Real estate	–	–	179	179
Derivatives and other	–	20	–	20

Description	Fair Value Measurements at October 2, 2010			
	Level 1	Level 2	Level 3	Total
Cash	13	71	–	84
Total	$2,102	$2,916	$977	$5,995

Changes in Level 3 assets for the years ended October 1, 2011 and October 2, 2010 are as follows:

	Alternative Investments					
	Diversified	Distressed	Private Equity	Venture Capital	Real Estate	Total
Balance at October 3, 2009	$109	$106	$274	$56	$142	$687
Additions	46	80	97	9	70	302
Distributions	(3)	(14)	(25)	(7)	(14)	(63)
Unrealized Gain (Loss)	14	24	31	1	(19)	51
Balance at October 2, 2010	$166	$196	$377	$59	$179	$977
Additions	7	34	148	10	66	265
Distributions	(6)	(24)	(66)	(3)	(21)	(120)
Unrealized Gain (Loss)	4	22	33	9	39	107
Balance at October 1, 2011	$171	$228	$492	$75	$263	$1,229

Uncalled Capital Commitments

Alternative investments held by the master trust include interests in certain limited partnerships that have rights to make capital calls to the limited partner investors. In such cases, the Master Trust would be contractually obligated to make a cash capital contribution to the limited partnership at the time of a capital call. At October 1, 2011, the total committed capital still uncalled and unpaid was $462 million.

Plan Contributions

During fiscal 2011, the Company made contributions to its pension and postretirement medical plans totaling $935 million, which included discretionary contributions above the minimum requirements for pension plans. The Company currently expects pension and postretirement medical plan contributions in fiscal 2012 to total approximately $325 million to $375 million. Final minimum funding requirements for fiscal 2012 will be determined based on our January 1, 2012 funding actuarial valuation which will be available in late fiscal 2012.

Estimated Future Benefit Payments

The following table presents estimated future benefit payments for the next ten fiscal years:

	Pension Plans	Postretirement Medical Plans[1]
2012	$273	$39
2013	293	42
2014	319	46
2015	342	49
2016	368	53
2017 - 2021	2,333	340

[1] Estimated future benefit payments are net of expected Medicare subsidy receipts of $64 million.

Assumptions

Actuarial assumptions, such as the discount rate, long-term rate of return on plan assets and the healthcare cost trend rate, have a significant effect on the amounts reported for net periodic benefit cost as well as the related benefit obligations.

Discount rate—The assumed discount rate for pension and postretirement medical plans reflects the market rates for high-quality corporate bonds currently available. The Company's discount rate was determined by considering the average of pension yield curves constructed of a large population of high quality corporate bonds. The resulting discount rate reflects the matching of plan liability cash flows to the yield curves.

Long-term rate of return on plan assets—The long-term rate of return on plan assets represents an estimate of long-term returns on an investment portfolio consisting of a mixture of equities, fixed income and alternative investments. When determining the long-term rate of return on plan assets, the Company considers long-term rates of return on the asset classes (both historical and forecasted) in which the Company expects the pension funds to be invested. The following long-term rates of return by asset class were considered in setting the long-term rate of return on plan assets assumption:

Equity Securities	9% - 11%
Debt Securities	4% - 7%
Alternative Investments	6% - 14%

Healthcare cost trend rate—The Company reviews external data and its own historical trends for healthcare costs to determine the healthcare cost trend rates for the postretirement medical benefit plans. For the 2011 actuarial valuation, we assumed an 8.00% annual rate of increase in the per capita cost of covered healthcare claims with the rate decreasing in even increments over fourteen years until reaching 4.50%.

Sensitivity—A one percentage point (ppt) change in the key assumptions would have had the following effects on the projected benefit obligations as of October 1, 2011 and on cost for fiscal 2012:

	Discount Rate		Expected Long-Term Rate of Return On Assets	Assumed Healthcare Cost Trend Rate	
Increase/(decrease)	Benefit Expense	Projected Benefit Obligations	Benefit Expense	Net Periodic Postretirement Medical Cost	Projected Benefit Obligations
1 ppt decrease	$223	$1,876	$ 9	$(38)	$(228)
1 ppt increase	(193)	(1,589)	(69)	54	285

Multi-employer Plans

The Company participates in various multi-employer pension plans under union and industry-wide agreements. In fiscal 2011, 2010 and 2009, the contributions to these plans, which are expensed as incurred, were $59 million, $60 million and $52 million, respectively.

Defined Contribution Plans

The Company has savings and investment plans that allow eligible employees to allocate up to 50% of their salary through payroll deductions depending on the plan in which the employee participates. The Company matches 50% of the employee's pre-tax contribution up to plan limits. In fiscal 2011, 2010 and 2009, the costs of these plans were $59 million, $54 million and $51 million, respectively.

Schlumberger
2011 Annual Report

18. Pension and Other Benefit Plans Pension Plans

Schlumberger sponsors several defined benefit pension plans that cover substantially all US employees hired prior to October 1, 2004. The benefits are based on years of service and compensation, on a career-average pay basis.

In addition to the United States defined benefit pension plans, Schlumberger sponsors several other international defined benefit pension plans. The most significant of these international plans are the International Staff Pension Plan and the UK pension plan (collectively, the "International plans"). The International Staff Pension Plan covers certain international employees and is based on years of service and compensation on a career-average pay basis. The UK plan covers employees hired prior to April 1, 1999, and is based on years of service and compensation, on a final salary basis.

The weighted-average assumed discount rate, compensation increases and the expected long-term rate of return on plan assets used to determine the net pension cost for the US and International plans were as follows:

	US			International		
	2011	*2010*	*2009*	*2011*	*2010*	*2009*
Discount rate	**5.50%**	6.00%	6.94%	**5.47%**	5.89%	6.81%

	US			International		
Compensation increases	**4.00%**	4.00%	4.00%	**4.91%**	4.93%	4.93%
Return on plan assets	**7.50%**	8.50%	8.50%	**7.50%**	8.00%	8.00%

Net pension cost for 2011, 2010 and 2009 included the following components:

(Stated in millions)

	US			International		
	2011	2010	2009	**2011**	2010	2009
Service cost-benefits earned during the period	**$59**	$56	$52	**$64**	$51	$67
Interest cost on projected benefit obligation	**150**	142	143	**226**	208	189
Expected return on plan assets	**(170)**	(191)	(166)	**(279)**	(228)	(181)
Amortization of net loss	**90**	60	29	**31**	19	–
Amortization of prior service cost	**12**	4	5	**120**	113	117
	141	71	63	**162**	163	192
Curtailment charge	–	–	32	–	–	98
	$141	$71	$95	**$162**	$163	$290

During 2009, due to the actions taken by Schlumberger to reduce its global workforce (See Note 3—*Charges and Credits*), Schlumberger experienced a significant reduction in the expected aggregate years of future service of its employees in certain of its pension plans and its postretirement medical plan. Accordingly, Schlumberger recorded a curtailment charge of $136 million during the second quarter of 2009 ($130 million relating to the pension plans and $6 million relating to the postretirement medical plan). The curtailment charge includes recognition of the change in benefit obligations as well as a portion of the previously unrecognized prior service costs, reflecting the reduction in expected future service for the impacted plans. As a result of the curtailment, Schlumberger performed a remeasurement of the impacted plans using a discount rate of 7.25%.

The weighted-average assumed discount rate and compensation increases used to determine the projected benefit obligations for the U.S. and International plans were as follows:

	US		International	
	2011	2010	**2011**	2010
Discount rate	**5.00 %**	5.50 %	**4.95 %**	5.47 %
Compensation increases	**4.00 %**	4.00 %	**4.91 %**	4.91 %

The changes in the projected benefit obligation, plan assets and funded status of the plans were as follows:

	US		International	
			(Stated in millions)	
	2011	*2010*	*2011*	*2010*
Change in Projected Benefit Obligations				
Projected benefit obligation at beginning of year	**$2,769**	$2,439	**$4,088**	$3,518
Service cost	**59**	56	**64**	51
Interest cost	**150**	142	**226**	208
Contributions by plan participants	–	–	**102**	76
Actuarial losses	**225**	172	**321**	310
Currency effect	–	–	**(8)**	(28)
Benefits paid	**(130)**	(122)	**(127)**	(121)
Plan amendments	–	82	–	74
Projected benefit obligation at end of year	**$3,073**	$2,769	**$4,666**	$4,088
Change in Plan Assets				
Plan assets at fair value at beginning of year	**$2,635**	$2,254	**$3,764**	$2,976
Actual return on plan assets	**78**	316	–	426
Currency effect	–	–	**(6)**	(26)
Company contributions	**72**	187	**364**	433
Contributions by plan participants	–	–	**102**	76
Benefits paid	**(130)**	(122)	**(127)**	(121)
Plan assets at fair value at end of year	**$2,655**	$2,635	**$4,097**	$3,764
Unfunded Liability	**$(418)**	$(134)	**$(569)**	$(324)
Amounts Recognized in Balance Sheet				
Postretirement Benefits	**$(418)**	$(134)	**$(569)**	$(367)
Other Assets	–	–	–	43
	$(418)	$(134)	**$(569)**	$(324)
Amounts Recognized in Accumulated Other Comprehensive Loss				
Actuarial losses	**$1,048**	$819	**$1,002**	$447
Prior service cost	**101**	114	**729**	840
	$1,149	$933	**$1,731**	$1,287
Accumulated benefit obligation	**$2,861**	$2,568	**$4,336**	$3,785

The unfunded liability represents the difference between the plan assets and the projected benefit obligation ("PBO"). The PBO represents the actuarial present value of benefits based on employee service and compensation and includes an assumption about future compensation levels. The accumulated benefit obligation represents the actuarial present value of benefits based on employee service and compensation, but does not include an assumption about future compensation levels.

The weighted-average allocation of plan assets and the target allocation by asset category are as follows:

	US			International		
	Target	*2011*	*2010*	*Target*	*2011*	*2010*
Equity securities	45 - 50%	47%	52%	50 - 70%	51%	61%
Debt securities	33 -43	39	40	25 - 35	38	31
Cash and cash equivalents	0 - 2	6	2	0 - 2	4	3
Alternative investments	0 - 10	8	6	0 - 20	7	5
	100%	100	100	100	100	100

Schlumberger's investment policy includes various guidelines and procedures designed to ensure that assets are prudently invested in a manner necessary to meet the future benefit obligation of the pension plans. The policy does not permit the direct investment of plan assets in any Schlumberger security. Schlumberger's investment horizon is long-term and accordingly the target asset allocations encompass a strategic, long-term perspective of capital markets, expected risk and return behavior and perceived future economic conditions. The key investment principles of diversification, assessment of risk and targeting the optimal expected returns for given levels of risk are applied. The target asset allocation is reviewed periodically and is determined based on a long-term projection of capital market outcomes, inflation rates, fixed income yields, returns, volatilities and correlation relationships. The inclusion of any given asset class in the target asset allocation is considered in relation to its impact on the overall risk/return characteristics as well as its impact on the overall investment return. As part of its strategy, Schlumberger may utilize certain derivative instruments, such as options, futures, swaps and forwards, within the plans to manage risks (currency, interest rate, etc.), as a substitute for physical securities or to obtain exposure to different markets.

Asset performance is monitored frequently with an overall expectation that plan assets will meet or exceed the weighted index of its target asset allocation and component benchmark over rolling five-year periods.

The expected long-term rate of return on assets assumptions reflect the average rate of earnings expected on funds invested or to be invested. The assumptions have been determined by reflecting expectations regarding future rates of return for the portfolio considering the asset allocation and related historical rates of return. The appropriateness of the assumptions is reviewed annually.

The fair value of Schlumberger's pension plan assets at December 31, 2011 and 2010, by asset category, are presented below and were determined based on valuation techniques categorized as follows:

- Level One: The use of quoted prices in active markets for identical instruments.

- Level Two: The use of quoted prices for similar instruments in active markets or quoted prices for identical or similar instruments in markets that are not active or other inputs that are observable in the market or can be corroborated by observable market data.

- Level Three: The use of significantly unobservable inputs that typically require the use of management's estimates of assumptions that market participants would use in pricing.

(Stated in millions)

| | US Plan Assets | | | | | | | |
| | 2011 | | | | 2010 | | | |
	Total	Level One	Level Two	Level Three	Total	Level One	Level Two	Level Three
Asset Category:								
Cash and Cash Equivalents	$147	$39	$108	–	$ 67	$35	$32	–
Equity Securities:								
US[a]	806	471	335		885	635	250	
International[b]	453	369	84		473	370	103	
Debt Securities:								
Corporate bonds[c]	340		340		220		220	
Government and government-related debt securities[d]	545	146	399		554	148	406	
Government agency collateralized mortgage obligations and mortgage backed securities[e]	96		96		201		201	
Other collateralized mortgage obligations and mortgage-backed securities[f]	58		58		67		67	
Alternative Investments:								
Private equity[g]	160		160		128		128	
Real estate[h]	50		50		40		40	
Total	$2,655	$1,025	$1,420	$210	$2,635	$1,188	$1,279	$168

(Stated in millions)

	International Plan Assets							
	2011				**2010**			
	Total	**Level One**	**Level Two**	**Level Three**	Total	Level One	Level Two	Level Three
Asset Category:								
Cash and Cash Equivalents	$152	$152	$ –	$ –	$106	$106	$ –	$ –
Equity Securities:								
US[a]	1,170	1,018	152		1,268	1,117	151	
International[b]	937	651	286		1,031	1,031		
Debt Securities:								
Corporate bonds[c]	399		399		289	15	274	
Government and governmentrelated[d]	808	551	257		693	365	328	
Government agency collateralized mortgage obligations and mortgage backed securities[e]	268	190	78		125	44	81	
Other collateralized mortgage obligations and mortgage-backed securities[f]	93		93		74		74	
Alternative Investments:								
Private equity[g]	150			150	114			114
Real estate[h]	62			62	64			64
Other	58			58				
Total	**$4,097**	**$2,562**	**$1,265**	**$270**	$3,764	$2,678	$908	$178

[a] US equities include companies that are well diversified by industry sector and equity style (i.e., growth and value strategies). Active and passive management strategies are employed. Investments are primarily in large capitalization stocks and, to a lesser extent, mid- and small-cap stocks.

[b] International equities are invested in companies that are traded on exchanges outside the US and are well diversified by industry sector, country and equity style. Active and passive strategies are employed. The vast majority of the investments are made in companies in developed markets with a small percentage in emerging markets.

[c] Corporate bonds consist primarily of investment grade bonds from diversified industries.

[d] Government and government-related debt securities are comprised primarily of inflation protected US treasuries and, to a lesser extent, other government-related securities.

[e] Government agency collateralized mortgage obligations and mortgage backed-securities are debt obligations that represent claims to the cash flows from pools of mortgage loans which are purchased from banks, mortgage companies, and other originators and then assembled into pools by governmental and quasi-governmental entities.

[f] Other collateralized mortgage obligations and mortgage-backed securities are debt obligations that represent claims to the cash flows from pools of mortgage loans which are purchased from banks, mortgage companies, and other originators and then assembled into pools by private entities.

[g] Private equity includes investments in several fund of funds limited partnerships.

[h] Real estate primarily includes investments in real estate limited partnerships, concentrated in commercial real estate.

The funding policy is to annually contribute amounts that are based upon a number of factors including the actuarial accrued liability, amounts that are deductible for income tax purposes, legal funding requirements and available cash flow. Schlumberger currently anticipates contributing approximately $600 million to its postretirement benefit plans in 2012, subject to market and business conditions.

Postretirement Benefits Other than Pensions

Schlumberger provides certain health care benefits to former US employees who have retired. The actuarial assumptions used to determine the accumulated postretirement benefit obligation and net periodic benefit cost for the US postretirement medical plan were as follows:

	Benefit Obligation at December 31,		Net Periodic Benefit Cost for the Year		
	2011	2010	**2011**	2010	2009
Discount rate	**5.00%**	5.50%	**5.50%**	6.00%	6.94%
Return on plan assets	–	–	**7.00%**	8.00%	8.00%
Current medical cost trend rate	**8.00%**	8.00%	**8.00%**	8.00%	8.00%
Ultimate medical cost trend rate	**5.00%**	5.00%	**5.00%**	5.00%	5.00%
Year that the rate reaches the ultimate trend rate	**2018**	2017	**2017**	2016	2015

The net periodic benefit cost for the US postretirement medical plan included the following components:

(Stated in millions)	**2011**	2010	2009
Service cost - benefits earned during the period	**$24**	$23	$19
Interest cost on projected benefit obligation	**57**	58	56
Expected return on plan assets	**(20)**	(6)	(2)
Amortization of prior service credit	**(12)**	(21)	(25)
Amortization of net loss	**13**	11	3
	62	65	51
Curtailment charge	–	–	6
	$62	$65	$57

The changes in the accumulated postretirement benefit obligation, plan assets and funded status were as follows:

(Stated in millions)	**2011**	2010
Change in Accumulated Postretirement Benefit Obligation		
Benefit obligation at beginning of year	**$1,051**	$991
Service cost	**24**	23

(Stated in millions)	2011	2010
Interest cost	57	58
Contributions by plan participants	6	4
Actuarial losses	90	8
Benefits paid	(40)	(33)
Benefit obligation at end of year	$1,188	$1,051
Change in Plan Assets		
Plan assets at fair value at beginning of year	$290	$58
Company contributions	165	248
Contributions by plan participants	6	5
Benefits paid	(40)	(33)
Actual return on plan assets	22	12
Plan assets at fair value at end of year	$443	$290
Unfunded Liability	(745)	(761)
Amounts Recognized in Accumulated Other Comprehensive Loss		
Actuarial losses	$286	$212
Prior service cost	(24)	(35)
	$262	$177

The unfunded liability is included in Postretirement Benefits in the Consolidated Balance Sheet. The assets of the US postretirement medical plan are invested 60% in US equity securities and 40% in government and government-related debt securities. The fair value of these assets were determined based on quoted prices in active markets for identical instruments.

Assumed health care cost trend rates have a significant effect on the amounts reported for the US postretirement medical plan. A one percentage point change in assumed health care cost trend rates would have the following effects:

(Stated in millions)	One percentage point increase	One percentage point decrease
Effect on total service and interest cost components	$16	$(13)
Effect on accumulated postretirement benefit obligation	$196	$(160)

Other Information

The expected benefits to be paid under the US and International pension plans as well as the postretirement medical plan (which is disclosed net of the annual Medicare Part D subsidy, which ranges from $3 million to $6 million per year) were as follows:

(Stated in millions)	Pension Benefits		Postretirement Medical Plan
	US	International	
2012	$135	$156	$45
2013	139	168	49

(Stated in millions)	Pension Benefits		Postretirement Medical Plan
	US	International	
2014	143	183	52
2015	149	197	55
2016	155	215	59
2017- 2021	911	1,250	352

Included in *Accumulated other comprehensive loss* at December 31, 2011 are non-cash pretax charges which have not yet been recognized in net periodic benefit cost. The estimated amounts that will be amortized from the estimated portion of each component of Accumulated other comprehensive loss which is expected to be recognized as a component of net periodic benefit cost during the year-ending December 31, 2012 are as follows:

(Stated in millions)	Pension Plans	Postretirement Medical Plan
Net actuarial losses	$104	$18
Prior service cost (credit)	$132	$(8)

In addition to providing defined pension benefits and a postretirement medical plan, Schlumberger and its subsidiaries have other deferred benefit programs, primarily profit sharing and defined contribution pension plans. Expenses for these programs were $582 million, $403 million and $418 million in 2011, 2010 and 2009, respectively.

Hanesbrands
2010 Annual Report

15. Defined Benefit Pension Plans

At January 1, 2011, the Company's pension plans consisted of the Hanesbrands Inc. Pension Plan, various nonqualified retirement plans and international plans. Benefits under the Hanesbrands Inc. Pension Plan were frozen effective December 31, 2005.

The annual cost (income) incurred by the Company for these defined benefit plans in 2010, 2009 and 2008, was $14,806, $21,293 and $(11,801), respectively. The components of net periodic benefit cost and other amounts recognized in other comprehensive loss of the Company's noncontributory defined benefit pension plans were as follows:

	Years Ended		
	January 1, 2011	January 2, 2010	January 3, 2009
Service cost	$ 1,225	$ 1,198	$ 1,136
Interest cost	49,337	50,755	51,412
Expected return on assets	(44,094)	(39,832)	(64,549)
Settlement cost	139	–	–

| | Years Ended | | |
	January 1, 2011	January 2, 2010	January 3, 2009
Amortization of:			
Prior service cost	26	26	39
Net actuarial loss	8,173	9,146	161
Net periodic benefit cost (income)	$ 14,806	$ 21,293	$ (11,801)
Other Changes in Plan Assets and Benefit Obligations Recognized in Other Comprehensive Income (Loss)			
Net (gain) loss	$ 6,605	$ (11,947)	$ 300,127
Prior service cost	(26)	(26)	(140)
Total recognized in other comprehensive loss (income)	6,579	(11,973)	299,987
Total recognized in net periodic benefit cost and other comprehensive loss (income)	$ 21,385	$ 9,320	$ 288,186

The estimated net loss and prior service credit for the defined benefit pension plans that will be amortized from accumulated other comprehensive loss into net periodic benefit cost in 2011 are $9,111 and $29, respectively.

The funded status of the Company's defined benefit pension plans at the respective year ends was as follows:

	January 1, 2011	January 2, 2010
Accumulated benefit obligation:		
Beginning of year	$ 899,208	$ 854,414
Service cost	1,225	1,198
Interest cost	49,337	50,755
Benefits paid	(56,859)	(57,782)
Impact of exchange rate change	1,939	2,711
Settlements	(1,284)	(5,394)
Actuarial loss	38,055	53,306
End of year	931,621	899,208
Fair value of plan assets:		
Beginning of year	612,590	564,705
Actual return on plan assets	67,624	92,805
Employer contributions	11,956	16,052
Benefits paid	(56,859)	(57,782)
Settlements	(1,284)	(5,744)
Impact of exchange rate change	1,141	2,554
End of year	635,168	612,590
Funded status	$ (296,453)	$ (286,618)

In the fourth quarter of 2010, the Company recognized a one-time out of period adjustment resulting from a review of census data for the Hanesbrands

Inc. Pension Plan, which reduced the accumulated benefit obligation by $18,892 and accumulated other comprehensive loss by $11,359 (net of taxes). The impact of the adjustment was not considered material to any current year or prior year periods.

The total accumulated benefit obligation and the accumulated benefit obligation and fair value of plan assets for the Company's pension plans with accumulated benefit obligations in excess of plan assets are as follows:

	January 1, 2011	January 2, 2010
Accumulated benefit obligation	$ 931,621	$ 899,208
Plans with accumulated benefit obligation in excess of plan assets		
Accumulated benefit obligation	931,621	898,997
Fair value of plan assets	635,168	612,317

Amounts recognized in the Company's Consolidated Balance Sheets consist of:

	January 1, 2011	January 2, 2010
Noncurrent assets	$ –	$ 51
Current liabilities	(2,177)	(3,591)
Noncurrent liabilities	(294,276)	(283,078)
Accumulated other comprehensive loss	(339,846)	(332,370)

Amounts recognized in accumulated other comprehensive loss consist of:

	January 1, 2011	January 2, 2010
Prior service cost	$ 139	$ 165
Actuarial loss	339,707	332,205
	$ 339,846	$ 332,370

Accrued benefit costs related to the Company's defined benefit pension plans are reported in the "Other noncurrent assets", "Accrued liabilities—Payroll and employee benefits" and "Pension and postretirement benefits" lines of the Consolidated Balance Sheets.

(a) Measurement Date and Assumptions

A December 31 measurement date is used to value plan assets and obligations for the pension plans. In determining the discount rate, the Company utilizes, as a general benchmark, the single discount rate equivalent to discounting the expected cash flows from each plan using the yields at each duration from a published yield curve as of the measurement date. The expected long-term rate of return on plan assets was based on the Company's investment policy target allocation of the asset portfolio between various asset classes and the expected real returns of each asset class over various periods of time. The weighted average actuarial assumptions used in measuring the net periodic benefit cost and plan obligations for the periods presented were as follows:

	January 1, 2011	January 2, 2010	January 3, 2009
Net periodic benefit cost:			
Discount rate	5.78 %	6.11 %	6.34 %
Long-term rate of return on plan assets	7.48	7.41	8.03
Rate of compensation increase[1]	3.70	3.38	3.63
Plan obligations:			
Discount rate	5.27 %	5.78 %	6.11 %
Rate of compensation increase[1]	3.75	3.70	3.38

[1] The compensation increase assumption applies to the international plans and portions of the nonqualified retirement plans, as benefits under these plans were not frozen at January 1, 2011, January 2, 2010 and January 3, 2009.

(b) Plan Assets, Expected Benefit Payments, and Funding

The allocation of pension plan assets as of the respective period end measurement dates is as follows:

	January 1, 2011	January 2, 2010
Asset category:		
Hedge fund of funds	43 %	42 %
U.S. equity securities	25	23
Debt securities	18	19
Foreign equity securities	10	11
Real estate	4	3
Cash and other	–	2

The Company's asset strategy and primary investment objective are to maximize the principal value of the plan assets to meet current and future benefit obligations to plan participants and their beneficiaries. To accomplish this goal, the assets of the plan are broadly diversified to protect against large investment losses and to reduce the likelihood of excessive volatility of returns. Diversification of assets is achieved through strategic allocations to various asset classes, as well as various investment styles within these asset classes, and by retaining multiple, third-party investment management firms with complementary investment styles and philosophies to implement these allocations. The Company has established a target asset allocation based upon analysis of risk/return tradeoffs and correlations of asset mixes given long-term historical data, prospective capital market returns and forecasted liabilities of the plans. The target asset allocation approximates the actual asset allocation as of January 1, 2011. In addition to volatility protection, diversification enables the assets of the plan the best opportunity to provide adequate returns in order to meet the Company's investment return objectives. These objectives include, over a rolling five-year period, to achieve a total return which exceeds the required actuarial rate of return for the plan and to outperform a passive portfolio, consisting of a similar asset allocation.

The Company utilizes market data or assumptions that market participants would use in pricing the pension plan assets. Effective January 2, 2010, the Company adopted new pension disclosure rules. In accordance with these rules, a three-tier fair value hierarchy, which prioritizes the inputs used in measuring fair value, is utilized for disclosing the fair value of the Company's pension plan assets. At January 1, 2011, the Company had $202,604 classified as Level 1 assets, $133,734 classified as Level 2 assets and $298,830 classified as Level 3 assets. At January 2, 2010, the Company had $201,571 classified as Level 1 assets, $135,817 classified as Level 2 assets and $275,202 classified as Level 3 assets. The Level 1 assets consisted primarily of U.S. equity securities, certain debt securities, certain foreign equity securities and cash and cash equivalents, Level 2 assets consisted primarily of certain debt securities and certain foreign equity securities, and Level 3 assets consisted primarily of hedge fund of funds and real estate investments. Refer to Note 14 for the Company's complete disclosure of the fair value of pension plan assets.

The Company expects to make a $7 million to $9 million contribution to the Hanesbrands Inc. Pension Plan in 2011 based on a preliminary calculation by its actuary. Expected benefit payments are as follows: $50,993 in 2011, $50,430 in 2012, $50,341 in 2013, $52,510 in 2014, $53,392 in 2015 and $280,310 thereafter.

Helmerich and Payne
2010 Annual Report

Note 11. Employee Benefit Plans

We maintain a domestic noncontributory defined benefit pension plan covering certain U.S. employees who meet certain age and service requirements. In July 2003, we revised the Helmerich & Payne, Inc. Employee Retirement Plan ("Pension Plan") to close the Pension Plan to new participants effective October 1, 2003, and reduce benefit accruals for current participants through September 30, 2006, at which time benefit accruals were discontinued and the Pension Plan was frozen.

The following table provides a reconciliation of the changes in the pension benefit obligations and fair value of Pension Plan assets over the two-year period ended September 30, 2010 and a statement of the funded status as of September 30, 2010 and 2009 (in thousands):

	2010	2009
Accumulated Benefit Obligation	$ 102,097	$ 89,996
Changes in Projected Benefit Obligations		
Projected benefit obligation at beginning of year	$ 89,996	$ 69,475
Interest cost	4,825	4,988
Actuarial gain (loss)	11,482	18,977
Benefits paid	(4,206)	(3,444)
Projected benefit obligation at end of year	$ 102,097	$ 89,996

	2010	2009
Change in plan assets		
Fair value of plan assets at beginning of year	$ 57,181	$ 59,605
Actual return on plan assets	5,005	270
Employer contribution	3,408	750
Benefits paid	(4,206)	(3,444)
Fair value of plan assets at end of year	$ 61,388	$ 57,181
Funded status of the plan at end of year	$ (40,709)	$ (32,815)

September 30,	2010	2009
Amounts Recognized in the Consolidated Balance Sheets (in thousands):		
Accrued liabilities	$ (181)	$ (40)
Noncurrent liabilities-other	(40,528)	(32,775)
Net amount recognized	$ (40,709)	$ (32,815)
The amounts recognized in Accumulated Other Comprehensive Income at September 30, 2010 and 2009, and not yet reflected in net periodic benefit cost, are as follows (in thousands):		
Net actuarial gain (loss)	$ (38,001)	$ (29,267)
Prior service cost	(2)	(1)
Total	$ (38,003)	$ (29,268)

The amount recognized in Accumulated Other Comprehensive Income and not yet reflected in periodic benefit cost expected to be amortized in next year's periodic benefit cost is a net actuarial loss of $3.0 million.

The weighted average assumptions used for the pension calculations were as follows:

Years Ended September 30,	2010	2009	2008
Discount rate for net periodic benefit costs	5.42%	7.25%	6.25%
Discount rate for year-end obligations	4.48%	5.42%	7.25%
Expected return on plan assets	8.00%	8.00%	8.00%

We contributed $3.4 million to the Pension Plan in fiscal 2010 to fund distributions in lieu of liquidating pension assets. We estimate contributing at least $0.6 million in fiscal 2011 to meet the minimum contribution required by law and expect to make additional contributions to continue funding distributions. Additional contributions will be made if needed to fund unexpected distributions.

Components of the net periodic pension expense (benefit) were as follows (in thousands):

Years Ended September 30,	2010	2009	2008
Interest cost	$ 4,825	$ 4,988	$ 4,919
Expected return on plan assets	(4,552)	(4,643)	(5,990)
Amortization of prior service cost	–	(1)	–
Recognized net actuarial loss	2,295	3	9
Net pension expense (benefit)	$ 2,568	$ 347	$ (1,062)

The following table reflects the expected benefits to be paid from the Pension Plan in each of the next five fiscal years and in the aggregate for the five years thereafter (in thousands).

Years Ended September 30,						
2011	2012	2013	2014	2015	2016-2020	Total
$ 4,907	$ 6,035	$ 5,707	$ 5,613	$ 6,901	$36,170	$ 65,333

INVESTMENT STRATEGY AND ASSET ALLOCATION

Our investment policy and strategies are established with a long-term view in mind. The investment strategy is intended to help pay the cost of the Plan while providing adequate security to meet the benefits promised under the Plan. We maintain a diversified asset mix to minimize the risk of a material loss to the portfolio value that might occur from devaluation of any one investment. In determining the appropriate asset mix, our financial strength and ability to fund potential shortfalls are considered. Plan assets are invested in portfolios of diversified public-market equity securities and fixed income securities. The plan holds no securities of the Company.

The expected long-term rate of return on plan assets is based on historical and projected rates of return for current and planned asset classes in the Plans' investment portfolio after analyzing historical experience and future expectations of the return and volatility of various asset classes.

Schlumberger NV
2010 Annual Report

18. Pension and Other Benefit Plans

Pension plans

Schlumberger sponsors several defined benefit pension plans that cover substantially all U.S. employees hired prior to October 1, 2004. The benefits are based on years of service and compensation, on a career-average pay basis.

In addition to the United States defined benefit pension plans, Schlumberger sponsors several other international defined benefit pension plans. The most significant of these international plans are the international staff pension plan, which was converted from a defined contribution plan to a defined benefit pension plan during the fourth quarter of 2008, and the U.K. pension plan (collectively, the "international plans"). The international staff pension plan covers certain international employees and is based on years of service and compensation on a career-average pay basis. The U.K. plan covers employees hired prior to April 1, 1999, and is based on years of service and compensation, on a final salary basis.

The weighted-average assumed discount rate, compensation increases and the expected long-term rate of return on plan assets used to determine the net pension cost for the U.S. and international plans were as follows:

	U.S.			International		
	2010	2009	2008	2010	2009	2008
Discount rate	6.00%	6.94%	6.50%	5.89%	6.81%	5.80%
Compensation increases	4.00%	4.00%	4.00%	4.93%	4.93%	4.90%
Return on plan assets	8.50%	8.50%	8.50%	8.00%	8.00%	8.00%

Net pension cost for 2010, 2009 and 2008 included the following components:

(Stated in millions)

	U.S.			International		
	2010	2009	2008	2010	2009	2008
Service cost - benefits earned during the period	$ 56	$ 52	$ 56	$ 51	$ 67	$ 33
Interest cost on projected benefit obligation	142	143	130	208	189	58
Expected return on plan assets	(191)	(166)	(162)	(228)	(181)	(75)
Amortization of net loss	60	29	13	19	–	11
Amortization of prior service cost	4	5	7	113	117	1
	71	63	44	163	192	28
Curtailment charge	–	32	–	–	98	–
	$ 71	$ 95	$ 44	$ 163	$ 290	$ 28

During 2009, due to the actions taken by Schlumberger to reduce its global workforce (see note 3—*charges and credits*), Schlumberger experienced a signifi- cant reduction in the expected aggregate years of future service of its employees in certain of its pension plans and its postretirement medical plan. Accordingly, Schlumberger recorded a curtailment charge of $136 million during the second quarter of 2009 ($130 million relating to the pension plans and $6 million relating to the postretirement medical plan). The curtailment charge includes recognition of the change in benefit obligations as well as a portion of the previously unrecognized prior service costs, reflecting the reduction in expected future service for the impacted plans. As a result of the curtailment, Schlumberger performed a remeasurement of the impacted plans using a discount rate of 7.25% (as compared to 6.50% at December 31, 2008). All other significant assumptions were unchanged from December 31, 2008 measurement date.

As the international staff pension plan was converted to a defined benefit pension plan during the fourth quarter of 2008, the net pension cost for this plan was not significant in 2008.

The weighted-average assumed discount rate and compensation increases used to determine the projected benefit obligations for the U.S. and international plans were as follows:

	U.S.		International	
	2010	2009	2010	2009
Discount rate	5.50%	**6.00%**	5.47%	**5.89%**
Compensation increases	4.00%	**4.00%**	4.91%	**4.93%**

The changes in the projected benefit obligation, plan assets and funded status of the plans were as follows:

(stated in millions)	U.S.		International	
	2010	2009	2010	2009
Change in Projected Benefit Obligations				
Projected benefit obligation at beginning of year	$ 2,439	**$ 2,150**	$ 3,518	**$ 2,767**
Service cost	56	**52**	51	**67**
Interest cost	142	**143**	208	**189**
Contributions by plan participants	–	–	76	**61**
Actuarial losses	172	**191**	310	**449**
Currency effect	–	–	(28)	**69**
Benefits paid	(122)	**(110)**	(121)	**(97)**
Plan amendments	82	–	74	**16**
Impact of curtailment	–	**13**	–	**(3)**
Projected benefit obligation at end of year	$ 2,769	**$ 2,439**	$ 4,088	**$ 3,518**
Change in Plan Assets				
Plan assets at fair value at beginning of year	$ 2,254	**$ 1,490**	$ 2,976	**$ 1,913**
Actual return on plan assets	316	**358**	426	**444**
Currency effect	–	–	(26)	**69**
Company contributions	187	**516**	433	**586**
Contributions by plan participants	–	–	76	**61**
Benefits paid	(122)	**(110)**	(121)	**(97)**
Plan assets at fair value at end of year	$ 2,635	**$ 2,254**	$ 3,764	**$ 2,976**
Unfunded Liability	$ (134)	**$ (185)**	$ (324)	**$ (542)**
Amounts Recognized in Balance Sheet				
Postretirement benefits	$ (134)	**$ (185)**	$ (367)	**$ (542)**
Other assets	–	–	43	–
	$ (134)	**$ (185)**	$ (324)	**$ (542)**
Amounts Recognized in Accumulated Other Comprehensive Income				
Actuarial losses	$ 819	**$ 833**	$ 447	**$ 335**

(stated in millions)	U.S.		International	
	2010	2009	2010	2009
Prior service cost	114	**36**	840	**881**
	$ 933	**$ 869**	$ 1,287	**$ 1,216**
Accumulated benefit obligation	$ 2,568	**$ 2,226**	$ 3,785	**$ 3,257**

The funded status position represents the difference between the plan assets and the projected benefit obligation ("PBO"). The PBO represents the actuarial present value of benefits based on employee service and compensation and includes an assumption about future compensation levels. The accumulated benefit obligation represents the actuarial present value of benefits based on employee service and compensation, but does not include an assumption about future compensation levels.

The weighted-average allocation of plan assets and the target allocation by asset category are as follows:

	U.S.			International		
	Target	2010	2009	Target	2010	2009
Equity securities	50 - 60%	52%	**48%**	55 - 70%	61%	**59%**
Debt securities	28 - 38	40	**38**	20 - 35	31	**32**
Cash and cash equivalents	–	2	**8**	–	3	**4**
Other investments	0 - 12	6	**6**	0 - 10	5	**5**
	100%	100%	**100%**	100%	100%	**100%**

Schlumberger's investment policy includes various guidelines and procedures designed to ensure that assets are prudently invested in a manner necessary to meet the future benefit obligation of the pension plans. The policy does not permit the direct investment of plan assets in any Schlumberger security. Schlumberger's investment horizon is long-term and accordingly the target asset allocations encompass a strategic, long-term perspective of capital markets, expected risk and return behavior and perceived future economic conditions. The key investment principles of diversification, assessment of risk and targeting the optimal expected returns for given levels of risk are applied. The target asset allocation is reviewed periodically and is determined based on a long-term projection of capital market outcomes, inflation rates, fixed income yields, returns, volatilities and correlation relationships. The inclusion of any given asset class in the target asset allocation is considered in relation to its impact on the overall risk/return characteristics as well as its impact on the overall investment return. As part of its strategy, Schlumberger may utilize certain derivative instruments, such as options, futures, swaps and forwards, within the plans to manage risks (currency, interest rate, etc.) or as a substitute for physical securities or to obtain exposure to different markets.

Asset performance is monitored frequently with an overall expectation that plan assets will meet or exceed the weighted index of its target asset allocation and component benchmark over rolling five year periods.

The expected long-term rate of return on assets assumptions reflect the average rate of earnings expected on funds invested or to be invested. The assumptions have been determined by reflecting expectations regarding future rates of return for the portfolio considering the asset allocation and related historical rates of return. The appropriateness of the assumptions is reviewed annually.

The fair value of Schlumberger's pension plan assets at December 31, 2010, by asset category, was as follows:

The fair values presented below were determined based on valuation techniques categorized as follows:

- Level one: the use of quoted prices in active markets for identical instruments.

- Level two: the use of quoted prices for similar instruments in active markets or quoted prices for identical or similar instruments in markets that are not active or other inputs that are observable in the market or can be corroborated by observable market data.

- Level three: the use of significantly unobservable inputs that typically require the use of management's estimates of assumptions that market participants would use in pricing.

(stated in millions)	U.S. Plan Assets							
	2010				2009			
	Total	Level One	Level Two	Level Three	Total	Level One	Level Two	Level Three
Asset Category:								
Cash and Cash Equivalents	$ 67	$ 35	$ 32	$ –	$ 191	$ 191	$ –	$ –
Equity Securities:								
US(a)	885	885			710	710		
International(b)	473	370	103		355	280	75	
Debt securities:								
Corporate bonds(c)	220		220		193		193	
Government and government-related debt securities(d)	554	148	406		462	161	301	
Government agency collateralized mortgage obligations and mortgage backed securities(e)	201		201		136		136	
	67		67		71		71	
Other Investments:								
Private equity(g)	128			128	99			99
Real estate(h)	40			40	37			37
Total	$ 2,635	$ 1,438	$ 1,029	$ 168	$ 2,254	$ 1,342	$ 776	$ 136

(stated in millions)	International Plan Assets							
	2010				2009			
	Total	Level One	Level Two	Level Three	Total	Level One	Level Two	Level Three
Asset Category:								
Cash and Cash Equivalents	$ 106	$ 106	$ –	$ –	$ 111	$ 111	$ –	$ –
Equity Securities:								
US[a]	1,268	1,268			1,113	1,113		
International[b]	1,031	1,031			643	643		
Debt securities:								
Corporate bonds[c]	289	15	274		257	11	246	
Government and government-related[d]	693	522	171		492	378	114	
Government agency collateralized mortgage obligations and mortgage backed securities[e]	125	44	81		137	20	117	
Other collateralized mortgage obligations and mortgage-backed securities[f]	74		74		70		70	
Other Investments:								
Private equity[g]	114			114	87			87
Real estate[h]	64			64	66			66
Total	$ 3,764	$ 2,986	$ 600	$ 178	$ 2,976	$ 2,276	$ 547	$ 153

[a] U.S. equities include companies that are well diversified by industry sector and equity style (i.e., growth and value strategies). Active and passive management strategies are employed. Investments are primarily in large capitalization stocks and, to a lesser extent, mid- and small-cap stocks.

[b] International equities are invested in companies that are traded on exchanges outside the U.S. and are well diversified by industry sector, country and equity style. Active and passive strategies are employed. The vast majority of the investments are made in companies in developed markets with a small percentage in emerging markets.

[c] Corporate bonds consist primarily of investment grade bonds from diversified industries.

[d] Government and government-related debt securities are comprised primarily of inflation protected us treasuries and, to a lesser extent, other government-related securities.

(e) Government agency collateralized mortgage obligations and mortgage backed-securities are debt obligations that represent claims to the cash flows from pools of mortgage loans which are purchased from banks, mortgage companies, and other originators and then assembled into pools by governmental and quasi-governmental entities.

(f) Other collateralized mortgage obligations and mortgage-backed securities are debt obligations that represent claims to the cash flows from pools of mortgage loans which are purchased from banks, mortgage companies, and other originators and then assembled into pools by private entities.

(g) Private equity includes investments in several fund of funds limited partnerships.

(h) Real estate primarily includes investments in real estate limited partnerships, concentrated in commercial real estate.

The funding policy is to annually contribute amounts that are based upon a number of factors including the actuarial accrued liability, amounts that are deductible for income tax purposes, legal funding requirements and available cash flow. Schlumberger currently anticipates contributing approximately $600 million to $650 million to its postretirement benefit plans in 2011, subject to market and business conditions.

Postretirement benefits other than pensions

Schlumberger provides certain health care benefits to former U.S. employees who have retired.

The actuarial assumptions used to determine the accumulated postretirement benefit obligation and net periodic benefit cost for the U.S. postretirement medical plan were as follows:

	Benefit Obligation at December 31,		Net Periodic Benefit Cost for the year		
	2010	2009	2010	2009	2008
Discount rate	5.50%	6.00%	6.00%	6.94%	6.50%
Return on plan assets	–	–	8.00%	8.00%	8.00%
Current medical cost trend rate	8.00%	8.00%	8.00%	8.00%	9.00%
Ultimate medical cost trend rate	5.00%	5.00%	5.00%	5.00%	5.00%
Year that the rate reaches the ultimate trend rate	2017	2016	2016	2015	2012

The net periodic benefit cost for the U.S. postretirement medical plan included the following components:

(stated in millions)	2010	2009	2008
Service cost - benefits earned during the period	$ 23	$ 19	$ 23
Interest cost on projected benefit obligation	58	56	52
Expected return on plan assets	(6)	(2)	(3)
Amortization of prior service credit	(21)	(25)	(27)
Amortization of net loss	11	3	10
	65	51	55
Curtailment charge	–	6	–
	$ 65	$ 57	$ 55

The changes in the accumulated postretirement benefit obligation, plan assets and funded status were as follows:

(stated in millions)	2010	2009
Change in Accumulated Postretirement Benefit Obligation		
Benefit obligation at beginning of year	$ 991	$ 862

(stated in millions)	2010	2009
Service cost	23	19
Interest cost	58	56
Contributions by plan participants	4	5
Actuarial losses	8	67
Benefits paid	(33)	(31)
Impact of curtailment	–	13
Benefit obligation at end of year	**$ 1,051**	**$ 991**
Change in Plan Assets		
Plan assets at fair value at beginning of year	$ 58	$ 29
Company contributions	248	47
Contributions by plan participants	5	5
Benefits paid	(33)	(31)
Actual return on plan assets	12	8
Plan assets at fair value at end of year	$ 290	$ 58
Unfunded Liability	$ (761)	$ (933)
Amounts Recognized in Accumulated		
Other Comprehensive Income		
Actuarial losses	$ 212	$ 223
Prior service cost	(35)	(56)
	$ 177	$ 167

The unfunded position is included in *postretirement benefits* in the *consolidated balance sheet*.

The assets of the U.S. postretirement medical plan are invested 60% in us equity securities and 40% in government and government-related debt securities. The fair value of these assets was determined based on quoted prices in active markets for identical instruments.

Assumed health care cost trend rates have a significant effect on the amounts reported for the U.S. postretirement medical plan. A one percentage point change in assumed health care cost trend rates would have the following effects:

(stated in millions)	One Percentage Point Increase	One Percentage Point Decrease
Effect on total service and interest cost components	$ 15	$ (12)
Effect on accumulated postretirement benefit obligation	$ 177	$ (145)

Other information

The expected benefits to be paid under the U.S. and International pension plans as well as the postretirement medical plan (which is disclosed net of the annual Medicare Part D subsidy, which ranges from $3 million to $7 million per year) were as follows:

(stated in millions)	Pension Benefits U.S.	Pension Benefits International	Postretirement Medical Plan
2011	$ 125	$ 134	$ 40
2012	129	146	43
2013	134	158	46
2014	139	170	50
2015	145	182	53
2016 - 2020	856	1,083	312

Included in *accumulated other comprehensive income* at December 31, 2010 are non-cash pretax charges which have not yet been recognized in net periodic benefit cost. The estimated amounts that will be amortized from the estimated portion of each component of *accumulated other comprehensive income* which is expected to be recognized as a component of net periodic benefit cost during the year-ending December 31, 2011 are as follows:

(stated in millions)	Pension Plans	Postretirement Medical Plan
Net actuarial losses	$ 89	$ 11
Prior service cost/(credit)	$ 132	$ (12)

In addition to providing defined pension benefits and a postretirement medical plan, Schlumberger and its subsidiaries have other deferred benefit programs, primarily profit sharing and defined contribution pension plans. Expenses for these programs were $403 million, $418 million and $482 million in 2010, 2009 and 2008, respectively.

Coca-Cola
2009 Annual Report

Note 10: Pension and Other Postretirement Benefit Plans

Our Company sponsors and/or contributes to pension and postretirement health care and life insurance benefit plans covering substantially all U.S. employees.

We also sponsor nonqualified, unfunded defined benefit pension plans for certain associates. In addition, our Company and its subsidiaries have various pension plans and other forms of postretirement arrangements outside the United States.

Obligations and Funded Status

The following table sets forth the changes in benefit obligations and the fair value of plan assets for our benefit plans (in millions):

	Pension Benefits		Other Benefits	
	2009	*2008*	*2009*	*2008*
Benefit obligation at January 1,[1]	$3,618	$3,517	$430	$438
Service cost	113	114	21	20
Interest cost	213	205	29	26
Foreign currency exchange rate changes	161	(141)	3	(3)
Amendments	1	(13)	(1)	–
Actuarial loss (gain)	89	125	23	(220)
Benefits paid[2]	(206)	(199)	(30)	(27)
Business combinations	–	–	–	–
Settlements	(2)	(3)	–	–
Curtailments	–	(1)	(1)	(6)
Special termination benefits	9	11	4	–
Other	–	3	5	2
Benefit obligation at December 31,[1]	$3,996	$3,618	$483	$430
Fair value of plan assets at January 1,	$2,290	$3,428	$175	$246
Actual return on plan assets	501	(961)	20	(47)
Employer contributions	269	96	1	–
Foreign currency exchange rate changes	121	(118)	–	–
Benefits paid	(149)	(155)	(26)	(25)
Business combinations	–	–	–	–
Settlements	–	(3)	–	–
Other	–	3	3	1
Fair value of plan assets at December 31,	$3,032	$ 2,290	$ 173	$ 175
Net liability recognized	$ (964)	$(1,328)	$(310)	$(255)

---

[1] For pension benefit plans, the benefit obligation is the projected benefit obligation. For other benefit plans, the benefit obligation is the accumulated postretirement benefit obligation. The accumulated benefit obligation for our pension plans was $3,657 million and $3,209 million as of December 31, 2009 and 2008, respectively.

[2] Benefits paid to pension plan participants during 2009 and 2008 included approximately $57 million and $44 million, respectively, in payments related to unfunded pension plans that were paid from Company assets. Benefits paid to participants of other benefit plans during 2009 and 2008 included approximately $4 million and $2 million, respectively, that were paid from Company assets.

Pension and other benefit amounts recognized in our consolidated balance sheets are as follows (in millions):

December 31,	Pension Benefits		Other Benefits	
	2009	2008	2009	2008
Noncurrent assets	$ 65	$ 37	$ –	$ –
Current liability	(42)	(39)	(1)	–
Long-term liability	(987)	(1,326)	(309)	(255)
Net liability recognized	$(964)	$(1,328)	$(310)	$(255)

In December 2008, the Company decided to modify the primary U.S. defined benefit pension plan. Beginning in 2010, the plan will have a two-part formula to determine pension benefits. The first part will retain the current final average pay structure, where service will freeze as of January 1, 2010, with pay escalating for the lesser of 10 years or until termination. The second part of the formula will be a cash balance account which will commence January 1, 2010, under which employees may receive credits based on age, service, pay and interest. The plan was also modified to allow lump sum distributions. These changes, as well as related changes to other U.S. plans, reduced pension obligations as of December 31, 2008, by approximately $21 million. In addition, the U.S. retiree medical plan was amended to close the plan to new hires effective January 1, 2009.

In February and October of 2007, the Company amended its U.S. retiree medical plan to limit the Company's exposure to increases in retiree medical costs associated with current and future retirees. Based on the significance of the change in liability resulting from the amendments, we remeasured the assets and liabilities of the U.S. retiree medical plan effective February 28, 2007, and October 31, 2007. As a result of the remeasurements, the Company reduced its liabilities for the U.S. retiree medical plan by approximately $435 million.

Certain of our pension plans have projected benefit obligations in excess of the fair value of plan assets. For these plans, the projected benefit obligations and the fair value of plan assets were as follows (in millions):

December 31,	2009	2008
Projected benefit obligation	$3,718	$3,416
Fair value of plan assets	2,687	2,051

Certain of our pension plans have accumulated benefit obligations in excess of the fair value of plan assets. For these plans, the accumulated benefit obligations and the fair value of plan assets were as follows (in millions):

December 31,	2009	2008
Accumulated benefit obligation	$3,139	$2,881
Fair value of plan assets	2,418	1,885

Pension Plan Assets

The following table presents total pension assets for our U.S. and non-U.S. plans (in millions):

	U.S. Plans		Non-U.S. Plans	
December 31,	2009	2008	2009	2008
Cash and cash equivalents	$ 169	$ 70	$ 41	$ 28
Equity securities:				
U.S.-based companies	744	561	–	1
International-based companies	154	111	11	8
Fixed income securities:				
Government bonds	61	53	164	115
Corporate bonds and debt securities	339	266	16	7
Mutual, pooled and commingled funds[1]	256	175	736	544
Hedge funds/limited partnerships	80	58	–	–
Real estate	107	157	46	41
Other	65	49	43	46
Total pension plan assets[2]	$1,975	$1,500	$1,057	$790

[1] Mutual, pooled and commingled funds include investments in equity securities, fixed income securities and combinations of both. There are a significant number of mutual and pooled funds from which investors can choose. The selection of the type of fund is dictated by the specific investment objectives and needs of a given plan. These objectives and needs vary greatly between plans.

[2] Fair value disclosures related to our pension assets are included in Note 13. Fair value disclosures include, but are not limited to, the level within the fair value hierarchy on which the fair value measurements in their entirety fall, a reconciliation of the beginning and ending balances of Level 3 assets and information about the valuation techniques and inputs used to measure the fair value of our pension and other postretirement assets.

U.S. Pension Plan Investment Strategy

The Company utilizes the services of investment managers to actively manage the pension assets of our primary U.S. plan. We have established asset allocation targets and investment guidelines with each investment manager. Our asset allocation targets promote optimal expected return and volatility characteristics given the long-term time horizon for fulfilling the obligations of the plan. Selection of the targeted asset allocation for U.S. plan assets was based upon a review of the expected return and risk characteristics of each asset class, as well as the correlation of returns among asset classes. Our target allocation is a mix of approximately 60 percent equity investments, 30 percent fixed income investments and 10 percent in alternative investments. Furthermore, we believe that our target allocation will enable us to achieve the following long-term investment objectives:

1. Optimize the long-term return on plan assets at an acceptable level of risk;

2. Maintain a broad diversification across asset classes and among investment managers;

3. Maintain careful control of the risk level within each asset class; and

4. Focus on a long-term return objective.

The guidelines that have been established with each investment manager provide parameters within which the investment managers agree to operate, including criteria that determine eligible and ineligible securities, diversification requirements and credit quality standards, where applicable. Unless exceptions have been approved, investment managers are prohibited from buying or selling commodities, futures or option contracts, as well as from short selling of securities. Additionally, investment managers agree to obtain written approval for deviations from stated investment style or guidelines. As of December 31, 2009, no investment manager was responsible for more than 10 percent of total U.S. plan assets.

Our target allocation of 60 percent equity investments is composed of approximately 33 percent domestic large-cap securities, 33 percent domestic small-cap securities, 19 percent international securities and 15 percent domestic mid-cap securities. Optimal returns through our investments in domestic large-cap securities are achieved through security selection and sector diversification. Investments in common stock of our Company accounted for approximately

25 percent of our investments in domestic large-cap securities and 5 percent of total plan assets. Our investments in domestic mid-cap and small-cap securities are expected to experience larger swings in their market value on a periodic basis. We select our investments in these asset classes based on capital appreciation potential. Our investments in international securities are intended to provide equity-like returns, while at the same time helping to diversify our overall equity investment portfolio.

Our target allocation of 30 percent fixed income investments are composed of 50 percent long-duration bonds and 50 percent high-yield bonds. Long-duration bonds provide a stable rate of return through investments in high-quality publicly traded debt securities. We diversify our investments in long-duration bonds to mitigate duration and credit exposure. High-yield bonds are investments in lower-rated and non-rated debt securities, which generally produce higher returns compared to long-duration bonds. Investments in high-yield bonds also help diversify our fixed income portfolio.

In addition to investments in equity securities and fixed income investments, we have a target allocation of 10 percent in alternative investments. These alternative investments include hedge funds, private equity limited partnerships, leveraged buyout funds, international venture capital partnerships and real estate. The objective of investing in hedge funds, private equity limited partnerships, leveraged buyout funds and international venture capital partnerships is to provide a higher rate of return than that available from publicly traded equity securities. This objective is achieved through investing in limited partnerships that require capital for rapidly growing businesses. These investments are inherently illiquid and require a long-term perspective in evaluating investment performance. Investments in real estate have two objectives. First, investments in real estate help diversify our overall portfolio due to the low historical correlation with traditional stocks and fixed income investments. The secondary objective is to provide stable investment returns from income-producing properties.

Non-U.S. Pension Plan Investment Strategy

The majority of our international subsidiaries' pension plan assets are invested in mutual, pooled and commingled funds. As of December 31, 2009, mutual, pooled and commingled funds were composed of approximately 45 percent pooled equity securities, 35 percent pooled fixed income securities and 20 percent mutual and commingled funds. The investment strategies of our international subsidiaries differ greatly, and in some instances are influenced by local law. None of our pension plans outside the United States is individually significant for separate disclosure.

Other Postretirement Benefit Plan Assets

Plan assets associated with other benefits represent funding of the primary U.S. postretirement benefit plan. In late 2006, we established and contributed $216 million to a U.S. Voluntary Employee Beneficiary Association (' 'VEBA''), a tax-qualified trust. The VEBA assets remain segregated from the primary U.S. pension master trust and are primarily invested in liquid assets due to the level of expected future benefit payments.

The following table presents total assets for our other postretirement benefit plans (in millions):

December 31,	2009	2008
Cash and cash equivalents	$ 86	$108
Equity securities:		
U.S.-based companies	62	47
International-based companies	13	9
Fixed income securities:		
Government bonds	1	11
Corporate bonds and debt securities	5	4
Mutual, pooled and commingled funds	2	2
Hedge funds/limited partnerships	1	1
Real estate	2	2

December 31,	*2009*	2008
Other	**1**	1
Total other postretirement benefit plan assets[1]	**$173**	$175

[1] Fair value disclosures related to our other postretirement assets are included in Note 13. Fair value disclosures include, but are not limited to, the level within the fair value hierarchy on which the fair value measurements in their entirety fall, a reconciliation of the beginning and ending balances of Level 3 assets and information about the valuation techniques and inputs used to measure the fair value of our pension and other postretirement assets.

Components of Net Periodic Benefit Cost

Net periodic benefit cost for our pension and other postretirement benefit plans consisted of the following (in millions):

	Pension Benefits			Other Benefits		
Year Ended December 31,	*2009*	2008	2007	*2009*	2008	2007
Service cost	**$ 113**	$ 114	$ 123	**$ 21**	$ 20	$ 40
Interest cost	**213**	205	191	**29**	26	34
Expected return on plan assets	**(214)**	(249)	(231)	**(8)**	(20)	(20)
Amortization of prior service cost (credit)	**5**	10	7	**(61)**	(61)	(42)
Amortization of actuarial loss	**86**	10	18	–	–	1
Net periodic benefit cost (credit)	**203**	90	108	**(19)**	(35)	13
Settlement charge	**5**	14	3	–	–	–
Curtailment charge (credit)	**1**	–	2	–	(6)	–
Special termination benefits[1]	**9**	11	–	**4**	–	–
Total cost (credit) recognized in the statements of income	**$ 218**	$ 115	$ 113	**$(15)**	$(41)	$ 13

[1] The special termination benefits primarily relate to several restructuring plans, including the Company's ongoing productivity initiatives. Refer to Note 15 for additional information related to our restructuring plans and productivity initiatives.

The following table sets forth the changes in AOCI for our benefit plans (in millions, pretax):

	Pension Benefits		Other Benefits	
December 31,	*2009*	2008	*2009*	2008
Beginning balance in AOCI	**$(1,389)**	$(108)	**$189**	$297
Recognized prior service cost (credit)	**6**	10	**(61)**	(61)
Recognized net actuarial loss (gain)	**91**	24	–	–

December 31,	Pension Benefits		Other Benefits	
	2009	2008	**2009**	2008
Prior service credit (cost) arising in current year	**(1)**	13	**1**	–
Net actuarial (loss) gain arising in current year	**198**	(1,335)	**(11)**	(47)
Translation gain (loss)	**(24)**	7	**–**	–
Ending balance in AOCI	**$(1,119)**	$(1,389)	**$118**	$189

The following table sets forth amounts in AOCI for our benefit plans (in millions, pretax):

December 31,	Pension Benefits		Other Benefits	
	2009	2008	**2009**	2008
Prior service credit (cost)	**$ (58)**	$ (56)	**$184**	$244
Net actuarial loss	**(1,061)**	(1,333)	**(66)**	(55)
Ending balance in AOCI	**$(1,119)**	$ (1,389)	**$118**	$189

Amounts in AOCI expected to be recognized as components of net periodic pension cost in 2010 are as follows (in millions, pretax):

	Pension Benefits	Other Benefits
Amortization of prior service cost (credit)	$ 6	$(61)
Amortization of actuarial loss	58	2
	$64	$(59)

Assumptions

Certain weighted-average assumptions used in computing the benefit obligations are as follows:

December 31,	Pension Benefits		Other Benefits	
	2009	2008	**2009**	2008
Discount rate	**$5^3/4$%**	6%	**$5^3/4$%**	$6^1/4$%
Rate of increase in compensation levels	**$3^3/4$%**	$3^3/4$%	**N/A**	N/A

Certain weighted-average assumptions used in computing net periodic benefit cost are as follows:

	Pension Benefits			Other Benefits		
December 31,	**2009**	2008	2007	**2009**	2008	2007
Discount rate	**6%**	6%	5^1/$_2$%	**6^1/$_4$%**	6^1/$_4$%	6%
Rate of increase in compensation levels	**3^3/$_4$%**	4^1/$_4$%	4^1/$_4$%	**N/A**	N/A	N/A
Expected long-term rate of return on plan assets	**8%**	8%	7^3/$_4$%	**4^3/$_4$%**	8^1/$_2$%	8^1/$_2$%

The expected long-term rate of return assumption for U.S. pension plan assets is based upon the target asset allocation and is determined using forward-looking assumptions in the context of historical returns and volatilities for each asset class, as well as correlations among asset classes. We evaluate the rate of return assumption on an annual basis. The expected long-term rate of return assumption used in computing 2009 net periodic pension cost for the U.S. plans was 8.5 percent. As of December 31, 2009, the 10-year annualized return on plan assets in the primary U.S. plan was 3.1 percent, the 15-year annualized return was 8.5 percent, and the annualized return since inception was 11.0 percent.

The assumed health care cost trend rates are as follows:

December 31,	**2009**	2008
Health care cost trend rate assumed for next year	**7^1/$_2$%**	9%
Rate to which the cost trend rate is assumed to decline (the ultimate trend rate)	**5^1/$_4$%**	5^1/$_4$%
Year that the rate reaches the ultimate trend rate	**2012**	2012

During 2007, the Company amended its U.S. retiree medical plan to limit the Company's exposure to increases in retiree medical costs for both current and future retirees. As a result, the effects of a 1 percentage point change in the assumed health care cost trend rate would not be significant to the Company.

The discount rate assumptions used to account for pension and other postretirement benefit plans reflect the rates at which the benefit obligations could be effectively settled. Rates for each of our U.S. plans at December 31, 2009, were determined using a cash flow matching technique whereby the rates of a yield curve, developed from high-quality debt securities, were applied to the benefit obligations to determine the appropriate discount rate. For our non-U.S. plans, we base the discount rate on comparable indices within each of the non-U.S. countries. The rate of compensation increase assumption is determined by the Company based upon annual reviews. We review external data and our own historical trends for health care costs to determine the health care cost trend rate assumptions.

Cash Flows

Our estimated future benefit payments for funded and unfunded plans are as follows (in millions):

Year Ended December 31,	2010	2011	2012	2013	2014	2015-2019
Pension benefit payments	$230	$232	$242	$252	$263	$1,541
Other benefit payments[1]	33	35	38	39	40	208
Total estimated benefit payments	$263	$267	$280	$291	$303	$1,749

[1] The expected benefit payments for our other postretirement benefit plans are net of estimated federal subsidies expected to be received under the Medicare Prescription Drug, Improvement and Modernization Act of 2003. Federal subsidies are estimated to be approximately $10 million annually for the period 2010-2014, and $15 million annually for the period 2015-2019.

We anticipate making contributions in 2010 of approximately $73 million, primarily to our non-U.S. pension plans.

Defined Contribution Plans

Our Company sponsors qualified defined contribution plans covering substantially all U.S. employees. Under the primary plan, we match 100 percent of participants' contributions up to a maximum of 3 percent of compensation, subject to certain limitations. Company costs related to the U.S. plans were approximately $27 million, $22 million and $29 million in 2009, 2008 and 2007, respectively. We also sponsor defined contribution plans in certain locations outside the United States. Company costs associated with those plans were approximately $36 million, $20 million and $25 million in 2009, 2008 and 2007, respectively.

Helmerich & Payne
2009 Annual Report

Note 10. Employee Benefit Plans

We maintain a domestic noncontributory defined benefit pension plan covering certain U.S. employees who meet certain age and service requirements. In July 2003, we revised the Helmerich & Payne, Inc. Employee Retirement Plan ("Pension Plan") to close the Pension Plan to new participants effective October 1, 2003, and reduce benefit accruals for current participants through September 30, 2006, at which time benefit accruals were discontinued and the Pension Plan was frozen.

On September 30, 2007, we adopted the provisions of ASC 715, "Compensation—Retirement Benefits". This statement requires employers to a) recognize the funded status of a benefit plan, determined as the difference between the fair value of plan assets and the benefit obligation, as an asset or liability in the statement of financial position, b) recognize as a component of other comprehensive income, net of tax, the gains or losses and prior service costs or credits that arise during the period but are not recognized as components of net periodic benefit cost, c) measure the defined benefit plan assets and obligations as of the date of the employer's fiscal year-end, which we have used historically, and d) include additional disclosures in the notes to the financial statements about effects on net periodic benefit cost that arise from delayed recognition of the gains or losses, prior service costs or credits, and transition assets or obligations.

The following table provides a reconciliation of the changes in the pension benefit obligations and fair value of Pension Plan assets over the two-year period ended September 30, 2009 and a statement of the funded status as of September 30, 2009 and 2008 (in thousands):

	2009	2008
Accumulated Benefit Obligation ("ABO")	$ 89,996	$ 69,475
Changes in Projected Benefit Obligations ("PBO")		
Projected benefit obligation at beginning of year	$ 69,475	$ 78,247
Interest cost	4,988	4,919
Actuarial gain (loss)	18,977	(8,975)
Benefits paid	(3,444)	(4,716)
Projected benefit obligation at end of year	$ 89,996	$ 69,475
Change in plan asset		
Fair value of plan assets at beginning of year	$ 59,605	$ 74,877
Actual return on plan assets	270	(13,662)
Employer contribution	750	3,106
Benefits paid	(3,444)	(4,716)
Fair value of plan assets at end of year	$ 57,181	$ 59,605
Funded status of the plan at end of year	$ (32,815)	$ (9,870)

September 30,	2009	2008
Amounts Recognized in the Consolidated Balance Sheets (in thousands):		
Accrued liabilities	$ (40)	$ (43)
Noncurrent liabilities-other	(32,775)	(9,827)
Net amount recognized	$(32,815)	$(9,870)
The amounts recognized in Accumulated Other Comprehensive Income at September 2009 and 2008, and not yet reflected in net periodic benefit cost, are as follows (in thousands):		
Net actuarial gain (loss)	$(29,267)	$(5,919)
Prior service cost	(1)	(1)
Total	$(29,268)	$(5,920)

The amount recognized in Accumulated Other Comprehensive Income and not yet reflected in periodic benefit cost expected to be amortized in next year's periodic benefit cost is a net actuarial loss of $2.1 million.

The weighted average assumptions used for the pension calculations were as follows:

Years Ended September 30,	2009	2008	2007
Discount rate for net periodic benefit costs	7.25%	6.25%	5.75%
Discount rate for year-end obligations	5.42%	7.25%	6.25%
Expected return on plan assets	8.00%	8.00%	8.00%

We contributed $0.8 million to the Pension Plan in fiscal 2009 to fund distributions in lieu of liquidating pension assets. We estimate contributing at least $3.0 million in fiscal 2010 to meet the minimum contribution required by law and expect to make additional contributions to continue funding distributions. Subsequent to September 30, 2009, we contributed $1.0 million to the plan. With the unpredictability in the equity, debt and global markets, it is possible that contributions in fiscal 2010 will be greater than expected.

Components of the net periodic pension expense (benefit) were as follows (in thousands):

Years Ended September 30,	2009	2008	2007
Interest cost	$ 4,988	$ 4,919	$4,865
Expected return on plan assets	(4,643)	(5,990)	(5,123)
Amortization of prior service costs	(1)	–	–
Recognized net actuarial loss	3	9	139
Net pension expense (benefit)	$ 347	$(1,062)	$ (119)

The following table reflects the expected benefits to be paid from the Pension Plan in each of the next five fiscal years and in the aggregate for the five years thereafter (in thousands).

			Years Ended September 30,			
2010	2011	2012	2013	2014	2015-2019	Total
$3,789	$3,977	$4,439	$4,824	$5,041	$28,492	$50,562

Included in the Pension Plan is an unfunded supplemental executive retirement plan.

INVESTMENT STRATEGY AND ASSET ALLOCATION

Our investment policy and strategies are established with a long-term view in mind. The investment strategy is intended to help pay the cost of the Plan while providing adequate security to meet the benefits promised under the Plan. We maintain a diversified asset mix to minimize the risk of a material loss to the portfolio value that might occur from devaluation of any one investment. In determining the appropriate asset mix, our financial strength and ability to fund potential shortfalls are considered.

The expected long-term rate of return on plan assets is based on historical and projected rates of return for current and planned asset classes in the Plans' investment portfolio after analyzing historical experience and future expectations of the return and volatility of various asset classes.

The target allocation for 2010 and the asset allocation for the Pension Plan at the end of fiscal 2009 and 2008, by asset category, follow:

Asset Category	Target Allocation 2010	Percentage of Plan Assets At September 30, 2009	Percentage of Plan Assets At September 30, 2008
U.S. equities	56%	27%	58%
International equities	14	15	15
Fixed income	25	27	24
Real estate and other	5	1	3
Total	100%	100%	100%

DEFINED CONTRIBUTION PLAN

Substantially all employees on the United States payroll may elect to participate in the 401(k)/Thrift Plan by contributing a portion of their earnings. We contribute an amount equal to 100 percent of the first five percent of the participant's compensation subject to certain limitations. The annual expense incurred for this defined contribution plan was $14.3 million, $15.0 million, and $10.9 million in fiscal 2009, 2008 and 2007, respectively.

FOREIGN PLAN

We maintain an unfunded pension plan in one of our international subsidiaries. Pension expense was approximately $0.4 million, $0.4 million and $0.3 million in fiscal 2009, 2008 and 2007, respectively. The pension liability at September 30, 2009 and 2008 was $5.0 million.

Humana Inc.
2009 Annual Report

13. Employee Benefit Plans

Employee Savings Plan

We have defined contribution retirement and savings plans covering eligible employees. Our contribution to these plans is based on various percentages of compensation, and in some instances, on the amount of our employees' contributions to the plans. The cost of these plans amounted to approximately $102.5 million in 2009, $79.6 million in 2008, and $69.7 million in 2007, all of which was funded currently to the extent it was deductible for federal income tax purposes. The Company's cash match is invested pursuant to the participant's contribution direction. Based on the closing stock price of $43.89 on December 31, 2009, approximately 15% of the retirement and savings plan's assets were invested in our common stock, or approximately 4.5 million shares, representing 3% of the shares outstanding as of December 31, 2009. At December 31, 2009, approximately 7.9 million shares of our common stock were reserved for issuance under our defined contribution retirement and savings plans.

Stock-Based Compensation

We have plans under which options to purchase our common stock and restricted stock awards have been granted to executive officers, directors and key employees. The terms and vesting schedules for stock-based awards vary by type of grant. Generally, the awards vest upon time-based conditions. For prospective grants of stock options or restricted stock awards on or after January 1, 2010, our equity award program includes a retirement provision that treats all employees with a combination of age and years of service with the Company totaling 65 or greater, with a minimum required age of 55 and a minimum requirement of 5 years of service, as retirement-eligible. Upon exercise, stock-based compensation awards are settled with authorized but unissued company stock. The compensation expense that has been charged against income for these plans was as follows for the years ended December 31, 2009, 2008, and 2007:

(in thousands)	2009	2008	2007
Stock-based compensation expense by type:			
Stock options	$19,555	$18,202	$15,408
Restricted stock awards	46,315	37,167	26,724
Total stock-based compensation expense	65,870	55,369	42,132
Tax benefit recognized	(24,128)	(20,282)	(15,568)
Stock-based compensation expense, net of tax	$41,742	$35,087	$26,564

The tax benefit recognized in our consolidated financial statements is based on the amount of compensation expense recorded for book purposes. The actual tax benefit realized in our tax return is based on the intrinsic value, or the excess of the market value over the exercise or purchase price, of stock options exercised and restricted stock awards vested during the period. The actual tax benefit realized for the deductions taken on our tax returns from option exercises and restricted stock vesting totaled $16.3 million in 2009, $16.9 million in 2008, and $48.0 million in 2007. There was no capitalized stock-based compensation expense.

The stock plans provide that one restricted share is equivalent to 1.7 stock options. At December 31, 2009, there were 12,818,855 shares reserved for stock award plans, including 4,797,304 shares of common stock available for future grants assuming all stock options or 2,821,944 shares available for future grants assuming all restricted shares.

Stock Options

Stock options are granted with an exercise price equal to the average market value of the underlying common stock on the date of grant. Our stock plans, as approved by the Board of Directors and stockholders, define average market value as the average of the highest and lowest stock prices reported by the New York Stock Exchange on a given date. Exercise provisions vary, but most options vest in whole or in part 1 to 3 years after grant and expire 7 to 10 years after grant. Upon grant, stock options are assigned a fair value based on the Black-

Scholes valuation model. Compensation expense is recognized on a straight-line basis over the total requisite service period, generally the total vesting period, for the entire award. For stock options granted on or after January 1, 2010 to retirement eligible employees, the compensation expense is recognized on a straight-line basis over the shorter of the requisite service period or the period from the date of grant to an employee's eligible retirement date.

The weighted-average fair value of each option granted during 2009, 2008, and 2007 is provided below. The fair value was estimated on the date of grant using the Black-Scholes pricing model with the weighted-average assumptions indicated below:

	2009	2008	2007
Weighted-average fair value at grant date	$14.24	$17.95	$21.07
Expected option life (years)	4.6	5.1	4.8
Expected volatility	39.2%	28.2%	28.9%
Risk-free interest rate at grant date	1.9%	2.9%	4.5%
Dividend yield	None	None	None

When valuing employee stock options, we stratify the employee population into three homogenous groups that historically have exhibited similar exercise behaviors. These groups are executive officers, directors, and all other employees. We value the stock options based on the unique assumptions for each of these employee groups.

We calculate the expected term for our employee stock options based on historical employee exercise behavior and base the risk-free interest rate on a traded zero-coupon U.S. Treasury bond with a term substantially equal to the option's expected term.

The volatility used to value employee stock options is based on historical volatility. We calculate historical volatility using a simple-average calculation methodology based on daily price intervals as measured over the expected term of the option.

Activity for our option plans was as follows for the year ended December 31, 2009:

	Shares Under Option	Weighted-Average Exercise Price
Options outstanding at December 31, 2008	5,777,115	$42.70
Granted	1,460,742	40.11
Exercised	(1,052,855)	17.43
Expired	(34,137)	60.48
Forfeited	(92,544)	60.67
Options outstanding at December 31, 2009	6,058,321	$46.10
Options exercisable at December 31, 2009	3,383,787	$44.09

As of December 31, 2009, outstanding stock options had an aggregate intrinsic value of $33.5 million, and a weighted-average remaining contractual term of 4.3 years. As of December 31, 2009, exercisable stock options had an aggregate intrinsic value of $27.3 million, and a weighted-average remaining contractual term of 3.2 years. The total intrinsic value of stock options exercised during 2009 was $23.7 million, compared with $18.3 million during 2008 and $133.9 million during 2007. Cash received from stock option exercises totaled $18.4 million in 2009, $12.1 million in 2008, and $62.7 million in 2007.

Total compensation expense not yet recognized related to nonvested options was $25.5 million at December 31, 2009. We expect to recognize this compensation expense over a weighted-average period of approximately 2.0 years.

Restricted Stock Awards

Restricted stock awards are granted with a fair value equal to the market price of our common stock on the date of grant. Compensation expense is recorded straight-line over the vesting period, generally three years from the date of grant. For restricted stock awards granted on or after January 1, 2010 to retirement eligible employees, the compensation expense is recognized on a straight-line basis over the shorter of the vesting period or the period from the date of grant to an employee's eligible retirement date.

The weighted-average grant date fair value of our restricted stock awards was $41.16 in 2009, $68.10 in 2008, and $63.59 in 2007. Activity for our restricted stock awards was as follows for the year ended December 31, 2009:

	Shares	Weighted-Average Exercise Price
Nonvested restricted stock at December 31, 2008	2,007,301	$62.12
Granted	978,064	41.16
Vested	(656,054)	54.34
Forfeited	(86,484)	57.46
Nonvested restricted stock at December 31, 2009	2,242,827	$55.44

The fair value of shares vested during the years ended was $35.6 million in 2009, $28.7 million in 2008, and $3.4 million in 2007. Beginning in 2005, a greater proportion of stock awards granted to employees, excluding executive officers, were restricted stock awards with a three-year vesting schedule as opposed to stock options, which resulted in an increase in the fair value of shares vested from 2007 to 2008. Total compensation expense not yet recognized related to nonvested restricted stock awards was $42.9 million at December 31, 2009. We expect to recognize this compensation expense over a weighted-average period of approximately 1.7 years. There are no other contractual terms covering restricted stock awards once vested.

In addition to restricted stock awards, we granted 36,746 restricted stock units to directors in 2009 with a weighted-average grant date fair value of $33.95.

As of December 31, 2009, 102,728 restricted stock units were outstanding, primarily associated with director compensation.

14. Earnings per Common Share Computation

Detail supporting the computation of basic and diluted earnings per common share was as follows for the years ended December 31, 2009, 2008 and 2007:

(in thousands, except per share results)	2009	2008	2007
Net income available for common stockholders	$1,039,675	$647,154	$833,684
Weighted-average outstanding shares of common stock used to compute basic earnings per common share	167,364	167,172	166,871
Dilutive effect of:			
Employee stock options	677	1,173	2,251
Restricted stock	1,030	842	698
Shares used to compute diluted earnings per common share	169,071	169,187	169,820
Basic earnings per common share	$ 6.21	$ 3.87	$ 5.00
Diluted earnings per common share	$ 6.15	$ 3.83	$ 4.91

Restricted stock and stock options to purchase 5,675,241 shares in 2009, 3,243,933 shares in 2008, and 1,017,381 shares in 2007 were anti-dilutive and, therefore, were not included in the computations of diluted earnings per common share.

Goodyear Tire & Rubber 2008 Annual Report

Note 14. Pension, Other Postretirement Benefit and Savings Plans

We adopted SFAS No. 158, "Employers' Accounting for Defined Benefit Pension and Other Postretirement Plans" ("SFAS No. 158") effective December 31, 2006. The impact of the adoption of SFAS No. 158 has been reflected within our consolidated financial statements as of December 31, 2006.

We provide employees with defined benefit pension or defined contribution plans. Our principal domestic hourly pension plan provides benefits based on length of service. The principal domestic pension plans covering salaried employees provide benefits based on final five-year average earnings formulas. Salaried employees who made voluntary contributions to these plans receive higher benefits. Effective January 1, 2005, the domestic pension plans covering salaried employees were closed to newly hired salaried employees in the United States, and those employees are eligible for Company-funded contributions into our defined contribution savings plan. Effective December 31, 2008, we froze our

U.S. salaried pension plans and, effective January 1, 2009, implemented improvements to our defined contribution savings plan, as discussed below.

In addition, we provide substantially all domestic employees and employees at certain non-U.S. subsidiaries with health care benefits or life insurance benefits upon retirement. Insurance companies provide life insurance and certain health care benefits through premiums based on expected benefits to be paid during the year. Substantial portions of the health care benefits for domestic retirees are not insured and are funded from operations.

Effective August 22, 2008, health care benefits for current and future domestic retirees who were represented by the United Steelworkers ("USW") became the responsibility of an independent Voluntary Employees' Beneficiary Association ("VEBA"). We made a one-time cash contribution of $980 million to the VEBA on August 27, 2008 and a one-time cash contribution of $27 million to a VEBA for USW retirees of our former Engineered Products business ("EPD VEBA") on December 4, 2008. As a result of these actions, we remeasured the benefit obligation of the affected plans. The discount rate used to measure the benefit obligations of our U.S. other postretirement health care plans for USW retirees was 6.75% at August 27, 2008, compared to 6.00% at December 31, 2007. The $980 million cash contribution to the VEBA was considered plan assets from August 27, 2008 until the appeals period expired in September 2008.

Responsibility for providing retiree healthcare for current and future domestic USW retirees has been transferred permanently to the VEBA and the EPD VEBA and we recorded a $9 million charge for settlement of the related obligations in 2008, which included $8 million of transactional costs incurred related to the VEBA settlement. The funding of the VEBA and subsequent settlement accounting reduced the OPEB liability by $1,107 million, of which $108 million was previously recognized in accumulated other comprehensive loss.

On February 28, 2007, we announced that we will freeze our U.S. salaried pension plans effective December 31, 2008 and will implement improvements to our defined contribution savings plan effective January 1, 2009. As a result of these actions, we recognized a curtailment charge of $64 million during the first quarter of 2007. On February 28, 2007, we also announced changes to our U.S. salaried other postretirement benefit plans effective January 1, 2008, including increasing the amounts that salaried retirees contribute toward the cost of their medical benefits, redesigning retiree medical benefit plans to minimize the cost impact on premiums, and discontinuing company-paid life insurance for retirees. As a result of these actions, we were required to remeasure the benefit obligations of the affected plans. The discount rate used to measure the benefit obligations of our U.S. salaried pension plan at February 28, 2007 and December 31, 2006 was 5.75%. The discount rate used to measure the benefit obligation of our U.S. salaried other postretirement benefit plans at February 28, 2007 was 5.50% compared to 5.75% at December 31, 2006.

During the fourth quarter of 2007, we recognized a settlement charge of $14 million for our U.S. salaried pension plan. This settlement charge resulted from total 2007 lump sum payments from the salaried pension plan exceeding 2007 service and interest cost for the plan. These payments primarily related to employees who terminated service as a result of the sale of our Engineered Products business. As such, $11 million of the charge was included in Discontinued Operations.

Effective March 1, 2006, all active participants in the Brazil pension plan were converted to a defined contribution savings plan, resulting in the recognition of a curtailment gain. The announcement of the elimination of tire production at our Tyler, Texas and Valleyfield, Quebec facilities resulted in the recognition of curtailment and termination charges for both pensions and other postretirement benefit plans during 2006. Other pension plans provide benefits similar to the principal domestic plans as well as termination indemnity plans at certain non-U.S. subsidiaries.

We use a December 31 measurement date for all plans.

Total benefits cost and amounts recognized in other comprehensive loss (income) follows:

| | Pension Plans | | | | | | Other Benefits | | |
| | U.S. | | | Non-U.S. | | | | | |
(In millions)	2008	2007	2006	2008	2007	2006	2008	2007	2006
Benefits cost:									
Service cost	$ 60	$ 84	$ 91	$ 32	$ 41	$ 49	$ 11	$ 14	$ 21
Interest cost	312	306	295	162	152	133	84	109	133
Expected return on plan assets	(371)	(351)	(295)	(139)	(130)	(112)	(5)	–	–
Amortization of prior service cost (credit)	36	40	59	2	2	4	(19)	(5)	42
Net losses	38	56	91	49	76	73	7	8	9
Net periodic cost	75	135	241	106	141	147	78	126	205
Curtailments/ settlements	4	67	20	3	1	(9)	9	–	31
Termination benefits	1	–	10	–	–	26	–	–	30
Total benefits cost	$ 80	$202	$271	$109	$142	$164	$ 87	$126	$266
Recognized in other comprehensive loss (income) before tax and minority:									
Prior service cost (credit) from plan amendments	$ –	$ 10		$ –	$ –			$ –	$(501)

(In millions)	Pension Plans						Other Benefits		
	U.S.			Non-U.S.					
	2008	2007	2006	2008	2007	2006	2008	2007	2006
Increase (decrease) in net actuarial losses	1,656	(215)		(145)	(140)		(80)	(139)	
Amortization of prior service (cost) credit in net periodic cost	(36)	(40)		(2)	(3)		19	5	
Amortization of net losses in net periodic cost	(38)	(56)		(53)	(74)		(7)	(8)	
Immediate recognition of prior service cost and unrecognized gains and losses due to curtailments, settlements and divestitures	(4)	(145)		(2)	(36)		(50)	32	
Total recognized in other comprehensive loss (income) before tax and minority	1,578	(446)		(02)	(253)		(118)	(611)	
Total recognized in total benefits cost and other comprehensive loss (income) before tax and minority	$1,658	$(244)		$ (93)	$(111)		$ (31)	$(485)	

Other Benefits total benefits cost was $70 million, $106 million and $232 million for our U.S. plans in 2008, 2007 and 2006, respectively, and $17 million, $20 million and $34 million for our Non-U.S. plans in 2008, 2007 and 2006, respectively.

We use the fair value of our pension assets in the calculation of pension expense for substantially all of our pension plans.

The estimated prior service cost and net actuarial loss for the defined benefit pension plans that will be amortized from AOCL into benefits cost in 2009 are $33 million and $157 million, respectively, for our U.S. plans and $2 million and $28 million, respectively for our non-U.S. plans.

The estimated prior service credit and net actuarial loss for the postretirement benefit plans that will be amortized from AOCL into benefits cost in 2009 are a benefit of $38 million and expense of $7 million, respectively.

The change in benefit obligation and plan assets for 2008 and 2007 and the amounts recognized in our Consolidated Balance Sheets at December 31, 2008 and 2007 are as follows:

	Pension Plans				Other Benefits	
	U.S.		Non-U.S.			
(In millions)	2008	2007	2008	2007	2008	2007
Change in benefit obligation:						
Beginning balance	$(5,105)	$(5,417)	$ (2,923)	$(2,927)	$(1,762)	$(2,456)
Service cost— benefits earned	(60)	(87)	(32)	(41)	(11)	(15)
Interest cost	(312)	(306)	(162)	(152)	(84)	(110)
Plan amendments	–	(10)	–	–	–	501
Actuarial gain	80	207	234	235	22	125
Participant contributions	(8)	(9)	(5)	(5)	(47)	(41)
Curtailments/ settlements	11	190	12	27	1,107	–
Termination benefits	(1)	(3)	–	–	–	–
Divestitures	–	–	–	4	–	–
Foreign currency translation	–	–	563	(214)	45	(32)
Benefit payments	379	330	151	150	216	266
Ending balance	$(5,016)	$(5,105)	$(2,162)	$(2,923)	$ (514)	$(1,762)

(In millions)	Pension Plans				Other Benefits	
	U.S.		Non-U.S.			
	2008	2007	2008	2007	2008	2007
Change in plan assets:						
Beginning balance	$ 4,456	$ 4,050	$ 2,110	$ 1,850	$ 4	$ 4
Actual return on plan assets	(1,366)	332	(138)	96	6	–
Company contributions to plan assets	159	519	149	158	1,009	2
Cash funding of direct participant payments	20	12	36	30	167	223
Participant contributions	8	9	5	5	47	41
Curtailments/settlements	(11)	(136)	(12)	(24)	(1,012)	–
Foreign currency translation	–	–	(456)	145	(1)	–
Benefit payments	(379)	(330)	(151)	(150)	(216)	(266)
Ending balance	$ 2,887	$ 4,456	1,543	$ 2,110	$ 4	$ 4
Funded status at end of year	$(2,129)	$ (649)	$ (619)	$ (813)	$ (510)	$(1,758)

Other Benefits funded status was $(352) million and $(1,530) million for our U.S. plans at December 31, 2008 and 2007, respectively, and $(158) million and $(228) million for our Non-U.S. plans at December 31, 2008 and 2007, respectively.

Amounts recognized in the Consolidated Balance Sheets consist of:

(In millions)	Pension Plans				Other Benefits	
	U.S.		Non-U.S.			
	2008	2007	2008	2007	2008	2007
Noncurrent assets	$ –	$ 1	$ 35	$ 61	$ –	$ –
Current liabilities	(17)	(23)	(21)	(22)	(61)	(193)
Noncurrent liabilities	(2,112)	(306)	(633)	(852)	(449)	(1,565)
Net amount recognized	$ (2,129)	$ (649)	$(619)	$(813)	$(510)	$(1,758)

Amounts recognized in accumulated other comprehensive loss, net of tax and minority, consist of:

(In millions)	Pension Plans U.S. 2008	U.S. 2007	Pension Plans Non-U.S. 2008	Non-U.S. 2007	Other Benefits 2008	Other Benefits 2007
Prior service cost (credit)	$ 200	$ 236	$ 8	$ 12	$ (318)	$(183)
Net actuarial loss	2,550	936	624	822	109	92
Gross amount recognized	2,750	1,172	632	834	(209)	(91)
Deferred income taxes	(210)	(210)	(68)	(91)	1	2
Minority shareholders' equity	(51)	(19)	(101)	(149)	5	15
Net amount recognized	$2,489	$ 943	$ 463	$ 594	$(203)	$ (74)

The following table presents significant weighted average assumptions used to determine benefit obligations at December 31:

(In millions)	Pension Plans 2008	Pension Plans 2007	Other Benefits 2008	Other Benefits 2007
Discount rate:				
—U.S.	6.50%	6.25%	6.50%	6.00%
—Non-U.S.	6.31	5.84	7.71	6.55
Rate of compensation increase:				
—U.S.	–	4.04	–	–
—Non-U.S.	3.71	3.81	4.20	4.26

The following table presents significant weighted average assumptions used to determine benefits cost for the years ended December 31:

(In millions)	Pension Plans 2008	Pension Plans 2007	Pension Plans 2006	Other Benefits 2008	Other Benefits 2007	Other Benefits 2006
Discount rate:						
—U.S.	6.25%	5.75%	5.50%	6.08%	5.75%	5.50%
—Non-U.S.	5.84	5.01	4.95	6.55	5.76	6.18
Expected long term return on plan assets:						
—U.S.	8.50	8.50	8.50	6.75	–	–
—Non-U.S.	7.03	6.69	6.92	12.00	12.50	10.25

(In millions)	Pension Plans			Other Benefits		
	2008	2007	2006	2008	2007	2006
Rate of compensation increase:						
—U.S.	4.04	4.04	4.04	–	4.00	4.08
—Non-U.S.	3.81	3.63	3.64	4.26	4.32	4.28

For 2008, an assumed discount rate of 6.25% was used for the U.S. pension plans. This rate was developed from a portfolio of bonds from issuers rated AA- or higher by Standard & Poor's as of December 31, 2007, with cash flows similar to the timing of our expected benefit payment cash flows. For our non-U.S. locations, a weighted average discount rate of 5.84% was used. This rate was developed based on the nature of the liabilities and local environments, using available bond indices, yield curves, and long term inflation.

For 2008, an expected long term rate of return of 8.50% was used for the U.S. pension plans. In developing this rate, we evaluated the compound annualized returns of our U.S. pension fund over a period of 15 years or more through December 31, 2007. In addition, we evaluated input from our pension fund consultant on asset class return expectations and long term inflation. For our non-U.S. locations, a weighted average assumed long term rate of return of 7.03% was used. Input from local pension fund consultants concerning asset class return expectations and long-term inflation form the basis of this assumption.

The following table presents estimated future benefit payments from the plans as of December 31, 2008. Benefit payments for other postretirement benefits are presented net of retiree contributions:

	Pension Plans		Other Benefits	
(In millions)	U.S.	Non-U.S	Without Medicare Part D Subsidy	Medicare Part D Subsidy Receipts
2009	$ 383	$125	$ 67	$ (5)
2010	382	125	62	(5)
2011	407	140	58	(4)
2012	395	133	54	(4)
2013	395	139	51	(4)
2014–2018	2,036	756	219	(17)

The following table presents selected information on our pension plans:

(In millions)	U.S.		Non-U.S.	
	2008	2007	2008	2007
All plans:				
Accumulated benefit obligation	$5,012	$5,092	$2,038	$2,766
Plans not fully-funded:				
Projected benefit obligation	$5,016	$4,993	$1,815	$2,413

(In millions)	U.S.		Non-U.S.	
	2008	2007	2008	2007
Accumulated benefit obligation	5,012	4,981	1,716	2,290
Fair value of plan assets	2,887	4,343	1,164	1,544

Certain non-U.S. subsidiaries maintain unfunded pension plans consistent with local practices and requirements. At December 31, 2008, these plans accounted for $237 million of our accumulated pension benefit obligation, $254 million of our projected pension benefit obligation, and $24 million of our AOCL adjustment. At December 31, 2007, these plans accounted for $268 million of our accumulated pension benefit obligation, $288 million of our projected pension benefit obligation, and $37 million of our AOCL adjustment.

Our pension plan weighted average asset allocation at December 31, by asset category, follows:

	U.S.		Non-U.S.	
	2008	2007	2008	2007
Equity securities	64%	68%	31%	41%
Debt securities	35	32	63	52
Real estate	–	–	1	1
Cash and short term securities	1	–	5	6
Total	100%	100%	100%	100%

At December 31, 2008 and 2007, the Plans did not directly hold any of our Common Stock.

Our pension investment policy recognizes the long term nature of pension liabilities, the benefits of diversification across asset classes and the effects of inflation. The diversified portfolio is designed to maximize returns consistent with levels of liquidity and investment risk that are prudent and reasonable. All assets are managed externally according to guidelines we have established individually with investment managers. The manager guidelines prohibit the use of any type of investment derivative without our prior approval. Portfolio risk is controlled by having managers comply with guidelines, establishing the maximum size of any single holding in their portfolios and by using managers with different investment styles. We periodically undertake asset and liability modeling studies to determine the appropriateness of the investments. The portfolio includes holdings of domestic, non-U.S., and private equities, global high quality and high yield fixed income securities, and short term interest bearing deposits. The target asset allocation of the U.S. pension fund is 70% equities and 30% fixed income. Actual U.S. pension fund asset allocations are reviewed on a monthly basis and the pension fund is rebalanced to target ranges on an as needed basis.

We expect to contribute approximately $350 million to $400 million to our funded U.S. and non-U.S. pension plans in 2009.

Assumed health care cost trend rates at December 31 follow:

	2008	2007
Health care cost trend rate assumed for the next year	9.70%	10.50%
Rate to which the cost trend rate is assumed to decline (the ultimate trend rate)	5.0	5.0
Year that the rate reaches the ultimate trend rate	2014	2014

A 1% change in the assumed health care cost trend would have increased (decreased) the accumulated postretirement benefit obligation at December 31, 2008 and the aggregate service and interest cost for the year then ended as follows:

(In millions)	1% Increase	1% Decrease
Accumulated postretirement benefit obligation	$22	$(18)
Aggregate service and interest cost	2	(2)

Savings Plans

Substantially all employees in the U.S. and employees of certain non-U.S. locations are eligible to participate in a defined contribution savings plan. Expenses recognized for contributions to these plans were $37 million, $32 million and $26 million for 2008, 2007 and 2006, respectively.

Black and Decker
2007 Annual Report

Note 12. Postretirement Benefits

As disclosed in Note 1 of Notes to Consolidated Financial Statements, SFAS No. 158, adopted by the Corporation effective December 31, 2006, requires the recognition of the overfunded or underfunded status of a defined benefit postretirement plan as an asset or liability in the balance sheet, with changes in the funded status recorded through other comprehensive income (loss). The Corporation uses a measurement date of September 30 for the majority of its defined benefit pension and postretirement plans. Defined postretirement benefits consist of several unfunded health care plans that provide certain postretirement medical, dental, and life insurance benefits for most United States employees. The postretirement medical benefits are contributory and include certain cost-sharing features, such as deductibles and co-payments. The following tables set forth the funded status of the defined benefit pension and postretirement plans, and amounts recognized in the Consolidated Balance Sheet, in millions of dollars.

	2007			2006		
	Pension Benefits Plans in the United States	*Pension Benefits Plans Outside of the United States*	*Other Post-Retirement Benefits All Plans*	*Pension Benefits Plans in the United States*	*Pension Benefits Plans Outside of the United States*	*Other Post-Retirement Benefits All Plans*
CHANGE IN BENEFIT OBLIGATION						
Benefit obligation at beginning of year	$1,074.8	$ 794.0	$88.8	$1,045.7	$757.1	$103.8
Service Cost	24.8	14.7	0.8	23.5	14.7	1.0
Interest cost	62.5	39.6	5.3	58.4	38.4	5.9
Plan participants' contributions	–	1.4	3.6	–	1.6	3.5
Actuarial (gains) losses	(83.5)	(76.6)	2.4	9.7	(76.7)	(10.0)
Foreign currency exchange rate changes	–	54.2	1.1	–	90.0	0.4
Benefits paid	(65.4)	(34.3)	(15.1)	(62.7)	(31.1)	(15.1)
Plan amendments	–	.1	–	.2	–	(0.7)
Benefit obligation at end of year	1,013.2	793.1	86.9	1,074.8	794.0	88.8
CHANGE IN PLAN ASSETS						
Fair value of plan assets at beginning of year	914.2	566.0	–	890.4	468.4	–
Actual return on plan assets	139.0	58.8	–	88.8	51.6	–
Expenses	(6.5)	(1.5)	–	(7.1)	(1.2)	–
Benefits paid	(65.4)	(32.8)	(15.1)	(62.7)	(29.9)	(15.1)
Employer contributions	6.5	16.0	11.5	4.8	15.0	11.6
Contributions by plan participants	–	1.4	3.6	–	1.6	3.5
Foreign currency exchange rate changes	–	35.7	–	–	60.5	–
Fair value of plan assets at end of year	987.8	643.6	–	914.2	566.0	–
Funded status	(25.4)	(149.5)	(86.9)	(160.6)	(228.0)	(88.8)
Contributions subsequent to measurement date	.1	4.5	–	–	3.3	–
Accrued benefit cost at December 31	$ (25.3)	$(145.0)	$(86.9)	$ (160.6)	$ (224.7)	$ (88.8)
AMOUNTS RECOGNIZED IN THE CONSOLIDATED BALANCE SHEET						
Noncurrent assets	$ 75.6	$ .9	–	$ 31.3	–	–

	2007			2006		
	Pension Benefits Plans in the United States	Pension Benefits Plans Outside of the United States	Other Post-Retirement Benefits All Plans	Pension Benefits Plans in the United States	Pension Benefits Plans Outside of the United States	Other Post-Retirement Benefits All Plans
Current liabilities	(7.6)	(5.2)	(9.6)	(9.3)	(4.4)	(9.3)
Postretirement benefits	(93.3)	(140.7)	(77.3)	(182.6)	(220.3)	(79.5)
Net amount recognized at December 31	$ (25.3)	$(145.0)	$(86.9)	$(160.6)	$(224.7)	$ (88.8)

WEIGHTED-AVERAGE ASSUMPTIONS USED TO DETERMINE BENEFIT OBLIGATIONS AS OF MEASUREMENT DATE

Discount rate	6.50%	5.67%	6.00%	6.00%	4.93%	6.25%
Rate of compensation increase	3.95%	3.65%	–	3.93%	3.65%	–

The amounts recognized in accumulated other comprehensive income (loss) as of December 31, 2007 and 2006, are as follows:

December 31, 2007	Pension Benefits Plans in the United States	Pension Benefits Plans Outside of the United States	Other Postretirement Benefits All Plans	Total
Prior service cost (credit)	$ 11.8	$ 10.8	$(26.3)	$ (3.7)
Net loss	196.7	93.1	11.8	301.6
Total	$208.5	$103.9	$(14.5)	$297.9
December 31, 2006				
Prior service cost (credit)	$ 14.7	$ 11.8	$(30.9)	$ (4.4)
Net loss	363.9	193.1	9.8	566.8
Total	$378.6	$204.9	$(21.1)	$562.4

The amounts in accumulated other comprehensive loss as of December 31, 2007, that are expected to be recognized as components of net periodic benefit cost (credit) during 2008 are as follows:

	Pension Benefits Plans in the United States	Pension Benefits Plans Outside of the United States	Other Postretirement Benefits All Plans	Total
Prior service cost (credit)	$ 2.1	$1.5	$(3.6)	$ –
Net loss	15.1	5.1	0.4	20.6
Total	$17.2	$6.6	$(3.2)	$20.6

The allocation, by asset category, of assets of defined benefit pension plans in the United States at September 30, 2007 and 2006, respectively, were as follows:

Plan Assets at September 30	2007	2006
Equity Securities	69%	69%
Fixed Income Securities	28%	28%
Alternative Investments	3%	3%
	100%	100%

At September 30, 2007, the Corporation's targeted allocation, by asset category, of assets of defined benefit pension plans in the United States is equity securities—65% (comprised of 50% U.S. and 15% non-U.S. equities); fixed income securities—30%; and alternative investments—5%.

The allocation, by asset category, of assets of defined benefit pension plans outside of the United States at September 30, 2007 and 2006, respectively, were as follows:

Plan Assets at September 30	2007	2006
Equity Securities	72%	72%
Fixed Income Securities	20%	21%
Real Estate	7%	5%
Other	1%	2%
	100%	100%

At September 30, 2007, the Corporation's targeted allocation, by asset category, of assets of defined benefit pension plans outside of the United States is equity securities—68%; fixed income securities—25%; and real estate—7%.

To the extent that the actual allocation of plan assets differs from the targeted allocation by more than 5% for any category, plan assets are rebalanced within three months.

The Corporation establishes its estimated long-term return on plan assets considering various factors, which include the targeted asset allocation percentages, historic returns, and expected future returns. Specifically, the factors are considered in the fourth quarter of the year preceding the year for which those assumptions are applied. The accumulated benefit obligation related to all defined benefit pension plans and information related to unfunded and underfunded defined benefit pension plans at the end of each year, in millions of dollars, follows:

	Pension Benefits Plans in the United States		Pension Benefits Plans Outside of the United States	
	2007	2006	2007	2006
All defined benefit plans:				
Accumulated benefit obligation	$948.3	$ 983.9	$746.4	$742.6

	Pension Benefits Plans in the United States		Pension Benefits Plans Outside of the United States	
	2007	2006	2007	2006
Unfunded defined benefit plans:				
Projected benefit obligation	100.9	107.4	126.9	119.5
Accumulated benefit obligation	82.3	85.3	116.6	109.7
Defined benefit plans with an accumulated benefit obligation in excess of the fair value of plan assets:				
Projected benefit obligation	100.9	1,032.0	126.9	780.7
Accumulated benefit obligation	82.3	941.0	116.6	730.1
Fair value of plan assets	–	840.0	–	553.4

The following table sets forth, in millions of dollars, benefit payments, which reflect expected future service, as appropriate, expected to be paid in the periods indicated.

	Pension Benefits Plans in the United States	Pension Benefits Plans Outside of the United States	Other Postretirement Benefits All Plans
2008	$ 68.1	$ 37.8	$ 9.9
2009	69.6	39.1	8.7
2010	70.6	40.7	8.7
2011	70.8	41.6	8.6
2012	70.2	42.9	8.3
2013–2017	387.6	234.7	38.2

The net periodic cost (benefit) related to the defined benefit pension plans included the following components, in millions of dollars:

	Pension Benefits Plans in the United States			Pension Benefits Plans Outside of the United States		
	2007	2006	2005	2007	2006	2005
Service cost	$26.0	24.8	$24.4	$14.7	$14.7	$13.7
Interest cost	62.5	58.4	57.9	39.6	38.4	37.5
Expected return on plan assets	(75.6)	(76.7)	(80.6)	(39.3)	(34.6)	(34.9)
Amortization of the unrecognized transition obligation	–	–	–	–	.1	.1
Amortization of prior service cost	2.1	3.3	1.2	1.7	1.6	1.4
Amortization of net actuarial loss	26.3	24.8	21.3	12.9	17.2	12.0
Net periodic cost	$41.3	$ 4.6	$24.2	$29.6	$37.4	$29.8

WEIGHTED-AVERAGE ASSUMPTIONS USED IN DETERMINING NET PERIODIC COST FOR YEAR:

Discount rate	6.00%	5.75%	6.00%	4.93%	4.87%	5.44%

	Pension Benefits Plans in the United States			Pension Benefits Plans Outside of the United States		
	2007	2006	2005	2007	2006	2005
Expected return on plan assets	8.75%	8.75%	8.75%	7.49%	7.49%	7.50%
Rate of compensation increase	3.95%	0.40%	4.00%	3.65%	3.86%	3.85%

The net periodic cost related to the defined benefit postretirement plans included the following components, in millions of dollars:

	2007	2006	2005
Service cost	$ .8	$ 1.0	$ .8
Interest cost	5.3	5.9	8.4
Amortization of prior service cost	(4.5)	(4.6)	(1.7)
Amortization of net actuarial loss	0.2	0.9	0.9
Curtailment gain	–	(0.3)	(0.6)
Net periodic cost	$1.8	$ 2.9	$ 7.8
Weighted-average discount rate used in determining net periodic cost for year	6.25%	6.00%	6.25%

The health care cost trend rate used to determine the postretirement benefit obligation was 9.0% for participants under 65 and 7.75% for participants 65 and older in 2007. This rate decreases gradually to an ultimate rate of 5.0% in 2013, and remains at that level thereafter. The trend rate is a significant factor in determining the amounts reported. A one-percentage-point change in these assumed health care cost trend rates would have the following effects, in millions of dollars:

One Percentage-Point	Increase	(Decrease)
Effect on total of service and interest cost components	$ .3	$ (.3)
Effect on postretirement benefit obligation	3.8	(3.6)

In 2008, the Corporation expects to make cash contributions of approximately $27 million to its defined benefit pension plans. The amounts principally represent contributions required by funding regulations or laws or those related to unfunded plans necessary to fund current benefits. In addition, the Corporation expects to continue to make contributions in 2008 sufficient to fund benefits paid under its other postretirement benefit plans during that year, net of contributions by plan participants. The Corporation expects that such contributions will be approximately $10 million in 2008.

Expense for defined contribution plans amounted to $12.4 million, $12.5 million, and $12.7 million in 2007, 2006, and 2005, respectively.

Schlumberger
2007 Annual Report

19. Pension and Other Benefit Plans

Adoption of SFAS 158

Effective December 31, 2006, Schlumberger adopted the provisions of SFAS 158 (*Employer's Accounting for Defined Benefit Pension and Other Postretirement Plans, an amendment of FASB Statements No. 87, 88, 106 and 132(R)*). SFAS 158 requires Schlumberger to recognize the funded status (i.e., the difference between the fair value of plan assets and the benefit obligation) of its defined benefit pension and other postretirement plans (collectively "postretirement benefit plans") in its *Consolidated Balance Sheet*, with a corresponding adjustment to *Accumulated Other Comprehensive Income*, net of tax.

The adjustment to *Accumulated Other Comprehensive Income* at adoption represents the net unrecognized actuarial losses and unrecognized prior service costs which were previously netted against Schlumberger's postretirement benefit plans' funded status in the *Consolidated Balance Sheet* pursuant to the provisions of SFAS 87 (*Employers' Accounting for Pensions*) and SFAS 106 (*Employer's Accounting for Postretirement Benefits Other Than Pensions*). These amounts are subsequently recognized as net periodic postretirement cost consistent with Schlumberger's historical accounting policy for amortizing such amounts. The adoption of SFAS 158 had no effect on Schlumberger's *Consolidated Statement of Income* for any prior periods, and it will not affect Schlumberger's operating results in future periods.

Upon the adoption of SFAS 158 on December 31, 2006, Schlumberger's total liabilities increased by approximately 2% and stockholders' equity decreased by approximately 3%. The impact on Schlumberger's total assets was insignificant.

United States Defined Benefit Pension Plans

Schlumberger and its United States subsidiary sponsor several defined benefit pension plans that cover substantially all employees hired prior to October 1, 2004. The benefits are based on years of service and compensation on a career-average pay basis. The funding policy with respect to qualified pension plans is to annually contribute amounts that are based upon a number of factors including the actuarial accrued liability, amounts that are deductible for income tax purposes, legal funding requirements and available cash flow.

The assumed discount rate, compensation increases and return on plan assets used to determine pension expense were as follows:

	2007	2006	2005
Assumed discount rate	6.00%	5.75%	6.00%
Compensation increases	4.00%	3.00%	3.00%
Return on plan assets	8.50%	8.50%	8.50%

Net pension cost in the United States for 2007, 2006 and 2005, included the following components:

(Stated-in-millions)	2007	2006	2005
Service cost—benefits earned during the period	58	$ 59	$ 53
Interest cost on projected benefit obligation	120	112	108
Expected return on plan assets [actual return: 2007—$212; 2006—$224; 2005—$132]	(147)	(134)	(109)
Amortization of prior service cost	7	8	8
Amortization of net loss	26	27	25
Net pension cost	$ 64	$ 72	$ 85

Included in *Accumulated Other Comprehensive Income* at December 31, 2007 are the following non-cash pretax charges which have not yet been recognized in net periodic pension cost. Also presented is the estimated portion of each component of *Accumulated Other Comprehensive Income* which is expected to be recognized as a component of net periodic benefit cost during the year ending December 31, 2008.

(Stated in millions)	Amt. Recognized in Acc. Other Comp. Income at Dec 31, 2007	Amount Expected to Be Charged to Net Periodic Cost in 2008
Net actuarial losses	$111	$11
Prior service cost	$ 53	$ 7

The changes in the projected benefit obligation, plan assets and funded status of the plans on December 31, 2007 and 2006, were as follows:

(Stated-in-millions)	2007	2006
Projected benefit obligation at beginning of the year	$2,006	$1,984
Service cost	58	59
Interest cost	120	112
Actuarial (gain)/losses	(57)	(89)
Benefits paid	(97)	(95)
Amendments	–	2
Other	–	33
Projected benefit obligation at end of the year	$2,030	$2,006
Plan assets at market value at beginning of the year	$1,913	$1,588
Actual return on plan assets	212	224
Contributions	152	204
Benefits paid	(97)	(95)
Administrative expense	(10)	(8)
Plan assets at market value at end of the year	$2,170	$1,913
Overfunded/(underfunded) position at end of year	$ 140	($ 93)

The overfunded/(underfunded) position represents the difference between the plan assets and the projected benefit obligation ("PBO"). The PBO represents the actuarial present value of benefits based on employee service and compensation and includes an assumption about future compensation levels.

The $140 million overfunded position of the United States defined benefit pension plan at December 31, 2007 is included in *Other Assets* in the accompanying *Consolidated Balance Sheet*.

The $93 million underfunded position at December 31, 2006 is included in *Postretirement Benefits* in the accompanying *Consolidated Balance Sheet*.

The assumed discount rate, the rate of compensation increases and the expected long-term rate of return on plan assets used to determine the projected benefit obligations were as follows:

	2007	2006
Assumed discount rate	6.50%	6.00%
Compensation increases	4.00%	3.00%
Return on plan assets	8.50%	8.50%

The following is a breakdown of the plan assets:

(Stated in millions)	2007	2006
US equity securities	$ 990	$ 905
Non-US equity securities	433	449
Fixed income securities	563	374
Cash and cash equivalents	38	85
Other investments	146	100
	$2,170	$1,913

The asset allocation objectives are to diversify the portfolio among several asset classes to reduce volatility while maintaining an asset mix that provides the highest expected rate of return consistent with an acceptable level of risk. The investment strategies include a rebalancing of the asset mix as necessary to the previously defined levels and reassessing funding levels and asset allocation strategy at least annually.

As at December 31, 2007, there was no investment of plan assets in Schlumberger common stock.

The expected long-term rate of return on assets is 8.5%. This assumption represents the rate of return on plan assets reflecting the average rate of earnings expected on the funds invested or to be invested to provide for the benefits included in the projected benefit obligation. The assumption has been determined by reflecting expectations regarding future rates of return for the portfolio considering the asset distribution and related historical rates of return. The appropriateness of the assumption is reviewed annually.

The expected benefits to be paid under the plan are as follows:

(Stated-in-millions)	
2008	$ 99
2009	$100
2010	$102
2011	$105
2012	$109
2013–2017	$616

No plan assets are expected to be returned to Schlumberger during the year ending December 31, 2008.

Although not required to make any contributions to its US qualified pension plans in 2008, Schlumberger currently expects to make contributions in 2008 of between $50 million and $100 million.

Other Defined Benefit Pension Plans

In addition to the previously disclosed United States defined benefit pension plans, Schlumberger sponsors several other defined benefit pension plans. Charges to expense for these plans were $58 million, $49 million and $50 million in 2007, 2006 and 2005, respectively, and are based upon costs computed by actuaries.

The most significant of these other defined benefit pension plans is in the UK, which covers employees hired prior to April 1, 1999.

The assumed discount rate, compensation increases and return on plan assets used to determine pension expense were as follows:

	2007	2006	2005
Assumed discount rate	5.20%	4.90%	5.40%
Compensation increases	4.50%	4.20%	4.10%
Return plan assets	8.00%	8.00%	8.00%

Net pension cost in the UK plan for 2007, 2006 and 2005 (translated into US dollars at the average exchange rate for the periods), included the following components:

Included in *Accumulated Other Comprehensive Income* at December 31, 2007 are the following non-cash pretax charges which have not yet been recognized in net periodic pension cost. Also presented is the estimated portion of each component of *Accumulated Other Comprehensive Income* which is expected to be recognized as a component of net periodic benefit cost during the year ending December 31, 2008.

(Stated in millions)	Amt. Recognized in Acc. Other Comp. Income at Dec 31, 2007	Amount Expected to Be Charged to Net Periodic Cost in 2008
Net actuarial losses	$251	$12
Prior service cost	$ 5	$ 1

The changes in the projected benefit obligation, plan assets and funded status of the plan (translated into US dollars at year-end exchange rates) were as follows:

(Stated in millions)	2007	2006
Projected benefit obligation at beginning of the year	$ 991	$ 801
Service cost	35	26
Interest cost	52	42
Contributions by Plan participants	2	2
Actuarial (gain) losses	(30)	33
Currency effect	26	109
Benefits paid	(25)	(23)
Other	12	1
Projected benefit obligation at end of the year	$1,063	$ 991
Plan assets at market value at beginning of the year	$ 810	$ 647
Actual return on plan assets	57	50
Currency effect	21	87
Employer contributions	98	47
Employee contributions	2	2
Benefits paid	(25)	(23)
Other	14	–
Plan assets at market value at end of the year	$ 977	$ 810
Underfunded position at end of year	$ (86)	$ (181)

The underfunded position of the UK defined benefit pension plans is included in *Postretirement Benefits* in the accompanying *Consolidated Balance Sheet* at December 31, 2007 and 2006, respectively.

The assumed discount rate and rate of compensation increases used to determine the projected benefit obligation were as follows:

	2007	2006
Assumed discount rate	5.80%	5.20%
Compensation increases	4.90%	4.50%

The following is a breakdown of the plan assets:

(Stated in millions)	2007	2006
Equity securities	$652	$542
Fixed income securities	197	155
Index linked gilts	102	74

(Stated in millions)	2007	2006
Other investments	26	39
	$977	$810

The expected benefits to be paid under the plan are as follows:

(Stated in millions)	
2008	$ 21
2009	$ 23
2010	$ 26
2011	$ 28
2012	$ 31
2013–2017	$206

Contributions to the UK plan in 2008 are expected to be between $40 million and $80 million.

Other Deferred Benefits

In addition to providing defined pension benefits, Schlumberger and its subsidiaries have other deferred benefit programs, primarily profit sharing and defined contribution pension plans. Expenses for these programs were $408 million, $351 million and $280 million in 2007, 2006 and 2005, respectively.

Health Care Benefits

Schlumberger and its United States subsidiary provide health care benefits for certain active employees. The costs of providing these benefits are expensed when incurred, and aggregated $80 million, $72 million and $65 million in 2007, 2006 and 2005, respectively. Outside the United States, such benefits are mostly provided through government-sponsored programs.

Postretirement Benefits Other than Pensions

Schlumberger and its United States subsidiary provide certain health care benefits to former employees who have retired.

The principal actuarial assumptions used to measure costs were a discount rate of 6.00% in 2007, 5.75% in 2006 and 6.00% in 2005. The overall medical cost trend rate assumption is 9% graded to 6% over the next four years and 5% thereafter.

Net periodic postretirement benefit cost in the United States for 2007, 2006 and 2005, included the following components:

(Stated in millions)	2007	2006	2005
Service cost—benefits earned during the period	$ 22	$ 26	$ 29
Interest cost on accumulated postretirement benefit obligation	47	45	45
Expected return on plan assets	(2)	–	–

(Stated in millions)	2007	2006	2005
Amortization of prior service cost	(27)	(28)	(14)
Amortization of net loss	13	16	11
	$ 53	$ 59	$ 71

Included in *Accumulated Other Comprehensive Income* at December 31, 2007 are the following non-cash pretax charges which have not yet been recognized in net periodic postretirement benefit cost. Also presented is the estimated portion of each component of *Accumulated Other Comprehensive Income* which is expected to be recognized as a component of net periodic postretirement benefit cost during the year ending December 31, 2008.

(Stated in millions)	Amt. recognized in Acc. Other Comp. Income at Dec. 31, 2007	Amount expected to be charged to net periodic cost in 2008
Net actuarial losses	$ 142	$ 7
Prior service cost	$(119)	$(27)

The change in accumulated postretirement benefit obligation and funded status on December 31, 2007 and 2006, was as follows:

(Stated in millions)	2007	2006
Accumulated postretirement benefit obligation at beginning of the year	$ 785	$ 785
Service cost	22	26
Interest cost	48	45
Actuarial gains	(35)	(40)
Benefits paid	(28)	(31)
Accumulated postretirement benefit obligation at the end of the year	$ 792	$ 785
Plan assets at market value at beginning of the year	$ 23	–
Contributions	42	53
Actual return on plan assets	2	1
Benefits paid	(28)	(31)
Plan assets at market value at the end of the year	$ 39	$ 23
Underfunded position at end of year	$(753)	$(762)

The underfunded position is included in *Postretirement Benefits* in the *Consolidated Balance Sheet*.

The components of the accumulated postretirement benefit obligation on December 31, 2007 and 2006, were as follows:

(*Stated in millions*)	2007	2006
Retirees	$403	$418
Fully eligible	255	217
Actives	134	150
	$792	$785

The assumed discount rate used to determine the accumulated postretirement benefit obligation was 6.50% for 2007 and 6.00% for 2006.

The overall medical cost trend rate assumption used to determine the accumulated postretirement benefit obligation for both 2007 and 2006 was 9% graded to 6% over the next four years and 5% thereafter.

If the assumed medical cost trend rate was increased by one percentage point per annum, health care cost in 2007 would have been $68 million, and the accumulated postretirement benefit obligation would have been $929 million on December 31, 2007.

If the assumed medical cost trend rate was decreased by one percentage point per annum, health care cost in 2007 would have been $45 million, and the accumulated postretirement benefit obligation would have been $712 million on December 31, 2007.

The expected payments to be paid under the plan are as follows and are net of the annual Medicare Part D subsidy, which ranges from $3 million to $6 million per year:

(*Stated in millions*)	
2008	$ 35
2009	$ 37
2010	$ 40
2011	$ 43
2012	$ 45
2013–2017	$263

Emerson Electric
2005 Annual Report

(10) Retirement Plans

Retirement plan expense includes the following components:

	U.S. Plans			Non-U.S. Plans		
	2003	2004	**2005**	2003	2004	2005
Defined benefit plans:						
Service cost (benefits earned during the period)	$ 41	49	**48**	11	15	14

Retirement plan expense includes the following components:

	U.S. Plans			Non-U.S. Plans		
	2003	2004	2005	2003	2004	2005
Interest cost	136	136	145	22	27	31
Expected return on plan assets	(187)	(196)	(207)	(22)	(21)	(27)
Net amortization	34	65	64	3	14	13
Net periodic pension expense	24	54	50	14	35	31
Defined contribution and multiemployer plans	60	66	69	22	22	23
Total retirement plan expense	$ 84	120	119	36	57	54

The reconciliations of the actuarial present value of the projected benefit obligations and of the fair value of plan assets for defined benefit pension plans follow:

	U.S. Plans		Non-U.S. Plans	
	2004	2005	2004	2005
Projected benefit obligation, beginning	$2,264	2,330	526	607
Service cost	49	48	15	14
Interest cost	136	145	27	31
Actuarial loss (gain)	(82)	320	2	101
Benefits paid	(108)	(118)	(16)	(27)
Acquisitions/divestitures, net	67	19	6	--
Foreign currency translation and other	4	3	47	(19)
Projected benefit obligation, ending	$2,330	$2,747	607	707
Fair value of plan assets, beginning	$1,962	2,292	326	433
Actual return on plan assets	318	258	30	47
Employer contributions	67	122	60	52
Benefits paid	(108)	(118)	(16)	(27)
Acquisitions/divestitures, net	51	10	4	–
Foreign currency translation and other	2	2	29	(13)
Fair value of plan assets, ending	$2,292	2,566	433	492
Plan assets in excess of (less than) benefit obligation as of June 30				
Unrecognized net loss	$ (38)	(181)	(174)	(215)
Unrecognized prior service cost (benefit)	872	1,079	176	240

	U.S. Plans		Non-U.S. Plans	
	2004	*2005*	*2004*	*2005*
Adjustment for fourth quarter contributions	10	**9**	(3)	(3)
Net amount recognized in the balance sheet	51	**1**	1	1
	$ 895	**908**	–	23
Accumulated benefit obligation	$2,151	**$2,535**	540	595

	U.S. Plans			Non-U.S. Plans		
	2003	*2004*	*2005*	*2003*	*2004*	*2005*
Weighted average assumptions used to determine net pension expense:						
Discount rate	7.25%	6.00%	**6.25%**	5.8%	5.2%	**5.4%**
Expected return on plan assets	9.00%	8.50%	**8.50%**	8.3%	7.2%	**7.4%**
Rate of compensation increase	3.75%	3.25%	**3.25%**	3.4%	3.3%	**3.1%**
Weighted average assumptions used to determine benefit obligations as of June 30:						
Discount rate	6.00%	6.25%	**5.25%**	5.2%	5.4%	**4.7%**
Rate of compensation increase	3.25%	3.25%	**3.00%**	3.3%	3.1%	**3.0%**

At September 30, 2005 and 2004, the pension assets recognized in the balance sheet were $925 and $883, and the pension liabilities recognized in the balance sheet were $276 and $242, respectively; in addition, $282 and $254 were included in accumulated other comprehensive income at September 30, 2005 and 2004, respectively. As of the plans' June 30 measurement date, the projected benefit obligation, accumulated benefit obligation, and fair value of plan assets for the retirement plans with accumulated benefit obligations in excess of plan assets were $1,006, $938 and $656, respectively, for 2005, and $1,009, $934 and $694, respectively, for 2004. As of the June 30, 2005 measurement date, the fair value of plan assets exceeded the accumulated benefit obligation for the primary defined benefit pension plan by approximately $150. If the performance of the equity and bond markets in 2006 eliminates the excess, the Company could be required to record an after-tax charge to equity of approximately $530. Effective for 2006, the Company adjusted the discount rate for the U.S. retirement plans to 5.25 percent and adjusted the expected long-term rate of return on plan assets to 8.0 percent. Defined benefit pension plan expense is expected to increase approximately $60 in 2006.

The primary objectives for the investment of plan assets is to secure partici-pant retirement benefits, while earning a reasonable rate of return. Plan assets are invested consistent with the provisions of prudence and diversification rules of ERISA and with a long-term investment horizon. The expected return on plan assets assumption is determined by reviewing the investment return of the plans for the past ten years and the historical return (since 1926) of an asset mix approximating Emerson's current asset allocation targets and evaluating these returns in relation to expectations of various investment organizations to determine whether long-term future returns are expected to differ significantly from the past. The Company's pension plan asset allocations at June 30, 2004 and 2005, and target weighted-average allocations are as follows:

	U.S. Plans			Non-U.S. Plans		
	2004	**2005**	Target	2004	**2005**	Target
Asset category						
Equity securities	70%	**69%**	66–70%	53%	**56%**	50–60%
Debt securities	30%	**27%**	26–32%	37%	**37%**	30–40%
Other	–	**4%**	2–5%	10%	**7%**	5–10%
	100%	**100%**	100%	100%	**100%**	100%

The Company estimates that future benefit payments for the U.S. plans will be as follows: $119 in 2006, $125 in 2007, $132 in 2008, $138 in 2009, $145 in 2010 and $838 in total over the five years 2011 through 2015. Using foreign exchange rates as of September 30, 2005, the Company estimates that future benefit payments for the non-U.S. plans will be as follows: $23 in 2006, $23 in 2007, $25 in 2008, $26 in 2009, $28 in 2010 and $169 in total over the five years 2011 through 2015. In 2006, the Company expects to contribute approximately $75 to $150 to the retirement plans.

(11) Postretirement Plans

The Company sponsors unfunded postretirement benefit plans (primarily health care) for U.S. retirees and their dependents. Net postretirement plan expense for the years ended September 30 follows:

	2003	2004	2005
Service cost	$ 7	5	6
Interest cost	27	25	27
Net amortization	8	19	21
Net postretirement plans expense	$42	49	54

The reconciliations of the actuarial present value of accumulated postretirement benefit obligations follow:

	2004	2005
Benefit obligation, beginning	$426	444
Service cost	5	6
Interest cost	25	27
Actuarial loss	30	55
Benefits paid	(37)	(43)

	2004	2005
Acquisitions/divestitures and other	(5)	13
Benefit obligation, ending	444	502
Unrecognized net loss	(101)	(134)
Unrecognized prior service benefit	8	7
Postretirement benefit liability recognized in the balance sheet	$351	375

The assumed discount rates used in measuring the obligations as of September 30, 2005, 2004 and 2003, were 5.25 percent, 5.75 percent and 6.00 percent, respectively. The assumed health care cost trend rate for 2006 was 9.5 percent, declining to 5.0 percent in the year 2014. The assumed health care cost trend rate for 2005 was 9.5 percent, declining to 5.0 percent in the year 2013. A one-percentage-point increase or decrease in the assumed health care cost trend rate for each year would increase or decrease the obligation as of September 30, 2005, and the 2005 postretirement plan expense by less than 5 percent. The Company estimates that future benefit payments will be $42 annually for 2006 through 2010 and $209 in total over the five years 2011 through 2015.

Winn-Dixie Stores
2005 Annual Report

12. Retirement Plans

Profit Sharing/401(k) Plan

The Company has a Profit Sharing/401(k) Plan that has a noncontributory, trusteed profit-sharing feature and a contributory, trusteed 401(k) feature. The plan is in effect for eligible associates and may be amended or terminated at any time. Charges to operations for plan contributions amounted to $11,283, $13,034 and $13,907 in 2005, 2004 and 2003, respectively. The assets and liabilities of this plan are excluded from the Chapter 11 proceedings and from the accompanying Consolidated Balance Sheets.

Defined Benefit and Retiree Medical Plans

The Company has a management security plan, which is a non-qualified defined benefit plan (the "Defined Benefit Plan") that provides retirement and death benefits to certain executives and members of management. Effective July 1, 2003, the eligibility criteria were modified to limit the number of active participants in the plan. The plan is a non-funded contributory plan. Effective February 21, 2005, no additional benefits will be credited and associate contributions ceased. A liability of $101.4 million was included in liabilities subject to compromise as of June 29, 2005. A liability of $68.8 million was separately reported as of June 30, 2004.

The Company also has a retiree medical plan that provides medical benefits until age 65 to associates who terminate employment after attaining 55 years of age and ten years of full-time service with the Company. Associates terminating employment after attaining 55 years of age and completion of ten years of service continue to be eligible to participate in the plan, but those meeting the criteria subsequent to July 1, 2002 are assessed the full cost of coverage.

The components of expense for the Defined Benefit Plan and retiree medical plan consisted of the following:

	Defined Benefit Plan			Retiree Medical		
	2005	2004	2003	2005	2004	2003
Service cost	$ 582	762	1,405	–	–	–
Interest cost	4,482	4,070	4,392	993	1,009	1,197
Amortization of prior service cost	–	–	–	2,088	2,088	876
Recognized net actuarial loss (gain)	1,349	2,193	1,781	(8)	(68)	(92)
Participant contributions	(35)	(364)	(472)	–	–	–
Net periodic benefit expense	$6,378	6,661	$7,106	3,073	3,029	1,981

The following summarizes the changes in the projected benefit obligation and post-retirement benefit obligation:

	Defined Benefit Plan		Retiree Medical	
	2005	2004	2005	2004
Beginning of year benefit obligation	$ 68,827	67,233	16,968	17,660
Service cost	582	762	–	–
Interest cost	4,482	4,070	993	1,009
Actuarial loss	31,870	1,661	1,052	282
Benefits paid	(4,399)	(4,899)	(1,616)	(1,983)
End of year benefit obligation	101,362	68,827	17,397	16,968
Unrecognized prior service cost	–	–	(14,616)	(16,704)
Unrecognized prior service cost (loss) gain	(41,637)	(11,113)	1,181	2,241
Additional minimum liability	41,637	11,113	–	–
Accrued benefit cost	$101,362	68,827	3,962	2,505

The accumulated benefit obligation for the Defined Benefit Plan was $101,362 and $68,827 as of June 29, 2005 and June 30, 2004, respectively.

	Defined Benefit Plan			Retiree Medical		
Additional information:	2005	2004	2003	2005	2004	2003
Minimum pension liability adjustment included in other comprehensive loss	$30,524	(533)	11,646	$ –	–	–
Discount rate used to determine benefit obligation	4.75%	6.00%	6.00%	4.75%	6.00%	6.00%

Additional information:	Defined Benefit Plan			Retiree Medical		
	2005	2004	2003	2005	2004	2003
Discount rate used to determine net periodic benefit expense	6.00%	6.00%	6.00%	6.00%	6.00%	6.00%

Assumed health care cost rates have a significant effect on the amounts reported for the retiree medical plan. The health care cost trend rates assumed for 2005 and 2004 were 11.0% and 11.50%, respectively. The rate to which the cost trend is assumed to decline (the ultimate trend rate) is 5.5%, which will be reached in 2016. A one-percentage-point change in assumed health care cost trend rates would have the following effects:

	1-Percentage- Point Increase	1-Percentage- Point Decrease
Effect on total of service and interest cost	$ 37	$ (36)
Effect on post-retirement benefit obligation	704	(671)

The following benefit payments, which reflect expected future service, as appropriate, are expected to be paid during the indicated fiscal years.

	Defined Benefit Plan	Retiree Medical
2006	$ 5,942	$2,600
2007	6,526	2,700
2008	6,960	2,800
2009	7,117	2,700
2010	7,360	2,600
Years 2011–2015	36,477	6,300

Supplemental Retirement Plan

The Company has a defined contribution, deferred compensation supplemental retirement plan in effect for eligible management associates. Effective February 21, 2005, contributions from associates were suspended, and are expected to remain suspended through the pendency of the Chapter 11 cases. As of June 29, 2005, a liability of $15.9 million was included in liabilities subject to compromise. As of June 30, 2004, a liability of $16.4 million was included in other liabilities. Charges to operations for plan contributions amounted to less than $0.5 million per year in 2005, 2004 and 2003.

Walt Disney
2004 Annual Report

Note 8. Pension and Other Benefit Programs

The Company maintains pension plans and postretirement medical benefit plans covering most of its domestic employees not covered by union or industry-wide plans. Employees hired after January 1, 1994 and ABC employees generally hired after January 1, 1987 are not eligible for postretirement medical benefits. With respect to its qualified defined benefit pension plans, the Company's policy is to fund, at a minimum, the amount necessary on an actuarial basis to provide for benefits in accordance with the requirements of the Employee Retirement Income Security Act of 1974. Pension benefits are generally based on years of service and/or compensation. The following chart summarizes the balance sheet impact, as well as the benefit obligations, assets, funded status and rate assumptions associated with the pension and postretirement medical benefit plans.

	Pension Plans		Postretirement Medical Plans	
	2004	2003	**2004**	2003
Reconciliation of funded status of the plans and the amounts included in the Company's Consolidated Balance Sheets:				
Projected benefit obligations				
Beginning obligations	**$(3,747)**	$(2,889)	**$(1,035)**	$ (680)
Service cost	**(150)**	(115)	**(35)**	(23)
Interest cost	**(216)**	(204)	**(60)**	(48)
Plan amendments	–	–	–	–
Actuarial gain/(loss)	**224**	(651)	**152**	(302)
Benefits paid	**120**	112	**24**	18
Ending obligations	**$(3,769)**	$(3,747)	**$ (954)**	$(1,035)
Fair value of plans' assets				
Beginning fair value	**$ 2,655**	$ 2,660	**$ 197**	$ 199
Actual return on plan assets	**465**	96	**24**	5
Employer contributions	**155**	26	**18**	11
Benefits paid	**(120)**	(112)	**(24)**	(18)
Expenses	**(16)**	(15)	–	–
Ending fair value	**$ 3,139**	$ 2,655	**$ 215**	$ 197
Funded status of the plans	**$ (630)**	$(1,092)	**$ (739)**	$ (838)
Unrecognized net loss	**697**	1,231	**307**	535
Unrecognized prior service cost (benefit)	**21**	23	**(18)**	(20)
Contributions after measurement date	**2**	6	–	–
Net balance sheet impact	**$ 90**	$ 168	**$ (450)**	$ (323)
Amounts recognized in the balance sheet consist of				
Prepaid benefit cost	**$ 69**	$ 42	**$–**	$ 17
Accrued benefit liability	**(394)**	(843)	**(450)**	(340)
Additional minimum pension liability adjustment	**415**	969	–	–
	$ 90	$ 168	**$ (450)**	$ (323)

The components of net periodic benefit cost are as follows:

	Pension Plans			Postretirement Medical Plans		
	2004	2003	2002	**2004**	2003	2002
Service costs	**$149**	$114	$97	**$ 35**	$23	$22
Interest costs	**216**	204	157	**60**	48	43
Expected return on plan assets	**(215)**	(262)	(241)	**(15)**	(19)	(21)
Amortization of prior year service costs	**2**	2	1	**(1)**	(1)	1
Recognized net actuarial loss	**77**	(1)	–	**66**	23	12
Net periodic benefit cost	**$229**	$ 57	$14	**$145**	$74	$57
Assumptions:						
Discount rate	**6.30%**	5.85%	7.20%	**6.30%**	5.85%	7.20%
Rate of return on plan assets	**7.50%**	7.50%	8.50%	**7.50%**	7.50%	8.50%
Salary increases	**4.00%**	3.75%	4.65%	**n/a**	n/a	n/a
Year 1 increase in cost of benefits	**n/a**	n/a	n/a	**10.00%**	10.00%	10.0%

Net periodic benefit cost for the current year is based on assumptions from the prior year.

PLAN FUNDED STATUS

As a result of pension plan asset performance below expected returns in fiscal 2002 and 2003 and a reduction in the discount rate over the last two years, a number of the Company's pension plans were under-funded at September 30, 2004, having accumulated benefit obligations exceeding the fair value of plan assets. For these plans, the fair value of plan assets aggregated $2.4 billion, the accumulated benefit obligations aggregated $2.8 billion and the projected benefit obligations aggregated $3.0 billion. As a result, the Company has recorded additional minimum pension liability adjustments of $415 million and $969 million as of September 30, 2004 and September 30, 2003, respectively. The decrease in the additional minimum pension liability adjustment of $554 million in the current year was primarily due to an increase in the discount rate from 5.85% at September 30, 2003 to 6.30% at September 30, 2004 and improved plan asset performance. This decrease resulted in an after-tax adjustment of $347 million that was recorded as an increase of shareholders' equity through accumulated other comprehensive income in fiscal 2004.

The Company's total accumulated pension benefit obligations at September 30, 2004 and September 30, 2003 were $3.5 billion and $3.5 billion, respectively, of which 95.2% and 98.6%, respectively, were vested.

The accumulated postretirement medical benefit obligations and fair value of plan assets for postretirement medical plans with accumulated postretirement medical benefit obligations in excess of plan assets were $954 million and $215 million, respectively, for 2004 and $1,035 million, and $197 million, respectively, for 2003.

PLAN ASSETS

The assets of the Company's defined benefit plans are managed on a commingled basis in a third party Master Trust. The investment policy and allocation of the assets in the Master Trust were approved by the Company's Investment and Administrative Committee, which has oversight responsibility for the Company's retirement plans. The investment policy ranges for each major asset class are as follows:

	Minimum	Maximum
Equity Securities.	40%	60%
Debt Securities	25%	35%
Alternative Investments	10%	30%
Cash	0%	5%

Alternative investments include venture capital funds, private equity funds, and real estate, among other things. The Company's pension plan asset mix at June 30, 2004 and 2003 (the Plan measurement date), by asset class, is as follows:

Asset Category	2004	2003
Equity Securities	57%	53%
Debt Securities	27	25
Alternative Investments.	15	21
Cash.	1	1
Total	100%	100%

Equity securities include $63 million (2% of total plan assets) and $56 million (2% of total plan assets) of Company common stock at September 30, 2004 and September 30, 2003, respectively.

PLAN CONTRIBUTIONS

During fiscal 2004, the Company contributed $155 million and $18 million to its pension and postretirement plans, respectively. The Company expects to contribute $148 million to its pension plans and $17 million to its postretirement medical plans during fiscal 2005.

ESTIMATED FUTURE BENEFIT PAYMENTS

The following table presents estimated future benefit payments:

	Pension Plans	Postretirement Medical Plans
2005	$ 129	$ 25
2006	139	27
2007	149	27
2008	161	29
2009	173	31
2010–2014	1,119	188
Total	$1,870	$327

MULTI-EMPLOYER PLANS
The Company participates in various multi-employer pension plans under union and industry-wide agreements. In 2004, 2003, and 2002, the contributions to these plans which are generally expensed as incurred were $38 million, $37 million, and $41 million, respectively.

ASSUMPTIONS
Certain actuarial assumptions, such as the discount rate, long-term rate of return and the healthcare cost trend rate have a significant effect on the amounts reported for postretirement medical benefit and net periodic pension expense as well as the respective benefit obligation amounts.

Discount Rate—The assumed discount rate for pension plans represents the market rate for high-quality fixed income investments or a long-term high quality corporate bond rate. For 2004, we increased our rate to 6.30% to reflect market interest rate conditions.

Long-term return on assets—The assumed rate of return on plan assets represents an estimate of long-term returns on an investment portfolio consisting of a mixture of equities, fixed income, and alternative investments. When determining the expected return on plan assets, the Company considers long-term rates of return on the asset classes (both historical and forecasted) in which the Company expects the pension funds to be invested. The following rates of return by asset class were considered in setting the long-term return on assets assumption:

Equity Securities	9%–10%
Debt Securities	5%–7%
Alternative Investments	8%–10%

Healthcare cost trend rate—The Company reviews external data and its own historical trends for healthcare costs to determine the healthcare cost trend rates for the postretirement medical benefit plans. For 2004, we assumed a 10.0% annual rate of increase in the per capita cost of covered healthcare claims with the rate decreasing in even increments over seven years until reaching 5.0%.

The effects of a one percentage point change in the key assumptions would have had the following effects increase/(decrease) in cost and/or obligation on the results for fiscal year 2004:

	Assumed Healthcare Cost Trend Rate		Pension Plans Discount Rate		Expected Long-Term Rate of Return on Assets
	Total Service and Interest Costs	Post-retirement Medical Obligations	Total Service and Interest Costs	Projected Benefit Obligations	Net Periodic Cost
1% point decrease	$(20)	$(188)	$31	$620	$29
1% point increase	27	245	(29)	(515)	(29)

DEFINED CONTRIBUTION PLANS

The Company has savings and investment plans that allow eligible employees to allocate up to 20% of salary through payroll deductions depending on the plan in which the employee participates. The Company matches 50% of the employee's pre-tax contributions, up to plan limits. In 2004, 2003 and 2002, the costs of these plans were $33 million, $32 million, and $29 million, respectively.

MEDICARE MODERNIZATION ACT

In May 2004, the FASB issued FASB Staff Position No.106-2, *Accounting and Disclosure Requirements Related to the Medicare Prescription Drug, Improvement and Modernization Act of 2003* (FSP 106-2) in response to a new law regarding prescription drug benefits under Medicare as well as a federal subsidy to sponsors of retiree healthcare benefit plans. We expect that the impact of this act will not be material.

Genuine Parts
2004 Annual Report

9. Employee Benefit Plans

The Company's defined benefit pension plans cover substantially all of its employees in the U.S. and Canada. The plan covering U.S. employees is noncontributory and benefits are based on the employees' compensation during the highest five of their last ten years of credited service. The Canadian plan is contributory and benefits are based on career average compensation. The Company's funding policy is to fund amounts deductible for income tax purposes.

The Company also sponsors unfunded supplemental retirement plans covering employee postretirement benefit plans. The Company uses a measurement date of December 31 for its pension and other postretirement benefit plans.

(in thousands)	Pension Benefits 2004	Pension Benefits 2003	Other Postretirement Benefits 2004	Other Postretirement Benefits 2003
Changes in benefit obligation				
Benefit obligation at beginning of year	$ 943,023	$827,379	$24,408	$10,018
Service cost	35,740	32,488	460	90
Interest cost	60,039	57,520	1,256	481
Plan participants' contributions	2,338	2,005	3,297	3,209
Plan amendments	–	–	–	(2,104)
Actuarial loss/(gain)	21,255	41,793	(483)	17,689
Exchange rate loss	6,496	12,641	–	–
Curtailments	–	(64)	–	–
Gross benefits paid	(33,033)	(30,739)	(6,233)	(4,975)
Benefit obligation at end of year	$1,035,858	$943,023	$22,705	$24,408

The total accumulated benefit obligation for the Company's defined benefit pension plans was approximately $841,392,000 and $731,025,000 at December 31, 2004 and 2003, respectively.

The assumptions used to measure the pension and other postretirement plan obligations for the plans at December 31, 2004 and 2003 were:

	Pension Benefits		Other Postretirement Benefits	
	2004	2003	2004	2003
Weighted-average discount rate	6.00%	6.25%	6.00%	6.25%
Rate of increase in future compensation levels	3.50%	3.25%	–	–

A 10% annual rate of increase in the per capita cost of covered health care benefits was assumed for 2005. The rate was assumed to decrease ratably to 5% in 2010 and thereafter.

	Pension Benefits		Other Postretirement Benefits	
(in thousands)	2004	2003	2004	2003
Changes in plan assets				
Fair value of plan assets at beginning of year	$834,015	$716,008	$ –	$ –
Actual return on plan assets	90,385	103,712	–	–
Exchange rate gain	6,429	13,274	–	–
Employer contributions	62,737	29,755	2,936	1,766
Plan participants' contribution	2,338	2,005	3,297	3,209
Gross benefits paid	(33,033)	(30,739)	(6,233)	(4,975)
Fair value of plan assets at end of year	$962,871	$834,015	$ –	$ –

The fair values of plan assets for the Company's U.S. pension plans included in the above were $875,236,000 and $757,684,000 at December 31, 2004 and 2003, respectively.

Following are the asset allocations for the Company's funded pension plans at December 31, 2004 and 2003, and the target allocation for 2005, by asset category:

	Target Allocation	Percentage of Plan Assets at December 31	
Asset Category	2005	2004	2003
Equity securities	65%	64%	62%
Debt securities	35%	33%	35%
Real estate and other	–	3%	3%
	100%	100%	100%

At December 31, 2004 and 2003, the plan held 2,016,932 shares and 1,619,480 shares, respectively, of common stock of the Company with a market value of approximately $88,866,024 and $53,767,000, respectively. Dividend payments received by the plan on Company stock totaled approximately $2,147,542 and $1,903,000 in 2004 and 2003, respectively. Fees paid during the year for services rendered by parties-in-interest were based on customary and reasonable rates for such services.

The Company's benefit plan committees in the U.S. and Canada establish investment policies and strategies and regularly monitor the performance of the funds. The pension plan strategy implemented by the Company's management is to achieve long-term objectives and invest the pension assets in accordance with the applicable pension legislation in the U.S. and Canada, as well as fiduciary standards. The long-term primary objectives for the pension plan are to provide for a reasonable amount of long-term growth of capital, without undue exposure to risk, protect the assets from erosion of purchasing power, and provide invest-ment results that meet or exceed the pension plan's actuarially assumed long term rate of return.

Based on the investment policy for the pension plans, as well as an asset study that was performed based on the Company's asset allocations and future expectations, the Company's expected rate of return on plan assets for measuring 2005 pension expense or income is 8.5% for the plans. The asset study forecasted expected rates of return for the approximate duration of the Company's benefit obligations, using capital market data and historical relationships.

The following table sets forth the funded status of the plans and the amounts recognized in the consolidated balance sheets at December 31:

	Pension Benefits		Other Postretirement Benefits	
(in thousands)	2004	2003	2004	2003
Funded status at end of year	$(72,987)	$(109,008)	$(22,705)	$(24,408)
Unrecognized net actuarial loss	341,262	340,416	19,309	20,788
Unrecognized prior service (income) cost	(1,115)	(2,191)	2,646	3,017
Net asset (liability) recognized at end of year	$267,160	229,217	$ (750)	$ (603)
Prepaid benefit cost	$297,496	$ 256,668	$ –	$ –
Accrued benefit cost	(30,336)	(27,451)	(750)	(603)
Additional minimum liability	(14,112)	–	–	–
Intangible asset	688	–	–	–
Accumulated other comprehensive income	13,424	–	–	–
Net asset (liability) recognized at end of year	$267,160	$ 229,217	$ (750)	$ (603)

For the pension benefits, the following table reflects the total benefits ex-pected to be paid from the plans' or the Company's assets. Of the pension benefits expected to be paid in 2005, $1,898,000 is expected to be paid from employer assets. Expected contributions reflect amounts expected to be contrib-uted to funded plans. For other postretirement benefits, the above table reflects only the Company's share of the benefit cost without regard to income from federal subsidy payments received pursuant to the Medicare Prescription Drug

Improvement and Modernization Act of 2003 (MMA). Expected MMA subsidy payments, which will reduce the Company's cost for the plan, are shown separately.

Information about the expected cash flows for the pension plans and other post retirement benefit plans follows:

		Other Postretirement Benefits	
(in thousands)	Pension Benefits	Net Employer Contribution (Excluding MMA Subsidy)	Value Due to MMA Subsidy
Employer Contribution			
2005 (expected)	31,235	$ –	$ –
Expected Benefit Payments			
2005	31,794	3,014	–
2006	33,802	3,124	(736)
2007	36,384	3,082	(797)
2008	39,442	3,020	(856)
2009	43,254	2,821	(477)
2010 through 2014	288,424	10,483	(432)

Net periodic benefit cost included the following components:

(in thousands)	Pension Benefits			Other Postretirement Benefits		
	2004	2003	2002	2004	2003	2002
Service cost	$35,740	$ 32,488	$ 27,021	$ 460	$ 90	$ 235
Interest cost	60,039	57,520	53,220	1,256	481	877
Expected return on plan assets	(81,962)	(77,763)	(77,690)	–	–	–
Amortization of prior service cost	(1,006)	(3,145)	(2,864)	371	372	487
Amortization of actuarial loss	13,600	8,588	974	996	150	268
Net periodic benefit cost	$26,411	$ 17,688	$ 661	$3,083	1,093	$1,867

The assumptions used in measuring the net periodic benefit costs for the plans follow:

(in thousands)	Pension Benefits			Other Postretirement Benefits		
	2004	2003	2002	2004	2003	2002
Weighted average discount rate	6.25%	6.75%	7.35%	6.25%	6.75%	7.35%
Rate of increase in future compensation levels	3.25%	4.15%	4.15%	–	–	–

(in thousands)	Pension Benefits			Other Postretirement Benefits		
	2004	2003	2002	2004	2003	2002
Expected long-term rate of return on plan assets	8.75%	8.95%	9.45%	–	–	–
Health care cost trend covered charges	–	–	–	10.00%	10.00%	6.50%

The effect of a one-percentage point change in the 2004 assumed health care cost trend is as follows:

(in thousands)	Decrease	Increase
Total service and interest cost components on 2004 net periodic postretirement health care benefit cost	$(364)	$573
Accumulated postretirement benefit obligation for health care benefits at December 31, 2004	(3,900)	5,861

The MMA was signed December 8, 2003 to make additional voluntary benefits available through Medicare. The federal government will begin making subsidy payments to qualifying employers in 2006. Effective July 1, 2004, the Company adopted FASB Staff Position No. 106-2 (FSP 106-2), Accounting and Disclosure Requirements Related to the Medicare Prescription Drug, Improvement and Modernization Act of 2003 (which superseded FSP No. 106-1). FSP 106-2 provides authoritative guidance on accounting for the federal subsidy and other provisions of MMA. The adoption of FSP 106-2 reduced the Company's accumulated postretirement benefit obligations by approximately $6.2 million and resulted in an unrecognized actuarial gain of a similar amount. The adoption resulted in approximately a $417,000 reduction in postretirement benefit cost for the year ended December 31, 2004.

The Company has a defined contribution plan that covers substantially all of its domestic employees. The Company's contributions are determined based on 20% of the first 6% of the covered employee's salary. Total plan expense was approximately $6,034,000 in 2004, $5,674,000 in 2003, and $6,112,000 in 2002.

Tommy Hilfiger
2005 Annual Report

Note 14–Retirement Plans

The Company maintains employee savings plans for eligible U.S. employees. The Company's contributions to the plans are discretionary with matching contributions of up to 50% of employee contributions up to a maximum of 6% of an employee's compensation. For the years ended March 31, 2005, 2004 and 2003, the Company made plan contributions of $2,029, $18,20 and $2,043, respectively.

The Company also operates a collective pension plan, through its European subsidiary, for employees who have been employed with TH Europe for at least one year, provided they meet certain criteria. The pension plan is a defined contribution plan and TH Europe pays 50% of the pension contributions for the employee, which can range between 3% and 5% of the employee's salary depending on the employee's age. TH Europe contributed approximately $803, $1,118 and $259 for the fiscal years ended March 31, 2005, 2004 and 2003, respectively.

The Company maintains a supplemental executive retirement plan which provides certain members of senior management with a supplemental pension. The supplemental executive retirement plan is an unfunded plan for purposes of both the Internal Revenue Code of 1986 and the Employee Retirement Income Security Act of 1974.

The following provides a reconciliation of the benefit obligation and funded status of the supplemental executive retirement plan:

	March 31,	
	2005	**2004**
Change in benefit obligation:		
Benefit obligation at beginning of year	$ 12,820	$ 11,565
Service cost	948	904
Interest cost	752	646
Benefits paid	(185)	(3)
Actuarial (gain) or loss	(130)	(292)
Benefit obligation at end of year	$ 14,205	$ 12,820
Reconciliation of funded status:		
Funded status	$ 14,205	$(12,820)
Unrecognized actuarial (gain) or loss	1,327	1,460
Unrecognized prior service cost	1,524	1,832
Net amount recognized at year-end	$ (11,354)	$ (9,528)
Amounts recognized in the Consolidated Balance Sheets consists of:		
Accrued benefit liability	$(11,354)	$ (9,843)
Intangible asset	–	315
Net amount recognized at year-end	$(11,354)	$(9,528)
Additional year-end information for pension plans with accumulated benefit obligations in excess of plan assets:		
Projected benefit obligation	$ 14,205	$ 12,820
Accumulated benefit obligation	11,096	9,843
Unfunded accumulated benefit obligation	11,096	9,843

The components of net periodic benefit cost for the last three fiscal years are as follows:

	Fiscal Year Ended March 31,		
	2005	2004	2003
Service cost	$ 948	$ 904	$ 811
Interest cost	752	646	583
Amortization of prior service cost	308	309	309
Amortization of actuarial (gain) or loss	3	–	–
Net periodic benefits cost	$ 2,011	$ 1,859	$ 1,703

Actuarial assumptions used to determine costs and benefit obligations for the supplemental executive retirement plan as follows:

	Fiscal Year Ended March 31,		
	2005	2004	2003
Discount rate	6.00%	6.00%	6.25%
Expected long-term rate of return on plan assets	N/A	N/A	N/A
Rate of compensation increase	5.00%	5.00%	5.00%

The Company currently estimates total payments under the supplemental executive retirement plan will be $500 in each in each of fiscal years 2006 through 2010, and $2,300 in the aggregate for fiscal years 201 through 2014.

On October 22, 2004, the President signed the American Jobs Creation Act of 2004 (the "AJCA"), which changes the tax laws governing the operation of deferred compensation plans such as the SERP. Although the AJCA imposes numerous requirements on deferred compensation plans, these new requirements do not apply to benefits accrued and vested as of December 31, 2004 (unless the plan is "materially modified" thereafter).

In order to preserve the favorable tax treatment with respect to grandfathered SERP benefits and to ensure the SERP is not materially modified, the Company recently proposed amendments to the SERP that "froze" the SERP effective as of December 31, 2004. This means that, effective as of January 1, 2005, participants will no longer earn or accrue any additional benefits under the SERP and any future salary increases will not be taken into account under the SERP benefit formula. This freezing of the SERP in no way impacts or reduces the SERP benefit accrued as of December 31, 2004 at such time or times a distribution is permitted under the terms of the SERP in effect prior to 2005.

The Company maintains a voluntary deferred compensation plan which provides certain members of senior management with an opportunity to defer a portion of base salary or bonus pursuant to the terms of the plan. The voluntary deferred compensation plan is an unfunded plan for purposes of both the Internal Revenue Code of 1986 and the Employee Retirement Income Security Act of 1974. Included in accrued expenses and other current liabilities is $716 and $640 at March 31, 2005 and 2004, respectively, related to this plan.

Woodhead Industries
2005 Annual Report

15. Benefit Plans

We have defined contribution, defined benefit and government mandated plans covering eligible non-bargaining unit employees.

The annual profit-sharing contributions, which are the lesser of (i) a percentage of income defined in the plans, or (ii) 15% of the aggregate compensation paid to participants during the year, were $0.7 million, $0.6 million and $0.6 million in 2005, 2004 and 2003, respectively.

We make matching contributions of 50% of employees' contributions, up to 4% of compensation, to a 401(k) plan. Matching contributions were $0.3 million in 2005, 2004 and 2003.

Pension benefits are fully vested after five years and are based upon years of service and highest five-year average compensation. It has been our policy to fund our pension costs by making annual contributions based upon minimum funding provisions of the *Employee Retirement Income Security Act of 1974*. We contributed an additional $1.5 million, $0.9 million and $2.0 million in 2005, 2004 and 2003, respectively, to improve the funded status of our plan. Our total pension expense for company-sponsored qualified plans was $0.7 million, $1.0 million, and $0.4 million in 2005, 2004 and 2003, respectively. The 2004 pension expense of $1.0 million included $0.4 million of pension settlement expense triggered by reduced employment levels that required us to recognize past gains and losses in our pension accounts. This $0.4 million settlement expense was included in the Aero-Motive restructuring charge.

In 1990 we adopted a supplemental retirement benefit plan for certain key executive officers which will provide supplemental payments upon retirement, disability or death. The obligations are not funded apart from our general assets. We charged $0.4 million in 2005 and $0.2 million in both 2004 and 2003 to expense under the plan.

The projected benefit obligation, accumulated benefit obligation and fair value of plan assets for the plans with accumulated benefit obligations in excess of plan assets were $2.0 million, $1.8 million and $0, respectively in 2005; $1.8 million, $1.6 million and $0, respectively in 2004; and $1.1 million, $1.0 million and $0, respectively, in 2003.

The components of net periodic pension cost for the non-union plans were:

	2005	2004	2003
Service cost-benefits earned during the year .	$ 664	$ 600	$ 496
Interest cost on projected benefit obligation . .	608	595	508
Expected return on plan assets	(616)	(610)	(486)
Amortization of prior service cost	27	27	27
Amortization of transitional asset	2	1	1
Recognized actuarial loss	331	196	50

	2005	2004	2003
Additional loss recognized due to settlement .	99	430	–
Periodic pension cost, net	$1,115	$1,239	$ 596

The measurement date used to determine pension benefits was September 30, 2005. We used the following assumptions in accounting for the pension plans.

	2005	2004	2003
Discount rate	5.5%	5.8%	6.3%
Rate of increase in compensation levels .	4.5%	4.5%	4.5%
Expected long-term rate of return on plan assets	8.0%	8.0%	8.0%

The following table reconciles the plans' funded status and the amount recorded on our consolidated balance sheets for our non-union plans:

	2005	2004
Change in benefit obligation:		
Benefit obligation at beginning of year	$10,413	$ 9,048
Service cost	664	600
Interest cost	608	595
Benefits paid	(917)	(255)
Settlement payments	(375)	(1,304)
Actuarial loss	1,148	1,729
Benefit obligation at end of year	11,541	10,413
Change in plan assets:		
Fair value of plan assets at beginning of year	7,256	7,059
Actual return on plan assets	755	811
Employer contributions	1,920	945
Benefits paid	(917)	(255)
Settlement payments	(375)	(1,304)
Fair value of plan assets at end of year	8,639	7,256
Reconciliation of funded status:		
Underfunded status	2,902	3,157
Unrecognized actuarial loss	(4,168)	(3,590)
Unrecognized transition obligation	(2)	(3)
Unrecognized prior service cost	(138)	(165)
Prepaid pension cost included in the consolidated balance sheets	$ (1,406)	$ (601)

Amounts recorded on the consolidated balance sheets were:

	2005	2004
Prepaid benefit cost	$(2,582)	$(1,783)
Accrued benefit liability	1,816	1,646
Intangible asset	(95)	(110)
Accumulated other comprehensive income	(545)	(354)
Prepared pension cost included in the consolidate balance sheets	$(1,406)	$ (601)

Our investment policies employ an approach whereby a mix of equities and fixed income investments are used to maximize the long-term return of plan assets for a prudent level of risk. The investment portfolio contains a diversified blend of equity and fixed income investments. Equity investments are diversified across domestic and international stocks, as well as growth, value and small to large capitalizations. Fixed income investments have an average duration of three to seven years. Investment and market risks are measured and monitored on an ongoing basis through regular portfolio reviews, annual liability measurements and periodic asset/liability studies. We rebalance asset allocations as appropriate in order to stay within a targeted range of allocation for each asset category. Investment in certain derivatives is permitted.

The plan asset targeted and actual allocations by category were:

	Targeted 2005	2005	2004
Domestic equities	30%–755	54%	41%
International equities	5%–25%	15%	17%
Fixed income	10%–65%	20%	30%
Cash		11%	12%
Total		100%	100%

The expected return on plan assets is based on our expectation of the long-term average rate of return of the capital markets in which the plan invests. The expected return reflects the investment policy target asset mix and considers the historical returns earned for each asset category.

We do not expect to contribute to the non-union qualified plan in 2006.

The following benefit payments, which reflect expected future service, as appropriate, are expected to be paid:

Fiscal Year	Payment
2006	$ 304
2007	312
2008	359
2009	402
2010	420
2011–2015	$2,968

Although we have the right to improve, change or terminate the plans, they are intended to be permanent.

Our union employees are covered by union-sponsored, collectively bargained, multi-employer pension plans. For such plans, we contributed and charged to expense $0.1 million in 2005 and $0.2 million in both 2004 and 2003.

These contributions are determined in accordance with the provisions of negotiated labor contracts and generally are based on the number of man-hours worked. Information from the union plans' administrators is not available to permit us to determine our share of unfunded vested benefits.

We provide an optional retiree medical program to a majority of our U.S. salaried and non-union retirees. Beginning in April 2003, the plan was modified to require participants to fund the total cost of the retiree medical program. At September 28, 2002 we had an accrued postretirement benefit cost, which was included in our consolidated balance sheet in the amount of $2.3 million. At December 27, 2003 we had no liability for any of these postretirement benefit costs and the reduction of the $2.3 million liability was amortized over the period from April 1, 2003 to December 27, 2003.

These postretirement benefits are unfunded. Cost components of these postretirement benefits, principally health care, were:

	2005	2004	2003
Service cost	–	$(1,497)	$ 67
Interest cost	–	–	166
Amortization of transition obligation	–	–	(2,895)
Recognized actuarial loss	–	719	1,493
Total cost	–	$ (778)	$(1,169)

We used an assumed discount rate of 6.3% in 2003 for these plans.

We provide certain post-employment benefits to former or inactive employees before retirement. The costs associated with those benefits are immaterial.

John Deere
2004 Annual Report

3. Pension and Other Postretirement Benefits

The company has several defined benefit pension plans covering its U.S. employees and employees in certain foreign countries. The company also has several defined benefit health care and life insurance plans for retired employees in the U.S. and Canada. The company uses an October 31 measurement date for these plans.

The worldwide components of net periodic pension cost and the assumptions related to the cost consisted of the following in millions of dollars and in percents:

	2004	2003	2002
Pensions			
Service cost	$130	$111	$107
Interest cost	454	450	448
Expected return on plan assets	(619)	(558)	(619)
Amortization of actuarial loss	49	40	2
Amortization of prior service cost	41	40	30
Amortization of net transition asset			(1)
Special early-retirement benefits	3		3
Settlements/curtailments			6
Net cost (income)	$ 58	$ 83	$ (24)
Weighted-average assumptions			
Discount rates	6.0%	6.7%	7.2%
Rate of compensation increase	3.9%	3.9%	3.9%
Expected long-term rates of return	8.5%	8.5%	9.7%

The worldwide components of net periodic postretirement benefits cost and the assumptions related to the cost consisted of the following in millions of dollars and in percents:

	2004	2003	2002
Health care and life insurance			
Service cost	$ 99	$ 88	$ 83
Interest cost	314	287	224
Expected returns on plan assets	(52)	(39)	(44)
Amortization of actuarial loss	304	176	46
Amortization of prior service cost	(129)	(2)	(6)
Special early-retirement benefits	2		
Net cost	$ 538	$ 510	$ 303
Weighted-average assumptions			
Discount rates	6.1%	6.8%	7.2%
Expected long-term rates of return	8.5%	8.5%	9.7%

The following is the percentage allocation for the total pension and health care plan assets (similar for both plans) at October 31:

	Allocation Percent	
	2004	2003
Equity securities	56%	61%
Debt securities	25	21

	Allocation Percent	
	2004	*2003*
Real estate	4	4
Other	15	14

The primary investment objective is to maximize the growth of the pension and health care plan assets to meet the projected obligations to the beneficiaries over a long period of time, and to do so in a manner that is consistent with the company's earnings strength and risk tolerance. Asset allocation policy is the most important decision in managing the assets and it is reviewed regularly. The asset allocation policy considers the company's financial strength and long-term asset class risk/return expectations since the obligations are long-term in nature. The target allocations are approximately 60 percent for equity securities, 20 percent for debt securities, 4 percent for real estate, and 16 percent for other. The assets are well diversified and are managed by professional investment firms as well as by investment professionals who are company employees.

The expected long-term rate of return on plan assets reflects management's expectations of long-term average rates of return on funds invested to provide for benefits included in the projected benefit obligations. The expected return is based on the outlook for inflation, fixed income returns and equity returns, while also considering historical returns, asset allocation and investment strategy. Although not a guarantee of future results, the average annual return of the company's U.S. pension fund was 11 percent during the past ten years and 12 percent during the past 20 years. The discount rate assumption is based on investment yields available on AA rated long-term corporate bonds.

The company expects to contribute approximately $130 million to its pension plans and approximately $680 million to its health care and life insurance plans in 2005, which include direct benefit payments on unfunded plans. These expected contributions also include voluntary contributions to the U.S. pension plans of approximately $100 million and the health care plans of approximately $400 million during 2005.

A worldwide reconciliation of the funded status of the benefit plans and the assumptions related to the obligations at October 31 in millions of dollars follows:

	Pensions		Health Care and Life Insurance	
	2004	*2003*	*2004*	*2003*
Change in benefit obligations				
Beginning of year balance	$(7,790)	$(6,840)	$(5,408)	$(4,108)
Service cost	(130)	(111)	(99)	(88)
Interest cost	(454)	(450)	(314)	(287)
Actuarial loss	(474)	(534)	(209)	(1,578)
Amendments	(3)	(190)	92	424
Benefits paid	516	484	260	238

	Pensions		Health Care and Life Insurance	
	2004	**2003**	**2004**	**2003**
Special early-retirement benefits	(3)		(2)	
Foreign exchange and other	(65)	(149)	(10)	(9)
End of year balance	(8,403)	(7,790)	(5,690)	(5,408)
Change in plan assets (fair value)				
Beginning of year balance	5,987	5,024	577	410
Actual return on plan assets	594	958	60	92
Employer contribution	1,548	432	304	313
Benefits paid	(516)	(484)	(260)	(238)
Foreign exchange and other	22	57	5	
End of year balance	7,635	5,987	686	577
Plan obligation more than plan assets	(768)	(1,803)	(5,004)	(4,831)
Unrecognized actuarial loss	2,551	2,094	2,768	2,869
Unrecognized prior service (credit) cost	217	254	(387)	(423)
Net amount recognized	$2,000	$ 545	$(2,623)	$(2,385)
Minimum pension liability adjustment	(106)	(1,964)		
Net asset (liability) recognized	$1,894	$(1,419)	$(2,623)	$(2,385)
Amounts recognized in balance sheet				
Prepaid benefit cost	$2,493	$63		
Accrued benefit liability	(599)	(1,482)	$(2,623)	$(2,385)
Intangible asset	18	250		
Accumulated pretax charge to other comprehensive income	88	1,714		
Net amount recognized	$2,000	$ 545	$(2,623)	$(2,385)
Weighted-average assumptions				
Discount rates	5.5%	6.0%	5.5%	6.0%
Rate of compensation increase	3.9%	3.9%		

The annual rates of increase in the per capita cost of covered health care benefits (the health care cost trend rates) used to determine benefit obligations at October 31, 2004 were assumed to be 9.0 percent for 2005 graded down evenly to 5.0 percent for 2009 and all future years. The obligations at October 31, 2003 assumed 10.0 percent for 2004 graded down evenly to 5.0 percent for 2009. An increase of one percentage point in the assumed health care cost trend rate would increase the accumulated postretirement benefit obligations at October 31, 2004 by $724 million and the aggregate of service and interest cost component of net periodic postretirement benefits cost for the year by $66 million. A decrease of one percentage point would decrease the obligations by $636 million and the cost by $56 million.

The benefits expected to be paid from the benefit plans, which reflect expected future years of service, and the Medicare subsidy expected to be received are as follows in millions of dollars.

	Pensions	Health Care and Life Insurance	Health Care Subsidy Receipts*
2005	$ 520	$ 277	
2006	531	296	$ (10)
2007	535	314	(12)
2008	543	330	(12)
2009	542	343	(12)
2010 to 2014	2,910	1,929	(62)

* See Note 1 for Medicare subsidy

The total accumulated benefit obligations for all pension plans at October 31, 2004 and 2003 was $7,954 million and $7,390 million, respectively.

The accumulated benefit obligations and fair value of plan assets for pension plans with accumulated benefit obligations in excess of plan assets were $732 million and $141 million, respectively, at October 31, 2004 and $7,186 million and $5,745 million, respectively, at October 31, 2003. The projected benefit obligations and fair value of plan assets for pension plans with projected benefit obligations in excess of plan assets were $4,725 million and $3,773 million, respectively, at October 31, 2004 and $7,569 million and $5,745 million, respectively, at October 31, 2003.

The minimum pension liability adjustment recorded by the company was $106 million and $1,964 million as of October 31, 2004 and 2003, respectively. The decrease in the adjustment, compared to last year, was a result of an increase in the fair value of plan assets due to voluntary company contributions and the return on plan assets during 2004.

See Note 23 for defined contribution plans related to employee investment and savings.

Chapter 15
Income Tax Accounting

CONTENTS

Under ASC 740-10-05-1 through 05-10, *Income Taxes: Overall,* income tax allocation is required. Temporary differences take place between book income and taxable income. The deferred tax liability or asset is measured at the tax rate that will arise when the temporary difference reverses. In determining the tax rate the fact that different rates exist for ordinary income and capital gains must be considered. The deferred tax liability or asset must be adjusted for changes in tax law or in tax rate. As a result, the asset and liability method (hereafter referred to simply as the liability method) must be used to account for deferred income taxes. The liability method is balance sheet oriented because the major goal is to present the estimated actual taxes to be paid in future years. Comprehensive deferred tax accounting is followed, meaning that all income tax effects of all revenues, expenses, gains, losses, and other items creating differences between tax and financial reporting are considered. Tax expense equals taxes payable plus the tax impact of all temporary differences. In other words, the total provision for income taxes is the sum of the amount of tax currently payable (current tax expense) and the net change in the deferred tax assets and deferred tax liabilities (deferred tax expense or benefit). Interperiod tax allocation is followed to account for temporary differences affecting the current year's results. Tax effects of future events should be reflected in the year they occur. Besides temporary differences, ASC 740-10-05-1 through 05-10 deals with the recognition of taxes currently payable or refundable.

Deferred tax assets and liabilities also take into account operating loss carryforwards for tax reporting purposes. Deferred tax assets are reduced by a valuation allowance account representing the amount of tax benefits not expected to be realized. In effect, the tax provision is basically the residual amount computed as the current tax provision plus the difference between the beginning and ending deferred tax balances.

If tax rates are graduated based on taxable income, aggregate calculations may be made using an estimated average rate.

This applies to federal, state, local, and foreign income taxes; consolidated and combined financial statements; investments under the equity method; and foreign companies issuing their financial statements in conformity with generally accepted accounting principles (GAAP).

Of note to the reader is the FASB Implementation Guide, *Accounting for Income Taxes*, providing questions and answers regarding the implementation of ASC 740-10-05-1 through 05-10.

TEMPORARY DIFFERENCES

Most transactions entered into by a company are accounted for in the same way for financial and tax reporting purposes. However, some transactions are accounted for differently. Temporary differences apply to the period in which revenue or expenses will be recognized. Temporary differences can be caused by four types of transactions as follows:

1. Revenue is included on the tax return after being presented on the books (financial records). An example is an installment sale that is recognized for the books in the year of sale but is recognized for tax purposes when cash collections are received. Another example is using the percentage-of-completion construction contract method on the books but the completed contract method on the tax return. This also occurs if the equity method is used by the investor, because the investees' earnings are recognized for book purposes by the investor but the investor recognizes only the investees' dividends for tax reporting.

2. Revenue is included on the tax return before being presented on the books. An example is deferred (unearned) revenue, such as an advance payment (retainer) that is recognized for tax purposes when the advance payment is received but is not recognized for book purposes until the services are performed.

3. Expenses are deducted on the tax return after being deducted on the books. For example, bad debts are deducted on the books in the year of sale (allowance method) but are not deductible on the tax return until the customer's balance is uncollectible (direct write-off method). Warranty expense is deducted on the books in the year of sale but is deducted on the tax return when paid. Another example is a contingent loss accrual for book purposes before being deductible for tax purposes. Sales returns and allowances are accrued for book purposes but not deducted on the tax return until the product is returned.

4. Expenses are deducted on the tax return before being deducted on the books. An example is accelerated depreciation on the tax return but straight-line depreciation on the books. Another example is a shorter depreciable life of fixed assets for tax purposes relative to book purposes. A deferred tax liability also arises when certain pre- operating costs and certain capital interest costs are deductible for tax purposes in the current year.

Other examples of temporary differences are:

☐ Unrealized losses or gains on trading securities or available-for-sale securities that are recorded for financial reporting purposes (on the tax return, losses or gains are recognized only when the securities are sold).

☐ Items relating to foreign-currency-denominated assets and liabilities.

☐ Use of the equity method for book purposes but the cost method for tax reporting.

☐ Gross profit recognized on the cost recovery method for book purposes but on the cash basis for tax purposes.

☐ Use of the capital lease method for book purposes but the operating method for tax reporting.

☐ Amortizing capitalized leases over different time periods for book and tax purposes.

☐ Gains or losses on fixed assets recognized for book purposes but deferred for tax purposes because of a trade-in on similar fixed assets.

☐ Gains on appreciation in assets distributed associated with a liquidation recognized for financial reporting and on distribution for tax purposes.

☐ Use of different amortization periods for intangible assets for book and tax purposes.

☐ Use of cost depletion for financial reporting while using statutory depletion for tax purposes.

☐ Net capital loss recognized in the current year for book purposes but carried forward to offset future capital gains on the tax return.

☐ Excess charitable contribution carried over to future years for tax reporting.

☐ Deferred compensation accrued for books while employee services are performed but not deductible on the tax return until actually paid.

☐ Amortization of bond issue costs under the interest method for book purposes but the straight-line method on the tax return.

☐ Accrual of sick or vacation pay as employee services are rendered for book purposes but when paid on the tax return.

☐ Deferral of intangible drilling costs for book purposes while expensing them on the tax return.

☐ Interest revenue used to offset capitalized interest on the books but recognized as income on the tax return.

☐ Inventories valued at the lower of cost or market value for books but at cost for tax reporting.

☐ Loss provision for obsolete inventory for books but not deductible on the tax return until the inventory is available for sale at discounted values or discarded.

☐ Inventory-related costs deducted on the books but capitalized for tax reporting.

☐ Use of the accrual basis for book purposes but the cash basis on the tax return.

☐ Effect of a change from the cash basis to the accrual basis recognized equally over four years for tax purposes.

☐ Imputed interest for book purposes that differs from the amount recognized for tax purposes.

☐ Reduction in the tax basis of depreciable assets due to tax credits.

☐ Increase in the tax basis of assets due to indexing whenever the local currency is the functional currency.

☐ Tax basis difference that results from the issuance of convertible debt with a beneficial conversion feature, as specified by ASC 740-10-55-51, *Income Taxes: Overall*. Under the EITF, the deferred taxes recognized should be adjusted to paid-in-capital.

☐ Tax consequences of differences between the assigned values and the tax bases of assets and liabilities in a purchase business combination.

☐ Tax basis adjustments required by the tax law.

Some items may be considered temporary differences in one case but not in another. For example, the amount by which the cash surrender value of life insurance exceeds insurance premiums paid is a temporary difference if there is an anticipation that the cash surrender value will be recovered. It is not a temporary difference if it is anticipated that the cash surrender value will not be recovered when the insured dies.

DEFERRED TAX LIABILITY

If book income (BI) exceeds taxable income (TI), then tax expense (TE) exceeds tax payable (TP), resulting in a deferred tax liability (credit). The deferred tax liability may also be calculated by multiplying the temporary difference by the applicable tax rate.

EXAMPLE

Book income and taxable income are both $200,000. Depreciation expense for book purposes is $20,000 using the straight-line method, but depreciation for tax purposes is $30,000 using an accelerated depreciation method. Assuming a 30% tax rate, the entry is:

Income tax expense ($180,000 × 30%)	54,000	
Income tax payable ($170,000 × 30%)		51,000
Deferred tax liability ($10,000 × 30%)		3,000

At the end of the life of the asset, the deferred tax liability of $3,000 will be completely reversed.

EXAMPLE

Interperiod Tax Allocation with Temporary Difference

XYZ Corporation's pretax financial income is $500,000 for year 20X1. It has a $200,000 temporary difference at the end of 20X1 that will reverse and result in taxable amounts as follows:

Year	Taxable Amount
20X2	$40,000
20X3	$70,000
20X4	$90,000

The tax rate is 30% for all years. There were no deferred taxes at the beginning of year 20X1.

The taxes payable for year 20X1 are calculated as follows:

Pretax financial income for 20X1	$500,000
Temporary difference at end of 20X1	(200,000)
Taxable income for 20X1	$300,000
Tax rate	30%
Taxes payable for 20X1	$ 90,000

The deferred tax liability is calculated as follows:

	20X2	20X3	20X4	Total
Future taxable amount	$40,000	$70,000	$90,000	$200,000
Tax rate	30%	30%	30%	30%

	20X2	20X3	20X4	Total
Deferred tax liability	$12,000	$21,000	$27,000	$ 60,000

Total tax expense for year 20X1 is as follows:

Current tax expense for 20X1	$ 90,000
Deferred tax liability for 20X1	$ 60,000
Total tax expense for 20X1	$150,000

The journal entry to record tax expense is:

Income tax expense	150,000	
Income tax payable		90,000
Deferred tax liability		60,000

EXAMPLE

Interperiod Tax Allocation with Temporary Difference and Beginning Deferred Taxes

XYZ Corporation's pretax financial income is $600,000 and taxable income is $450,000 for year 20X1. Its beginning deferred tax liability account has a balance of $75,000. Its cumulative temporary difference for year end 20X1 is equal to $300,000 and will reverse and result in taxable amounts as follows:

Year	Taxable Amount
20X2	$100,000
20X3	$ 75,000
20X4	$125,000

The tax rate is 30% for all years.

The taxes payable for year 20X1 are calculated as follows:

Pretax financial income for 20X1	$600,000
Temporary difference at end of 20X1	(50,000)
Taxable income for 20X1	$550,000
Tax rate	30%
Taxes payable for 20X1	$165,000

The deferred tax liability is calculated as follows:

	20X2	20X3	20X4	Total
Future taxable amount	$100,000	$75,000	$125,000	$300,000
Tax rate	30%	30%	30%	30%
Deferred tax liability	$ 30,000	$22,500	$ 37,500	$ 90,000

Total tax expense for year 20X1 is as follows:

Current tax expense for 20X1		$165,000
Deferred tax liability at end of 20X1	$90,000	
Deferred tax liability at beginning of 20X1	75,000	
Deferred tax expense for 20X1 (additional)		15,000
Total tax expense for 20X1($600,000 × 30%)		$180,000

The journal entry to record tax expense is:

Income tax expense	150,000	
Income tax payable		135,000
Deferred tax liability		15,000

EXAMPLE

On January 1, 20X0, Levita Company purchased an $800,000 machine with an estimated useful life of 10 years with no salvage value. The machine was depreciated using a accelerated method for both book and tax purposes. On December 31, 20X2, the carrying value of the machine was $380,000. At the beginning of the next year (January 1, 20X3), Levita changed to the straight-line method for financial statement purposes. Levita's tax rate was 40%. On January 1, 20X3, what amount should Levita report as a deferred income tax liability as a result of the change?

After the change in accounting method was made (to the straight-line method), there would be a temporary difference because the machine was being depreciated using the straight-line method for financial statement purposes and an accelerated method for tax purposes. The temporary difference may be computed in the following manner*:

Carrying amount of the machine for financial statement purposes after the change on 1/1/20X3	
$800,000 − (3/10 × $800,000)	$560,000
Less: carrying amount of machine for tax purposes on 1/1/20X3	380,000
Temporary difference—(future taxable amount)	$180,000

Because the machine was being depreciated using the straight-line method for financial statement purposes and an accelerated method for tax purposes, the temporary difference represents a future taxable amount and therefore results in a deferred tax liability. ASC 740-10-05-1 through 05-10 requires that the deferred tax liability be measured by multiplying the amount of the temporary difference by the tax rate scheduled to be in effect when the temporary difference reverses. Therefore, the deferred income tax liability is computed in the following way:

Deferred income tax liability, January 1, 19X9:	
$180,000 × .4 =	$72,000

*The carrying value of the machine was the same for both financial statement purposes and tax purposes prior to the change because during that period the machine was depreciated using an accelerated method for both book and tax purposes.

DEFERRED TAX ASSET

If book income (BI) is less than taxable income (TI), then tax expense (TE) is less than tax payable (TP), causing a deferred tax asset (charge). The deferred tax asset equals the temporary difference multiplied by the tax rate scheduled to be in effect when the difference reverses.

A net deferred tax asset may be recorded if it is more likely than not (more than a 50% probability) that the tax benefit will be realized in the future. The gross deferred tax asset is reduced by a valuation allowance (contra account) if it is more likely than not that some or all of the gross deferred tax asset will not be realized. The net deferred tax asset represents the amount likely to be realized. The deferred tax asset is presented in the following balance sheet, assuming a temporary difference of $500,000, a tax rate of 40%, and $350,000 of the tax benefit having more than a 50% probability of being realized.

Gross deferred tax asset ($500,000 × .40)	$200,000
Less: valuation allowance ($150,000 × .40)	60,000
Net deferred tax asset ($350,000 × .40)	$140,000

EXAMPLE

There is a temporary difference of $300,000, a 30% tax rate, and the entire temporary difference has more than a 50% probability of being realized. The balance sheet presentation follows:

Gross deferred tax asset ($300,000 × .30)	$90,000
Less: valuation allowance	0
Net deferred tax asset ($300,000 × .30)	$90,000

EXAMPLE

If in the previous example the entire deferred tax asset of $300,000 had less than a 50% probability of being realized, the balance sheet presentation would be as follows:

Gross deferred tax asset ($300,000 × .30)	$90,000
Less: valuation allowance ($300,000 × .30)	90,000
Net deferred tax asset	$ 0

The following factors are reflective of there being more than a 50% probability of future realization of a temporary difference presented as a deferred tax asset:

☐ There has been a relatively consistent strong earnings history.

☐ Future earnings are assured.

☐ There is expected adequate future taxable income arising from the reversal of a temporary difference (deferred tax liability) to realize the benefit of the tax asset.

☐ Sound and prudent tax planning strategies are in place that would allow for the realization of the deferred tax asset.

☐ The amount per books of asset values exceeds their tax bases sufficient to realize the deferred tax asset.

☐ Lucrative contracts exist.

☐ There is a significant sales backlog.

The following factors indicate that there is a 50% or less probability of future realization of a deferred tax asset:

☐ A history of losses in prior years.

☐ An expectation of future operating losses even though prior years showed profitability.

☐ Tax benefits that have expired.

☐ Significant contingencies and uncertainties, such as lawsuits that could have a disastrous effect on the business.

The valuation allowance reduces the deferred tax asset to its realizable value. The determination of whether a valuation allowance is necessary involves considering the positive and negative factors related to whether the deferred tax asset is more likely than not to be realized. The valuation allowance account should be evaluated periodically at each year-end to determine whether any adjustments are required. For example, the valuation allowance account would be eliminated in full if positive evidence now exists indicating that the deferred tax asset is no longer impaired. Any entry required to the valuation allowance account is coupled with a related adjustment to income tax expense. For example, if the valuation allowance account is increased, so is income tax expense. The entry is to debit income tax expense and credit valuation allowance.

EXAMPLE

XYZ Company has income before taxes of $1,100,000. The only temporary difference is warranty expense, which is recorded at $100,000 on the books based on sales but is recognized for tax purposes at $30,000 (which is based on the amount paid). The tax rate is 34%. Therefore, the amount of the temporary difference is $70,000 ($100,000 – $30,000). It is concluded that $60,000 of this temporary difference has a greater than 50% probability of being realized, and $10,000 of the temporary difference has a 50% or less probability of being realized. Relevant computations follow:

	Book Income	Tax Income
Income before taxes	$1,100,000	$1,100,000
Warranty expense	100,000	30,000
Income	$1,000,000	$1,070,000

The journal entry to record the temporary difference is:

Income tax expense (.34 × $1,000,000)	340,000	
Deferred tax asset (.34 × $70,000)	23,800	
Income tax payable (.34 × $1,070,000)		363,800

The entry to record the valuation allowance is:

Income tax expense (.34 × $10,000)	3,400	
Valuation allowance (.34 × $10,000)		3,400

The balance sheet presentation follows:

Gross deferred tax asset (.34 × $70,000)	$23,800
Less: valuation allowance (.34 × $10,000)	3,400
Net deferred tax asset (.34 × $60,000)	$20,400

The valuation allowance for a particular tax jurisdiction should be allocated proportionately (pro rata) between the current and noncurrent deferred tax assets for that jurisdiction.

EXAMPLE

Temporary differences at year-end related to accounts receivable and fixed assets were $40,000 and $10,000, respectively. The company determines that the valuation allowance should be $8,000 at year-end. The tax rate is 30%. Therefore, the valuation allowance must be proportionately allocated between current and noncurrent deferred tax assets as follows:

		Percent	Allocation
Amount			
Current:			
Deferred tax asset (for accounts receivable):			
$40,000 × .30	$12,000	80%	$6,400
Noncurrent:			
Deferred tax asset (for fixed assets):			
$10,000 × .30	3,000	20%	1,600
	$15,000	100%	$8,000

At year-end, the amounts presented in the balance sheet follow:

Current:	
Deferred tax asset	$12,000
Less: valuation allowance	6,400
Net deferred tax asset	$5,600

Noncurrent:	
Deferred tax asset	$3,000
Less: valuation allowance	1,600
Net deferred tax asset	$1,400

A deferred tax asset may be recognized up to an existing deferred tax liability balance.

EXAMPLE

In 20X3, a company sold a fixed asset at a gain of $40,000 for book purposes, which was deferred for tax purposes (installment method) until 20X4. Also in 20X3, $25,000 of deferred revenue was received. The income was reflected on the current year's tax return but was deferred for book purposes until the next year. The deferred tax asset may be recognized because the deductible amount in the future ($25,000) offsets the taxable amount ($40,000). Using a 25% tax rate and income taxes payable of $42,000, the entry in 20X3 is

Income tax expense (balancing figure)	45,750	
Deferred tax asset ($25,000 × .25)	6,250	
Deferred tax liability ($40,000 × .25)		10,000
Income tax payable		42,000

A deferred tax asset can also be recognized for the tax benefit of deductible amounts realizable by carrying back a loss from future years to lower taxes paid in the current year or in prior years.

A deferred tax asset is recognized for the excess of the tax basis over the amount for book purposes of an investment in a subsidiary or joint venture that is permanent in nature if it is expected that the temporary difference will reverse in the future years.

ASC 740-10-15-2A, *Income Taxes: Overall*, clarifies the accounting for uncertainty in income taxes recognized in a company's financial statements in accordance with ASC 740-10-05-1 through 05-10.

There is a two-step process involved in appraising a tax position. The first step is *recognition*. The company determines if it is more likely than not that a tax position will be sustained upon examination. Consideration is given to the merits of any litigation or appeal. The second step is *measurement*. A tax position that satisfies the more-likely-than-not recognition threshold is measured to calculate the amount of benefit to be recognized. The tax position is measured at the largest amount of benefit that is greater than 50% likely of being realized upon ultimate settlement.

ASC 740-10-25-9, *Income Taxes: Overall, Definition of Settlement in FASB Interpretation No. 48*), provides guidance on how a company may determine when a previously unrecognized tax position may be recognized. Companies must assess if a tax position is *more likely than not* to be sustained on review and to recognize in its financial statements only the largest benefit amount from the tax position that is greater than 50% likely to be realized.

Previously, the company could also recognize a tax position when the tax matter was eventually settled through negotiation or litigation. Under ASC 740-10-25-9, the position may be recognized upon effective settlement, which takes into account:

1. The exam procedure has been completed by the taxing authority.

2. The company does not intend to appeal or litigate the tax position of the taxing authority.

3. It is remote that the taxing authority would examine or reexamine any aspect of the tax position.

The difference between the tax shown on the tax return compared to the tax reported on the financial statements will arise from one of the following:

1. An increase in the deferred tax liability or a reduction in the deferred tax asset.

2. An increase in income taxes payable or a reduction in the income tax refund receivable.

3. Both (1) and (2).

A liability for unrecognized tax benefits should be classified as current to the degree that the company expects making payment within one year or the operating cycle, if longer. An income tax liability should not be classified as a deferred tax liability unless it results from a taxable temporary difference. The liability for unrecognized tax benefits (or reduction in amounts refundable) shall *not* be combined with deferred tax liabilities or assets.

If the company's tax position is considered 50% or less probable of being realized, then interest must be accrued. Interest equals the tax rate multiplied by the difference between the tax position taken on the tax return and the tax position likely to be ultimately upheld by the taxing body. In addition, the company may take a position on the tax return that does not satisfy the minimum statutory threshold for avoiding the penalty. In this situation, the company records an expense for the penalty. A company has discretion as to the categorization of interest and penalties.

In the event that the more-likely-than-not recognition threshold is not satisfied in the period for which a tax position is taken, the company should recognize the benefit of the tax position in the first interim period that meets any of the following conditions:

1. The tax matter is ultimately resolved through litigation or negotiation.

2. The statute of limitations to examine the tax position has expired.

3. The more-likely-than-not recognition threshold is met by the reporting date.

Interest expense on an underpayment of income taxes should be recognized in the first period the interest would begin accruing.

A company must disclose the following:

1. Policy of classifying interest and penalties.

2. Tabular reconciliation of the total amounts of unrecognized tax benefits at the beginning and end of year. There should be disclosure of the amounts of decreases in the unrecognized tax benefits applicable to settlements with taxing authorities or a lapse in the statutory time period.

3. The total amount of unrecognized tax benefits impacting the effective tax rates.

4. The nature of any significant uncertainties affecting taxes, including a range in the dollar amount associated with an ultimate resolution.

5. Tax years being examined.

PERMANENT DIFFERENCES

Permanent differences do not reverse in subsequent years and therefore do not require tax allocation. They affect either book income or taxable income, but not both. Examples of expenses that are not tax deductible are penalties and fines. Premiums paid on an officer's life insurance policy for which the company is the beneficiary are not tax deductible. Some organization and start-up costs are not deductible for tax purposes (e.g., costs associated with raising capital). The amount of wages used to derive the jobs credit is not tax deductible. An example of an expense that is only partly deductible on the tax return is 50% for meals and entertainment. An example of tax-exempt income is interest on municipal bonds. The proceeds of life insurance arising from an officer's death for which the company is the beneficiary are not subject to tax. An example of income that is fully or partly nontaxable is dividends received by a corporation.

EXAMPLE

Roberta Company began its operation in 20X2. In that year, it reported income before operations of $425,000. In 20X2, Roberta Company's tax depreciation exceeded its book depreciation by $55,000. Roberta's tax rate for 20X2 was 35%. Recent legislation that was enacted boosted this rate to 40% for years after 20X2. *Roberta Company also had nondeductible book expenses of $20,000 related to permanent differences.* According to ASC 740, *Income Taxes*, what amount of deferred income tax liability should be reported by Roberta in its December 31, 20X2 balance sheet?

ASC 740 requires that a deferred tax liability be measured by multiplying the amount of temporary tax difference by the tax rate that is scheduled to be in effect when the temporary difference reverses. In the problem at hand, tax depreciation exceeded book depreciation by $55,000. That is, there are future taxable amounts of $55,000, which will result in a deferred tax liability currently that will reverse in the future (after 20X2). Computing the amount of the deferred tax liability requires the following:

$55,000 × 40% (the enacted tax rate after 20X2) = $22,000

Thus, the deferred tax liability is $22,000. As was noted previously, permanent differences do not reverse in subsequent years and therefore do not require tax allocation. They affect either book income or taxable income, but not both. In this case, the $20,000 represents a permanent difference and as such should be ignored in computing the deferred income tax liability.

Some permanent differences arise because of different bases used for financial and tax purposes. Examples are investments in a leveraged lease, the excess of the tax bases of assets in a buyer's tax jurisdiction over the financial bases of assets as presented in consolidated financial statements, and different bases for tax versus book arising from foreign currency remeasurements.

A permanent difference is the permanent excess of the amount for financial reporting over that for tax reporting of an investment in a foreign subsidiary or a foreign corporate joint venture.

INTRAPERIOD TAX ALLOCATION

Intraperiod tax allocation occurs when tax expense is presented in different parts of the financial statements for the current year. The income statement shows the tax impact of income from continuing operations, of income from discontinued operations, of extraordinary items, and of the cumulative effect of a change in accounting principle. In the retained earnings statement, prior-period adjustments are shown net of tax.

EXAMPLE

Intraperiod Tax Allocation

XYZ Corporation's financial information for year ended December 31, 20X2, is as follows:

Income from continuing operations	$600,000
Loss from discontinued operations	(150,000)
Extraordinary gain	80,000
Correction of accounting error	(30,000)
Taxable income	$500,000

There are $150,000 in deductible temporary differences at year-end December 31, 20X1. No change occurs in year 20X2. $10,000 of tax credit is available for year 20X2. The tax rate structure is as follows:

Taxable Income	Rate
1 to 100,000	20%
100,001 to 200,000	25%
200,001 to 300,000	40%
300,001 and above	50%

Future tax rates are expected to increase from 25% on December 31, 20X1, to 35% on December 31, 20X2.

Tax on income from continuing operations is $225,000 (including a credit of $10,000). Based on taxable income of $500,000 and a credit of $10,000, the tax due is $175,000. The $50,000 difference should be allocated between discontinued operations, extraordinary gain, and correction of error. Deferred taxes are adjusted by $15,000 [$150,000 × (35% − 25%)] for the increase in estimate of expected tax rate.

The combined statement of income and retained earnings is as follows:

Income from continuing operations, before taxes		$600,000
Tax on income from continuing operations		
Current	$235,000	
Deferred	(15,000)	
Tax credits	(10,000)	
		210,000
Income from continuing operations, net of taxes		$390,000
Loss from discontinued operations, net of tax benefit of $75,000		(75,000)
Extraordinary gain, net of tax of $40,000		40,000
Net income		$355,000
Retained earnings, January 1, 20X2		435,000
Correction of accounting error, net of tax of $15,000		(15,000)
Retained earnings, December 31, 20X2		$775,000

BALANCE SHEET PRESENTATION

ASC 740-10-45-7, *Income Taxes: Overall*, deals with balance sheet classification of deferred income taxes. In the balance sheet, deferred tax assets are offset against deferred tax liabilities and shown as (1) net current or (2) net noncurrent. However, a current account cannot be offset against a noncurrent account. Further, (net) current or noncurrent accounts cannot be offset for different tax-paying components or for different tax jurisdictions (e.g., federal versus local) because offsetting is prohibited unless there is a legal right of set-off.

Deferred tax assets or deferred tax liabilities are classified based on the related asset or liability they apply to. For example, a deferred tax liability due to depreciation on a fixed asset would be presented as noncurrent. A deferred tax asset related to accounts receivable would be classified as current.

Deferred taxes not related to specific assets or liabilities are classified as current or noncurrent, depending on the anticipated reversal dates of the temporary differences. Temporary differences reversing within one year are current, but those reversing after one year are noncurrent. In some cases, a given temporary difference may be a mix of current and noncurrent, such as a three-year warranty in which the first year is shown as a current account while years 2 and 3 are presented as a noncurrent account. Other examples are deferred tax assets related to a loss carryforward, and deferred tax liabilities arising when a long-term contract is accounted for by the percentage-of-completion method for financial reporting and by the completed contract method for tax purposes. Under the latter circumstances, the temporary difference becomes taxable when the contract is completed.

If a valuation allowance account exists as a reduction of a gross deferred tax asset, there must be a proration of the valuation allowance between current and noncurrent relative to the classification of the gross deferred tax asset.

INCOME STATEMENT PRESENTATION

Income tax expense should be presented in the income statement as two components—namely, the tax currently payable (the liability) and the deferred portion (portion of the expense based on temporary differences). The total income tax expense provision is based on financial reporting income excluding permanent differences. Presentation of these two expense portions would be as follows:

Income tax expense:		
Amount currently payable	$40,000	
Deferred portion	(32,000)	8,000

The amount currently payable is the current year's taxable income multiplied by the current year's tax rate. The deferred portion equals the temporary difference times the tax rate, or the change in the deferred tax balance during the year (ending balance less beginning balance).

As indicated previously, the deferred tax provision is added to the current tax provision to derive the total tax provision for the year. The current tax provision is the income taxes for the year as reported on the tax return.

LOSS CARRYBACKS

Tax effects of net operating loss carrybacks are allocated to the loss period (the current year). A company may carry back a net operating loss two years and receive a tax refund for taxes paid in profitable years. The tax benefit is recognized as a receivable for the refundable amount. Further, the tax benefit reduces the current year's tax expense, but the amount is based on the tax rates in effect in the carryback period. The loss is first applied to the earliest year, with any remaining loss carried forward. (A company may elect to forgo the carryback.) Loss carryforwards are discussed in the next section.

The presentation of a loss carryback with recognition of the refund during the loss year follows:

Loss before refundable income taxes	$120,000
Refund of prior years' income taxes arising from carryback of operating loss	40,000
Net loss	$ 80,000

Note: The refund should be computed at the amount actually refundable regardless of current tax rates.

EXAMPLE

In 20X3, a net loss of $100,000 occurred. Prior years' net incomes were $250,000 in 20X1 and $80,000 in 20X2. The tax rates over the years were 30% in 20X1, 31% in 20X2, and 32% in 20X3.

The 20X3 net loss may be carried back starting in 20X1. The loss carryback of $100,000 can be used in 20X1 because the net profit that year was higher. The tax benefit of the carryback is calculated based on the 20X1 tax rate of 30%, since 20X1 was when the tax was paid. The amount of the tax benefit is $30,000 ($100,000 × 30%). The journal entry in 20X3 to recognize the loss carryback benefit is:

Receivable from the IRS	30,000	
Income tax expense		30,000

EXAMPLE

The same facts as in the previous example are again assumed, except that the net income in 20X1 was $75,000. In that case, the tax benefit of the carryback loss is first applied to 20X1 with the balance ($25,000) in 20X2. The relevant computations follow:

20X1 $75,000 × 30%	$22,500
20X2 $25,000 × 31%	7,750
Total	$30,250

The journal entry in 20X3 to reflect the loss carryback benefit is:

Receivable from the IRS	30,250	
Income tax expense		30,250

LOSS CARRYFORWARDS

A net operating loss may be carried forward up to 20 years. A loss carryforward may be recognized to the extent that there are net taxable amounts in the carryforward period (deferred tax liabilities) to absorb them. A loss carryforward benefit may also be recognized if there exists more than a 50% probability of future realization. In this case, a net deferred tax asset may be recorded for the tax benefit (the gross deferred tax asset amount becomes the net deferred tax asset balance because the valuation allowance is zero). In other words, the tax benefit of a loss carryforward is recognized as a deferred tax asset if the loss is to be carried forward to offset future amounts of taxable income. The tax benefit is measured at the tax rates scheduled to be in effect for the carryforward period. When the net deferred tax asset is recorded, income tax expense is reduced. In later years, as income is realized, the deferred tax asset is reduced. If there is a 50% or less probability of future realization, a net deferred tax asset is not recorded (the valuation allowance equals the gross deferred tax asset, resulting in a zero balance in the net deferred tax asset). In this case, the tax effect of the operating loss carryforward cannot be recognized until the year realized (the year in which the tax liability is reduced). In other words, the amount of the gross deferred tax asset is reduced by a valuation allowance if it is more likely than not that some or all of the benefit of the loss carryforward will not be realized (that is, sufficient taxable income will not be earned in the carryforward period). When the tax benefit of a loss carryforward is recognized upon being realized in a later year, it is classified in the same way as the income-enabling recognition (typically reducing tax expense).

Presentation of the loss carryforward with recognition of benefit in the year realized follows:

Income tax expense:		
Without carryforward	$50,000	
Reduction of income taxes arising from carryforward of prior years' operating losses	(30,000)	$20,000

Special rules and exceptions exist. The tax benefit of operating losses arising in a business combination accounted for under the purchase method subsequent to the acquisition date should be applied first to reduce goodwill and other noncurrent intangible assets related to the purchase to zero. The tax benefits of carryforwards related to contributed capital and expenses for employee stock options should be allocated to the relate equity components. The tax benefit of operating losses as of the date of a quasi-reorganization that are later recognized usually should be added to contributed capital.

There should be footnote disclosure of the amount and expiration dates of operating loss carryforwards.

TAX RATES

Deferred taxes are recorded at the amounts of settlement when the temporary differences reverse.

EXAMPLE

Assume that in 20X2 a total temporary difference of $300,000 will reverse in later years, resulting in the following taxable amounts and tax rate:

	20X3	20X4	20X5	Total
Reversals	$110,000	$140,000	$50,000	$300,000
× Tax rate	× .30	× .28	× .25	
Deferred tax liability	$ 33,000	$ 39,200	$12,500	$ 84,700

On 12/31/20X2, the deferred tax liability has an $84,700 balance.

According to federal tax law, there is a graduated tax rate structure (tax rates increase when taxable income reaches the next tax level). However, GAAP requires deferred federal taxes to be based on a flat tax rate (currently 35%) unless the effect of the graduated rate is significant or special rates apply to the temporary difference.

If the use of a flat tax rate results in a more significant difference than if graduated tax rates were used, an average tax rate should apply in computing deferred taxes. The average tax rate equals the tax divided by taxable income.

EXAMPLE

It is assumed that the first $100,000 of income is taxed at 15%, the next $100,000 is taxed at 25%, and income above $200,000 is taxed at 35%. If taxable income in the next year is estimated at $240,000, the expected average graduated tax rate is computed as follows:

Tax Computation

$100,000 × .15	$15,000
$100,000 × .25	25,000
$ 40,000 × .35	14,000
Total tax	$54,000
Average tax rate = $54,000/$240,000 = 22.5%	

The use of a single average graduated tax rate based on average estimated annual taxable income during the reversal period will usually suffice.

EXAMPLE

A company has a taxable temporary difference of $400,000. The difference is anticipated to reverse $300,000 in year 1 and $100,000 in year 2. The company also anticipates $120,000 of taxable income from other sources per year. The relevant computations follow:

Year 1: expected taxable income ($300,000 + $120,000)	$420,000
Year 2: expected taxable income ($100,000 + $120,000)	$220,000
Average taxable income = ($420,000 + $220,000)/2 =	$320,000

The company should use an average graduated tax rate based on the estimated annual taxable income of $320,000. This is computed as follows:

$100,000 × .15	$15,000
$100,000 × .25	25,000
$120,000 × .35	42,000
Total Tax	$82,000
Average tax rate = $82,000/$320,000 = 25.63%	

A change in tax rate or other provisions of the tax law (e.g., tax deductibility of expenses) must immediately be reflected by adjusting tax expense and deferred taxes. If less taxes are owed, tax expense and deferred taxes will be decreased. If more taxes are owed, tax expense and deferred taxes will be increased.

EXAMPLE

On December 31, 20X2, a new tax law increases the tax rate from 28% to 33%. The effective date of the increase is January 1, 20X4. If the temporary difference is expected to reverse in 20X4, the company should calculate the deferred tax liability at December 31, 20X2, at the newly enacted tax rate of 33%.

EXAMPLE

At the end of 20X4, a new tax law reduces the tax rate from 36% to 30% starting in 20X6. In 20X4, the business had a deferred profit of $400,000 and showed a deferred tax liability of $144,000. The gross profit is to be reflected equally in 20X5, 20X6, 20X7, and 20X8. Thus, the deferred tax liability at year-end 20X4 of $18,000 is derived as follows:

	20X5	20X6	20X7	20X8	Total
Reversals	$100,000	$100,000	$100,000	$100,000	$400,000
× Tax rate	× .36	× .30	× .30	× .30	
Deferred tax liability	$36,000	$30,000	$30,000	$30,000	$126,000

The required journal entry in 20X4 is:

Deferred tax liability	18,000	
Income tax expense ($144,000 – $126,000)		18,000

A short-cut to obtain $18,000 follows:

Income subject to change in tax rate	$300,000
× Change in tax rate	.06
Adjustment	$18,000

If a new tax law occurs after year-end but before the audit report date, the company should use the tax rate in effect at the year-end financial statement date but disclose in a footnote as a subsequent event the new rate.

EXAMPLE

After December 31, 20X2, but before the financial statements are issued, a new tax law reduces the tax rate from 32% to 31%. The decrease in rate is effective January 1, 20X5. The 32% tax rate should be used in computing the deferred tax liability at December 31, 20X2, because that is the rate expected to be in effect in 20X5 based on the tax law in effect on the balance sheet date. However, the effect of the rate change should be a subsequent event footnote disclosure in the December 31, 20X2 financial statements. Of course, on the December 31, 20X3 financial statements, the company should compute the deferred tax liability at the newly enacted tax rate of 31%.

MULTIPLE TAX JURISDICTIONS

The determination of tax liability for federal reporting purposes may differ from that of state or city reporting requirements. As a consequence, temporary differences, permanent differences, and loss carrybacks or carryforwards may be different between federal and local reporting. If the temporary differences are significant, separate deferred tax calculations and recording will be required.

If temporary differences are treated the same for federal and local reporting purposes, a combined tax rate may be used in determining deferred taxes. The combined tax rate equals:

Federal tax rate × (1 – state tax rate) + state tax rate

TAX CREDITS

According to ASC 740-10-25-39 and 25-40, *Income Taxes: Overall*, if a company pays a dividend, any tax credit associated with it acts to reduce income tax expense.

According to ASC 718-740-45-8, *Compensation—Stock Compensation: Income Taxes*, tax benefits of dividends on unvested restricted stock are to be recognized in equity as "excess tax benefits." If the related awards are forfeited or are no longer expected to vest, the benefits from equity to the income statement should be reclassified.

TAX STATUS CHANGES

The effect of any change in tax status affecting a company requires an immediate adjustment to deferred tax liabilities (or assets) and to income tax expense. For example, if a company changes to S corporation status, a tax advantage generally arises, resulting in a reduction in both the deferred tax liability and income tax expense. Another example of a tax status change requiring an adjustment on the accounts is a company electing C corporation status. There should be a footnote explaining the nature of the status change and its affect on the accounts.

If an entity's tax status changes from nontaxable to taxable, a deferred tax asset or liability should be recorded for any temporary differences at the time the status changes. On the other hand, if the status change is from taxable to nontaxable, any deferred tax asset or liability should be eliminated.

BUSINESS INVESTMENTS

If the market value method is used to account for an investment in the common stock of other companies, no temporary difference arises. However, if the equity method is used to account for an investment in another company, a temporary difference arises because, as discussed in Chapter 10, the investor recognizes in its earnings the profit of the investee but recognizes for tax purposes the dividends received from the investee. As a result, the investor's book income exceeds its tax income because profit is usually in excess of dividends. In consequence, a deferred tax liability will likely arise.

BUSINESS COMBINATIONS

In a business combination accounted for under the grandfathered purchase method or the acquisition method, the fair values assigned to the acquired company's net assets may differ from the valuation of those net assets on the tax return. This may result in a temporary difference arising in either a deferred tax liability or deferred tax asset reported on the acquirer's consolidated financial statements.

In some cases, companies may have unrecognized tax benefits associated with operating losses or tax credits arising from a business combination accounted for under the grandfathered purchase method or the acquisition method. This may give rise to other similar tax advantages subsequent to the date of combination. In the absence of a provision in the tax law to the contrary, the tax benefits realized should be apportioned for book reporting between pre- and postacquisition tax benefits.

EXAMPLE

Tax Effects of Purchase Business Combination

XYZ Corporation's information about a nontaxable acquisition method business combination is as follows:

☐ The fair value of consideration transferred is $800,000.

☐ The fair value of assets acquired is $950,000 and XYZ's carryforward tax bases is $700,000.

☐ The $250,000 difference between the fair and tax carryforward bases of assets acquired consists of taxable temporary differences of $350,000 and deductible temporary differences of $100,000.

☐ The fair and carryforward tax bases of liabilities assumed is $150,000.

☐ Assume deductible temporary differences will be realized.

☐ The tax rate is a flat 30%.

The allocation of the purchase price is as follows:

Purchase price		$800,000
Allocation to Identifiable assets and (liabilities)		
Fair value of assets	$950,000	
Fair value of liabilities	(150,000)	
Deferred tax benefits	30,000	
Deferred tax obligations	(105,000)	
		725,000
Allocation to goodwill		$ 75,000

EXAMPLE

On 1/1/20X2, XYZ Company bought ABC Company for $4,000,000 in a business combination accounted for under the acquisition method. Goodwill was not involved. The tax basis of the net assets is $12,000,000. Therefore, deductible temporary differences equal $8,000,000. The tax rate is 40%. It has been determined that a valuation allowance for the entire amount of the deferred tax asset is required. However, at year-end 20X3, it is determined that the valuation allowance account is no longer needed. Income results for 20X2 and 20X3 are as follows:

	20X2	20X3
Before-tax for book income	$3,000,000	$1,800,000
Reversal of acquired deductible temporary differences	(3,000,000)	(1,800,000)
Taxable income	0	0

On the purchase date, the deferred tax asset is recorded at $3,200,000 ($8,000,000 × 40%), with a valuation allowance for $3,200,000. On 12/31/20X2, the deferred tax asset is $2,000,000 equal to 40% of $5,000,000 ($8,000,000 – $3,000,000), with a valuation allowance for the same amount ($2,000,000). On 12/31/20X3 the valuation allowance account, which is no longer required, is eliminated, resulting in a deferred tax benefit or in a reduction of deferred tax expense. **Caution:** If goodwill arose in the purchase business combination, the tax benefit would first reduce goodwill to zero, with any residual balance left reducing to zero any acquired intangible assets.

The journal entries applicable to deferred taxes follow:

1/1/20X2 (date of purchase combination)		
Net assets	4,000,000	
Deferred tax asset	3,200,000	
Cash		4,000,000
Valuation allowance		3,200,000
12/31/20X2		
Valuation allowance	1,200,000	
Deferred tax asset		1,200,000
$3,200,000 – $2,000,000		
12/31/20X3		
Valuation allowance	2,000,000	
Deferred tax asset		720,000
Income tax benefit deferred		1,280,000

SEPARATE FINANCIAL STATEMENTS OF A SUBSIDIARY

If separate financial statements are prepared, the consolidated income tax expense should be allocated to each of the subsidiaries. The allocation basis should be logical and in conformity with the liability method of tax allocation.

LEASES

Components of a leveraged lease have to be recomputed from the beginning of the rental when modifications occur in tax laws or other relevant financial variables (e.g., cash flows). The effects of a change must be accounted for and reflected in the income statement for the year of change. Lease calculations must incorporate the impact of the alternative minimum tax.

CONVERTIBLE DEBT

ASC 740-10-55-51, *Income Taxes: Overall*, deals with accounting for convertible debt issued with a non-detachable conversion feature that is "in-the-money," and requires that this beneficial conversion feature be accounted for separately. The feature is recognized and measured separately by allocating to additional paid-in-capital a portion of the proceeds equal to its intrinsic value.

EMPLOYEE STOCK OWNERSHIP PLANS (ESOPs)

Retained earnings are increased for the tax benefit arising from deductible dividends paid on unallocated shares held by an ESOP. However, dividends paid on allocated shares are includable in income tax expense.

QUASI-REORGANIZATION

The tax benefits associated with deductible temporary differences and carryforwards on the date of a quasi-reorganization should typically be recorded as an increase in paid-in-capital if the tax benefits will occur in later years.

JOBS ACT

ASC 740-10-55, 27-30, *Income Taxes: Overall*, applies to the special tax deduction allowed under the Jobs Act for income from qualified domestic production activities. The impact of the deduction is to be reported in the year in which the deduction is claimed on the U.S. tax return. The Act states that the manufacturer's deduction should be accounted for as a special deduction as earned instead of as a tax rate change. The special deduction will not affect deferred tax assets and liabilities existing at the enactment date. This deduction equals 3% of qualified income for the years 2005 and 2006, then increases to a 6% deduction for years 2007 through 2009, and finally increases to a 9% deduction beginning in 2010. Under the Jobs Act, there is a special one-time dividends received deduction on certain foreign earnings repatriated to qualifying U.S. taxpayers during a one-year period. To qualify for this deduction the profit must be reinvested in the U.S. pursuant to a domestic reinvestment plan. A company taking advantage of the Jobs Act will reduce its federal income tax rate on dividends from non-U.S. subsidiaries.

HEALTH CARE ACT

According to Accounting Standards Update (ASU) No. 2010-12 (ASC 740, *Income Taxes*), *Accounting for Certain Tax Effects of the 2010 Health Care Reform Acts*, the measurement of present and deferred tax obligations and assets are based on enacted tax law. The two health care acts should be taken together for financial reporting purposes. (ASC 740-10-S99-4)

DISCLOSURES

Disclosure is required of:

- ☐ Current tax expense or benefit.
- ☐ Deferred tax expense or benefit.
- ☐ Types of temporary differences and cumulative amounts.
- ☐ Reconciliation between tax expense per books and tax payable per the tax return.
- ☐ Reconciliation between the actual and expected tax rates.
- ☐ Components of the net deferred tax liability or asset.
- ☐ Valuation allowance provision and changes therein during the year. (The reasons for the changes should be specified.)
- ☐ Factors considered in determining the realizability of deferred tax assets.
- ☐ Adjustments to tax expense due to a change in tax law, tax rates, or tax status.
- ☐ Operating loss carryforwards and their tax benefits, including expiration dates.
- ☐ Amount of any unrecognized deferred tax liability because of undistributed foreign earnings.
- ☐ Amount of any unrecognized deferred tax liability for temporary differences applicable to undistributed domestic earnings.
- ☐ Tax expense arising from allocating tax benefits to contributed capital or to reduce the goodwill of an acquired company.
- ☐ Major aspects of the method used by which consolidated tax expense is allocated to subsidiaries.
- ☐ Method to account for the sale or purchase of tax benefits arising through tax leases.
- ☐ Government grants that reduce tax expense.
- ☐ Intercorporate tax sharing arrangements.
- ☐ Tax-related balances due to or from affiliates.

ASC 605-45-15-2, *Revenue Recognition: Principal Agent Considerations*, requires disclosure of a company's accounting policy with respect to the presentation of taxes collected on a revenue-producing transaction between a seller and a customer (e.g., sales, use, value-added, and some excise taxes, on either a gross [included in revenue and costs] or net [excluded from revenue] basis). Disclosure should be made of the taxes included in the financial statements.

INDEFINITE REVERSAL

Deferred taxes should not be recognized for the following types of temporary differences unless it is evident that they will reverse in the future years:

☐ Temporary differences applicable to an investment in a foreign subsidiary or foreign corporate joint venture that is permanent in nature.

☐ Undistributed earnings of a domestic subsidiary or domestic joint venture that is permanent in nature that arose in fiscal years beginning on or before December 15, 1992.

Comprehensive Example

ABC Company uses the accelerated depreciation method for tax reporting and the straight-line depreciation method for financial reporting. At December 31, 20X2, there was a taxable temporary difference of $250,000, which will reverse equally over 20X3 and 20X4. The current and expected future tax rate is 30%. Therefore, on December 31, 20X2 the company presented a noncurrent deferred tax liability of $75,000 ($250,000 × 30%) for this temporary difference.

During 20X3, ABC earned book income of $600,000. The following five differences arose between financial and tax reporting:

1. Nondeductible officers' life insurance premiums recorded in 20X3 were $30,000.

2. Gross profit on installment sales in 20X3 of $150,000 will be taxed evenly in 20X4, 20X5, and 20X6.

3. Depreciation for books exceed that for tax by $125,000 in 20X3. This represents the reversal of 50% of the $250,000 temporary difference referred to previously as of December 31, 20X2.

4. An estimated loss provision was made in 20X3 for $40,000. The loss is deductible in 20X5 for tax purposes because that is when it will be paid. Of course, as on December 31, 20X3, the accrued liability is a noncurrent liability.

5. A valuation allowance is not required at December 31, 20X3.

A schedule follows, presenting the taxable income and the current portion of income tax expense for 20X3:

Pretax financial statement income	$ 600,000
Reversal of 20X2 depreciation temporary difference	125,000
Deferral of gross profit on installment sales	(150,000)
Contingent loss	40,000
Officers' life insurance premium	30,000
Taxable income	$ 645,000

Current income tax expense and liability equals:

$$645,000 \times 30\% = 193,500$$

The deferred tax liability at December 31, 20X3, is $70,500 calculated as follows:

Depreciation temporary difference ($250,000 − $125,000)	$125,000
Deferred gross profit on installment sales	150,000
Contingent loss	(40,000)

Net temporary difference	$235,000
Deferred tax liability $235,000 × 30%	$ 70,500

The deferred portion of tax expense as of December 31, 20X3, is $4,500 calculated as follows:

Deferred tax liability—12/31/20X2	$75,000
Deferred tax liability—12/31/20X3	70,500
Net change in deferred tax liability (expense credit)	$ 4,500

Total income tax expense for the year ended December 31, 20X3, is $189,000 computed as follows:

Current portion	$193,500
Deferred portion (credit)	(4,500)
Total income tax expense	$189,000

The composition of the deferred tax liability as of December 31, 20X3, follows:

Current portion (based on the installment sales temporary difference) $150,000 × 30%		$45,000
Noncurrent portion:		
Depreciation temporary difference $125,000 × 30%	$37,500	
Less contingent loss temporary difference $40,000 × 30%	12,000	25,500
Total deferred tax liability—12/31/20X3		$70,500

On December 31, 20X3, the following journal entry is made:

Income tax expense	189,000	
Deferred tax liability (noncurrent)	49,500	
Income taxes payable		193,500
Deferred tax liability (current)*		45,000

* $150,000 × 30% = $45,000.

With respect to the journal entry, note the following:

☐ The $49,500 charge to deferred tax liability (noncurrent) adjusts the December 31, 20X2 balance of $75,000 to the required $25,500 net noncurrent balance at December 31, 20X3. The two elements of this account are noncurrent because they apply to items classified as noncurrent in the balance sheet (the depreciation difference applying to fixed assets, and the loss contingency applying to a reversal in more than one year).

☐ The deferred tax liability (current) of $45,000 applies to the installment sales temporary difference. A current classification is appropriate because installment receivables are typically considered current based on the operating cycle of the business.

OTHER

According to ASC 718-740-45-8 through 45-12, *Compensation—Stock Compensation: Income Taxes*, unrealized income tax benefits from dividends on equity-classified employee share-based payment awards should be excluded from the pool of excess tax benefits available to absorb tax deficiencies on share-based payment awards.

PROPERTY TAXES

Accounting Requirements

Real and personal property taxes are based, by law, on the assessed valuation of property as of a particular date. Although the states differ as to when this date should be, generally taxes are recognized on the date on which they are assessed by the taxing authority. Although the exact amount owed may not be known on the assessment date, a reasonable estimate should be made by the taxpayer (on that date) so that the expected amount of taxes and related liability may be accrued and recognized. The entry should be accounted for as a debit to the deferred property taxes account and a credit to a property taxes payable account, a current liability. After this entry is made (on the assessment date), a portion of the property taxes should be recognized in income by amortizing the deferred property taxes account over the fiscal period of the taxing authority.

When the exact amount of property taxes is determined, an adjustment to the estimated tax liability of the prior year is made. Frequently, this adjustment is made to the current year's property tax provision (either increasing it or reducing it) in the current income statement (the year in which the exact amount of the tax liability is determined) or as a separate item there.

Property taxes assessed on property that will be sold to customers or under construction for an entity's own use are generally capitalized as part of the cost of these items.

Reporting Requirements

Because real and personal taxes are considered bona fide expenses of doing business, they should be disclosed and reported as:

☐ Expenses allocated to other related expense accounts, such as manufacturing, overhead, and, general and administrative expenses,

☐ Operating expenses, or

☐ Deductions from income.

Real and property taxes should not be combined with income taxes.

EXAMPLE

On October 1, 20X3, Levita Company is assessed property taxes of $24,000 for the city's fiscal period from October 1, 20X3 through September 30, 20X3. Levita Company's accounting and financial reporting year ends December 31, 20X3.

Levita Company should record its property taxes on October 1, 20X3, the assessment day, and make the following entry:

October 1, 20X3:	Deferred property taxes	24,000	
	Property taxes payable		24,000

Each month a portion of the deferred property taxes should be amortized, providing recognition for the appropriate amount of property tax expense. The entry that should be made follows:

Property tax expense	2,000 (1/12 × $24,000)
Deferred property taxes	2,000

ANNUAL REPORT REFERENCES

Campbell Soup
2011 Annual Report

12. Taxes on Earnings

The provision for income taxes on earnings from continuing operations consists of the following:

	2011	2010	2009
Income taxes:			
Currently payable			
Federal	$215	$253	$145
State	27	46	12
Non-U.S.	78	45	46
	320	344	203
Deferred			
Federal	47	38	142
State	(2)	1	9
Non-U.S.	1	15	(7)
	46	54	144
	$366	$398	$347
Earnings from continuing operations before income taxes:			
United States	$944	$1,051	$976
Non-U.S.	224	191	103
	$1,168	$1,242	$1,079

The following is a reconciliation of the effective income tax rate on continuing operations with the U.S. federal statutory income tax rate:

	2011	2010	2009
Federal statutory income tax rate	35.0 %	35.0 %	35.0 %
State income taxes (net of federal tax benefit)	1.4	2.5	1.7
Tax effect of international items	(2.1)	(2.5)	(0.8)
Settlement of tax contingencies	(0.5)	(0.7)	(1.0)
Federal manufacturing deduction	(1.8)	(1.3)	(1.0)
Other	(0.7)	(1.0)	(1.7)
Effective income tax rate	31.3 %	32.0 %	32.2 %

During 2011, the company recorded a tax benefit of $8 following the finalization of tax audits.

In the third quarter of 2010, the company recorded deferred tax expense of $10 due to the enactment of U.S. health care legislation in March 2010. The law changed the tax treatment of subsidies to companies that provide prescription drug benefits to retirees. Accordingly, the company recorded the non-cash charge to reduce the value of the deferred tax asset associated with the subsidy.

In 2010, the company recorded a tax benefit of $9 following the finalization of tax audits. The company recorded an additional tax benefit of $2 during the year related to the resolution of other tax contingencies.

In 2009, the company recorded a tax benefit of $11 following the finalization of tax audits.

Deferred tax liabilities and assets are comprised of the following:

	2011	2010
Depreciation	$ 253	$ 221
Amortization	474	449
Other	14	13
Deferred tax liabilities	741	683
Benefits and compensation	307	319
Pension benefits	93	134
Tax loss carryforwards	84	67
Capital loss carryforwards	122	101
Other	83	76
Gross deferred tax assets	689	697
Deferred tax asset valuation allowance	(156)	(123)
Net deferred tax assets	533	574
Net deferred tax liability	$ 208	$ 109

At July 31, 2011, U.S. and non-U.S. subsidiaries of the company have tax loss carryforwards of approximately $395. Of these carryforwards, $163 expire between 2012 and 2028, and $232 may be carried forward indefinitely. The current statutory tax rates in these countries range from 20% to 35%. At July 31, 2011, deferred tax asset valuation allowances have been established to offset $132 of these tax loss carryforwards. Additionally, at July 31, 2011, non-U.S. subsidiaries of the company have capital loss carryforwards of approximately $406, which are fully offset by deferred tax asset valuation allowances.

The net change in the deferred tax asset valuation allowance in 2011 was an increase of $33. The increase was primarily due to the impact of currency and recognition of additional valuation allowances on foreign loss carryforwards. The net change in the valuation allowance in 2010 was an increase of $15. The increase was primarily due to the impact of currency and the recognition of additional valuation allowances on foreign loss carryforwards that are not expected to be utilized prior to the expiration date. The net change in the valuation allowance in 2009 was a decrease of $7, primarily due to currency.

As of July 31, 2011, U.S. income taxes have not been provided on approximately $420 of undistributed earnings of non-U.S. subsidiaries, which are deemed to be permanently reinvested. It is not practical to estimate the tax liability that might be incurred if such earnings were remitted to the U.S.

A reconciliation of the activity related to unrecognized tax benefits follows:

	2011	2010	2009
Balance at beginning of year	$ 36	$ 42	$ 54
Increases related to prior-year tax positions	6	14	–
Decreases related to prior-year tax positions	(4)	(11)	(11)
Increases related to current-year tax positions	9	4	4
Settlements	–	(11)	(2)
Lapse of statute	(4)	(2)	(3)
Balance at end of year	$ 43	$ 36	$ 42

As of July 31, 2011, August 1, 2010, and August 2, 2009, there were $17, $22, and $28, respectively, of unrecognized tax benefits that if recognized would affect the annual effective tax rate. The total amount of unrecognized tax benefits can change due to audit settlements, tax examination activities, statute expirations and the recognition and measurement criteria under accounting for uncertainty in income taxes. The company is unable to estimate what this change could be within the next twelve months, but does not believe it would be material to the financial statements.

The company's accounting policy with respect to interest and penalties attributable to income taxes is to reflect any expense or benefit as a component of its income tax provision. The total amount of interest and penalties recognized in the Consolidated Statements of Earnings was a benefit of $1 in 2011, an expense of $2 in 2010 and a benefit of $1 in 2009. The total amount of interest and penalties recognized in the Consolidated Balance Sheets as of July 31, 2011, and August 1, 2010, was $8 and $9, respectively.

None of the unrecognized tax benefit liabilities, including interest and penalties, are expected to be settled within the next twelve months. The $51 and $45 of unrecognized tax benefit liabilities, including interest and penalties, were reported as other non-current liabilities in the Consolidated Balance Sheets as of July 31, 2011, and August 1, 2010, respectively.

The company does business globally and, as a result, files income tax returns in the U.S. federal jurisdiction and various state and non-U.S. jurisdictions. In the normal course of business, the company is subject to examination by taxing authorities throughout the world, including such major jurisdictions as the United States, Australia, Canada, Belgium, France and Germany. The 2011 tax year is currently under audit by the IRS. In addition, several state income tax examinations are in progress for fiscal years 2001 to 2009.

With limited exceptions, the company has been audited for income tax purposes in Canada and France through fiscal year 2005, in Germany through fiscal year 2007, and in Belgium and Australia through fiscal year 2009.

Cisco Systems
2011 Annual Report

15. Income Taxes

(a) Provision for Income Taxes

The provision for income taxes consists of the following (in millions):

Years Ended	July 30, 2011	July 31, 2010	July 25, 2009
Federal:			
Current	914	1,469	1,615
Deferred	(168)	(435)	(397)
	746	1,034	1,218
State:			
Current	49	186	132
Deferred	83	–	(30)
	132	186	102
Foreign:			
Current	529	470	386
Deferred	(72)	(42)	(147)
	457	428	239
Total	$ 1,335	$ 1,648	$ 1,559

Income before provision for income taxes consists of the following (in millions):

Years Ended	July 30, 2011	July 31, 2010	July 25, 2009
United States	$ 1,214	$ 1,102	$ 1,650
International	6,611	8,313	6,043
Total	$ 7,825	$ 9,415	$ 7,963

The items accounting for the difference between income taxes computed at the federal statutory rate and the provision for income taxes consist of the following:

Years Ended	July 30, 2011	July 31, 2010	July 25, 2009
Federal statutory rate	35.0 %	35.0 %	35.0 %
Effect of:			
State taxes, net of federal tax benefit	1.5	1.4	1.3
Foreign income at other than U.S. rates	(19.4)	(19.3)	(18.9)
Tax credits	(3.0)	(0.5)	(2.4)
Transfer pricing adjustment related to share-based compensation	–	(1.7)	2.3
Nondeductible compensation	2.5	2.0	2.6
Other, net	0.5	0.6	0.4
Total	17.1 %	17.5 %	20.3 %

In the second quarter of fiscal 2011, the Tax Relief, Unemployment Insurance Reauthorization, and Job Creation Act of 2010 reinstated the U.S. federal R&D tax credit, retroactive to January 1, 2010. As a result, the tax provision in fiscal 2011 includes a tax benefit of $65 million related to the R&D tax credit for fiscal 2010.

During fiscal 2010, the U.S. Court of Appeals for the Ninth Circuit (the "Ninth Circuit") withdrew its prior holding and reaffirmed the 2005 U.S. Tax Court ruling in *Xilinx, Inc. v. Commissioner*. This final decision impacted the tax treatment of share-based compensation expenses for the purpose of determining intangible development costs under a company's research and development cost sharing arrangement. While the Company was not a named party to the case, this decision resulted in a change in the Company's tax benefits recognized in its financial statements. As a result of the decision, the Company recognized in fiscal 2011 a combined tax benefit of $724 million, of which $158 million was recorded as a reduction to the provision for income taxes and $566 million was recorded as an increase to additional paid-in capital. These tax benefits effectively reversed the related charges that the Company incurred during fiscal 2009. The tax provision in fiscal 2009 also included a net tax benefit of $106 million, related to the R&D tax credit for fiscal 2008, as a result of the Tax Extenders and Alternative Minimum Tax Relief Act of 2008 which reinstated the U.S. federal R&D tax credit retroactive to January 1, 2008.

U.S. income taxes and foreign withholding taxes associated with the repatriation of earnings of foreign subsidiaries were not provided for on a cumulative total of $36.7 billion of undistributed earnings for certain foreign subsidiaries as of the end of fiscal 2011. The Company intends to reinvest these earnings indefinitely in its foreign subsidiaries. If these earnings were distributed to the United States in the form of dividends or otherwise, or if the shares of the relevant foreign subsidiaries were sold or otherwise transferred, the Company would be subject to additional U.S. income taxes (subject to an adjustment for foreign tax credits) and foreign withholding taxes. Determination of the amount of unrecognized deferred income tax liability related to these earnings is not practicable.

As a result of certain employment and capital investment actions, the Company's income in certain foreign countries is subject to reduced tax rates and in some cases is wholly exempt from taxes. A portion of these tax incentives will expire at the end of fiscal 2015 and the majority of the remaining balance will expire at the end of fiscal 2025. As of the end of the respective fiscal years, the gross income tax benefits attributable to these tax incentives were estimated to be $1.3 billion ($0.24 per diluted share) in fiscal 2011, $1.7 billion ($0.30 per diluted share) in fiscal 2010, and $1.3 billion ($0.22 per diluted share) in fiscal 2009. These gross income tax benefits for the respective years were partially offset by accruals of U.S. income taxes on undistributed earnings.

(b) Unrecognized Tax Benefits

The aggregate changes in the balance of gross unrecognized tax benefits were as follows (in millions):

Years Ended	July 30, 2011	July 31, 2010	July 25, 2009
Beginning balance	$ 2,677	$ 2,816	$ 2,505
Additions based on tax positions related to the current year	374	246	190
Additions for tax positions of prior years	93	60	307
Reductions for tax positions of prior years	(60)	(250)	(17)
Settlements	(56)	(140)	(109)
Lapse of statute of limitations	(80)	(55)	(60)
Ending balance	$ 2,948	$ 2,677	$ 2,816

As of July 30, 2011, $2.6 billion of the unrecognized tax benefits would affect the effective tax rate if realized. During fiscal 2011, the Company recognized $38 million of net interest expense and $9 million of penalties. During fiscal 2010, the Company recognized $167 million of net interest income and $5 million of penalties. The Company's total accrual for interest and penalties was $214 million and $167 million as of the end of fiscal 2011 and 2010, respectively. The Company is no longer subject to U.S. federal income tax audit for returns covering tax years through fiscal 2001. With limited exceptions, the Company is no longer subject to state and local or foreign income tax audits for returns covering tax years through fiscal 1997.

During fiscal 2010, the Ninth Circuit withdrew its prior holding and reaffirmed the 2005 U.S. Tax Court ruling in Xilinx, Inc. v. Commissioner. As a result of this final decision in fiscal 2010, the Company decreased the amount of gross unrecognized tax benefits by approximately $220 million and decreased the amount of accrued interest by $218 million, which effectively reversed a similar amount that was recorded as an increase in the unrecognized tax benefits during fiscal 2009 as a result of the Ninth Circuit's initial decision.

The Company regularly engages in discussions and negotiations with tax authorities regarding tax matters in various jurisdictions. The Company believes it is reasonably possible that certain federal, foreign, and state tax matters may be concluded in the next 12 months. Specific positions that may be resolved include issues involving transfer pricing and various other matters. The Company estimates that the unrecognized tax benefits at July 30, 2011 could be reduced by approximately $350 million in the next 12 months.

(c) Deferred Tax Assets and Liabilities

The following table presents the breakdown between current and noncurrent net deferred tax assets (in millions):

	July 30, 2011	July 31, 2010
Deferred tax assets—current	$ 2,410	$ 2,126
Deferred tax liabilities—current	(131)	(87)
Deferred tax assets—noncurrent	1,864	2,079
Deferred tax liabilities—noncurrent	(264)	(276)
Total net deferred tax assets	$ 3,879	$ 3,842

The components of the deferred tax assets and liabilities are as follows (in millions):

	July 30, 2011	July 31, 2010
ASSETS		
Allowance for doubtful accounts and returns	$ 413	$ 248
Sales-type and direct-financing leases	178	224
Inventory write-downs and capitalization	160	176
Investment provisions	226	329
IPR&D, goodwill, and purchased intangible assets	106	191

	July 30, 2011	July 31, 2010
Deferred revenue	1,634	1,752
Credits and net operating loss carryforwards	713	752
Share-based compensation expense	1,084	970
Accrued compensation	507	339
Other	590	517
Gross deferred tax assets	5,611	5,498
Valuation allowance	(82)	(76)
Total deferred tax assets	5,529	5,422
LIABILITIES		
Purchased intangible assets	(997)	(1,224)
Depreciation	(298)	(120)
Unrealized gains on investments	(265)	(185)
Other	(90)	(51)
Total deferred tax liabilities	(1,650)	(1,580)
Total net deferred tax assets	$ 3,879	$ 3,842

As of July 30, 2011, the Company's federal, state, and foreign net operating loss carryforwards for income tax purposes were $334 million, $1.7 billion, and $298 million, respectively. If not utilized, the federal net operating loss carryforwards will begin to expire in fiscal 2019, the state net operating loss carryforwards will begin to expire in fiscal 2012, and the foreign net operating loss carryforwards will begin to expire in fiscal 2012. As of July 30, 2011, the Company's federal and state tax credit carryforwards for income tax purposes were approximately $5 million and $531 million, respectively. If not utilized, the federal and state tax credit carryforwards will begin to expire in fiscal 2013 and fiscal 2012, respectively.

Ariba
2011 Annual Report

Note 8—Income Taxes

The provision for income taxes for the years ended September 30, 2011, 2010 and 2009 was comprised of the following (in thousands):

	Current	Deferred	Total
2011:			
Federal	$ –	$ –	$ –
State	214	–	214
Foreign	1,357	(975)	382
Total	$1,571	$(975)	$596

	Current	Deferred	Total
2010:			
Federal	$ –	$ –	$ –
State	118	–	118
Foreign	1,620	(470)	1,150
Total	$1,738	$(470)	$1,268
2009:			
Federal	$ –	$ –	$ –
State	42	–	42
Foreign	1,076	(14)	1,062
Total	$1,118	$(14)	$1,104

The Company's (loss) income from continuing operations before income taxes for the years ended September 30, 2011, 2010 and 2009 consisted of the following components (in thousands):

	2011	2010	2009
Domestic	$(23,603)	$11,577	$ 566
Foreign	21,216	2,916	2,194
(Loss) income from continuing operations before income taxes	$ (2,387)	$14,493	$2,760

The reconciliation between the amount computed by applying the United States federal statutory tax rate of 35% to the income from continuing operations before income taxes and actual income tax expense for the years ended September 30, 2011, 2010 and 2009 is as follows (in thousands):

	2011	2010	2009
Computed tax benefit	$ (835)	$ 5,073	$ 966
State taxes, net of federal benefit	(818)	864	427
Nondeductible expenses and other permanent differences	8,236	5,102	805
Foreign taxes	(7,043)	105	274
Provision to return adjustments	5,039	3,712	4,337
Other	999	494	161
Change in valuation allowance	(4,982)	(14,082)	(5,866)
Provision for income taxes	$ 596	$ 1,268	$1,104

Included in tax expense from discontinued operations is a decrease in valuation allowance and corresponding utilization of net operating losses of $15.0 million, $1.0 million, and $2.0 million for the years ended September 30, 2011, 2010, and 2009, respectively.

The tax effects of temporary differences that give rise to significant portions of net deferred tax assets as of September 30, 2011 and 2010 are as follows (in thousands):

Included in tax expense from discontinued operations is a decrease in valuation allowance and corresponding utilization of net operating losses of $15.0 million, $1.0 million, and $2.0 million for the years ended September 30, 2011, 2010, and 2009, respectively.

The tax effects of temporary differences that give rise to significant portions of net deferred tax assets as of September 30, 2011 and 2010 are as follows (in thousands):

	2011	2010
Deferred Tax Assets		
Accruals and allowances	$ 68,750	$ 65,906
Capitalized research and experimentation costs	64,880	81,868
Depreciation and amortization	73,305	85,193
Credit carryforwards	64,850	64,871
Net operating loss and other carryforwards	588,123	584,934
Deferred tax assets	859,908	882,772
Valuation allowance	(855,509)	(875,553)
Deferred tax assets, net of valuation allowance	4,399	7,219
Deferred Tax Liabilities		
Unremitted earnings of foreign subsidiaries	–	(832)
Acquired intangibles	(1,571)	(5,189)
Net deferred tax assets	2,828	1,198
Recorded As:		
Current deferred tax asset	$ 31,879	$ 39,298
Valuation allowance	(30,130)	(38,852)
Net current deferred tax asset	1,749	446
Non-current deferred tax asset	828,031	843,475
Valuation allowance	(825,381)	(836,702)
Net non-current deferred tax asset	2,650	6,773
Current deferred tax liability	–	(832)
Non-current deferred tax liability	(1,571)	(5,189)
Net deferred tax assets	$ 2,828	$ 1,198

The Company has provided a valuation allowance due to the uncertainty of generating future profits that would allow for the realization of such deferred tax assets. The net decrease in the total valuation allowance for the year ended September 30, 2011 was $20.0 million. The net decrease in the total valuation allowance for the year ended September 30, 2010 was $15.1 million. Utilization of the Company's net operating loss and tax credit carryforwards may be subject to a substantial annual limitation due to the ownership change limitations imposed by Internal Revenue Code Sections 382 and 383 and similar state provisions. Such an annual limitation could result in the expiration of the Company's federal and state net operating loss and tax credit carryforwards before utilization.

As of September 30, 2011, the Company had net operating loss carryforwards for federal, state and foreign tax purposes of approximately $1.5 billion, $784.0 million and $2.0 million, respectively, before consideration of any annual limitation as described above. These federal, state and foreign net operating loss carryforwards expire in various years from fiscal year 2012 through fiscal year 2031, from fiscal year 2012 through fiscal year 2031 and from fiscal year 2012 through fiscal year 2014, respectively. As of September 30, 2011, the Company had research credit carryforwards for federal and state tax purposes of approximately $39.0 million and $25.0 million, respectively. If not utilized, the federal research credit carryforwards will expire in various years from fiscal year 2012 through fiscal year 2024. The state research credit carryforwards will continue indefinitely.

The Company also had manufacturer's credit carryforwards as of September 30, 2011 for state tax purposes of approximately $119,000, which will expire in fiscal year 2012. The Company's net operating loss and tax credit carryforwards include net operating loss and research credit carryforwards of approximately $270.0 million and $4.8 million, respectively, generated by FreeMarkets, which are subject to annual limitations which could reduce or defer the utilization of those losses and credits.

The undistributed earnings of the foreign subsidiaries are approximately $48.9 million as of September 30, 2011. The Company has decided to permanently reinvest those earnings and accordingly has not provided for any taxes thereon. Determination of the amount of unrecognized deferred U.S. income tax liability on these undistributed earnings is not practicable.

The aggregate changes in the balances of the Company's gross unrecognized tax benefits were as follows (in thousands):

	Year Ended September 30, 2011	Year Ended September 30, 2010
Gross unrecognized tax benefits as of October 1	$ 4,698	$ 4,718
Increases related to tax positions from prior fiscal years, including acquisitions	512	–
Decreases related to tax positions from prior fiscal years	–	–
Increases related to tax positions taken during the fiscal year	260	133
Lapses of statutes of limitations	(3,106)	(312)
Changes in unrecognized tax benefits due to foreign currency translation	(555)	159
Total gross unrecognized tax benefits as of September 30	$ 1,809	$ 4,698

The Company does not expect any significant changes to the unrecognized tax benefits in the next twelve months.

As of September 30, 2011, approximately $1.8 million of unrecognized benefits would affect the Company's effective tax rate if realized. The Company released interest and penalties related to lapses of statute of limitations of uncertain tax positions of $1.0 million during fiscal year 2011. Interest and penalties were insignificant in fiscal years 2010 and 2009. The gross amount of interest and penalties accrued as of September 30, 2011 and 2010 was $568,000 and $1.7 million, respectively. Interest and penalties are recorded in the provision for income taxes in the statement of operations.

The Company has numerous tax audits in progress globally which could affect its unrecognized tax benefits. At this time, the Company cannot reasonably predict the outcomes of those audits or the impacts on its unrecognized tax benefits. The Company believes that it has adequately provided for any reasonably foreseeable outcomes related to the Company's tax audits. However, there can be no assurances as to the possible outcomes. The Company's United States federal income tax return is open to examination for the fiscal year ended September 30, 2008 and forward. Globally, the Company's income tax returns are open to examination among various jurisdictions ranging from fiscal year ended September 30, 2005 and forward.

Qualcomm
2011 Annual Report

Note 6. Income Taxes

The components of the income tax provision were as follows (in millions):

	2011	2010	2009
Current provision:			
Federal	$179	$1,514	$268
State	57	242	71
Foreign	670	389	291
	906	2,145	630
Deferred provision:			
Federal	170	(1,139)	(72)
State	62	(26)	72
Foreign	(6)	(7)	(19)
	226	(1,172)	(19)
	$1,132	$973	$611

The foreign component of the income tax provision consists primarily of foreign withholding taxes on royalty income included in United States earnings.

The components of income from continuing operations before income taxes by United States and foreign jurisdictions were as follows (in millions):

	2011	2010	2009
United States	$2,984	$2,195	$1,368
Foreign	2,703	2,298	1,035
	$5,687	$4,493	$2,403

The following is a reconciliation of the expected statutory federal income tax provision to the Company's actual income tax provision for continuing operations (in millions):

	2011	2010	2009
Expected income tax provision at federal statutory tax rate	$1,991	$1,573	$841
State income tax provision, net of federal benefit	283	226	113
Foreign income taxed at other than U.S. rates	(1,074)	(897)	(407)
Tax audit impacts, net	1	3	(155)
Tax credits	(151)	(55)	(112)
Valuation allowance	42	(40)	227
Revaluation of deferred taxes	69	152	74
Other	(29)	11	30
	$1,132	$973	$611

The revaluation of deferred taxes represents the impact of paying current taxes at a higher state effective tax rate than the effective tax rate that will be in effect when the resulting deferred tax asset or liability is scheduled to reverse. The Company has not recorded a deferred tax liability of approximately $4.7 billion related to the United States federal and state income taxes and foreign withholding taxes on approximately $13.5 billion of undistributed earnings of certain non-United States subsidiaries indefinitely invested outside the United States. Should the Company decide to repatriate the foreign earnings, the Company would have to adjust the income tax provision in the period management determined that the earnings will no longer be indefinitely invested outside the United States.

The Company files income tax returns in the United States federal jurisdiction and various state and foreign jurisdictions. Tax audit impacts, net reflects adjustments to the Company's prior year estimates of uncertain tax positions as a result of various federal, state and foreign tax audits. The Company is currently a participant in the Internal Revenue Service (IRS) Compliance Assurance Process, whereby the IRS and the Company endeavor to agree on the treatment of all tax issues prior to the tax return being filed. The IRS completed its examination of the Company's tax return for fiscal 2008 and issued a full acceptance letter for fiscal 2009 during the third quarter of fiscal 2010, resulting in an increase to the tax provision of $20 million. The Company is no longer subject to United States federal income tax examinations for years prior to fiscal 2010. The Company is subject to examination by the California Franchise Tax Board for fiscal years after 2004 and is currently under examination for fiscal 2005 through 2008. The Company is also subject to income taxes in other taxing jurisdictions in the United States and around the world, many of which are open to tax examinations for periods after fiscal 2000.

The Company had deferred tax assets and deferred tax liabilities as follows (in millions):

	September 25, 2011	September 26, 2010
Accrued liabilities, reserves and other	$205	$287
Share-based compensation	592	615
Capitalized start-up and organizational costs	91	102
Unearned revenues	1,269	1,311
Unrealized losses on marketable securities	309	341
Unrealized losses on other investments	28	27
Capital loss carryover	40	37
Tax credits	145	54
Unused net operating losses	97	64
Other basis differences	30	10
Total gross deferred assets	2,806	2,848
Valuation allowance	(98)	(39)
Total net deferred assets	2,708	2,809
Purchased intangible assets	(174)	(108)
Deferred contract costs	(7)	(6)
Unrealized gains on marketable securities	(206)	(352)
Property, plant and equipment	(85)	(100)
Total deferred liabilities	(472)	(566)
Net deferred assets	$2,236	$2,243
Reported as:		
Current deferred tax assets	$537	$321
Non-current deferred tax assets	1,703	1,922
Current deferred tax liabilities[1]	(2)	–
Non-current deferred tax liabilities[1]	(2)	–
	$2,236	$2,243

(1) Current deferred tax liabilities and non-current deferred tax liabilities are included in other current liabilities and other liabilities, respectively, in the consolidated balance sheets.

At September 25, 2011, the Company had unused federal net operating loss carryforwards of $167 million expiring from 2021 through 2029, unused state net operating loss carryforwards of $352 million expiring from 2012 through 2031, and unused foreign net operating loss carryforwards of $76 million, which expire from 2012 through 2020. At September 25, 2011, the Company had unused tax credits of $20 million in foreign jurisdictions, which expire in 2013.

The Company does not expect its federal net operating loss carryforwards and its state income tax credits to expire unused.

The Company believes, more likely than not, that it will have sufficient taxable income after stock option related deductions to utilize the majority of its deferred tax assets. At September 25, 2011, the Company has provided a valuation allowance on certain foreign deferred tax assets, state net operating losses and net capital losses of $76 million, $10 million and $12 million, respectively. The valuation allowances reflect the uncertainties surrounding the Company's ability to generate sufficient future taxable income in certain foreign and state tax jurisdictions to utilize its net operating losses and the Company's ability to generate sufficient capital gains to utilize all capital losses.

A summary of the changes in the amount of unrecognized tax benefits for fiscal 2011, 2010 and 2009 follows (in millions):

	2011	2010	2009
Beginning balance of unrecognized tax benefits	$353	$84	$244
Additions based on prior year tax positions	64	223	39
Reductions for prior year tax positions	(10)	(58)	(202)
Additions for current year tax positions	12	165	3
Settlements with taxing authorities	(323)	(61)	–
Ending balance of unrecognized tax benefits	$96	$353	$84

At September 25, 2011, the Company does not expect any unrecognized tax benefits to result in cash payment in fiscal 2012. Unrecognized tax benefits at September 25, 2011 include $88 million for tax positions that, if recognized, would impact the effective tax rate. The unrecognized tax benefits differ from the amount that would affect the Company's effective tax rate primarily because the unrecognized tax benefits are included on a gross basis and do not reflect secondary impacts such as the federal deduction for state taxes, adjustments to deferred tax assets and the valuation allowance that might be required if the Company's tax positions are sustained. The decrease in unrecognized tax benefits in fiscal 2011 was primarily due to an agreement reached on a component of the Company's fiscal 2006 through fiscal 2010 state tax returns related to the method used by the Company to apportion income to states for such periods, which is partially offset by an increase resulting from the acquisition of Atheros (Note 12). The Company does not believe that it is reasonably possible that the total amounts of unrecognized tax benefits at September 25, 2011 will significantly increase or decrease in fiscal 2012. Interest expense related to uncertain tax positions was negligible in fiscal 2011, 2010 and 2009. The amount of accrued interest and penalties was negligible at September 25, 2011 and September 26, 2010.

Cash amounts paid for income taxes, net of refunds received, were $2.1 billion, $671 million and $516 million for fiscal 2011, 2010 and 2009 , respectively.

International Game Technology
2010 Annual Report

17. Income Taxes

Income Tax Provision

Distribution of income before tax

Years ended September 30, (In millions)	2010	2009	2008
U.S.	$ 224.9	$ 157.3	$ 484.9
Non - U.S.	88.1	62.0	92.7
Total income from continuing operations before tax	$ 313.0	$ 219.3	$ 577.6

Reconciliation of statutory federal rate to effective rate for continuing operations

Years ended September 30,	2010	2009	2008
Federal statutory tax	35.0%	35.0%	35.0%
State income tax, net	0.7%	1.4%	2.0%
Foreign subsidiaries tax, net	-0.4%	0.6%	-0.1%
Domestic production activities	-1.4%	-2.5%	-1.2%
Change in income tax contingencies	-10.4%	-3.5%	0.0%
Changes in valuation allowance	2.4%	0.9%	1.7%
Other, net	2.4%	-1.4%	4.7%
Effective rate	28.3%	30.5%	42.1%

Components of income tax provision

Years ended September 30, (In millions)	2010	2009	2008
Federal	$ 16.2	$ 51.5	$ 206.4
State	8.1	9.6	16.1
Foreign	22.4	23.2	33.7
Total current	46.7	84.3	256.2

Years ended September 30, (In millions)	2010	2009	2008
Federal	41.2	(10.3)	(8.9)
State	(4.3)	(4.7)	1.2
Foreign	5.1	(2.5)	(5.2)
Total deferred	42.0	(17.5)	(12.9)
Total income tax provision from continuing operations	$ 88.7	$ 66.8	$ 243.3

Income Taxes Receivable

Presented as a component of current other assets and deferred costs, income taxes receivable is comprised of prepaid US taxes on intercompany sales, as well as tax overpayments in various US and foreign jurisdictions. Income taxes receivable increased to $104.6 million at September 30, 2010 from $53.1 million at September 30, 2009, primarily due to a favorable US tax law change enacted near the end of fiscal 2010.

Deferred Income Taxes

Significant Components of Deferred Income Taxes

September 30, (In millions)	2010	2009
Deferred Tax Assets		
Reserves	$ 90.7	$ 70.5
Jackpot payment timing difference	128.8	142.3
Share-based compensation	27.6	22.9
Net operating loss carry forwards	33.5	32.5
State income taxes, net	18.8	14.9
Foreign	20.1	27.5
Property, plant and equipment	2.3	10.0
Goodwill and intangibles	31.3	34.7
Capital loss carryover	19.9	1.0
Other	14.6	29.5
Total deferred income tax assets	387.6	385.8
Valuation allowance	(62.6)	(37.1)
Total deferred income tax assets, net	325.0	348.7
Deferred Tax Liabilities		
Interest expense on convertible debt	(35.6)	(22.4)
Foreign	(2.6)	(3.8)
Intangibles	(51.4)	(61.7)
Other	(14.3)	(5.8)
Total deferred income tax liabilities	(103.9)	(93.7)
Net deferred income tax assets	$ 221.1	$ 255.0

Net operating loss carry forwards at September 30, 2010 of $13.9 million for the US and $77.3 million for foreign countries expire in tax years 2012 through

2020. Capital loss carryover at September 30, 2010 of $57.3 million expire in tax years 2012 through 2015.

Our valuation allowance is based on our assessment that it is more likely than not that certain deferred tax assets will not be realized in the foreseeable future. The valuation allowance increased by $25.5 million in fiscal 2010, primarily due to foreign operating losses and capital losses not expected to be fully realized, of which $7.5 million was reflected in continuing operations.

At September 30, 2010, we had not provided for US deferred income taxes or foreign withholding taxes on $179.7 million in unrecognized temporary differences related to the basis of our investments in foreign subsidiaries expected to be permanently reinvested in operations outside the US. Determination of the amount of any unrecognized deferred income tax liability on these undistributed earnings is not practicable.

Unrecognized Tax Benefits

Under the accounting guidance for uncertain tax positions, we are required to recognize uncertain tax positions taken or expected to be taken, when they are "more likely than not" to be sustained upon examination. This assessment further presumes that tax authorities evaluate the technical merits of transactions individually with full knowledge of all facts and circumstances surrounding the issue. The adoption of this guidance, as of the beginning of fiscal 2008, increased our unrecognized tax benefits and related interest and penalties $107.0 million, increased deferred tax assets $55.4 million, increased other non-current assets $17.1 million and decreased retained earnings $34.5 million.

Aggregate changes in the balance of unrecognized tax benefits

Years ended September 30, (In millions)	2010	2009	2008
Balance at beginning of year	$ 91.5	$ 106.2	$ 109.3
Increases related to prior year tax positions	23.6	4.4	8.9
Decreases related to prior year tax positions	(1.6)	(27.6)	(0.1)
Increases related to current year tax positions	11.6	13.8	5.0
Decreases related to current year tax positions	(5.8)	(1.9)	(16.9)
Reductions for settlements with taxing authorities	(35.5)	(3.4)	–
Balance at year end	$ 83.8	$ 91.5	$ 106.2

The amount of unrecognized tax benefits which would impact our effective tax rate totaled $65.6 million at September 30, 2010 and $70.2 million at September 30, 2009. During 2010, the IRS closed its examination of our tax returns for fiscal 2002 through 2005. In connection with the settlement of our fiscal 2002 through 2005 examinations, we paid the IRS approximately $12.4 million, including interest of $4.3 million. In general, we are no longer subject to any significant US federal, state, local or foreign income tax examination by tax authorities for years before fiscal 2004. Our unrecognized tax benefits decreased $7.7 million during fiscal 2010, primarily due to the IRS settlement, partially offset by current year additions. We do not believe our total unrecognized tax benefits will change significantly during the next twelve months.

Interest and penalties related to unrecognized tax benefits are included in our income tax provision. During fiscal 2010, we recognized a $15.1 million benefit primarily for the reversal of interest and penalties related to settlements with tax authorities, partially offset by current year additions. In fiscal 2009, we recognized $2.9 million benefit for the reversal of interest and penalties related to settlements with tax authorities and an accounting method change. Accrued interest and penalties related to uncertain tax positions totaled $22.7 million at September 30, 2010 and $46.5 million at September 30, 2009.

Jacobs Engineering Group
2010 Annual Report

9. Income Taxes

The following table presents the components of our consolidated income tax expense for each of the last three fiscal years (in thousands):

	2010	2009	2008
Current income tax expense:			
Federal	$ 123,154	$ 146,865	$ 145,483
State	23,477	30,137	17,255
Foreign	22,909	42,597	71,625
Total current tax expense	169,540	219,599	234,363
Deferred income tax expense (benefit):			
Federal	(19,518)	(733)	(8,005)
State	(675)	397	1,695
Foreign	(3,700)	5,656	8,616
Total deferred tax expense (benefit)	(23,893)	5,320	2,306
Consolidated income tax expense	$ 145,647	$ 224,919	$ 236,669

Deferred taxes reflect the tax effects of the differences between the amounts recorded as assets and liabilities for financial reporting purposes and the comparable amounts recorded for income tax purposes. Deferred tax assets and liabilities are measured using the enacted tax rates and laws that will be in effect when the differences are expected to reverse. The following table presents the components of our net deferred tax assets at October 1, 2010 and October 2, 2009 (in thousands):

	2010	2009
Deferred tax assets:		
Obligations relating to:		
Defined benefit pension plans	$ 108,826	$ 83,734
Other employee benefit plans	137,810	129,279
Self-insurance programs	19,481	26,213

	2010	2009
Contract revenues and costs	13,602	15,102
Foreign tax credits carryforward	14,305	–
Office closings / consolidations	–	1,076
Other	10,719	17,631
Gross deferred tax assets	304,743	273,035
Deferred tax liabilities:		
Depreciation and amortization	(81,693)	(91,501)
Residual U.S. tax on unremitted, non-U.S. earnings	–	(222)
Other, net	(792)	(1,954)
Gross deferred tax liabilities	(82,485)	(93,677)
Net deferred tax assets	$ 222,258	$ 179,358

The following table presents the income tax benefits realized from the exercise of nonqualified stock options, and disqualifying dispositions of stock sold under our employee stock purchase plans during each of the last three fiscal years (in millions):

	2010	2009	2008
Income tax benefits realized under stock plans	$ 4.0	$ 4.7	$ 51.1

The reconciliation of total income tax expense using the statutory U.S. federal income tax rate to the consolidated income tax expense shown in the accompanying Consolidated Statements of Earnings for each of the last three fiscal years follows (dollars in thousands):

	2010	2009	2008
Statutory amount (computed using 35%)	$ 137,177	$ 218,446	$ 230,289
State taxes, net of the federal benefit	14,821	19,848	12,317
Utilization of foreign tax credit carryover	–	(5,856)	(6,703)
Tax differential on foreign earnings	(7,178)	(9,838)	(5,565)
Other, net	827	2,319	6,331
Consolidated income tax expense	$ 145,647	$ 224,919	$ 236,669
Rates used to compute statutory amount	35.0 %	35.0 %	35.0 %
Consolidated effective income tax rate	37.2 %	36.0 %	36.0 %

The following table presents income tax payments made during each of the last three fiscal years (in millions):

	2010	2009	2008
Income tax payments	$ 170.8	$ 255.5	$ 177.7

The following table presents the components of our consolidated earnings before taxes for each of the last three fiscal years (in thousands):

	2010	2009	2008
United States earnings	$ 295,144	$ 449,065	$ 394,191
Foreign earnings	96,790	175,067	263,777
	$ 391,934	$ 624,132	$ 657,968

United States income taxes, net of applicable credits, have been provided on the undistributed earnings of the Company's foreign subsidiaries, except in those instances where the earnings are expected to be permanently reinvested. At October 1, 2010, approximately $26.1 million of such undistributed earnings of certain foreign subsidiaries was expected to be permanently reinvested. Should these earnings be repatriated, approximately $7.5 million of income taxes would be payable.

Sonic Foundry
2010 Annual Report

6. Income Taxes

The provision for income taxes consists of the following (in thousands):

	Years Ended September 30,	
	2010	2009
Federal income tax	$ 240	$ 142
Federal income tax refundable research credit	(15)	–
Deferred income tax expense (benefit)	1,373	(1,033)
Change in valuation allowance	(1,373)	1,033
Provision for income taxes	$ 225	$ 142

The reconciliation of income tax expense (benefit) computed at the U.S. federal statutory rate to income tax expense (benefit) is as follows (in thousands):

	Years Ended September 30,	
	2010	2009
Income tax expense (benefit) at U.S. statutory rate of 34%	$ 35	$ (851)
Federal income tax refundable research credit	(15)	–
State income tax expense (benefit)	5	(130)
Permanent differences, net	13	14
Adjustment of temporary differences to income tax returns	1,560	76
Change in valuation allowance	(1,373)	1,033
Income tax expense	$ 225	$ 142

The significant components of the deferred tax accounts recognized for financial reporting purposes are as follows (in thousands):

	September 30,	
	2010	2009
Deferred tax assets:		
Net operating loss and other carryforwards	$ 34,663	$ 34,566
Common stock warrants	398	1,997

	September 30,	
	2010	2009
Allowance for doubtful accounts	41	41
Other	117	74
Total deferred tax assets	35,219	36,678
Valuation allowance	(35,219)	(36,678)
Goodwill amortization	(1,490)	(1,250)
Deferred tax liability for goodwill amortization	$ (1,490)	$ (1,250)

At September 30, 2010, the Company had net operating loss carryforwards of approximately $88 million for both U.S. Federal and state tax purposes. For Federal tax purposes, the carryforwards expire in varying amounts between 2018 and 2030. For State tax purposes, the carryforwards expire in varying amounts between 2013 and 2025. Utilization of the Company's net operating loss may be subject to substantial annual limitation due to the ownership change limitations provided by the Internal Revenue Code and similar state provisions. Such an annual limitation could result in the expiration of the net operating loss carryforwards before utilization. In addition, the Company has research and development tax credit carryforwards of approximately $530 thousand, which expire in varying amounts between 2017 and 2020. The Company's net deferred tax asset has been offset by a valuation allowance of the same amount. The valuation allowance has been recorded due to the uncertainty of realization of the deferred tax asset.

Beginning with an acquisition in fiscal year 2002, the Company has amortized Goodwill for tax purposes over a 15 year life. Goodwill is not amortized for book purposes. Annual impairment tests are performed for book purposes and the balance of goodwill is to be written down if impairment occurs. The impairment tests have not indicated any goodwill impairment.

In accordance with accounting guidance for uncertainty in income taxes, the Company has concluded that a reserve for income tax contingencies is not necessary. The Company's practice is to recognize interest and/or penalties related to income tax matters in income tax expense. The Company had no accruals for interest and penalties on the Company's Consolidated balance sheets at September 30, 2010 and 2009, and has not recognized any interest or penalties in the Consolidated statement of operations for the years ended September 30, 2010 or 2009.

The Company is subject to taxation in the U.S. and various state jurisdictions. All of the Company's tax years are subject to examination by the U.S. and state tax authorities due to the carryforward of unutilized net operating losses.

Texas Instruments
2010 Annual Report

5. Income Taxes.

Income before income taxes	U.S.	Non-U.S.	Total
2010	**$ 3,769**	**$ 782**	**$ 4,551**
2009	1,375	642	2,017
2008	1,749	732	2,481

Provision (benefit) for income taxes	U.S. Federal	Non-U.S.	U.S. State	Total
2010:				
Current	**$ 1,347**	**$ 146**	**$ 18**	**$ 1,511**
Deferred	**(128)**	**(62)**	**2**	**(188)**
Total	**$ 1,219**	**$ 84**	**$ 20**	**$ 1,323**
2009:				
Current	$ 334	$ 63	$ 4	$ 401
Deferred	117	30	(1)	146
Total	$ 451	$ 93	$ 3	$ 547
2008:				
Current	$ 646	$ 89	$ 8	$ 743
Deferred	(214)	43	(11)	(182)
Total	$ 432	$ 132	$ (3)	$ 561

Principal reconciling items from income tax computed at the statutory federal rate follow:

	2010	2009	2008
Computed tax at statutory rate	**$ 1,593**	$ 706	$ 868
Effect of non-U.S. rates	**(182)**	(101)	(197)
Research and development tax credits	**(54)**	(28)	(75)
U.S. tax benefits for manufacturing	**(63)**	(21)	(18)
Other	**29**	(9)	(17)
Total provision for income taxes	**$ 1,323**	$ 547	$ 561

The primary components of deferred income tax assets and liabilities were as follows:

	December 31,	
	2010	2009
Deferred income tax assets:		
Inventories and related reserves	**$ 525**	$ 347
Postretirement benefit costs recognized in AOCI	**404**	380
Stock-based compensation	**357**	339
Accrued expenses	**251**	219
Deferred loss and tax credit carryforwards	**220**	201
Intangibles	**62**	71

	December 31,	
	2010	2009
Investments	**43**	49
Other	**103**	98
	1,965	1,704
Less valuation allowance	**(3)**	(2)
	1,962	1,702
Deferred income tax liabilities:		
Accrued retirement costs (defined benefit and retiree health care)	**(190)**	(176)
Property, plant and equipment	**(83)**	(53)
Other	**(78)**	(68)
	(351)	(297)
Net deferred income tax asset	**$ 1,611**	$ 1,405

As of December 31, 2010 and 2009, net deferred income tax assets of $1.61 billion and $1.41 billion were presented in the balance sheets, based on tax jurisdiction, as deferred income tax assets of $1.70 billion and $1.47 billion and deferred income tax liabilities of $86 million and $67 million. The increase in net deferred income tax assets from December 31, 2009, to December 31, 2010, exceeds the $188 million deferred tax provision due to the recording of deferred tax assets associated with postretirement benefit costs recognized in Accumulated other comprehensive income (AOCI). We make an ongoing assessment regarding the realization of U.S. and non-U.S. deferred tax assets. While these assets are not assured of realization, our assessment is that a valuation allowance is not required for the remaining balance of the deferred tax assets. This assessment is based on our evaluation of relevant criteria including the existence of (a) deferred tax liabilities that can be used to absorb deferred tax assets, (b) taxable income in prior carryback years and (c) expectations for future taxable income.

We have U.S. and non-U.S. tax loss carryforwards of approximately $257 million, of which $134 million expire through the year 2024.

Provision has been made for deferred taxes on undistributed earnings of non-U.S. subsidiaries to the extent that dividend payments from these subsidiaries are expected to result in additional tax liability. The remaining undistributed earnings (approximately $3.44 billion at December 31, 2010) have been indefinitely reinvested; therefore, no provision has been made for taxes due upon remittance of these earnings. It is not practicable to determine the amount of unrecognized deferred tax liability on these unremitted earnings.

Cash payments made for income taxes (net of refunds) were $1.47 billion, $331 million and $772 million for the years ended December 31, 2010, 2009 and 2008.

Uncertain tax positions: We operate in a number of tax jurisdictions and are subject to examination of our income tax returns by tax authorities in those jurisdictions who may challenge any item on these tax returns. Because the matters challenged by authorities are typically complex, their ultimate outcome is uncertain. We recognize accrued interest related to uncertain tax positions and penalties as components of OI&E. Before any benefit can be recorded in the financial statements, we must determine that it is "more likely than not" that a tax position will be sustained by the appropriate tax authorities.

The following table summarizes the changes in the total amounts of uncertain tax positions for 2010 and 2009:

	2010	2009
Balance, January 1	$ 56	$ 148
Additions based on tax positions related to the current year	12	10
Additions for tax positions of prior years	50	6
Reductions for tax positions of prior years	(12)	(18)
Settlements with tax authorities	(3)	(90)
Balance, December 31	$ 103	$ 56
Interest expense recognized in the year ended December 31	$ 2	$ –
Accrued interest receivable as of December 31	$ 5	$ 9

The liability for uncertain tax positions is a component of Deferred credits and other liabilities, and accrued interest receivable is a component of Other assets on our balance sheets.

Within the $103 million liability for uncertain tax positions as of December 31, 2010, are uncertain tax positions totaling $136 million that, if recognized, would impact the effective tax rate. If these tax liabilities are ultimately realized, $101 million of deferred tax assets would also be realized, primarily related to refunds from counterparty jurisdictions resulting from procedures for relief from double taxation.

As of December 31, 2010, the statute of limitations remains open for U.S. federal tax returns for 1999 and following years. Our returns for the years 2000 through 2006 are the subject of tax treaty procedures for relief from double taxation.

In foreign jurisdictions, the years open to audit represent the years still subject to the statute of limitations. Years still open to audit by foreign tax authorities in major jurisdictions include Germany (2005 onward), France (2008 onward), Japan (2003 onward) and Taiwan (2005 onward).

We are unable to estimate the range of any reasonably possible increase or decrease in uncertain tax positions that may occur within the next 12 months resulting from the eventual outcome of the years currently under audit or appeal. However, we do not anticipate any such outcome will result in a material change to our financial condition or results of operations.

J & J Snack Foods
2009 Annual Report

Note I—Income Taxes

Income tax expense (benefit) is as follows:

	Fiscal year ended		
(in thousands)	September 26, 2009	September 27, 2008	September 29, 2007
Current			
U.S. Federal	$18,574	$11,417	$15,485
Foreign	706	844	423
State	3,744	2,270	2,581
	23,024	14,531	18,489
Deferred			
U.S. Federal	3,106	2,983	474
Foreign	109	(168)	–
State	658	631	83
	3,873	3,446	557
	$26,897	$17,977	$19,046

The provisions for income taxes differ from the amounts computed by applying the statutory federal income tax rate of approximately 35% to earnings before income taxes for the following reasons:

	Fiscal year ended		
(in thousands)	September 26, 2009	September 27, 2008	September 29, 2007
Income taxes at statutory rates	$23,873	$16,059	$17,905
Increase (decrease) in taxes resulting from:			
State income taxes, net of federal income tax benefit	2,958	1,918	1,819
Other, net	66	–	(678)
	$26,897	$17,977	$19,046

Deferred tax assets and liabilities consist of the following:

	September 26, 2009	September 27, 2008
Deferred tax assets		
Vacation accrual	$ 1,233	$ 1,117
Insurance accrual	2,943	2,634
Deferred income	67	105
Allowances	1,902	1,865
Inventory capitalization	499	519
Share-based compensation	1,113	896
Other, net	65	104

(in thousands)	September 26, 2009	September 27, 2008
	7,822	7,240
Deferred tax liabilities		
Amortization of goodwill and other intangible assets	13,388	11,899
Depreciation of property and equipment	17,793	14,818
Other, net	15	24
	31,196	26,741
	$23,374	$19,501

Sherwin-Williams
2009 Annual Report

Note 15—Income Taxes

Deferred income taxes reflect the net tax effects of temporary differences between the carrying amounts of assets and liabilities for financial reporting purposes and the amounts used for income tax purposes using the enacted tax rates and laws that are currently in effect. Significant components of the Company's deferred tax assets and liabilities as of December 31, 2009, 2008 and 2007 were as follows:

	2009	2008	2007
Deferred tax assets:			
Exit costs, environmental and other similar items	$ 82,378	$ 76,237	$ 77,725
Deferred employee benefit items	65,550	61,340	
Other items (each less than 5 percent of total assets)	111,094	106,341	122,938
Total deferred tax assets	$259,022	$243,918	$200,663
Deferred tax liabilities:			
Depreciation and amortization	$161,916	$144,715	$111,311
Deferred employee benefit items			16,227
Total deferred tax liabilities	$161,916	$144,715	$127,538

Netted against the Company's other deferred tax assets were valuation reserves of $15,735, $6,611 and $3,728 at December 31, 2009, 2008 and 2007, respectively, resulting from the uncertainty as to the realization of the tax benefits from certain foreign net operating losses and certain other foreign assets.

Significant components of the provisions for income taxes were as follows:

	2009	2008	2007
Current:			
Federal	$151,492	$144,789	$208,508
Foreign	25,964	34,367	28,388
State and local	18,118	28,078	27,485
Total current	195,574	207,234	264,381
Deferred:			
Federal	(4,887)	25,668	24,770
Foreign	(1,592)	(666)	3,602
State and local	(2,126)	5,363	4,612
Total deferred	(8,605)	30,365	32,984
Total provisions for income taxes	$186,969	$237,599	$297,365

The provisions for income taxes included estimated taxes payable on that portion of retained earnings of foreign subsidiaries expected to be received by the Company. The effect of the repatriation provisions of the American Jobs Creation Act of 2004 and the provisions of the Income Taxes Topic of the ASC was $1,899 in 2009, $(1,337) in 2008 and $1,925 in 2007. A provision was not made with respect to $14,971 of retained earnings at December 31, 2009 that have been invested by foreign subsidiaries. It was not practicable to estimate the amount of unrecognized deferred tax liability for undistributed foreign earnings.

Significant components of income before income taxes as used for income tax purposes, were as follows:

	2009	2008	2007
Domestic	$591,558	$602,934	$802,211
Foreign	31,259	111,541	110,732
	$622,817	$714,475	$912,943

A reconciliation of the statutory federal income tax rate to the effective tax rate follows:

	2009	2008	2007
Statutory federal income tax rate	35.0%	35.0%	35.0%
Effects of:			
State and local income taxes	1.7	3.0	2.3
Investment vehicles	(3.6)	(1.9)	(1.1)
ESOP dividends	(2.0)	(1.8)	(1.6)
Other—net	(1.1)	(1.0)	(2.0)
Effective tax rate	30.0%	33.3%	32.6%

The 2009 state and local income tax component of the effective tax rate decreased compared to 2008 primarily due to the impact of favorable audit settlements, favorable tax deductions available to the Company and the benefits of state tax credits. The increase in the tax deduction related to investment vehicles was the result of an increase in the impact of investments in tax favorable vehicles in 2009 compared to 2008.

The Company and its subsidiaries file income tax returns in the U.S. federal jurisdiction, and various state and foreign jurisdictions. The Internal Revenue Service (IRS) commenced an examination of the Company's U.S. income tax returns for the 2006 and 2007 tax years in the fourth quarter of 2008. Fieldwork is anticipated to be completed prior to December 31, 2010. At this time, the Company has determined that $3,135 of additional tax is due. The only open issue for the period 2004 to 2005 relates to the Company's ESOP. As of December 31, 2009, the Company is subject to non-U.S. income tax examinations for the tax years of 2002 through 2009. In addition, the Company is subject to state and local income tax examinations for the tax years 1992 through 2009.

Effective January 1, 2007, the Company adopted FIN No. 48, "Accounting for Uncertainty in Income Taxes," which is now codified in the Income Taxes Topic of the ASC. As a result, the Company recognized a cumulative-effect adjustment of $3.4 million, increasing its liability for unrecognized tax benefits, interest and penalties and reducing the January 1, 2007 balance of Retained Earnings. A reconciliation of the beginning and ending amount of unrecognized tax benefits in 2009, 2008 and 2007 is as follows:

	2009	*2008*	*2007*
Balance at beginning of year	**$38,051**	$39,378	$37,807
Additions based on tax positions related to the current year	**3,357**	3,709	5,570
Additions for tax positions of prior years	**9,170**	4,212	4,070
Reductions for tax positions of prior years	**(4,111)**	(3,863)	(4,998)
Settlements	**(7,937)**	(3,212)	(1,915)
Lapses of Statutes of Limitations	**(1,567)**	(2,173)	(1,156)
Balance at end of year	**$36,963**	$38,051	$39,378

Included in the balance of unrecognized tax benefits at December 31, 2009, 2008 and 2007 is $32,543, $32,420 and $34,235 in unrecognized tax benefits, the recognition of which would have an affect on the effective tax rate. This amount differs from the gross unrecognized tax benefits presented in the table due to the decrease in U.S. federal income taxes which would occur upon recognition of the state tax benefits included therein.

Included in the balance of unrecognized tax benefits at December 31, 2009 is $9,586 related to tax positions for which it is reasonably possible that the total amounts could significantly change during the next twelve months. This amount represents a decrease in unrecognized tax benefits comprised primarily of items related to a payment related to a federal audit of a partnership investment, assessed state income tax audits, the receipt of outstanding partnership investment filings and state settlement negotiations currently in progress and expiring statutes in foreign jurisdictions.

The Company classifies all income tax related interest and penalties as income tax expense. During the tax year ended December 31, 2009 and 2008 the Company recognized a release of $3,157 and $215, respectively, in income tax interest and penalties. During the tax year ended December 31, 2007, the Company recognized a net increase of $1,095 in income tax interest and penalties. As of December 31, 2009, 2008 and 2007, the Company has accrued $11,783, $15,563 and $15,812, respectively, for the potential payment of interest and penalties.

NCR
2008 Annual Report

Note 7. Income Taxes

For the years ended December 31, income from continuing operations before income taxes consisted of the following:

In millions	2008	2007	2006
Income before income taxes			
United States	$ 80	$141	$ 87
Foreign	209	91	72
Total income from continuing operations before income taxes	$289	$232	$159

For the years ended December 31, income tax (benefit) expense consisted of the following:

In millions	2008	2007	2006
Income tax (benefit) expense			
Current			
Federal	$(15)	$ 8	$ (46)
State and local	(1)	2	6
Foreign	74	58	40
Deferred			
Federal	25	$ 75	$ 62
State and local	1	(4)	(6)
Foreign	(26)	(78)	(48)
Total income tax expense	$ 58	$ 61	$ 8

The following table presents the principal components of the difference between the effective tax rate and the U.S. federal statutory income tax rate for the years ended December 31:

In millions	2008	2007	2006
Income tax expense at the U.S. federal tax rate of 35%	$101	$ 81	$ 56
Foreign income tax differential	(42)	(68)	(58)
U.S. permanent book to tax differences	1	(2)	1
Tax audit settlements	(19)	–	6
Change in liability for unrecognized tax benefits	18	35	–
Prior period corrections—Note 1	–	10	–
Other, net	(1)	5	3
Total income tax expense	$ 59	$ 61	$ 8

NCR's tax provisions include a provision for income taxes in certain tax jurisdictions where its subsidiaries are profitable, but reflect only a portion of the tax benefits related to certain foreign subsidiaries' tax losses due to the uncertainty of the ultimate realization of future benefits from these losses. During 2008, we favorably settled examinations with the Internal Revenue Service (IRS) for the tax years of 2000 through 2006 that resulted in a $19 million tax benefit. In addition, income tax expense was benefited in 2008 by $26 million from the repatriation of earnings from international subsidiaries at an effective tax rate lower than previously estimated.

Deferred income tax assets and liabilities included in the Consolidated Balance Sheets as of December 31 were as follows:

In millions	2008	2007
Deferred income tax assets		
Employee pensions and other benefits	$ 604	$ –
Other balance sheet reserves and allowances	72	140
Tax loss and credit carryforwards	406	399
Capitalized research and development	50	71
Property, plant and equipment	21	79
Other	44	59
Total deferred income tax assets	1,197	748
Valuation allowance	(478)	(441)
Net deferred income tax assets	719	307
Deferred income tax liabilities		
Property, plant and equipment	10	13
Employee pensions and other benefits	–	20
Other	5	49

In millions	2008	2007
Total deferred income tax liabilities	15	82
Total net deferred income tax assets	$ 704	$ 225

Our total, net deferred income tax assets increased $479 million to $704 million as of December 31, 2008. This increase in net deferred income tax assets is primarily related to the tax effect of the adjustment to other comprehensive income as a result of the significant declines in the fair values of our pension plan assets due to market conditions.

NCR recorded valuation allowances related to certain deferred income tax assets due to the uncertainty of the ultimate realization of the future benefits from those assets. The valuation allowances cover deferred tax assets, primarily tax loss carryforwards, in tax jurisdictions where there is uncertainty as to the ultimate realization of a benefit from those tax losses. As of December 31, 2008, NCR had U.S. federal and foreign tax loss carryforwards of approximately $1,049 million. The tax loss carryforwards, subject to expiration, expire in the years 2009 through 2027.

As described in Note 1, "Description of Business and Significant Accounting Policies", the Company adopted FIN 48 as of January 1, 2007. Under FIN 48, the Company may recognize the tax benefit from an uncertain tax position only if it is more likely than not that the tax position will be sustained on examination by the taxing authorities, based on the technical merits of the position. The tax benefits recognized in the financial statements from such a position are measured based on the largest benefit that has a greater than fifty percent likelihood of being realized upon settlement.

The aggregate changes in the balance of our gross unrecognized tax benefits were as follows for the years ended December 31:

In millions	2008	2007
Gross unrecognized tax benefits—January 1	$ 319	$ 296
Increase related to tax positions from prior years	76	31
Decreases related to tax positions from prior years	(54)	(17)
Increases related to tax positions taken during current year	56	42
Settlements with tax authorities	(106)	(25)
Lapses of statutes of limitation	(4)	(8)
Total gross unrecognized tax benefits—December 31	$ 287	$ 319

In 2008, the $106 million decrease in gross unrecognized tax benefits due to settlements with tax authorities is primarily related to the settlement with the IRS for the tax years of 2000 through 2006. The total amount of gross unrecognized tax benefits as of December 31, 2008 was $287 million, of which, up to $79 million would affect NCR's effective tax rate if realized.

We recognized interest and penalties associated with uncertain tax positions as part of the provision for income taxes in our Consolidated Statements of Operations of $4 million and $19 million for the years ended December 31, 2008 and 2007, respectively. The gross amount of interest and penalties accrued as of December 31, 2008 and 2007 was $57 million and $53 million, respectively.

In the U.S., NCR files consolidated federal and state income tax returns where statutes of limitations generally range from three to five years. Although the Company resolved examinations for the tax years of 2000 through 2006 with the IRS in 2008, U.S. federal tax years are open from 2003 forward. NCR and its subsidiaries also file income tax returns in international jurisdictions where statutes of limitations generally range from three to five years. Years beginning after 1995 are still open to examination by certain foreign taxing authorities, including several major taxing jurisdictions. In Canada, we are open to examination from 1997 onward. In Japan, we are open to examination from 2001 onward. At this time, the Company does not expect any significant changes in unrecognized tax benefits in the next year.

NCR did not provide for U.S. federal income taxes or foreign withholding taxes in 2008 on approximately $797 million of undistributed earnings of its foreign subsidiaries as such earnings are intended to be reinvested indefinitely. Quantification of the deferred tax liability, if any, associated with these undistributed earnings is not practicable.

See the Consolidated Statements of Changes in Stockholders' Equity for details of the tax effects on the components of other comprehensive income and Note 9, "Employee Benefit Plans".

Sherwin-Williams
2008 Annual Report

Note 14. Income Taxes

Deferred income taxes reflect the net tax effects of temporary differences between the carrying amounts of assets and liabilities for financial reporting purposes and the amounts used for income tax purposes using the enacted tax rates and laws that are currently in effect. Significant components of the Company's deferred tax assets and liabilities as of December 31, 2008, 2007 and 2006 were as follows:

	2008	2007	2006
Deferred tax assets:			
Exit costs, environmental and other similar items	$ 76,237	$ 77,725	$ 56,914
Deferred employee benefit items	61,340		
Other items (each less than 5 percent of total assets)	106,341	122,938	161,447
Total deferred tax assets	$243,918	$200,663	$218,361
Deferred tax liabilities:			
Depreciation and amortization	$144,715	$111,311	$ 98,445

	2008	2007	2006
Deferred employee benefit items		16,227	171
Total deferred tax liabilities	$144,715	$127,538	$ 98,616

Netted against the Company's other deferred tax assets were valuation reserves of $6,611, $3,728 and $739 at December 31, 2008, 2007 and 2006, respectively, resulting from the uncertainty as to the realization of the tax benefits from certain foreign net operating losses and certain other foreign assets.

Significant components of the provisions for income taxes were as follows:

	2008	2007	2006
Current:			
Federal	$142,985	$213,767	$208,835
Foreign	34,367	28,388	22,684
State and local	28,078	27,485	38,087
Total current	205,430	269,640	269,606
Deferred:			
Federal	27,472	19,511	(8,129)
Foreign	(666)	3,602	(2,705)
State and local	5,363	4,612	(518)
Total deferred	32,169	27,725	(11,352)
Total provisions for income taxes	$237,599	$297,365	$258,254

The provisions for income taxes included estimated taxes payable on that portion of retained earnings of foreign subsidiaries expected to be received by the Company. The effect of the repatriation provisions of the American Jobs Creation Act of 2004 and the provisions of APBO No. 23, "Accounting for Income Taxes—Special Areas," was $(1,337) in 2008, $1,925 in 2007 and $1,834 in 2006. A provision was not made with respect to $14,845 of retained earnings at December 31, 2008 that have been invested by foreign subsidiaries. It was not practicable to estimate the amount of unrecognized deferred tax liability for undistributed foreign earnings.

Significant components of income before income taxes as used for income tax purposes, were as follows:

	2008	2007	2006
Domestic	$602,934	$802,211	$736,875
Foreign	111,541	110,732	97,437
	$714,475	$912,943	834,312

A reconciliation of the statutory federal income tax rate to the effective tax rate follows:

	2008	2007	2006
Statutory federal income tax rate			
Effect of:	35.0%	35.0%	35.0%
State and local income taxes	3.0	2.3	2.9
Investment vehicles	(1.9)	(1.1)	(2.8)
ESOP dividends	(1.8)	(1.6)	(2.6)
Other—net	(1.0)	(2.0)	(1.5)
Effective tax rate	33.3%	32.6%	31.0%

The 2008 state and local income tax component of the effective tax rate increased compared to 2007 primarily due to the impact of prior audit settlements and the effects of current state law changes. The increase in the tax deduction related to investment vehicles was the result of an increase in the impact of investments in tax favorable vehicles in 2008 compared to 2007.

The Company and its subsidiaries file income tax returns in the U.S. federal jurisdiction, and various state and foreign jurisdictions. The Internal Revenue Service (IRS) commenced an examination of the Company's U.S. income tax returns for the 2006 and 2007 tax years in the fourth quarter of 2008. Fieldwork is anticipated to be completed prior to December 31, 2009. At this time, the Company cannot determine if an additional payment may be due. The IRS substantially completed the audit of the 2004 and 2005 tax years. The Company has paid $1,298 to date related to the audit. The 2004 and 2005 audit remains open as it relates to the Company's ESOP. As of December 31, 2008, the Company is subject to non-U.S. income tax examinations for the tax years of 2001 through 2008. In addition, the Company is subject to state and local income tax examinations for the tax years 1992 through 2008.

Effective January 1, 2007, the Company adopted FIN No. 48, "Accounting for Uncertainty in Income Taxes." In accordance with FIN No. 48, the Company recognized a cumulative-effect adjustment of $3.4 million, increasing its liability for unrecognized tax benefits, interest and penalties and reducing the January 1, 2007 balance of Retained Earnings. A reconciliation of the beginning and ending amount of unrecognized tax benefits in 2008 and 2007 is as follows:

	2008	2007
Balance at beginning of year	$39,378	$37,807
Additions based on tax positions related to the current year	3,709	5,570
Additions for tax positions of prior years	4,212	4,070
Reductions for tax positions of prior years	(3,863)	(4,998)
Settlements	(3,212)	(1,915)
Lapses of Statutes of Limitations	(2,173)	(1,156)
Balance at end of year	$38,051	$39,378

Included in the balance of unrecognized tax benefits at December 31, 2008 and 2007, is $32,420 and $34,235 in unrecognized tax benefits, the recognition of which would have an affect on the effective tax rate. This amount differs from the gross unrecognized tax benefits presented in the table due to the decrease in U.S. federal income taxes, which would occur upon recognition of the state tax benefits included therein. Included in the balance of unrecognized tax benefits at December 31, 2008 is $7,486 related to tax positions for which it is reasonably possible that the total amounts could significantly change during the next twelve months. This amount represents a decrease in unrecognized tax benefits comprised primarily of items related to a payment related to a federal audit of a partnership investment, assessed state income tax audits, state settlement negotiations currently in progress and expiring statutes in foreign jurisdictions.

The Company classifies all income tax related interest and penalties as income tax expense. During the tax year ended December 31, 2008, the Company recognized a net release of $215 in income tax interest and penalties and during the tax year ended December 31, 2007 the Company recognized a net increase of $1,095 in income tax interest and penalties. As of December 31, 2008 and 2007, the Company has accrued $15,563 and $15,812 for the potential payment of interest and penalties.

Humana
2008 Annual Report

10. Income Taxes

The provision for income taxes consisted of the following for the years ended December 31, 2008, 2007 and 2006:

(in thousands)	2008	2007	2006
Current provision:			
Federal	$336,870	$452,286	$192,878
States and Puerto Rico	30,829	36,066	11,722
Total current provision	367,699	488,352	204,600
Deferred benefit	(22,005)	(32,736)	70,062
Provision for income taxes	$345,694	$455,616	$274,662

The provision for income taxes was different from the amount computed using the federal statutory rate for the years ended December 31, 2008, 2007 and 2006 due to the following:

(in thousands)	2008	2007	2006
Income tax provision at federal statutory rate	$347,497	$451,255	$266,730
State, net of federal benefit and Puerto Rico	12,412	23,377	18,301
Tax exempt investment income	(21,253)	(20,254)	(15,713)
Contingent tax reserves (benefits)	–	–	1,570
Other, net	7,038	1,238	3,774
Provision for income taxes	$345,694	$455,616	$274,662

Deferred income tax balances reflect the impact of temporary differences between the tax bases of assets or liabilities and their reported amounts in our consolidated financial statements, and are stated at enacted tax rates expected to be in effect when the reported amounts are actually recovered or settled. Principal components of our net deferred tax balances at December 31, 2008 and 2007 were as follows:

	Assets (Liabilities)	
(in thousands)	2008	2007
Compensation and other accrued expenses	$ 117,037	$ 98,852
Future policy benefits payable	121,259	65,919
Investment securities	113,854	7,739
Net operating loss carryforward	60,342	39,842
Unearned premiums	25,203	22,894
Professional liability risks	10,331	13,235
Capital loss carryforward	9,272	–
Benefits payable	1,543	–
Total deferred income tax assets	458,841	248,481
Valuation allowance	(28,063)	–
Total deferred income tax assets, net of valuation allowance	430,778	248,481
Depreciable property and intangible assets	(211,012)	(186,673)
Prepaid expenses and other	(68,612)	(75,029)
Investment securities	–	(6,894)
Benefits payable	–	(605)
Total deferred income tax liabilities	(279,624)	(269,201)
Total net deferred income tax assets (liabilities)	$ 151,154	$ (20,720)
Amounts recognized in the consolidated balance sheet:		
Other current assets	$ 96,349	$ 14,986

(in thousands)	Assets (Liabilities) 2008	2007
Other long-term assets	54,805	(35,706)
Total net deferred income tax assets	$ 151,154	$ (20,720)

At December 31, 2008, we had approximately $164.7 million of net operating losses to carry forward related to prior acquisitions. These net operating loss carryforwards, if not used to offset future taxable income, will expire from 2009 through 2026. Due to limitations and uncertainty regarding our ability to use some of the carryforwards, a valuation allowance was established on $76.6 million of net operating loss carryforwards ("SRLY NOLs") related to our 2007 acquisition of KMG. For the remainder of the net operating loss carryforwards, based on our historical record of producing taxable income and profitability, we have concluded that future operating income will be sufficient to give rise to tax expense to recover all deferred tax assets.

We file income tax returns in the United States and certain foreign jurisdictions. In 2007, the Internal Revenue Service (IRS) completed its examination of our U.S. income tax returns for 2003 and 2004 which did not result in any material adjustments. With few exceptions, which are immaterial in the aggregate, we are no longer subject to state, local and foreign tax examinations by tax authorities for years before 2005. The IRS commenced an examination of our U.S. income tax returns for 2005 and 2006 during 2007 that is anticipated to be completed in 2009. As of December 31, 2008, we are not aware of any material adjustments the IRS may propose.

We adopted the provisions of FASB Interpretation No. 48, Accounting for Uncertainty in Income Taxes, on January 1, 2007. We recognize interest accrued related to unrecognized tax benefits and penalties in tax expense. The liability for unrecognized tax benefits was $16.8 million and $16.0 million at December 31, 2008 and 2007, respectively all of which would affect the effective tax rate if recognized. The only change to the liability during the twelve months ended December 31, 2008, was accrued interest. The Company believes it is reasonably possible that its liability for unrecognized tax benefits will decrease in the next twelve months by approximately $16.8 million as a result of audit settlements.

Corning 2007 Annual Report

6. Income Taxes

Income (loss) from continuing operations before income taxes follows (in millions):

	Years ended December 31,		
	2007	2006	2005
U.S. companies	$ 235	$175	$(213)
Non-U.S. companies	1,056	786	772
Income from continuing operations before income taxes	$1,291	$961	$559

The current and deferred amounts of the provision (benefit) for income taxes follow (in millions):

	Years ended December 31,		
	2007	2006	2005
Current:			
Federal			$ (14)
State and municipal	$ 2	$ (8)	
Foreign	176	164	167
Deferred:			
Federal			443
State and municipal	(3)		
Foreign	(95)	(101)	(18)
Provision for income taxes	$ 80	$ 55	$ 578

Amounts are reflected in the preceding tables based on the location of the taxing authorities.

Reconciliation of the U.S. statutory income tax rate to our effective tax rate for continuing operations follows:

	Years ended December 31,		
	2007	2006	2005
Statutory U.S. income tax (benefit) rate	35.0%	35.0%	35.0%
State income tax (benefit), net of federal benefit	0.5	(0.2)	(1.9)
Worthless stock deduction	(12.1)	(1.4)	(272.7)[2]
Tax holidays[6]	(1.7)	(10.1)	(8.9)
Investment & other tax credits[7]	(3.1)	(3.6)	(12.7)
Rate difference on foreign earnings		6.1	10.2
Minimum pension obligation			(14.6)[8]
Currency translation adjustment			(5.2)
Tax rate changes	13.2[9]		
Valuation allowances:			
Provision (release) of prior period valuation allowances	(12.4)[5]	(8.6)[5]	94.0[1]
Tax (expenses) benefits not recorded on (income) losses	(13.5)[4]	(13.4)[4]	280.0[2][3]
Other items, net	0.3	1.9	0.2
Effective income tax rate	6.2%	5.7%	103.4%

Significant items that cause our effective tax rate to vary from the U.S. statutory rate of 35% are as follows:

(1) In 2004, significant events occurred which required us to increase our valuation allowance against our U.S. deferred tax assets. At that time, we believed that it was more likely than not that we could realize the remaining net U.S. deferred tax assets of approximately $525 million through a tax planning strategy involving the sale of our investment in Dow Corning, a non-strategic appreciated asset, if we were faced with expiring net operating loss carryforwards. During 2005, Dow Corning's performance was much stronger than expected and Dow Corning resumed paying a dividend; both of which are expected to continue in the future. Due to this improved performance, we concluded that Dow Corning provides strong financial, geographic and market balance to Corning's portfolio of businesses, the profitability of which has become more concentrated due to the success of the display operating segment. As a result, we considered Dow Corning to be a strategic investment and could no longer assert that a potential tax planning strategy involving the sale of Dow Corning would be prudent, as required by FAS 109. Therefore, we no longer believed, in the fourth quarter of 2005, that it was more likely than not that we would realize the remaining net deferred tax assets. Accordingly, we increased our valuation allowance by $525 million to fully reserve our net U.S. deferred tax assets in the fourth quarter of 2005, which increased our effective tax rate by 94%.

(2) During the third quarter of 2005, Corning filed its 2004 consolidated U.S. Federal income tax return, which included a $3.9 billion worthless stock deduction for the loss on our investment in the photonic technologies business associated with the Pirelli acquisition. This acquisition was completed in December 2000 and was substantially impaired in the second quarter of 2001. Prior to the third quarter of 2005, we did not record a deferred tax asset for this item as the ultimate realization of such deduction was uncertain, and consistent with the requirements of SFAS 5, recognition of an asset prior to the time management determines the realization of the asset is probable is prohibited. On September 2, 2005, Corning and the Commissioner of the IRS entered into a closing agreement under section 7121 of the Internal Revenue Code of 1986 which provides that Corning is entitled to this worthless stock deduction. We recorded a $1.5 billion deferred tax asset for this item in the third quarter, which was concurrently offset by a valuation allowance of an equal amount due to our inability to record tax benefits for U.S. net operating losses. The net result had no impact of our effective tax rate for 2005.

(3) We were unable to record tax benefits on net operating losses generated in the U.S. and certain foreign jurisdictions, resulting in an increase in the effective tax rate of 7.3% for 2005.

(4) In both 2007 and 2006, we generated income from continuing operations in the U.S. The tax expense on such income was fully offset by the tax benefit of releasing a portion of the valuation allowance to reflect the realization of deferred taxes resulting from the generation of U.S. income. The impact of the release of valuation allowance and, thus, not recording tax expense on income generated in the U.S. is a reduction in the rate of 14.2% for both 2007 and 2006, respectively.

(5) In 2004, we recorded valuation allowances against our entire German and Australian deferred tax assets due to losses in recent years. In 2007, due to sustained profitability and positive earnings projections for our overall German operations, we have concluded that it is more likely than not that the German national deferred tax assets are realizable and that the related valuation allowance is no longer required. In 2006, due to sustained profitability and positive earnings projections in Australia and at certain of our German operations, we concluded that it was more likely than not that a portion of the German local and the entire Australian deferred tax assets were realizable and that the related valuation allowances were no longer required. The impact of the release of the valuation allowances on our effective rate is a reduction in the rate of 12.4% and 8.7% for 2007 and 2006, respectively.

(6) Certain foreign subsidiaries in China, South Africa and Taiwan are operating under tax holiday arrangements. The nature and extent of such arrangements vary, and the benefits of existing arrangements phase out in future years (through 2011) according to the specific terms and schedules of the relevant taxing jurisdictions. The impact of the tax holidays on our effective rate is a reduction in the rate of 12.1%, 10.1% and 8.9% for 2007, 2006 and 2005, respectively.

(7) Taiwan grants investment tax credits for investments in qualifying machinery and equipment. The impact of such credits on our effective tax rate is a reduction in the rate of 0.4%, 3.1%, and 12.3%, for 2007, 2006, and 2005, respectively.

(8) The elimination of our minimum pension liability for the domestic qualified plan in 2005 resulted in a decrease in the effective tax rate of 14.6%.

(9) In 2007, U.S. and German deferred taxes were revised for enacted law changes. The impact on the effective rate is an increase of 13.2%.

The tax effects of temporary differences and carryforwards that gave rise to significant portions of the deferred tax assets and liabilities follows (in millions):

	December 31,	
	2007	2006
Loss and tax credit carryforwards	$ 2,145	$ 2,399
Capitalized research and development	106	142
Restructuring reserves	194	215
Postretirement medical and life benefits	303	309
Inventory	39	63
Intangible and other assets	64	64
Other accrued liabilities	398	339
Other employee benefits	117	182
Other		17
Gross deferred tax assets	3,366	3,730
Valuation allowance	(3,091)	(3,542)
Total deferred tax assets	275	188
Fixed assets	(40)	(50)
Total deferred tax liabilities	(40)	(50)
Net deferred tax assets	$ 235	$ 138

The net deferred tax assets are included in (in millions):

	December 31,	
	2007	2006
Current assets	$ 54	$ 47
Other assets	202	114
Other current liabilities		(1)
Other noncurrent liabilities	(21)	(22)
Net deferred tax assets	$235	$138

Details on deferred tax assets for loss and tax credit carryforwards at December 31, 2007 follow (in millions):

			Expiration		
	Amount	2008–2012	2013–2017	2018–2026	Indefinite
Net operating losses	$1,829	$ 42	$ 40	$1,539	$208
Capital losses	55	55			
Contributions	8	8			
Tax credits	253	82	77	52	42
Total as of December 31, 2007	$2,145	$187	$117	$1,591	$250

FAS 123 (R) prohibits the recognition of windfall tax benefits from stock-based compensation deducted on the tax return until realized through a reduction of income tax payable. Cumulative tax benefits totaling $202 million will be recorded in additional paid-in-capital when the net operating loss carryforward is utilized and the windfall tax benefit can be realized.

SFAS No. 109 provides that deferred tax assets are to be reduced by a valuation allowance if, based on the weight of available positive and negative evidence, it is more likely than not (a likelihood of greater than 50 percent) that some portion or all of the deferred tax assets will not be realized. SFAS No. 109 further requires that in assessing the realizability of deferred tax assets, objective evidence (e.g., actual, historical information) should be given greater weight than subjective evidence (e.g., the outlook for future profitability). The valuation allowance should be sufficient to reduce the deferred tax assets to the amount that is more likely than not to be realized.

In both 2006 and 2007, we generated income from continuing operations in the U.S. The tax expense on such income was fully offset by the tax benefit of releasing a portion of the valuation allowance to reflect the realization of deferred taxes resulting from the generation of U.S. income. The impact of the release of the valuation allowances, and thus not recording tax expense on income generated in the U.S., is a reduction in our effective tax rate of 14.2% for both 2007 and 2006.

We continue to provide a full valuation allowance against all of our U.S. deferred tax assets as of December 31, 2007 because we do not believe it is more likely than not that we will be able to generate in the future sufficient levels of profitability in the U.S. to realize some or all of the deferred tax assets. U.S. profits of approximately $8.3 billion dollars would be required to fully realize the deferred tax assets as of December 31, 2007. Of that amount, $4.2 billion of U.S. profits would be required over the next 19 years to fully realize the deferred tax assets associated with federal net operating loss carry forwards. Our evaluation of the realizability of our deferred tax assets is inherently subjective and is based on our analysis and weighting of all positive and negative evidence available to us. This evaluation includes estimates and assumptions about a number of market, execution and economic variables. Our judgment as of December 31, 2007 has been formed based on these variables which include:

- We had a taxable loss in the U.S. in 2005 and, absent nonrecurring items, we would have also had a taxable loss in the U.S. in 2006. 2007 is the only year in the last three years in which we have generated income in the U.S. when considering only recurring items.

- Although our consolidated net income has reached record levels, we have continued to incur losses or have generated only marginal profitability in the U.S. because (a) Display Technologies, the key driver of our consolidated profitability, is largely a foreign-based business with only net royalty income occurring in the U.S.; (b) our Environmental and Life Sciences segments have lost money or have been only marginally profitable due to very significant U.S.-based factory start-up costs and developmental spending; and (c) improvement in our Telecommunications segment has been more than offset by higher U.S.-based research, development, and engineering, stock and incentive compensation and other administrative expenses.

- A significant factor in our forecasts of future U.S. taxable profitability is the amount of assumed royalties to be paid by our Display Technologies businesses to the U.S. The amount of such royalties could decline if our sales of LCD glass are impacted by:

  — Manufacturing capacity constraints;

  — Reduced demand due to the slowing of corporate information technology and consumer spending or (b) challenges to pricing, both of which may arise from global economic pressures; or

  — Shifts in the global market share of our customers which manufacture flat panel TV and computer monitors.

  Additionally, a change in our judgment regarding the sustainability of the level of these royalties in accordance with the principles of FIN 48, "Accounting for Uncertainty in Income Taxes" may also impact our forecasts of U.S. profitability.

Although we remain optimistic about our consolidated outlook for 2008 and beyond, as of December 31, 2007, we are sufficiently uncertain about our U.S.-based results, primarily due to the current economic uncertainty, but also due to a number of market and execution risks in our operating segments, particularly those pertaining to Display Technologies, as noted above that we have concluded that the positive evidence supporting realization of our U.S. deferred tax assets does not sufficiently outweigh the negative evidence that we will not realize our U.S. deferred tax assets.

We will update our assessment of the realizability of our U.S. deferred tax assets on a quarterly basis in 2008, taking into account year-to-date actual as well as forecasted U.S. results. If, after considering the actual results and the potential impact of the economic uncertainties and business risks considered in our 2007 year-end assessment as well as our FIN 48 assessment of the Display Technologies U.S. royalties we conclude that it is more likely than not that we will be profitable in the U.S. in 2008 and future years, we will quantify the portion of our U.S. deferred tax assets we believe to be realizable and reduce our valuation allowance accordingly. Until that time, we will continue to adjust the valuation allowance to offset the current U.S. income tax expense (or benefit) that would otherwise be recorded on income (or losses) in the U.S. and, therefore, reflect no net U.S. income tax expense.

We do not provide income taxes on the post-1992 earnings of domestic subsidiaries that we expect to recover tax-free without significant cost. Income taxes have been provided for post-1992 unremitted earnings of domestic corporate joint ventures that we do not expect to recover tax-free. Unremitted earnings of domestic subsidiaries and corporate joint ventures that arose in fiscal years beginning on or before December 31, 1992 have been indefinitely reinvested. We currently provide income taxes on the earnings of foreign subsidiaries and affiliated companies to the extent these earnings are currently taxable or expected to be remitted. As of December 31, 2007, taxes have not been provided on approximately $4.0 billion of accumulated foreign unremitted earnings which are expected to remain invested indefinitely.

We adopted the provisions of FASB Interpretation (FIN) No. 48, "Accounting for Uncertainty in Income Taxes," (FIN 48) effective January 1, 2007. As a result of the implementation of FIN 48, we recognized a $25 million increase in the liability for unrecognized tax benefits and a decrease to the January 1, 2007, balance of retained earnings of $4 million. A reconciliation of the beginning and ending amount of unrecognized tax benefits is as follows (in millions):

Balance at January 1, 2007	$ 56
Additions based on tax positions related to the current year	2
Additions for tax positions of prior years	13
Reductions for tax positions of prior years	(23)
Settlements and lapse of statue of limitations	(8)
Balance at December 31, 2007	$ 40

Included in the balance at December 31, 2007 is $25 million of unrecognized tax benefits which would impact our effective tax rate if recognized.

We recognize accrued interest and penalties associated with uncertain tax positions as part of tax expense. During the years ended December 31, 2007, 2006, and 2005, we recognized approximately $1 million of interest expense, $0.5 million and $2.6 million in interest income, respectively. We had approximately $7.1 million and $4.1 million accrued at December 31 2007 and 2006, respectively, for the payment of interest and penalties.

Corning Incorporated, as the common parent company, and all 80%-or-more-owned U.S. subsidiaries join in the filing of consolidated U.S. federal income tax returns. All such returns for periods ended through December 31, 2004, have been audited by and settled with the Internal Revenue Service (IRS). We expect the IRS to begin the examination of our consolidated U.S. federal income tax returns for the years ended December 31, 2005 and December 31, 2006 in the first quarter of 2008.

Corning Incorporated and U.S. subsidiaries file income tax returns on a combined, unitary or stand-alone basis in multiple state and local jurisdictions, which generally have statutes of limitations ranging from 3 to 5 years. Various state income tax returns are currently in the process of examination or administrative appeal.

Our foreign subsidiaries file income tax returns in the countries in which they have operations. Generally, these countries have statutes of limitations ranging from 3 to 7 years. Years still open to examination by foreign tax authorities in major jurisdictions include Japan (2000 onward) and Taiwan (2004 onward).

While we expect the amount of unrecognized tax benefits to change in the next 12 months, we do not expect the change to have a significant impact on the results of operations or our financial position.

Schlumberger 2007 Annual Report

15. Income Tax Expense

Schlumberger and its subsidiaries operate in more than 100 taxing jurisdictions where statutory tax rates generally vary from 0% to 50%.

As more fully described in Note 3 *Charges and Credits*, Schlumberger recorded a pretax credit outside the United States in 2007 of $25 million, pretax charges in 2006 of $46 million ($19 million in the United States; $27 million outside the United States) and net pretax credits in 2005 of $172 million ($19 million of net credits in the United States; $153 million of credits outside the United States).

Pretax book income subject to United States and non-United States income taxes for each of the three years ended December 31, was as follows:

(Stated in millions)	2007	2006	2005
United States	$1,754	$1,582	$ 892
Outside United States	4,870	3,366	2,080
Pretax income	$6,624	$4,948	$2,972

The components of net deferred tax assets were as follows:

(Stated in millions)	2007	2006
Postretirement and other long-term benefits	$244	$394
Current employee benefits	29	31
Fixed assets, inventory and other	124	151
	$397	$576

The above deferred tax assets at December 31, 2007 and 2006 are net of valuation allowances relating to net operating losses in certain countries of $214 million and $218 million, respectively. The deferred tax assets are also net of valuation allowances relating to a capital loss carryforward of $144 million at

December 31, 2007 ($151 million at December 31, 2006) which expires in 2009 and 2010, and a foreign tax credit carryforward of $55 million at December 31, 2007 ($55 million at December 31, 2006) which expires in 2009 through 2012.

The components of consolidated income tax expense were as follows:

(Stated in millions)	2007	2006	2005
Current:			
United States—Federal	$ 538	$ 495	$256
United States—State	54	49	24
Outside United States	834	641	372
	$1,426	$1,185	$652
Deferred:			
United States—Federal	$ (3)	8	$ 12
United States—State	8	12	2
Outside United States	38	(10)	77
Valuation allowance	(21)	(5)	(61)
	$ 22	$ 5	$ 30
Consolidated taxes on income	$1,448	$1,190	$682

A reconciliation of the United States statutory federal tax rate (35%) to the consolidated effective tax rate is:

(Stated in millions)	2007	2006	2005
US statutory federal rate	35%	35%	35%
US state income taxes	1	1	1
Non-US income taxed at different rates	(12)	(10)	(8)
Effect of equity method investment	(1)	(1)	(1)
Minority partner's share of LLC earnings	–	–	(1)
Charges and credits	–	–	(2)
Other	(1)	(1)	(1)
Effective income tax rate	22%	24%	23%

Schlumberger adopted the provisions of FASB Interpretation No. 48, *Accounting for Uncertainty in Income Taxes–an Interpretation of FASB Statement No. 109* ("FIN 48") on January 1, 2007. This interpretation clarifies the accounting for uncertain tax positions and requires companies to recognize the impact of a tax position in their financial statements, if that position is more likely than not of being sustained on audit, based on the technical merits of the position. The adoption of FIN 48 did not have any impact on the total liabilities or stockholders' equity of Schlumberger.

A reconciliation of the beginning and ending amount of liabilities associated with uncertain tax positions is as follows:

(Stated in millions)	
Balance at January 1, 2007	$730
Additions based on tax positions related to the current year	187
Additions for tax positions of prior years	16
Impact of changes in exchange rates	21
Settlements with tax authorities	(8)
Reductions for tax positions of prior years	(55)
Reductions due to the lapse of the applicable statute of limitations	(33)
Balance at December 31, 2007	$858

Included in the Schlumberger *Consolidated Balance Sheet* at December 31, 2007 is approximately $858 million of liabilities associated with uncertain tax positions in the over 100 jurisdictions in which Schlumberger conducts business, a number of which have tax laws that are not fully defined and are evolving. This amount excludes $130 million of accrued interest and penalties. All but $25 million of the unrecognized tax benefits, if recognized, would impact the Schlumberger effective tax rate.

Schlumberger classifies interest and penalties relating to uncertain tax positions within *Taxes on income* in the *Consolidated Statement of Income*. During 2007, Schlumberger recognized approximately $36 million in interest and penalties.

The following table summarizes the tax years that are either currently under audit or remain open and subject to examination by the tax authorities in the most significant jurisdictions in which Schlumberger operates:

(Stated in millions)	
Canada	2002–2007
Mexico	2002–2007
Russia	2004–2007
Saudi Arabia	2001–2007
United Kingdom	2004–2007
United States	2003–2007

In certain of the jurisdictions noted above, Schlumberger operates through more than one legal entity, each of which has different open years subject to examination. The table above presents the open years subject to examination for the most material of the legal entities in each jurisdiction. Additionally, it is important to note that tax years are technically not closed until the statute of limitations in each jurisdiction expires. In the jurisdictions noted above, the statute of limitations can extend beyond the open years subject to examination.

Due to the geographic breadth of the Schlumberger operations, numerous tax audits may be ongoing throughout the world at any point in time. Tax liabilities are recorded based on estimates of additional taxes which will be due upon the conclusion of these audits. Estimates of these tax liabilities are made based upon prior experience and are updated in light of changes in facts and circumstances. However, due to the uncertain and complex application of tax regulations, it is possible that the ultimate resolution of audits may result in liabilities which could be materially different from these estimates. In such an event, Schlumberger will record additional tax expense or tax benefit in the period in which such resolution occurs.

WM. Wrigley Jr. 2007 Annual Report

13. Income Taxes

Income taxes are based on pretax earnings, which were distributed geographically as follows:

	2007	2006	2005
Domestic	$102,849	90,835	140,762
Foreign	829,314	678,212	613,898
Total	$932,163	769,047	754,660

Reconciliation of the provision for income taxes computed at the U.S. federal statutory rate of 35% to the reported provision for income taxes is as follows:

	2007	2006	2005
Provision at U.S. federal statutory rate	$326,257	269,166	264,131
State taxes—net	2,404	2,272	4,134
Foreign tax rates	(72,552)	(51,893)	(35,767)
Foreign earnings remitted to parent	49,188	33,801	10,761
Tax credits	(3,200)	(3,500)	(3,590)
Other—net	(1,939)	(10,176)	(2,261)
Total	$300,158	239,670	237,408

Foreign earnings remitted to parent includes estimated taxes provided on foreign sourced earnings remitted or expected to be remitted, net, to the parent company after considering financial and operational requirements of the parent and foreign affiliate.

The Other—net in 2005 includes the incremental income tax expense of $5,500 due to the repatriation of foreign earnings.

The components of the provisions for income taxes were:

	Current	Deferred	Total
2007			
Federal	$ 12,302	35,292	47,594
Foreign	253,460	(7,766)	245,694
State	5,890	980	6,870
Total	$271,652	28,506	300,158

	Current	Deferred	Total
2006			
Federal	$ 14,871	5,305	20,176
Foreign	217,650	(4,927)	212,723
State	6,630	141	6,771
Total	$239,151	519	239,670
2005			
Federal	$ 16,469	7,570	24,039
Foreign	207,451	(1,275)	206,176
State	7,392	(199)	7,193
Total	$231,312	6,096	237,408

The Company or one of its subsidiaries files income tax returns in the U.S. federal jurisdiction and various states and foreign jurisdictions. With certain exceptions, the Company is no longer subject to U.S. federal, state and local or non-U.S. income tax examinations by tax authorities for years prior to 2004. The Company adopted the provisions of FIN 48, "Accounting for Uncertainty in Income Taxes—an interpretation of FASB Statement No. 109" on January 1, 2007 with no material impact to the financial statements. A reconciliation of the beginning and ending balance of unrecognized tax benefits is as follows:

	2007
Balance at January 1	$37,054
Additions based on tax positions related to the current year	13,938
Additions for tax positions of prior years	641
Reduction for tax positions of prior years	(2,397)
Settlements	(6,119)
Foreign currency translation	1,867
Balance at December 31	$44,984

Approximately $30,700 of the total amount of unrecognized tax benefits at December 31, 2007 would affect the annual effective tax rate, if recognized. See Note 3 discussion of SFAS No. 141(R) for pending accounting rule changes. Further, the Company is unaware of any positions for which it is reasonably possible that the total amounts of unrecognized tax benefits will significantly increase or decrease within the next twelve months.

The Company recognizes interest accrued and penalties related to unrecognized tax benefits in income tax expense. The total amount of accrued interest and penalties at December 31, 2007 and 2006 was approximately $2,900.

The following table summarizes components of deferred tax assets and (liabilities) at December 31:

	2007	2006
Accrued compensation, pension and post-retirement benefits	$127,448	$121,438
Depreciation	(37,352)	(24,625)
Goodwill and intangibles	(75,727)	(46,586)
Accrued liabilities and other items—net	(1,365)	12,701
Net deferred tax asset (liability)	$ 13,004	$ 62,928

The following table summarizes the balance sheet classification of deferred tax assets and (liabilities) at December 31:

	2007	2006
Deferred Tax Asset		
Current	$ 33,446	40,661
Noncurrent	25,526	36,480
Deferred Tax Liability		
Current	(2,017)	(1,511)
Noncurrent	(43,951)	(12,702)
Net deferred tax asset (liability)	$ 13,004	62,928

Applicable U.S. income and foreign withholding taxes have not been provided on approximately $958,600 of undistributed earnings of international associated companies at December 31, 2007. These earnings are considered to be permanently invested and, under certain tax laws, are not subject to taxes until distributed as dividends. Tax on such potential distributions would be substantially offset by foreign tax credits. If the earnings were not considered permanently invested, approximately $210,500 of deferred income taxes would need to be provided.

United Technologies 2007 Annual Report

Note 9. Taxes on Income

(in millions of dollars)	2007	2006	2005
Current:			
United States:			
Federal	$ 490	$ 667	$ 230
State	82	11	64
Foreign	1,206	1,030	697
	1,778	1,708	991
Future:			
United States:			
Federal	$ 220	($ 82)	$ 135
State	(60)	38	6

(in millions of dollars)	2007	2006	2005
Foreign	(102)	(170)	121
	58	(214)	262
Income tax expense	$1,836	$1,494	$1,253
Attributable to items (charged) credited to equity and goodwill	($ 493)	$1,287	($ 597)

Future income taxes represent the tax effects of transactions, which are reported in different periods for tax and financial reporting purposes. These amounts consist of the tax effects of temporary differences between the tax and financial reporting balance sheets and tax carryforwards. Pursuant to SFAS 109, "Accounting for Income Taxes," current and non-current future income tax benefits and payables within the same tax jurisdiction are generally offset for presentation in the Consolidated Balance Sheet.

The tax effects of net temporary differences and tax carryforwards which gave rise to future income tax benefits and payables at December 31, 2007 and 2006 are as follows:

(in millions of dollars)	2007	2006
Future income tax benefits:		
Insurance and employee benefits	$ 755	$1,279
Other asset basis differences	(332)	(303)
Other liability basis differences	1,266	1,339
Tax loss carryforwards	549	523
Tax credit carryforwards	700	638
Valuation-allowance	(545)	(525)
	$2,393	$2,951
Future income taxes payable:		
Fixed assets	$ 630	$ 330
Other items, net	192	272
	$ 822	$ 602

Valuation allowances have been established primarily for tax credit, tax loss carryforwards, and certain foreign temporary differences to reduce the future income tax benefits to expected realizable amounts. Of the total valuation allowance amount of $545 million, $245 million was established in purchase accounting, relating primarily to the purchase of Chubb. Subsequently recognized tax benefits associated with a valuation allowance recorded in a business combination will be recorded as an adjustment to goodwill. However, upon the January 1, 2009 adoption of SFAS 141(R), changes in deferred tax asset valuation allowances and income tax uncertainties after the acquisition date generally will affect income tax expense including those associated with acquisitions that closed prior to the effective date of SFAS 141(R).

The sources of income from continuing operations before income taxes and minority interests are:

(in millions of dollars)	2007	2006	2005
United States	$2,786	$2,410	$1,936
Foreign	3,598	3,082	2,748
	$6,384	$5,492	$4,684

U.S. income taxes have not been provided on undistributed earnings of international subsidiaries. It is not practicable to estimate the amount of tax that might be payable. Our intention is to reinvest these earnings permanently or to repatriate the earnings only when it is tax effective to do so. Accordingly, we believe that any U.S. tax on repatriated earnings would be substantially offset by U.S. foreign tax credits.

The American Jobs Creation Act, signed into law in October of 2004, provided an opportunity in 2005 to repatriate up to $500 million of reinvested foreign earnings and to claim an 85% dividend received deduction against the repatriated amount. We evaluated the potential effects of the repatriation provision and determined not to repatriate earnings under this provision.

Differences between effective income tax rates and the statutory U.S. federal income tax rates are as follows:

	2007	2006	2005
Statutory U.S. federal income tax rate	35.0%	35.0%	35.0%
Tax on international activities including exports	(5.2)%	(7.8)%	(4.9)%
Benefit of prior period foreign tax credits	–	–	2.9%
Tax audit settlements	(0.6)%	(0.6)%	(1.4)%
Other	(0.4)%	0.6%	1.0%
Effective income tax rate	28.8%	27.2%	26.8%

The effective tax rates for 2007, 2006 and 2005 reflect the tax benefits associated with lower tax rates on international earnings, which we intend to permanently reinvest outside the United States. The 2007 effective tax rate reflects approximately $80 million of tax expense reductions, principally relating to re-evaluation of our liabilities and contingencies based upon global examination activity including IRS completion of 2000 through 2003 examination field-work and related protest filing, and development of claims for research and development tax credits. Principal adverse tax impacts to the 2007 effective tax rate related to the EU Fine and enacted tax law changes outside the United States.

The 2005 effective tax rate reflects an approximately $66 million reduction in tax expense primarily as a result of the re-evaluation of our liabilities and contingencies in light of the completion and commencement of exam cycles. In 2006, a residual disputed issue related to the 1999 disposition of a business segment was settled with the Appeals Division of the IRS and was reviewed by the U.S. Congress Joint Committee on Taxation. The settlement resulted in an approximately $35 million reduction in tax expense.

The 2005 effective rate also reflects a benefit of approximately $135 million related to an amended return, filed in 2005, which claimed credits for 2003 foreign taxes previously recognized as deductions. The 2005 effective tax rate also reflects a tax benefit of approximately $19 million associated with non-core business divestitures. We recognized a tax cost related to the tax gain from the sale of a Hamilton Sundstrand division, and tax benefits related to tax losses from the sale of a Carrier refrigeration operation and the sale and liquidation of a Pratt & Whitney subsidiary. The third-party sales did not result in significant pre-tax gains or losses for financial reporting purposes. In the normal course of business, various tax authorities examine us, including the IRS. In 2007, the IRS completed the examination phase of the 2000 through 2003 audit and UTC is discussing disputed adjustments with the Appeals Division of the IRS. Separately, the IRS commenced an examination of tax years 2004 and 2005. Although the outcome of these matters cannot currently be determined, we believe adequate provision has been made for any potential unfavorable financial statement impact.

At December 31, 2007, tax credit carryforwards, principally state and federal, were $700 million, of which $314 million expire as follows: $23 million expire from 2008–2012, $137 million from 2013–2017, and $154 million from 2018–2027.

At December 31, 2007, tax loss carryforwards, principally state and foreign, were $2,183 million, of which $971 million expire as follows: $442 million from 2008–2012, $151 million from 2013–2017, and $378 million from 2018–2027.

As disclosed in Note 1, we adopted the provisions of FIN 48 as of January 1, 2007. At December 31, 2007, we had gross tax-affected unrecognized tax benefits of $798 million of which $613 million, if recognized, would impact the effective tax rate. During the years ended December 31, 2007, 2006, and 2005, we recorded interest related to unrecognized tax benefits of approximately $56 million, $38 million, and $25 million, respectively. Total accrued interest at December 31, 2007 and 2006 was approximately $174 million and $142 million, respectively. A reconciliation of the beginning and ending amount of unrecognized tax benefits is as follows:

(in millions of dollars)	
Balance as of January 1, 2007	$815
Additions for tax positions related to the current year	78
Additions for tax positions of prior years	93
Reductions for tax positions of prior years	(48)
Settlements	(140)
Balance as of December 31, 2007	$ 798

Included in the balance at December 31, 2007, are $63 million of tax positions whose tax characterization is highly certain but for which there is uncertainty about the timing of tax return inclusion. Because of the impact of deferred tax accounting, other than interest and penalties, the timing would not impact the annual effective tax rate but could accelerate the payment of cash to the taxing authority to an earlier period.

We conduct business globally and, as a result, UTC or one or more of our subsidiaries file income tax returns in the U.S. federal jurisdiction and various state and foreign jurisdictions. In the normal course of business, we are subject to examination by taxing authorities throughout the world, including such major jurisdictions as Australia, Canada, China, France, Germany, Hong Kong, Italy, Japan, Korea, Singapore, Spain, the United Kingdom and the United States. With few exceptions, we are no longer subject to U.S. federal, state and local, or non-U.S. income tax examinations for years before 1998.

It is reasonably possible that a reduction in a range of $25 million to $75 million of unrecognized tax benefits may occur within 12 months as a result of projected resolutions of worldwide tax disputes.

Clorox 2006 Annual Report

Note 18. Income Taxes

The provision for income taxes on continuing operations, by tax jurisdiction, consisted of the following for the fiscal years ended June 30:

	2006	2005	2004
Current			
Federal	$178	$209	$186
State	20	24	19
Foreign	40	26	32
Total current	238	259	237
Deferred			
Federal	(15)	(62)	29
Federal—American Jobs Creation	8	12	–
State	(1)	(5)	(4)
Foreign	(4)	8	–
Total deferred	(28)	(47)	(25)
Total	$210	$212	$262

The components of earnings from continuing operations before income taxes, by tax jurisdiction, were as follows for the fiscal years ended June 30:

	2006	2005	2004
United States	$516	$587	$639
Foreign	137	142	113
Total	$653	$729	$752

A reconciliation of the statutory federal income tax rate to the Company's effective tax rate on continuing operations follows for the fiscal years ended June 30:

	2006	2005	2004
Statutory federal tax rate	35.0%	35.0%	35.0%
State taxes (net of federal tax benefits)	1.4	1.7	1.9
Tax differential on foreign earnings	(2.4)	(0.6)	(1.2)
Net adjustment of prior year federal and state tax accruals	1.9	(2.9)	0.5
Change in valuation allowance	(0.6)	(1.4)	(0.4)
Low-income housing tax credits	(1.4)	(0.9)	(1.1)
Other differences	(1.8)	(1.8)	0.2
Effective tax rate	32.1%	29.1%	34.9%

Applicable U.S. income and foreign withholding taxes have not been provided on approximately $23 of undistributed earnings of certain foreign subsidiaries at June 30, 2006, since these earnings are considered indefinitely reinvested. The net federal income tax liability that would arise if these earnings were not indefinitely reinvested is approximately $3. Applicable U.S. income and foreign withholding taxes have been provided on these earnings in the periods in which they are repatriated.

During fiscal year 2006, the Company repatriated approximately $265 of cash previously held in foreign entities. Of this amount, $111 represented dividends paid under the terms of the American Jobs Creation Act (AJCA) that the Company plans to use for reinvestment in certain qualified activities. All entities whose earnings had been designated as indefinitely reinvested prior to remitting qualified dividends under the terms of the AJCA have reverted back to indefinite reinvestment status as of June 30, 2006.

With respect to the Company's stock option plans, realized tax benefits in excess of tax benefits recognized in net earnings are recorded as increases to additional paid-in capital. Excess tax benefits of approximately $17, $22 and $32 were realized and recorded to additional paid in capital for the fiscal years 2006, 2005 and 2004, respectively. In addition, previously recognized tax benefits of $5, relating to the cumulative charge described at Note 15, were reclassified from additional paid-in capital to income tax expense during the fiscal year 2006.

The components of deferred tax assets and liabilities at June 30 are shown below:

	2006	2005
Deferred tax assets		
Compensation and benefit programs	$ 84	$ 55
Basis difference related to Venture Agreement (Note 11)	30	34
Net operating loss and tax credit carryforwards	20	26
Minimum pension funding obligation	4	75
Other	67	33
Subtotal	205	223
Valuation allowance	(26)	(33)
Total deferred tax assets	179	190
Deferred tax liabilities		
Fixed and intangible assets	(168)	(173)
Low-income housing partnerships	(24)	(24)
Accruals and reserves	(14)	(9)
Other	(69)	(43)
Total deferred tax liabilities	(275)	(249)
Net deferred tax liabilities	$ (96	$ (59)

The net deferred tax assets and liabilities included in the consolidated balance sheet at June 30 were as follows:

	2006	2005
Current deferred tax assets	$ 24	$ 16
Noncurrent deferred tax assets	9	8
Current deferred tax liabilities	–	(1)
Noncurrent deferred tax liabilities	(129)	(82)
Net deferred tax liabilities	$ (96)	$ (59)

The Company periodically reviews its deferred tax assets for recoverability. A valuation allowance is established when the Company believes that it is more likely than not that some portion of its deferred tax assets will not be realized. Valuation allowances have been provided to reduce deferred tax assets to amounts considered recoverable. Details of the valuation allowance at June 30 were as follows:

	2006	2005
Valuation allowance at beginning of year	$ (33)	$ (39)
Other	7	6
Valuation allowance at end of year	$(26)	$(33)

At June 30, 2006, the Company had federal foreign tax credit carryforwards of $5 with an expiration date in fiscal year 2016. In addition, the Company had income tax credit carryforwards in foreign jurisdictions of $1 with an expiration date in fiscal year 2008. Tax benefits from foreign net operating loss carryforwards of $11 have expiration dates between fiscal years 2007 and 2016. Tax benefits from foreign net operating loss carryforwards of $3 may be carried forward indefinitely.

In April 2005, the Company reached an agreement with the IRS resolving certain tax issues originally arising in the period from 1997 through 2000. As a result of the settlement agreement, the Company paid $94 (excluding $6 of tax benefits) in fiscal year 2005 and $151 (excluding $13 of tax benefits) in fiscal year 2006, respectively. The Company had previously accrued for this contingency and released approximately $23 in tax accruals related to this matter in fiscal year 2005.

The IRS has now completed audits of the Company's income tax returns through fiscal year 2002, and additional tax matters related to these audits are now being reviewed at the IRS appeals level. Resolution of these matters is not expected to have a material impact to earnings.

Nike 2006 Annual Report

Note 8—Income Taxes

Income before income taxes is as follows:

	Year Ended May 31,		
	2006	2005	2004
	(In millions)		
Income before income taxes:			
United States	838.6	755.5	607.7
Foreign	1,303.0	1,104.3	842.3
	2,141.6	1,859.8	1,450.0

The provision for income taxes is as follows:

	Year Ended May 31,		
	2006	2005	2004
	(In millions)		
Current:			
United States			
Federal	$359.0	$279.6	$185.3
State	60.6	50.7	43.3
Foreign	356.0	292.5	266.8
	775.6	622.8	495.4

	Year Ended May 31,		
	2006	2005	2004
	(In millions)		
Deferred:			
United States			
Federal	(4.2)	21.9	3.9
State	(6.8)	(5.3)	2.4
Foreign	(15.0)	8.8	2.7
	(26.0)	25.4	9.0
	$749.6	$648.2	$504.4

Deferred tax (assets) and liabilities are comprised of the following:

	May 31,	
	2006	2005
	(In Millions)	
Deferred tax assets:		
Allowance for doubtful accounts	$ (10.9)	$ (15.7)
Inventories	(43.9)	(29.7)
Sales return reserves	(39.4)	(31.5)
Deferred compensation	(110.6)	(89.2)
Reserves and accrued liabilities	(50.6)	(20.2)
Property, plant, and equipment	(28.6)	(26.4)
Foreign loss carryforwards	(29.2)	(28.9)
Foreign tax credit carryforwards	(9.5)	(34.4)
Hedges	(25.5)	(3.7)
Other	29.1	22.7
Total deferred tax assets	377.3	302.4
Valuation allowance	36.6	29.1
Total deferred tax assets after valuation allowance	340.7	273.3
Deferred tax liabilities:		
Undistributed earnings of foreign subsidiaries	135.3	130
Property, plant and equipment	91.4	94.9
Intangibles	96.8	101.6
Hedges	7.8	4
Other	12.5	13.1
Total deferred tax liabilities	343.8	343.6
Net deferred tax liability	$ 3.1	$ 70.3

A reconciliation from the U.S. statutory federal income tax rate to the effective income tax rate follows:

| | Year Ended May 31, | | |
	2006	2005	2004
Federal income tax rate	35.0%	35.0%	35.0%
State taxes, net of federal benefit	1.5	1.8	2.1
Foreign earnings	(1.5)	(2.8)	(0.6)
Other, net	–	0.9	(1.7)
Effective income tax rate	35.0%	34.9%	34.8%

During the quarter ending November 30, 2005, the Company's CEO and Board of Directors approved a domestic reinvestment plan as required by the American Jobs Creation Act of 2004 (the "Act") to repatriate $500 million of foreign earnings in fiscal 2006. The Act creates a temporary incentive for U.S. multinational corporations to repatriate accumulated income earned outside the U.S. by providing an 85% dividend received deduction for certain dividends from controlled foreign corporations. A $500 million repatriation was made during the quarter ending May 31, 2006 comprised of both foreign earnings for which U.S. taxes has previously been provided and foreign earnings that had been designated as permanently reinvested. Accordingly, the provisions made did not have a material impact on the Company's income tax expense or effective tax rate for the years ended May 31, 2006 and 2005.

The Company has indefinitely reinvested approximately $850.0 million of the cumulative undistributed earnings of certain foreign subsidiaries. Such earnings would be subject to U.S. taxation if repatriated to the U.S. The amount of unrecognized deferred tax liability associated with the permanently reinvested cumulative undistributed earnings was approximately $154.6 million.

Deferred tax assets at May 31, 2006 and 2005 were reduced by a valuation allowance relating to tax benefits of certain foreign subsidiaries with operating losses where it is more likely than not that the deferred tax assets will not be realized.

A deferred tax asset has been recorded for foreign tax credit carryforwards of $9.5 million at May 31, 2006 which expire by the year ended May 31, 2016.

During the years ended May 31, 2006, 2005, and 2004, income tax benefits attributable to employee stock option transactions of $54.2 million, $63.1 million, and $47.2 million, respectively, were allocated to shareholders' equity.

H. J. Heinz 2006 Annual Report

7. Income Taxes

The following table summarizes the provision/(benefit) for U.S. federal, state and foreign taxes on income from continuing operations.

	2006	2005	2004
	(Dollars in thousands)		
Current:			
U.S. federal	$ 71,533	$ 65,905	$ 67,401
State	14,944	9,128	7,119
Foreign	225,498	169,629	180,815
	311,975	247,662	255,340
Deferred:			
U.S. federal	(54,957)	45,020	59,394
State	3,015	3,144	3,606
Foreign	(9,333)	3,685	33,777
	(61,275)	51,849	96,777
Provision for income taxes	$250,700	$299,511	$352,117

Tax benefits related to stock options and other equity instruments recorded directly to additional capital totaled $6.7 million in Fiscal 2006, $10.5 million in Fiscal 2005 and $4.4 million in Fiscal 2004. The components of income from continuing operations before income taxes consist of the following:

	2006	2005	2004
	(Dollars in thousands)		
Domestic	$ 87,409	$385,926	$ 332,010
Foreign	606,052	601,589	735,558
From continuing operations	$693,461	$987,515	$1,067,568

The differences between the U.S. federal statutory tax rate and the Company's consolidated effective tax rate on continuing operations are as follows:

	2006	2005	2004
	(Dollars in thousands)		
U.S. federal statutory tax rate	35.0%	35.0%	35.0%
Tax on income of foreign subsidiaries	(5.9)	(7.9)	(3.7)
State income taxes (net of federal benefit)	1.8	0.9	0.8
Earnings repatriation	4.3	(0.5)	1.6
Losses (recognized)/not recognized for tax	2.7	3.7	(1.0)
Other	(1.7)	(0.9)	0.3
Effective tax rate	36.2%	30.3%	33.0%

The increase in the effective tax rate in Fiscal 2006 is primarily the result of increased costs of repatriation including the effects of the AJCA, a reduction in tax benefits associated with tax planning, increased costs associated with audit settlements and the write-off of investment in affiliates for which no tax benefit could be recognized, offset by the reversal of valuation allowances, the benefit of increased profits in lower tax rate jurisdictions and a reduction in tax reserves. The Fiscal 2005 effective tax rate was favorably impacted by changes to the capital structure in certain foreign subsidiaries, tax credits resulting from tax planning associated with a change in certain foreign tax legislation, reduction of the charge associated with remittance of foreign dividends and the settlement of tax audits, partially offset by impairment charges for Hain, an e-commerce business venture, and other operating losses for which no tax benefit can currently be recorded. The Fiscal 2004 effective tax rate was unfavorably impacted by 0.4 percentage points due to the sale of the Northern Europe bakery business.

The following table and note summarize deferred tax (assets) and deferred tax liabilities as of May 3, 2006 and April 27, 2005.

	2006	2005
	(Dollars in thousands)	
Depreciation/amortization	$582,543	$ 470,758
Benefit plans	155,052	141,888
Other	47,314	106,409
Deferred tax liabilities	784,909	719,055
Operating loss carryforwards	(70,192)	(56,044)
Benefit plans	(140,810)	(105,467)
Investments	(18,904)	(27,434)
Tax credit carryforwards	(54,897)	(36,243)
Other	(74,388)	(90,834)
Deferred tax assets	(359,191)	(316,022)
Valuation allowance	30,950	70,248
Net deferred tax liabilities	$456,668	$473,281

The Company also has foreign deferred tax assets and valuation allowances of $128.2 million each, related to statutory increases in the capital tax bases of certain internally generated intangible assets for which the probability of realization is remote.

The Company records valuation allowances to reduce deferred tax assets to the amount that is more likely than not to be realized. When assessing the need for valuation allowances, the Company considers future taxable income and ongoing prudent and feasible tax planning strategies. Should a change in circumstances lead to a change in judgment about the realizability of deferred tax assets in future years, the Company would adjust related valuation allowances in the period that the change in circumstances occurs, along with a corresponding increase or charge to income.

The resolution of tax reserves and changes in valuation allowances could be material to the Company's results of operations for any period, but is not expected to be material to the Company's financial position.

The net change in the Fiscal 2006 valuation allowance shown above is a decrease of $39.3 million. The decrease was primarily due to the reversal of valuation allowances of $27.3 million in continuing operations related to the non-cash asset impairment charges recorded in Fiscal 2005 on the cost and equity investments discussed above. The net change in the Fiscal 2005 valuation allowance shown above is an increase of $50.6 million. The increase was primarily due to increases in the valuation allowance related to additional deferred tax assets for loss carryforwards of $43.8 million. The net change in the Fiscal 2004 valuation allowance was a decrease of $43.2 million. This decrease was primarily due to a decrease in deferred tax assets for foreign tax credit and loss carryforwards.

At the end of Fiscal 2006, foreign operating loss carryforwards totaled $200.7 million. Of that amount, $128.6 million expire between 2007 and 2016; the other $72.1 million do not expire. Deferred tax assets of $9.7 million have been recorded for state operating loss carryforwards. These losses expire between 2007 and 2026. Foreign tax credit carryforwards total $54.9 million and expire between 2013 and 2015.

Undistributed earnings of foreign subsidiaries considered to be indefinitely reinvested amounted to $2.5 billion at May 3, 2006.

During the third quarter of Fiscal 2004, the Company reorganized certain of its foreign operations, resulting in a step-up in the tax basis of certain assets. As a consequence, the Company incurred a foreign income tax liability of $125 million, which was offset by an equal amount of a prepaid tax asset. The tax liability was paid in the third quarter of Fiscal 2005. The prepaid tax asset is being amortized to tax expense to match the amortization of the stepped up tax basis in the assets. As a result of the step-up, the Company expects to realize a tax benefit in excess of the tax liability paid. Accordingly, cash flow and tax expense are expected to improve by $120 million over the amortization period. Also during the third quarter of Fiscal 2004, the Company filed suit seeking a refund of federal income tax related to a transaction completed in Fiscal 1995. Receipt of the refund would have a positive effect on the Company's cash flow. The tax effect of the refund would be credited to additional paid-in capital, except for any interest allowed which would be credited to tax expense.

Tidewater 2006 Annual Report

(4) Income Taxes

Earnings before income taxes derived from United States and international operations for the years ended March 31 are as follows:

(In thousands)	2006	2005	2004
United States	$126,533	(4,505)	(52,590)
International	196,979	104,301	107,093
Expected life in years	$323,512	99,795	54,503

Income tax expense for the years ended March 31 consists of the following:

(In thousands)	U.S. Federal	State	International	Total
2006				
Current	$ 4,153	(340)	28,383	32,196
Deferred	56,916	–	(1,356)	55,560
	$ 61,069	(340)	27,027	87,756
2005				
Current	$ (3,339)	57	35,605	32,323
Deferred	(32,066)	–	(1,801)	(33,867)
	$(35,405)	57	33,804	(1,544)
2004				
Current	$ 346	504	28,625	29,475
Deferred	(14,671)	–	(1,963)	(16,634)
	$ (14,325)	504	26,662	12,841

The actual income tax expense for the years ended March 31, 2006, 2005, and 2004 differs from the amounts computed by applying the U.S. federal statutory tax rate of 35% to pre-tax earnings as a result of the following:

(In thousands)	2006	2005	2004
Computed "expected" tax expense	$113,229	34,928	19,076
Increase (reduction) resulting from:			
Foreign income taxed at different rates	(19,158)	–	–
Foreign tax credits not previously recognized	(1,356)	(1,801)	(1,963)
Overaccrual of prior year taxes on certain foreign earnings	–	(579)	(2,500)
Utilization of net operating loss carryforwards	–	(4)	(1)
Current foreign earnings not subject to taxation	(879)	(1,810)	(2,100)
Expenses which are not deductible for tax purposes	97	124	118
State taxes	(221)	37	328

(In thousands)	2006	2005	2004
Effect of reversal of previously recorded deferred taxes on timing differences of non-U.S. subsidiaries	–	(31,772)	–
Other, net	(3,956)	(667)	(117)
	$ 87,756	(1,544)	12,841

The company's fiscal 2006, 2005 and 2004 effective annual tax rate was 27.1%, (1.6%) and 23.6%, respectively.

The tax effects of temporary differences that give rise to significant portions of the deferred tax assets and deferred tax liabilities at March 31, 2006 and 2005 are as follows:

(In thousands)	2006	2005
Deferred tax assets:		
Financial provisions not deducted for tax purposes	$ 21,972	19,145
Domestic net operating loss carryforwards	–	46,601
Tax credit carryforwards	13,117	31,811
Other	381	381
Gross deferred tax assets	35,470	98,224
Less valuation allowance	–	–
Net deferred tax assets	35,470	98,224
Deferred tax liabilities:		
Depreciation and amortization	(174,615)	(183,359)
Other	(652)	(1,051)
Gross deferred tax liabilities	(175,267)	(184,410)
Net deferred tax liabilities	$(139,797)	(86,186)

The provisions of the American Jobs Creation Act of 2004 (the Act), were effective for the company as of April 1, 2005, and allowed the company to omit recording deferred tax assets or liabilities on future undistributed earnings of most non-U.S. subsidiaries and business ventures that it considers indefinitely reinvested abroad. At March 31, 2005, the company reversed all previously recorded deferred tax assets and liabilities related to timing differences, foreign tax credits, or prior undistributed earnings of these entities whose future and prior earnings are now anticipated to be indefinitely reinvested abroad. This resulted in an approximate $31.8 million reduction of income tax expense in the fourth quarter of fiscal 2005.

The company has not recognized a U.S. deferred tax liability associated with temporary differences related to investments in foreign subsidiaries that are essentially permanent in duration. The differences relate primarily to undistributed earnings and stock basis differences. Though the company does not anticipate repatriation of funds, a current U.S. tax liability would be recognized when the company receives those foreign funds in a taxable manner such as through receipt of dividends or sale of investments. As of March 31, 2006, the total amount for which U.S. deferred taxes have not been recognized is approximately $265.3 million. A determination of the unrecognized deferred tax liability for temporary differences related to investments in foreign subsidiaries is not practicable due to uncertainty regarding the use of foreign tax credits which would become available as a result of a transaction. The American Jobs Creation Act of 2004 provides for a special one-time tax deduction of 85% of certain foreign earnings that are repatriated in either fiscal 2005 or 2006. The company has evaluated the repatriation provision, and consistent with its decision to reinvest all future earnings of its foreign subsidiaries, has concluded that the repatriation of unremitted foreign earnings provides no benefit to the company, and has no effect on income tax expense as reported.

As of March 31, 2006, the company has foreign tax credit carry-forwards approximating $12.0 million that expire in 2014 through 2015.

The company receives a tax benefit that is generated by certain employee stock benefit plan transactions. This benefit is recorded directly to additional paid-in-capital and does not reduce the company's effective income tax rate. The tax benefit for the years ended March 31, 2006, 2005 and 2004 totaled approximately $4.1 million, $0.8 million and $0.7 million, respectively.

Energizer Holdings 2006 Annual Report

4. Income Taxes

The provisions for income taxes consisted of the following for the years ended September 30:

	2006	2005	2004
Currently payable:			
United States—Federal	$63.7	$ 71.4	$62.6
State	3.6	5.3	5.1
Foreign	51.7	46.9	37.3
Total current	119	123.6	105.0
Deferred:			
United States—Federal	(15.8)	(12.3)	(5.1)
State	(0.6)	(1.7)	(1.5)
Foreign	(6.9)	(1.6)	(11.6)
Total deferred	(23.3)	(15.6)	(18.2)
Provision for income taxes	$95.7	$108.0	$86.8

The source of pre-tax earnings was:

	2006	2005	2004
United States	$160.2	$150.6	$156.2
Foreign	196.4	238.1	191.6
Pre-tax earnings	$356.6	$388.7	$347.8

A reconciliation of income taxes with the amounts computed at the statutory federal rate follows:

	2006		2005		2004	
Computed tax at federal statutory rate	$124.8	35.0%	$136.0	35.0%	$121.7	35.0%
State income taxes, net of federal tax benefit	1.9	0.5	3.0	0.8	3.0	0.9
Foreign tax less than the federal rate	(17.7)	(5.0)	(27.4)	(7.0)	(26.1)	(7.5)
Foreign benefits recognized related to prior years' losses	(5.7)	(1.6)	(14.7)	(3.8)	(16.2)	(4.7)
Adjustments to prior year tax accruals	(10.9)	(3.1)	(10.6)	(2.7)	(8.5)	(2.4)
Taxes on repatriation of foreign earnings under provisions of the American Jobs Creation Act	–	–	9.0	2.3	–	–
Other taxes on repatriation of foreign earnings	4.5	1.3	9.4	2.4	10.7	3.1
Other, net	(1.2)	(0.3)	3.3	0.8	2.2	0.6
Total	$ 95.7	26.8%	$108.0	27.8%	$ 86.8	25.0%

In 2006, 2005 and 2004, $5.7, $14.7 and $16.2, respectively, of tax benefits related to prior years' losses were recorded. These benefits related to foreign countries where our subsidiary subsequently began to generate earnings and could reasonably expect future profitability sufficient to utilize tax loss carryforwards prior to expiration. Improved profitability in Mexico, Germany and Switzerland account for the bulk of the amount recognized in 2006, 2005 and 2004, respectively.

Adjustments were recorded in each of the three years to revise previously recorded tax accruals to reflect refinement of tax attribute estimates to amounts in filed returns, settlement of tax audits and changes in estimates related to uncertain tax positions in a number of jurisdictions. Such adjustments decreased the income tax provision by $10.9, $10.6 and $8.5 in 2006, 2005 and 2004, respectively.

The American Jobs Creation Act of 2004 (AJCA) introduced a special one-time dividends received deduction on the repatriation of certain foreign earnings to a U.S. taxpayer. The repatriation of foreign earnings following the criteria prescribed by the AJCA generated an additional tax provision in fiscal 2005 of $9.0.

The deferred tax assets and deferred tax liabilities recorded on the balance sheet as of September 30 are as follows and include current and non-current amounts:

	2006	2005
Deferred tax liabilities:		
Depreciation and property differences	$(80.8)	$(87.8)
Intangible assets	(41.7)	(38.5)
Pension plans	(30.9)	(39.0)
Other tax liabilities	(3.2)	(4.8)
Gross deferred tax liabilities	(156.6)	(170.1)
Deferred tax assets:		
Accrued liabilities	63.9	62.2
Deferred and stock-related compensation	69.7	57.5
Tax loss carryforwards and tax credits	24.0	29.1
Intangible assets	36.7	42.1
Postretirement benefits other than pensions	28.4	29.9
Inventory differences	18.9	18.1
Other tax assets	31.2	31.2
Gross deferred tax assets	272.8	270.1
Valuation allowance	(10.7)	(15.1)
Net deferred tax assets	$105.5	$ 84.9

There were no tax loss carryforwards that expired in 2006. Future expirations of tax loss carryforwards and tax credits, if not utilized, are as follows: 2007, $0.3; 2008, $0.2; 2009, $1.0; 2010, $1.3; 2011, $10.6; thereafter or no expiration, $10.6. The valuation allowance is attributed to tax loss carryforwards and tax credits outside the U.S. The valuation allowance decreased $4.4 in 2006 primarily due to projected utilization in future years that are deemed more likely than not, partially offset by additional deferred tax assets deemed unlikely to be realized.

At September 30, 2006, approximately $235 of foreign subsidiary net earnings was considered permanently invested in those businesses. U.S. income taxes have not been provided for such earnings. It is not practicable to determine the amount of unrecognized deferred tax liabilities associated with such earnings.

Smucker's
2005 Annual Report

Note Q: Income Taxes

Deferred income taxes reflect the tax effects of temporary differences between the carrying amounts of assets and liabilities for financial reporting purpose and the amount used for income tax reporting. Significant components of the Company's deferred tax assets and liabilities are as follows:

	April 30,	
	2005	*2004*
Deferred tax liabilities:		
Intangible assets	**$130,711**	$115,433
Depreciation and amortization	**68,228**	35,575
Other (each less than five percent of total liabilities)	**13,816**	7,396
Total deferred tax liabilities	**212,755**	158,404
Deferred tax assets:		
Loss carryforwards	**$ 64,160**	**$ 256**
Employee benefits	**41,237**	18,510
Tax credit carryforwards	**12,139**	–
Intangible assets	**7,103**	1,860
Other (each less than five percent of total assets)	**13,109**	3,949
Total deferred tax assets	**$137,748**	$ 24,575
Valuation allowance for deferred tax assets	**(24,280)**	(266)
Total deferred tax assets less allowance	**$113,468**	$ 24,309
New deferred tax liability	**$ 99,287**	$134,095

The Company acquired a number of tax loss and credit carryforwards as a result of the Multifoods acquisition. The valuation allowance for deferred tax assets at April 30, 2005, primarily relates to these acquired deferred tax assets.

The following table summarizes domestic and foreign loss carryforwards at April 30, 2005.

	Related Tax Deduction	*Deferred Tax Asset*	*Expiration Date*
Loss carryforwards:			
Federal net operating loss	$141,462	$49,512	2021 to 2024
Federal capital loss	19,779	7,322	2009 to 2010
State net operating loss	101,936	6,959	2006 to 2027
Foreign net operating loss	1,117	367	2011 to 2014
Total loss carryforwards	$264,294	$64,160	

The following table summarizes tax credit carryforwards at April 30, 2005:

	Deferred Tax Asset	*Expiration Date*
Tax credit carryforwards		
Foreign tax credit	$ 9,448	2010 to 2015
Alternative minimum tax credit	2,691	Indefinite
Total tax credit carryforwards	$12,139	

The valuation allowance at April 30, includes approximately $23,195 for the above domestic and foreign loss and tax credit carryforwards.

Domestic income and foreign withholding taxes have not been recorded on undistributed earnings of foreign subsidiaries since these amounts are considered to be permanently reinvested. Any additional taxes payable on the earnings of foreign subsidiaries, if remitted, would be partially offset by domestic tax credits and deductions for foreign taxes already paid.

Income from continuing operations before income taxes is as follows:

	Year Ended April 30,		
	2005	2004	2003
Domestic	$187,707	$169,004	$147,581
Foreign	19,907	8,166	4,129
Income from continuing operations before income taxes	$207,614	$177,170	$151,710

The components of the provision for income taxes are as follows:

	Year Ended April 30,		
	2005	2004	2003
Current:			
Federal	$28,645	$52,604	$53,767
Foreign	4,490	2,692	1,331
State and local	4,772	4,463	6,080
Deferred	36,247	6,113	(3,680)
Total income tax expense— continuing operations	$74,154	$65,872	$57,498
Total income tax expense— discontinued operations	$ 4,725	$ 1,597	$ 1,549

A reconciliation of the statutory federal income tax rate and the effective income tax rate follows:

	Year Ended April 30,		
Percent of Pretax Income	2005	2004	2003
Statutory federal income tax rate	35.0%	35.0%	35.0%
Increase (decrease) in income taxes resulting from:			
State and local income taxes, net of federal income tax benefit	1.8	0.7	2.5
Research credits	–	–	–
Other items	(0.6)	1.5	0.5
Effective income tax rate	36.2%	37.2%	37.9%
Income taxes paid	$60,359	$70,927	$45,052

Saks Incorporated
2005 Annual Report

Note 7—Income Taxes

The components of income tax expense were as follows:

| | | Restated | |
	2004	2003	2002
Current:			
Federal	$ 13,616	$ 5,688	$ 2,215
State	2,793	3,103	324
	16,409	8,791	2,539
Deferred:			
Federal	23,770	17,062	35,762
State	(17,026)	(4,021)	899
	6,744	13,041	36,661
Total expense	$ 25,153	$ 21,832	$39,200

Components of the net deferred tax asset or liability recognized in the consolidated balance sheets were as follows:

| | Restated | |
	January 29, 2005	January 31, 2004
Current:		
Deferred tax assets:		
Accrued expenses	$ 52,302	$ 49,622
NOL carryforwards	142,578	39,943
Valuation allowance	(6,508)	(4,629)
Deferred tax liabilities:		
Inventory	(9,814)	(8,334)
Net current deferred asset	$178,558	$ 76,602
Non-current:		
Deferred tax assets:		
Capital leases	$ 29,087	$ 26,417
Other long-term liabilities	100,014	79,138
AMT credit carryforwards	16,317	13,291
NOL carryforwards	172,193	267,335
Valuation allowance	(59,000)	(162,912)
Deferred tax liabilities:		
Property and equipment	(78,922)	(93,403)
Other assets	(13,325)	(9,524)
Net non-current deferred tax asset	$166,364	$120,342

As January 29, 2005, the Company has $593,405 of federal net operating loss carryforwards ("NOLs"). This amount considers the fact the the carryforwards are restricted under federal income tax change-in-ownership rules. The carryforwards will expire between 2005 and 2018. The Company believes it will be sufficiently profitable during the periods from 2005 to 2018 to utilize all of its federal NOLs and a significant portion of its existing state NOLs and a valuation allowance has been established against that portion that the Company currently does not anticipate being able to utilize based on current projections.

During 2004, the Company re-analyzed certain deferred tax assets related to the acquisition of Carson's, specifically those that are attributable to the period when Carson's reorganized under the Bankruptcy Code and are accounted for in accordance with Statement of Position No. 90-7 (SOP9-7), Financial Reporting by Entities in Reorganization Under the Bankruptcy Code. AOP 90-7 states that benefits realized from deferred taxes should be reported as an addition to paid-in capital. Based on the analysis, the Company released a portion of its valuation allowance and the net realizable value of the asset was credited to Shareholder's Equity. In addition, the Company analyzed its state NOLs by jurisdiction and determined that the deferred tax rate applicable to state corresponding increase to the valuation allowance.

As noted above, a valuation allowance has been established against a portion of the Company's existing NOLs. During 2004, the valuation allowance was reduced by $20,638 based on projections of future profitability, which include a gain related to the sale of the Proffitts business in 2005. Of this amount $10,138 was recorded as an income tax benefit and the remaining $10,500 was credited to Shareholders' Equity.

Income tax expense varies from the amount computed by applying the statutory federal income tax rate to income before taxes. The reasons for this difference were as follows:

		Restated	
	2004	2003	2002
Expected federal income taxes at 35%	$29,483	$32,968	$17,954
State income taxes, net of federal benefit	1,936	299	194
Amortization of goodwill	–	–	15,957
Reduction of valuation allowance against state NOL's	(10,138)	–	–
Deferred tax asset for AMT credit carryforwards	–	(4,474)	–

		Restated	
	2004	*2003*	*2002*
Effect of setting tax exams and other tax reserve adjustments .	2,555	(7,187)	1,156
Effect of deductibility of tax reserve interest	–	1,132	2,759
Other items, net	(683)	(906)	1,180
Provision for income taxes	$23,153	$21,832	$39,200

During 2004, the statue of limitations expired with respect to certain tax examination periods. This resulted in a reduction of $4,586 to the Company's reserve for tax exposures which was credited to Shareholder's Equity in accordance with SOP 90-7. In addition, the Company re-assessed its uncertain federal and state tax filing positions in accordance with FAS #5, Accounting for Contingencies. This resulted in an increase to its reserve for tax exposures of $2,555.

During 2003 and 2002, the Company favorably concluded a number of tax examinations, many of which addressed corporate organization changes that had occurred over the previous five years in conjunction with the Company's multiple acquisitions. In 2003, the effect of the favorable conclusion of tax examinations was an income tax benefit of $7,187 and a credit to Shareholder's Equity of $3,923. In 2002, the effect of the favorable conclusion of the tax examination and the related corporate organization changes was to reduce the asset representing the state tax benefit of tax basis differences ($18,883), and to reduce the liability representing exposures associated with various state and federal tax positions (37,800).

The Company made income tax payments, net of refunds received of $1,939, $4,485 and $1,134 during 2004, 2003 and 2002, respectively.

Proctor & Gamble
2005 Annual Report

Note 9—Income Taxes

Under SFAS No. 109, "Accounting for Income Taxes," income taxes are recognized for the amount of taxes payable for the current year end for the impact of deferred tax liabilities and assets, which represent future tax consequences of events that have been recognized differently in the financial statements than for tax purposes. Deferred tax assets and liabilities are established using the enacted statutory tax rates and are adjusted for changes in such rates in the period of changes.

Earning before income taxes consisted of the following:

| | Years ended June 30 | | |
	2005	2004	2003
United States	$ 6,543	$6,023	$4,920
International	3,896	3,327	2,610
	10,439	9,350	7,530

Management judgment is required in determining tax provisions and evaluating tax positions. Management believes its tax positions and related provisions reflected in the consolidated financial statements are fully supportable. We establish reserves for additional income taxes that may be challenged by local authorities and may not be fully sustained, despite out belief that the underlying tax positions are fully supportable. In such cases, the reserves for additional taxes are based on management's best estimate of the ultimate outcome. These reserves are reviewed on an ongoing basis and are adjusted in light of changing facts and circumstances, including progress on tax audits, changes in interpretations of tax laws, developments in case law and closing of statutes of limitations. Our tax provision includes the impact of recording reserves and any changes thereto. We have a number of tax audits in process and have open tax years with various significant taxing jurisdictions that range primarily from 1993 to 2005. Although the results of current tax audits and adjustments from other tax positions related to open tax years have not been finalized, we believe based on currently available information that the ultimate outcomes will have a material adverse effect on our financial position, results of operations or cash flows.

The income tax provision consisted of the following:

| | Years ended June 30 | | |
	2005	2004	2003
Current Tax Expense	$1,491	$1,508	$1,595
U.S. Federal	898	830	588
International	143	116	98
U.S. State and Local	2,532	2,454	2,281
Deferred Tax Expense			
U.S. Federal	294	348	125
International and other	356	67	(62)
	650	415	63
Total Tax Expense	3,182	2,869	2,344

A reconciliation of the U.S. federal statutory income tax rate to our actual income tax rate is provided below:

| | Years ended June 30 | | |
	2005	2004	2003
U.S. Federal statutory income tax rate	35.0%	35.0%	35.0%
Country mix impacts of foreign operations	−4.9%	−4.1%	−3.0%
AJCA repatriation tax charge	2.8%	–	–
Income tax reserve reversals	−2.3%	–	−1.4%
Other	−0.1%	−0.2%	0.5%
Effective income tax rate	**30.5%**	30.7%	31.1%

Taxes impacted shareholders' equity with credits of $275 and $351 for the years ended June 30, 2005 and 2004, respectively. These primarily relate to the tax effects of net investment hedges and the minimum pension liability and tax benefits from the exercise of stock options.

The American Jobs Creation Act of 2004 (the "AJCA") permits U.S. corporations to repatriate earnings of foreign subsidiaries at a one-time favorable effective federal statutory tax rate of 5.25% as compared to the highest corporate tax rate of 35%. We plan to repatriate approximately $7.2 billion in earnings previously considered indefinitely invested. The income tax expense associated with this repatriation is $295 for the year ended June 30, 2005.

We have undistributed earnings of foreign subsidiaries of approximately $10.3 billion at June 30, 2005, for which deferred taxes have not been provided. Such earnings are considered indefinitely invested in the foreign subsidiaries. If such earnings were repatriated, additional tax expense may result, although the calculation of such additional taxes is not practicable. The amount of unremitted earnings for which no tax has been provided decreased in 2005 due to our repatriation plan under the AJCA.

Deferred income tax assets and liabilities were comprised of the following:

| | June 30 | |
	2005	2004
Deferred Tax Assets		
Unrealized loss on financial and foreign exchange transactions	$ 503	$ 436
Loss and other carryforwards	406	365
Advance payments	257	226
Pension and postretirement benefits	295	95
Accrued marketing and promotion expense	137	81
Fixed assets	127	134
Other	900	986
Valuation allowances	(386)	(342)
Total	2,239	1,981
Deferred Tax Liabilities		
Fixed assets	(1,487)	(1,437)

| | June 30 | |
	2005	*2004*
Goodwill and other intangible assets	**(1,396)**	(1,281)
AJCA repatriation	**(303)**	–
Other	**(597)**	(352)
Total	**(3,783)**	(3,070)

Net operating loss carryforwards were $1,418 and $1,398 at June 30, 2005 and June 30, 2004, respectively. If unused, $505 will expire between 2006 and 2025. The remainder, totaling $913 at June 30, 2005, may be carried forward indefinitely.

Walt Disney
2004 Annual Report

Note 7. Income Taxes

	2004	*2003*	*2002*
Income Before Income Taxes, Minority Interests and the Cumulative Effect of Accounting Change			
Domestic (including U.S. exports)	**$3,279**	$1,802	$1,832
Foreign subsidiaries	**460**	452	358
	$3,739	$2,254	$2,190
Income Tax (Benefit) Provision			
Current			
Federal	**$ 835**	$ (55)	$ 137
State	**90**	39	55
Foreign (including withholding)	**350**	317	257
	1,275	301	449
Deferred			
Federal	**(103)**	448	372
State	**25**	40	32
	(78)	488	404
	$1,197	$ 789	$853
Components of Deferred Tax Assets and Liabilities			
Deferred tax assets			
Accrued liabilities	**$(1,412)**	$(1,255)	
Foreign subsidiaries	**(842)**	(269)	
Retirement benefits	**(22)**	(193)	
Loss and credit carry forwards	**(30)**	(80)	

	2004	*2003*	*2002*
Other, net	–	(17)	
Total deferred tax assets	**(2,306)**	(1,814)	
Deferred tax liabilities			
Depreciable, amortizable and other property	**3,818**	3,036	
Licensing revenues	**214**	132	
Leveraged leases	**261**	312	
Investment in Euro Disney	–	298	
Other, net	**117**	–	
Total deferred tax liabilities	**4,410**	3,778	
Net deferred tax liability before valuation allowance	**2,104**	1,964	
Valuation allowance	**74**	74	
Net deferred tax liability	**$2,178**	$2,038	
Reconciliation of Effective Income Tax Rate			
Federal income tax rate	**35.0%**	35.0%	35.0%
State taxes, net of federal benefit	**2.0**	2.3	2.6
Dispositions	–	0.4	–
Impact of audit settlements	**(3.2)**	(2.5)	–
Foreign sales corporation and extraterritorial income	**(2.6)**	(3.1)	(3.1)
Other, including tax reserves and related interest	**0.8**	2.9	4.4
	32.0%	35.0%	38.9%

Deferred tax assets at September 30, 2004 and 2003 were reduced by a valuation allowance relating to a portion of the tax benefits attributable to certain net operating losses (NOLs) reflected on state tax returns of Infoseek and its subsidiaries for periods prior to the Infoseek acquisition on November 18, 1999 where applicable state laws limit the utilization of such NOLs. In addition, deferred tax assets at September 30, 2004 and 2003 were reduced by a valuation allowance relating to a portion of the tax benefits attributable to certain NOLs reflected on tax returns of ABC Family Worldwide, Inc. and its subsidiaries for periods prior to the ABC Family acquisition on October 24, 2001 (see Note 3). Since the valuation allowances associated with both acquisitions relate to acquired deferred tax assets, the subsequent realization of these tax benefits would result in adjustments to the allowance amount being applied as reductions to goodwill. In addition, at September 30, 2004, approximately $42 million of other acquired NOL carry forwards from the acquisition of ABC Family are available to offset future taxable income through the year 2022.

In 2004, 2003, and 2002, income tax benefits attributable to employee stock option transactions of $25 million, $5 million, and $8 million, respectively, were allocated to shareholders' equity.

In 2004, the Company derived tax benefits of $97 million from an exclusion provided under U.S. income tax laws with respect to certain extraterritorial income attributable to foreign trading gross receipts ("FTGRs"). This exclusion was repealed as part of the American Jobs Creation Act of 2004 (the "Act"), which was enacted on October 22, 2004. The Act provides for a phase-out such that the exclusion for the Company's otherwise qualifying FTGRs generated in fiscal 2005, 2006, and 2007 will be limited to approximately 85%, 65%, and 15%, respectively. No exclusion will be available in fiscal years 2008 and thereafter.

The Act makes a number of other changes to the income tax laws which will affect the Company in future years, the most significant of which is a new deduction for qualifying domestic production activities. The impact of this and other changes made by the Act cannot be quantified at this time.

As a matter of course, the Company is regularly audited by federal, state and foreign tax authorities. From time to time, these audits result in proposed assessments. During the fourth quarter of fiscal 2004, the Company reached a settlement with the Internal Revenue Service regarding all assessments proposed with respect to the Company's federal income tax returns for 1993 through 1995. This settlement resulted in the Company releasing $120 million in tax reserves which are no longer required with respect to these matters. This release of reserves is reflected in the current year income tax provision. During the fourth quarter of fiscal 2003, the Company resolved certain state income tax audit issues and the corresponding release of $56 million of related tax reserves is reflected in the 2003 income tax provision.

Mylan Laboratories
2005 Annual Report

Note 9. Income Taxes

Income taxes consist of the following components:

(in thousands) Fiscal year ended March 31,	2005	2004	2003
Federal:	**$134,994**	$133,223	$156,823
Current	**(34,513)**	30,549	(18,127)
Deferred	**100,481**	163,772	138,696
State and Puerto Rico:			
Current	**10,560**	12,501	17,211
Deferred	**(2,386)**	1,726	(1,747)
	8,174	14,227	15,464
Income taxes	**$108,655**	$177,999	$154,160
Pretax earnings	**$312,247**	$512,608	$426,513
Effective tax rate	**34.8%**	34.7%	36.1%

Temporary differences and carryforwards that result in the deferred tax assets and liabilities are as follows at March 31:

(in thousands)	2005	2004
Deferred tax assets:		
Employee benefits	$ 10,301	$ 9,824
Contractual agreements	–	–
Intangible assets	10,615	9,721
Accounts receivable allowances	113,267	75,301
Inventories	3,587	1,852
Investments	6,003	8,099
Federal tax loss carryforwards	–	–
Tax credit carryforwards	–	–
Other	1,117	656
Total deferred tax assets	144,890	105,453
Deferred tax liabilities:		
Plant and equipments	22,848	19,271
Intangible assets	25,946	27,915
Investments	1,569	2,394
Other	105	–
Total deferred tax liabilities	50,486	49,580
Deferred tax asset, net	$ 94,422	$ 55,873
Classification in the consolidated Balance Sheets:		
Deferred income tax benefit-current	$119,327	$ 78,477
Deferred income tax liability-noncurrent	24,905	22,604
Deferred tax asset, net	$ 94,422	$ 55,873

Deferred tax assets relating to net operating loss carryforwards and research and development tax credit carryforwards were acquired in fiscal 1999 with the acquisition of Penederm. The utilization of these assets is subject to certain limitations set forth in the U.S. Internal Revenue Code. In fiscal 2003, the Company utilized approximately $10,709,000 of acquired federal net operating loss $2,707,000 and federal tax credit carryforwards of $2,092,000.

Federal research and development tax credits of $567,000 that were deferred at March 31, due to tax law changes, were applied for and received in fiscal 2004.

A reconciliation of the statutory tax rate to the effective tax rate is as follows:

Fiscal year ended March 31,	2005	2004	2003
Statutory tax rate	35.0%	35.0%	35.0%
State and Puerto Rico income taxes	2.8%	2.7%	3.3%
State and Puerto Rico tax credits	(1.3%)	(0.7%)	(0.7%)
Federal tax credits	(2.1%)	(1.8%)	(1.8%)
Other items	0.4%	(0.5%)	0.3%
Effective income tax rate	34.8%	34.7%	36.1%

Federal tax credits result principally from operations in Puerto Rico and from qualified research and development expenditures, including orphan drug research. State tax credits are comprised mainly of awards for expansion and wage credits at our manufacturing facilities and research credits awarded by certain states. State income taxes and state tax credits are shown net of the federal tax effect.

Operations in Puerto Rico benefit from incentive grants from the government of Puerto Rico, which partially exempt the Company extending tax incentives until fiscal 2010. This grant exempts all earnings during this grant period from tollgate tax upon repatriation of cash to the United States. In fiscal 2004, $100,000,000 of cash from post-fiscal 2000 earnings was repatriated to the United States. Pursuant to the terms of our new tax grant, no tollgate tax was due for this repatriation.

Under Section 936 of the U.S. Internal Revenue Code, Mylan is a "grandfathered" entity and is entitled to the benefits under such statute through fiscal 2006. Our Section 936 federal tax credits totaled approximately $3,874,000 in fiscal 2005 and $4,732,000 each year in fiscal 2004 and 2003.

Our federal income tax returns have been audited by the Internal Revenue Service through fiscal 2000. We are currently under audit by the Internal Revenue Service for fiscal year 2002 through 2004.

Rockwell Automation
2005 Annual Report

16. Income Taxes

The components of the income tax provision are as follows (in millions):

	2005	2004	2003
Current:			
United States	$ 50.8	$ 32.3	$(35.4)
Non-United States	56.6	(5.8)	28.7
State and local	(4.6)	(6.1)	(3.5)
Total current	102.8	20.4	(10.2)
Deferred:			
United States	112.0	53.4	23.3
Non-United States	(5.8)	6.0	(0.3)
State and local	9.6	4.2	3.4
Total deferred	115.8	63.6	26.4
Income tax provision	$218.6	$ 84.0	$ 16.2

During 2005, we recognized a net tax benefit of $19.7 million in income from continuing operations and $21.6 million in income from discontinued operations related to current and former businesses. The net tax benefits included in income from continuing operations are primarily related to the resolution of claims and other tax matters in connection with the closure of the federal audit cycle for the years 1998 through 2002. In addition, these net tax benefits include the effect of the true-up of estimated tax audit contingency accruals in connection with closure of the 1998 through 2002 audit. The net tax benefits included in discontinued operations relate primarily to the closure of the 1998 through 2002 audit ($7.5 million), a prior year state tax refund of a divested business ($11.3 million) and the resolution of various other tax matters of divested businesses ($2.8 million).

During 2004, we recognized tax benefits of $46.3 million in income from continuing operations and $18.4 million in income from discontinued operations related to the following items:

☐ $34.5 million resulting from the resolution of certain tax matters, in part related to former businesses. A majority of the benefits recognized related to non-U.S. tax matters in addition to an agreement with a taxing authority related to the treatment of an investment. Of this amount, $11.5 million is reflected as a reduction of the United States income tax provision; $21.3 million is reflected as a reduction of the non-United States income tax provision; and $1.7 million is reflected as reduction of the state and local income tax provision;

☐ $4.3 million related to additional state tax benefits associated with the U.S. research and experimentation credit refund claim in 2003 (see discussion below); and,

☐ $25.9 million related to a refund from the State of California for the period 1989 to 1991. Of this amount, $7.5 million is included as a reduction in the income tax provision and $18.4 million is included in Income from discontinued operations.

During 2003, we recognized in earnings a tax benefit of $69.4 million related to a federal research and experimentation credit refund claim for the years 1997 through 2001. Of this amount, $66.4 million is reflected as a reduction of the United States income tax provision and $3.0 million is reflected as a reduction of the state and local income tax provision.

Net current deferred income tax assets in September 30, 2005 and 2004 consist of the tax effects of temporary differences related to the following (in millions):

	2005	2004
Compensation and benefits	$ 56.3	$ 20.5
Product warranty costs	12.9	11.3
Inventory	25.7	26.4
Allowance for doubtful accounts	12.3	11.1
Net operating loss carryforwards	3.5	3.5
State tax credit carryforwards	1.3	1.1

	2005	2004
Other—net	57.4	58.8
Current deferred income tax assets	$169.4	$132.7

Net long-term deferred income tax assets/(liabilities) at September 30, 2005 and 2004 consist of the tax effects of temporary differences related to the following (in millions):

	2005	2004
Retirement benefits	$ 152.6	$ 135.0
Property	(105.4)	(125.2)
Intangible assets	(30.2)	(22.1)
Net operating loss carryforwards	31.6	19.4
Capital loss carryforwards	46.5	58.4
State tax credit carryforwards	11.9	9.1
Other—net	14.8	0.5
Subtotal	121.8	75.1
Valuation allowance	(55.5)	(63.0)
Long-term deferred income tax assets	$ 66.3	$ 12.1

Total deferred tax assets were $426.8 million at September 30, 2005 and $355.1 million at September 30, 2004. Total deferred tax liabilities were $135.6 million at September 30, 2005 and $147.3 million at September 30, 2004.

We reclassified our tax audit accrual as of September 30, 2004 from Deferred income taxes (non-current) to Other liabilities in the Consolidated Balance Sheet. The reclassification resulted in a remaining net non-current deferred tax asset of $12.1 million at September 30, 2004, which is reported as a non-current asset in the Consolidated Balance Sheet.

We believe it is more likely than not that we will realize current and long-term deferred tax assets through the reduction of future taxable income, other than as reflected below for tax attributes to be carried forward. Significant factors we considered in determining the probability of the realization of the deferred tax assets include: (a) our historical operating results ($261.0 million of United States taxable income over the past three years), (b) expected future earnings, and (c) the extended period of time over which the retiree medical benefits will be paid.

	Tax Benefit Amount	Valuation Allowance	Carryforward Period Ends
Non-United States net operating loss . . .	$ 2.2	$ (2.2)	2008-2012
Non-United States net operating loss . . .	17.5	(7.3)	Indefinite
Non-United States capital loss	29.8	(29.1)	Indefinite

	Tax Benefit Amount	Valuation Allowance	Carryforward Period Ends
United States net operating loss	1.7	–	2019-2025
United States capital loss	16.7	(16.7)	2007-2009
State and local net operating loss	13.7	(0.2)	2006-2025
State tax credit	13.2	–	2006-2020
Total	$94.8	$(55.5)	

We have a valuation allowance at September 30, 2005 as noted above for carryforwards for which future use is uncertain.

During 2005, the valuation allowance decreased by $7.5 million as a result of a basis adjustment in connection with the filing of the 2004 income tax return related to the sale of FirstPoint Contact and the recording of a valuation allowance for non-U.S. net operating losses.

We operate in numerous taxing jurisdictions and are subject to regular examinations by various U.S. Federal, state and foreign jurisdictions for various tax periods. Additionally, we have retained tax liabilities and the rights to tax refunds in connection with various divestitures of businesses in prior years. Our income tax positions are based on research and interpretations of the income tax laws and rulings in each of the jurisdictions in which we do business. Due to the subjectivity of interpretations of laws and rulings in each jurisdiction, the differences and interplay in tax laws between those jurisdictions as well as the inherent uncertainty in estimating the final resolution of complex tax audit matters, our estimates of income tax liabilities may differ from actual payments or assessments.

Cross jurisdictional transactions between our subsidiaries involving the transfer price for products, services, and/or intellectual property as well as various U.S. state tax matters comprise our more significant income tax exposures. We regularly assess our position with regard to tax exposures and record liabilities for these uncertain tax positions and related interest and penalties, if any, according to the principles of SFAS No. 5, *Accounting for Contingencies*. We have recorded an accrual of $103.1 million and $111.7 million at September 30, 2005 and 2004, respectively, that reflects our estimate of the likely outcome of current and future audits and is recorded in Other liabilities in our Consolidated Balance Sheet. The change in the accrual reflects a reduction of $34.6 million related primarily to settlement of the 1998 - 2002 U.S. federal audit, offset by an increase of $26.0 million to the accrual for changes in estimates and additional interest related to previously identified income tax exposures. A final determination of these tax audits or changes in our estimates may result in additional future income tax expense or benefit.

The effective income tax rate differed from the United States statutory tax rate for the reason set forth below:

	2005	2004	2003
Statutory tax rate	35.0%	35.0%	35.0%
State and local income taxes	2.1	2.8	1.3
Non-United States taxes	(0.5)	(3.0)	0.6
Foreign tax credit utilization	(0.9)	(0.2)	(0.8)
Employee stock ownership plan benefit	(0.5)	(0.9)	(1.4)
Tax refund claims	(1.6)	(3.7)	(2.4)
Utilization of foreign loss carryforwards	(0.1)	(0.3)	(1.0)
Utilization of capital loss carryforwards	–	0.8	(1.7)
Tax benefits on export sales	(0.9)	(2.1)	(0.8)
Research and experimentation refund claim	–	(2.3)	(23.3)
Resolution of prior period tax matters	(4.2)	(8.3)	0.6
Other	1.3	1.4	(0.7)
Effective income tax rate	29.7%	19.2%	5.4%

We calculated the income tax provisions based upon the following components of income from continuing operations before income taxes (in millions):

	2005	2004	2003
United States income	$610.0	$319.8	$205.6
Non-United States income	127.0	118.3	92.0
Total	$737.0	$438.1	297.6

We have not provided U.S. deferred taxes on cumulative earnings of non-U.S. affiliates that have been reinvested indefinitely. These earnings relate to ongoing operations and at September 30, 2005, were approximately $510.0 million. Because of the availability of U.S. foreign tax credits, it is not practicable to determine the U.S. or state income tax liabilities that would be payable if such earnings were not reinvested indefinitely. Deferred taxes are provided for non-U.S. affiliates when we plan to remit those earnings. Income taxes paid were $134.8 million during 2005, $30.0 million during 2004 and $84.5 million during 2003.

Microsoft
2005 Annual Report

Note 10. Income Taxes

The components of the provision for income taxes are as follows:

(In millions) Year Ended June 30	2003	2004	2005
Current taxes:			
U.S. federal	$(3,708)	$3,766	$3,401
U.S. state and local	153	174	152

(In millions) Year Ended June 30	2003	2004	2005
International	808	1,056	911
Current taxes	4,669	4,996	4,464
Deferred taxes	(1,146)	(968)	(90)
Provision for income taxes	$(3,523)	$4,028	$4,374

U.S. and international components of income before income taxes are as follows:

(In millions) Year Ended June 30	2003	2004	2005
U.S.	$ 7,674	$ 8,088	$ 9,806
International	3,380	4,108	6,822
Income before income taxes	$11,054	$12,196	$16,628

The items accounting for the difference between income taxes computed at the federal statutory rate and the provision for income taxes are as follows:

Year Ended June 30	2003	2004	2005
Federal statutory rate	35.0%	35.0%	35.0%
Effect of:			
IRS examination settlement	–	–	(4.7)
Foreign earnings taxed at lower rates	(1.3)	(1.7)	(3.1)
Extraterritorial income exclusion	(1.6)	(0.9)	(1.3)
Other reconciling items	–	0.6	0.4
Effective rate	32.1%	33.0%	26.3%

The 2005 other reconciling items include a $179 million repatriation tax benefit. The 2004 other reconciling items include the $208 million benefit from the resolution of the issue remanded by the Ninth Circuit Court of Appeals and the impact of the $605 million non-deductible European Commission fine.

The components of the deferred tax assets and liabilities are as follows:

(In millions) June 30	2004	2005
Deferred income tax assets:		
Unearned revenue	$ 1,746	$ 915
Impaired investments	1,246	861
Stock-based compensation expense	3,749	3,994
Other revenue items	286	213
Other expense items	1,308	1,751

(In millions)		
Other	–	173
Deferred income tax assets	$ 8,335	$ 7,907
Deferred income tax liabilities:		
Unrealized gain on investments	$(1,087)	$(1,169)
International earnings	(1,327)	(1,393)
Other	(16)	(23)
Deferred income tax liabilities	(2,430)	(2,585)
Net deferred income tax assets	$ 5,905	$ 5,322
Reported as:		
Current deferred tax assets	$ 2,097	$ 1,701
Long-term deferred tax assets	3,808	3,621
Net deferred income tax assets	$ 5,905	$ 5,322

Deferred income tax balances reflect the effects of temporary differences between the carrying amounts of assets and liabilities and their tax bases and are stated at enacted tax rates expected to be in effect when taxes are actually paid or recovered.

We have not provided for U.S. deferred income taxes or foreign withholding taxes on $4.1 billion of our undistributed earnings for certain non-U.S. subsidiaries, all of which relate to fiscal 2002 through 2005 earnings, because these earnings are intended to be permanently reinvested in operations outside the United States.

The American Jobs Creation Act of 2004 (the "Act") was enacted in October 2004. The Act creates a temporary incentive for U.S. corporations to repatriate foreign subsidiary earnings by providing an elective 85% dividends received deduction for certain dividends from controlled foreign corporations. The deduction is subject to a number of limitations and requirements, including adoption of a specific domestic reinvestment plan for the repatriated funds. Based on our current understanding of the Act and subsequent guidance published by the U.S. Treasury, we have determined that we are eligible and intend to repatriate approximately $780 million in dividends subject to the elective 85% dividends received deduction. Accordingly, we recorded a corresponding tax provision benefit of $179 million from the reversal of previously provided U.S. deferred tax liabilities on these unremitted foreign subsidiary earnings. We intend to pay this dividend in fiscal year 2006.

Income taxes paid were $2.8 billion in fiscal year 2003, $2.5 billion in fiscal year 2004, and $4.3 billion in fiscal year 2005.

Tax Contingencies. We are subject to income taxes in the United States and numerous foreign jurisdictions. Significant judgment is required in determining our worldwide provision for income taxes and recording the related assets and liabilities. In the ordinary course of our business, there are many transactions and calculations where the ultimate tax determination is uncertain. We are regularly under audit by tax authorities. Accruals for tax contingencies are provided for in accordance with the requirements of SFAS No. 5, *Accounting for Contingencies.*

The Internal Revenue Service (IRS) has completed and closed its audits of our consolidated federal income tax returns through 1996. We recently entered into a closing agreement with the IRS for tax years 1997 through 1999 resulting in certain adjustments to our federal income tax liability for those years. Accordingly, our fiscal year 2005 tax provision has been reduced by $776 million as a result of reversing previously established reserves in excess of the additional tax liability assessed by the IRS for the 1997–1999 tax years. The IRS is currently conducting an audit of our consolidated federal income tax return for tax years 2000 through 2003.

Although we believe we have appropriate support for the positions taken on our tax returns, we have recorded a liability for our best estimate of the probable loss on certain of these positions, the non-current portion of which is included in other long-term liabilities. We believe that our accruals for tax liabilities are adequate for all open years, based on our assessment of many factors including past experience and interpretations of tax law applied to the facts of each matter, which matters result primarily from intercompany transfer pricing, tax benefits from the Foreign Sales Corporation and Extra Territorial Income tax rules and the amount of research and experimentation tax credits claimed. Although we believe our recorded assets and liabilities are reasonable, tax regulations are subject to interpretation and tax litigation is inherently uncertain; therefore our assessments can involve both a series of complex judgments about future events and rely heavily on estimates and assumptions. Although we believe that the estimates and assumptions supporting our assessments are reasonable, the final determination of tax audits and any related litigation could be materially different than that which is reflected in historical income tax provisions and recorded assets and liabilities. Based on the results of an audit or litigation a material effect on our income tax provision, net income, or cash flows in the period or periods for which that determination is made could result. Due to the complexity involved we are not able to estimate the range of reasonably possible losses in excess of amounts recorded.

Dell
2005 Annual Report

Note 3—Income Taxes

The provision for income taxes consists of the following:

	Fiscal Year Ended		
	January 28, 2005	January 30, 2004	January 31, 2003
	(in millions)		
Current:			
Domestic	$ 984	$ 969	$702
Foreign	209	132	94

	Fiscal Year Ended		
	January 28, 2005	*January 30, 2004*	*January 31, 2003*
Tax repatriation charge	280	–	–
Deferred	(71)	(22)	109
Provision for income taxes	$1,402	$1,079	$905

Income before income taxes included approximately $2.4 billion, $1.6 billion, and $968 million related to foreign operations in Fiscal 2005, 2004, and 2003, respectively. On October 22, 2004, the American Jobs Creation Act of 2004 (the "Act") was signed into law. Among other items, the Act creates a temporary incentive for U.S. multinationals to repatriate accumulated income earned outside the U.S. at a tax rate of 5.25%, versus the U.S. federal statutory rate of 35%. Although the Act contains a number of limitations related to the repatriation and some uncertainty remains, as of January 28, 2005 Dell believes that it has the information necessary to make an informed decision regarding the impact of the Act on its repatriation plans. Based on this new legislation, and subsequent guidance issued by the Department of Treasury, Dell determined during the fourth quarter of Fiscal 2005 that it will repatriate $4.1 billion in foreign earnings. Accordingly, Dell recognized a tax repatriation charge of $280 million in accordance with SFAS No. 109, *Accounting for Income Taxes*. This tax charge includes an amount relating to an apparent drafting oversight that Congressional leaders indicate will be fixed by a Technical Corrections Bill sometime during calendar year 2005. The fiscal 2005 tax repatriation charge will be reduced in the quarter that the Technical Corrections Bill becomes law. In addition, at the time of repatriation further adjustment may be required depending upon a number of factors, including geographic location of cash, mix of foreign earnings, and statutory tax rates in effect at the time of the repatriation. The repatriation is required to be completed by the end of fiscal 2006. This tax repatriation charge increased Dell's effective tax rate by 6.3% for fiscal 2005.

Deferred taxes have not been provided on excess book basis in the amount of approximately $2.9 billion in the shares of certain foreign subsidiaries because these basis differences are not expected to reverse in the foreseeable future and are essentially permanent in duration. These basis differences arose primarily through the undistributed book earnings of the subsidiaries that Dell intends to reinvest indefinitely. The basis differences could reverse through a sale of the subsidiaries, the receipt of dividends from the subsidiaries as well as various other events. Net of available foreign tax credits, residual income tax of approximately $740 million would be due upon a reversal of this excess book basis. The excess book basis of $2.9 billion excludes the $4.1 billion to be repatriated under the Act. The components of Dell's net deferred tax asset are as follows:

	January 28, 2005	January 30, 2004
	(in millions)	
Deferred tax assets:	$ 241	$ 86
Deferred revenue	232	260
Inventory and warranty provisions	23	39
Investment impairments and unrealized gains	22	21
Provisions for product returns and doubtful accounts	6	96
Capital loss	–	69
Leasing	99	104
Other	623	675
Deferred tax liabilities:	(156)	(129)
Fixed assets	(10)	–
Leasing	(26)	(74)
Other	(192)	(203)
Net deferred tax assets	$ 431	$ 472
Current portion (included in other current assets)	425	339
Non-current portion (included in other non-current assets)	6	133
Net deferred tax assets	431	472

A portion of Dell's operations operate at a reduced tax rate or free of tax under various tax holidays which expire in whole or in part during fiscal 2012 through 2019. Many of these holidays may be extended when certain conditions are met. The income tax benefits attributable to the tax status of these subsidiaries were estimated to be approximately $280 million ($0.11 per share) in fiscal 2005, $210 million ($0.08 per share) in fiscal 2004, and $137 million ($0.05 per share) in fiscal 2003.

The effective tax rate differed from the statutory U.S. federal income tax rate as follows:

	Fiscal Year Ended		
	January 28, 2005	January 30, 2004	January 31, 2003
U.S. Federal statutory rate	35.0%	35.0%	35.0%
Foreign income taxed at different rates	(11.6)	(7.3)	(7.9)
Tax repatriation charge	6.3	–	–
Other	1.8	1.3	2.8
Effective tax rate	31.5%	29.0%	29.9%

The increase in Dell's fiscal 2005 effective tax rate, compared to fiscal 2004 and fiscal 2003, is due to the aforementioned tax repatriation charge, partially offset by a higher proportion of operating profits attributable to foreign jurisdictions.

QLogic
2005 Annual Report

Note 12. Income Taxes

Income before income taxes consists of the following components:

	2005	2004	2003
		(In thousands)	
United States	$242,019	$216,127	$159,276
Foreign	340	(526)	(57)
	$242,359	$215,601	$159,219

The components of the income tax provision are as follows:

	2005	2004	2003
		(In thousands)	
Current:			
Federal	$70,330	$57,770	$42,220
State	16,060	8,896	7,609
Foreign	14	(158)	–
Total current	86,404	66,508	49,809
Deferred:			
Federal	(1,570)	13,550	6,174
State	(77)	1,870	(237)
Foreign	6	–	–
Total deferred	(1,641)	(15,420)	(5,937)
Total income tax provision	$84,763	$81,928	$55,746

The tax benefits associated with dispositions from employee stock compensation plans of approximately $2.4 million, $10.6 million and $6.0 million in Nscal 2005, 2004 and 2003, respectively, were recorded directly to additional paid-in capital.

A reconciliation of the income tax provision with the amount computed by applying the federal statutory tax rate to income before income taxes is as follows:

	2005	2004	2003
		(In thousands)	
Expected income tax provision at the statutory rate	$84,826	$75,460	$55,727
State income taxes, net of federal tax benefit .	10,389	6,998	4,792
Benefit from research and other credits	(1,668)	(1,759)	(2,500)

	2005	2004	2003
		(In thousands)	
Benefit from export sales	(3,147)	(3,185)	(3,465)
Nondeductible business combination related costs	2,119	3,841	2,246
Reversal of taxes previously accrued	(8,253)	–	–
Tax exempt income	(275)	(161)	(358)
Other, net	772	734	(696)
	$84,763	$81,928	$55,746

The tax effects of temporary differences that give rise to significant portions of the deferred tax assets and liabilities are as follows:

	2005	2004
	(In thousands)	
Deferred tax assets:		
Reserves and accruals not currently deductible .	$18,459	$14,701
Net operating loss carryforwards	3,822	4,675
State taxes	4,343	2,706
Acquired in-process technology	1,730	1,930
Research credits	857	701
Property and equipment	–	461
Unrealized losses on investment	1,854	–
Other	16	278
Total gross deferred tax assets	$31,081	$25,452
Deferred tax liabilities:		
Research and development expenditures	5,367	4,512
Property and equipment	1,279	–
Unrealized gains on investments	–	–
Total gross deferred tax liabilities	6,646	6,901
Net deferred tax assets	$24,435	$18,551

Based upon the Company's current and historical pre-tax earnings, management believes it is more likely than not that the Company will realize the benefit of the existing net deferred tax assets as of April 3, 2005. Management believes the existing net deductible temporary differences will reverse during periods in which the Company generates net taxable income or that there would be sufficient tax carry backs available; however, there can be no assurance that the Company will generate any earnings or any specific level of continuing earnings in future years.

As of April 3, 2005, the Company has federal net operating loss carryforwards of approximately $10.1 million and aggregate state net operating loss carryforwards of approximately $3.8 million. The federal net operating loss carryforwards expire on various dates between 2011 and 2020. The aggregate state net operating loss carryforwards expire on various dates between 2006 and 2015. All net operating loss carryforwards relate to acquired companies and are subject to limitations on their utilization.

As of April 3, 2005, the Company has state tax credit carryforwards of approximately $1.3 million. If not utilized, the state tax credit carryforwards will begin to expire in 2014. Approximately $0.3 million of the state tax credits carryforwards relate to acquired companies and are subject to limitations on their utilization.

The Company's California combined income tax returns for the 2000, 2001 and 2002 fiscal years are presently under review by the Franchise Tax Board. Management does not expect a material impact on the consolidated material statements from this review.

Oracle
2003 Annual Report

14. Income Taxes

The following is a geographical breakdown of income before the provision for income taxes:

		Year Ended May 31,	
(Dollars in millions)	2003	2002	2001
Domestic	$1,925	$2,131	$2,661
Foreign	1,500	1,277	1,310
Total	$3,425	$3,408	$3,971
The provision for income taxes consists of the following:			
Current provision:			
Federal	$ 546	$ 831	$ 954
State	100	97	119
Foreign	382	416	496
Total current provision	1,028	1,344	1,569
Deferred provision (benefit):			
Federal	120	(132)	(139)
State	(15)	(33)	(11)
Foreign	(15)	5	(9)
Total deferred provision (benefit)	90	(160)	(159)
Total provision for income taxes	$1,118	$1,184	$1,410
Effective income tax rate	32.6%	34.7%	5.5%

The provision for income taxes differs from the amount computed by applying the federal statutory rate to our income before taxes as follows:

| | Year Ended May 31, | | |
(Dollars in millions)	2003	2002	2001
Tax provision at statutory rate	$1,199	$1,193	$1,390
Foreign earnings at other than United States rates	(214)	(133)	(77)
State tax expense, net of federal benefit	68	88	104
Other, net	65	36	(7)
Provision for income taxes	$1,118	$1,184	$1,410

The components of the deferred tax assets and liabilities, as reflected on the consolidated balance sheets, consist of the following:

| | Year Ended May 31, | |
(Dollars in millions)	2003	2002
Deferred tax liabilities:		
Unrealized gain on stock	$(178)	$(194)
Other	(8)	(56)
Total deferred tax liabilities	(186)	(250)
Deferred tax assets:		
Accruals and allowances	269	235
Differences in timing of revenue recognition	98	96
Depreciation and amortization	63	71
Foreign tax credits	6	94
Employee compensation and benefits	79	70
Other	63	168
Total deferred tax assets	578	734
Valuation allowance	–	(3)
Net deferred tax asset	$ 392	$ 481
Recorded as:		
Current deferred tax assets	$ 381	$ 452
Non-current deferred tax assets	197	233
Non-current deferred tax liabilities	(186)	(204)
Net deferred tax asset	392	$ 481

Under FASB Statement No. 109, *Accounting for Income Taxes*, deferred tax assets and liabilities are determined based on differences between financial reporting and tax bases of assets and liabilities, and are measured using the enacted tax rates and laws that will be in effect when the differences are expected to reverse. Statement 109 provides for the recognition of deferred tax assets if realization of such assets is more likely than not. We evaluate the realizability of the deferred tax assets on a quarterly basis.

We provide for United States income taxes on the earnings of foreign subsidiaries unless they are considered permanently invested outside the United States. At May 31, 2003, the cumulative earnings upon which United States income taxes have not been provided for were approximately $3.1 billion. If these earnings were repatriated in the United States, they would generate foreign tax credits that could reduce the Federal tax liability associated with the foreign dividend. Assuming a full utilization of the foreign tax credits, the potential deferred tax liability for these earnings would be $690.7 million.

At May 31, 2003, we had net operating loss carryforwards, resulting in a $10.9 million deferred tax asset, which originated from acquired domestic subsidiaries. We expect to utilize all of these loss carryforwards, which expire between 2004 and 2019. We also have loss carryforwards of $71.5 million in certain foreign subsidiaries, resulting in deferred tax assets of approximately $21.3 million, which expire at various dates: $2.4 million in 2005, $11.4 million in 2007, $8.4 million in 2008, $1.7 million in 2010, $9.6 million in 2011, $6.1 in 2013 and the remaining balance of $31.9 million has no expiration.

The Internal Revenue Service has examined our federal tax returns for all years through 1995 without any material adjustment of additional taxes due. The IRS is currently examining our United States income tax returns for 1996 through 1999. We do not believe that the outcome of these matters will have a material adverse effect on our consolidated results of operations or consolidated financial position.

Our intercompany transfer prices are currently being reviewed by the IRS and by foreign tax jurisdictions and will likely be subject to additional audits in the future. We previously negotiated two Advance Pricing Agreements with the IRS that cover many of our intercompany transfer prices and preclude the IRS from making a transfer pricing adjustment within the scope of these agreements. The agreements, however, are only effective through May 31, 2001, do not cover all elements of our transfer pricing and do not bind tax authorities outside the United States. We are currently negotiating bilateral and unilateral Advance Pricing Agreements to cover the period from June 1, 2001 to May 31, 2006.

Rite Aid
2005 Annual Report

Income Taxes

The provision for income taxes was as follows:

	Year Ended		
	February 26, 2005	February 28, 2004	March 1, 2003
Current tax expense (benefit)			
Federal	$ 1,405	$(41,140)	$(44,011)
State	14,092	5,766	2,071
	15,497	(35,374)	(41,940)

	Year Ended		
	February 26, 2005	February 28, 2004	March 1, 2003
Deferred tax (benefit)			
Federal	$(176,031)	$(13,421)	–
State	(7,937)	–	–
	(183,968)	(13,421)	–
Total income tax (benefit)	(168,471)	(48,795)	(41,940)

A reconciliation of the expected statutory federal tax and the total income tax benefit is as follows:

	Year Ended		
	February 26, 2005	February 28, 2004	March 1, 2003
Expected federal statutory expense (benefit) at 35%	$ 46,903	$ 12,083	$(58,660)
Nondeductible compensation ...	99	2,375	940
Other nondeductible expenses ..	2,974	981	1,693
State income taxes, net	4,001	1,962	(10,726)
Recoverable federal tax and reduction of previously recorded liabilities	–	(56,663)	–
Other	–	–	–
Valuation allowance	(222,448)	(9,533)	24,134
Total income tax benefit	(168,471)	(48,795)	(41,940)

The income tax benefit for fiscal 2005 includes $179,538 related to the reduction of the valuation allowance on federal and state net deferred tax assets that have an expected future utilization and were fully reserved prior to fiscal 2005.

The income tax benefit for fiscal 2004 includes $54,561 primarily representing recoverable federal and state income taxes and interest as well as a reduction of previously recorded liabilities related to the conclusions of the Internal Revenue Service examination of fiscal years 1996 through 2000.

The income tax benefit for fiscal 2003 includes $44,011 arising from enacted federal law extending the net operating loss carryback period from two to five years.

The tax effect of temporary differences that give rise to significant components of deferred tax assets and liabilities consist of the following at February 26, 2005 and February 28, 2004:

	2005	2004
Deferred tax assets:		
Accounts receivable	$ 68,572	$ 18,511
Accrued expenses	69,061	91,838
Liability for lease exit costs	91,037	101,492
Pension, retirement and other benefits	185,660	150,647
Investment impairment	28,782	34,296
Long-lived assets	139,514	121,919
Credits	81,922	75,332
Net operating loses	1,079,521	1,142,937
Total gross deferred tax assets	1,744,069	1,736,972
Valuation allowance	(1,436,570)	(1,650,967)
Net deferred tax assets	307,499	86,005
Deferred tax liabilities		
Inventory	115,176	83,384
Other	3,052	2,621
Total gross deferred tax liabilities	118,228	86,005
Net deferred tax assets	189,271	–

As a result of the conclusions of the Internal Revenue Service examination cycle for fiscal years 1996 through 2000, components of the net deferred tax assets were adjusted and reclassified in fiscal years 2005 and 2004. The Company continues to be examined by state taxing authorities for the above tax years and management believes there are adequate reserves for remaining federal and state income taxes.

Net Operating Losses, Capital Losses and Tax Credits

At February 26, 2005, the Company had federal net operating loss (NOL) carryforwards of approximately $2,330,000, the majority of which expire between fiscal 2019 and 2022. The Company underwent an ownership change for statutory tax purposes during fiscal 2002, which resulted in a limitation on the future use of net operating loss carryforwards. This limitation was considered when the valuation allowance was established.

At February 26, 2005 the Company had state NOL carryforwards of approximately $3,488,000, the majority of which will expire between fiscal 2015 and 2022.

At February 26, 2005, the Company had a capital loss carryforward of $680,144 which will expire, if not offset by future capital gains, between fiscal 2006 and 2008.

At February 26, 2005, the Company had federal business tax credit carryforwards of $52,229, the majority of which expire between fiscal 2013 and 2025. In addition to these credits, the Company has alternative minimum tax credit carryforwards of $7,964.

Valuation Allowances

The valuation allowances as of February 26, 2005 and February 28, 2004 apply to the net deferred tax assets of the Company. Until the fourth quarter of fiscal 2005, the Company provided a full valuation allowance against its net deferred tax assets. Based upon a review of a number of factors, including the Company's historical operating performance and its expectation that it can generate sustainable consolidated taxable income for the foreseeable future, the Company now believes it is more likely than not that a portion of these deferred tax assets will be utilized. Based upon the Company's expected future utilization, a portion of the valuation allowance at year end was reduced resulting in a non-cash tax benefit of $179,538 during fiscal 2005. An additional reduction in the valuation allowance of $5,293 was recorded as additional paid-in capital in fiscal 2005 to reflect the tax benefit associated with previously recorded stock based compensation. The Company continues to maintain a valuation allowance of $1,436,570 against remaining net deferred tax assets at fiscal year end 2005.

ArvinMeritor
2004 Annual Report

21. Income Taxes

The components of the Provision for Income Taxes are summarized as follows (in millions):

	2004	2003	2002
Current tax expense (benefit):			
U.S.	$16	$25	$(13)
Foreign	8	61	84
State and local	1	(5)	(2)
Total current tax (benefit) expense	25	81	69
Deferred tax expense (benefit):			
U.S.	(28)	16	11
Foreign	38	(53)	(44)
State and local	9	1	(3)
Total deferred tax (benefit) expense	19	(36)	(36)
Provision for Income Taxes	$44	$45	$33

The deferred tax expense or benefit represents tax effects of current year deductions or items of income that will be recognized in future periods for tax purposes. The deferred tax benefit primarily represents the tax benefit of current year net operating losses and tax credits carried forward.

Net current deferred income tax assets included in the consolidated balance sheet consist of the tax effects of temporary differences related to the following (in millions):

	September 30,	
	2004	*2003*
Compensation and benefits	$55	$50
Product warranties	23	20
Inventories	(3)	(9)
Receivables	12	6
Other, net	10	13
Net current deferred income taxes asset	$97	$80

Net non-current deferred income tax assets included in the consolidated balance sheet consist of the tax effects of temporary differences related to the following (in millions):

	September 30,	
	2004	*2003*
Retiree medical liability	$87	$90
Loss and tax credit carry forwards	388	285
Pension liability	53	76
Taxes on undistributed income	(55)	(53)
Property	(27)	(14)
Intangible assets	3	34
Other, net	13	59
Subtotal	462	447
Valuation allowance	(93)	(62)
Net non-current deferred income taxes—asset	$369	$415

Net deferred current and non-current deferred income tax assets are included in the consolidated balance sheet as follows (in millions):

	September 30,	
	2004	*2003*
Other current asset (see Note 9)	$117	$ 89
Other current liabilities (see Note 13)	(20)	(9)
Net current deferred income taxes—asset	97	80
Other assets (see Note 11)	428	462
Other liabilities (see Note 14)	(59)	(47)
Net non-current deferred income taxes—asset	$369	$415

Management believes it is more likely than not that current and non-current deferred tax assets will reduce future income tax payments. Significant factors considered by management in its determination of the probability of the realization of the deferred tax benefits include: (a) historical operating results, (b) expectations of future earnings, and (c) the extended period of time over which the retirement medical and pension liabilities will be paid. The valuation allowance represents the amount of tax benefits related to net operating loss and tax credit carry forwards, which management believes are not likely to be realized. The carry forward periods for $251 million of net operating losses and tax credit carry forwards expire between fiscal 2005 and 2024. The carry forward period for the remaining net operating losses and tax credits is indefinite. The company's effective tax rate was different from the U.S. statutory rate for the reasons set forth below:

	2004	2003	2002
Statutory tax rate	35.0%	35.0%	35.0%
State and local income taxes	(3.5)	(3.1)	(2.5)
Foreign income taxes	(11.9)	(5.4)	(9.6)
Tax audit settlements	–	(3.7)	–
Recognition of basis differences	(14.7)	(22.1)	(1.4)
Tax on undistributed foreign earnings	2.0	4.1	1.9
Valuation allowance	19.6	19.9	2.6
Other	(1.9)	5.3	(2.4)
Effective tax rate	24.6%	30.0%	23.6%

For Fiscal 2004, the significant benefit for recognition of basis differences was related to the following items:(a) favorable book and tax basis differences on the sale of APA, (b) favorable impact of recently issued IRS regulations supporting recoverability of previously disallowed capital losses, and (c) utilization of previously unrecognized capital losses associated with our Brazilian restructuring. For Fiscal 2003, the significant benefit was primarily due to a restructuring of certain Brazilian operations which increased the long-term deferred tax asset associated with intangible assets.

The income tax provisions were calculated based upon the following components of income before income taxes (in millions):

	2004	2003	2002
U.S. income	$ 17	$ 31	$ 28
Foreign income	162	119	112
Total	$179	$150	$140

For fiscal 2004 and 2003, no provision has been made for U.S., state or additional foreign income taxes related to approximately $665 million and $406 million, respectively of undistributed earnings of foreign subsidiaries that have been or are intended to be permanently reinvested.

Hormel Foods
2004 Annual Report

Note G

Income Taxes

The components of the provision for income taxes are as follows:

(In Thousands)	2004	2003	2002
Current:			
U.S. Federal	**$133,882**	$97,855	$91,590
State	**13,794**	8,908	9,798
Foreign	**880**	1,381	208
Total Current	**148,556**	108,144	101,596
Deferred:			
U.S. Federal	**(12,931)**	(4,533)	2,882
State	**(2,723)**	(59)	170
Total Deferred	**(15,654)**	(4,592)	3,052
Total Provision for Income Taxes	**$132,902**	$103,552	$104,648

Deferred income taxes reflect the net tax effects of temporary differences between the carrying amounts of assets and liabilities for financial reporting purposes and the amounts used for income tax purposes. The company believes that, based upon its lengthy and consistent history of profitable operations, it is probable that the net deferred tax assets of $24.9 million will be realized on future tax returns, primarily from the generation of future taxable income. Significant components of the deferred income tax liabilities and assets are as follows:

(In Thousands)	October 30, 2004	October 25, 2003
Deferred tax liabilities:		
Prepaid pension	**$(60,306)**	$(52,802)
Tax over book depreciation	**(53,985)**	(48,237)
Book/tax basis difference from acquisition	**(35,227)**	(35,889)
Other, net	**(35,766)**	(27,477)
Deferred tax assets:		
Postretirement benefits	**100,064**	94,842
Pension accrual	**15,889**	13,609
Deferred compensation	**13,825**	11,845
Supplemental pension accrual	**9,902**	6,624
Insurance accruals	**6,062**	5,773
Vacation accrual	**6,182**	5,606
Other, net	**58,290**	29,876
Net Deferred Tax Assets	**$ 24,930**	$ 3,770

Reconciliation of the statutory federal income tax rate to the company's effective tax rate is as follows:

	2004	2003	2002
U.S. statutory rate	35.0%	35.0%	35.0%
State taxes on income, net of federal tax benefit	2.0	2.0	2.2

	2004	2003	2002
All other, net	(0.5)	(1.2)	(1.6)
Effective Tax Rate	36.5%	35.8%	35.6%

In fiscal 2004, the company received a $9.0 million cash distribution from a foreign subsidiary under the provisions of the American Job Creation Act. The provisions of the Act provide for a one-time repatriation of foreign earnings of an affiliate at a net 5.25%tax rate if the earnings are repatriated under a Qualified Domestic Reinvestment Plan.

U.S. income taxes have not been provided on remaining undistributed earnings of foreign subsidiaries, which were approximately $24.6 million as of October 30, 2004. The company has reinvested such earnings overseas in foreign operations indefinitely and expects that future earnings will also be reinvested overseas indefinitely.

Total income taxes paid during fiscal 2004, 2003, and 2002 were $138.8 million, $76.4 million, and $101.3 million, respectively.

Solectron
2003 Annual Report

Note 10. Income Taxes

The components of income taxes (benefit) from continuing operations for the fiscal periods included in this report are as follows:

	2003	2002	2001
Current:			
Federal	$21.5	$(186.6)	$11.9
State	3.2	3.5	2.6
Foreign	17.9	17.3	39.2
	42.6	(165.8)	53.7
Deferred:			
Federal	464.8	(212.5)	(78.9)
State	63.5	(53.5)	(14.3)
Foreign	10.1	(51.2)	5.3
	538.4	(317.2)	(87.9)
Total	$581.0	$(483.0)	$(34.2)

The overall effective income tax rate (expressed as a percentage of financial statement loss from continuing operations and before income taxes) varied from the United States statutory income tax rate for all fiscal years presented as follows:

	2003	2002	2001
Federal tax rate	35.0%	35.0%	35.0%
State income tax, net of federal tax benefit	(1.7)	0.9	7.0
Income of international subsidiaries taxed at different rates	(1.9)	(0.7)	(47.1)
Tax holiday	0.5	1.6	59.4
Tax exempt interest income	–	–	4.0
Nondeductible goodwill and acquisition costs	(15.9)	(18.2)	(11.1)
Loss for which no benefit is currently realized	(22.3)	(5.5)	(10.6)
Intercompany interest charges	–	–	(4.9)
Change in beginning valuation allowance	(18.2)	–	–
Other	1.5	0.2	(0.7)
Effective income tax rate	(23.0)%	13.3%	31.0%

The tax effects of temporary differences from continuing operations that gave rise to significant portions of deferred tax assets and liabilities as of August 31, 2003 and 2002 were as follows (in millions):

	2003	2002
Deferred tax assets:		
Accruals and allowances	$ 86.4	$ 240.2
State income tax	52.0	60.6
Acquired intangible assets	487.4	319.5
Depreciation	–	4.4
Net operating loss carryforward and credits	798.3	227.3
Restructuring accruals	34.3	70.7
Other	32.6	–
Deferred tax assets	1,491.0	922.7
Valuation allowance	(1,433.6)	(314.1)
Total deferred tax assets	$ 57.4	$ 608.6
Deferred tax liabilities:		
Foreign inventories expensed for tax	$ –	$ (35.2)
Depreciation	(12.6)	–
Realized translation gains	–	(8.0)
Other	–	(5.7)
Total deferred tax liabilities	(12.6)	(48.9)
Net deferred tax assets	$ 44.8	$ 559.7

Net deferred tax assets were recorded in other assets in the accompanying consolidated balance sheet.

The Company has U.S. federal net operating loss carryforwards arising from continuing operations in its U.S. consolidated group of approximately $864 million. The net operating loss carryforwards, if not utilized, will expire in 2021 through 2023.

As a result of various business acquisitions, the Company had acquired additional U.S. federal net operating loss carryforwards arising from continuing operations from U.S. subsidiaries totaling approximately $105 million, which will expire if not utilized beginning in 2004 through 2021. The annual utilization of these net operating losses is limited under the ownership change provisions of the U.S. Internal Revenue Code.

The Company also has California state net operating losses in its unitary group of approximately $367 million, which will expire if not utilized in 2011 through 2013.

The Company has net operating loss carryforwards in various foreign jurisdictions. A summary of significant foreign net operating loss carryforwards follows (in millions):

Jurisdiction	Amount	Expiration
Brazil	$120.6	Indefinite
Canada	218.6	2004–2010
France	279.4	2004–2008
Germany	83.9	Indefinite
Ireland	62.7	Indefinite
Japan	82.7	2006–2008
Malaysia	81.8	Indefinite
Singapore	71.5	Indefinite
United Kingdom	190.9	Indefinite
Other	240.8	Various

Management has determined that a valuation allowance in the amount of approximately $1.4 billion is required with respect to deferred tax assets. Management believes that it is more likely than not that the remaining deferred tax assets will be realized, principally through carrybacks to taxable income in prior years. In the event the tax benefits relating to the valuation allowance are realized, $14 million of such benefits would reduce goodwill and $13 million would be credited to other comprehensive loss.

Worldwide income (loss) from continuing operations before taxes for all fiscal years presented consisted of the following (in millions):

	2003	2002	2001
U.S	$ (305.0)	$(3,872.8)	$(239.7)
Non-U.S	(2,218.9)	251.7	129.5
Total	$(2,523.9)	$(3,621.1)	$(110.2)

Cumulative undistributed earnings of the international subsidiaries amounted to $630 million as of August 29, 2003, all of which is intended to be permanently reinvested. The amount of deferred income tax liability that would result had such earnings been repatriated is estimated to be approximately $171 million which would be absorbed by a corresponding reversal in valuation allowance.

Solectron has been granted a tax holiday for its Malaysian sites which is effective through July 31, 2011, subject to certain conditions. In addition, Solectron has been granted a tax holiday for certain manufacturing operations in Singapore which is effective through March 2011, subject to certain conditions. Solectron has also been granted various tax holidays in China, which are effective for various terms and are subject to certain conditions. The net impact of these tax holidays was to decrease local country taxes by $45 million ($0.05 per diluted share) in 2003, $37 million ($0.05 per diluted share) in 2002, and $58 million ($0.09 per diluted share) in 2001.

Part III

FOREIGN OPERATIONS AND DERIVATIVE INSTRUMENTS

Chapter 16
Foreign Currency Translation and Transactions

CONTENTS

This chapter discusses the process of translating financial statements from foreign currency into U.S. dollars. It also covers the accounting and reporting of foreign currency transactions. Forward contracts may be entered into for hedging or speculative purposes. A sale or liquidation of an investment in a foreign entity may occur. The tax impact related to foreign currency dealings is also presented. Footnote disclosures are necessary so readers can properly appraise a company's exposure in overseas operations to variability in foreign exchange rates.

ASC 830-10-15, *Foreign Currency Matters: Overall*, requires that the assets, liabilities, and operations of an entity be measured in the functional currency of that business. The pronouncement applies to:

☐ Foreign currency financial statements of divisions, branches, and other investees included in the financial statements of a U.S. company by consolidation, combination, or the equity method.

☐ Foreign currency transactions, including imports and exports denominated in a currency other than the company's functional currency.

An essential purpose in translating foreign currency is to preserve the financial performance and relationships expressed in the foreign currency. This is achieved by using the foreign entity's functional currency. The functional currency is then converted into the reporting entity's reporting currency. It is presumed under ASC 830-10-15 that the reporting currency for a company is U.S.

dollars; however, it is possible that the reporting currency may be other than U.S. dollars.

A U.S. company should usually include the profits from foreign activities in its financial statements only to the degree that it receives funds in the United States or has unrestricted funds available to be transferred to the United States. If losses are expected, they should be provided for. In accounting and reporting of assets located in foreign countries, consideration should be given to possible problems of expropriation or restriction, if any exist.

ASC 946-830-05, *Financial Services—Investment Companies: Foreign Currency Matters*, deals with foreign currency accounting and financial statement presentation for investment companies.

TERMINOLOGY

Key terms in foreign dealings are defined as follows:

Foreign Entity. An operation (e.g., division, subsidiary, branch, joint venture) whose financial statements are prepared in a currency other than the reporting currency of the reporting entity.

Spot Rate The exchange rate for immediate delivery of currencies exchanged.

Conversion. The exchange of one currency for another.

Exchange Ratio. The ratio of one unit of a currency to that of another at a given date. If a temporary lack of exchangeability exists between the two currencies at the transaction date or balance sheet date, the first rate available thereafter should be used.

Foreign Currency Translation. Stating in a company's reporting currency those amounts denominated or measured in a different currency.

Measure. Translating into a currency other than the original reporting currency. Foreign financial statements are expressed in U.S. dollars by using the relevant exchange rate.

Denominate. To pay or receive in the same foreign currency. The account can be denominated only in one currency (e.g., lira). It is a real account (asset or liability) fixed in terms of a foreign currency regardless of the exchange rate.

Local Currency. The currency of a particular foreign country.

Reporting Currency. The currency the business prepares its financial statements in, typically U.S. dollars.

Foreign Currency. A currency other than the functional currency of a business. For example, the dollar could be a foreign currency for a foreign entity. Composites of currencies (e.g., special drawing rights) may be used to establish prices or denominate amounts of loans.

Foreign Currency Transactions. Transactions in which the terms are denominated in a currency other than the entity's functional currency. Foreign currency transactions occur when a company (1) purchases (imports) or sells (exports) on credit merchandise or services the prices being denominated in a foreign currency; (2) buys or sells assets or incurs or settles liabilities denominated in foreign currency; (3) takes out or gives international loans in which the amounts payable or receivable are denominated in a foreign currency; (4) is a participant in an unperformed forward exchange contract; and (5) borrows or lends money, and the amounts payable or receivable are expressed in a foreign currency.

Currency Swap. The exchange between two business entities of the currencies of two different countries in accordance with a contract to re-exchange the two currencies at the same exchange rate at an agreed upon future date.

Functional Currency. A company's functional currency is the currency of the primary economic environment in which the company operates. It is usually the currency of the environment in which the business mostly receives and pays cash. Once determined, the functional currency should be used consistently unless significant changes clearly indicate a change. **Note:** The currency of a highly inflationary environment (three-year rate of 100% or more) is not stable enough to be used for this purpose. In such circumstances, the U.S. dollar is the functional currency. The functional currency of a foreign operation may be the same as that of a related affiliate where a foreign activity is a "key" component or extension of a related affiliate.

If remeasurement (restatement) of a subsidiary's foreign currency financial statements is required before translation can be accomplished (i.e., when the functional currency is the U.S. dollar), a transaction gain or loss results.

Foreign Currency Statements. Financial statements using as the measuring unit a functional currency other than the reporting currency of the business.

Translation Adjustments. Adjustments derived from translating financial statements from the entity's functional currency into the reporting one.

Monetary Assets and Liabilities. Cash, receivables, and obligations to pay a fixed amount of debt.

Nonmonetary Items. All balance sheet items except for cash, claims to cash, and cash obligations.

Transaction Gain or Loss. Transaction gain or loss is produced from redeeming receivables/payables that are fixed in terms of amounts of foreign currency received/paid. An example is a French subsidiary having a receivable denominated in francs from a Swiss customer. A transaction gain or loss takes place when there is a change in exchange rates between the functional currency and the currency in which a foreign currency transaction is denominated. It constitutes an increase or decrease in (1) the actual functional currency cash flows realized upon settlement of foreign currency transactions and (2) the expected functional currency cash flows on unsettled foreign currency transactions.

THE FUNCTIONAL CURRENCY

In most instances, the functional currency is the currency of the country in which the company is located. In other instances, it may be the currency of another country. For example, if a foreign subsidiary's activities are situated within one country, are basically self-contained, and do not rely on the parent's economic environment, the subsidiary's functional currency is the currency of the country in which it is located.

EXAMPLE

If a foreign subsidiary is an independent entity and received cash and incurred expenses in France, the franc is the functional currency.

Conversely, if a foreign subsidiary's daily activities are a direct and important element of the parent's operations and environment, the parent's currency will be the functional currency. If the company carries out major operations in more than one currency, management must determine which currency to use as the functional currency. However, a company may have more than one distinct operation (e.g., branch, division). If conducted in different economic settings, each operation may have a different functional currency.

Before financial statements from a company's functional currency can be translated into the reporting currency, the foreign country figures must be remeasured in the functional currency.

There should be consistent use of the functional currency unless significant economic changes required a change. A change in the functional currency is accounted for as a change in estimate. Previously issued financial statements are not restated for a change in the functional currency. Further, when there is a change in functional currency, the translation adjustments for previous years are still kept as a separate component of stockholders' equity.

If a company's books are not maintained in the functional currency, remeasurement into the functional currency is required. The remeasurement process takes place prior to translation into the reporting currency. When a foreign entity's functional currency is the reporting currency, remeasurement into the reporting currency obviates translation (remeasurement is necessary to account for timing differences). The objective of the remeasurement process is to generate the same result as if the company's books had been kept in the functional currency.

EXAMPLE

A foreign entity's records are maintained in Mexican pesos, but the functional currency is Canadian dollars. The foreign entity's accounts must be remeasured into Canadian dollars before the financial statements are translated into the reporting entity's currency. An ensuing translation gain or loss from Mexican pesos to Canadian dollars is included in the remeasured net profit. However, if the foreign entity's functional currency is the Mexican peso, there is only a need to translate to the reporting currency. If the foreign entity's functional currency is the same as that of the reporting entity, remeasurement is only from the Mexican peso to the reporting currency.

The following guidelines are used to determine the functional currency of a foreign activity:

☐ *Market.* The functional currency is the foreign currency when the foreign activity has a strong local sales market for products or services, even though a substantial amount of exports may arise. The functional currency is the parent's currency when the foreign operation's sales market is primarily in the parent's country.

☐ *Financing.* The functional currency is the foreign currency if financing the foreign activity is in foreign currency and funds obtained by the foreign activity are adequate to meet debt obligations. The functional currency is the parent's currency when financing of foreign activity is provided by the parent or occurs in U.S. dollars. Funds received by the foreign activity are adequate to meet debt requirements.

☐ *Selling Price.* The functional currency is the foreign currency when the foreign operations' selling prices of products or services arise from local factors such as competition and government law. It is not because of changes in exchange rate. The functional currency is the parent's currency when the foreign operation's selling prices mostly apply in the short term to variability in the exchange rate owing to international reasons such as global competition.

☐ *Expenses.* The functional currency is the foreign currency when the foreign operation's manufacturing costs or services are typically incurred locally. However, some foreign imports may exist. The functional currency is the parent's currency when the foreign operations' manufacturing and service costs are mostly component costs obtained from the parent's country.

☐ *Intercompany Transactions.* If there is a limited number of intercompany transactions, the functional currency is the foreign currency—that is, when minor interrelationship occurs between the activities of the parent and foreign entity except for competitive advantages (e.g., patents, trademarks). Conversely, if there are many intercompany transactions, the functional currency is the parent's currency—that is, when substantial interrelationship exists between the parent and foreign entity.

☐ *Cash Flow.* The functional currency is the foreign currency when the foreign operation's cash flows are mostly in foreign currency not directly impacting the parent's cash flow. The functional currency is the parent's currency when the foreign operation's cash flows directly affect the parent's cash flows. Cash flows are typically available for remittance via intercompany accounting settlement.

FOREIGN CURRENCY TRANSACTIONS

Foreign currency transactions may result in receivables or payables fixed in the amount of foreign currency to be received or paid. A foreign currency transaction requires payment in a currency other than the reporting entity's functional currency.

When a transaction is entered into, each asset, liability, revenue, expense, gain, or loss arising from that transaction should be measured and recorded based on the reporting company's functional currency at the exchange rate on that date. At each balance sheet date, balances that will be settled should be brought up to date at the current exchange rate.

A change in exchange rates between the functional currency and the currency in which a transaction is denominated increases or decreases the expected amount of functional currency cash flows upon settlement of the transaction.

The change in expected functional currency cash flows is a foreign currency transaction gain or loss that is presented separately as an element of income from continuing operations in the income statement for the period in which the exchange rate changed. In other words, if the exchange rate changes between the date of a purchase or sale and the time of actual payment or receipt, a foreign exchange transaction gain or loss arises.

EXAMPLE

A transaction may result in a gain or loss when an Italian subsidiary has a receivable denominated in Euros from a Canadian customer. In other words, a transaction gain or loss (measured from the transaction date or the most recent intervening balance sheet date, whichever is later) realized upon settlement of a foreign currency transaction should typically be included in arriving at net income for the period in which the transaction is settled.

EXAMPLE

An exchange gain or loss takes place when the exchange rate changes between the purchase and payment dates. Merchandise is purchased for 300,000 Euros. The exchange rate is 3 Euros to 1 dollar. The journal entry is:

Purchases	$100,000	
Accounts payable		$100,000

300,000 Euros/3 = $100,000

When the goods are paid for, the exchange rate is 3.5 Euros to 1 dollar. The journal entry is:

Accounts payable	$100,000	
Cash		$85,714
Foreign exchange gain		14,286

300,000 Euros/3.5 = $85,714

The $85,714, using an exchange rate of 3.5 to 1, can buy 300,000 Euros. The transaction gain is the difference between the cash required of $85,714 and the initial liability of $100,000.

EXAMPLE

On January 15, 20X1, ABC Company, which uses a perpetual inventory system, shipped merchandise costing $45,000 to XYZ Company, a German company, for 100,000 Euros. On February 15, 20X1, ABC Company received a draft for 100,000 Euros from XYZ Company. The draft was immediately converted. The spot rates were as follows:

	1 Euro =	
	Buying Rate	*Selling Rate*
January 15, 20X1	0.60	0.65
January 31, 20X1	0.65	0.70
February 15, 20X1	0.55	0.60

Assuming that monthly statements are prepared, ABC Company will make the following journal entries:

1/15/20X1 Accounts receivable		
[100,000 Euros × $.60]	$60,000	
Sales		$60,000
1/15/20X1 Cost of goods sold	$45,000	
Inventory		$45,000
1/31/20X1 Accounts receivable	$ 5,000	
[100,000 Euros × ($0.65 – $0.60)]		
Transaction gain or loss		$ 5,000
2/15/20X1 Cash [100,000 Euros × 0.55]	$55,000	
Transaction gain or loss	$10,000	
Accounts receivable [$60,000 + $5,000]		$65,000

EXAMPLE

Klemer Corporation bought merchandise for 240,000 pesos when the exchange rate was 12 pesos to a dollar. The journal entry expressed in dollars follows:

Purchases	$20,000	
Accounts payable		$20,000

When the merchandise is paid for, the exchange rate changes to 15:1. The journal entry in dollars is:

Accounts payable	$20,000	
Cash		$18,667
Foreign exchange gain		$ 1,333

At a 15:1 exchange rate the $18,667 can buy 240,000 pesos. The difference between the $18,667 and the initial liability of $20,000 represents a foreign exchange gain. If payment is made when the exchange rate is below 12 pesos to a dollar, a foreign exchange loss would arise.

EXAMPLE

On September 1, 20X0, a U.S. company bought foreign goods requiring payment in Euros in 30 days after their receipt. Title to the merchandise passed on November 15, 20X0. The goods were still in transit on November 30, 20X0, the fiscal year-end. The exchange rates were one dollar to 22 Euros, 20 Euros, and 21 Euros on September 1, November 15, and November 30, 20X0, respectively.

The transaction was recorded on November 15, 20X0, when title to the merchandise passed, and was recorded at an exchange rate of one dollar to 20 Euros (i.e., it would cost $.05 to buy one Euro). At November 30, 20X0, the exchange rate increased to 21 Euros (it would cost less than $.05 to buy one Euro). Because the dollar equivalent of the liability declined from November 15 to November 30, it gave rise to a gain included in income before extraordinary items.

Note: A foreign transaction gain or loss needs to be determined at each balance sheet date on all recorded foreign transactions that have not been settled. The difference between the exchange rate that would have settled the transaction at the date it occurred and the exchange rate that could be used to settle the transaction at a later balance sheet date is the gain or loss to be recorded.

EXAMPLE

A U.S. company sells merchandise to a customer in Italy on 10/1/20X1, for 20,000 Euros. The exchange rate is 1 Euro to $.40. Hence, the transaction is valued at $8,000 (20,000 Euros × $.40). The terms of sale require payment in four months. The journal entry for the sale is:

10/1/20X1

Accounts receivable—Italy	$8,000	
Sales		$8,000

Accounts receivable and sales are measured in U.S. dollars at the transaction date using the spot rate. Even though the accounts receivable are measured and reported in U.S. dollars, the receivable is fixed in Euros. Hence, a transaction gain or loss can occur if the exchange rate changes between the date of sale (10/1/20X1) and the settlement date (2/1/20X2).

Because the financial statements are prepared between the transaction date (date of sale) and settlement date, receivables denominated in a currency other than the functional currency (U.S. dollar) must be restated to reflect the spot rate on the balance sheet date. On 12/31/20X1, the exchange rate is 1 Euro equals $.45. Thus, 20,000 Euros are now valued at 9,000 (20,000 × $.45). In consequence, the accounts receivable denominated in Euros should be increased by $1,000.

The journal entry to do this on 12/31/20X1 is:

Accounts receivable—Italy	$1,000	
Foreign exchange gain		$1,000

The income statement for the year ended 12/31/20X1, shows an exchange gain of $1,000. It should be pointed out that sales is not affected by the exchange gain because sales relates to operational activity.

On 2/1/20X2, the spot rate is 1 Euro equals $.43. The journal entry is:

Cash	$8,600*	
Foreign exchange loss	$ 400	
Accounts receivable—Italy		$9,000

* 20,000 Euros × $.43 = $8,600

The 20X2 income statement presents an exchange loss $400.

EXAMPLE

On September 14, 20X0, ABC Company bought goods from an unaffiliated foreign company for 30,000 units of the foreign company's local currency. On that date, the spot rate was $.57. ABC paid the bill in full on March 27, 20X1, when the spot rate was $.64. The spot rate was $.68 on December 31, 20X0. ABC should report as a foreign currency transaction loss $3,300 in its income statement for the year ended December 31, 20X0, calculated as follows:

Liability—12/31/20X0: 30,000 × $.68	$20,400
Liability—9/22/20X0: 30,000 × $.57	17,100
Foreign currency transaction loss at 12/31/20X0: 30,000 × $.11	$ 3,300

Exception: Gains or losses on some types of foreign currency transactions are not included in profit but rather are treated as translation adjustments. Such gains and losses include:

☐ Intercompany foreign currency transactions of a long-term investment nature (settlement is not planned or anticipated in the foreseeable future), when the entities to the transactions are consolidated, combined, or accounted for under the equity method in the reporting company's financial statements.

☐ Foreign currency transactions engaged in as economic hedges of a net investment in a foreign entity, beginning as of the designation date.

A foreign currency transaction is deemed a hedge of an identifiable foreign currency commitment provided both of the following two conditions exist:

1. The foreign currency commitment is firm.

2. The foreign currency transaction is intended as a hedge.

Note: A dealer in foreign exchange may account for transaction gains or losses as dealer gains or losses.

In conclusion, when the balance sheet falls between the transaction and final settlement dates, receivables/payables must be adjusted to the dollar equivalent as of the balance sheet date; the difference is an exchange gain or loss. Upon settlement of the transaction, there will be a further gain or loss based on the recorded balance at that time.

TRANSLATION PROCESS

Translation of foreign currency statements is usually needed when a foreign subsidiary's statements or equity-method investee has a functional currency other than the U.S. dollar included in a domestic company's financial statements, such as through consolidation or using the equity method.

If a foreign entity's functional currency is the U.S. dollar and the parent's currency is also the U.S. dollar, no translation adjustment is required. A translation adjustment occurs only if the foreign entity's functional currency is different from that of the parent.

The objectives of translation include:

☐ *Preserving the operating results and relationships measured in the foreign currency.* This is achieved by measuring assets, liabilities, and operating results in the foreign entity's functional currency and, when required, converting them to the parent's reporting currency.

☐ *Providing information in consolidated financial statements about the financial performance of each foreign consolidated entity.*

☐ *Providing information on the anticipated effects of changes in exchange rates on cash flow and equity.*

The following steps are required in translating the foreign country's financial statements into U.S. reporting requirements:

1. The foreign currency financial statements must be made to conform with U.S. GAAP before they are translated to the functional or reporting currency.

2. The functional currency of the foreign entity is ascertained.

3. The financial statements are remeasured in the functional currency, if required. Gain or loss from remeasurement is included in the remeasured net income.

   Note: If the foreign company keeps its records in a currency other than the functional or reporting currency, its balance sheet and income statement accounts have to be remeasured into the functional currency before translation into the reporting currency. For example, a parent maintains its financial statements in U.S. dollars and owns a foreign subsidiary whose functional currency is British pounds. If some or all of the foreign subsidiary's records are kept in Italian lira, its financial statements must be remeasured into British pounds before translation into U.S. dollars.

4. Foreign (functional) currency is converted into U.S. dollars (reporting currency). If a foreign company's functional currency is other than the reporting currency, translation into the reporting currency is necessary before the entity may be consolidated, combined, or accounted for on the equity method.

   Note: A permanent impairment of a foreign investment must be provided for before translation and consolidation.

In the usual case, when the foreign currency is the functional currency, balance sheet items (assets and liabilities) are translated at the current exchange rate at the balance sheet date of the foreign entity. Capital accounts are translated using the historical exchange rate in effect when the foreign entity's stock was issued, or reacquired retained earnings are translated at the translated amount at year-end of the previous year, plus the translated amount of net income for the current year, less the translated amount of dividends during the current year. If the current exchange rate is unavailable at the balance sheet date, the first available exchange rate after that date should be used. The current method is required under ASC 830-10-45 (except when there is a highly inflationary environment, to be discussed shortly). The current method ensures that financial relationships remain the same in both local currency and U.S. dollars.

In the statement of cash flows, cash flows are translated based on the exchange rates in existence at the time of the cash flows. If reasonable and practical, a weighted-average rate for the year may be used, as long as the result is similar. Disclosure should be made in the statement of cash flows for the impact of any exchange rate changes on cash flow.

In the usual case (when high inflation does not exist), income statement items (revenue, expenses, gains, and losses) are translated at the exchange rate at the dates those items are recognized. Because translation at the exchange rates at the dates of many revenues, expenses, gains, and losses is usually impractical, a weighted-average exchange rate for the year is typically used in translating income statement items. However, average quarterly or monthly rates may be used if significant revenues and expenses occur at particular times during the year.

If a company's functional currency is a foreign currency, translation adjustments occur from translating the company's financial statements into the reporting currency. Translation adjustments are unrealized. They are reported separately as a component of "other comprehensive income" in the income statement for the current year amount with the cumulative translation adjustment reported as "accumulated other comprehensive income" in the stockholders' equity section of the balance sheet. Translation adjustments shall not be included in net income unless and until there is a sale or liquidation of the investment in the foreign entity.

Exception: If remeasurement from the recording currency to the functional currency is needed before translation, the gain or loss is included in the income statement.

EXAMPLE

Blake Company's wholly owned subsidiary, David Company, keeps its records in German marks. Because David Company's branch offices are located in Switzerland, its functional currency is the Swiss franc. Remeasurement of David Company's 20X2 financial statements resulted in an $8,700 gain, and translation of its financial statements resulted in a $9,200 gain. Blake should report as a foreign exchange gain $8,700 in its income statement for the year ended December 31, 20X2. The translation gain of $9,200 should be included in "other comprehensive income" and the cumulative translation adjustment, which is a separate component of stockholders' equity.

HIGHLY INFLATIONARY ENVIRONMENT IN FOREIGN COUNTRY

According to ASC 830-10-45-12, a highly inflationary environment is one with a cumulative inflation rate exceeding 100% over a three-year period. In other words, the inflation rate must be increasing at an average rate of about 26% per year for three consecutive years, given compounding. **Note:** The International Monetary Fund of Washington, D.C. publishes information about the international inflation rates. **Tip:** In some cases, the inflation trend may be as important as the absolute rate of inflation.

The foreign entity's financial statements in a very inflationary environment are unstable and should be remeasured as if the functional currency were the reporting currency. In this case, the investor's reporting currency is used directly. Consequently, if a foreign entity's financial statements in a highly inflationary economy are expressed in a currency different from the reporting currency, they have to be remeasured into the reporting currency.

If the U.S. dollar is used directly as the functional currency because of high inflation, balance sheet conversion would be as follows:

☐ Cash, receivables, and payables are converted at the foreign exchange rate in effect at the balance sheet date.

☐ Other assets and liabilities are converted at foreign exchange rates (historical rates) in effect at the date of transaction, except that the exchange rate in effect at the balance sheet date is used to translate assets and liabilities that are accounted for on the basis of current prices, such as marketable securities carried at market and estimated warranty obligations.

If the U.S. dollar is used as the functional currency because of high inflation, translation of income statement items is based on the weighted average rate for the period. However, revenues and expenses that relate to assets and liabilities translated at historical rates should be translated at such historical rates. Examples are depreciation on fixed assets, amortization expense on intangible assets, and amortized revenue arising from deferred revenue.

In a highly inflationary environment in a foreign country requiring the use of the reporting currency directly, gains and losses from converting foreign currency financial statements into reporting currency financial statements are recognized in net income rather than reported in stockholders' equity.

According to ASC 830-10-45-15, *Foreign Currency Matters: Overall*, when a foreign subsidiary's environment is no longer highly inflationary, the entity must convert the amounts expressed in the reporting currency into the local currency based on the exchange rates on the date of change.

EXAMPLE

Remeasuring Accounts of a Foreign Subsidiary

FNC is a wholly owned German subsidiary of MNC. The functional currency is U.S. dollars. The following accounts, for year ended December 31, 20X2, are stated in Euros.

Rent expense	150,000
Allowance for doubtful accounts	60,000
Patent amortization expense*	85,000

* Acquired on March 23, 20X0

The exchange rates for the Euros for various dates and time periods are as follows:

March 23, 20X0	0.65
December 31, 20X2	0.55
Average for year ended December 31, 20X2	0.6

The remeasured accounts in U.S. dollars are as follows:

	Euros	Exchange Rate	U.S. Dollars
Rent expense	150,000	0.60	$ 90,000
Allowance for doubtful accounts	60,000	0.55	33,000
Patent amortization expense	85,000	0.65	55,250
	295,000		$178,250

EXAMPLE

Remeasuring Accounts of a Foreign Subsidiary

The trial balance of the German branch of XYZ Corporation for its first month of operations in Euros is as follows:

XYZ Corporation German Branch Trial Balance (in Euros) January 31, 20X2		
Cash	50,000	
Accounts receivable	250,000	
Inventory	500,000	
Investment in German branch		700,000
Sales		1,200,000
Cost of goods sold	650,000	
Selling expenses	125,000	
Administrative expenses	325,000	
	1,900,000	1,900,000

Inventory was shipped from the main office on January 1, 20X2, when the exchange rate was 1 Euro = $0.65. The exchange rate on January 31, 20X2 was 1 Euro = $0.55. The average exchange rate for the month of January 20X2 was .60.

The investment in German branch appears on XYZ Corporation's at $105,000 on January 31, 20X2.

The remeasured trial balance of the German branch in the functional currency (U.S. dollars) is as follows:

	Balance in Euros debit/(credit)	Exchange Rate	Balance in U.S. Dollars debit/(credit)
Cash	50,000	0.55	$ 27,500
Accounts receivable	250,000	0.55	137,500
Inventory	500,000	0.65	325,000
Investment in German branch	(700,000)		−105,000
Sales	(1,200,000)	0.60	−720,000
Cost of goods sold	650,000	0.65	422,500
Selling expenses	125,000	0.60	75,000
Administrative expenses	325,000	0.60	195,000
	$0		$357,500
Transaction gain	$0		($357,500)
Total	$0		$ 0

According to Accounting Standards Update (ASU) No. 2010-19 (May 2010) (ASC 830, *Foreign Currency*), *Foreign Currency Issues*, in the case of a foreign company's financial statements in a highly inflationary environment, there should be a remeasurement, assuming the functional currency is the reporting currency. If there is a difference existing before using the mandates of a highly inflationary accounting between the financial reporting balances and the U.S. dollar denominated balances, it should be reflected in the profit and loss statement.

Disclosure should be made of translation and remeasurement rates, why U.S. dollar denominated balances are different from financial reporting balances and the reasons why different rates were employed for translation and remeasurement. (ASC 830-30-S99-1)

HEDGING

Foreign currency transaction gains and losses on assets and liabilities, denominated in a currency other than the entity's functional currency, can be hedged if the U.S. company enters into a forward exchange contract or a foreign currency option.

An entity may enter into hedging transactions to minimize the adverse effects of changes in exchange rates on cash flows and net income. An entity's aim is to recognize a gain or loss from the hedge in the same period as the loss or gain on the risk being hedged.

ASC 815-10-05, *Derivatives and Hedging: Overall*, and ASC 815-20-25, *Derivatives and Hedging: Hedging—General*, permit hedge accounting for foreign currency derivatives only if the following three conditions are satisfied:

1. The derivative is used to hedge either a fair value exposure or a cash flow exposure.

2. The derivative is highly effective in offsetting changes in the fair value or cash flows.

3. The derivative is documented as a hedge.

A fair-value exposure exists if changes in exchange rates can affect the fair value of assets or liabilities. If the exposure is not hedged, it must have the potential to affect net income. A fair value hedge also may exist for foreign currency firm commitments.

A cash flow exposure exists if changes in exchange rates can affect the amount of cash flow that will be realized from a transaction, where changes in cash flow are reflected in net income.

To use hedge accounting, derivatives must be designated as either a fair value hedge or a cash flow hedge. An entity may use either a fair value hedge or a cash flow hedge for:

☐ Recognized foreign currency assets and liabilities.

☐ Foreign currency firm commitments.

Hedges of forecasted foreign currency transactions can only qualify for a cash flow hedge. Gains or losses on fair value hedges are recognized immediately in net income, whereas gains or losses on cash flow hedges are included in other comprehensive income.

To use hedge accounting, the hedge must be expected to be highly effective in offsetting gains and losses on the items being hedged. Critical terms of the hedging instrument, such as currency type, amount, and settlement date should match those of the hedged item. The hedging entity should document the:

☐ Hedged item;

☐ Hedging instrument;

☐ Nature of risk;

☐ Means of assessing the hedging instrument's effectiveness; and

☐ Management's objectives and strategies for undertaking the hedge.

SALE OR LIQUIDATION OF AN INVESTMENT IN A FOREIGN ENTITY

If there is a sale or liquidation of an investment in a foreign entity, the amount attributable to that entity and accumulated in the translation adjustment component of equity is removed from the stockholders' equity section. It is considered a part of the gain or loss on sale or liquidation of the investment in the income statement for the period during which the sale or liquidation occurs.

As per ASC 830-30-40-2, *Foreign Currency Matters: Translation of Financial Statements*, sale of an investment in a foreign entity may include a partial sale of an ownership interest. In that event, a proportionate amount of the cumulative translation adjustment reflected as a stockholders' equity component is included in determining the gain or loss on sale.

EXAMPLE

If a business sells 30% ownership in a foreign investment, 30% of the translation adjustment applicable to it is included in computing gain or loss on sale of that ownership interest.

ASC 830-30-45-13, *Foreign Currency Matters: Translation of Financial Statements*, provides that a company that plans to dispose of an equity method investment in a foreign operation or a consolidated foreign subsidiary should include in the book value of the investment both the foreign currency translation adjustments associated with the foreign entity's disposal as well as the part of the foreign currency translation adjustments applicable to the gain or loss from the hedge of the company's net investment in the foreign operation.

INTERCOMPANY PROFITS

In the elimination of intercompany profits, the company should use the exchange rate in existence at the date of the intercompany transaction. A transaction is either at the date of sale or transfer. However, a reasonable average or estimated rate may be used when there are frequent intercompany transactions during the year.

ASC 970-470-05-2, *Real Estate—General: Debt*, covers the hedging of intercompany foreign currency risks.

EXCLUDING A FOREIGN ENTITY FROM FINANCIAL STATEMENTS

In some cases, a foreign entity may be excluded from consolidated or combined financial statements. This may arise if serious political problems exist in the foreign country (e.g., civil war) or if exchange restrictions are extremely restrictive, inhibiting any reliability to exchange rates. In this situation, profits of a foreign activity should be included in the financial statements only to the degree of receipt of unrestricted cash. When the foreign entity is excluded from the financial statements, proper disclosure should be made of the reasons therefor, other pertinent information, and dollar effect. Such disclosure may be in a supplemental schedule or in footnote form.

FOREIGN OPERATIONS IN THE UNITED STATES

An entity in the United States may be a subsidiary of a parent company domiciled in a foreign country. In this case, the local company's financial statements may be presented separately in the United States or combined with the financial statements in the foreign country.

TAXES

Deferred taxes will typically be recorded for the future tax impact of temporary differences, resulting in taxable translation and/or transaction gains or losses. Tax effects may be presented in either the income statement or stockholders' equity section, depending on the nature of the taxable item. However, deferred taxes may not need to be recorded for a foreign subsidiary's unremitted earnings. In such a case, proper disclosure should be made.

According to ASC 830-740-25-2 and 25-3 and 830-740-45-2, *Foreign Currency Matters: Income Taxes*, deferred taxes on temporary differences arising because of a change in the functional currency are accounted for as an adjustment to the cumulative translation adjustments presented in stockholders' equity.

DISCLOSURES

Footnote disclosure is required of:

☐ Profits earned from overseas. This also includes the amount of foreign earnings in excess of amounts received in the United States.

☐ Foreign currency transaction gains or losses, including that associated with forward exchange contracts.

☐ The impact on unsettled balances regarding foreign currency transactions.

☐ Cumulative translation adjustments reported in stockholders' equity. This includes the reasons for the change in the balance from the beginning to the end of the year.

☐ Gains or losses arising from hedging a foreign currency position.

☐ Effect of exchange rate changes on operating results and financial position. This disclosure includes the impact of a change in exchanges rates from the prior year to the current year associated with translation of revenues and expenses. It also includes the effect of a change in exchange rate on revenue and cost components, such as sales volume, sales price, and cost of sales. The nature of restated figures should be noted.

☐ A significant change in exchange rate taking place after year-end and before the audit report date. This is a subsequent event disclosure.

SUMMARY

If the foreign statements have any accounts expressed in a currency other than their own, they have to be converted into the foreign statement's currency prior to translation into U.S. dollars or any other reporting currency.

In most cases, assets and liabilities are translated at the current exchange rate at the balance sheet date. Revenue and expenses are usually translated at the weighted-average exchange rate for the period. Translation adjustments are reported as a part of comprehensive income and ultimately as a separate component of stockholders' equity as accumulated other comprehensive income. Foreign currency transaction gains and losses are reported in the income statement.

ANNUAL REPORT REFERENCES

Johnson & Johnson
2011 Annual Report

14. International Currency Translation

For translation of its subsidiaries operating in non-U.S. Dollar currencies, the Company has determined that the local currencies of its international subsidiaries are the functional currencies except those in highly inflationary economies, which are defined as those which have had compound cumulative rates of inflation of 100% or more during the past three years, or where a substantial portion of its cash flows are not in the local currency.

In consolidating international subsidiaries, balance sheet currency effects are recorded as a component of accumulated other comprehensive income. This equity account includes the results of translating all balance sheet assets and liabilities at current exchange rates, except for those located in highly inflationary economies. The translation of balance sheet accounts for highly inflationary economies are reflected in the operating results.

An analysis of the changes during 2011, 2010 and 2009 for foreign currency translation adjustments is included in Note 13.

Net currency transaction gains and losses included in Other (income) expense were losses of $10 million, $130 million and $210 million in 2011, 2010 and 2009, respectively.

Shaw Group
2005 Annual Report

Note 17—Foreign Currency Translation and Transactions

As of August 31, 2005, all of our significant foreign subsidiaries maintained their accounting records in their local currency (primary British pounds, Venezuelan Bolivars, Canadian dollars, and the Euro). The currencies are converted to U.S. dollars at exchange rates as of the balance sheet date with the effect of the foreign currency translation reflected in "accumulated other comprehensive income (loss," a component of shareholders equity, in accordance with SFAS No. 52, "Foreign Currency Translation," and SFAS No. 130, "Reporting Comprehensive Income." Foreign currency transaction gains or losses are credited or charged to income. At August 31, 2005 and 2004, cumulative foreign currency translation adjustment related to these subsidiaries reflected as a reduction to shareholders' equity amounted to $7.3 million and $3.5 million, respectively; transaction gains and losses reflected in income were a gain of $0.9 million during fiscal 2005, a loss of $2.7 million during fiscal 2004 and a gain of $0.1 million during fiscal 2003, respectively.

Varian
2004 Annual Report

Note 4. Forward Exchange Contracts

The Company enters into foreign exchange forward contracts to minimize the short-term impact of foreign currency fluctuations on assets and liabilities denominated in non-functional currencies. These contracts are accounted for under SFAS 133, Accounting for Derivative Instruments and Hedging Activities. The Company records these contracts at fair value with the related gains and losses recorded in general and administrative expenses. The gains and losses on these contracts are substantially offset by transaction losses and gains on the underlying balance being hedged.

From time to time, the Company also enters into foreign exchange forward contracts to minimize the impact of foreign currency fluctuations on forecasted transactions. These contracts are designated as cash flow hedges under SFAS 133. During the year ended October 1, 2004, there were no outstanding foreign exchange forward contracts designated as cash flow hedges of forecasted transactions. During the year ended October 1, 2004, no foreign exchange gains or losses from hedge ineffectiveness were recognized.

The Company's foreign exchange forward contracts generally range from one to 12 months in original maturity. A summary of all foreign exchange forward contracts that were outstanding as of October 1, 2004 follows:

	Notional Value Sold	Notional Value Purchased
(in thousands)		
Euro	$ –	$45,525
Australian dollar	–	13,610
Japanese yen	9,415	–
Canadian dollar	4,945	–
British pound	–	3,295
Swedish krona	792	–
Total	$15,152	$62,430

IBM
2003 Annual Report

Translation of Non-U.S. Currency Amounts

Assets and liabilities of non-U.S. subsidiaries that operate in a local currency environment are translated to U.S. dollars at year-end exchange rates. Income and expense items are translated at weighted-average rates of exchange prevailing during the year. Translation adjustments are recorded in Accumulated gains and (losses) not affecting retained earnings within Stockholders' equity.

Inventories, Plant, rental machines and other property-net, and other non-monetary assets and liabilities of non-U.S. subsidiaries and branches that operate in U.S. dollars, or whose economic environment is highly inflationary, are translated at approximate exchange rates prevailing when the company acquired the assets or liabilities. All other assets and liabilities are translated at year-end exchange rates. Cost of sales and depreciation are translated at historical exchange rates. All other income and expense items are translated at the weighted-average rates of exchange prevailing during the year. Gains and losses that result from translation are included in net income.

Dell Computer
2003 Annual Report

Foreign Currency Instruments

The Company uses purchased option contracts and forward contracts designated as cash flow hedges to protect against the foreign currency exchange risk inherent in its forecasted transactions denominated in currencies other than U.S. dollar. Hedged transactions include international sales by U.S. dollar functional currency entities, foreign currency denominated purchases of certain components and intercompany shipments to some international subsidiaries. The risk of loss associated with purchased options is limited to premium amounts paid for the option contracts. The risk of loss associated with forward contracts is equal to the exchange rate differential from the time the contract is entered into until the time it is settled. These contracts generally expire in twelve months or less.

The Company also uses forward contracts to hedge monetary assets and liabilities, primarily receivables and payables, denominated in a foreign currency. These contracts are not designated as hedging instruments under generally accepted accounting principles, and therefore, the change in the instrument's fair value is recognized currently in earnings and is reported as a component of investment and other income (loss), net. The change in the fair value of these instruments represents a natural hedge as their gains and losses offset the changes in the underlying fair value of the monetary assets and liabilities due to movements in currency exchange rates. These contracts generally expire in three months or less.

If the derivative is designated as a cash flow hedge, the effective portion of the change in the fair value of the derivative is initially deferred in other comprehensive income. These amounts are subsequently recognized in income as a component of net revenue or cost of revenue in the same period the hedged transaction affects earnings. The ineffective portion of the change in the fair value of cash flow hedge is recognized currently in earnings and is reported as a component of investment and other income (loss), net. Hedge effectiveness is measured by comparing the hedging instrument's cumulative change in fair value from inception to maturity to the forecasted transaction's terminal value. During fiscal years 2003 and 2002, the Company did not discontinue any cash flow hedges as substantially all forecasted foreign currency transactions were realized in the Company's actual results. Furthermore, hedge ineffectiveness was not material.

At January 31, 2003, the Company held purchased option contracts with a notional amount of $2 billion, a net asset value of $31 million and a net unrealized deferred loss of $37 million, net of taxes. At January 31, 2003, the Company held forward contracts with a notional amount of $2 billion, a net liability value of $140 million and a net unrealized loss of $25 million, net of taxes.

At February 1, 2002, the Company held purchased option contracts with a notional amount of $2 billion, a net asset value of $83 million and a net unrealized deferred gain of $11 million, net of taxes. At February 1, 2002, the Company held forward contracts with a notional amount of $2 billion, a net asset value of $95 million and a net unrealized gain of $28 million, net of taxes.

Black & Decker
2002 Annual Report

Foreign Currency Translation: The financial statements of subsidiaries located outside of the United States, except those subsidiaries operating in highly inflationary economies, generally are measured using the local currency as the functional currency. Assets, including goodwill, and liabilities of these subsidiaries are translated at the rates of exchange at the balance sheet date. The resultant translation adjustments are included in accumulated other comprehensive income (loss), a separate component of stockholders' equity. Income and expense items are translated at average monthly rates of exchange. Gains and losses from foreign currency transactions of these subsidiaries are included in net earnings. For subsidiaries operating in highly inflationary economies, gains and losses from balance sheet translation adjustments are included in net earnings.

NCR
2002 Annual Report

Foreign Currency   For many NCR international operations, the local currency is designated as the functional currency. Accordingly, assets and liabilities are translated into U.S. dollars a year-end exchange rates, and revenues and expenses are translated at average exchange rates prevailing during the year. Currency translation adjustments resulting from fluctuations in exchange rates are recorded in other comprehensive income.

In the normal course of business, NCR enters into various financial instruments, including derivative financial instruments. NCR uses foreign exchange forward contracts and options to reduce the Company's exposure to changes in currency exchange rates, primarily as it relates to inventory purchases by marketing units and inventory sales by manufacturing units. Derivatives used as a part of NCR's risk management strategy, which are designated at inception as cash-flow hedges, are measured for effectiveness both at inception and on an ongoing basis. For foreign exchange contracts designated as cash-flow hedges, the gains or losses are deferred in other comprehensive income and recognized in the determination of income as adjustments of carrying amounts when the underlying hedged transaction is realized, canceled or otherwise terminated. For the year ended December 31, 2002, NCR reclassified net losses of $1 million to other income as a result of discontinuance of cash-flow hedges. The net impact related to the ineffectiveness of all cash-flow hedges was not material during 2002. At December 31, 2002, before-tax deferred net losses recorded in other comprehensive income related to cash-flow hedges were $9 million, and are expected to be reclassified to earnings during the next 12 months.

Kodak
2002 Annual Report

Foreign Currency

For most subsidiaries and branches outside the U.S., the local currency is the functional currency. In accordance with the Statement of financial Accounting Standards (SFAS) No. 52, "Foreign Currency Translation," the financial statements of these subsidiaries and branches are translated into U.S. dollars as follows: assets and liabilities at year-end exchange rates; income, expenses and cash flows at average exchange rates; and shareholders' equity at historical exchange rates. For those subsidiaries for which the local currency is the functional currency, the resulting translation adjustment is recorded as a component of accumulated other comprehensive income in the accompanying Consolidated Statement of Financial Position. Translation adjustments are not tax-effected since they relate to investments, which are permanent in nature.

For certain other subsidiaries and branches, operations are conducted primarily in U.S. dollars, which is therefore the functional currency. Monetary assets and liabilities, and the related revenue, expense, gain and loss accounts, of these foreign subsidiaries and branches are remeasured at year-end exchange rates. Non-monetary assets and liabilities, and the related revenue, expense, gain and loss accounts, are remeasured at historical rates.

Foreign exchange gains and losses arising from transactions denominated in a currency other than the functional currency of the entity involved are included in income. The effects of foreign currency transactions, including related hedging activities, were losses of $19 million, $9 million, and $13 million in the years 2002, 2001, and 2000, respectively, and are included in other (charges) income in the accompanying Consolidated Statement of Earnings.

DuPont
2002 Annual Report

Foreign Currency Translation

The U.S. dollar is the functional currency of most of the company's worldwide operations. For subsidiaries where the U.S. dollar is the functional currency, all foreign currency asset and liability amounts are remeasured into U.S. dollars at end-of-period exchange rates, except for inventories, prepaid expenses, property, plant and equipment, and intangible assets, which are remeasured at historical rates. Foreign currency income and expenses are remeasured at average exchange rates in effect during the year, except for expenses related to balance sheet amounts remeasured at historical exchange rates. Exchange gains and losses arising from remeasurement of foreign currency-denominated monetary assets and liabilities are included in income in the period in which they occur.

For subsidiaries where the local currency is the functional currency, assets and liabilities denominated in local currencies are translated into U.S. dollars at end-of-period exchange rates, and the resultant translation adjustments are reported, net of their related tax effects, as a component of Accumulated Other Comprehensive Income (Loss) in stockholders' equity. Assets and liabilities denominated in other than the local currency are remeasured into the local currency prior to translation into U.S. dollars, and the resultant exchange gains or losses are included in income in the period in which they occur. Income and expenses are translated into U.S. dollars at average exchange rates in effect during the period.

Dana
2003 Annual Report

Foreign Currency Translation

The financial statements of subsidiaries and equity affiliates outside the United States (U.S.) located in non-highly inflationary economies are measured using the currency of the primary economic environment in which they operate as the functional currency, which for the most part is the local currency. Transaction gains and losses which result from translating assets and liabilities of these entities into the functional currency are included in net earnings. Other income includes transaction gains of $3 in 2003, $19 in 2002 and $8 in 2001. When translating into U.S. dollars, income and expense items are translated at average monthly rates of exchange and assets and liabilities are translated at the rates of exchange at the balance sheet date. Translation adjustments resulting from translating the functional currency into U.S. dollars are deferred as a component of accumulated other comprehensive income in shareholders' equity. For affiliates operating in highly inflationary economies, non-monetary assets are translated into U.S. dollars at historical exchange rates and monetary assets are translated at current exchange rates. Translation adjustments for these affiliates are included in net earnings.

Monsanto
2003 Annual Report

Foreign Currency Translation

The financial statements for most of Monsanto's ex-U.S. operations are translated into U.S. dollars at current exchange rates. For assets and liabilities the year-end rate is used. For revenues, expenses, gains and losses the average rate for the period is used. Unrealized currency adjustments in the Statement of Consolidated Financial Position are accumulated in equity as a component of accumulated other comprehensive loss. The financial statements of ex-U.S. operations in highly inflationary economies are translated at either current or historical exchange rates, in accordance with SFAS No. 52, *Foreign Currency Translation*. These currency adjustments are included in net income. As of Jan. 1, 2003, Monsanto identified Turkey, Russia, Romania and Ukraine as hyperinflationary countries in which it has operations.

Significant translation exposures are the Brazilian real, the euro, and the Canadian dollar. Other translation exposures include the Polish zloty, the U.K. pound sterling, and the Australian dollar. For all periods presented, Monsanto designated the U.S. dollar as the functional currency in Argentina. In January 2002, Argentina formally abandoned the fixed exchange rate regime between the Argentine peso and the U.S. dollar, and the peso subsequently was devalued by approximately 70 percent. Argentina simultaneously imposed various banking and exchange controls, and the government has instituted additional controls since that time. Included in the net transaction loss were losses of $34 million in 2002 and $15 million in 2001. These amounts reflect the effect of this devaluation on Argentine peso-denominated transaction exposures (primarily value-added taxes and other taxes due to or recoverable by Monsanto). See Note 20—Commitments and Contingencies—for further details on the Argentine devaluation. Currency restrictions, with a possible exception in Argentina, are not expected to have a significant effect on Monsanto's cash flow, liquidity, or capital resources.

United Technologies
2004 Annual Report

Note 12—Foreign Exchange

UTC conducts business in many different currencies and, accordingly, is subject to the inherent risks associated with foreign exchange rate movements. The financial position and results of operations of substantially all of UTC's foreign subsidiaries are measured using the local currency as the functional currency. Foreign currency denominated assets and liabilities are translated into U.S. dollars at the exchange rates existing at the respective balance sheet dates, and income and expense items are translated at the average exchange rates during the respective periods. The aggregate effects of translating the balance sheets of these subsidiaries are deferred as a separate component of Shareowners' Equity. UTC had foreign currency net assets in more than forty currencies, aggregating $8.5 billion and $6.5 billion at December 31, 2004 and 2003, respectively.

The notional amount of foreign exchange contracts hedging foreign currency transactions was $5.7 billion and $4.9 billion at December 31, 2004 and 2003, respectively.

Note 13—Financial Instruments

UTC operates internationally and, in the normal course of business, is exposed to fluctuations in interest rates, foreign exchange rates, and commodity prices. These fluctuations can increase the costs of financing, investing and operating the business. UTC manages its foreign currency transaction risks and some commodity exposures to acceptable limits through the use of derivatives designated as hedges.

By nature, all financial instruments involve market and credit risks. UTC enters into derivative and other financial instruments with major investment grade financial institutions and has policies to monitor the credit risk of those counterparties. UTC limits counterparty exposure and concentration of risk by diversifying counterparties. UTC does not anticipate non-performance by any of these counterparties.

The non-shareowner changes in equity associated with hedging activity for the twelve months ended December 31, 2004 and 2003 were as follows:

(millions of dollars)	2004	2003
Balance at January 1	$55	$ 4
Cash flow hedging gain, net	86	66
Net (gain) reclassified to sales or cost of products sold	(76)	(15)
Balance at December 31	$65	$55

Of the amount recorded in Shareowners' Equity, a $67 million pre-tax gain is expected to be reclassified into sales or cost of products sold to reflect the fixed prices obtained from hedging within the next twelve months. Gains and losses recognized in earnings related to the discontinuance or the ineffectiveness of cash flow and fair value hedges were immaterial for the years ended December 31, 2004 and 2003. At December 31, 2004, all derivative contracts accounted for as cash flow hedges mature by October 2009.

All derivative instruments are recorded on the balance sheet at fair value. At December 31, 2004 and 2003, the fair value of derivatives recorded as assets is $165 million and $162 million, respectively, and the fair value of derivatives recorded as liabilities is $43 million and $56 million, respectively. UTC uses derivatives to hedge forecasted cash flows associated with foreign currency commitments or forecasted commodity purchases, which are accounted for as cash flow hedges. In addition, UTC uses derivatives, such as interest rate swaps, which are accounted for as fair value hedges.

The carrying amounts and fair values of financial instruments at December 31 are as follows:

(in millions of dollars)	2004		2003	
	Carrying Amount	Fair Value	Carrying Amount	Fair Value
Financial Assets and Liabilities				
Marketable equity securities	$746	$746	$79	$79
Long-term receivables	170	166	128	125
Customer financing Note receivables	483	465	439	425
Short-term borrowing	(1,320)	(1,320)	(669)	(669)
Long-term debt	(4,243)	(4,941)	(4,614)	(5,363)

The above fair values were computed based on comparable transactions, quoted market prices, discounted future cash flows or an estimate of the amount to be received or paid to terminate or settle the agreement, as applicable.

The values of marketable equity securities represent UTC's investment in Common Stock that is classified as available as available for sale and is accounted for at fair value. The increase in marketable equity securities primarily reflects the initial purchases of Kidde shares.

UTC had outstanding financial and rental commitments totaling $838 million at December 31, 2004. Risks associated with changes in interest rates on these commitments are mitigated by the fact that interest rates are variable during the commitment term and are set at the date of funding based on current market conditions, the fair value of the underlying collateral and the credit worthiness of the customers. As a result, the fair value of these financings is expected to equal the amounts funded.

The fair value of the commitment itself is not readily determinable and is not considered significant itself is not readily determinable and is not considered significant. Additional information pertaining to these commitments is included in Note 4.

Caterpillar
2004 Annual Report

3. Derivative Financial Instruments and Risk Management

A. Foreign currency exchange rate risk

Foreign currency exchange rate movements create a degree of risk by affecting the U.S. dollar value of sales made and costs incurred in foreign currencies. Movements in foreign currency rates also affect our competitive position as these changes may affect business practices and/or pricing strategies of non-U.S.-based competitors. Additionally, we have balance sheet positions denominated in foreign currency, thereby creating exposure to movements in exchange rates.

Our Machinery and Engines operations purchase, manufacture and sell products in many locations around the world. As we have a diversified revenue and cost base, we manage our future foreign currency cash flow exposure on a net basis. We use foreign currency forward and option contracts to manage unmatched foreign currency cash inflow and outflow. Our objective is to minimize the risk of exchange rate movements that would reduce the U.S. dollar value of our foreign currency cash flow. Our policy allows for man-aging anticipated foreign currency cash flow for up to four years.

We generally designate as cash flow hedges at inception of the contract any Australian dollar, Brazilian real, British pound, Canadian dollar, euro, Japanese yen, Mexican peso, or Singapore dollar forward or option contracts that exceed 90 days in duration. Designation is performed on a specific exposure basis to support hedge accounting. The remainder of Machinery and Engines foreign currency contracts are undesignated.

As of December 31, 2004, $102 million of deferred net gains included in equity ("Accumulated other comprehensive income" in Statement 3), related to Machinery and Engines foreign currency contracts designated as cash flow hedges, is expected to be reclassified to current earnings ["Other income (expense)"] over the next twelve months. There were no circumstances where hedge treatment was discontinued during 2004, 2003 or 2002.

In managing foreign currency risk for our Financial Products operations, our objective is to minimize earnings volatility resulting from conversion and the remeasurement of net foreign currency balance sheet positions. Our policy allows the use of foreign currency forward contracts to offset the risk of currency mismatch between our receivables and debt. All such foreign currency forward contracts are undesignated.

(Losses) included in current earnings [Other income (expense)] on undesignated contracts:

(Millions of dollars)	*2004*	*2003*	*2002*
Machinery and Engines:			
On undesignated contracts	**$ (9)**	$ (1)	$ –
Due to changes in time and volatility value on options	–	–	$ (1)
Financial Products: On undesignated contracts	**$(46)**	$(121)	$(96)
	$(55)	$(122)	$(97)

Gains and losses on the Financial Products contracts above are substantially offset by balance sheet remeasurement and conversion gains and losses.

B. Interest rate risk

Interest rate movements create a degree of risk by affecting the amount of our interest payments and the value of our fixed rate debt. Our policy is to use interest rate swap agreements and forward rate agreements to manage our exposure to interest rate changes and lower the cost of borrowed funds.

Machinery and Engines operations generally use fixed rate debt as a source of funding. Our objective is to minimize the cost of borrowed funds. Our policy allows us to enter fixed-to-floating interest rate swaps and forward rate agreements to meet that objective with the intent to designate as fair value hedges at inception of the contract all fixed-to-floating interest rate swaps. Designation as a hedge of the fair value of our fixed rate debt is performed to support hedge accounting. During 2001, our Machinery and Engines operations liquidated all fixed-to-floating interest rate swaps. Deferred gains on liquidated fixed-to-floating interest rate swaps, which were previously designated as fair value hedges, are being amortized to earnings ratably over the remaining life of the hedged debt. We designate as cash flow hedges at inception of the contract all forward rate agreements. Designation as a hedge of the anticipated issuance of debt is performed to support hedge accounting. Machinery and Engines forward rate agreements are 100% effective.

Financial Products operations have a "match funding" objective whereby, within specified boundaries, the interest rate profile interest rate profile of their receivables. In connection with that objective, we use interest rate derivative instruments to modify the debt structure to match the receivable portfolio. This "match funding" reduces the volatility of margins between interest-bearing assets and interest-bearing liabilities, regardless of which direction interest rates move. We also use these instruments to gain an economic and/or competitive advantage through a lower cost of borrowed funds. This is accomplished by changing the characteristics of existing debt instruments or entering into new agreements in combination with the issuance of new debt.

Our policy allows us to issue floating-to-fixed, fixed-to-floating, and floating-to-floating interest rate swaps to meet the "match funding" objective. To support hedge accounting, we designate fixed-to-floating interest rate swaps as fair value hedges of the fair value of our fixed rate debt at inception of the swap contract. Financial Products policy is to designate most floating-to-fixed interest rate swaps as cash flow hedges of the variability of future cash flows at inception of the swap contract. Designation as a hedge of the variability of cash flow is performed to support hedge accounting. During 2004, Financial Products operations liquidated three fixed-to-floating interest rate swaps and during 2002, Financial Products liquidated four such swaps. As a result, the fair value adjustment of the original debt is being amortized to earnings ratably over the remaining life of the hedged debt.

Gains (losses) included in current earnings [Other income (expense)]:

(Millions of dollars)	2004	2003	2002
Fixed-to-floating interest rate swaps			
Machinery and Engines:			
Gain on liquidated swaps	$5	$6	$8
Financial Products:			
Gain/(loss) on designated interest rate derivatives	(28)	(20)	17
Gain/(loss) on hedged debt	28	(20)	(17)
Gain on liquidated swaps—included in interest expense	2	2	1
	$7	$8	$9

As of December 31, 2004, $3 million of deferred net losses included in equity ("Accumulated other comprehensive income" in Statement 3), related to Financial Products floating-to-fixed interest rate swaps, is expected to be reclassified to current earnings ("Interest expense of Financial Products") over the next twelve months. There were no circumstances where hedge treatment was discontinued during 2004, 2003 or 2002 in either Machinery and Engines or Financial Products.

C. Commodity price risk

Commodity price movements create a degree of risk by affecting the price we must pay for certain raw material. Our policy is to use commodity forward and option contracts to manage the commodity risk and reduce the cost of purchased materials.

Our Machinery and Engines operations purchase aluminum, copper and nickel embedded in the components we purchase from suppliers. Our suppliers pass on to us price changes in the commodity portion of the component cost.

Our objective is to minimize volatility in the price of these commodities. Our policy allows us to enter commodity forward and option contracts to lock in the purchase price of the commodities within a four-year horizon. All such commodity forward and option contracts are undesignated. Gains on the undesignated contracts of $15 million, $27 million, and $1 million were recorded in current earnings ["Other income (expense)"] for 2004, 2003, and 2002, respectively.

Chapter 17

Derivatives, Repurchase Agreements, and Disclosures of Credit Risk and Fair Values: Accounting, Reporting, and Disclosures*

CONTENTS

This chapter addresses the accounting and disclosure requirements related to derivative financial instruments (derivatives), including those specific to mort-

---

*This chapter was co-authored by Jeffrey Satenstein, MS, CPA, Managing Director (retired), JPMorgan Chase Investment Bank, Lecturer, Accounting & Information Systems, Queens College—CUNY.

gage servicing and repurchase agreements. This chapter should be read in conjunction with the previous chapter on foreign currency translation and transactions. Also addressed are selected disclosure requirements for other financial instruments, primarily those related to fair value and concentrations of credit risk.

TERMINOLOGY

Accounting Loss. Loss recorded on the financial books due to changes in the market, credit, or other risk arising from a financial instrument.

Arbitrage. The simultaneous purchase and sale of similar financial instruments with the purpose of taking advantage of perceived disparities in the relative value of these instruments.

Cap, Collar, or Floor. An option contract that provides the purchaser with protection against price movements outside a predefined range (e.g., an interest rate cap protects the purchaser from interest rate increases above a certain level).

Carrying Amount (Carrying Value). Amount recorded on the financial books.

Compound Instrument. A financial instrument that contains two or more embedded financial instruments. For example, a callable bond consists of a bond and a call option.

Comprehensive Income. Change in equity (net asset) arising from either transactions or other occurrences with non-owners. For more information, see Chapter 1.

Contractual Rights and Obligations. Specific legal obligations of the parties to an agreement. Based on the contract terms, rights may result in an asset being recorded, obligations may result in a liability, or an off-balance-sheet contingency may exist.

Counterparty Risk. Counterparty (default) risk is the risk to each contract participant that the counterparty will not abide to its commitments. Such risk applies to each individual or entity in an agreement such as a sales contract. Counterparty risk may be controlled by utilizing a central counterparty.

In counterparty risk there is the risk that a business entity will not pay a bond, credit derivative, or other type of transaction. It is also possible that a company that has purchased credit insurance still has the uncertainty that the insurer will not be able to pay because of financial problems.

An example of counterparty risk is when company X lends funds to company Y. The default risk is that company Y will not pay back the loan or company X will cease giving further loans. Another example is when a company fails to provide agreed-upon securities.

Credit Derivatives. Bilateral financial contracts that isolate specific aspects of credit risk from an underlying instrument and can be used to transfer risk of default from the holder of the instrument to a counterparty that will be compensated for assuming that risk.

Credit Risk. Risk of a loss caused by the failure of a counterparty to perform as per contractual terms.

Derivative Financial Instrument (derivative). Contract in which the value is tied to the return on stocks, debt, currencies, or commodities. Thus, there may be an underlying interest rate, commodity price, stock price index, foreign exchange rate, or other variable.

Duration. The expected actual life, in years, that an asset or a liability will be outstanding. For example, when long-term interest rates are declining, prepayments of home mortgages will significantly shorten their expected duration.

Equity Instrument. A security evidencing ownership interest in a business.

Fair Value. A price set in the ordinary course of business by willing buyers and sellers who are not under duress to buy or sell. The best measure of fair value is a quoted market price when the market is liquid. If a quoted price does not exist, an estimate of fair value is used. When possible, such estimate should take into account quoted market prices for comparable instruments. If comparable instruments with quoted prices are not available, other valuation approaches can be used, including the discounted value of expected future cash flows (using a suitable discount rate), or model-derived prices (option-pricing models, matrix pricing, fundamental analysis, option-adjusted spread models). In arriving at a valuation, consideration should be given to expectations regarding: future revenues, future expenses, interest rates, and volatility. In valuing foreign currency forward contracts by discounting techniques, expected cash flows generally are based on the forward rate (not the spot rate). In valuing liabilities by discounting, the discount rate generally is based on a rate the company would need to pay a financially sound third party to assume a similar obligation.

Financial Asset. Cash, an ownership interest in another company, or a contract to receive cash or another asset from a third party.

Financial Instrument. Financial assets and liabilities. Includes derivatives and non-derivatives.

Financial Liability. Obligation to deliver cash or another financial asset to a third party.

Firm Commitment. Legal agreement or other binding obligation to perform. The failure to perform results in possible damages. The terms of the commitment should be stated, such as price, date and amount.

Forecasted Transaction. Expected transaction, but without firm commitment. A forecasted transaction does not give the company current rights to later benefits or duties for future sacrifices.

Forward Contract. An over-the-counter contract similar to futures. Unlike a futures contract, a forward contract is not uniform or standardized, and is not traded on an exchange. In such a contract, the contract is settled when the underlying is actually delivered or received at a future date—or, if the parties agree, settlement may be in cash, based on the change in value of the underlying. A forward contract may be based on a commodity or a financial instrument. The contract fixes the quantity, price, and date of purchase or sale. In most cases, money is not paid until the delivery date.

Forward Exchange Rate. Agreed-upon rate at which two currencies will be exchanged at some future date, usually 30, 90, or 180 days from the day the forward exchange contract is entered into.

Futures Contract. Agreement to buy or sell a specified amount of a commodity or financial instrument at a particular future date at a given price. With futures, physical delivery of the underlying asset almost never occurs; the position instead is closed out by the purchase of an offsetting contract. The contracts are standardized and traded on an exchange, usually subject to daily margin requirements. Examples of the underlying include commodities, debt instruments, composite stock indexes, or foreign currencies.

Hedge. An action taken to reduce risk, e.g., exposure to market price volatility. For example the purchase of an equity put option can protect the holder against a declining stock price.

Interest Rate Swap. Agreement to exchange future cash flows based on a reference rate. In a single currency interest rate swap, one party pays a fixed interest rate and one party pays a floating interest rate (e.g., LIBOR plus a spread) based on a notional principle amount.

LIBOR. London Inter-Bank Offered Rate. Floating-rate index that can be contrasted with the prime rate in the U.S.

Market Risk. Risk associated with changes in market value of financial instruments.

Market Risk Valuation Adjustments. A valuation adjustment may be used to account for uncertainty in a market price or model-derived value. Such uncertainties include high concentrations in a particular security, or liquidity concerns when trading for a particular security is thin.

Notional Amount. Number of shares, currency, or goods stated in a contract (e.g., the number of bushels in a corn futures contract).

Option Contract. Giving buyers the right, but not the obligation, to purchase ("call") or sell ("put") a specified amount of an asset at a set price for a given time period. The value of an option is typically a minor percentage of the underlying value of the asset.

Permanent Impairment. Decline in the market price of an asset viewed to be other than temporary. The permanent impairment reduces the carrying value of the asset, and establishes a new "cost" basis.

Realized Gain (Loss). Excess (or deficiency) in selling price relative to carrying value of a financial instrument. For instruments that are not marked to market, realized gains or losses are included in net income in the year of the sale.

Repurchase Agreement (Repo). Contract in which the company sells a security to a third party for cash and at the same time commits to repurchase that security at a later date at a stated price plus interest. Interest is due for the period of transfer. Examples of securities involved might be mortgage-backed securities and U.S. Treasuries. "Dollar roll" repurchase agreements are contracts to sell and repurchase similar but not identical securities; the securities are collateralized by different, but similar, mortgage pools and will typically have different principal amounts. These transactions are also referred to as collateralized borrowings.

Reverse Repo.. A security purchased under the agreement to resell. A repurchase agreement contract from the perspective of the company that purchases the security.

Risk of Accounting Loss. Likelihood of loss arising from changes in credit, market or operational risks.

Spot (or Cash) Rate. Exchange rate for a foreign currency for immediate delivery in accordance with normal market conventions.

Securities Lending. Similar to a repurchase agreement except that the company that lends (sells) the security may accept other securities or other financial instruments as collateral, instead of cash.

Swap. Contractual agreement to exchange something, usually obligations to pay streams of money. Typically, there is no exchange of the underlying instrument itself. A swap may be tied to various underlying financial instruments, indices, or commodities. Examples are currency swaps and interest rate swaps. A swap is not publicly traded on an exchange.

Swaption. Option on a swap giving the holder the right but not the obligation to enter into a swap at a particular future date at specified terms or to lengthen or terminate an existing swap.

Underlying. Price, interest rate, share price, foreign exchange rate, index of prices, or other variable applied to a notional amount to compute cash settlement or other exchange per the derivative contract provisions. Although an underlying may be the price of an asset or liability, it is not itself an asset or liability of the derivative holder.

Unrealized Gain (Loss). Difference between market price and carrying (book) value of an unsold financial instrument.

Valuation Adjustments (holdbacks). Adjustments to model-derived values to arrive at fair value. This can be necessary because of such factors as systems limitations, structural complexity of the instrument, hedging costs. For derivatives that are marked to market, models that are used to derive fair value often do not take into account changes in the counterparties' creditworthiness, or certain operational costs. For example, a portion of the initial model-generated mark-to-market may be deferred to take into account potential credit losses. This deferred income is recognized in revenue over time to create a matching of revenue and expense at the portfolio level. A similar treatment may be used to account for normal, recurring operations costs that are not factored into the valuation model.

Value at Risk. A measure of expressing a potential gain or loss on a financial instrument due to market risk over a period of time with a degree of probability.

Warrants. Refers to a call option in the company's stock. Typically, warrants have longer terms than other call options. For transactions in the company's own stock, see Chapter 5 on stockholders' equity.

BACKGROUND

ASC 825 *Financial Instruments* (ASC Glossary—"Financial Instrument"), defines a financial instrument as cash (including currencies of other countries), evidence of an ownership interest in another company (e.g., common or preferred stock), or a contract that both:

☐ Imposes on one company the obligation to (1) deliver cash or another financial instrument to another company or (2) exchange financial instruments with another company on potentially unfavorable terms, and

☐ Conveys to the other company the right (1) to receive cash or another financial instrument from the first company, or (2) exchange other financial instruments on potentially favorable terms with the first company.

From the preceding definition, conventional assets and liabilities (e.g. accounts and notes receivable, accounts and notes payable, investment in equity and debt securities, and bonds payable) are deemed to be financial instruments. The definition also encompasses many derivative contracts, such as options, swaps, caps, and futures. Exhibit 17-1 provides examples of conventional and derivative financial instruments.

Exhibit 17-1: Conventional and Derivative Financial Instruments

Conventional Financial Instruments	Derivative Financial Instruments
Corporate bonds and notes	Interest rate swaps and options
Commercial loans	Credit default swaps
Corporate equities	Stock-index futures and options
Municipal bonds	Fixed rate loan commitments
Mortgages	Mortgage servicing rights
Foreign currencies	Currency futures and options
Accounts receivable and payable	Swaptions
Bank certificates of deposit	Commodity futures and options
Treasury bonds, bills and notes	Interest rate caps, floors, and collars

DERIVATIVE FINANCIAL INSTRUMENTS

A derivative financial instrument has *all* of the following characteristics: (1) it has an underlying interest rate, security or commodity price, foreign exchange rate, or index with one or more notional amounts; (2) it has no initial cash outlay; and (3) the terms permit net settlement between counterparties.

A primary purpose of using derivative financial instruments is to reduce risk, such as risk of changes in market price of interest rates, currency exchange rates, and fluctuations in commodity prices. Derivatives are contracts that may hedge the company from adverse movement in the underlying base. However, derivatives are not without their own risks. If used for speculation, they can be extremely risky. If leveraged, minor adverse price or interest rate changes can result in huge gains or losses. Leverage significantly multiplies return or losses.

Other risks besides leverage exist, such as:

☐ *Credit risk* The risk that the other party to a contract may default. Investors in hedge funds rely on the ability of the fund to meet its obligations.

☐ *Market risk* The risk of loss in the market value of the underlying instrument.

☐ *Operational (business) risk* The risk of internal operational errors (such as failure to accurately reflect counterparty obligations) or poor internal controls.

☐ *Legal risk* A judge may rule the contract illegal or invalid.

☐ *Valuation risk* The risk that an unrealized profit or loss from a transaction is misstated.

☐ *Liquidity risk* Inability to sell a financial instrument quickly because of an illiquid market.

☐ *Correlation risk* Risk that the value of a hedge (e.g., in derivatives, conventional securities) will not react in the same manner as the item being hedged.

☐ *Systemic risk* A problem with a particular instrument that may disrupt the entire market.

☐ *Settlement risk* Risk of not receiving timely payment on a contract.

Derivatives can be either on the balance sheet or off the balance sheet (recorded as a commitment). They include:

☐ Futures.

☐ Option contracts.

☐ Fixed-rate loan commitments.

☐ Interest rate caps and floors.

☐ Interest rate collars.

☐ Forward contracts.

☐ Forward interest rate agreements.

☐ Swaps.

☐ Instruments with similar characteristics.

The FASB's current definition of derivatives excludes on-balance-sheet receivables and payables, such as:

☐ Principal-only ("zero coupon") obligations.

☐ Interest-only ("strips") obligations.

☐ Indexed debt.

☐ Mortgage-backed securities.

☐ Other optional attributes incorporated within those receivables and Payables (e.g., convertible debt conversion or call provisions).

The FASB definition of a derivative excludes (1) security purchases and sales on exchanges that provide standard settlement terms, (2) normal purchases and sales of something other than a financial instrument, (3) certain insurance contracts, and (4) financial guarantees.

A company enters into derivative contracts for either trading (speculative) or hedging purposes. However, only certain hedges qualify to be treated as hedges for accounting purposes. Therefore, a company may enter into a derivative contract as an economic hedge of an item that is not carried at fair value, but the contract is required to be marked to market. For such contracts, the timing of the recognition of the mark-to-market value of the derivative will not match the timing of the recognition of the changes in value of the hedged item. If the hedge is serving its intended purpose, eventually these timing differences will offset, although it will be in different reporting periods.

If the derivative is entered into for trading purposes or hedge accounting is not allowed, then the instrument is recorded at fair value (marked to market) and any unrealized gain or loss is recorded in income. Generally, an end user of derivatives will obtain the fair value of a derivative by getting a quote from a market maker. Market makers will use either observed market transaction prices or models based on discounted cash flows to calculate fair value. If the cash instrument underlying the derivative is illiquid, market risk adjustments may be used to reduce the model-derived value to net realizable value. In addition, valuation adjustments, or holdbacks, may be used to take into account operational costs or changes in counterparty credit risk that are not contemplated in the models. Fair values are also used to evaluate hedge effectiveness.

Accounting loss may arise from writing off a contractual right or from settling a contractual obligation applicable to a financial instrument. An accounting loss that may arise from credit or market risk is required to be footnoted. Credit risk is the possibility that a loss may occur because of the failure of another party to carry out the terms of a derivatives contract. An example is a derivative counterparty's failure to pay the net settlement amount on a contract when due. Market risk is the possibility that future changes in market prices may cause a financial instrument to decline in value. An example is a decline in the price of a financial futures contract.

It is possible that accounting risk associated with a financial instrument may already be reflected in the balance sheet. In other instances, the risk exceeds the amount recorded, which is called unrecorded risk, or off-balance-sheet risk. An example is a guarantee of another company's debt. The estimated amount of potential credit losses is set up as an allowance for bad debts on the balance sheet. For recorded risks, the bad debt allowance is shown as a contra asset. For unrecorded risks, the allowance is classified in liabilities. Credit risk is generally limited to the amount recorded on the balance sheet, whereas market risk is unlimited. Exhibit 17–2 lists certain derivative financial instruments with off-balance-sheet risk.

Cash positions (e.g., securities, loans) have little or no off-balance-sheet risk, although they expose the company to credit and market risks. Accounting loss is limited to the amount recorded on the balance sheet. Thus, there can be no present credit loss if no asset is recorded. However, market risk often exists—that is, the market value the next day may be lower, thereby causing the company to record a loss. Many disclosures relate to communicating risk of loss to financial statement users.

In recent years, the market for credit derivatives products has grown substantially. Simply stated, a credit derivative contract is an agreement between two counterparties to transfer the risk of default of an obligor (as in a commercial loan made by a bank or a corporate bond) from the holder of the instrument (e.g., loan) to another entity that, for a fee, is willing to accept that risk. The fair value of a credit derivative is based on the changing credit risk of the underlying financial instrument. In practice, credit default swaps are the most frequently traded of the various credit derivative products. The main participants in the credit derivatives markets are insurance companies, banks, pension funds, corporations, and hedge funds. As with interest rate derivative products, credit derivatives may be used to reduce the risk of holding a financial instrument, or can be entered into for speculative purposes. It should be remembered that the holder (purchaser) of a credit derivative is now exposed to the credit risk of the protection seller, should the protection seller be unable to pay in the event of a credit default by the obligor on the underlying financial instrument.

An embedded derivative refers to either implicit or explicit terms that affect some or all of the cash flows or the value of other exchanges required by a contract in a manner similar to a derivative instrument.

In Accounting Standards Update (ASU) No. 2010-11 (March 2010) (ASC 815, *Derivatives and Hedging*), *Scope Exception Related to Embedded Credit Derivatives*, the following items do not meet the scope exception for embedded credit derivatives:

1. The possible future payments due to factors excluding subordination.

2. A derivative characteristic applied to a different risk included in a securitized security. (ASC 815-15-15-9)

A company may select the fair value option for a securitized security. A change in fair value over an accounting period is recognized in the income statement. (ASC 815-10-65-5)

ASC 815 abandons the historical accounting approach in that it no longer permits companies to defer gains and losses on derivatives, even on hedge contracts.

Exhibit 17-2: Examples of Derivative Financial Instruments with Off-Balance-Sheet Risk

Financial Instrument	Risk of Accounting Loss to Reporting Company	
	Credit Risk	Market Risk
Over-the-Counter Contracts—marked to market		
In a gain position (i.e., receivable)	Yes	Yes
In a loss position (i.e., payable)	No	Yes

Financial Instrument	Risk of Accounting Loss to Reporting Company	
	Credit Risk	Market Risk
Over-the-Counter Contracts, settled net under a qualifying netting arrangement		
In a net gain position	Yes	Yes
In a net loss position	No	Yes
Exchange-Traded Contracts—marked to market		
In a gain position	Yes, but minimal credit risk if margin settles daily	Yes
In a loss position	No	Yes

CONCENTRATIONS OF CREDIT RISK FOR ALL FINANCIAL INSTRUMENTS

A company must footnote the following for each category of financial instrument with off-balance-sheet credit risk:

☐ The company's collateral policy and access to the collateral. (Disclosure includes a summary description of the collateral plus any other information that may prove useful in helping to understand the extent of market risk.) And,

☐ The amount of accounting loss due to a party's failure to perform, after consideration of the value of available collateral. Additional disclosures are encouraged.

A distinction is to be made between financial instruments held or issued for trading purposes from those held or issued for other purposes for credit risk disclosures.

A company must disclose concentrations of credit risk for financial instruments that could cause the company to be adversely impacted by economic conditions. Examples of credit risk concentrations are sales to companies concentrated in one industry or locality. In this case, disclosures includes:

☐ The amount of possible accounting loss,

☐ The policy regarding security or collateral, and

☐ Particulars regarding the area of concentration (e.g., economic sector, class of customer, geographic region, and activity).

The amount of possible accounting loss must be presented on a gross basis, before consideration of netting agreements. The company then will be required to disclose the nature of netting agreements and how they impact the credit exposure. See the discussion later in this chapter regarding netting agreements under "Offsetting Assets and Obligations."

ASC 815, *DERIVATIVES AND HEDGING*

The following is required by accounting under GAAP:

1. All derivatives are recorded on the balance sheet at fair value—that is, marked to market.

2. Changes in the fair value of derivatives must be recognized in the financial statements as they occur:

   — Changes in value of *qualified* hedges of foreign currency translation exposure are reported as part of comprehensive income (not as part of the income statement).

   — Changes in value of other *qualified* hedges will be recognized in income along with an offsetting adjustment to the item being hedged.

   — Changes in value of all other derivatives are recognized income.

Three types of qualified hedges are discussed in ASC 815-20, *Derivatives and Hedging: Hedging—General*, fair value hedges, cash flow hedges, and foreign currency hedges.

Simply stated, a *fair value hedge* is protection against adverse changes in the value of an existing asset, liability, or unrecognized firm commitment.

A *cash flow hedge* protects against changes in the value of future cash flows— for instance, interest payments on fixed rate debt, if the company is concerned about falling interest rates and the fact that it would not be able to renegotiate the terms of the debt to capitalize on lower rates.

A *foreign currency hedge* protects against adverse movement of exchange rates impacting any foreign currency exposure. A foreign currency hedge can, for example, involve either fair value or cash flow hedges in foreign currency or a net investment in a foreign business activity when there is concern over the impact that a devaluation of a foreign currency would have on the company's investment in an overseas subsidiary.

In all of these three hedges, a hedge effectiveness test must be met in order to achieve hedge accounting. This test is described in further detail in the next section, where illustrations of the accounting are provided.

Exhibit 17-3 lists some common derivative-like contracts, along with whether they are covered by ASC 815.

Exhibit 17-3: Impact of ASC 815 on Selected Financial Instruments

What financial instruments are covered by ASC 815?

	Yes	No
Interest rate caps, floor, collars	✓	
Interest rate and currency swaps	✓	
Financial guarantees		✓
Financial futures contracts	✓	
Forward contracts with no net settlement		✓
Mortgage backed security		✓

What financial instruments are covered by ASC 815?

	Yes	No
Option to purchase securities	✓	
Adjustable rate loan		✓
Variable annuity contract		✓
Swaptions	✓	
Commodities	✓	

ASC 815 requires that many derivatives that are components of a compound instrument be bifurcated (separated into component parts) and accounted for under the new rules. An exception is provided if:

☐ The instrument is subject to mark-to-market accounting,

☐ The embedded derivative does not meet the definition of a derivative, or

☐ The embedded derivative is "clearly and closely" related to the embedded cash instrument. For example, if a deposit pays an interest rate based on a stock index, the deposit must be bifurcated such that the deposit is separated from the embedded stock index because the embedded derivative is not "clearly and closely" related.

Fair Value Hedges

If a hedge qualifies as reducing the risk of changes in value of an on-balance-sheet asset or liability or an unrecognized firm commitment, both the hedge and the underlying risk exposure are marked to market through the income statement. In the case of a qualifying hedge, the gain or loss on the hedging derivative instrument will offset the impact of the valuation of the exposure that is being hedged. For a nonqualifying hedge, any "breakage" between the valuation of the hedge and the underlying risk exposure will flow through earnings.

The following example illustrates the ASC 815 accounting for interest rate swaps used to hedge the fair value of fixed-rate debt.

EXAMPLE

On June 1, 20X2, ABC Corporation enters into an agreement with its bank to borrow $ 10 million over 3 years at a fixed interest rate of 7%, with no prepayment permitted. ABC wishes to convert this debt to floating rate so as to not run the risk of paying an above market interest rate, if the general level of interest rate declines.

An interest rate swap is structured that will require ABC's counterparty to pay it a fixed rate of interest (assumed to be 7%) equal to what ABC owes its bank. In return, ABC will pay its counterparty a floating market rate of interest based on a six-month LIBOR. This effectively converts ABC's fixed-rate debt to floating-rate debt. The expiration of the swap matches the maturity of the borrowing, and the periodic payments under the swap are made with the same frequency as payments required under the borrowing agreement.

The changes in fair value of the fixed-rate debt and the interest rate swap are assumed to move in equal and opposite directions. When interest rates rise, the fair value of the fixed-rate debt increases (ABC is receiving cheaper funding than the market level of interest rates) while the fair value of the interest rate swap decreases (ABC is paying a market interest rate—LIBOR—that is higher than when the swap was originally contracted).

The following value of the swap and the debt is assumed:

	Value of Swap	Value of Debt
June 30, 20X2	+$200,000	$10,200,000
December 31, 20X2	–$100,000	$9,900,000

The calculation of the periodic six-month settlements on the interest rate swap, assuming LIBOR rates in effect as indicated, is:

Date	Pay Six-Month LIBOR	Receive Fixed Rate	Notional Amount	Net Settlement
June 20X2	6%	7%	$10 million	$ 50,000
July 20X2—December 20X2	7$1/4$%	7%	$10 million	$ (12,500)

Accounting Entries

June 30, 20X2:

| Dr. Interest expense | $350,000 | |
| Cr. Accrued interest payable | | $350,000 |

To accrue six months contractual interest due on outstanding debt.

| Dr. Funds borrowed | $200,000 | |
| Cr. Gain on valuation of debt | | $200,000 |

To record gain in the value of fixed-rate debt in a rising interest rate environment.

| Dr. Loss on swap hedge | $200,000 | |
| Cr. Swap hedge (balance sheet liability) | | $200,000 |

To record loss in value of the qualifying swap hedge contract that is marked to market.

| Dr. Cash | $50,000 | |
| Cr. Interest expense | | $50,000 |

To record six-month settlement of the swap as a reduction of interest expense.

December 31, 20X2:

| Dr. Interest expense | $350,000 | |
| Cr. Accrued interest payable | | $350,000 |

To record contractual interest due.

| Dr. Loss on valuation of debt | $300,000 | |
| Cr. Funds borrowed | | $300,000 |

To record the cumulative loss in the value of the fixed-rate debt in a falling interest rate environment.

| Dr. Swap hedge (balance sheet asset) | $300,000 | |
| Cr. Gain on swap hedge | | $300,000 |

To record gain in value of swap hedge contract that is marked to market.

December 31, 20X2:		
Dr. Interest expense	$12,500	
Cr. Cash		$12,500
To record cash payment on semi-annual settlement of the swap as an adjustment to (i.e., increase in), interest expense.		

Cash Flow Hedges

Companies are often interested in protecting (hedging) the value of future cash flows that they will either receive or pay. The nature of cash flows that require protection is one where there is variability/uncertainty of what those future flows will be. In some instances transactions that are hedged relate to contractual future cash flows, whereas in other instances they may relate to forecasted transactions.

Examples of transactions that may be eligible for cash flow hedge treatment include:

☐ A hedge of future cash interest outflows associated with floating rate debt.

☐ A hedge of a forecasted future purchase of a commodity to protect against rising prices.

☐ A hedge to protect against rising rates for prime-based mortgages.

☐ A hedge to lock in the future cost of borrowing for the company.

☐ A hedge to anticipate future repricings of certificates of deposit.

Accounting for cash flow hedges involves reporting the effective portion of the hedge in Other Comprehensive Income. It is later reclassified into earnings in the same period as the contractual or forecasted cash flow affects earnings. Any ineffective portion of the hedge is reported as earnings. This will be clear in the example below.

EXAMPLE

XYZ Corporation has issued $100 million of six-month fixed-interest-rate commercial paper that is rolled over at each expiration date. Rising interest rates will increase its cost of funds when the commercial paper comes up for repricing and this is an exposure XYZ wishes to minimize.

Because XYZ is attempting to take action to protect its future cash interest outflows, in this example there is a cash flow hedge. To hedge its interest rate risk, XYZ sells 100 Treasury bill futures contracts (sold in contract units of $1 million). Management has determined that this strategy meets the hedge effectiveness test—discussed later in this chapter—and thereby qualifies for hedge accounting treatment under ASC-815.

The following changes in interest rates and their impact on future cash flows are assumed:

- ☐ Six-month commercial paper is issued January 1, 20X2 at 6% interest, due June 30.
- ☐ At June 30, 20X2, interest rates increase to 6.5%, resulting in an additional cost of funds of. 5% or $250,000 for the second half of the year.
- ☐ The future contract is removed at June 30 and has a gain of $240,000.

For simplicity purposes, this example does not deal with any initial or variation margin that would be required on the futures contract.

The following financial accounting entries reflect this transaction:

January 1, 20X2		
Dr. Cash	$100,000,000	
Cr. Commercial paper outstanding		$100,000,000
To record issuance of commercial paper.		

June 30, 20X2		
Dr. Interest expense	$3,000,000	
Cr. Accrued interest payable		$3,000,000
To record contractual interest due for six months.		
Dr. Cash	$240,000	
Cr. Other comprehensive income		$240,000
To record gain on the settlement of the futures contract. The entire futures contract is assumed to be an effective hedge.		

July 31, 20X2		
Dr. Interest expense	$541,667	
Cr. Accrued interest payable		$541,667
To record one month of interest after the rollover of the commercial paper to 6.5%.		
Dr. Other comprehensive income	$40,000	
Cr. Interest income		$40,000
To reclassify one month of hedge gain as a reduction of interest expense on the rolled over commercial paper debt.		

The result of the cash flow hedge is that interest expense beginning at the rollover date of the commercial paper has been reduced from what it otherwise would have been if the hedge had not been put in place. In the example, the effective interest rate after the rollover comes to 6.02% (6.5% − .48% hedge gain).

Foreign Currency Hedges

With respect to foreign currency hedges:

1. ASC 815 permits the company to hedge *forecasted transactions* with foreign currency forward contracts, and

2. It permits the company to hedge an exposure with a *tandem currency,* assuming hedge effectiveness can be proven.

(See also Chapter 16, "Foreign Currency Translation and Transactions.")

Hedge Effectiveness Criteria

In order to receive the benefit of hedge accounting, there must be a highly effective relationship between the item to be hedged and the hedging instrument. This effective relationship must exist both at the initiation of the hedge, and throughout the life of the hedge. The relationship must be evaluated quarterly and whenever financial statements for the company are issued.

The company must indicate how hedge effectiveness is defined and measured, and then stay with the criteria. It must also be able to measure the ineffective part of the hedge. Statistical methods, including regression analysis, are a means of assessing initial and ongoing effectiveness. For a hedging relationship to qualify as "highly effective," the change in fair value or cash flows of the hedge must fall between 80% and 125% of the opposite change in fair value or cash flows of the exposure that is hedged.

If a transaction no longer meets the "highly effective" test, hedge accounting is to be terminated.

Disclosure Requirements

Both qualitative and quantitative disclosures are required under ASC 815. The company must provide qualitative disclosures of:

☐ The business reason for holding or issuing derivatives, for both trading and hedging. Discussion of hedging should differentiate by hedge type (fair value hedge, cash flow hedge, and hedges of a foreign currency exposure of a net investment in a foreign operation).

☐ The company's risk management strategy and which risks are hedged with derivatives. The discussion should differentiate by hedge type and detail the items or transactions for which the company hedges risks. A discussion of the company's overall risk management strategy is encouraged.

Similar separate qualitative disclosures should be made for non-derivative instruments used for hedging purposes.

The company's quantitative disclosures for derivatives and non-derivatives by hedge type (for cash flow hedges and fair value hedges) should include the amount of gains or losses recognized in earnings because: (1) They are a result of hedge ineffectiveness, or (2) they are related to the derivative but are excluded in assessing hedge effectiveness. The company should disclose the income statement classification. In addition:

☐ For fair value hedges, the company should disclose the amount recognized that resulted from previously hedged firm commitments that are no longer firm along with the amount of hedge ineffectiveness.

☐ For cash flow hedges, the company should disclose the amount of gains or losses currently included in other comprehensive income that is expected to be recognized in the income statement within the next 12 months. The disclosure should include a discussion of the: (1) events that would cause the earnings to be recognized, and (2) expected maximum duration of hedges of forecasted transactions other than those related to outstanding floating-rate financial instruments. The company should disclose the amount recognized that resulted from previously hedged firm commitments that are no longer firm. The company's comprehensive earnings include the net gain or loss on derivative instruments designated and qualifying as cash flow hedging instruments. Consistent with ASC 220, *Comprehensive Income,* the company must present a reconciliation of changes in the accumulated derivative gain or loss, including, the net change related to hedging transactions, and the net amount recognized in earnings.

For hedges of the net investment in a foreign operation, the company should disclose the amount of gains or losses included in the cumulative translation adjustment.

The company is encouraged to provide quantitative disclosures that provide the context for derivatives by activity.

OFFSETTING OF ASSETS AND LIABILITIES ARISING FROM DERIVATIVE FINANCIAL INSTRUMENTS AND REPURCHASE AGREEMENTS

Offsetting (netting) of assets and liabilities is not permitted unless all of the following four criteria are satisfied:

1. Each of two parties owes the other determinable amounts.
2. The company has the right to set off the amount it owes with the amount owed by the other party.
3. The company intends to set off.
4. The right of set-off is enforceable under law.

ASC 210-20-45-1 states that the requirements for offsetting also relate to conditional contracts and to exchange contracts, such as options, currency swaps, forward contracts, and interest rate swaps, caps, or collars. In a conditional contract, obligations or rights depend on a future occurrence. In an exchange contract, these will be a future exchange of assets or liabilities. Unless the criteria for the right of setoff are satisfied, the fair value of conditional contracts in a gain position should not be offset against other contracts with a loss position. In a similar vein, accrued receivables and payables from conditional or exchange contracts should not be offset against each other unless the preceding four conditions are met.

Recorded amounts, whether accrued or at fair value associated with conditional or exchange contracts, are assets and liabilities in their own right. The fair value of conditional or exchange contracts recognized and executed with the same counterparty may be offset under a master netting agreement. In a master netting arrangement, a reporting company has multiple contracts, with one counterparty stipulating net settlement of all contracts in a single sum in one currency if default or cancellation of any one contract takes place. The contracts need not be of the same type. The offsetting in a master netting situation results in recording one asset or liability constituting the net fair value of all positions for all contracts with the same counterparty.

Similar agreements to master netting arrangements described above include:

1. Derivative clearing agreements;

2. Global master repurchase agreements; and

3. Global master securities lending agreements.

ASC 210-20-45-11 permits (but does not require) offsetting of payables under repurchase arrangements against receivables under reverse repurchase agreements if all six of the following criteria are satisfied:

1. The securities underlying the repurchase and reverse repurchase contracts are in "book entry" form and can be transferred only by means of entries in the records of the transfer system operator or securities custodian.

2. The repurchase and reverse repurchase agreements are with the same counterparty.

3. The repurchase and reverse repurchase agreements are executed under a master netting arrangement.

4. The company expects to use the same account at the clearing bank on the settlement date in transacting the cash flows from both the reverse repurchase agreement and the offsetting repurchase agreement.

5. The repurchase and the reverse repurchase agreements have the same explicit settlement date when initiated.

6. The repurchase and reverse repurchase agreements will be settled on a qualifying securities transfer system that allows for daylight overdrafts or a comparable settlement facility.

The company's offsetting policy must be consistently followed. It is possible that measurement of instruments subject to offset may have differing accounting methods. For example, repurchase agreements are measured at amortized cost, while derivatives are measured at fair value. Any difference in the measurement basis for offset amounts should be described in the related footnote disclosures.

Disclosure Requirements

Accounting Standards Update 2011-11, issued in December 2011, requires the following converged disclosures (identical with IFRS requirements) for annual periods beginning on or after January 1, 2013, and interim periods within those annual periods. Note that the reporting entity, once adopting this standard, must present the following disclosures retrospectively for all periods presented:

1. The gross amounts of recognized assets and liabilities for financial instruments and derivative financial instruments that are either offset (netted on the balance sheet) in accordance with the above described netting criteria, or are subject to an enforceable master netting arrangement or similar agreement, whether or not they have been offset.

2. The amounts offset in accordance with the above described netting criteria.

3. The net amounts presented on the balance sheet.

4. The amounts subject to an enforceable master netting arrangement or similar agreement (not included in 2. above) that either:

   a. Relate to recognized financial and derivative instruments that either management chooses not to offset or does not meet the above netting criteria; or

   b. Relate to financial collateral (including cash collateral).

5. The net amounts after deducting the amounts in 4b. above from 3.

It is recommended that the information above be presented in a table, separately for assets and liabilities. All amounts in the above disclosure must be reconciled with the individual line items presented on the balance sheet. The fair value of any cash or financial instrument held as collateral must be disclosed along with any restriction on the ability to use the collateral to offset obligations of the counterparty. Additionally, the entity must provide a description of the rights of setoff associated with a master netting arrangement, including the nature of those rights.

TRANSFERS AND SERVICING OF FINANCIAL ASSETS AND EXTINGUISHMENTS OF LIABILITIES

Most transfers of financial assets involve the transfer of control over an asset to the buyer/transferee and are accounted for as sales and purchases by the respective parties. Each company recognizes the financial and servicing assets it controls and derecognizes liabilities it extinguishes. The transferor may continue to be involved with assets transferred either through servicing arrangements or agreements to repurchase assets prior to maturity. ASC 860-50-25, *Transfers and Servicing: Servicing Assets and Liabilities*, provides accounting guidance with respect to certain mortgage servicing rights and collateral pledged in repurchase agreements and securities lending arrangements.

Accounting Standards Update (ASU) No. 2011-03 (April 2011) (ASC 860, *Transfers and Servicing*), *Reconsideration of Effective Control for Repurchase Agreements*, removes from the evaluation of effective control the criterion mandating the transferor to have the ability to repurchase financial assets on agreed terms, even when the transferee defaults. A transferor is considered to have kept effective control over transferred financial assets (and therefore has to account for the transaction as a secured borrowing) for agreements that require the transferor to repurchase financial assets before their maturity date if all of the following conditions exist:

- The agreement is made in contemplation of the transfer.

- The repurchase will be made prior to maturity at a determinable price.

- The repurchased financial assets are the same as those transferred.

This update withdraws the previous requirement that the transferor have sufficient collateral to fund most of the cost to buy replaced financial assets. The update also improves the accounting for repurchase agreements (repos).

Mortgage Servicing Rights

Typical transfer and servicing transactions include collateralized mortgage obligations, securitizations, options for repurchase, transfers of loans with recourse, loan participations, and factoring arrangements. For example, a bank that has mortgages may wish to sell those receivables to another financial institution.

A pool of mortgages that are bundled together to form a negotiable instrument is referred to as a mortgage-backed security. Car loans, credit cards, and other assets pooled together are called asset-backed securities. However, in selling these receivables, the bank may retain the rights to service the loans (collect the principal, interest, and escrow payments and pay taxes and insurance payments from the escrow). Servicing activities that generate revenue in excess of the costs of the servicing activity are called *servicing assets,* and they are termed *servicing liabilities* if the costs are more than the revenues. Therefore, the financial components of a loan receivable might include as assets the following: cash, calls or puts, servicing assets, and swaps. The liability components may include servicing liabilities and recourse obligations.

If the company is required to service financial assets, it should record a servicing asset or a servicing obligation for the servicing contract. Servicing may include such activities as collecting principal, interest and escrow payments from the borrower, following up on delinquencies, remitting taxes and insurance out of escrow accounts. Accounting for the servicing of financial assets is as follows:

☐ Servicing assets or servicing liabilities are recorded at fair value.

☐ The balance sheet should present separately servicing assets and servicing liabilities.

☐ Servicing assets retained in the sale or securitization of the assets being serviced are presented at their allocated previous carrying amount based on proportionate fair values.

☐ Servicing assets are amortized proportionately to, and over the period of, estimated net servicing income.

☐ Impairment of servicing assets are recorded in a valuation allowance account and adjusted subsequently as measurement of the impairment changes. This can occur when the future servicing costs exceeds future servicing income.

☐ Servicing liabilities are amortized proportionately to estimated net servicing loss. However, if later events cause an increase in the fair value of the servicing liability, an expense provision should be made. An example is a sudden and drastic increase in servicing expenses.

☐ Rights to future interest income derived from serviced assets exceeding agreed-upon servicing fees should be shown separately from servicing assets.

In the case of previously recognized servicing receivables exceeding fees specified in the contract, they should be reclassified as interest-only strips receivable.

The company must disclose the following information for its servicing as sets and servicing liabilities: (1) amounts recognized and amortized, (2) fair values, (3) risk factors of the underlying financial assets, and (4) movement of the balances in the valuation allowance for impaired activities.

Collateral Pledged in Repurchase Agreements and Securities Lending Arrangements

The principal question with a repurchase agreement is whether it should be treated as a sale or as a collateralized borrowing by the transferor of the securities. In a typical transaction, an entity will "sell" financial assets to a counterparty with an agreement to purchase the same or equivalent assets before their contractual maturity. Financial assets subject to these agreements are typically securities issued by the U.S. Treasury, mortgage-backed securities, or corporate debt. For the transferor, it is an efficient way to raise cash on a short-term basis. If the transferor maintains effective control of the collateral, a sale has not taken place.

Under ASC 860, assets received as collateral in repurchase agreements and securities lending arrangements are considered assets of the company (secured party) if:

☐ The company is able to sell or repledge the collateral, *and*

☐ The party pledging the collateral does *not* have the ability to redeem the collateral on short notice by substituting other collateral or terminating the contract.

In that case, the company recognizes the collateral and an obligation to return the collateral, and the pledging party reclassifies the securities pledged as securities receivable, as in Exhibit 17-4.

Exhibit 17-4: Accounting for Collateral in Certain Repurchase Transactions

Secured Party (Reverse Repo)		Pledging Party (Repo)

Dr. Securities Purchased under Resale Agreements
  Cr. Cash
	Cash →	Dr. Cash
		  Cr. Securities Sold under Repurchase Agreements

Dr. Trading Securities—Collateral Received Cr. Trading Liabilities—Liability to Return Collateral	← Collateral	(Securities are reclassified to a segregated Securities Pledged Asset account)

In April 2011, as a result of the FASB's study of the impact on financial reporting by companies during the "Great Recession" of 2007-2008 in the United States, a significant change (prospective application effective for fiscal years ending on or after December 15, 2011) was adopted. Specifically the FASB has eliminated from the definition of effective control, the criterion requiring the transferor to have the ability to repurchase or redeem the financial assets on substantially the agreed terms and the collateral maintenance implementation guidance related to that criterion. This appears to be a specific response by the FASB to the Lehman Brothers "Repo 105 transactions," which were treated as sales (rather than borrowings) by Lehman because of their over-collateralization of the money they were obligated to return under repurchase agreements. (ASC 860-10-40-22 through ASC 860-10-40-26) The result is that effective control should focus on a transferor's contractual rights or obligations with respect to the transferred assets, not on whether the transferor has the practical ability to perform in accordance with those rights and obligations.

OPTIONS ON ISSUER'S SECURITIES

A company may sign contracts that are tied to, and/or settled in, its own stock. Examples are written put or call options, purchased put or call options, and forward sale or purchase contracts. These contracts may be settled using various the following approaches:

☐ *Physical settlement* The buyer pays cash while the seller delivers the shares.

☐ *Net cash settlement* The party incurring a loss delivers to the party having a gain the cash payment equal to the gain.

☐ *Net share settlement* The party incurring a loss delivers to the party having a gain the shares with a current fair value equal to the gain.

☐ A combination of the preceding.

Such derivatives are excluded from the scope of ASC 815 if they are indexed to the company's stock and classified in Stockholders' Equity.

AUTHORITATIVE LITERATURE

ASC 480-10-65-1 clarifies the difference between liabilities and equity. It mandates an issuing company to classify the financial instruments as liabilities or, when applicable, assets:

☐ A financial instrument of mandatorily redeemable shares that involves an unconditional obligation requiring the issuing entity to redeem it by transferring assets.

☐ A financial instrument, not in the form of an outstanding share, that when issued represents a commitment to reacquire the issuer's stock, or is indexed to such an obligation, and mandates that the issuer satisfy that obligation by transferring assets. Examples are a written put option or forward purchase contract on the issuing company's equity shares that is to be settled in cash or with other assets.

☐ A financial instrument other than an outstanding share that the issuer is unconditionally obligated to settle by issuing a variable number of equity shares provided that the value of the obligation is based on (1) factors inversely tied to changes in the fair value of the issuer's stock (e.g., a written put option), (2) variations in something except the fair value of the issuer's stock (e.g., a financial instrument indexed to the Dow Jones 30 Average), or (3) a fixed dollar amount stated at inception.

Forward contracts to reacquire a company's equity securities that must be settled in cash are initially recorded at the fair value of the shares at inception.

ASC 480-10 is not applicable to features embedded in a financial instrument that is not fully derivative.

Disclosure should be made of the terms of the financial instruments and alternative settlement arrangements. This includes the number of shares, along with their fair values, that would have to be issued and the amount of payments required. In the case of a forward contract or option, disclosure must be made of the forward price or option strike price, the number of the issuer's shares indexed under the contract, and the contractual settlement dates.

Note: Many financial instruments that were previously classified as equity are now considered liabilities under ASC 480-10.

ASC 480-10-55-33 states that freestanding warrants and other similar instruments on shares that are puttable (under option to sell) or mandatorily redeemable include obligations to transfer assets and should be accounted for as liabilities. In the case of puttable shares, the issuer is contingently obligated to transfer assets if the warrant is exercised and the shares are put to the issuer. For mandatorily redeemable shares, the issuer is contingently liable to transfer assets when the holder exercises the warrant. In both instances, the warrant should be accounted for as a liability.

Accounting for Certain Hybrid Financial Instruments

ASC 815-15-25-4 and 25-5 allows for the fair value option to be elected for the measurement of any hybrid instrument containing an embedded derivative that otherwise would require bifurcation. This Codification section clarifies which principal-only and interest-only strips are not subject to the requirements of ASC 815. ASC 815-155 states that concentration of credit risk in the form of subordination is *not* embedded derivatives. The statement requires the appraisal of interests in securitized financial assets to identify interests that are freestanding derivatives or that are hybrid financial instruments having an embedded derivative requiring bifurcation.

Accounting for Servicing of Financial Assets

ASC 860-50-35-3 deals with respect to the accounting for separately recognized servicing assets and liabilities. A servicing asset (liability) is a contract to service financial assets under which the estimated future revenues from specified servicing fees, late charges, and other ancillary revenues are *not* expected to more than compensate for performing services.

A company recognizes a servicing asset or liability each time it is obligated to service a financial asset by agreeing to a service contract in any of the following cases:

- An acquisition or committing to an obligation to service a financial asset that does not apply to financial assets of the servicer or its consolidated affiliates.

- A transfer of the servicer's financial assets that satisfies the requirements for sale accounting.

- A transfer of the servicer's financial assets to a special-purpose entity in a guaranteed mortgage securitization in which the transferor keeps all of the securities and classifies them as either trading or available-for-sale. (*Securitization* is the process by which financial assets are transformed into securities).

ASC 860-10-65-3 requires that all separately recognized servicing assets and liabilities be initially measured at fair value if practicable. The company is allowed to use one of the following subsequent measurement methods:

- *Fair value method* The fair value of the servicing assets or liabilities is used for each reporting date. A change in fair value during the period is recognized in earnings.

- *Amortization method* Servicing assets or liabilities is amortized in proportion to and over the period of estimated net servicing income (loss). At the end of each reporting period, servicing assets or liabilities must be checked for any impairment or increased obligation based on fair value.

ASC 860-50-50-3 mandates separate presentation of servicing assets and liabilities subsequently measured at fair value on the balance sheet. Appropriate disclosures should also be made for separately recognized servicing assets and liabilities.

A change that utilizes derivatives to reduce the risks associated with servicing assets and liabilities must account for those derivative instruments at fair value.

An interest-only strip is the right to receive the interest due on a bond, mortgage loan, or other interest-bearing financial asset.

A transfer is the conveyance of a noncash financial asset by and to someone other than the issuer of that financial asset. Therefore, a transfer includes selling a receivable, collateralizing a receivable, or putting the receivable into a securitization trust. However, the term *transfer* excludes the origination of a receivable, the settlement of a receivable, or the restructuring of a receivable into a securitization in a troubled debt restructuring.

ANNUAL REPORT REFERENCES

Oshkosh
2011 Annual Report

14. Derivative Financial Instruments and Hedging Activities

The Company has used forward foreign currency exchange contracts ("derivatives") to reduce the exchange rate risk of specific foreign currency denominated transactions. These derivatives typically require the exchange of a foreign currency for U.S. dollars at a fixed rate at a future date. At times, the Company has designated these hedges as either cash flow hedges or fair value hedges under FASB ASC Topic 815, *Derivatives and Hedging,* as follows:

Fair Value Hedging Strategy—The Company enters into forward foreign exchange contracts to hedge certain firm commitments denominated in foreign currencies, primarily the Euro. The purpose of the Company's foreign currency hedging activities is to protect the Company from risk that the eventual U.S. dollar-equivalent cash flows from the sale of products to international customers will be adversely affected by changes in the exchange rates.

Cash Flow Hedging Strategy—To protect against an increase in the cost of forecasted purchases of foreign-sourced component parts payable in Euro, the Company has a foreign currency cash flow hedging program. The Company hedges portions of its forecasted purchases denominated in Euro with forward contracts. When the U.S. dollar weakens against the Euro, increased foreign currency payments are offset by gains in the value of the forward contracts. Conversely, when the U.S. dollar strengthens against the Euro, reduced foreign currency payments are offset by losses in the value of the forward contracts.

At September 30, 2011 and 2010, the Company had no forward foreign exchange contracts designated as hedges.

To manage a portion of the Company's exposure to changes in LIBOR-based interest rates on its variable-rate debt, the Company entered into an amortizing interest rate swap agreement that effectively fixes the interest payments on a portion of the Company's variable-rate debt. The swap has been designated as a cash flow hedge of 3-month LIBOR-based interest payments and, accordingly, derivative gains or losses are reflected as a component of accumulated other comprehensive income (loss) and are amortized to interest expense over the respective lives of the borrowings. During fiscal 2011, 2010 and 2009, $16.6 million, $41.6 million and $48.3 million of expense, respectively, was recorded in the Consolidated Statements of Operations as amortization of interest rate derivative gains and losses. At September 30, 2011, $2.1 million of net unrealized losses remained deferred in "Accumulated other comprehensive income (loss)." See Note 11 of the Notes to Consolidated Financial Statements for information regarding the interest rate swap.

The Company has entered into forward foreign currency exchange contracts to create an economic hedge to manage foreign exchange risk exposure associated with non-functional currency denominated payables resulting from global sourcing activities. The Company has not designated these derivative contracts as hedge transactions under ASC Topic 815, and accordingly, the mark-to-market impact of these derivatives is recorded each period in current earnings. The fair value of foreign currency related derivatives is included in the Consolidated Balance Sheets in "Other current assets" and "Other current liabilities." At September 30, 2011, the U.S. dollar equivalent of these outstanding forward foreign exchange contracts totaled $154.5 million in notional amounts, including $69.1 million in contracts to sell Euro, $65.0 million in contracts to sell Australian dollars, $18.2 million in contracts to sell U.K. pounds sterling and buy Euro with the remaining contracts covering a variety of foreign currencies.

Fair Market Value of Financial Instruments—The fair values of all open derivative instruments in the Consolidated Balance Sheets were as follows (in millions):

	September 30, 2011			September 30, 2010		
	Other Current Assets	Other Current Liabilities	Other Long-term Liabilities	Other Current Assets	Other Current Liabilities	Other Long-term Liabilities
Designated as hedging instruments:						
Interest rate contracts	$ –	$ 2.1	$ –	$ –	$ 15.6	$ 2.8
Not designated as hedging instruments:						
Foreign exchange contracts	0.8	0.2	–	0.3	0.8	–
	$ 0.8	$ 2.3	$ –	$ 0.3	$16.4	$ 2.8

The pre-tax effects of derivative instruments on the Consolidated Statements of Operations consisted of the following (in millions):

		Fiscal Year Ended September 30,	
	Classification of Gains (Losses)	2011	2010
Cash flow hedges:			
Reclassified from other comprehensive income (effective portion):			
Interest rate contracts	Interest expense	$(16.6)	$(40.7)
Foreign exchange contracts	Cost of sales	–	(0.3)
Not designated as hedges:			
Interest rate contracts	Interest expense	–	(0.9)
Foreign exchange contracts	Miscellaneous, net	2.0	2.8
		$(14.6)	$(39.1)

Hormel Foods
2011 Annual Report

Note M. DERIVATIVES AND HEDGING

The Company uses hedging programs to manage price risk associated with commodity purchases. These programs utilize futures contracts and swaps to manage the Company's exposure to price fluctuations in the commodities markets. The Company has determined that its programs which are designated as hedges are highly effective in offsetting the changes in fair value or cash flows generated by the items hedged.

Cash Flow Hedges: The Company utilizes corn and soybean meal futures to offset the price fluctuation in the Company's future direct grain purchases, and has entered into various swaps to hedge the purchases of grain and natural gas at certain plant locations. The financial instruments are designated and accounted for as cash flow hedges, and the Company measures the effectiveness of the hedges on a regular basis. Effective gains or losses related to these cash flow hedges are reported in accumulated other comprehensive loss and reclassified into earnings, through cost of products sold, in the period or periods in which the hedged transactions affect earnings. Any gains or losses related to hedge ineffectiveness are recognized in the current period cost of products sold. The Company typically does not hedge its grain or natural gas exposure beyond the next two upcoming fiscal years. As of October 30, 2011, and October 31, 2010, the Company had the following outstanding commodity futures contracts and swaps that were entered into to hedge forecasted purchases:

Commodity	Volume	
	October 30, 2011	October 31, 2010
Corn	**20.8 million bushels**	21.1 million bushels
Soybean meal	–	190,400 tons
Natural gas	**0.5 million MMBTU's**	1.6 million MMBTU's

As of October 30, 2011, the Company has included in accumulated other comprehensive loss, hedging gains of $27.3 million (before tax) relating to its positions, compared to gains of $32.9 million (before tax) as of October 31, 2010. The Company expects to recognize the majority of these gains over the next 12 months. The balance as of October 30, 2011, includes gains of $6.9 million related to the Company's soybean meal futures contracts. These contracts were de-designated as cash flow hedges effective January 30, 2011, as they were no longer highly effective. These gains will remain in AOCL until the hedged transactions occur or it is probable the hedged transactions will not occur. Gains or losses related to these contracts after the date of de-designation have been recognized in earnings as incurred.

Fair Value Hedges: The Company utilizes futures to minimize the price risk assumed when forward priced contracts are offered to the Company's commodity suppliers. The intent of the program is to make the forward priced commodities cost nearly the same as cash market purchases at the date of delivery. The futures contracts are designated and accounted for as fair value hedges, and the Company measures the effectiveness of the hedges on a regular basis. Changes in the fair value of the futures contracts, along with the gain or loss on the hedged purchase commitment, are marked-to-market through earnings and are recorded on the Consolidated Statement of Financial Position as a current asset and liability, respectively. Effective gains or losses related to these fair value hedges are recognized through cost of products sold in the period or periods in which the hedged transactions affect earnings. Any gains or losses related to hedge ineffectiveness are recognized in the current period cost of products sold. As of October 30, 2011, and October 31, 2010, the Company had the following outstanding commodity futures contracts designated as fair value hedges:

Commodity	Volume	
	October 30, 2011	October 31, 2010
Corn	**12.4 million bushels**	9.9 million bushels
Lean hogs	**1.3 million cwt**	1.1 million cwt

Other Derivatives: During fiscal years 2011 and 2010, the Company has held certain futures and options contract positions as part of a merchandising program and to manage the Company's exposure to fluctuations in commodity markets and foreign currencies. The Company has not applied hedge accounting to these positions.

Additionally, as of January 30, 2011, the Company de-designated its soybean meal futures contracts that were previously designated as cash flow hedges, as these contracts were no longer highly effective. Hedge accounting is no longer being applied to these contracts, and gains or losses occurring after the date of de-designation have been recognized in earnings as incurred.

As of October 30, 2011, and October 31, 2010, the Company had the following outstanding futures and options contracts related to other programs:

Commodity	Volume	
	October 30, 2011	October 31, 2010
Corn	–	1.5 million bushels
Soybean meal	**4,300 tons**	1,200 tons

Fair Values: The fair values of the Company's derivative instruments (in thousands) as of October 30, 2011, and October 31, 2010, were as follows:

	Location on Consolidated Statement of Financial Position	Fair Value[1]	
		October 30, 2011	October 31, 2010
Asset Derivatives:			
Derivatives Designated as Hedges:			
Commodity contracts	Other current assets	**$ 58,753**	$ 54,395
Derivatives Not Designated as Hedges:			
Commodity contracts	Other current assets	**121**	2,137
Total Asset Derivatives		**$ 58,874**	$ 56,532
Liability Derivatives:			
Derivatives Designated as Hedges:			
Commodity contracts	Accounts payable	**$ 351**	$ 6,390

	Location on Consolidated Statement of Financial Position	Fair Value[1]	
		October 30, 2011	October 31, 2010
Total Liability Derivatives		$ 351	$ 6,390

[1] Amounts represent the gross fair value of derivative assets and liabilities. The Company nets the derivative assets and liabilities for each of its hedging programs, including cash collateral, when a master netting arrangement exists between the Company and the counterparty to the derivative contract. The amount or timing of cash collateral balances may impact the classification of the derivative in the Consolidated Statement of Financial Position. See Note N - Fair Value Measurements for a discussion of these net amounts as reported in the Consolidated Statements of Financial Position.

Derivative Gains and Losses: Gains or losses (before tax, in thousands) related to the Company's derivative instruments for the fiscal year ended October 30, 2011, and October 31, 2010, were as follows:

	Gain/(Loss) Recognized in Accumulated Other Comprehensive Loss (AOCL) (Effective Portion)[1]			Gain/(Loss) Recognized in Earnings (Effective Portion)[4]		Gain/(Loss) Recognized in Earnings (Ineffective Portion)[2][5]	
	Fiscal Year Ended			Fiscal Year Ended		Fiscal Year Ended	
Cash Flow Hedges:	October 30, 2011	October 31, 2010	Location on Consolidated Statement of Operations	October 30, 2011	October 31, 2010	October 30, 2011	October 31, 2010
Commodity contracts	$39,480	$23,511M	Cost of products sold	$45,103	$(28,672)	$(8,704)	$9,947

[1] Amounts represent gains or losses in AOCL before tax. See Note B for the after tax impact of these gains or losses on net earnings.
[2] There were no gains or losses excluded from the assessment of hedge effectiveness during the fiscal year.
[3] There were no gains or losses resulting from the discontinuance of cash flow hedges during the fiscal year. However, effective January 30, 2011, the Company de-designated and discontinued hedge accounting for its soybean meal futures contracts. At the date of de-designation of these hedges, gains of $17.7 million (before tax) were deferred in AOCL, with $6.9 million (before tax) remaining as of October 30, 2011. These gains will remain in AOCL until the hedged transactions occur or it is probable the hedged transactions will not occur. Gains or losses related to these contracts after the date of de-designation have been recognized in earnings as incurred.
[4] Amounts represent losses on commodity contracts designated as fair value hedges that were closed during the fiscal year, which were offset by a corresponding gain on the underlying hedged purchase commitment. Additional gains or losses related to changes in the fair value of open commodity contracts, along with the offsetting gain or loss on the hedged purchase commitment, are also marked-to-market through earnings with no impact on a net basis.
[5] There were no gains or losses recognized as a result of a hedged firm commitment no longer qualifying as a fair value hedge during the fiscal year.

		Gain/(Loss) Recognized in Earnings	
		Fiscal Year Ended	
Derivatives Not Designated as Hedges:	Location on Consolidated Statement of Operations	October 30, 2011	October 31, 2010
Commodity contracts	Cost of products sold	$(1,981)	$ (86)
Commodity contracts	Net sales	$(129)	$ (1)
Option contracts	Cost of products sold	$ –	$1,883

Navistar
2011 Annual Report

13. Fair value measurements

For assets and liabilities measured at fair value on a recurring and nonrecurring basis, a three-level hierarchy of measurements based upon observable and unobservable inputs is used to arrive at fair value. Observable inputs are independent market data, while unobservable inputs reflect our assumptions about valuation. Depending on the inputs, we classify each fair value measurement as follows:

- Level 1—based upon quoted prices for *identical* instruments in active markets,

- Level 2—based upon quoted prices for similar instruments, prices for identical or *similar* instruments in markets that are not active, or model-derived valuations, all of whose significant inputs are observable, and

- Level 3—based upon one or more significant unobservable inputs.

The following section describes key inputs and assumptions in our valuation methodologies:

Cash Equivalents and Restricted Cash Equivalents—We classify highly liquid investments, with a maturity of 90 days or less at the date of purchase, including U.S. Treasury bills, federal agency securities, and commercial paper, as cash equivalents. We use quoted prices to determine fair value.

Marketable Securities—Our marketable securities portfolios are classified as available-for-sale and primarily include investments in U.S. government and commercial paper with a maturity of greater than 90 days at the date of purchase. We use quoted prices from active markets to determine fair value.

Derivative Assets and Liabilities—We measure the fair value of derivatives assuming that the unit of account is an individual derivative transaction and that each derivative could be sold or transferred on a stand-alone basis. We classify within Level 2 our derivatives that are traded over-the-counter and valued using internal models based on observable market inputs. In certain cases, market data is not available and we estimate inputs such as in situations where trading in a particular commodity is not active. Measurements based upon these unobservable assumptions are classified within Level 3. For more information regarding derivatives, see Note 14, *Financial instruments and commodity contracts.*

Retained Interests—We retain certain interests in receivables sold in off-balance sheet securitization transactions prior to November 1, 2010. We estimate the fair value of retained interests using internal valuation models that incorporate market inputs and our own assumptions about future cash flows. The fair value of retained interests is estimated based on the present value of monthly collections on the sold finance receivables in excess of amounts accruing to investors and other obligations arising in securitization transactions. In addition to the amount of debt and collateral held by the securitization vehicle, the three key inputs that affect the valuation of the retained interests include credit losses, payment speed, and the discount rate. We classify these assets within Level 3. For more information regarding retained interests, see Note 4, *Finance receivables.*

Guarantees—We provide certain guarantees of payments and residual values to specific counterparties. Fair value of these guarantees is based upon internally developed models that utilize current market-based assumptions and historical data. We classify these liabilities within Level 3. For more information regarding guarantees, see Note 15, *Commitments and contingencies.*

The following table presents the financial instruments measured at fair value on a recurring basis as of October 31, 2011:

(in millions)	Level 1	Level 2	Level 3	Total
Assets				
Marketable securities				
U.S. Treasury bills	$ 283	$ –	$ –	$ 283
Other U.S and non-U.S. government bonds	415	–	–	415
Other	20	–	–	20
Derivative financial instruments				
Foreign currency contracts	–	–	1	1
Commodity contracts	–	3	–	3
Total assets	$ 718	$ 3	$ 1	$ 722
Liabilities				
Derivative financial instruments				
Foreign currency contracts	–	4	–	4
Commodity contracts	–	3	63	36
Guarantees	–	–	6	6
Total liabilities	$ –	$ 7	$ 9	$ 16

The following table presents the financial instruments measured at fair value on a recurring basis as of October 31, 2010:

(in millions)	Level 1	Level 2	Level 3	Total
Assets				
Marketable securities				
U.S. Treasury bills	$ 159	$ –	$ –	$ 159
Other U.S and non-U.S. government bonds	407	–	–	407
Other	20	–	–	20
Derivative financial instruments				
Commodity contracts	–	–	2	2
Foreign currency contracts	–	8	–	8
Retained interests	–	–	53	53
Total assets	$ 586	$ 8	$ 55	$ 649
Liabilities				
Derivative financial instruments				
Commodity contracts	–	4	–	4
Total liabilities	$ –	$ 4	$ –	$ 4

The table below presents the changes for those financial instruments classified within Level 3 of the valuation hierarchy:

		2011			2010	
				Interest rate		
		Retained	Commodity	swap assets and	Retained	Commodity
(in millions)	Guarantees	interests	contracts	liabilities	interests	contracts
Year Ended October 31						
Balance at November 1	$ –	$ 53	$ 2	$ 1	$ 291	$ –
Total gains (losses) (realized/ unrealized) included in earnings(A)	–	–	2	(1)	4	2
Purchases, issuances, and settlements	6	(53)	(6)	–	(242)	–
Balance at October 31	$ 6	$ –	$ (2)	$ –	$ 53	$ 2

(A) For interest rate swap assets and liabilities, gains (losses) are included in *Interest expense.* For commodity contracts, gains (losses) are included in *Cost of products sold.* For retained interests, gains recognized are included in *Finance revenues.*

The following table presents the financial instruments measured at fair value on a nonrecurring basis as of October 31:

| | Level 2 | |
	2011	2010
(in millions)		
Finance receivables(A)	$ 5	$ 27

(A) Certain impaired finance receivables are measured at fair value on a nonrecurring basis. An impairment charge is recorded for the amount by which the carrying value of the receivables exceeds the fair value of the underlying collateral, net of remarketing costs. As of October 31, 2011, impaired receivables with a carrying amount of $15 million had specific loss reserves of $10 million and a fair value of $5 million. As of October 31, 2010, impaired receivables with a carrying amount of $50 million had specific loss reserves of $23 million and a fair value of $27 million. Fair values of the underlying collateral are determined by reference to dealer vehicle value publications adjusted for certain market factors.

For the purpose of impairment evaluation, the Company measured the fair values of certain long-lived assets, including intangible assets, utilizing the fair value measurement guidance. The following table presents the non-financial instruments measured at fair value on a nonrecurring basis:

| | Level 3 |
	2011
(in millions)	
Assets	
Property and equipment(A)	$ 54
Intangible assets(B)	30
Total assets	$ 84

(A) Certain impaired property and equipment with a carrying amount of $64 million were written down to their fair value of $54 million, resulting in an impairment charge of $10 million, which was included in *Impairment of property and equipment and intangible assets* during the three months ended July 31, 2011. We utilized the market and cost approach to determine the fair value of these assets.

(B) Intangible assets with a carrying amount of $84 million were written down to their fair value of $30 million, resulting in an impairment charge of $54 million, which was included in *Impairment of property and equipment and intangible assets* during the three months ended July 31, 2011. We utilized the income and market approach to determine the fair value of these assets.

In addition to the methods and assumptions we use for the financial instruments recorded at fair value as discussed above, we use the following methods and assumptions to estimate the fair value for our other financial instruments that are not marked to market on a recurring basis. The carrying amounts of cash and cash equivalents, restricted cash and cash equivalents, and accounts payable approximate fair values because of the short-term maturity and highly liquid nature of these instruments. The carrying amounts of customer receivables and retail and wholesale accounts approximate fair values as a result of the short-term nature of the receivables. Due to the nature of the aforementioned financial instruments, they have been excluded from the fair value amounts presented in the table below. The fair values of our finance receivables are estimated by discounting expected cash flows at estimated current market rates. We also use quoted market prices, when available, or the present value of estimated future cash flows to determine fair values of debt instruments.

The carrying values and estimated fair values of financial instruments as of October 31, 2011 and 2010 are summarized in the table below:

	October 31, 2011 Carrying Value	Estimated Fair Value	October 31, 2010 Carrying Value	Estimated Fair Value
(in millions)				
Assets				
Finance receivables	$ 2,141	$ 2,085	$ 2,465	$ 2,349
Notes receivable	47	47	40	40
Liabilities				
Debt:				
Manufacturing operations				
8.25% Senior Notes, due 2021	967	1,131	965	1,141
3.0% Senior Subordinated Convertible Notes, due 2014(A)	497	633	476	684
Debt of majority-owned dealerships	94	88	66	63
Financing arrangements	114	112	203	197
Loan Agreement related to 6.5% Tax Exempt Bonds, due 2040	225	234	225	234

| | October 31, 2011 | | | October 31, 2010 | |
	Carrying Value	Estimated Fair Value	Carrying Value	Estimated Fair Value
Promissory Note	40	39	–	–
Other	39	26	33	29
Financial services operations				
Asset-backed debt issued by consolidated SPEs, at various rates, due serially through 2018	1,664	1,695	1,731	1,773
Bank revolvers, at fixed and variable rates, due dates from 2012 through 2018	1,072	1,091	974	984
Commercial paper, at variable rates, due serially through 2012	70	70	67	67
Borrowings secured by operating and finance leases, at various rates, due serially through 2017	70	70	112	113

(A) The carrying value represents the financial statement amount of the debt after allocation of the conversion feature to equity, while the fair value is based on quoted market prices for the convertible note which includes the equity feature.

14. Financial instruments and commodity contracts

Derivative Financial Instruments

We use derivative financial instruments as part of our overall interest rate, foreign currency, and commodity risk management strategies to reduce our interest rate exposure, reduce exchange rate risk for transactional exposures denominated in currencies other than the functional currency, and minimize the effect of commodity price volatility. From time to time, we use foreign currency forward and option contracts to manage the risk of exchange rate movements that would reduce the value of our foreign currency cash flows. Foreign currency exchange rate movements create a degree of risk by affecting the value of sales made and costs incurred in currencies other than the functional currency. From time to time, we also use commodity forward contracts to manage our exposure to variability in certain commodity prices. In connection with the sale of the Convertible Notes, the Company purchased call options for $125 million. The call options are intended to minimize share dilution associated with the Convertible Notes. As the call options and warrants are indexed to our common stock, we recognized them in permanent equity in *Additional paid in capital*, and will not recognize subsequent changes in fair value as long as the instruments remain classified as equity. For additional information on the purchased call options, see Note 10, *Debt*.

We generally do not enter into derivative financial instruments for speculative or trading purposes and did not during the years ended October 31, 2011,

2010 and 2009. None of our derivatives qualified for hedge accounting treatment in 2011, 2010 and 2009.

Certain of our derivative contracts contain provisions that require us to provide collateral if certain thresholds are exceeded. No collateral was provided at October 31, 2011 or October 31, 2010. Collateral is not required to be provided by our counter-parties for derivative contracts. We manage exposure to counter-party credit risk by entering into derivative financial instruments with various major financial institutions that can be expected to fully perform under the terms of such instruments.

We do not anticipate nonperformance by any of the counter-parties. Our exposure to credit risk in the event of nonperformance by the counter-parties is limited to those gains that have been recorded, but have not yet been received in cash. At October 31, 2011 and October 31, 2010, our exposure to the credit risk of others was $4 million and $10 million, respectively.

Our financial services operations manage exposure to fluctuations in interest rates by limiting the amount of fixed rate assets funded with variable rate debt. This is accomplished by funding fixed rate receivables utilizing a combination of fixed rate and variable rate debt and derivative financial instruments to convert variable rate debt to fixed. These derivative financial instruments may include interest rate swaps, interest rate caps, and forward contracts. The fair value of these instruments is estimated by discounting expected future monthly settlements and is subject to market risk, as the instruments may become less valuable due to changes in market conditions, interest rates, or credit spreads of counter-parties. There were no such derivative financial instruments outstanding as of October 31, 2011. Notional amounts of derivative financial instruments do not represent exposure to credit risk.

The fair values of all derivatives are recorded as assets or liabilities on a gross basis in our Consolidated Balance Sheets. At October 31, 2011 and 2010, the fair values of our derivatives and their respective balance sheet locations are presented in the following table:

As of October 31, 2011				
Asset Derivatives			*Liability Derivatives*	
Location in Consolidated Balance Sheets		*Fair Value*	*Location in Consolidated Balance Sheets*	*Fair Value*
(in millions)				
Foreign currency contracts	Other current assets	$ 3	Other current liabilities	$ –
Cross currency swaps	Other current assets	–	Other current liabilities	4
Commodity contracts	Other current assets	1	Other current liabilities	6
Total fair value		$ 4		$ 10

| | As of October 31, 2010 | | | |
| | Asset Derivatives | | Liability Derivatives | |
Location in Consolidated Balance Sheets		Fair Value	Location in Consolidated Balance Sheets	Fair Value
(in millions)				
Foreign currency contracts	Other current assets	$ 8	Other current liabilities	$ –
Commodity contracts	Other current assets	2	Other current liabilities	4
Total fair value		$ 10		$ 4

The location and amount of gain (loss) recognized in income on derivatives are as follows for the years ended October 31:

| Location in Consolidated Statements of Operations | | Amount of Gain (Loss) Recognized | | |
		2011	2010	2009
(in millions)				
Interest rate swaps	Interest expense	$ –	$ (5)	$ (44)
Interest rate caps purchased	Interest expense	–	(3)	2
Interest rate caps sold	Interest expense	–	3	(1)
Cross currency swaps	Other income, net	(8)	–	–
Foreign currency contracts	Other income, net	4	8	5
Commodity forward contracts	Costs of products sold	14	1	(6)
Total gain (loss)		$ 10	$ 4	$ (44)

Foreign Currency Contracts

During 2011 and 2010, we entered into foreign exchange forward and option contracts as economic hedges of anticipated cash flows denominated in Canadian dollars, Indian rupees, Brazilian reais, and Euros. As of October 31, 2011, we had forward exchange contracts with notional amounts of C $6 million Canadian dollars with a maturity date of January 2012 and € 54 million Euros with maturity dates ranging from November 2011 through August 2012. As of October 31, 2010, we had outstanding forward exchange contracts with notional amounts of € 49 million Euros and C $24 million Canadian dollars. All of these contracts were entered into to protect against the risk that the eventual cash flows resulting from certain transactions will be affected by changes in exchange rates between the U.S. dollar and the respective foreign currency.

Commodity Forward Contracts

During 2011 and 2010, we entered into commodity forward contracts as economic hedges of our exposure to variability in commodity prices for diesel fuel,
lead, steel, and natural rubber. As of October 31, 2011, we had outstanding diesel
fuel contracts with aggregate notional values of $19 million, outstanding lead
contracts with aggregate notional values of $1 million, outstanding steel con-
tracts with aggregate notional values of $41 million, and outstanding natural
rubber contracts with aggregate notional values of $14 million. The commodity
forward contracts have maturity dates ranging from December 2011 to December
2012. As of October 31, 2010, we had outstanding diesel fuel contracts with
aggregate notional values of $21 million, outstanding lead contracts with aggre-
gate notional values of $1 million, and outstanding steel contracts with aggregate
notional values of $80 million. All of these contracts were entered into to protect
against the risk that the eventual cash flows related to purchases of the commodities will be affected by changes in prices.

Interest-Rate Contracts

We may enter into various interest-rate contracts, including interest-rate swaps
and cross currency interest-rate swaps. Interest-rate swaps involve the exchange
of fixed for floating rate or floating for fixed rate interest payments based on the
contractual notional amounts in a single currency. Cross currency interest-rate
swaps involve the exchange of notional amounts and interest payments in
different currencies. We are exposed to interest rate and exchange rate risk
caused by market volatility as a result of our borrowing activities. The objective
of these contracts is to mitigate the fluctuations on earnings, cash flows, and fair
value of borrowings. As of October 31, 2011, the notional amount of our outstanding interest-rate contracts was $50 million.

International Game Technology
2011 Annual Report

10. FAIR VALUE MEASUREMENTS

Financial Assets (Liabilities) Carried at Fair Value

	Fair Value	Level 1	Level 2	Level 3
September 30, 2011				
Money market funds	$ 76.9	$ 76.9	$ –	$ –
Investments in unconsolidated affiliates	9.3	–	–	9.3
Derivative assets	90.8	–	90.8	–
Derivative liabilities	(93.2)	–	(93.2)	–

	Fair Value	Level 1	Level 2	Level 3
September 30, 2010				
Money market funds	137.5	137.5	–	–
Investments in unconsolidated affiliates	34.0	12.7	–	21.3
Derivative assets	52.1	–	52.1	–
Derivative liabilities	(54.3)	–	(54.3)	–

Reconciliation of Items Carried at Fair Value Using Significant Unobservable Inputs (Level 3)

	2011	2010		2009	
	Investments in Unconsolidated Affiliates	Investments in Unconsolidated Affiliates	Investments in ARS and Put Rights	Investments in Unconsolidated Affiliates	Investments in ARS and Put Rights
Beginning balance	$ 21.3	$ 78.4	$ 21.3	$ 80.4	$ 19.6
Total gain (loss):					
Included in other income (expense) - other	(2.1)	(19.5)	0.3	(1.7)	(0.3)
Included in other comprehensive income	0.1	(0.7)	–	2.8	2.0
Purchases, issuances, accretion, settlements	(10.0)	(36.9)	(21.6)	(3.1)	–
Ending balance	$ 9.3	$ 21.3	$ –	$ 78.4	$ 21.3
Net change in unrealized gain (loss) included in earnings related to instruments still held	$ (2.1)	$ (19.5)	$ –	$ –	$ (0.3)

Valuation Techniques and Balance Sheet Presentation

Money market funds were valued based on quoted market prices in active markets and are primarily money market securities.

Investments in unconsolidated affiliates were valued using quoted market prices when available or DCF models incorporating market participant assumptions for credit quality and market interest rates and a Black-Scholes or integrated lattice model with assumptions for stock price volatility and default recovery rates. These investments are presented as a component of other noncurrent assets. See Note 2.

Investments in ARS were valued using DCF, with certain assumptions related to lack of liquidity and observable market transactions. Related put rights were valued based on the difference between the ARS par and fair value, discounted for the broker's non-performance risk and the time remaining until the exercise period. Our entire portfolio of ARS was sold during 2010.

Derivative assets and liabilities were valued using quoted forward pricing from bank counterparties, LIBOR credit default swap rates for non-performance risk, and net settlement amounts where appropriate. These are presented primarily as components of other assets, other liabilities, and notes payable. See Note 11.

Financial Assets (Liabilities) Not Carried at Fair Value

	Carrying Value	Fair Value	Unrealized	
			Gain	Loss
September 30, 2011				
Jackpot investments	$ 387.8	$ 458.9	$ 71.1	$ –
Contracts & notes receivable	293.5	294.6	1.1	–
Jackpot liabilities	(508.4)	(521.6)	–	13.2
Debt	(1,553.1)	(1,879.5)	–	326.4
September 30, 2010				
Jackpot investments	$ 425.9	$ 495.2	$ 73.1	$ 3.8
Contracts & notes receivable	356.0	$ 356.8	0.8	–
Jackpot liabilities	(570.9)	(567.5)	3.4	–
Debt	(1,622.2)	(1,933.2)	–	311.0

Valuation Techniques and Balance Sheet Presentation

Jackpot investments were valued based on quoted market prices.

Contracts and notes receivable were valued using DCF incorporating expected payments and current market interest rates relative to the credit risk of each customer.

Jackpot liabilities were valued using DCF models incorporating estimated funding rates, future payment timing, and IGT's nonperformance credit risk.

Debt was valued using quoted market prices or dealer quotes, when available, for the identical financial instrument when traded as an asset in an active market. Otherwise, fair value was determined using DCF models of expected payments on outstanding borrowings at current borrowing rates. Carrying values above excluded swap adjustments and equity components of convertible debt.

11. FINANCIAL DERIVATIVES

Foreign Currency Hedging

We hedge our net foreign currency exposure related to monetary assets and liabilities denominated in nonfunctional currency. The notional amount of foreign currency contracts hedging this exposure totaled $13.9 million at September 30, 2011and $26.7 million at September 30, 2010.

In May 2007, we executed five-year forward contracts designated as a fair value hedge to protect a portion of the US dollar value of our Hong Kong dollar investment in the CLS convertible note (See Note 2). In conjunction with the early redemption of our CLS investment negotiated in September 2010, we executed additional contracts which effectively reduced the cumulative amount of forward contracts. The notional amount of foreign currency contracts hedging this exposure totaled $6.4 million at September 30, 2011 and $15.0 million at September 30, 2010 for which there was no ineffectiveness for years 2011 and 2010.

Interest Rate Management

In conjunction with our 7.5% Bonds issued in June 2009, we executed $250.0 million notional value of interest rate swaps that exchange 7.5% fixed interest payments for variable rate interest payments at one-month LIBOR plus 342 bps reset two business days before the 15th of each month. In April 2011, we additionally executed $250.0 million notional value interest rate swaps that exchange the remaining fixed interest payments on our 7.5% Bonds for variable rate interest payments based on six-month LIBOR plus 409 bps reset in arrears two business days before June 15 and December 15 each year. All of these swaps terminate on June 15, 2019.

In conjunction with our 5.5% Bonds issued in June 2010, we executed $300.0 million notional value of interest rate swaps that terminate on June 15, 2020. These swaps effectively exchange 5.5% fixed interest payments for variable rate interest payments based on the six-month LIBOR plus 186 bps reset in arrears two business days before June 15 and December 15 each year. These swaps terminate on June 15, 2020.

All of our interest rate swaps are designated fair value hedges against changes in the fair value of a portion of their related bonds. Net amounts receivable or payable under our swaps settle semiannually on June 15 and December 15. Our assessments have determined that our interest rate swaps are highly effective.

Presentation of Derivative Amounts

Balance Sheet Location and Fair Value at September 30,	*2011*	*2010*
Non-designated Hedges		
Foreign currency contracts: Other assets and deferred costs (current)	$ 0.4	$ –
Foreign currency contracts: Other accrued liabilities	–	2.2
Designated Hedges		
Interest rate swaps: Other assets and deferred costs (noncurrent)	$ 90.4	$ 52.1
Interest rate swaps: Long-term debt	93.2	52.1

Income Statement Location and Gain (loss) For Fiscal Years	2011	2010	2009
Non-designated Hedges			
Foreign currency contracts: Other income (expense)	$ 2.6	$ (1.5)	$ (0.9)
Designated Hedges			
Foreign currency contracts: Other income (expense)	$ –	$ 0.2	$ 0.3
Interest rate swap - ineffectiveness: Other income (expense)	(2.9)	0.4	(0.3)
Interest rate swap - effectiveness: Interest expense	22.1	12.4	2.9

Arvinmeritor
2010 Annual Report

17. Financial Instruments

The company's financial instruments include cash and cash equivalents, short-term debt, long-term debt, interest rate swaps, interest rate cap and foreign exchange forward contracts. The company uses derivatives for hedging and non-trading purposes in order to manage its interest rate and foreign exchange rate exposures.

Foreign Exchange Contracts

As a result of the company's substantial international operations, it is exposed to foreign currency risks that arise from normal business operations, including in connection with transactions that are denominated in foreign currencies. In addition, the company translates sales and financial results denominated in foreign currencies into U.S. dollars for purposes of its consolidated financial statements. As a result, appreciation of the U.S. dollar against these foreign currencies generally will have a negative impact on reported revenues and operating income while depreciation of the U.S. dollar against these foreign currencies will generally have a positive effect on reported revenues and operating income. For fiscal years 2008 and 2010, the company's reported financial results have benefited from depreciation of the U.S. dollar against foreign currencies whereas during fiscal year 2009, reported financial results have been adversely affected by appreciation of the U.S. dollar against foreign currencies.

The company has a foreign currency cash flow hedging program to reduce the company's exposure to changes in exchange rates on foreign currency purchases and sales. The company uses foreign currency forward contracts to manage the company's exposures arising from foreign currency exchange risk. Gains and losses on the underlying foreign currency exposures are partially offset with gains and losses on the foreign currency forward contracts. Under this foreign currency cash flow hedging program, the company has designated the foreign exchange contracts (the "contracts") as cash flow hedges of underlying forecasted foreign currency purchases and sales. The effective portion of changes in the fair value of the contracts is recorded in Accumulated Other Comprehensive Loss (AOCL) in the consolidated balance sheet and is recognized in operating income when the underlying forecasted transaction impacts earnings. The terms of the foreign exchange contracts require the company to place cash on deposit as collateral if the fair value of these contracts represents a liability for the company at any time. The fair values of the foreign exchange derivative instruments and any related collateral cash deposits are presented on a net basis as the derivative contracts are subject to master netting arrangements. The company's foreign exchange contracts generally mature within twelve months.

At September 30, 2010, the company had no foreign exchange contracts outstanding under its foreign currency cash flow hedging program. At September 30, 2009, the company had outstanding contracts with notional amounts of $89 million. These notional values consisted primarily of contracts for the European euro, Australian dollar and Swedish krona, and are stated in U.S. dollar equivalents at spot exchange rates at the respective dates. At September 30, 2010 there was no income or loss recorded in AOCL and at September 30, 2009 there was a loss of $2 million recorded in AOCL.

The company classifies the cash flows associated with the contracts in cash flows from operating activities in the consolidated statement of cash flows. This is consistent with the classification of the cash flows associated with the underlying hedged item.

The company generally has not hedged against its foreign currency exposure related to translations to U.S. dollars of financial results denominated in foreign currencies. In the fourth quarter of fiscal year 2010, due to the volatility of the Brazilian real as compared to the U.S. dollar, the company entered into foreign currency option contracts to reduce volatility in the translation of Brazilian real earnings to U.S. dollars. Gains and losses on these option contracts are recorded in other income (expense), net, in the consolidated statement of operations, generally reducing the exposure to translation volatility during a full-year period. The impact of these option contracts was not significant to the company's fiscal year 2010 results of operations or financial position.

Fair Value

Fair values of financial instruments are summarized as follows (in millions):

	September 30, 2010		September 30, 2009	
	Carrying Value	*Fair Value*	*Carrying Value*	*Fair Value*
Cash and cash equivalents	$ 343	$ 343	$ 95	$ 95
Foreign exchange contracts—asset (liability)	–	–	(3)	(3)
Short-term debt	–	–	97	97
Long-term debt	1,029	1,132	995	885

Cash and cash equivalents—All highly liquid investments purchased with an original maturity of three months or less are considered to be cash equivalents.

The carrying value approximates fair value because of the short maturity of these instruments.

Foreign exchange forward contracts—The company uses foreign exchange forward purchase and sale contracts with terms of one year or less to hedge its exposure to changes in foreign currency exchange rates. The fair value of foreign exchange forward contracts is based on a model which incorporates observable inputs including quoted spot rates, forward exchange rates and discounted future expected cash flows utilizing market interest rates with similar quality and maturity characteristics.

Short-term debt and long-term debt—Fair values are based on interest rates that would be currently available to the company for issuance of similar types of debt instruments with similar terms and remaining maturities.

Navistar International
2010 Annual Report

16. Financial Instruments and Commodity Contracts

Derivative Financial Instruments

We use derivative financial instruments as part of our overall interest rate, foreign currency and commodity risk management strategies to reduce our interest rate exposure, to potentially increase the return on invested funds, to reduce exchange rate risk for transactional exposures denominated in currencies other than the functional currency and to minimize commodity price volatility. From time to time, we use foreign currency forward and option contracts to manage the risk of exchange rate movements that would reduce the value of our foreign currency cash flows. Foreign currency exchange rate movements create a degree of risk by affecting the value of sales made and costs incurred in currencies other than the functional currency. From time to time, we also use commodity forward contracts to manage variability related to exposure to certain commodity price risk. In connection with the sale of the Convertible Notes, the Company purchased call options for $125 million. The call options are intended to minimize share dilution associated with the Convertible Notes. As the call options and warrants are indexed to our common stock, we recognized them in permanent equity in *Additional paid in capital*, and will not recognize subsequent changes in fair value as long as the instruments remain classified as equity. For additional information on the purchased call options, see Note 12, *Debt*. We generally do not enter into derivative financial instruments for speculative or trading purposes and did not during the years ended October 31, 2010, 2009, or 2008. None of our derivatives qualified for hedge accounting treatment in 2010, 2009, or 2008.

Certain of our derivative contracts contain provisions that require us to provide collateral only if certain thresholds are exceeded. No collateral was provided at October 31, 2010 and 2009. Collateral is not required to be provided by our counter-parties for derivative contracts. We manage exposure to counter-party credit risk by entering into derivative financial instruments with various major financial institutions that can be expected to fully perform under the terms of such agreements. We do not anticipate nonperformance by any of the counter-parties. Our exposure to credit risk in the event of nonperformance by the counter-parties is limited to those gains that have been recorded, but have not yet been received in cash. At October 31, 2010 and 2009, our exposure to credit risk was $10 million and $38 million, respectively.

Our financial services operations manage exposure to fluctuations in interest rates by limiting the amount of fixed rate assets funded with variable rate debt. This is accomplished by funding fixed rate receivables utilizing a combination of fixed rate and variable rate debt and derivative financial instruments to convert variable rate debt to fixed. These derivative financial instruments may include interest rate swaps, interest rate caps, and forward contracts. The fair value of these instruments is estimated by discounting expected future monthly settle-ments and is subject to market risk, as the instruments may become less valuable due to changes in market conditions, interest rates, or credit spreads of counterparties. Notional amounts of derivative financial instruments do not represent exposure to credit loss.

The fair values of all derivatives are recorded as assets or liabilities on a gross basis in our Consolidated Balance Sheets. At October 31, 2010 and 2009, the fair values of our derivatives and their respective balance sheet locations are presented in the following table:

	Asset Derivatives		Liability Derivatives	
As of October 31, 2010	Location in Consolidated Balance Sheets	Fair Value	Location in Consolidated Balance Sheets	Fair Value
(in millions)				
Foreign Currency Contracts:				
Current portion	Other current assets	$ 8	Other current liabilities	$ –
Noncurrent portion	Other noncurrent assets	–	Other noncurrent liabilities	–
Commodity contracts	Other current assets	2	Other current liabilities	4
Total fair value		10		4
Less: Current portion		10		4
Noncurrent portion		$ –		$ –

	Asset Derivatives		Liability Derivatives	
As of October 31, 2009	Location in Consolidated Balance Sheets	Fair Value	Location in Consolidated Balance Sheets	Fair Value
(in millions)				
Interest rate swaps:				
Current portion	Other current assets	$ 5	Other current liabilities	$ 9
Noncurrent portion	Other noncurrent assets	27	Other noncurrent liabilities	52
Interest rate caps purchased	Other noncurrent assets	5	Other noncurrent liabilities	–
Interest rate caps sold	Other noncurrent assets	–	Other noncurrent liabilities	4
Commodity contracts	Other current assets	1	Other current liabilities	1
Total fair value		38		66
Less: Current portion		(6)		(10)
Noncurrent portion		$ 32		$ 56

The location and amount of gain (loss) recognized in income on derivatives are as follows for the years ended October 31:

(in millions)	Location in Consolidated Statements of Operations	Amount of Gain (Loss) Recognized		
		2010	2009	2008
Interest rate swaps	Interest expense	$ (5)	$ (44)	$ (57)
Interest rate caps purchased	Interest expense	(3)	2	1
Interest rate caps sold	Interest expense	3	(1)	(1)
Foreign currency contracts	Other (income) expenses, net	8	5	–
Commodity forward contracts	Costs of products sold	1	(6)	1
Total gain (loss)		$ 4	$ (44)	$ (56)

Interest Rate Swaps and Caps

In September 2008, we entered into two floating-to-floating interest rate swaps ("basis swaps") to economically hedge a portion of the floating interest rate associated with our $1.5 billion five-year term loan facility and synthetic revolving facility. The basis swaps had an aggregate notional amount of $1.1 billion and became effective October 30, 2008. The basis swaps matured on January 30, 2009. For the year ended October 31, 2009, we recognized a loss of $2 million under these arrangements.

In June 2005, TRIP entered into a $500 million revolving facility that matured and was paid in June 2010. Under the terms of this agreement, TRIP purchases and holds fixed rate retail notes and finance leases from NFC. TRIP finances such purchases with its revolving facility. TRIP purchased interest caps with a notional amount of $500 million to protect it against the potential of rising commercial paper interest rates. To offset the economic cost of these caps, NFC sold identical interest rate caps. As of October 31, 2010, there were no interest rate caps outstanding.

NFC previously entered into various interest rate swap agreements in connection with the sale of retail notes and lease receivables. The purpose and structure of these swaps is to convert the floating rate portion of the asset-backed securities into fixed rate swap interest to match the interest basis of the receivables pool sold to the owner trust in those periods, and to protect NFC from interest rate volatility. As of October 31, 2009, the aggregate notional amount of the outstanding interest rate swaps was $3.4 billion. As of October 31, 2010, there were no interest rate swaps outstanding.

Foreign Currency Contracts

In 2010, we entered into forward exchange contracts as economic hedges of anticipated cash flows denominated in Canadian dollars, Indian rupees, and Euros. In 2009, we also entered into forward exchange contracts as economic hedges of anticipated cash flows denominated in Indian rupees and South African rand. All of these contracts were entered into to protect against the risk that the eventual cash flows resulting from such transactions will be adversely affected by changes in exchange rates between the U.S. dollar and the respective foreign currency. In 2009, we entered into put option contracts for Canadian dollars as economic hedges of anticipated cash flows denominated in Canadian dollars to also protect the revenue of certain contracts denominated in Canadian dollars. The put option contracts for Canadian dollars had staggered maturity dates, and the final contract matured in June 2010. As of October 31, 2010, we had outstanding forward exchange contracts with notional amounts of €49 million Euros and C$24 million Canadian dollars and maturity dates ranging from January 2011 to May 2011.

Commodity Forward Contracts

In 2010, we entered into commodity forward contracts as economic hedges of exposure to variability of commodity prices for diesel fuel, lead, and steel. These contracts were entered into to protect against the risk that the eventual cash flows related to purchases of the commodities will be adversely affected by future changes in prices. As of October 31, 2010, we had outstanding diesel fuel contracts with aggregate notional values of $21 million, outstanding lead contracts with aggregate notional values of $1 million, and outstanding steel contracts with aggregate notional values of $80 million. As of October 31, 2009, we had outstanding diesel fuel commodity forward contracts with aggregate notional amounts of $2 million and outstanding steel contracts with aggregate notional amounts of $39 million. The commodity forward contracts have several maturity dates ranging from February 2011 to October 2011.

Walt Disney
2010 Annual Report

17. Derivative Instruments

The company manages its exposure to various risks relating to its ongoing business operations according to a risk management policy. The primary risks managed with derivative instruments are interest rate risk and foreign exchange risk.

The following table summarizes the gross fair value of the company's derivative positions as of October 2, 2010:

	Current Assets	Other Assets	Other Accrued Liabilities	Other Long-Term Liabilities
Derivatives designated as hedges				
Foreign exchange	$ 78	$ 65	$ (210)	$ (104)
Interest rate	13	218	–	–
Derivatives not designated as hedges				
Foreign exchange	80	181	(140)	(36)
Interest rate	–	–	–	(22)
Other	–	–	–	–
Gross fair value of derivatives	171	464	(350)	(162)
Counterparty netting	(121)	(85)	130	76
Total Derivatives[1]	$ 50	$ 379	$ (220)	$ (86)

The following table summarizes the gross fair value of the company's derivative positions as of October 3, 2009:

	Current Assets	Other Assets	Other Accrued Liabilities	Other Long-Term Liabilities
Derivatives designated as hedges				
Foreign exchange	$ 84	$ 111	$ (115)	$ (55)
Interest rate	4	186	–	–
Derivatives not designated as hedges				
Foreign exchange	37	127	(70)	(37)
Interest rate	–	–	–	(18)
Other	–	–	(2)	–
Gross fair value of derivatives	125	424	(187)	(110)
Counterparty netting	(98)	(72)	103	67
Total Derivatives[1]	$ 27	$ 352	$ (84)	$ (43)

[1] Refer to note 16 for further information on derivative fair values and counterparty netting.

Interest rate risk management

The company is exposed to the impact of interest rate changes primarily through its borrowing activities. The company's objective is to mitigate the impact of interest rate changes on earnings and cash flows and on the market value of its borrowings. In accordance with its policy, the company targets its fixed-rate debt as a percentage of its net debt between a minimum and maximum percentage. The company typically uses pay-floating and pay-fixed interest rate swaps to facilitate its interest rate management activities.

The company designates pay-floating interest rate swaps as fair value hedges of fixed-rate borrowings effectively converting fixed-rate borrowings to variable rate borrowings indexed to LIBOR. As of October 2, 2010 and October 3, 2009, the total notional amount of the company's pay-floating interest rate swaps was $1.5 billion and $1.6 billion, respectively. The following table summarizes adjustments related to fair value hedges included in net interest expense in the consolidated statements of income.

	2010	2009
Gain (loss) on interest rate swaps	$ 41	$ 105
Gain (loss) on hedged borrowings	(41)	(105)

The company may designate pay-fixed interest rate swaps as cash flow hedges of interest payments on floating-rate borrowings. Pay-fixed swaps effectively convert floating rate borrowings to fixed-rate borrowings. The unrealized gains or losses from these cash flow hedges are deferred in accumulated other comprehensive income (AOCI) and recognized as the interest payments occur. The company did not have pay-fixed interest rate swaps that were designated as cash flow hedges of interest payments at October 2, 2010 nor at October 3, 2009.

Foreign exchange risk management

The company transacts business globally and is subject to risks associated with changing foreign currency exchange rates. The company's objective is to reduce earnings and cash flow fluctuations associated with foreign currency exchange rate changes, enabling management to focus on core business issues and challenges.

The company enters into option and forward contracts that change in value as foreign currency exchange rates change to protect the value of its existing foreign currency assets, liabilities, firm commitments and forecasted but not firmly committed foreign currency transactions. In accordance with policy, the company hedges its forecasted foreign currency transactions for periods generally not to exceed five years within an established minimum and maximum range of annual exposure. The gains and losses on these contracts offset changes in the U.S. dollar equivalent value of the related forecasted transaction, asset, liability or firm commitment. The principal currencies hedged are the euro, British pound, Japanese yen and Canadian dollar. Cross-currency swaps are used to effectively convert foreign currency-denominated borrowings into U.S. dollar denominated borrowings.

The company designates foreign exchange forward and option contracts as cash flow hedges of firmly committed and forecasted foreign currency transactions. As of both October 2, 2010 and October 3, 2009, the notional amount of the company's net foreign exchange cash flow hedges was $2.8 billion. Mark to market gains and losses on these contracts are deferred in AOCI and are recognized in earnings when the hedged transactions occur, offsetting changes in the value of the foreign currency transactions. Gains and losses recognized related to ineffectiveness for the years ended October 2, 2010 and October 3, 2009 were not material. Deferred losses recorded in AOCI for contracts that will mature in the next twelve months totaled $132 million. The following table summarizes the pre-tax adjustments to AOCI for foreign exchange cash flow hedges.

	2010	2009
Gain (loss) recorded in AOCI	$ (187)	$ 81
Reclassification of (gains) losses from AOCI into revenues and costs and expenses	(7)	(183)
Net change in AOCI	$ (194)	$ (102)

Foreign exchange risk management contracts with respect to foreign currency assets and liabilities are not designated as hedges and do not qualify for hedge accounting. The notional amount of these foreign exchange contracts at October 2, 2010 and October 3, 2009 was $2.2 billion and $2.1 billion, respectively. For the years ended October 2, 2010 and October 3, 2009, the company recognized a net gain of $102 million and $140 million, respectively, in costs and expenses on these foreign exchange contracts which offset a net loss of $173 million and $137 million of the related economic exposures for the years ended October 2, 2010 and October 3, 2009, respectively.

Commodity price risk management

The company is subject to the volatility of commodities prices and designates certain commodity forward contracts as cash flow hedges of forecasted commodity purchases. Mark to market gains and losses on these contracts are deferred in AOCI and are recognized in earnings when the hedged transactions occur, offsetting changes in the value of commodity purchases. The fair value of commodity hedging contracts was not material at October 2, 2010.

Risk management—other derivatives not designated as hedges

The company enters into certain other risk management contracts that are not designated as hedges and do not qualify for hedge accounting. These contracts, which include pay fixed interest rate swaps, commodity swap contracts and credit default swaps, are intended to offset economic exposures of the company and are carried at market value with any changes in value recorded in earnings.

The notional amount of these contracts at October 2, 2010 and October 3, 2009 was $218 million and $253 million, respectively. The gains or losses recognized in income for fiscal 2010 and fiscal 2009 were not material.

Contingent features

The company's derivative financial instruments may require the company to post collateral in the event that a net liability position with a counterparty exceeds limits defined by contract and that vary with Disney's credit rating. If the company's credit ratings were to fall below investment grade, such counterparties would have the right to terminate our derivative contracts, which could lead to a net payment to or from the company for the aggregate net value by counterparty of our derivative contracts. The aggregate fair value of all derivative instruments with credit-risk-related contingent features that are in a net liability position by counterparty on October 2, 2010 and October 3, 2009 were $306 million and $125 million, respectively.

Schlumberger
2009 Annual Report

12. Derivative Instruments and Hedging Activities

Schlumberger is exposed to market risks related to fluctuations in foreign currency exchange rates, commodity prices and interest rates. To mitigate these risks, Schlumberger utilizes derivative instruments. Schlumberger does not enter into derivatives for speculative purposes.

Foreign Currency Exchange Rate Risk As a multinational company, Schlumberger conducts its business in approximately 80 countries.

Schlumberger's functional currency is primarily the US dollar, which is consistent with the oil and gas industry. Approximately 80% of Schlumberger's revenue in 2009 was denominated in US dollars. However, outside the United States, a significant portion of Schlumberger's expenses is incurred in foreign currencies. Therefore, when the US dollar weakens (strengthens) in relation to the foreign currencies of the countries in which Schlumberger conducts business, the US dollar—reported expenses will increase (decrease).

Schlumberger is exposed to risks on future cash flows to the extent that local currency expenses exceed revenues denominated in local currency that are other than the functional currency. Schlumberger uses foreign currency forward contracts and foreign currency options to provide a hedge against a portion of these cash flow risks. These contracts are accounted for as cash flow hedges, with the effective portion of changes in the fair value of the hedge recorded on the Consolidated Balance Sheet and in Other Comprehensive Income (Loss). Amounts recorded in Other Comprehensive Income (Loss) are reclassified into earnings in the same period or periods that the hedged item is recognized in earnings. The ineffective portion of changes in the fair value of hedging instruments, if any, is recorded directly to earnings.

At December 31, 2009, Schlumberger recognized a cumulative net $40 million gain in Accumulated other comprehensive loss relating to revaluation of foreign currency forward contracts and foreign currency options designated as cash flow hedges, the majority of which is expected to be reclassified into earnings within the next twelve months.

Schlumberger is also exposed to changes in the fair value of assets and liabilities, including certain of its long-term debt, which are denominated in currencies other than the functional currency. Schlumberger uses foreign currency forward contracts and foreign currency options to hedge this exposure as it relates to certain currencies. These contracts are accounted for as fair value hedges with the fair value of the contracts recorded on the Consolidated Balance Sheet and changes in the fair value recognized in the Consolidated Statement of Income along with the change in fair value of the hedged item.

At December 31, 2009, contracts were outstanding for the US dollar equivalent of $4.3 billion in various foreign currencies.

Commodity Price Risk Schlumberger is exposed to the impact of market fluctuations in the price of certain commodities, such as metals and fuel. Schlumberger utilizes forward contracts to manage a small percentage of the price risk associated with forecasted metal purchases. The objective of these contracts is to reduce the variability of cash flows associated with the forecasted purchase of those commodities. These contracts do not qualify for hedge accounting treatment and therefore, changes in the fair value of the forward contracts are recorded directly to earnings.

At December 31, 2009, $4 million of commodity forward contracts were outstanding.

Interest Rate Risk Schlumberger is subject to interest rate risk on its debt and its investment portfolio. Schlumberger maintains an interest rate risk management strategy that uses a mix of variable and fixed rate debt combined with its investment portfolio and interest rate swaps to mitigate the exposure to changes in interest rates.

During the third quarter of 2009, Schlumberger entered into interest rate swaps relating to two of its debt instruments. The first swap was for a notional amount of $600 million in order to hedge a portion of the changes in fair value of Schlumberger's $650 million 6.50% Notes due 2012. Under the terms of this swap agreement, Schlumberger will receive interest at a fixed rate of 6.5% semiannually and will pay interest semiannually at a floating rate of one-month LIBOR plus a spread of 4.84%. The second swap was for a notional amount of $450 million in order to hedge changes in the fair value of Schlumberger's $450 million 3.00% Notes due 2013. Under the terms of this swap, Schlumberger will receive interest at a fixed rate of 3.00% annually and will pay interest quarterly at a floating rate of three-month LIBOR plus a spread of 0.765%.

These interest rate swaps are designated as fair value hedges of the underlying debt. These derivative instruments are marked to market with gains and losses recognized currently in income to offset the respective losses and gains recognized on changes in the fair value of the hedged debt. This results in no net gain or loss being recognized in the Consolidated Statement of Income.

At December 31, 2009, Schlumberger had fixed rate debt aggregating approximately $3.2 billion and variable rate debt aggregating approximately $2.3 billion, after taking into account the effects of the interest rate swaps.

The fair values of outstanding derivative instruments are summarized as follows:

(Stated in millions)	Fair Value of Derivatives		Classification
	Dec. 31 2009	Dec. 31 2008	
Derivative assets			
Derivative designated as hedges:			
Foreign exchange contracts	**$14**	$62	*Other current assets*
Foreign exchange contracts	81	3	*Other Assets*
	$95	$65	

(Stated in millions)	Fair Value of Derivatives		Classification
Derivative not designated as hedges:			
Commodity contracts	$1	$ –	Other current assets
Foreign exchange contracts	11	30	Other current assets
Foreign exchange contracts	28	8	Other Assets
	$40	$38	
	$135	$103	
Derivative liabilities			
Derivative designated as hedges:			
Foreign exchange contracts	$15	$148	Accounts payable and accrued liabilities
Foreign exchange contracts	51	53	Other Liabilities
	$66	$201	
Derivative not designated as hedges:			
Commodity contracts	$3	$4	Accounts payable and accrued liabilities
Foreign exchange contracts	–	5	Accounts payable and accrued liabilities
Foreign exchange contracts	25	–	Other Liabilities
	$28	$9	
	$94	$210	

The fair value of all outstanding derivatives is determined using a model with inputs that are observable in the market or can be derived from or corroborated by observable data.

The effect of derivative instruments designated as fair value hedges and not designated as hedges on the Consolidated Statement of Income was as follows:

(Stated in millions)	Gain/(Loss) Recognized in Income		Classification
	2009	2008	
Derivatives designated as fair value hedges:			
Foreign exchange contracts	$105	$(122)	Cost of revenue
Interest rate swaps	6	–	Interest expense
	$111	$(122)	
Derivatives not designated as hedges:			
Foreign exchange contracts	$32	$(11)	Cost of revenue

(Stated in millions)	Gain/(Loss) Recognized in Income		Classification
	2009	*2008*	
Commodity contracts	2	(6)	Cost of revenue
	$34	$(17)	

The effect of derivative instruments in cash flow hedging relationships on income and other comprehensive income (OCI) was as follows:

(Stated in millions)	Gain (Loss) Reclassified from Accumulated OCI into Income		Classification
	2009	*2008*	
Foreign exchange contracts	$ 95	$(19)	Cost of revenue
Foreign exchange contracts	(15)	5	Research & engineering
	$ 80	$(14)	

(Stated in millions)	Gain (Loss) Recognized in OCI	
	2009	*2008*
Foreign exchange contracts	**$223**	$(149)

Whirlpool Corporation
2009 Annual Report

(7) Hedges and Derivative Financial Instruments

Derivative instruments are accounted for at fair value. The accounting for changes in the fair value of a derivative depends on the intended use and designation of the derivative instrument. For a derivative instrument designated as a fair value hedge, the gain or loss on the derivative is recognized in earnings in the period of change in fair value together with the offsetting gain or loss on the hedged item. For a derivative instrument designated as a cash flow hedge, the effective portion of the derivative's gain or loss is initially reported as a component of Other Comprehensive Income ("OCI") and is subsequently recognized in earnings when the hedged exposure affects earnings. The ineffective portion of the gain or loss is recognized in earnings. Gains and losses from changes in fair values of derivatives that are not designated as hedges for accounting purposes are recognized in earnings.

Using derivative instruments means assuming counterparty credit risk. Counterparty credit risk relates to the loss we could incur if a counterparty were to default on a derivative contract. We deal with investment grade counterparties and monitor the overall credit risk and exposure to individual counterparties. We do not anticipate nonperformance by any counterparties. The amount of counterparty credit exposure is the unrealized gains, if any, on such derivative contracts. We do not require, nor do we post, collateral or security on such contracts.

Hedging Strategy We are exposed to certain risks relating to our ongoing business operations. As a result, we enter into derivative transactions to manage certain of these exposures that arise in the normal course of business. The primary risks managed by using derivative instruments are foreign currency exchange rate, commodity price and domestic and foreign interest rate risks. Fluctuations in these rates and prices can affect our operating results and financial condition. We manage the exposure to these market risks through operating and financing activities and through the use of derivative financial instruments. We do not enter into derivative financial instruments for trading or speculative purposes.

Foreign currency exchange rate risk We incur expenses associated with the procurement and production of products in a limited number of countries, while we sell in the local currencies of a large number of countries. Our primary foreign currency exchange exposures result from cross-currency sales of products. As a result, we enter into foreign exchange contracts to hedge certain firm commitments and forecasted transactions to acquire products and services that are denominated in foreign currencies.

We enter into certain undesignated non-functional currency asset and liability hedges that relate primarily to short-term payables, receivables, inventory and intercompany loans. These forecasted cross-currency cash flows relate primarily to foreign currency denominated expenditures and intercompany financing agreements, royalty agreements and dividends.

Commodity price risk We enter into forward contracts on various commodities to manage the price risk associated with forecasted purchases of materials used in our manufacturing process. The objective of the hedges is to reduce the variability of cash flows associated with the forecasted purchase of those commodities.

Interest rate risk We enter into interest rate swap agreements to manage interest rate risk exposure. Our interest rate swap agreements effectively modify our exposure to interest rate risk, primarily through converting certain of our floating rate debt to a fixed rate basis, and certain fixed rate debt to a floating rate basis, thus reducing the impact of interest rate changes on future interest expense. These agreements involve either the receipt or payment of floating rate amounts in exchange for fixed rate interest payments or receipts, respectively, over the life of the agreements without an exchange of the underlying principal amounts.

The following table summarizes our outstanding derivative contracts and their effects on our Consolidated Balance Sheet at December 31, 2009:

| Millions of dollars | Notional Amount | Fair Value of [1] | | Type of Hedge [2] | Terms |
		Hedge Assets	Hedge Liabilities		
Designated derivatives					
Foreign exchange forwards/options	$1,090	$ 40	$54	(CF)/ (FV)	Various, up to 15 months
Commodity swaps/ options	486	109	2	(CF)/ (FV)	Various, up to 29 months

Millions of dollars	Notional Amount	Fair Value of [1]		Type of Hedge [2]	Terms
		Hedge Assets	Hedge Liabilities		
Total designated derivatives		$149	$56		
Undesignated derivatives					
Foreign exchange forwards/options	$ 801	$ 6	$ 4		Various, up to 5 months
Commodity swaps/options	24	4	2		Various, up to 24 months
Total undesignated derivatives		10	6		
Total derivatives		$159	$62		

[1] Periodic adjustments from fair valuing hedge assets and liabilities are recorded in other current assets and other assets or other current liabilities and other liabilities. As of December 31, 2009, hedge assets of $119 million and $40 million were recorded in other current assets and other assets, respectively, and hedge liabilities of $61 million and $1 million were recorded in other current liabilities and other liabilities, respectively.

[2] Designated derivatives are either considered cash flow (CF) or fair value hedges (FV).

The effects of derivative instruments on our Consolidated Statement of Income for the year ended December 31, 2009 are as follows:

Cash Flow Hedges—Millions of dollars	Gain (Loss) Recognized in OCI (Effective Portion)	Gain (Loss) Reclassified from Accumulated OCI into Income (Effective Portion)[1]	Gain (Loss) Recognized in Income (Ineffective Portion)[2]
Foreign exchange forwards/options	$ (23)	$ 8[a] [b]	$1
Commodity swaps/options	196	(101)[b]	2
Interest rate swaps	1	1[c]	–
	$174	$ (92)	$3

[1] Gains and losses reclassified from accumulated OCI into income are recorded in (a) interest and sundry income (expense), (b) cost of products sold or (c) interest expense.

[2] Gains and losses recognized in income related to the ineffective portion of hedges are recorded in interest and sundry income (expense).

Fair Value Hedges—Millions of dollars	Gain (Loss) Recognized on Derivative[3]	Gain (Loss) Recognized on Related Hedged Items[3]	Hedged Item
Foreign exchange forwards/options	$(7)	$7	Non-functional currency assets and liabilities

[3] Gains and losses recognized in income are recorded in interest and sundry income (expense).

Undesignated Hedges—Millions of Dollars	Gain (Loss) Recognized on Undesignated Hedges[4]
Foreign exchange forwards/options	$(70)
Commodity swaps	(6)
	$64

[4] Mark to market gains and losses are recorded in interest and sundry income (expense).

The net amount of unrealized gain or loss on derivative instruments included in accumulated other comprehensive income related to contracts maturing, and expected to be realized during the next twelve months is a gain of $57 million at December 31, 2009.

Early Hedge Settlement

During November and December 2008, we cash settled certain foreign currency derivative contracts prior to their scheduled settlement dates. As a result of these transactions, we received $82 million in cash, which represented the fair value of these contracts at the date of settlement. Effective gains of $82 million were initially recorded in accumulated OCI until the hedged forecasted transactions affected earnings, then the gains were recorded as a reduction in cost of products sold on our Consolidated Statements of Income. Approximately $10 million of these gains were recorded in earnings during 2008 and the remainder was recorded in earnings in 2009. There was no ineffectiveness related to these settled foreign currency derivative contracts.

United States Steel 2009 Annual Report

15. Derivative Instruments

U.S. Steel is exposed to foreign currency exchange rate risks as a result of our European and Canadian operations. USSE's revenues are primarily in euros and costs are primarily in U.S. dollars, euros and Serbian dinars. Prior to Slovakia's entry into the Eurozone as of January 1, 2009, the USSE segment also had foreign currency exchange rate risks related to the Slovak koruna. USSC's revenues and costs are denominated in both Canadian and U.S. dollars.

In addition, the acquisition of USSC was funded from the United States and through the reinvestment of undistributed earnings from USSE, creating intercompany monetary assets and liabilities in currencies other than the functional currency of the entities involved, which can have a non-cash impact on income when remeasured at the end of each quarter. An $892 million U.S. dollar-denominated intercompany loan (the Intercompany Loan) from a U.S. subsidiary to a European subsidiary was the primary exposure at December 31, 2009.

U.S. Steel holds or purchases derivative financial instruments for purposes other than trading to mitigate foreign currency exchange rate risk. U.S. Steel uses euro forward sales contracts with maturities no longer than 12 months to exchange euros for U.S. dollars to manage our exposure to foreign currency exchange rate fluctuations. The gains and losses recognized on these euro-forward sales contracts may also partially offset gains and losses recognized on the Intercompany Loan.

As of December 31, 2009, U.S. Steel held euro forward sales contracts with a total notional value of approximately $185 million. We mitigate the risk of concentration of counterparty credit risk by purchasing our forward sales contracts from several counterparties.

Derivative instruments are required to be recognized at fair value in the balance sheet. U. S. Steel has not elected to designate these foreign currency forward contracts as hedges. Therefore, changes in the fair value of these forward contracts are recognized immediately in the results of operations.

Additionally, we routinely enter into fixed-price forward physical purchase contracts to partially manage our exposure to price risk related to the purchases of natural gas and certain nonferrous metals used in the production process. Historically, the forward physical purchase contracts for natural gas and nonferrous metals have qualified for the normal purchases and normal sales exemption in ASC Topic 815. However, due to reduced natural gas consumption in 2009, we net settled some of our excess natural gas purchase contracts for certain facilities. Therefore, the remaining contracts for natural gas at those facilities no longer met the exemption criteria and were therefore subject to mark-to-market accounting.

As of December 31, 2009, there are no longer natural gas purchase contracts subject to mark-to-market accounting. Fixed-price forward physical purchase contracts entered into for 2010 to partially manage our exposure to natural gas price risk qualify for the normal purchases normal sales exemption. As of December 31, 2008, U.S. Steel held commodity contracts for natural gas with a total notional value of approximately $33 million that were subject to mark-to-market accounting.

The following summarizes the location and amounts of the fair values and gains or losses related to derivatives included in U.S. Steel's financial statements as of and for the years ended December 31, 2009 and 2008:

(In millions)	Location of Fair Value in Balance Sheet	Fair Value December 31, 2009	Fair Value December 31, 2008
Foreign exchange forward contracts	Accounts (payable) receivable	($ 2)	$ 14
Forward physical purchase contracts	Accounts payable	$–	($ 18)

	Location of Gain (Loss) on Derivative in Statement of Operations	Amount of Gain(Loss) Year ended December 31, 2009	Amount of Gain(Loss) Year ended December 31, 2009
Forward physical purchase contracts	Cost of Sales	($ 20)	($ 18)
Foreign exchange forward contracts	Other financial costs	$7	$ 38

There were no gains or losses related to forward physical purchase contracts and there was an immaterial loss related to foreign exchange forward contracts included in U.S. Steel's financial statements for the year ended December 31, 2007.

In accordance with ASC Topic 820 on fair value measurements and disclosures, the fair value of our foreign currency derivatives is determined using Level 2 inputs, which are defined as "significant other observable" inputs. The inputs used are from market sources that aggregate data based upon market transactions. The fair value of our forward physical purchase contracts for natural gas is also determined using Level 2 inputs. The inputs used include forward prices derived from the New York Mercantile Exchange.

Coca-Cola
2008 Annual Report

Note 11. Hedging Transactions and Derivative Financial Instruments

When deemed appropriate, our Company uses derivative financial instruments primarily to reduce our exposure to adverse fluctuations in interest rates and foreign currency exchange rates, commodity prices and other market risks. The Company formally designates and documents the financial instrument as a hedge of a specific underlying exposure, as well as the risk management objectives and strategies for undertaking the hedge transactions. The Company formally assesses, both at the inception and at least quarterly thereafter, whether the financial instruments that are used in hedging transactions are effective at offsetting changes in either the fair value or cash flows of the related underlying exposure. Because of the high degree of effectiveness between the hedging instrument and the underlying exposure being hedged, fluctuations in the value of the derivative instruments are generally offset by changes in the fair values or cash flows of the underlying exposures being hedged. Any ineffective portion of a financial instrument's change in fair value is immediately recognized in earnings. Virtually all of our derivatives are straightforward over-the-counter instruments with liquid markets. Our Company does not enter into derivative financial instruments for trading purposes.

The fair values of derivatives used to hedge or modify our risks fluctuate over time, and are determined in accordance with SFAS No. 157. Refer to Note 12. We do not view these fair value amounts in isolation, but rather in relation to the fair values or cash flows of the underlying hedged transactions or other exposures. The notional amounts of the derivative financial instruments do not necessarily represent amounts exchanged by the parties and, therefore, are not a direct measure of our exposure to the financial risks described above. The amounts exchanged are calculated by reference to the notional amounts and by other terms of the derivatives, such as interest rates, foreign currency exchange rates or other financial indices.

Our Company recognizes all derivative instruments as either assets or liabilities in our consolidated balance sheets at fair value. The accounting for changes in fair value of a derivative instrument depends on whether it has been designated and qualifies as part of a hedging relationship and, further, on the type of hedging relationship. At the inception of the hedging relationship, the Company must designate the instrument as a fair value hedge, a cash flow hedge, or a hedge of a net investment in a foreign operation. This designation is based upon the exposure being hedged.

We have established strict counterparty credit guidelines and enter into transactions only with financial institutions of investment grade or better. We monitor counterparty exposures daily and review any downgrade in credit rating immediately. If a downgrade in the credit rating of a counterparty were to occur, we have provisions requiring collateral in the form of U.S. government securities for substantially all of our transactions. To mitigate presettlement risk, minimum credit standards become more stringent as the duration of the derivative financial instrument increases. To minimize the concentration of credit risk, we enter into derivative transactions with a portfolio of financial institutions. The Company has master netting agreements with most of the financial institutions that are counterparties to the derivative instruments. These agreements allow for the net settlement of assets and liabilities arising from different transactions with the same counterparty. Based on these factors, we consider the risk of counterparty default to be minimal.

Interest Rate Management

Our Company monitors our mix of fixed-rate and variable-rate debt as well as our mix of short-term debt versus long-term debt. This monitoring includes a review of business and other financial risks. From time to time, in anticipation of future debt issuances, we may manage our risk to interest rate fluctuations through the use of derivative financial instruments. During 2008, the Company discontinued a cash flow hedging relationship on interest rate locks, as it was no longer probable that we would issue the long-term debt for which these hedges were designated. As a result, the Company reclassified a previously unrecognized gain of approximately $17 million from AOCI to earnings as a reduction to interest expense. Additionally, during 2008 the Company recognized losses of approximately $9 million related to the portion of cash flow hedges deemed to be ineffective as an increase to interest expense.

Any ineffective portion, which was not significant, of these instruments during 2007 and 2006 was immediately recognized in net income.

Foreign Currency Management

The purpose of our foreign currency hedging activities is to reduce the risk that our eventual U.S. dollar net cash inflows resulting from sales outside the United States will be adversely affected by changes in foreign currency exchange rates.

We enter into forward exchange contracts and purchase foreign currency options (principally euro and Japanese yen) and collars to hedge certain portions of forecasted cash flows denominated in foreign currencies. The effective portion of the changes in fair value for these contracts, which have been designated as foreign currency cash flow hedges, was reported in AOCI and reclassified into earnings in the same financial statement line item and in the same period or periods during which the hedged transaction affects earnings. The Company did not discontinue any foreign currency cash flow hedging relationships during the years ended December 31, 2008, 2007 and 2006. Any ineffective portion, which was not significant in 2008, 2007 or 2006, of the change in the fair value of these instruments was immediately recognized in net income.

Additionally, the Company enters into forward exchange contracts that are effective economic hedges and are not designated as hedging instruments under SFAS No. 133. These instruments are used to offset the earnings impact relating to the variability in foreign currency exchange rates on certain monetary assets and liabilities denominated in nonfunctional currencies. Changes in the fair value of these instruments are immediately recognized in earnings in the line item other income (loss)—net in our consolidated statements of income to offset the effect of remeasurement of the monetary assets and liabilities.

The Company also enters into forward exchange contracts to hedge its net investment position in certain major currencies. Under SFAS No. 133, changes in the fair value of these instruments are recognized in foreign currency translation adjustment, a component of AOCI, to offset the change in the value of the net investment being hedged. For the years ended December 31, 2008, 2007 and 2006, we recorded net gain (loss) in foreign currency translation adjustment related to those instruments of approximately $3 million, $(7) million and $3 million, respectively.

Commodities

The Company enters into commodity futures and other derivative instruments to mitigate exposure to fluctuations in commodity prices and other market risks.

We purchase commodity futures to hedge forecasted cash flows related to future purchases of certain commodities. The effective portion of the changes in fair value for these contracts, which have been designated as commodity cash flow hedges, are reported in AOCI and reclassified into earnings in the same financial statement line item and in the same period or periods during which the hedged transaction affects earnings. The Company did not discontinue any commodity cash flow hedging relationships during the years ended December 31, 2008, 2007 and 2006. Any ineffective portion, which was not significant in 2008, 2007 or 2006, of the change in the fair value of these instruments was immediately recognized in net income.

The following tables present the carrying values, fair values and maturities of the Company's derivative instruments outstanding as of December 31, 2008 and 2007 (in millions):

2008	Carrying Values Assets/(Liabilities)[1]	Fair Values Assets/(Liabilities)[1]	Maturity
Foreign currency forward contracts	$(124)	$(124)	2009-2010
Foreign currency options and collars	12	12	2009-2010
Interest rate locks	(43)	(43)	2009
Commodity futures	(42)	(420)	2009-2010
Other derivative instruments	(17)	(17)	2009
	$(214)	$(214)	

[1] Does not include the impact of approximately $8 million of cash collateral held or placed with the same counterparties.

2007	Carrying Values Assets/(Liabilities)	Fair Values Assets/(Liabilities)	Maturity
Foreign currency forward contracts	$(58)	$(58)	2008-2009
Foreign currency options and collars	46	46	2008
Interest rate locks	–	–	N/A
Commodity futures	1	1	2008
Other derivative instruments	28	28	2008
	$ 17	$ 17	

The Company estimates the fair values of its derivatives based on quoted market prices or pricing models using current market rates, and records them as prepaid expenses and other assets or accounts payable and accrued expenses in our consolidated balance sheets. The amounts recorded reflect the effect of legally enforceable master netting agreements that allow the Company to settle positive and negative positions and cash collateral held or placed with the same counterparties. As of December 31, 2008, we had approximately $5 million reflected in prepaid expenses and other assets and $211 million reflected in accounts payable and accrued expenses. Refer to Note 12.

Summary of AOCI

For the years ended December 31, 2008, 2007 and 2006, we recorded a net gain (loss) to AOCI of approximately $(6) million, $(59) million and $(31) million, respectively, net of both income taxes and reclassifications to earnings, primarily related to gains and losses on foreign currency cash flow hedges. These items will generally offset the variability of the cash flows relating to the underlying exposures being hedged in future periods. The Company estimates that it will reclassify into earnings during the next 12 months losses of approximately $31 million from the after-tax amount recorded in AOCI as of December 31, 2008, as the anticipated cash flows occur.

The following table summarizes activity in AOCI related to derivatives designated as cash flow hedges held by the Company during the applicable periods (in millions):

2008	Before-Tax Amount	Income Tax	After-Tax Amount
Accumulated derivative net gains (losses) as of January 1, 2008	$(112)	$43	$(69)
Net changes in fair value of derivatives	(62)	23	(39)
Net reclassification from AOCI into earnings	53	(20)	33
Accumulated derivative net gains (losses) as of December 31, 2008	$(121)	$46	$(75)

2007	Before-Tax Amount	Income Tax	After-Tax Amount
Accumulated derivative net gains (losses) as of January 1, 2007	$ (16)	$ 6	$(10)
Net changes in fair value of derivatives	(158)	61	(97)
Net reclassification from AOCI into earnings	62	(24)	38
Accumulated derivative net gains (losses) as of December 31, 2007	$(112)	$43	$(69)

2006	Before-Tax Amount	Income Tax	After-Tax Amount
Accumulated derivative net gains (losses) as of January 1, 2006	$ 35	$(14)	$ 21
Net changes in fair value of derivatives	(38)	15	(23)
Net reclassification from AOCI into earnings	13	5	(8)
Accumulated derivative net gains (losses) as of December 31, 2006	$(16)	$ 6	$(10)

Note 12. Fair Value Measurements

Effective January 1, 2008, the Company adopted SFAS No. 157, which defines fair value as the exchange price that would be received for an asset or paid to transfer a liability (an exit price) in the principal or most advantageous market for the asset or liability in an orderly transaction between market participants at the measurement date. FSP FAS 157-2 delayed the effective date for all nonfinancial assets and liabilities until January 1, 2009, except those that are recognized or disclosed at fair value in the financial statements on a recurring basis. SFAS No. 157 establishes a three-level fair value hierarchy that prioritizes the inputs used to measure fair value. This hierarchy requires entities to maximize the use of observable inputs and minimize the use of unobservable inputs. The three levels of inputs used to measure fair value are as follows:

- Level 1—Quoted prices in active markets for identical assets or liabilities.
- Level 2—Observable inputs other than quoted prices included in level 1, such as quoted prices for similar assets and liabilities in active markets; quoted prices for identical or similar assets and liabilities in markets that are not active; or other inputs that are observable or can be corroborated by observable market data.

Hershey
2008 Annual Report

7. Financial Instruments

The carrying amounts of financial instruments including cash and cash equivalents, accounts receivable, accounts payable and short-term debt approximated fair value as of December 31, 2008 and 2007, because of the relatively short maturity of these instruments.

The carrying value of long-term debt, including the current portion, was $1,524.3 million as of December 31, 2008, compared with a fair value of $1,595.0 million based on quoted market prices for the same or similar debt issues. The carrying value of long-term debt, including the current portion, was $1,286.1 million as of December 31, 2007 compared with a fair value of $1,331.1 million.

Foreign Exchange Forward Contracts

For information on the objectives, strategies and accounting polices related to our use of foreign exchange forward contracts, see Note 5, Derivative Instruments and Hedging Activities.

The following table summarizes our foreign exchange activity:

December 31,	2008		2007	
In millions of dollars	Contract Amount	Primary Currencies	Contract Amount	Primary Currencies
Foreign exchange forward contracts to purchase foreign currencies	$ 0.8	Euros Swiss francs Mexican pesos	$13.8	British pounds Australian dollars Euros
Foreign exchange forward contracts to sell foreign currencies	$68.1	Canadian dollars Australian dollars	$86.7	Canadian dollars Brazilian reais Mexican pesos

The fair value of foreign exchange forward contracts is included in prepaid expenses and other current assets, other non-current assets, accrued liabilities or other long-term liabilities, as appropriate.

We define the fair value of foreign exchange forward contracts as the amount of the difference between contracted and current market foreign currency exchange rates at the end of the period. On a quarterly basis, we estimate the fair value of foreign exchange forward contracts by obtaining market quotes of spot and forward rates for contracts with similar terms, adjusted where necessary for maturity differences.

The combined fair value of our foreign exchange forward contracts included in prepaid expenses and other current assets, other non-current assets, accrued liabilities or other long-term liabilities on the Consolidated Balance Sheets was as follows:

December 31, In millions of dollars	2008	2007
Fair value of foreign exchange forward contracts, net—asset (liability)	$10.3	$(2.1)

Tellabs
2008 Annual Report

7. Derivative Financial Instruments

Financial Contracts and Market Risk We conduct business on a global basis in U.S. and foreign currencies, so our financial results are subject to risks associated with fluctuating foreign exchange rates. To mitigate these risks, we have a foreign currency exposure management program, which uses derivative foreign exchange contracts to address nonfunctional currency exposures that are expected to be settled in one year or less. We enter into derivative foreign exchange contracts only to the extent necessary to meet our goal of mitigating nonfunctional foreign currency exposures. We do not enter into hedging transactions for speculative purposes. The derivative foreign exchange contracts consist of foreign currency forward and option contracts.

Derivative financial contracts involve elements of market and credit risk not recognized in the financial statements. The market risk that results from these contracts relates to changes in foreign currency exchange rates, which generally are offset by changes in the value of the underlying assets or liabilities being held. Credit risk relates to the risk of nonperformance by a counterparty to one of our derivative contracts. We do not believe there is a significant credit risk associated with our hedging activities. We monitor the counterparties' credit ratings and other market data to minimize credit risk. In addition, we also limit the aggregate contract amount entered into with any one financial institution to mitigate credit risk.

Non-Designated Hedges

We use derivative contracts to manage overall foreign currency exposures that are remeasured through income. We record these contracts on the balance sheet at fair value. Changes in the fair value of these contracts, excluding forward points, are included in earnings as part of Other expense, net. We had net losses of $2.4 million in 2008, net gains of $2.2 million in 2007 and net gains of $9.0 million in 2006. Receivables resulting from the contracts are included in Miscellaneous receivables and other current assets, while payables from the contracts are included as part of Other accrued liabilities. We recorded expense related to forward points in Other expense, net of $1.5 million in 2008, $1.0 million in 2007 and $1.5 million in 2006. We do not engage in hedging specific individual transactions. We held derivatives designated as non-designated hedges at the end of the year.

Our net foreign currency exposure is diversified among a broad number of currencies. The notional amounts reflected in the following table represent the U.S. dollar values of the agreed-upon amounts that will be delivered to a third party on the agreed-upon date:

In millions	Notional Value of Forward Contracts[1]	
	1/2/09	12/28/07
Related forward contracts to sell foreign currencies for Euro	$ 78.6	$146.3
Related forward contracts to buy foreign currencies for Euro	3.2	57.6
Related forward contracts to buy foreign currencies for Australian dollar	25.0	11.6
Related forward contracts to sell foreign currencies for British pound	15.1	15.8
Related forward contracts to buy foreign currencies for Brazil real	14.6	–
Related forward contracts to sell foreign currencies for U.S. dollar	11.2	13.8
Related forward contracts to buy foreign currencies for U.S. dollar	2.8	2.1
Related forward contracts to sell foreign currencies for Singapore dollar	1.1	1.3

In millions	Notional Value of Forward Contracts[1]	
	1/2/09	12/28/07
Related forward contracts to buy foreign currencies for Philippine peso	0.8	–
Total	$152.4	$248.5

[1] Pursuant to our policy, we entered into the above contracts immediately prior to the respective year-ends. Accordingly, the fair value of such contracts was nominal as of January 2, 2009, and December 28, 2007.

Cash Flow Hedges

We use derivative contracts designated as cash flow hedges to mitigate currency risk related to an imbalance of nonfunctional currency denominated costs and related revenue. We conducted monthly effectiveness tests of our derivative contracts on a spot-to-spot basis, which excludes forward points. We recorded expense related to forward points in Other expense, net of $0.5 million in 2008, $0.4 million in 2007 and income of $0.4 million in 2006. Effective gains and losses from derivative contracts are recorded in Accumulated other comprehensive income until the underlying transactions are realized, at which point they are reclassified to Total cost of revenue. Ineffectiveness of derivative contracts is recorded to Other expense, net. We did not have any ineffective derivative contracts in 2008. We recorded a nominal amount of ineffectiveness in 2007. If it becomes probable that an anticipated transaction that is hedged will not occur, we immediately reclassify the gains or losses related to that hedge from Accumulated other comprehensive income to Other expense, net. At January 2, 2009, we had net unrealized gain of $2.9 million in Accumulated other comprehensive income, which is expected to be reclassified to income within the next 12 months at the prevailing market rate. We held derivatives designated as cash flow hedges at the end of the year.

In millions	Notional Value of Forward Contracts[1]	
	1/2/09	12/28/07
Related forward contracts to buy foreign currencies for Euro	$43.4	$66.7
Related option contracts to buy foreign currencies for Euro	$ –	$15.6

[1] Pursuant to our policy, we entered into the above contracts immediately prior to the respective year-ends. Accordingly, the fair value of such contracts was $3.4 million as of January 2, 2009, and nominal as of December 28, 2007.

Net Investment Hedges

During 2008, we entered into foreign currency forward contracts to hedge a portion of our net investment in one of our foreign subsidiaries to reduce economic currency risk. Changes in the fair value of these contracts due to Euro exchange rate fluctuations are recorded as foreign currency translation adjustments within Accumulated other comprehensive income. As of January 2, 2009, we had a net unrealized gain of $7.4 million in Accumulated other comprehensive income. We recorded expense related to forward points in Other expense, net of $0.6 million in 2008. We held net investment hedges for the aggregate contract amount of 100 million Euros at January 2, 2009.

In millions	Notional Value of Forward Contracts[1]	
	1/2/09	12/28/07
Related forward contracts to sell foreign currencies for U.S. dollar	$139.7	$–

[1] Pursuant to our policy, we entered into the above contracts immediately prior to the respective year-end. Accordingly, the fair value of such contracts was nominal as of January 2, 2009.

IBM
2008 Annual Report

Note L. Derivatives and Hedging Transactions

The company operates in multiple functional currencies and is a significant borrower and lender in the global markets. In the normal course of business, the company is exposed to the impact of interest rate changes and foreign currency fluctuations, and to a lesser extent equity price changes and client credit risk. The company limits these risks by following established risk management policies and procedures, including the use of derivatives, and, where cost effective, financing with debt in the currencies in which assets are denominated. For interest rate exposures, derivatives are used to align rate movements between the interest rates associated with the company's lease and other financial assets and the interest rates associated with its financing debt. Derivatives are also used to manage the related cost of debt. For foreign currency exposures, derivatives are used to limit the effects of foreign exchange rate fluctuations on financial results.

As a result of the use of derivative instruments, the company is exposed to the risk that counterparties to derivative contracts will fail to meet their contractual obligations. To mitigate the counterparty credit risk, the company has a policy of only entering into contracts with carefully selected major financial institutions based upon their credit ratings and other factors, and maintains strict dollar limits that correspond to each institution's credit rating. The company's established policies and procedures for mitigating credit risk on principal transactions include reviewing and establishing limits for credit exposure and continually assessing the creditworthiness of counterparties. Master agreements with counterparties include master netting arrangements as further mitigation of credit exposure to counterparties. These arrangements permit the company to net amounts due from the company to a counterparty with amounts due to the company from a counterparty reducing the maximum loss from credit risk in the event of counterparty default.

The company employs derivative instruments to hedge the volatility in stockholders' equity resulting from changes in currency exchange rates of significant foreign subsidiaries of the company with respect to the U.S. dollar. These instruments, designated as net investment hedges in accordance with SFAS No. 133, expose the company to liquidity risk as the derivatives have an immediate cash flow impact upon maturity which is not offset by the translation of the underlying hedged equity. The company monitors the cash loss potential on an ongoing basis and may discontinue some of these hedging relationships by de-designating the derivative instrument to manage this liquidity risk. Although not designated as accounting hedges, the company may utilize derivatives to offset the changes in fair value of the de-designated instruments from the date of de-designation until maturity. The company expended $546 million and $258 million related to maturities of derivative instruments that existed in qualifying net investment hedge relationships in 2008 and 2007, respectively. At December 31, 2008, the company had net liabilities of $244 million, representing the fair value of derivative instruments in qualifying net investment hedge relationships. Of this amount, $50 million is expected to mature in fiscal 2009. In addition, at December 31, 2008, the company had net liabilities of $458 million, representing the fair value of derivative instruments that were designated in qualifying net investment hedging relationships as of December 31, 2007, but were subsequently de-designated in fiscal 2008. This amount will fully mature in fiscal 2009. At December 31, 2008 the weighted-average remaining maturity of all derivative instruments designated as net investment hedges was approximately 2.4 years as compared to 1.5 years at December 31, 2007.

In its hedging programs, the company uses forward contracts, futures contracts, interest-rate swaps and currency swaps, depending upon the underlying exposure.

A brief description of the major hedging programs follows.

DEBT RISK MANAGEMENT

The company issues debt in the global capital markets, principally to fund its financing lease and loan portfolio. Access to cost-effective financing can result in interest rate and/or currency mismatches with the underlying assets. To manage these mismatches and to reduce overall interest cost, the company uses interest-rate swaps to convert specific fixed-rate debt into variable-rate (or "floating-rate") debt (i.e., fair value hedges) and to convert specific variable-rate debt into fixed-rate debt (i.e., cash flow hedges).

The company is exposed to exchange rate volatility on foreign currency denominated debt. To manage this risk, the company employs cross-currency swaps to convert fixed-rate foreign currency denominated debt to fixed-rate debt denominated in the functional currency of the borrowing entity. These swaps are accounted for as cash flow hedges.

The company is exposed to interest rate volatility on forecasted debt issuances. To manage this risk, the company may use forward starting interest-rate swaps to lock in a portion of the rate on the interest payments related to the forecasted debt issuance. These swaps are accounted for as cash flow hedges.

At December 31, 2008 and 2007, the weighted-average remaining maturity of all swaps in the debt risk management program was approximately five years.

LONG-TERM INVESTMENTS IN FOREIGN SUBSIDIARIES (NET INVESTMENT)

A significant portion of the company's foreign currency denominated debt portfolio is designated as a hedge of net investment which reduces the volatility in stockholders' equity caused by changes in foreign currency exchange rates in the functional currency of major foreign subsidiaries with respect to the U.S. dollar. The company also uses cross-currency interest rate swaps and foreign exchange forward contracts for this risk management purpose. The currency effects of these hedges (approximately $243 million losses in 2008, $880 million losses in 2007 and $350 million losses in 2006, net of tax) were reflected in accumulated gains and (losses) not affecting retained earnings within the Consolidated Statement of Stockholders' Equity, thereby offsetting a portion of the translation adjustment of the applicable foreign subsidiaries' net assets.

ANTICIPATED ROYALTIES AND COST TRANSACTIONS

The company's operations generate significant nonfunctional currency, third-party vendor payments and intercompany payments for royalties and goods and services among the company's non-U.S. subsidiaries and with the parent company. In anticipation of these foreign currency cash flows and in view of the volatility of the currency markets, the company selectively employs foreign exchange forward contracts to manage its currency risk. These forwards are accounted for as cash flow hedges. The maximum length of time over which the company is hedging its exposure to the variability in future cash flows is approximately four years. At December 31, 2008, the weighted-average remaining maturity of these derivative instruments was approximately 446 days as compared to 281 days at December 31, 2007.

SUBSIDIARY CASH AND FOREIGN CURRENCY ASSET/LIABILITY MANAGEMENT

The company uses its Global Treasury Centers to manage the cash of its subsidiaries. These centers principally use currency swaps to convert cash flows in a cost-effective manner. In addition, the company uses foreign exchange forward contracts to economically hedge, on a net basis, the foreign currency exposure of a portion of the company's nonfunctional currency assets and liabilities. The terms of these forward and swap contracts are generally less than six months. The changes in the fair values of these contracts and of the underlying hedged exposures are generally offsetting and are recorded in other (income) and expense in the Consolidated Statement of Earnings.

EQUITY RISK MANAGEMENT

The company is exposed to equity price changes related to certain obligations to employees. These equity exposures are primarily related to market price movements in certain broad equity market indices and in the company's common stock. Changes in the overall value of these employee compensation obligations are recorded in SG&A expense in the Consolidated Statement of Earnings. Although not designated as accounting hedges, the company utilizes equity derivatives, including equity swaps and futures, to economically hedge the exposures related to certain employee compensation obligations. The derivatives are linked to the total return on certain broad equity market indices or the total return on the company's common stock. They are recorded at fair value with gains or losses also reported in SG&A expense in the Consolidated Statement of Earnings.

OTHER DERIVATIVES

The company holds warrants in connection with certain investments that are deemed derivatives because they contain net share or net cash settlement provisions. The company records the changes in the fair value of these warrants in other (income) and expense in the Consolidated Statement of Earnings.

The company is exposed to a potential loss if a client fails to pay amounts due under contractual terms (credit risk). The company utilizes credit default swaps to economically hedge its credit exposures. The swaps are recorded at fair value with gains and losses reported in other (income) and expense in the Consolidated Statement of Earnings. The company had no credit default swaps outstanding at December 31, 2008.

To economically hedge its foreign exchange exposure not covered by any of the previously discussed programs, the company also uses certain forward contracts that are not designated as accounting hedges. These derivatives are recorded at fair value with gains and losses reported in other (income) and expense in the Consolidated Statement of Earnings.

The tables on page 93 summarize the net fair value of the derivative instruments and the carrying value of foreign currency denominated debt designated as a hedge of net investment at December 31, 2008 and 2007 (included in the Consolidated Statement of financial Position).

| ($ In millions) | | Hedge Designation | | |
At December 31, 2008	Fair Value	Cash Flow	Net Investment	Non-Hedge/ Other
Derivatives—net asset/ (liability):				
Debt risk management	$848	$ 19	$ –	$ 77
Long-term investments in foreign subsidiaries (net investments)	–	–	(244)	(458)
Anticipated royalties and cost transactions	–	(404)	–	–
Subsidiary cash and foreign currency asset/liability management	–	–	–	(88)
Equity risk management	–	–	–	24
Other derivatives	–	–	–	–
Total derivatives	848[a]	(385)[b]	(244)[c]	(445)[d]
Debt:				
Long-term investments in foreign subsidiaries (net investments)	–	–	(3,819)[e]	–
TOTAL	$848	$(385)	$(4,063)	$(445)

(a) Comprises assets of $858 million and liabilities of $10 million.
(b) Comprises assets of $593 million and liabilities of $978 million.
(c) Comprises assets of $109 million and liabilities of $353 million.
(d) Comprises assets of $330 million and liabilities of $775 million.
(e) Represents foreign currency denominated debt formally designated as a hedge of net investment.

| ($ In millions) | | Hedge Designation | | |
At December 31, 2008	Fair Value	Cash Flow	Net Investment	Non-Hedge/ Other
Derivatives—net asset/ (liability):				
Debt risk management	$167	$291	$ –	$ 50
Long-term investments in foreign subsidiaries (net investments)	–	–	(937)	–
Anticipated royalties and cost transactions	–	(203)	–	–
Subsidiary cash and foreign currency asset/liability management	–	–	–	(56)
Equity risk management	–	–	–	30
Other derivatives	–	–	–	6
Total derivatives	167(a)	88(b)	(937)(c)	30(d)
Debt:				
Long-term investments in foreign subsidiaries (net investments)	–	–	(2,787)(e)	–
TOTAL	$167	$ 88	$(3,724)	$ 30

(a) Comprises assets of $181 million and liabilities of $14 million.
(b) Comprises assets of $526 million and liabilities of $438 million.
(c) Comprises liabilities of $937 million.
(d) Comprises assets of $90 million and liabilities of $60 million.
(e) Represents foreign currency denominated debt formally designated as a hedge of net investment.

ACCUMULATED DERIVATIVE GAINS OR LOSSES

At December 31, 2008, in connection with its cash flow hedges of anticipated royalties and cost transactions, the company recorded net gains of $88 million, net of tax, in accumulated gains and (losses) not affecting retained earnings. Of this amount, $235 million of gains are expected to be reclassified to net income within the next year, providing an offsetting economic impact against the under-lying anticipated transactions. At December 31, 2008, net losses of approximately $14 million, net of tax, were recorded in accumulated gains and (losses) not affecting retained earnings in connection with cash flow hedges of the company's borrowings. Of this amount, $10 million of gains are expected to be reclassified to net income within the next year, providing an offsetting economic impact against the underlying transactions.

The following table summarizes activity in the accumulated gains and (losses) not affecting retained earnings section of the Consolidated Statement of Stockholders' Equity related to all derivatives classified as cash flow hedges.

($ In millions, net of tax)	(Credit)/Debit
December 31, 2005	$(238)
Net gains reclassified into earnings from equity during 2006	205
Changes in fair value of derivatives in 2006	138
December 31, 2006	104
Net losses reclassified into earnings from equity during 2007	(116)
Changes in fair value of derivatives in 2007	239
December 31, 2007	227
Net losses reclassified into earnings from equity during 2008	(303)
Changes in fair value of derivatives in 2008	2
December 31, 2008	$ (74)

For the years ending December 31, 2008, 2007 and 2006, there were no significant gains or losses recognized in earnings representing hedge ineffectiveness or excluded from the assessment of hedge effectiveness (for fair value hedges and cash flow hedges), or associated with an underlying exposure that did not or was not expected to occur (for cash flow hedges); nor are there any anticipated in the normal course of business.

U.S. Steel
2008 Annual Report

14. Derivative Instruments

In March 2008, the FASB issued FAS No. 161, "Disclosures about Derivative Instruments and Hedging Activities—an amendment of FASB Statement No. 133" (FAS 161). FAS 161 amends and expands the disclosure requirements of FAS No. 133, "Accounting for Derivative Instruments and Hedging Activities" (FAS 133), to provide qualitative and quantitative information on how and why an entity uses derivative instruments, how derivative instruments and related hedged items are accounted for under FAS 133 and its related interpretations, and how derivative instruments and related hedged items affect an entity's financial position, financial performance and cash flows. FAS 161 is effective for U. S. Steel as of January 1, 2009; however, we chose to adopt FAS 161 in the first quarter of 2008.

U.S. Steel is exposed to foreign currency exchange risks as a result of our European and Canadian operations. USSE's revenues are primarily in euros and costs are primarily in U.S. dollars, Slovak koruna, Serbian dinars and euros. USSC's revenues are denominated in both Canadian and U.S. dollars. While most of USSC's costs are in Canadian dollars, it makes significant raw material purchases in U.S. dollars. In addition, the acquisition of USSC was funded from the United States and through the reinvestment of undistributed earnings from USSE, creating intercompany monetary assets and liabilities in currencies other than the functional currency of the entities involved, which can impact income when remeasured at the end of each quarter. An $815 million U.S. dollar-denominated intercompany loan (the Intercompany Loan) to a European subsidiary was the primary exposure at December 31, 2008.

U.S. Steel holds or purchases derivative financial instruments for purposes other than trading to mitigate foreign currency exchange rate risk. U.S. Steel uses euro forward sales contracts with maturities no longer than 18 months to exchange euros for U.S. dollars to manage our exposure to foreign currency price fluctuations. The gains and losses recognized on these euro forward sales contracts may partially offset gains and losses recognized on the Intercompany Loan.

As of December 31, 2008, U.S. Steel held euro forward sales contracts with a total notional value of approximately $363 million. We mitigate the risk of concentration of counterparty credit risk by purchasing our forward sales contracts from several counterparties. FAS 133 requires derivative instruments to be recognized at fair value in the balance sheet. U.S. Steel has not elected to designate these foreign currency forward contracts as hedges under FAS 133. Therefore, changes in the fair value of these contracts are recognized immediately in the results of operations.

Additionally, we routinely enter into contracts to hedge a portion of our purchase commitments for natural gas to lower our financial exposure related to commodity price fluctuations. As part of this strategy, we routinely utilize fixed-price forward physical purchase contracts. Historically, these forward physical purchase contracts have qualified for the normal purchases and normal sales exemption under FAS 133. However, due to the idling of certain facilities in December 2008, some of these contracts no longer meet the exemption criteria and are therefore subject to mark-to-market accounting. As of December 31, 2008, U.S. Steel held commodity contracts for natural gas with a total notional value of approximately $33 million that qualified as derivatives. See Note 1 to the financial statements for a summary of accounting policies related to derivative financial instruments.

The following summarizes the location and amounts of the fair values and gains or losses related to derivatives included in U. S. Steel's financial statements as of and for the year ended December 31, 2008:

(In millions)	Location of Fair Value in Balance Sheet	Fair Value December 31, 2008
Foreign exchange forward contracts	Accounts receivable	$14
Forward physical purchase contracts	Accounts payable	$18

	Location of Gain (Loss) on Derivative in Statement of Operations	Amount of Gain (Loss) Year ended December 31, 2008
Forward physical purchase contracts	Cost of sales	($18)
Foreign exchange forward contracts	Other financial costs	$38

In accordance with FAS 157, the fair value of our foreign currency derivatives is determined using Level 2 inputs, which are defined as "significant other observable" inputs. The inputs used include quotes from counterparties that are corroborated with market sources. The fair value of our natural gas derivatives is also determined using Level 2 inputs. The inputs used include forward prices derived from the New York Mercantile Exchange.

Kellogg's
2008 Annual Report

Note 12. Financial Instruments and Credit Risk Concentration

The carrying values of the Company's short-term items, including cash, cash equivalents, accounts receivable, accounts payable and notes payable approximate fair value. The fair value of long-term debt is calculated based on incremental borrowing rates currently available on loans with similar terms and maturities. The fair value of the Company's long-term debt at January 3, 2009 exceeded its carrying value by approximately $246 million.

The Company is exposed to certain market risks which exist as a part of its ongoing business operations. Management uses derivative financial and commodity instruments, where appropriate, to manage these risks. In general, instruments used as hedges must be effective at reducing the risk associated with the exposure being hedged and must be designated as a hedge at the inception of the contract. In accordance with SFAS No. 133, the Company designates derivatives as cash flow hedges, fair value hedges, net investment hedges, or other contracts used to reduce volatility in the translation of foreign currency earnings to U.S. dollars. The fair values of all hedges are recorded in accounts receivable, other assets, other current liabilities and other liabilities. Gains and losses representing either hedge ineffectiveness, hedge components excluded from the assessment of effectiveness, or hedges of translational exposure are recorded in other income (expense), net. Within the Consolidated Statement of Cash Flows, settlements of cash flow and fair value hedges are classified as an operating activity; settlements of all other derivatives are classified as a financing activity.

Cash flow hedges

Qualifying derivatives are accounted for as cash flow hedges when the hedged item is a forecasted transaction. Gains and losses on these instruments are recorded in other comprehensive income until the underlying transaction is recorded in earnings. When the hedged item is realized, gains or losses are reclassified from accumulated other comprehensive income to the Consolidated Statement of Earnings on the same line item as the underlying transaction. For all cash flow hedges, gains and losses representing either hedge ineffectiveness or hedge components excluded from the assessment of effectiveness were insignificant during the periods presented.

The cumulative net loss attributable to cash flow hedges recorded in accumulated other comprehensive income at January 3, 2009, was $24 million, related to forward interest rate contracts settled during 2001 and 2003 in conjunction with fixed rate long-term debt issuances, 10-year natural gas price swaps entered into in 2006, and commodity price cash flow hedges, partially offset by gains on foreign currency cash flow hedges. The interest rate contract losses will be reclassified into interest expense over the next 23 years. The natural gas swap losses will be reclassified to cost of goods sold over the next 8 years. Gains and losses related to foreign currency and commodity price cash flow hedges will be reclassified into earnings during the next 18 months.

Fair value hedges

Qualifying derivatives are accounted for as fair value hedges when the hedged item is a recognized asset, liability, or firm commitment. Gains and losses on these instruments are recorded in earnings, offsetting gains and losses on the hedged item. For all fair value hedges, gains and losses representing either hedge ineffectiveness or hedge components excluded from the assessment of effectiveness were insignificant during the periods presented.

Net investment hedges

Qualifying derivative and nonderivative financial instruments are accounted for as net investment hedges when the hedged item is a nonfunctional currency investment in a subsidiary. Gains and losses on these instruments are included in foreign currency translation adjustments in other comprehensive income.

Other contracts

The Company also periodically enters into foreign currency forward contracts and options to reduce volatility in the translation of foreign currency earnings to U.S. dollars. Gains and losses on these instruments are recorded in other income (expense), net, generally reducing the exposure to translation volatility during a full-year period.

Foreign exchange risk

The Company is exposed to fluctuations in foreign currency cash flows related primarily to third-party purchases, intercompany transactions and nonfunctional currency denominated third-party debt. The Company is also exposed to fluctuations in the value of foreign currency investments in subsidiaries and cash flows related to repatriation of these investments. Additionally, the Company is exposed to volatility in the translation of foreign currency earnings to U.S. dollars. Management assesses foreign currency risk based on transactional cash flows and translational volatility and enters into forward contracts, options, and currency swaps to reduce fluctuations in net long or short currency positions. Forward contracts and options are generally less than 18 months duration. Currency swap agreements are established in conjunction with the term of underlying debt issues.

For foreign currency cash flow and fair value hedges, the assessment of effectiveness is generally based on changes in spot rates. Changes in time value are reported in other income (expense), net.

Interest rate risk

The Company is exposed to interest rate volatility with regard to future issuances of fixed rate debt and existing issuances of variable rate debt. The Company periodically uses interest rate swaps, including forward starting swaps, to reduce interest rate volatility and funding costs associated with certain debt issues, and to achieve a desired proportion of variable versus fixed rate debt, based on current and projected market conditions.

Variable-to-fixed interest rate swaps are accounted for as cash flow hedges and the assessment of effectiveness is based on changes in the present value of interest payments on the underlying debt. Fixed-to-variable interest rate swaps are accounted for as fair value hedges and the assessment of effectiveness is based on changes in the fair value of the underlying debt, using incremental borrowing rates currently available on loans with similar terms and maturities.

Price risk

The Company is exposed to price fluctuations primarily as a result of anticipated purchases of raw and packaging materials, fuel, and energy. The Company has historically used the combination of long-term contracts with suppliers, and exchange-traded futures and option contracts to reduce price fluctuations in a desired percentage of forecasted raw material purchases over a duration of generally less than 18 months. During 2006, the Company entered into two separate 10-year over-the-counter commodity swap transactions to reduce fluctuations in the price of natural gas used principally in its manufacturing processes.

Commodity contracts are accounted for as cash flow hedges. The assessment of effectiveness for exchange-traded instruments is based on changes in futures prices. The assessment of effectiveness for over-the-counter transactions is based on changes in designated indexes.

Credit risk concentration

The Company is exposed to credit loss in the event of nonperformance by counterparties on derivative financial and commodity contracts. This credit loss is limited to the cost of replacing these contracts at current market rates. In some instances the Company has reciprocal collateralization agreements with counterparties regarding fair value positions in excess of certain thresholds. These agreements call for the posting of collateral in the form of cash, treasury securities or letters of credit if a fair value loss position to the Company or its counterparties exceeds a certain amount. There were no collateral balance requirements at January 3, 2009 or December 29, 2007.

Financial instruments, which potentially subject the Company to concentrations of credit risk are primarily cash, cash equivalents, and accounts receivable. The Company places its investments in highly rated financial institutions and investment-grade short-term debt instruments, and limits the amount of credit exposure to any one entity. Management believes concentrations of credit risk with respect to accounts receivable is limited due to the generally high credit quality of the Company's major customers, as well as the large number and geographic dispersion of smaller customers. However, the Company conducts a disproportionate amount of business with a small number of large multinational grocery retailers, with the five largest accounts comprising approximately 30% of consolidated accounts receivable at January 3, 2009.

Whirlpool
2007 Annual Report

(9) Hedges and Derivative Financial Instruments

We are exposed to market risk from changes in foreign currency exchange rates, domestic and foreign interest rates, and commodity prices. Fluctuations in these rates and prices can affect our operating results and financial condition. We manage the exposure to these market risks through operating and financing activities and through the use of derivative financial instruments. We do not enter into derivative financial instruments for speculative or trading purposes.

Using derivative markets means assuming counterparty credit risk. Counterparty credit risk relates to the loss we could incur if a counterparty defaulted on a derivative contract. We primarily deal with investment-grade counterparties and monitor the overall credit risk and exposure to individual counterparties. We do not anticipate nonperformance by any counterparties. The amount of counterparty credit exposure is the unrealized gains on such derivative contracts. We do not require, nor do we post, collateral or security on such contracts.

The following table summarizes our outstanding derivative contracts at December 31, 2007 and 2006:

Exposure	Derivative	Notional Amount in Millions of Dollars		Hedge Type	Term
		2007	2006		
Forecasted cross currency cash flows	Foreign exchange forwards/ options	$2,023	$1,313	Cash flow or fair value hedge	Various, up to 28 months
Non-functional currency asset/liability	Foreign exchange forwards/ options	$1,154	$ 608	Undesignated	Various, up to 9 months
Raw material purchases	Commodity swaps	$ 294	$ 297	Cash flow or fair value hedge	Various, up to 15 months
Raw material purchases	Commodity swaps	$ 23	$ 19	Undesignated	Various, up to 11 months
Fixed rate debt	Interest rate swaps	100	100	Fair value hedge	2008
Floating rate debt	Interest rate swaps	150	150	Cash flow hedge	2008

		Notional Amount in Millions of Dollars			
Exposure	Derivative	2007	2006	Hedge Type	Term
Floating rate debt	Interest rate swap	50	50	Cash flow hedge	2009
Receivables	Credit put	1	–	Fair value hedge	2008

Forecasted cross currency cash flows relate primarily to foreign currency denominated expenditures and intercompany financing agreements, royalty agreements and dividends. Non-functional currency asset and liability hedges are undesignated but relate primarily to short term payables and receivables and intercompany loans. Commodity swaps relate to raw material purchases (for example, copper and aluminum) used in the manufacturing process. Unrealized gains and losses relating to these foreign exchange forwards/options and commodity swaps were a loss of $3 million and a gain of $70 million at December 31, 2007 and 2006, respectively.

Interest rate swaps with a notional amount of $100 million maturing in 2008 are designated and accounted for as a fair value hedge on fixed rate debt. The fair values of these contracts were a loss of $0.5 million and $1.7 million as of December 31, 2007 and 2006, respectively.

Interest rate swaps with a notional amount of $150 million maturing in 2008 are designated and accounted for as a cash flow hedge on floating rate debt. The fair values of these contracts were a loss of $2.3 million and $0.3 million as of December 31, 2007 and 2006, respectively.

An interest rate swap with a notional amount of $50 million maturing in 2009 is designated and accounted for as a cash flow hedge on future cash payments. The fair value of this contract was a loss of $0.6 million and $0.2 million as of December 31, 2007 and 2006, respectively.

Gains and losses related to the ineffective portion of our hedging instruments were immaterial for the years ended December 31, 2007, 2006 and 2005.

The amount of unrealized gain on derivative instruments included in other comprehensive income related to contracts maturing, and expected to be realized during 2008 is approximately $2 million at December 31, 2007.

Black & Decker
2007 Annual Report

Note 9. Derivative Financial Instruments

The Corporation is exposed to market risks arising from changes in interest rates. With products and services marketed in over 100 countries and with manufacturing sites in 11 countries, the Corporation also is exposed to risks arising from changes in foreign exchange rates.

Credit Exposure: The Corporation is exposed to credit-related losses in the event of nonperformance by counterparties to certain derivative financial instruments.

The Corporation monitors the creditworthiness of the counterparties and presently does not expect default by any of the counterparties. The Corporation does not obtain collateral in connection with its derivative financial instruments.

The credit exposure that results from interest rate and foreign exchange contracts is the fair value of contracts with a positive fair value as of the reporting date. Some derivatives are not subject to credit exposures. The fair value of all financial instruments is summarized in Note 10.

Interest Rate Risk Management: The Corporation manages its interest rate risk, primarily through the use of interest rate swap agreements, in order to achieve a cost-effective mix of fixed and variable rate indebtedness. It seeks to issue debt opportunistically, whether at fixed or variable rates, at the lowest possible costs. The Corporation may, based upon its assessment of the future interest rate environment, elect to manage its interest rate risk associated with changes in the fair value of its indebtedness, or the future cash flows associated with its indebtedness, through the use of interest rate swaps.

The amounts exchanged by the counterparties to interest rate swap agreements normally are based upon the notional amounts and other terms, generally related to interest rates, of the derivatives. While notional amounts of interest rate swaps form part of the basis for the amounts exchanged by the counterparties, the notional amounts are not themselves exchanged and, therefore, do not represent a measure of the Corporation's exposure as an end user of derivative financial instruments.

The Corporation's portfolio of interest rate swap instruments at December 31, 2007 and 2006, consisted of $325.0 million notional and $400.0 million notional amounts of fixed-to-variable rate swaps with a weighted-average fixed rate receipt of 5.08% and 5.11%, respectively. The basis of the variable rate paid is LIBOR.

Credit exposure on the Corporation's interest rate derivatives at December 31, 2007 and 2006, was $11.6 million and $4.7 million, respectively.

Foreign Currency Management: The Corporation enters into various foreign currency contracts in managing its foreign currency exchange risk. Generally, the foreign currency contracts have maturity dates of less than twenty-four months. The contractual amounts of foreign currency derivatives, principally forward exchange contracts, generally are exchanged by the counterparties. The Corporation's foreign currency derivatives are designated to, and generally are denominated in the currencies of, the underlying exposures. To minimize the volatility of reported equity, the Corporation may hedge, on a limited basis, a portion of its net investment in subsidiaries located outside the United States through the use of foreign currency forward contracts and purchased foreign currency options.

The Corporation seeks to minimize its foreign currency cash flow risk and hedges its foreign currency transaction exposures (that is, currency exposures related to assets and liabilities) as well as certain forecasted foreign currency exposures. Hedges of forecasted foreign currency exposures principally relate to the cash flow risk relating to the sales of products manufactured or purchased in a currency different from that of the selling subsidiary. The Corporation hedges its foreign currency cash flow risk through the use of forward exchange contracts and, to a small extent, options. Some of the forward exchange contracts involve the exchange of two foreign currencies according to the local needs of the subsidiaries. Some natural hedges also are used to mitigate risks associated with transaction and forecasted exposures. The Corporation also responds to foreign exchange movements through various means, such as pricing actions, changes in cost structure, and changes in hedging strategies.

The following table summarizes the contractual amounts of forward exchange contracts as of December 31, 2007 and 2006, in millions of dollars, including details by major currency as of December 31, 2007. Foreign currency amounts were translated at current rates as of the reporting date. The "Buy" amounts represent the United States dollar equivalent of commitments to purchase currencies, and the "Sell" amounts represent the United States dollar equivalent of commitments to sell currencies.

AS OF DECEMBER 31, 2007	BUY	SELL
United States dollar	$2,246.8	$ (1,510.1)
Pound sterling	1,001.4	(1,295.1)
Euro	767.9	(832.6)
Canadian dollar	–	(318.6)
Australian dollar	73.6	(94.9)
Czech koruna	64.2	–
Japanese yen	15.2	(24.6)
Swedish krona	67.3	(90.6)
New Zealand dollar	13.7	(5.2)
Swiss franc	12.1	(27.5)
Norwegian krone	–	(34.0)
Danish krone	9.9	(75.9)
Other	21.7	(18.8)
Total	$4,293.8	$ (4,327.9)

AS OF DECEMBER 31, 2006		
Total	$5,096.4	$ (5,081.6)

No options to buy or sell currencies were outstanding at December 31, 2007. Credit exposure on foreign currency derivatives as of December 31, 2007 and 2006, was $18.0 million and $32.7 million, respectively.

Hedge ineffectiveness and the portion of derivative gains and losses excluded from the assessment of hedge effectiveness related to the Corporation's cash flow hedges that were recorded to earnings during 2007, 2006, and 2005 were not significant.

Amounts deferred in accumulated other comprehensive income (loss) at December 31, 2007, that are expected to be re-classified into earnings during 2008 represent an after-tax loss of $21.4 million. The amount expected to be reclassified into earnings in the next twelve months includes unrealized gains and losses related to open foreign currency contracts. Accordingly, the amount that is ultimately reclassified into earnings may differ materially.

Note 10: Fair Value of Financial Instruments

The fair value of a financial instrument represents the amount at which the instrument could be exchanged in a current transaction between willing parties, other than in a forced sale or liquidation. Significant differences can arise between the fair value and carrying amount of financial instruments that are recognized at historical cost amounts.

The following methods and assumptions were used by the Corporation in estimating fair value disclosures for financial instruments:

- Cash and cash equivalents, trade receivables, certain other current assets, short-term borrowings, and current maturities of long-term debt: The amounts reported in the Consolidated Balance Sheet approximate fair value.

- Long-term debt: Publicly traded debt is valued based on quoted market values. The fair value of other long-term debt is estimated based on quoted market prices for the same or similar issues or on the current rates offered to the Corporation for debt of the same remaining maturities.

- Interest rate hedges: The fair value of interest rate hedges reflects the estimated amounts that the Corporation would receive or pay to terminate the contracts at the reporting date.

- Foreign currency contracts: The fair value of forward exchange contracts and options is estimated using prices established by financial institutions for comparable instruments.

The following table sets forth, in millions of dollars, the carrying amounts and fair values of the Corporation's financial instruments, except for those noted above for which carrying amounts approximate fair values:

Assets (Liabilities) As of December 31, 2007	Carrying Amount	Fair Value
Non-derivatives:		
Long-term debt	$(1,179)	$(1,146)
Derivatives relating to:		
Debt		
Assets	11.6	11.6
Foreign Currency		
Assets	18.0	18.0
Liabilities	(44.0)	(44.0)

Assets (Liabilities) As of December 31, 2006	Carrying Amount	Fair Value
Non-derivatives:		
Long-term debt	$(1,170)	$(1,149)
Derivatives relating to:		
Debt		
Assets	4.7	4.7

Assets (Liabilities) As of December 31, 2006	Carrying Amount	Fair Value
Liabilities	(6.0)	(6.0)
Foreign Currency		
Assets	32.7	32.7
Liabilities	(29.6)	(29.6)

Darden Restaurants
2006 Annual Report

Note 9. Derivative Instruments and Hedging Activities

We use interest rate related derivative instruments to manage our exposure on debt instruments, as well as commodities derivatives to manage our exposure to commodity price fluctuations. We also use equity related derivative instruments to manage our exposure on cash compensation arrangements indexed to the market price of our common stock. By using these instruments, we expose ourselves, from time to time, to credit risk and market risk. Credit risk is the failure of the counterparty to perform under the terms of the derivative contract. When the fair value of a derivative contract is positive, the counterparty owes us, which creates credit risk for us. We minimize this credit risk by entering into transactions with high quality counterparties. Market risk is the adverse effect on the value of a financial instrument that results from a change in interest rates, commodity prices, or market price of our common stock. We minimize this market risk by establishing and monitoring parameters that limit the types and degree of market risk that may be undertaken.

Option Contracts and Commodity Swaps

During fiscal 2006 and 2005, we entered into option contracts and commodity swaps to reduce the risk of natural gas price fluctuations. To the extent these derivatives are effective in offsetting the variability of the hedged cash flows, changes in the derivatives' fair value are not included in current earnings but are reported as accumulated other comprehensive income (loss). These changes in fair value are subsequently reclassified into earnings when the natural gas is purchased and used by us in our operations. Net gains (losses) of $4,281 and ($311) related to these derivatives were reclassified to earnings during fiscal 2006 and 2005, respectively, in connection with the settlement of our contracts. The fair value of these contracts was a net loss of $3,042 at May 28, 2006 and is expected to be reclassified from accumulated other comprehensive income (loss) into restaurant expenses during fiscal 2007. To the extent these derivatives are not effective, changes in their fair value are immediately recognized in current earnings. The fair value of outstanding derivatives is included in other current assets or other current liabilities.

At May 28, 2006, the maximum length of time over which we are hedging our exposure to the variability in future natural gas cash flows is 12 months. No gains or losses were reclassified into earnings during fiscal 2006 or fiscal 2005 as a result of the discontinuance of natural gas cash flow hedges.

Interest Rate Lock Agreement

During fiscal 2002, we entered into a treasury interest rate lock agreement (treasury lock) to hedge the risk that the cost of a future issuance of fixed-rate debt may be adversely affected by interest rate fluctuations. The treasury lock, which had a $75,000 notional principal amount of indebtedness, was used to hedge a portion of the interest payments associated with $150,000 of debt subsequently issued in March 2002. The treasury lock was settled at the time of the related debt issuance with a net gain of $267 being recognized in other comprehensive income (loss). The net gain on the treasury lock is being amortized into earnings as an adjustment to interest expense over the same period in which the related interest costs on the new debt issuance are being recognized in earnings. Annual amortization of $53 was recognized in earnings as an adjustment to interest expense during fiscal 2006, 2005 and 2004. We expect that the remaining $40 of this gain will be recognized in earnings as an adjustment to interest expense during fiscal 2007.

Interest Rate Swaps

During fiscal 2005 and fiscal 2004, we entered into interest rate swap agreements (swaps) to hedge the risk of changes in interest rates on the cost of a future issuance of fixed-rate debt. The swaps, which had a $100,000 notional principal amount of indebtedness, were used to hedge a portion of the interest payments associated with $150,000 of unsecured 4.875 percent senior notes due in August 2010, which were issued in August 2005. The interest rate swaps were settled at the time of the related debt issuance with a net loss of $1,177 being recognized in accumulated other comprehensive income (loss). The net loss on the interest rate swaps is being amortized into earnings as an adjustment to interest expense over the same period in which the related interest costs on the new debt issuance are being recognized in earnings. A loss of $177 was recognized in earnings during fiscal 2006 as an adjustment to interest expense.

We also had interest rate swaps with a notional amount of $200,000, which we used to convert variable rates on our long-term debt to fixed rates effective May 30, 1995, related to the issuance of our $150,000 6.375 percent notes due February 2006 and our $100,000 7.125 percent debentures due February 2016. We received the one-month commercial paper interest rate and paid fixed-rate interest ranging from 7.51 percent to 7.89 percent. The interest rate swaps were settled during January 1996 at a cost to us of $27,670. A portion of the cost was recognized as an adjustment to interest expense over the term of our 10-year 6.375 percent notes that were settled at maturity in February 2006. The remaining portion continues to be recognized as an adjustment to interest expense over the term of our 20-year 7.125 percent debentures due 2016.

Equity Forwards

During fiscal 2006 and 2005, we entered into equity forward contracts to hedge the risk of changes in future cash flows associated with the unvested unrecognized Darden stock units granted during the first quarters of fiscal 2006 and 2005 (see Note 16—Stock Plans for additional information). The equity forward contracts will be settled at the end of the vesting periods of their underlying Darden stock units, which range between four and five years. In total, the equity forward contracts are indexed to 330 shares of our common stock, have an $8,264 notional amount and can only be net settled in cash. To the extent the equity forward contracts are effective in offsetting the variability of the hedged cash flows, changes in the fair value of the equity forward contracts are not included in current earnings but are reported as accumulated other comprehensive income (loss). A deferred gain of $2,348 related to the equity forward contracts was recognized in accumulated other comprehensive income (loss) at May 28, 2006. As the Darden stock units vest, we will effectively de-designate that portion of the equity forward contract that no longer qualifies for hedge accounting and changes in fair value associated with that portion of the equity forward contract will be recognized in current earnings. Gains of $965 and $471 were Darden Restaurants 2006 Annual Report recognized in earnings as a component of restaurant labor during fiscal 2006 and 2005, respectively.

During May 2006, we entered into an equity forward contract to hedge the risk of changes in future cash flows associated with employee directed investments in Darden stock within the non-qualified deferred compensation plan (see Note 15—Retirement Plans for additional information). The equity forward contract is indexed to 100 shares of our common stock, has a $3,744 notional amount, can only be net settled in cash and expires in May 2011. We did not elect hedge accounting with the expectation that changes in the fair value of the equity forward contract would offset changes in the fair value of the Darden stock investments in the non-qualified deferred compensation plan within net earnings in our consolidated statements of earnings. A loss of $93 related to the equity forward contract was recognized in net earnings during fiscal 2006.

Note 10. Financial Instruments

The fair values of cash equivalents, accounts receivable, accounts payable and short-term debt approximate their carrying amounts due to their short duration.

The carrying value and fair value of long-term debt at May 28, 2006 was $644,601 and $645,600, respectively. The carrying value and fair value of long-term debt at May 29, 2005 was $650,247 and $686,040, respectively. The fair value of long-term debt is determined based on market prices or, if market prices are not available, the present value of the underlying cash flows discounted at our incremental borrowing rates.

General Mills
2006 Annual Report

6. Financial Instruments and Risk Management Activities

Financial Instruments   The carrying values of cash and cash equivalents, receivables, accounts payable, other current liabilities and notes payable approximate fair value. Marketable securities are carried at fair value. As of May 28, 2006, a comparison of cost and market values of our marketable debt and equity securities is as follows:

In Millions	Cost	Market Value	Gross Gains	Gross Losses
Held to Maturity:				
Equity securities	$ 2	$ 2	$–	$–
Total	$ 2	$ 2	$–	
Available for sale:				
Debt securities	$20	$20	$–	$–
Equity securities	4	8	4	–
Total	$24	$28	$4	$–

Earnings include realized gains from sales of available-for-sale marketable securities of less than $1 million in fiscal 2006, $2 million in fiscal 2005 and $20 million in fiscal 2004. Gains and losses are determined by specific identification. The aggregate unrealized gains and losses on available-for-sale securities, net of tax effects, are classified in Accumulated Other Comprehensive Income within Stockholders' Equity. At May 28, 2006, we owned twenty marketable securities with a fair market value less than cost. The fair market value of these securities was $0.3 million below their cost.

Scheduled maturities of our marketable securities are as follows:

In Millions	Held to Maturity		Available for Sale	
	Cost	Market Value	Cost	Market Value
Under one year (current)	$–	$–	$5	$5
From 1 to 3 years	–	–	5	5
From 4 to 7 years	–	–	2	2
Over 7 years	–	–	8	8
Equity securities	2	2	4	8
Total	$2	$2	$24	$28

Cash, cash equivalents and marketable securities totaling $48 million as of May 28, 2006, and $63 million as of May 29, 2005, were pledged as collateral. These assets are primarily pledged as collateral for certain derivative contracts.

The fair values and carrying amounts of long-term debt, including the current portion, were $4,566 million and $4,546 million at May 28, 2006, and $6,074 million and $5,893 million at May 29, 2005. The fair value of long-term debt was estimated using discounted cash flows based on our current incremental borrowing rates for similar types of instruments.

Risk Management Activities As a part of our ongoing business operations, we are exposed to market risks such as changes in interest rates, foreign currency exchange rates and commodity prices. To manage these risks, we may enter into various derivative transactions (e.g., futures, options and swaps) pursuant to our established policies.

Interest Rate Risk—We are exposed to interest rate volatility with regard to existing variable-rate debt and planned future issuances of fixed-rate debt. We use a combination of interest rate swaps and forward-starting swaps to reduce interest rate volatility and to achieve a desired proportion of variable versus fixed-rate debt, based on current and projected market conditions.

Variable Interest Rate Exposures—Except as discussed below, variable-to-fixed interest rate swaps are accounted for as cash flow hedges, as are all hedges of forecasted issuances of debt. Effectiveness is assessed based on either the perfectly effective hypothetical derivative method or changes in the present value of interest payments on the underlying debt. Amounts deferred to Accumulated Other Comprehensive Income are reclassified into earnings over the life of the associated debt. The amount of hedge ineffectiveness was less than $1 million in fiscal 2006, 2005 and 2004.

Fixed Interest Rate Exposures—Fixed-to-variable interest rate swaps are accounted for as fair value hedges with effectiveness assessed based on changes in the fair value of the underlying debt, using incremental borrowing rates currently available on loans with similar terms and maturities. Effective gains and losses on these derivatives and the underlying hedged items are recorded as interest expense. The amount of hedge ineffectiveness was less than $1 million in fiscal 2006, 2005 and 2004.

In anticipation of the Pillsbury acquisition and other financing needs, we entered into pay-fixed interest rate swap contracts during fiscal 2001 and fiscal 2002 totaling $7.1 billion to lock in our interest payments on the associated debt. During fiscal 2004, $750 million of these swaps matured. In fiscal 2005, $2 billion of these swaps matured. At May 28, 2006, we still owned $3.15 billion of Pillsbury-related pay-fixed swaps that were previously neutralized with offsetting pay-floating swaps in fiscal 2002. At May 28, 2006, $500 million of our pay-floating interest rate swaps were designated as a fair value hedge of our 2.625 percent notes due October 2006.

In May 2006, we entered into a $100 million pay-fixed, forward-starting interest rate swap with a fixed rate of 5.7 percent in anticipation of fixed-rate debt refinancing probable of occurring in fiscal 2007. Subsequent to May 28, 2006, we entered into an additional $600 million of pay-fixed, forward-starting interest rate swaps with an average fixed rate of 5.7 percent.

The following table summarizes the notional amounts and weighted average interest rates of our interest rate swaps. As discussed above, we have neutralized all of our pay-fixed swaps with pay-floating swaps; however, we cannot present them on a net basis in the following table because the offsetting occurred with different counterparties. Average variable rates are based on rates as of the end of the reporting period.

In Millions	May 28, 2006	May 29, 2005
Pay-floating swaps—notional amount	$3,770	$3,795
Average receive rate	4.8%	4.8%
Average pay rate	5.1%	3.1%

In Millions	May 28, 2006	May 29, 2005
Pay-fixed swaps—notional amount	$3,250	$3,150
Average receive rate	5.1%	3.1%
Average pay rate	6.8%	6.9%

The swap contracts mature at various dates from 2007 to 2015, as follows:

In Millions Fiscal Year Maturity Date	Pay Floating	Pay Fixed
2007	$1,923	$1,400
2008	22	–
2009	20	–
2010	20	–
2011	18	–
Beyond 2011	1,767	1,850
Total	$3,770	$3,250

Foreign Exchange Transaction Risk—We are exposed to fluctuations in foreign currency cash flows related primarily to third-party purchases, intercompany product shipments and intercompany loans. Our primary U.S. dollar exchange rate exposures are with the Canadian dollar, the euro, the Australian dollar, the Mexican peso and the British pound. Forward contracts of generally less than 12 months duration are used to hedge some of these risks. Hedge effectiveness is assessed based on changes in forward rates. The amount of hedge ineffectiveness was $1 million or less in fiscal 2006, 2005 and 2004.

Commodity Price Risk—We are exposed to price fluctuations primarily as a result of anticipated purchases of ingredient and packaging materials. The principal raw materials that we use are cereal grains, sugar, dairy products, vegetables, fruits, meats, vegetable oils, and other agricultural products as well as paper and plastic packaging materials, operating supplies and energy. We use a combination of long cash positions with suppliers, exchange-traded futures and option contracts and over-the-counter hedging mechanisms to reduce price fluctuations in a desired percentage of forecasted purchases over a period of less than two years. Except as discussed below, commodity derivatives are accounted for as cash flow hedges, with effectiveness assessed based on changes in futures prices. The amount of hedge ineffectiveness was a gain of $3 million in fiscal 2006, and were losses of $1 million or less in fiscal 2005 and 2004.

Other Risk Management Activities—We enter into certain derivative contracts in accordance with our risk management strategy that do not meet the criteria for hedge accounting, including those in our grain merchandising operation, certain foreign currency derivatives and offsetting interest rate swaps as discussed above. Even though they may not qualify as hedges, these derivatives have the economic impact of largely mitigating the associated risks. These derivatives were not acquired for trading purposes and are recorded at fair value with changes in fair value recognized in earnings each period.

Our grain merchandising operation provides us efficient access to and more informed knowledge of various commodities markets. This operation uses futures and options to hedge its net inventory position to minimize market exposure. As of May 28, 2006, our grain merchandising operation had futures and options contracts that essentially hedged its net inventory position. None of the contracts extended beyond May 2007. All futures contracts and options are exchange-based instruments with ready liquidity and determinable market values. Neither the results of operations nor the year-end positions of our grain merchandising operation were material.

Unrealized losses from cash flow hedges recorded in Accumulated Other Comprehensive Income as of May 28, 2006, totaled $92 million, primarily related to interest rate swaps we entered into in contemplation of future borrowings and other financing requirements (primarily related to the Pillsbury acquisition), which are being reclassified into interest expense over the lives of the hedged forecasted transactions. The majority of the remaining gains and losses from cash flow hedges recorded in Accumulated Other Comprehensive Income as of May 28, 2006, were related to foreign currency contracts. The net amount of the gains and losses in Accumulated Other Comprehensive Income as of May 28, 2006, that is expected to be reclassified into earnings within the next twelve months is $39 million in expense. See Note Seven for the impact of these reclassifications on interest expense.

Concentrations of Credit Risk—We enter into interest rate, foreign exchange, and certain commodity and equity derivatives primarily with a diversified group of highly rated counterparties. We continually monitor our positions and the credit ratings of the counterparties involved and, by policy, limit the amount of credit exposure to any one party. These transactions may expose us to potential losses due to the credit risk of nonperformance by these counterparties; however, we have not incurred a material loss nor are losses anticipated. We also enter into commodity futures transactions through various regulated exchanges.

Our top five customers in the U.S. Retail segment account for 47 percent of the segment's net sales. Payment terms vary depending on product categories and markets. We establish and monitor credit limits to manage our credit risk. We have not incurred a material loss nor are any such losses anticipated.

Dell Inc.
2006 Annual Report

Note 2—Financial Instruments

Disclosures About Fair Values of Financial Instruments

The fair value of investments, long-term debt, and related interest rate derivative instruments has been estimated based upon market quotes from brokers. The fair value of foreign currency forward contracts has been estimated using market quoted rates of foreign currencies at the applicable balance sheet date. The estimated fair value of foreign currency purchased option contracts is based on market quoted rates at the applicable balance sheet date and the Black-Scholes option pricing model. The estimates presented herein are not necessarily indicative of the amounts that Dell could realize in a current market exchange. Changes in assumptions could significantly affect the estimates.

Cash and cash equivalents, accounts receivable, accounts payable, and accrued and other liabilities are reflected in the accompanying consolidated statement of financial position at cost, which approximates fair value because of the short-term maturity of these assets and liabilities.

Investments

The following table summarizes by major security type the fair value and cost of Dell's investments. All investments with remaining maturities in excess of one year are recorded as long-term investments in the accompanying consolidated statement of financial position.

	February 3, 2006			January 28, 2005		
	Fair Value	Cost	Unrealized Gain (Loss)	Fair Value	Cost	Unrealized Gain (Loss)
			(In millions)			
Debt securities:						
U.S. government and agencies	$2,501	$2,547	$(46)	$7,973	$8,012	$(39)
U.S. corporate	1,638	1,657	(19)	1,012	1,021	(9)
International corporate	352	359	(7)	243	245	(2)
State and municipal governments	115	115	–	25	25	–
Total debt securities	4,606	4,678	(72)	9,253	9,303	(50)
Equity and other securities	101	101	–	101	98	3
Total investments	$4,707	$4,779	$(72)	$9,354	$9,401	$(47)
Short-term	$2,016	$2,028	$(12)	$5,060	$5,068	$ (8)
Long-term	2,691	2,751	(60)	4,294	4,333	(39)
Total investments	$4,707	$4,779	$(72)	$9,354	$9,401	$(47)

As of February 3, 2006, Dell had approximately 385 debt investment positions that had fair values below their carrying values for a period of less than 12 months. The fair value and unrealized losses on these investment positions totaled $2 billion and $27 million, respectively, as of February 3, 2006. As of February 3, 2006, Dell had approximately 660 investment positions that had fair values below their carrying values for a period of more than 12 months. The fair value and unrealized losses on these investment positions totaled $2 billion and $45 million, respectively, as of February 3, 2006. The unrealized losses are due to changes in interest rates and are expected to be recovered over the contractual term of the instrument.

The following table summarizes Dell's recognized gains and losses on investments, including impairments of certain investments:

	Fiscal Year Ended		
	February 3, 2006	January 28, 2005	January 30, 2004
		(In millions)	
Gains	$13	$40	$94
Losses	(9)	(34)	(78)
Not recognized gains	$ 4	$ 6	$16

Dell routinely enters into securities lending agreements with financial institutions in order to enhance investment income. Dell requires that the loaned securities be collateralized in the form of cash or securities for values which generally exceed the value of the loaned security. As of February 3, 2006, there were no securities on loan.

Foreign Currency Instruments

Dell uses purchased option contracts and forward contracts designated as cash flow hedges to protect against the foreign currency exchange risk inherent in its forecasted transactions denominated in currencies other than the U.S. dollar. Hedged transactions include international sales by U.S. dollar functional currency entities, foreign currency denominated purchases of certain components and intercompany shipments to some international subsidiaries. The risk of loss associated with purchased options is limited to premium amounts paid for the option contracts. The risk of loss associated with forward contracts is equal to the exchange rate differential from the time the contract is entered into until the time it is settled. These contracts generally expire in twelve months or less.

Dell also uses forward contracts to hedge monetary assets and liabilities, primarily receivables and payables, denominated in a foreign currency. These contracts are not designated as hedging instruments under GAAP, and therefore, the change in the instrument's fair value is recognized currently in earnings and is reported as a component of investment and other income, net. The change in the fair value of these instruments represents a natural hedge as their gains and losses offset the changes in the underlying fair value of the monetary assets and liabilities due to movements in currency exchange rates. These contracts generally expire in three months or less.

If the derivative is designated as a cash flow hedge, the effective portion of the change in the fair value of the derivative is initially deferred in other comprehensive income (loss) net of tax. These amounts are subsequently recognized in income as a component of net revenue or cost of revenue in the same period the hedged transaction affects earnings. The ineffective portion of the change in the fair value of a cash flow hedge is recognized currently in earnings and is reported as a component of investment and other income, net. Hedge effectiveness is measured by comparing the hedging instrument's cumulative change in fair value from inception to maturity to the forecasted transaction's terminal value. During fiscal 2006, 2005, and 2004, Dell did not discontinue any cash flow hedges as substantially all forecasted foreign currency transactions were realized in Dell's actual results. Furthermore, hedge ineffectiveness was not material.

At February 3, 2006, Dell held purchased foreign currency option contracts with a notional amount of approximately $3.3 billion, a net asset value of $145 million and a net unrealized deferred gain of $1 million, net of taxes. At February 3, 2006, Dell held foreign currency forward contracts with a notional amount of approximately $3.3 billion, a net asset value of $1 million and a net unrealized deferred loss of $20 million, net of taxes.

At January 28, 2005, Dell held purchased foreign currency option contracts with a notional amount of approximately $2.0 billion, a net asset value of $53 million and a net unrealized deferred loss of $52 million, net of taxes. At January 28, 2005, Dell held foreign currency forward contracts with a notional amount of approximately $3.0 billion, a net liability value of $146 million and a net unrealized deferred gain of $21 million, net of taxes.

Long-Term Debt and Interest Rate Risk Management

In April 1998, Dell issued $200 million 6.55% fixed rate senior notes due April 15, 2008 (the "Senior Notes") and $300 million 7.10% fixed rate senior debentures due April 15, 2028 (the "Senior Debentures"). Interest on the Senior Notes and Senior Debentures is paid semi-annually, on April 15 and October 15. The Senior Notes and Senior Debentures rank pari passu and are redeemable, in whole or in part, at the election of Dell for principal, any accrued interest and a redemption premium based on the present value of interest to be paid over the term of the debt agreements. The Senior Notes and Senior Debentures generally contain no restrictive covenants, other than a limitation on liens on Dell's assets and a limitation on sale-leaseback transactions involving Dell property.

Concurrent with the issuance of the Senior Notes and Senior Debentures, Dell entered into interest rate swap agreements converting Dell's interest rate exposure from a fixed rate to a floating rate basis to better align the associated interest rate characteristics to its cash and investments portfolio. The interest rate swap agreements have an aggregate notional amount of $200 million maturing April 15, 2008 and $300 million maturing April 15, 2028. The floating rates are based on three-month London Interbank Offered Rates plus 0.41% and 0.79% for the Senior Notes and Senior Debentures, respectively. As a result of the interest rate swap agreements, Dell's effective interest rates for the Senior Notes and Senior Debentures were 4.108% and 4.448%, respectively, for fiscal 2006.

The interest rate swap agreements are designated as fair value hedges, and the terms of the swap agreements and hedged items are such that effectiveness can be measured using the short-cut method defined in SFAS No. 133. The differential to be paid or received on the interest rate swap agreements is accrued and recognized as an adjustment to interest expense as interest rates change. The difference between Dell's carrying amounts and fair value of its long-term debt and related interest rate swaps was not material at February 3, 2006 and January 28, 2005.

H.J. Heinz
2006 Annual Report

14. Derivative Financial Instruments and Hedging Activities

The Company operates internationally, with manufacturing and sales facilities in various locations around the world, and utilizes certain derivative financial instruments to manage its foreign currency and interest rate exposures.

At May 3, 2006, the Company had outstanding currency exchange and interest rate derivative contracts with notional amounts of $3.01 billion and $2.72 billion, respectively. At April 27, 2005, the Company had outstanding currency exchange and interest rate derivative contracts with notional amounts of $1.27 billion and $2.88 billion, respectively. The fair value of derivative financial instruments was a net (liability)/asset of $(48) million and $177 million at May 3, 2006 and April 27, 2005, respectively.

Foreign Currency Hedging

The Company uses forward contracts and to a lesser extent, option contracts to mitigate its foreign currency exchange rate exposure due to forecasted purchases of raw materials and sales of finished goods, and future settlement of foreign currency denominated assets and liabilities. Derivatives used to hedge forecasted transactions and specific cash flows associated with foreign currency denominated financial assets and liabilities that meet the criteria for hedge accounting are designated as cash flow hedges. Consequently, the effective portion of gains and losses is deferred as a component of accumulated other comprehensive loss/(income) and is recognized in earnings at the time the hedged item affects earnings, in the same line item as the underlying hedged item.

In Fiscal 2006, the Company entered into cross currency swaps with a total notional amount of $1.9 billion as of May 3, 2006, which were designated as net investment hedges of foreign operations. These contracts mature within two years. The Company assesses hedge effectiveness for these contracts based on changes in fair value attributable to changes in spot prices. Losses of $16.3 million (net of income taxes of $10.3 million) which represented effective hedges of net investments, were reported as a component of accumulated other comprehensive loss/(income) within unrealized translation adjustment for Fiscal 2006. Gains of $5.5 million, which represented the changes in fair value excluded from the assessment of hedge effectiveness, were included in current period earnings as a component of interest expense for Fiscal 2006.

The Company has used certain foreign currency debt instruments as net investment hedges of foreign operations. Losses of $32.2 million (net of income taxes of $18.9 million) and $13.4 million (net of income taxes of $7.8 million), which represented effective hedges of net investments, were reported as a component of accumulated other comprehensive loss/(income) within unrealized translation adjustment for the years ended April 27, 2005 and April 28, 2004, respectively.

Interest Rate Hedging

The Company uses interest rate swaps to manage interest rate exposure. These derivatives may be designated as cash flow hedges or fair value hedges depending on the nature of the risk being hedged. Derivatives used to hedge risk associated with changes in the fair value of certain fixed-rate debt obligations are primarily designated as fair value hedges. Consequently, changes in the fair value of these derivatives, along with changes in the fair value of the hedged debt obligations that are attributable to the hedged risk, are recognized in current period earnings.

Hedge Ineffectiveness

Hedge ineffectiveness related to cash flow hedges, which is reported in current period earnings as other income and expense, was not significant for the years ended May 3, 2006 and April 27, 2005 and was a net gain of $0.5 million for the year ended April 28, 2004. The Company excludes the time value component of option contracts from the assessment of hedge effectiveness.

Deferred Hedging Gains and Losses

As of May 3, 2006, the Company is hedging forecasted transactions for periods not exceeding two years. During the next 12 months, the Company expects $4.1 million of net deferred losses reported in accumulated other comprehensive loss/(income) to be reclassified to earnings, assuming market rates remain constant through contract maturities. Net deferred losses reclassified to earnings because the hedged transaction was no longer expected to occur were not significant for the years ended May 3, 2006, April 27, 2005, and April 28, 2004.

Other Activities

The Company enters into certain derivative contracts in accordance with its risk management strategy that do not meet the criteria for hedge accounting. Although these derivatives do not qualify as hedges, they have the economic impact of largely mitigating foreign currency or interest rate exposures. These derivative financial instruments are accounted for on a full mark to market basis through current earnings even though they were not acquired for trading purposes.

Concentration of Credit Risk

Counterparties to currency exchange and interest rate derivatives consist of major international financial institutions. The Company continually monitors its positions and the credit ratings of the counterparties involved and, by policy, limits the amount of credit exposure to any one party. While the Company may be exposed to potential losses due to the credit risk of non-performance by these counterparties, losses are not anticipated. During Fiscal 2006, no single customer represented more than 10% of the Company's sales.

Del Monte Foods
2006 Annual Report

Note 8. Derivative Financial Instruments

The Company uses interest rate swaps as well as futures and option contracts to hedge market risks relating to possible adverse changes in interest rates and commodity and other prices, which affect interest expense on the Company's floating-rate obligations as well as the cost of its raw materials and other inputs, respectively.

Interest Rates. The Company's debt primarily consists of fixed rate notes and floating rate term loans. The Company also uses its floating rate revolving credit facility to fund seasonal working capital needs. Interest expense on the Company's floating rate debt is typically calculated based on a fixed spread over a reference rate, such as LIBOR. Therefore, fluctuations in market interest rates will cause interest expense increases or decreases on a given amount of floating rate debt.

All interest rate swaps that have been entered into by the Company are used to hedge interest payments on floating rate debt. On February 24, 2003, the Company entered into six interest rate swaps, with a combined notional amount of $300.0, as the fixed rate-payer. A formal cash flow hedge accounting relationship was established between the six swaps and a portion of the Company's interest payments on floating rate debt. These six swaps expired on April 28, 2006. We had two interest rate swaps with a combined notional amount of $125.0 which were entered into by pre-Merger DMC. On December 31, 2002, a formal cash flow hedge accounting relationship was established between the two swaps and a portion of our interest payments on our floating rate debt. These two interest rate swaps expired on September 30, 2004.

In fiscal 2006, the Company's interest rate cash flow hedges resulted in a $2.0 decrease to OCI and a $1.3 decrease to deferred tax liabilities. The interest rate cash flow hedges did not have an impact on other expense. In fiscal 2005, the Company's interest rate cash flow hedges resulted in a $1.8 increase to OCI, a $1.2 increase to deferred tax liabilities and a $0.3 decrease to other expense. In fiscal 2004, the Company's interest rate cash flow hedges resulted in a $1.6 increase to OCI, a $1.0 decrease to deferred tax assets and a $0.2 decrease to other income.

During fiscal 2005 and fiscal 2004, the Company reduced interest expense by $1.4 and $4.2, respectively, resulting from the amortization of a $6.9 swap liability that existed prior to formal hedge designation of two interest rate swaps on December 31, 2002. At the end of fiscal 2005, the swap liability was fully amortized in conjunction with the expiration of the interest rate swaps with a combined notional amount of $125.0 on September 30, 2004.

On May 1, 2005, the fair values of the Company's interest rate swaps were recorded as current assets of $3.4.

Commodities. Certain commodities such as corn, wheat, soybean meal and soybean oil are used in the production of the Company's products. Generally these commodities are purchased based upon market prices that are established with the vendor as part of the purchase process. The Company uses futures or options contracts, as deemed appropriate to reduce the effect of price fluctuations on anticipated purchases of some commodities for up to one year. The Company accounted for these commodities derivatives as either cash flow or economic hedges. For cash flow hedges, the effective portion of derivative gains and losses is recognized as part of cost of products sold and the ineffective portion is recognized as other income or expense. Changes in the value of economic hedges are recorded directly in earnings. These contracts generally have a term of less than eighteen months.

On April 30, 2006, the fair values of the Company's commodities hedges were recorded as current assets of $0.8 and current liabilities of $0.1. The fair values of the Company's commodities hedges were recorded as current assets of $1.4 and current liabilities of $0.3 at May 1, 2005.

Other. During the first and second quarters of fiscal 2006, the price of fuel rose substantially in comparison to prior periods. As a result, in the second quarter of 2006, the Company began a hedging program for heating oil as a proxy for fluctuations in diesel fuel prices. During the second, third and fourth quarters, the Company entered into futures contracts to cover a portion of its projected diesel fuel costs for the respective quarters. These contracts generally have a term of less than three months and did not qualify as cash flow hedges for accounting purposes. Accordingly, associated gains or losses are recorded directly as other income or expense. As of April 30, 2006 all such contracts were closed.

During the fourth quarter of fiscal 2006, the Company began a hedging program for natural gas. The Company accounted for these natural gas derivatives as either cash flow or economic hedges. These contracts generally have a term of 15 months or less. For cash flow hedges, the effective portion of derivative gains and losses is recognized as part of cost of products sold and the ineffective portion is recognized as other income or expense. Changes in the value of economic hedges are recorded directly in earnings. As of April 30, 2006, the fair values of the Company's natural gas hedges were recorded as current assets of $0.6 and current liabilities of $1.2.

Gains and losses related to commodity and other hedges reported in OCI are expected to be reclassified into earnings within the next twelve months.

The table below presents the changes in the following balance sheet accounts and impact on statement of income accounts of our commodities and other activities:

	Fiscal 2006	Fiscal 2005	Fiscal 2004
(Increase) decrease in other comprehensive income[a]	$0.5	$0.1	$(0.7)
(Increase) decrease in deferred tax liabilities	0.3	–	0.5
Increase (decrease) in cost of products sold	(0.1)	2.9	(0.9)
Increase (decrease) in other expense	–	1.5	(3.2)

[a] The change in other comprehensive income is net of related taxes.

Sara Lee
2006 Annual Report

Note 18—Financial Instruments and Risk Management

Interest Rate and Currency Swaps—To manage interest rate risk, the corporation has entered into interest rate swaps that effectively convert certain fixed-rate debt instruments into floating-rate instruments or fix the interest payments of certain floating-rate debt instruments. The corporation has issued certain foreign-denominated debt instruments and utilizes currency swaps to reduce the variability of functional currency cash flows related to the foreign currency debt.

Interest rate swap agreements that are effective at hedging the fair value of fixed-rate debt agreements are designated and accounted for as fair value hedges.

Currency swap agreements that are effective at hedging the variability of foreign-denominated cash flows are designated and accounted for as cash flow hedges. The effective portion of the gains or losses of currency swaps that are recorded as cash flow hedges is recorded in accumulated other comprehensive income and reclassified into earnings to offset the gain or loss arising from the remeasurement of the hedged item.

The fair value of interest rate and currency swaps is determined based upon externally developed pricing models, using financial data obtained from swap dealers.

	Notional Principal [1]	Weighted Average Interest Rates [2]	
		Receive	Pay
Interest Rate Swaps			
2006 Receive fixed—pay variable	$1,316	5.1%	5.8%
2005 Receive fixed—pay variable	1,644	4.8	4.4
2004 Receive fixed—pay variable	1,725	4.9	3.1
Currency Swaps			
2006 Receive fixed—pay fixed	$ 771	5.1%	5.0%
2005 Receive fixed—pay fixed	680	5.1	5.0
2004 Receive fixed—pay fixed	683	5.1	5.0
Receive variable—pay variable	248	2.5	1.7

[1] The notional principal is the amount used for the calculation of interest payments that are exchanged over the life of the swap transaction and is equal to the amount of foreign currency or dollar principal exchanged at maturity, if applicable.

[2] The weighted average interest rates are as of the respective balance sheet dates.

Forward Exchange, Futures and Option Contracts—The corporation uses forward exchange and option contracts to reduce the effect of fluctuating foreign currencies on short-term foreign-currency-denominated intercompany transactions, third-party product-sourcing transactions, foreign-denominated investments and other known foreign currency exposures. Gains and losses on the derivative are intended to offset losses and gains on the hedged transaction in an effort to reduce the earnings volatility resulting from fluctuating foreign currency exchange rates. The principal currencies hedged by the corporation include the European euro, Mexican peso, Swiss franc, Canadian dollar, British pound and Hungarian forint.

The corporation uses futures contracts to hedge commodity price risk. The principal commodities hedged by the corporation include hogs, beef, coffee, wheat, butter and corn. The corporation does not use significant levels of commodity financial instruments to hedge commodity prices. In circumstances where commodity-derivative instruments are used, there is a high correlation between the commodity costs and the derivative instrument.

The following table summarizes by major currency the contractual amounts of the corporation's forward exchange contracts used in continuing operations in U.S. dollars. The bought amounts represent the net U.S. dollar equivalent of commitments to purchase foreign currencies, and the sold amounts represent the net U.S. dollar equivalent of commitments to sell foreign currencies. The foreign currency amounts have been translated into a U.S. dollar equivalent value using the exchange rate at the reporting date. Forward exchange contracts mature at the anticipated cash requirement date of the hedged transaction, generally within one year.

	2006	2005	2004
Foreign Currency—Bought (Sold)			
European euro	$89	$1,553	$1,684
British pound	(66)	109	140
Swiss franc	25	137	95
Canadian dollar	(36)	25	(66)
Hungarian forint	188	170	71
Mexican peso	(26)	(19)	23
Other	(32)	27	66

The corporation held foreign exchange option contracts to reduce the foreign exchange fluctuations on anticipated purchase transactions. The following table summarizes the notional amount of option contracts relating to continuing operations to sell foreign currency, in U.S. dollars:

	2006	2005	2004
Foreign Currency—Sold			
European euro	$558	$548	$792
Other	6	–	–

The following table summarizes the net derivative gains or losses deferred into accumulated other comprehensive income and reclassified to earnings in 2006, 2005 and 2004:

	2006	2005	2004
Net accumulated derivative gain (loss) deferred at beginning of year	$(14)	$(14)	$(17)
Deferral of net derivative gain (loss) in accumulated other comprehensive income	(38)	(10)	(38)
Reclassification of net derivative (gain) loss to income	10	10	41
Net accumulated derivative gain (loss) at end of year	$(42)	$(14)	$(14)

At July 1, 2006, the maximum maturity date of any cash flow hedge was 1.0 year, excluding any forward exchange, option or swap contracts related to the payment of variable interest on existing financial instruments. The corporation expects to reclassify into earnings during the next 12 months net losses from accumulated other comprehensive income of $24 at the time the underlying hedged transactions are realized. In 2006 and 2004, hedge ineffectiveness was insignificant. During 2005, the corporation recognized an expense of $7 for hedge ineffectiveness related to cash flow hedges, which is recorded in the "Selling, general and administrative expenses" line of the Consolidated Statements of Income. In 2006, 2005 and 2004, derivative losses excluded from the assessment of effectiveness, and gains or losses resulting from the disqualification of hedge accounting are insignificant in each of these periods.

Non-U.S. Dollar Financing Transactions—The corporation uses non-U.S. dollar financing transactions as net investment hedges of long-term investments in the corresponding foreign currency. Hedges that meet the effectiveness requirements are accounted for under net investment hedging rules. For the year ended July 1, 2006, a net loss of $70 arising from effective hedges of net investments has been reflected in the cumulative translation adjustment account within common stockholders' equity.

Fair Values—The carrying amounts of cash and equivalents, trade accounts receivable, notes payable and accounts payable approximated fair value as of July 1, 2006 and July 2, 2005. The fair value of the remaining financial instruments recognized in continuing operations on the Consolidated Balance Sheets of the corporation at the respective year-ends were:

	2006	2005
Long-term debt, including current portion	$4,120	$4,764
Interest rate swaps	(30)	18
Currency swaps	(206)	(170)
Foreign currency forwards	(30)	(2)
Foreign currency options	(17)	24

The fair value of the corporation's long-term debt, including the current portion, is estimated using discounted cash flows based on the corporation's current incremental borrowing rates for similar types of borrowing arrangements. The fair value of interest rate and currency swaps is determined based upon externally developed pricing models, using financial market data obtained from swap dealers. The fair value of foreign currency forwards and options is based upon currency forward rates obtained from third-party institutions.

Concentrations of Credit Risk—A large number of major international financial institutions are counterparties to the corporation's financial instruments. The corporation enters into financial instrument agreements only with counterparties meeting very stringent credit standards, limiting the amount of agreements or contracts it enters into with any one party and, where legally available, executing master netting agreements. These positions are continuously monitored. While the corporation may be exposed to credit losses in the event of nonperformance by these counterparties, it does not anticipate material losses because of these control procedures.

Trade accounts receivable due from customers that the corporation considers highly leveraged were $234 at July 1, 2006 and $197 at July 2, 2005. The financial position of these businesses has been considered in determining allowances for doubtful accounts.

Johnson Controls
2005 Annual Report

11. Financial Instruments

The fair values of cash and cash equivalents, accounts receivable, short-term debt and accounts payable approximate their carrying values. The fair value of long-term debt, which was $1.7 billion and $1.9 billion at September 30, 2005 and 2004, respectively, was determined using market interest rates and discounted future cash flows.

The Company selectively uses derivative instruments to reduce market risk associated with changes in foreign currency and interest rates. The use of derivatives is restricted to those intended for hedging purposes; the use of any derivative instrument for trading purposes is strictly prohibited. See the Summary of Significant Accounting Policies for additional information regarding the Company's objectives for holding certain derivative instruments, its strategies for achieving those objectives, and its risk management and accounting policies applicable to these instruments.

The Company has global operations and participates in the foreign exchange markets to minimize its risk of loss from fluctuations in currency exchange rates. The Company primarily uses foreign currency exchange contracts to hedge certain of its foreign currency exposure.

The Company selectively uses interest rate swaps to reduce market risk associated with changes in interest rates (cash flow or fair value hedges). In May 2002, the Company entered into a four-and-a-half-year interest rate swap to hedge a portion of the Company's 5% notes maturing in November 2006. Under the swap, the Company receives interest based on a fixed U.S. dollar rate of 5% and pays interest based on a floating three-month U.S. dollar LIBOR rate plus 14.75 basis points. Terms of the four-and-a-half-year swap were modified since inception of the swap resulting in a decrease of notional amount of $100 million from the original $250 million. In October 2003, the Company entered into a four-year and three-month interest rate swap to hedge the Company's 6.3% notes maturing in February 2008. Under the swap, the Company receives interest based on a fixed U.S. dollar rate of 6.3% and pays interest based on a floating three-month U.S. dollar LIBOR rate plus 283.5 basis points.

In September 2005, the Company entered into three forward treasury lock agreements to reduce the market risk associated with changes in interest rates associated with the Company's anticipated fixed-rate bond issuance to finance the acquisition of York International Corporation (cash flow hedge; see Note 23). The three forward treasury lock agreements, which have a combined notional amount of $1.3 billion, fix a portion of the future interest cost for 5-year, 10-year and 30-year bonds. The fair value of each treasury lock agreement, or the difference between the treasury lock reference rate and the fixed rate at time of bond issuance, will be amortized to interest expense over the life of the respective bond issuance.

The Company also selectively uses cross-currency interest rate swaps to hedge the foreign currency exposure associated with its net investment in certain foreign operations (net investment hedges). Under the swaps, the Company receives interest based on a variable U.S. dollar rate and pays interest based on variable yen and euro rates on the outstanding notional principal amounts in dollars, yen and euro, respectively.

In addition, the Company selectively uses equity swaps to reduce market risk associated with its stock-based compensation plans, such as its deferred compensation plans and stock appreciation rights. These equity compensation liabilities increase as the Company's stock price increases and decrease as the Company's stock price decreases. In contrast, the value of the swap agreement moves in the opposite direction of these liabilities, allowing the Company to fix a portion of the liabilities at a stated amount. In March 2004, the Company entered into an equity swap agreement. In connection with the swap agreement, a third party may purchase shares of the Company's stock in the market or in privately negotiated transactions up to an amount equal to $135 million in aggregate market value at any given time. Although the Swap Agreement has a stated expiration date, the Company's intention is to continually renew the Swap Agreement with Citibank, N.A.'s consent. The Swap Agreement's impact on the Company's earnings for the year ended September 30, 2005 was not material.

The Company's derivative instruments are recorded at fair value in the Consolidated Statement of Financial Position as follows:

| | September 30, | | | |
| | 2005 | | 2004 | |
	Notional Amount	Fair Value Asset (Liability)	Notional Amount	Fair Value Asset (Liability)
(U.S. dollar equivalents, in millions)				
Other current assets				
Treasury look agreements	$1,275	$31	$ –	$ –
Foreign currency exchange contracts	2,988	20	1,219	1
Cross-currency interest rate swaps .	737	58	–	–
Equity swap	107	3	97	3
Other noncurrent assets				
Interest rate swaps	–	–	325	9
Other noncurrent liabilities				
Interest rate swaps	325	(2)	–	–
Cross-currency interest rate swaps .	–	–	816	(24)

It is important to note that the Company's derivative instruments are hedges protecting against underlying changes in foreign currency and interest rates. Accordingly, the implied gains/losses associated with the fair values of foreign currency exchange contracts and cross-currency interest rate swaps would be offset by gains/losses on underlying payables, receivables and net investments in foreign subsidiaries. Similarly, implied gains/losses associated with interest rate swaps offset changes in interest rates and the fair value of long-term debt.

The fair values of interest rate and cross-currency interest rate swaps were determined using dealer quotes and market interest rates. The fair values of foreign currency exchange contracts were determined using market exchange rates.

Clorox
2005 Annual Report

10. Fair Value of Financial Instruments

The Company's derivative financial instruments were recorded at fair value in the consolidated balance sheets as assets at June 30 as follows:

	2005	2004
Current assets:		
Commodity purchase contracts	$ 7	–
Foreign exchange contracts	–	$ 1
Other assets:		
Commodity purchase contracts	5	3

In fiscal year 2004, the Company discontinued hedge accounting treatment for its resin commodity contracts since the contracts no longer met the accounting requirements for a cash flow hedge. These contracts are used as an economic hedge of resin prices and changes in the fair value of these contracts are recorded to other (income) expense. The pretax effect on net earnings from these contracts was a gain of $2 in both fiscal year 2005 and 2004. All instruments accorded hedge accounting treatment are considered effective.

In fiscal year 2004, the Company terminated the interest rate swap agreements associated with its senior unsecured note maturing in February 2011. The fair value of these swaps, which totaled $24 upon termination, is being recognized in net earnings on a straight-line basis over the remaining life of the note.

The Company uses commodity futures, swap, and option contracts to fix the price of a portion of its raw material requirements. Contract maturities, which extend to fiscal year 2007, are matched to the length of the raw materials. The estimated amount of existing pretax net gains for commodity contracts in accumulated other comprehensive net income that is expected to be reclassified into net earning during the year ending June 30, 2006 is $6.

The Company also enters into certain foreign-currency related derivative contracts with no specific hedge designations. These contracts, which have been entered into to manage a portion of the Company's foreign exchange risk, are accounted for adjusting the carrying amount of the contracts to market value and recognizing any gain or loss in other (income) expense.

The notional and estimated fair values of the Company's derivative instruments are summarized below as of June 30:

	2005		2004	
	Notional	Fair Value	Notional	Fair Value
Derivative Instruments				
Foreign exchange contracts	$32	–	$36	$1
Commodity purchase contracts . .	73	$12	43	3
Commodity option contracts	–	–	2	–

The carrying values of cash, short-term investments, accounts receivable and accounts payable approximate their fair values at June 30, 2005 and 2004 due to the short maturity and nature of those balances. See Note 9 for fair values of notes and loans payable and long-term debt.

Smucker's
2005 Annual Report

Note O: Derivative Financial Instruments

The Company is exposed to market risks, such as changes in interest rates, currency exchange rates, and commodity pricing. To manage the volatility relating to these exposures, the Company enters into various derivative transactions.

Commodity Price Management: In connection with the purchase of raw materials used by the Company's flour and baking business in Canada, and the consumer oils and baking business in the United States, the Company enters into commodity futures and options contracts to manage the price volatility and reduce the variability of future cash flows related to anticipated inventory purchases of wheat, flour, and edible oils. The Company also enters into commodity futures and options related to the delivery of natural gas to the manufacturing plants in the United States. The derivative instruments generally have maturities of less than one year. Certain of the derivative instruments associated with the Company's oils business meet the hedge criteria according to Statement of Financial Accounting Standards No. 133, *Accounting for Derivative Instruments and Hedging Activities,* and are accounted for as cash flow hedges. The mark-to-market gains or losses on qualifying hedges are deferred and included as a component of other comprehensive income or loss to the extent effective, and reclassified into cost of products sold in the period during which the hedged transaction affects earnings.

In order to qualify as a hedge of commodity price risk, it must be demonstrated that the changes in the fair value of the commodities futures contracts are highly effective in hedging price risks associated with the commodity purchased. Hedge ineffectiveness is measured on a quarterly basis. The mark-to-market gains or losses on nonqualifying, excluded, and ineffective portions of hedges are recognized in cost of products sold immediately.

The mark-to-market value of all derivative commodity instruments is included in current assets on the Consolidated Balance Sheets. As of April 30, 2005 and 2004, the deferred gain, net of tax, included in accumulated other comprehensive loss was $916 and $1,237, respectively. This entire amount at April 30, 2005, is expected to be recognized in earnings as the related commodity is utilized during 2006. The impact of commodities futures contracts and options recognized in earnings was a loss of $10,915 in 2005, and a gain of $3,967 and $4,050, in 2004 and 2003, respectively. Included in these amounts are amounts related to nonqualifying, excluded, and ineffective portions of hedges resulting in a loss of $2,389 in 2005, and a gain of $351 and $3,226, in 2004 and 2003, respectively.

Interest Rate Hedging: The Company's policy is to manage interest cost using a mix of fixed-and variable-rate debt. To manage this mix in a cost efficient manner, the Company may periodically enter into interest rate swaps in which the Company agrees to exchange, at specified intervals, the difference between fixed and variable interest amounts calculated by reference to an agreed-upon notional principal amount. The interest rate swap agreements effectively modify the Company's exposure to interest risk by converting a portion of the Company's fixed-rate debt to a floating rate. The interest rate swap and the instrument being hedged is marked to market in the balance sheet. The mark-to-market value of both the fair value hedging instruments and the underlying debt obligations are recorded as equal and offsetting gains or losses in other income or expense. No other cash payments are made unless the contract is terminated prior to maturity, in which case the amount paid or received in settlement is established by agreement at the time of termination, and usually represents the net present value, at current rates of interest, of the remaining obligations to exchange payments under the terms of the contract. Any gains or losses upon the early termination of the interest rate swap contracts are deferred and recognized over the remaining life of the contract.

During 2004 and 2003, the Company terminated its interest rate swap agreements prior to maturity. As a result of the early terminations, the Company received $924 and $4,092 in cash in 2004 and 2003, respectively, and realized corresponding gains, which have been deferred. These deferred gains will be recognized in earnings over the remaining lives of the original swap agreements as a reduction of future interest expense. At April 30, 2005 and 2004, the balance of the deferred gains related to the terminated swaps was $2,334 and $3,530, respectively, and is included in other noncurrent liabilities on the Consolidated Balance Sheets.

Foreign Exchange Rate Hedging: The Company utilizes forward currency exchange contracts with maturities of less than one year. These contracts are used to hedge the effect of foreign exchange fluctuations on future cash payments related to purchases of certain assets. These contracts are accounted for as cash-flow hedges with associated mark-to-market gains and losses deferred and included as a component of other comprehensive income or loss. These gains or losses are reclassified to earnings in the period the futures contracts are executed. The mark-to-market value of all foreign exchange rate derivatives are included in other current assets on the Consolidated Balance Sheets. Included in accumulated other comprehensive loss was a deferred gain, net of tax, of $8 and a deferred loss, net of tax, of $47 at April 30, 2005 and 2004, respectively. The entire amount at April 30, 2005, is expected to be recognized in earnings during 2006.

Note P: Other Financial Instruments:

Financial instruments, other than derivatives, that potentially subject the Company to significant concentrations of credit risk consist principally of cash investments, marketable securities, and trade receivables. The Company places its cash investments with high quality financial institutions and limits the amount of credit exposure to any one institution. The Company's marketable securities are in debt securities. Under the Company's investment policy, it will invest in securities deemed to be investment grade at time of purchase. Currently, these investments are defined as government-backed mortgage obligations, corporate bonds, municipal bonds, and commercial paper. The Company determines the appropriate categorization of its debt securities at the time of purchase and reevaluates such designation at each balance sheet date. The Company has categorized all debt securities as available for sale because it currently has the intent to convert these investments into cash if and when needed. With respect to trade receivables, concentration of credit risk is limited due to the large number of customers. The Company does not require collateral from its customers. The fair value of the Company's financial instruments, other than certain of its fixed-rate long-term debt, approximates their carrying amounts. The fair value of the Company's fixed-rate long-term debt, estimated using current market rates and a discounted cash flow analysis, was approximately $465,797 at April 30, 2005.

The following table provides information on the carrying amount and fair value of financial instruments, including derivative financial instruments.

	April 30, 2005		April 30, 2004	
	Carrying Amount	Fair Value	Carrying Amount	Fair Value
Marketable securities				
Current	$ 17,739	$ 17,739	$15,074	$15,074
Noncurrent	59,074	59,074	41,589	41,589
Long-term debt				
6.77% Senior Notes due June 1, 2009	75,000	82,185	75,000	75,906
7.70% Series A Senior Notes due September 1, 2005	17,000	17,347	17,000	16,943
7.87% Series B Senior Notes due September 1, 2007	33,000	36,051	33,000	35,061
7.94% Series C Senior Notes due September 1, 2010	10,000	11,654	10,000	11,105
4.78% Senior Notes due June 1, 2014	100,000	98,892	–	–
6.60% Senior Notes due November 13, 2009	213,560	219,668	–	–
Derivative financial instruments	1,754	1,754	(424)	(424)

Carnival Corporation
2004 Annual Report

Note 11—Financial Instruments

We estimated the fair value of our financial instruments through the use of public market prices, quotes from financial institutions and other available information. Considerable judgment is required in interpreting data to develop estimates of fair value and, accordingly, amounts are not necessarily indicative of the amounts that we could realize in a current market exchange. Our financial instruments are not held for trading or other speculative purposes.

Cash and Cash Equivalents and Short-Term Investments

The carrying amounts of our cash and cash equivalents and short-term investments approximate their fair values due to their short maturities or variable interest rates.

Other Assets

At November 30, 2004 and 2003, long-term other assets included marketable securities held in rabbi trusts for certain of our nonqualified benefit plans and notes and other receivables. These assets had carrying and fair values of $240 million and $227 million at November 30, 2004, respectively, and carrying and fair values of $200 million at November 30, 2003. Fair values were based on public market prices, estimated discounted future cash flows or estimated fair value of collateral.

Debt

The fair values of our non-convertible debt and convertible notes were $6.32 billion and $2.53 billion, respectively, at November 30, 2004 and $5.83 billion and $1.92 billion at November 30, 2003. These fair values were greater than the related carrying values by $100 million and $790 million, respectively, at November 30, 2004 and by $140 million and $205 million at November 30, 2003. The net difference between the fair value of our debt and its carrying value was due primarily to our issuance of debt obligations at fixed interest rates that are above market interest rates in existence at the measurement dates. The net difference between the fair value of our convertible notes is largely due to the impact of changes in the Carnival Corporation common stock value on the value of our convertible notes on those dates. The fair values of our unsecured fixed rate public notes, convertible notes, sterling bonds and unsecured 5.57% euro notes were based on their public market prices. The fair values of our other debt were estimated based on appropriate market interest rates being applied to this debt.

Foreign Currency Swaps and Other Hedging Instruments

We have foreign currency swaps that are designated as foreign currency fair value hedges for three of our euro denominated shipbuilding contracts (see Note 7). At November 30, 2004 and 2003, the fair value of the foreign currency swaps related to our shipbuilding commitments was an unrealized gain of $219 million and $363 million, respectively. These foreign currency swaps mature through 2006.

We have foreign currency swaps totaling $887 million that are effectively designated as hedges of our net investments in foreign subsidiaries, which have euro and sterling denominated functional currencies. These foreign currency swaps were entered into to effectively convert $251 million and $466 million of U.S. dollar denominated debt into sterling debt and euro debt, respectively, and $170 million of euro denominated debt into sterling debt. At November 30, 2004, the fair value of these foreign currency swaps was an unrealized loss of $137 million, which is included in the cumulative translation adjustment component of AOCI. These currency swaps mature through 2012.

The fair values of these foreign currency swaps were estimated based on prices quoted by financial institutions for these instruments.

Finally, we have designated $1.1 billion of our out-standing euro and sterling debt and other obligations, which are nonderivatives and mature through 2012, as hedges of our net investments in foreign operations and, accordingly, have included $194 million of foreign currency transaction losses in the cumulative translation adjustment component of AOCI at November 30, 2004.

Interest Rate Swaps

We have interest rate swap agreements designated as fair value hedges whereby we receive fixed interest rate payments in exchange for making variable interest rate payments. At November 30, 2004 and 2003, these interest rate swap agreements effectively changed $929 million and $1.19 billion of fixed rate debt to Libor-based floating rate debt.

In addition, we also have interest rate swap agreements designated as cash flow hedges whereby we receive variable interest rate payments in exchange for making fixed interest rate payments. At November 30, 2004 and 2003, these interest rate swap agreements effectively changed $828 million and $760 million, respectively, of euribor floating rate debt to fixed rate debt.

These interest rate swap agreements mature through 2008. At November 30, 2004 and 2003, the fair value of our interest rate swaps designated as cash flow hedges was an unrealized loss of $22 million and $6 million, respectively. The fair values of our interest rate swap agreements were estimated based on prices quoted by financial institutions for these instruments.

Walt Disney
2005 Annual Report

12. Financial Instruments

Interest Rate Risk Management The Company is exposed to the impact of interest rate changes primarily through its borrowing activities. The Company's objective is to mitigate the impact of interest rate changes on earnings and cash flows and on the market value of its investments and borrowings. In accordance with policy, the Company maintains its fixed rate debt expressed as a percentage of its net debt between a minimum and maximum percentage.

The Company typically uses pay-floating and pay-fixed interest rate swaps to facilitate its interest rate risk management activities. Pay-floating swaps effectively convert fixed rate medium and long-term obligations to variable rate instruments indexed to LIBOR. Pay-floating swap agreements in place at year-end expire in one to 17 years. Pay-fixed swaps effectively convert floating rate obligations to fixed rate instruments. The pay-fixed swaps in place at year-end expire in one to ten years. As of October 1, 2005 and September 30, 2004 respectively, the Company held $151 million and $148 million notional value of pay-fixed swaps that do not qualify as hedges. The changes in market values of all swaps that do not qualify as hedges have been included in earnings.

The impact of hedge ineffectiveness was not significant for fiscal 2005, 2004 and 2003. The net amount of deferred gains in AOCI from interest rate risk management transactions was $8 million and $10 million at October 1, 2005 and September 30, 2004 respectively.

Foreign Exchange Risk Management The Company transacts business globally and is subject to risks associated with changing foreign exchange rates. The Company's objective is to reduce earnings and cash flow fluctuations associated with foreign exchange rate changes thereby enabling management to focus attention on core business issues and challenges.

The Company enters into various contracts that change in value as foreign exchange rates change to protect the value of its existing foreign currency assets, liabilities, firm commitments and forecasted but not firmly committed foreign currency transactions. The Company uses option strategies and forward contracts to hedge forecasted transactions. In accordance with policy, the Company hedges its forecasted foreign currency transactions for periods generally not to exceed five years within an established minimum and maximum range of annual exposure. The Company uses forward contracts to hedge foreign currency assets, liabilities and firm commitments. The gains and losses on these contracts offset changes in the U.S. dollar equivalent value of the related forecasted transaction, asset, liability or firm commitment. The principal currencies hedged are the Euro, British pound, Japanese yen and Canadian dollar. Cross-currency swaps are used to effectively convert foreign currency-denominated borrowings to U.S. dollars.

Mark to market gains and losses on contracts hedging forecasted foreign currency transactions are initially recorded to AOCI and are reclassified to current earnings when the hedged transactions are realized, offsetting changes in the value of the foreign currency transactions. At October 1, 2005 and September 30, 2004, the Company had pre-tax deferred gains of $114 million and $45 million, respectively, and pre-tax deferred losses of $69 million and $147 million, respectively, related to foreign currency hedges on forecasted foreign currency transactions.

Deferred amounts to be recognized change with market conditions and will be substantially offset by changes in the value of the related hedged transactions. Deferred losses recorded in AOCI for contracts that will mature in the next twelve months totaled $21 million. The Company reclassified after-tax losses of $108 million and $144 million from AOCI to earnings during fiscal 2005 and 2004, respectively. These losses were offset by changes in the U.S. dollar equivalent value of the items being hedged.

At October 1, 2005 and September 30, 2004, changes in value related to cash flow hedges included in AOCI were a pre-tax gain of $45 million and a pre-tax loss of $102 million, respectively. During fiscal 2005 and 2004, the Company recorded the change in fair market value related to fair value hedges and the ineffectiveness related to cash flow hedges to earnings. The amounts of hedge ineffectiveness on fair value and cash flow hedges were not material for fiscal 2005, fiscal 2004 and fiscal 2003. The impact of foreign exchange risk management activities on operating income in 2005, 2004 and 2003 was a loss of $168 million, $277 million and $273 million, respectively. The net losses from these hedges offset changes in the U.S. dollar equivalent value of the related exposures being hedged.

Fair Value of Financial Instruments At October 1, 2005 and September 30, 2004, the Company's financial instruments included cash, cash equivalents, investments, receivables, accounts payable, borrowings and interest rate and foreign exchange risk management contracts.

At October 1, 2005 and September 30, 2004, the fair values of cash and cash equivalents, receivables and accounts payable approximated the carrying values because of the short-term nature of these instruments. The estimated fair values of other financial instruments subject to fair value disclosures, determined based on broker quotes or quoted market prices or interest rates for the same or similar instruments and the related carrying amounts are as follows:

	2005		2004	
	Carrying Amount	*Fair Value*	*Carrying Amount*	*Fair Value*
Investments	**$ 62**	**$ 62**	$ 60	$ 60
Borrowings	**(12,467)**	**(12,733)**	(13,488)	(13,811)
Risk management				
Contracts:				
Foreign exchange forwards	**$ 76**	**$ 76**	$ (54)	$ (54)
Foreign exchange Options	**6**	**6**	(26)	(26)
Interest rate Swaps	**22**	**22**	66	66
Cross-currency Swaps	**3**	**3**	86	86

Credit Concentrations The Company continually monitors its positions with, and the credit quality of, the financial institutions that are counterparties to its financial instruments and does not anticipate nonperformance by the counterparties.

The Company would not realize a material loss as of October 1, 2005 in the event of nonperformance by any single counterparty. The Company enters into transactions only with financial institution counterparties that have a credit rating of A- or better. The Company's current policy regarding agreements with financial institution counterparties is generally to require collateral in the event credit ratings fall below A- or in the event aggregate exposures exceed limits as defined by contract. In addition, the Company limits the amount of investment credit exposure with any one institution.

The Company's trade receivables and investments do not represent a significant concentration of credit risk at October 1, 2005 due to the wide variety of customers and markets into which the Company's products are sold, their dispersion across geographic areas, and the diversification of the Company's portfolio among issuers.

ORACLE
2005 Annual Report

13. Derivative Financial Instruments

FASB Statement No. 133, *Accounting for Derivative Instruments and Hedging Activities,* as amended, establishes accounting and reporting standards requiring that every derivative instrument be recorded in the balance sheet as either an asset or liability measured at its fair value. Statement 133 also requires that changes in the derivative's fair value be recognized currently in earnings unless specific hedge accounting criteria are met and that a company must formally document, designate and assess the effectiveness of transactions that receive hedge accounting. We use derivatives to manage foreign currency and interest rate risk.

Net Investment Hedges

Periodically, we hedge the net assets of certain international subsidiaries (net investment hedges) using foreign currency forward contracts to offset the translation and economic exposures related to our investments in these subsidiaries. We measure the ineffectiveness of net investment hedges by using the changes in spot exchange rates because this method reflects our risk management strategies, the economics of those strategies in our financial statements and better manages interest rate differentials between different countries. Under this method, the change in fair value of the forward contract attributable to the changes in spot exchange rates (the effective portion) is reported in stockholders' equity to offset the translation results on the net investments. The remaining change in fair value of the forward contract (the ineffective portion) is recognized in non-operating income, net.

Net losses on investment hedges reported in stockholders' equity were $23.1 million, $38.4 million and $44.7 million in fiscal 2005, 2004 and 2003, respectively. The net gain on investment hedges reported in non-operating income, net were $13.6 million, $7.5 million and $8.9 million in fiscal 2005, 2004 and 2003, respectively.

At May 31, 2005, we had one net investment hedge in Japanese Yen. The Yen investment hedge minimizes currency risk arising from net assets held in Yen as a result of equity capital raised during the initial public offering and secondary offering of Oracle Japan. The fair value of our Yen investment hedge was $0.5 million and $1.4 million as of May 31, 2005 and 2004. The Yen investment hedge has a notional amount of $615.5 million and an exchange rate of 107.23 Yen for each United States dollar.

Foreign Currency Forward Contracts

We transact business in various foreign currencies and have established a program that primarily utilizes foreign currency forward contracts to offset the risk associated with the effects of certain foreign currency exposures. Under this program, increases or decreases in our foreign currency exposures are offset by gains or losses on the forward contracts, to mitigate the possibility of foreign currency transaction gains or losses. These foreign currency exposures typically arise from intercompany sublicense fees and other intercompany transactions. Our forward contracts generally have terms of 90 days or less. We do not use forward contracts for trading purposes. All outstanding foreign currency forward contracts used in this program are marked to market at the end of the period with unrealized gains and losses included in non-operating income, net. Our ultimate realized gain or loss with respect to currency fluctuations will depend on the currency exchange rates and other factors in effect as the contracts mature. Net foreign exchange transaction losses included in non-operating income, net in the accompanying consolidated statements of operations were $27.2 million, $20.9 million and $1.0 million in fiscal 2005, 2004 and 2003, respectively. The fair values of foreign currency forward contracts were not individually significant and approximated $0.2 million and $(0.7) million as of May 31, 2005 and 2004. These amounts are included in other assets in the accompanying consolidated balance sheets.

Interest Rate Swap

We have $150 million in 6.91% senior notes due in February 2007. In February 2002, we entered into an interestrate swap agreement that has the economic effect of modifying the interest obligations associated with these senior notes so that the interest payable on the senior notes effectively becomes variable based on the three month LIBOR set quarterly until maturity. The notional amount of the interest rate swap and the termination date match the principal amounts and maturity date of the outstanding senior notes. Our interest rate swap reduced the effective interest rate on our 6.91% senior notes to 5.23% as of May 31, 2005. The fair value of the interest rate swap was $3.1 million and $7.2 million at May 31, 2005 and May 31, 2004 and is included in other assets in the accompanying consolidated balance sheets.

International Rectifier
2005 Annual Report

3. Derivative Financial Instruments

The Company is exposed to various risks, including fluctuations in interest and foreign currency rates. In the normal course of business, the Company also faces risks that are either non-financial or non-quantifiable. Such risks principally include country risk, credit risk and legal risk and are not discussed or quantified in the following analyses.

Interest Rate Risk

In December 2001, the Company entered into interest rate swap transaction (the "Transaction") with an investment bank, JP Morgan Chase Bank (the "Bank"), to modify the Company's effective interest payable with respect to $412.5 million of its $550 million outstanding convertible debt (the "Debt") (see Note 4, "Bank Loans and Long-Term Debt"). In April 2004, the Company entered into an interest rate swap transaction (the "April 2004 Transaction") with the Bank to modify the effective interest payable with respect to the remaining $137.5 million of the Debt. The Company will receive from the Bank fixed payments equal to 4.25 percent of the notional amount, payable on January 15 and July 15. In exchange, the Company will pay to the Bank floating rate payments based upon the London InterBank Offered Rate ("LIBOR") multiplied by the notional amount. At the inception of the Transaction, interest rates were lower than that of the Debt and the Company believed that interest rates would remain lower for an extended period of time. The variable interest rate paid since the inception of the swaps has averaged 2.47 percent, compared to a coupon of 4.25 percent on the Debt. During the fiscal years ended June 30, 2005, 2004 and 2003, these arrangements reduced interest expense by $8.0 million, $12.9 million and $10.4 million, respectively. Accounted for as a fair value hedge under SFAS No. 133, the mark-to-market adjustments of the Transaction and April 2004 Transaction were offset by the mark-to-market adjustments on the Debt, resulting in no material impact to earnings. The market value of the Transaction was a $0.3 million liability and a $13.1 million asset position at June 30, 2005 and 2004, respectively. The market value of the April 2004 Transaction was a $3.4 million and a $1.3 million liability position at June 30, 2005 and 2004, respectively.

Both transactions terminate on July 15, 2007 ("Termination Date"), subject to certain early termination provisions. On or after July 18, 2003 and prior to July 14, 2007, if the ten-day average closing price of the Company's common stock equals or exceeds $77.63, the Transaction and the April 2004 Transaction will terminate. Depending on the timing of the early termination event, the Bank would be obligated to pay the Company an amount equal to the redemption premium called for under the terms of the Debt.

In support of the Company's obligation under the two transactions, the Company is required to obtain irrevocable standby letters of credit in favor of the Bank, totaling $7.5 million plus a collateral requirement for the Transaction and April 2004 Transaction, as determined periodically. At June 30, 2005, $12.0 million in letters of credit were outstanding related to both transactions.

The Transaction and the April 2004 Transaction qualify as fair value hedges under SFAS No. 133. To test effectiveness of the hedge, regression analysis is performed quarterly comparing the change in fair value of the two transactions and the Debt. The fair values of the transactions and the Debt are calculated quarterly as the present value of the contractual cash flows to the expected maturity date, where the expected maturity date is based on probability-weighted analysis of interest rates relating to the five-year LIBOR curve and the Company's stock prices. For the fiscal years ended June 30, 2005, 2004 and 2003, the hedges were highly effective and therefore, the ineffective portion did not have a material impact on earnings.

In April 2002, the Company entered into an interest rate contract (the "Contract") with an investment bank, Lehman Brothers ("Lehman"), to reduce the variable interest rate risk of the Transaction. The notional amount of the Contract is $412.0 million, representing approximately 75 percent of the Debt. Under the terms of the Contract, the Company has the option to receive a payout from Lehman covering our exposure to LIBOR fluctuations between 5.5 percent and 7.5 percent for any four designated quarters. The market value of the Contract at June 30, 2005 and 2004 was $0.1 million and $0.9 million, respectively, and was included in other long-term assets. Interest expense was increased by mark-to-market losses of $0.8 million, $0.5 million and $3.1 million for the fiscal years ended 2005, 2004 and 2003, respectively.

Foreign Currency Risk

The Company conducts business on a global basis in several foreign currencies, and at various times, is exposed to fluctuations with the British Pound Sterling, the Euro and the Japanese Yen. The Company's risk to the European currencies is partially offset by the natural hedge of manufacturing and selling goods in both U.S. dollars and the European currencies. Considering its specific foreign currency exposures, the Company has the greatest exposure to the Japanese Yen, since it has significant yen-based revenues without the yen-based manufacturing costs. The Company has established a foreign-currency hedging program using foreign exchange forward contracts, including the Forward Contract described below, to hedge certain foreign currency transaction exposures. To protect against reductions in value and volatility of future cash flows caused by changes in currency exchange rates, it has established revenue, expense and balance sheet hedging programs. Currency forward contracts and local Yen and Euro borrowings are used in these hedging programs. The Company's hedging programs reduce, but do not always eliminate, the impact of currency exchange rate movements.

In March 2001, the Company entered into a five-year foreign exchange forward contract (the "Forward Contract") for the purpose of reducing the effect of exchange rate fluctuations on forecasted inter-company purchases by our subsidiary in Japan. The Company has designated the Forward Contract as a cash flow hedge under which mark-to-market adjustments are recorded in accumulated other comprehensive income, a separate component of stockholders' equity, until the forecasted transactions are recorded in earnings. Under the terms of the Forward Contract, the Company is required to exchange 1.2 billion yen for $11.0 million on a quarterly basis from June 2001 to March 2006. At June 30, 2005, three quarterly payments of 1.2 billion yen remained to be swapped at a forward exchange rate of 109.32 yen per U.S. dollar. The market value of the forward contract was a $0.1 million asset and a ($2.2) million liability at June 30, 2005 and 2004, respectively. The mark-to-market gains (losses), net of tax, of $0.7 million, (4.0) million and $4.0 million for the fiscal years ended June 30, 2005, 2004 and 2003, respectively, were included in other comprehensive income. Based on effectiveness tests comparing forecasted transactions through the Forward Contract expiration date to its cash flow requirements, the Company does not expect to incur a material charge to income during the next twelve months as a result of the Forward Contract.

The Company had approximately $75.9 million and $62.4 million in notional amounts of forward contracts not designated as accounting hedges under SFAS No. 133 at June 30, 2005 and 2004, respectively. Net realized and unrealized foreign-currency net gains recognized in earnings were $1.4 million for the fiscal year ended June 30, 2005 and less than $1 million for the fiscal years ended June 30, 2004 and 2003.

Wal-Mart
2005 Annual Report

3 Financial Instruments

The company uses derivative financial instruments for hedging and non-trading purposes to manage its exposure to interest and foreign exchange rates. Use of derivative financial instruments in hedging programs subjects the company to certain risks, such as market and credit risks. Market risk represents the possibility that the value of the derivative instrument will change. In a hedging relationship, the change in the value of the derivative is offset to a great extent by the change in the value of the underlying hedged item. Credit risk related to derivatives represents the possibility that the counterparty will not fulfill the terms of the contract. The notional, or contractual, amount of the company's derivative financial instruments is used to measure interest to be paid or received and does not represent the company's exposure due to credit risk. Credit risk is monitored through established approval procedures, including setting concentration limits by counterparty, reviewing credit ratings and requiring collateral (generally cash) when appropriate. The majority of the company's transactions are with counterparties rated "AA-" or better by nationally recognized credit rating agencies.

Fair Value Instruments

The company enters into interest rate swaps to minimize the risks and costs associated with its financing activities. Under the swap agreements, the company pays variable-rate interest and receives fixed-rate interest payments periodically over the life of the instruments. The notional amounts are used to measure interest to be paid or received and do not represent the exposure due to credit loss. All of the company's interest rate swaps that receive fixed interest rate payments and pay variable interest rate payments are designated as fair value hedges. As the specific terms and notional amounts of the derivative instruments exactly match those of the instruments being hedged, the derivative instruments were assumed to be perfect hedges and all changes in fair value of the hedges were recorded on the balance sheet with no net impact on the income statement.

Net Investment Instruments

At January 31, 2005, the company is party to cross-currency interest rate swaps that hedge its net investments in the United Kingdom and Japan. The agreements are contracts to exchange fixed-rate payments in one currency for fixed-rate payments in another currency. The company also has outstanding approximately £2.0 billion of debt that is designated as a hedge of the company's net investment in the United Kingdom. All changes in the fair value of these instruments are recorded in other comprehensive income, offsetting the foreign currency translation adjustment that is also recorded in other comprehensive income.

Cash Flow Instruments

The company is party to a cross-currency interest rate swap to hedge the foreign currency risk of certain foreign-denominated debt. The swap is designated as a cash flow hedge of foreign currency exchange risk. The agreement is a contract to exchange fixed-rate payments in one currency for fixed-rate payments in another currency. Changes in the foreign currency spot exchange rate result in reclassification of amounts from other accumulated comprehensive income to earnings to offset transaction gains or losses on foreign-denominated debt. The instrument matures in fiscal 2007.

The company expects that the amount of gain or loss existing in other accumulated comprehensive income to be reclassified into earnings within the next 12 months will not be significant.

Fair Value of Financial Instruments

Instrument	Notional Amount		Fair Value	
Fiscal Year Ended January 31, (in millions)	**2005**	2004	2005	2004
Derivative financial instruments designated for hedging:				
Receive fixed-rate, pay floating rate interest rate swaps designated as fair value hedges	**$ 8,042**	$ 8,292	**$ 477**	$ 697

Instrument Fiscal Year Ended January 31, (in millions)	Notional Amount		Fair Value	
	2005	2004	2005	2004
Receive fixed-rate, pay fixed-rate cross-currency interest rate swaps designated as net investment hedges (Cross-currency notional amount: GBP 795 at 1/31/2005 and 1/31/2004)	**1.250**	1.250	**(14)**	29
Receive fixed-rate, pay fixed-rate cross-currency interest rate swaps designated as a cash flow hedge (Cross-currency notional amount: CAD 503 at 1/31/2005 and 1/31/2004)	**325**	325	**(87)**	(54)
Receive fixed-rate, pay fixed-rate cross-currency interest rate swaps designated as a net investment hedge (Cross-currency notional amount: ☐ 52,056 at 1/31/2005 and 1/31/2004)	**432**	432	**(68)**	(46)
Receive floating rate, pay fixed-rate interest rate swap designated as a cash flow hedge	**1,500**	1,500	**(5)**	(16)
	$11,549	$11,799	**$ 303**	$ 610
Non-derivative financial instruments: Long-term debt	**$23,846**	$20,006	**$ 25,016**	$21,349

Hedging instruments with a favorable fair value are recorded on the Consolidated Balance Sheets as other current assets or other assets and deferred charges, based on maturity date. Those instruments with an unfavorable fair value are recorded in accrued liabilities or deferred income taxes and other, based on maturity date.

Cash and cash equivalents: The carrying amount approximates fair value due to the short maturity of these instruments.

Long-term debt: Fair value is based on the company's current incremental borrowing rate for similar types of borrowing arrangements.

Interest rate instruments and net investment instruments: The fair values are estimated amounts the company would receive or pay to terminate the agreements as of the reporting dates.

Anheuser-Busch
2004 Annual Report

3. Derivatives and Other Financial Instruments
Derivatives

Under FAS 133, Anheuser-Busch appropriately defers the recognition of most unrealized derivatives gains or losses until the related underlying hedged transactions occur. Gains and losses that relate to any portion of a hedge that is not 100% effective at offsetting price movements in the hedged exposure are immediately recognized in the income statement.

The following table shows (in millions) derivatives gains and losses deferred as of December 31, 2004, 2003, and 2002. The amounts shown for 2003 and 2002 were recognized in the income statement the next year. For the gains and losses deferred as of December 31, 2004, the majority are expected to be recognized in cost of sales in 2005, when the underlying transaction occurs. However, the amounts ultimately recognized may differ, favorably or unfavorably, from those shown because many of the company's derivative positions are not yet settled and therefore remain subject to ongoing market price fluctuations in 2005. The company had deferred option premium costs of $6.5 million, $26.2 million, and $9.5 million at the end of 2004, 2003, and 2002, respectively.

Also shown below are net amounts recognized in earnings as ineffective during the year. The gain for 2004 includes $19.5 million reported in other income related to the sale of commodity hedges that had been in place for future years. The hedges were originally placed using estimates of costs to be contained in the renewal of supply contracts. Anheuser-Busch lowered its cost estimates during the first quarter after negotiating the agreements, resulting in significant hedge ineffectiveness in compliance with FAS 133. Due to the hedge ineffectiveness, the company sold these hedges and recorded the ineffective portion of the gain.

	2004	2003	2002
Deferred gains	$ 2.8	$ 86.0	$ 20.5
Deferred losses	(4.9)	(26.2)	(19.4)
Net deferred gains/(losses)	$ (2.1)	$ 59.8	$ 1.1
Net ineffective gains/(losses) recognized in earnings	$ 26.5	$ 1.3	$ (0.4)

The table below summarizes the notional transaction amounts and fair values for the company's outstanding derivatives, by risk category and instrument type, at December 31 (in millions). Because the company hedges only with derivatives that have high correlation with the underlying transaction pricing, changes in derivatives fair values and the underlying prices are expected to essentially offset.

	2004		2003	
	Notional Amount	Fair Value	Notional Amount	Fair Value
Foreign Currency:				
Forwards	$114.7	$ 0.7	$ 87.3	$ 1.0
Options	151.0	3.8	161.2	5.4
	265.7	4.5	248.5	6.4
Interest Rate:				
Swaps	150.0	5.6	401.0	19.2

	2004		2003	
	Notional Amount	**Fair Value**	Notional Amount	Fair Value
Commodity Price:				
Swaps	**22.0**	**(2.9)**	235.5	28.5
Futures and forwards	**14.6**	**(0.9)**	21.5	1.2
Options	**58.32**	**.4**	461.4	54.0
	94.9	**(1.4)**	718.4	83.7
Total outstanding derivatives	**$510.6**	**$ 8.7**	$1,367.9	$109.3

Anheuser-Busch's primary foreign currency exposures are to transactions and investments denominated in Mexican and Argentine pesos, Chinese renminbi, Canadian dollars, British pounds sterling, and euros. Hedged commodity exposures include aluminum, rice, corn, natural gas, and diesel fuel. The primary foreign currency exposures are long, meaning the company generates a surplus of these currencies, while the commodity exposures are short, meaning the company must acquire additional quantities to meet its operating needs.

Concentration of Credit Risk

The company does not have a material concentration of credit risk.

Nonderivative Financial Instruments

Nonderivative financial instruments included in the balance sheet are cash, accounts receivable, accounts payable, and long-term debt. Accounts receivable include allowances for doubtful accounts of $12.5 million and $6.6 million, at December 31, 2004 and 2003, respectively. The fair value of long-term debt, excluding commercial paper, and estimated based on future cash flows discounted at interest rates currently available to the company for debt with similar maturities and characteristics, was $7.7 billion and $7.2 billion at December 31, 2004 and 2003, respectively.

General Electric
2002 Annual Report

Note 28: Derivatives and Other Financial Instruments

Derivatives and Hedging

Our global business activities routinely deal with fluctuations in interest rates, currency exchange rates and commodity and other asset prices. We apply strict policies to managing each of these risks, including prohibitions on derivatives trading, derivatives market-making or other speculative activities. These policies require the use of derivative instruments in concert with other techniques to reduce or eliminate these risks.

Cash flow hedges

Under SFAS 133, cash flow hedges are hedges that use simple derivatives to offset the variability of expected future cash flows. Variability can appear in floating rate assets, floating rate liabilities or from certain types of forecasted transactions, and can arise from changes in interest rates or currency exchange rates. For example, GECS often borrows at a variable rate of interest to fund our financial services businesses. If Commercial Finance needs the funds to make a floating rate loan, there is no exposure to interest rate changes, and no hedge is necessary. However, if a fixed rate loan is made, we will contractually commit to pay a fixed rate of interest to a counterparty who will pay us a variable rate of interest (an "interest rate swap"). This swap will then be designated as a cash flow hedge of the associated variable rate borrowing. If, as would be expected, the derivative is perfectly effective in offsetting variable interest in the borrowing, changes in its fair value are recorded in a separate component in equity and released to earnings contemporaneously with the earnings effects of the hedged item. Further information about hedge effectiveness is provided below.

We use currency forwards and options to manage exposures to changes in currency exchange rates associated with commercial purchase and sale transactions. These instruments permit us to eliminate the cash flow variability, in local currency, of costs or selling prices denominated in currencies other than the functional currency. In addition, we use these instruments, along with interest rate and currency swaps, to optimize borrowing costs and investment returns. For example, currency swaps and non-functional currency borrowings together provide lower funding costs than could be achieved by issuing debt directly in a given currency.

At December 31, 2002, amounts related to derivatives qualifying as cash flow hedges amounted to a reduction of equity of $2,112 million, of which $519 million was expected to be transferred to earnings in 2003 along with the earnings effects of the related forecasted transactions. In 2002, there were no forecasted transactions that failed to occur. At December 31, 2002, the maximum term of derivative instruments that hedge forecasted transactions was 24 months.

Fair value hedges

Under SFAS 133, fair value hedges are hedges that eliminate the risk of changes in the fair values of assets, liabilities and certain types of firm commitments. For example, we will use an interest rate swap in which we receive a fixed rate of interest and pay a variable rate of interest to change the cash flow profile of a fixed rate borrowing to match the variable rate financial asset that it is funding. Changes in fair value of derivatives designated and effective as fair value hedges are recorded in earnings and are offset by corresponding changes in the fair value of the hedged item.

We use interest rate swaps, currency swaps and interest rate and currency forwards to hedge the effect of interest rate and currency exchange rate changes on local and nonfunctional currency denominated fixed rate borrowings and certain types of fixed rate assets. Equity options are used to hedge price changes in investment securities and equity-indexed annuity liabilities at Insurance.

Net investment hedges

The net investment hedge designation under SFAS 133 refers to the use of derivative contracts or cash instruments to hedge the foreign currency exposure of a net investment in a foreign operation. We manage currency exposures that result from net investments in affiliates principally by funding assets denominated in local currency with debt denominated in that same currency. In certain circumstances, we manage such exposures with currency forwards and currency swaps.

Derivatives not designated as hedges

SFAS 133 specifies criteria that must be met in order to apply any of the three forms of hedge accounting. For example, hedge accounting is not permitted for hedged items that are marked to market through earnings. We use derivatives to hedge exposures when it makes economic sense to do so, including circumstances in which the hedging relationship does not qualify for hedge accounting as described below. We also will occasionally receive derivatives, such as equity warrants, in the ordinary course of business. Under SFAS 133, derivatives that do not qualify for hedge accounting are marked to market through earnings.

We use option contracts, including caps, floors and collars, as an economic hedge of changes in interest rates, currency exchange rates and equity prices on certain types of assets and liabilities. For example, Insurance uses equity options to hedge the risk of changes in equity prices embedded in liabilities associated with annuity contracts it writes. We also use interest rate swaps, purchased options and futures as an economic hedge of the fair value of mortgage servicing rights. We occasionally obtain equity warrants as part of sourcing or financing transactions. Although these instruments are considered to be derivatives under SFAS 133, their economic risk is similar to, and managed on the same basis as, other equity instruments we hold.

Earnings effects of derivatives

The table that follows provides additional information about the earnings effects of derivatives. In the context of hedging relationships, "effectiveness" refers to the degree to which fair value changes in the hedging instrument offset the corresponding expected earnings effects of the hedged item. Certain elements of hedge positions cannot qualify for hedge accounting under SFAS 133 whether effective or not, and must therefore be marked to market through earnings. Time value of purchased options is the most common example of such elements in instruments we use. Pre-tax earnings effects of such items are shown in the following table as "amounts excluded from the measure of effectiveness."

December 31 (In millions)	2002	2001
CASH FLOW HEDGES		
Ineffectiveness	**$(24)**	$1
Amounts excluded from the measure of effectiveness	–	(1)
FAIR VALUE HEDGES		
Ineffectiveness	**3**	26
Amounts excluded from the measure of effectiveness	**3**	(16)

Counterparty credit risk

The risk that counterparties to derivative contracts will be financially unable to make payments to us according to the terms of the agreements is counterparty credit risk. We manage counterparty credit risk on an individual counterparty basis, which means that we net gains and losses for each counterparty to determine the amount at risk. When a counterparty exceeds credit exposure limits in terms of amounts they owe us (see table below), typically as a result of changes in market conditions, no additional transactions are permitted to be executed until the exposure with that counterparty is reduced to an amount that is within the established limit. All swaps are required to be executed under master swap agreements containing mutual credit downgrade provisions that provide the ability to require assignment or termination in the event either party is downgraded below A3 or A-. If the downgrade provisions had been triggered at December 31, 2002, we could have been required to disburse up to $4.0 billion and could have claimed $1.9 billion from counterparties—the net fair value losses and gains. At December 31, 2002 and 2001, gross fair value gains amounted to $5.0 billion and $3.3 billion, respectively. At December 31, 2002 and 2001, gross fair value losses amounted to $7.1 billion and $5.4 billion, respectively.

As part of its ongoing activities, our financial services businesses enter into swaps that are integrated into investments in or loans to particular customers. Such integrated swaps not involving assumption of third-party credit risk are evaluated and monitored like their associated investments or loans and are therefore not subject to the same credit criteria that would apply to a stand-alone position. Except for such positions, all other swaps, purchased options and forwards with contractual maturities longer than one year are conducted within the credit policy constraints provided in the table below. Foreign exchange forwards with contractual maturities shorter than one year must be executed with counterparties having an A-1/P-1 credit rating and the credit limit for exposures on these transactions is $150 million.

Counterparty Credit Criteria

| | Credit Rating | |
	Moody's	S&P
Term of transaction		
Between one and five years	Aa3	AA–
Greater than five years	Aaa	AAA
Credit exposure limits		
Up to $50 million	Aa3	AA–
Up to $75 million	Aaa	AAA

Financial Instruments
(Table on next page)

Assets and liabilities that are reflected in the accompanying financial statements at fair value are not included in the following disclosures; such items include cash and equivalents, investment securities, separate accounts and derivative financial instruments. Other assets and liabilities—those not carried at fair value—are discussed below. Apart from certain of our borrowings and certain marketable securities, few of the instruments discussed below are actively traded and their fair values must often be determined using models. Although we have made every effort to develop the fairest representation of fair value for this section, it would be unusual if the estimates could actually have been realized at December 31, 2002 or 2001.

December 31 (In millions)	2002 Assets (Liabilities)				2001 Assets (Liabilities)			
	Notional Amount	Carrying amount (net)	Estimated High	Fair Value Low	Notional Amount	Carrying Amount (net)	Estimated High	Fair Value Low
GE(a)								
Investments and notes receivable	$(b)	$567	$567	$567	$(b)	$570	$568	$568
Borrowings(c)(d)	(b)	(9,756)	(9,816)	(9,816)	(b)	(2,509)	(2,509)	(2,509)
GECS(a)								
Assets								
Time sales and loans	(b)	138,695	141,784	138,834	(b)	115,773	117,159	115,135
Other commercial and residential mortgages	(b)	8,093	8,504	8,417	(b)	6,505	6,671	6,636
Other financial instruments(b)	(b)	6,702	6,772	6,634	(b)	4,742	4,806	4,734
Liabilities								
Borrowings(c)(d)(f)	(b)	(270,347)	(286,824)	(273,717)	(b)	(240,519)	(249,516)	(240,519)
Investment contract benefits	(b)	(37,814)	(37,731)	(37,312)	(b)	(32,427)	(32,192)	(31,815)
Insurance—financial guarantees and credit life(e)	312,489	(3,614)	(3,475)	(3,564)	278,941	(2,941)	(2,983)	(3,091)
Other financial instruments	(b)	(369)	(369)	(369)	(b)	(629)	(590)	(590)
Other firm commitments								
Ordinary course of business lending commitments	11,956	–	–	–	10,279	–	–	–
Unused revolving credit lines Commercial	28,525	–	–	–	27,770	–	–	–
Consumer—principally credit cards	259,085	–	–	–	222,929	–	–	–

(a) As a result of the adoption of FIN 45, guarantees within its scope are disclosed within notes 29 and 30.
(b) These financial instruments do not have notional amounts.
(c) Includes effects of interest rate and currency swaps.
(d) See note 18.
(e) See note 19.
(f) Estimated fair values in 2001 have been re-evaluated consistent with our current methodology.

A description of how we estimate fair values follows.

Time sales and loans

Based on quoted market prices, recent transactions and/or discounted future cash flows, using rates at which similar loans would have been made to similar borrowers.

Borrowings

Based on market quotes or comparables.

Investment contract benefits

Based on expected future cash flows, discounted at currently offered discount rates for immediate annuity contracts or cash surrender values for single premium deferred annuities.

Financial guarantees and credit life

Based on expected future cash flows, considering expected renewal premiums, claims, refunds and servicing costs, discounted at a current market rate.

All other instruments

Based on comparable market transactions, discounted future cash flows, quoted market prices, and/or estimates of the cost to terminate or otherwise settle obligations.

Unused credit lines and lending commitments at December 31, 2002, were as follows:

(In millions)	Fixed Rate	Variable Rate	Total
Ordinary course of business lending commitments	$ 842	$ 11,114	$ 11,956
Unused revolving credit lines Commercial	8,879	19,646	28,525
Consumer—principally credit cards	136,249	122,836	259,085

Applied Materials
2005 Annual Report

Note 2 Financial Instruments

Investments

Short-term investments by security type at October 30, 2005 were as follows:

	Cost	Gross Unrealized Gains	Gross Unrealized Losses	Estimated Fair Value
		(In thousands)		
Obligations of states and political subdivisions	$ 1,362,456	$ 194	$ 4,720	$ 1,357,930

	Cost	Gross Unrealized Gains	Gross Unrealized Losses	Estimated Fair Value
U.S. commercial paper, corporate bonds and medium-term notes	1,069,556	1,429	7,806	1,063
Bank Certificates of deposit	63,847	–	–	63,847
U.S. Treasury and agency securities . .	1,671,396	134	16,339	1,671,396
Other debt securities .	816,424	764	12,335	816,424
	$4,983,679	$2,520	$41,200	$4,983,679

Short-term investments by security type at October 31, 2004 were as follows:

	Cost	Gross Unrealized Gains	Gross Unrealized Losses	Estimated Fair Value
		(In thousands)		
Obligations of states and political subdivisions	$1,246,46	$ 2,732	$1,277	$ 1,247,91
U.S. commercial paper, corporate bonds and medium-term notes	1,157,123	6,185	1,970	1,521,338
Bank Certificates of deposit	116,933	–	–	116,933
U.S. Treasury and agency securities . .	1,501,897	3,609	2,771	1,502,735
Other debt securities .	693,579	4,704	2,536	695,747
	$5,076,028	$17,230	$8,554	$5,084,704

Cash and cash equivalents included investments in debt and other securities of $719 million at October 31, 2004 and $608 million at October 30, 2005.

Contractual maturities of short-term investments at October 30, 2005 were as follows:

	Cost	Estimated Fair Value
	(In thousands)	
Due in one year or less	$1,724,984	$1,719,315
Due after one through three years	1,136,017	1,123,831
Due after three years	1,297,957	1,289,056

	Cost	Estimated Fair Value
	(In thousands)	
No single maturity date*	824,721	812,797
	$4,983,679	$4,944,999

* Securities with no single maturity date include mortgage- and asset-backed securities.

Applied manages its cash equivalents and short-term investments as a single portfolio of highly marketable securities that is intended to be available to meet Applied's current cash requirements. For fiscal 2004, gross realized gains on sales of short-term investments were $15 million, and gross realized losses were $7 million. For fiscal 2005, gross realized gains on sales of short-term investments were $3 million, and gross realized losses were $8 million.

The following table provides the breakdown of the short-term investments with unrealized losses at October 30, 2005:

	In Loss Position for Less Than 12 Months		In Loss Position for 12 Months or Greater		Total	
	Fair Value	Gross Unrealized Losses	Fair Value	Gross Unrealized Losses	Fair Value	Gross Unrealized Losses
	(In thousands)					
Obligations of states and political subdivisions . .	$ 536,069	$ 3,939	$ 20,028	$ 781	$556,097	$ 4,720
U.S. commercial paper, corporate bonds and medium-term notes	571,797	4,744	147,774	3,062	719,571	7,806
U.S. Treasury and agency securities . . .	1,188,798	10,932	294,453	5,407	1,483,251	16,339
Other debt securities . . .	537,875	7,510	176,713	4,825	714,588	12,335
	$2,834,539	$27,125	$638,968	$14,075	3,473,507	412,200

The gross unrealized losses related to short-term investments are primarily due to a decrease in the fair value of debt securities as a result of an increase in interest rates during fiscal 2005. Applied has determined that the gross unrealized losses on its short-term investment at October 30, 2005 are temporary in nature. Applied reviews its investment portfolio to identify and evaluate investments that have indications of possible impairment. Factors considered in determining whether a loss is temporary include the length of time and extent to which fair value has been less than the cost basis, the financial condition and near-term prospects of the investee, credit quality and Applied's ability to hold the investment for a period of time sufficient to allow for any anticipated recovery in market value.

Derivative Financial Instruments Derivative instruments and hedging activities, including foreign currency exchange contracts, are recognized on the balance sheet at fair value. Changes in the fair value of derivatives that do not qualify for hedge treatment, as well the ineffective portion of any hedges, are recognized currently in earnings. All of Applied's derivative financial instruments are recorded at their fair value in other current assets or accounts payable and accrued expenses.

Applied conducts business in a number of foreign countries, with certain transactions denominated in local currencies, such as Japanese yen, British pound, euro and Israeli shekel. The purpose of Applied's foreign currency management is to mitigate the effect of exchange rate fluctuations on certain foreign currency denominated revenues, costs and eventual cash flows. The terms of currency instruments used for hedging purposes are generally consistent with the timing of the transactions being hedged.

Applied uses derivative financial instruments, such as forward exchange contracts and currency option contracts, to hedge certain forecasted foreign currency denominated transactions expected to occur within the next 12 months. Hedges related to anticipated transactions are designated and documented at the inceptions of the hedge as cash flow hedges, and are evaluated for effectiveness quarterly. The effective portion of the gain or loss on these hedges is reported as a component of accumulated other comprehensive income in stockholders' equity, and is reclassified into earnings when the hedged transaction affects earnings. Amounts included in accumulated other comprehensive income at October 30, 2005 will generally be reclassified into earnings within 12 months. Changes in the fair value of currency forward exchange and option contracts due to changes in time value are excluded from the assessment of effectiveness, and are recognized in cost of products sold. The change in option and forward time value was not material for fiscal 2003, 2004, or 2005. If the transaction being hedged fails to occur, or if a portion of any derivative is ineffective, Applied promptly recognizes the gain or loss on the associated financial instrument in general and administrative expenses. The amounts recognized due to anticipated transactions failing to occur were not material for all periods presented.

Forward exchange contracts are generally used to hedge certain foreign currency denominated assets or liabilities. These derivatives are not designated for hedge accounting treatment. Accordingly, changes in the fair value of these hedges are recorded promptly in earnings to offset the changes in the fair value of the assets or liabilities being hedged.

Derivative-related activity in accumulated other comprehensive income was as follows:

	2004	2005
	(In thousands)	
Unrealized gain, net, on derivative instruments at beginning of period	$ 1,929	$ 646

	2004	2005
Increase in fair value of derivative instruments	13,701	10,105
Gains reclassified into earnings, net	(14,984)	(1,544)
Unrealized gain, net, on derivative instruments at end of period	$ 646	$ 9,207

Fair Value of Financial Instruments The carrying amounts of Applied's financial instruments, including cash and cash equivalents, accounts receivable, notes payable, and accounts payable and accrued expenses, approximate fair value due to the short maturities of these financial instruments. At October 31, 2004, the carrying amount of long-term debt was $456 million, and the estimated fair value was $510 million. At October 30, 2005, the carrying amount of long-term debt was $415 million, and the estimated fair value was $432 million. The estimated fair value of long-term debt is based primarily on quoted market prices for the same or similar issues.

Honeywell
2004 Annual Report

Note 17—Financial Instruments

As a result of our global operating and financing activities, we are exposed to market risks from changes in interest and foreign currency exchange rates and commodity prices, which may adversely affect our operating results and financial position. We minimize our risks from interest and foreign currency exchange rate and commodity price fluctuations through our normal operating and financing activities and, when deemed appropriate, through the use of derivative financial instruments.

Credit and Market Risk—Financial instruments, including derivatives, expose us to counterparty credit risk for nonperformance and to market risk related to changes in interest or currency exchange rates. We manage our exposure to counterparty credit risk through specific minimum credit standards, diversification of counterparties, and procedures to monitor concentrations of credit risk. Our counterparties in derivative transactions are substantial investment and commercial banks with significant experience using such derivative instruments.

We monitor the impact of market risk on the fair value and cash flows of our derivative and other financial instruments considering reasonably possible changes in interest and currency exchange rates and restrict the use of derivative financial instruments to hedging activities. We do not use derivative financial instruments for trading or other speculative purposes and do not use leveraged derivative financial instruments. We continually monitor the creditworthiness of our customers to which we grant credit terms in the normal course of business. While concentrations of credit risk associated with our trade accounts and notes receivable are considered minimal due to our diverse customer base, a significant portion of our customers are in the commercial air transport industry (aircraft manufacturers and airlines) accounting for approximately 13 percent of our consolidated sales in 2004. The terms and conditions of our credit sales are designed to mitigate or eliminate concentrations of credit risk with any single customer. Our sales are not materially dependent on a single customer or a small group of customers.

Foreign Currency Risk Management—We conduct our business on a multinational basis in a wide variety of foreign currencies. Our exposure to market risk for changes in foreign currency exchange rates arises from international financing activities between subsidiaries, foreign currency denominated monetary assets and liabilities and anticipated transactions arising from international trade. Our objective is to preserve the economic value of non-functional currency denominated cash flows. We attempt to have all transaction exposures hedged with natural offsets to the fullest extent possible and, once these opportunities have been exhausted, through foreign currency forward and option agreements with third parties. Our principal currency exposures relate to the Euro, the British pound, the Canadian dollar, and the U.S. dollar.

We hedge monetary assets and liabilities denominated in non-functional currencies. Prior to conversion into U.S dollars, these assets and liabilities are remeasured at spot exchange rates in effect on the balance sheet date. The effects of changes in spot rates are recognized in earnings and included in Other (Income) Expense. We hedge our exposure to changes in foreign exchange rates principally with forward contracts. Forward contracts are marked-to-market with the resulting gains and losses similarly recognized in earnings offsetting the gains and losses on the non-functional currency denominated monetary assets and liabilities being hedged.

We partially hedge forecasted 2005 sales and purchases denominated in non-functional currencies with currency forward contracts. When a functional currency strengthens against non-functional currencies, the decline in value of forecasted non-functional currency cash inflows (sales) or outflows (purchases) is partially offset by the recognition of gains (sales) and losses (purchases), respectively, in the value of the forward contracts designated as hedges. Conversely, when a functional currency weakens against non-functional currencies, the increase in value of forecasted non-functional currency cash inflows (sales) or outflows (purchases) is partially offset by the recognition of losses (sales) and gains (purchases), respectively, in the value of the forward contracts designated as hedges. Market value gains and losses on these contracts are recognized in earnings when the hedged transaction is recognized. All open forward contracts mature by December 31, 2005.

At December 31, 2004 and 2003, we had contracts with notional amounts of $790 and $641 million, respectively, to exchange foreign currencies, principally in the Euro countries and Great Britain.

Commodity Price Risk Management—Our exposure to market risk for commodity prices arises from changes in our cost of production. We mitigate our exposure to commodity price risk through the use of long-term, firm-price contracts with our suppliers and forward commodity purchase agreements with third parties hedging anticipated purchases of several commodities (principally natural gas). Forward commodity purchase agreements are marked-to-market, with the resulting gains and losses recognized in earnings when the hedged transaction is recognized.

Interest Rate Risk Management—We use a combination of financial instruments, including medium-term and short-term financing, variable-rate commercial paper, and interest rate swaps to manage the interest rate mix of our total debt portfolio and related overall cost of borrowing. At December 31, 2004 and 2003, interest rate swap agreements designated as fair value hedges effectively changed $1,218 and $1,189 million, respectively, of fixed rate debt at an average rate of 6.42 and 6.45 percent, respectively, to LIBOR based floating rate debt. Our interest rate swaps mature through 2007.

Fair Value of Financial Instruments—The carrying value of cash and cash equivalents, trade accounts and notes receivables, payables, commercial paper and short-term borrowings contained in the Consolidated Balance Sheet approximates fair value. Summarized below are the carrying values and fair values of our other financial instruments at December 31, 2004 and 2003. The fair values are based on the quoted market prices for the issues (if traded), current rates offered to us for debt of the same remaining maturity and characteristics, or other valuation techniques, as appropriate.

	December 31, 2004		December 31, 2003	
	Carrying Value	Fair Value	Carrying Value	Fair Value
Assets				
Long-term receivables	$ 237	$ 218	$ 388	$ 369
Interest rate swap agreements	39	39	67	67
Foreign currency exchange contracts	22	22	12	12
Forward commodity contracts	10	10	18	18
Liabilities				
Long-term debt and related current maturities	$(5,025)	$(5,411)	$(5,008)	$(5,508)
Foreign currency exchange contracts	(6)	(6)	(11)	(11)
Forward commodity contracts	(2)	(2)	–	–

Microsoft
2003 Annual Report

Note 11—Derivatives

For fiscal 2001, investment income included a net unrealized loss of $592 million, comprised of a $214 million gain for changes in the time value of options for fair value hedges, $211 million loss for changes in the time value of options for cash flow hedges, and $595 million loss for changes in the fair value of derivative instruments not designated as hedging instruments. For fiscal 2002, investment income included a net unrealized loss of $480 million, comprised of a $30 million gain for changes in the time value of options for fair value hedges, a $331 million loss for changes in the time value of options for cash flow hedges, and a $179 million net loss for changes in the fair value of derivative instruments not designated as hedging instruments. For fiscal 2003, investment income included a net unrealized loss of $141 million, comprised of a $74 million loss for changes in the time value of options for fair value hedges, a $229 million loss for changes in the time value of options for cash flow hedges, and a $162 million gain for changes in the fair value of derivative instruments not designated as hedging instruments.

Derivative gains and losses included in OCI are reclassified into earnings at the time forecasted revenue or the sale of an equity investment is recognized. During fiscal 2001, $214 million of derivative gains were reclassified to revenue and $416 million of derivative losses were reclassified to investment income/ (loss). During fiscal 2002, $234 million of derivative gains were reclassified to revenue and $10 million of derivative losses were reclassified to investment income/(loss). During fiscal 2003, $40 million of derivative gains were reclassified to revenue and $2 million of derivative gains were reclassified to investment income/(loss). We estimate that $22 million of net derivative gains included in other comprehensive income will be reclassified into earnings within the next twelve months.

For instruments designated as hedges, hedge ineffectiveness, determined in accordance with SFAS 133, had no significant impact on earnings for the fiscal years 2001, 2002, and 2003. No significant fair value hedges or cash flow hedges were derecognized or discontinued for fiscal years 2001, 2002, and 2003.

IBM
2004 Annual Report

(Dollars in millions) AT DECEMBER 31:	2004	2003
Unused lines:		
From the committed global credit facility	$ 9,804	$ 9,907
From other committed and uncommitted lines	6,477	5,976
Total unused lines of credit	$16,281	$15,883

I. Derivatives and Hedging Transactions

The company operates in approximately 35 functional currencies and is a significant lender and borrower in the global markets. In the normal course of business, the company is exposed to the impact of interest rate changes and foreign currency fluctuations, and to a lesser extent equity price changes and client credit risk. The company limits these risks by following established risk management policies and procedures including the use of derivatives and, where cost-effective, financing with debt in the currencies in which assets are denominated. For interest rate exposures, derivatives are used to align rate movements between the interest rates associated with the company's lease and other financial assets and the interest rates associated with its financing debt. Derivatives are also used to manage the related cost of debt. For foreign currency exposures, derivatives are used to limit the effects of foreign exchange rate fluctuations on financial results.

The company does not use derivatives for trading or speculative purposes, nor is it a party to leveraged derivatives. Further, the company has a policy of only entering into contracts with carefully selected major financial institutions based upon their credit ratings and other factors, and maintains strict dollar and term limits that correspond to the institution's credit rating.

In its hedging programs, the company employs the use of forward contracts, futures contracts, interest rate and currency swaps, options, caps, floors or a combination thereof depending upon the underlying exposure.

A brief description of the major hedging programs follows.

Debt Risk Management

The company issues debt in the global capital markets, principally to fund its financing lease and loan portfolio. Access to cost-effective financing can result in interest rate and/or currency mismatches with the underlying assets. To manage these mismatches and to reduce overall interest cost, the company primarily uses interest-rate and currency instruments, principally swaps, to convert specific fixed-rate debt issuances into variable-rate debt (i.e., fair value hedges) and to convert specific variable-rate debt and anticipated commercial paper issuances to fixed rate (i.e., cash flow hedges). The resulting cost of funds is lower than that which would have been available if debt with matching characteristics was issued directly. At December 31, 2004, the weighted-average remaining maturity of all swaps in the debt risk management program was approximately three years.

Long-Term Investments in Foreign Subsidiaries (Net Investment)

A significant portion of the company's foreign currency denominated debt portfolio is designated as a hedge of net investment to reduce the volatility in stockholders' equity caused by changes in foreign currency exchange rates in the functional currency of major foreign subsidiaries with respect to the U.S. dollar. The company also uses currency swaps and foreign exchange forward contracts for this risk management purpose. The currency effects of these hedges (approximately $156 million in 2004 and approximately $200 million in 2003, net of tax) are reflected as a loss in the Accumulated gains and (losses) not affecting retained earnings section of the Consolidated Statement of Stockholders' Equity, thereby offsetting a portion of the translation adjustment of the applicable foreign subsidiaries' net assets. anticipated royalties and cost transactions The company's operations generate significant nonfunctional currency, third-party vendor payments and inter company payments for royalties, and goods and services among the company's non-U.S. subsidiaries and with the parent company. In anticipation of these foreign currency cash flows and in view of the volatility of the currency markets, the company selectively employs foreign exchange forward and option contracts to manage its currency risk. In general, these hedges have maturities of one year or less, but from time to time extend beyond one year commensurate with the underlying hedged anticipated cash flow. At December

31, 2004, the weighted-average remaining maturity of these derivative instruments was approximately one year.

Subsidiary Cash and Foreign Currency Asset/Liability Management

The company uses its Global Treasury Centers to manage the cash of its subsidiaries. These centers principally use currency swaps to convert cash flows in a cost-effective manner. In addition, the company uses foreign exchange forward contracts to hedge, on a net basis, the foreign currency exposure of a portion of the company's nonfunctional currency assets and liabilities. The terms of these forward and swap contracts are generally less than one year. The changes in fair value from these contracts and from the underlying hedged exposures are generally offsetting and are recorded in Other (income) and expense in the Consolidated Statement of Earnings.

Equity Risk Management

The company is exposed to certain equity price changes related to certain obligations to employees. These equity exposures are primarily related to market value movements in certain broad equity market indices and in the company's own stock. Changes in the overall value of this employee compensation obligation are recorded in SG&A expense in the Consolidated Statement of Earnings. Although not designated as accounting hedges, the company utilizes equity derivatives, including equity swaps and futures to economically hedge the equity exposures relating to this employee compensation obligation. To match the exposures relating to this employee compensation obligation, these derivatives are linked to the total return of certain broad equity market indices and/or the total return of the company 's common stock. These derivatives are recorded at fair value with gains or losses also reported in SG&A expense in the Consolidated Statement of Earnings.

Other Derivatives

The company holds warrants in connection with certain investments that, although not designated as hedging instruments, are deemed derivatives since they contain net share settlement clauses. During the year, the company recorded the change in the fair value of these warrants in net income.

The company is exposed to a potential loss if a client fails to pay amounts due the company under contractual terms ("credit risk"). The company has established policies and procedures for mitigating credit risk on principal transactions, including reviewing and establishing limits for credit exposure, maintaining collateral land continually assessing the credit worthiness of counterparties. Master agreements with counterparties include master netting arrangements as further mitigation of credit exposure to counterparties. These arrangements permit the company to net amounts due from the company to a counter party with amounts due to the company from a counterparty reducing the maximum loss from credit risk in the event of counterparty default. Also, in 2003, the company began utilizing credit default swaps to economically hedge certain credit exposures. These derivatives have terms of two years. The swaps are not designated as accounting hedges and are recorded at fair value with gains and losses reported in SG&A expense in the Consolidated Statement of Earnings.

The following table and the table on page 67 summarize the net fair value of the company's derivative and other risk management instruments at December 31, 2004 and 2003 (included in the Consolidated Statement of Financial Position).

Risk Management Program

(Dollars in millions)	Hedge Designation			
AT DECEMBER 31, 2004	Fair Value	Cash Flow	Net Investment	Non-Hedge/ Other
Derivatives—net asset/(liability):				
Debt risk management	$221	$ (53)	$ –	$(14)
Long-term investments in foreign subsidiaries (net investments)	–	–	(58)	–
Anticipated royalties and cost transactions	–	(939)	–	–
Subsidiary cash and foreign currency asset/liability management	–	–	–	(19)
Equity risk management	–	–	–	(7)
Total derivatives	22[a]	(992)[b]	(58)[c]	(40)[d]
Debt:				
Long-term investments in foreign subsidiaries (net investments)	–	–	(2,490)[e]	–
Total	$221	$(992)	$(2,548)	$(40)

[a] Comprises assets of $440 million and liabilities of $219 million.
[b] Comprises assets of $12 million and liabilities of $1,004 million.
[c] Comprises liabilities of $58 million.
[d] Comprises assets of $60 million and liabilities of $100 million.
[e] Represents fair value of foreign denominated debt issuances formally designated as a hedge of net investment.

(Dollars in millions)	Hedge Designation			
AT DECEMBER 31, 2004	Fair Value	Cash Flow	Net Investment	Non-Hedge/ Other
Derivatives—net asset/(liability):				
Debt risk management	297	$ (23)	$ –	$(10)
Long-term investments in foreign subsidiaries (net investments)	–	–	(27)	–
Anticipated royalties and cost transactions	–	(643)	–	–
Subsidiary cash and foreign currency asset/liability management	–	–	–	(31)
Equity risk management	–	–	–	39
Other derivatives	–	–	–	8
Total derivatives	297[a]	(666)[b]	(27)[c]	6[d]

(Dollars in millions)	Hedge Designation			
AT DECEMBER 31, 2004	Fair Value	Cash Flow	Net Investment	Non-Hedge/ Other
Debt:				
Long-term investments in foreign subsidiaries (net investments)	–	–	(2,470)[(e)]	–
Total	$297	$(666)	$(2,497)	$ 6

[(a)] Comprises assets of $1,083 million and liabilities of $786 million.
[(b)] Comprises liabilities of $666 million.
[(c)] Comprises liabilities of $27 million.
[(d)] Comprises assets of $73 million and liabilities of $67 million.
[(e)] Represents fair value of foreign denominated debt issuances formally designated as a hedge of net investment.

Accumulated Derivative Gains or Losses

As illustrated above, the company makes extensive use of cash flow hedges, principally in the Anticipated royalties and cost transactions risk management program. In connection with the company's cash flow hedges, it has recorded approximately $653 million of net losses in Accumulated gains and (losses) not affecting retained earnings as of December 31, 2004, net of tax, of which approximately $492 million is expected to be reclassified to net income within the next year, providing an offsetting economic impact against the underlying anticipated cash flows hedged.

The following table summarizes activity in the Accumulated gains and (losses) not affecting retained earnings section of the Consolidated Statement of Stockholders' Equity related to all derivatives classified as cash flow hedges held by the company during the periods January 1, 2001 (the date of the company's adoption of SFAS No.133) through December 31, 2004:

(Dollars in millions, net of tax)	Debit/(Credit)
December 31, 2001	$(296)
Net losses reclassified into earnings from equity during 2002	(5)
Changes in fair value of derivatives in 2002	664
December 31, 2002	$ 63
Net losses reclassified into earnings from equity during 2003	(713)
Changes in fair value of derivatives in 2003	804
December 31, 2003	$ 454
Net losses reclassified into earnings from equity during 2004	(463)
Changes in fair value of derivatives in 2004	662
December 31, 2004	$ 653

For the years ending December 31, 2004 and 2003, respectively, there were no significant gains or losses on derivative transactions or portions thereof that were either ineffective as hedges, excluded from the assessment of hedge effectiveness, or associated with an underlying exposure that did not or was not expected to occur; nor are there any anticipated in the normal course of business.

The Chase Manhattan Corporation

19. Derivative and Foreign Exchange Contracts

Chase utilizes derivative and foreign exchange financial instruments for both trading and non-trading activities, such as ALM. A discussion of the credit and market risks involved with these instruments is included in the first six paragraphs of the Derivative and Foreign Exchange Contracts section of the Management's Discussion and Analysis ("MD&A"), and paragraphs one through four of the Market Risk Management section of the MD&A.

Derivative and Foreign Exchange Instruments Used for Trading Purposes

The credit risk associated with Chase's trading activities is recorded on the balance sheet. The effects of any market risk (gains or losses) on Chase's trading activities have been reflected in trading revenue, as the trading instruments are marked-to-market daily. See Summary of Significant Accounting Policies.

Derivative and Foreign Exchange Instruments Used for ALM Activities

A discussion of Chase's objectives and strategies for using these instruments for ALM activities is included in the first four paragraphs of the Asset/Liability Management discussion of the MD&A in Market Risk Management.

Chase believes the best measure of credit risk is the mark-to-market exposure amount of the derivative or foreign exchange contract. This is also referred to as repayment risk or the replacement cost.

While notional principal is the most commonly used volume measure in the derivative and foreign exchange markets, it is not a useful measure of credit or market risk. The notional principal typically does not change hands, but is simply a quantity upon which interest and other payments are calculated. The notional principal amounts of Chase's derivative and foreign exchange products greatly exceed the possible credit and market loss that could arise from such transactions.

The following table summarizes the aggregate notional amounts of derivative and foreign exchange contracts as well as the credit exposure related to these instruments (after taking into account the effects of legally enforceable master netting agreements).

December 31 (in billions)	Notional Amounts[a]		Credit Exposure	
	1998	1997	1998	1997
Interest Rate Contracts				
Interest Rate Swaps				
Trading	$4,882.4	$3,206.0	$10.8	$14.0
ALM	97.8	98.2	0.3	0.6

December 31 (in billions)	Notional Amounts[a]		Credit Exposure	
	1998	1997	1998	1997
Futures, Forwards and Forward Rate Agreements				
Trading	2,090.0	1,643.7	0.4	0.3
ALM	74.6	42.6	–	–
Purchased Options				
Trading	443.8	316.1	1.5	1.7
ALM	52.6	13.1	–	–
Written Options				
Trading	503.2	395.7	–	–
ALM	27.5	0.2	–	–
Total Interest Rate Contracts	$8,171.9	$5,715.6	$13.0	$16.6
Foreign Exchange Contracts				
Spot, Forward and Futures Contracts				
Trading	$1,532.6	$1,521.7	$11.0	$14.4
ALM	54.0	72.6	–	–
Other Foreign Exchange Contracts[b]				
Trading	449.8	358.7	5.0	5.8
ALM	4.2	5.2	–	–
Total Foreign Exchange Contracts	$2,040.6	$1,958.2	$16.0	$20.2
Debt, Equity, Commodity and Other Contracts				
Trading	$140.5	$64.4	$4.3	$1.6
Total Debt, Equity, Commodity and Other Contracts	$140.5	$64.4	$4.3	$1.6
Total Credit Exposure Recorded on the Balance Sheet			$33.3	$38.4

[a] The notional amounts of exchange-traded interest rate contracts, foreign exchange contracts, and equity, commodity and other contracts were $699.3 billion, $3.3 billion and $3.9 billion, respectively, at December 31, 1998, compared with $691.2 billion, $22.8 billion and $6.1 billion, respectively, at December 31, 1997. The credit risk for these contracts was minimal as exchange-traded contracts principally settle daily in cash.

[b] Includes notional amounts of purchased options, written options and cross-currency interest rate swaps of $137.0 billion, $137.9 billion and $179.1 billion, respectively, at December 31, 1998, compared with $123.9 billion, $126.6 billion and $113.4 billion, respectively, at December 31, 1997.

Classes of Derivative and Foreign Exchange Instruments

The following instruments are used by Chase for purposes of both trading and ALM activities.

Derivative and foreign exchange instruments may be broadly categorized as exchange-traded or over-the-counter ("OTC"). Exchange-traded instruments are executed through a recognized exchange as standardized contracts, and are primarily futures and options. OTC contracts are executed between two counterparties who negotiate specific agreement terms, including the underlying instrument, notional amount, exercise price and maturity. In this context the underlying instrument may include interest rates, foreign exchange rates, commodities, debt or equity instruments.

Interest rate swaps are contracts in which a series of interest rate flows in a single currency are exchanged over a prescribed period. Interest rate swaps are the most common type of derivative contract that Chase utilizes for both assets and liabilities. An example of a situation in which Chase would utilize an interest rate swap would be to convert its fixed-rate debt to a variable rate. By entering into the swap, the principal amount of the debt would remain unchanged but the interest streams would change. Cross-currency interest rate swaps are contracts that generally involve the exchange of both interest and principal amounts in two different currencies.

Interest rate futures and forwards are contracts for the delayed delivery of securities or money market instruments. The selling party agrees to deliver on a specified future date, a specified instrument, at a specified price or yield.

Forward rate agreements are contracts to exchange payments on a specified future date, based on a market change in interest rates from trade date to contract settlement date.

Interest rate options, including caps and floors, are contracts to modify interest rate risk in exchange for the payment of a premium when the contract is initiated. As a writer of interest rate options, Chase receives a premium in exchange for bearing the risk of unfavorable changes in interest rates. Conversely, as a purchaser of an option, Chase pays a premium for the right, but not the obligation, to buy or sell a financial instrument or currency at predetermined terms in the future. Foreign currency options are similar to interest rate options, except that they are based on foreign exchange rates.

Chase's use of written options as part of its ALM activities is permitted only in those circumstances where they are specifically linked to purchased options. All unmatched written options are included in the trading portfolio at fair value.

Foreign exchange contracts are used for the future receipt or delivery of foreign currency at previously agreed-upon terms.

Debt, equity, commodity and other contracts include swaps and options and are similar to interest rate contracts, except that the underlying instrument is debt, equity or commodity-related. Credit derivatives are considered debt-related and are included in this category of derivatives.

These instruments are all subject to market risk, representing potential loss due to adverse movements in the underlying instrument. Credit risk arises primarily from OTC contracts, since exchange-traded contracts are generally settled daily.

Market risk is reduced by entering into offsetting positions using other financial instruments.

Credit risk is reduced significantly by entering into legally enforceable master netting agreements. To further reduce exposure, management may deem it necessary to obtain collateral. The amount and nature of the collateral obtained is based on management's credit evaluation of the customer. Collateral held varies, but may include cash, securities, accounts receivable, inventory, property, plant and equipment and real estate.

Texas Instruments
2004 Annual Report

9. Financial Instruments and Risk Concentration

Financial Instruments: The carrying amounts and related estimated fair values of the Company's significant financial instruments at December 31, 2004 and 2003 were:

	December 31, 2004		December 31, 2003	
	Carrying Value	Fair Value	Carrying Value	Fair Value
Assets/(liabilities)				
Long-term debt[a]	$(379)	$(394)	$(826)	$(871)
Forward purchase contract[b]	2	2	3	3
Interest rate swaps[c]	13	13	32	32

[a] Fair value of long-term debt was determined primarily by calculating the net present value of the expected cash flows using current market interest rates.

[b] The Company uses a forward purchase contract for shares of the Company's common stock to minimize the adverse earnings impact from the effect of stock market value fluctuations on the portion of the Company's deferred compensation obligations denominated in TI stock. Fair value was based on quoted market price of TI common stock. (See Note 14 for discussion of Deferred Compensation Arrangements.)

[c] The Company uses interest rate swaps on long-term debt to change the characteristics of the interest rate payments from fixed rates to short-term variable rates. Fair value was determined by calculating the net present value of the expected cash flows using current market interest rates and represents current market settlement values.

The Company has other derivative financial instruments such as call options embedded in a convertible note, investment warrants and forward currency exchange contracts, the carrying value and fair values of which were not significant as of December 31, 2004 or 2003. The forward currency exchange contracts outstanding at December 31, 2004 had a notional or face value of $270 million to hedge net balance sheet exposures (including $139 million to buy euros, $28 million to buy Taiwan dollars, and $28 million to sell Japanese yen). At December 31, 2003, the Company had forward currency exchange contracts outstanding with a notional or face value of $315 million to hedge net balance sheet exposures (including $223 million to buy euros, $25 million to buy Taiwan dollars, and $16 million to sell pound sterling). Short-term cash investments are carried at fair value. The carrying values for other current financial assets and liabilities, such as accounts receivable and accounts payable, approximate fair value due to the short maturity of such instruments.

Risk Concentration: Financial instruments that potentially subject the Company to concentrations of credit risk are primarily cash investments, accounts receivable and equity investments. The Company places its cash investments in investment-grade debt securities and limits the amount of credit exposure to any one commercial issuer.

Concentrations of credit risk with respect to the receivables are limited due to the large number of customers in the Company's customer base and their dispersion across different industries and geographic areas. The Company maintains an allowance for losses based upon the expected collectibility of accounts receivable.

In order to minimize its exposure to credit risk, the Company limits its counterparties on the forward currency exchange contracts and interest rate swaps to investment-grade rated financial institutions.

TRW
2001 Annual Report

Financial Instruments

Fair values of financial instruments—at December 31

(In millions)	2001 Carrying Value	2001 Fair Value	2000 Carrying Value	2000 Fair Value
Cash and cash equivalents	$ 240	$ 240	$ 267	$ 1267
Short-term debt	115	115	1,450	1,450
Floating rate long-term debt	815	813	492	489
Fixed rate long-term debt	4,779	4,807	4,762	4,439
Foreign currency forward contracts–(liability) asset	(46)	(46)	12	11
Interest rate swaps–(liability)	(11)	(11)	–	(6)
Forward share sale agreements–(liability)				
Liability portion	(212)	(227)	(197)	(205)
Hedge portion	144	144	121	101

The fair value of long-term debt was estimated using a discounted cash flow analysis based on the Company's current borrowing rates for similar types of borrowing arrangements. The fair value of interest rate hedges was estimated based on quoted market prices of offsetting contracts. The fair value of the foreign currency forward contracts was estimated using a discounted cash flow analysis based on quoted market prices of offsetting contracts. The fair value of the liability portion of the forward share sale agreements was estimated using a discounted cash flow analysis. The hedge portion was valued by analyzing the floor and ceiling options with a BlackScholes option pricing model.

At December 31, 2001, the Company had hedging relationships designated as cash flow hedges which were as follows:

Foreign currency forward contracts—The Company manufactures and sells its products in countries throughout the world. As a result, it is exposed to fluctuations in foreign currency exchange rates. The Company enters into forward contracts and, to a lesser extent, purchased currency options to hedge portions of its foreign currency denominated forecasted revenues, purchases and the subsequent cash flows. The critical terms of the hedges are the same as the underlying forecasted transactions, and the hedges are considered to be perfectly effective to offset the changes in fair value of cash flows from the hedged transactions. Gains or losses on these instruments, which mature at various dates through April 2007, are generally recorded in other comprehensive income (loss) until the underlying transaction is recognized in net earnings. The earnings impact is reported in either sales, cost of sales, or other (income) expense-net, to match the underlying transaction.

The amount of gains and losses reclassified into net earnings in 2001 as a result of the discontinuance of cash flow hedges was immaterial. Foreign currency cash flow hedges with a combined fair value of a $5 million loss after tax at December 31, 2001 are expected to be recognized in net earnings in 2002.

In addition, the Company enters into certain foreign currency forward contracts that are not treated as hedges under SFAS 133 to hedge recognized foreign currency transactions. Gains and losses on these contracts are recorded in net earnings and are substantially offset by the earnings effect of the revaluation of the underlying foreign currency denominated transaction.

Interest rate swap agreements—The Company enters into interest rate swaps to manage the risks and costs associated with its financing activities. The net payments or receipts under the agreements are recognized as an adjustment to interest expense. At December 31, 2001, the Company had $100 million notional principal amount of interest rate swaps outstanding that converted a portion of its variable rate debt to a fixed rate through August 2005. The agreements were entered into with major financial institutions. No collateral is held in relation to the interest rate swaps, and the Company anticipates that the financial institutions will satisfy their obligations under the agreements.

Forward share sale agreements—The Company hedges certain equity investments in publicly traded companies. These instruments protect the forecasted cash flows resulting from the sale of shares in the Company's investments in RF Micro Devices, Inc. (RFMD) and Applera Corporation-Celera Genomics Group (Celera).

In 2000, the Company monetized a portion of its holdings in RFMD through the execution of three forward share sale agreements. The Company received cash proceeds of $168 million in consideration for its agreement to deliver up to 4 million shares of RFMD common stock, in the aggregate, upon maturity of the contracts. Also in 2000, the Company similarly monetized its holdings of 229,354 shares in Celera through an agreement maturing in December 2003. The Company received cash proceeds of $18.6 million in consideration for its agreement to deliver up to 229,354 shares of Celera common stock, in the aggregate, upon maturity of the contract. The actual number of shares to be delivered will be determined on the basis of a formula in the agreements. Through the setting of a floor and ceiling price, these agreements eliminate the Company's exposure to downside market risk, while enabling the Company to retain potential market appreciation up to the respective ceiling price. Certain terms of the agreements are summarized below:

	RFMD			Celera
Maturity dates	February 2003	August 2003	February 2004	December 2003
Number of shares	1,333,334	1,333,334	1,333,332	229,354
Floor price per share	$54	$54	$54	$102
Ceiling price per share	79	86	93	176
Up-front proceeds as a percent of floor price	80%	78%	75%	80%

The investment in RFMD and Celera and the related hedge portion of the forward share sale agreements are carried at fair market value. Changes in fair market value of the Company's shares of RFMD and Celera, including the shares monetized, are recorded in the other comprehensive income (loss) component of shareholders' investment. Any gains or losses reported in other comprehensive income (expense) will be reclassified to net earnings at the maturity of these agreements.

The Company sold 18.7 million shares of RFMD for $453 million in 2001 and 5.3 million shares for $225 million in 2000. At December 31, 2001, the Company owned approximately 4.5 million shares, including the 4 million shares pledged to secure its obligations under the forward share sale agreements. The fair value of the RFMD shares at December 31, 2001 and 2000, excluding the effect of the forward share sale agreements, was approximately $89 million and $635 million, respectively. The fair value of the Celera shares at December 31, 2001 and 2000, excluding the effect of the forward share sale agreement, was approximately $6 million and $8 million, respectively. Both investments are included in the Balance Sheets in investments in affiliated companies. During 2001, these hedges on forward share sales agreements were redesignated to cash flow hedges. Prior to their redesignation, a $10 million gain representing the hedges' ineffectiveness was recorded in other (income) expense-net. The fair market value of these hedges as of December 31, 2001 was a $144 million gain.

The following table represents the movement of amounts reported in other comprehensive income(loss) of deferred cash flow hedges, net of tax.

(In millions)	2001
Balance at December 31, 2000	$ –
Net change in derivative fair value and other movements during the year	(10)
Amounts reclassified to earnings during the year	8
Other comprehensive income(loss)	$ (2)

Hershey Foods
2004 Annual Report

8. Financial Instruments

The carrying amounts of financial instruments including cash and cash equivalents, accounts receivable, accounts payable and short-term debt approximated fair value as of December 31, 2004 and 2003, because of the relatively short maturity of these instruments. The carrying value of long-term debt, including the current portion, was $969.6 million as of December 31, 2004, compared to a fair value of $1,094.3 million based on quoted market prices for the same or similar debt issues. The carrying value of long-term debt, including the current portion, was $969.0 million as of December 31, 2003, compared to a fair value of $1,100.9 million.

As of December 31, 2004, the Company had foreign exchange forward contracts and options maturing in 2005 and 2006 to purchase $103.1 million in foreign currency, primarily Australian dollars, Canadian dollars, and euros, and to sell $30.8 million in foreign currency, primarily Mexican pesos and Japanese yen, at contracted forward rates.

As of December 31, 2003, the Company had foreign exchange forward contracts and options maturing in 2004 and 2005 to purchase $57.7 million in foreign currency, primarily Canadian dollars, and to sell $18.0 million in foreign currency, primarily Japanese yen, at contracted forward rates.

The fair value of foreign exchange forward contracts and options is estimated by obtaining quotes for future contracts with similar terms, adjusted where necessary for maturity differences. The fair value of foreign exchange forward contracts and options included in prepaid expenses and other current assets was $4.4 million and $1.6 million as of December 31, 2004 and 2003, respectively. The Company does not hold or issue financial instruments for trading purposes.

In order to minimize its financing costs and to manage interest rate exposure, the Company, from time to time, centers into interest rate swap agreements. In October 2003, the Company entered into interest rate swap agreements to effectively convert interest payments on long-term debt from fixed to variable rates. Interest payments on $200.0 million of 6.7% Notes due in October 2005 and $150.0 million of 6.95% Notes due in March 2007 were converted from the respective fixed rates to variable rates based on LIBOR. In March 2004, the Company terminated these agreements, resulting in cash receipts totaling $5.2

million, with a corresponding increase to the carrying value of the long-term debt. This increase is being amortized over the remaining term of the respective long-term debt as a reduction to interest expense.

In February 2001, the Company entered into interest rate swap agreements that effectively converted variable-interest-rate payments on certain leases from a variable to a fixed rate of 6.1%. The fair value of variable to fixed interest rate swaps was a liability of $1.7 million and $5.2 million as of December 31, 2004 and 2003, respectively.

Varian Inc.
2005 Annual Report

Note 5. Forward Exchange Contract

The Company enters into foreign exchange forward contracts to minimize the short-term impact of foreign currency fluctuations on assets and liabilities de-nominated in non-functional currencies. These contracts are accounted for under SFAS 133, *Accounting for Derivative Instruments and Hedging Activities.* The Company records these contracts at fair value with the related gains and losses recorded in selling, general and administrative expenses. The gains and losses on these contracts are substantially offset by transaction losses and gains on the underlying balance being hedged.

From time to time, the Company also enters into foreign exchange forward contracts to minimize the impact of foreign currency fluctuations on forecasted transactions. These contracts are designated as cash flow hedges under SFAS 133. There were no outstanding foreign exchange forward contracts designated as cash flow hedges of forecasted transactions as of September 30, 2005 or October 1, 2004. In addition, no foreign exchange gains or losses from hedge ineffective-ness were recognized during fiscal years 2005 or 2004. During fiscal year 2003, a loss of $0.1 million from hedge ineffectiveness was recognized and included in selling, general and administrative expenses.

The Company's foreign exchange forward contracts generally range from one to 12 months in original maturity. A summary of all foreign exchange forward contracts that were outstanding as of September 30, 2005 follows:

	Notional Value Sold	Notional Value Purchased
(In thousands)		
Euro	$ –	$ –
British pound	20,050	10,105
Australian dollar	–	(1,544)
Canadian dollar	5,789	$ 9,207
Japanese yen	1,832	–
Danish krone	1,197	–
Swiss franc	–	925
Total	$ 28,868	$ 52,982

Corning
2005 Annual Report

We operate and conduct business in many foreign countries and as a result are exposed to movements in foreign currency exchange rates. Our exposure to exchange rate effects includes:

- exchange rate movements on financial instruments and transactions denominated in foreign currencies which impact earnings, and

- exchange rate movements upon conversion of net assets in foreign subsidiaries for which the functional currency is not the U.S. dollar, which impact our net equity.

Our most significant foreign currency exposures relate to Japan, Korea, Taiwan and western European countries. We selectively enter into foreign exchange forward and option contracts with durations generally 15 months or less to hedge our exposure to exchange rate risk on foreign source income and purchases. The hedges are scheduled to mature coincident with the timing of the underlying foreign currency commitments and transactions. The objective of these contracts is to neutralize the impact of exchange rate movements on our operating results.

We engage in foreign currency hedging activities to reduce the risk that changes in exchange rates will adversely affect the eventual net cash flows resulting from the sale of products to foreign customers and purchases from foreign suppliers. The hedge contracts reduce the exposure to fluctuations in exchange rate movements because the gains and losses associated with foreign currency balances and transactions are generally offset with gains and losses of the hedge contracts. Because the impact of movements in foreign exchange rates on the value of hedge contracts offsets the related impact on the underlying items being hedged, these financial instruments help alleviate the risk that might otherwise result from currency exchange rate fluctuations.

The following table summarizes the notional amounts and respective fair values of Corning's derivative financial instruments, which mature at varying dates, at December 31, 2005 (in millions):

	Notional Amount	Fair Value
Foreign exchange forward contracts	$ 829	$ 11
Foreign exchange option contracts	$ 374	$ 10

The forward and option contracts we use in managing our foreign currency exposures contain an element of risk in that the counterparties may be unable to meet the terms of the agreements. However, we minimize this risk by limiting the counterparties to a diverse group of highly-rated major domestic and international financial institutions with which we have other financial relationships. We are exposed to potential losses in the event of non-performance by these counterparties; however, we do not expect to record any losses as a result of counterparty default. We do not require and are not required to place collateral for these financial instruments.

In the second quarter of 2005, Corning began using derivative instruments (forwards) to limit the exposure to foreign currency fluctuations associated with certain monetary assets and liabilities. These derivative instruments are not designated as hedging instruments for accounting purposes and, as such, are referred to as undesignated hedges.

Changes in the fair value of undesignated hedges are recorded in current period earnings in the other income, net component, along with the foreign currency gains and losses arising from the underlying monetary assets or liabilities, in the consolidated statement of operations. At December 31, 2005, the notional amount of the undesignated derivatives was $366 million.

Cash Flow Hedges

Corning has cash flow hedges that relate to foreign exchange forward and option contracts. The critical terms of each cash flow hedge are identical to the critical terms of the hedged item. Therefore, Corning utilizes the critical terms test under SFAS 133, "Accounting for Derivative Instruments and Hedging Activities" (SFAS 133), and the presumption is that there is no hedge ineffectiveness as long as the critical terms of the hedge and the hedged item do not change. During the life of each hedge, the critical terms of the hedge and the hedged item did not change. We did not have any gain or loss from hedge ineffectiveness. We did not exclude any components of a hedge's gain or loss from the assessment of hedge effectiveness.

Corning defers net gains and losses from cash flow hedges into accumulated other comprehensive income (loss) on the consolidated balance sheet, until such time as the hedged item impacts earnings. At that time Corning reclassifies net gains and losses from cash flow hedges into the same line item of the consolidated statement of operations as where the effects of the hedged item are recorded, typically sales or cost of sales. Amounts are reclassified from accumulated other comprehensive income (loss) when the underlying hedged item impacts earnings. At December 31, 2005, the amount of net gains expected to be reclassified into earnings within the next 12 months is $22 million.

Fair Value Hedges

In March and April of 2002, we entered into three interest rate swaps that are fair value hedges and economically exchanged a notional amount of $275 million of fixed rate long-term debt to floating rate debt. Under the terms of the swap agreements, we paid the counterparty a floating rate that is indexed to the six month LIBOR rate and received the fixed rates of 8.3% to 8.875%, which are the stated interest rates on the long-term debt instruments. As a result of these transactions, Corning was exposed to the impact of interest rate changes.

Each fair value hedge (swap) had identical terms to the critical terms of the hedged item. Therefore, Corning utilized the short-cut method allowed under FAS 133 which presumes that there is no hedge ineffectiveness as long as the critical terms of the hedge and the hedged item do not change. During the life of each hedge, the critical terms of the hedge and the hedged item did not change. We did not have any gain or loss from hedge ineffectiveness.

We did not exclude any components of a hedge's gain or loss from the assessment of hedge ineffectiveness.

In 2004 and 2003, we terminated the interest rate swap agreements described above. The termination of these swaps resulted in gains of $5 million in 2004 and $15 million in 2003 which we will amortize to earnings as a reduction of interest expense over the remaining life of the debt. The cash proceeds from the termination of the swaps total $8 million in 2004 and $17 million in 2003 and are included in the financing section of our consolidated statement of cash flows.

Corning records net gains and losses from fair value hedges into the same line item of the consolidated statement of operations as where the effects of the hedged item are recorded.

Net Investment in Foreign Operations

We have issued foreign currency denominated debt that has been designated as a hedge of the net investment in a foreign operation. The effective portion of the changes in fair value of the debt is reflected as a component of other accumulated comprehensive income (loss) as part of the foreign currency translation adjustment. Net losses included in the cumulative translation adjustment at December 31, 2005 and 2004, were $107 million and $166 million, respectively.

Chapter 18
International Financial Reporting Standards (IFRS): An Examination of Accounting Convergence

CONTENTS

For several years, major accounting and reporting differences have existed between U.S. GAAP and international reporting standards.[*] However, in a 2002 Memorandum of Understanding (MOU) between the Financial Accounting Standards Board (FASB) and the International Accounting Standards Board (IASB), commonly known as the "Norwalk Agreement" (http://72.3.243.42/news/memorandum.pdf), the two accounting standard-setting bodies made a firm

[*] This chapter was authored by Benjamin Silliman, CPA, Associate Professor of Accounting and Taxation at St. John's University, Queens, NY

commitment to develop high quality accounting standards that converge. In effect, this effort has been a movement toward a globalization of accounting standards. In this MOU, the two boards agreed to several joint projects in an effort to converge accounting standards. Since the Norwalk Agreement, the FASB and IASB have issued new standards that closely converged and revised many existing ones in order to attain a near-uniform set of accounting standards. While the challenge for practitioners is to learn and eventually implement this new set of global accounting standards, the benefits of a single set of worldwide standards is expected to produce financial reporting that is more comparable, transparent, and achieves greater understandability. The American Institute of Certified Public Accountants (AICPA) amended Rules 202 and 203 of the AICPA Code of Professional Conduct by inserting the IASB into the allowable rules.

As of this writing, the SEC has temporarily halted early implementation of IFRS. In the United States, registered companies were scheduled to issue financial statements using IFRS in 2014 as part of a proposed "road map." The original timeline for IFRS convergence with U.S. GAAP is as follows: U.S. companies registered with the United States Securities and Exchange Commission (SEC) are currently required to file financial statements in accordance with U.S. generally accepted accounting principles (GAAP). In 2008, foreign private issuers were allowed to issue financial statements in accordance with IFRS without footnote reconciliation to U.S. GAAP. On August 27, 2008, the SEC then voted unanimously to adopt a road map for conversion of accounting standards, thus implementing IFRS in the United States by as early as 2010 and requiring all companies to file financial statements under IFRS by 2014. However, on February 24, 2010, the SEC withdrew proposed rules that would have allowed early implementation of IFRS and announced it would table the decision until 2011. In addition, the SEC indicated that it was not ruling out the possibility that registered companies could be permitted to select to issue financial statements using U.S. GAAP or IFRS [*Originally, in January 2009, the SEC had announced that registered companies were required to file with a two-year dual-reporting beginning in 2012; by 2014, all large U.S. companies were required to file financial statements using IFRS, with smaller U.S. companies delaying IFRS filing until 2016*]. SEC Chairman Mary Schapiro formally announced that the Commission was expected to issue its recommendation sometime in 2011. As of this writing, no action has been taken by the SEC.

As this chapter goes to print, the FASB-IASB joint project has realized progress as well as some modest delays, as convergence was scheduled for completion in early 2011. The boards recently issued new guidance on fair value measurement and disclosure requirements in May 2011 (ASC 820), and have partially completed the joint conceptual framework project in October 2010. On June 16, 2011, the FASB announced the issuance of an updated standard on the presentation of comprehensive income (ASC 220), which will briefly be addressed in this chapter. However, the movement toward convergence has slowed somewhat due to the boards' inability to reach a conclusion on remaining guidance from the joint project, including revenue recognition, insurance contracts, leases, and financial instruments. These projects were expected to be concluded by the end of the June 2011, but have been delayed. Furthermore, the

FASB-IASB re-exposed the revenue recognition proposals on June 15, 2011, in order to allow for comment on some remaining issues. It is, therefore, not known if these delays will keep the SEC from taking action on IFRS implementation until the components of the FASB-IASB joint project are resolved.

In an effort to better understand how convergence will affect financial reporting in the United States, depending on the IFRS implementation action taken by the SEC, this chapter examines some of the material differences that currently exist between U.S. GAAP and IFRS.

REQUIRED FINANCIAL STATEMENTS AND STRUCTURAL DIFFERENCES IN PRIMARY FINANCIAL REPORTING

Financial statements required under U.S. GAAP and IFRS are somewhat similar. IFRS require a Statement of Financial Position similar to U.S. GAAP, but its format is not based on order of liquidity of assets, an income statement, a Statement of Changes in Equity or a Statement of Recognized Income and Expense (reported as a separate financial statement), Statement of Cash Flows, and disclosure notes including a Summary of Significant Accounting Policies. Under U.S. GAAP, comprehensive income and changes in equity are reported as a separate financial statement (allowable under IFRS—and is reported as a Statement of Changes in Equity) or reported in the notes to the financial statements (not allowed under IFRS). However, U.S. GAAP allows for a combined statement of income and comprehensive income, which is not allowed under IFRS.

Unlike U.S. GAAP, IFRS require comparative information on each financial statement for the preceding period only, with the option of providing additional years of comparable reporting. SEC registrants are required to present current and prior years information on the balance sheet, while other financial statements are required to report three years of comparable results.

In addition, in regard to consolidated financial reporting, under U.S. GAAP, the parent firm must present consolidated financial statements. However, IFRS allows for exemptions if the parent is a wholly owned or partially owned subsidiary, the parent does not trade bond or equity instruments in the public market, or it did not file (or will not file) financial statements with a regulatory agency.

Lastly, U.S. GAAP currently allows both multi-step and single-step income statement formats, whereas under IFRS, the single-step format is not used. In addition, U.S. GAAP defines the four elements on an income statement as revenues, expenses, gains and losses, while IFRS provides only two elements, income and expenses. In addition, under IFRS, revenues and gains are reported as income, which increase economic benefits; and expenses include both expenses and losses, which decrease economic benefits. With the IFRS approach, all items are reported as income from operations, therefore, ignoring unusual or irregular activity. Extraordinary item reporting is prohibited under IFRS, whereas discontinued operations reporting is allowed, with some differences to U.S. GAAP. In addition, U.S. GAAP presents expenses using a functional classification, which is required by the SEC, while on IFRS-produced income statements, expenses are presented using a nature of expense classification, which prohibit allocations and requires more specificity.

Financial Statement Presentation—Joint Project of the FASB and IASB

In addition to the current structure of financial reporting under U.S. GAAP and IFRS, one of the goals contained in a 2007 Memorandum of Understanding was to develop a common standard for financial statement presentation that focuses on relationships across financial statements, disaggregating information on each financial statement to allow for better efforts of predicting an operation's future cash flows, and to improve a user's ability to assess an entity's liquidity and financial strength. While two of the three phases have been completed, the proposed changes will affect financial reporting in the United States and world-wide when convergence of standards occurs beginning in 2011.

Phase A of the project proposes four financial statements and requires no less than two years of comparative data to be presented in such statements. The proposed financial statements include: a Statement of Comprehensive Income, a Statement of Financial Position, a Statement of Cash Flows, and a Statement of Changes in Equity. While many of the features of financial reporting will continue, the proposal recommends including a new parallel classification structure across three of the four proposed financial statements (excluding the Changes in Equity Statement). *Phase B* of the project led the two boards to issue three proposed objectives of information that should be presented in financial statements "in a manner that":

☐ Portrays a cohesive financial picture of an entity's activities, which means "that the relationship between items across financial statements is clear and that an entity's financial statements complement each other as much as possible."

☐ Assists users in assessing future cash flows by "assessing the amount, timing, and uncertainty of future cash flows" by requiring that financial information be "disaggregated reasonably homogeneous groups of items"; however, should items differ economically, users may report "differently in predicting future cash flows."

☐ Helps users assess an entity's liquidity and financial flexibility by providing information concerning liquidity, which will assist users in assessing the entity's ability to "meet its financial commitments as they become due . . . [and allows users to assess] the entity's ability to invest in business opportunities and respond to unexpected needs."

The Statements of Comprehensive Income, Financial Position, and Cash Flows will each contain a Business section, which will report operating activities and investing activities of the specific statement. For example, the Statement of Comprehensive Income's Business section will contain operating income and expenses as well as investing income and expenses; the Statement of Financial Position's Business section will report operating assets and liabilities, and investing assets and liabilities.

In addition to the Business section, in three of the four statements (excluding the Changes in Equity Statement), a Financing section is provided as well as a section on taxes and discontinued operations (net of taxes). There are many other provisions in the proposed structure of the financial statements, which is in its preliminary stage and no final outcome has been determined; the joint project (IASB and FASB) staff are currently reviewing public responses to the proposed financial statements as this book goes to press. Current information on the status of the proposed financial statements and other issues regarding the joint project may be accessed at: http://www.fasb.org/project/financial statement_presentation.shtml.

IFRS DIFFERENCES AFFECTING THE STATEMENT OF FINANCIAL POSITION

Cash and Cash Equivalents

Cash and cash equivalents are defined similarly under IFRS and U.S. GAAP. However, U.S. GAAP does not allow bank overdraft offsets to the cash account and reports them as a liability. The only exception where offsetting is allowable is in the case of two accounts held by the same bank; an overdrawn account may be offset against another account in the same institution. IFRS allows offsetting of overdrafts to cash as long as it is integral to the entity's cash management.

Receivables

Under U.S. GAAP, receivables are not reported at fair value. However, under IFRS they are initially reported at fair value, with subsequent adjustments accounted for using amortized cost (effective interest method). In addition, under U.S. GAAP, an estimate of bad debts impacts earnings on the income statement. When a receivable is deemed uncollectible using the allowance method for accounting for bad debts, the write-off of the specific account does not impact earnings; any recovery of a previously written-off account also does not impact earnings. Under IFRS, impairment losses previously recognized on the income statement may be reversed in subsequent years, adjusting earnings. U.S. GAAP prohibits reversals of impairment losses on bad debts.

In the case of derecognition of receivables, two transaction scenarios can occur. Under the first, a concern can sell (factor) a receivable to another company, transferring all of the risks and rewards of ownership, warranting derecognition of the receivable by the transferor. Under the second scenario, if a receivable no longer possesses any contractual rights to future cash flows, derecognition is warranted and the receivable is removed from the balance sheet. Under U.S. GAAP, a receivable is derecognized when there exists a loss of control of the receivable, whereas under IFRS, if substantially all of the risks and rewards are not transferred, the receivable is treated as a secured borrowing. U.S. GAAP disallows partial derecognition of receivables.

Inventories

U.S. GAAP generally measures inventory at lower of cost or market; under IFRS, inventory is measured at lower of cost or net realizable value (estimated selling price less estimated costs of completion and sale). IFRS includes distribution and marketing costs in its cost of sales, whereas U.S. GAAP excludes marketing costs in determining cost of sale.

Inventory write-downs under GAAP are normally determined either on an item-by-item, group, or categorical basis. IFRS writes inventory down to net realizable value (floor) on an item-by-item basis, but allows write-downs to occur by groups of similar products in special circumstances. In addition, any inventory write-downs under U.S. GAAP cannot subsequently be reversed, whereas IFRS allows previous inventory write-down reversals to be recognized in the same period as the write-down.

U.S. GAAP allows for the cost of inventory to be calculated using FIFO, LIFO, or a weighted-average calculation. IFRS allows FIFO and weighted-average, but prohibits use of LIFO.

Investments

Accounting for trading, available-for-sale, and held-to-maturity instruments is similar between U.S. GAAP and IFRS. One clarifying difference is that under IFRS, securities are called "assets," which is a much broader category. As with securities (asset) classification, under IFRS, any non-trading financial asset is classified as available-for-sale; under U.S. GAAP, only debt securities and marketable equity securities are classified as available-for-sale investments. Another major difference exists with unrealized gains and losses of available-for-sale securities, which are reported in comprehensive income under U.S. GAAP, whereas under IFRS, such gains and losses are reported in the equity section of the balance sheet. In addition, IFRS allows for impairment reversals for only available-for-sale debt (not equity) securities and held-to-maturity securities, while U.S. GAAP does not permit impairment reversals of any investments.

Another key difference is with debt security impairment. Under U.S. GAAP, a debt security is classified as other than temporarily impaired (OTTI) if the entity has the positive intent to sell an impaired debt security, or if the entity does not expect to recover the full amortized cost basis of the security and more likely than not the concern will be required to sell the security prior to its recovery, or if the debt security has a credit loss. Under IFRS, a debt security is deemed to be impaired if there is objective evidence of impairment and the estimated future cash flows if the security is adversely affected. IFRS requires that impairment losses on debt securities are recognized in current earnings, whereas U.S. GAAP records other-than-temporarily impaired debt securities in other comprehensive income. Lastly, under U.S. GAAP, an equity security is other-than-temporarily impaired if the decline is considered significant *and* prolonged, whereas under IFRS, impairment is recorded if the decline is significant *or* prolonged. Note that as of this writing, the FASB-IFRS joint project dealing with financial instruments is expected to be issued in the third quarter of 2011 and may converge many of these differences as well as introduce new treatments.

Equity-Method Investments

Both U.S. GAAP and IFRS account for investments where the investor possesses significant influence over the investee, holding at least 20% and up to 50% of an investee's outstanding stock, lacking control over the entity. IFRS refers to an equity investment as an investment in associates. Additionally, IFRS requires that the investee and investor firms follow the same accounting policies, where U.S. GAAP does not require such a practice.

Property, Plant and Equipment

In general, U.S. GAAP and IFRS treat the accounting for property, plant and equipment similarly, including the initial accounting for all costs necessary to bring the asset to its intended use. Under IFRS, IAS 16.16(b) describes costs of property, plant and equipment as "any costs directly attributable to bring an asset to the location and condition necessary for it to be capable of operating in a manner intended by management." Additionally, there are no differences in depreciation methods used. Differences exist primarily in the treatment of capitalized interest, the components approach for depreciation, and the subsequent revaluation of the asset's fair value.

Interest incurred is capitalized under U.S. GAAP only during construction of a qualifying asset. Under IFRS, interest costs of borrowing may either be capitalized for the acquisition, construction, or production of a qualifying asset or expensed in the period incurred. Whichever method selected must be consistently applied.

IAS 16 requires that upon initial recognition of a depreciable asset, costs are allocated to significant components of the assets (including non-physical components). Each component is then separately depreciated. For example, a roof would be one component and the remainder of the structure would be a separate component—each having different useful lives and depreciated separately. In addition, subsequent expenditures must be capitalized to the asset as long as probable future economic benefits will flow to the entity and the costs can be reliably measured. U.S. GAAP does not follow the components approach to depreciation.

Another difference between U.S. GAAP and IFRS is in the revaluation of property, plant and equipment. U.S. GAAP requires property, plant and equipment be accounted for using the cost method. Under IFRS, property, plant and equipment is reported on a company's books at fair value less accumulated depreciation and impairment losses (if any). The accumulated depreciation account is used to revalue plant and equipment with the permission of two treatments, which use a revaluation surplus account. When a depreciable asset is revalued, depreciation is also revalued over the remaining useful life of the asset.

IAS 16 allows for two revaluation alternatives: Revaluation of specific assets regularly or revaluation of assets of the same class. When revaluation occurs under IFRS, and the revaluation requires a write-up (increase) to the asset (assuming no previous downward revaluation), the asset is debited and the incremental increase is credited to a surplus account (revaluation surplus account), which is an equity account. If there is a write-down (decrease) to the asset (assuming no previous upward revaluation), such downward revaluation is debited to an expense and the asset's book value is credited. If there had been a previous upward revaluation (causing surplus recognition) and a current downward revaluation occurs, the write-down cannot exceed the amount in the revaluation surplus account. Examples of a land revaluation are provided below.

EXAMPLE

Assume in Year 1, QRS Corp. owns land costing $500,000 with a current fair value of $550,000. The journal entry to adjust the book value of the land to reflect its fair value is:

Land	50,000	
Revaluation surplus—Land		50,000

Any subsequent decreases in the fair value of the land would be offset against the revaluation surplus account, with any excess charged to an expense.

EXAMPLE

Assume in the following year (Year 2), the fair value of QRS Corp.'s land has decreased to $480,000. The journal entry to adjust the book value of the land to reflect its fair value (with previous upward revaluation) is:

Revaluation surplus—Land	50,000	
Loss on Revaluation—Land*	20,000	
Land		70,000

* The loss on revaluation is treated as an expense of the period.

For previous revaluation that had resulted in the recognition of an expense, any subsequent revaluations resulting in an increase to the fair value of the asset, such incremental increases should be recognized as income to the extent of the previously recognized expense; any excess revaluation increase would be credited to the revaluation surplus account.

EXAMPLE

Assume in Year 3, the fair value of QRS Corp.'s land is $510,000. Given that there was a recent downward revaluation in Year 2, the journal entry to adjust the book value of the land to reflect its fair value is:

Land	30,000	
Revaluation surplus—Land		10,000
Gain on revaluation—Land*		20,000

* The gain on revaluation is recognized as income in Year 3 to the extent of expense recognition in the previous year(s).

Revaluations Involving Depreciable Assets

When depreciable assets are revalued annually, IAS 16 allows for two permissible treatments. The first is offsetting accumulated depreciation against the gross book value of the depreciable asset, with the difference restated to reflect the revalued amount of the asset.

EXAMPLE

Assume KRF Corp. owns a building that cost $2,000,000 and has accumulated depreciation of $400,000, with a book value of $1,600,000. Assume KRF Corp. revalues the building to reflect its fair value of $1,800,000. Under this treatment, KRF Corp. would first remove its accumulated depreciation of $400,000, reducing the building by that amount of expired cost. Then, in the second entry, the building would be debited for $200,000 and the revaluation surplus credited, reflecting the net amount that is being restated. The entries are:

Accumulated depreciation—Building	400,000	
Building		400,000
Building	200,000	
Revaluation surplus—Building		200,000

The second permissible treatment is accumulated depreciation is proportionately restated with the change in the revalued asset; the result is the book value of the asset, after revaluation, equaling the revalued amount of the asset:

EXAMPLE

Assume KRF Corp. owns a building that cost $2,000,000 and has accumulated depreciation of $400,000, with a book value of $1,600,000. Assume KRF Corp. revalues the building to reflect its fair value of $1,800,000. KRF Corp. would restate the building account and accumulated depreciation based on the ratio of net book value to the revalued assets, which is 80% ($1,600,000/$2,000,000), and the entry is:

Building	250,000*	
Accumulated depreciation—Building		50,000
Revaluation surplus—Building		200,000

* $200,000 ÷ 80% = $250,000

The result of the above entry will provide a book value that equals the revalued amount of the building.

Intangible Assets and Goodwill

U.S. GAAP and IFRS are similar in their definition of an intangible asset, which lacks physical substance and is not viewed as a financial asset. In addition, U.S. GAAP and IFRS consider intangibles as identifiable assets if they are separable or as a result of contractual or legal rights. Goodwill, in particular, is viewed similarly by both as a residual that arises from a business combination and is not amortized but is tested annually for impairment. Some significant differences exist. While U.S. GAAP bases amortization of intangibles based on historical cost less any impairment, IFRS allows revaluation of the value of the intangible by crediting any upward revision to the asset to a revaluation surplus account and adjusted against equity; downward revisions to fair value reduce the revaluation surplus account (until the account declines to zero). In addition, impairment for intangibles is treated differently under U.S. GAAP and IFRS (see the Impairment section below).

Regarding research and development costs, such costs are segregated into two types: research phase costs and developmental phase costs. Under both U.S. GAAP and IFRS, research phase costs are expensed in the period incurred. Developmental phase costs are expensed in the period incurred under U.S. GAAP. Under IFRS, such costs are similarly expensed unless technological feasibility is achieved. If technical feasibility results, such development costs are capitalized only if there is an intention to complete the developed asset, if there exists an ability to either use or sell the asset, if future economic benefits are reasonably expected to result, and if the entity provides adequate resources to finish development of the asset. With regard to in-process research and development costs that are acquired as part of a business combination, U.S. GAAP and IFRS standards have converged, where acquired in-process research and development costs are capitalized and amortized, with annual testing for impairment.

Contingent Liabilities

U.S. GAAP and IFRS measure contingent liabilities similarly in that such a liability can only be recognized if the outcome is probable and can be reasonably estimated. However, IFRS contains a slight difference in estimating the contingent liability. While U.S. GAAP uses a more conservative (low-end) estimate in recording the liability, IFRS recognizes a contingent liability at the mid-point of the estimate range.

Defined Benefit Plans

Under U.S. GAAP, prior service costs are retroactive benefits from a plan amendment based on the expected future service life of such participants. These prior service costs are often amortized proportionately (or using straight-line) over the expected future period of service. IFRS uses the terminology *past service costs* and recognizes such costs using a straight-line basis over the average remaining service period until the amended benefits are vested. Therefore, under IFRS, entities are amortizing past service costs over a shorter period of time. Under IAS 19.96, should any past service costs be vested at the time the plan is amended, the entity must recognize them in the period of the amendment. U.S. GAAP makes no distinction whether the employees are vested or not vested.

Another area yet to be converged in regard to defined benefit plans is the issue of actuarial valuations and the measurement date. Under U.S. GAAP, actuarial valuations are required to be performed annually and are mandated by ERISA regulations. In addition, the measurement date for valuation of the plan assets and the projected benefit obligation is the balance sheet date, unless a specific event causes for re-measurement. Under IFRS, there is no mandate as to the frequency of actuarial valuations; however, IAS 19.77 requires valuation results to be updated as of the balance sheet date for any significant changes since the previous valuation.

In addition to prior (past) service cost treatment, there are differences in procedures on handling actuarial gains and losses. Actuarial gains and losses are the differences between the actual and expected result in the valuation of the projected benefit obligation and plan assets. U.S. GAAP and IFRS allow a choice for recognition of actuarial gains and losses. Under U.S. GAAP, any actuarial gains and losses measured can be reflected as part of Other Comprehensive Income (OCI) to the extent they are not recognized in earnings on the income statement. Alternatively, such gains and losses are permitted to be recognized in earnings in a systematic and rational method resulting in more rapid recognition than if the corridor method is used. Actuarial gains and losses that are recognized in Accumulated Other Comprehensive Income (AOCI) are reclassified to current earnings using a corridor approach (or using an alternative approach if it results in faster recognition). IFRS allows actuarial gains and losses to be either recognized completely in either OCI, in earnings of the period, or recognized in earnings using a corridor method (or using an alternative approach if it results in faster recognition).

U.S. GAAP also requires recognition of the funded status of the pension, either as a net pension asset or net pension liability. IFRS does not require funded status recognition on the balance sheet. As for asset ceilings, U.S. GAAP does not limit the amount of net pension assets, whereas under IFRS, the prepaid pension amount is limited by an asset ceiling.

Income Tax Deferrals

In accounting for deferred income tax differences, U.S. GAAP and IFRS use the asset and liability approach in recognizing future tax differences arising from present transactions. There are a few differences in approaches. First, U.S. GAAP's recognition of a deferred tax asset (or liability) is based on the assumption that the underlying asset or liability will eventually be reversed (recovered or settled) in a manner consistent with its use in the business. IFRS recognizes deferred taxes based on the expected manner of settlement or recovery. Second, U.S. GAAP employs an Asset Valuation account to the extent that it is *more likely than not* that the deferred tax asset will eventually be realized (reversed) at a future date. Under IFRS, a deferred tax asset is recognized if it is *probable* that it will eventually be realized (reversed) in the future. Therefore, IFRS has a higher recognition threshold.

Third, U.S. GAAP allows for a deferred tax asset or liability classification to be either current or noncurrent, based on the classification of the related asset or liability. IFRS instead classifies all deferred tax differences as noncurrent. Lastly, IFRS measures the deferred tax based on tax rates that are enacted or substantively enacted at the reporting date, whereas U.S. GAAP uses only the enacted tax rates at the reporting date (and ignores estimated future tax rate adjustments).

Fourth, one of the more relatively pervasive concerns is the temporary book-tax differences with regard to revaluations of property, plant, and equipment. IFRS requires that such temporary differences be recognized directly into equity; U.S. GAAP currently does not allow for such revaluations, so no deferred tax differences would exist.

Fifth, under U.S. GAAP, intercompany profits are derived using the seller's tax rate, whereas under IFRS, such intercompany profits are calculated using the buyer's tax rate. In addition, under U.S. GAAP, deferred tax liabilities are recognized on domestic subsidiaries if greater than 80%-owned; IFRS does not recognize deferred taxes for joint ventures or investments in subsidiaries if the parent controls the timing of the deferred tax reversal and it is probable that the temporary difference is not expected to immediately reverse. Finally, the last substantive difference exists with foreign nonmonetary assets. Under IFRS, deferred taxes are recognized for any differences related to foreign nonmonetary assets remeasured from the local to functional currency, whereas under U.S. GAAP, deferred taxes are not recognized for such functional currency remeasurements.

Lease Accounting

U.S. GAAP and IFRS recognize the economic substance of recording leases of both the lessor and lessee. However, there are some relatively significant differences in the accounting treatments. While U.S. GAAP refers to *capital lease* treatment, IFRS terminology refers to such leases as *finance leases*. Under U.S. GAAP, leased assets consist of only property, plant, and equipment, whereas under IFRS, the leased asset can consist of other types of assets including leases to explore mineral or natural resources and other licensing agreements (e.g., motion pictures, plays, and manuscripts). U.S. GAAP is more rules-based; for example, four criteria are used by the lessee and lessor (plus two required additional criteria for lessor) in determining if a lease should be capitalized. Many of these criteria are quantitative thresholds. IFRS similarly focuses on recording a lease where it transfers substantially all of the risks and rewards of ownership from the lessor to the lessee. Unlike the specific quantitative criteria under U.S. GAAP, IFRS provides a series of indicators that are used to determine if a lease is classified as a finance lease. This criteria determination is much more general than U.S. GAAP and is not rules-based.

Another difference involves the accounting for executory costs. U.S. GAAP expenses and excludes specific costs from the calculation of minimum lease payments, including insurance, maintenance and taxes, whereas IFRS excludes costs for services and taxes from minimum lease payments. Lastly, the present value of the minimum lease payment by the lessee are computed under U.S. GAAP as the *lower of* the lessor's implicit rate (if known by the lessee) or the lessee's incremental borrowing rate. IFRS uses the interest rate implicit in the lease if known by lessee. If the lessee lacks knowledge of such rate, then the lessee uses its incremental borrowing rate.

Equity

There are several differences in the classification of items in the equity section of the Statement of Financial Position under U.S. GAAP and IFRS. First, "common stock" is referred to as "share capital" under IFRS, "additional paid-in capital" is reported as "share premium" under IFRS, and "retained earnings" are often referred to as "accumulated profit and loss" or "retained profits." Similar to U.S. GAAP, treasury stock under IFRS is reported as a reduction to shareholders' equity; however, IFRS allows treasury stock amounts to be offset against specific equity accounts. Further, IFRS does not recognize gains or losses on the disposition of treasury shares and, instead, makes an adjustment to equity. Under U.S. GAAP, using the cost method, proceeds in excess of the purchase price are generally credited to a specific paid-in capital account from treasury stock, while subsequent losses are reduced from the paid-in capital account (to the extent of its balance) and then any residual is deducted from retained earnings.

In addition to the standard items classified in the Equity section of the Statement of Financial Position, two other common classification issues exist: the treatment of convertible bonds and the reporting of noncontrolling (minority) interest in a subsidiary. For corporate bonds that are convertible into common shares, U.S. GAAP reports such financial instruments as debt. However, under IFRS, proceeds of a debt instrument that are convertible into common shares are allocated between debt (reported at fair value) and equity (reported at residual value). As for reporting on noncontrolling interest in a subsidiary, U.S. GAAP reported minority interest in the "mezzanine section" of the balance sheet. However, U.S. GAAP and IFRS methods recently converged and now report noncontrolling interest in a subsidiary in the Equity section.

IFRS DIFFERENCES AFFECTING THE INCOME STATEMENT

Revenue Recognition

One of the more complex differences between U.S. GAAP and IFRS is in the area of revenue recognition. IAS 18 deals with revenue recognition issues, specifically when to recognize revenues from the sale of goods or services, interest, dividend income, and royalties. Other revenue recognition issues are reflected in other IFRS pronouncements. For the most part, under IFRS, income is the framework, with revenue being a subset of income. Conversely, under U.S. GAAP, revenue is considered an element of the income statement, whereas income is not considered an element, but a calculated result. Under U.S. GAAP, revenue is generally recognized when a product has been delivered or a service performed, the sales price is fixed and determinable, and collectability is reasonably assured. Following are some specific U.S. GAAP-IFRS differences involving revenue recognition. Note that as of this writing, the FASB-IFRS joint project dealing with revenue recognition is expected to be issued in the third quarter of 2011 and may converge many of these differences as well as introduce new treatments.

Sale of Goods

Revenue recognition principles appear in several areas of authority within the literature, particularly with the application of the concepts of *realized*, *recognized*, and *earned* revenue. In addition, the SEC offers specific guidance on revenue recognition for listed companies. The IASB does not receive guidance from a regulatory body such as the SEC. Further, U.S. GAAP has several areas of specific industry guidance with regard to revenue recognition; IFRS has no industry guidance.

IFRS uses a risks and reward model when applying revenue recognition under IAS 18. In applying IFRS, revenue is generally recognized when probable economic benefits exist, the item(s) of revenue *and* costs can be reliably measured, the significant risks and rewards of ownership are conveyed from the seller to the buyer, and the seller does not retain managerial involvement to the degree of ownership or retain effective control over the buyer. According to ASC 605-10-S99, if there is to be revenue recognition from the sale of goods, there needs to be persuasive evidence of an arrangement, collectability of the revenue is reasonably assured, the sales price is fixed and determinable, and the delivery occurred or services were rendered. Under IFRS, collectability is not mentioned in IAS 18, but is considered inherent in the standard by the mention of the receipt of probable future economic benefits.

Bill-and-Hold Transactions

Under U.S. GAAP, revenue is recognized under bill-and-hold transactions after:

☐ The risks of ownership have passed to the buyer,

☐ The customer has a fixed commitment to purchase the goods,

☐ The buyer requests that the transaction be processed on a bill-and-hold basis,

☐ The buyer has a substantial business purpose for placing the order on a buy and hold basis,

☐ The seller cannot retain any performance obligations that would taint the completion of the earnings process,

☐ The acquired goods have to be held separate from the seller's inventory and not be used to fill orders,

☐ The product is ready for delivery, and

☐ There is a fixed schedule for delivery to the buyer that includes the date of delivery consistent with the buyer's business purpose.

Under IFRS, revenue recognition for bill-and-hold arrangements occurs when the buyer takes title, provided it is probable that delivery will occur; goods are on hand, identified, and ready for delivery to the buyer; the buyer acknowledges deferred delivery arrangements; and usual payment terms exist. However, one noteworthy aspect to both U.S. GAAP and IFRS, any time a buyer requests a delay in the delivery of goods, but takes title and acknowledges receipt of the invoice, revenue is not yet recognized. The seller still has to pay for storage, delivery, and insurance costs on the goods, so the significant risks and rewards have not yet passed to the buyer. Under IFRS, written orders are not required; however, U.S. GAAP requires that if written orders are customary business practices, then that format would be needed as evidence of the transaction.

Multiple Element Arrangements

A multiple element contract involves goods sold with subsequent maintenance or support offered for no additional cost (such as a warranty). Under IFRS, revenue is recognized under IAS 18 based on separability of identifiable components of a transaction and revenue is allocated to each component usually based on relative fair market value. IAS 18, par. 19, requires full revenue recognition and an accrual of costs. This approach ignores the matching principle.

U.S. GAAP (ASC 605-25-25) provides criteria for separating the contract components in such arrangements. In general, the total consideration received should be allocated to each element of the contract based on relative fair values.

Long-Term Construction Contracts

U.S. GAAP (ASC 605-35-25) permits, with specific guidance, the use of either the percentage-of-completion method, completed-contract method (on a limited basis), or zero-profit method for recognition of gross profits for long-term construction contracts. Corresponding revenues and expenses related to the construction project are recognized on the income statement either by computing a ratio of stages of completion (using a cost-to-cost approach or other reasonable method) or basing recognition on the actual costs incurred of the project and deferring revenue recognition until project completion.

Under IFRS, IAS 11 permits use of either the percentage-of-completion method or zero-profit method to account for long-term construction contracts. IAS 11 does not permit the completed-contract method; therefore, revenues are recognized only by computing a ratio of stages of completion and costs are expensed in the period incurred. In addition, IAS 11 includes the fair value of receivables in recognizing revenues. U.S. GAAP uses fair value only if the receivable is at fair value; otherwise, the amount of revenue is based on the negotiated amount (undiscounted). In addition, SOP 81-1 does not permit construction accounting standard application to service contracts and must instead be accounted for based on the type of service provided. To contrast, IFRS allows either the percentage-of-completion method or zero-profit method for service contracts.

In the discussion above, in the case of real estate sales, according to IFRIC 15, if the agreement is a construction contract, IAS 11 applies and revenue is accounted for using the rules described. However, if the real estate agreement is not a construction contract, then IAS 18 would apply and revenue recognition would occur based on sale of goods or services criteria. The criteria in IFRIC 15 as to whether an agreement is a real estate contract centers on one criteria: if the agreement specifies major structural elements of design before or during construction, it is accounted for using IAS 11. If it does not specify major structural elements of design, but the contract specifies control and risks and rewards being transferred as the contract work progresses, then IAS 18 is used, but revenue is recognized in stages; otherwise, the contract is accounted for as a sale of goods under IAS 18.

Customer Loyalty Programs

There are variations on how companies account for rewards programs granted to their customers. U.S. GAAP has mixed practices. ASC 605-25-25 may apply to such arrangements, where entities account for these programs similar to a product warranty approach, accruing the incremental estimated cost of providing the goods or services that are to be redeemed. IFRIC 13 requires companies to estimate the value of points to the customer and defer the revenue as a liability until the concern has fulfilled its obligation to supply awards. IFRIC 13 requires awards to be recognized as a separate component of the sale if any consideration received is allocated to the loyalty program based on relative fair value or using a residual method.

In addition, IFRS includes gains in the definition of revenue, which are not reported separately on the income statement, whereas U.S. GAAP records gains separate from revenue and defines it as a specific element on the income statement.

Discontinued Operations

Currently, the definition of "discontinued operations" in ASC 360 does not converge with IFRS 5. Under U.S. GAAP, discontinued operations apply to asset groups, whereas under IFRS, discontinued operations apply to major lines of business or geographical areas of operation. In addition, U.S. GAAP provides specific guidance on continuing involvement, where there is minimal guidance under IFRS. In presentation of discontinued operations under U.S. GAAP, disclosure of revenues, pre-tax profit (or loss), gain (or loss) on disposal of the unit, and the tax effect of discontinued operations is presented below income from continuing operations. Under IFRS, the same items are presented as under U.S. GAAP with the exception of also disclosing the expenses associated with the revenue segregated as part of the discontinued operation. Further, IFRS 5 requires that cash flows related to discontinued operations be separately presented by categories (i.e., operating, investing, and financing activities). U.S. GAAP has no cash flows disclosure requirement.

Share-Based Payment

U.S. GAAP and IFRS standards have closely converged in the accounting of share-based payment, where the fair value of shares and options that are awarded to employees are recognized over their period of service (period of benefit). One significant difference that remains regarding share-based payment is that under U.S. GAAP, ASC 718 applies to employee and non-employee share-based payments, whereas IFRS 2 generally only applies to employees of the concern. Share-based payments are classified as a liability under ASC 718 if the grantor can be compelled to deliver cash or other assets and no equity holder relationship is established. IFRS 2 classifies share-based payment awards as separated into components: cash-settled (the extent the liability will be settled in cash or other assets) and equity-settled (which is the award's fair value over the liability incurred).

In addition, there are differences in the treatment of the grant date under U.S. GAAP and IFRS. Under ASC 718, the grant date is the date the employer and employee have a mutual understanding of the terms and conditions of the stock-based award and the employee begins to benefit from or be negatively impacted by the changes in the employer's share price. Under IFRS 2, the grant date is the date the entity and the employee agree to a share-based payment arrangement and possess a mutual understanding of the terms and conditions of the arrangement.

Impairment

Intangible Impairment

U.S. GAAP measures impairment as the excess of the intangible's carrying value over its fair value (expected future cash flows, undiscounted); IFRS recognizes impairment if the intangible's carrying value exceeds its recoverable amount (which is the higher of the intangible's fair value less costs to dispose of the asset and its value in use). Under U.S. GAAP, recorded impairment losses are not reversed in subsequent periods, as the intangible's revised basis for amortization reflects the written-down asset after impairment loss recognition. Under IFRS, IAS 36 allows for recovery of impairment losses (other than goodwill) in subsequent periods if there has been a change in economic conditions or a change in the expected use of the asset. Such allowable impairment recoveries (or asset write-ups) are limited to the intangible's pre-impairment carrying value.

For goodwill, U.S. GAAP tests for impairment annually (or more often if evidence of impairment exists) and is based on a two-step, recoverability test and impairment assessment. IFRS uses a one-step process in testing for goodwill impairment, where an impairment loss is recognized if the asset's carrying value is greater than its discounted fair value, less cost to sell and its discounted value in use.

Property, Plant and Equipment Impairment

According to U.S. GAAP and IFRS, a company must record an asset impairment when the book value of an asset is not recoverable. U.S. GAAP relies on a recoverability test to determine whether impairment has occurred. If the sum of expected future cash flows (undiscounted) is less than the carrying amount of the asset, the asset is considered impaired. Such an impairment loss is measured as the difference between the carrying amount of the asset and its fair value. U.S. GAAP prohibits subsequent impairment reversals.

Under IAS 36, an asset is impaired when its recoverable amount is less than its carrying amount. The recoverable amount is the greater of net selling price and its value in use. The net selling price is the market value of the asset less any disposal costs. Value in use is the present value of expected future net cash flows over the remaining useful life of the asset. The impairment loss is the difference between the asset's book value and its recoverable amount, which is recognized in income. IFRS permits asset write-ups for subsequent recoveries of impairments.

Earnings per Share

The calculations of basic and diluted earnings per share (EPS) are similar under U.S. GAAP and IFRS, with some minor differences. First, both require EPS to be reported on the face of the income statement if the shares are traded publicly. U.S. GAAP and IFRS each report EPS for income from continuing operations and for net income or loss; however, U.S. GAAP requires EPS for discontinued operations and extraordinary items. In addition, under U.S. GAAP, if the treasury stock method of calculating incremental shares is used, a quarterly calculation of the average stock price is used. IFRS calculates the incremental shares based on a weighted-average at the end of the accounting period, not at the end of each quarter. This topic is one that the two boards are jointly working on in order to converge accounting treatments.

Subsequent Events

Under U.S. GAAP, ASC 855 deals with accounting and disclosure requirements for subsequent events. Specifically, subsequent events are considered through the date the financial statements are issued or are available to be issued. In addition, SEC registrants are not required to disclose the date through which the subsequent events have been evaluated. Under IFRS, IAS 10 defines subsequent events through the date of financial statement authorization; the date of authorization of financial statement issue is disclosed.

Comprehensive Income

The FASB recently issued Accounting Standards Update (ASU) No. 2011-05 (*ASC 220, Comprehensive Income*), *Presentation of Comprehensive Income*. The ASU is intended to increase the prominence of other comprehensive income in financial statements and will supersede some of the guidance in ASC 220.

The central changes contained in the ASU provide that an entity that reports items in other comprehensive income have the option to present comprehensive income in either one or two consecutive financial statements as follows:

1. As a single statement approach by presenting the components of net income and total net income, the components of other comprehensive income and total other comprehensive income, and a total for comprehensive income.

2. In a two-statement approach, where an entity must present the components of net income and total net income in the first statement. That statement must be immediately followed by a financial statement that presents the components of other comprehensive income, a total for other comprehensive income, and a total for comprehensive income.

This ASU disallows the presentation of other comprehensive income in the statement of changes in equity. It also conforms very closely to IFRS.

Conceptual Framework Project

One of the unique features of the FASB was its issuance of a conceptual framework to assist in solving and narrowing accounting treatment differences. Since 1978 when the first concept statement was issued, the board has used the conceptual framework to develop and modify existing accounting guidance. Since the FASB and IASB jointly decided to converge accounting standards, in October 2004, the boards added to their agendas a joint project to develop an improved, common conceptual framework that builds on their existing frameworks (i.e., the IASB's *Framework for the Preparation and Presentation of Financial Statements* and the FASB's *Statements of Financial Accounting Concepts*). The project will do the following:

1. Focus on changes in the environment since the original frameworks were issued, as well as omissions in the original frameworks, in order to efficiently and effectively improve, complete, and converge the existing frameworks.

2. Give priority to addressing and deliberating those issues within each phase that are likely to yield benefits to the boards in the short term; that is, cross-cutting issues that affect a number of their projects for new or revised standards. Thus, work on several phases of the project will be conducted simultaneously and the boards expect to benefit from work being conducted on other projects.

3. Initially consider concepts applicable to private sector business entities. Later, the boards will jointly consider the applicability of those concepts to private sector not-for-profit organizations. Representatives of public sector (governmental) standard-setting boards are monitoring the project and, in some cases, considering the potential consequences of private sector deliberations for public sector entities.

The objective of the joint FASB-IASB conceptual framework project is to develop an improved common conceptual framework that provides a sound foundation for developing future accounting standards. Such a framework is essential to fulfilling the boards' goal of developing standards that are principles-based, internally consistent, and internationally converged and that lead to financial reporting that provides the information capital providers need to make decisions in their capacity as capital providers. The new framework, once completely finalized, will deal with a wide range of issues and will build on the existing IASB and FASB frameworks and consider developments subsequent to the issuance of those frameworks.

In September 2010, the boards jointly completed a portion of the conceptual framework, *Chapter 1, Objective of General Purpose of Financial Reporting, and Chapter 3, Qualitative Characteristics of Useful Financial Information*. The two boards are still deliberating on Elements and Recognition, Measurement, and Reporting Entity in order to complete the project. Information on the joint conceptual framework project is at http://www.fasb.org/project/conceptual_framework.shtml.

Objective of General Purpose of Financial Reporting

According to Concept Statement No. 8, *the objective of financial reporting states that financial reporting is to provide financial information about the reporting entity that is useful to existing and potential investors, lenders, and other creditors in making decisions about providing resources to the entity. Those decisions involve buying, selling, or holding equity and debt instruments and providing or settling loans and other forms of credit.* This revised concept chapter replaces the former three-pronged objectives.

Qualitative Characteristics of Useful Financial Information

There were significant changes that the joint boards made to the hierarchy of accounting qualities. The first significant adjustment was changing the fundamental qualities from relevance and reliability to relevance and full representation. The ingredients of fundamental qualities under relevance are now predictive value and confirmatory value, which is information that is capable of making a difference in one of those decisions only if it will help users to make new predictions, confirm or correct prior predictions, or both.

In addition to relevance, faithful representation (which replaces reliability) includes three ingredients: completeness, neutrality, and free from error. The joint boards concluded that there was a lack of a common understanding to the term reliability. According to the revised concept statement, faithful representation means that financial information represents the substance of an economic phenomenon rather than merely representing its legal form. Substance over form is, therefore, not considered a separate component of faithful representation because it would be redundant.

The enhancing qualities are comparability, verifiability (which used to be a secondary ingredient), timeliness (which used to be a secondary ingredient), and understandability. Some of these changes are significant and have altered the definitions of many of the contents of this part of the conceptual framework for both the FASB and IASB. The remainder of the conceptual framework project will deal with definitions of the elements and recognition in financial reporting, measurement, and reporting entity and are expected to be resolved by the joint boards in the near future.

Part IV

GAAP IN SPECIALIZED INDUSTRIES

Chapter 19
Accounting in Specialized Industries

CONTENTS

BROADCASTING INDUSTRY

Sources of Authoritative Guidance

The sources of authoritative guidance in the broadcasting industry are:

☐ ASC 920, *Entertainment—Broadcasters*.

☐ ASC 820, *Fair Value Measurements and Disclosures*.

Abstract and Introduction

A license agreement for program material generally includes specials, features, series, or cartoons. The agreement covers a package consisting of several programs granting a television station (or group), network, pay television, or cable television (licensee) the right to broadcast either an unlimited or specified number of showings over a license period (specified by parties) for a given fee. The agreement usually consists of separate licenses for each program in the package. The licensee must pay the required fee for the program materials even though the rights may not be used. If the rights of use are not exercised, they revert to the licensor with no refund to the licensee. The license period specified in the license agreement defines a reasonable period of time within which the licensee can exercise its purchased rights for programming use. It does not delineate the period of time in which a licensee may use programming material on a continuing basis.

A broadcaster's acquisition of a license agreement to broadcast program material should be accounted for as a group of rights or privileges. The rights that have been acquired and the related obligation incurred should be reported by the licensee as an asset and liability. They may be shown at either the gross amount or the present value of the liability when the license period begins and certain other conditions are satisfied. Broadcasters may also participate in barter transactions. That is, they exchange unsold advertising time for programs, fixed assets, merchandise, travel and hotel arrangements, entertainment and other products, or services. These events generally should be accounted for as nonmonetary transactions and therefore their recognition and disclosure must adhere to the guidance of ASC 845-10-05, *Nonmonetary Transactions: Overall*. A network affiliation agreement should be accounted for as an intangible asset. If a broadcaster owns the program material that it will show on its network, cable, or television station, it must follow guidance of ASC 926-10-15-2, *Entertainment—Films: Overall*.

Authoritative Guidance

Program License Agreements

ASC 920-350-25, *Entertainment—Broadcasters: Intangibles—Goodwill and Other*, requires that a broadcaster's acquisition of a license agreement for program material should be reported as an asset purchased and liability incurred when the license period commences and all of the following conditions have been satisfied:

☐ The program material has been accepted by the licensee in accordance with the conditions of the license agreement.

☐ The cost of each program constituting the program package is known or is reasonably determinable.

☐ The program is available for its first showing or telecast. This condition is not met when a conflicting license prevents program broadcasting. However, any restriction under this license or another license with the same licensor regarding programming should not be construed as causing this condition to fail.

Any program license agreement that has been executed but has not met the aforementioned three criteria and was not reported as an asset and liability should be fully disclosed in the notes to the financial statements.

GAAP requires that the license program agreement be classified as a current and noncurrent asset based on its estimated future usage. The related liability should also be dichotomously classified as current or noncurrent based on the future payment terms.

The amount of the recorded asset and liability that is to be reported by the licensee for a broadcast license agreement should be shown at either (1) the gross amount of the liability or (2) the present value of the liability computed. If the latter option is chosen, the difference between the gross and net liability shall be accounted for as interest (ASC 920-350-25).

Cost Allocation and Amortization of Capitalized Program License Agreement

The total capitalized cost of the program license agreement should be proportionally allocated to the individual programs that compose it based on the relative value of each program to the broadcaster. These amounts are commonly specified in the program license agreement contract. Amortization of the allocated cost should then be based on the estimated number of future showings of each program. If a particular program license provides for an unlimited number of showings, as is usually the case for cartoons and related types of programming, the amortization of the costs should take place over the period of the license agreement because the number of showings cannot be determined.

License agreements for feature programs should be amortized on a program-by-program basis. Program series and other syndicated products should be amortized as a series. Because television series license agreements commonly provide for rerun rights, the licensee must also ascertain whether the first showing of the series is more valuable to the station than its reruns. If so, the amortization should be based on an accelerated method. If all showings are considered equally valuable, the straight-line method may be used.

Balance Sheet Valuation of Capitalized Program License Agreement

The capitalized program license agreement should be reported on the balance sheet of the licensee at the lower of amortized cost or estimated net realizable value. Each component of the license agreement (programs, series, packages, dayparts [collection of programs broadcast during a particular time of the day, such as daytime, evening, and late night]) should be valued separately. If the licensee's management decides that the usefulness of a program, series, package, or daypart is to be revised downward, amortized cost may have to be written down to a lower estimated realizable value. This lower amount then becomes the new cost basis of the capitalized program license agreement. Once written down to a new cost basis, the asset cannot later be written up for a recovery in value.

Network Affiliation Agreements

A broadcaster may be affiliated with a network under a network affiliation agreement. If a station has signed such an agreement, it receives compensation for the network programming that it carries based on a pre-agreed formula. This formula is designed to compensate the station for advertising sold on a network basis that is included in network programming. Program costs for stations that have network affiliation agreements are generally lower than those for an independent station because the affiliate does not have to incur costs for network programs. These programs generally represent a major expense for television stations.

Network affiliation agreements should be classified as intangible assets. If a network affiliation agreement is terminated and is not immediately replaced or under agreement to be replaced, any remaining unamortized capitalized cost should be charged to expense. However, if there is immediate replacement or there is an agreement for such a replacement, a loss should be recognized equal to the excess of the unamortized cost of the terminated affiliation agreement over the fair value of the new affiliation agreement that replaced it. If, on the other hand, the fair value of the replacement agreement exceeds the unamortized cost of the terminated affiliation agreement, no gain should be recognized in the accounting record or disclosed in the financial statements.

Broadcaster Barter Transactions

Broadcasters commonly exchange unsold advertising time for products or services. That is, they frequently engage in barter transactions in which no material amounts of cash exchange hands between the parties involved. All barter transactions (with the exception of trading advertising time for network programming) should be accounted for at the estimated fair value of the products or services received or advertising time given up, whichever is more clearly determinable. The accounting parameters that must be followed in these transactions may be found in ASC 845-10-05. Barter revenue should be recognized when commercials are broadcast, and merchandise or services received should be reported when received or used. Thus, if advertising time is broadcast before the products or services are compensatorily received, a receivable should be recorded at the same time that the advertising revenue is reported. Correspondingly, if merchandise or services are received prior to the broadcast of an advertising commercial, a liability should be recorded.

BANKING AND THRIFT INDUSTRY

Sources of Authoritative Guidance

The sources of authoritative guidance in the banking and thrift industry are:

☐ ASC 740-30-05, *Income Taxes: Other Considerations or Special Areas.*

☐ ASC 310-20-05-2, *Receivables: Nonrefundable Fees and Other Costs.*

☐ ASC 230, *Statement of Cash Flows.*

☐ ASC 740, *Income Taxes.*

☐ ASC 320, *Investments—Debt and Equity Securities.*

☐ ASC 360-10-05-4, *Property, Plant, and Equipment: Overall.*

☐ ASC 942-10, *Financial Services—Depository and Lending: Overall.*

☐ ASC 948-310-35, *Financial Services—Mortgage Banking: Receivables.*

Abstract and Introduction

Previously, under ASC 948-10-15-3, *Financial Services—Mortgage Banking: Overall,* guidance for acquisitions of banks and thrifts was industry based. GAAP required that these financial institutions recognize any excess of fair value of liabilities assumed over the fair value of tangible and identifiable intangible assets acquired as an unidentifiable intangible asset. In addition, the unidentifiable intangible asset was required to be subsequently amortized. Under the guidance of ASC 805-10-10-1, these requirements are removed (except for such transactions between two or more mutual entities). Acquisitions of financial institutions must now be accounted for in accordance with ASC 805, *Business Combinations*, and ASC 350, *Intangibles—Goodwill and Other*. ASC 805-10-10-1 also modifies ASC 360-10-05-4, *Property, Plant, and Equipment: Overall*, which now requires that its scope be augmented to include financial institution long-term intangible assets such as depositor-and borrower-relationship assets and credit cardholder intangible assets. These intangible assets must now be tested using the undiscounted cash flow recoverability test and other impairment measurement requirements for the purpose of recognizing and recording any impairment loss that may have occurred during the period. In addition, ASC 948-10-15-3 also requires that acquisitions of a branch (i.e., a less-than-whole financial institution) should be accounted for as a business combination if it meets the definition of a business. If it does not satisfy the definition, it should be accounted for as an acquisition of net assets that does not generate the recognition of goodwill.

The benefit of these changes is that now acquisitions of financial institutions (except for mutual companies—where the old rules still prevail) will be accounted for (as are other business acquisitions) in accordance with ASC 805, *Business Combinations*, and ASC 350, *Intangibles—Goodwill and Other*. The requirements of ASC 805-10-10-1 clearly result in an improvement to financial reporting comparability.

Members of the Federal Home Loan Banking System should account for distributions of preferred stock received from Federal Home Loan Mortgage Corporation at fair market value as of December 31, 1984.

Authoritative Guidance

Acquiring Banking and Thrift Institutions

A full or partial acquisition of a financial institution that constitutes a business combination should be accounted for by the purchase method, as required by ASC 805-10-05, *Business Combinations: Overall*. ASC 805-10-05 defines a business combination in the following way:

> [A] business combination occurs when an entity acquires net assets that constitute a business or acquires equity interests of one or more other entities and obtains control over that entity or entities ... provisions apply equally to a business combination in which (a) one or more entities are merged or become subsidiaries, (b) one entity transfers net assets, or its owners transfer their equity interests to another, or (c) all entities transfer net assets or the owners of those entities transfer their equity interests to a newly formed entity (some of which are referred to as roll-up or put-together transactions) ... An exchange of a business for a business also is a business combination.

If the acquisition is not a business combination, then the transactions should be recorded (in general) at fair value and should not give rise to goodwill.

Accounting for the Impairment and Disposal of Long-Term Customer Relationship Intangible Assets

The scope of ASC 360-10-05-4, *Property, Plant, and Equipment: Overall*, now includes long-term customer-relationship intangible financial institution related assets that are recognized when a financial institution is acquired. These assets include depositor-and borrower-relationship intangible assets, credit cardholder intangible assets, and servicing assets. These first two assets should not be tested for impairment under ASC 360-10-05-4. The last, servicing assets, are tested for impairment under ASC 860-10-05-3, *Transfers and Servicing: Overall.*

Savings and Loan Associations' Bad Debts Reserves

Governmental regulatory bodies require that stock and mutual savings and loan associations restrict part of their earnings to general reserves as a means of protecting depositors against the possibility of loss. In addition, the IRS allows these entities to deduct an amount as a reserve for bad debts in determining taxable income. This amount is generally different from the amount that is deducted on the income statement in determining pretax financial income (i.e., under GAAP for financial accounting purposes). Therefore, as would be assumed, taxable income and pretax financial income will differ. Under GAAP, a savings and loan association is precluded from providing deferred taxes on the difference between taxable income and pretax accounting income attributable to its bad debts reserve that arose in tax years beginning December 31, 1987 (the base-year amount). However, if circumstances indicate that an association is likely to pay income taxes, either currently or in later years (because of known or expected reductions in the bad debts reserve), income taxes attributable to that reduction should be accrued as tax expense for the current period. The income tax expense that is accrued in this manner should not be accounted for as an extraordinary item.

Nonrefundable Fees and Costs Associated with Lending Activities and Loan Purchases

Standards of financial reporting and reporting for nonrefundable fees and costs associated with lending activities and loan purchases are very important to the activities of banking and thrift institutions. Primary guidance in this area is derived from ASC 310-20-05-2, *Receivables: Nonrefundable Fees and Other Costs.* The following salient lending guidance relating to the banking and thrift activities are enumerated below:

1. Loan origination fees should be deferred and recognized over the life of the related loan. It should be recognized in the form of interest income as an adjustment of the loan's yield. Loan origination fees consist of:

   a. Fees charged to borrowers as prepaid interest or buy-downs that reduce the loan's nominal amount.

   b. Lender reimbursement for origination activities.

   c. Fees charged to the borrower that relate directly to making a loan that is approved quickly or that is complex.

   d. Fees that are yield adjustments to rates that would not have otherwise been extended without the fee.

2. Direct loan origination costs are defined as the incremental costs of loan origination with independent third parties for a loan that represents costs directly related to specified activities performed by the lender for that loan. These activities may consist of:

   a. Evaluating the prospective borrower's financial condition

    b. Evaluating and recording guarantees, collateral, and other security arrangement

    c. Negotiating loan terms

    d. Preparing and processing loan documents and

    e. Closing the transaction

3. Direct loan origination fees should be deferred and recognized as a reduction in the yield of the loan. For any given loan, loan origination fees and related direct loan origination costs should be offset and only the net amount should be deferred and amortized. ASC 310 specifically prohibits the practice of recognizing a portion of loan origination fees in a given period for the express purpose of offsetting all or part of the cost of origination.

4. Fees received for a commitment to originate or purchase a loan or group or loans should be deferred. If the commitment is exercised, then the fees should be recognized over the life of the loan as an adjustment to yield. If the commitment expires unexercised, the fees should be recognized in income upon expiration of the commitment. If the probability of exercise is remote, then the commitment fee should be recognized as service fee income over the commitment period amortized on a straight-line basis. If exercise does occur, then the remaining unamortized commitment fee should be recognized over the life of the loan as an adjustment to yield. If the commitment fee is determined retrospectively as a percentage of the unused line credit that is available, and if the percentage rate of the fee is nominal in relation to the stated rate of interest on the borrowing, and the loan is made at the market rate of interest at the date the loan is made, then the commitment fee should be recognized as service fee income.

5. If a loan or group of loans is purchased, the initial investment generally includes the amount paid to the seller as well as any fees that were paid or less any fees that were received. Therefore, the initial investment will differ from the related loan's principal amount when the purchase was made. The discrepancy should be accounted for as an adjustment of yield over the life of the loan. Any other costs incurred in either acquiring the loan or committing to it should be charged to expense in the period incurred.

6. In general, any amounts that are required to be recognized as yield adjustments over the life of the related loan (e.g., net fees and costs) should be computed using the interest method based on its contractual terms of the loan. The use of the effective interest method is used to insure that interest income (and recognition of related fees and costs) is recognized in a manner that produces a constant effective yield on the net investment in the receivable.

7. Investments in financial instruments that may be prepaid or settled in a way that would preclude the investor from not recovering all of its recorded investment (e.g., loans, receivables, retained interests in securi-

tizations, and interest-only strips) should be accounted for as available-for-sale debt securities.

8. For financial statement disclosure, any unamortized amounts of loan origination, commitment, and other costs and fees that are being recognized as an adjustment of yield should be recorded on the balance sheet as a part of the loan to which it relates. The portion of these amounts that has been recognized as an adjustment to yield should be reported as part of interest income. Commitment fees (or other fees) that are being amortized over the commitment period on a straight-line basis or included in income when the commitment expires, should be shown as service fee income.

Specialized Disclosure Requirements—Cash Flows Statement

ASC 230-10-45, *Statement of Cash Flows: Overall*, amends ASC 230, *Statement of Cash Flows*, regarding the specialized disclosure requirements relating to the Cash Flows Statement of banking and thrift associations.

Banks, savings institutions, and credit unions are not required to report the gross amounts of cash receipts and cash payments for the following:

1. Deposits placed with other financial institutions and withdrawals of deposits.

2. Loans made to customers and principal collections of loans.

3. Time deposits accepted and repayments of deposits.

When a banking or thrift association is part of a consolidated entity, net amounts of cash receipts and cash payments for deposit and lending activities of these entities should be reported separately from the gross amounts of cash receipts and payments for the other investing and financing activities of the consolidated entity. This guidance also applies to parts of a consolidated entity such as a subsidiary of a bank, savings institution, or credit union that is not a bank, savings institution, or credit union.

CABLE TELEVISION

Sources of Authoritative Guidance

The sources of authoritative guidance in the cable television industry are:

☐ ASC 922, *Entertainment—Cable Television*.

☐ ASC 280, *Segment Reporting*.

☐ ASC 350, *Intangibles—Goodwill and Other*.

☐ ASC 360-10-05-4, *Property, Plant, and Equipment: Overall*.

Abstract and Introduction

ASC 922 presents the standards of financial reporting and disclosure for certain revenues and expenses related to cable television systems. The emphasis of this statement is on special accounting rules applicable to the prematurity period. During this period, a cablevision television system is partly in use and partly under construction. The prematurity period generally begins with the first earned subscriber revenue and ends when the first major construction period has been completed or the achievement of a specified predetermined subscriber level has been reached. Prematurity status is very common in this industry. For example, over time it is usual for cable companies to expand throughout the geographical area that they have franchised. For large and medium-size entities, this effort results in many parts of their system being "energized" while construction progresses in others. Thus, except for the smallest systems, programming is delivered to parts of the area being serviced (with revenues being earned) before construction of the entire system is complete. Thus, virtually every medium-size and large franchise cable television system experiences a prematurity period during which it receives some revenue while continuing to incur substantial costs related to its completion. During the prematurity period, costs incurred that relate to both current and future operations shall be partially capitalized and partially expensed.

Authoritative Guidance

Establishment of the Prematurity Period

Before revenue is earned from the first subscriber, the management of a cable television entity should establish the beginning and end of the prematurity period. By definition, the prematurity period begins with the first earned subscriber revenue. Its end will vary with the circumstances of the system but will be determined based on plans for completion of the system's first major construction period. The end of the prematurity period can also be based on the achievement of a specified predetermined subscriber level at which no additional investment will be required for other than cable television plants. Under GAAP, the prematurity period is not to exceed two years. A longer period is justified only in major urban markets. After its establishment, a premature period should not be changed except under highly unusual circumstances. The part of the cable television system that is in the prematurity period should be accounted for separately from the rest of the system and should be clearly distinguished from it. The portion that is in the prematurity period should have most of the following characteristics:

☐ It should be in a geographically different area or different franchise area.

☐ It should have mechanical differences, such as different equipment and facilities. For example, it might have separate equipment used to receive the signals of distant television or radio stations whether directly from a transmitter or from a microwave relay system. Equipment used to receive television and radio signals, called headend, may also include separate studio facilities required for operator originated programming if such activities take place in this portion of the cable television system.

☐ There should be timing differences. For example, its construction or marketing should start at dates significantly different from the other portions of the system.

☐ There should be investment decision differences. The portion of the cable television system that is in the prematurity period should have different breakeven and return-on-investment analyses or different construction start approvals.

☐ It should have separate accounting records, separate budgets and forecasts, or other accountability differences.

Accounting for Costs During the Prematurity Period

In general, costs incurred by the system should be charged to the portion of the cable television system in the prematurity period only if they are specifically identified with the operations of that portion. Separate projections for the portion shall be developed, and the portion's capitalized costs should be evaluated separately during the prematurity period for recoverability. Other guidance related to accounting in the prematurity period includes the following:

☐ Subscriber-related costs and general and administrative expenses shall be expensed as period costs. Subscriber-related costs are those costs incurred to obtaining and retaining subscribers to the cable television system. They include:

— Cost of billing and collection.

— Bad debts.

— Mailings.

— Repairs and maintenance of subscriber connections.

— Franchise fees related to revenue or the number of subscribers.

— Salary of the system manager and office rent.

— Programming cost for additional channels used in the marketing effort or costs related to revenues from, or the number of subscribers to, channels or program services.

— Direct selling costs.

☐ Costs of the cable television plant should be capitalized in full. These include materials, direct labor, and construction overhead.

☐ Programming and other systems costs that are incurred in anticipation of servicing a fully operating system should be allocated between current and future operations. These costs do not change based on the number of subscribers. They include such items as property taxes based on valuation of the cable entity as a fully operating system; pole, underground duct, antenna site, and microwave rental based on rental costs for a fully operating system; and local origination programming to satisfy franchise requirements.

The proportion attributable to current operations shall be expensed currently, and the remainder of the expenditures should be capitalized. The amount that should be expensed in the current period is derived by multiplying the total expenditures for the month by the following fraction:

The greatest of a, b, or c

Total numbers of subscribers expected at end of prematurity period

where:

a = the average number of subscribers expected that month as estimated at the beginning of the prematurity period

b = the average number of subscribers that would be attained using at least equal (straight-line) monthly progress in adding new subscribers towards the estimate of subscribers that would be attained at the end of the prematurity period

c = the average number of actual subscribers

The preceding fraction should be determined each month of the prematurity period.

In addition, depreciation and amortization expense should be determined by multiplying the monthly depreciation and amortization based on total capitalized costs expected on completion of the prematurity period by the aforementioned fraction using the depreciation that will be applied by the entity after the prematurity period.

Capitalization of Interest Costs During the Prematurity Period

The interest costs that should be capitalized during the prematurity period should be done in accordance with ASC 835-20-05, *Interest: Capitalization of Interest*. ASC 835-20-05 requires that interest costs to be capitalized be determined by multiplying an interest capitalization rate to the average amount of qualifying assets for the system during the period. During the prematurity period, a portion of the system is in use in the earnings activity of the enterprise and therefore is not eligible for interest capitalization. In addition, interest should not be capitalized on phases of the project that are complete and ready for service. In total, the amount of interest cost that is capitalized should not exceed the total amount of interest cost incurred by the total cablevision system for the period.

Recognition of Hookup Revenue and Amortization of Capitalized Costs

Hookup revenue should be recognized as revenue to the extent of the direct selling costs incurred. Direct selling costs include:

1. Commissions.

2. The portion of a salesperson's compensation other than commissions for obtaining new subscribers.

3. Local advertising targeted for acquisition of new subscribers.

4. Costs of processing documents related to new subscribers acquired.

Direct selling costs do not include supervisory and administrative expenses or indirect expenses such as rent and costs of facilities.

Subscriber installation costs, including material, labor, and overhead costs, should be capitalized and depreciated over a period no longer than the depreciation period used for the cable television plant. Costs of subsequently disconnecting and reconnecting should be charged to expense of the current period.

The cost of a successful franchise application should be capitalized and subsequently amortized in accordance with ASC 350-10-05-1. Unsuccessful franchise applications and abandoned franchises should be expensed given their lack of future benefits.

Franchise Applications

Costs incurred in pursuance of successful franchise applications should be capitalized and amortized in accordance with ASC 350, *Intangibles—Goodwill and Other*. If a franchise application is deemed unsuccessful or a decision is made to abandon the franchise altogether, its costs should be charged to expense.

Recoupment of Capitalized Assets

The carrying amounts of the capitalized assets and identifiable intangible assets are subject to the requirement of ASC 360-10-05-4, *Property, Plant, and Equipment: Overall*. Other intangible assets require the guidance of ASC 350. Even if it is determined that the entity's capitalized costs are unrecoverable, capitalization of costs should not cease. Instead, the provision required to reduce capitalized costs to their recoverable value should also be increased.

DEVELOPMENT OF COMPUTER SOFTWARE TO BE SOLD, LEASED, OR OTHERWISE MARKETED

Sources of Authoritative Guidance

The sources of authoritative guidance relating to the development of computer software to be sold, leased, or otherwise marketed are:

- ASC 730-10-05, *Research and Development: Overall*.
- ASC 985-20-15, *Software: Costs of Software to Be Sold, Leased, or Marketed*.
- Additional Guidance: Related FASB Staff Positions and/or Questions and Answers Previously Issued as FASB Staff Implementation Guides.

Abstract and Introduction

ASC 985-20 is the primary source of guidance in the area of accounting for the costs of computer software to be sold, leased, or otherwise marketed. The guidance of this statement relates to software that has been internally created or purchased that is to be externally marketed. GAAP requires that costs that have been incurred in the development of a computer software product be expensed when incurred to research and development costs until technological feasibility for the product has been established. Technological feasibility is deemed established when a detailed program design or working model for the product is completed. All software production costs incurred after that point should be capitalized and amortized to current and future periods. In computing amortization expense, companies are required to use the greater of the ratio of current revenues to current and anticipated revenues or the amount derived through straight-line amortization computed over the remaining estimated economic life of the computer product. With respect to financial statement disclosure, computer software costs should be reported in the financial statements at the lower of amortized cost or net realizable value.

Authoritative Guidance

ASC 985-20 discusses the accounting for the costs of computer software to be sold, leased, or otherwise marketed as a separate product or as part of a product or process. It applies to computer software developed internally and to purchased software. It does not address the accounting and reporting of costs incurred for computer software created for the internal use of an entity or for the development of software for others under a contractual arrangement.

A software product has the following characteristics:

☐ It is complete and has exchange value.

☐ It consists of a collection of programs (e.g., a series of instructions or statements enabling the computer to perform its function) that interact.

Embedded software, sometimes called "firmware," should be accounted for as described in this section. This type of software is sold as part of a product; for example, there may be software embedded in a personal digital assistant (PDA). Other instances, such as when time-sharing services are provided, also would fall under the scope of this section, as it would not be possible to provide these services without the software.

Research and Development Costs

All costs incurred in establishing the technological feasibility of a computer software product to be sold, leased, or otherwise marketed should be charged to research and development expense when incurred. A computer software product's technological feasibility is established when the developing entity has performed all planning, designing, coding, and test activities that are required to meet its design specifications. Such specifications generally include the product's technical performance, functions, and features. Coding refers to generating the software product's detailed instructions in computer language. These make the computer perform all that has been called for in the detailed program design. Testing refers to performing the steps necessary to ensure that the coded computer software is doing what it was designed to do.

At a minimum, the entity developing the software product must perform the following specific activities before evidence is provided that technological feasibility has been achieved. These activities are broken into two categories based on whether or not a detailed program design has been created. A detail program design is a blueprint of a computer product's function, features, and technological requirements derived to their most detailed, logical form. The specific activities that evince technological feasibility are:

☐ If the software product development process includes a detail program design:

— The product design and detail program design are completed, and the entity developing the software has established that the necessary skills, hardware, and software technology are available to it to produce the product. The product design is a logical enumeration of all the product functions and serves as the product specifications.

— The consistency between the product design and detail program design and the completeness of the latter has been confirmed by documenting and tracing the detail program design to the product specifications found in the product design.

— The detail program design has been reviewed for what are termed high-risk development issues, such as novel, unique, or unproven functions and features and technological innovations. Assurance has been derived that any uncertainties related to these issues have been resolved through coding and testing.

☐ If the software product development process does not have a detail program design:

— A product design and working model has been completed. A working model is an operative version of the computer software product that will be marketed. It is written in the same software language as the computer software product and performs all the functions planned for the product.

— The completeness of the working model and its consistency with the product design have been confirmed by testing.

A company is required to capitalize its software costs upon the completion of the working model. A company may not use a more stringent criterion or impose additional criteria.

If a company has established technological feasibility and subsequently a high-risk development issue arises, then it should be accounted for as a change in accounting estimate. Previously, capitalized costs should thus be charged to research and development expense.

Capitalization of Computer Software Subsequent to the Establishment of Technological Feasibility

Product master production costs incurred subsequent to the establishment of technological feasibility should be capitalized. These costs generally include the performance of coding and testing. 985-20-25-3, *Software: Costs of Software to Be Sold, Leased, or Marketed* indicates that no software production costs shall be capitalized until technological feasibility has been established for the software and all R&D activities for the other components of the product or process have been completed. The capitalization process should be discontinued when the product is ready and available for general release to customers.

Maintenance and customer support costs should be charged to expense when these costs are incurred or the related revenue is recognized from the product's sale. When the sales price of a computer software product includes customer support for several periods and the price of that support is not separately stated, the estimated cost of the customer support should be accrued in the same period that the sales revenue is recognized.

Technological feasibility of a software product is based on the product as a whole and not on its various modules, unless the modules are individually saleable.

Indirect product costs, such as overhead related to programming and facilities, should be capitalized as part of the production costs of computer software. On the other hand, general and administrative overhead are period costs and hence should not be capitalized.

The costs to revise and modify system software to keep current with changes in hardware technology are considered maintenance expenses and should be expensed as incurred.

Purchased Computer Software with No Alternative Future Uses

The cost of purchased computer software that is to be sold, leased, or otherwise marketed and that has no alternative future uses should be charged to expense in the period of acquisition like R&D expenditures. If, on the other hand, the purchased software has alternative future uses, it should be capitalized and amortized based on its future expected application.

Amortization of Capitalized Software Costs

Capitalized software computer costs should be amortized on a product-by-product basis. Annual amortization that is recognized should be based on the greater of the following two computations after the product is available for general release to customers:

1. Result derived by computing the ratio of current gross revenues of the product to its current and anticipated gross revenues.

2. The straight-line method taken over the remaining estimated economic life of the product, including the period being reported on.

Straight-line amortization for the software is computed over the remaining estimated economic life of the product. Estimates of future revenues or the remaining economic life for a product can change over time; therefore, most recent information should be used to determine whether changes to estimates should be made. Amortization expense of capitalized software costs should be charged to cost of sales.

Companies must disclose the total amount charged to expense for amortization and amounts written down to net realizable value. These amounts may be combined for the purpose of disclosure.

Capitalized software costs represent amortizable intangible assets and should be presented in the balance sheet as "Other Assets" if the software costs have a life of more than one year or one operating cycle.

Costs incurred for product enhancements should be expensed as research and development until the technological feasibility of the enhancement has been established.

The estimated life of the enhancement, including any costs carried over from the original product, should be amortized over the enhancement's estimated useful life.

Duplication Costs Charged to Inventory

All costs incurred in duplicating the computer software and related materials (e.g., documentation and training materials) from the product masters as well as the physical packaging needed for its distribution should be recorded as inventory on a unit-specific basis. When the sale of the unit is recognized, the cost of the inventory should also be recognized and charged to the cost of sales. If the unit is unsold, its costs remain as unsold inventory.

End-of-Period Evaluation and Disclosure on the Financial Statements

At each balance date, the unamortized capitalized costs of the computer software product should be compared to its net realizable value. Any excess of the unamortized capitalized computer product over its net realizable value should be written off. The amount of the write-off should not be subsequently restored. In addition, the remaining unamortized capitalized computer software costs at the close of the entity's annual fiscal period then become its new cost for subsequent accounting periods.

The following disclosure requirements should be satisfied relating to computer software costs each period:

☐ Unamortized computer software costs should be included in each balance sheet presented. The software costs should be presented in the "other asset" section of the balance sheet, assuming the asset's useful life is more that one year or the operating cycle, whichever is longer.

☐ The total amount that was charged to expense should be disclosed in each income statement presented (e.g., amortization of capitalized computer software costs as well as the amounts that were written off in bringing the amortized costs down to their net realizable values).

ACCOUNTING BY FRANCHISORS

Sources of Authoritative Guidance

The sources of authoritative guidance in accounting by franchisors are:

☐ ASC 952-605-25, *Franchisors: Revenue Recognition.*
☐ ASC 805-10-05, *Business Combinations: Overall.*

Abstract and Introduction

A franchise is a written business agreement in which a franchisor, for a specified period and delineated geographical area, allows a franchisee to use certain tradenames and trademarks, sell certain products, and perform certain services for which the franchisor has exclusive legal rights. The franchisor is the entity that grants the rights under the franchise contract to the franchisee, who then operates the franchised business and, in turn, compensates the franchisor for the privilege. ASC 952-605-25 discusses the accounting and reporting requirements from the perspective of the franchisor. Individual and area franchise sales should be recognized as franchise fee revenue when all material services or conditions related to the sale have been substantially performed and satisfied by the franchisor. Other areas of the standard for which guidance is rendered are contractual arrangements between franchisor and franchisee, allocation of initial franchise fee, continuing franchise fees, product sales made to franchisee on a continuing basis, agency sales, franchising costs, repossessed franchises, business combinations, and required disclosures.

Authoritative Guidance

Accounting for Revenue from Individual Franchise Sales

Franchise fee revenue from individual franchise sales should be recognized when the franchisor has substantially performed and satisfied all material services or conditions relating to the sale. ASC 952-10-05-1 indicates that *substantial perform- ance on the part of the franchisor* means:

☐ There is no obligation or intent to refund any cash received or forgive any unpaid notes or receivables.

☐ All initial services that the franchisor was contractually required to do by the signed franchise agreement have been completed.

☐ No significant responsibilities related to substantial performance by the franchisor remain.

In addition, a provision for estimated uncollectible initial franchise fees should be recorded to ensure a proper matching of revenues and costs. In exceptional cases, when franchise fee revenue is collected over an extended period and no reasonable basis exists for estimating collectibility, it may be necessary to use the installment or cost recovery methods to account for revenue recognition.

Unless there are unusual circumstances, substantial performance cannot take place before the franchisee starts his or her operation. Often, a franchise agree- ment calls for a large initial franchise fee and relatively small continuing franchise fees providing for future services that the franchisor agrees to perform throughout the term of the franchise agreement. If it is determined that the continuing fee will not cover the cost of the continuing services performed by the franchisor as well as earning a reasonable profit, then a portion of the initial franchise fee should be deferred and subsequently amortized over the life of the franchise. That is, the portion of the initial franchise fee that is deferred should be sufficient to cover the estimated cost in excess of continuing franchise fees and the earning of a reasonable profit on the continuing services themselves.

Accounting for Revenue from Area Franchise Sales

An area franchise is an agreement that transfers franchise rights within a geo- graphical area, permitting the opening of a number of franchised outlets. A franchisor may sell an area franchise to a franchisee, who may decide to operate the franchised outlets, or the franchisor may sell an area franchise to an intermediary franchisee, who then may decide to sell the individual franchises to other franchisees who will operate the outlets.

Sometimes the cost and efforts relating to the initial services performed by the franchisor are not affected by the number of outlets opened in an area, and therefore the area franchise sale is very similar to an individual franchise sale. In that situation, any initial franchise fees relating to area franchise sales should be accounted for in the same manner as individual franchise sales, and substantial performance on the part of the franchisor should be evaluated using the same parameters.

However, when the efforts and total cost related to the initial services are materially affected by the number of outlets opened in an area, it may be necessary to view the area franchise agreement differently. In this circumstance, an area franchise agreement should be viewed as a divisible contract, and area franchise fees should be recognized in proportion to the number of outlets opened. For example, the more outlets that are opened, the proportionally greater part of the area franchise fee should be recognized (assuming substantial performance has taken place). This may require an estimate on the part of the franchisor regarding the expected number of outlets guided by, perhaps, the minimum or maximum outlets indicated in the franchise contract. Any change in estimate resulting from a change in circumstance should result in recognizing the remaining fees as revenues in proportion to the remaining services that have yet to be performed.

Contractual Arrangements Between Franchisor and Franchisee

A franchisor and franchisee may have several contractual business relationships outstanding at any given point in time. For example, a franchisor may have guaranteed the borrowings of a franchisee, have a creditor interest in the franchisee, or control a franchisee's operations by sales or other agreements. The extent of these associations may effectively make the franchisee an affiliate of the franchisor. This relationship (between franchisor and franchisee) does not change the GAAP requirement that revenue should not be recognized if all material services, conditions, or obligations relating to the sale have not been substantially performed or satisfied.

A franchisor may have an option (delineated in the franchise agreement) to purchase a franchisee's business. A franchisor may choose to repurchase a franchise business because it is profitable or because it is having financial difficulties or other problems that may tarnish the reputation and goodwill of the entire franchise system. If such an option exists, the likelihood of the franchisor's acquiring the franchised business should be considered in accounting for the initial franchise fee. If it is probable that the franchisor will eventually repurchase the franchise, the initial fee must be deferred and considered as a reduction of the repurchase price when the option is exercised.

Allocation of Initial Franchise Fee

A franchise agreement commonly establishes an initial franchise fee that is to be paid to a franchisor for the franchise rights and services that are to be performed by the franchisor. However, that fee may also include the sale of such tangible property as franchise signs, equipment, inventory, land, and buildings. In this situation, a portion of the fee related to the sale of the tangible assets based on their fair market value may be recognized before or after recognizing the portion applicable to the initial services. For example, a franchisor may recognize a portion of the fee related to the sale of specific tangible assets when their title passes although the balance of the fee relating to services would be recognized as revenue when those services have been substantially performed or satisfied.

A franchise agreement may specify that certain portions of the franchise fee relate to specific services that the franchisor will provide the franchisee. If, however, the services that the franchisor will provide are interrelated to such an extent that the amount that applies to each service cannot be objectively segregated, the revenue for a specific purpose should not be recognized until all services noted by the franchise agreement are substantially performed. If, on the other hand, transaction prices for the services are available, a part of the revenue may be recognized when that service is performed.

Continuing Franchise Fees

A franchisee may be contractually required to pay continuing franchise fees to a franchisor for the continued use of the franchised rights as well as for services performed by the franchisor. These fees should be reported by the franchisor as revenue as the fees are earned and become a receivable to the franchisor. In addition, any costs incurred by the franchisor related to the franchise fees should be expensed as incurred. The earnings process must be honored even though a portion of the continuing fee is designated for a particular purpose, such as an advertising program. It should not be recognized as revenue until the fee is earned and becomes receivable from the franchisee. An exception exists when a franchise arrangement is an agency arrangement under which a portion of the continuing fee is required to be segregated and used for a special purpose. In this situation, the segregated amount should be recorded as a liability by the franchisor against which costs incurred by the franchisee would be charged.

Product Sales Made to Franchisee on a Continuing Basis

In the course of franchisee operations, the franchisee may purchase some or all of its supplies and equipment from the franchisor. As part of this arrangement, the franchisee may be given the right to purchase these items at a bargain price. If this price is lower than the selling price of the product to other customers or the price that is paid does not generate a reasonable profit on the equipment or supplies, a portion of the initial franchise fee should be deferred and accounted for as an adjustment of the selling price when the equipment or supplies are purchased. The portion deferred should be one of the following:

☐ The difference between the selling price of the equipment or products and the bargain purchase price that the franchisee is receiving.

☐ An amount that would cover any cost in excess of the bargain purchase price and provide a reasonable profit to the franchisor.

Accounting for Agency Sales

Some franchisors may act as an agent for franchisees by placing orders for inventory and equipment and selling them to franchisees at no profit. Franchisors involved in such transactions should account for these transactions as receivables and payables and not as revenues and expenses.

Franchising Costs

Direct costs relating to franchise sales should be recognized in the same accounting period as the revenue that they helped generate. If revenue is not yet recognized, costs incurred should be deferred until it is. However, deferred costs shall not exceed anticipated revenue less estimated additional estimated costs. Indirect costs of a regular and recurring nature that are incurred independent of the level of sales—such as general, administrative, and selling costs—should be expensed as incurred.

Repossessed Franchises

If a franchisee decides not to open a franchise business, a franchisor may recover the franchise rights through repossession. If repossession occurs, two possible outcomes may occur. The franchisor may decide to refund or not refund the money received from the franchisee. A description of the contingencies follows:

☐ *A refund is made.* If the franchisor refunds the franchisee's money, the original sale is canceled and the revenue previously recognized is accounted for as a reduction in revenue in the period in which the franchise is repossessed.

☐ *No refund is made.* If the franchisor does not refund the franchisee's money:

— The transaction should be regarded as a canceled sale.

— No adjustment should be made to any previously recognized revenue.

— Any uncollectible amounts resulting from receivables that have not been paid should be accounted for and a provision for bad debts should be provided for.

— Any money that was previously received and accounted for as deferred revenue should now be recognized as earned revenue.

Business Combinations

If a franchisor acquires an operating business from a franchisee, it should be accounted for as a business combination. However, if such an acquisition results in the cancellation of an original franchise, then it should be accounted for as a repossessed franchise. (See previous section, "Repossessed Franchises.")

Required Disclosures on the Financial Statements or Notes

The following information should be disclosed in the body of the franchisor's financial statements or notes:

☐ The nature of all significant commitments and obligations resulting from the franchise agreement, including a description of the services that the franchisor has agreed to provide but has not yet substantially performed.

☐ If no basis exists for estimating the collectibility of specific franchise fees, the notes to the financial statements should disclose:

— Whether the installment or cost recovery method is being used to account for the related franchise fee revenue.

— The sales price of the franchise.

— Revenue and related costs deferred both currently and on a cumulative basis.

— The periods in which the franchise fees become payable by the franchisee.

— Amounts that were originally deferred but later recognized because the uncertainty relating to the franchise fee's collectibility was resolved.

☐ If material, initial franchise fees should be separated from other franchise revenue.

☐ Predictable decline in future initial franchise fee revenues because sales have reached a saturation point. (This disclosure is desirable but not required.)

☐ Separate disclosure of the amount of initial franchise fees relative to the amount of net income when such amounts are not apparent. (This disclosure is desirable but not required.)

☐ Revenue and costs related to franchisor-related businesses should be shown separately from those related to franchisee related businesses when practicable.

☐ If there are significant changes in the ownership of franchisor-owned outlets or franchised outlets during the period, the following should be disclosed:

— Number of franchises sold.

— Number of franchises purchased during the period.

— Number of franchised outlets in operation during the fiscal year.

— Number of franchisor-owned outlets in operation during the fiscal year.

INSURANCE INDUSTRY

Sources of Authoritative Guidance

The sources of authoritative guidance in the insurance industry are:

☐ ASC 450, *Contingencies*.

☐ ASC 944-20, *Financial Services—Insurance: Insurance Activities*.

☐ ASC 310-20-05-2, *Receivables: Nonrefundable Fees and Other Costs*.

☐ ASC 944-20-05-20, *Financial Services—Insurance: Insurance Activities.*

☐ ASC 740, *Income Taxes.*

☐ ASC 944-20-05-38, *Financial Services—Insurance: Insurance Activities.*

☐ ASC 310-10-35-2, *Receivables: Overall.*

☐ ASC 320, *Investments—Debt and Equity Securities.*

☐ ASC 944-20-15-11, *Financial Services—Insurance: Insurance Activities.*

☐ ASC 958-320, *Not-for-Profit Entities: Investments—Debt and Equity Securities.*

☐ ASC 815, *Derivatives and Hedging.*

☐ ASC 470-50-45-1, *Debt: Modifications and Extinguishments.*

☐ ASC 860, *Transfers and Servicing.*

☐ ASC 360-10-05-4, *Property, Plant, and Equipment: Overall.*

☐ ASC 860-50, *Transfers and Servicing: Servicing Assets and Liabilities.*

☐ ASC 944-20-15-66, *Financial Services—Insurance: Insurance Activities.*

☐ ASC 944-10-15, *Financial Services—Insurance: Overall.*

☐ Accounting Standards Update (ASU) 2010-15, *Financial Services-Insurance (Topic 944), How Investments Held through Separate Accounts Affect an Insurer's Consolidation Analysis of Those Investments.*

Abstract and Introduction

Insurance is purchased to provide economic protection from identified risks occurring within a specified period. Types of risks usually covered by insurance include death, damage, injury to others, and business interruption. In general, an insurance transaction may be identified as one in which (1) the purchaser of an insurance contract makes an initial payment or deposit to the insurance company in advance of the possible occurrence or contingency and (2) the insurance company does not know if, how much, or when amounts will be payable to the insured when the insurance contract is consummated.

Insurance contracts also may be classified as either short-duration or long-duration contracts. Long-duration insurance contracts are expected to remain in force for an extended period, such as whole life, universal life, guaranteed renewable term life, endowment, annuity, title insurance, and participating life insurance contracts. Long-duration contracts with terms that are not fixed and guaranteed (i.e., more flexible contracts) are called universal-life-type contracts. Short-duration contracts (the remainder) consist mainly of property and liability contracts.

Insurance contracts that do not involve the assumption of significant insurance risks by the insurance company are referred to as investment contracts and are not accounted for as insurance. These should be accounted for as interest-bearing financial instruments.

Premiums from long-duration contracts that are not universal-life-type contracts are recognized as revenue when they are due from policyholders over the premium paying periods. Premiums that are collected on universal life-type contracts are not recognized nor reported as revenue. Rather, contract services assessments (based on contract benefits for policyholders) are recognized as revenue in the period of assessment. Amounts that policyholders are assessed representing compensation for the insurer's performance of future periods should be reported as unearned revenue and recognized in the period benefited. Short-term duration contract premiums are recognized as revenue evenly as insurance protection is provided. Claim costs (including estimates of costs for claims relating to events that have occurred but have not been reported to the insurer) are recognized when the insured event occurs.

Universal-life type contract acquisition costs are capitalized and amortized in proportion to the gross profit amounts that are derived from the operations of these contracts. Any costs that are incurred relating to the acquisition of insurance contracts other than universal-life type contracts should also be capitalized. However, these costs should be charged to expense in proportion to the premium revenue derived from these contracts.

Insurance companies that reinsure insurance contracts should account for their reinsurance receivables and prepaid reinsurance premiums as assets. Guidelines for the accounting and reporting standards used in recording and disclosing these types of transactions are fully described.

Authoritative Guidance

Classification of Insurance Contracts

In general, insurance contracts are classified as short-duration or long-duration (including universal-life-type contracts). Each category is discussed in the following paragraphs.

Short-duration contracts. Most property and liability insurance contracts are considered short duration. These contracts cover expected claim costs resulting from insured events that occur during a fixed period of short duration. The insurance company, in this situation, has the right to cancel the contract or revise the premium at the beginning of each contract period covering insured events. This enables the insurer to adjust the amount of the premiums charged or coverage provided at the end of each period. As was noted, short-duration contracts include most property and liability insurance contracts. They also include certain term life insurance contracts, such as credit life insurance. (Credit life insurance is decreasing term insurance issued on the lives of borrowers to cover the payment of debt of the insured.) Accident and health insurance contracts, for example, may be short duration or long duration, depending on whether the contract is expected to remain in force for an extended period. *Premiums from short-duration contracts are earned and recognized as revenue evenly as the insurance protection is consumed.*

Long-duration contracts. Long-duration contracts are expected to remain in force for an extended period, such as whole life, universal life, guaranteed renewable term life, endowment, annuity, title insurance, and participating life insurance contracts. These types of contracts are generally not subject to unilateral changes in their provisions. For example, policies that are of long duration may be noncancelable or may be a guaranteed renewable contract. Premiums from long-duration insurance contracts are generally level even though the policy benefits and services provided do not occur evenly over the contract periods. They are recognized as revenue throughout the pay periods of the contract. Because this premium revenue generally exceeds the policy benefits that will be derived in the early years of the contract, the insurer is required to accrue a liability for the costs that are expected to be paid in the later years of the contract. Thus, for most types of long-duration contracts, a liability is accrued for current and expected renewal contract periods. The amount of the liability is equal to the present value of estimated future policy benefits to be paid policyholders less the present value of estimated future net premiums to be collected from policyholders. These estimates are based on several assumptions, such as investment yields, mortality, morbidity (the incidence of disability caused by disease or physical impairment), terminations, and other expenses.

Universal-life-type contracts. These long-duration insurance contracts lack the fixed or guaranteed terms that are characteristic of most of the life insurance policies. They provide either death or annuity benefits and have any one of the following features:

☐ One or more of the amounts assessed by the insurer against the policyholder, such as amounts for mortality coverage, contract administration, initiation, or surrender, are not fixed or guaranteed by the terms of the contract.

☐ Amounts accruing to the policyholder, such as accrued interest on policy balances, are not fixed or guaranteed by the contract terms.

☐ The policyholder may vary the premiums within the contract limits and without the permission of the insurer.

Premium Revenue Recognition for Short-Duration Contracts

Premiums received from short-duration contracts should be recognized as revenue in proportion to the amount of insurance protection provided over the insurance contract period. However, if the period of risk differs significantly from the contract period, revenue should be recognized in proportion to the amount of insurance provided over the period of risk. As a result, premiums are generally recognized as revenue evenly over the contract period (or period of risk if that differs from the contract period). The only exception to the generalization is if the insurance protection declines according to some predetermined schedule.

Under certain circumstances, premiums may be subject to adjustment. For example, certain insurance contracts may be experience rated. That is, the premium may be determined after the period of the contract based on the insured's claim experience. In such a situation, the premium revenue should be recognized in accordance with the following guidelines:

☐ If the ultimate premium can be reasonably estimated, it should be recognized as revenue over the contract period with appropriate revision to reflect the experience of the insurance company.

☐ If the ultimate premium cannot be reasonably estimated, the cost recovery method or deposit method should be used until the ultimate premium is reasonably estimable. Under the cost recovery method, premiums are recognized as revenue in an amount equal to estimated claim costs as insured events occur. Under the deposit method, the recognition of income is deferred until the ultimate premium can be reasonably estimated. That is, premiums are not recognized as revenue and claim costs are not correspondingly recorded as expenses until a reasonable estimate is derived of the ultimate premium that will be earned by the insurer.

Premium Revenue Recognition for Long-Duration Contracts

Premiums received from long-duration contracts should be recognized as revenue when they are due from policyholders. Long-duration contracts that typically require this recognition include whole-life contracts, guaranteed renewable term life, and title insurance contracts. In the case of title insurance, for example, the premium is considered due from policyholders on the effective date of the insurance policy. It is on this date that premium revenue should be recognized. If the binder date (the date a commitment to issue the policy is given by the insurer) is earlier, it may be used as the date of premium revenue recognition.

Premiums collected on universal-life-type contracts should be recognized as revenue in the period in which the amounts were assessed against policyholders unless the amounts collected represent compensation to the insurer for more than one period. If this is the case, the amounts received for future services should be accounted for as unearned revenue and as income in the period earned.

Recognition of Claim Costs

Unpaid claim costs, including estimates of cost relating to claims that have been incurred but not reported, should be accrued when the insured events occur. The exception to this is title insurance contracts, in which estimated claim costs (including estimates of costs) are incurred but not reported. Such claims should be accrued when title insurance premiums are recognized as revenue.

The recorded liability for unpaid claims should be based on the cost of settling the claim, which, in turn, should be based on past experience adjusted for current trends as well as any other factors that would help make past experiences more current and realistic. Changes in the estimates of claim costs due to differences between estimates and payments for claims should be recognized in the period in which the estimates are changed or payments are made. Estimated recoveries from unsettled claims, such as from salvage, subrogation, or potential interests from real estate, should be evaluated for their estimated realizable value and deducted from the recorded liability for unpaid claims. Any estimated recoveries on settled claims (other than mortgage guaranty and title insurance claims) should also be deducted from the liability on unpaid claims.

In the settlement of mortgage guaranty and title insurance claims, real estate is often acquired by the insurer. The real estate should be reported at its fair value. This is the amount that could be expected to be received in a current sale between a buyer and seller. If market value is unavailable, expected cash flows (anticipated sales price less maintenance and selling costs of the real estate) may be used in estimating the fair value of the asset. The real estate acquired in settling claims should be reported in the balance sheet separately and not categorized as an investment. If there are any subsequent reductions in the reported amount of real estate or if gains or losses are realized as a result of its sale in settling claims, these amounts should be used as an adjustment of the claim costs incurred.

In Accounting Standards Update (ASU) No. 2011-06 (July 2011), *Other Expenses* (Topic 720), *Fees Paid to the Federal Government by Health Insurers,* the liability for fees required by the Patient Protection and Affordable Care Act should be recorded when the entity provides qualifying health insurance in the year the fee is payable with a corresponding deferred cost that is amortized to expense using a straight-line allocation method. The annual fee is presented as an operating expense.

Accounting for Catastrophe Losses by Property and Liability Insurance Enterprises

Property and liability insurance enterprises are entities that issue insurance contracts that protect against (1) damage to or loss of property caused by perils such as fire and theft or (2) legal liability resulting from injuries to other persons or to their property. Typically, property and liability insurance enterprises are fire and casualty insurance entities.

When a property and liability insurance entity issues an insurance policy against loss from catastrophes, it assumes a contingency relating to the risk of loss from such events. That is, it assumes the risk of loss from the occurrence of covered catastrophes that may occur during the period of the insurance contract. It incurs no potential asset impairment or liability incurrence with respect to any catastrophes that may occur beyond the insurance term.

An estimated loss from a contingency should be accrued by a charge against income if both of the following conditions occur:

☐ Information becomes known prior to the issuance of the financial statements that indicates that it is probable that an asset had been impaired or a liability had been incurred at the date of the financial statements.

☐ The amount of the loss can be reasonably estimated.

Thus, in order for a loss contingency to be accrued, the possibility of catastrophic occurrence must be reasonably predictable within the insurance contract period and the amount of the loss must be reasonably estimable. Actuarial techniques are utilized by insurance companies to predict the rate of occurrence and amounts that would have to be paid as a result of losses from catastrophes over long periods of time for insurance rate-setting purposes. Predictions over relatively short periods of time, such as an individual accounting period or the periods of coverage of a large number of outstanding insurance contracts, are subject to significant deviations. Thus, the assumption of risk of loss by accrual (by property and liability insurance companies) relating to catastrophes fails the criteria. In addition, deferral of unearned premiums within the coverage periods of "in force" insurance policies represents the unknown liability for unpaid claims, including catastrophe claim liabilities. An accrual, therefore, of an additional liability for potential losses is inappropriate. Disclosure, however, of the loss contingency is required. An insurance entity should accrue a net loss on insurance contracts that will probably be incurred in excess of deferred premiums when the liability can be reasonably estimated.

Liability Accrual for Future Policy Benefits

When premium revenue is recognized, a liability for long-duration contracts (other than title insurance contracts or universal insurance) should be accrued. The liability equals the present value of future benefits to be paid to policyholders and related expenses less the present value of future net premiums (portion of gross premiums required to provide all benefits and expenses). The liability is estimated based on expected investment yields, mortality, morbidity (the relative incidence of disability caused by disease and impairment), terminations, and other applicable expenses that are incurred at the time that the insurance contracts are consummated. Changes in the liability for future policy benefits that result from periodic estimation for financial reporting purposes should be recognized in the period in which the changes occur. It is assumed that all original assumptions continue into subsequent accounting periods for purposes of determining the liability for future policy benefits.

Liability Accrual for Universal-Life-Type Contracts

The liability for policy benefits for universal-life-type contracts should be equal to the sum of the following components:

☐ The balance that accrues to the benefit of policyholders at the date of the financial statements.

☐ Any amounts that have been assessed against policyholders to compensate the insurer for services to be performed over future periods.

☐ Any amounts that have previously been assessed against policyholders that are refundable as a result of the termination of the contract.

☐ Any probable loss (premium deficiency).

Amounts that have been assessed against policyholders in a given period that represent services to be provided in future periods are not considered to be earned in the period assessed. Such amounts should be reported as an unearned revenue liability and recognized in income only over the periods benefited. The FASB rejected the use of this account as a means of achieving a smoothing level of reported earnings for the insurance enterprise. It noted that an amount might be considered an unearned revenue liability if the substance of the insurance contract clearly indicates that the financing of the contract differs from the performance of services. In addition, an amount may be considered unearned if it assessed only in certain contract periods or in a manner that is expected to result in current profit and future losses. For example, amounts assessed for mortality protection often produces a much larger profit margin in early years than is produced for those amounts assessed in later years. In this situation, it is believed that a portion of early mortality assessments represent compensation for services to be provided in future periods. The recognition of an unearned revenue liability is required when the insurance enterprise makes premium assessments that result in profits in the early years and losses in subsequent years from the insurance benefit function. However, this does not limit the recognition of an unearned revenue liability to this case.

Acquisition Costs

Accounting Standards Update (ASU) 2010-26 provides guidance on accounting for costs associated with acquiring or renewing insurance contracts. FASB Accounting Standards Codification's Master Glossary defines acquisition costs as "costs that are related directly to the successful acquisition of new or renewal insurance contracts." These costs are generally referred to as deferred acquisition costs and are often recognized as assets. The Master Glossary defines incremental direct cost of a contract acquisition as "A cost to acquire an insurance contract that has both of the following characteristics: (a) It results directly from and is essential to the contract transaction(s), and (b) it would not have been incurred by the insurance entity had the contract transaction(s) not occurred."

These costs should be capitalized and charged to expense in proportion to the revenue that is recognized. To ensure a proper matching, acquisition costs should be allocated by the insurer by categories of insurance contracts. Unamortized acquisition costs are classified on the balance sheet as an asset.

For universal-life-type contracts, capitalized acquisition costs should be amortized over the life of a book of universal-life-type contracts at a constant rate based on the present value of the estimated gross profit amounts expected to be realized over the life of such book of contracts.

The present value of estimated gross profits should be computed using the specified contract rate (i.e., the rate of interest that accrues to policyholder balances).

An insurance entity is only allowed to capitalize acquisition costs that are directly related to the successful acquisition of new or renewal insurance contracts. Only the following costs may be capitalized:

- Incremental direct costs related to the contract.

- Total compensation of employees, including payroll-related fringe benefits, for time spent on (a) underwriting, (b) policy issuance and processing, (c) medical and inspection, and (d) sales force contract selling. Only a portion of the compensation that is for a contract that has actually been acquired may be capitalized; if the above costs were incurred for an unsuccessful contract acquisition, then those costs must be expensed.

- Other relevant costs such as, transportation and hotel expenditures or itemized communication costs, related to (a) underwriting, (b) policy issuance and processing, (c) medical and inspection, and (d) sales force contract selling that were incurred only due to contract acquisition.

- Advertising costs meeting the criteria of ASC 340-20-25-4.

An insurance entity must charge to expense all costs that do the meet the capitalization criteria. Such costs typically include: soliciting potential customers (other than through direct-response advertising, which may be capitalized in accordance with ASC 944-30-25-1A(d)), market research, training, administration, product development, or other unsuccessful acquisition or renewal efforts.

Indirect costs, such as administrative costs, rent, depreciation, occupancy costs and general overhead, must also be expensed.

Accounting Standards Update No. 2010-26 specifies that an insurance entity may apply its guidance either:

- Prospectively for fiscal years beginning after December 15, 2011, and interim periods within those fiscal years, or

- Retrospectively to all prior periods.

Premium Deficiency Recognition

Short-duration contracts. A short-duration contract premium deficiency occurs if unearned premiums do not exceed the sum of related expected claim costs and claim adjustment expenses, expected dividends to policyholders, unamortized acquisition costs, and maintenance costs. The premium deficiency should first be recognized by expensing any unamortized acquisition costs to the extent required to eliminate the deficiency. If the premium deficiency is greater than the unamortized acquisition costs, a liability should be accrued for the excess deficiency.

Long-duration contracts. A long-duration contract premium deficiency exists if the insurer's actual experience with respect to investment yields, mortality, morbidity, terminations, or expenses indicates that existing contract liabilities, together with the present value of future gross premiums, will not be sufficient to:

- ☐ Cover the present value (PV) of future benefits to be paid to or on behalf of policyholders as well as settlement and maintenance relating to long-duration contracts.

- ☐ Recoup any unamortized acquisition costs.

A premium deficiency should be computed as follows:

PV of future payments for benefits and related settlements and maintenance costs, determined by using revised assumptions based on actual and anticipated experience	$XXXX
Less: PV of future gross premiums, determined by using revised assumptions based on actual and anticipated experience	XXXX
Liability for future policy benefits using revised assumptions	$XXXX
Less: Liability for future policy benefits at the valuation date, reduced by unamortized acquisition costs	XXXX
Premium deficiency	$XXXX

The premium deficiency should be recorded by a charge to income and (1) a reduction of unamortized costs or (2) an increase in the liability for future policy benefits. If a premium deficiency does occur, future changes in the liability should be based on the insurer's revised assumptions. In addition, no loss should be recognized if it ultimately results in creating future income.

Replacement Transactions

Universal-life-type contracts are often purchased as replacements for other insurance contracts issued by the same insurer. A policyholder commonly uses the cash surrender value of the previous contract to pay an initial lump-sum premium for the new replacement contract. When a replacement occurs with a universal-life-type contract, any unamortized acquisition costs associated with the replaced contract and any difference between the cash surrender value and its previously recorded liability should not be deferred in connection with the replacement.

Accounting for Policyholder Dividends

Policyholder dividends are paid on participating insurance contracts of life insurance enterprises. These contracts allow the policyholder to participate in the earnings or surplus of the insurance entity. Policyholder dividends should be accrued using an estimate of the amount that will be paid. Two situations prevail here:

1. For life insurance companies that use life insurance dividend scales unrelated to actual net income earned, policyholder dividends should be accrued over the premium paying periods of the contract.

2. If limitations exist on the amount of net income from participating insurance contracts that may be distributed to stockholders, the amount of the policyholder's share of net income that cannot be distributed to stockholders should be excluded from stockholders' equity by a charge to current operations and a credit to a liability relating to participating policyholders funds. Dividends declared or paid to participating policyholders should then reduce this liability. Any dividends declared or paid in excess of the liability should be charged to current operations.

Contingent Commission Arrangements

Experience-rated insurance contracts sometimes provide that an insurance agent should be paid additional commissions under an experience refund arrangement. For example, if a particular policy that an insurance agent sold has had a positive experience in a given period, that agent is due additional commission. Income in any period should not include amounts that are expected to be paid to agents in the form of experience refunds or additional commissions. Instead, contingent commissions payables or receivables should be accrued over the period in which related income is recognized.

Accounting for Insurance Entity Investments

An insurance enterprise should account for its investments in debt and equity securities that have readily determinable fair values in accordance with ASC 320, *Investments—Debt and Equity Securities*.

Investments that do not have a readily determinable fair value should also be reported at fair value, with changes in such values accounted for as unrealized gains and losses and reported net of taxes in other comprehensive income. However, all or a portion of the unrealized gain or loss of a security that is designated as being hedged in a fair value hedge shall be recognized in earnings during the period of the hedge.

Mortgage loans should be reported at their outstanding principal balance if acquired at par value. When purchased at a discount or premium, they should be reported at amortized cost with an allowance for estimated uncollectible amounts. Amortization of the discount or premium and related charges or credits is charged or credited to investment income.

Investments in assets in which the holder would not recover substantially its recorded investment (e.g., interest-only strips, loans, other receivables, retained interests in securitizations) should be classified as investments in debt securities and reported in the available-for-sale or trading portfolio.

Real estate investments should be reported at their cost less any accumulated depreciation. Depreciation and related charges or credits should be charged or credited to investment income.

Real Estate Used in the Business

Real estate acquired by an insurance enterprise is classified in one of two ways: as an investment or as real estate that is being used in the entity's operations. Thus, depreciation and other real estate operating expenses should be classified either as investment expenses or as operating expenses, depending how the real estate is categorized.

When Are Separate Accounts Used by an Insurance Entity?

Insurance entities frequently maintain separate assets and liabilities accounts for a contract holder for purposes of funding fixed-benefit plans, pension plans, and variable annuity contracts. The insurance enterprise, in this circumstance, receives a fee for investment management, administrative expenses, and other related functions. It is the contract holder, however, who assumes the investment risk, as it is he or she who directs the portfolio management.

Investments in the separate accounts described previously should be reported at market value except for those with guaranteed investment returns. For those separate accounts, the related assets should be reported as investments of the insurance enterprise described in the investments section previously noted. In addition, the assets and liabilities of separate accounts should be reported as summary totals in the insurance entity's financial statements.

Separate account interests held for the benefit of policy holders should not be considered to be in the interest of the insurer. The insurer also should not combine any separate accounts held for the benefit of policy holders with the insurer's general account interest in the same investment. This does not apply to separate account interests held for the benefit of a related party (ASC 810-10-25-43, *Consolidation—Overall—Recognition*) policy holder. Related-party policy holder accounts must be combined with the insurer's general account interest for variable interest entities as required by ASC 810-10, *Consolidation—Overall*).

When consolidating an insurer's investment fund with a portion of a fund that is owned by the insurer's separate account, fund assets constituting the contract holder's interests should be included as separate account assets and liabilities (ASC 944-80-25-3, *Financial Services—Insurance—Separate Accounts—Recognition*). Remaining fund assets should be included on a line-by-line basis in the general account of the insurer. Noncontrolling interests should be classified as a liability or equity and should not be included in the separate account liability.

Income Tax Considerations

Insurance enterprises are required to recognize a deferred tax liability or asset for the deferred tax consequences of temporary differences necessitated by ASC 740. However, an insurance entity should not recognize deferred taxes on taxable temporary differences related to policyholder's surplus that arose in fiscal years beginning December 15, 1992. If, on the other hand, there is an expected reduction in policyholders' surplus, and it is likely that the insurance entity will pay income taxes either currently or in subsequent years, the income tax expense attributable to this reduction should be accrued and recognized in the current period.

Reinsurance

Insurance entities frequently seek to obtain indemnification against loss or liability from claims associated with contracts they wrote. They do this by entering into a reinsurance contract with another insurance entity called the reinsurer or assuming entity. In general, any transaction that provides indemnification to an insurer in this manner should be accounted for as a reinsurance contract. When such a contract is consummated, the original insurer, known as the ceding enterprise, pays an amount to the reinsurer and the latter agrees to reimburse the insurer for a specified portion of the claims paid under the reinsurance contract. The legal rights of the insured remain unaffected by the reinsurance transaction. Although the insurer is indemnified for contracted losses under this arrangement, it is not relieved of obligation to the original policyholder, who, incidentally, is usually unaware of the reinsurance arrangement. In addition, the reinsurer may enter into reinsurance contracts with other reinsurers to be indemnified for loss and liability in a process known as retrocession.

Indemnification against Loss or Liability Relating to Insurance Risk through Reinsurance Contracts

Ascertaining whether an reinsurer's insurance contract with a ceding enterprise provides indemnification against loss or liability relating to insurance risk requires an understanding of the arrangement between the parties involved.

Short-duration contracts. In a short-duration contract, the reinsurer is required to assume significant insurance risk under the reinsured portions of the underlying insurance contracts. In this situation, it is assumed that both the timing and amount of the reinsurer's payments will depend on and vary directly with the amounts and timing of claims settled under the reinsured contract. Provisions in the reinsurance contract that delay timely reimbursement to the ceding entity would prevent the assumption of significant risk by the reinsurer. Contractual features may also prevent the reinsurer's payments from directly varying with the claims settled under the reinsured contract.

There must be a reasonable possibility (more than remote and less than probable) that the reinsurer may realize a significant loss from the transaction. The risk transfer assessments should be made at the contract's inception, based on all the information and facts known at that time. Toward this end, very careful judgment and evaluation must be exercised to determine whether it is reasonably possible that significant loss may be realized by the reinsurer. To determine the significance of loss, the present value of all cash flows between the ceding and assuming entities under reasonable possible outcomes are compared using an appropriate and reasonable interest rate. If this comparison indicates that the reinsurer is not exposed to the reasonable possibility of significant loss, the ceding entity may be considered indemnified against loss only if substantially all of the insurance risk relating to the reinsured portions of the underlying insurance contracts has been assumed by the reinsurer. This risk transfer should be reevaluated, under ASC 944-20-05-40, when and if the terms of the reinsurance contract are amended.

Long-duration contracts. There must be a reasonable possibility that the reinsurer will realize a significant loss from indemnifying a ceding insurance entity against loss or liability in assuming the insurance risk in a reinsurance contract. Long-duration contracts that do not subject the insurance enterprise to mortality or morbidity risks should be classified as investment contracts rather than insurance contracts.

Reinsurance Transactions

Reinsurance contracts that are legal replacements of one insurer by another eradicate the ceding entity's liability to the policyholder and result in the removal of related assets and liabilities from that entity's financial statements. Some reinsurance contracts do not extinguish the ceding entity's legal liability to the policyholder. In this situation, the ceding entity should not remove the related assets and liabilities from its financial statements.

Estimated reinsurance receivables arising from those contracts with enterprises that reinsure insurers should be reported separately as assets. In addition, amounts prepaid to the reinsurer relating to reinsurance contracts should also be reported as assets.

Receivables and payables between a reinsurer and the ceded entity should be offset only when a right of set-off exists. Earned premiums ceded (paid to the reinsurer) and recoveries recognized under reinsurance contracts should be reported in either the statement of earnings or the footnotes to the financial statements.

Recognition of Revenues and Costs for Reinsurance Contracts

The parameters for revenue and cost recognition relating to reinsurance by the insurer depend on whether the contract is in fact a bona fide reinsurance contract (see section on indemnification against loss or liability relating to insurance risk). Recognition also depends on whether the contract is of a short or long duration.

Contracts That Do Not Meet the Conditions for Reinsurance Accounting

If, despite its form, the reinsurance contract does not provide for indemnification of the ceding entity against loss and liabilities, the premiums paid less the premium that is to be retained by the reinsurer should be accounted for as a deposit by the ceding entity. A net credit that results from the contract is reported as a liability by the ceding entity. A net charge resulting from the contract, on the other hand, should be reported as an asset by the reinsurer.

In addition, proceeds from reinsurance transactions that represent recovery of acquisition costs should reduce unamortized acquisition costs so that net acquisition costs are capitalized and charged to expense in proportion to net revenue recognized. If the ceded entity has agreed to service all related insurance contracts without reasonable compensation, a liability should be accrued for estimated excess servicing costs under the reinsurance contract. Any net cost should be accounted for as an acquisition cost.

Contracts That Meet the Conditions for Reinsurance Accounting

Short-duration contracts. Amounts paid for prospective reinsurance by the ceded enterprise should be accounted for and reported as prepaid insurance premiums and amortized over the remaining contract period in proportion to the amount of insurance protection provided. If the amounts paid in are subject to adjustment, the basis for amortization should be the amount that is estimated to be paid.

Amounts that are paid for retroactive reinsurance should be reported as reinsurance receivables to the extent those amounts do not exceed the recorded liabilities relating to the underlying reinsured contracts. If the recorded liabilities, in fact, exceed the amounts paid, the reinsurance receivables should be increased to reflect the difference and the resulting gain that is deferred. This gain is then amortized over the estimated remaining settlement period. (The settlement period is the estimated period over which the ceding entity expects to recover amounts from the reinsurer under the terms of the reinsurance contract.) If the amounts and timing of the reinsurance recoveries can be reasonably estimated, the gain should be amortized using the interest method. The recovery method is used when amounts and timing of recoveries cannot be estimated. The recovery method bases the amount of amortization on the proportion of actual recoveries to the total estimated recoveries. If the amount that was paid for retroactive reinsurance exceeds the recorded liabilities relating to the reinsured contracts, the ceding entity should increase the related liabilities, reduce the reinsurance receivable, or do both at the time the reinsurance contract has been effected so that the excess is charged to earnings.

The amortization of deferred amounts (under both the interest method and recovery method) should be based on estimates of the ceding entity's estimates of the expected timing and amounts of cash flows. The timing of changes in these estimates should not change the recognition of revenues and reinsurance costs.

ASC 944-20-05-40 requires that any changes in estimates relating to the amount that will be recovered from the insurer be accounted for consistently at both the beginning of and after the reinsurance transactions. Changes in the estimated amount of liabilities relating to the underlying insurance contracts should be recognized in income in the period of the change. Reinsurance receivables must reflect any adjustment in the amount recoverable from the reinsurer, and a gain should be adjusted or established.

Reinsurance contracts include both prospective and retroactive provisions. The difference between prospective and retroactive reinsurance is predicated on whether the reinsurance contract reinsures future or past insured events covered by the underlying insurance contract. In order for a claim to be covered by the underlying policy in claims-made insurance, the insured event must be reported to the insurer within the period of time covered by that policy. ASC 944-20-05-40 notes that if a reinsurance contract is entered into by the insurer, any claim made to the reinsurer in a future period as a result of insured events that occurred prior to entering the reinsurance contract is considered a retroactive contract. For example, a given reinsurance contract may insure liabilities relating to contracts applying to one or more prior years and may at the same time insure losses under contracts covering one or more future periods. In addition, a reinsurer may make an adjustment in which new or additional coverage is provided for past insurable events. To illustrate, if a reinsurer adjusts future year's premiums, which create additional coverage for previous accident years, the new additional coverage is considered retroactive although the original coverage for those same years was initially considered prospective. When possible, prospective and retroactive provisions should be accounted for separately. If separate accounting within a single contract is impracticable, the contract should be accounted for as a retroactive contract.

Long-duration contracts. The insurance enterprise should amortize the estimated cost of reinsurance of long-duration contracts over the remaining life of the underlying reinsured contracts. This compares to the cost of reinsurance of short-duration contracts where the cost is amortized over the reinsurance contract period. Determining whether an insurance contract that reinsures a long-duration contract is long or short duration is a matter of professional judgment. Nevertheless, the assumptions relating to accounting for reinsurance costs should be consistent with those used for the reinsured contract. Any difference between the amount paid for a reinsurance contract and the amount of liabilities for policy benefits relating to the underlying reinsured contract is part of the estimated cost to be amortized.

Disclosure Requirements

GAAP requires that insurance entities disclose the following information in their financial statements:

1. The basis for estimating liabilities for unpaid claims and claim adjustment expenses.

2. The methods and assumptions used in estimating the liability for future policy benefits. This should include the disclosure of the average rate of assumed investment yields in effect for the current year.

3. The nature and type of acquisition costs that were capitalized. In addition, the method of amortizing those costs and the amount that was amortized for the period should be shown.

4. The carrying amount of liabilities for unpaid claims and claim adjustment expenses on short-duration contracts. These should be presented at their present value in the financial statements with the range of interest rates that were used to discount those liabilities.

5. Determination of whether the insurance entity considered anticipated investment income in determining whether a short-duration contract premium deficiency exists.

6. The relative percentage of participating insurance, the method of accounting for policyholder dividends, the amount of dividends, and the amount of any additional income that was allocated to participating policyholders.

7. The amount of statutory capital and surplus.

8. The amount of statutory capital and surplus needed to satisfy regulatory requirements based on current operations if material in relation to the entity's statutory capital and surplus.

9. The nature of statutory restrictions on the payment of dividends and the amount of retained earnings that are not available for payment to stockholders.

10. The nature, purpose, and effect of any ceded reinsurance transactions on the insurance entity's operations. In addition, the ceded enterprise must disclose the fact that it is not relieved of its primary obligation to the policyholder in a given reinsurance transaction.

11. For short-duration contracts, premiums from direct business; reinsurance assumed; and reinsurance ceded on both a written and earned basis.

12. For long-duration contracts, premiums and amounts assessed against policyholders from direct business; reinsurance assumed and ceded; and premiums and amounts earned.

13. Methods used for income recognition on reinsurance contracts.

Ceding insurance entities are required to disclose concentrations of credit risk associated with reinsurance receivables and prepaid reinsurance premiums.

Accounting for Financial Guarantee Insurance Contracts

The purpose of these standards is to reduce the diversity in the accounting for financial guarantee insurance contracts by insurance enterprises. Additional disclosure guidelines are also provided in this statement. Enterprises included within this scope are:

☐ Stock life insurance enterprises;

☐ Property and liability insurances enterprises;

☐ Title insurance enterprises;

☐ Mutual life insurance enterprises;

☐ Assessment enterprises;

☐ Fraternal benefit societies; and

☐ Mortgage guaranty insurance enterprises (except for sections on premium revenue and claim cost recognition and acquisition costs).

This should be applied on a "contract-by-contract" basis and only apply to contracts that are not accounted for as derivative instruments. This statement does not apply to financial guarantee contracts, such as some financial institutions and government-sponsored enterprises.

Financial guarantee insurance (and reinsurance) contracts provide protection in the event of a default to holders of financial obligations. For instance, municipal bonds or asset-backed securities may be insured to provide protection in the event of a default. The direct or indirect beneficiary of the contract is the holder of the insured financial obligation. The policyholder is sometimes the issuer of the insured financial obligation (such as a municipality or a corporation) seeking to enhance its credit standing. Other times, the policyholder is both the holder of the insured financial obligation as well as the beneficiary.

At the start of a financial guarantee insurance contract, a liability for unearned premiums should be recorded by the insurance enterprise. In most instances, unearned premium revenue should be recorded at the present value of the premium due. The discount rate for determining the present value of premiums due or expected to be collected should be based upon the risk-free rate at the start of the insurance contract.

Generally, the expected period of risk equals the contract period. However, when the expected period of risk is significantly shorter than the full contract period due to expected prepayments, then the expected period may be used only if a homogenous pool of assets underlying the insured financial obligation is contractually pre-payable.

When the expected period is used to measure unearned premium revenue, an insurance enterprise should adjust pre-payment assumptions as they change. Adjustment to unearned premium revenue should equal the adjustment to premium receivable; it should have no effect on earnings at the time of adjustment.

The insurance enterprise should assess whether premiums expected to be collected are fully collectible. Premiums receivable should be adjusted for uncollectible premiums by adjusting earnings. When the contract period is used as the period of the financial guarantee insurance contract, the insurance enterprise should adjust unearned premium revenue to reflect early principal payments.

Insurance protection provided is assumed to be directly related to the insured principal amount outstanding. Hence, premium revenue from financial guarantee insurance contracts should be recognized over the period of the contract in proportion to the amount of insurance protection provided. As premium revenue is recognized, unearned premium revenue should be decreased. The proportion of premium revenue to be recognized should be a constant rate based on the insured principal amount outstanding in a given period compared with the sum of each of the insured principal amounts outstanding for all periods.

In some instances (such as zero coupon bonds), the insured financial obligation accretes to the principal amount over its life and has a single principal payment at maturity. The ratio to calculate the amount of revenue to be recognized should be based on the unearned premium revenue divided by the sum of all insured accreted principal amounts outstanding during each reporting period.

Sometimes, the issuer of the insured financial obligation will retire the obligation before its maturity and replace it with a new financial obligation. This refunding situation typically occurs when the interest rates have declined. In such instances, the insurance enterprise should immediately recognize any nonrefundable unearned premium revenue and associated acquisition costs that were previously deferred. If the insured enterprise will be insuring the new financial obligation, it should recognize unearned premium revenue in a manner similar to a separate transaction. If the premium charged for the new transaction is different from the premium that would normally be charged in such a transaction, the difference should be recognized in current earnings.

A claim liability should be recognized if the insurance enterprise expects that a claim loss will exceed the unearned premium revenue. The claim liability should be valued at the present value of expected cash flows to be paid using a current risk-free discount rate. Expected net cash flows are simply probability weighted.

In periods subsequent to the initial recognition of a claim liability, the insurance enterprise should update the discount rate each reporting period. All revisions to the claim liability in subsequent periods should be recognized as a claim expense in the period of the change, as a change in accounting estimate.

The insurance enterprise is required to disclose information that would enable users to understand the factors affecting present and future recognition and measurement. The insurance enterprise should disclose the following information for each annual period, and interim period if a significant change has occurred:

☐ The insurance enterprise should disclose as of the date(s) of statement of financial position, including the line item on the statement of financial position where the amounts are reported:

— If premiums are received over the period of contract rather than at its start, the premium receivable and the unearned revenue liability.

— The amount of accretion on the premium receivable.

— The weighted-average risk-free rate used to discount the premiums expected to be collected and the weighted-average period of the premium receivable.

☐ A schedule of premiums expected to be collected in the next four quarters of the subsequent annual period, and for each of the next four annual periods. The remaining periods should be aggregated in five-year increments.

☐ A roll-forward of the premium receivable for the period, including the premium receivable at the beginning of the period, premium payments received, new business written, adjustment to premium receivable, and ending premium receivable.

☐ If premium revenue recognition has been accelerated, the amount and reason for acceleration.

☐ The weighted-average risk-free rate used to discount the claim liability, as well as significant components of the change in claim liability.

☐ A disclosure of the enterprises risk management activities used to track the deteriorating insured financial obligations.

The insurance enterprise shall also disclose:

☐ Number of issued and outstanding financial guarantee insurance contracts.

☐ Remaining weighted-average contract periods.

☐ Insured contractual payments outstanding, segregated by principal and interest.

☐ Gross claim liability.

☐ Gross potential recoveries.

☐ Discount, net (both claim liability and potential recoveries).

☐ Net claim liability.

☐ Reinsurance recoverables.

☐ Unearned premium revenue.

MOTION PICTURE INDUSTRY

Sources of Authoritative Guidance

The source of authoritative guidance in the motion picture industry is ASC 926-10-15-2, *Entertainment—Films: Overall*.

Abstract and Introduction

An entity should recognize revenue from a sale or licensing arrangement of a film when five conditions are met. If a licensing arrangement of a single film provides that an entity will receive a flat fee, the entity should recognize this fee as revenue only when it has met all five criteria. The costs of producing a film and bringing that film to market consists of film costs, participation costs, and manufacturing costs. An entity should report its film costs as a separate asset on its balance sheet. An entity should amortize film costs and accrue participation costs using the individual-film-forecast-computation method, which amortizes or accrues (expenses) in the same ratio that current period actual revenue (numerator) bears to estimated remaining unrecognized ultimate revenue as of the beginning of the current fiscal year (denominator). An entity should account for advertising costs in accordance with ASC 720-35, *Other Expenses: Advertising Costs*. All other exploitation costs, including marketing costs, should be expensed when incurred. An entity should charge manufacturing costs and duplication costs of products for sale, such as videocassettes and digital video discs, to expense on a unit- specific basis when the related product revenue is recognized.

Authoritative Guidance

Revenue Recognition-Basic Principles

An entity may license films to such customers as distributors, theaters, exhibitors, or other licensees on either an exclusive or nonexclusive basis in a particular market and territory.[*] The license fee may be fixed (flat fee) or based on a percentage of a customer's revenue (variable fee). A variable-fee arrangement may include a nonrefundable guarantee that may be paid in advance or over a license period.

Revenue from a sale or licensing arrangement of a film should be recognized when all of the following conditions are met:

☐ Persuasive evidence exists of a sale or licensing arrangement with a customer.

☐ The film is complete and has been delivered or is available for immediate and unconditional delivery (in accordance with the terms of the arrangement).

☐ The license period of the arrangement has begun and the customer can begin its exploitation, exhibition, or sale.

☐ The fee that has been arranged for is fixed or determinable.

☐ Collection of the fee is reasonably assured.

If one or more of the preceding conditions are not met, the entity should defer recognizing revenue until all of the conditions are met.

If a receivable is recognized on the accounting records of an entity for advances presently due or cash payments are received prior to revenue recognition, the entity should also recognize an equivalent liability for deferred revenue until the entity satisfies all five conditions of revenue recognition. If that receivable is transferred to a third party, the liability for deferred revenue should not be reduced and the revenue for the film should not be recognized until all conditions of revenue recognition are met.

Discussion of Revenue Recognition Considerations

Persuasive evidence of an arrangement is generally provided only by a contract or other enforceable document that indicates the license period that is applicable, the film or films that are affected, the rights transferred, and the consideration

---

[*] The following discussion is based on "Accounting Changes for the Film Industry," by Marc H. Levine and Joel Siegel (*The CPA Journal*), October 2001, pp. 32–38.

that will be exchanged. If these factors somehow raise doubt regarding the obligation or ability of either party to perform under the terms of the arrangement, revenue should not be recognized by the entity. Based on the aforementioned, forms of verifiable evidence (e.g., a written contract, purchase order, or on-line authorization) to document the contract arrangements should be presented. This evidence should clearly show that there is in fact a mutual agreement between the entity and the customer or that actions by the customer are in accordance with such an agreement.

Delivery. Revenue recognition should not occur until the product is delivered, assuming the licensing agreement requires such an agreement. If no such requirement exists, it is assumed that physical delivery is required in order to recognize revenue. Some licensing agreements do not require the delivery of the film to the customer. If the arrangement gives the customer immediate and unconditional access to the film print or authorization to make the film immediately and unconditionally available for the customer's use, the delivery condition for revenue recognition is considered met. If the licensing agreement requires that the entity make significant changes to a film after its initial availability to a customer, the delivery condition is not deemed to be met. Revenue should not be recognized until these significant changes are met as well as the other conditions for revenue recognition previously discussed. Significant changes are additions of new or revised content to the film after it is initially available to the customer. Costs for reshooting a scene or adding special effects, for example, should be added to the film costs and charged to expense when the entity recognizes the related revenue. Insignificant changes consist of insertions or additions of preexisting film footage, additions of dubbing or subtitles (done to existing footage), removal of offensive language, reformatting a film, and adjustments to allow for the insertions of commercials. These changes do not preclude the recognition of revenue by the entity prior to their completion and should be accrued and charged to expense if the entity begins to recognize revenue from the agreement before incurring those costs.

Availability. Some arrangements in a given contract will restrict a customer from initiating its exploitation, exhibition, or sale of a given film. For example, a contract may restrict a customer from selling or displaying a given home video product until months in the future, or a film may be restricted from exploitation, exhibition, or sale in a given territory or market for a period of time. In these situations, revenue should not be recognized until the restrictions lapse or expire and the conditions of revenue recognition previously noted are satisfied.

Fixed or determinable fee. If a single film arrangement provides that an entity will receive a flat fee, that entire fee (considered fixed and determinable) should be recognized revenue when the entity has met all of the other revenue recognition conditions. In a multiple-films arrangement (including films not yet produced or completed), the entity should allocate the fixed or determinable fee to each individual film by market or territory, based on relative fair values of the rights to exploit each film under the licensing agreement. Allocations to a film or films not yet produced or completed should be based on the amounts refundable if the entity does not ultimately complete and deliver the films to the customer.

The remaining flat fee is allocated to the completed films based on their relative fair values of the rights to exploit them. Once an allocation is made, it should not be adjusted later. If relative fair values of films exploitation in a licensing arrangement cannot be ascertained, the fee is not fixed or determinable and the entity should not recognize revenue until such a determination can be made and all other conditions of revenue recognition are met. In determining the fair value of the rights to exploit an individual film that is part of a multiple-film arrangement, an entity must use the best information available in the circumstances with the objective of measuring the amount the entity believes it would have received had it entered into a license agreement that grants the same rights to the film separately rather than as a part of a multiple-film arrangement.

Variable fees. If the entity's fee arrangement is predicated on a percentage or share of customer's revenue from the exhibition or other exploitation of a film, recognition of revenue should be based on meeting the conditions of revenue recognition previously noted as the customer exhibits or exploits the film.

Nonrefundable minimum guarantees. In licensing arrangements that have a variable-fee structure, a customer may guarantee to pay an entity, a nonrefundable minimum amount, that is to be applied against the variable fee on a film or films that are not cross-collateralized. The nonrefundable minimum guarantee should be considered fixed and determinable and should be recognized as revenue by the entity when all of the other conditions of revenue recognition are satisfied. If the nonrefundable minimum amount is applied against variable fees from a group of films on a cross-collateralized basis, the amount of the minimum guarantee applicable to each film cannot be objectively determined. Revenue recognition during the license period should be recognized when the revenue recognition conditions previously noted are all satisfied. If at the end of the license period, a portion of the nonrefundable minimum guarantee remains unearned, an entity should recognize the remaining guarantee as revenue by allocating it to the individual films based on their relative performance.

Barter revenue. If a licensing agreement to television stations provides programming in exchange for a specified amount of advertising on that station, the transaction is deemed a nonmonetary transaction. The accounting for this type of transaction should be in accordance with ASC 845, *Nonmonetary Transactions*.

Returns and price concession. If the contract arrangement between the customer and the entity includes a right-of-return provision or the entity's past practices allow for such a procedure, then in order for the entity to recognize revenue, it must meet several conditions.

Revenue recognition when right of return exists. For example, in the home video business, customers are frequently granted price protection on previously purchased and unsold products if the entity subsequently reduces its wholesale prices. At the date of revenue recognition, in this case, the entity is required to account for allowances given the possibility of price reduction. If future price concessions cannot be reasonably and reliably estimated (or there are some uncertainties regarding the entity's ability to maintain its prices), the revenue to be recognized is not considered fixed and determinable. The entity, in this situation, should not recognize revenue until it can make reasonable and reliable estimates of future price changes.

Licensing of film-related products. An entity should recognize revenue from licensing arrangements of film-related products only after it releases the film itself.

Present value. The amount of revenue recognized in connection with a licensing agreement should represent the present value of the licensing fee as of the date that the entity first recognizes the revenue.

Costs and Expenses

By definition, the costs of producing a film and bringing that film to market consists of:

☐ Participation costs,

☐ Exploitation costs, and

☐ Manufacturing costs.

Discussion of Cost and Expenses Considerations

Capitalization of film costs. Film costs include all direct costs incurred in the physical production of a film. They include expenditures such as the costs of story and scenario; film rights to books, stage plays, or original screenplays; compensation of cast, directors, producers, and extras; costs of set construction, operations, and wardrobe; costs of sound synchronization; rental facilities on location; and post production costs (music, special effects, and editing). They also include allocations of production overhead and capitalized interest costs. Production overhead consists of the costs of individuals or departments that have a significant (or exclusive) responsibility for the production of films. These costs should not include administrative and general expenses and the costs of certain "overall deals." An entity may enter an arrangement called an overall deal, in which a producer or the like is compensated for his or her creative services. If the costs of overall deals cannot be associated with specific projects, they should be charged to expense as they are incurred over the related period of time. In general, an entity should record a reasonable proportion of costs of overall deals as specific project film costs to the extent that these costs are directly related to the acquisition, adaptation, or development of specific projects.

The cost of adaptation or development should also be added to the cost of a particular property. The entity should periodically review properties in development to see if they will be used in the production of a film. If it is determined that a property in development will be disposed of, the entity should recognize a loss on these costs by charging them to the current-period income statement. The guideline to follow in these situations is that it is assumed that an entity will dispose of a property either by sale or abandonment if it has not been set for production within three years from the time of the first capitalized transaction. The amount of the loss is the amount by which the carrying amount of the project exceeds its carrying value. Amounts that have been written off should not be recapitalized. The costs of producing a film and bringing it to market should be reported as a separate asset on the entity's balance sheet.

Additional guidance for film costs is required for an episodic television series. Ultimate revenue for an episodic television series generally includes estimates from initial and secondary markets. The initial market is the first market of exploitation in each territory. That market may include a distribution channel, such as a broadcast or cable television network or first-run syndication. Secondary markets, by definition, are markets other than the initial market. Until an entity can establish estimates of secondary market revenue, the capitalized costs for each episode produced should not exceed the amount equal to the amount of revenue contracted for that episode. Any costs incurred in excess of this limitation on an episode-by-episode basis should be expensed as film costs incurred and not restored as capitalized film costs. As an entity recognizes the revenue for each television episode, the related capitalized costs of production (including the costs of sets) should be expensed. However, once the entity can estimate its secondary market revenue, it should capitalize all subsequent film costs. These capitalized expenditures, however, should be amortized and periodically evaluated for impairment.

Film costs amortization and participation costs accruals. An entity is required to amortize film costs and accrue participation costs using the individual-film-forecast-computation method. The method amortizes or accrues film costs in the following ratio:

$$\frac{\text{Current period actual revenue}}{\substack{\text{Estimated remaining unrecognized ultimate revenue* as of the beginning} \\ \text{of the current fiscal year}}}$$

* The concept of ultimate revenue will be discussed in detail later.

To calculate the amount of film costs that should be amortized for the period, the unamortized film costs as of the beginning of the current fiscal year are multiplied by the individual-film-forecast-computation method fraction. In addition, unaccrued ultimate participation costs that have to be recorded for the period are expensed by multiplying the individual-film-forecast-computation method fraction by the unaccrued ultimate participation costs at the beginning of the current fiscal year. Using this technique ensures that, in the absence of changes in estimates, film costs are amortized and participation costs are accrued in a manner that generates a constant rate of profit over the ultimate period for each period before exploitation costs (marketing, advertising, publicity, promotion, and other distribution expenses, manufacturing costs, and other period costs.) Participation costs are contingent payments paid to parties involved in the production of a film based on contractual formulas (participations) and by contingent amounts derived under the provisions of collective bargaining agreements (residuals).

Those that collect such amounts are called participants and these costs are collectively called participation costs. Participants generally include creative talent, such as actors, writers, or entities, from whom distribution rights are licensed. In general, an entity should accrue a liability for participation costs only if it is probable that there will be a sacrifice of assets to settle its obligation under the terms of a participation agreement.

EXAMPLE

Individual-Film-Forecast Method of Amortization for a Film in Its Initial Year of Release

Given: Film cost—$62,500

   Estimated ultimate revenue—$125,000

   Actual revenue earned in Year 1—$75,000

   Estimated ultimate participation costs—$12,500

Film Cost Amortization in Year 1:

$$\frac{\$75{,}000 \text{ earned revenue}}{\$125{,}000 \text{ ultimate revenue}} \times \$62{,}500 \text{ film costs} = \$37{,}500$$

Participation costs accrued in Year 1:

$$\frac{\$75{,}000 \text{ earned revenue}}{\$125{,}000 \text{ ultimate revenue}} \times \$12{,}500 \text{ ultimate film costs} = \$7{,}500$$

   Actual results may very well vary from those that were estimated. Therefore, at each reporting date, the entity should review and revise estimates of ultimate revenue and participation costs to reflect the most available information. If revisions take place, the entity should determine a new denominator that includes only the ultimate revenue from the beginning of the fiscal year of the change (the ultimate revenue changes are treated prospectively as of the beginning of the fiscal year of change). The numerator (revenue for the current fiscal year) is unaffected by the change. The entity should apply the revised fraction to the net carrying amount of unamortized film costs and to the film's unaccrued ultimate participation costs as of the beginning of the fiscal year, and the difference between expenses determined using the new estimates and any amounts previously expensed during that fiscal year should be charged or credited to the income statement in the fiscal year of the revised estimates.

EXAMPLE

Individual-Film-Forecast Method of Amortization Where Estimates Are Revised Subsequent to the Initial Year of Release

Given: Film cost—$100,000

Estimated ultimate revenue:

Year 1—$200,000

Year 2—$180,000 (This is not the remaining revenue starting from this year.)

   Actual Revenue earned:

   In Year 1—$120,000

   In Year 2—$20,000

Estimated ultimate participation costs:

Year 1—$20,000

Year 2—$18,000

For Year 1, film costs amortization was $60,000 and participation costs accrued were $12,000

Film cost amortization in Year 2:

$$\frac{\$20,000 \text{ earned revenue}}{\$60,000 \text{ remaining ultimate revenue}^2} \times \$40,000^1 \text{ unamortized film costs}$$

$$= \$13,333$$

Participation costs accrued in Year 2:

$$\frac{\$20,000 \text{ earned revenue}}{\$60,000 \text{ remaining ultimate revenue}} \times \$6,000^3 \text{ remaining ultimate participation costs}$$

$$= \$2,000$$

---

[1] Film cost of $100,000 minus cumulative prior amortization of $60,000.
[2] Year 2 revised ultimate revenue of $180,000 minus cumulative prior earned revenue of $120,000.
[3] Year 2 revised ultimate participation expense of $18,000 minus cumulative prior accrued costs of $12,000.

Ultimate revenue. The ultimate revenue that was included in the individual-film-forecast-computation method fraction just illustrated includes estimates of revenue that are expected to be recognized by an entity from the exploitation, exhibition, and sale in all markets and territories. However, the following constraints apply:

☐ For films other than an episodic television series, ultimate revenue should include estimates over a period not to exceed 10 years following the date of the film's release.

☐ For an episodic television series, ultimate revenue should include estimates of revenue over a period not to exceed 10 years from the date of delivery of the first episode.

☐ For an episodic television series still in production, ultimate revenue should include estimates of revenue over a period not to exceed five years from the date of delivery of the most recent episode (if later than the date of delivery of the first episode).

☐ Ultimate revenue for an episodic television series should include estimates of all secondary market revenue only if the entity can show that it will be able to successfully license those episodes already produced and those committed to be produced in the secondary market.

☐ For previously released film acquired as part of a film library, ultimate revenue should include estimates over a period not to exceed 20 years from the date of acquisition. A film library consists of, for purposes of this guidance, those films whose initial release dates were at least three years prior to the acquisition date.

☐ If persuasive evidence exists that revenue can be generated from a market or territory or a history of such earnings exists, this revenue should be included in estimates of ultimate revenue. Use estimates of revenue from newly developing territories only if an existing arrangement provides convincing evidence that the entity will, in fact, realize such amounts.

☐ If convincing evidence exists that revenue can be generated from licensing arrangements with third parties to market film-related products (e.g., a contract between the entity and third party exists giving the entity a nonrefundable minimum guarantee or nonrefundable advance), then estimates of such revenue should be included in ultimate revenue.

☐ Ultimate revenue should include estimates of the portion of wholesale or retail revenue from an entity's sale of such items as toys and apparel (peripheral items) that are attributable to the exploitation of themes, characters, or features of a film if the entity can show that there is a history of such revenue generation from, for example, similar kinds of films.

☐ Estimates of revenue from unproven or undeveloped technologies should not be included in ultimate revenue.

☐ Estimates of wholesale promotion or advertising reimbursement from third parties should not be included in ultimate revenue. These amounts should be offset against exploitation costs incurred by the entity.

☐ Estimates of amounts related to the sale of film rights for the following periods should not be included in ultimate revenue:

— For films other than episodic television series, estimates exceeding a period of 10 years following the date of the film's initial release.

— For episodic television series, estimates exceeding a period of 10 years from the date of delivery of the first episode or, if still in production, a period exceeding five years from the date of delivery of the most recent episode, if later.

☐ Ultimate revenue should be discounted to its present value. All foreign currency estimates of future revenues should be predicated on current spot rates. In addition, ultimate revenue should not include projections for current inflation.

Ultimate participation costs. Estimates of unaccrued ultimate participation costs are used in the individual-film-forecast-computation method to arrive at current period participation cost expense. As was noted, such costs are derived based on estimates of film costs, exploitation costs, and ultimate revenue. If at any balance sheet date, the recognized participation costs liability exceeds the estimated unpaid ultimate participation costs for an individual film, the excess liability should be reduced with an offsetting credit to unamortized film costs. To the extent that an excess liability exceeds unamortized costs for that film, it should be credited to income. If a film continues to generate revenue after its film costs are fully amortized, the entity should accrue associated participation costs as the additional revenue is recognized. That is, associated participation costs should be recognized when additional revenue is recorded on fully amortized films.

EXAMPLE

Participation Liability That Is in Excess of a Revised Estimate of Amounts Ultimately Payable

As previously indicated, a participation liability that exceeds the unpaid amount expected to be ultimately payable should be offset against the remaining carrying value of the corresponding film. This situation can result from the changes in ultimate revenue and cost estimates that result in reduced expectations of ultimate participation costs.

Given: Film cost—$100,000

    Estimated ultimate revenue:

        Year 1—$200,000

        Year 2—$160,000

    Actual revenue earned:

        Year 1—$120,000

        Year 2—$120,000

    Estimated ultimate participation costs:

        Year 1—$20,000

        Year 2—$0

In Year 1, film cost amortization was $60,000 and participation costs accrued were $12,000.

Adjustments of participation liability and film costs in Year 2:

	Unamortized Film Costs	Participation Liability
Balance at end of Year 1	$ 40,000[1]	$ 12,000
Adjustment to eliminate excess liability	(12,000)	(12,000)
Adjusted balances	$ 28,000	$ 0

---

[1] Film cost of $ 100,000 minus film cost amorization of $60,000 in Year 1.

    Film Cost amortization in Year 2:

$$\frac{\$20,000 \text{ earned revenue}}{\$40,000 \text{ remaining ultimate revenue[3]}} \times \$28,000[2] = \$14,000$$

Participation costs accrued in Year 2:

$$\frac{\$20{,}000 \text{ earned revenue}}{\$40{,}000 \text{ remaining}} \times \$0 \text{ remaining ultimate revenue}[4] = \$0$$
$$\text{ultimate revenue}$$

[2] Film costs of $100,000 minus cumulative prior amortization of $60,000 minus the excess participation liability adjustment of $12,000.

[3] Year 2 revised ultimate revenue of $160,000 minus cumulative prior earned revenue of $120,000.

[4] Estimated ultimate participation costs were reduced to $0 in Year 2. Therefore, the excess liability was reduced and no further accruals were required.

Film costs valuation. The following circumstances require an assessment by an entity of the possibility that the fair value of a film, regardless of its completion, is less than its amortized costs:

☐ There is an adverse change in the expected performance of the film prior to its release.

☐ Actual costs substantially exceed budgeted costs.

☐ There are significant delays in its completion or release schedules.

☐ There is a reduction in the initial release pattern or changes in other release patterns.

☐ There are insufficient resources (funding) to complete the film and market it effectively.

☐ Actual performance subsequent to release does not meet prior expectations.

If one or more of these indications or others like them imply that the fair value of a film is less than its unamortized costs, the fair value of the film should be determined. This determination should be influenced by estimated future exploitation costs still to be incurred. The entity should then compare the fair value of the film to the unamortized capitalized costs and write off to the income statement the amount by which the unamortized capitalized costs of the film exceed its fair value. After writing down a film to fair value, the costs that have been written off should never be restored in subsequent periods.

It is common to use a discounted cash flow model to estimate fair value. In estimating the future cash flows for a given film, the following should be considered:

☐ The public's perception of the film's story, director, producer, and cast.

☐ Historical results of similar films.

☐ Historical results of the cast, director, or producer in prior films.

☐ If previously released, the film's performance in prior markets.

☐ The running time of the film.

☐ The degree of cash outflows necessary to generate the film's cash inflows. The entity should incorporate estimates of future costs to complete the film, future exploitation, participation costs, and other necessary cash outflows in determining fair value.

When determining the fair value of a film using a traditional discounted cash flow approach, the following additional guidelines should be considered:

☐ The discount rates should not be an entity's incremental borrow rates, liability settlement rates, or weighed average cost of capital. These rates do not consider the risks associated with a film asset.

☐ The discount rates used should consider the time value of money and expectations about possible variations in the amount or timing of the most likely cash flows. This rate should also be adjusted to incorporate the uncertainty inherent in a film asset including illiquidity and market imperfections.

Subsequent evidence leading to a write-down of unamortized film costs. If a film is released around the entity's balance sheet date and evidence exists that a write-down of the film's unamortized costs is required, then, if the entity has not issued its financial statements, it should adjust its financial statements for the effect of any changes in estimates resulting from the use of subsequent evidence. The entity is not required to take such action during the subsequent period if it can be shown that the conditions leading to the write-off did not exist at the date of the balance sheet.

Accounting for film advertising costs. Advertising costs incurred by an entity should be accounted for in accordance with ASC 720-35-05, *Other Expenses: Advertising Costs*. Marketing costs and all other exploitation costs should be expensed as incurred.

Incurrence of manufacturing costs. The costs of products for sale, such as videocassettes and digital video discs, should be expensed on a unit-specific basis and charged to manufacturing and/or duplication of products for sale when the related product revenue is recognized. At the balance sheet date, the entity should evaluate its inventory of these products to determine whether adjustments are required when considering their net realizable value and obsolescence exposures. In addition, the costs of theatrical film prints should be expensed over the period that these costs benefit.

Disclosure. Film costs should be disclosed as noncurrent assets on the balance sheet if the entity presents a classified balance sheet. Regardless of whether or not the entity's balance sheet is presented as classified, the portion of unamortized costs of its completed films that will be written off during its upcoming presumably 12-month operating cycle should be disclosed in the financial statements. In addition, the components of film costs should be separately shown as theatrical films and direct-to-television products. These film costs (within each of the two categories) should be further divided into the following classifications including: released; completed and not released; in production; or in development or preproduction.

An entity should disclose the percentage of unamortized film costs for released films (excluding acquired film libraries) that it plans to amortize within three years from the entity's balance sheet date. If the percentage is less than 80%, the entity must disclose the period required to reach that amortization level (80%). For acquired film libraries, an entity must disclose the amount of unamortized costs that remains, the method of amortization, and the amortization period that is being used.

The following miscellaneous disclosure guidelines should also be followed:

☐ The amount of accrued participation liabilities that an entity expects to pay during the upcoming operating cycle should be disclosed.

☐ Cash flows for film costs, participation costs, exploitation costs, and manufacturing costs should be disclosed by the entity in the operating activities section of its Cash Flow Statement. The amortization of film costs in the reconciliation of net income to net cash flow from operating activities should also be shown.

☐ The method of accounting for revenue, film costs, participation costs, and exploitation costs should be disclosed.

☐ The entity should disclose the effect on income before extraordinary items, net income, and related per-share amounts of the current fiscal period for a change in estimate that affects several future periods.

☐ Events occurring subsequent to the date of the balance sheet that do not require an adjustment to the financial statements but require disclosure so as to keep the financial statements from being misleading should be shown.

RECORD AND MUSIC INDUSTRY

Sources of Authoritative Guidance

The source of authoritative guidance in the record and music industry is ASC 928, *Entertainment—Music*.

Abstract and Introduction

ASC 928-10-05-1, *Entertainment—Music: Overall*, discusses the standards of financial accounting and reporting for licensors and licensees in the record and music industry. A licensor of a music copyright or the owner of a record master should recognize license fees as revenue if a license agreement is, in substance, an outright sale and collectibility of the licensing fees is reasonably assured. A licensee, paying minimum guarantees to a licensor, should record them as assets and charge them to expense in accordance with the terms of the license agreement. Compensation paid to artists in the form of royalties should be adjusted for anticipated returns and charged to expense in the period in which the sale of the recording takes place.

Authoritative Guidance

Accounting for Licensors

An entity may generate a significant amount of revenue by licensing the rights of ownership in a record master or music copyright. A record master is the master tape of the performance of an artist. It is used to produce the molds used for commercial record production and other CDs and tapes for use in making cartridges, cassettes, and reel tapes. In a licensing agreement, the licensor (owner of a record master or music copyright) grants the licensee the right to sell or distribute records or music for a fixed fee (paid to the licensor) or for a fee based on the sales of records or music. In many instances, a license agreement is, in substance, an outright sale. ASC 928-605-25-2, *Entertainment—Music: Revenue Recognition*, requires the earnings process regarding licensing fees relating to such agreements (licensor agreements) to be considered complete and reported as revenue if collectibility of the full fee is reasonably assured and the following criteria relating to the licensor has been met. The licensor must have:

☐ Signed a noncancelable contract.

☐ Agreed to a fixed fee.

☐ Delivered the rights to the licensee who is free to exercise them.

☐ In addition, there must be no remaining significant obligations to furnish music or records.

A minimum guarantee is commonly paid by a licensee. The licensor should report such a payment as a liability initially and recognize the guarantee as revenue as the license fee is earned. If the amount of license fee earned cannot be ascertained, the guarantee should be recognized equally over the remaining period of the license agreement. Other fees (such as free records distributed by a record club in excess of a predetermined amount) that are required by a license agreement and are not fixed in amount prior to the expiration date of the agreement should be recognized as revenue only when reasonable estimates of such amounts can be made or when the agreement has expired.

Compensation to Artists

Royalties earned by recording artists should be adjusted for anticipated returns and charged to expense in the period in which the sale of the recording takes place. If an advance royalty is paid to an artist, it should be reported as an asset if the artist's current popularity and past performance provide a valid basis for estimating the amount of the advance that will be recoverable from future royalties to be earned by the artist. Advances should be charged to expense as subsequent royalties are earned by the artist. If it appears that a portion of future royalties is not recoverable from future royalties to be earned by the artist, such portion should be charged to expense in the period in which the loss becomes apparent. Advance royalties should be classified as either current or noncurrent assets.

Cost of Record Masters Incurred by a Record Company

Costs for record masters incurred by a record company should be reported as an asset if the current popularity and past performance of the artist indicate a sound basis for estimating the recovery of cost from future sales. If not, the cost should be expensed. Costs that are recognized as assets should be amortized over the estimated life of the recorded performance using a method that reasonably matches the amount of net revenue to be realized.

The part of the cost of record masters (incurred by the record company) that is recoverable from the royalties of an artist should be accounted for as an advance royalty, as discussed in the section on compensation to artists.

Accounting by Licensees

Minimum guarantees are commonly paid in advance by a licensee. This amount should be reported by a licensee as an asset and subsequently charged to expense. If all or a portion of the recorded guarantee appears not to be expense. If all or a portion of the recorded guarantee appears not to be recoverable through the future use of rights derived from the license, then that amount deemed unrecoverable should be charged to expense. Any other fees that must be paid (e.g., free records distributed by a record club in excess of a predetermined amount) that are not fixed in amount prior to the expiration date of the license agreement should be estimated and accrued by the licensee on a license-by-license basis.

Disclosure Requirements

ASC 928 requires that the following be disclosed by a record entity:

1. Commitments for artist advances that are payable in future years and future royalty guarantees.

2. The recorded cost of record masters incurred by the record company that are recorded as assets.

GOVERNMENT CONTRACTS—ACCOUNTING FOR THE CONTRACTOR

Sources of Authoritative Guidance

The source of authoritative guidance in government contracts—accounting for the contractor is:

☐ ASC 912, *Contractors—Federal Government*.

Abstract and Introduction

ASC 912-605-05-2 deals with the accounting problems arising under cost-plus-fixed-fee (CPFF) contracts. Fees received under government CPFF contracts should be credited to income on the basis of partial performance, assuming reasonable assurance that realization has taken place. Billable fees may also be accrued as income unless the accrual is not reasonably related to the proportionate performance of the total work or services.

Contractor profit in a fixed-price supply contract that is unilaterally terminated by the government accrues as of the effective date of the termination. That is, the contractor in such a situation is entitled to reimbursement for all costs plus a fair portion of the fixed contractual fee.

Authoritative Guidance

Government contracts are generally prepared on a CPFF structure, which allows for possible renegotiation if the government believes that the contract has been generating excess profits. In addition, the government usually reserves the right in these agreements to terminate the contract at its convenience.

CPFF contracts allow the contractor to collect a fixed fee from the government as well as all costs incurred required to satisfy the contract. The government, in contracting for the construction of some product or the performance of services, may choose at its discretion to withhold a certain percentage of payments due on the contract while the work is being performed. If the government should choose to terminate the contract for a given reason, the contractor is entitled to be repaid for all costs incurred as well as a proportionate part of the contracted fixed fee.

From the contractor's point of view, the primary accounting problem is when to recognize profits on CPFF contracts with the government. A contractor should not recognize any profits on CPFF contracts until the services have been fully performed and accepted unconditionally by the government or the product that has been manufactured has been deemed to meet the government's contractual standards. However, if a government contract is expected to last over an extended number of years, the contractor should use the percentage-of-completion method.

When accounting for CPFF contracts, two general rules prevail:

1. When the contract calls for only the performance of services by the contractor, all fees charged should be included in the contractor's revenue account.

2. When the contract involves the manufacture of goods and products, contractor's sales and revenue accounts should include the fees generated on the project as well as all reimbursable costs.

Renegotiating Government Contracts

As previously noted, most government CPFF contracts allow the government to make adjustments of the original sales price of the contract when excessive profits are being generated by the contractor. Generally, an estimate is made and an adjustment provision is accounted for. The basis for the estimate is predicated on the government's past experiences in the industry as well as the contractor's past experiences. If a reasonable estimate cannot be made and a renegotiation of sales revenue cannot be reached, that fact should be fully disclosed in the footnotes of the contractor's financial statements. The estimate of the reduction of sales revenue should be shown in the (contractor's) income statement as either contra-sales or contra-income. The adjustment provision should be shown as a current liability on the balance sheet, assuming it will be satisfied in one year or in the operating cycle, whichever is longer. In the next accounting period, if it is determined that the estimate accounted for in the prior period was incorrect relative to the final adjustment, the change that is required should be shown in the income statement in the period in which final resolution is determined.

A contractor should account for revenue on CPFF contracts using the installment method or the cost recovery method, if it is deemed that collections from the government will not be reasonably assured. However, this situation is generally very unusual.

Government Contract Disclosures

When a material portion of an enterprise's revenue is derived from government contracts, that fact must be disclosed in the financial statements or in the notes of the contractor. Specifically, disclosure is required if at least 10% of the entity's revenue is generated from contracts with the federal, state, local, or foreign government. In addition, the following disclosures should be made:

- ☐ Uncertainty exists that the provision that was made for renegotiation of the contract by the government is insufficient and additional charges may be required.

- ☐ The basis for ascertaining the provision for renegotiation should be disclosed (e.g., past experience, industry experience).

Terminated War and Defense Contracts

War and defense contracts have generally been made on both a CPFF and fixed-price basis. If the government terminates a war or defense contract, the determination of the extent of profit that should be accounted for should be made as of the effective date of the termination. The contractor, on this date, has the right to accrue any amount due from the government on the part of the contract that has been canceled. The amount of profit that should be accrued is the difference between all allowable costs that have been incurred by the contractor and the amount of the termination claim. However, most of the contracts that are signed with the government provide a minimum-profit-percentage formula that should be used if an agreement regarding what should be paid by the government cannot be reached.

If a reasonable estimate of the termination claim cannot be made for reporting purposes, this fact should be fully disclosed in the notes to the financial statements, including the uncertainty involved.

Termination claims on the accounting records of the contractor should be shown as current assets. Prior to receiving these notices, advances that are paid should be deducted from termination claims receivable. Correspondingly, any loans that are received by the contractor based on the termination claims or security of the governmental contract should be disclosed separately on the contractor's balance sheet as current debt.

Sometimes a contractor reacquires items that were included in the termination claim. These items, known as disposal credits, should be recorded as a new purchase and applied as a reduction of the termination claim.

Termination Claims Disclosure Requirements

Termination claims based on governmental contracts should be classified as receivables on the balance sheet of the contractor. However, if material in amount, they must be separately disclosed from other receivables in the financial statements.

Contractors should fairly estimate the amount of the termination claim by determining the amounts that are collectible. In addition, provision should be made for those amounts whose collectibility are questionable. Of course, these items should be fully disclosed in the financial statements.

OIL- AND GAS-PRODUCING ACTIVITIES

Sources of Authoritative Guidance

The sources of authoritative guidance in oil- and gas-producing enterprises are:

☐ ASC 932-10-05-2, *Extractive Activities—Oil and Gas: Overall.*

☐ ASC 932-235-55, *Extractive Activities—Oil and Gas: Notes to Financial Statements.*

☐ ASC 230, *Statement of Cash Flows.*

☐ ASC 740, *Income Taxes.*

☐ ASC 280-10-05-2, *Segment Reporting: Overall.*

☐ ASC 410-20, *Asset Retirement and Environmental Obligations: Asset Retirement Obligations.*

☐ ASC 360-10-05-4, *Property, Plant, and Equipment: Overall.*

☐ ASC 470-50-45, *Debt: Modifications and Extinguishments.*

☐ ASC 932-360-25-10, *Extractive Activities—Oil and Gas: Property, Plant, and Equipment.*

☐ ASC 932-360-25-18, *Extractive Activities—Oil and Gas: Property, Plant, and Equipment.*

☐ ASC 275-10-05-2, *Risks and Uncertainties—Overall—Background.*

☐ Accounting Standards Update (ASU) 2010-03, *Extractive Activities—Oil and Gas (Topic 932), Oil and Gas Reserve Estimation and Disclosures.*

☐ Accounting Standards Update (ASU) 2010-14, *Accounting for Extractive Activities—Oil and Gas.*

Abstract and Introduction

Oil and gas entities are required to follow the successful efforts approach. After strong opposition from small oil and gas producers, the SEC examined both the successful efforts approach and the full cost approach and found both methodologies to be lacking. In place of them, the SEC believed that an alternative method would be appropriate. This alternative, entitled Reserve Recognition Accounting (RRA), had not yet been fully developed. In response to the SEC's decisions, the FASB suspended the requirement that the successful efforts approach be used. However, because of many insurmountable estimation problems relating to the RRA method, the SEC abandoned its choice and established guidelines that allowed oil and gas companies to use either the successful efforts approach or the full cost approach. (The full cost method of accounting requires that all exploratory costs be capitalized because these represent integral costs of locating the existence of productive wells. Smaller exploration-oriented oil companies generally use the full cost method. The successful efforts method of accounting requires that only exploratory costs of successful wells be capitalized; exploratory costs of unsuccessful wells are expensed. Many successful, large oil companies use the successful efforts approach.) However, because of the importance of value-based disclosures relating to oil and gas reserves advocated by the RRA method, current value disclosures relating to oil-and gas-producing activities was required.

SEC has disclosure requirements relating to oil- and gas-producing. Comprehensive guidelines relating to the full cost approach are described in regulations published by the SEC. With respect to the results of operations for oil- and gas-producing activities, the following information should be presented for the year:

☐ Revenues.

☐ Production (lifting) costs.

☐ Explorations expenses.

☐ Depreciation, depletion, amortization, and valuation provisions.

☐ Income tax expenses.

☐ Results of operations for oil- and gas-producing activities (excluding corporate overhead and interest costs).

Publicly traded enterprises with significant oil and gas activities should disclose the following as supplementary information with their financial statements:

☐ Proved oil and gas reserve quantities.

☐ Capitalized costs relating to oil- and gas-producing activities.

☐ Costs incurred in oil and gas property acquisition, exploration, and development activities.

☐ Results of operations for oil- and gas-producing activities.

☐ A standardized measure of discounted future net cash flows relating to proved oil and gas reserve quantities.

Costs of drilling exploratory wells should be capitalized pending determination of proved reserves. If the well has found proved reserves, the capitalized costs become part of the enterprise's wells, equipment, and facilities. On the other hand, if the well has not found proved reserves, the capitalized costs (net of any salvage value) of drilling the well should be expensed.

Sometimes reserves found in an exploratory well cannot be classified as proved until drilling is completed. To classify as proved reserves, there must be reasonable certainty that the geological and engineering data supporting the quantities of reserves are recoverable under existing economic and operating conditions.

Exploratory well costs should be capitalized when the well has found a sufficient quantity of reserves to justify its completion as a producing well.

If there is substantial doubt about the economic or operational viability of the project, the exploratory well or exploratory-type stratigraphic well should be assumed to be impaired. Its costs, net of any salvage value, should be charged to expense.

An enterprise cannot continue to capitalize the costs of an exploratory well if there is a chance that market conditions will change or technology will be developed to make the development of the project economically and operationally viable.

The following is a list of some of the factors that an enterprise should consider in determining sufficient progress on assessing the reserves and the economic and operating viability of the project. This list is not exhaustive and no single indicator is determinative. All relevant facts and circumstances should be considered when making the determination:

1. Commitment of appropriately skilled project personnel.

2. Costs incurred to assess the reserves and their potential development.

3. Consideration of the economic, legal, political, and environmental aspects.

4. Sales contracts with customers for the oil and gas.

5. Agreements with governments, lenders, and venture partners.

6. Requests for proposals for development of required facilities.

7. Existence of plans, timetables, or contractual commitments.

8. Progress made on contractual arrangements allowing for future development.

9. Existing transportation and other infrastructure available for the project.

Long delays in the assessment or development plan may raise concerns about progress to continue the capitalization of a exploratory well after the completion of drilling.

Oil- and gas-producing activities include searching for crude oil, including condensate and natural gas liquids or natural gas in their natural states and original locations. They involve acquiring property rights or properties to extract oil and gas, or for exploratory purposes. In addition, they are comprised of construction, drilling, and production activities necessary to retrieve oil and gas, as well as the extraction of saleable hydrocarbons intended to be upgraded into synthetic oil or gas.

Oil- and gas-producing activities do not include transporting, refining, or marketing activities. Moreover, processing of produced oil, gas, or natural resources that can be upgraded into synthetic oil or gas by an entity that does not serve as a producer of such natural resources is not considered an oil or gas activity. Activities concerning production of natural resources, other than oil, gas, or natural resources from which synthetic oil and gases can be extracted, are also not considered oil or gas activities.

Authoritative Guidance

Types of Assets Utilized in Oil- and Gas-Producing Activities

An oil- and gas-producing entity is involved in activities that require special types of assets. The costs of these assets should be capitalized when they are incurred. The following are definitions of the special types of assets that are used in the oil- and gas-producing industry:

Mineral interests in properties. Generally referred to as *properties*, these include fee ownership or a lease, concession, or other interest that provides the legal right to produce, or a revenue interest in the production of oil or gas. Properties may also include royalty interests, production payments that are payable in oil or gas, and agreements with foreign governments under which an entity participates in the operation of the properties or serves as producer of the underlying reserves. Properties do not include other supply agreements or contracts that represent the right to purchase rather than extract oil and gas. Properties are classified as being proved or unproved.

Proved properties. Proved properties are properties with proved reserves. Proved reserves consist of proved oil and gas reserves, proved developed oil and gas reserves, and proved undeveloped reserves. A discussion of these three components follows.

Proved oil and gas reserves are those that are expected to be recovered either through:

☐ Existing wells with existing equipment and operating methods or when the cost of additional equipment is relatively insignificant with respect to the cost of a new well.

☐ Installed extraction equipment and infrastructure, which must be operational at the time of the reserve estimate, if the extraction does not involve a well.

Oil and gas reserves may be classified as "proved" using geoscience analysis and engineering data if it can be estimated with reasonable certainty that they are economically producible given:

☐ Existing economic conditions;

☐ Operating methods; and

☐ Government regulations (before the time the contract expires, unless evidence supports with reasonable certainty that the contract will be renewed).

Either the project to extract hydrocarbons should have started or it should be reasonably certain that it will start within a reasonable time. "Proved" areas of the reservoir include:

☐ Any area identified by drilling, and limited by fluid contact (if any); or

☐ Adjacent undrilled areas of the reservoir judged with reasonable certainty to be continuous with, and contain economically producible oil and gas based on, geoscience and engineering data.

If data on fluid contact is lacking, proved quantities in a reservoir are limited by the lowest known amount of hydrocarbons as seen in a well penetration, unless a lower contact is established with reasonable certainty using geoscience, engineering, or performance data.

Proved oil reserves may be assigned in the structurally higher portions of the reservoir when direct observation from well penetrations has defined a highest known oil elevation and the potential exists for an associated gas cap, if geoscience, engineering, or performance data establish the higher contact with reasonable certainty.

Economic producibility from a reservoir is based on existing economic conditions, including cost and prices. The price is calculated as the average price during the 12-month period before the ending date of the period covered by the report, determined as unweighted arithmetic average of the first day of the month price for each month within such a period, unless prices are defined by contractual arrangements, excluding escalations based upon future conditions.

Proved undeveloped reserves are reserves that are expected to be recovered from new wells on undrilled acreage, or from existing wells for which a relatively major expenditure is required for recompletion. Reserves on undrilled acreage should be limited to those directly offsetting development spacing areas that are reasonably certain of production when drilled, unless reliable technology provides evidence that it is reasonably certain that it will have economic producibility at greater distances.

Unproved properties. These are properties with no proved reserves.

Wells and related equipment and facilities. These include the costs of items incurred to:

☐ Drill and equip the exploratory wells and exploratory-type stratigraphic test wells that have found proved reserves. Stratigraphic test wells are drilling projects that are geologically directed to obtain information pertaining to specific geological information.

☐ Obtain access to proved reserves and provide facilities for extracting, treating, gathering, and storing the oil and gas, including the drilling and equipping of development wells (a productive well drilled within the proved area of an oil or gas reservoir drilled down to the stratigraphic horizon) and development-type stratigraphic test wells and service wells (a well drilled for the purpose of supporting production in an existing field).

Support equipment and facilities used in oil- and gas-producing activities. These include such items as drilling equipment, construction and grading equipment, seismic equipment, vehicles, repair shops, warehouses, and supply points.

Uncompleted wells, equipment, and facilities. The costs of these assets include those incurred to (1) drill and equip wells that are not yet completed and (2) acquire or construct equipment and facilities that are not yet completed and installed.

Accounting for Incurred Costs

ASC 932-360-25-5, *Extractive Activities—Oil and Gas: Property, Plant, and Equipment*, requires that acquisition costs that are incurred to acquire a property (whether unproved or proved) through purchase, lease, or otherwise must be capitalized when incurred. Examples of these expenditures include:

☐ Lease bonuses.

☐ Options to purchase or lease properties.

☐ Portions of costs applicable to minerals when land including minerals rights is purchased.

☐ Brokers' and legal fees.

☐ Other related acquisition costs.

Exploration. Exploration involves:

☐ Identifying those areas that warrant examination.

☐ Examining those areas that have been determined to contain oil and gas reserves.

Exploration costs may be incurred both before acquiring a given property (prospecting costs) and after its acquisition. The principal types of exploration costs (including depreciation and operating costs of support equipment and facilities; see the subsequent section on support equipment and facilities) and other costs of exploration activities consist of:

☐ Geological and geophysical costs, such as topographical and geophysical studies, rights of access to properties to conduct these studies, and salaries of geologists.

☐ Costs of carrying and retaining undeveloped properties.

☐ Dry hole contributions and bottom hole contributions.

☐ Costs of drilling and equipping exploratory wells.

☐ Costs of drilling exploratory-type stratigraphic test wells.

Other exploration costs. Geological and geophysical exploration costs and the costs of carrying and retaining undeveloped properties should be charged to expense when they are incurred.

The costs of drilling exploratory wells and the costs of drilling exploratory-type stratigraphic test wells should be capitalized as part of the entity's uncompleted wells, equipment, and facilities pending determination of whether the well has found proved reserves. Based on what is found, the following accounting procedures should be followed:

☐ If proved reserves have been found by the well, the capitalized costs of drilling the well should become part of the entity's wells and related equipment and facilities.

☐ If proved reserves have not been found by the well, the capitalized costs of drilling the well, net of salvage value, should be charged to expense.

It is common for an oil- and gas-producing entity to perform exploration activities on a property owned by another in exchange for the contractual right to receive an interest in the property if proved reserves are found to exist. If, in fact, proved reserves are found, the costs should become part of the proved property acquired. Alternatively, if proved reserves are not found, the entity performing the exploration activities is due reimbursement for the costs incurred and should account for them as a receivable.

Development. Development costs are incurred by oil- and gas-producing companies to obtain access to proved reserves and to provide facilities for extracting, treating, gathering, and storing the oil and gas. Development costs are incurred to:

☐ Prepare and allow for access to well locations for drilling, including determining specific drilling sites, clearing ground, draining, road building, and relocating public roads, gas lines, and power lines, and other considerations necessary in the development of proved reserves.

☐ Drill and equip development wells, development-type stratigraphic wells, and service wells, including the costs of platforms and well equipment such as casing, tubing, pumping equipment, and the wellhead assembly.

☐ Acquire, construct, and install production facilities. These include lease flow lines, separators, treaters, heaters, manifolds, measuring devices, production storage tanks, natural gas cycling and processing plants, and utility and waste disposal systems.

☐ Provide improved recovery systems.

ASC 932-360-25-5 notes that all costs incurred to drill and equip development wells, development-type test wells, and service wells are, in fact, development costs and should be capitalized whether or not the well is successful. All costs incurred in the drilling of those wells as well as the costs of constructing equipment and facilities should be included in the entity's uncompleted wells, equipment, and facilities until drilling or construction is completed. At completion, the costs become part of these assets costs.

Costs of production. The production process involves bringing the oil and gas to the surface as well as gathering, treating, field processing, and storing them. Production costs include those costs needed to operate and maintain an entity's wells, related equipment, and facilities; depreciation; and other costs of operating support equipment and facilities. These costs become part of the oil and gas that is produced. The following are examples of production costs incurred in lifting gas and oil to the surface:

☐ Costs of labor to operate the wells and related equipment and facilities.

☐ Repairs and maintenance.

☐ Materials, supplies, and fuel consumed, and services utilized in operating the wells and related equipment and facilities.

☐ Property taxes and insurance applicable to proved properties and wells and related equipment and facilities.

☐ Severance taxes.

In addition to the aforementioned production costs, depreciation, depletion, amortization of capitalized acquisition, exploration, and development costs also become part of the cost of oil and gas produced.

Support equipment and facilities. Support equipment and facilities include such items as seismic equipment; construction and grading equipment; vehicles; repair shops; warehouses; supply points; camps; and division, district, or field offices. All costs of acquiring or constructing support equipment and facilities should be capitalized. Some support equipment or facilities may have been acquired or constructed for a single activity, including exploration, development, or production. Others may serve two or more of these activities and may also serve in the transportation, refining, and marketing activities of the enterprise. If support equipment and facilities are used in oil- and gas-producing activities, their depreciation and operating costs are considered exploration, development, or production costs based on the specific use.

Disposition of Acquisition Costs after Capitalization

Acquisition costs of proved properties and the costs of wells and related equipment and facilities should be amortized and become part of the cost of oil and gas that is produced. In general, if impairment of unproved properties is found to exist, it should be recognized. In addition, the costs of exploratory wells or exploratory-type stratigraphic test wells should be charged to expense if it is ascertained that the wells have not realized proved reserves. The following discussion of GAAP augments these concepts related to the disposition of capitalized acquisition costs.

Assessment and reclassification of unproved properties. A periodic assessment of unproved properties should be made to ascertain whether impairment has occurred. Impairment is likely to have occurred if, for example, a dry hole has been drilled on it and the entity has no plans to continue drilling in the future. In general, if drilling has not begun on the property or nearby properties, the probability of its partial or total impairment increases as the expiration of the lease term approaches. If, in fact, impairment is indicated in a periodic assessment, a loss should be recognized through the use of a valuation allowance account.

A property should be reclassified from an unproved to a proved property when proved reserves are discovered on or are otherwise attributed to the property.

Depletion, Amortization, and Depreciation Considerations

Depletion of proved properties. Capitalized acquisition cost of proved properties should be depleted (amortized) by the unit-of-production method. By doing so, each unit-of-production is assigned a pro rata portion of the unamortized acquisition costs. The unit-of-production method may be applied on a property-by-property basis or on the basis of some reasonable aggregation of properties with a common geological structural feature or stratigraphic condition, such as a reservoir or field. The unit cost should be computed on the basis of the total estimated units of proved oil and gas reserves. The total amount of depletion is then computed based on the number of units produced in the current period. Unit-of-production depletion rates should be reevaluated whenever needed, but at least once a year. All such revisions should be accounted for prospectively as changes of accounting estimates.

Assessing the reserves and accounting for an exploratory well or exploratory-type stratigraphic well when drilling is completed. As was noted previously, the costs of drilling an exploratory strategic well or exploratory-type stratigraphic well are capitalized as part of the entity's uncompleted wells, equipment, and facilities. A determination must then be made of whether the well has proved reserves. If these are found, the costs of drilling the well should be capitalized and reclassified as part of the entity's wells, equipment, and facilities. If they are not found, the costs are expensed. There may be circumstances in which it is ascertained that a well has oil and gas reserves that cannot, when the drilling is completed, be characterized as proved. The costs of drilling such a well should continue to be capitalized if it is determined that (1) the well has a sufficient quantity of reserves to justify its completion as a producing well and (2) progress is being made in assessing its reserves and economic viability. If the entity obtains information that places in doubt the economic viability of the well, or either of the two aforementioned criteria is not met, the well should be viewed as being impaired and its net costs expensed. In addition, an exploratory well or exploratory-type stratigraphic well's costs should not continue to be capitalized predicated on the possibility that current market conditions will change (i.e., improve) or technology that has not yet been developed will materialize, thus guaranteeing that the well is economically feasible.

In evaluating the progress being made on the assessment of a project's reserves and economic feasibility, some important determinants may be used:

☐ The entity has an ongoing assessment process in progress to appraise the economic, legal, political, and economic aspects of the well's development.

☐ Costs are currently being incurred to evaluate the potential of the well's reserves.

☐ Sales contracts with customers for the oil and gas currently exist or are in the process of being negotiated for.

☐ Contractual progress is being made that will permit the development of the reserves.

☐ There are outstanding requests for development of facilities that will be needed to develop the reserves.

☐ Contractual agreements with governments, lenders, and venture partners relating to the oil and gas currently exist that are in the process of being negotiated for.

☐ There is a clear commitment of appropriate-level project personnel who have the requisite skills required for the development of the reserves.

☐ Plans, established timetables, and contractual commitments relating to the wells all exist and include seismic testing and drilling of additional exploratory wells.

☐ Transportation and other related infrastructure is available or will be available for the project.

The existence of inordinate delays in the assessment of the well's reserves indicates doubt that sufficient progress is being made and that capitalization of the well's costs after completion of the drilling should continue. Moreover, if substantial assessment activities have not taken place, or such activities have been suspended, any costs of the well that have been capitalized, net of salvage value, should be expensed. Thereafter, the continuation of the process of capitalization of costs associated with exploratory wells or exploratory-type stratigraphic wells should not take place without the occurrence of substantial reserve assessment activities. However, it is important to note that brief interruptions in assessment activities on the part of the entity do not require the expensing of capitalized well costs.

Amortization and depreciation of exploratory drilling and development costs. The units-of-production method should be used to amortize (depreciate) the capitalized cost of exploratory wells or exploratory-type stratigraphic wells that have proved reserves and development costs. The computation should be performed on a property-by-property basis or on an aggregation of properties basis such as on a reservoir or field. With respect to natural gas cycling and processing plants, a method other than the units-of-production method of depreciation may be preferable.

The unit-of-production calculation should be predicated on the basis of the total estimated units of proved developed reserves rather than all proved reserves. Proved reserves are the basis for depleting the acquisition costs of proved properties. Proved developed reserves that may materialize only after large additional development costs are incurred (e.g., construction of improved recovery systems for the wells) should be excluded from the amortization rate. In addition, future development costs should never be anticipated in calculating the appropriate amortization rate. The units of production amortization rate should be reevaluated at least once a year; however, revisions should be done sooner if circumstances indicate such a need. ASC 250-10-45-17, *Accounting Changes and Error Corrections: Overall*, requires such revisions be accounted for prospectively as changes in accounting estimates.

Depreciation of support equipment and facilities. Depreciation of support equipment and facilities should be accounted for as either exploration cost, development cost, or production cost based on the assets' specific use.

Dismantlement, restoration, and abandonment costs. Obligations for these costs must be accounted for in accordance with ASC 410-20-25-2, *Asset Retirement and Environmental Obligations: Asset Retirement Obligations*. Salvage values must be considered in determining amortization and depreciation rates.

Amortization of Oil and Gas Reserve Costs That Are Produced Jointly

Many properties contain a combination of oil and gas reserves. This presents a problem for amortizing capitalized costs using the unit-of-production method, which requires that the number of current units of oil or gas produced be determined and be compared to the total units of gas or oil reserves in a property or group of properties to be estimated. In those cases where a combination of oil and gas resources is present, the gas and oil produced should be converted to a common unit of measure on the basis of their approximate relative energy content without considering their relative sales value.

If, on the other hand, the relative proportion of gas and oil extracted in the current period is expected to be the same throughout the remaining life of the property, the unit-of-production methodology may be computed on the basis of only one of the minerals. In addition, if either oil or gas dominates both the reserves and current production (evaluated on the basis of relative energy content), the unit-of-production process should be computed on the basis of the dominant mineral only.

Information that surfaces after the balance sheet date. Any information that becomes known after the balance sheet date but before the financial statements are issued should be considered as having existed at the balance sheet date. For example, information that may be ascertained regarding the assessment of an unproved property during the period subsequent to year-end but prior to the financial statements issuance should be considered to have existed at the balance sheet date and should be disclosed. In addition, if an exploratory well is in progress at the end of a financial period and is determined not to have any proved reserves before the financial statements are issued, the costs incurred up until the end of the period, net of any salvage, should be charged to expense for this period. However, previously issued financial statements should not be retroactively restated for this new information.

Surrender or abandonment of properties. ASC 932-360-25-5 requires that when an unproved property is surrendered, abandoned, or determined to be worthless, all capitalized acquisition costs should be charged off against the related allowance that has been provided for impairment. When the allowance is insufficient, a loss should be recognized.

If only a single well or piece of equipment is abandoned or retired as part of an individual property or group of proved properties (constituting an overall amortization base), and the remainder (of the property or group) continues to produce oil or gas, then no gain or loss should be recognized on the abandonment or retirement. Instead, the assets being abandoned or retired should be considered to be fully amortized and their cost should be charged to accumulated depreciation, depletion, or amortization. When the last well on an individual property or group of properties (on which amortization is aggregately computed) ceases to produce and the entire property or group is abandoned, a gain or loss should be recognized. A loss is also recognized if a partial abandonment or retirement of a proved property or group of proved properties, or the abandonment or retirement of wells or related equipment, results from a catastrophic event or other major abnormality.

Mineral property conveyances. Mineral interests in properties are commonly conveyed to others. This may be due to a desire to obtain financing, spread risks, improve operating efficiency, and achieve tax benefits. Conveyances may involve the transfer of all or part of the rights and responsibilities of operating a property. Similarly, the transfer may be of a non-operating interest to another party with full retention of the property's operation.

ASC 932-360-25-5 requires that a gain or loss should not be recognized at the time of conveyance when:

☐ Assets used in oil- and gas-producing activities (including both proved and unproved properties) are transferred in exchange for other assets also used in oil and gas production. If proved properties are transferred in exchange for others also used in gas- and oil-producing activities, and if an impairment loss is found, the guidance of ASC 360-10-15-3, *Property, Plant, and Equipment: Overall*, must be followed regarding its recognition in accounting.

☐ Assets in a joint undertaking are jointly pooled with the intention of finding, developing, or producing oil or gas from a particular property or group of properties.

ASC 932-360-25-5 also requires that a gain not be recognized at the time of conveyance when:

☐ A part of an interest owned is sold and substantial uncertainty exists about the recovery of costs applicable to the retained interests.

☐ A part of an interest owned is sold and the seller has a substantial obligation for future performance (e.g., obligation to drill a well or operate the property without reimbursement for the portion of drilling or costs to the interest that was sold).

If a conveyance is not classified as one of the transactions described in the aforementioned sections, then a gain or loss would ordinarily be recognized unless other aspects of the transaction would prohibit such recognition under GAAP.

Accounting for income taxes. Oil- and gas-producing companies are required to follow ASC 740, *Income Taxes*. These entities incur many transactions (e.g., intangible drilling and development costs that are deductible in determining taxable income when incurred but are capitalized and amortized for financial accounting purposes for successful exploratory wells and development wells) that enter into the determination of taxable income and pretax accounting income in different periods. These transactions generate temporary differences that result in deferred income tax consequences. In applying ASC 740 to the gas and oil industry, the possibility that statutory depletion in future periods will reduce or eliminate taxable income in future years should be considered. This is important in determining the likelihood that the tax benefits of deferred tax assets will be realized. However, the tax benefit of the excess of statutory depletion over cost depletion for tax purposes should not be recognized until the period in which the excess is deducted for income tax purposes.

Capitalizing interest costs under the full cost method. For oil- and gas- producing operations accounted for by the full cost method, assets that are in use in the earnings process of the entity do not quality for capitalization of interest cost. Unusually significant investments in unproved properties and major development projects that are not currently being used (and as a result are not being depreciated, depleted, or amortized) and on which exploration or development activities are in progress qualify for capitalization of interest costs. In addition, a cost center with no production, significant properties, and projects on which exploration or development activities are in progress represents assets qualifying for capitalization of interest costs.

Disclosure. All oil-and gas-producing enterprises must disclose in their financial statements the method of accounting for costs incurred in their oil- and gas-producing activities and the manner of disposing of capitalized costs relating to those activities.

For purposes of this section, an entity is considered to have *significant* oil- and gas-producing activities if it satisfies one or more of the following criteria:

☐ Revenues from oil- and gas-producing activities are 10% or more of the combined revenues of all of the entity's industry segments.

☐ The results of operations for oil and gas activities, including equity earnings or losses from oil- and gas-producing activities, excluding income taxes, are 10% or more of the greater of:

— The combined operating profit (including equity earnings) of all industry segments that did not incur an operating loss.

— The combined operating loss of all industry segments that did incur an operating loss.

☐ The identifiable assets, including the investment balance in the oil- and gas-producing activities of equity method investees, relating to oil and gas activities are 10% or more of the combined identifiable assets of the enterprise, excluding assets used exclusively for general corporate purposes.

This determination should be applied separately for each year for which a complete set of annual financial statements are presented (e.g., a statement of financial position, an income statement, and statement of cash flows including necessary footnotes).

The aforementioned disclosures are required only for complete sets of annual financial statements; they are not required in interim financial reports. Interim financial reports should, however, include information about a major discovery or other favorable or adverse events that cause a significant change from the information relating to oil and gas reserve quantities presented in the most recent annual financial report issued.

An entity that engaged in oil- and gas-producing activities must disclose information about continued capitalization of exploratory well costs as part of its complete set of annual financial statements. Moreover, such disclosure is not deemed to be supplementary information. In the notes of the financial statements, the entity should disclose management's application of judgment in its evaluation of a project's capitalized exploratory well costs. While these disclosures are not normally required in interim financial statements, any significant changes should be disclosed in these statements. Any impairment of capitalized exploratory well costs (capitalized for a period of greater than one year after the completion of drilling at the most recent annual balance sheet date) are considered significant and should be disclosed in interim financial statements. In addition, the following disclosures are required:

☐ Amount of capitalized exploratory well costs pending the determination of proved reserves. For each annual period that an income statement is presented, the reporting entity is also required to disclose:

— Additions in capitalized exploratory well costs resulting from pending determination of proved reserves.

— Changes in capitalized exploratory well costs due to reclassification to wells, equipment, and facilities based on the determination of proved reserves.

— Capitalized exploratory well costs that were expensed.

☐ Amount of exploratory well costs that have been capitalized:

— For a period greater than one year after the completion of drilling at the most recent balance sheet date.

— The number of projects.

— An aging schedule should be provided for exploratory costs that have been capitalized for a period greater than one year after the completion of drilling at the most recent balance sheet date. The aging schedule should include exploratory costs classified by year or range of years and the number of projects related to such costs.

☐ For exploratory well costs capitalized for more than a year after the completion of drilling at the time of the most recent balance sheet date, a description of the projects and an evaluation about classifying the reserved as proved.

A publicly traded entity is not required to make disaggregated disclosures about its equity method investments if they were acquired before December 31, 2009, it is unable to obtain the information needed for the disclosure, and it has made an exhaustive effort to try to obtain the information. Otherwise, the entity must provide the required disclosure or explain why it has not been able to provide the disaggregated disclosure information.

Publicly traded entities that have significant oil- and gas-producing activities are required to disclose with their complete sets of annual financial statements the following information, which is considered to be of a supplementary nature:

☐ Proved oil and gas reserve quantities.

☐ Capitalized costs relating to oil- and gas-producing activities.

☐ Costs incurred for property acquisition, exploration, and development activities.

☐ Results of operations for oil- and gas-producing activities.

☐ A standardized measure of discounted future net cash flows relating proved oil and gas reserve quantities.

Details relating to these categories are discussed next.

Disclosures relating to proved oil and gas reserve quantities. Publicly traded entities that have significant oil and gas production activities are required to disclose the following supplemental information relating to proved oil and gas quantities:

☐ Net quantities of the entity's interests in proved oil and gas reserves and proved developed oil and gas reserves and proved undeveloped oil and gas reserves (including condensate and natural gas liquids, synthetic oil, synthetic gas, and other nonrenewable natural resources that are intended to be upgraded to synthetic oil and gas). Net quantities should include reserves relating to royalty interests owned if the necessary information is available to the entity. If this information is unavailable, that fact and the entity's share of oil and gas produced for those royalty interests should be disclosed for the year. Net quantities should not include interests of others in properties owned by the entity.

☐ Changes in net quantities or an entity's proved reserves of oil and gas. The following should be disclosed with an explanation:

— Revisions of previous estimates either upward or downward resulting from new information derived from development drilling.

— Changes in reserve estimates resulting from the application of improved recovery techniques.

— Purchases of minerals in place.

— Additions to proved reserves that result from (1) extension of proved acreage through additional drilling in periods subsequent to discovery and (2) discovery of new fields with proved reserves.

— Production.

— Sales of minerals in place.

☐ The entity shall disclose net quantities of proved reserves of oil and gas and changes in them in the aggregate and separately by geographic region. If proved reserves are located entirely within the entity's home country, such information should also be disclosed. A geographic region may be an individual country, a group of countries within a continent, or a continent. All facts and circumstances, not only the quantity of reserves, should be considered in determining whether the reserves are significant. The disclosure should be made for each country or geographic area that contains 15% or more than an entity's proved reserves (expressed on an oil-equivalent-barrels basis). An entity's proportionate share of reserves, when using the equity method of investment, should be included when determining an entity's reserves.

☐ Quantities of oil and gas liquid reserves and any changes in them should be disclosed in barrels and cubic feet, respectively.

☐ Important economic consideration or significant uncertainties affecting an entity's proved reserves should be disclosed. Examples are unusually expensive development or lifting costs, and the necessity of building major pipeline or other major facilities before reserve production could begin.

☐ Proved reserves do not have to be disclosed when disclosure is prohibited by the country in which the reserves are located. In addition, proved reserves need not be disclosed when the country prohibits disclosing a particular field and the disclosure would have the effect of disclosing reserves in a particular field. If disclosure of reserves is prohibited by a government, but the government does not prohibit the inclusion of the reserve as part of a more aggregated total quantity, the entity should include the reserve in the total, most disaggregated geographic area that is permissible.

☐ The entity should indicate that the disclosed reserve estimates or amounts do not include amounts for a specific country if that country's government restricts the disclosure of estimated reserves for properties under its authority or of amounts under long-term supply, purchase, or similar agreements or contracts. If the government requires disclosure of reserves other than proved, the entity must disclose that the reserve estimates do not include amounts for that specific country or that reserve estimates include reserves other than proved.

Disclosures relating to capitalized costs of oil- and gas-producing activities. An entity must disclose the aggregate capitalized cost relating to its oil- and gas-producing activities as well as the aggregate related accumulated depreciation, depletion, amortization, and valuation allowances at the end of the year. In general, balances of major classes of depreciable assets should be disclosed by nature or function. Thus, there should be separate disclosure of capitalized costs for mineral interests in properties, wells and related equipment and facilities, support equipment and facilities used in oil- and gas-producing activities, and uncompleted wells, equipment, and facilities. In addition, combinations of these categories may be appropriate.

If material, capitalized costs of unproved properties should also be disclosed. If the entity's financial statements include investments that are accounted for by the equity method, aggregate capitalized costs about an entity's oil and gas activities and the related accumulated depreciation, depletion, amortization, and valuation allowances as of year-end should be disclosed. In addition, capitalized costs of unproved properties, if significant, should be disclosed separately.

This information should also be separately disclosed for both the consolidated entities and the entity's share of equity method investees when an entity's investments are accounted for using the equity method.

Disclosures relating to oil and gas property acquisition, exploration, and development activities. Information relating to property acquisition costs, exploration costs, and development costs (whether they are capitalized or charged to expense at the time incurred) are required supplemental disclosures of publicly traded entities that have significant oil and gas production activities.

If the entity accounts for investments using the equity method, the entity's share of the investees's property acquisition, exploration, and development costs should be separately disclosed for the year, in the aggregate, and for each geographical area for which reserve quantities are disclosed.

Presentation of results of operations for oil- and gas-producing activities. Information relating to the results of operations for oil- and gas-producing activities of an entity should be disclosed for the year. This information should be shown in the aggregate and for each geographic area for which reserve quantities are disclosed. Information relating to the following areas should be presented:

☐ Revenues.

☐ Production (lifting) costs.

☐ Exploration expenses. (It is important to note that entities using the full cost method of accounting generally do not have exploration expenses. Exploration costs incurred using the full cost method of accounting must be capitalized when incurred and therefore are presented in earnings in the form of depreciation, depletion, amortization, and valuation provisions. Usually, only entities that disclose exploration expenses are those that utilize the successful efforts method.)

☐ Depreciation, depletion, amortization, and valuation provisions.

☐ Income tax expense.

☐ Results of operations for oil- and gas-producing activities (excluding corporate overhead and interest costs).

Disclosure of a standardized measure of discounted future net cash flows related to proved oil and gas reserve quantities. Information relating to a standardized measure of discounted future net cash flows regarding an entity's interest's in (1) proved oil and gas reserves and (2) oil and gas subject to purchase under long-term supply, purchase, or similar agreements and contracts in which the entity participates in the operation of the properties should be disclosed at the end of the period as part of the supplemental disclosures requirement for publicly traded entities that have significant oil and gas production activities. The following information should be shown in the aggregate and for each geographic area for which quantities are disclosed:

☐ *Future cash inflows*—Future cash inflows should be computed by applying the prices used in estimating the entity's proved oil and gas reserves to the year-end quantities of those reserves. Future price changes should only be considered to the extent provided by contractual arrangements in existence at year-end.

☐ *Future development and production costs*—Future development and production costs should be computed by estimating the expenditures to be incurred in developing and producing the proved oil and gas reserves at the end of the period based on year-end costs and assuming the continuation of existing economic conditions. If estimated development expenditures are significant, they should be disclosed separately from estimated production costs.

☐ *Future income taxes*—Future income taxes are derived by applying the appropriate year-end statutory tax rates to the future pretax net cash flows relating to the entity's proved oil and gas reserves less the tax basis of the properties involved.

☐ *Future net cash flows*—Future net cash flows are determined by subtracting future development production costs and future income tax expense from future cash inflows.

☐ *Discount*—The discount amount is derived by using a discount rate of 10% a year to reflect the timing of future net cash flows relating to proved oil and gas reserves.

☐ *Standardized measure of discounted future net cash flows*—This measure is determined by subtracting future net cash flows less the computed discount.

☐ *The aggregate change in the standardized measure of discounted cash flow*—The following sources of change relating to this measure should be disclosed separately if individually significant:

In computing the aforementioned nine amounts, the following guidelines should be followed:

— Net change in sales and transfer prices and in production (lifting) costs related to future production.

— Changes in estimated future development costs.

— Sales and transfers of oil and gas produced during the period.

— Net change due to extensions, discoveries, and improved recovery.

— Net change due to purchases and sales of minerals in place.

— Net change to revisions in quantity estimates.

— Previously estimated development costs incurred during the period.

— Accretion of discount.

— Net change in income taxes.

— The effects of changes in prices and costs should be computed before the effects of changes in quantities. As a result, changes in quantities should be stated at prices used in estimating proved oil and gas reserves and year-end costs.

— The change in computed income taxes should reflect the effect of income taxes incurred during the period as well as the change in future income tax expenses.

— All changes except income taxes should be reported on a pretax basis.

☐ Any additional information that must be provided in preventing the disclosure of the standardized discounted cash flow from being misleading should be included.

Other Disclosure Requirements

Disclosure should be provided to users of financial statements about management's evaluation of capitalized exploratory well costs. An enterprise is required to disclose the amount of capitalized exploratory well costs that is pending the determination of proved reserves. In addition, it is also required to disclose for each annual period in the income statement changes to capitalized exploratory well costs arising from:

1. Additions to capitalized exploratory well costs pending determination of proved reserves.

2. Capitalized exploratory well costs reclassified to wells, equipment, and other facilities resulting from proved reserves.

3. Capitalized exploratory well costs that were expensed.

REAL ESTATE SALES TRANSACTIONS

Sources of Authoritative Guidance

The sources of authoritative guidance relating to real estate sales transactions are:

☐ ASC 976-605-25-4, *Real Estate—Retail Land: Revenue Recognition*.

☐ ASC 840, *Leases*.

☐ ASC 860-10-05-3, *Transfers and Servicing: Overall*.

☐ ASC 360-10-05-4, *Property, Plant, and Equipment: Overall*.

☐ ASC 978, *Real Estate—Time-Sharing Activities*.

☐ ASC 360-20, *Property, Plant, and Equipment: Real Estate Sales*.

Abstract and Introduction

GAAP distinguishes between retail land sales and real estate sales other than retail land sales. (See descriptions in the Primary GAAP sections.) Under the full accrual method of accounting for land sales, the following must be satisfied before profits may be determined and recognized.

☐ The seller's receivables from sales must be collectible as demonstrated by the buyer's commitment to pay.

☐ The earnings process is deemed complete because the seller has no significant remaining obligations for construction or development.

Retail land sales not accounted for by the full accrual method should be accounted for and reported using the percentage-of-completion or the installment method. The criteria for their applicability are based on the collectibility of the seller's receivable from the land sales and the seller's remaining obligations.

Profit recognition for other sales of real estate by the full accrual and several other methods is delineated in the subsequent discussions. ASC 976-605-25-1, *Real Estate—Retail Land: Revenue Recognition*, notes that recognition is dependent on whether a sale has been consummated, the degree of the buyer's investment in the property being sold, whether the sellers' receivable is subject to future subordination, and the extent of the seller's continuing involvement with the property after the sale.

Authoritative Guidance

GAAP enumerates the standards for recognition of profit on all real estate sales transactions, including real estate with property improvements and integral equipment, without regard to the nature of the seller's business. ASC 360-20-15-3, *Property, Plant, and Equipment: Real Estate Sales*, notes that property improvements and integral equipment refer to any physical structures or equipment attached to the real estate that cannot be removed and used separately without incurring significant costs (e.g., an office building, a manufacturing facility, a power plant, timberlands or farms [land with trees or crops attached to it]). Natural assets that have been extracted from the land, such as soil, gas, and coal, are excluded from this guidance. The following transactions are also excluded from this guidance:

☐ The sale of the net assets or stock of a subsidiary or component of an entity if the assets of that subsidiary or that component, as applicable, contain real estate, unless the transaction is, in substance, the sale of real estate.

☐ The sale of securities that are accounted for in accordance with ASC 320-10-35, *Investments—Debt and Equity Securities: Overall*.

☐ The sale of property improvements or integral equipment only without the sale of the underlying land.

The provisions of GAAP in this area distinguish between retail land sales and real estate sales other than retail land sales. ASC 976-605-25-1 notes that the former are sales, on a volume basis, of lots that are subdivisions of large tracts of land. They are characterized by (1) very small down payments; (2) the inability of the seller to enforce the sales contract or the buyer's note against the buyer's general credit; (3) return of the buyer's down payment if the cancellation is made within an established cancellation period; and (4) defaults by the buyer after the cancellation, resulting in recovery of the land by the seller and forfeiture of at least some of the principal payments by the buyer. Amounts retained by the seller are determined by federal and state laws.

Examples of real estate sales transactions that are not retail land sales are:

☐ Sales of lots to builders.

☐ Sales of homes, buildings, and parcels of land to builders and others.

☐ Sales of corporate stock of enterprises with substantial real estate.

☐ Sales of a partnership interest that is in substance a sale of real estate (for example, an enterprise that forms a partnership, arranging for the partnership to acquire the property directly from third parties, and selling an interest in the partnership to investors, who then become limited partners).

☐ Sales of time-sharing interests (time-sharing real estate interests represent the right to occupy a dwelling for a designated period each year). ASC 978, *Real Estate—Time-Sharing Activities*, specifically notes that real estate time-sharing transactions should be accounted for as nonretail land sales. ASC 978-10-05, *Real Estate—Time-Sharing Activities: Overall*, provides additional guidance on accounting for real estate time-sharing transactions.

Real Estate Sales Revenue Recognition Methodologies

Some important considerations relating to profit recognition methodologies in real estate sales other than retail land sales and in retail land sales are:

☐ *Full accrual method*—The use of the full accrual method in accounting for real estate transactions is specifically based on the parameters set by ASC 976-605-25-1. In general, the use of the full accrual method requires full profit recognition at the time of sale. In accordance with the revenue recognition principle of GAAP, profit under the accrual method is recognized when two conditions are satisfied. First, the revenue must be realized and second, the earnings process must have taken place. Generally, at the date of sale, confirmation of revenue recognition is achieved. In a sale of real estate other than retail land sales, for example, these are satisfied when four criteria (to be discussed later in this chapter) are met. If this occurs, the seller must account for the transaction using the full accrual method and must recognize the entire profit when the sale is made.

☐ *Installment method*—The installment method of accounting for profit recognition should be used only when a reasonable estimate of the collectibility of the seller's receivable cannot be made. That is, the seller is not reasonably assured of collecting the sales price. Under the installment method, profit is not recognized until cash is collected. Thus, profit recognition in the installment method is cash based, not accrual based. Each payment received is considered a partial recovery of cost and profit. That is, the payment is apportioned in the same ratio as the total cost and total gross profit bear to the sales value. The seller recognizes profit each time the buyer makes a payment to the seller, and on debt primarily assumed by the buyer.

☐ *Cost recovery method*—This method should be used when there is uncertainty regarding the recovery of the seller's cost (as a result of a buyer default). ASC 976-605-25-4 notes that under the cost recovery method, no profit is recognized until the cash payments made by the buyer due the seller, including principal and interest on debt due the seller and on existing debt assumed by the buyer, exceed the seller's cost for the property that was sold. Thus, profit is recognized by the seller when cash payments are received after the property's cost is recovered. The cost recovery method, like the installment method, is cash not accrual based.

☐ *Deposit method*—This method is used when there is significant uncertainty regarding the viability of the real estate sales contract and collectibility of the contact sales price. These circumstances require unusual accounting profit recognition procedures. For example, the following is required when the deposit method is used and payments are received by the seller:

— Payments made by the buyer to the seller are regarded as deposit receipts.

— The seller does not recognize any profit.

— A note receivable is not to be recorded on the seller's books.

— The seller continues to report the property that was sold and the related existing debt (even if the buyer has assumed it) on its books. The seller must also disclose these items as being subject to a sales contract in the financial statements.

— The seller must continue to record depreciation as a period cost even though the property has been sold. (An exception here is if the property has been classified as held for sale under ASC 360-10-05-5).

☐ *Percentage-of-completion method*—The amount of profit recognized each period is predicated on the relationship of costs incurred to date to the total cost expected to be incurred. An important application of the percentage-of-completion method is in recording profit recognition in retail land sales. It is used, in this scenario, if all the criteria for the use of the full accrual method are satisfied for profit recognition on retail land sales (see the discussion of the full accrual method in the following section titled "Retail Land Sales") except one: the seller is not obligated to complete improvements of lots sold or to construct amenities or other facilities relating to them. This requirement is replaced with two other requirements relating to the improvement and development of the project (described in a discussion of the percentage-of-completion method in the section titled "Retail Land Sales").

☐ *Reduced profit method*—This method provides for the initial recognition of a reduced amount of profit based on guidance described in ASC 976-605-25-1. The reduced profit is based on discounting the receivable from the buyer to the present value of the lowest level of annual payments required by the sales contract over a maximum period specified by ASC 976-605-25-1. The statement specifies a period of no more than 20 years for debt on land and the customary amortization of a first mortgage loan by an independent established lending institution for other real estate. This method was designed to ensure the quality of a buyer's continuing investment in the real estate transaction. The recognition of the remaining profit on the contract is postponed until a lump sum or other payments are made.

Real Estate Sales Other Than Retail Land Sales

For real estate sales other than real land sales, the recognition of profit by the full accrual method and other aforementioned methodologies is dependent on whether a sale has been consummated; the extent of the buyer's investment in the property that is being sold; whether the seller's receivable is subject to future subordination; and the seller's involvement with the property after the sale.

Use of the full accrual method. The full accrual method should be used if:

☐ The sale has been fully consummated. A sale has been fully consummated when:

— All consideration specified in the contract has been exchanged.

— The parties to the contract are fully bound by the contract.

— All requirements that had to be satisfied to close the sale of property have been satisfied (e.g., inspections, land surveys, title policies).

— Any permanent financing that is required of the seller has been arranged.

☐ The buyer's initial and continuing investments in the property are considered sufficient commitments to pay for the property.

The initial investment in the property is considered to be met by ASC 976-605-25-1 for purposes of sufficiency if it is at least equivalent to that which an independent lending institution would require for a loan on the same type of property at the same price. For example, the following are some examples of the minimum initial investments expressed as a percentage of sales value that would have to be paid in to satisfy the requirements of ASC 976-605-25-1 that an adequate initial investment be made.

Property	Percentage of Sales to be Paid In
Land—Held for commercial, industrial, or residential development to commence within two years after sale	20
Held for commercial, industrial, residential, development to commence after two years	25
Multifamily residence:	
Primary residence:	
Cash flow currently sufficient to service all indebtedness	10
Start-up situations or current deficiencies in cash flow	15
Secondary or recreational residence:	
Cash flow currently sufficient to service all indebtedness	15
Start-up situations or current deficiencies in cash flow	25
Single-family residential property (including condominium or cooperative housing)	
Primary residence of the buyer	5
Secondary or recreational residence	10

It is not uncommon for real estate land agreements to provide for the continuous release of land (in sections or in total) from debt liens to the buyer. ASC 360-20-55-2 notes that a contract to sell land or other property may allow the property, in total or in part, to be released from liens by one of the two following payment scenarios: (1) payment of a release price or (2) payments by the buyer may be assigned to the released property first. If either (1) or (2) exists in the contract, the buyer's initial investment shall be deemed sufficient to:

— Any cash that was paid as a down payment.

— The purchaser's notes payable to the seller together with irrevocable letters of credit from established lending institutions.

— Any payments by the buyer to third parties to reduce any existing debt that may remain on the property.

— Additional cash proceeds that were paid by the buyer as a required part of the sales contract (e.g., points, prepaid interest).

— Any other payments or considerations that have been sold or converted to cash to the seller.

— Pay release prices on property released at the date of sale, and

— Be considered an adequate initial investment on property not released or not subject to release at that time for purposes of being considered an adequate initial investment for the property.

☐ The receivable is not subject to future subordination. The seller's receivable should not be subordinate to any other debt in the property except (1) a first mortgage loan existing at the date of sale or (2) a future loan or existing permanent loan commitment provided for in the sales agreement assuming that any proceeds for loan repayment will be applied first to the receivable of the seller.

☐ The sale of the property fully constitutes a transfer of all the risks and rewards of property ownership without any future seller involvement in the property. The fact that the seller has some sort of involvement may be indicative of the fact that the risks and rewards of property ownership have not, in fact, been transferred and a bona fide sale has not been made. For example, the seller may guarantee the buyer some purchase price rebate if a minimum return is not generated for the new buyer.

EXAMPLE

Full Accrual Method

A company that develops land lots enters into a sales agreement with a contractor to purchase the land lots for $600,000. The agreement calls for the contractor to pay the development company $150,000 cash and a note for $450,000. The note is due in four equal installments, pays interest at the rate of 8%, is not subordinate to any new loans on the property, and is backed by an irrevocable letter of credit from an independent established lending institution. Land and development costs on the part of the development company equal $400,000. The land development company would make the following entry on the sale of the developed lots:

Cash	150,000	
Note receivable	450,000	
Sales from lots		600,000
Cost of lots	400,000	
Land and development capitalized costs		400,000

The full accrual method should be used when the aforementioned noted criteria have been met. If they have not been met, the method of accounting that should be used depends on the criteria that have not been met. The following are examples of methods that should be used when certain criteria have not been met.

Nonconsummation of the sale. If the real estate sale has not been consummated, the seller should use the deposit method of accounting. However, when office buildings, apartments, condominiums, shopping centers, and similar structures are being built, the percentage-of-completion method may be used because of the relatively long construction period.

Buyer's initial investment is insufficient and does not qualify. If the buyer's initial investment is insufficient but recovery of the cost of the property is reasonably assured in the contingency of a default by the buyer, the sale should be accounted for using the installment method. However, if the recovery of the property's cost is uncertain or if the cost has already been recovered and collection of additional amounts is uncertain, the cost recovery method or the deposit method should be used. The cost recovery method can be used to account for real estate for which the installment method would be acceptable.

It is possible for the seller of the property that has accounted for the sale under the installment method or cost recovery method to subsequently change to the full accrual method if the requirements for the full accrual method are satisfied. The accounting for the change consists of recognizing in income the remaining profit that had not been recognized under the installment or cost recovery method.

Buyer's continuing investment is insufficient for the full accrual method and does not qualify. If the purchaser's initial investment is sufficient to satisfy the full accrual method, but it is not sufficient to recognize profit under that method because the continuing investment is not sufficient, the seller should use the reduced profit method, installment method, or cost recovery method. The reduced profit method should be used when the purchaser's annual payments made to the seller are large enough to cover (1) principal and interest on the maximum first mortgage loan that could be obtained on the property and (2) interest, at the market rates, on the excess of the actual total debt on the property over such a maximum first mortgage loan. If these criteria are not both met, the seller should recognize profit by the either the installment method or the cost recovery method.

Receivable accepted by the seller subject to future subordination. If the seller receivable is subject to future subordination, its recoverability is not assured, because the seller would not have an unequivocal right to the property if the buyer defaults. In this situation, the seller should use the cost recovery method when its receivable is subject to future subordination, except when (1) a first mortgage loan exists on the date of the sale or (2) a future loan provided for in the sales agreement if the loan proceed will be applied first to pay the seller's receivable.

Seller's continuing involvement exists after property is sold. If the transfer of the risks and rewards of ownership to the purchaser has not occurred because the seller still maintains a continuing involvement with the property, the full accrual method of accounting should not be used. If the sellers' loss of profit because of his or her continuing involvement with the property is limited by the terms of the sales contract, profit may be recognized but should be reduced by the seller's maximum exposure to loss. In all other situations, if the seller has some other form of continuing involvement with the property, the transaction should be accounted for in accordance with the extent and nature of the seller's involvement rather than as a sale (e.g., profit sharing, financing, leasing).

A brief discussion follows of different forms of continuing involvement with the property and the accounting methods that should be used:

☐ The seller has partially sold the property. Partial sales consist of those in which the seller maintains an ownership interest in the property or has an ownership interest in the buyer. In this situation, profit should be recognized only when:

— The buyer and seller are independent of each other. If the seller has a noncontrolling interest in the buyer, the seller should recognize profit in proportion to the outside ownership of the purchaser. However, if the seller has a controlling interest in the buyer, no profit should be recorded until it is realized by a sale to an independent party or by profits from continuing operations.

— The sales price is reasonably assured of being collectible. If the sale is not reasonably assured, the installment method or cost recovery method should be used.

— The seller is not obligated to support the operations of the property or its obligations to an extent greater than its ownership interest. If, in fact, the seller has to support the operations of the property or its obligations and the transaction is in substance a sale, the seller should record profit to the extent that the proceeds from the sale exceed all the costs related to the property that are the responsibility of the seller.

☐ The seller is required to repurchase the property, or the contract contains an option that may be exercised by the buyer requiring that the seller repurchase the property. In substance, therefore, this transaction should be accounted for as a financing, leasing, or profit-sharing contract rather than a sale of real property.

☐ The seller is required to support the operations of the property. If the degree of support provided by the seller is only for a limited amount of time, profit on the sale should be recognized on the basis of the services performed. This assumes, however, that profit should not be recognized until there is reasonable assurance that future receipts will exceed operating expenses, debt payments, and other contractual obligations. On the other hand, if the seller is required to support operations for an extended period of time, the transaction should be accounted for as a financing, leasing, or profit-sharing agreement rather than a sale. If the support period is not specified in the sales contract, it is presumed for at least two years beyond the date that rental operations begin. Revenue should be recognized on the degree of performance of the seller in this situation. If actual rental proceeds exceed operating expenses, debt service, and other contractual payments before the two-year period ends, profit may be recognized at an earlier date. If the sales agreement requires that the seller manage the property without any compensation at all or less than the going rates expected for such services, compensation should be estimated as income as the services are performed over the contract term when the sale is recognized.

☐ The seller is a general partner in a limited partnership that has acquired an interest in the property and the seller holds a receivable from the buyer for a material portion of the sales price. In this situation, the transaction should be accounted for as a financing, leasing, or profit-sharing agreement rather than a sale of property.

☐ The seller leases back all or a part of the property for the remaining life of the property. This transaction should be accounted for as a financing, leasing, or profit-sharing arrangement rather than a sale.

☐ The seller contractually guarantees a return of the buyer's investment in the property or guarantees some return on the investment for an extended period of time. The transaction is a financing, leasing, or profit-sharing arrangement rather than a sale. **Note:** If the guarantee of investment return is for a limited period of time, the deposit method of accounting should be used until operations of the property cover the operating expenses, debt service, and contractual payments. Profit should only be recognized subsequently when required services are performed.

☐ On sales of condominiums or time-sharing interests, profits should be recognized based on the percentage-of-completion method. The percentage-of-completion method should be used on the sale of individual units (of condominium units or time sharing interests) if the following criteria are met:

— The buyer can no longer require a refund (except for nondelivery of the unit or interest).

— Construction is beyond the preliminary stage.

— Sales prices are deemed to be collectible.

— Enough units of the building project have been sold so that it may be assumed that the project will not become a rental property.

— Total sales revenues and costs can be reasonably estimated.

If any of the aforementioned criteria were not met, the deposit method should be used. When all are met, the percentage-of-completion method should be used.

☐ Although the form of the agreement appears to be a sale, the purchaser of the property has an option to buy the property. In this situation, generally, the buyer makes a down payment and is not required to make any more payments on the property until certain conditions are resolved, such as obtaining a building permit or zoning modification. These transactions should be accounted for using the deposit method, and the funds from the sale are accounted for as a liability and recognized as income when the purchaser exercises the option or allows it to expire.

☐ The seller sells building improvements and leases the land underlying the improvements to the buyer. In this situation, the entire transaction is accounted for as a lease if the land lease does not cover the entire economic life of the improvements or is not for a substantial period. If both of these criteria are met, profit should be recognized on the sale of the improvements at the time of the sale and measured by (1) the present value of the lease rental payments (not in excess of the cost of the land) plus (2) the sales value of the improvements less (3) the carrying value of the improvements and the land. The seller should record profit on the buyer's rent payments that are made if they exceed the land's cost and the rent is received after the primary debt on the improvements is paid off. The profits should be recognized when:

— The land is sold, or

— The rents in excess of the seller's cost of the land are earned under the lease.

— The sales contract requires that the seller is obligated to develop the property in the future. In this case, if such obligation exists, or the seller is required to extend the facilities in any way, the percentage-of-completion method is commonly used to account for the sale.

— The sales agreement calls for the seller to partake in the future profits of the property without the risk of any loss. In general, if this transaction qualifies for the full accrual method of accounting and the seller partakes in future profits in the property without risk of loss, then the risks and rewards of ownership and the lack of continuing involvement are considered to be met. Future profit is recorded in the accounting period when the profits are in fact realized. All costs of the sale are recognized at the time of the sale. Specifically, no costs are deferred to periods when contingent profits are realized.

A summary of the applicability of each methodology, in the form of a decision tree, for sales of real estate other than retail land sales may be found in ASC 976-605-25-1. Comprehensive calculations for the recognition of profit may be found in Appendix C.

Retail Land Sales

Retail land sales consist of large amounts of residential lot sales of subdivisions of large tracts of land. The developer of the land attempts to provide the buyer with financing terms that require a lower down payment than would be possible if the buyer would attempt to obtain the financing from outside financial institutions. In the latter situation, for example, financial institutions would require that the buyer's note be purchased only at a significant discount. In general, the land developer is also required to provide the buyer with a refund period in which a full refund would be received and the sales contract would be considered null and void.

ASC 360-20-55, *Property, Plant, and Equipment: Real Estate Sales*, defines a retail land project as a homogenous, reasonably contiguous area of land that may, for development and marketing, be subdivided in accordance with a master plan. With respect to a retail land project, a single method of recognizing profit is required to be applied to all sales transactions within a retail land project that has been consummated. The following is a discussion of the methods used to account for profits from retail land sales:

☐ *Full accrual method.* The full accrual method should be utilized when these five criteria are met:

— Before the cancellation and refund period has expired, the purchaser has made the required down payment and all other payments required by the contract.

— The payments that are made cumulatively (principal and interest) must equal no less than 10% of the full contract price.

— The seller's collection experience should be that at least 90% of the receivables from contracts from the land sale project, if they are not canceled within six months following the sales contract date, will be collected in total. The criteria may be alternatively met if a down payment of at least 20% on the contract price is received.

— The receivable from the sale of the land sale must not be subordinate to any new loans on the property.

— The seller is not obligated to complete improvements of the lots sold or to build any other facilities to lots that have been sold. In accounting for the full accrual method, sales must be recognized at the amount contracted for, an allowance of doubtful collectibles must be provided for, the cost of the lots that are sold must be transferred from the seller's inventory account, and an allowance for discounts (contra contracts receivable account) must be recorded to reduce the receivable account to the present value of all required payments. If the seller has initiated programs that are designed to accelerate the collection of receivables, any profit on the sale should be reduced by the charges for anticipated discounts being offered as a result of incentives. Sales discounts as a result of infrequently offered incentives should be debited against income in the period in which they are granted.

☐ *Percentage-of-completion method.* If a retail land sale that satisfies all the conditions for the accrual method except the last (i.e., the seller is not obligated to complete all improvements or construction on the lots that are sold), the percentage-of-completion method should be used if the two following conditions are met:

— It is believed that the land can be developed for the purposes expected and that the properties can be used for these purposes at the end of the expected payment period.

— The improvements and construction that are required on the property have been initiated and are in progress. There is every reason to believe, based on the work that has already been performed, that all improvements and construction will be completed according to the agreed-upon plan. There do not appear to be any extenuating circumstances, such as delays or additional costs, that would mean the project will not be completed as expected.

Accounting for the percentage-of-completion method is as one would expect. Revenue should be recorded by computing the ratio of costs incurred to date to the total estimated costs expected to be incurred. This fraction is then multiplied by the net sales number. Costs incurred and total cost to be incurred include the following: land cost, interest and project carrying costs incurred prior to the sale (previously charged to expense), and selling costs associated with the project. Estimates for future improvement costs should be based on amounts that are expected in the construction industry in the area. Estimates of future improvements should be reviewed yearly and the percentage-of-completion should be recalculated when cost estimates are revised.

☐ *Installment Method*. If a retail land sale has gone beyond its refund period, has had its cumulative payments equal no less than 10% of the full contract price, and does not meet any of the other criteria for the full accrual method or percentage-of-completion methods, it should be accounted for under the installment method if the following two conditions are met regarding the financial condition of the seller:

— The seller is able to provide both land improvement and any offsite construction that was committed to in the contract.

— The seller is satisfying all other commitments made in the contract, including ensuring the completion of the improvements of the project.

A seller originally accounting for a retail land sale by the installment method may adopt the percentage-of-completion method if the land sale subsequently satisfies all the conditions required of this method. In this situation, the seller may utilize the percentage-of-completion method for the whole project (both prior and current sales) and account for the change in methodology as a change in accounting estimate.

☐ *Deposit Method*. A retail land sale that fails to satisfy the conditions required for the full accrual method, percentage-of-completion method, and the installment method should be accounted for under the deposit method.

A summary of the applicability of each methodology, in the form of a decision tree, for retail land sales may be found in ASC 976-605-25-1. Comprehensive calculations for the recognition of profit may be found in Appendix D.

Disclosure Requirements

Real estate transactions—other than retail land sales. The following are the disclosure requirements for some of the methods of accounting for real estate transactions:

Installment method—Under this method, the income statement (or notes) in the period of the sale should disclose the sales value, the deferred gross profit, and the total cost of the sale. Revenue and the cost of the sales should be shown as separate items on the income statement or should be shown in the notes when the profit is recognized.

Cost recovery method—Under this method, the income statement for the period including the sales date should disclose the sales value, the deferred gross profit, and the total cost of the sale. The gross profit that has not yet been recognized should be offset against the related receivable on the balance sheet. Gross profit should be presented as a separate revenue item on the income statement when it is recognized.

Deposit method—Under this method, the nonrecourse debt that has been assumed by the purchaser should be disclosed as a liability in the balance sheet of the seller. It should not be offset against the related asset.

Retail land sales. The following are the disclosure requirements for enterprises involved in retail land sales:

☐ Accounts receivable that mature for each of the five years following the date of the financial statements.

☐ The weighted average of stated interest rates and range of receivables.

☐ The balance of delinquent accounts receivable as well as the method used by the seller for determining the delinquency.

☐ An estimate of the total costs and estimated dates of expenditures for contractual improvements for major areas from which sales are being generated for each of the five years after the date of the balance sheet.

☐ Recorded debts for contractual improvements that must be made.

NOT-FOR-PROFIT ORGANIZATIONS

Sources of Authoritative Guidance

The sources of authoritative guidance in not-for-profit organizations are:

☐ ASC 958-605-05-3, *Not-for-Profit Entities: Revenue Recognition.*

☐ ASC 958-205-05-5, *Not-for-Profit Entities: Presentation of Financial Statements.*

☐ ASC 958-320-05-2, *Not-for-Profit Entities: Investments—Debt and Equity Securities.*

☐ ASC 815, *Derivatives and Hedging.*

☐ ASC 958-20-15-3, *Not-for-Profit Entities: Financially Interrelated Entities.*

☐ ASC 360-10-05-4, *Property, Plant, and Equipment: Overall.*

☐ ASC 820-10-05, *Fair Value Measurements and Disclosures: Overall.*

☐ ASC 825-10-10, *Financial Instruments: Overall.*

Abstract and Introduction

In general, GAAP requires not-for-profit organizations to issue a statement of financial position, a statement of activities, and a statement of cash flows. Not-for-profit organizations' classification of net assets, revenues, expenses, gains, and losses are based on whether there are restrictions by donors. Net assets in the statement of financial position must be categorized as being permanently restricted, temporarily restricted, or unrestricted. The amount of change in each of these classes must also be disclosed in a statement of activities. In addition, expiration of donor-imposed restrictions is required to be disclosed in the period in which the restrictions expire as are restrictions that increase one class of net assets and decrease another (reclassifications). The latter should be reported separately from other transactions in the statement of activities. Investments in equity securities with readily determinable fair values and all investments in debt securities should be reported at fair value with gains and losses disclosed in the statement of activities.

The use of the term *fund balance* is not prohibited. However, the term *net assets* is used to describe the residual remaining after liabilities are subtracted from assets. Considerable flexibility is allowed in formatting the financial statements. The fund accounting format emphasizes the purpose for which the assets may be used.

Authoritative Guidance

Under GAAP, a complete set of financial statements for a not-for-profit organization (NFPO) consists of a statement of financial position (SFP) as of the end of the reporting period, a statement of activities (SOA), and a statement of cash flows (SCF) for the reporting period, and accompanying notes to the financial statements. A voluntary health and welfare organization (VHWO) must also provide a statement of functional expenses, which reports expenses by functional as well as natural classification. VHWOs are tax exempt, are supported by public donations, and operate on a not-for-profit basis. They are primarily designed to solve the health and welfare problems of individuals and overall society.

Statement of Financial Position

The SFP reports the pertinent data about the entity's assets, liabilities, and net assets as well as their interrelationship to each other at a cumulative point in time. This information (together with data from other financial statements and disclosures) assists donors, creditors, members of the organization itself, and others to determine the entity's ability to continue to provide services. In addition, it allows for the assessment of the NFPO's liquidity, solvency, and financial flexibility needed to obtain external financing and satisfy its day-to-day debts.

An NFPO's SFP must report amounts for each of three classes of net assets: permanently restricted net assets, temporarily restricted net assets, and unrestricted net assets. Each of these classes are discussed below:

☐ *Permanently restricted net assets.* That part of an NFPO's net assets that result from:

— Contributions and other inflows of assets whose use by the organization is limited by donor-imposed restrictions that do not expire or cannot be satisfied or removed by actions taken by the organization.

— Other asset increases and reductions that are also so restricted.

— Reclassifications from or to other net asset classifications as a result of donor-imposed terms.

☐ *Temporarily restricted net assets.* That part of an NFPO's net assets that results from:

— Contributions and other inflows of assets whose use by the organization is limited by donor-imposed restrictions that either expire by the passage of time or can be satisfied or removed by actions taken by the organization.

— Other asset augmentations and reductions that occur as a result of the conditions just described.

— Reclassifications from or to other net asset classifications are a result of donor-imposed terms, expiration as a passage of time, or satisfaction and removal by actions of the organization.

☐ *Unrestricted net assets.* That part of the net assets of an NFPO's net assets that are neither permanently nor temporarily restricted by requests of the donor.

Information relating to the nature and amounts of varying permanent restrictions or temporary restrictions should be shown by reporting their amounts on the face of the SFP or including such data in the notes to the entity's financial statements.

Unrestricted net assets are generally constrained only by broad limits resulting from the nature of the organization, its operating environment, legal restrictions specified in the entity's articles of incorporation, or any contracts that the entity might have signed during the course of doing business. Any such constraints, together with self-imposed limits by the organization itself, should be shown in the notes of the financial statements.

When classifying endowment funds, the source of funds must be considered separately. The primary sources of endowment funds are the original gift, gains and losses, and interest and dividends. Unless restricted by donor stipulations or by law, each source is considered unrestricted. Restrictions by donor or by law may be temporary or permanent.

Generally, donors explicitly state any restrictions on the original gift and future interests and dividends. However, the donor may be silent with respect to gains or losses. In many states, the Uniform Management of Institutional Funds Act provides the relevant law for endowment funds. In the absence of donor stipulations or laws to the contrary, losses on the investments of a donor-restricted endowment fund reduce temporarily restricted net assets to the extent that the donor-imposed temporary restrictions on net appreciation of the fund have not been met before the loss occurs. Other loss reduces unrestricted net assets.

Statement of Activities

The SOA (together with disclosures and information in the NFPO's other financial statements and note disclosures) enables donors, creditors, and other readers to:

☐ Determine the entity's performance during a given period of time.

☐ Gauge the organization's service efforts and its ability to continue to perform services.

☐ Appraise the success or failure of management's performance.

Specifically, the SOA measures:

☐ The results of transactions and other occurrences that change the amount and nature of the NFPO's net assets.

☐ The relationship of those transactions and occurrences to each other.

☐ How the entity's resources are being used in relation to its ongoing programs and services.

The SOA reports the amount of change in permanently restricted net assets, temporary restricted net assets, and unrestricted net assets for the period. Expirations of donor-imposed restrictions that increase one class of net assets and decrease another through reclassification are required to be reported as separate items. Revenues should be reported as increases in unrestricted net assets unless use of the assets received is limited by donor-imposed restrictions. In addition, an SOA should report expenses as decreases in unrestricted net assets. It should also report gains and losses recognized on investments and other assets (or liabilities) as increases or decreases in unrestricted net assets unless restricted by law or donor requests. An NFPO is not prevented from classifying its revenues, expenses, gains, or losses within classes of net assets with additional classifying captions within the SOA (e.g., operating, nonoperating, expendable, nonexpendable). If an intermediate determinant of operations is reported (e.g., operating income, operating surplus, operating profit, operating deficit), this information should be reported in a financial statement that, at the very least, reports the change in unrestricted net assets for the period.

To ensure that readers of the SOA clearly understand the NFPO's major operations and activities, the SOA should report the gross amount of its revenues and expenses. Investment revenues, on the other hand, may be shown net of related expenses, such as custodial fees or advisory costs. However, they must be disclosed either on the face of the SOA or in the notes to the financial statements. Costs of services, consumption of resources, and information about expenses should be reported by their functional classification, such as major classes of program services (activities resulting in goods and services being distributed to beneficiaries or customers, for example, that satisfy the objectives of the NFPO) and supporting activities (all activities other than program services, such as management and general activities, fund-raising, and membership activities). VHWOs should report this information by natural classification, such as salaries, rent, utilities, interest expense, and depreciation.

NEPOs should classify the costs of soliciting contributed services as fund raising costs.

Statement of Cash Flows

The SCF provides readers with data regarding the cash receipts and cash payments of the organization during the year. Guidelines regarding the information that is provided to users of an NFPO's SCF and the standards for its preparation are discussed in the SCF section of this volume relating to a business enterprise (see Chapter 6).

Contributions Received

When contributions are received by an NFPO, they must be classified as permanently restricted, temporarily restricted, or without donor-imposed limitations. Contributions that are restricted increase permanently or temporarily restricted net assets, and those that do not have donor-imposed stipulations increase unrestricted net assets. Unconditional promises to make contributions (make payments) that are expected in future periods should be classified as restricted support unless the donor clearly indicated the money is to be used for activities in the current period. Specifically, unless indicated otherwise, receipts of unconditional support of cash in the future generally increase temporarily restricted net assets.

Expiration of Donor-Imposed Restrictions

The expiration of a donor-imposed restriction on a contribution should be recognized in the period in which the restriction expires. This occurs when (1) the purpose for which the resource was restricted has been satisfied, (2) the time of the imposed restriction has elapsed, or (3) both of these criteria occur. For example, a donor established a memorial fund for a loved one that requires that the money (accounted for as revenue or a gain in the period in which it was received) be invested in a certain type of investment (i.e., bonds) for 10 years. The contribution must be classified as restricted support in the period of receipt. After the donor-imposed restriction is satisfied (i.e., after the 10 years have passed), the entity must report a reclassification that shows that its unrestricted net assets have increased and temporarily restricted net assets of the entity has decreased.

Investments Held by NFPO

The following discussion relating to accounting for investments held by NFPOs does not apply to the following situations:

 ☐ Investments in equity securities that are accounted for under the equity method.

 ☐ Investments in consolidated subsidiaries.

 ☐ Investments in derivative instruments that are subject to ASC 815, *Derivatives and Hedging*, and related pronouncements.

Fair value should be used to value investments in equity securities (with determinable fair values) and all debt securities on the balance sheet. In general, quoted market prices are the best sources of this measure. If a fair value cannot be obtained for a debt security, a reasonable estimate (using market prices for similar securities, present value of expected future cash flows, and other such techniques) should be made for those debt securities for which fair value cannot easily be obtained because they are limitedly traded.

Organizations are required to value all investments in equity securities with readily determinable fair values and all investments in debt securities should be measured at fair value in the statement of financial position.

An NFPO concerned about the comparability of its financial statements with those of business entities in the same industry may report investment in debt and certain equity securities by identifying securities as available-for-sale or held-to-maturity. The not-for-profit organization may also exclude unrealized gains or losses on those securities from an operating measure with the statement of activities.

Disclosing Investment Income, Gains, and Losses

Gains and losses on investments must be reported in the SOA as increases or decreases in unrestricted net assets unless their use is temporarily or permanently restricted by the donor or by law. Similarly, interest, dividends, and other investment income must be reported as increases in unrestricted net assets in the period earned unless the use of the underlying assets that were received were restricted by the donor. Investment income that is restricted (depending on the type of restriction mandated by the donor) must be reported as an increase in temporarily restricted net assets or permanently restricted net assets. If restrictions relating to gains and investment income are satisfied in the same reporting period as these items are recognized, the gains and income limited by donor-restricted stipulations may be reported as increases in unrestricted net assets.

Endowment Funds That Are Donor Restricted

In a donor-restricted endowment fund, the donor stipulates that a gift must be invested in perpetuity or for a specified period of time. Gains and losses on investments of donor-restricted endowments should be reported as changes in unrestricted net assets unless the gains and losses are temporarily or permanently restricted by the donor or by law. That is, if a donor requires that a particular investment be permanently restricted, the gains and losses on this investment must also be permanently restricted unless otherwise specifically stipulated. On the other hand, if the donor does not require that the investment be held in such a manner—that is the organization is allowed to choose whatever investments it desires—the gains are not permanently restricted unless the donor or law requires such a restriction. In general, losses on the investments of a donor-restricted endowment fund should be used to reduce temporarily restricted net assets to the extent that donor-imposed temporary restrictions on net appreciation of the fund have not been met before the loss occurs. Any loss that remains after this shall be used to reduce unrestricted net assets. If a donor-restricted endowment fund is reduced by losses below the level required by the donor or law, any gains that restore the fair value of the assets of the endowment fund to that minimally required level should be classified as increases in unrestricted net assets.

The board of directors of the NFPO may create an endowment of unrestricted monies. Losses on investments of such a fund are classified in unrestricted net assets. All sources of such an endowment fund, including the original investment, gains and losses, interest and dividends, do not have any donor restrictions.

Financial Statement Disclosures

Statement of activities. The SOA of an NFPO is required to have the following disclosures for each period presented:

☐ The details of the NFPO's investment return for the period, including:

— Investment income.

— Net realized gains or losses on investments reported at other than fair value.

— Net gains or losses on investments reported at fair value.

☐ If investment return is separated into operating and nonoperating amounts, a reconciliation of this return to amounts reported in the statement of activities.

☐ A description of the policy used to determine the amount that is included in measuring operations and, if a change was made in that policy, a discussion of the cause leading to such a change.

Statement of financial position. The SFP of an NFPO is required to present the following disclosures for each period:

☐ Carrying amounts of investments disclosed in the aggregate and classified by major types, including equity securities, U.S. Treasury securities, corporate debt securities, mortgage-backed securities, real estate, and oil and gas properties.

☐ A description of how the basis was determined for the carrying amounts for all debt and investments other than equity securities with readily determinable fair values.

☐ A description of the significant assumptions and methods used to estimate the fair values of investments other than financial instruments if those other investments are reported at fair value.

☐ Where the fair value of the assets at the reporting date for all donor-restricted endowment funds is less than the level required by donor restriction or law, the aggregate amount of these deficiencies.

Other Disclosure Requirements

Concentration of credit risk. An NFPO is required (for the most recent period for which an SFP is presented) to enumerate the nature of and carrying amount for each individual investment or group of investments that represents a significant concentration of market risk that results from lack of diversity of industry currency, geographic location, or nature of the investments itself. An entity is required to disclose all significant concentrations of credit risk arising from financial instruments, whether from an individual counterparty or groups of counterparties. Group concentrations of credit risk exist if a number of counterparties are engaged in similar activities and have similar economic characteristics that would cause their ability to meet contractual obligations to be similarly affected by changes in economic or other conditions (e.g., if all an NFPO's receivables were from customers in the same industry or same region of the nation). If an economic downturn occurred affecting that industry or region, the collectibility of those receivables would be significantly reduced.

Transfers of assets by an NFPO to a charitable trust or another NFPO that raises or holds contributions for others. If an NFPO transfers assets to another organization (the recipient organization) and specifies itself or another as the beneficiary or its affiliate, the following disclosures must be presented in its SFP for each period:

☐ Recognition of the recipient organization of the transfer.

☐ Recognition of whether that recipient organization was given variance power and the terms of such power.

☐ The terms under which amounts will be distributed to the resource provider or its affiliate.

☐ The aggregate amount recognized in the SFP for those transfers and determination of whether that amount is recorded as an interest in the net assets of the recipient organization or as another asset (e.g., refundable advance or beneficial interest in assets held by others).

FINANCE INDUSTRY

Sources of Authoritative Guidance

The sources of authoritative guidance in the finance industry are:

☐ ASC 310-20-05-2, *Receivables: Nonrefundable Fees and Other Costs.*

☐ ASC 958-320-05, *Not-for-Profit Entities: Investments—Debt and Equity Securities.*

☐ ASC 860-10-05-3, *Transfers and Servicing: Overall.*

Abstract and Introduction

Accounting in the finance industry relates to accounting for nonrefundable fees associated with lending or purchasing a loan or a group of loans. The concepts enumerated here apply to all types of loans or lenders. Overall, following are the salient matters of the area:

☐ Loan origination fees should be recognized over the term of the related loan as an adjustment of yield.

☐ Some direct loan origination costs should be recognized over the term of the related loan as a reduction of its yield.

☐ In general, all loan commitment fees should be deferred except for certain retrospectively determined fees. Specifically, commitment fees that meet certain conditions should be recognized over the loan commitment period. All other commitment fees should be recognized as an adjustment of the yield over the related loan life. If the commitment expires and is not exercised by the lender, the loan commitment fee should be recognized in income at the date of the commitment's expiration.

☐ The following should be recognized as an adjustment of yield by the interest method based on the contractual terms of the loan: loan fees, certain direct loan origination costs, and purchase premiums and discounts on loans.

Authoritative Guidance

Loan Origination Fees and Related Costs

An entity may acquire a loan by lending or by purchasing. Acquiring a loan by lending is called originating a loan. Acquiring one by purchasing is known as acquiring the loan from a party or other borrower. Loan origination fees should be deferred and recognized over the life of the loan as an adjustment of its yield resulting in an adjustment of interest income. Direct loan origination costs should also be deferred and recognized as a reduction in the yield of the loan. Direct loan origination costs should include only the following:

☐ Incremental direct costs of the loan origination incurred in transactions with independent third parties for that loan.

☐ Certain costs directly related to the loan performed by the lender, such as evaluating the potential buyer's borrower's financial condition, evaluating and recording guarantees, collateral, and other security arrangements.

All other lending-related costs include costs related to activities performed by the lender for such activities as advertising, soliciting potential borrowers, servicing existing loans, and other activities related to establishing and monitoring credit policies, supervision, and administration. These costs should be charged to expense as incurred.

Commitment Fees and Costs

In general, fees received for a commitment to originate or purchase a loan or group of loans should be deferred and, if the commitment is exercised, recognized over the life of the loan as an adjustment of the related loan's yield. If the commitment expires unused, the fee should be recognized in income at the date of the expiration of the commitment. There are two exceptions to this general rule:

1. If the amount of the commitment fee is determined retrospectively as a percentage of the line of credit available but unused in a previous period; if that percentage is nominal in relation to the stated interest rate on any related borrowing; and if that borrowing will bear a market interest rate at the date the loan is made, the commitment should be recognized as service fee income as of the determination date.

2. If it is determined by the lending entity that the likelihood of commitment exercise is remote, the commitment fee should be recognized over the commitment period on a straight-line basis as service fee income. If the commitment is, in fact, subsequently exercised over the commitment period, the remaining unamortized commitment fee at the time of exercise should be recognized over the term of the loan as an adjustment of its yield.

Direct loan origination costs incurred to make a commitment to originate a loan should be offset against any related commitment fee and the net amount recognized as a commitment fee, described previously.

Purchase of a Loan or Group of Loans

If a loan or a group of loans are purchased, the initial investment should include the amount paid to the seller plus any fees paid or less any fees received. The initial investment frequently differs from the related loan's principal amount at the date of the purchase. The amount (difference) should be recognized as an adjustment of the yield over the life of the loan. All other costs incurred in connection with acquiring a purchased loan or committing to purchase loans should be charged to expense as incurred. If loans are purchased as a group, the purchaser may either allocate the initial investment to the individual loans making up the group or may account for the initial investment in the aggregate. Deferred net fees or costs should not be amortized during the periods in which interest income on a loan is not being recognized because of concerns about the realization of loan principal or interest.

Measurement of Loans Subject to Prepayment

Interest-only strips, loans, other receivables, or retained interests in securitizations that can be contractually prepaid or otherwise settled in such a way that the holder would not recover substantially all of its recorded investment should be subsequently measured in debt securities and classified as available-for-sale securities or as trading securities.

Accounting for the Capitalized Cost of a Purchased Servicing Right When Mortgage Loans are Refinanced

A mortgage servicing right is a contractual relationship between the mortgage servicer and the investor in the loan. A relationship between the servicer and the borrower does not exist. Thus, an enterprise should not consider the estimated future net servicing income from a new (refinanced) loan when determining amortization of capitalized costs from the old loan.

Income Statement Classification

Loan origination, commitment, and other fees and costs that are recognized as an adjustment of loan yield should be reported as interest income. Amortization fees, such as commitment fees that are being amortized on a straight-line basis over the commitment period or included in income when the commitment expires should be reported as service fee income.

Balance Sheet Classification

Unamortized balance of loan origination, commitment, and other fees and costs and purchase premiums and discounts that are being recognized as an adjustment of yield should be reported on the balance sheet of the enterprise as part of the loan balance that it relates to.

MORTGAGE BANKING INDUSTRY

Sources of Authoritative Guidance

The sources of authoritative guidance in the mortgage banking industry are:

- ☐ ASC 948, *Financial Services—Mortgage Banking.*
- ☐ ASC 310-20-05-2, *Receivables: Nonrefundable Fees and Other Costs.*
- ☐ ASC 320, *Investments—Debt and Equity Securities.*
- ☐ ASC 958-320, *Not-for-Profit Entities: Investments—Debt and Equity Securities.*
- ☐ ASC 815, *Derivatives and Hedging.*
- ☐ ASC 860-10-05-3, *Transfers and Servicing: Overall.*

☐ ASC 815, *Derivatives and Hedging*.

☐ ASC 820, *Fair Value Measurements and Disclosures*.

☐ ASC 860-50-35-17, *Transfers and Servicing: Servicing Assets and Liabilities*.

GAAP Abstract and Introduction

Mortgage banking consists of the purchase or origination of mortgage loans and sale of the loans to such investors as insurance companies, commercial savings banks, pension plans, and real estate investment trusts. (These investors, known as permanent investors, invest in mortgage loans for their own account.) In addition, mortgage banking entities also retain the right to service mortgage loans that they sell to investors. A servicing fee is received for this function.

In general, mortgage loans that are held for sale should be disclosed at the lower of cost or market value. In addition, any direct loan origination costs and origination fees for loans held for sale should be capitalized as part of the carrying amount of the related loan. These costs should not be amortized.

If loans are held for investments, any direct loan origination costs and origination fees should be deferred and recognized as an adjustment to yield. If there are also loan commitment fees, these should be deferred and recognized over the life of the loan or until the loan is sold. In general, any fees that are paid to permanent investors should be recorded as expenses when the loans are sold. In addition, any fees for services performed by a third party and loan placement fees should be recognized when all the major services have been performed.

Authoritative Guidance

Mortgage Loans and Mortgage-Backed Securities

GAAP requires that mortgage loans held for sale should be disclosed at the lower of cost or market value. In the case of a fair value hedge in which a mortgage loan is the hedged item, the cost of the loan (for the purpose of disclosing the lower of cost or market) should be adjusted in accordance with ASC 815, *Derivatives and Hedging*. ASC 820-10-05-1 requires that the amount of the hedged item be adjusted for the change in its fair value (gain or loss) attributable to the hedged risk. It also requires that the gain or loss be recognized in earnings and be accounted for using a valuation allowance. Thus, changes in the valuation allowance from period to period should be included in net income in the period of the change.

ASC 948 prohibits purchase discounts on mortgage loans from being amortized as interest revenue in the period in which the loans are being held for sale.

ASC 948-10-05-4 requires that a mortgage loan not be classified as a long-term investment unless the mortgage banking entity has the ability and intent to hold the loan until maturity. In accounting for the transference to long-term status, the mortgage loan should be accounted for at the lower of cost or fair value on the transfer date. Any difference that exists between the carrying amount of the loan and its outstanding principal balance should be recorded as an adjustment to yield by the interest method. If a mortgage loan held for sale is securitized, any retained mortgage-backed securities should be classified in accordance with ASC 320-10-25-1. If a mortgage banking entity commits to sell any retained mortgage-backed securities before or during the securitization process, it must classify such securities as trading.

If a mortgage loan that is held for sale as a long-term investment is deemed impaired (beyond temporary status), the carrying amount of the loan should be reduced to the amount that the entity expects to receive. A loss should be recorded and the amount expected to be collected should become the security's new cost basis. A gain on recovery should not be recorded. However, upon maturity, sale, or other disposition of the security, a gain may be recognized and reported.

Ascertaining the fair value of mortgage loans and mortgage-backed securities held for sale is a function of loan type. For example, separate market determinations should be made for residential and commercial mortgage loans. In addition, for each type of loan, the lower of cost or fair value should be determined using either the aggregate or individual loan basis.

The fair value of uncommitted loans (loans held on a speculative basis), uncommitted mortgage-backed securities, and committed loans (loans subject to investor purchase commitments) should be determined separately using the following parameters:

☐ *Uncommitted loans.* Fair value is based on the market in which the mortgage banking entity regularly operates. Determination of market value should consider:

— The market prices and yields determined by the entity's normal operating outlets.

— Security prices from the Government National Mortgage Association (GNMA) or other long-term mortgage rates from other public market quotations.

— Current delivery prices of the Federal Home Loan Mortgage Corporation (FHLMC) and Federal National Mortgage Association (FNMA).

☐ *Uncommitted mortgage-backed securities.* Uncommitted mortgage-backed securities that are collateralized by a mortgage banking entity's own loans should be based on the fair value of the securities. If the trust that holds these loans may be terminated and the loans sold directly, fair value of the securities should be based on the value of the loans or securities. Other mortgage-backed securities should be based on the yields of published mortgage-backed securities.

☐ *Committed loans and mortgage-backed securities.* The market value of these securities (mortgage loans that are covered by investor commitments) should be based on fair value.

In general, capitalized costs of acquiring rights to service mortgage loans associated with the purchase or origination of mortgage loans should be excluded from the cost of mortgage loans for the purpose of determining lower of cost or fair value.

Loan and Commitment Fees

Mortgage banks may receive or pay nonrefundable loan or commitment fees representing various sources of compensation. These fees may include, for example, an adjustment of the interest yield on the loan, a fee for designating funds for the borrower, or an offset of loan origination costs. Loan and commitment fees should be accounted for in the following manner:

☐ *Loan origination fees and costs.* If the loan is held for resale, loan origination costs should be deferred until the related loan is sold. If the loan is held for investment, such fees and costs should be deferred and recognized as an adjustment of yield.

☐ *Service fees.* Fees for the reimbursement for the costs of specific services performed by third parties with respect to originating a loan, such as appraisal fees, should be recognized as revenue when the services have been performed.

☐ *Fees relating to loans held for sale.* In general, fees received for guaranteeing the funding of mortgage loans to borrowers, builders, or developers should be deferred and recognized over the life of the loan as an adjustment of yield if the commitment is exercised. If the commitment is unexercised and expires, it should be recognized in income upon expiration. Fees paid to permanent investors to ensure the sale of loans (residential or commercial loan commitment fees) should be recognized as expense when the loans are sold to permanent investors or when it appears that the commitment will not be used. In general, residential loan commitment fees relate to blocks of loans; therefore, fees recognized as revenue or expense as a result of individual loans transactions should be based on the ratio of the individual loan amount to the total commitment amount.

☐ Loan placement fees—that is, fees generated for arranging a commitment directly between a permanent investor and a borrower—should be recognized as revenue when all significant services have been performed. In another situation, if a mortgage banking entity obtains a commitment from a permanent investor before or at the time a related commitment is made to a borrower and if the commitment to the borrower requires that the following conditions occur, then the related fees should also be accounted for as loan placement fees. The two conditions that must be satisfied are:

— Simultaneous assignment of the commitment to the investor.

— Simultaneous transfer to the borrower of the amount received from the investor.

☐ *Fees relating to investment loans (loans not held for sale).* Fees relating to the origination or acquisition of loans for investment should be deferred and recognized as an adjustment of yield.

☐ *Loans repaid before repayment date or commitment expiration.* If a loan is paid before its repayment date or if a loan commitment expires without a loan occurring, then any related fees that have not been recognized should be recognized as revenue or expense at the time of that occurrence.

Balance Sheet Classification and Disclosures

Mortgage banks' balance sheet presentation must distinguish between (1) mortgage loans held for sale and (2) mortgage loans held as long-term investments.

The method that the mortgage bank entity used in determining the lower of cost or market value of mortgage loans (either in the aggregate or on an individual loans basis) should be disclosed.

Index

ANN

DEF

DIS

FIN

INS

L

LON

M

RET

SHA

T

SOFTWARE LICENSE AGREEMENT FOR ELECTRONIC FILES TO ACCOMPANY GAAP 2013 HANDBOOK OF POLICIES AND PROCEDURES (THE "BOOK").